CARDIOPULMONARY BYPASS

BYPASS

PRINCIPLES AND PRACTICE

CARDIOPULMONARY BYPASS

PRINCIPLES AND PRACTICE

Editors

Glenn P. Gravlee, M.D.
Professor of Anesthesia
Head, Section on Cardiothoracic Anesthesia
Bowman Gray School of Medicine
Wake Forest University
Winston-Salem, North Carolina

Richard F. Davis, M.D.
Professor of Anesthesiology
Oregon Health Sciences University
Chief, Anesthesiology Service
Portland Veterans Affairs Medical Center
Portland, Oregon

Joe R. Utley, M.D.
Chief, Cardiac Surgery Division
Spartanburg Regional Medical Center
Spartanburg, South Carolina
Clinical Professor of Surgery
Medical University of South Carolina
Charleston, South Carolina
and University of South Carolina School of Medicine
Columbia, South Carolina

Williams & Wilkins

BALTIMORE • PHILADELPHIA • HONG KONG
LONDON • MUNICH • SYDNEY • TOKYO

A WAVERLY COMPANY

Editor: Timothy H. Grayson
Managing Editor: Marjorie Kidd Keating
Copy Editor: E. Ann Donaldson
Designer: Wilma E. Rosenberger
Illustration Planner: Wayne Hubbel
Production Coordinator: Raymond E. Reter
Cover Designer: Wilma E. Rosenberger

Copyright © 1993
Williams & Wilkins
428 East Preston Street
Baltimore, Maryland 21202, USA

Accurate indications, adverse reactions, and dosage schedules for drugs are provided in this book, but it is possible that they may change. The reader is urged to review the package information data of the manufacturers of the medications mentioned.

Printed in the United States of America

Chapter reprints are available from the publisher.

Library of Congress Cataloging-in-Publication Data

Cardiopulmonary bypass : principles and practice / editors, Glenn P.
Gravlee, Richard F. Davis, Joe R. Utley.
    p.   cm.
  Includes bibliographical references and index.
  ISBN 0-683-03720-X
  1. Cardiopulmonary bypass. I. Gravlee, Glenn P. II. Davis,
Richard F. (Richard Franklin), 1947–   III. Utley, Joe R.
  [DNLM: 1. Cardiopulmonary Bypass. WG 168 C2662]
RD598.C3544 1993
617.4'12059—dc20
DNLM/DLC
for Library of Congress   92-48697
                                                CIP
                                  94 95 96
                             5 6 7 8 9 10

FOREWORD

Cardiopulmonary bypass has long been recognized as the technique by which the circulation of blood by the heart and the functions of the lung are replaced temporarily by passing blood of the patient through an extracorporeal device that both oxygenates and returns the blood to the arterial system of the patient. John Gibbon first successfully used the pump oxygenator in 1953 to repair an atrial septal defect and subsequently reported this in 1954. Thus, the entrance of cardiopulmonary bypass into the field of cardiac surgery essentially opened the door for many repairs of intracardiac and intravascular lesions. Very quickly the mechanical devices used for cardiopulmonary bypass improved and today it is a routine procedure practiced in essentially all parts of the world.

One of the difficulties with cardiopulmonary bypass in this generation is that it has become so effective and so efficient that many surgeons in training essentially are not aware of many of the physiologic and pathologic alterations that occur in a patient during this period of extracorporeal circulation. The current book, *Cardiopulmonary Bypass: Principles and Practice*, is extremely timely as it refreshes our memories and provides us with a considerable amount of the historic background and evolving knowledge that have accumulated over the last 40 years of experience with this modality. Essentially all aspects of the physiologic derangements that potentially occur to the body during cardiopulmonary bypass are well described in this book. The alterations that occur in body function dur-

ing cardiopulmonary bypass are so diverse and can be of such magnitude that it continues to amaze me that most patients tolerate these alterations and make rapid readjustments following the period of bypass quite easily. The effects of various medications and anesthetic agents are altered by the process; the ability to rapidly change body temperatures with bypass also alters physiologic, metabolic, and pharmacologic function; and the still-present effect of cardiopulmonary bypass on leukocyte and red cell function is an everyday alteration that, again, is reasonably well tolerated. This book is extremely timely and quite complete since almost every aspect of altered body function related to cardiopulmonary bypass is discussed.

The editors have organized this wide array of material into five sections that address not only the physiologic, pathophysiologic, and pharmacologic alterations, but also describe the varying types of components that may comprise a cardiopulmonary bypass system. Many individual variations and applications of cardiopulmonary bypass are described, and how these may be implemented is discussed. This quite complete textbook should serve as a reference for the experienced practitioner and certainly as an excellent learning text for the medical student and resident. In no other current location will one be able to obtain such a detailed discussion of the techniques, methodology, and physiologic abnormalities associated with the use of cardiopulmonary bypass.

Paul A. Ebert, M.D., F.A.C.S.

v

PREFACE

The rapidly expanding scope of medical knowledge threatens to overwhelm even our most diligent efforts to remain current, even within a discrete specialty arena. In a lecture reflecting on his noteworthy academic career in anesthesiology spanning over four decades, Dr. Joseph Artusio noted that there were just three English-language textbooks relevant to anesthesiology during his residency in the 1940s. He went on to say, "And now, there's a new book every week."[a] Amid this scenario, one might reasonably ask whether this, or any other new medical text, offers something new and worthwhile. This book was designed to provide comprehensive and scholarly discussion of cardiopulmonary bypass with a comprehensive multidisciplinary scope and a structure that differ considerably from previous texts in the field.

Current annual oxygenator utilization is estimated at 350,000 patients in the United States, and 650,000 patients worldwide, so the number of patients affected by this intervention is not insignificant. These numbers reflect continued growth in oxygenator utilization, and the complexity of disease present in patients undergoing cardiopulmonary bypass continues to escalate. Although cardiac surgical procedures account for the vast majority of oxygenators consumed, other indications for cardiopul-

monary bypass are either emerging (e.g., cardiac arrest and supported angioplasty) or re-emerging (e.g., pulmonary support). In the United States, the number of hospitals offering cardiopulmonary bypass is also rapidly expanding.

The clinical management of cardiopulmonary bypass for cardiac surgery represents a team effort involving perfusionists, surgeons, and anesthesiologists. Our goal has been to provide a textbook representing the perspectives of each of those professions while addressing both practical and reference needs for practitioners and trainees. We also hope to assist cardiologists, neonatologists, and intensive care specialists who manage patients undergoing or recovering from cardiopulmonary bypass. We hope that scholarly pathophysiologic discussions will enhance the understanding and application of patient care after cardiopulmonary bypass. Like most multiauthor textbooks, some redundancy exists between individual chapters. We strove to minimize this, but elected to retain any overlap that appeared to enhance the understanding of the primary subject covered in a given chapter or represented an author's unique perspective on that particular subject. As with most medical subjects, when discussing cardiopulmonary bypass, the border between fact and opinion is often indistinct. Such is the nature of medicine as an imperfect science.

Glenn P. Gravlee, M.D.
Richard F. Davis, M.D.
Joe R. Utley, M.D.

[a]Artusio Jr JF: Rovenstine Lecture, 1991 New York Postgraduate Assembly of Anesthesiologists, New York Society of Anesthesiologists, New York, New York.

ACKNOWLEDGMENTS

Glenn P. Gravlee, M.D., thanks his wife, Joyce, and children, Brent and Sarah, for their support and patience during preparation of this book. Special thanks go to Philips Hallowell, M.D., whose teaching inspired his interest in cardiopulmonary bypass. Terri Barkley, Adele Larrimore, and Wilson Somerville are gratefully acknowledged for administrative and editorial assistance.

Richard F. Davis, M.D., thanks his wife and family for their consistent support. He also gratefully acknowledges Sue Gardner and Deborah Heideman for their steadfast support with manuscript preparation, editing, correspondence, and general communication.

Joe R. Utley, M.D., thanks Connie Wilde for her invaluable assistance with manuscript processing, correspondence, and communication.

CONTRIBUTORS

Nabil Aboud, M.D.
Assistant Professor of Clinical Anesthesia
Jewish Hospital at
Washington University Medical Center
St. Louis, Missouri

Francisco A. Arabia, M.D.
Department of Cardiovascular and
Thoracic Surgery
University of Arizona Health Sciences
Center
Tucson, Arizona

Thomas X. Aufiero, M.D.
Assistant Professor of Surgery
Division of Cardiothoracic Surgery
The Pennsylvania State University
College of Medicine
The Milton S. Hershey Medical Center
Hershey, Pennsylvania

Robert H. Bartlett, M.D.
Professor of Surgery
University of Michigan Medical Center
Ann Arbor, Michigan

Gerard Bashein, M.D.
Associate Professor of Anesthesiology
University of Washington Medical
Center
Seattle, Washington

Dan E. Berkowitz, M.D.
Cardiac Anesthesia Fellow
Division of Cardiac Anesthesia
Department of Anesthesiology
Duke University Medical Center
Durham, North Carolina

Bruce D. Butler, Ph.D.
Associate Professor
Department of Anesthesiology
The University of Texas Medical School
Houston, Texas

John F. Butterworth IV, M.D.
Associate Professor of Cardiothoracic
Anesthesia
Department of Anesthesia
Bowman Gray School of Medicine of
Wake Forest University
Winston-Salem, North Carolina

Frederick W. Campbell III, M.D.
Professor and Vice Chairman
Department of Anesthesiology
Medical College of Pennsylvania
Philadelphia, Pennsylvania

Henry Casson, M.D.
Associate Professor of Anesthesiology
Oregon Health Sciences University
Portland, Oregon

Robert E. Cilley, M.D.
Assistant Professor of Surgery and
Pediatrics
Division of Pediatric Surgery
The Milton S. Hershey Medical Center
Hershey, Pennsylvania

Marilyn R. Cleavinger, M.S.
Assistant Director
Artificial Heart Program
University Medical Center
Tucson, Arizona

John R. Cooper, Jr., M.D.
Clinical Assistant Professor
University of Texas Health Science
Center, Houston
Attending Anesthesiologist
Texas Heart Institute
Houston, Texas

Jack G. Copeland, M.D.
Professor and Chief
Section of Cardiovascular and Thoracic
Surgery
Michael Drummond Distinguished
Professor of Surgery
University of Arizona Health Sciences
Center
Tuscon, Arizona

Christine Kozyra Cushen, C.C.P.
Senior Perfusionist
UCLA School of Medicine
Los Angeles, California

Laurie K. Davies, M.D.
Associate Professor of Anesthesiology
University of Florida College of
Medicine
Gainesville, Florida

Richard F. Davis, M.D.
Professor of Anesthesiology
Oregon Health Sciences University
Chief, Anesthesiology Service
Portland Veterans Affairs Medical Center
Portland, Oregon

Jeri L. Dobbs, P.A., C.C.P.
Assistant Professor
Cardiopulmonary Surgery
Oregon Health Sciences University
Portland, Oregon

L. Henry Edmunds, Jr., M.D.
Julian Johnson Professor of
Cardiothoracic Surgery
Chief, Division of Cardiothoracic
Surgery
University of Pennsylvania
Philadelphia, Pennsylvania

Richard N. Gates, M.D.
Chief Resident
Division of Cardiothoracic Surgery
UCLA School of Medicine
Los Angeles, California

James F. George, Ph.D.
Assistant Professor of Surgery
Division of Cardiothoracic Surgery
The University of Alabama at
Birmingham
Birmingham, Alabama

Glenn P. Gravlee, M.D.
Professor of Anesthesia
Head, Section on Cardiothoracic
Anesthesia
Bowman Gray School of Medicine of
Wake Forest University
Winston-Salem, North Carolina

John W. Hammon, M.D.
Howard Holt Bradshaw Professor and
Chairman
Department of Cardiothoracic Surgery
Bowman Gray School of Medicine of
Wake Forest University
Winston-Salem, North Carolina

Hugh C. Hemmings, Jr., M.D., Ph.D.
Assistant Professor of Anesthesiology
and Pharmacology
Cornell University Medical College
Assistant Attending Anesthesiologist
New York Hospital
New York, New York

Eugene A. Hessel II, M.D.
Associate Professor of Anesthesiology
University of Kentucky School of
Medicine
Lexington, Kentucky

Kane M. High, M.D.
Associate Professor of Anesthesia
The Pennsylvania State University
College of Medicine
The Milton S. Hershey Medical Center
Hershey, Pennsylvania

David R. Hockmuth, M.D.
Attending Cardiac Surgeon
Mercy Hospital Medical Center
Des Moines, Iowa

William Holman, M.D.
Associate Professor of Surgery
Division of Cardiothoracic Surgery
The University of Alabama at
Birmingham
Birmingham, Alabama

Jan C. Horrow, M.D.
Director, Cardiothoracic Anestheisa
Professor and Deputy Chairman of
Anesthesiology
Hahnemann University
Philadelphia, Pennsylvania

James K. Kirklin, M.D.
Professor of Surgery
Director of Cardiac Transplantation
Division of Cardiothoracic Surgery
The University of Alabama at
Birmingham
Birmingham, Alabama

William R. Klausing, C.C.P.
Chief Perfusionist
Jewish Hospital at
Washington University Medical Center
St. Louis, Missouri

Nicholas T. Kouchoukos, M.D.
John M. Schoenberg Professor of
Cardiovascular Surgery
Washington University School of
Medicine
Surgeon in Chief
Jewish Hospital at
Washington University Medical Center
St. Louis, Missouri

Mark Kurusz, C.C.P.
Chief Perfusionist
Assistant Professor of Surgery
Department of Surgery
University of Texas Medical Branch
Galveston, Texas

Hillel Laks, M.D.
Professor and Chief
Cardiothoracic Surgery
UCLA School of Medicine
Los Angeles, California

Douglas F. Larson, Ph.D., C.C.P.
Associate Professor of Surgery
University of Arizona
University Heart Center
Tucson, Arizona

Glenn W. Laub, M.D.
Attending Surgeon
Deborah Heart and Lung Center
Browns Mills, New Jersey
Assistant Professor of Surgery
University of Medicine and Dentistry of
New Jersey
Robert Wood Johnson Medical School
New Brunswick, New Jersey

C. Walton Lillehei, Ph.D., M.D.
Professor of Surgery
University of Minnesota Medical Center
Minneapolis, Minnesota

Edward Lowenstein, M.D.
Professor of Anaesthesia
Harvard Medical School
Anesthetist-in-Chief
Department of Anesthesia and Critical
Care
Beth Israel Hospital
Boston, Massachusetts

Noel L. Mills, M.D.
Surgical Director
West Jefferson General Hospital
New Orleans, Louisiana

Roger A. Moore, M.D.
Chairman, Department of
Anesthesiology
Deborah Heart and Lung Center
Browns Mills, New Jersey
Associate Professor of Anesthesia
University of Pennsylvania
Philadelphia, Pennsylvania

Rita M. Moorman, M.D.
Instructor in Anaesthesia
Harvard Medical School
Associate Anesthetist
Beth Israel Hospital
Boston, Massachusetts

Michael J. Murray, M.D., Ph.D.
Assistant Professor, Anesthesiology
Mayo Medical School
Associate Director of Critical Care
Service
Chair, Division of Intensive Care and
Respiratory Therapy
Mayo Clinic and Foundation
Rochester, Minnesota

Stanton P. Newman, D.Phil., Dip.
Psych.
Adjunct Research Associate Professor
Department of Anesthesia
Bowman Gray School of Medicine of
Wake Forest University
Winston-Salem, North Carolina

Walter E. Pae, Jr., M.D.
Associate Professor of Surgery
Division of Cardiothoracic Surgery
The Pennsylvania State University
College of Medicine
The Milton S. Hershey Medical Center
Hershey, Pennsylvania

Daniel M. Philbin, M.D.
Professor of Anaesthesia
Harvard Medical School
Anesthetist, Department of Anesthesia
Massachusetts General Hospital
Boston, Massachusetts

Donald S. Prough, M.D.
Chairman, Department of Anesthesia
University of Texas Medical Branch
Galveston, Texas

Anne T. Rogers, M.B.Ch.B.,
F.R.C.P.(C)
Associate Professor of Cardiothoracic
Anesthesia
Bowman Gray School of Medicine of
Wake Forest University
Winston-Salem, North Carolina

Carl E. Rosow, M.D., Ph.D.
Associate Professor Anaesthesia
Harvard Medical School
Associate Anesthetist
Massachusetts General Hospital
Boston, Massachusetts

Robert E. Shangraw, M.D., Ph.D.
Assistant Professor of Anesthesiology
Oregon Health Sciences University
Portland, Oregon

Robert N. Sladen, M.D.
Associate Professor of Anesthesiology
and Surgery
Vice Chairman, Department of
Anesthesiology
Co-Director, Surgical Intensive Care
Unit
Duke University Medical Center
Durham, North Carolina

Stephen Slogoff, M.D.
Co-Director, Cullen Cardiovascular
Research Laboratories
Chairman, Research Committee, Texas
Heart Institute
Attending Anesthesiologist
Clinical Professor, University of Texas
Health Science Center
Houston, Texas

Richard G. Smith, M.S.E.E., C.C.E.
Technical Director
Artificial Heart Program
University Medical Center
Tucson, Arizona

Michael T. Snider, M.D., Ph.D.
Professor of Anesthesia
Director, Division of
Respiratory/Intensive Care
Associate Professor of Cellular and
Molecular Physiology
The Pennsylvania State University
College of Medicine
The Milton S. Hershey Medical Center
Hershey, Pennsylvania

David A. Stump, Ph.D.

Research Associate Professor of
Anesthesia
Bowman Gray School of Medicine of
Wake Forest University
Winston-Salem, North Carolina

Julie A. Swain, M.D.

Chief, Division of Cardiovascular
Surgery
Vice-Chairman, Department of
Surgery
University of Nevada School of
Medicine
Las Vegas, Nevada

Stephen J. Thomas, M.D.

Professor of Anesthesiology
Vice Chairman, Department of
Anesthesiology
Attending Anesthesiologist
New York Hospital Cornell Medical
Center
New York, New York

Joe R. Utley, M.D.

Chief, Cardiac Surgery Division
Spartanburg Regional Medical Center
Spartanburg, South Carolina
Clinical Professor of Surgery
Medical University of South Carolina
Charleston, South Carolina
and University of South Carolina
School of Medicine
Columbia, South Carolina

Jakob Vinten-Johansen, Ph.D.

Associate Professor of Cardiothoracic
Surgery and Physiology
Associate Research Professor of
Anesthesia
Bowman Gray School of Medicine of
Wake Forest University
Winston-Salem, North Carolina

Warren M. Zapol, M.D.

Reginald Professor of Anaesthesia
Harvard Medical School
Massachusetts General Hospital
Boston, Massachusetts

CONTENTS

=========================== Section III ===========================
Coagulation Management During Cardiopulmonary Bypass

1

HISTORICAL DEVELOPMENT OF CARDIOPULMONARY BYPASS

C. Walton Lillehei

A physician at the bedside of a child dying of an intracardiac malformation as recently as 1952 could only pray for a recovery! Today, with the heart-lung machine, correction is routine.

As a result, open heart surgery has been widely regarded as one of the most important medical advances of the 20th century. Today, its application is so widespread (2000 such surgeries performed every 24 hours worldwide) and it is performed so effortlessly and with such low risk at all ages from neonates to octogenarians that it may be very difficult for the current generation of cardiologists and cardiac surgeons, much less the lay public, to appreciate that just 40 years ago, the outer wall of the living human heart presented an impenetrable anatomical barrier to the surgeon's knife and to the truly incredible therapeutic accomplishments that are so commonplace today.

The keystone to this astonishing progress has been cardiopulmonary bypass (CPB) by extracorporeal circulation (ECC). These methods for ECC have allowed surgeons to empty the heart of blood, stop its beat as necessary, open any desired chamber, and safely carry out reparative procedures or even total replacement in an unhurried manner.

Beginning in 1951, a number of the developments that made the transition from the research laboratory to clinical open heart surgery possible and successful occurred in the Department of Surgery at the University of Minnesota (Table 1.1). This institution boasted two unequaled assets. One was the world's first heart hospital devoted entirely to the medical and surgical treatment of heart diseases. This 80-bed facility for pediatric and adult patients was donated to the University of Minnesota by the Variety Club of the Northwest and opened its doors to patients on July 1, 1951.

The second and perhaps even more important advantage was the presence of Owen H. Wangensteen, a truly visionary surgeon, as Chairman of the Department of Surgery. He was not a cardiac surgeon, but he had made immense contributions in the field of general surgery by his innovative work in the treatment and prevention of bowel obstruction.

Over the years, beginning in 1930, he had evolved the unique "Wangensteen system" for the training of young surgeons. He placed a heavy emphasis on in-depth knowledge of the basic sciences and in research. He believed that this combination of a thorough grounding in the basic sciences and the insights gained by research gave young surgeons the confidence to disregard or abandon previously held ideas and traditions and to go forward on the basis of their own judgment and knowledge.

Table 1.1.   Original Open Heart Operations and Techniques Developed at the University of Minnesota, 1952 to 1957

Operation/Technique	Date[a]	Technique
Atrial septal defect closure	September 2, 1952	General hypothermia
Ventricular septal defect closure	March 26, 1954	Cardiopulmonary bypass (by cross-circulation)
Atrioventricularis communis correction	August 6, 1954	Same as above
Tetralogy of Fallot intracardiac correction	August 31, 1954	Same as above
Disposable Bubble Oxygenator for CPB	May 13, 1955	
First use of direct cardiac stimulation by myocardial electrodes with a pacemaker for complete heart block	January 30, 1957	

[a]Dates indicate the first successful use in patients.

Proverbial, also, was his ability to spot talent and capabilities in his younger men, whose aptitudes were not at all obvious to others—often not even to themselves. He would then proceed to develop that student using a combination of intellectual stimulation and material assistance.

THE OPEN HEART ERA IS BORN

Hypothermia

In this stimulating milieu, major accomplishments were soon forthcoming. The first of these occurred on September 2, 1952, when Dr. F. John Lewis, a medical school classmate and close personal friend of the author, after a period of laboratory research on dogs, successfully closed an atrial secundum defect (ASD)(1) in a 5-year-old girl under direct vision utilizing inflow stasis and moderate total-body hypothermia (Fig. 1.1).[a] The date has considerable historical significance because that operation was the world's first successful operation within the open human heart under direct vision. Dr. Lewis had been inspired by Bigelow's experimental studies (2) upon

general body hypothermia as a technique for open heart repairs. Such operations became routine at the University of Minnesota Hospital, and news of these successes spread rapidly throughout the medical world. Swan was the next surgeon to report successful direct vision intracardiac operations in man utilizing general hypothermia and inflow stasis (3).

Hypothermia with inflow stasis proved to be an excellent method for simple atrial defects. Lewis reported in 1954 that eight of his first nine patients had their atrial septal defects successfully closed, with only one death (4). Later in 1954, Lewis, Varco, and Taufic (5) reported on closure of ASD in 11 patients with a mortality of only 18% (Table 1.2).

By 1955, Lewis reported 33 atrial septal defects closed at a 12.1% mortality rate compared to Gross's 30.2% mortality using blind technics (atrial well) (6). Also, the blind atrial well provided significantly fewer complete corrections (6).

Hypothermia also proved excellent for isolated congenital pulmonic or aortic stenoses (3). However, failure was uniform when this technique was applied to more complex lesions such as ostium primum, atrioventricularis communis, or ventricular septal defect (VSD). These experiences reconfirmed the oft-predicted need for a perfusion method for the more complex intracardiac lesions.

---

[a]This first patient had a normal postoperative heart catheterization. She is now the mother of two healthy children and remains entirely well, 40 years after her operation.

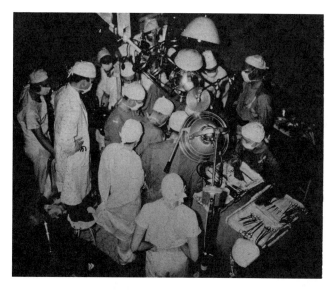

Figure 1.1. Scene in the University of Minnesota Hospital operating room on September 2, 1952, near the end of the first successful open heart operation in medical history. On that date, Dr. F. John Lewis closed by suture an atrial secundum defect (2 cm in diameter) under direct visualization, utilizing inflow stasis and moderate total body hypothermia (26°C), in a 5-year-old girl who remains alive and well today. Postoperative heart catheterization confirmed a complete closure. She is the mother of two normal children.

Table 1.2. Direct Vision Closure Atrial (Secundum) Defect Systemic Hypothermia and Caval Occlusion[a]

Patients	Defects Closed	Deaths
11[b]	10	2 (18%)

[a]Surgery performed by F. J. Lewis, M.D., at the University of Minnesota, 1952 to 1953 (5).
[b]One patient developed ventricular fibrillation and was not repaired, but recovered.

CARDIOPULMONARY BYPASS

Beginning Efforts, Then Discouragement

The first attempts to use a heart-lung machine for total CPB to permit intracardiac surgery in humans were also carried out at the University of Minnesota Hospital by Dennis and colleagues on April 5, 1951 (7). Two patients were operated on within a month's time, but both died in the operating room. The first patient had an erroneous preoperative diagnosis despite two heart catheterizations and finger exploration of the heart's interior 5 months earlier. Instead of the anticipated atrial secundum defect, she had an unexpected partial atrioventricularis communis lesion. This pathology was baffling at the time. The second patient, operated on 2 weeks later, had an atrial secundum defect repaired, but died intraoperatively from massive air embolism (8).

In both of these operations, the failures were related to the high perfusion rates that were considered necessary. In the first patient, in addition to the unfamiliar pathology, Drs. Dennis and Varco stated that they were visually handicapped by "an amazing amount of blood" lost from the coronary sinus and thebesian vein, and "adjacent tissue anteriorly was employed to attempt closure in spite of the recognition of a good deal of encroachment upon the tricuspid orifice" (7). The cardiac specimen was studied by Dr. Jesse Edwards, the world-renowned cardiac pathologist, who found the tricuspid orifice had been severely stenosed in the attempt to close the ostium primum defect (9). In the second patient, the arterial reservoir was emptied suddenly (by the high flow), resulting in air being pumped into the patient's systemic circuit (8). Later in 1951, Dr. Dennis and many of his team moved to the University of New York (Brooklyn) to continue their work.

The next milestone was reached in May 1953 by Dr. John Gibbon, who had started working on a pump oxygenator in

1937 (10). He had developed his apparatus and techniques to the point where 12 of 20 dogs survived the closure of a surgically created VSD for 1 week to 6 months (11). By 1953 he believed he was ready to venture into the clinical area. His first patient had died,[b] but the second case, with an atrial (secundum) defect, was operated on May 6, 1953, and was a complete success (12). This success was well received in a report in the lay press 12 days later (13), but aroused surprisingly little enthusiasm or interest among cardiologists and cardiac surgeons at the time. There were several reasons for this. First, Dr. Gibbon had been able to duplicate only once Dr. Lewis' successes beginning 8 months earlier, and had not been able to repeat or extend his one success (12, 14). Second, Dr. Lewis was regularly closing ASD, under direct vision using inflow stasis and moderate hypothermia with excellent results (1, 4–6). Swan and others (3, 15) were also duplicating these excellent results with ASD.

---

[b]Similar to the experience of Dennis, Gibbon's first patient selected for intracardiac surgery to close an atrial septal defect was a 15-month-old infant with an erroneous preoperative diagnosis. At operation, no septal defect was found. Autopsy disclosed a large unrecognized patent ductus arteriosus. Case 2 was the 18-year-old girl with the successful atrial defect closure. Cases 3 and 4 were both 5½-year-old girls operated on in July 1953, and both died intraoperatively. Case 3 had an ASD, and repair was attempted. Case 4 had been diagnosed preoperatively as having an atrial septal defect, but also had a VSD and small patent ductus. Dr. Gibbon stated that "None of the defects could be repaired because of the flooding of the intracardiac field by blood" inside the bypassed heart (12). Kirklin (14) has written (and also confirmed in a letter to this author) that Gibbon operated on four patients after his May 1953 success and none survived. These last two patients were never reported by Gibbon or associates, and details are not available.

Third, and perhaps most importantly, was the fact that Dr. Gibbon, not being able to repeat his one success with the ASD or to achieve success with the more complex VSD, became so discouraged after five failures (Table 1.3) that he abandoned open heart surgery as a means of repair of human heart lesions. That decision by the dean of the pioneering surgeons at that time had a profound, chilling effect on the minds of many investigators upon the future of open heart surgery.

From 1951 to early 1954, there were many reported—and many more unreported—attempts to utilize CPB for intracardiac operations (Table 1.4). In all of these reported clinical attempts at open heart operations, there was a common scenario: good-to-acceptable survival in the experimental animals, but universal failure when the same apparatus and techniques were applied to humans. Thus, virtually all of the most experienced investigators of that era concluded with seemingly impeccable logic that the problems were not with the perfusion techniques or the heart-lung machines, but that the "sick human heart," ravaged by failure, could not possibly be expected to tolerate the magnitude of the operations required and then recover immediately, with adequate output as occurred when the same machines and techniques were applied to dogs with healthy hearts.

Thus, discouragement was rampant, and pessimism about the future of open heart surgery became widespread.

The prevalent belief was that the concept of open heart repair, however attractive, was doomed for patients with the more complex pathological conditions who urgently required and would benefit the most from corrective procedures. What was necessary, many thought, was a means of mechanical support for the heart during its recovery period. Even today, more than 3 decades later, prolonged mechanical support of the failing heart during recovery still presents many unsolved problems.

Table 1.3. Clinical Experience by J. H. Gibbon with Total Cardiopulmonary Bypass Using His Screen Oxygenator (12, 13)

Patient	Age	Date of Operation	Diagnosis Preop[a]	Postop Results[a]
1	15 months	1953	ASD	Had PDA (only); died in OR
2	18 years	May 6, 1953	ASD	Lived (long term)
3	5½ years	July 1953	ASD	Died in OR
4	5½ years	July 1953	ASD	Had also VSD, PDA; died in OR
5	Data NA[b]	Data NA[b]	Data NA[b]	Died
6	Data NA[b]	Data NA[b]	Data NA[b]	Died
Total: 6 patients				1 *Lived* (ASD), 5 *Died*

[a]PDA, patent ductus arteriosus; VSD, ventricular septal defect; ASD, atrial secundum.
[b]NA, not available.

CARDIOPULMONARY BYPASS— A NEW OUTLOOK

During some canine experiments in which the cavae were temporarily occluded to test tolerance limits of the brain and heart to ischemia (20), we discovered that if the azygos vein was not clamped (but all other inflow to the heart was), the resulting very small cardiac output (measured at 8 to 14 ml/kg body weight per minute) (21), was sufficient to sustain the vital organs safely in *every* animal for a minimum of 30 minutes at normothermia. To even mention, at that time, that such a low flow might be adequate for perfusions was heresy; thus, we were pleased to learn of a similar observation in 1952 in England by Andreason and Watson (22). Both of these studies agreed that only about 10% of the so-called basal cardiac output was needed to sustain animals unimpaired physiologically for a reasonable period of time at normothermia.

From the earliest days, the universally accepted *minimum flow* for cardiopulmonary bypass (at normothermia) was considered by the "authorities" at that time to be 100 to 165 ml/kg per body weight per minute in animals and man (7, 12, 16, 19, 23). Our findings of this remarkable tolerance to drastically lower the flows of only 8 to 14 ml/kg/min was very surprising, but the animal (dog) results were unmistakably clear. In analyzing these findings, we described at that time (1954) at least three identifiable important physiologic adjustments that were occurring in response to lowered blood flow (21). These compensating readjustments were additive, and in their entirety at normal body temperatures accounted very well for the fact that these animals survived for 30 minutes or longer with their vital organs (brain, liver, heart, and kidneys) well protected.

At that time in our studies, we quickly found that "low flow" was a pejorative term, and that advocacy of systemic flows much lower than the so-called basal cardiac output of 100 to 120 ml/kg/min was considered "totally wrong." What most clinicians and even physiologists did not appreciate was the simple fact that with the basal cardiac output, venous blood was returning with 65 to 75% of its oxygen content *unused*. There was no physiologic harm whatsoever in fully utilizing the oxygen contained in the blood. Thus, the "azygos flow was really not low flow, but *physiologic flow*."

Reducing the volume of blood necessary to be pumped had immediate and immense benefits. It has been observed repeatedly that one of the universal problems responsible in a very large part for the early failures with extracorporeal circulation by Dennis (7), Gibbon et al. (12), Helmsworth et al. (16), and others was the enormous and unexpected blood return out of the open hearts due to well-developed systemic-to-pulmonary collaterals that made

Table 1.4. Open Heart Surgery With Total Cardiopulmonary Bypass[a]

Physician	Patients	Age Range	Defects[b]	Method	Date	Died	Lived
						Result	
Dennis (7, 8)	2	6–8 years	ASD, AV Canal	Film oxygenator	1951	2	0
Gibbon (12–14)	6	15 months–18 years	PDA, ASD (2), ASD and VSD (1), NA (2)	Film oxygenator	1953	5	1 (ASD)
Helmsworth (16)	1	4 years	ASD	Bubble oxygenator	1952	1	0
Dodrill (17)	1	NA	Pulmonary stenosis	Autogenous lung	1953	1	0
Mustard (18)	5	10 months–11 years	Tetralogy	Monkey lungs	1951–53	5	0
Clowes (19)	3	Neonate–55 years	Lung disease, AO stenosis, left atrial myxoma	Bubble oxygenator	1953	3	0
Total:	18					Died: 17 (11 O.R.) Lived: 1 (5½%)	

[a]All reported cases from 1951 to 1954, prior to cross-circulation, March 26, 1954.
[b]ASD, atrial secundum; AV canal, atrioventricularis communis; PDA, patent ductus; VSD, ventricular septal defect; NA, not available.

6

accurate vision almost impossible. Also, these unanticipated losses often made the perfusions physiologically precarious.

We immediately appreciated that the discovery of the "azygos flow concept" represented the sword that would eventually sever the Gordian knot of complexity that had garrotted perfusion technology. I was convinced that some simple way could be found to successfully perfuse at only 20 to 25 ml/kg/min, which we set as a desirable flow rate with a comfortable safety margin. This low flow or physiologic flow quantity was only 10 to 20% of what others deemed necessary. Consequently, armed with this information in 1952, I believed that successful open heart surgery was not only possible, but inevitable in the near future.

THE AUTOGENOUS LUNG FOR CPB

The low-flow principle made autogenous lung oxygenation much simpler and thus attractive. However, we found that the extra cannulae and tubing in the operative field were sensitive to even slight displacements, with the subsequent rapid onset of pulmonary edema. This rather frequent complication in our animal studies dampened our enthusiasm for potential clinical use (24). However, these venous drainage kinking problems led directly to the idea of moving these extra pulmonary cannulae completely out of the operative field by utilizing a separate donor animal for oxygenation (cross-circulation).

These experimental studies (24) convinced us that the autogenous lung was not a feasible route to pursue clinically, even with the significant advantages offered by the azygos flow concept.

THE DODRILL EXPERIENCE WITH AUTOGENOUS LUNG PUMP BYPASS

Dodrill et al. (25), in collaboration with the General Motors Corporation engi-

neers in Detroit, had developed a blood pump for animal and clinical use as a right, left, or combined heart bypass with autogenous lung oxygenator. All of their reported clinical experiences have been summarized in Table 1.5. In their series of four patients, three had partial heart bypasses (two left sides, one right side). All three of these lived, but in only one (patient 2) was a therapeutic procedure (pulmonary valvuloplasty) carried out (27). The fourth (patient 3 in Table 1.5) had bypass of both sides of the heart, but did not survive pulmonary valvuloplasty.

In their patients, Dodrill and colleagues used high flow rates (4500 ml/m² or about 56 to 64 ml/kg per body weight. Those perfusion rates led to a significant amount of collateral flow within the bypassed heart making it difficult to open the heart without sizeable blood losses, which made therapeutic maneuvers difficult or impossible. For this and various other reasons, they did not report any further clinical work.

Controlled Cross-Circulation for CPB

Initially, our extracorporeal perfusions using cross-circulation in dogs had been intended only as an interim method to permit some open heart experience in animals without the need for a complex conventional pump-oxygenator, which was unavailable to us at the time. The term controlled refers to the use of a pump to precisely control the balance of the volume of blood flowing into and out of the donor and the patient. However, as the experiments progressed, it became apparent that the dogs undergoing a 30-minute open heart interval utilizing physiologic flow with cross-circulation not only survived at a far higher rate, but recovered far more rapidly when compared with the dogs we had observed undergoing a similar period of

Table 1.5. Dodrill's Clinical Experience With Autogenous Lung-Pump Bypass

Patient	Diagnosis	Date	Procedure	Operation	Postop Result
Male, 41 years	Mitral regurgitation	7/3/52	Pump bypass of left ventricle, 50 minutes	Heart not opened (26); finger exploration of valve	Lived
Male, 16 years	Pulmonary stenosis	10/21/52	Right heart bypass, 25 minutes	Pulmonary (27) valvuloplasty, direct vision	Lived (RV 190 mm, to 59 mm, by catheter)
Unknown	Pulmonary stenosis	Before 9/16/53 (17)	Bypass both sides of heart, autogenous lungs	Pulmonary valvuloplasty	Died (4th day)
Unknown	Mitral disease	Before 9/16/53 (17)	Pump bypass of left ventricle	Mitral valve exposed	Lived

high-flow pump-oxygenator perfusions.[c] The differences were truly astonishing and, for the first time, we realized that this might be the simple and effective clinical method for intracardiac operations for which we were searching. The experimental and clinical data on cross-circulation perfusions, and the reduced or physiological perfusion flow rates based on the azygos flow studies have been documented elsewhere (28, 29).

CROSS-CIRCULATION—CLINICAL APPLICATION

Cross-circulation for clinical intracardiac operations was an immense departure from established surgical practice at the time (1954). The thought of taking a normal human being to the operating room to provide a donor circulation (with potential risks, however small), even temporarily, was considered unacceptable and even "immoral" by some critics. However, we had begun to suspect that there were massive physiological disturbances evoked by total body perfusion and open cardiotomy, about which we knew very little, and that by temporarily instituting a "placental" circulation, we might minimize or even correct those to permit successful operations that would have otherwise been impossible (Figs. 1.1 and 1.2).

The continued lack of any success in the other centers around the world that were working actively on heart-lung bypass (Table 1.4) and the widespread doubt about the feasibility of open heart surgery in man contributed to our decision to go ahead clinically on March 26, 1954 (29) (Fig. 1.3).

The cross-circulation technique was a dramatic success in humans (29–37). In the months that followed its first use to

close a VSD, a rapid succession of surgical firsts occurred for correction of congenital heart defects that previously had been inoperable (Table 1.1). Cross-circulation as the means for extracorporeal circulation to permit work inside the human heart was utilized for 45 operations (Table 1.6). There was no donor mortality and no long-lasting donor sequelae (37).

Almost overnight, the "sick human heart theory" was refuted because the patients operated on with cross-circulation, mostly infants in terminal congestive failure, could not have been worse operative risks. Thus, after 15 years in the experimental laboratory, open heart surgery moved permanently into the clinical arena.

A THREE-DECADE FOLLOW-UP

The follow-up of a minimum of 30 years on these first patients—with VSD, atrioventricularis communis, infundibular pulmonic stenosis, and tetralogy of Fallot—to have successful intracardiac corrections has been particularly informative and impressively sanguine (37). Twenty-eight of the 45 (62%) patients undergoing extracorporeal circulation survived their operations and were discharged from the hospital. Even more impressive was the finding that only six of these survivors had died in 30 years. Thus, 22 of the 45 patients (49%) initially operated on were alive 30 years later, and all were in good health.

The 27 patients with VSDs constituted the largest category to have repair, and 17 (63%) were living and well 30 or more years later. There were only two later VSD patient deaths in all of the years following hospital discharge. Both occurred in patients with closed defects, but inexorable progression of their pulmonary vascular disease.

Similarly, the late follow-up on the more complex tetralogy patients has been equally rewarding (36–39).

Cross-circulation was so successful because the donor automatically corrected

---

[c] In the years 1950 and 1951, Dr. C. Dennis and Dr. C.W. Lillehei had experimental laboratories next door to each other in the attic of the physiology building (Millard Hall) at the University of Minnesota Medical School.

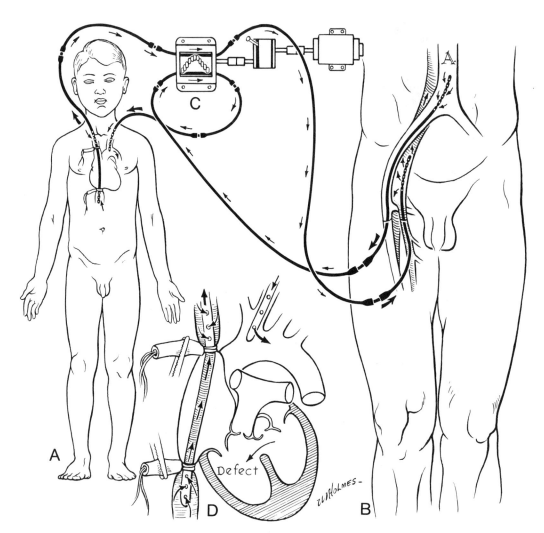

Figure 1.2. A depiction of the method of direct-vision intracardiac surgery utilizing extracorporeal circulation by means of controlled cross-circulation. **A.** The patient, showing sites of arterial and venous cannulations. **B.** The donor, showing sites of arterial and venous (superficial femoral and great saphenous) cannulations. **C.** The single Sigmamotor pump controlling precisely the reciprocal exchange of blood between the patient and donor. **D.** Close-up of the patient's heart, showing the vena caval catheter positioned to draw venous blood from both the superior and inferior venae cavae during the cardiac bypass interval. The arterial blood from the donor was circulated to the patient's body through the catheter that was inserted into the left subclavian artery.

all of the various hematological and metabolic derangements. At that time, we had no idea what these physiological aberrations were, and thus no knowledge about measuring them, much less treating them. In 1954 to 1955, pH and blood gases were not available clinically. Even emergency plasma electrolytes took 4 to 6 hours. There was no respiratory assistance equipment for infants or children, and there were no intensive care units, much less any monitors, pacemakers, or external defibrillators. In temporarily reconstituting the placental circulation with cross-circulation, we rediscovered the world's greatest ICU: "the intrauterine environment." It was some years before we could duplicate these remarkable results in equally sick patients using the pump oxygenator.

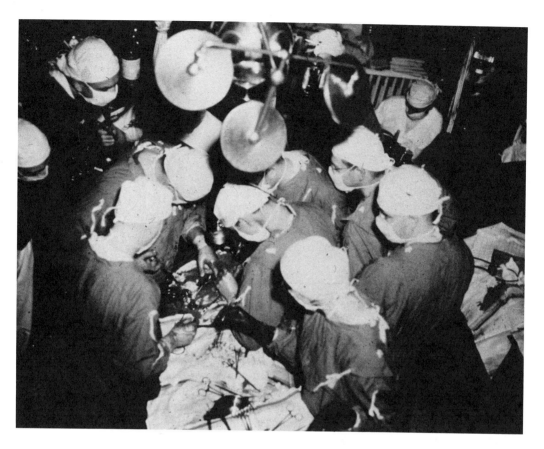

Figure 1.3. The scene on March 26, 1954, in Operating Room B, University of Minnesota Medical Center, during the first controlled cross-circulation operation. At that time a ventricular septal defect was successfully visualized by ventricular cardiotomy and closed in a 12-month-old infant. The lightly anesthetized donor (the patient's father), with the groin cannulations serving as the extracorporeal oxygenator, may be seen to the far right (the patient is in the left foreground). Dr. C. W. Lillehei is immediately to the right of the scrub nurse, and opposite him is Dr. R. L. Varco. Behind Dr. Lillehei is Dr. H. E. Warden, and next to him, looking over the shoulder of the scrub nurse, is Dr. M. Cohen. Drs. Cohen and Warden are the two residents who had perfected this technique in the experimental dog laboratory. To Dr. Varco's right is Dr. J. B. Aust, an assistant resident. Behind Dr. Varco, at the left upper corner, is Dr. V. L. Gott, the surgical intern. Also, behind Dr. Varco is an observer, Dr. Norman Shumway, who was an assistant resident at the time. The VSD was closed by direct suture during a bypass interval of 19 minutes. The average flow rate was 40 ml/kg per body weight per minute at normothermia. The Sigmamotor pump that served to control the interchange of blood is located on Dr. Warden's right between donor and patient. It is not visible in this photo.

PROBLEMS REQUIRING SOLUTIONS FOR SUCCESSFUL OPEN HEART SURGERY

For open intracardiac operations in humans to be regularly successful, workable solutions had to be identified for the three major obstacles that had stalled progress for so long. The first thing needed was an effective method for safely emptying the heart of blood for a reasonable length of time. Extracorporeal circulation by cross-circulation fulfilled that need. Next, having gained access to the interior of the living human heart, it was soon evident that these malformations existed in a very broad spectrum, and in many forms not yet described or even recognized by clinicians or patholo-

Table 1.6.   Results of Direct-Vision Intracardiac Operations With CPB By Cross-Circulation in 45 Patients, from March 26, 1954, to July 9, 1955[a]

Abnormality	Corrective Operations	Patients	Mortality Hospital	Mortality Late (30 years)
VSD	Suture closure	27	8	2
PDA (with severe pulmonary hypertension)	Exploratory ventriculotomy; division of ductus	1	0	0
Tetralogy of Fallot	Closure of VSD; correction of infundibular/valvular pulmonary stenosis	10	5	3
Atrioventricularis communis	Closure of ostium primum, VSD; repair of valvular deformities	5	3	1
Isolated infundibular pulmonary stenosis	Resection of infundibulum	1	0	0
Pulmonary stenosis, ASD, anomalous pulmonary venous return	Pulmonary valvotomy; ventricular and atrial cardiotomies; transposition of anomalous pulmonary veins; closure of septal defects	1	1	0
Totals		45	17	6

[a]Cross-circulation was used exclusively from its inception through February 1955. Beginning March 1, 1955, other bypass methods (bubble oxygenator, dog-lung oxygenator, arterial reservoir) were employed for lower-risk patients. Cross-circulation was reserved for high-risk patients. By July 1955, the bubble oxygenator had become the sole method. VSD, ventricular septal defect; PDA, patent ductus arteriosus; ASD, atrial (secundum) septal defect.

gists. Surgical methods for dealing with these unfamiliar lesions required rapid technical development, often improvised on the spot, and sometimes with poignant failures. Moreover, given the existing state of technology, the preoperative diagnoses were often wrong or incomplete. Finally, these patients, often critically ill preoperatively, required postoperative care on a much higher level of sophistication than was known or available at the time.

Knowing now what we did not know in 1951 through 1954, it seems very probable that the only method for extracorporeal circulation that could possibly have succeeded so rapidly in the face of such formidable problems, in the face of such limited knowledge, and in the many high-risk infants and children with complex anatomical lesions was cross-circulation. The homeostatic mechanisms of the donor automatically corrected the untold number of mostly unknown physiological aberrations evoked by total body perfusion.

Thirty years ago we wrote that "clinical experience with cross-circulation has made it apparent that it is unlikely that a technique for total cardiopulmonary bypass will be developed which excels this one for the patients' safety" (33). The spectacular success of clinical cross-circulation operations stimulated intensive laboratory work on alternative methods for CPB without the need for a living human donor.

Heterologous Biologic Oxygenators

Beginning on March 1, 1955, a series of clinical open heart operations was started at the University of Minnesota utilizing a pair of canine lungs as oxygenators. Twelve patients were operated on and there were four long-term survivors (40, 41). Subsequent to those two reports, two more patients were operated on, to give a total of 14, with 5 long-term survivors. In none of these patients were the deaths attributable to oxygenator dysfunction. The only other attempt to use heterologous lungs at that time was the report of Mustard and associates (18, 42) using monkey lungs. In their series of seven patients, there were no survivors. Mustard and Thomson (18) subsequently reported on surgery utilizing monkey lungs in 21 infants and children having ECC, between 1952 and 1956; there were three survivors in this series.

Extracorporeal Circulation from a Reservoir of Oxygenated Blood

Beginning March 3, 1955, the first of a series of five patients were operated on at the University of Minnesota for intracardiac repairs of VSD or transposition of the great vessels by continuous perfusion from a reservoir of oxygenated blood (30, 43, 44). This very simple technique was particularly applicable to infants needing relatively simple intracardiac repairs, thereby requiring lesser blood requirements.[d] The arterialized venous blood for perfusion was drawn in the blood bank a few hours preoperatively utilizing an ordinary venipuncture in donors whose arms had been immersed in water heated to 45°C for 15 minutes prior to collection, which effectively oxygenated the venous blood.

THE MECHANICAL PUMP OXYGENATOR FOR CPB— BEGINNING OF AN ERA

In two publications in 1955 from the Mayo Clinic, Jones et al. (45) and Donald et al. (46) described their experimental results utilizing the design of the Gibbon-type pump oxygenator as originally built by International Business Machines Corporation (IBM) and modified by the Mayo Clinic (Fig. 1.4). Their first clinical application

---

[d]The patient was operated on utilizing reservoir perfusion March 29, 1955, at age 6 months, weighing 4.7 kg, for closure of a ventricular septal defect. This patient reported upon in 1955 (30, 44) has now been followed 37 years. He was recatheterized in 1964 with findings of normal pulmonary pressures and a completely closed defect. He graduated from college and was a Federal Bureau of Investigation agent for 20 years. He presently heads a private security company.

was March 22, 1955, and a report followed on their first eight patients undergoing open heart surgery (47). Two of their four survivors had ventricular septal defects, one had an atrial septal defect, one had an atrioventricularis communis canal. The four deaths occurred in patients with VSD (two), tetralogy (one), or atrioventricularis communis canal (one) (Table 1.7). Their flow rates varied from 100 to 200 ml per kg body weight. By September 1958, 245 patients had been operated on at the Mayo Clinic by Kirklin and associates (48). In the skillful and thoughtful hands of Dr. John Kirklin and his associates, their initial high mortality declined rapidly.

Advent of the DeWall-Lillehei Bubble Oxygenator

Prior to 1955, there was universal agreement among the world's authorities on extracorporeal circulation that the one way that blood *could not* be arterialized for clinical CPB was by a bubble oxygenator because of potential problems with air embolism. On May 13, 1955, DeWall and Lillehei, based upon their dog laboratory research, began routine clinical use of a simple, disposable bubble oxygenator (Fig. 1.5A). In their first report, Lillehei et al. (49) described surgery for seven patients with closure VSD, five of whom were longtime survivors. The operations took place at normothermia with perfusion rates [utilizing a Sigmamotor pump, (SIGMAMOTOR, INC., Middleport, NY)], of 25 to 30 ml/kg per body weight. All of the seven patients awoke postoperatively, and there was no evidence of neurologic, hepatic, or renal impairment of even a temporary nature.

In an addendum to their paper (49), Lillehei and colleagues reported that a total of 36 patients ranging in age from 16 weeks to 21 years had their hearts and lungs totally bypassed for intracardiac correction utilizing their bubble oxygenator with similar

Figure 1.4.   The Mayo Clinic-Gibbon Screen Oxygenator. This model was used in 1955 during the first series of open heart operations performed by Dr. John Kirklin and associates at the Mayo Clinic, Rochester, Minnesota. (Photo courtesy of J. W. Kirklin).

Table 1.7.   Mayo Clinic Open Heart Experience[a]

Defect	No. of Patients	Lived	Hospital Deaths
Atrial (secundum)	1	1	0
Ventricular	4	2	2
AV Canal[b]	2	1	1
Tetralogy	1	0	1
Totals	8	4	4 (50%)

[a]First Series (March to May 1955) with Mayo-Gibbon Screen Oxygenator (47)
[b]Atrioventricularis communis.

excellent results. The congenital defects successfully corrected were VSD, tetralogy of Fallot, atrioventricularis communis canal, complete transposition, and atrial secundum defects. As the number of patients having open heart surgery by ECC increased rapidly, the bubble oxygenator was refined to increase capacity for adult patients (50) (Figs. 1.5B and C and 1.6).

In the early clinical open heart operations, considerable physiologic and biochemical data (51) were collected, ana-lyzed, and compared to the earlier animal studies (52). This information confirmed the excellence of the patients' physiologic status while undergoing perfusions from the bubble oxygenator at the lower (more physiologic) flow rates based on the azygos flow concept. Tests done by psychologists and neurologists on our patients before and after perfusion detected no significant abnormalities in cerebral function attributable to the perfusions (53).

In a 26 to 31 year follow-up of 106 patients operated on for correction of tetralogy (38), 34 (32%) had college or graduate degrees, including two M.D.s, two Ph.D.s, and one lawyer (LLB). Obviously, putting people on the bubble oxygenator could not be expected to increase intelligence, but these figures were far beyond the average for a random group from the general population, and at the very least confirmed the absence of any significant cerebral dysfunction.

The DeWall-Lillehei bubble oxygenator was an instant success where it was tried because it had so many practical advantages. It was efficient, inexpensive, heat sterilizable, easy to assemble and check, and it had no moving parts. Since it could be assembled from commercially available materials at a small material cost, it was also disposable (Figs. 1.5 and 1.6). The development of the self-contained, unitized plastic sheet oxygenator (Figs. 1.5C and 1.7) in 1956 by Gott and others (54, 55) further improved this system, and played an important role in the tremendous expansion of open heart surgery that occurred after 1956. The revelation that safe perfusion of the body could be maintained with several lengths of plastic tubing, a few clamps, and some oxygen had an explosive effect upon the worldwide development of cardiac surgery (Fig. 1.8). The surgeon's dream of routinely performing intracardiac correction in the open heart had become a reality (56) (Table 1.8).

In the year 1954, there was only one place in the world doing regularly scheduled open heart surgery by extracorporeal circulation, and that center was the University of Minnesota Hospital in Minneapolis (utilizing cross-circulation). Beginning in May of 1955 and well into 1956, there were only two places in the world performing these operations, the University of Minnesota in Minneapolis, and the Mayo Clinic in Rochester, Minnesota, only 90 miles apart. Visitors from all parts of the world traveled to these two places to observe open heart surgery. On the one hand, there was the Mayo Clinic-Gibbon apparatus, which was very expensive, handcrafted, and very impressive in appearance, but difficult to use and maintain. On the other hand, there was the unbelievably simple, disposable, heat-sterilized bubble-oxygenator of DeWall and Lillehei, costing only a few dollars to assemble. It is no wonder, as Professor Naef (57) has written that, "Many surgeons left these two clinics with their minds in a totally confused state as to which method they should seek to pursue."

Dr. Denton Cooley (58), an early visitor and observer in June of 1955, was to later write,

"The contrast between the two institutions and the two surgeons was striking. We observed

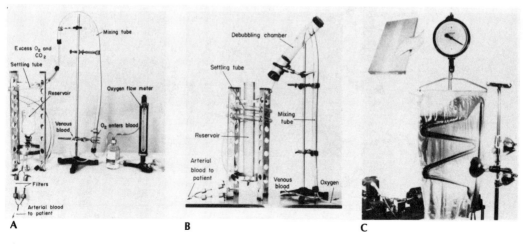

A   B   C

Figure 1.5. Evolution of the simple disposable DeWall-Lillehei bubble oxygenator for open heart surgery. **A.** The first 1955 clinical model; it was successful in infants and small children. **B.** Later in 1955, helix reservoir model with adult capacity was developed. **C.** A 1956 commercially manufactured model, shipped sterile in a package (left upper inset), ready to hang up and use.

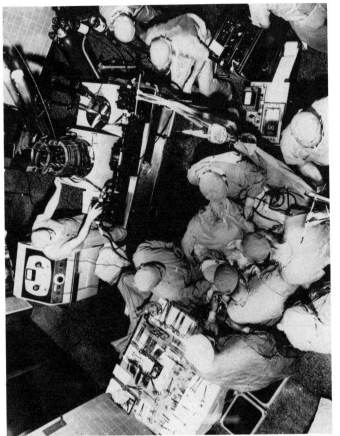

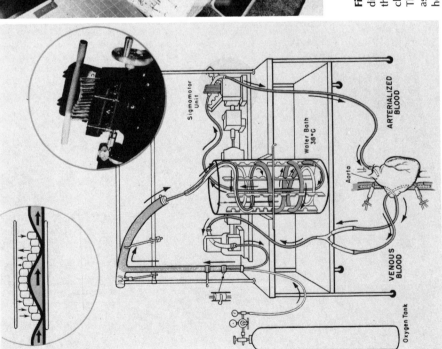

Figure 1.6. *Left.* A diagrammatic portrayal of the 1955 DeWall-Lillehei helix reservoir, disposable bubble oxygenator with adult capacity. The upright oxygenating column with the venous blood mixing with oxygen bubbles formed at the base, transverse debubbling chamber, and the spiral (helix) debubbling reservoir immersed in a water bath are evident. The two insets show the wave-like pattern of the Sigmamotor pump's 12 metallic "fingers" as they stroke the blood through the plastic tubing without direct contact. *Right.* An open heart operation in an adult patient at the University of Minnesota Hospital in 1956.

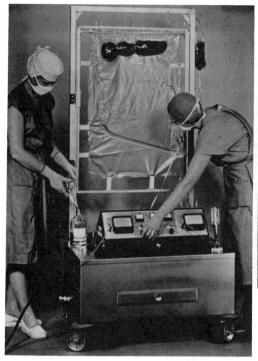

Figure 1.7. *Left.* A DeWall-Lillehei unitized plastic, sheet oxygenator, commercially manufactured and shipped sterile ready to hang up, prime, and use as shown here. (Photo courtesy D. A. Cooley). *Right.* The Temptrol disposable bubble oxygenator with self-contained heat exchanger during a perfusion. In this unit, Dr. DeWall introduced the rigid, presterilized plastic outer shell, which has been the basis of all subsequent oxygenator designs for both bubble and membrane units.

Lillehei and a team composed mostly of house staff correct a ventricular septal defect using cross-circulation. During the visit, we also saw an oxygenator developed by Richard DeWall at the University of Minnesota. The next day we observed John Kirklin and his impressive team in Rochester that was made up of physiologists, biochemists, cardiologists, and others as they performed operations using the Mayo-Gibbon apparatus. Such a device was beyond my organizational capacity and financial reach. Thus I was deeply disappointed on our return to Houston when Dr. McNamara stated that he would not permit me to operate on his patients unless I had a Mayo-Gibbon apparatus."

However, Cooley succeeded in convincing some of his cardiologists that, "the era of open heart surgery had arrived," and in 1956 began to perform open heart surgery utilizing the DeWall-Lillehei bubble oxygenator with considerable success.

Professor Naef (57) also later wrote, "The homemade helix reservoir bubble ox-ygenator of DeWall and Lillehei, first used clinically on May 13, 1955, went on to conquer the world and helped many teams to embark on the correction of malformations inside the heart in a precise and unhurried manner. The road to open-heart surgery had been opened."

The Rotating Disc Film Oxygenator (Kay-Cross).

After finishing his surgical training at the University of Minnesota in 1953,[e] Dr. Frederick Cross moved to Cleveland, where

---

[e] Dr. Fred Cross was one of the surgery residents at the University of Minnesota who assisted on the world's first successful open heart operation, closure of an ASD under hypothermia, on September 2, 1952 (1).

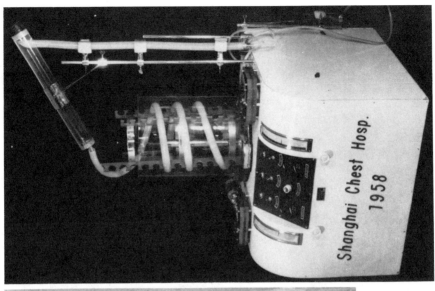

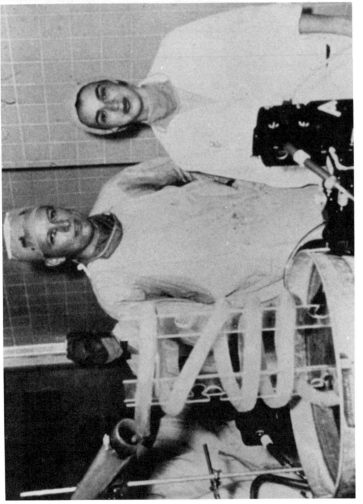

Figure 1.8. The ready availability of the simple and effective, disposable Helix Reservoir Bubble Oxygenator had an explosive effect upon worldwide growth of open heart surgery. *Left.* Dr. Denton Cooley with a perfusionist after an atrial septal defect closure, September 12, 1957, in Caracas, Venezuela. *Right.* The equipment utilized by Professor Pan Chih and associates for many successful open heart operations at the Shanghai Chest Hospital in China, 1957 to 1958. The first successful cardiac operations utilizing CPB in both China and Japan were done with the DeWall-Lillehei bubble oxygenator.

he developed with Earl Kay in 1956 a rotating disc oxygenator that had wide use in the later 1950s, particularly in the U.S. This oxygenator, called the Kay-Cross apparatus (59, 60), was based on the earlier experimental work of Bjork (61). It had multiple vertical discs placed on a horizontal axis that rotated, with the discs dipping into a pool of venous blood, creating a film on the discs in an atmosphere of oxygen. This filming unit, like the Mayo Clinic-Gibbon film oxygenator, was capable of good oxygenation, but both, being nondisposable, shared similar problems: cumbersome to use, large priming volumes, very difficult and tedious to clean and sterilize, and rapid loss of efficiency if hemodilution was attempted. However, the Kay-Cross unit became commercially available in contrast to the Mayo Clinic-Gibbon machine, which

was extremely expensive to handcraft and was not available commercially in those early years. Although this oxygenator certainly accomplished its purpose, the rotating disc mechanism had clinical limitations, in addition to its cumbersome assembly and maintenance. Disc oxygenation was later supplanted everywhere by bubble oxygenation and perfusionists no longer had to plan to spend all day setting up for the next surgery. The blood bank personnel were equally grateful at its passing.

Robert E. Gross, who pioneered cardiac surgery in 1938 with his brilliantly conceived ligation of patent ductus, began open heart surgery with CPB at the Boston Children's Hospital in 1956 (Table 1.9). For his first patient, who died after a pulmonary valvuloplasty, he had utilized a screen pump oxygenator modeled after the Gibbon machine, but constructed in the Harvard laboratories by an engineer, Mr. Savage.

Dr. Dwight Harken, who also used this oxygenator, has told the author that the unit was cumbersome, not heat sterilizable, required a very large priming volume, was inefficient as an oxygenator, and was extremely noisy (62).

Gross was also disturbed by the performance of this device, and instituted a

Table 1.8. Open Cardiotomy: Summary of the Early Clinical Experience at the University of Minnesota Hospitals (56)

Method	Period	No. of Patients
Hypothermia only	1952–1956	70
Cross-circulation	1954–1955	45
Arterial reservoir	1955	5
Dog-lung oxygenator	1955	14
Bubble oxygenator	1955–1966	2581
Total		2715

Table 1.9. Open Heart Surgery by Extracorporeal Circulation[a]

Patient/Age (years)			Date of Surgery	Procedure[b]	Result	
1	F	6	5/24/56	Pulmonary valvuloplasty	Died	
2	F	10	1/13/57	Aortic valvuloplasty	Died	
3	M	12	1/17/57	ASD closure		Lived
4	F	13	2/14/57	Pulmonary valvuloplasty		Lived
5	F	7	2/21/57	ASD closure		Lived
6	F	9	2/26/57	ASD closure	Died	
7	M	8	4/2/57	Pulmonary valvuloplasty		Lived
8	F	6	4/4/57	VSD closure	Died	
9	M	8	4/11/57	VSD closure	Died	
10	F	3	4/18/57	VSD closure	Died	
11	F	9	4/20/57	VSD closure, pulmonary valvuloplasty	Died	
12	F	14	4/25/57	VSD closure	Died	
Totals					8 Died (67%)	4 Lived

[a]Early experience of R. E. Gross (63), Boston Children's Hospital. The first patient was operated upon utilizing the Harvard screen oxygenator, and the remaining with the Kay-Cross rotating disc film oxygenator.
[b]ASD, atrial septal defect; VSD, ventricular septal defect.

moratorium on open heart surgery in his unit for almost 8 months. He restarted CPB in January 1957, utilizing the Kay-Cross oxygenator with high flow (2.3 to 2.5 liters/m²/min) at normothermia and without hemodilution. In the next 3½ months, a total of 11 patients had been operated on with a disastrously high mortality rate of 67% (Table 1.9).

Gross persisted with the same equipment and methods, and even at the time of his Shattuck Lecture to the Massachusetts Medical Society in Boston on May 20, 1959, his operative mortality remained very high. He reported a 13% early mortality for pulmonary valvuloplasty, a 40% mortality for VSD closure, and recommended against intracardiac correction in cyanotic tetralogies (64).

Looking at these results is a clear reiteration of a lesson that many pioneer cardiac surgeons had to learn, "that even consummate surgical skill could not compensate for deficiencies in perfusion physiology."

The Kay-Cross filming unit appealed to the cardiac surgeons who at that time could not or refused to believe that bubble oxygenation was more efficient, safer, ideally adapted for hemodilution, yet vastly simpler to use and less expensive than the filming units. Even the Mayo Clinic had by 1971 converted almost entirely to the use of the bubble oxygenator (65). By 1976 it was estimated that 90% of all open heart operations worldwide involved the use of a bubble oxygenator (66).

Other oxygenators for CPB that were publicly known and worthy of mention, but had moderate to ephemeral clinical applications, were those of Rygg and Kyvsgaard[f] (67) (bubble), Dennis (8) (film), Clark et al. (68) (bubble), Craaford and Senning (69) (film and bubble), Clowes et al. (19) (bubble), Clowes and Neville (70) (membrane), Melrose (71) (film), and Gerbode et al. (72) (membrane). For more information on these devices, the reader is referred to the references cited as a starting point, and also to two fine review articles by DeWall and colleagues (73, 74).

MEMBRANE OXYGENATORS

Kolff and associates (75) described a disposable membrane oxygenator for experimental use in 1956. Clowes and Neville (70) described their experimental studies with membrane oxygenation and a complex apparatus they considered suitable for clinical perfusions in 1958. The belief that membrane oxygenation gives a better perfusion than the bubble or film oxygenators has been clear only with perfusions exceeding 8 hours in duration. Confusion has arisen over the innumerable comparative studies of membrane versus bubble oxygenators in shorter perfusions. With perfusions lasting 6 to 8 hours, the membrane oxygenator is associated with less reduction of platelets, less complement activation, less postoperative bleeding, and fewer microemboli. Since ECC times for most cardiac procedures are 2 to 3 hours or less, it has been difficult to prove that these changes, which are for the most part readily reversible, have any permanent side effects. Some studies have failed to show the theoretical benefits of membrane over bubble oxygenation (76–78), while other published data demonstrate improved hematologic tolerance of CPB with membrane oxygenators (79–81). The author, with Lande and others (82), described in 1967 the first compact, disposable, commercially manufactured membrane oxygenator for clinical use.

FURTHER DEVELOPMENTS IN BUBBLE OXYGENATION

In 1966, DeWall et al. (83) made a very significant advance in oxygenator de-

[f]The Rygg bubble oxygenator (67) was a replica of the DeWall-Lillehei technology that was manufactured in Denmark, and had usage particularly in countries where U.S. patents did not apply.

sign with the introduction of a hard-shell bubble oxygenator with an integrated oxygenator and omnithermic heat exchanger in a disposable, presterilized, polycarbonate unit (Fig. 1.7). The adequacy of oxygenation and acid-base balance was amply documented (84, 85). The integrated hard-shell concept has been the basis of all subsequent refinements, both in the bubble and membrane oxygenators (Fig. 1.9).

In the early days of open heart surgery, postoperative cerebral dysfunction was a subject of intense interest. As the major causes were identified and resolved (53), concern over this matter decreased. However, there has been a resurgence of interest in the detection and prevention of more subtle changes in personality and intellect that may be associated with an otherwise successful CPB (86–89). The reality and frequency of these changes, as well as the need for continuous EEG monitoring for immediate correction of problems, are under study (90).

HEMODILUTION

One of the major technologic advances that has had an astonishing effect upon the growth of ECC was the knowledge that the pump oxygenators could be primed with nonblood solutions, thereby immensely reducing the need for blood donors, and at the same time improving the quality of perfusions by a reduction in viscosity and the safety by reducing foreign blood. Zuhdi and colleagues developed the theory and process of hemodilution in 1961 (91–93); they had trained in cardiac surgery at the University of Minnesota. DeWall and colleagues (94, 95) confirmed the benefits of hypothermic hemodilution in ECC. Other hemodilution studies were reported from the Minnesota group that confirmed the value of low molecular weight dextran (96–98). Other comparative studies were carried out that demonstrated the value of hemodilution with differing perfusates for improving renal blood flow and lessening hemolysis (99, 100). Further, the beneficial effects of hemodilution and antiadrenergic drugs on the prevention of renal ischemia during ECC were confirmed (101, 102).

Figure 1.9. The Maxima (Medtronic) hollow fiber membrane oxygenator is a widely used state-of-the-art device. This disposable unit and similar competitive devices such as those of Cobe, Terumo, Sarns, Shiley, and Bard, have rigid outer shells with integrated heat exchangers, easily attached venous reservoirs and cardiotomy suction chambers, low priming volumes, and efficient gas transfer. Their ease of use and more competitive price differentials versus the bubblers have resulted in increasing use for routine open heart procedures.

PROGRESS IN PUMP DESIGN

In the earliest days of ECC, the multicam-activated, Sigmamotor pump was used. Then the roller pumps, because of their ease of use and reliability, gained popularity. In more recent years, the centrifugal pump described by Rafferty and coworkers in 1968 (103) has become commercially available as the Biomedicus Biopump[g] (Fig. 1.10). Some of the advantages of this pump are reliability, ease of use over a wide range of flows, less likelihood to pump air, absence of spallation, and low hemolysis. This pump was originally developed and used for perfusions lasting hours or days. However, surgeons in growing numbers have been impressed by the centrifugal pump's performance and advantages and have begun in increasing numbers to use it for routine ECC.

As extracorporeal circulation became predictably reliable for a wide variety of congenital malformations, beginning in 1956 open cardiotomy was successfully applied to revolutionize the treatment of patients with acquired valvular heart disease (104, 105) and, subsequently, to the treatment of an even larger group afflicted with coronary arteriosclerosis (106, 107). By 1967, the ultimate landmark of successful human heart transplantation was reached by two surgeons, Drs. Barnard and Shumway, who had trained together in the late 1950s

---

[g]The Biopump is marketed by BioMedicus, Inc., a division of Medtronic, Inc., 7000 Central Avenue NE, Minneapolis, MN 55432.

in the author's cardiac program at the University of Minnesota.

Today, the primary challenge is the need to further widen the benefits of heart replacement by both increasing the availability of donors and by an effective permanent intracorporeal mechanical heart. This latter seems a likelihood in the foreseeable future. Because of the shortage of donors, only 10 to 12% of potential recipients are being served. Short of a breakthrough with xenotransplantation (which is quite possible), the gap inevitably will have to be filled by a reliable, practical, fully implantable, total artificial heart.

SUMMARY

Cardiopulmonary bypass by extracorporeal circulation for open heart surgery, and even replacement of the heart itself, were just dreams only 40 years ago. Today, after millions of total body perfusions, CPB has become a standard, widely used, low-risk procedure with immense benefits to mankind.

This chapter has attempted to tell how we got where we are today by a worldwide catalytic combination of research, heterodoxy, and serendipity.

Figure 1.10.   The BioMedicus disposable centrifugal flow blood pump, with ease of use over a wide range of flows, and a number of other advantages (see text), has gained steadily increasing acceptance for routine open heart operations, and also for longer time circulatory support. Three sizes are available.

REFERENCES

1. Lewis FJ, Taufic M. Closure of atrial septal defects with the aid of hypothermia; experimental accomplishments and the report of one successful case. Surgery 1953;33:52–59.
2. Bigelow, WG, Callaghan JC, Hopps JA. General hypothermia for experimental intracardiac surgery. Ann Surg 1950;132:531–539.
3. Swan H. Zeavin I, Blount SG Jr, Virtue RW. Surgery by direct vision in the open heart during hypothermia. JAMA 1953;1081–1085.
4. Lewis FJ. In discussion: Bigelow WG, Mustard WT, Evans JG. Some physiologic concepts of hypothermia and their applications to cardiac surgery. J Thorac Surg 1954;28:463–480.
5. Lewis FJ, Varco RL, Taufic M. Repair of atrial septal defects in man under direct vision with the aid of hypothermia. Surgery 1954;36:538–556.
6. Lewis FJ. In discussion: Watkins E, Gross RE: Experiences with surgical repair of atrial septal defects. J Thorac Surg 1955;30:469–491.
7. Dennis C, Spreng DS Jr, Nelson GE, et al. Development of a pump-oxygenator to replace the heart and lungs; an apparatus applicable to human patients and application to one case. Ann Surg 1951;134:709–721.
8. Dennis C. Perspective in review: one group's struggle with development of a pump-oxygenator. Trans Am Soc Artif Intern Organs 1985; 31:1–11.
9. Edwards JE. Personal communication, 1951.
10. Gibbon JH Jr. Artificial maintenance of circulation during experimental occlusion of pulmonary artery. Arch Surg 1937;34:1105–1131.
11. Gibbon JH Jr, Miller BJ, Dobell AR, Engell HC, Voight GB. The closure of interventricular septal defects in dogs during open cardiotomy with the maintenance of the cardiorespiratory functions by a pump oxygenator. J Thorac Surg 1954;28:235–240.
12. Gibbon JH Jr. Application of a mechanical heart and lung apparatus to cardiac surgery. Minn Med 1954;37:171–185.
13. Historic Operation. Time News Magazine, May 1953:70.
14. Kirklin JW. Open heart surgery at the Mayo Clinic—the 25th Anniversary. Mayo Clinic Proc 1980;50:339.
15. Swan H. In discussion: Lewis FJ, Varco RL, Taufic M. Repair of atrial septal defects in men under direct vision with the aid of hypothermia. Surgery 1954;36:538–556.
16. Helmsworth JA, Clark LC Jr, Kaplan S, Sherman RT. An oxygenator pump for use in total bypass of heart and lungs. J Thorac Surg 1953;26:617–631.
17. Dodrill FD. In discussion: Gibbon JH Jr. Artificial maintenance of circulation during experimental occlusion of pulmonary artery. Arch Surg 1937;34:1105–1131.
18. Mustard WT, Thomson JA. Clinical experience with the artificial heart lung preparation. J Can Med Assoc 1957;76:265–269.
19. Clowes GHA Jr, Neville WE, Hopkins A, Anzola J, Simeone A. Factors contributing to the success of failure in the use of a pump oxygenator for complete bypass of the heart and lung, experimental and clinical. Surgery 1954;36: 557–579.
20. Cohen M, Hammerstrom RW, Spellman MW, Varco RL, Lillehei CW. The tolerance of the canine heart to temporary complete vena caval occlusion. Surg Forum 1952;3:172–177.
21. Cohen M, Lillehei CW. A quantitative study of the "azygos factor" during vena caval occlusion in the dog. Surg Gynecol Obstet 1954;98:225.
22. Andreason AT, Watson F. Experimental cardiovascular surgery. Br J Surg 1952;39:548.
23. Gibbon JH Jr. The maintenance of life during experimental occlusion of the pulmonary artery followed by survival. Surg Genecol Obstet 1939;69:602.
24. Cohen M, Lillehei CW. Autogenous lung oxygenator with total cardiac bypass for intracardiac surgery. In: Surgical Forum, Clinical Congress of the American College of Surgeons, Philadelphia: WB Saunders, 1953;4:34–40.
25. Dodrill FD, Hill E, Gerish RA. Some physiologic aspects of the artificial heart problem. J Thorac Surg 1952;24:134–150.
26. Dodrill ARC, Hill E, Gerish A. Temporary mechanical substitute for the left ventricle in man. JAMA 1952;150:642–644.
27. Dodrill FD, Hill E, Gerisch RA, Johnson A, et al. Pulmonary valvuloplasty under direct vision using the mechanical heart for a complete bypass of the right heart in a patient with congenital pulmonary stenosis. J Thorac Surg 1953;26:584–597.
28. Warden HE, Cohen M, DeWall RA, Schultz EA, Buckley JJ, Read RC, Lillehei CW. Experimental closure of intraventricular septal defects and further physiologic studies on controlled cross circulation. Surg Forum 1954;5:22–28.
29. Warden HE, Cohen M, Read RC, Lillehei CW. Controlled cross circulation for open intracardiac surgery. J Thorac Surg 1954;28:331.
30. Lillehei CW, Cohen M, Warden HE, et al. In: Proceedings of Henry Ford Hospital Symposium. Direct Vision Intracardiac Surgery. By Means of Controlled Cross Circulation or Continuous Arterial Reservoir Perfusion for Correction of Ventricular Septal Defects, Atrioventricularis Communis, Isolated Infundibular Pulmonic Stenosis, and Tetralogy of Fallot. Philadelphia: WB Saunders, 1955;371–392.
31. Lillehei CW. Controlled cross circulation for

direct vision intracardiac surgery correction of ventricular septal defects, atrioventricularis communis, and tetralogy of Fallot. Postgrad Med 1955;17:388–396.

32. Lillehei CW, Cohen M, Warden HEE, Varco RL. The direct vision intracardiac correction of congenital anomalies by controlled cross circulation; results in 32 patients with ventricular septal defects, tetralogy of Fallot, and atrioventricular communis defects. Surgery 1955; 38:11.

33. Lillehei CW, Cohen M, Warden HE, et al. Direct vision intracardiac surgical correction of the tetralogy of Fallot, pentalogy of Fallot, and pulmonary atresia defects; report of first ten cases. Ann Surg 1955;142:418.

34. Lillehei CW, Cohen M, Warden HE, et al. The results of direct vision closure of ventricular septal defects in eight patients by means of controlled cross circulation. Surg Gynecol Obstet 1955;101:446.

35. Lillehei CW, Cohen M, Warden HE, Varco RL. Complete anatomical correction of the tetralogy of Fallot defects: report of a successful surgical case. Arch Surg 1956;73:526.

36. Lillehei CW. A personalized history of extracorporeal circulation. ASAIO J 1982;28:5–16.

37. Lillehei CW, Varco RL, Cohen M, et al. The first open heart repairs of ventricular septal defect, atrioventricular communis, and tetralogy of Fallot using extracorporeal circulation by cross circulation: a 30-year follow-up. Ann Thorac Surg 1986;41:4–21.

38. Lillehei CW, Varco RL, Cohen M, et al. The first open heart corrections of tetralogy of Fallot. A 26-31 year follow-up of 106 patients. Ann Surg 1986;204:490–502.

39. Gott VL. C. Walton Lillehei and total correction of tetralogy of Fallot. Ann Thorac Surg 1990;49:328–332.

40. Campbell GS, Crisp NW, Brown EB. Total cardiac bypass in humans utilizing a pump and heterologous lung oxygenator (dog lungs). Surgery 1956;40:364.

41. Campbell GS, Vernier R, Varco RL, Lillehei CW. Traumatic ventricular septal defect. Report of two cases. J Thorac Surg 1959;37:496.

42. Mustard WT, Chute AL, Keith JD, Sirek A, Rowe RD, Valad P. A surgical approach to transposition of the great vessels with extracorporeal circuit. Surgery 1954;36:39.

43. Warden HE, DeWall RA, Read RC, et al. Total cardiac bypass utilizing continuous perfusion from a reservoir of oxygenated blood. Proc Soc Exp Biol Med 1955;90:246–250.

44. Warden HE, Read RC, DeWall RA, et al. Direct vision intracardiac surgery by means of a reservoir of "arterialized venous" blood. J Thorac Surg 1955;30:649–657.

45. Jones RE, Donald DE, Swan HJC, Harshbarger HG, Kirklin JW, Wood EH. Apparatus of the Gibbon type for mechanical bypass of the heart and lungs. Mayo Clinic Proc 1955;30:105.

46. Donald DE, Harshbarger HG, Hetzel PS, Patrick RT, Wood EH, Kirklin JW. Experiences with a heart lung bypass (Gibbon type) in the experimental laboratory. Mayo Clinic Proc 1955; 30:113.

47. Kirklin JW, DuShane JW, Patrick RT, et al. Intracardiac surgery with the aid of a mechanical pump oxygenator system (Gibbon type): report of eight cases. Mayo Clinic Proc 1955;30:201.

48. Kirklin JW, McGoon DC, Patrick RT, Theye RT. What is adequate perfusion. In: Moore FD, Morrow AG, Swan H, eds. Extracorporeal Circulation. Springfield, IL: Charles C Thomas, 1958.

49. Lillehei CW, DeWall RA, Read RC, Warden HE, Varco RL. Direct vision intracardiac surgery in man using a simple, disposable artificial oxygenator. Dis Chest 1956;29:1–8.

50. DeWall RA, Warden HE, Read RC, et al. A simple, expendable, artificial oxygenator for open heart surgery. Surg Clin North Am 1956;1025–1034.

51. DeWall RA, Warden HE, Gott VL, Read RC, Varco RL, Lillehei CW. Total body perfusion for open cardiotomy utilizing the bubble oxygenator. J Thorac Surg 1956;32:591–603.

52. DeWall RA, Warden HE, Varco RL, Lillehei CW. The helix reservoir pump-oxygenator. Surg Gynecol Obstet 1957;104:699–710.

53. Hodges PC, Sellers RD, Story JL, Stanley PH, Torres F, Lillehei CW. The effects of total cardiopulmonary bypass procedures upon cerebral function evaluated by the electroencephalogram and a blood brain barrier test. In: Moore FD, Morrow AG, Swan H, eds. Extracorporeal Circulation. Springfield, IL: Charles C Thomas, 1958:279–294.

54. Gott VL, DeWall RA, Paneth M, et al. A self-contained, disposable oxygenator of plastic sheet for intracardiac surgery. Thorax 1957; 12:1–9.

55. Gott VL, Sellers RD, DeWall RA, Varco RL, Lillehei CW. A disposable unitized plastic sheet oxygenator for open heart surgery. Dis Chest 1957;32:615–625.

56. Lillehei CW, Varco RL, Ferlic RM, Sellers RD. Results in the first 2,500 patients undergoing open heart surgery at the University of Minnesota Medical Center. Surgery 1967;62: 819–832.

57. Naef AP. The story of thoracic surgery. Toronto: Hografe and Huber, 1990:113–119.5

58. Cooley DA. Recollections of early development and later trends in cardiac surgery. J Thorac Cardiovasc Surg 1989;98:817–822.

59. Cross FS, Berne RM, Hirsoe Y, Kay EB. Descrip-

tion and evaluation of a rotating disc type reservoir oxygenator. Surgical Forum 1956;7:274.

60. Kay EB, Zimmerman HA, Berne RM, Hirose Y, Jones RD, Cross FS. Certain clinical aspects in the use of the pump oxygenator. JAMA 1956; 162,639.

61. Bjork VO. Brain perfusions in dogs with artificially oxygenated blood. Acta Chir Scand 1948;96(suppl):137.

62. Harken DE, personal communication, May 1992.

63. Gross RE, unpublished data, 1992.

64. Gross RE. Shattuck lecture. Open heart surgery for repair of congenital defects. N Engl J Med 1959;260:1047–1057.

65. Barnhorst DE, Moffitt EA, McGoon DC. Clinical use of the Bentley-Temptrol oxygenator system. In: Ionescu MI, Wooler GH, eds. Current Techniques in Extracorporeal Circulation. London: Butterworths, 1976.

66. Bartlett RH, Harken DE. Instrumentation for cardiopulmonary bypass-past, present, and future. Med Instrum 1976;10:119–124.

67. Rygg IH, Kyvsgaard E. A disposable polyethylene oxygenator system applied in a heart-lung machine. Acta Chir Scand 1956;112: 433.

68. Clark LC Jr, Gollan F, Gupta VB. The oxygenation of blood by gas dispersion. Science 1950;111:85–87.

69. Craaford CA, Senning A. Utvecklingen av extracorporeal cirkulation med hjart-lungmaskin. Nordisk Med 1956;56:1263.

70. Clowes GHA Jr, Neville WE. The membrane oxygenator. In Allen JG, ed. Extracorporeal Circulation. Springfield, IL: Charles C Thomas, 1958;81–100.

71. Melrose DM. A mechanical heart-lung for use in man. Br Med J 1953;2:57–66.

72. Gerbode F, Osborn JJ, Bramson ML. Experiences in the development of a membrane heart-lung machine. Am J Surg 1967;114:16.

73. DeWall RA, Grage TB, McFee AS, Chiechi MA. Theme and variations on blood oxygenators. Surgery 1961;50:931–940.

74. DeWall RA, Grage TB, McFee AS, Chiechi MA. Theme and variation on blood oxygenators. II. Film oxygenators. Surgery 1962;51:251–257.

75. Kolff WJ, Effler DB, Groves LJ, Peereboom G, Moraca PP. Disposable membrane oxygenator (heart-lung machine) and its use in experimental surgery. Cleve Clin Q 1956;23:69–97.

76. Edmunds LH Jr, Ellison N, Colman RW, et al. Platelet function during cardiac operations. Comparison of membrane and bubble oxygenators. J Thorac Cardiovasc Surg 1982;83: 805–812.

77. Sade RM, Bartles DM, Dearing JP, Campbell LJ,

Loadholt CB. A prospective randomized study of membrane and bubble oxygenators in children. Ann Thorac Surg 1980;29:502–511.

78. Trumbell HR, Howe J, Mottl K, Nicoloff DM. A comparison of the effects of membrane and bubble oxygenators on platelet counts and platelet size in elective cardiac operations. Ann Thorac Surg 1980;30:52–57.

79. van den Dungen JAM, Karlicek GF, Brenken U, Homan van der Heide JN, Wildevuur CRH. Clinical study of blood trauma during perfusion with membrane and bubble oxygenators. J Thorac Cardiovasc Surg 1982;83:108–116.

80. Van Deveren W, Kazatchkine VDW, Descamps-Latscha B, et al. Deleterious effects of cardiopulmonary bypass. A prospective study of bubble versus membrane oxygenation. J Thorac Cardiovasc Surg 1985;89:888–889.

81. Boers M, van den Dungen JJAM, Karlicek GF, Brenken U, Homan van der Heide JN, Wildevuur CRH. Two membrane oxygenators and a bubbler. A clinical comparison. Ann Thorac Surg 1983;35:455–462.

82. Lande AJ, Dos SJ, Carlson RG, et al. A new membrane oxygenator-dialyzer. Surg Clin North Am 1967;47:1461–1470.

83. DeWall RA, Bentley DJ, Hirose M, Battung V, Najafi H, Roden T. A temperature controlling (omnithermic) disposable bubble oxygenator for total body perfusion. Dis Chest 1966; 49,207.

84. DeWall RA, Najafi H, Roden T. A hard shell temperature controlling disposable blood oxygenator. JAMA 1966;197:1065.

85. Kalke BR, Castaneda A, Lillehei CW. A clinical evaluation of the new Temptrol (Bentley) disposable blood oxygenator. J Thorac Cardiovasc Surg 1969;57:679.

86. Aberg T, Kihlgren M, Jonsson L, et al. Improved cerebral protection during open-heart surgery. A psychometric investigation on 339 patients. In: Becker R, et al., eds. Psychopathological and neurological dysfunctions following open-heart surgery. Berlin: Springer-Verlag, 1982; 343–351.

87. Aberg T, Ahlund P, Kihlgren M. Intellectual function late after open heart operation. Ann Thorac Surg 1983;36:680–683.

88. Henriksen L. Evidence suggestive of diffuse brain damage following cardiac operations. Lancet 1984;1:816–820.

89. Shaw PJ, Bates D, Carlidge NEF, et al. Early neurological complications of coronary artery bypass surgery. Br Med J 1985;291:1384–1387.

90. Arom KV, Cohen DE, Strobl FT. Effect of intraoperative intervention on neurological outcome based on electroencephalographic monitoring during cardiopulmonary bypass. Ann Thorac Surg 1989;48:476–483.

91. Zuhdi N, McCollough B, Carey J, Krieger K, Greer A. Hypothermic perfusion for open heart surgical procedures—report of the use of a heart lung machine primed with five percent dextrose in water inducing hemodilution. J Int Coll Surg 1961;35:319.

92. Zuhdi N, McCollough B, Carey J, Greer A. Double helical reservoir heart lung machine designed for hypothermic perfusion primed with five percent glucose in water inducing hemodilution. Arch Surg 1961;82:320.

93. Zuhdi N. Discussion of paper by YEH TJ, Ellison LT, Ellison RG. Hemodynamic and Metabolic Responses to Cardiopulmonary Bypass (JTH & C.V Surg 1961;42:782–792.) J Thorac Cardiovasc Surg 1961;42:827.

94. DeWall R, Lillehei CW. Simplified total body perfusion-reduced flows, moderate hypothermia, and hemodilution. JAMA 1962;179:430.

95. DeWall R, Lillehei R, Sellers R. Hemodilution perfusions for open heart surgery. N Engl J Med 1962;266:1078.

96. Lillehei CW. Hemodilution perfusions for open heart surgery. Use of low molecular dextran and 5 per cent dextrose. Surgery 1962; 52:30–31.

97. Cuello-Mainardi L, Bhanganada K, Mack JD, Lillehei CW. Hemodilution in extracorporeal circulation: comparative study of low molecular weight dextran and 5 percent dextrose. Surgery 1964;56:349–354.

98. Long DM Jr, Todd DB, Indeglia RA, Varco RL, Lillehei CW. Clinical use of dextran-40 in extracorporeal circulation—a summary of 5 years experience. Transfusion 1966;6:401–403.

99. Todd DB, Indeglia RA, Simmons RL, Levy MJ, Lillehei CW. Comparative clinical study of hemolysis and renal function accompanying extracorporeal circulation utilizing hemodilution with different perfusates. Am J Cardiol 1965;15:149.

100. Nakib A, Lillehei CW. Assessment of different priming solutions for oxygenators by renal blood flow and metabolism. Ann Thorac Surg 1966;2:814–822.

101. Lillehei CW, Simmons RL, Miller ID, Bonnabeau RC Jr. Role of hemodilution and phenoxybenzamine (dibenzyline) in prevention of renal ischemia during cardiopulmonary bypass. Circulation 1965;31,32(supp 2):138.

102. Todd DB Jr, Indeglia RA, Lillehei RC, Lillehei CW. An analysis of some factors influencing renal function following open heart surgery utilizing hemodilution and antiadrenergic drugs. Am J Cardiol 1967;19:154.

103. Rafferty EH, Kletschka HD, Wynyard M, Larkin JT, Smith LV. Cheathem B: Artificial heart: application of nonpulsatile force-vortex principle. Minn Med 1968;51:11.

104. Lillehei CW, Gott VL, DeWall RA, et al. Surgical correction of pure mitral insufficiency by annuloplasty under direct vision. Lancet 1957; 77:446–449.

105. Lillehei CW, Gott VL, DeWall RA, et al. The surgical treatment of stenotic or regurgitant lesions of the mitral and aortic valves by direct vision utilizing a pump oxygenator. J Thorac Surg 1958;35:154–191.

106. Favaloro RG. Saphenous vein graft in the surgical treatment of coronary artery disease, operative technique. J Thorac Cardiovasc Surg 1969;58:178–185.

107. Johnson WD, Flemma RS, Lepley D Jr. Direct coronary surgery utilizing multiple-vein bypass grafts. Ann Thorac Surg 1970;9: 436–444.

Section I

Physiologic and Engineering Foundations of Cardiopulmonary Bypass

2

Principles of Oxygenator Function: Gas Exchange, Heat Transfer, and Blood-Artificial Surface Interaction

Kane M. High, Michael T. Snider, and Gerard Bashein

Through common clinical usage, the term "oxygenator" has come to mean that portion of the perfusion apparatus that subserves the functions of the patient's natural lungs during the period of extracorporeal circulation. More correctly, the device should be called a gas exchanger, since it also transports carbon dioxide, anesthetics, and possibly other gases into and out of the circulation. In addition, most modern oxygenators have integral heat exchangers, and bubble oxygenators also serve as the main reservoir and as a filter for blood returned from the cardiotomy suction. Thus, the oxygenator performs all of the major functions of the natural lungs except for their endocrine function, which can be suspended for a short time without major ill effects.

As Chapter 1 indicated, designing a practical oxygenator constituted one of the major challenges faced by early pioneers of cardiopulmonary bypass (CPB), and it was only after disposable and relatively inexpensive oxygenators were developed that widespread practice of open heart surgery became possible. Table 2.1 shows the trends in the use of oxygenators over the past 8 years in the United States. The shift from bubble toward membrane oxygenators probably reflects progressive improve-

ments in both performance and cost of membrane oxygenators, and a growing awareness of the theoretical advantages that they offer over bubble oxygenators for reducing blood trauma and the risk of embolization.

Oxygenator designers strive to maximize the amount of oxygen, carbon dioxide, and other gases that can be transferred at a given blood flow rate, to make gas transport easy for the perfusionist to regulate, to maximize heat-transfer efficiency, to minimize blood trauma, and to minimize the priming volume, i.e., the amount of liquid that must be added to fill the oxygenator prior to operation. Table 2.2 illustrates some of the reasons why engineers have such a formidable task in attempting to duplicate the functions of the natural lung. First, red blood cells pass through pulmonary capillaries one at a time, making the

Table 2.1. Comparison of Oxygenator Sales in the United States in 1983 and 1991[a]

Year	Bubble Oxygenators	Membrane Oxygenators
1983	150,000	50,000
1990	29,000	285,000

[a]Data obtained from Kurusz M. Gaseous microemboli: sources, causes, and clinical considerations. Medical Instrumentation 1985;19:73–76.

Table 2.2. Comparison of Physical Characteristics of a Membrane Lung and Natural Lung

Characteristic	Membrane Lung[a]	Natural Lung[b]
Surface area (m²)	0.5–4	70
Blood path width (microns)	200	8
Blood path length (microns)	250,000	200
Membrane thickness (microns)	150	0.5
Maximum O_2 transfer (ml/min, STP)	400–600	2,000

[a]Data for a Sci-Med Spiral Coil Membrane Lung (Sci-Med Life Systems, Minneapolis, MN).
[b]Data obtained from Guyton AC. Textbook of medical physiology. Philadelphia: WB Saunders Co., 1976.

distance for O_2 diffusion much shorter than has ever been achieved in an artificial lung. The rate of oxygen transfer in natural lungs is not limited by diffusion, except in the case of severe lung disease or extreme exercise. Indeed, the difference between gas tensions measured in the natural alveoli and in the blood are mostly due to ventilation/perfusion mismatching. In contrast, in artificial lungs operating under normal conditions, a significant difference in partial pressures occurs between the gas and blood phases.

A second disadvantage to the artificial lung is a much smaller surface area over which to exchange gases (typically less than 10% of the natural lung's area). Current membrane lungs compensate for these shortcomings by increasing the blood path length (the distance that the blood travels past the gas exchange surface), thereby increasing the time available for blood exposure to the gas exchange surface (i.e., an increased dwell time). In addition, secondary flows are induced in artificial lungs to promote mixing and bring deoxygenated blood closer to the exchange surface (see "Enhancing Gas Transport with Secondary Flows"). Artificial lungs can be ventilated with 100% O_2 to maximize the driving pressure difference for O_2 diffusion, without the toxic effects that would occur in the natural

lung, and the artificial lung can be ventilated with a high flow of fresh gas to keep the CO_2 fraction in the gas phase low. Even the best available artificial lungs are incapable of achieving anywhere near the gas exchange of the natural lung (Table 2.2). Fortunately, hypothermia, muscle paralysis, and anesthesia all reduce the patient's metabolic requirements to the point where gas exchange requirements can ordinarily be met by one of these devices.

In what follows, we review the physical principles that determine how gas and heat transfer occurs in oxygenators and how these principles are utilized in the design of generic bubble and membrane oxygenators. We also review studies examining interactions of blood with artificial surfaces and bubbles. Then we discuss how these considerations translate into the performance differences of membrane and bubble oxygenators. Finally, we discuss clinical considerations in the use of bubble and membrane oxygenators and techniques for safe practice.

PERTINENT PHYSICAL PRINCIPLES

Regardless of the type of oxygenator, gas transfer from the gas to the liquid phase (or the opposite direction) is driven by diffusion according to the partial pressure difference of the particular gas. Gas transfer is limited by the resistance to diffusion of the particular gas through the primary substance, whether it is a synthetic membrane, blood, or the gas phase itself. Other factors that come into play are the physical size and structure of the oxygenator and how the blood flow and gas flow affect these driving forces and resistances.

Determinants of the P_{O_2} and P_{CO_2} in Gas and Blood

The partial pressure of gases present in a mixture of gases occupying a volume acts as if each individual gas is occupying the volume independently (Dalton's law), and the sum of the individual gas partial pressures equals the total gas pressure. This applies for gases occupying a space by themselves or dissolved in solution, i.e., blood. Thus, when blood equilibrates at atmospheric pressure, the partial pressures or gas tensions of all of the gases dissolved in blood must add up to 760 mm Hg at sea level. In the gas phase, the partial pressure (P), the concentration (C), and the mole fraction are equivalent.

The fact that CO_2 and O_2 blood content does not derive simply from these gases being dissolved in solution complicates analysis of gas transfer in oxygenators. The well-known oxyhemoglobin dissociation curve (1) shown in Figure 2.1 reflects the

nonlinear binding of O_2 by hemoglobin. The CO_2 in the blood combines chemically with different moieties (Fig. 2.2) to form bicarbonate, the major carrier of CO_2 in blood, and to amino groups of proteins, primarily hemoglobin and is not linearly related to the partial pressure of CO_2 (2). Because of the chemical combination of CO_2 and O_2 to hemoglobin and the other moieties just described, both are present in much higher concentrations than would be possible simply by physical solution.

Diffusion of Gases Through Liquids and Solids

Diffusion is best considered at the molecular level. The random motion of the

Figure 2.1. Oxyhemoglobin dissociation curve reflecting the nonlinear relationship between hemoglobin saturation and oxygen partial pressure.

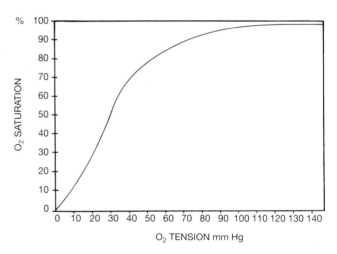

Figure 2.2. Carbon dioxide solubility in blood is not a linear function of the partial pressure of carbon dioxide because of its chemical combination to form carbonate and its binding to hemoglobin.

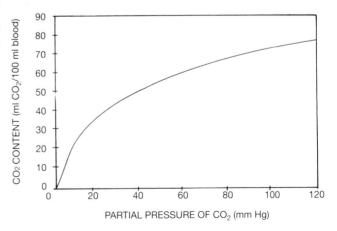

atoms or molecules of the diffusing gas move from regions of higher concentration to regions of lower concentration. Fick's law describes the rate at which gases diffuse through gases, liquids, and solids. This law states that the rate of diffusion is proportional to the partial pressure gradient of the gas in the direction of diffusion, i.e., the change in the partial pressure of the gas per unit distance. Mathematically, the rate of diffusion per unit area, J, at a particular location, x, along the diffusion path would be described as:

$$J = -D \cdot \delta P /_{\delta x} \qquad (1)$$

where D = the diffusivity constant (a characteristic of the material and gas) and P = the partial pressure of the gas at any particular location, x. The negative sign in the equation is the result of the negative value of the partial pressure difference, a result of the decreasing pressure in the direction of increasing distance, x.

Several inferences can be made from this relationship. The rate of total gas transfer can be increased by increasing the partial pressure difference (represented by δP) or the surface area available for diffusion. The rate of gas transfer can also be increased by decreasing the distance through which the gas must diffuse (represented by δx). These important concepts will be discussed in the section on oxygenator function and design. Of course there are practical limits to how far these concepts can be taken, as they will lead to an increased oxygenator priming volume or increased pressure drop across the oxygenator as membranes are brought closer together.

The diffusivity, D, is constant for a particular gas and diffusion barrier material at a constant temperature. Kinetic theory dictates that the diffusivity is related to the molecular speed of the gas molecules and, according to Graham's law, is inversely pro-

portional to the square root of the molecular weight of the gas. The diffusivity of a gas is related to the solubility of the gas, since increasing solubility enhances movement of the gas through a solid or liquid. This later factor complicates the analysis of gas transfer (3, 4).

Gas diffusion in blood, particularly oxygen diffusion, is somewhat more complicated than predicted by Fick's law. In addition to simple diffusion through the blood plasma, the absorption of oxygen by red blood cells must be considered. While detailed mathematical derivation of this process is beyond this scope of this book, if one assumes, as Marx et al. (3) have done, that local variations of o_2 around the red cell are small compared to the overall o_2 gradient, a second-order differential equation can be derived that describes diffusion of oxygen in blood as a nonlinear function of distance and time. It is not difficult to imagine that the o_2 concentration within a volume of blood will increase as the exposure time of blood to either a bubble or membrane interface increases. Thus, time, i.e., red cell dwell time within the oxygenator, becomes an important factor when considering gas transport in the blood phase. Furthermore, diffusion of o_2 within the red blood cell is not well-elucidated because the shape of the cell and the packing of the hemoglobin make this analysis difficult.

Diffusion of Momentum in a Flowing Fluid, and Generation of the Stagnant Boundary Layer

Blood or any other viscous fluid flowing past either a stationary surface or a bubble will have variations in velocity from zero at the interface surface to that of the free stream. This region in which this variation occurs is defined as the boundary layer. If the main stream of the fluid has a different velocity than the interface surface (a bubble could flow within the blood flow),[a] a velocity gradient will be formed in which the fluid velocity varies from zero at the interface to V_s, the velocity in the main stream as shown in Figure 2.3A. This may be conceptualized as layers of fluid slipping or dragging over one another. Hence, as the distance from the wall increases, each subsequent layer has a greater velocity and momentum (momentum is the product of mass times velocity). Momentum thus varies from a maximum in the free stream to zero at the wall, which may be conceptualized as a momentum flux from the free stream through each layer to the surface. This is comparable to a flux of gas undergoing diffusion or heat transfer (see "The Analogs of Momentum, Mass, and Heat Transfer"). As Figure 2.3A shows, as the flow continues along a surface, the boundary layer widens (known as the developing boundary layer). If the boundary layer widens to the point that it meets the growing boundary layer from the other side of the flow channel, then the flow is said to be fully developed.

The contour of the velocity boundary layer is important because it determines the overall resistance to flow or the pressure drop that occurs. At any place within the boundary layer the shear stress, τ, is proportional to the rate of change of velocity in the direction perpendicular to the main flow (the partial derivative of velocity, $\delta u/\delta x$) with the proportionality constant being the viscosity, μ, or:

$$\tau = -\mu^{\delta u}/_{\delta x} \qquad (2)$$

Thus, as the velocity gradient increases, the shear stress increases.[b] The viscosity, μ, is constant for most fluids. Such fluids are referred to as Newtonian fluids. However, some fluids, including blood, do not have a constant viscosity, i.e., the viscosity changes depending on the nature of the flow; these are called non-Newtonian fluids. The primary determinant of blood viscosity is the concentration of red blood cells, i.e., the hematocrit, which tends to vary within boundary layers. At the wall, the shear stress, τ_w, is also related to the steepness of this velocity gradient, as shown in Figure 2.3A. The integral or summation of all of the wall shear stresses over the entire wall surface area is what determines the pressure drop of any viscous flow.

Velocity profiles vary with the nature of the flow stream to produce either laminar or turbulent flow. Turbulent flow generates spontaneous eddies from flow instabilities within the flow. Such a flow would have a high Reynolds number[c] (a nondimensional number used to predict the transition from laminar to turbulent flow). Turbulence can also result from an irregularity in the flow path, creating eddies within the flow (see "Enhancing Gas Transport with Secondary Flows"). Figure 2.3B shows how turbulence changes the boundary layer velocity profile by moving higher velocity fluid into the boundary layer closer to the surface, causing a steeper rise in the velocity profile (shear rate) and in shear stress.

---

[a]From a fluid mechanics viewpoint, it does not matter whether the blood is moving past the surface or the surface of a bubble past the blood. It is the relative velocity that affects the velocity boundary layer and possibly the diffusion boundary layer.

[b]Note that shear stress, τ, is a force applied to a unit area and thus has units of pressure. The force, however, is applied tangentially to or across the area, unlike pressure, in which the force is applied perpendicular to the area. Furthermore, note that the velocity gradient, $\delta u/\delta x$, is usually referred to as the shear rate.

[c]The Reynolds number is defined as the ratio of inertial to viscous forces, or $Re = \rho \cdot U \cdot d/\mu$.

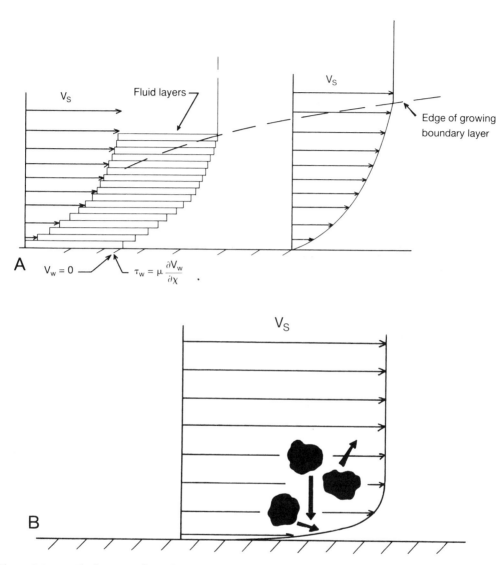

Figure 2.3.   A. The laminar velocity boundary layer of fluid showing layers of fluid dragging each other along with greater velocity and momentum as the free stream velocity, V_s, is approached. Note the increasing thickness of the boundary layer as the flow continues along the surface from left to right. The wall shear stress, τ_w, is shown as equal to the product of the viscosity, μ, multiplied by the velocity gradient, $\delta Vw/\delta x$. **B.** Turbulent velocity profile, showing the steeper rise in velocity because of the movement of aliquots of fluid having a higher velocity into the boundary layer. Note that the velocity profile represents the *average velocity* throughout this turbulent flow.

As a fluid flows past a surface through which diffusion is occurring, a diffusion boundary is generated that is layer-similar to the velocity boundary and depends on Fick's law. For oxygen diffusion typical of a membrane lung, as shown in Figure 2.4, the oxygen partial pressure in the fluid varies from P_w, the partial pressure of oxygen at the interface with the blood, to P_s, the partial pressure within the stream not yet affected by the diffusion of gas to or from the wall. Note that in Figure 2.4, the O_2 partial

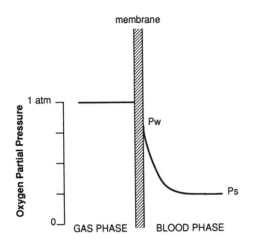

Figure 2.4. Typical variation of oxygen partial pressure from the membrane of an artificial lung to the free stream of blood. (See text for details.)

pressure decreases slightly in the membrane itself, but rapidly decreases in the blood. This graphically represents the actual physical condition. In modern membrane oxygenators, the majority of the resistance to O_2 diffusion occurs in the blood (estimates are >90%) due to the low diffusivity of O_2 in blood. As the blood stream flows along the interface, the boundary layer of O_2 grows in a manner similar to that described for the velocity boundary layer. As the width of this boundary layer increases, the diffusion distance increases and, hence, the rate of gas diffusion decreases because of the greater diffusion distance.

Principles of Heat Transfer

Discussion of heat transfer traditionally begins with consideration of the molecular basis of this form of energy transfer. Heat transfer represents the transfer of kinetic energy from molecules with a higher energy (higher temperature) to molecules with a lower energy (lower temperature). This transfer actually represents the transfer of kinetic energy from the higher energy source to the lower.

Heat transfer is possible in one of three forms: conduction (through solids), convection (from solids to liquids, with motion of the liquid carrying fluid away from the solid-liquid interface), and radiation (an electromagnetic mechanism). Within the CPB heat exchanger, the major forms of heat transfer are forced convection (the water and blood of the heat exchanger are actively pumped past the stainless steel interface; hence, the term forced) and conduction within the stainless steel.

The flow of energy or heat, Q, is related to the temperature difference by the thermal conductivity, K, a constitutive property of any material, such that:

$$Q = -K \cdot {}^{\delta T}/_{\delta x} \qquad (3)$$

where $T =$ the temperature at any point and $x =$ distance. This equation is the one-dimensional form of Fourier's law of heat conduction. In a similar manner to that already discussed for the other boundary layers, as blood flows past the heat exchanger surface, a thermal boundary layer is generated in which the temperature varies from the temperature of the wall to that of the free stream yet unaffected by the heat exchanger.

The Analogs of Momentum, Mass, and Heat Transfer

It provides insight to consider the similarities between the various forms of mass and energy transfer that have just been discussed: diffusion, momentum transfer, and heat transfer (5). Marked similarity exists between the apparent movement of momentum in the velocity boundary layer, gas diffusion, and heat transfer in the heat exchanger. Table 2.3 summarizes these similarities. The most striking feature is the resemblance of the defining equations as shown in the right column. While these equations are simpler than the actual equa-

Table 2.3. Comparison of Momentum Transfer, Heat Transfer, and Mass Transfer (Diffusion)

Transfer	Driving Force	Flow	Defining Equation[a]
Momentum	Velocity gradient	Momentum	$\tau = -\mu^{\delta u}/_{\delta x}$
Heat	Temperature gradient	Heat (energy)	$Q = -K^{\delta T}/_{\delta x}$
Mass (Diffusion)	Concentration gradient	Mass (diffusing gas)	$J = -D^{\delta P}/_{\delta x}$

[a]The negative signs in these equations are the result of standard conventions used in defining positive and negative directions.

tions needed to describe the physical situations, they provide insight into the nature of the equations.

Enhancing Gas Transport with Secondary Flows

The major resistance to gas diffusion occurs in the blood phase (6). Efforts to improve gas exchange have focused on reducing this diffusion barrier (7, 8). As mentioned earlier, the primary methods for enhancing gas diffusion are increasing the driving gradient and dwell time, or decreasing the diffusion path. Increasing the driving gradient is limited to 760 mm Hg minus the oxygen tension in the blood, because pressures above atmospheric pressure risk bulk gas transport across the membrane with resultant gas embolization. Increasing the dwell time is limited by the requirement for increased priming volume as the size of the oxygenator increases.

However, decreasing the diffusion path has been used very successfully to enhance gas transfer. First, the blood path thickness has been minimized as much as technically feasible by placing the membranes as close together as possible without causing an excessive pressure drop across the oxygenator. *The major advance has been the utilization of induced eddies or secondary flows of the blood (9) from the*

primary stream (Fig. 2.5) into the diffusion boundary layer, thus decreasing the thickness of this layer and increasing the gas transfer. Eddies have been generated in several different ways. Some possible methods include making the surface of the membrane irregular, e.g., dimpled (10), or positioning the elements within the flow stream to disrupt the smooth flow.

This bulk movement of venous blood into the diffusion boundary layer also impacts on the blood velocity boundary layer, thus increasing the shear stresses within the boundary layer and at the wall. This has two negative effects. First, the increased shear stress within the boundary layer can lead to increased formed element destruction, as discussed later. Furthermore, increasing wall shear stresses (membrane oxygenators) increases the blood pressure drop across the oxygenator. These factors must be balanced in the design of the blood flow pattern within a membrane oxygenator.

BUBBLE OXYGENATORS

Standard Design

Although the concepts of both bubble and membrane oxygenation were well-appreciated by the early developers of CPB, the inherent simplicity of bubble oxygenation led to the earlier development of a practical device. Structurally, a typical bubble oxygenator is divided into two sections (Fig. 2.6). Venous blood first enters a mixing chamber, where fresh gas flows into the blood through a screen, which causes small bubbles to form. The blood and bubbles coalesce; sufficient time is allowed in this section for adequate gas exchange to occur prior to defoaming in the second section.

One of the major advantages of bubble oxygenators is their low pressure drop, which allows them to be placed upstream of the CPB pump where they can also act as the reservoir for the system. The flow

Figure 2.5. Conceptualization of the blood flow past hollow fibers, showing the effect of an eddy on the boundary layer (cross-section) of a downstream fiber. An eddy current impacts on the boundary layer of the fiber on the right, disrupting its development and reducing its thickness. This phenomenon occurs much more frequently and on a smaller scale than indicated here, causing continuous inhibition of the boundary layer development.

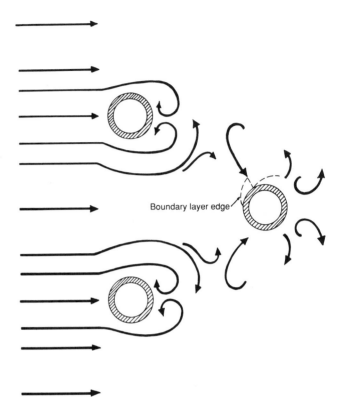

Boundary layer edge

through a bubble oxygenator is driven primarily by the hydrostatic pressure head generated in the venous perfusion tubing (which explains why CPB machines are designed to stay close to the floor). However, the mixing chamber is designed so that the blood flows through it in an upward direction, exploiting the tendency of the rising bubbles to facilitate blood flow and reduce the pressure drop. Generally, the pressure drop through a bubble oxygenator is less than 30 cm of water, in contrast to the 100 cm of water pressure drop typically found in membrane oxygenators.

The hydrostatic pressure and drag from the bubbles carry the blood over the top of a separator and into the heat exchanger, bubble remover, and reservoir. As the heat exchanger functions similarly for both bubble and membrane oxygenators, it is described in a later section. An advantage to having the heat exchanger downstream from the bubble chamber is that gas exchange continues while heat transfer occurs. Blood is first defoamed by silicone antifoam-A, which consists of the liquid polymer dimethylpolysiloxane (96%) and particulate silica (4%). Dimethylpolysiloxane, the active defoaming agent, is mounted on the silica [which acts to disperse it in blood (11)] and destabilizes the bubbles, causing them to collapse. Bubbles are also mechanically restrained by the mesh net through which the blood and bubbles must pass.

The reservoir section has several purposes. First, it compensates for inevitable flow discrepancies between the passively flowing venous tubing and the pump-driven arterial tubing, and it allows the perfusionist some time to react to these changes. Unlike membrane oxygenators, bubble oxygenators do not require a separate venous or arterial reservoir. Second, the reservoir also serves a debubbling function by allowing time for the blood to briefly stagnate and thus facilitate bubble elimination by allowing them to float to the top of the reservoir. Blood exits from the reservoir through the bottom, away from any bubbles floating to the top.

Bubble Considerations

Gas bubbles are eliminated from the oxygenated blood both by separation (as described above) and by absorption into the blood. The absorption of the gas in a bubble depends upon the difference in partial pressures between the gas in the bubble and the liquid. In the case of oxygen bubbles coming from the oxygenator, the net pressure difference tending to drive absorption is the sum of the ambient pressure of the blood and the surface tension of the bubble minus the sum of the partial pressure of CO_2 in the bubble and the oxygen partial pressure within the blood. This difference becomes more favorable for absorption when the bubbles are compressed by the high ambient pressure of the blood present in the arterial infusion tubing. Absorption of bubbles will be inhibited as the arterial P_{O_2} increases.

Bubble size also affects the rate of CO_2 and O_2 exchange. For a specified flow of oxygen into the mixing chamber, decreasing the size of the bubbles by injecting the gas through smaller holes will increase the total amount of surface area of the blood-gas interface. As Table 2.4 shows, for a given total gas volume, the total area available for gas transfer is inversely proportional to the bubble diameter (assuming all of the bubbles are the same diameter). Thus, as the bubble diameter decreases from 100 μm to 10 μm, the surface area per cubic centimeter of total gas increases 10-fold from 300 cm² to 3000 cm². However, as Galletti and Brecher (12) pointed out, there is a difficulty with smaller bubbles: the CO_2 tension within them will rise faster, limiting the total carbon dioxide transfer. One can imagine a limiting case where bubbles containing only a few oxygen molecules are injected, resulting in excellent blood oxygenation without any carbon dioxide diffusing into them whatsoever! Manufacturers have assessed this trade-off between oxygenation and carbon dioxide elimination and have selected bubble sizes that provide the best compromise, generally with a respiratory

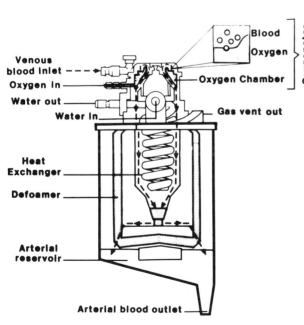

Figure 2.6. Schematic of a typical bubble oxygenator showing the mixing chamber, heat exchanger, defoamer, and arterial reservoir. (Reprinted with permission from High KM, Williams DR, Kurusz M. Cardiopulmonary bypass circuits and design. In: Hensley FA, Martin DE, eds. The practice of cardiac anesthesia. Boston: Little, Brown & Co., 1990.)

Table 2.4. Total Blood-Gas Interface for 1 cm³ of Gas Separated Into Various Blood Sizes[a]

Bubble Diameter (μm)	Number of Bubbles ($\times 10^{+3}$)	Total Surface Area (cm²)
10	238,700	3000
50	1,910	600
100	239	300
200	29.8	150
400	3.73	75

[a]Numbers calculated based on equations for volume of a sphere ($V = 4/3\pi r^3$) and surface areas of a sphere ($A = 4\pi r^2$).

quotient (ratio of CO_2 elimination to O_2 uptake) of 0.8 under standard operating conditions.

Operation and Control

Control of oxygenation in bubble oxygenators is made more complicated by the interaction between oxygenation and carbon dioxide removal. This situation contrasts with natural lungs or artificial membrane lungs, where independent change in carbon dioxide elimination can be accomplished by simply changing the ventilating gas flow rate. Increasing the flow of oxygen into a bubble oxygenator will increase the number of bubbles generated and the surface available for gas transfer, resulting in increased P_{O_2} in the blood. In lieu of adding more oxygen, attempts have been made (13) to add so-called "inert gases" to the ventilating gas in an attempt to control the oxygenation and carbon dioxide elimination independently. The perfusionist could then adjust the ratio of the oxygen and inert gas, i.e., nitrogen or helium, thus maintaining a constant flow of oxygen while varying the total ventilating flow. However, this is dangerous because the higher total ventilating flow increases the risk of gas emboli. Furthermore, inert gases in the bubbles would absorb more slowly than the oxygen, which avidly combines with hemoglobin. Inert gases are not generally used.

One vital aspect of using a bubble oxygenator is maintaining an adequate volume of blood in the reservoir. As mentioned above, this reservoir enhances debubbling of the blood by giving the bubbles the opportunity to rise to the top of the blood pool. This volume of blood also acts as a compliance chamber for the system, giving the perfusionist time to add volume, warn surgeons of decreased venous return, and/or temporarily decrease blood pump flow rate.

MEMBRANE OXYGENATORS

Standard Design—"True" versus Microporous Membranes

Membrane lungs attempt to achieve separation between blood and gas in a manner analogous to the natural lung. "True" membrane lungs provide a complete barrier between the gas and blood phases so that gas transfer depends totally on diffusion of gas through the membrane material. True membrane lungs are costly to manufacture and have a large priming volume, and as a result, most of the membrane lungs used for surgery today have micropores. The only true membrane oxygenator currently in production is the Sci-Med Spiral Coil Membrane Lung (Sci-Med Life Systems, Inc., Minneapolis, MN). This lung is utilized primarily in extracorporeal membrane oxygenation (ECMO) because of its ability to maintain stable CO_2 and O_2 for long periods of time (weeks) without the decrement in gas transfer that is commonly seen with microporous membrane lungs. As depicted in Figure 2.7, the Sci-Med membrane lung consists of a silicone membrane in the shape of an envelope that is coiled on itself. Blood flows through the integral heat exchanger and then past the membrane. This oxygenator is available in gas exchange surface area sizes from 0.5 m² to 4.5 m² to provide ECMO to patients ranging from neonates with congenital lung disease to adults with adult respiratory distress syndrome and conventional CPB.

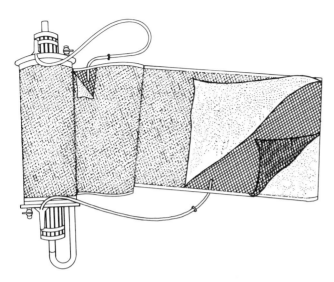

Figure 2.7. An unfolded view of a Sci-Med coiled membrane oxygenator showing the coiled silicone envelope with a mesh screen separating the membranes in the gas phase of the oxygenator. Fresh gas is supplied to the envelope by several silicone tubes (one is depicted in the figure) and removed in a similar manner. (Reproduced with permission from Snider MT, High KM, Campbell DB, Williams DR. Extracorporeal membrane oxygenation. In: Hensley FA, Martin DE, eds. The practice of cardiac anesthesia. Boston: Little, Brown & Co., 1990.)

Microporous membranes allow at least a transient direct blood-gas interfacing at the initiation of CPB. After a short time, protein coating of the membrane and gas interface takes place, and no further direct blood and gas contact exists. Typically, the surface tension of the blood prevents large amounts of fluid from traversing the small micropores during CPB. The micropores provide conduits through the polypropylene membrane that give sufficient diffusion capability to the membrane for both oxygen and CO_2 exchange.

However, over several hours of use, the functional capacity of micropore membrane oxygenators decreases because of evaporation and subsequent condensation of serum that leaks through the micropores (14–16). It has been suggested that this transfer may be reduced by heating the membrane lung and the gas entering it (15), the premise being that the condensation within the fibers can be minimized by maintaining the ventilating gas temperature above blood temperature to minimize condensation. Although currently unconfirmed, the initial results of this approach appear promising. Blood surface tension prevents gas leakage into the blood (provided excessive gas pressures do not occur).

Membrane Configuration and the Manifolding of Gas and Blood Flow

Two primary designs of microporous membrane structure are currently being used: the hollow fiber design originally described by Bodell et al. (17), and others of the folded envelope design. Hollow polypropylene fibers are extruded, annealed, and stretched to produce the micropores and then heated to stabilize the structure of the polymer (18). Pore size is less than 1 micron, although the size depends upon the manufacturing process used. Pores less than 1 micron are required to inhibit both gas and serum leakage across the membrane.

The widespread use of membrane lungs depended on the development of the microporous membrane. Prior to this innovation, available materials with the necessary structural integrity (Teflon, cellulose) were incapable of sufficient gas exchange without excess surface areas. The microporous membrane provides the necessary gas transfer capability via the micropores, where there is a direct blood-gas interface with minimal resistance to diffusion.

Two basic types of hollow fiber membrane lungs have been made: those with the blood phase on the inside or outside of the fibers. Decreased oxygenator function from thrombosis within the fibers has occurred with the former design (19). However, satisfactory clinical performance continues to be achieved with both blood flow patterns. For oxygenators with blood flow outside the fiber, blood flows either perpendicular to the fiber bundle (cross-current) or in the direction of the fibers. In the latter case, blood usually flows in the opposite direction to the gas flow (counter-current). Cross-current blood flow offers the advantage of naturally induced secondary flow generation. The fibers tend to "trip" the flow, inducing eddies downstream of each fiber (Figs. 2.5 and 2.8). This flow alteration reduces the diffusion boundary layer of downstream fibers, thereby enhancing gas exchange.

Elimination of blood streamlining (direct flow through the oxygenator without gas exchange) through the oxygenator constitutes a key feature to ensuring optimal lung performance. Therefore, in hollow fiber designs where blood flows outside the fibers, adequate manifolding (the blood flow channel in and out of the oxygenator) of both the inlet and outlet blood flow is critical, as is the flow pattern within the oxygenator itself. In hollow fiber designs where blood flows inside the fibers, reducing fiber occlusions from thrombosis has been the key to successful design.

Operation and Control of Membrane Oxygenators

In contrast to bubble oxygenators, control of ventilation and oxygenation is relatively independent in membrane oxygenators. Increasing the total gas flow rate changes ventilation (CO_2 elimination) by reducing the gas phase CO_2 partial pressures and probably by decreasing the gas

Figure 2.8. Schematic diagram of a typical membrane lung. In this case, the heat exchanger (shown in detail in the upper left of the figure) incorporates fins that act as channels through which the blood flows. The blood first passes through the heat exchanger and then through the gas exchange portion of the membrane lung. Both the heat exchanger and gas exchanger portions contain manifolding that distribute blood flow evenly to minimize shunting within the device.

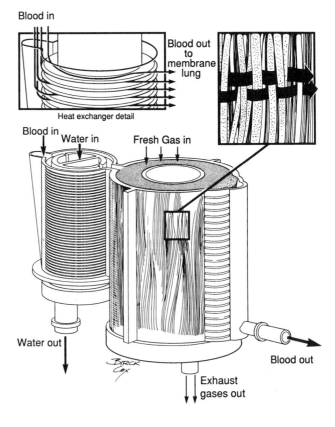

phase boundary layers for CO_2 transfer. Gas flow is adjusted by a flow controller upstream of the oxygenator, such that some pressurization of the gas occurs (generally only a few centimeters of water pressure).

Blood oxygenation control is accomplished simply by increasing (or decreasing) the fraction of O_2 in the gas supplied to the oxygenator. Because the membrane oxygenator separates the blood and gas phases and does not introduce gas bubbles into the blood, the addition of nitrogen to the gas flows does not increase the risk of gas emboli to the patient (as it does with bubble oxygenators). Some experts have commended the ability of membrane oxygenators to function with a reduced supply of gas oxygen fraction as an indicator of efficiency, although this capability has limited clinical relevance, except in the rare instance of a hypermetabolic patient.

QUANTIFICATION OF OXYGENATOR PERFORMANCE

Measurement of Gas Transfer

It is not common practice at this time to measure the amount of O_2 and CO_2 that is transferred across the artificial lung. However, situations can arise (20) in which determination of oxygenator gas exchange is critical and perhaps lifesaving. In the case of oxygenator dysfunction, it is vital to distinguish between primary oxygenator dysfunction and hypermetabolic states of the patient. The gas exchange of the oxygenator can rapidly be determined using either blood or gas phase measurements.

In the blood phase, gas transfer can be calculated by application of conservation of mass (Fick's principle). This assumes that the transfer of O_2 across the membrane or bubble interface causes the difference between the oxygen content flowing into and emerging from the oxygenator. Thus, the oxygen content of the arterial and venous perfusion tubes is determined by continuous in-line monitors or blood gas determi-

nations, and the difference is multiplied by the flow rate of blood (pump flow rate) as shown in equation 4:

$$VO_2 = Q \cdot (C_a - C_v) \qquad (4)$$

where VO_2 = the oxygen transport, Q = the blood flow rate, and C = the oxygen content, with a and v representing the arterial and venous values, respectively.

Gas transfer can also be determined in the gas phase, perhaps more accurately and rapidly in some cases than blood phase measurements. Using the operating room mass spectrometer, the gas concentrations of the gas flowing into and from the oxygenator can be sampled and gas fractions determined. The difference of O_2 in inlet and outlet gas concentrations can then be multiplied by the total gas flow rate to determine the O_2 transfer rate:

$$VO_2 = Q \cdot (FiO_2 - FeO_2) \qquad (5)$$

In this case, Q = gas flow rate and FiO_2 and FeO_2 are in inlet and outlet gas oxygen fractions, respectively.

This method introduces what is usually a minor inaccuracy in the calculations. Because the rate of transfer of O_2 and CO_2 is not necessarily the same, the flow rate of the gas entering the oxygenator is slightly different than the exiting flow rate. If more accurate gas transfer rates are desired, then a dilutional gas can be added to the supply gas. Typically, a relatively inert and insoluble gas such as helium is added in a low concentration of 5–10%. Helium in the gas phase rapidly comes into equilibrium with blood-phase helium, so that after a short time the net transmembrane helium flux is zero. Again by continuity, the helium flow into the oxygenator equals the flow out of the oxygenator. This can be rearranged so that the outflow can be calculated by:

$$Q_e = (Fi_{He} / Fe_{He}) \cdot Q_i \qquad (6)$$

where Q_i and Q_e are the total gas flow rates in and out, respectively, and the subscripts Fi_{He} and Fe_{He} represent helium gas fractions in and out, respectively. The rate of oxygen transport can be calculated from conservation of mass by subtracting the amount of oxygen leaving the oxygenator from that entering:

$$\mathrm{V_{O_2}} = Q_i \cdot Fi_{O_2} - Q_e \cdot Fe_{O_2} \quad (7)$$

or by substituting equation 6 in equation 7 and rearranging terms:

$$\mathrm{V_{O_2}} = Q_i \cdot [Fi_{O_2} - (Fi_{He}/Fe_{He}) \cdot Fe_{O_2}] \quad (8)$$

Thus, oxygen transfer within the oxygenator can be calculated by measuring only one flow and inlet and outlet gas concentrations. Similar equations can be derived for CO_2, which are usually simplified because $Fi_{CO_2} = O$.

Industrial Standardization of Gas Transfer and Blood Flows

The industrial method for describing oxygenator performance relates to standards outlined by American Association of Medical Instrumentation (Arlington, VA). Some of the more pertinent reference conditions are as follows:

Carbon Dioxide Reference Blood Flow. This is the flow rate of normothermic whole blood having a hemoglobin content of 12 g/100 ml, zero base excess, and oxygen saturation of 65%, that has its carbon dioxide content decreased by 38 ml carbon dioxide (standard pressure and temperature [STP]) per liter of blood flow by direct passage through the blood oxygenator.

Oxygen Reference Blood Flow. This is the flow rate of normothermic whole blood having a hemoglobin content of 12 g/100 ml, zero base excess and oxygen saturation of 65%, that has its oxygen content increased by 45 ml O_2 (STP) per liter of blood flow by passage through the blood oxygenator.

Reference Blood Flow. This is the lowest of the following: oxygen reference blood flow, carbon dioxide reference blood flow, the manufacturer's recommended blood flow, or a blood flow of 6 liters per minute.

Index of Hemolysis. Quantity (in milligrams) of plasma-hemoglobin generated in the in vitro cellular damage test per 100 liters of blood flow through the circuit containing the oxygenator less the quantity generated in the circuit without the oxygenator.

Initial Priming Volume. Static volume of blood (in milliliters) to fill the blood phase of the device to the manufacturer's recommended minimal running level. With bubble oxygenators, this is measured with the reference oxygen flow recommended by the manufacturer for the start of perfusion.

Maximum Operating Volume. Volume of blood contained in the device at the maximum reservoir level recommended by the manufacture at reference blood flow and reference oxygen flow.

Minimum Operating Volume. Volume contained in the device at the minimum reservoir level recommended by manufacturer at the reference blood flow and reference oxygen flow.

BLOOD-ARTIFICIAL SURFACE INTERACTIONS: THE EFFECTS OF MEMBRANE AND BUBBLE OXYGENATORS ON PROTEINS AND FORMED ELEMENTS OF THE BLOOD

Although all of the chemical processes involved in blood-surface interactions are not clearly understood, it is relatively well-established (21, 22) that when blood comes into contact with a foreign surface, a predicted chain of events occur. Almost immediately at the onset of contact, protein deposition begins. Deposition of a thin protein covering (approximately 50 Å) occurs within a few seconds. The primary proteins involved are albumin, fibrinogen, and glob-ulin. This protein coat gradually thickens and changes its composition, which is somewhat dependent upon the polymer surface. This protein adhesion is followed by platelet deposition (as shown in Fig. 2.9) and white cell chemotaxis to the pro-tein coat. Platelet adhesion would begin even without the protein coat by utilizing proteins on the surface of the platelet. This mass of protein and platelets is commonly referred to as a white clot. Red cells are en-trapped as this mass extends into the blood flow, resulting in a red clot.

Baier (21) describes three basic modi-fiers of the interface surface: texture, sur-face charge, and surface chemistry. Surface irregularities less than 1 micron in size do not affect compatibility with blood (23), assuming that surfaces are prewetted to re-move pockets of gas from the blood inter-face. Plasma protein adherence to the pros-thetic surface tends to level these irregulari-ties, thus reducing their effect. Some have suggested that surfaces having a net nega-tive surface charge slowly erode during contact with blood (24, 25) and are antithrombogenic. Furthermore, Baier sug-gested that the chemical characteristics of the foreign surface affect the manner of pro-tein deposition.

The interaction of gas bubbles in blood has been described by Butler (26). Gas bubbles in blood cause the formation of a "capsule" around the bubble consisting of platelets, a lipoidal material, and a protein layer containing clotting factors. Butler de-scribes other blood-bubble interactions, which include red blood cell agglutina-tion, leukocyte activation, denaturation of plasma proteins, release of vasoactive sub-stances (serotonin, histamine, kinins, and prostaglandins), and changes in capillary permeability.

Hemolysis during cardiopulmonary bypass (27, 28) is most commonly associ-ated with the roller or centrifugal pump, or suctioning into the cardiotomy reservoir. However, shear stresses induced by flow through the oxygenator will impart some damage to red cells. Nevaril et al. (27) util-ized a concentric cylinder viscometer, which consists of an outer rotating cylinder and an inner stationary cylinder. They deter-mined that for human blood a threshold shear stress of 3000 dyne·cm^{-2} existed (ex-posure period of 2 minutes). Hemolysis was relatively constant for long time periods. Leverett et al. (28) identified a threshold shear stress of 1500 dyne·cm^{-2} and a time dependency for hemolysis at higher stress rates.

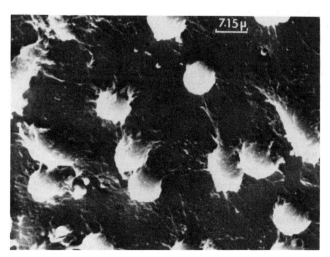

Figure 2.9. Scanning electron micro-scope view of platelet adhesion to poly-urethane sac from a circulatory assist de-vice. Note the aggregated platelets and incorporation of white cells into the growing thrombus. (×1880) (Photograph courtesy of Dr. William Pierce, Hershey Medical Center, Hershey, PA.)

Damage to platelets can occur either as a result of contact with the interface surfaces or from shear stresses within the blood (29–31). Platelet damage manifests either as alterations in platelet structure or aggregation. Brown et al. (29) utilized a rotational viscometer and demonstrated that when platelets were exposed to a threshold shear stress of 150 dyne·cm^{-2} for several minutes, significant loss of platelets and platelet function occurred. There was some return of platelet count and function when these measurements were made again 4 hours after platelet exposure, suggesting a reversible component to the platelet damage and to the platelet aggregation that contributed to the decreased platelet count. Colantuoni et al. (30) injected platelet-rich plasma through a capillary tube, thus exposing the platelets to high shear stresses for very short periods. For exposure times of approximately 1 msec, platelet exposure to shear stresses of 7,000 to 15,000 dyne·cm^{-2} were required to produce increases in plasma serotonin and decreases in platelet count and impaired aggregation to adenosine diphosphate.

Sorting out whether these changes are caused by shear stress directly or wall contact is difficult. Bernstein et al. (31) confirmed these earlier results by an injection of platelet-rich plasma into a stagnant pool, but suggested that differences in the shear stress required to induce abnormal platelets were caused by differences in the test systems and the exposure times. While it is difficult to delineate whether shear stress or wall contact is the primary irritant, increasing exposure time and shear stresses (increased turbulence in the boundary layer) increases platelet damage.

At blood-gas interfaces, globular proteins denature (32, 33), i.e., undergo conformational changes of secondary or tertiary structure without changes to the primary amino acid sequence. Dipolar molecules orient themselves with hydrophilic portions extending into the plasma, but coiled. However, folded proteins with polar groups on the external surface are physically altered to orient in such a fashion. Devices such as bubble oxygenators denature proteins, resulting in decreased protein solubility and increased exposure of the nonpolar protein and reactive side chains. This makes the protein available to the surface of erythrocytes, chylomicrons, and platelets. The resulting aggregates of blood cells and activated platelets can cause sludging in the microcirculation, and are postulated as an etiology of the postperfusion lung syndrome. The coagulopathy associated with prolonged perfusion may be, in part, related to the consumption of coagulation factors by this denaturation. Decreased immune mechanisms have been studied, and some evidence supports increased susceptibility to bacterial growth after clinical CPB (34) (see Chapter 10). All of these effects appear to depend on the length of the total exposure, i.e., the length of CPB and the amount of the exposure.

HEAT TRANSFER DURING CARDIOPULMONARY BYPASS

Heat Exchangers

The design of heat exchangers for cooling and rewarming blood in the oxygenator centers around making a biologically inert surface capable of achieving the desired rate of heat exchange, without producing any localized overheating of the blood. Generally, the energy transfer into and out of the heat exchanger is provided by nonsterile water that is circulated through a heater/cooler unit, which is part of the perfusion apparatus. When cooling is desired, the water is passed through an ice bath, and when warming is desired, it is heated by electric resistance heaters. Use of water as the heat transfer fluid is simple, reliable, and provides an even temperature distribution across the surface of the heat exchanger without localized hot spots, which might occur, for example, if the electric heating element were built into the oxygenator itself.

The heat transfer surface is usually made of stainless steel or aluminum. Both materials have good thermal conductivity and are readily coated with polymers to minimize blood interactions. To maximize heat efficiency of heat transfer, designers try to maximize the available surface area for heat exchange, either by making a larger heat exchanger (at the cost of increasing the priming volume) or by using fins extending into the blood. "Finning" also allows for a reduced number of water channels (Fig. 2.8), which in turn simplifies construction of the heat exchanger and decreases the potential number of sites at which fluid leaks might occur. Many presently used heat exchangers consist simply of a coiled tubing, wound so that the resulting cylinder acts as the blood conduit. This design has the advantages of simplicity and a low risk of leakage. Heat exchange is also enhanced in most devices by flowing the blood and water in opposite directions (Counter-current heat exchange).

Constraints on Rate of Heat Transfer

The temperature difference between the circulating water and the blood drives heat transfer. A thermal boundary layer exists in the blood flowing just beside the wall of the heat exchanger (i.e., the wall separating blood and water), an area where the temperature varies from the wall temperature to the free stream temperature (35). The exact temperature profile in the boundary layer depends on the nature of the velocity boundary layer, but a typical profile would appear similar to the curves shown earlier for gas concentrations during diffusion (Fig. 2.3). Rapid cooling is commonly employed at the onset of CPB, when the circulating water is cooled to temperatures approaching 0°C by an ice bath, thus rapidly cooling the blood. Typically, the rate of cooling at the onset of CPB is limited only by this thermal boundary layer and the temperature difference between the water and the blood.

On the other hand, at the conclusion of CPB the rate of rewarming is limited not by physical constraints, but by concerns regarding blood damage due to overheating and bubble formation because of the lower gas solubility of warmer blood. Blood damage, in the form of protein denaturation, limits the *absolute* maximum temperature (42°C) that can be safely achieved in the blood (36). In addition, the maximum *difference* in temperature between the water and the venous blood is limited in order to prevent bubble formation due to the rapidly decreasing gas solubility. It has been shown in vitro and in clinical CPB (37) that gaseous microemboli formation can be avoided by limiting the water/blood temperature difference to 10°C. Some manufacturers of membrane oxygenators have taken the additional precaution of placing the warmer upstream from the gas exchanger (where lower oxygen tensions are present). The actual advantage of this approach has not been demonstrated, and this configuration is not used by all manufacturers. Furthermore, it cannot be readily used in bubble oxygenators.

Determination of Rate of Heat Transfer

The amount of heat being transferred is readily quantifiable (38, 39) by simple energy balance as defined by the first law of thermodynamics. This relationship requires that the amount of heat transferred to the blood equals the thermal energy in the blood leaving the oxygenator less the thermal energy of the blood entering the heat exchanger. The thermal energy of blood can be determined by multiplication of the specific heat of blood, C, (0.90 kcal·kg^{-1}·°C) (40) by the absolute temperature. Thus, the heat transfer can be calculated by:

$$H = C \cdot F \cdot (T_i - T_o) \qquad (9)$$

where C = the specific heat, F = blood flow rate, and T_i and T_o are the inlet and outlet temperatures, respectively. This provides the instantaneous heat transfer (heat/unit time usually expressed in kilocalories per minute). If this quantity is then integrated either continuously or in a finite manner over discrete time intervals, the total amount of heat transferred into or from the patient can be determined. This may provide an alternative method of assessing the adequacy of rewarming during CPB in the future.

PERFORMANCE COMPARISON OF BUBBLE VERSUS MEMBRANE OXYGENATORS

The advantages of membrane oxygenators over bubble oxygenators have been clearly established in patients undergoing long-term extracorporeal perfusion for pulmonary insufficiency. However, in patients undergoing cardiac operations having short perfusion times, it remains a subject of debate whether the theoretical advantages of membrane oxygenators translate into a measurably improved clinical outcome.

Although the sale of oxygenators for cardiac surgery is a multimillion dollar annual business in the United States, large-scale evaluative studies of the available products are not ordinarily performed by governmental or other independent testing laboratories. Thus, it is usually left to clinicians to conduct the comparative trials of oxygenators in their practices. Since major granting agencies will seldom support evaluations of medical devices, those studies conducted are often done on very limited budgets and thus tend to evaluate only a small number of types of oxygenators with only a few performance variables.

It is important to appreciate that a complete performance assessment of an oxygenator must include numerous measures, including efficiency of gas transfer, efficiency of heat transfer, priming volume, ease of setup and debubbling, blood compatibility, clinical outcomes, and cost. Two other points should be borne in mind when comparing bubble and membrane oxygenators. First, the two types of membrane oxygenators, microporous and true membranes, may differ importantly in their performance, particularly with respect to gas exchange and blood compatibility. Second, any conclusions drawn about the performance characteristics of any particular oxygenator may not apply to other oxygenators of the same type, even when they are similar in design and come from the same manufacturer.

Early Clinical Studies

Prior to the early 1980s, comparative studies of oxygenators concentrated on clinical outcome assessment and common clinical laboratory measurements to evaluate differences in oxygenator performance. An early prospective, randomized study found no major differences in two groups of 10 patients perfused for an average of more than 4 hours with either a bubble or membrane oxygenator (41). Clark et al. (42) performed the first large-scale, randomized comparison of blood trauma in bubble versus microporous Teflon oxygenators in two prospectively selected groups of 80 patients each: those having short perfusion times (averaging 109 minutes) and those with long perfusions (averaging 188 minutes). In the short perfusion group, the authors found no statistically significant differences in the hematologic and immunologic variables measured. However, in the long perfusion group, the membrane patients had lower plasma hemoglobin and white cell concentrations, much smaller losses of IgG, IgM, and C3, and less bleeding and transfusion. However, the membrane oxygenator patients had a greater loss of C4, a paradoxical result which the authors suggested may have resulted from binding of C4 by the Teflon membrane.

In 1980, Hessel et al. (43) prospectively studied 32 patients, randomized to have either a bubble or microporous membrane oxygenator according to the type of operation planned. With bypass runs averaging about 2 hours, the authors found no significant differences in cardiac outcome (infarction, creatine phosphokinase-MB levels), neurologic and mental function (by time to awakening and standardized examinations), pulmonary function (duration of mechanical ventilation, alveolar-arterial oxygen tension differences), renal function (urine output, blood urea nitrogen), overall outcome (intensive care and hospital stay), and most hematologic parameters (bleeding, blood administration, plasma-free hemoglobin, gross hemoglobinuria). However, the platelet count (expressed as a fraction of the control count) was higher immediately after bypass in the patients undergoing solitary coronary artery surgery. This difference disappeared by 18 hours postoperatively. A subsequent study in dogs found increased platelet lysis with bubble oxygenators as compared to the membrane oxygenator (44). However, a human study found less platelet destruction with bubble oxygenators and no difference between oxygenator types in bleeding time, tests of platelet aggregation, or postoperative blood loss (45).

Blood Cell Damage

It is well-known that bubble oxygenators tend to hemolyze red blood cells to a greater extent than do membrane oxygenators, probably through the mechanism of high shear stresses induced around the bubbles (46). Recent studies (47–49) have confirmed the results of numerous earlier ones finding greater increases in plasma-free hemoglobin after perfusion with bubble oxygenators, suggesting that design improvements in the modern bubble oxygenators have not eliminated the hemolysis problem. A related question is whether the red cells surviving a perfusion run have a diminished life span. This was studied in dogs by withdrawing an aliquot of blood from each animal, tagging the red cells with a radioactive tracer, and then exposing the specimen to perfusion with a bubble or membrane oxygenator or else to a control period of extracorporeal incubation (50). Red cell survival over the ensuing 30 days was found to be adversely affected by the duration of perfusion, but not by the oxygenator type.

The results of early studies examining the effect of oxygenator type on platelets were contradictory. In a dog model using radiolabeled platelets, Peterson et al. (44) convincingly demonstrated a greater decrease in platelet numbers, more platelet destruction, and more deposition of platelets on the artificial surfaces of a bubble oxygenator as compared to a membrane oxygenator. On the other hand, Edmunds et al. (45) found no significant differences in platelet counts, in vitro platelet function tests, or bleeding times between oxygenators in a clinical comparison. More recent clinical evaluations have tended to indicate that membrane oxygenators do preserve platelets better than bubble oxygenators, although this effect has not been accompanied by significant differences in postoperative blood loss between oxygenator types (47, 51). White blood cell destruction during and after bypass occurs largely because of activation of the complement system; this will be discussed in the next section. The general topic of blood cell activation during bypass has been extensively reviewed by Royston (52).

Complement Activation and the Inflammatory Response

The emphasis on which variables to study when comparing oxygenators appears to have shifted in the early 1980s when a group from the University of Alabama called attention to the problem of complement activation during bypass (53) (see also Chapter 9). The authors studied 15 patients perfused with a bubble oxygenator and found significant elevations of C3a levels, beginning within 10 minutes of starting bypass, while the plasma levels of C5a did not change significantly. However, after bypass they found statistically significant circulating neutrophilia and transpulmonary neutropenia, which they believed might have resulted from pulmonary sequestration of C5a-activated granulocytes. They also demonstrated that both bubble oxygenation and incubation of blood with the nylon mesh liner of the bubble oxygenators promoted complement activation. Although they did not establish a causal relationship between the actions of the anaphylatoxins and major organ dysfunction after surgery, they suggested that measurements of complement activation might be used to facilitate redesign of clinical oxygenators. Several manufacturers have reportedly replaced the nylon mesh in their oxygenators with polyester or polypropylene (54).

Subsequently, this group extended their findings in a group of 116 patients undergoing cardiopulmonary bypass by relating postoperative C3a levels to postoperative cardiac dysfunction, pulmonary dysfunction, renal dysfunction, abnormal bleeding, and overall morbidity (55). They were also among the first to implicate heparin/protamine complexes as causing complement activation and potentially confounding the assessment of complement activation by oxygenators (56). The hypothesis of a "whole-body inflammatory reaction of variable magnitude" to cardiopulmonary bypass evolved from these studies and earlier work. Subsequent studies in monkeys and humans suggest that membrane oxygenators activate complement predominantly by the alternative pathway, while bubble oxygenators activate it primarily through the classic pathway (57).

Cavarocchi et al. (58) investigated the possibility that high-dose steroid administration might compensate for the added complement activation apparently caused by bubble oxygenators. The study randomly assigned 91 patients to a silicone membrane oxygenator group or to bubble oxygenator groups, with or without pretreatment with methylprednisolone sodium succinate (30 mg/kg). The C3a activation and leukocyte sequestration in the bubble oxygenator group without methylprednisolone exceeded that in either the membrane oxygenator group or in the bubble oxygenator group with methylprednisolone. However, no clinical differences in postoperative organ function were found among the treatment groups.

In a dog model in which the surgical wound was deliberately sprayed with an aerosol of *Staphylococcus aureus,* infection developed only in the animals perfused with a bubble oxygenator (59). Host defenses were mildly impaired by use of cardiotomy suction with a membrane oxygenator and markedly impaired in the group with bubble oxygenators, whether or not cardiotomy suction was used.

An extensive recent study employing in vitro circuits illustrates the complexities involved in attempting to assess the response of the complement system to cardiopulmonary bypass. In this study, fresh human blood was circulated through six different membrane and bubble oxygenators for 1 hour (60). To eliminate the effect of the gas-blood interface, no oxygen was run into the oxygenators. Complement activation was assessed by measuring levels of both C3a and the terminal complement complex (C5-C9). The authors found a similar increase in terminal complement activation with all of the oxygenators. In addition, no significant C3 activation was observed in the hollow fiber membrane and soft-shell bubble oxygenators, while similar increases in C3 were induced by the capillary membrane, sheet membrane, nonporous membrane, and hard-shell bubble oxygenators. The authors were unable to explain the differences in C3 activation among the oxygenators, either on the basis of the types of materials employed or the amount of surface area exposed to the blood. Neither the perfusion tubing nor the arterial line filter appeared to contribute significantly to complement activation. In a randomized clinical trial (61) subsequently reported by the same group, two bubble oxygenators and a nonporous silicone membrane oxygenator again produced similar elevations in terminal complement complex, although both of the bubblers produced greater increases in C3 activation. The authors emphasized the importance of testing for activation products at both the initial and terminal parts of the complement cascade when evaluating oxygenators. Some of the important issues to be considered in assessing complement activation in the setting of bypass were discussed by Volanakis (62).

Nilsson et al. (63) studied 96 patients, randomly assigned to two bubble and two microporous membrane oxygenators, and 7 thoracotomy patients who served as controls. Complement activation during bypass was measured as changes in the ratio of C3d/C3, to correct for hemodilution. No significant differences were observed among the oxygenators studied. Similarly, tests of the classic and alternative pathway showed markedly decreasing complement levels during bypass, without significant differences between oxygenator groups.

The studies mentioned above (and others reviewed by Nilsson et al.) are often contradictory about the degree of complement activation with bubble versus membrane oxygenators. There is a clear suggestion that the amount of complement activation depends heavily on the materials used in a particular oxygenator, as well as its other design features and the method of testing employed. Thus, it does not appear that any general conclusions can be drawn about the superiority of either oxygenator type in regards to complement activation. Furthermore, much remains to be learned about the degree to which complement activation influences patient morbidity after cardiac surgery.

Lung Injury

Possible oxygenator-type influences on postoperative lung function have been assessed in humans directly by gas exchange measurements and indirectly by measurements of pulmonary lung water and the degranulation of white cells, a process implicated in the genesis of the adult respiratory distress syndrome. In one randomized study of 30 patients (64) having perfusions of unspecified duration, extravascular lung water and pulmonary gas exchange were found to be no different between bubble oxygenator and membrane oxygenator patients for 5 hours postperfusion. However, Nilsson et al. (48) found an increased alveolar gradient occurring 3 hours after bypass in patients perfused with a bubble oxygenator for more than 2 hours. In this same group of patients, two serum protein markers of white cell degranulation, lactoferrin and myeloperoxidase, were both found to be more elevated with the bubble than with the membrane oxygenators (63). Elevated lactoferrin levels have been associated with the adult respiratory distress syndrome. Since the syndrome occurs so infrequently after routine cardiac surgery today, it would be difficult to determine whether its incidence is related to the type of oxygenator employed. More convincing evidence of the benefit of membrane oxygenators comes from a recent dog study in which bubble oxygenators produced greater pulmonary sequestration of platelets and white cells and more profound pathological changes in the lung during reperfusion following bypass (65).

Brain Microembolism and Injury

Although brain injury has been recognized as a complication of extracorporeal perfusion since the middle 1950s, its exact causes, incidence, severity, and duration remain a subject of debate. Anatomic evidence of injury has been produced with a number of imaging modalities. For example, in a heterogeneous series of 64 infants and children, computed tomography demonstrated decreases in brain mass after cardiac surgery in 31% of patients in whom a bubble oxygenator and 40-μm arterial line filter were used, whereas no such changes were found in patients perfused with either a membrane oxygenator or a bubble oxygenator with a 20-μm arterial filter (66). Although these changes suggest microembolism as the cause of the loss of brain mass, none of the patients with computed tomographic changes had clinical evidence of brain injury, and the tomographic changes disappeared after a follow-up of 6 to 11 months.

A group from the Hammersmith Hospital in London have quantitated microembolization by performing digital subtraction of an intraoperative angiogram (taken 5 minutes before weaning from CPB) and an angiogram recorded preoperatively (67). In comparing coronary bypass patients perfused with a bubble and a flat-sheet membrane oxygenator, marked differences were found in the incidence of retinal embolization (100% with the bubble oxygenator versus 44% with the membrane oxygenator), the number of ischemic lesions, and the area of retinal ischemia. Arterial filtration (40 μm) was used with both groups of patients, which may explain why most of the occluded vessels measured 20 μm or less in diameter. Whether the degree of retinal embolization is related to neuropsychological dysfunction after surgery is currently under investigation by this group.

Using transcranial Doppler ultrasound, Padayachee and co-workers (68) observed irregular signals suggestive of emboli during bypass in patients in whom a bubble oxygenator was used without arterial filtration. The rate of occurrence of these signals was related to the gas flow rate through the bubble oxygenator. On the other hand, no embolic-type signals were observed during perfusion with a membrane oxygenator and arterial line filter.

Similar results were obtained independently by Pedersen et al. (69).

From the above reports, it appears clear that much less cerebral microembolization occurs with unfiltered membrane oxygenators than with unfiltered bubble oxygenators. However, it has been much more difficult to prove whether the excess of embolization that occurs with bubble oxygenators actually causes harm to patients.

Recent Clinical Studies

The design of both membrane and bubble oxygenators has improved through continuous evolution over the years. With this in mind, one is led to give greater weight to the more recent oxygenator studies. In one recent study performed for the Procurement Directorate of the British National Health Service, Pearson (51) randomly assigned seven bubble and nine membrane oxygenator types to 180 patients and assessed their performance in terms of blood gas control, gaseous microemboli, and hematology. Taken as a group, it was easier for the perfusionist to achieve the targeted blood-gas values with the membrane oxygenators than with the bubble oxygenators. As expected, gaseous microemboli were also far fewer in number with the membrane oxygenators, but there was a surprising degree of variability in microemboli delivery among the bubble oxygenators. It was suggested that membrane oxygenators were inherently safer than hard-shell bubble oxygenators as far as inadvertently pumping air, although the membrane oxygenators, and not the bubble oxygenators, were thought to be more likely to embolize air left over from improper priming.

With regard to platelet counts, there was generally a smaller decrement from before to after bypass with the membrane oxygenators; indeed, some membrane oxygenators actually produced a rise in the platelet count. There was also a greater rise in β-thromboglobulin, a marker of platelet activation, among patients with bubble oxygenators. However, neither the white blood count, platelet aggregation, nor postoperative blood loss were significantly different between oxygenator types. The variability in performance observed within the groups of oxygenators underscores the importance of evaluating each oxygenator design individually and of not considering the performance of a single oxygenator of each type as representative of the performance of the groups as a whole.

A further report by Nilsson et al. (47) from the study of the four oxygenators, mentioned above (48), confirms Pearson's findings of better preservation of platelet function and less release of β-thromboglobulin with membrane oxygenators. In addition, this study also found less hemolysis and less degranulation of white cells with the bubble oxygenator.

In summary, there appears to be a growing body of evidence favoring membrane oxygenators in terms of their ability to minimize embolization and the abnormalities in laboratory indices of blood function and immune response associated with cardiopulmonary bypass. However, clear evidence not been found for the clinical superiority of the membrane oxygenator for operations having short perfusion times. Nevertheless, as improved manufacturing techniques have reduced the cost difference between oxygenator types, there appears to be a trend toward routine use of membrane oxygenators in all cardiac surgery.

OXYGENATOR-RELATED CPB ACCIDENTS

In a retrospective study of CPB accidents in approximately 573,000 patients, Kurusz et al. (70) reported that oxygenator failure was the third leading cause, following protamine reactions and hypoperfusion. Oxygenator failure occurred in 506 cases (an incidence of 1 in 13,362 cases) and caused life-threatening hypoxia in 156 patients and permanent damage or death in 42 patients. These accidents occurred with almost equal frequency with membrane and bubble oxygenators. In the 1970s, a time of predominant bubble oxygenator use, Stoney et al. (71) reported a survey of 374,000 CPB cases. Of 1419 accidents reported, 24% involved the oxygenator, with specific problems including leakage (16%), clotting (4%), pressurization (1%), burst (1%), contamination (1%), and chemical injury (1%).

An iatrogenic cause of oxygenator failure involves isoflurane that is spilled onto either bubble (72) or membrane (73) oxygenators, while filling a vaporizer resulting in cracks in the polycarbonate shell or venous connector. Simply avoiding the physical placement of the vaporizer over the oxygenator eliminates this risk.

SUMMARY

This chapter has delved into the principles that control the exchange of carbon dioxide and oxygen in membrane and bubble oxygenators. These principles form the basis upon which design modifications have been predicated and comparisons have been made between membrane and bubble oxygenators. Descriptions, photographs, and operating characteristics of specific oxygenators have not been included as these are readily available from the manufacturers.

While membrane oxygenators are the only type suitable for long-term perfusion, it has been difficult to demonstrate any clear-cut superiority of membrane oxygenators for a typical 2-hour perfusion time for cardiac surgery. In the majority of studies, membrane oxygenators appear to lessen derangements in several hematologic variables, notably red cell damage and granulocyte and platelet activation. Similarly, a majority of studies show less complement activation with membrane oxygenators, although the picture is clouded by different indices of complement activation measured among the various studies and by numerous other potentially confounding factors. Furthermore, although a number of deleterious effects have been associated with complement activation in man, direct proof of its influence on morbidity in the cardiac surgery patient is lacking. In particular, the incidence of infection or lung or renal injury does not appear to be associated with the type of oxygenator employed. Likewise, membrane oxygenator use reduces embolization to the cerebral circulation and brain mass reduction (by computed tomography) in children, but both of these findings were eliminated by adding an arterial filter to a the bubble oxygenator circuit.

There appears to be general agreement that benefits may be realized from using membrane oxygenators in long perfusions in adults and possibly in all perfusions in infants and small children. In adults having short perfusion times, it remains unproven whether it is worthwhile to minimize subclinical abnormalities by substituting a membrane oxygenator for a bubble oxygenator. However, since technological advances have reduced the cost difference between membrane and bubble oxygenators, a trend toward the routine use of membrane oxygenators for all cardiopulmonary bypass has developed.

REFERENCES

1. Bjork VO, Sternlieb JJ, Davenport C. From the spinning disc to the membrane oxygenator for open-heart surgery. Scand J Thorac Cardiovasc Surg 1985;19:207–216.
2. Boers M, van den Dungen JJ, Karliczek GF, Brenken U, van der Heide JN, Wildevuur CR. Two membrane oxygenators and a bubbler: a clinical comparison. Ann Thorac Surg 1983;35:455–462.
3. Marx TI, Snyder WE, St. John AD, Moeller CE. Diffusion of oxygen into a film of whole blood. J Appl Physiol 1960;15:1123–1129.
4. Zapol WM, Qvist J. Artificial lungs for acute respiratory failure. New York: Academic Press, 1976.
5. Bird RB, Stewart WE, Lightfoor EN. Transport phenomena. New York: John Wiley & Sons, 1960.
6. Marx TI, Baldwin BR, Miller DR. Factors influencing oxygen uptake by blood in membrane oxygenators: report of a study. Ann Surg 1962;156:204–213.
7. Gaylor JDS. Membrane oxygenators: current developments in design and application. J Biomed Eng 1988;10:541–547.
8. Bartlett RH, Kittredge D, Noyes BS Jr, Willard RH III, Drinker PA, Harken DE. Development of a membrane oxygenator: overcoming blood diffusion limitation. J Thorac Cardiovasc Surg 58:795–800.
9. Drinker PA, Bartlett RH, Bialer RM, Noyes BS Jr. Augmentation of membrane gas transfer by induced secondary flows. Surgery 1969;66:775–781.
10. Dorrington KL, Gardaz J-P, Bellhouse BJ, Sykes MK. Extracorporeal oxygen and CO_2 transfer of a polypropylene dimpled membrane lung with variable secondary flows: partial bypass in the dog. J Biomed Eng 1986;8:36–42.
11. Smith WT. Cerebral lesions due to emboli of silicone antifoam in dogs subjected to cardiopulmonary bypass. J Pathol Bacteriol 1960;80:9–18.
12. Galletti PM, Brecher GH. Heart lung bypass: principles and techniques of extracorporeal circulation. New York: Grune & Stratton, 1962.
13. Groom RC, Kramer M, Reed CC. Use of a sweep gas in bubble oxygenators to obtain independent control of blood carbon dioxide levels. Proc Am Acad Cardiovasc Perfusion 1982;3:69–72.
14. Murphy W, Trundell LA, Freidman LI, et al. Laboratory and clinical experience with a microporous membrane oxygenator. Trans Am Soc Artif Intern Organs 1974;20A:278.
15. Mottaghy K, Oedekoven H, Starmans H, et al. Technical aspects of plasma leakage prevention in microporous membrane oxygenators. Trans Am Soc Artif Intern Organs 1989;35:640–643.
16. Gile JP, Trudell L, Snider MT, Borsanyi AS, Galletti PM. Capability of the microporous membrane-lined, capillary oxygenator in hypercapnic dogs. Trans Am Soc Artif Intern Organs 1970;16:365–374.
17. Bodell BR, Head JM, Head LR, Formolo AJ, Head JR. A capillary membrane oxygenator. J Thorac Cardiovasc Surg 1963;46:639–649.
18. Bierenbaum HS, Isaacson RB, Druin ML, Plovan SG. Microporous polymeric films. Ind Eng Chem Prod Res Develop 1974;13:2–9.
19. Dutton RC, Edmunds LH Jr. Formation of platelet aggregate emboli in a prototype hollow-fiber membrane oxygenator. J Biomed Mater Res 1974;8:163.
20. Quin RD, Pae WE, McGary SA, Wickey GS. Development of malignant hyperthermia during mitral

valve replacement. Ann Thorac Surg 1992;53: 1114–1116.

21. Baier RE. The organization of blood components near interfaces. Ann NY Acad Sci 1977; 283:17–36.

22. Lyman DJ, Knutson K, McNeil B, Shibatani K. The effects of chemical structure and surface properties of synthetic polymers on the coagulation of blood. IV. The relation between polymer morphology and protein adsorption. Trans Am Soc Artif Intern Organs 1975;21:49–54.

23. DePalma VA, Baier RE, Ford JW, Gott VL, Furuse A. Investigation of three surface properties of several metals and their relation to blood compatibility. In: Homsy C, Armeniades CD, eds. Biomaterials for skeletal and cardiovascular applications. New York, Interscience Publications, 1972:37–75.

24. Sawyer PN, Wu KT, Weslowski SA, Brattain WH, Boddy PJ. Bioelectric phenomena and intravascular thrombosis: the first 12 years. Surgery 1964;56:1020–1026.

25. Costello M, Stanczewski B, Vriesman P, Lucas T, Srinivasan S, Sawyer PN. Correlations between electrochemical and antithtombogenic characteristics of polyelectrolyte materials. Trans Am Soc Artif Intern Organs 1970;16:1–6.

26. Butler BD. Biophysical aspects of gas bubbles in blood. Med Instrum 1985;19:59–62.

27. Nevaril CG, Lynch EC, Alfrey CP, Hellums JD. Erythrocyte damage and destruction induced by shearing stress. J Lab Clin Med 1968; 71:784–790.

28. Leverett LB, Hellums JD, Alfrey CP, Lynch EC. Red blood cell damage by shear stress. Biophys J 1972;12:257–273.

29. Brown CH III, Lemuth RF, Hellums JD, Leverett LB, Alfrey CP. Response of human platelets to shear tress. Trans Am Soc Artif Intern Organs 1975;XXI:35–38.

30. Colantuoni G, Hellums JD, Moake JL, Alfrey CP Jr. The response of human platelets to shear stress at short exposure times. Trans Am Soc Artif Intern Organs 1977;XXIII:626–630.

31. Bernstein EF, Marzec U, Johnston GG. Structural correlates of platelet functional damage by physical forces. Trans Am Soc Artif Intern Organs 1977;XXIII:617–625.

32. Lee WH Jr, Hairston P. Structural effects on blood proteins at the gas-blood interface. Fed Proc 1971;30:1615–1620.

33. Wright ES, Sarkozy E, Harpur ER, Dobell ARC, Murphy DR. Plasma protein denaturation in extracorporeal circulation. J Thorac Cardiovasc Surg 1962;44:550–556.

34. Hairston P, Manos JP, Graber CD, Lee WH. Depression of immunologic surveillance by pump-oxygenator perfusion. J Surg Res 1969;9: 587–593.

35. Holman JP. Heat transfer. New York: McGraw-Hill Book Co., 1972.

36. Reed CC, Stafford TB. Cardiopulmonary bypass. Houston: Medical Press, 1985:327.

37. Clark RE, Dietz DR, Miller JG. Continuous detection of microemboli during cardiopulmonary bypass in animals and man. Circulation 1975; 54:74–78.

38. Jenkins I, Karliczek G, de Geus F, Brenken U. Postbypass hypothermia and its relationship to the energy balance of cardiopulmonary bypass. J Cardiothorac Vasc Anes 1991;5:135–138.

39. Davis FM, Parumelazhagan KN, Harris EA. Thermal balance during cardiopulmonary bypass with moderate hypothermia in man. Br J Anaesth 1977;49:1127–1132.

40. Mendelowitz M. The specific heat of human blood. Science 1948;107:97–98.

41. Chopra PS, Dufek JH, Kroncke GM et al. Clinical comparison of the General Electric-Peirce membrane lung and bubble oxygenator for prolonged cardiopulmonary bypass. Surgery 1973;74: 874–879.

42. Clark RE, Beauchamp RA, Magrath RA, Brooks JD, Ferguson TB, Weldon CS. Comparison of bubble and membrane oxygenators in short and long term perfusions. J Thorac Cardiovasc Surg 1979;78:655–666.

43. Hessel EA II, Johnson DD, Ivey TD, Miller DW Jr. Membrane versus bubble oxygenator for cardiac operations. J Thorac Cardiovasc Surg 1980;80: 111–122.

44. Peterson KA, Dewanjee MK, Kaye MP. Fate of indium 111-labeled platelets during cardiopulmonary bypass performed with membrane and bubble oxygenators. J Thorac Cardiovasc Surg 1982;84:39–43.

45. Edmunds LH Jr, Ellison N, Colman RW, et al. Platelet function during cardiac operation: comparison of membrane and bubble oxygenators. J Thorac Cardiovasc Surg 1982;83:805–812.

46. Hirayama T, Yamaguchi H, Allers M, Roberts D. Evaluation of red cell damage during cardiopulmonary bypass. Scand J Thorac Cardiovasc Surg 1985;19:263–265.

47. Nilsson L, Bagge L, Nystroem SO. Blood cell trauma and postoperative bleeding: comparison of bubble and membrane oxygenators and observations on coronary suction. Scand J Thorac Cardiovasc Surg 1990;24:65–69.

48. Nilsson L, Tyden H, Johansson O, et al. Bubble and membrane oxygenators—comparison of postoperative organ dysfunction with special reference to inflammatory activity. Scand J Thorac Cardiovasc Surg 1990;24:59–64.

49. Benedetti M, De Caterina R, Bionda A, et al. Blood—artificial surface interactions during cardiopulmonary bypass. A comparative study of

four oxygenators. Int J Artif Organs 1990; 13:488–497.

50. Tabak C, Eugene J, Stemmer EA. Erythrocyte survival following extracorporeal circulation. A question of membrane versus bubble oxygenator. J Thorac Cardiovasc Surg 1981;81:30–33.

51. Pearson DT. Gas exchange: bubble and membrane oxygenators. Semin Thorac Cardiovasc Surg 1990;2:213–319.

52. Royston D. Blood cell activation. Semin Thorac Cardiovasc Surg 1990;3:341–357.

53. Chenoweth DE, Cooper SW, Hugli TE, Stewart RW, Blackstone EH, Kirklin JW. Complement activation during cardiopulmonary bypass: evidence for generation of C3a and C5a anaphylatoxins. N Engl J Med 1981;304:497–503.

54. Kirklin JK. Prospects for understanding and eliminating the deleterious effects of cardiopulmonary bypass [Editorial]. Ann Thorac Surg 1991;51:529–531.

55. Kirklin JK, Westaby S, Blackstone EH, Kirklin JW, Chenoweth DE, Pacifico AD. Complement and the damaging effects of cardiopulmonary bypass. J Thorac Cardiovasc Surg 1983;86:845–857.

56. Kirklin JK, Chenoweth DE, Naftel DC, et al. Effects of protamine administration after cardiopulmonary bypass on complement, blood elements, and the hemodynamic state. Ann Thorac Surg 1986;41:193–199.

57. Tamiya T, Yamasaki M, Maeo Y, Yamashiro T, Ogoshi S, Fujimoto S. Complement activation in cardiopulmonary bypass, with special reference to anaphylatoxin production in membrane and bubble oxygenators. Ann Thorac Surg 1988;46:47–57.

58. Cavarocchi NC, Pluth JR, Schaff HV, et al. Complement activation during cardiopulmonary bypass. Comparison of bubble and membrane oxygenators. J Thorac Cardiovasc Surg 1986;91:252–258.

59. van Oeveren W, Dankert J, Wildevuur CR. Bubble oxygenation and cardiotomy suction impair the host defense during cardiopulmonary bypass: a study in dogs. Ann Thorac Surg 1987;44:523–528.

60. Videm V, Fosse E, Mollnes TE, Ellingsen O, Pedersen T, Karlsen H. Different oxygenators for cardiopulmonary bypass lead to varying degrees of human complement activation in vitro. J Thorac Cardiovasc Surg 1989;97:764–770.

61. Videm V, Fosse E, Mollnes TE, Garred P, Svennevig JL. Complement activation with bubble and membrane oxygenators in aortocoronary bypass grafting. Ann Thorac Surg 1990;50:387–391.

62. Volanakis JE. Complement activation caused by different oxygenators (invited letter). J Thorac Cardiovasc Surg 1989;98:292–295.

63. Nilsson L, Nilsson U, Venge P, et al. Inflammatory system activation during cardiopulmonary bypass as an indicator of biocompatibility: a randomized comparison of bubble and membrane oxygenators. Scand J Thorac Cardiovasc Surg 1990;24:53–58.

64. Boldt J, von Bormann B, Kling D, Ratthey K, Mulch J, Hempelmann G. New membrane oxygenator (LPM 50): influence on extravascular lung water and pulmonary function in comparison to bubble oxygenator. J Thorac Cardiovasc Surg 1986;92:798–800.

65. Gu YJ, Wang YS, Chiang BY, Gao XD, Ye CX, Wildevuur CR. Membrane oxygenator prevents lung reperfusion injury in canine cardiopulmonary bypass. Ann Thorac Surg 1991;51:573–578.

66. Muraoka R, Yokota M, Aoshima M, et al. Subclinical changes in brain morphology following cardiac operations as reflected by computed tomographic scans of the brain. J Thorac Cardiovasc Surg 1981;81:364–369.

67. Blauth C, Smith P, Newman S, et al. Retinal microembolism and neuropsychological deficit following clinical cardiopulmonary bypass: comparison of a membrane and a bubble oxygenator. A preliminary communication. Eur J Cardiothorac Surg 1989;3:135–138.

68. Padayachee TS, Parsons S, Theobold R, Linley J, Gosling RG, Deverall PB. The detection of microemboli in the middle cerebral artery during cardiopulmonary bypass: a transcranial Doppler ultrasound investigation using membrane and bubble oxygenator. Ann Thorac Surg 1987;44:298–302.

69. Pedersen TH, Karlsen HM, Semb G, Hatteland K. Comparison of bubble release from various types of oxygenators. An in vivo investigation. Scand J Thorac Cardiovasc Surg 1987;21:73–80.

70. Kurusz M, Conti VR, Aarens JF, Brown JP, Faulkner SC, Manning JV. Perfusion accident survey. Proc Am Acad Cardiovasc Perfusion 1986;7:57–65.

71. Stoney WS, Alford WC, Burrus GR, Glassford DM, Thomas CS. Air embolism and other accidents using pump oxygenators. Ann Thorac Surg 1980;29:336–340.

72. Walls JT, Curtis JJ, McClatchey BJ, Wood D. Adverse effects of anesthetic agents on polycarbonate plastic oxygenators [Letter to the Editor]. J Thorac Cardiovasc Surg 1988;96:667–672.

73. Cooper S, Levin R. Near catastrophic oxygenator failure [Letter to the Editor]. Anesthesiology 1987;66:101–102.

3

CARDIOPULMONARY BYPASS CIRCUITRY AND CANNULATION TECHNIQUES

Eugene A. Hessel, II

GENERAL SURVEY OF THE CIRCUIT

The primary function of cardiopulmonary bypass (CPB) is to divert blood away from the heart (both the right and left side, and, hence, usually the lungs as well) and return it to the systemic arterial system. Therefore, it must replace the function of both the lung (gas exchange) and heart (provide energy to assure circulation of blood). Typically, blood is drained by gravity via cannulae in the superior and inferior vena cavae (and/or right atrium) to the heart-lung machine where it passes through the artificial lung (bubble or membrane "oxygenator") and then is pumped (usually with a roller or centrifugal pump) back into the systemic arterial system via an arterial cannula that is usually placed in the ascending aorta.[a] When bubble oxygenators are used, the pump is usually placed after the oxygenator, while the pump is usually placed in front of a membrane oxygenator (Fig. 3.1).

Because of the need to offset the cooling during the extracorporeal passage of blood, as well as the frequent desire to intentionally cool and then rewarm the patient, a heat exchanger is included in the oxygenator, either prior to or contiguous with the gas exchange unit.

Peripheral cannulation, utilizing the femoral or other veins and arteries, is occasionally utilized electively for cardiac surgery when central cannulation is not technically possible, for initiating bypass prior to opening the chest, for emergent situations, for aortic surgery, and for extracorporeal membrane oxygenation. Left heart bypass or proximal aorta bypass (with "venous cannulation" of the left atrium, left ventricle, or proximal aorta) and distal infusion into the distal aorta or femoral artery, incorporating only an extracorporeal pump—commonly a centrifugal pump with minimal anticoagulation—is sometimes utilized for aortic surgery.

Besides the major venous and arterial connections and the oxygenator, heat exchanger and pump, there are many other components to the "heart-lung" machine when used for cardiac surgery (Fig. 3.2). An adjustable *clamp* guards the main venous drainage line and a separate definitive clamp is used on the arterial line whenever not on bypass to prevent backflow out of arterial cannula. The *venous reservoir* serves as a buffer for fluctuations in venous return and a source of fluid for rapid transfusion. It

---

[a]In rare circumstances, total body retrograde perfusion (perfusion into the vena cava, drain out of the aorta) may be utilized (see "Total Body Retrograde Perfusion" in the section entitled "Miscellaneous Topics.")

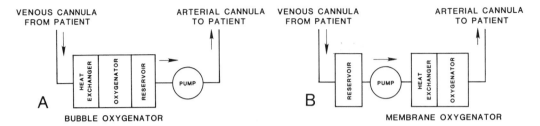

Figure 3.1. The usual pattern of cardiopulmonary bypass circuits with bubble (A) and membrane (B) oxygenators. The bubble oxygenators usually include an integral heat exchanger within the oxygenator. (venous) (Modified from Hensley FA Jr, Martin DE, eds. The Practice of Cardiac Anesthesia. Boston: Little, Brown and Company, 1990.)

usually is placed prior to a membrane oxygenator (prior to the pump) and following a bubble oxygenator, usually incorporated as part of the oxygenator, but prior to the pump. Various fluids, such as blood and crystalloids, and drugs may be added to this reservoir. Several *suction devices* and systems, usually utilizing one or more of the roller pumps, may aspirate blood and gas from the open heart chambers (hence, the term "cardiotomy suction"), surgical field,[b] aortic root (during aortic cross-clamping as a left ventricular vent, and after unclamping as an air vent), and *left ventricular vent.* This blood is then passed into the *cardiotomy reservoir,* from which it is returned to the venous reservoir, or bubble oxygenator.

A *cardioplegia delivery* and/or *coronary perfusion* system is another component that typically would use another one of the roller pumps for administering blood or the cardioplegia solution into the coronary arteries, aortic root, or coronary sinus. This circuit may include a separate heat exchanger and reservoir, and usually a recirculation line from the surgical field, which is used when cardioplegia is not being administered into the heart.

---

[b]It is more common now to use a "cell saver" or autotransfusion device suction to remove *extracardiac* blood and cardioplegia, thereby allowing the red blood cells to be washed, and debris and excess crystalloid to be discarded, before returning them to the extracorporeal circuit.

A source of oxygen, air, and sometimes carbon dioxide with appropriate *flow meters and blenders* supplies gas to the oxygenator, usually through an anesthetic gas vaporizer. Although at times hot and cold water is supplied from wall outlets to a temperature blender and regulator for adjusting water temperature in the heat exchanger, more commonly a dedicated stand-alone *water heater-cooler* is used for this purpose. A number of *filters* (macro or micro) are often included in various sites, e.g., cardiotomy reservoir, venous reservoir, oxygenator, and arterial line. Also included are *sampling ports* (pre- and postoxygenator); *pressure monitoring* in sites such as the cardioplegia-coronary perfusion delivery line and the arterial line (after the arterial pump, but before the arterial filter); arterial and venous *in-line blood gas monitors,* and *temperature monitoring sites,* such as water in-flow and out-flow for major heat exchanger, venous and arterial blood, i.e., before and after heat exchanger, cardioplegia fluid, and water bath.

Whenever a centrifugal pump is used, *a flow meter* must be included in the arterial outflow line. Various *safety devices* and *monitors,* besides those already mentioned, are frequently present, including a bubble trap on the arterial line—often incorporating a microfilter and a bubble purge line that passes through a one-way valve back to the cardiotomy reservoir, and a bypass line that goes around the arterial microfilter in case the latter becomes ob-

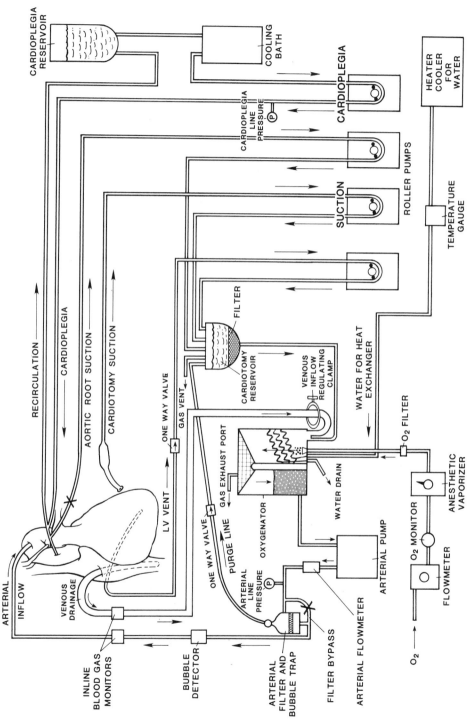

Figure 3.2. Detailed diagram of a cardiopulmonary bypass circuit employing a bubble oxygenator. The bubble oxygenator usually incorporates an integral heat exchanger within the gas exchange portion of the oxygenator, a defoaming chamber and reservoir. Only pure oxygen or an oxygen-carbon dioxide mixture is utilized, to which volatile anesthetic gas may be added. (Modified from Hensley FA Jr, Martin DE, eds. The practice of cardiac anesthesia. Boston: Little, Brown and Company, 1990.)

structed; a bubble detector on the arterial line; and a low-level alarm or weighing balance, on the venous reservoir. A *hemoconcentrator* is sometimes attached between the arterial line and the venous or cardiotomy reservoirs.

VENOUS CANNULATION AND DRAINAGE

Principles of Venous Drainage

Venous drainage is accomplished by siphonage. Early in the history of CPB, suction pumps were used for venous drainage, but were very difficult to control. Siphonage places two constraints on successful venous drainage: first, the venous reservoir must be below the level of the patient; and second, the lines must be full of blood (or fluid) or else an air lock will occur and disrupt the siphon. The amount of venous drainage is determined by the pressure in the central veins, the difference in height of the patient and the top of the blood level in the venous reservoir or entrance of venous line into a bubble oxygenator (gravity-negative pressure equals this height differential in centimeters of water), and the resistance

in the venous cannulae, venous line, and connectors—and venous clamp, if one is in use.

The central venous pressure is influenced by intravascular volume and venous compliance, which will be influenced by medications, sympathetic tone, and anesthesia. Excessive drainage, i.e., faster than the blood is returning to the central veins, which may be caused by an excessive negative pressure caused by gravity, may cause the compliant vein or atrial walls to collapse around the ends of the venous cannulae ("chattering" as "fluttering") and cause cessation of venous drainage. This may be ameliorated by partially occluding the clamp on the venous line, which may, paradoxically, increase venous drainage. Obviously, the ultimate limit to venous flow is the amount of blood returning to the great veins from the body.

Types of Cannulae and Size (Fig. 3.3)

Venous cannulae are either single or so-called two-stage ("cavoatrial"). The latter have a wider portion with holes designed to sit in the right atrium and a narrower tip designed to rest in the inferior

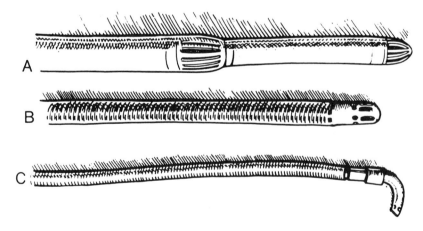

Figure 3.3.   Venous cannulae. **A.** Two-stage cannula. **B.** Wire-reinforced plastic cannula for atrial or caval cannulation. **C.** Cannula with right-angled tip usually constructed of metal because the thin wall optimizes the ratio of internal to external diameters. This type of venous cannula is often used for pediatric cases. May be inserted directly into the vena cava near its junction with the right atrium. (From Hensley FA Jr, Martin DE, eds. The Practice of Cardiac Anesthesia. Boston: Little, Brown, and Company, 1990.)

vena cava (IVC) (see "Single Atrial Cannulation" section). Cannulae are usually made of a flexible plastic; some are wire-reinforced to reduce the risk of kinking. They may be straight or right-angled. Some of the latter are constructed of hard plastic or metal for optimal inside diameter (ID) to outside diameter (OD) ratio. The venous cannulae are typically the narrowest component and, thus, a limiting factor for venous drainage. Knowing the flow characteristics of the particular catheter, which should be provided by the manufacturer, and the required flow [about one-third of total flow from superior vena cava (SVC) and two-thirds of total flow from IVC], one can select the appropriate venous cannula for a patient. For a 1.8 m² patient (total flow, 5.4 liter/min; SVC, 1.8 liter/min; IVC, 3.6 liter/min) at a siphon (gravity) gradient of 40 cm, this would require at least about a 30 French (F) SVC, a 34 F IVC, and a 38 F single catheter (1, 2). These requirements are easily met by various 36 to 51 F cavoatrial cannulae (3). Delius et al. (4) have offered a new method for describing the performance of cannulas used in cardiac surgery: the "M" number. They have reported the M numbers of several currently used cannulae and have provided a nomogram for determining the M number and for predicting the pressure gradient across of any cannula at any flow based upon its M number.

Connection to the Patient

Usually the venous connection for CPB is accomplished by inserting cannulae into the right atrium. Three basic approaches are used (Fig. 3.4): bicaval, in which separate cannulae are inserted into SVC and IVC; single atrial; and cavoatrial, or two-stage approach. The latter has a wider proximal section with holes that lie within the right atrium and a narrower extension with end and side holes that extends into the IVC (Fig. 3.3). When bicaval cannulae are used, tapes are frequently placed around the cavae and passed through small tubes so they may be cinched down as tourniquets or snares around the cannula, thereby forcing all of the venous return to pass out into the extracorporeal circuit, preventing any systemic venous blood from getting into the right heart and any air (if the right heart is opened) from getting into the venous lines. This is referred to as "caval occlusion."

Other ways of accomplishing this include the use of elastic tapes placed around the cavae and held together with vascular clips (5), the use of specially designed external clamps that go around the cavae and their contained cannulae (6), and the use of cuffed venous cannulae, either specially designed for this purpose or by use of cuffed endotracheal tubes (7, 8). The latter may be helpful in emergency cases and when dissection around the vena cava to place tapes could be particularly difficult or dangerous. When there is a hole in the atrium and it is not possible (or there is not enough time) to insert a purse-string suture, or the suture breaks, a cuffed endotracheal tube may also be used for venous drainage (9). After insertion, the cuff is inflated and gentle traction tamponades the hole in the atrium so adequate venous drainage may be provided.

Arom et al. (10) and Bennett et al. (11) have compared the efficiency of the various approaches for venous drainage (Table 3.1). *Bicaval cannulation with caval occlusion* is required anytime the right heart is going to be entered. This system may provide the best caval decompression *if properly positioned.* However, caval cannulae cause greater interference with venous flow (and, hence, cardiac output) when not on bypass, i.e., after cannulation but before going on bypass and following bypass but before decannulation. When the caval tapes are tightened, no provision for decompression of the right heart (atrium and ventricle) is provided. If the right ventricle is not able to eject, then coronary sinus blood returning to the right

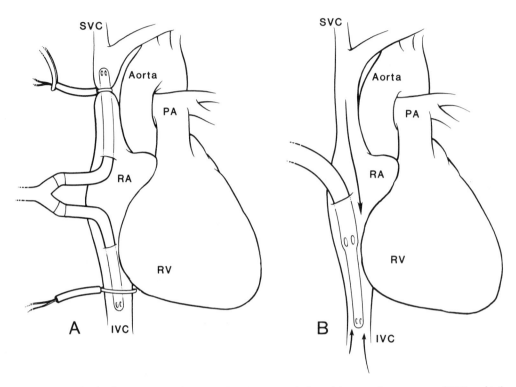

Figure 3.4. Methods of venous cannulation. **A.** Separate cannulation of the superior vena cava (SVC) and inferior vena cava (IVC). Note that there are loops placed around the cavae and venous cannulae and passed through tubing to act as tourniquets or snares. The tourniquet on the SVC has been tightened to divert all of the SVC flow into the SVC cannula and prevent communication with the right atrium (RA). **B.** Single cannulation of right atrium with a "two-stage" cannula. This is typically inserted through the right atrial appendage. Note that the narrower tip of the cannula is in the IVC, where it drains this vein. The wider portion, with additional holes, resides in the right atrium, where blood is received from the coronary sinus and SVC. The SVC must drain via the right atrium. RV, right ventricle; PA, pulmonary artery.

atrium must be removed by opening or venting the right heart or releasing the caval tourniquets. This would be aggravated by a left superior vena cava (see below). When the aorta is cross-clamped, coronary sinus flow is greatly reduced. However, the problem of right heart decompression recurs whenever cardioplegia or direct coronary perfusion is administered.

Bicaval cannulation without caval tourniquets is often preferred for mitral valve surgery because the retraction necessary often distorts the cavoatrial junctions interfering with venous drainage if only a single atrial cannula is used (see the next section). Right heart decompression is much better than when caval tourniquets

are used, but may not be as good as with atrial cannulation.

Single atrial cannulation has the advantage of being simpler, faster, and less traumatic, with one less incision, and provides fairly good drainage of both the cavae and the right heart. It interferes least with caval return when off bypass. However, the quality of its drainage of the cavae and right heart is very sensitive to positioning, especially with distortion of the heart, e.g., "circumflex position" when lifting the heart to make an anastomosis to posterior branches of the circumflex coronary arteries. The cavoatrial cannula enjoys many of the advantages of a simple right atrial cannula, but may provide superior drainage of the right heart, especially in the circumflex position, perhaps by providing some stability to the position of the atrial holes (11).

Although drainage of the IVC remains good with cavoatrial cannulation in the circumflex position, drainage of the SVC is often compromised. Proper location of the atrial holes is critical to optimal drainage by this cannula (10) and adequacy of decompression of the right heart and myocardial temperature must be monitored and appropriate adjustments made when needed. Some controversy has occurred regarding the effect of the type of venous cannulation on the adequacy of myocardial protection during aortic cross-clamping utilizing cardioplegic arrest. The concern is that with atrial cannulation alone, relatively warm (about 25–30° C) blood returning from the body may bathe the right heart and interfere with myocardial protection (12). Bennett et al. (13) studied the effects of venous drainage on myocardial preservation in a dog model and compared cavoatrial cannulation to biatrial cannulation with or without caval tourniquets. They observed the

greatest myocardial cooling, the slowest rewarming (between cardioplegic dosage), and the least evidence of myocardial ischemia with cavoatrial cannulation, which they attributed to superior decompression of the right heart. The fact that the majority of surgeons employ a cavoatrial cannula for coronary artery bypass grafting (CABG) surgery with apparent good results corroborates these observations.

Taylor and Effler (14) and Kirklin and Barratt-Boyes (2) have reviewed the surgical technique of venous cannulation. Single atrial cannulae are usually inserted through the right atrial appendage after placing a purse-string suture. Bicaval cannulae are usually placed through separate incisions, although some surgeons may place both through a single incision in the atrial appendage. The SVC cannula is usually passed through the right atrial appendage. The IVC cannula is usually passed through a purse-string suture placed in the posteroinferior portion of the lateral wall of the right atrium near the IVC and avoiding the right coronary artery. The cavoatrial

Table 3.1. Comparison of Venous Cannulation Methods[a]

	Bicaval		Single	
	With Tourniquet	Without Tourniquet	Atrial	Cavoatrial
Atrial incisions	2[b]	2[b]	1	1
Speed of cannulation	Slowest	Slow	Fast	Fast
Technical difficulty	Most difficult	Difficult	Easy	Moderately easy
Right heart exclusion	Complete	Incomplete	No	No
Coronary sinus return	Excluded	Partial	Included	Included
Right heart decompression	None	Fair	Good	Best
Right heart decompression with heart lifted up	Bad	Bad	Bad	Good
Caval drainage	Best	About as good	Good (less good for IVC)	Good
Caval drainage with heart lifted up	Good	Good	Bad	IVC okay; SVC bad
Adequate venous drainage for all types of surgery	Yes	Yes	No	No
Potential rewarming of heart by systemic venous return	No	Yes	Yes	Yes
Myocardial preservation	Best	Good	Suboptimal	Controversial[c]

[a]Multiple sources including Arom et al. (10), Bennett et al. (11, 13), Lake (129), and Casthely (206).
[b]Some surgeons place both catheters through a single atriotomy.
[c]See Bennett et al. (13).

junctions may be dangerously thin. Some surgeons place purse-string sutures directly in the SVC and IVC, but this could cause narrowing when closed.

At times, venous cannulation is accomplished *peripherally,* usually via the femoral or iliac veins. This is used for emergency closed cardiopulmonary assist, for support of particularly ill patients prior to induction of anesthesia, for management of bleeding complications during sternotomy for reoperations, and for certain types of aortic and thoracic surgery. The key to adequate flow rates with peripheral cannulation is use of as large a cannula as possible and advancing the catheter into the right atrium, if possible. Bahadir and Dietrich (15) described a commercially available catheter designed for this purpose. Smith et al. (16) described passing a 34 to 40 F Argyle chest tube over a guide wire that has been passed up to the right atrium (as confirmed by echocardiography or x-ray). They accomplish this maneuver by first inserting an angioplasty balloon catheter (7.5 F with 4 × 1 cm balloon) into the Argyle chest tube so that it just protrudes out the end of the tube, thereby providing a tapered leading edge that facilitates passage along the guide wire. Rosenbloom and Muskett (17) described a similar approach, but using a 14 F plastic catheter inside the venous drainage cannula, which facilitates its passage over the guide wire. (Such equipment is available preassembled from Research Medical, Inc., Salt Lake City, UT.) Alternatively, percutaneous venous catheters intended for percutaneous CPB may be utilized. Westaby (18) has suggested that in cases where IVC drainage alone does not provide adequate venous return, adding a 32 F cannula inserted into the SVC via a cutdown in the right internal jugular vein is effective.

Left Superior Vena Cava

A left SVC is present in about 2 to 4% of patients with congenital heart disease and about 0.3% of others (19–21). It is usually connected to the coronary sinus and, hence, drains into the right atrium. This causes obvious problems if the right heart is to be entered or with right heart decompression if bicaval cannulation is utilized. If an adequate-sized innominate vein is present, the left SVC can simply be occluded during bypass. If the innominate vein is absent, occlusion of the SVC may cause serious venous hypertension on the left side of the head; therefore, some arrangement for its drainage must be made. Use of cardiotomy suction may be adequate, but cannulation, usually via a cannula passed retrograde through the ostium of the coronary sinus, is preferred, with a caval tape placed around the left SVC. Alternatively, a cuffed caval cannula or endotracheal tube may be used (20).

Complications Associated with Achieving Venous Drainage

These include atrial arrhythmias, laceration and bleeding of the atrium, air embolization (especially if atrial pressure is low, which could cause systemic embolization if there are potential right to left shunts), laceration of the vena cavae (the IVC is particularly prone to this), and malposition of the tips or atrial portion of the cavoatrial catheter, including inserting the tips into the azygous, innominate, or hepatic veins or across an atrial septal defect into the left heart. Placement of the low atrial purse-string suture for cannulation of the IVC requires retraction of the heart, which may have adverse hemodynamic consequences and sometimes is deferred until the patient is placed on bypass with a single cannula (SVC). Placing tapes around the cavae may result in lacerations of the cavae themselves, or branches thereof, or, when encircling the SVC, the right pulmonary artery. Remember that once the venous cannulae are in place, they may interfere with venous return and cardiac output until bypass is initiated. Placing venous cannulae may displace central venous or pulmonary artery catheters (22). Caval tapes may occlude these monitor lines and, conversely, their presence may prevent tight caval occlusion by the tapes. Finally, these monitor lines may become caught in atrial purse-string sutures, causing malfunction and preventing their removal.

Causes of Low Venous Return

Reduced venous drainage may be due to reduced venous pressure, inadequate height of the patient above the reservoir, malposition of the venous cannulae (sometimes due to manipulation of heart), or obstruction or excess resistance of the lines and cannulae. Inadequate venous pressure may be caused by venodilation with drugs (e.g., nitroglycerine, inhalation anesthetics) or hypovolemia. Obstruction may be caused by kinks, air lock, insertion of a pulmonary artery balloon catheter into a cannula (23), or the cannulae may be too small.

ARTERIAL CANNULATION

Cannulae (Fig. 3.5).

Many different types of cannulae are available, made of various materials. Some that are designed for insertion into the ascending aorta have right-angled tips; some are tapered; and some have flanges to aid in fixation and prevent introduction of too great a length into the aorta. The arterial cannula is usually the narrowest part of the extracorporeal circuit. High flow through narrow cannulae may lead to high pressure gradients, high velocity of flow (jets), turbulence, and cavitation with undesirable consequences, which will be discussed below.

The key characteristic of an arterial cannula is its performance index (pressure gradient versus external diameter at any given flow) (24). The narrowest portion of the catheter that enters the aorta should be as short as compatible with safety, and thereafter the cannula size should enlarge to minimize the gradient. Long catheters with a uniform narrow diameter are undesirable. The use of metal or hard plastics for the tips provide the best ID to OD ratio. Pressure gradients exceeding 100 mm Hg are associated with excessive hemolysis and protein denaturation (25).

The jets produced by small cannulae may damage the aortic wall and dislodge atheroemboli and cause dissections as well as disturb flow into nearby vessels (see the discussion of the Coanda effect that follows in "Connection to the Patient"). Drews et al. (26) have suggested that in small-sized cannulae, the right angle configuration (as compared with straight configuration) may aggravate hemolysis. Thus, one needs to select a cannula that will provide adequate flow (e.g., 3 liter/min/m^2) with no more than 100 mm Hg pressure gradient.

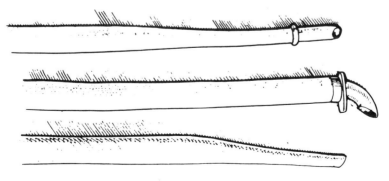

Figure 3.5. Examples of three types of arterial cannulae described in the text. (From Hensley FA Jr, Martin DE, eds. The practice of cardiac anesthesia. Boston: Little, Brown, and Company, 1990.)

Brodman et al. (24) evaluated 29 different types of arterial cannulae. They found the 8-mm OD high-flow aortic arch cannula (Sarns model 15235) and 8-mm OD aortic arch cannula with or without flange (USCI models 1858 and 1860) to be best (gradient <50 mm Hg at flows of 5 liters/min), while several others were unacceptable (gradient >100 mm Hg at flows of 4 liters/min). For cannulae not studied by them, one should refer to gradient-flow data provided by the manufacturer or conduct in vitro tests. Unfortunately, the data of Brodman et al. may underestimate in vivo gradients since they used water rather than blood as the fluid in their studies.

Connection to the Patient

In the early days of CPB, arterial inflow was via the subclavian or femoral artery (27), but currently it is usually via a cannula inserted into the ascending aorta (28). The advantages of this approach over the femoral or iliac arteries (Table 3.2) include ease, safety, and the fact that it does not require an additional incision. The surgical technique for aortic cannulation has been reviewed in detail by many others (2, 14, 29, 30). The site for cannulation is se-

lected based upon the type of cannula to be used, the operation planned (how much of the ascending aorta must be available), and the quality of the aortic wall (31).

Ohteki et al. (32) and Wareing et al. (33) have advocated the use of intraoperative ultrasonographic scanning of the ascending aorta as a much more sensitive and accurate method than palpation for detecting atheromatous disease and guiding cannulation sites. If possible, the intrapericardial aorta is chosen because this segment best resists tearing or dissection. Many surgeons insert two concentric purse-string sutures into the aortic wall. Surgeons differ as to whether these should be shallow, deep, or full-thickness bites (2, 34). Most surgeons then incise and dissect away the adventitia within the purse-string suture. Most avoid using a partial occluding clamp, except in pediatric patients, to minimize clamp trauma. Optimal arterial blood pressure (mean arterial pressure of about 80 to 100, systolic pressure of about 100 to 120 mm Hg) is important: if too high, there is a greater chance of tears and dissection, and blood loss and spray; if too low, the aorta tends to collapse, it is harder to make an incision and insert the cannula, and there is a greater risk of damaging the back wall of the

Table 3.2. Arterial Cannulation[a]

	Ascending Aorta or Arch	Femoral or Iliac
Accessibility	Easy	Difficult
Additional incision	No	Yes
Cannula size	Usually unlimited	Limited
Obstruct ascending aorta	Possible	No
Risk of malperfusion of arch vessels	Yes	No
Perfusion direction	Antegrade	Retrograde
Leg ischemia	No	Possible
Aortic dissection incidence	0.02–0.2%	0.2–3.0%
Leg wound and artery complications	0	~4%
Indications	Most cases	When aortic cannulation not feasible or desirable, peripheral cannulation under local anesthesia, bleeding complications during reentry
Contraindications	Ascending aortic aneurysms; diseased ascending aorta	When aortic cannulation feasible, occlusive disease of vessels

[a] From multiple sources including Lake (129); see text for details.

aorta. An appropriately long, full-thickness incision is then made—although Garcia-Rinaldi et al. (35) have suggested only incising down to the intima—and the leak is controlled with a finger, or by approximating the adventitia or by simultaneously inserting the cannula.

Dilators are routinely or selectively used. If a right-angled tip is used, it is often initially directed toward the heart and then rotated 180° to confirm intraluminal placement. Slight back bleeding is allowed to eliminate air and to further confirm intraluminal placement, which can be additionally confirmed by noting a pulsatile pressure in the arterial line pressure monitor on the heart-lung machine, which is at least as high as the radial artery pressure. Proper position of the cannula tip is critical (see below). Most surgeons insert only 1 to 2 cm of the tip into the aorta and direct it toward the middle of the transverse arch to avoid entering the arch vessels.

There are many potential *complications of aortic root cannulation* (27), including inability to introduce the cannula (interference by adventitia or plaques, too small an incision, fibrosis of wall, low arterial pressure), intramural placement, dislodgement of atheroemboli (31, 33), air embolism from the cannula or if the aortic pressure is very low, injury to the back wall of the aorta, persistent bleeding around the cannula or after its removal, malposition of the tip—retrograde and even across the aortic valve, against the vessel wall, or into the arch vessels (27), abnormal cerebral perfusion (36), obstruction of the aorta in infants (27), aortic dissection, and high line pressure. High line pressure may be a clue to malposition of the tip (against the vessel wall, into arch vessel), cannula occlusion by aortic cross-clamp, aortic dissection, a kink anywhere in the arterial in flow system, including a line clamp still on, or too small a cannula.

Inadvertent cannulation of the arch vessels or the direction of a jet into an arch vessel (27, 36, 37) may cause irreversible cerebral injury and reduced systemic perfusion (37–41). Suggestive evidence includes high arterial line pressure in the extracorporeal circuit, high pressure in the radial artery if supplied by cannulated vessel (27) (or low pressure if not supplied by the cannulated vessel), unilateral facial blanching when initiating bypass with a clear priming solution (39), asymmetric cooling of the neck during perfusion cooling (41), and unilateral hyperemia, edema, petechia, otorrhea, or dilated pupils. Prior to bypass, palpation of the carotids may reveal *asymmetric* pulsation (reduced on cannulated side) and the opposite may be observed during pulsatile bypass (increased pulsation on cannulated side) (41). Prior to bypass, the radial artery catheter may reveal sudden damping if the cannula is inserted in the arch vessel supplying the monitored radial artery (42).

It has been suggested that the Coanda effect—in which a jet stream adheres to the boundary wall and, hence, produces a lower pressure along the opposite wall—which has been shown experimentally to be associated with carotid hypoperfusion (43), may account for some cerebral dysfunction following CPB utilizing aortic cannulation. Salerno et al. (44) detected major electroencephalographic abnormalities due to malposition of a cannula in 3 of 84 patients undergoing arch perfusion, possibly on the basis of the Coanda effect.

Antegrade dissection associated with aortic cannulation has been reported to occur in between 0.022 and 0.23% of cases (30, 34, 45, 46) and to be more common in patients with abnormal aortic roots. Clues to diagnosis are discussed in the next section. Murphy et al. (45) and Still et al. (34) have discussed its prevention and management in detail. Bleeding and infected or noninfected false aneurysms are late complications of aortic cannulation.

Cannulation of the femoral or iliac arteries (exposed via a retroperitoneal suprainguinal approach) is indicated when there is an aneurysm of the ascending aorta or when it is otherwise unsatisfactory for cannulation (31, 33). It may also be indicated when there is no space available due to multiple procedures involving the ascending aorta; for peripheral cannulation under local anesthesia in unstable patients; during reoperations, especially if bleeding complications occur during re-entry; or when an antegrade dissection complicates aortic cannulation. Femoral cannulation requires a second incision and limits the size of the cannula that can be used; hence, the adverse consequences of a jet and high pressure gradients are more likely. Lees et al. (47) found no difference in the distribution of blood flow and vascular resistance between retrograde (femoral artery infusion) and antegrade (aortic root infusion) flow in monkeys.

Femoral cannulation is associated with many complications (28, 44). These include trauma to the cannulated vessel, such as tears, dissection, late stenosis or thrombosis, and bleeding, lymph fistula, and infection. Since the retrograde perfusion cannula usually totally occludes the blood supply to the cannulated limb, ischemic complications (acidosis, compartmental syndrome, muscle necrosis, neuropathy) may develop if cannulation exceeds 4 to 6 hours (48). The most serious complication of femoral cannulation is retrograde arterial dissection, which may lead to retroperitoneal hemorrhage or retrograde extension all the way to the aortic root. The incidence of this complication has been reported at between 0.2 to 0.9% (26, 49–51), although rates as high as 2 of 35 (6%) (52) and as low as 0 of 702 (44) have been reported. Retrograde arterial dissection is thought to be caused by either direct (cannula) or indirect (jet) trauma, and to be more likely in the presence of atherosclerosis or cystic medial necrosis and in patients over 40 years old (28). Aortic dissection should be suspected when there is a sudden decrease in venous return and arterial pressure, excessive loss of perfusate, increased arterial line pressure in the extra-corporeal circuit, evidence of decreased organ perfusion (oliguria, dilated pupil), electroencephalographic changes, ECG evidence of myocardial ischemia, blue discoloration of the aortic root (the differential diagnosis is subadventitial hematoma), and bleeding from needle or cannulation sites in the aortic root. Transesophageal echocardiography may be useful in establishing the diagnosis (53). Immediate discontinuation of bypass, if feasible, or transferring the arterial perfusion cannula to the ascending aorta may be life saving, although the mortality is about 50%.

When aortic root cannulation is undesirable or not feasible and femoral cannulation is also not possible (e.g., due to vascular disease), the subclavian artery may be used, but with the potential for cerebral or upper extremity ischemia. Also, antegrade aortic perfusion has been accomplished in this situation by cannulating through the left ventricular apex and passing the cannula (20 to 22 F) across the aortic valve into the aortic root (54–56). In this circumstance, Robicsek (56) has used a special padded vascular clamp (Heinrich Ulrich Co., Ulm, Germany) that allows clamping of the ascending aorta around the perfusion cannula. Both Robicsek (56) and Norman (55) have described the use of special double-lumen or double-barreled cannulae that allow for both aortic perfusion and venting of the left ventricle. Coselli and Crawford (57) described retrograde perfusion through a graft sewn onto the abdominal aorta when distal occlusive disease prevents femoral cannulation and when ascending aortic cannulation is not feasible.

TUBING AND CONNECTORS

Minimizing blood trauma, prime volume, and resistance to flow, as well as avoiding leaks (outward flow of blood, aspiration of air), are considerations in selection of tubing and connectors. To minimize blood trauma, one should strive to have smooth, nonwettable inside walls of nontoxic materials, to avoid velocities above 100 cm/sec, and avoid exceeding a critical Reynolds number (above 1000)[c] (Table 3.3). One also wishes to minimize the gradient necessary to propel the blood along the tubing (Table 3.3). The selection of wide tubing aids in achieving these objectives. On the other hand, the larger the tubing, the greater the priming volume (Table 3.3). Keeping tubing as short as possible will reduce prime volume, pressure gradient (resistance to flow), and blood trauma.

Desirable tubing characteristics include transparency, resilience (re-expands after compression), flexibility, kink resistance, hardness (resists collapse), toughness (resists cracking and rupture), low spallation rate, inertness, smooth and nonwettable inner surface, toleration for heat sterilization, and blood compatibility. Medical-grade polyvinyl chloride (e.g., Tygon) seems to meet these standards. Silicone and latex rubber tubing are sometimes used in roller pumps. New formulations of polyvinyl chloride are being developed for

---

[c] In general, turbulence occurs when disrupting forces (inertial) overcome the retaining forces (viscous). This relationship is expressed by the Reynolds number [= (density × velocity × diameter) ÷ viscosity]. Empirically, turbulence has been found to occur in blood when this number exceeds 1000, although its occurrence is also influenced by curvature, smoothness, and inlet conditions.

use in roller pumps to minimize spallation (see below).

Disposable hard plastic connectors (polycarbonate) with smooth, nonwettable hemocompatible inner surfaces that make smooth junctions with plastic tubing (to minimize turbulence) are desirable. Smooth curves rather than sharp-angled bends will minimize turbulence. Connections must be tight enough to prevent leakage of blood when exposed to positive pressures (up to 500 mm Hg beyond the arterial pump) and aspiration of air on the venous side, i.e., prior to the arterial pump. The friction of fluted connectors with a larger outside diameter than the inside diameter of the plastic tubing or cannula into which the connector is inserted may provide sufficient tightness; otherwise, plastic bands should be applied tightly around all such connections.

Most tubing and connectors are prepackaged and disposable for convenience and safety.

PUMPS

Types

Three types of pumps are currently used: roller, centrifugal, and ventricular. Only the first two types are in common use.

ROLLER PUMPS

Roller pumps (Fig. 3.6A) have been the most commonly used pumps for CPB for

Table 3.3. **Priming Volume and Maximum Flow Rates for Various Sizes of Tubing**

Tubing Size (ID)		Volume (ml/M)	To Avoid all Hemolysis[a]	Maximum Flow (liters/min)					
				To Keep					
				Pressure Gradient[a]		Reynolds Number[b]		Velocity[b]	
Inch	mm			<5 mm Hg	<10 mm Hg	<1000	<2000	<100 cm/sec	<200 cm/sec
3/16	4.5	15	<0.1	0.1	0.2	0.9	1.0	1.0	2.0
1/4	6	30	0.11	0.4	0.9	1.1	2.2	1.7	3.4
3/8	9	65	0.35	2.0	4.0	1.8	3.3	3.9	>6
1/2	12	115	0.5	3.8	7.0	2.0	4.0	>6	
3/4	18	255				3.0	6.0		

[a] Data adapted from Peirce (1).
[b] Calculated by the author.

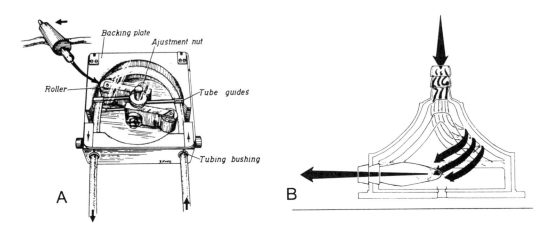

Figure 3.6. Arterial pumps. **A.** Roller pump. **B.** Centrifugal pump. See text for details of their function. (**A** is from Reed CC, Stafford TB. Cardiopulmonary Bypass. 2nd ed. Houston: Texas Medical Press, Inc., 1985. **B** is from Lake CL, ed. Pediatric Cardiac Anesthesia. Norwalk, Connecticut: Appleton and Lang, 1988.)

the past 30 years. They consist of a length of tubing located inside a curved raceway at the perimeter of the travel of rollers (usually two) mounted on the ends of rotating arms (usually two, 180° apart), arranged so that one roller is compressing the tubing at all times. Flow of blood is induced by compressing the tubing, thereby pushing the blood ahead of the moving roller. Flow rate depends upon the size of the tubing, length of the track, and rotation rate of the rollers (revolutions per minute). For a given pump and type and size of tubing, flow is proportional to pump speed (revolutions per minute). In vitro calibration curves must be constructed and checked periodically. This is done by measuring the output of the pump over a measured period of time at various pump settings in a mock circulation, preferably using blood.

Silastic rubber, latex rubber, and polyvinyl chloride (e.g., Tygon) tubing have been used in the raceway. The latter type is favored by many surgeons because it is an integral part of the circuit, is durable, and associated with acceptable rates of hemolysis (58). It does get stiff during hypothermia and is subject to release of particulate material (spallation). Latex rubber was associated with greater hemolysis, while

silastic rubber had less hemolysis when the pump was completely occlusive (58) (see below), and is said to resist fracture over long periods of time (59). Spallation refers to the release of microparticles of plastic from the inner walls of tubing due to compression by roller pumps (60, 61). Silicone releases more particles than polyvinylchloride (PVC) (59), while new formulations of PVC that release even less are being developed (62).

The degree of compression ("occlusiveness") of the tubing by the rollers can be adjusted and appears to be critical. Excessive compression aggravates hemolysis and tubing wear, while too little occlusion may also aggravate hemolysis but, more importantly, compromises forward output. Although there is some disagreement, most surgeons believe that least hemolysis occurs when compression is adjusted to be barely nonocclusive (58). This is accomplished by holding the outflow line vertically so the top of the fluid (blood or asanguinous) is about 60 to 75 cm (24 to 30 inches) above the pump, and then gradually decreasing the occlusiveness until the fluid level falls at a rate of 1 cm every 5 sec (58) to 1 cm/min (63). The tighter setting assures more accurate forward flow, makes the roller pump relatively insensitive to afterload, and may not be associated with more hemolysis.

Complications associated with roller pumps include malocclusion (with the consequences noted above), miscalibration, fracture of the pump tubing, "run away" (64) or loss of power, spallation, and pumping of gross air. If the outflow becomes occluded, pressure in the line will progressively rise until the tubing or connections break. If inflow becomes limited, the roller pumps will develop high negative pressures producing cavitation (microbubbles).

CENTRIFUGAL PUMPS

Centrifugal pumps (Fig. 3.6B) consist of a vaned impeller (Sarns and Aries) or a nest of smooth plastic cones that sit inside a plastic housing. The impellers or cones are magnetically coupled with an electric motor and, when rotated rapidly, generate a pressure differential that may cause the movement of blood. Unlike roller pumps, they are totally nonocclusive and afterload-dependent, i.e., an increase in downstream resistance decreases forward flow delivered to the patient. This has both favorable and unfavorable consequences. Flow is not determined by rotational rate alone, and, therefore, a flow meter must be incorporated in the arterial outflow to quantitate pump flow. Furthermore, when the pump is connected to the patient's arterial system but is not running, blood will flow backward through the pump and out of the patient unless the arterial line is clamped. This can cause exsanguination of the patient or aspiration of air into the arterial line (e.g., from around the purse-string sutures) (65). Thus, *whenever the centrifugal pump is not running, the arterial line must be clamped.* Kolff et al. (65) have described a check valve to prevent this problem. On the other hand, if the arterial line becomes occluded, these pumps will not generate excessive pressure (the maximum is only about 700 to 900 mm Hg) and will not rupture the arterial line. Likewise, they will not generate as much negative pressure (and, hence, as much cavitation and microembolus production—the maximum is only about -400 to -500 mm Hg) as a roller pump if inflow becomes occluded.

Another reputed advantage of centrifugal pumps over roller pumps is less risk of passing massive air emboli into the arterial line. This is because they will become "deprimed" and stop pumping if more than 32 to 52 ml of air is introduced into the circuit (but *they will pass smaller but still potentially lethal quantities of air*). Wheeldon et al. (66) compared the BioMedicus centrifugal pump with the Stockert roller pump in a prospective randomized study of 16 patients undergoing CABG. They found the centrifugal pump was associated with greater preservation of platelet numbers, decreased complement activation, and reduced microbubble transmission. Driessen et al. (67) noted no fall in white blood cell counts with centrifugal pumping, while they did fall with roller pumps during human bypass. Hoerr et al. (62), in a prolonged in vitro study, observed less hemolysis and loss of clottable fibrinogen with centrifugal as compared to roller pumps.

Some authors believe that centrifugal pumps require less anticoagulation (68–70). Centrifugal pumps are probably superior for use as temporary extracorporeal assist devices (71, 72) and for left heart bypass (68, 69, 73). On the other hand, roller pumps are simpler, cheaper (especially cheaper disposables), have a lower prime volume, and are easier to prime (deair), produce a predictable output that is independent of afterload, and are capable of generating greater degrees of pulsatile flow. Clinical studies to date (66, 67) have *not* documented superior outcome with use of centrifugal pumps.

Several types of centrifugal pumps are commercially available, including the BioMedicus Bio-pump, Sarns Delphin, and Aries Lifestream 2000 pumps. Leschinsky et al. (74) have analyzed the development of centrifugal pumps and made suggestions for future improvements. Qian et al. (75) described one such promising new impeller-type pump. Compared with the BioMedicus pump, which employs the nested cones constrained vortex principle, the Sarns and Aries pumps utilize a finned (vaned) impeller. The Sarns pump is said to be more efficient (fewer revolutions per minute to generate the same flow), require less prime volume (48 versus 80 ml), and to be easier to debubble at the start of the case. It also takes less air to deprime [i.e., 32 versus 52 ml to stop output], generates less negative and positive pressures, is capable of generating a modest pulsatile flow when operated in the pulsatile mode, and has a stronger outer chamber (polycarbonate versus acrylic).

Pacheco et al. (76) compared the Bio-Medicus, Sarns, and Aires pumps regarding depriming volumes and microembolus generation (when inflow was occluded). At a flow of 4 liters/min none generated microbubbles, but at 6 liters/min the Bio-pump generated the most and the Delphin the least. The deprime volumes were about 50 ml for the Lifestream (Aries), 40 ml for the Bio-pump (Biomedicus), and 30 ml for the Delphin (Sarns). Whether any of these features influence clinical outcome is unknown.

Pulsatile Bypass

The significance of pulsatile blood flow during CPB is discussed in Chapter 13. Methods available to generate pulsatile flow include an indwelling intraaortic balloon pump (77), an extracorporeal "balloon" [e.g., Pulsatile Assist Device (78)], ventricular-type pneumatic or hydraulic pumps [e.g., Keele pump (79), Polystan

pulsatile pump (80)], modified roller pumps [e.g., Sarns (81) and Stockert (82)], and modified centrifugal pumps [e.g., Sarns (67)]. Even conventional roller pumps produce some pulsatile flow (83). The Sarns centrifugal pulsatile pump produces a much lower pulse pressure amplitude than pulsatile roller pumps, but more than conventional roller pumps (67).

Wright (84) has compared the hydraulic power outputs of various pulsatile pumps and analyzed the factors that affect the hydraulic power output of one type of pulsatile roller pump (Stockert) (85). The marked differences in pulsatile power output with different pumps and bypass configurations might explain the dichotomy of results of comparative studies of pulsatile and nonpulsatile perfusion. Factors that favor maximal transfer of pulsatile power into the patient, besides optimal control settings on the pump, include use of a wide, stiff arterial line, large arterial cannula (≥ 24 F or 6.5 mm), and not having a microfilter or membrane oxygenator between the pulsatile pump and the patient (85, 86). Three types of hollow fiber membrane oxygenators (Sarns 16310, Bentley CM 50, Bard HF 4000) and a microarterial line filter (Pall Ultipore) had less damping effect than three flat-sheet membrane oxygenators (Cobe CML, SciMed SM35, and Shiley M200) (85, 87). For optimal transfer of pulsatile energy in a circuit employing a membrane oxygenator, a two-pump system with a simple recirculation line is necessary (see Fig. 3.8C). The pump perfusing the membrane oxygenator must run slightly faster than the pulsatile pump that perfuses the patient. This adds significantly to the complexity (and possibly to the risk of complications) of the circuit.

Ventricular-type pumps, while potentially more powerful, are rather cumbersome and have not been well accepted. The Pulsatile Assist Device exposes the patient to risk of air embolization. Patient factors, such as vascular tone and impedance, anesthetic state, and physiologic autoregulation, also influence the physiologic impact of pulsatile bypass (85, 86).

OXYGENATORS

Although numerous types of oxygenators have been used in the past, including heterologous and homologous biologic lungs, vertical screens, and disc oxygenators, currently only two varieties are in use: the bubble and membrane oxygenators (Fig. 3.7). The details concerning the function of these two types of oxygenators and the debate over whether the membrane oxygenator is superior is covered in Chapter 2. The oxygenator used does influence the configuration of the extracorporeal circuit (Fig. 3.8) (88), and often the oxygenator includes other components of the circuit. The heat exchanger is usually an integral part of the oxygenator and usually is situated just proximal to the gas exchanging section, or sometimes within the bubble chamber of a bubble oxygenator. Bubble oxygenators are positioned proximal to the pump and include an arterial reservoir, which is located distal to the oxygenating column and defoaming area and proximal to the arterial pump for which it serves as an "atrium." No additional venous reservoir is included in this circuit since the venous return empties directly into the oxygenating column of the oxygenator, as does the cardiotomy reservoir (Fig. 3.8A).

Membrane oxygenators are usually positioned after the pump because the resistance in most membrane oxygenators requires blood to be pumped through them (Fig. 3.8B). A venous reservoir receives the venous return, as well as the drainage from the cardiotomy reservoir, and serves as the atrium for the arterial pump, which pumps the blood through the oxygenator and into the patient (Fig. 3.8B). Some low-resistance membrane oxygenators may be adequately perfused by gravity drainage of venous blood and, hence, positioned like a bubble oxygenator (Fig. 3.8A). For pulsatile bypass with a membrane oxygenator circuit, a second (pulsatile pump) is placed beyond the membrane oxygenator to avoid the damping that would occur if it were placed proximal to the membrane oxygenator (Fig. 3.8C). This requires inclusion of a second (arterial) reservoir and a bypass line to handle the excess flow of the first (venous) pump, which must run slightly faster than the arterial pump. If there is no arterial reservoir between the membrane oxygenator and the arterial pump, there is a risk of drawing bubbles of gas across the membrane and into the bypass circuit (Fig. 3.8C).

Often to gain maximum benefit from the membrane oxygenator elimination of blood-gas interface, collapsible reservoirs are used in these circuits (see the "Venous/Arterial Reservoir" section). Membrane oxygenators do require additional time to debubble (de-air). This may be facilitated by filling the circuit with carbon dioxide before priming with fluid, since CO_2 is considerably more soluble than oxygen and nitrogen.

Oxygenators require a gas supply system. This requires at least a source of oxygen (but usually also air, and sometimes carbon dioxide), flow regulators, and flow meters. Often, when oxygen and air are used, a blender is utilized. An oxygen analyzer should be incorporated in the circuit (after the blender, if one is used) as well as a microfilter. One or more anesthetic vaporizers are usually incorporated in the gas supply line to the oxygenator. In this regard, one must beware that volatile anesthetic liquids may be destructive to the plastic components of extracorporeal circuits and, hence, one must consider the location of these vaporizers and use extreme care when filling them with anesthetic liquid so as to not "contaminate" any plastic (including tubing) component. When bubble oxygenators are employed, gas flow must be initiated before the oxy-

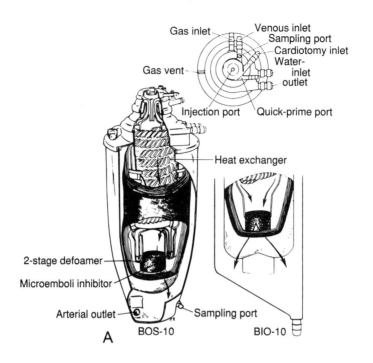

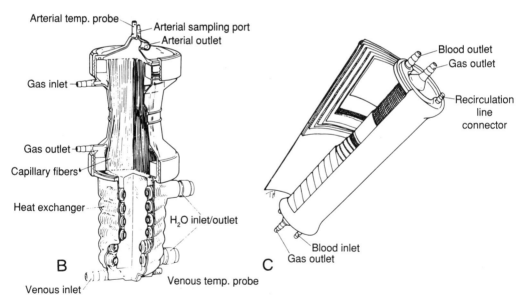

Figure 3.7. Oxygenators. **A.** A typical bubble oxygenator (Bentley BOS 10). Venous blood enters the top, where it is mixed with bubbles of oxygen and passes over an integral heat exchanger. It then passes through defoaming and debubbling stages and collects in the reservoir at the bottom. **B.** A capillary microporous membrane oxygenator (Bentley BOS CM 50). Venous blood enters the bottom, where it passes over the heat exchanger tubes and then into the oxygenating column where it passes around the multiple capillary tubes through which the fresh gas (oxygen ± air) passes and out the top as oxygenated blood. **C.** A silicone true membrane (sheet) oxygenator (Sci-Med). An envelope made up of a silicone rubber membrane enclosing a nylon screen separator is wound in a spiral fashion around a core. Blood passes within the envelope and the fresh gas passes on the outside of the envelope in a counter-current fashion (blood enters the bottom and goes out the top; fresh gas passes in the opposite direction). (From Reed CC, Stafford TB. Cardiopulmonary Bypass. Houston: Texas Medical Press, Inc., 1985.)

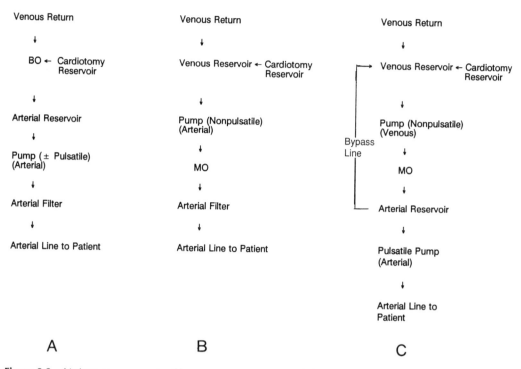

Figure 3.8. Various arrangements of bypass components. **A** with bubble oxygenator (BO); **B** with membrane oxygenator (MO); **C** with MO and pulsatile pump. (Modified from Kirson LE, Laurnen ME, Tornbene MA. Position of oxygenators in the bypass circuit [Letter]. J Cardiothorac Anesth 1989;3:817–818.)

genator is primed and continued thereafter to avoid back leakage of fluid through the bubble disperser plate, which may degrade its efficiency (89). Gravlee et al. (90) have called attention to the risk of hypoxemia during CPB caused by leaks in the gas supply system at various sites, and have described and advocated a low-pressure leak test. An obstructed oxygen line also will cause hypoxemia (91).

HEAT EXCHANGERS

Heat exchangers are designed to add or remove heat from the blood, thereby controlling body temperature. During its flow in the extracorporeal circuit, the blood cools and, hence, heat must be added to avoid patient cooling. In addition, the patient's temperature is often deliberately lowered and then needs to be restored to normothermia before discontinuing bypass.

Although in the past separate heat exchangers were used in extracorporeal circuits, currently they are invariably included as an integral part of the disposable oxygenators. The details concerning the function and performance of blood heat exchangers are discussed in Chapter 2. They are usually located proximal to the gas exchanging section of the circuit to minimize the risk of releasing microbubbles of gas from the blood, which could occur if the blood is warmed after being saturated with gas. An additional risk of heat exchangers is water leakage into the blood path, which might be manifested by the appearance of hemolysis.

A source of hot and cold water, a regulator/blender, and temperature sensors are supplemental requirements of heat exchangers. While hospital water supply may provide such a source, more frequently a dedicated free-standing water heater-cooler is utilized.

Separate heat exchangers are needed for administration of cardioplegia and/or blood for coronary perfusion. In the former case, the simplest system is to use bags of precooled (e.g., in a refrigerator or ice bucket) cardioplegia. Alternatively the cardioplegia is circulated through coils of plastic tubing that are placed in an ice bath or a warm water bath. For coronary artery perfusion, blood may be passed through a dedicated separate heat exchanger so that the temperature of the blood perfusing the coronary arteries may be different than that perfusing the rest of the body.

VENOUS/ARTERIAL RESERVOIR

A reservoir is placed immediately prior to the arterial pump to serve as its "holding tank" or atrium and act as a buffer for fluctuation and imbalances between venous return and arterial flow. It also serves as a high capacitance (i.e., low pressure) receiving chamber for venous return and, hence, facilitates gravity drainage of venous blood. Additionally, it is a place to store excess blood when the heart and lungs are exsanguinated. Additional venous blood may become available from the patient when CPB is initiated and systemic venous pressure is reduced to low levels; thus, as much as 1 to 3 liters of blood may need to be translocated from the patient to the extracorporeal circuit when full CPB begins, especially in a patient who has been in congestive heart failure. This reservoir may also serve as a gross bubble trap for air that enters the venous line; as the site where blood, fluids, or drugs may be added; into which the cardiotomy reservoir (see below) empties; and as a ready source of blood for transfusion into the patient. One of its most important functions, however, is to provide time for the perfusionist to act if venous drainage is sharply reduced or stopped, in order to avoid pumping the system dry and risking systemic air embolism. The reaction time is determined by the volume of blood in the reservoir and the

flow rate. At a flow of 4.3 liters/min (2.4 liters/min/m^2 in a 1.8 m^2 subject), a reservoir volume of 500 ml allows 7 seconds, and a volume of 1000 ml allows 14 seconds.

When a bubble oxygenator is utilized, the reservoir is placed beyond the oxygenating and defoaming chambers and is usually included as an integral part of the disposable bubble oxygenator. This may be referred to as an "arterial reservoir" (Fig. 3.8A). In this case, venous return and cardiotomy drainage enter directly into the oxygenating chamber of the bubble oxygenator; hence, this inlet must be as low as possible to facilitate venous return. With membrane oxygenators, the reservoir is the first component of the extracorporeal circuit, directly receiving the venous drainage as well as the cardiotomy drainage (Fig. 3.8B). Blood then passes through the arterial pump and then through the membrane oxygenator.

Reservoirs may be rigid (hard) plastic canisters or soft collapsible plastic bags. The rigid canisters have the advantages of making it easier to measure volume, handling venous air more effectively, often having a larger capacity, and being easier to prime, and often less expensive. The soft bags eliminate the blood-gas interface and reduce the risk of massive air embolism because they collapse when empty and do not permit air to enter the arterial pump.

CARDIOTOMY RESERVOIR AND FIELD SUCTION

During cardiac surgery it is necessary to aspirate variable but often large amounts of blood from the cardiac chambers and surgical field to prevent distension of cardiac chambers and air embolization and provide adequate exposure of the surgical field. It is not practical to discard the blood, and most of it is returned to the heart-lung machine via the cardiotomy reservoir.

The cardiotomy reservoir receives blood that has been aspirated from the heart or pericardium, or out of various vents (see "Venting of the Heart" section). They usually include a defoaming chamber containing a sponge impregnated with a substance that lowers surface tension, a storage chamber, and filters (macro and micro, see "Filters, Bubble Traps, and Microembolization" section). Blood is then returned, usually by gravity, to the arterial reservoir (with membrane oxygenator systems) or into the inflow of the bubble oxygenator, either intermittently or continuously.

The cardiotomy suction and reservoir have been found to be a major source of hemolysis, particulate and gaseous microemboli, fat globule formation, cellular aggregation, and platelet injury and loss (92–94). A major contributor to these adverse effects is the amount of air that is aspirated along with the blood. Not only does this add gaseous microemboli to the blood (which are particularly hard to dissipate because they mainly contain nitrogen, which is quite insoluble), but air-blood mixture causes turbulence and high shear stresses that injure both red blood cells and platelets. Pearson et al. (95) have analyzed the ability of various commercial cardiotomy reservoirs to remove bubbles from aspirated blood, and have described desirable features: direct injection of blood into the defoamer, avoidance of turbulence at the inlet, ensuring that all blood passes through the defoamer, avoiding free fall of blood into the reservoir, and incorporation of a micropore filter. Storing the blood in the cardiotomy reservoir for as long as possible rather than let it continuously flow into the main circuit will reduce the number of gaseous microemboli, as will reducing the air-to-blood ratio in the aspirated blood (95).

Edmunds, et al. (92) found that the fall in platelet count was proportional to the amount of cardiotomy suction, expressed as either total amount (liters per case) or as a fraction of total extracorporeal flow during CPB. de Jong et al. (96) observed progressively greater reduction in platelet number and function, and prolon-

gation of bleeding time with increasing amounts of air being aspirated along with blood during cardiotomy suction in a study in dogs. Boonstra et al. (97) noted less release of β-thromboglobulin ($p < 0.05$), less depression of adenosine diphosphate-induced platelet aggregation (not significant), and less prolongation of postoperative bleeding time (not significant) when they used an automatic controlled cardiotomy suction device that prevented aspiration of air with the blood, as compared to conventional ("uncontrolled") suction in a prospective study of patients undergoing CABG with a membrane oxygenator. Further, there was significantly less postoperative bleeding in patients in whom controlled suction was used if large volumes [>65 liters, usually longer (average, 3 hours) perfusion times] of cardiotomy suction were required. Wright and Sanderson (94) also documented the adverse effects of coaspiration of air on platelet count and formation of microaggregates (rise in screen filtration pressure).

The cardiotomy suction appears to be a principal source of hemolysis during cardiopulmonary bypass. This has been attributed to blood contact with the pericardium (although Wright and Sanderson did not find this to be true if it has been previously washed with saline), excessive negative pressure (98, 99), and, most importantly, the coaspiration of air (94, 96). Less hemolysis has been observed when a vacuum suction pump is used rather than a roller pump (94, 99).

The amount of cardiotomy suction is influenced by the type of surgery, being greater with surgery for valvular and congenital heart disease (especially if cyanotic) (92) as compared with coronary artery surgery. The amount of blood damage can be minimized by avoiding or minimizing coaspiration of air (i.e., the sucker tip should be kept below the blood level and the field not sucked "dry"), utilizing the slowest flow rates and largest suction tips possible, and avoiding generation of high degrees of negative pressure by not occluding the sucker tip and utilizing a controlled vacuum suction rather than a roller pump. The use of controlled vacuum suction, however, is somewhat more complicated and requires a closed system, increasing the risk of developing positive pressure in the cardiotomy reservoir and thereby risking systemic air embolism.

An alternative method of handling blood and fluid in the surgical field is the use of centrifugal cell washers (e.g., Haemonetics Cell Saver). These aspirate the blood with a controlled vacuum; the red cells are then automatically washed with saline and separated from the fluid by a centrifugation, and then the washed red blood cells may be returned to the extracorporeal circuit (see Chapter 4). The advantage of this method is that it removes undesirable materials (microaggregates, fat, gross air, tissue debris, potassium, bioactivators, etc.) and will hemoconcentrate, or raise the hematocrit of the perfusate. The disadvantage is the slow turn-around time and the loss of plasma proteins, coagulation factors, platelets, and other desirable substances that are in the blood. Many teams use both "cell saver" suction and cardiotomy suction, choosing one or the other depending upon the type of fluid (e.g., predominantly cardioplegic solution or ice melt versus predominantly blood) and location (e.g., pleural versus intracardiac).

VENTING OF THE HEART

The right heart is normally drained or vented by the venous cannulae. The relative efficiency of various types of venous lines at venting the right heart has been studied by Arom et al. (10) and Bennett et al. (11), and has been summarized in the "Venous Cannulation and Drainage" section and Table 3.1. When bicaval cannulation with caval occlusion is utilized, venting of the right heart is *not* provided, and if the right ventricle is not able to eject, the right heart must be vented by a cannula, cardiotomy

suction, or opening it up to drain into the pericardial sac. The rest of this discussion will relate to venting of the left ventricle.

Purpose of Venting the Left Ventricle

The purpose of left ventricular venting is to prevent distension of the ventricle, reduce myocardial rewarming, prevent ejection of air, and to facilitate surgical exposure, e.g., when working on the aortic valve. Prevention of distension of the left ventricle is desirable to prevent mechanical damage to the muscle from excessive stretching, improve myocardial preservation by decreasing myocardial oxygen demand (decreased wall tension due to decreased radius of ventricle), facilitating subendocardial perfusion (subendocardial perfusion pressure equals aortic pressure minus left ventricular pressure), and to prevent pulmonary venous hypertension, with possible pulmonary injury or edema with pulmonary artery hypertension.

Sources of Blood Returning to the Left Ventricle

The normal sources of blood returning to the left ventricle during CPB include bronchial and thebesian veins as well as blood returning to the right heart that passes throughout the pulmonary circuit. Abnormal sources include a left superior pulmonary vein that drains into the coronary sinus and right heart, patent ductus arteriosus or a systemic to pulmonary artery shunt (e.g., Blalock-Taussig or Waterston), anomalous systemic venous drainage into the left heart, and aortic regurgitation. Even if not present preoperatively, aortic regurgitation commonly occurs when administering cardioplegia into the aortic root and from distortion of aortic root with other surgical manipulations. Even hemodynamically mild aortic regurgitation (e.g., 1 liter/min) becomes catastrophic when the heart fibrillates during CPB yielding continuous aortic regurgitation without the ability of the left ventricle to empty itself. The bronchial blood flow to the periphery of the lung normally drains with the pulmonary veins. On bypass, this averages about 40 ± 182 ml/min (100) and the amount is influenced by the mean arterial pressure, which is one rationale for maintaining low perfusion pressures during CPB.

Patients with chronic lung infections or inflammatory lung disease (e.g., bronchiectasis) and cyanotic congenital heart disease have exaggerated bronchial blood flow. Coronary sinus flow into the right heart should greatly diminish with aortic cross-clamping except for noncoronary collateral flow [average, 48 ± 74 ml/min (100)], when cardioplegia (or coronary perfusion) is administered, and in the presence of a left superior vena cava. Most coronary sinus blood should be removed if the venous cannulae are working properly, unless bicaval cannulae with caval tourniquets are employed. When excessive return of blood to the left heart is encountered, improper function or placement of the venous cannulae, a left superior vena cava, a patent ductus arteriosus, or aortic regurgitation should be suspected.

Indications for Venting the Left Heart

Venting of the left heart is indicated whenever the left ventricle is unable to handle the amount of blood that is returning to it. This is assessed by direct inspection of the heart, monitoring the left atrial or pulmonary artery pressure, or by transesophageal echocardiography. There is considerable debate about the need to vent the left heart during cardiac surgery, especially in the era of cold cardioplegia and for coronary artery surgery (101–104). Excellent results have been reported without the use of venting in aortic (105) and coronary artery (106) surgery. On the other hand, experimental studies suggest optimal myocardial recovery after an ischemic in-

sult is best provided by full CPB and venting of the left ventricle (107). Otherwise, myocardial oxygen demand may be considerable *even though the left ventricular diastolic pressure is low* and the heart is not ejecting (107). Thus, left ventricular venting during reperfusion may be warranted in hearts with limited reserve, or which have been incompletely revascularized or have sustained a particularly severe ischemic insult.

Methods of Venting

During coronary artery surgery, either no venting or venting via the cardioplegia cannula in the aortic root (108, 109) is commonly practiced (Fig. 3.9A).[a] One of the limitations of aortic root venting is that it does not function while cardioplegia is being administered, and if there is any aortic regurgitation or excessive blood return to the left heart, it may be necessary to intermittently interrupt the administration of cardioplegia and apply suction to the vent with or without external compression of the left ventricle. When direct venting of the left ventricle is desired, this is most commonly accomplished by inserting a catheter through a purse-string suture placed at the junction of the right superior pulmonary vein and the left atrium, and advancing the catheter across the mitral valve into the left ventricle (Fig. 3.9B). Today, vents are seldom placed directly through the apex of the left ventricle (Fig. 3.9C). This approach has been largely abandoned because of the risk of hemorrhage and myocardial injury. Some surgeons insert vents into the left atrium only or into the pulmonary artery (Fig. 3.9D) (102, 110, 111), which eliminate some of the risks of direct left ventricular venting but exhibit variable effectiveness. The effectiveness of pulmo-

_____

[a]Special cardioplegia cannulae are available with a Y-arm, which may be connected to suction when cardioplegia is not being administered through the main arm of the cannula.

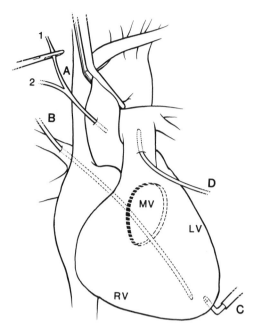

Figure 3.9.   Sites for venting the left ventricle (*LV*). *A,* the aortic root cannula; one limb of the "Y" (*1*) is connected to the cardioplegia administration system and the other limb (*2*) to suction for venting left heart. *B,* the cannula inserted at junction of right superior pulmonary vein and left atrium, and advanced through left atrium and mitral valve (*MV*) into the left ventricle. *C,* the cannula is inserted directly into the apex of left ventricle. *D,* the cannula is inserted into the pulmonary artery. *RV,* right ventricle. (Modified from Hensley FA Jr, Martin DE, eds. The Practice of Cardiac Anesthesia. Boston: Little, Brown and Company, 1990.)

nary artery venting may be improved by pulmonary vein occlusion (112), but this requires careful monitoring of the adequacy of pulmonary artery venting. Pulmonary artery venting may not prevent left ventricular distension in the presence of aortic valve insufficiency and mitral valve competence (111).

These vents are then attached to a suction device (roller pump or regulated wall suction) and the blood is returned to the cardiotomy reservoir. When the tip of the vent is in the ventricle, the degree of suction must be constantly adjusted to avoid excess suction (with collapse and trauma to the ventricle and the risk of aspirating air), or inadequate suction (with overdisten-

sion). For this reason, some surgeons employ gravity (siphon) drainage instead of suction. This requires that the drainage reservoir be placed well below the patient, and it may not provide adequate drainage if large volumes of blood are returning to the left heart. Some surgeons "Y the line" coming from the ventricular vent so that either gravity or suction drainage can be utilized.

Complications of Venting the Left Heart

Left ventricular venting is not without complications. These include introduction of air into the left heart and subsequent systemic air embolism. This is most likely to occur at the time of insertion or removal if the left heart volume is low. To minimize this risk, the heart is usually allowed to fill before insertion, and the vents are often removed while the insertion site is covered with fluid. Excessive suction is another source of air introduction. Finally, erroneous function of the suction (positive pressure in reservoir, misdirection of tubing into roller pump head, reversal of roller pump) may cause air to be pumped into the ventricle. The use of a one-way valve in the left ventricular vent line is advocated by some surgeons to prevent this complication. Most surgeons will test the function of the vent line to see if it aspirates fluid before attaching it to the heart. Other risks are bleeding and damage to the heart, including late left ventricular aneurysms (113). If there is a significant blood return through the left heart vent due to aortic regurgitation or bronchial blood flow, this steals systemic blood flow, which should be compensated for by increasing pump flow by an equivalent amount.

Aortic Root Air Venting

Any time the heart is entered, even simply by placing a catheter in a chamber, air may collect in the heart that, if not removed, will embolize. Even right heart air may pass into the left heart via septal defects or through the lungs. In addition to vigorous attempts at removal of all air before closing the left heart, the use of left heart vents, and repeated aspirations of left-sided chambers, the use of venting at the highest point of the aorta is considered the "final safety valve" against systemic air embolism (114). Brenner et al. (115) have analyzed the physiologic principles relevant to the efficiency of aortic root air vents and studied various systems in an in vitro model. They found that a freely bleeding stab wound containing a nonconstricted fenestrated 10 F plastic catheter connected to suction was most efficient (97%). A freely bleeding stab wound was almost as efficient (91%), but inserting a catheter, *not* connected to suction, into the stab wound decreased its efficiency to 79%. Freely bleeding needles and catheter vents not connected to suction were very inefficient (20 to 36%), but efficiency was improved (to about 90%) by applying suction. Marco and Barner (114) have demonstrated that the larger the vent needle area and the greater the flow out of the vent (suction), the greater its efficiency. There are obvious limits to this approach, including loss of forward flow and hemolysis.

FILTERS, BUBBLE TRAPS, AND MICROEMBOLIZATION

Gross and microembolic material are ever-present during CPB (93, 116) and are fully discussed in Chapter 6. Multiple strategies have been suggested to reduce the hazards of embolization (Table 3.4), but the most obvious is the use of micropore filters (117, 118).[e] Two types of micropore filters are available. The *depth filter* con-

---

sists of packed fibers or porous foam. The predominant example of this is the Swank dacron wool filter. It has no defined pore size, presents a tortuous large wetted surface, and filters by impaction and absorption. The *screen filters* are usually made of woven polymer thread that has a defined pore size and filters by interception, although the smallest pored screen filters (0.2 to 5.0 microns) are made of membranes. Screen filters vary in pore size, material used (principally polyester and nylon), and configuration. They not only block particulate emboli, but also gross and microscopic air emboli. The latter is accomplished because the pores are filled with liquid that is maintained by surface active forces. Excessive pressure could overcome this barrier by exceeding the so-called bubble point pressure.

Several studies have compared the performance of various micropore filters designed for cardiotomy (119, 120) or arterial lines (95, 121–125) and most have found the dacron wool (depth) filter to be the most effective (119, 120, 122, 123, 125). Gourlay et al. (121–123), in an in vitro study of 13 commercially available arterial line filters, found all to have a similar pressure drop (24 to 34 mm Hg at 5 liters/min flow), but to exhibit variable degrees of hemolysis and platelet loss and handling of gross and microscopic air that did not appear to be related to pore size or type of material, except that again, the dacron wool (Swank) was best at removal of both microscopic and gross air. For other filters there was no parallel between their effectiveness at handling gross or microscopic air. However, all were vastly superior to no filter in regards to interdiction of microemboli. Other authors have expressed concern that the dacron wool filter might cause significantly more hemolysis and thrombocytopenia, and develop channelling and saturation breakthrough (117). Gourlay et al. (121) did not note excessive hemolysis, and Ware et al. (120) determined that although platelet counts were lower following the

Table 3.4. Procedures and Practices that Have Been Proposed to Reduce the Amount of Microembolization

Membrane oxygenator (vs. bubble)

Centrifugal pump (vs. roller)

Micropore filter between cardiotomy reservoir and main circuit (≤40 micron)

Arterial line micropore filter (≤40 micron)
    Vented continuously to cardiotomy reservoir

Microfiltration of blood added to circuit

If Using Bubble Oxygenator
    Maintain high reservoir level
    Use lowest gas:blood flow ratio possible

Regarding Cardiotomy Suction
    Use as little as possible
    Aspirate as little air as possible
    Use lowest flow possible

Regarding Cardiotomy Reservoir
    Should have an integral micropore filter
    Maintain high reservoir volume
    Retain blood in reservoir as long as possible

If Using Roller Pump
    Set barely non-occlusive
    Use PVC vs. Silicone Rubber

During Priming
    Flush with carbon dioxide before prime
    Prime with warmed fluids
    Use prebypass micropore filter (5 micron)
    Prolonged recirculation with manual tapping of components

Keep temperature gradients during warming and cooling to less than 8–10°C

Use largest arterial cannula possible

Adequate anticoagulation

Keep purse-string sutures around cannula as tight as possible

Minimal acceptable suction on vents

Vigorous de-airing at end of any procedure if left heart has been opened

Avoid use of nitrous oxide during or after CPB

use of dacron wool cardiotomy filters, the number of functional platelets were the same (i.e., the screen filter allowed more dysfunctional platelets to pass). Some concern has also been expressed that nylon screen filters may activate or complement (117, 118). Recently, heparin-coated arterial line micropore filters have been introduced to reduce platelet aggregation and loss, and facilitate debubbling and priming (126). However, studies have shown that the heparin-benzalkonium coating may leak off during priming, rendering it ineffective or increasing the risk of passage of microscopic air (127).

Micropore filters may be used in several locations in the extracorporeal circuits, including as an integral part of cardiotomy reservoirs, in the arterial line, the gas flow line to the oxygenator, the cardioplegia line, as a prebypass filter (during priming), and in blood administration sets. A survey from 1981 to 1983 indicated that micropore filters were used in the cardiotomy suction circuit over 90% of the time; in fact, most commercial cardiotomy reservoirs now contain an integrated micropore filter. Since the cardiotomy suction is a major source of microemboli, and since a micropore filter is more effective if placed in the cardiotomy reservoir line than arterial line (95), this would appear to be a reasonable practice. With the demonstrated presence of various foreign particulate matter in the disposables used for extracorporeal circuits, it also seems reasonable to use a prebypass filter during priming. The need for micropore filters on the *cardioplegia delivery system* has been questioned by recent experimental studies (128).

The need for and benefits of arterial micropore filtration are still debated (129). In vitro and animal studies previously mentioned (95, 122–125) have documented that micropore arterial filtration does reduce the number of microemboli measured by ultrasound, and clinical studies have confirmed this (130–133). Brennan et al. (134) observed improved cerebral blood flow and metabolism in dogs when arterial microfiltration was used. Muraoka et al. (135) noted fewer (0 of 14) abnormal computed tomography scans when a 20-micron filter (Johnson and Johnson Intersept) was used, but just as many abnormal scans (3 of 8) when a 40-micron filter (Pall EC3840) was used as compared with no filter (1 of 5) during CPB in children with a bubble oxygenator. Blauth et al. (136) observed no reduction in microembolic retinal ischemia when a 40-micron arterial filter (Ultipore, Pall) was used in a bubble oxygenator circuit. Henriksen et al. (137) found that the use of arterial micropore filtration only modestly reduced the cerebral hyperemic response to bypass, which they had previously attributed to microembolization.

Several authors, using historical controls, have reported a reduced incidence of neurologic damage with the use of micropore filters (138–141). When compared to historical controls Garvey et al. (142) found no significant difference in functional impairment, as judged by psychometric testing with two arterial micropore filters (Pall, 40 micron, and Bentley, 25 micron) (8, 54). Three prospective controlled studies have failed to detect a difference in neurologic outcome with or without the use of micropore filters (143–145), and another observed no difference in performance on a sophisticated neuropsychometric test with the use of arterial micropore filtration (146). Ohri et al. (147) observed no difference in the incidence of intraabdominal complications with the use of arterial microfiltration. Only one prospective study utilizing concurrent controls has found improved outcome (performance on a battery of neuropsychometric tests) with the use of arterial micropore filtration, and this study was small and reported in only an abbreviated format (148). Thus, I cannot agree with Marshall that "the clinical efficacy (of micropore filtration) has been established" (118).

On the negative side, these filters add to the cost, may obstruct, are harder to de-air (and, therefore, may be a source of gaseous microemboli), may generate microemboli, cause hemolysis and platelet loss, and complement activation. However, the wide use and available studies suggest that there is little adverse effect from their use. Micropore arterial filters (Fig. 3.10) are excellent gross bubble traps and, on this basis alone, their routine use can probably be justified. If they are used for this purpose, however, they must have (unless they are self-venting) a continuously open purge line that goes from the filter to the cardiotomy reservoir to allow escape of trapped air, and a bypass safety line that goes around the filter and is usually clamped but can be opened in case the filter clogs.

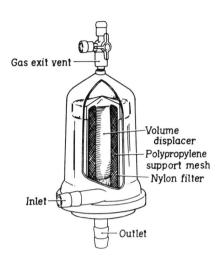

Gas exit vent

Volume
displacer
Polypropylene
support mesh
Nylon filter

Inlet

Outlet

Figure 3.10. An arterial line microfilter and bubble trap (Bentley AF-10). Blood enters tangentially at the bottom and swirls upward, encouraging bubbles to flow to the top, where they escape through a continuous purge line to the cardiotomy reservoir. Blood passes through a microfilter (25 microns) and out the bottom. (From Reed CC, Stafford TB. Cardiopulmonary Bypass. Houston: Texas Medical Press, Inc., 1985.)

HEMOCONCENTRATORS (HEMOFILTRATION, ULTRAFILTRATION)

Hemoconcentrators contain semipermeable membranes (typically hollow fibers) that permit passage of water and electrolytes out of the blood. They are used in lieu of diuretics to remove excess fluid or electrolytes (e.g., potassium) and to raise hematocrit. They can be connected to the extracorporeal circuit in several different configurations. Blood may be drawn from the venous line, the arterial or venous reservoirs, or the arterial line, and filtered blood may be returned to the venous line or the cardiotomy or venous reservoirs. Except when blood is taken from the arterial line, a pump must be utilized to drive blood through the device, and may be used to control flow even if blood comes from the arterial line. Most hemoconcentrators need to be primed (rinsed) with a clear electrolyte fluid. Pressure is generated within the

blood channels by resistance to flow through the capillaries or by a partially occluding clamp downstream. Suction may or may not be applied to the air side of the membrane to facilitate filtration. Fluid removal can be as great as 180 ml/min (at a 500 ml/min flow) (149). Various types of membranes are used. Molecules up to a molecular weight of 20,000 daltons are removed. At least some heparin is removed and, thus, adequacy of heparinization must be monitored. Because of blood viscosity considerations, caution should be exercised in raising the hematocrit during hypothermia.

The hemofilter can be used postbypass to concentrate the pump blood before it is given back to the patient. Advantages of their use compared to centrifugal cell washers (e.g., Cell Saver) are that they conserve platelets, albumin and coagulation factors (149), and may be cheaper. Potential adverse consequences (besides cost) are additional entrance into the circuit, potential for complement activation, retention of free hemoglobin and proteolytic enzymes (e.g., polymorphonuclear elastase), and loss of heparin and excessive rise in hematocrit. However, no adverse effects were encountered by Boldt et al. (149) These authors compared six different hemofiltration devices with the Cell Saver and identified some significant differences. Compared with diuretics, they are more easily controlled and do not cause excessive potassium losses (150). See Chapter 4 for a further discussion of these systems.

CARDIOPLEGIA COOLING AND DELIVERY SYSTEM AND CORONARY PERFUSION SYSTEMS

Myocardial protection is reviewed in detail in Chapter 7. Continuous direct coronary artery perfusion has virtually disappeared with the acceptance of antegrade, and now retrograde, cardioplegia. Occasionally, antegrade cardioplegia must be given by inserting hand-held cannulae into the coronary artery orifices. These come in various sizes and should fit snugly in the coronary ostia to avoid significant back leakage. Care must be taken not to injure the coronary artery or to insert the catheter in too far (and, hence, not perfuse critical branches). This is more likely with perfusion of the left main coronary artery in the presence of left dominance because the left main artery is shorter in this circumstance.

The simplest cardioplegia delivery system is a cold bag of clear crystalloid cardioplegia placed under external pressure. Care must be taken to avoid infusion of air. Probably most surgeons, however, deliver the cardioplegia from the heart-lung machine. Typically, the cardioplegia cannula is attached to a Y connector. One limb of the Y is connected to suction for venting out the aortic root when not administering cardioplegia; and the other limb of the Y is connected to the cardioplegia delivery line. The cardioplegia delivery line often has a return line back to the cardioplegia circuit so that the cardioplegia can be recirculated when not being administered. Automatic switching devices are available. The cardioplegia circuit also includes a reservoir, heat exchanger (often simply a plastic coil placed in a water bath), temperature monitors to monitor both water bath and cardioplegia temperature, a pressure gauge to monitor line pressure, a pump (usually roller), and some way of monitoring flow rates. If blood cardioplegia is utilized, a connection to a source of oxygenated blood in the extracorporeal circuit must be available. Some surgeons run two tubes of different sizes through a single pump head, one carrying crystalloid and the other oxygenated blood, so that the two are mixed in a 4:1 ratio (151).

Retrograde cardioplegia is delivered through the coronary sinus (152, 153). Special cannulae are designed for this purpose. All have an extra port near the tip for monitoring coronary sinus pressure and a balloon to prevent leak. These may require manual inflation or may autoinflate with infusion of the cardioplegia solution. They may be inserted blindly through an atrial purse-string suture, which may be aided by intraatrial palpation with a finger passed through a separate atrial purse-string suture. It is often easier to accomplish *before* the atrial cannulae are inserted and bypass has begun, but the patient may not tolerate this hemodynamically or electrically. When inserted during bypass, there may be problems with air entrainment and subsequent air lock. The same cardioplegia delivery systems are then employed as for antegrade cardioplegia.

SAFETY, RISK CONTAINMENT, CONTROL, AND MONITORING

Monitoring

Overall monitoring of the patient during cardiopulmonary bypass is covered in Chapter 22.

IN-LINE BLOOD GAS MONITORS

Noninvasive flow-through devices are available to measure blood gases in the arterial and venous lines (154–156). The arterial monitor provides continuous assessment of arterial oxygenation (like a pulse oximeter) and permits more rapid and precise control of blood gases (157, 158). Venous oximetry permits rapid assessment of the balances of oxygen supply and demand (159–161). Rubsamen (162), a medicolegal scholar, asserted that in-line blood gas monitoring is a standard of care that is essential both from the standpoint of patient safety and prevention of devastating malpractice suits. Unfortunately, there appears to be little scientific data documenting that this approach is superior (more safe) to the visual monitoring of arterial and venous lines plus periodic blood gas sampling. Further, currently available devices are imperfect and may provide misleading information (163).

Another approach at more timely monitoring of blood gases and various electrolytes is the use of automated operating room analyzers (164, 165), but the perfusion team or other individuals in the operating room must then accept responsibility for quality control and recognize their limitations (155, 164). One must also beware that blood drawn from the sampling port of some oxygenators may give misleading information (166).

Just as monitoring the oxygen content of gas being delivered to a patient under anesthesia is an American Society of Anesthesiologists standard of care, an oxygen analyzer should be included in the gas supply to the extracorporeal oxygenator (167).

ARTERIAL LINE PRESSURE

The pressure in the arterial line, following the pump but before the arterial line filter, should be monitored continuously to detect obstruction in the arterial line, malposition of the arterial cannula, dissection, or obstruction of the filter. This pressure must be interpreted in the context of the expected pressure drop across the arterial cannula at the indicated flow rate and the patient's monitored intraarterial pressure (4). It is also a useful guide to proper initial arterial cannulation, and as a monitor of central arterial pressure in the early postbypass period, when radial artery pressure may be misleading.

OTHER MONITORS

An arterial line flow meter is essential if a centrifugal pump is being used, and a helpful adjunct to confirm proper occlusiveness when a roller pump is used. Akers et al. (168) have compared four different extracorporeal blood flow meters and the influence of changing hematocrit. The differences they observed were small and do not appear clinically significant.

Monitoring the temperature of the water supplying the system and cardioplegia heat exchangers is essential for the safe conduct of perfusion, as is knowledge of the temperature of the venous (from body) and arterial (returning) blood.

Low-level alarms on arterial or venous reservoir and a bubble detector on the arterial line are considered desirable safety devices. Whether they should be connected to the pump controller to automatically turn off the pump is the subject of debate (faster response time versus risk of false alarms).

Automatic data collection systems are available to assist with the preoperative calculations and process and store data during bypass, which should free up the perfusionist to attend to more important tasks (169). Whether this will indeed improve outcome remains to be demonstrated (158, 170).

Incidence and Types of Critical Incidents

Four surveys conducted between 1972 and 1986 (171–174) found a life-threatening incident rate of 0.4 to 1% and a permanent injury or death rate attributed to such incidents of about 1 in 1000 to 1 in 1500 (172) (Table 3.5). Principal types of incidents were inadequate oxygenation, electrical failure, gas embolization, clotting, line separation, blood leaks, mechanical failure, and failure of blender-flow meter, while principal causes of permanent

Table 3.5. Incidence of Critical Incidents During Perfusion: Serious Incident, 0.4–1.0%; Permanent Injury or Death, 0.07–0.09%[a]

Type of Critical Incident	Incidence (per 1000)	Permanent Injury or Mortality (%)
Gas embolism	1.2	25
Electrical failure	0.9	1
Oxygenator failure	0.6	7
Mechanical failure	0.2	4
Reversed LV vent	0.05	

[a]Summary of data from four studies between the years of 1972–1986 as presented by Kurusz and Wheeldon (171, 172, 174).

injury or death were gas embolism, oxygenator failure, and clotting. Other reported incidents that may not be directly related to the cardiopulmonary bypass equipment per se include hypoperfusion, drug errors, and transfusion-related complications. Like most other adverse incidents, the majority of these are estimated to be due to human error, with only 20% attributed to device failure (172).

Gross and Massive Air Embolism (see also Chapter 11)

This is one of the most common serious adverse events associated with cardiopulmonary bypass (175–177), and is largely preventable. Principal causes include pumping air out of a dry or nearly empty reservoir (vortexing), disconnection, leaks, or oxygenator breaks or line occlusion prior to the arterial pump (with air entrainment or cavitation); incomplete deairing of circuit prior to bypass; reversal of arterial and venous lines, reversal of arterial pump head, or backflow into arterial cannula, if not occlusive, e.g., centrifugal pump (65); occlusion of the exhaust port of a membrane oxygenator (forcing air bubbles into the blood), development of positive pressure in a cardiotomy reservoir, which may force air back through the arterial filter bleed line or left ventricular or aortic root vents, injection of air into the aortic root from the cardioplegia delivery system, ejection of air from the heart, or introduction of air at the time of cannulation or decannulation of aorta or left heart. Air entrainment during the latter procedures may be aggravated by low arterial or left heart pressures. The deflation phase of intraaortic balloon pumping may aspirate air through an open aorta. Air may be entrained into the heart by the patient's own respiratory efforts (e.g., inadequate muscle paralysis) when the left heart is open or by injudicious mechanical ventilation if the pressures in the heart cavities fall precipitously during exhalation.

The pumping of air out of the reservoir is principally due to inattention on the part of the perfusionist, but will be aggravated by a sudden decline in venous return or a runaway pump. Ejection of air from the left ventricle occurs whenever air enters the left heart and is allowed to eject before adequate drainage. Insertion of lines and vents into the left heart, deep suction into the pulmonary arteries, reverse flow of air through a left-sided vent (due to reversal of pump head or development of positive pressure in the cardiotomy reservoir), and septal defects all may permit air to enter the left heart. Kurusz and Wheeldon (172) reported that 44% of 458 episodes of gas embolization came from the arterial line, and in half of these cases it was attributed to inattention on the part of the perfusionist. Nine percent of all cases were attributed to reversed left ventricular vent line, 10% to unexpected resumption of heart beat, and 5% to a pressurized cardiotomy reservoir.

Vigilance is the key to prevention. Other helpful components are protection of the venous lines by the surgical team and communication with the perfusionist when venous return is likely to be compromised (e.g., lifting the heart), maintaining a safe volume of blood in the reservoir, use of collapsible reservoirs, centrifugal pumps, arterial line filters/bubble traps with a continuously open air purge line guarded by a one-way valve, placement of one-way valves in left heart vent line, and use of low-level alarms and bubble detectors that may or may not be connected to automatic shut-off devices connected to the arterial pump.

Risk Containment (171–174)

Accidents are principally due to human error, although device failure accounts for some of them. A risk containment program therefore should include the following components.

Adequate education, practice, experience, training and certification (and recertification) (178) of all members of the team, and proper accreditation of training centers should be the primary concern. The well-trained, vigilant human is the key to risk containment. The development of and familiarity with protocols for all routine and emergency situations is also necessary. Emergency protocols and contingency plans should be periodically reviewed and practiced by all team members. The use of checklists fits closely with the development of protocols.

The risk prevention program should include the employment (and activation) of safety equipment and alarms—if not turned on, they will not help. Some of these features are listed in the "Monitoring" section under "Safety, Risk Containment, Control, and Monitoring." An appropriate preventive maintenance program is also necessary. It has been mentioned that power failure can occur. Therefore, evaluate the capabilities of all power supplies; know the capacity of outlets and beware of overloading, especially with heater-coolers.

Old equipment should be replaced when appropriate. When new equipment or components are added, team members must be thoroughly familiar ("inserviced") with it, and it should be tested.

Another safety point is to avoid distractions of any team member during the procedure. Each of the three key members of the team (surgeon, anesthesiologist, and perfusionist) must maintain communication with one another. In particular, they must mention any activity they engage in that may have impact upon the other two. Commands must be clear and must be verbally acknowledged.

MISCELLANEOUS TOPICS

Heparin-Coated Circuits (179)

Various methods of coating the surfaces of extracorporeal circuits with heparin are available, of which a proprietary method (Duraflow II, Bentley) seems most promising (126). Currently, all compo-

nents can be coated with heparin. The objective of heparin coating is to improve biocompatability, i.e., reduce surface activation of platelets, kallikrein, complement, clotting, and fibrinolytic systems. Hopefully, this will reduce the whole body inflammatory response to CPB, as well as to reduce or eliminate the need for heparin and, hence, blood loss. Clinical use of heparin-coated surfaces for CPB with full heparinization have been shown to reduce complement activation (180–182) and thrombin generation (thrombin-antithrombin III complexes) (181, 183), but not to significantly reduce pulmonary neutrophil sequestration, retinal microembolism or postoperative blood loss (181, 182. von Segesser et al. (184, 185) have demonstrated the feasibility of performing coronary artery surgery with low levels of systemic heparinization (100 units/kg loading; activated clotting time, >180 seconds, but with important constraints (e.g., no cardiotomy reservoir, avoid stagnant blood, cannulae must be vented). Utilizing this method, they observed a 50% reduction in blood loss and a 75% reduction in homologous blood administration (one-fourth).

Total Body Retrograde Perfusion

On special occasions, total body retrograde perfusion (i.e., infusion into the vena cava and drainage out of the aorta) may be used. Mills and Ochsner (176) first suggested temporary retrograde perfusion of the SVC (and sometimes even the IVC) at rates of 1–2 liters/min for 1 to 2 minutes to treat massive systemic air embolism. Yasuura et al. (186) have utilized retrograde perfusion of both SVC and IVC at flow rates of 300 to 600 ml/min at rectal temperatures of 20°C for up to 110 minutes as part of the extracorporeal circulation management of patients undergoing surgery for aortic dissection. Standard antegrade perfusion was used at the start and end of the perfusion to induce hypothermia and to rewarm. The SVC pressure was limited to 30 mm Hg and "venous drainage" (out of the aorta) was accomplished by suction into the venous reservoir. Venous valves in the neck apparently do not prevent retrograde flow and are apparently absent from the veins draining abdominal viscera, but probably preclude flow into the extremities. Further studies of this novel approach are needed before general applications can be recommended.

REFERENCES

1. Peirce EC II. Extracorporeal circulation for open-heart surgery. Springfield, Illinois: Charles C Thomas, 1969.
2. Kirklin JW, Barratt-Boyes BE. Cardiac surgery. Part I, Sections 1 and 2. New York: John Wiley and Sons, 1986:30–82.
3. Riley JB, Hardin SB, Winn BA, Hurdle MB. In vitro comparison of cavoatrial (dual stage) cannulae for use during cardiopulmonary bypass. Perfusion 1986;1:197–204.
4. Delius RF, Montoya JP, Merz SJ, et al. A new method for describing the performance of cardiac surgery cannulas. Ann Thorac Surg 1992;33:278–281.
5. Sadeghi AM, Rose EA, Michler RE, et al. A simplified method for the occlusion of the venae cavae during cardiopulmonary bypass. Ann Thorac Surg 1986;41:678.
6. Cooley DA. Caval occlusion clamps for temporary cardiopulmonary bypass. J Thorac Cardiovasc Surg 1970;59:292.
7. Phillips SJ, Romanowski E. A new designed venous cannula for cardiopulmonary bypass. J Thorac Cardiovasc Surg 1972;63:769–770.
8. Kirsh MM, Lemmer JH, Zwischenberger, JB. Rapid technique of occlusion of the venae cavae for total cardiopulmonary bypass during repeat cardiac operations. Ann Thorac Surg 1987;43:566–567.
9. Morritt GN, Holden MP. The cuffed endotracheal tube in emergency cardiopulmonary bypass operations. Ann Thor Surg 1981;31:287–288.
10. Arom KV, Ellestad C, Grover FL, Trinkle JK. Objective evaluation of the efficacy of various venous cannulas. J Thorac Cardiovasc Surg 1981;81:464–469.
11. Bennett EV Jr, Fewel JG, Ybarra J, et al. Comparison of flow differences among venous cannulas. Ann Thorac Surg 1983;36:59–65.
12. Rosenfeldt FL, Watson DA. Interference with local myocardial cooling by heat gain during aortic cross-clamping. Ann Thorac Surg 1979;27:13–16.
13. Bennett EV Jr, Fewel JG, Grover FL, Trinkle JK. Myocardial preservation: effect of venous drainage. Ann Thorac Surg 1983;36:132–42.
14. Taylor PC, Effler DB. Management of cannulation for cardiopulmonary bypass in patients with adult-acquired heart disease. Surg Clinic North Am 1975;55:1205–1215.
15. Bahadir I, Diethrich EB. A new venous cannula for use during CPB [Letter]. Ann Thorac Surg 1984;37:439.
16. Smith CR, Getrajdman Hsu DT. Venous cannulation for high-flow femoro-femoral bypass. Ann Thorac Surg 1990;49:674–675.
17. Rosenbloom M, Muskett AD. Simplified method for femoral venous cannulation. Ann Thorac Surg 1991;51:846–847.
18. Westaby S. Extrathoracic cannulation for urgent cardiopulmonary bypass in cardiac tamponade: use of internal jugular vein. J Cardiovasc Surg 1988;29:103–105.
19. Choudhry AK, Conacher ID, Hilton CJ, et al. Persistent left superior vena cava. J Cardiothorac Anesth 1989;3:616–619.
20. Harris AM, Shawkat S, Bailey JS. The use of an endotracheal tube for cannulation of left superior vena cava via coronary sinus for repair of a sinus venosus atrial septal defect. Br Heart J 1987;58:676–677.
21. Horrow JC, Lingaraju N. Unexpected persistent left superior vena cava: diagnostic clues during monitoring. J Cardiothorac Anesth 1989;3:611–615.
22. Ratnaraj J, Manohar G. Pulmonary artery catheter displacement during cannulation for CPB [Letter]. J Cardiothorac Vasc Anesth 1991;5:648.
23. Herrema IH, Winsser LJA. Flow directed pulmonary artery catheter obstructs venous drainage cannula of cardiopulmonary bypass machine [Letter]. Anaesthesia 1988;43:799.
24. Brodman R, Siegel H, Lesser M, Frater R. A comparison of flow gradients across disposable arterial perfusion cannulas. Ann Thorac Surg 1985;39:225–233.
25. Galletti PM, Brecher GA. Heart-lung bypass. New York: Grune & Stratton, 1962.
26. Drews JA, Cleveland RJ, Nelson RJ. An approach to aortic cannulation with a caution on hemolysis associated with angled cannulas. Rev Surg 1974;31:57–59.
27. Magner, JB. Complications of aortic cannulation for open-heart surgery. Thorax 1971;26:172–173.
28. McAlpine WA, Selman MW, Kawakami T. Routine use of aortic cannulation in open heart operations. Am J Surg 1967;114:831–834.
29. Davidson KG. Cannulation for cardiopulmonary bypass. In: Taylor KM, ed. Cardiopulmo-

nary bypass: principles and management. Ch 5. Baltimore: Williams & Wilkins, 1986:55–89.

30. Taylor PC, Groves LK, Loop FD, Effler DB. Cannulation of the ascending aorta for cardiopulmonary bypass. J Thorac Cardiovasc Surg 1976;71:255–258.

31. Mills NL, Everson CT. Atherosclerosis of the ascending aorta and coronary artery bypass: pathology, clinical correlates, and operative management. J Thorac Cardiovasc Surg 1991;102:546–553.

32. Ohteki H, Itoh T, Natsuaki M, et al. Intraoperative ultrasonic imaging of the ascending aorta in ischemic heart disease. Ann Thorac Surg 1990;50:539–542.

33. Wareing TH, Davilla-Roman VG, Barzilai B, et al. Management of the severely atherosclerotic ascending aorta during cardiac operations: A strategy for detection and treatment. J Thorac Cardiovasc Surg 1992;103:453–462.

34. Still RJ, Hilgenberg AD, Akins CW, et al. Intraoperative aortic dissection. Ann Thorac Surg 1992;53:374–380.

35. Garcia-Rinaldi R, Vaughan GD III, Revuelta JM, et al. Simplified aortic cannulation. Ann Thorac Surg 1983;36:226–227.

36. Parker R: Aortic cannulation. Thorax 1969;24:742–745.

37. Krous HF, Mansfield PB, Sauvage LR. Carotid artery hyperperfusion during open-heart surgery. J Thorac Cardiovasc Surg 1973;66:118–121.

38. Kulkarni MG. A complication of aortic cannulation. J Cardiovasc Surg 1968;9:207–208.

39. Dalal FY, Patel KD. Another sign of inadvertent carotid cannulation [Letter]. Anesthesiology 1981;55:487.

40. Ross WT Jr, Lake CL, Wallons HA. Cardiopulmonary bypass complicated by inadvertent carotid cannulation. Anesthesiology 1981;54:85–86.

41. Watson BG: Unilateral cold neck. Anaesthesia 1983;38:659–661.

42. McLeskey CH, Cheney FW. A correctable complication of cardiopulmonary bypass. Anesthesiology 1982;56:214–216.

43. Magilligan DJ Jr, Eastland MW, Lell WA, et al. Decreased carotid flow with ascending aortic cannulation. Circulation 1972;45(46:suppl):130–133.

44. Salerno TA, Lince DP, White DN, et al. Arch versus femoral artery perfusion during cardiopulmonary bypass. J Thorac Cardiovasc Surg 1978;78:681–684.

45. Murphy DA, Craver JM, Jones EL, et al. Recognition and management of ascending aortic dissection complicating cardiac surgical operations. J Thorac Cardiovasc Surg 1983;85:247–256.

46. Salama FD, Blesovsky A. Complications of cannulation of the ascending aorta for open heart surgery. Thorax 1970;25:604–607.

47. Lees MH, Herr RH, Hill JD, et al. Distribution of systemic blood flow of the rhesus monkey during cardiopulmonary bypass. J Thorac Cardiovasc Surg 1971;61:570–586.

48. Herman BE, Wallace HW, Gadboys HL, Litwak RS. Anterior crural syndrome as a complication of cardiopulmonary bypass. J Thorac Cardiovasc Surg 1966;52:755–758.

49. Benedict JS, Buhl TL, Henney, RP. Acute aortic dissection during cardiopulmonary bypass. Arch Surg 1974;108:810–813.

50. Bigutay AM, Garamella JJ, Danyluk M, Remucal HC. Retrograde aortic dissection occurring during cardiopulmonary bypass. JAMA 1976;236:465–468.

51. Carey JS, Skow JR, Scott C. Retrograde aortic dissection during cardiopulmonary bypass: "nonoperative" management. Ann Thorac Surg 1977;24:44–48.

52. Jones TW, Vetto RR, Winterscheid LC, et al. Arterial complications incident to cannulation in open-heart surgery. Ann Surg 1960;152:969–974.

53. Trojanos CA, Savino JS, Weiss RL. Transesophageal echocardiographic diagnosis of aortic dissection during cardiac surgery. Anesthesiology 1991;75:149–153.

54. Golding LAR. New cannulation technique for the severely calcified ascending aorta. J Thorac Cardiovasc Surg 1985;90:626–627.

55. Norman JC. A single cannula for aortic perfusion and left ventricular decompression. Chest 1970;58:378–379.

56. Robicsek F. Apical aortic cannulation: application of an old method with new paraphernalia. Ann Thorac Surg 1991;51:320–322.

57. Coselli JS, Crawford ES. Femoral artery perfusion for cardiopulmonary bypass in patients with aortoiliac artery obstruction. Ann Thorac Surg 1987;43:437–439.

58. Bernstein EF, Gleason LR. Factors influencing hemolysis with roller pumps. Surgery 1967;61:432–442.

59. Uretzky G, Landsburg G, Cohn D, et al. Analysis of microembolic particles originating in extracorporeal circuits. Perfusion 1987;2:9–17.

60. Hubbard LC, Kletchka HD, et al. Spallation using roller pumps and its clinical implications. Am SECT Proc 1975;3:27–32.

61. Kurusz M, Christman EW, Williams EH, et al. Roller pump induced tubing wear: another argument in favor of arterial line filtration. J Extra-Corpor Technol 1980;12:49–59.

62. Hoerr HR, Kraemer MF, Williams JL, et al. In vitro comparison of the blood handling by the

constrained vortex and twin roller blood pumps. J Extra-Corpor Technol 1987;19: 316–20.

63. Reed CC, Stafford TB: Cardiopulmonary bypass. 2nd ed. Houston: Medical Press, 1985.

64. Kurusz M, Shaffer CW, Christman EW. Runaway pump head. J Thorac Cardiovasc Surg 1979;77: 792–795.

65. Kolff J, McClurken JB, Alpern JB. Beware centrifugal pumps: not a one-way street, but a dangerous siphon! Perfusion 1990;5:225–226.

66. Wheeldon DR, Bethune DW, Gill RD. Vortex pumping for routine cardiac surgery: a comparative study. Perfusion 1990;5:135–143.

67. Driessen JJ, Fransen G, Rondelez L, et al. Comparison of the standard roller pump and a pulsatile centrifugal pump for extracorporeal circulation during routine coronary artery bypass grafting. Perfusion 1991;6:303–311.

68. Everts P, Schonberger JPAM, Steenbrink J, Bredee JJ. Partial left heart bypass with centrifugal pump and limited anticoagulation during the resection of coarctation of the aorta. Perfusion 1991;6:285–289.

69. Olivier HF Jr, Maher TD, Liebler GA, et al. Use of the BioMedicus centrifugal pump in traumatic tears of the thoracic aorta. Ann Thorac Surg 1984;38:586–591.

70. Dixon CM, Magovern GJ. Evaluation of the Bio-Pump for long term cardiac support without heparinization. J Extra-Corpor Technol 1982; 14:331.

71. Joyce LD, Kiser JC, Eales F, et al. Experience with the Sarns centrifugal pump as a ventricular assist device. ASAIO Trans 1990;36: M619–23.

72. Odom NJ, Richens D, Glenville BE, et al. Successful use of mechanical assist device for right ventricular failure after orthotopic heart transplantation. J Heart Lung Trans 1990;9: 652–653.

73. Walls JT, Crutis JJ, Boley T. Sarns centrifugal pump for repair of thoracic aortic injury: case reports. J Trauma 1989;29:1283–1285.

74. Leschinsky BM, Zimin NK. Centrifugal blood pumps—a brief analysis: development of new designs. Perfusion 1991;6:115–121.

75. Qian K, Jin Y, Lin K, et al. A new impeller blood pump design: in vitro and in vivo studies. Perfusion 1988;3:233–240.

76. Pacheco DA, Ingram JM, Pacheco SL. A comparison of three centrifugal pumps ability to expel micro-air under conditions of cavitation or bolus air injection. Presented at the American Academy of Cardiovascular Perfusion, Orlando, FL, February 1992.

77. Pappas G, Winter SD, Kopriva CJ, Steele PP. Improvement of myocardial and other vital organ

functions and metabolism with a simple method of pulsatile flow (IABP) during clinical cardiopulmonary bypass. Surgery 1975;77: 34–44.

78. Bregman D, Bailin M, Bowman FO Jr, et al. A pulsatile assist device (PAD) for use during cardiopulmonary bypass. Ann Thorac Surg 1977; 24:574–581.

79. Sanderson JM, Morton PG, Tolloczko TS, et al. The Morton-Keele pump—a hydraulically activated pulsatile pump for use in extracorporeal circulation. Med Biol Eng II:1973;182–190.

80. Waaben J, Andersen K, Husum B. Pulsatile flow during cardiopulmonary bypass. Scand J Thor Cardiovasc Surg 1985;19:149–153.

81. Adams S, Fleming J, Gourlay T, Taylor KM. Clincial experience with the Sarns pulsatile pump during open-heart surgery. Perfusion 1986;1:53–56.

82. Taylor KM, Bain WH, Maxted KJ, et al. Comparative studies of pulsatile and nonpulsatile bypass I: pulsatile system employed and its hematologic effects. J Thorac Cardiovasc Surg 1978;75:569–573.

83. James SD, Peters J, Maresca L, et al. The roller pump does produce pulsatile flow. J Extra-Corpor Technol 1987;19:376–383.

84. Wright G. The hydraulic power outputs of pulsatile and nonpulsatile cardiopulmonary bypass pumps. Perfusion 1988;3:251–262.

85. Wright G. Factors affecting the pulsatile hydraulic power output of the Stockert roller pump. Perfusion 1989;4:187–195.

86. Taylor KM. The hemodynamics of cardiopulmonary bypass. Semin Thorac Cardiovasc Surg 1990;2:300–312.

87. Gourlay T, Gibbons W, Taylor KM. Pulsatile flow capability of a group of membrane oxygenators. Perfusion 1987;2:115–126.

88. Kirson LE, Laurnen ME, Tornbene MA. Position of oxygenators in the bypass circuit [Letter]. J Cardiothorac Anesth 1989;3:817–318.

89. Dickson TA. Hypoxemia after intraluminal oxygen line obstruction during cardiopulmonary bypass [Letter]. Ann Thorac Surg 1990;49:512.

90. Gravlee GP, Wong AA, Charles DJ. Hypoxemia during cardiopulmonary bypass from leaks in the gas supply system [Letter]. Anesth Analg 1985;64:649–650.

91. Robblee JA, Crosby E, Keon WJ. Hypoxemia after intraluminal oxygen line obstruction during cardiopulmonary bypass. Ann Thorac Surg 1989;48:575–576.

92. Edmunds LH Jr, Saxena NC, Hillyer P, Wilson TJ. Relationship between platelet count and cardiotomy suction return. Ann Thorac Surg 1978;25:306–310.

93. Pearson DT. Micro-emboli: gaseous and particu-

late. In: Taylor KM, ed. Cardiopulmonary bypass: principles and management. Baltimore: Williams & Wilkins, 1986:313–354.

94. Wright G, Sanderson JM. Cellular aggregation and trauma in cardiotomy suction systems. Thorax 1979;34:621–628.

95. Pearson DT, Watson BG, Waterhouse PS. An ultrasonic analysis of the comparative efficiency of various cardiotomy reservoirs and micropore blood filters. Thorax 1978;33:352–358.

96. de Jong JCF, ten Duis HJ, Sibinga CT. Hematologic aspects of cardiotomy suction in cardiac operations. J Thorac Cardiovasc Surg 1980;79: 227–236.

97. Boonstra PW, van Imhoff GW, Eysman L, et al. Reduced platelet activation and improved hemostasis after controlled cardiotomy suction during clinical membrane oxygenator perfusions. J Thorac Cardiovasc Surg 1985;89: 900–906.

98. Wielogorski JW, Cross DE, Nwadike EVO. The effects of subatmospheric pressure on the hemolysis of blood. J Biomechanics 1975;8: 321–325.

99. Hirose T, Burman SD, O'Connor RA. Reduction of perfusion hemolysis by use of atraumatic low pressure suction. J Thorac Cardiovasc Surg 1964;47:242–247.

100. Baile EM, Ling IT, Heyworth JR, et al. Bronchopulmonary anastomotic and noncoronary collateral blood flow in humans during cardiopulmonary bypass. Chest 1985;87: 749–754.

101. Arom KV, Vinas JF, Fewel JE, et al: Is a left ventricular vent necessary during cardiopulmonary bypass? [Abstract] Ann Thorac Surg 1977;24:566–573.

102. Burton NA, Graeber GM, Zajtchuk R. An alternate method of ventricular venting—the pulmonary artery sump. Chest 1984;85:814–815.

103. Breyer RH, Meredith JW, Mills SA, et al. Is a left ventricular vent necessary for coronary artery bypass procedures performed with cardioplegic arrest? J Thorac Cardiovasc Surg 1983;86:338–349.

104. Buckberg GD. The importance of venting the left ventricle [Editorial]. Ann Thorac Surg 1975;20:488–490.

105. Najafi H, Javid H, Golding MD, Serry C. Aortic valve replacement without left heart decompression. Ann Thorac Surg 1976;21:131–133.

106. Salerno TA, Charrette EJP. Elimination of venting in coronary artery surgery. Ann Thorac Surg 1979;27:340–343.

107. Kanter KR, Schaff HV, Gott VL. Reduced oxygen consumption with effective left ventricular venting during postischemic reperfusion. Circulation 1982;66(suppl I):I50–I54.

108. Salomon NW, Copeland JG. Single catheter

109. Miller DW, Ivey TD, Bailey WW, et al. The practice of coronary artery bypass surgery in 1980. J Thorac Cardiovasc Surg 1981;81:423–427.

110. Little AG, Lin CY, Wernley JA, et al. Use of the pulmonary artery for left ventricular venting during cardiac operations. J Thorac Cardiovasc Surg 1984;87:532.

111. Roach GW, Bellows WH. Left ventricular distension during pulmonary artery venting in a patient undergoing coronary artery bypass surgery. Anesthesiology 1992;76:655–658.

112. Daily PO, Kinney T, Steinke TA. Pulmonary vein clamping during cardiopulmonary bypass: enhancement of operative field visualization and myocardial hypothermia. Ann Thorac Surg 1987;43:388–340.

113. Weesner KM, Byrum C, Rosenthal A. Left ventricular aneurysms associated with intraoperative venting of the cardiac apex in children. Am Heart J 1981;101:622–625.

114. Marco JD, Barner HB. Aortic venting: comparison of vent effectiveness. J Thorac Cardiovasc Surg 1977;73:287–292.

115. Brenner WI, Wallsh E, Spencer FC. Aortic vent efficiency: a quantitative evaluation. J Thorac Cardiovasc Surg 1971;61:258–264.

116. Butler BD, Kurusz M. Gaseous microemboli: a review. Perfusion 1990;5:81–99.

117. Berman L, Marin F: Micropore filtration during cardiopulmonary bypass. In: Taylor KM, ed. Cardiopulmonary bypass: principles and management. Baltimore: Williams & Wilkins, 1986:355–374.

118. Marshall L. Filtration in cardiopulmonary bypass: past, present and future. Perfusion 1988;3: 135–147.

119. Solis RT, Horak J. Evaluation of a new cardiotomy blood filter. Ann Thorac Surg 1979;28:487–488.

120. Ware JA, Scott MA, Horak JK, Solis RT. Platelet aggregation during and after cardiopulmonary bypass: effect of two different cardiotomy filters. Ann Thorac Surg 1982;34:204–206.

121. Gourlay T, Gibbons M, Fleming J, Taylor KM. Evaluation of a range of arterial line filters: Part I. Perfusion 1987;2:297–302.

122. Gourlay T, Gibbons M, Taylor KM. Evaluation of a range of arterial line filters. Part II. Perfusion 1988;3:29–35.

123. Gourlay T. The role of arterial line filters in perfusion safety. Perfusion 1988;3:195–204.

124. Patterson RH Jr, Wasser JS, Porro RS. The effect of various filters on microembolic cerebrovascular blockade following cardiopulmonary bypass. Ann Thorac Surg 1974;17:464–473.

125. Pedersen T, Hatteland K, Semb BKH. Bubble ex-

traction by various arterial filters measured in vitro with doppler ultrasound techniques. Ultrasound Med Biol 1982;8:71–81.

126. Hsu LC. Principles of heparin-coating techniques. Perfusion 1991;6:209–219.

127. Palanzo DA, Kurusz M, Butler BD. Surface tension effects of heparin coating on arterial line filters. Perfusion 1990;5:277–284.

128. Munsch C, Rosenfeldt F, Chang V. Absence of particle-induced coronary vasoconstriction during cardioplegic infusion: is it desirable to use a microfilter in the infusion line? J Thorac Cardiovasc Surg 1991;101:473–480.

129. Lake CL. Controversies in the management of cardiopulmonary bypass. In: Cardiothoracic and vascular anesthesia update. Vol 1. Ch 9. 1990:1–21.

130. Sellman M, Ivert T, Stensved P, et al. Doppler ultrasound estimation of microbubbles in the arterial line during extracorporeal circulation. Perfusion 1990;5:23–32.

131. Griffin S, Pugsley W, Treasure T. Microembolism during cardiopulmonary bypass: a comparison of bubble oxygenator with arterial line filter and membrane oxygenator along. Perfusion 1991;6:99–103.

132. Padayachee TS, Parsons S, Theobold R, et al. The effect of arterial filtration on reduction of gaseous microemboli in the middle cerebral artery during cardiopulmonary bypass. Ann Thorac Surg 1988;45:647–649.

133. Pugsley W. The use of Doppler ultrasound in the assessment of micro-emboli during cardiac surgery. Perfusion 1989;4:115–122.

134. Brennan RW, Patterson RH Jr, Kessler J. Cerebral blood flow and metabolism during cardiopulmonary bypass: evidence of microembolic encephalophathy. Neurology 1971;21:665–672.

135. Muraoka R, Yokota M, Aoshima M et al. Subclinical changes in brain morphology following cardiac operations as reflected by computed tomographic scans of the brain. J Thorac Cardiovasc Surg 1981;81:364–369.

136. Blauth CI, Smith PL, Arnold JV, et al. Influence of oxygenator type on the prevalence and extent of micro-emboli retinal ischemia during cardiopulmonary bypass. J Thorac Cardiovasc Surg 1990;99:61–69.

137. Henriksen L. Hjelms E. Cerebral blood flow during cardiopulmonary bypass in man: effect of arterial filtration. Thorax 1986;41:386–395.

138. Aberg T, Kihlgren M. Cerebral protection during open heart surgery. Thorax 1977;32:525–533.

139. Branthwaite MA. Prevention of neurological damage during open-heart surgery. Thorax 1975;30:258–261.

140. Hill JD, Osborn JJ, Swank RL, et al. Experience using a new dacron wool filter during extracorporeal circulation. Arch Surg 1970;101:649–652.

141. Skagseth E, Froysaker T, Refsum SB. Disposable filter for microemboli in cardiopulmonary bypass. J Cardiovasc Surg 1974;15:318–322.

142. Garvey JW, Willner A, Wolpowitz A, et al. The effect of arterial filtration during open heart surgery on cerebral function. Circulation 1983;64(suppl II):II125–II128.

143. Aris A, Solanes H, Camara ML, et al. Arterial line filtration during cardiopulmonary bypass. J Thorac Cardiovasc Surg 1986;91:526–533.

144. Loop F. Personal communication, 1971.

145. Mossing KA. Post cardiotomy delirium and microfiltration. University of Washington; 1975. Seattle, Washington: Dissertation.

146. Nussmeier NA, Fish KJ. Neuropsychologic dysfunction after cardiopulmonary bypass: a comparison of two institutions. J Cardiothorac Vasc Anesth 1991;5:584–588.

147. Ohri SK, Desai JB, Gaer JAR, et al. Intra-abdominal complications after cardiopulmonary bypass. Ann Thorac Surg 1991;52:826–831.

148. Treasure T. Interventions to reduce cerebral injury during cardiac surgery—the effect of arterial line filtration. Perfusion 1989;4:147–152.

149. Boldt J, Zickmann B, Fedderson B, et al. Six different hemofiltration devices for blood conservation in cardiac surgery. Ann Thorac Surg 1991;51:747–753.

150. High KM, Williams DR, Kurusz M. Cardiopulmonary bypass circuits and design. In: Hensley FA Jr, Martin DE, eds: The practice of cardiac anesthesia. Boston: Little, Brown and Co., 1990:583–601.

151. Munsch C. Blood cardioplegia. Perfusion 1991;6:245–252.

152. Arom KV, Emery RW. Retrograd cardioplegia: detail for coronary sinus cannulation technique. Ann Thorac Surg 1992;53:714–715.

153. Chitwood WR Jr: Retrograde cardioplegia: current methods. Ann Thorac Surg 1992;53:352–355.

154. Alston RP, Trew A. An in vitro assessment of a monitor for continuous in-line measurement of PO_2, PCO_2 and pH during cardiopulmonary bypass. Perfusion 1987;2:139–147.

155. Bashein G, Pino JA, Nessly ML, et al. Clinical assessment of a flow-through fluorometric blood gas monitor. J Clin Monit 1988;4:195–203.

156. Pino JA, Bashein G, Kenny MA. In vitro assessment of a flow-through fluorometric blood gas monitor. J Clin Monit 1989;4:186–194.

157. Pearson DT. Blood gas control during cardiopulmonary bypass. Perfusion 1988;3:113–133.

158. Justison GA, Parsons S. Improved quality control utilizing continuous blood gas monitoring and computerized perfusion systems. Proceedings of the 27th International Conference of the American Society for Extracorpeal Technology, 1989:83–87.
159. Baraka A, Barody M, Harous S, et al. Continuous venous oximetry during cardiopulmonary bypass: influence of temperature changes, perfusion flow and hematocrit level. J Cardiothorac Anesth 1990;4:35–38.
160. Philbin DM, Inada E, Sims N, et al. Oxygen consumption and on-line blood gas determinations during rewarming on cardiopulmonary bypass. Perfusion 1987;2:127–129.
161. Swan H, Sanchez M, Tyndall M, Koch C. Quality control of perfusion: monitoring venous blood oxygen tension to prevent hypoxic acidosis. J Thorac Cardiovasc Surg 1990;99:868–872.
162. Rubsamen DS. Continuous blood gas monitoring during cardiopulmonary bypass—how soon will it be the standard of care? [Editorial] J Cardiothorac Anesth 1990;4:1–4.
163. Mark JB, Fitzgerald D, Fenton T, et al. Continuous arterial and venous blood gas monitoring during cardiopulmonary bypass. J Thorac Cardiovasc Surg 1991;102:431–439.
164. Bashein G, Greydanus WK, Kenny MA. Evaluation of a blood gas and chemistry monitor for use during surgery. Anesthesiology 1989;70:123–127.
165. Nicolson SC, Jobes DR, Steven JM, Hillyer P, Handrrahan. Evaluation of a user-operated patient-side blood gas and chemistry monitor in children undergoing cardiac surgery. J Cardiothorac Anesth 1989;3:741–744.
166. Kent AP, Tarr JT, Fox MA. Where to sample during cardiopulmonary bypass [Letter]. J Cardiothorac Anesth 1989;3:136.
167. Kurusz M, Conti VR, Arens JF. Oxygenator failure [Letter]. Ann Thorac Surg 1990;49:511.
168. Akers T, Bolen G, Gomez J, et al. In vitro comparison of ECC blood flow measurement techniques. ExtraCorp Tech Proceedings, 28th International Conference 1990;17–22.
169. Berg E, Knudsen N. Automatic data collection for cardiopulmonary bypass. Perfusion 1988;3:263–270.
170. Gourlay T. Computers in perfusion practice. Perfusion 1987;2:79–85.
171. Kurusz M, Wheeldon DR. Perfusion safety. Perfusion 1988;3:97–112.
172. Kurusz M, Wheeldon DR. Risk containment during cardiopulmonary bypass. Semin Thorac Cardiovasc Surg 1990;2:400–491.
173. Reed CC, Kurusz M, Lawrence AE. Safety techniques in perfusion. Stafford, TX: Quali-Med, Inc., 1988.
174. Wheeldon DR: Safety during cardiopulmonary bypass. In: Taylor KM, ed. Cardiopulmonary bypass: principles and management. Baltimore: Williams & Wilkins, 1986:398–422.
175. Bayindir O, Paker T, Akpinar B, et al. Case conference: a 58-year old man had a massive air embolism during cardiopulmonary bypass. J Cardiothorac Vasc Anesth 1991;5:627–634.
176. Mills NL, Ochsner JL. Massive air embolism during cardiopulmonary bypass: causes, prevention, and management. J Thorac Cardiovasc Surg 1980;80:708–717.
177. Mills NL, Morris JM. Air embolism associated with cardiopulmonary bypass. In: Waldahausen JA, Orringer MB, eds. Complications in cardiothoracic surgery. St. Louis: Mosby Year Book, 1991:60–67.
178. Fosburg RG, Anderson RD, Nolan SP, Barner HB. Invited letter concerning: certification of perfusionists. J Thorac Cardiovasc Surg 1990;100:455.
179. von Segesser LK, Weiss BM, Turina M. Perfusion with heparin-coated equipment: potential for clinical use. Semin Thorac Cardiovasc Surg 1990;2:273–280.
180. Mollnes TE, Videm V, Gotze O, et al. Formation of C5a during cardiopulmonary bypass inhibition by precoating with heparin. Ann Thorac Surg 1991;52:92–97.
181. Pradhan MJ, Fleming JS, Nkere UU, et al. Clinical experience with heparin-coated cardiopulmonary bypass circuits. Perfusion 1991;6:235–243.
182. Videm V. Svennevig JL, Fosse E, et al. Reduced complement activation with heparin-coated oxygenator and tubing in coronary bypass operations. J Thorac Cardiovasc Surg 1992;103:808–813.
183. Gu YJ, van Oeveren W, van der Kamp KWHJ, et al. Heparin-coating of extracorporeal circuits reduces thrombin formation in patients undergoing cardiopulmonary bypass. Perfusion 1991;6:221–225.
184. von Segesser LK, Weiss BM, Garcia E, Turina MI. Clinical application of heparin-coated perfusion equipment with special emphasis on patients refusing homologous transfusions. Perfusion 1991;6:227–233.
185. von Segesser LK, Weiss BM, Garcia E, et al. Reduction and elimination of systemic heparinization during cardiopulmonary bypass. J Thorac Cardiovasc Surg 1992;103:790–799.
186. Yasuura K, Ogawa Y, Okamoto H, et al. Clinical applications of total body retrograde perfusion to operations for aortic dissection. Ann Thorac Surg 1992;53:655–658.

4

HEMOFILTRATION, DIALYSIS, AND BLOOD SALVAGE TECHNIQUES DURING CARDIOPULMONARY BYPASS

Roger A. Moore and Glenn W. Laub

ULTRAFILTRATION

Historic Perspective

The concept of removing excess fluid from the intravascular space of patients in renal failure by the filtration of blood through an ultraporous membrane dates back to 1928 (1). However, the clinical application of ultrafiltration technology did not occur until the 1950s (2) and 1960s (3), when filtering devices were developed for the effective removal of edema fluid in overhydrated patients with renal impairment. During the 1970s there was a refinement of ultrafiltration techniques (4, 5) as well as the first use of this technology as part of an open heart surgical procedure (6). The use of ultrafiltration during open heart surgery was initially restricted to the severely hemodiluted patient as a method for concentrating blood remaining in the extracorporeal circuit after cardiopulmonary bypass. Ultrafiltration under these circumstances was found to be efficacious in reducing hemodilution and producing higher postoperative hemoglobins. However, by 1979 the application of ultrafiltration techniques with extracorporeal circulation was extended to use *during* the bypass period, though this specific application was initially limited to patients with compromised renal function (7). For these patients, ultrafiltration was chosen as an alternative to hemodialysis for managing fluid homeostasis.

In the 1980s the use of ultrafiltration during open heart surgery spread from isolated academic centers into general clinical practice. The primary impetus that initially led to the more widespread use of ultrafiltration was the recognition that patients in renal failure could undergo open heart surgery safely. Ultrafiltration provided a simple, easy method for allowing volume control in these patients (8, 9). After the initial use in patients with renal failure, ultrafiltration was secondarily recognized as an excellent method for concentrating hemodiluted blood in normal patients who had been overhydrated (10–13). Further use of ultrafiltration devices finally led to the realization that not only was volume control possible, but ultrafiltration also served as an effective method for blood conservation through the preservation of platelets and coagulation factors (14–17). At present, ultrafiltration techniques have numerous advantageous applications, both during and after cardiopulmonary bypass. Benefits from the use of ultrafiltration can be obtained for nearly any patient undergoing extracorporeal circulation.

93

Basic Physiologic Principles

The primary principle governing ultrafiltration is the selective separation of plasma water and low molecular weight solutes from the intravascular cellular components and plasma proteins of blood, using a semipermeable membrane filter. Unlike hemodialysis, the ultrafiltration technique is simplified by eliminating the requirement for a dialysate solution. Rather than solute osmotic pressure, the driving force for ultrafiltration is provided by the hydrostatic pressure differential occurring across the ultrafiltration membrane (Fig. 4.1). The application of a negative pressure on the effluent side of the membrane or the use of an increased perfusion pressure applied to the blood side of the membrane results in improved solute and fluid filtration. The relationship between these pressures can be expressed by the following equation:

$$TMP = \frac{P_A + P_V}{2} + P_S$$

In this equation, TMP refers to the transmembrane pressure gradient, which is the ultimate determinant of filtration rate, while P_A is the arterial or inlet blood pressure into the ultrafilter (in millimeters of mercury), the P_V is the venous or outlet blood pressure from the ultrafiltration device (in millimeters of mercury), and P_S is the amount of negative pressure applied to the effluent side of the ultrafiltration membrane (in millimeters of mercury). The arterial to venous pressure difference is usually less than 100 mm Hg under normal circumstances; this fall in blood pressure is due primarily to the inherent resistance in the ultrafilter as blood flows through the filtering system. However, the arterial to venous blood pressure difference can also be affected by a variety of other variables, such as the hemoglobin, temperature, and rate of blood flow through the filter.

The range of transmembrane pressures for the normal function of any given ultrafiltration device varies, based upon the manufacturer's specifications. However, transmembrane pressures in the range of 100 to 500 mm Hg are typically suggested. At equal hemoglobin levels the resistance to blood flow through a filter is disproportionately greater when low flow is used as opposed to high flow circumstances (18). The reason for this is a basic rheologic flow dynamic principle, whereby the viscosity of blood under high shear circumstances (high flows) will be lower than in low flow conditions (19, 20). Another important principle is that the cooling of blood

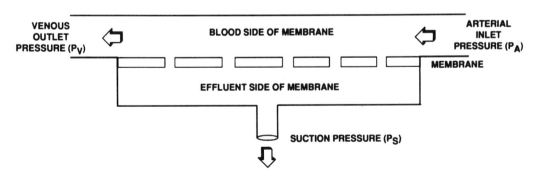

Figure 4.1. Ultrafiltration of free water and solutes across a semipermeable membrane occurs because of a combination of the blood pressure differential across the filter—the mean of the arterial inlet pressure (P_A) and the venous outlet pressure (P_V)—and any vacuum pressure placed on the effluent side of the membrane (P_S). The combination of these pressures is equal to the transmembrane pressure, which is the primary factor determining filtration rate.

leads to striking increases in viscosity, which in turn can increase the resistance of blood flow through the ultrafilter (Fig. 4.2) (20). Finally, the presence of high levels of serum protein is also a factor causing an increase in the arteriovenous transfilter pressure differential.

A variety of manufacturers produce ultrafiltration devices and each device varies as to its efficacy in producing ultrafiltration. This efficacy can be expressed as an ultrafiltration coefficient that is intrinsic to each device. The typical ultrafiltration membrane consists of a thin membrane skin that serves as the primary microfilter, placed over a thicker more porous substructure. Important characteristics in determining the ultrafiltration coefficient include the diameter of the pores in the membrane through which fluid and solutes will pass, the total number of pores on the membrane surface, and the length of the pores (membrane thickness) through which the solutes and fluids must pass. The ultrafiltration coefficient (U_C) is directly related to the efficiency of the ultrafiltration device's ability to remove fluid (Q_F), as described in the following equation:

$$Q_F = U_C \times (TMP - I_P)$$

In this equation I_P represents the protein oncotic pressure in the blood and TMP represents the transmembrane pressure. The higher the serum protein concentration, the slower the filtration rate. On the other hand, the higher the transmembrane pressure, the faster the filtration rate.

Aside from differences in ultrafiltration rate due to variations in the membrane structure, the hemoglobin concentration, and the fluid temperature, fluid removal through the membrane is primarily determined by the transmembrane pressure. Absolute ultrafiltration can be increased by providing either an increase in perfusion pressure into the filter, by partially clamping the blood flow from the filter thereby increasing outlet pressure, or by increasing the vacuum on the effluent side of the membrane. Typically, a relatively linear relationship exists between the transmembrane pressure and the ultrafiltration rate (Fig. 4.3). When the membrane limit is reached, a plateauing of filtration occurs. The plateau is a function of both the number of pores available for filtration and the accumulation of serum proteins on the membrane surface that occlude the ultrafiltration pores (7). By increasing the blood flow rate through the filter, the slope of the

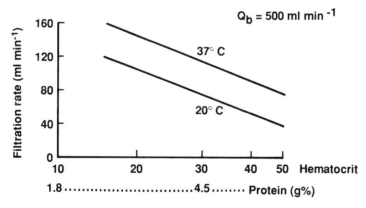

Figure 4.2. The filtration rate of an ultrafiltration device depends upon multiple factors. At a constant flow, decreases in filtration rate are observed at higher hematocrits, higher serum protein levels, and lower temperatures. Q_b, or blood flow in this representation, is kept constant at 500 ml/min. (From Wheeldon DR, Bethune DW. Blood conservation during cardiopulmonary bypass—autologous transfusion, cell saving and hemofiltration. In: Taylor KM, ed. Cardiopulmonary bypass. Baltimore: Williams & Wilkins, 1986.)

ultrafiltration curve can be increased (Fig. 4.3). The reason for this observed improvement in filtration at higher flow rates is a more rapid removal of the accumulated proteins on the membrane surface that obstruct fluid flow through the pores (7). The higher the protein content of the plasma, the greater this blood flow effect.

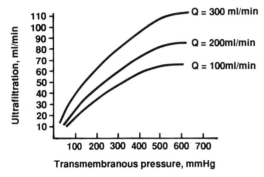

Figure 4.3. A relatively linear relationship exists between the transmembrane pressure and the ultrafiltration rate. Note that as the blood flow increases through the filter, the slope of the ultrafiltration to transmembrane pressure relationship becomes steeper. This is a result of more rapid removal of accumulated proteins on the membrane surface. Q represents blood flow through the ultrafiltering device. (Adapted from Darup J, Bleese N, Kalmar P, Lutz G, Pokar H, Polonius MJ. Hemofiltration during extracorporeal circulation. Thorac Cardiovasc Surg 1979; 27:227.)

Membrane pore size is important for determining what soluble plasma molecules will be removed with the plasma fluid. The pore size normally ranges between 10 and 35 angstroms, allowing molecules up to 20,000 daltons to undergo ultrafiltration. The efficiency of an ultrafiltration device to remove a soluble molecule is called the sieving coefficient and is directly related to molecular size (Fig. 4.4) (14). The larger the molecular size of a filtered substance, the less efficient the ultrafiltration device will be in its removal. Small molecules with molecular weights below 10,000 daltons, such as sodium, potassium, chloride, urea, creatinine and glucose, have a sieving coefficient of 1, meaning they are filtered at a rate equal to their concentration in the plasma. Large molecules, such as albumin (molecular weight, 69,000 daltons), hemoglobin (molecular weight, 68,000 daltons), and fibrinogen (molecular weight, 341,000 daltons) as well as the cellular components of blood (leukocytes, platelets, and red blood cells) are too large to traverse the pores and, therefore, remain within the blood. The result is a higher blood concentration of the nonfiltered elements following a period of ultrafiltration.

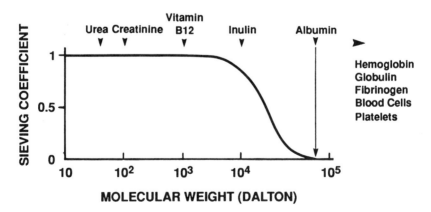

Figure 4.4. The sieving coefficient is a measure of the efficiency of an ultrafiltration device to remove a soluble molecule from the blood. The sieving coefficient is directly related to molecular size. Molecules with molecular weights below 11,000 daltons have a coefficient of 1, indicating that they are filtered at the same concentration as they exist in the blood. Large molecules that will not pass through the pores have a sieving coefficient of 0. (Adapted from Solem JO, Tengborn L, Steen S, Luhrs C. Cell saver versus hemofilter for concentration of oxygenator blood after cardiopulmonary bypass. Thorac Cardiovasc Surg 1987;35:46.)

Of interest, the heparin molecule, which is a mucopolysaccharide between 6,000 and 25,000 daltons in weight (21, 22), is removed during ultrafiltration (23). Because of this, intensified anticoagulation monitoring may be needed when ultrafiltration is used in conjunction with extracorporeal circulatory techniques (13). However, one investigator has found that no additional heparin supplementation is required, even when volumes as great as 15 liters are removed during cardiopulmonary bypass, possibly because the heparin *concentration* remains the same (11). Pharmacologic agents with low molecular weights, which the patient needs for physiologic stability, may have increased clearance from the plasma, and thereby may require supplementation.

Technical Concerns

Historically, ultrafiltration devices have either been developed as parallel membrane sheets, requiring a bulky mechanical framework for their support, or as hollow membrane fibers that are internally supported. The hollow fiber construction due to its less bulky nature, simplicity of use, and requirement for smaller priming volume, has become the most practical and widely used type of device for ultrafiltration. Hollow fiber filters are composed of thousands of hollow polysulfone, polyacrylonitrite, or cellulose acetate fibers, with each fiber having an internal diameter of approximately 200 microns. Examples of two hollow fiber devices are shown in Figure 4.5.

The placement of the ultrafiltration device within the extracorporeal circuit will partially depend upon whether the decision to use ultrafiltration is made before or after the institution of cardiopulmonary bypass, and whether a membrane or bubble oxygenator is to be employed in the extracorporeal circuitry. In the event that the use of ultrafiltration is decided upon before the

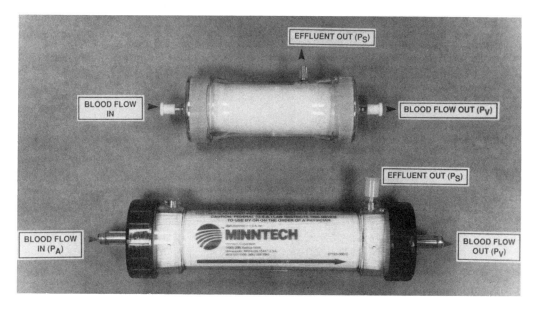

Figure 4.5. Two examples of hollow fiber ultrafilters presently on the market. The upper filter is the Diafilter-20 Hemofilter by Amicon, which has a overall unit length of 17.5 cm, a membrane area of 0.25 m², a priming blood volume of 20 ml, and a hemoconcentrating rate of 10 to 110 ml/min. The lower ultrafilter is the Hemocor Plus 950 Hemoconcentrator produced by Minntech. This unit's overall length is 21.5 cm, the membrane area is 0.95 m², the priming volume is 70 ml, the hemoconcentrating rate is 30 to 113 ml/min, and the molecular weight cutoff is 17,000 daltons.

initiation of cardiopulmonary bypass, the inlet tubing leading to the ultrafiltering device can be placed as a branch connection from the arterial line filter with both membrane and bubble oxygenators (Fig. 4.6). The outflow from the ultrafiltering device is returned to the cardiotomy reservoir with both oxygenators. A separate graduated collection container is attached to the effluent side of the filter for collection of ultrafiltration fluids and solutes for eventual measurement and disposal. The collection container for the fluids and solutes is placed on a variable pressure vacuum line allowing the adjustment of suction pressure. The advantage of this approach is that a single arterial pump head is used to perfuse the patient and the filter. The primary disadvantage of using a single pump head is that when blood flow to the patient is varied, the blood flow to the ultrafiltering device is varied. Also, pump head flow rates have to be increased to compensate for flow that is diverted from the patient to the ultrafilter.

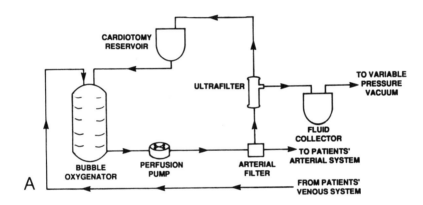

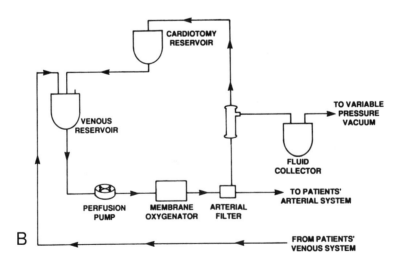

Figure 4.6.   If the use of an ultrafilter is decided upon before the initiation of cardiopulmonary bypass, and a bubble oxygenator is used, a branch connector from the arterial line filter is the easiest method for establishing ultrafiltration (**A**). With the use of a membrane oxygenator, a branch connection from the arterial line filter can also be used effectively, with return of the filtered blood to the cardiotomy reservoir (**B**). The effluent outlet in both cases is connected to a variable pressure vacuum.

The postbypass concentration of residual pump blood can be accomplished by clamping the arterial tubing distal to the side branch of the arterial filter leading to the patient, and simply recirculating blood through the ultrafilter device (10).

If use of the ultrafilter is decided upon after the institution of cardiopulmonary bypass and a bubble oxygenator is being used, an acceptable alternative for providing blood flow to the ultrafilter is to run tubing through an extra pump head from the coronary arterial port of the bubble oxygenator directly to the ultrafilter. In this situation, the separate, dedicated pump head provides the needed blood flow through the ultrafilter (Fig. 4.7A). Ultrafiltered blood will be returned to the pump oxygenator via the cardiotomy reservoir. In the case of a membrane oxygenator, when an ultrafilter is decided upon following the initiation of bypass, the simplest method is

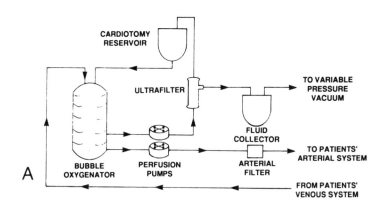

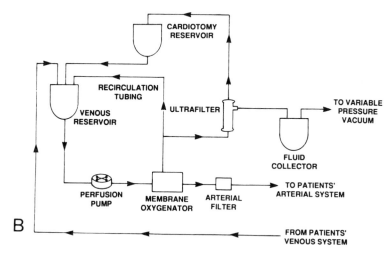

Figure 4.7. If the use of an an ultrafilter is decided upon after the institution of cardiopulmonary bypass, and a bubble oxygenator is used, a separate dedicated pump head can be utilized to direct blood from the coronary arterial port of the oxygenator into the ultrafilter (**A**). In the case of a membrane oxygenator (**B**), blood flow to the ultrafilter can be established by using a branch connector from the recirculation tubing. In this situation, the perfusion pump flow will have to be increased to compensate for perfusion that is redirected from the patient into the ultrafilter.

to establish a branch from the recirculation tubing directly to the ultrafilter (Fig. 4.7B). Since the same pump head is being used both for patient perfusion and ultrafilter perfusion, the pump speed will have to be increased to compensate for lost patient perfusion through the ultrafilter. With all of these approaches, ultrafiltration can be increased with partial cross-clamping of the ultrafilter venous outlet or with the initiation of suction on the effluent side of the ultrafilter membrane (24, 25).

Indications for Use of Ultrafiltration During Open Heart Surgery

Ultrafiltration has a growing list of acceptable therapeutic uses and clinical indications for patients undergoing cardiopulmonary bypass.

FREE WATER REMOVAL IN PATIENTS WITH COMPROMISED RENAL FUNCTION UNDERGOING OPEN HEART SURGERY

From its inception, hemofiltration has been recognized as a rapid and efficient method for managing fluid overload in patients with renal failure (24, 26, 27). The first clinical report of ultrafiltration use during open heart surgery for volume management occurred in 1975 by Darup and his colleagues (7). Effective control of excess fluid during cardiopulmonary bypass in the 10 patients studied resulted in minimal postoperative weight gain. Following their initial report, the efficacy of hemofiltration in the management of volume and electrolytes, in both the pediatric (9) and adult (8, 11, 13, 17) patient having open heart surgery and presenting with renal failure, has been substantiated. Since the patient in renal failure undergoing cardiopulmonary bypass is unable to concentrate hemodiluted intravascular volume through renal mechanisms, ultrafiltration serves as a useful method for reducing hemodilution secondary to excess pump prime, unscavenged cardioplegia solution, and preexist-

ing volume overload. Ultrafiltration also has minimal adverse effects on hemostasis (15, 28) and red blood cell integrity in these patients (11, 29). These advantages become particularly important when long-term hemofiltration (continuous slow ultrafiltration) is performed after open heart surgery in pediatric (9) and adult patients (30) being treated for acute renal failure.

FREE WATER REMOVAL IN PATIENTS WITH NORMAL RENAL FUNCTION UNDERGOING OPEN HEART SURGERY

Extensive hemodilution can occur in any patient during cardiopulmonary bypass due to a combination of pump prime dilution, crystalloid cardioplegia return into the pump, and prebypass fluid loading. Hemodilution during cardiopulmonary bypass has been related to postoperative increases in the extravascular water of the lungs (12) as well as other organs. The use of hemofiltration during cardiopulmonary bypass to remove free water from the intravascular space has been found to be efficacious in reducing extravascular water accumulation (10, 12, 31). The reduction of extravascular water is due to a combination of excess intravascular, free water removal, and an increase in intravascular colloid osmotic pressure (25, 32). Hemofiltration has repeatedly been shown to be an effective adjunct to cardiopulmonary bypass, as a mechanism for oxygenator volume control (23, 33, 34). At present, recommendations for the use of ultrafiltration extend from limiting this modality to only those patients with prolonged periods on bypass (longer than 2 hours) or preoperative evidence of excessive body water (edema) (10), all the way up to routinely using ultrafiltration during any open heart surgical procedure (17, 28).

Preservation Of Hemostasis

The newest and perhaps most important indication for hemofiltration is providing a means of hemoconcentration, while preserving intravascular coagulation factors and platelets. Whether ultrafiltration is utilized during or after extracorporeal circulation is not of importance, since preservation of hemostasis (14–16) and reduction in blood product requirements (14) occurs in either case. In one study of 100 patients undergoing ultrafiltration following cardiopulmonary bypass, platelet counts rose by 57%, fibrinogen by 102%, hemoglobin by 85%, and albumin by 91% (25). As might be predicted, the ability of ultrafiltration to concentrate and preserve both platelets and clotting factors provides for better postoperative hemostasis than techniques of cell washing, where platelets and coagulation factors are discarded (14–16, 28, 35).

Contraindications

At present no absolute contraindication exists for the use of ultrafiltration during or after open heart surgery. Theoretically, the passage of blood through a filtering system might lead to an increase in red blood cell damage. However, significant increases in the serum free hemoglobin concentration in patients undergoing ultrafiltration have not been observed (28, 29). Another potential concern is the activation of complement and the sequestration of leukocytes in the pulmonary circuit (36). Immunologic reactivity has been described when the material used in the ultrafilter construction includes cuprophan, or cellulose acetate, while membranes made from polyacrylonitrite or polysulfone do not seem to have immunologic reactivity. In spite of this potential for reactivity with the immunologic system, the occurrence of hypersensitivity reactions during or after ultrafiltration is extremely rare (12). Finally, serum elastase levels, along with other serum proteins, are elevated following hemofiltration (15). Elastase, which is released from activated polymorphonuclear leukocytes during extracorporeal circulation, may have a role in producing postoperative pulmonary dysfunction (36). However, the increase in elastase levels observed following open heart surgery, when hemofiltration is used, is transient. Within 5 hours following cardiopulmonary bypass, the elastase levels are undistinguishable from patients not receiving ultrafiltration (15). The use of ultrafiltration is safe, and the slight theoretical concern associated with its use is heavily outweighed by its proven value in reducing intravascular volume and preserving postoperative hemostasis.

HEMODIALYSIS

Historic Perspective

The first apparatus used for hemodialysis (described as "vividiffusion") was constructed in 1913 and used to treat uremic animals (37). It was composed of parallel rows of semipermeable celloidin tubes through which blood flowed, while a saline solution was infused outside the tubes for removal of diffusible impurities. Anticoagulation was imperfectly provided using hirudin. The clinical application of hemodialysis was delayed until the 1940s, when effective anticoagulation, as well as more efficient dialysis membranes became available. In 1944 with the use of heparin for anticoagulation and cellophane semipermeable membrane tubes, the first clinical use of hemodialysis in a patient was described (38). The patient had end-stage nephritis, and the use of dialysis provided periodic improvement during her 12-day hospital stay. On the 12th day, the inability to provide dialysis due to arterial access difficulties led to the patient succumbing to her disease process. Over the next 1½ decades, continued improvement occurred in the design and materials used in dialyzing units (39–41). The primary objective was to develop a dialyzer that was disposable, had a small blood volume capacity (low blood priming volume), showed high dialysis efficiency, was simple to set up, was safe to use, and was economic in both the personnel needed to run the dialyzer, as well as the equipment needed to provide dialysis.

In 1970 an animal experiment was performed, predating clinical consideration of the intraoperative use of hemodialysis, using a dialyzer in conjunction with extracorporeal cardiac and pulmonary support. This experiment showed that dialysis in conjunction with extracorporeal circulation could be used efficaciously (42). Also, during the 1970s the concept of offering open heart surgery to patients in chronic renal failure began to develop. Patients on hemodialysis were known to be at increased risk for developing advanced atherosclerotic heart disease (43–45). Mortality rates from heart disease in the hemodialysis patient were 5 times greater than in patients having hypertension without known renal disease (44). The causes for the accelerated atherosclerosis in these patients were felt to be related to multiple factors, including a high incidence of hypertensive disease, comparatively greater sustained cardiac output due to anemia, hypertriglyceridemia, abnormal carbohydrate metabolism, and increased vascular calcification (43, 46).

The primary circumstance that eventually brought patients with chronic renal failure into the operating room for open heart surgery was the limited ability to provide hemodialysis to a subset of these patients, secondary to severe anginal symptoms during the dialytic process. In 1974 the first report of coronary artery bypass grafting performed on a patient in chronic renal failure appeared in the literature (47). Soon after this report, numerous descriptions of the successful performance of open heart surgery, in spite of chronic renal failure, appeared in the literature (46, 48–53). The primary point these reports transmitted was that patients in chronic renal failure could have marked improvement in their New York Heart Association functional classification (46, 48, 53–55), while sustaining acceptably low operative mortality (53–57). Of interest, the long-term risk of death from coronary artery disease did not change for dialysis patients who had under-gone coronary artery bypass grafting, when compared to a similar cohort of patients without open heart surgery (55, 56, 58). In spite of actuarial mortality rates being similar, the primary difference remained that patients having undergone open heart surgery had substantial improvement in lifestyle and functional status. It was for this reason that operative intervention for these patients was considered to be justified. Though operative mortality was low, these patients did have increased postoperative morbidity, as shown by relatively longer periods of intubation and hemodynamic support, as well as longer stays in the intensive care unit and hospital (57).

The preoperative medical management of patients on chronic hemodialysis undergoing open heart surgery typically included preoperative red blood cell transfusion to hematocrits greater than 30% (46, 58) and the provision of hemodialysis for stabilization of electrolytes within 24 hours before the planned surgical procedure (50–52, 58). Following the operative procedure, hemodialysis was reinstituted either within 24 hours (50, 53, 59) or within the first few days immediately following surgery, based upon the potassium, blood urea nitrogen, and volume status (46, 58, 60). The primary concern for the early postoperative use of hemodialysis was an increased risk of bleeding because of the requirement for heparinization during the dialytic process. Regional heparinization, which entailed the addition of heparin to blood flowing into the dialyzer and protamine reversal of blood leaving the dialyzer, was one method used to alleviate this problem (58, 61).

One way of delaying immediate postoperative hemodialysis was the provision of dialysis *during* cardiopulmonary bypass (62, 63). In 1979 the first intraoperative use of hemodialysis during open heart surgery was successfully performed on a patient with severe aortic regurgitation, congestive heart failure, and volume overload unresponsive to daily hemodialysis (62).

The use of hemodialysis during cardiopulmonary bypass in this patient allowed postoperative hemodialysis to be delayed for 3 days. Since this report, other investigators have successfully used hemodialysis during extracorporeal circulation (11, 63–65) and during prolonged circulatory support with a left ventricular assist device (66).

Basic Physiologic Principles

Hemodialysis is similar to ultrafiltration in that a semipermeable membrane allows the differential passage of fluid and soluble molecules through pores of about 50 angstroms. Sodium, calcium, urea, creatinine, and glucose as well as indoles, phenols, and guanidines that accumulate in uremic patients, are able to diffuse through the membrane. Unlike ultrafiltration, which depends solely upon differential hydrostatic pressures to provide the driving force for removal of fluid and soluble molecules, hemodialysis also depends upon the concentration gradient for solutes existing between the blood and the dialysate. The clearance of a substance from the blood during dialysis is described by the following equation:

$$CS = \frac{S_A - S_V}{S_A} \times Q_F$$

where CS is the clearance of a substance from blood, S_A is the substance concentration entering the filter, S_V is the substance concentration leaving the filter and Q_F is the rate of blood flow through the filter.

As blood flow through the filter increases, clearance of the substance also increases. Also, as the serum concentration increases, the concentration gradient is greater, allowing better clearance (4). Obviously, clearance presupposes that the molecule being cleared is small enough to pass through the semipermeable membrane. Clearance rates also increase as the molecular weight of the substances decrease (Fig. 4.8) (11, 20).

Hemodialysis requires the use of a dialysate, which carries the fluids and solutes removed from the blood away from the semipermeable membrane (Fig. 4.9). The choice of the components constituting the dialysate will, in part, be determined by the concentration of the undesirable substances in the patient's serum. If the patient has an abnormally high serum potassium, a dialysate formula lacking potassium is chosen in order to maximize potassium clearance. In a similar respect, if fluid overload in the patient exists, the choice of a dialysate with a higher osmotic pressure can be made in order to maximize free water removal (38). The best use of the concentration differ-

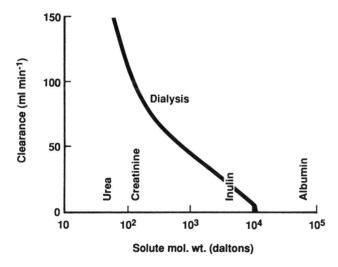

Figure 4.8. The clearance rate of a solute during dialysis decreases as the molecular weight of the soluble molecule increases. Note the high clearance rate of the small molecule, urea, compared to the poor clearance for the larger molecule, albumin. (Adapted from Hakim M, Wheeldon DW, Bethune BB, Milstein BB, English T, Wallwork J. Haemodialysis and haemofiltration on cardiopulmonary bypass. Thorax 1985; 40:101–106.)

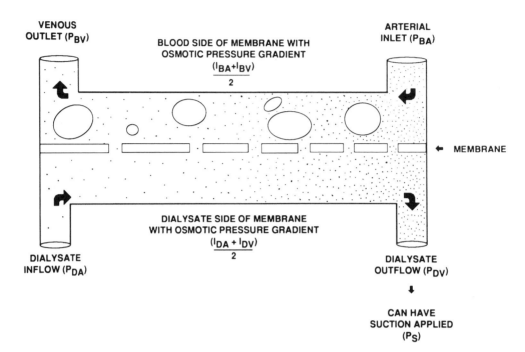

Figure 4.9. Hemodialysis occurs across a semipermeable membrane. Solutes and fluids leave the blood into the dialysate, as the blood travels from the arterial inlet to the venous outlet. The dialysate carries the solute away and the counter-current flow of blood and dialysate, as they travel by the semipermeable membrane, serves to increase total solute removal.

ence in the dialyzing apparatus is provided through the use of a counter-current flow mechanism (Fig. 4.9), where blood flow across the membrane occurs in one direction and dialysate flow occurs in the opposite direction. The concentration of the diffusible substance progressively decreases in the blood as it flows through the filter and encounters dialysate fluid with a progressively lower concentration of the substance. The counter-current mechanism allows a consistently higher relative diffusion gradient to be maintained throughout the filtering process and is similar to the loop of Henle in the glomerulus (67). Within a certain range, the faster the rate of dialysate flow through the filter, the more effective the solute removal (Fig. 4.10) (41, 68).

The semipermeable membrane used in various dialyzers is made from a variety of substances including cellophane, cellulose acetate, polyacrylonitrite, and polysulfone. These membranes allow high permeability

to molecules below 300 daltons in size and, to a lesser extent, molecules up to 10,000 daltons, as well as high free water movement. The primary determinant for the removal of free water is the hydrostatic and

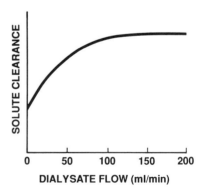

Figure 4.10. Within the specifications of the membrane, solute clearance is a direct function of dialysate flow. Plateauing of solute clearance with an increase in dialysate flow is related to the membrane coefficient, which is determined by the number, size, and depth of the membrane pores.

osmotic pressure differentials that exist between the plasma and dialysate compartments of the filter. This can be expressed in
the following equation:

$$TMP = \left(\frac{P_{BA} + P_{BV}}{2}\right) - \left(\frac{P_{DA} + P_{DV}}{2}\right)$$
$$+ \left(\frac{I_{DA} + I_{DV}}{2}\right) - \left(\frac{I_{BA} + I_{BV}}{2}\right) + P_S$$

where TMP is the transmembrane pressure
for fluid removal, P_{BA} is the blood pressure
at the inlet of the filter, P_{BV} is the blood
pressure at the outlet of the filter, P_{DA} is the
dialysate inlet pressure, P_{DV} is the dialysate
outlet pressure, I_{DA} is the dialysate inlet osmotic pressure, I_{DV} is the dialysate outlet
osmotic pressure, I_{BA} is the serum osmotic
pressure at the inlet of the filter, I_{BV} is the
serum oncotic pressure at the outlet of the
filter, and P_S is negative pressure at the dialysate side of the membrane.

Technical Concerns

The membranes of dialyzing devices
are typically arranged in one of three basic orientations: parallel plates, coils, or
hollow fibers (Fig. 4.11). The objective in
each of these designs is to provide the blood
flowing through the dialyzer with the
greatest possible surface area. Resistance to
blood flow is greatest in coil dialyzers,
while the hollow fiber dialyzers present the
lowest resistance to blood flow because of
the short path for blood flow and the thousands of fibers through which the blood can
flow. In spite of the small cross-sectional internal diameter of each individual hollow
fiber of only 200 microns, which would be
expected to have high resistance to blood
flow, the 10,000 or more fibers within each
filter insure an overall low resistance to
blood flow. The small size, simplicity of
use, and high efficiency of hollow fiber dialyzers make them readily adaptable for
intraoperative use during open heart surgery, as well as for continuous arteriove-

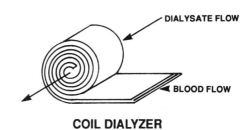

PLATE DIALYZER

COIL DIALYZER

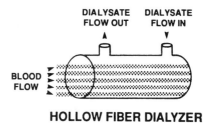

HOLLOW FIBER DIALYZER

Figure 4.11. Dialyzers have been developed with
the objective of providing the greatest blood to dialysate interface across the semipermeable membrane.
Three methods for increasing the interface include
using layers of parallel plates in the plate dialyzer, coil-
ing the blood-dialysate interface in the coil dialyzer,
and multiple small hollow fibers in the hollow fiber
dialyzer.

nous hemodialysis postoperatively (66–
70). An example of a hollow filter dialyzer
is shown in Figure 4.12.

Placement of the dialyzer in the extracorporeal bypass circuitry is similar to the
positioning of an ultrafiltration device. A
side branch of the arterial line filter, the
coronary perfusion port of the oxygenator,
or the recirculation line can each serve as
adequate access ports for dialyzer attachment. Blood from the dialyzer is returned in
each case to the cardiotomy reservoir. Perfusion of the dialyzer with dialysate is usually provided with a separate pump head,

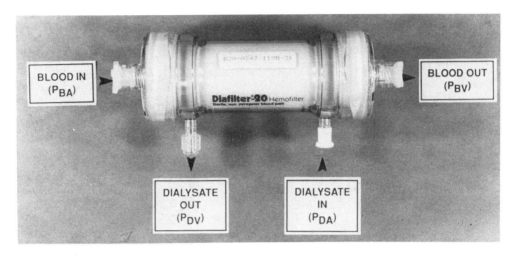

Figure 4.12.   An example of a hollow fiber dialyzer that shows the counter-current flow of blood and dialysate is the Diafilter-20 Hemofilter made by Amicon. This device can also function as an ultrafilter by eliminating the dialysate and providing effluent removal through the dialysate inlet.

though gravitational flow of dialysate can be used with some filters. Dialysate, which has traversed the filter, is collected in a graduated container for measurement of volume before discarding or recirculating through the filter (Fig. 4.13).

Many patients who have been on chronic hemodialysis will have a surgically placed arteriovenous fistula present in an extremity. Extreme caution must be taken with these patients to protect this shunt from reduced blood flow or pressure occlusion. A blood pressure cuff should not be placed on the arm containing an arteriovenous fistula (59), and that arm should be avoided during the placement of either intravenous or arterial catheters. In fact, avoiding the use of either arm in patients with chronic renal disease has been suggested in order to save the arm vessels as future access sites for hemodialysis (52).

Concern about maintaining adequate heparinization and other drug levels in patients undergoing hemodialysis exists because of the increased drug clearance occurring during the hemodialytic process. However, these concerns are no greater with hemodialysis than with ultrafiltration techniques (11, 13, 25).

Indications

CHRONIC RENAL FAILURE

Some 70,000 patients in the United States receive some form of chronic hemodialysis. Considering the accelerated atherosclerotic disease that occurs in these patients (43, 44, 45), it would not be unreasonable to expect that a fairly large percentage might require coronary artery bypass graft surgery at some point in their lives. Normally, the preoperative care of these patients can be adequately managed by providing hemodialysis the day before surgery, followed by postoperative hemodialysis at some point governed by the laboratory findings and the volume status of the patient (50, 53, 58). However, limitations in the ability to provide adequate preoperative dialysis due to severe anginal symptoms (55, 65) or the unexpected intraoperative exposure of the patient to a potassium overload from a massive blood transfusion (65) or poor retrieval of cardioplegic solution (71), may necessitate the intraoperative use of hemodialysis. Simple volume overload is more easily handled with ultrafiltration. However, a more frequent use of intraoperative hemodialysis is advocated by some as a

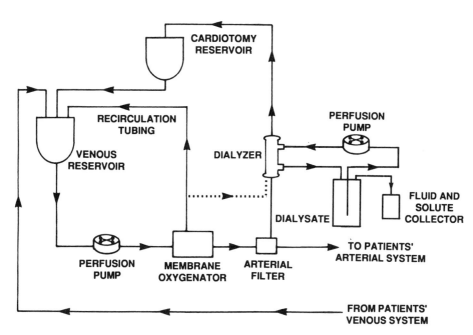

Figure 4.13.   Placement of the dialyzer in the extracorporeal circuit when a membrane oxygenator is used can be accomplished with a side branch from the arterial line filter or from the recirculation tubing. Dialysate flow is provided to the dialyzer with a separate perfusion pump or by gravitational flow.

method for avoiding hemodialysis in the 2- to 3-day period following open heart surgery (63). Anticoagulation for hemodialysis soon after surgery may increase the risk for postoperative bleeding.

ACUTE RENAL FAILURE

Renal compromise following the use of extracorporeal circulatory techniques is not uncommon, occurring with a reported incidence of between 1.5% (72) and 5.3% (73, 74). Preoperative left ventricular dysfunction (74), preoperative renal compromise (72, 74, 75), and duration of the surgical procedure (75) have all been related to the development of postoperative acute renal failure. Though the use of pulsatile flow (76, 77) as well as the early institution of low-dose dopamine infusions intraoperatively (78) may reduce the occurrence of postoperative acute renal failure in some patients, these modalities alone are unable to insure postoperative renal integrity. Patients who develop acute renal failure during extracorporeal circulation can be im-

mediately placed on continuous arteriovenous hemodialysis (66, 70). This intervention can be initiated intraoperatively and continued during the patient's intensive care unit stay. Continuous arteriovenous hemodialysis provides more efficient urea and creatinine clearance, as well as the removal of other toxic metabolites, compared to ultrafiltration techniques (70). The early institution of hemodialysis in patients with acute renal failure may have beneficial effects on long-term survival and return of normal renal function.

INTRAOPERATIVE BLOOD SALVAGE TECHNIQUES

Cardiac surgical procedures are a major source of the total amount of blood used for transfusion purposes in the United States (79–82). The propensity for major blood loss during open heart surgical procedures is due to a combination of the extensive intervention involving major vascular structures and the inherent derangement of hemostasis that accompanies the use of extracorporeal circulatory techniques (83–87). The destruction of both red blood cells and coagulation factors during cardiopulmonary bypass results in an increased need for blood and blood products with these procedures. However, there exists increasing pressure to reduce or eliminate the exposure of patients to blood and blood products because of the widespread recognition of the multiple dangers associated with homologous blood transfusion. These dangers mandate that alternative strategies be utilized to circumvent the need for homologous blood transfusion. A list of recognized dangers from homologous blood transfusion is provided in Table 4.1.

Two intraoperative strategies developed for reducing homologous blood usage are autologous donation with reinfusion and scavenging of shed blood with reinfusion. The use of these techniques not only

Table 4.1. Examples of Disadvantages Associated with Homologous Blood Use

1. Infection transmission
   Human immunodeficiency viruses
   Hepatitis viruses
   Cytomegalovirus
   Syphilis
   Malaria
   African trypanosomiasis
   American filariasis
   Leishmaniasis
   Toxoplasmosis
   Babesiosis
   Bacterial contamination
2. Incompatibility reactions
   Hemolytic Rh reactions
   Hemolytic ABO reactions
   Graft versus host reactions
3. Febrile reactions
   Leukocyte reaction
   Heat stable pyrogens
4. Deficiencies
   2,3-diphosphoglycerate
   Platelets
   Polymorphonucleocytes (loss of phagocytosis after 48 hours)
   Factors V and VIII, (decrease 10–20% in 24 hours)
5. Limited blood supply

reduces the burden that open heart surgical procedures place upon the limited blood supply, but also eliminates the many risks associated with homologous blood transfusion. Intraoperative autologous blood donation during the early phases of the surgical procedure and the intraoperative scavenging of shed blood during surgery both play an important role in reducing homologous blood transfusion requirements.

Autologous Blood Donation

HISTORIC PERSPECTIVE

Preoperative autologous blood donation for postoperative reinfusion was first successfully reported in 1921 (88), but was not adopted for routine use because of the advances in techniques for homologous blood collection. With the development of cardiovascular surgery, and the attendant substantial increases in the demand for homologous blood transfusion, interest in autologous blood donation reappeared. The use of 8 to 12 units of blood during each open heart surgical procedure was not uncommon (81, 89). In the early 1970s, as coronary bypass surgery became an accepted surgical intervention, there was concern that the nation's entire blood supply might be consumed by cardiac surgery alone (90). In addition, the complications and risks associated with homologous blood transfusion served as a further stimulus to find alternative methods for avoiding homologous blood transfusions (80, 90, 91). Early recognition that the best donor for a blood transfusion was the patient, gave primary impetus for the development of autologous blood transfusion techniques (92, 93). It was known that normal, healthy volunteers could be phlebotomized for 3 to 5 units of whole blood each week for as many as 23 weeks with maintenance of a stable hemoglobin, as long as iron supplementation was provided (94). Debilitated patients also could tolerate preoperative phlebotomy of up to 4 units of blood during the 10 days prior to the planned surgical procedure with maintenance of hemoglobins over 10 g/dL, with supplemental iron (95).

A boost to the concept of preoperative autologous blood collection was provided with the finding that patients readily tolerated hemodilution during cardiopulmonary bypass without long-term sequelae. From these observations an immediate interest developed for collecting autologous blood preoperatively whenever major intraoperative blood losses could be predicted (96–98). It was not long thereafter that the collection of autologous blood *intraoperatively* during the planned surgical procedure, utilizing hemodilution techniques, was recommended for reducing homologous blood usage (96, 97, 99–103).

Intraoperative autogolous blood donation not only avoided the risks of homologous blood exposure, but when reinfused, provided the patient with fresh blood that was richer in 2,3-diphosphoglycerate, platelets, and clotting factors than bank blood (104). By the reinfusion of the freshly collected autologous blood, a reduction in total operative blood requirements could be realized (96, 97, 103, 104). The primary method advocated for the intraoperative collection of autologous blood during open heart surgery was its removal prior to the initiation of cardiopulmonary bypass through hemodilution (96, 97, 104, 105).

BASIC PHYSIOLOGIC PRINCIPLES

Autologous blood transfusion can be conceptionally differentiated into several categories depending upon the method and timing of blood collection. If the blood is removed prior to the operative procedure, it is termed predeposit phlebotomy or predonation (94, 95). The preoperative donation of autologous blood is especially useful for patients with unusual serum antibodies for which a shortage of homologous blood exists. Much more common is the intraoperative collection of autologous blood, either before the institution of cardiopulmonary bypass or during the very early phases of the bypass process. The donated blood volume is usually replaced with isotonic intravenous fluid, resulting in hemodilution (96, 97, 104).

Intraoperative autologous blood donation for open heart surgery involves withdrawing several hundred milliliters of blood from the patient and storing it, prior to exposing the patient's blood to the deleterious effects of the heart-lung machine. Reinfused after termination of cardiopulmonary bypass, this fresh autologous blood is an excellent oxygen-carrying volume expander, containing a full complement of coagulation factors and platelets. Most cardiac surgical patients are candidates for intraoperative blood donation as long as they meet two important criteria: the patients must be hemodynamically stable and must have sufficient red blood cell mass to maintain adequate oxygen-carrying capacity once hemodilution has occurred. While the lowest acceptable hematocrit during cardiopulmonary bypass remains controversial, evidence exists that for most patients a hematocrit of 20% is safe (89, 90, 106–108). The reduced hemoglobin is offset by the decreased viscosity of the blood, which in turn decreases myocardial work and improves the coronary microcirculation (108–112).

In order to insure an adequate hemoglobin during bypass, it is essential to calculate what the patient's hemoglobin will be following the dilution occurring with prebypass donation and the dilution from the pump prime in the extracorporeal circuit. The hemoglobin after intraoperative donation can be estimated by the following equation:

$$Hb_d = Hb_i \left[\frac{V_b - V_d}{V_b} \right] \tag{1}$$

where Hb_d is the hemoglobin after dona-tion, Hb_i is the initial predonation hemo-globin, V_b is the total blood volume, and V_d is volume of blood donated. Typically, the patient's blood volume can be approxi-mated to be between 6 and 8% of the kilo-gram body weight depending on the age, size, gender, and clinical status of the pa-tient (113–115).

A patient's hemoglobin on bypass (Hb_b) after further dilution with the extra-corporeal prime will equal the postdo-nation hemoglobin (Hb_d), from equation one, multiplied by the proportion of the total blood volume (V_b) to the combined total blood volume and bypass prime volume (V_e).

$$Hb_b = Hb_d \left[\frac{V_b}{(V_b + V_e)} \right]$$

Combining the hemoglobin-reducing effects of blood donation and hemodilution from pump prime, the maximum volume of blood that can be donated ($V_{d(max)}$) to main-tain the hemoglobin above a predetermined minimal level ($Hb_{e(min)}$) can be calculated with the following equation:

$$V_{d_{MAX}} = V_b - (V_b + V_e) \left[\frac{Hb_{e_{MIN}}}{Hb_i} \right]$$

The extracorporeal circuit prime volume (V_e), the estimated blood volume of the pa-tient (V_b), and the initial hemoglobin (Hb_i) serve as the variable factors. In most cases it is possible to safely remove autologous blood equal to at least 10% of the patient's blood volume prior to bypass (90, 96, 97, 100). Harvesting smaller amounts of autol-ogous blood will decrease the quantity of hemostatic elements available with rein-fusion and decrease the impact on total red blood cell mass.

TECHNICAL CONCERNS

The objective of intraoperative predo-nation is the removal of the maximum quantity of blood possible, maintenance of that blood in satisfactory condition throughout the period of cardiopulmonary bypass, and reinfusion of the blood at the end of cardiopulmonary bypass. During do-nation, the blood must be removed in such a way as to maintain the patient's hemody-namic stability while preserving the hemo-globin at a clinically acceptable level. Elec-trocardiographic and hemodynamic moni-toring are essential during the donation process. It is important to obtain the blood isovolumically in order to prevent hemody-namic instability. Support of the intravas-cular volume with administration of crystal-loid or colloid solutions during the process of autologous blood removal is required. The blood's oxygen-carrying capacity must also be maintained at a sufficient level to prevent hypoxia.

Several techniques can be used for collecting blood intraoperatively. For each, blood is donated prior to or immediately after the initiation of cardiopulmonary by-pass. This minimizes the contact of blood and blood elements with the artificial sur-faces of the extracorporeal circuit. After ini-tiation of cardiopulmonary bypass, not only is the blood diluted with the prime, but co-agulation factors and platelets are exposed to the artificial surfaces, reducing the value of the blood for later hemostatic control (102, 116–118). Numerous techniques have been proposed for obtaining blood, but the most widely accepted access routes are through a central venous catheter, an ar-terial catheter, or the venous tubing of the heart-lung machine (119). Whichever tech-nique is utilized, maintenance of hemody-namic stability is essential throughout the donation process.

If blood is to be collected from a cen-tral venous catheter, the catheter is con-nected by a short segment of sterile intrave-nous tubing to a blood collection bag that contains an anticoagulant. The blood col-lection bag is placed below the level of the patient's right atrium, and the blood is allowed to collect into the bag by gravity

(Fig. 4.14A). Simultaneously, the patient's blood volume is replaced with crystalloid solution through a peripheral intravenous line. After the blood has been collected, it is labeled and usually left connected to the patient for later reinfusion. This technique is attractive for several reasons: it requires no complex equipment or training to accomplish; the blood loss is gradual and can be easily compensated for by intravenous fluid replacement; and the quantity of anticoagulant in the blood storage bag is usually small, causing a minimal effect on coagulation when the blood is reinfused. The major limitation of this technique is that it is relatively slow. In many operating room environments, time is of the essence, and the period from the start of anesthesia to the initiation of cardiopulmonary bypass may be relatively short. In addition, another disadvantage of this technique is that the anesthesiologist's attention may be diverted from the patient during the collection process, which may increase the potential for an adverse event.

Another method of blood collection is through an arterial cannula (Fig. 4.14B). An advantage for blood collection through this route is that donation can be accomplished fairly rapidly. Of course, there is an increased risk for transient hypovolemia and hypotension during the donation process. In addition, monitoring the blood pressure may be problematic if only one arterial line is in place.

Alternatively, the blood can be collected immediately prior to the initiation of cardiopulmonary bypass through a "Y" connector placed in the venous tubing, proximal to the venous reservoir of the extracorporeal circuit (Fig. 4.15). This connector allows blood either to pass unimpeded into the venous reservoir or to be diverted into a separate circuit draining into a blood collection bag. Immediately prior to the initiation of cardiopulmonary bypass, the limb of the "Y" connector leading to the collection bag is clamped, and the pump prime is allowed to drain into the reservoir until venous blood begins en-

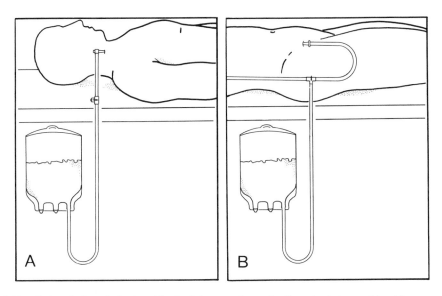

Figure 4.14. **A.** A technique is depicted for the intraoperative collection of autologous blood from a central venous catheter. The blood is collected in a anticoagulated blood collection bag placed below the level of the patient in order to allow gravity flow. **B.** A technique is depicted for the intraoperative collection of autologous blood from a femoral arterial catheter. The arterial pressures serve as the driving force, allowing the filling of the anticoagulated blood collection bag.

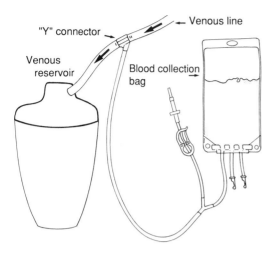

Figure 4.15. The technique for the intraoperative collection of autologous blood from the venous line of the extracorporeal circuit is depicted. During cardiopulmonary bypass, a side branch or "Y" connector allows the diversion of blood from the venous line into a blood collection bag. Since the blood is already heparinized, anticoagulant is not needed in the collection bag.

tering the reservoir. At that point, the venous return to the reservoir is clamped and blood is diverted into the collection bag. Simultaneously, pump prime is transfused through the arterial cannula to replace the volume loss. After a calculated quantity of blood has been harvested, the drainage tubing to the collection bag is clamped and the venous return is rediverted back to the reservoir. With this technique the blood collection bag does not have to be anticoagulated because of the patient's full heparinization. The bagged blood is labeled and can be reinfused into the extracorporeal circuit by the perfusionist should the hemoglobin on bypass become unacceptably low. If the blood is not returned during cardiopulmonary bypass, the anesthesiologist can reinfuse it later during the surgical procedure.

Immediate prebypass collection of blood is attractive because of the ability to rapidly sequester large volumes prior to the initiation of cardiopulmonary bypass. Also, it is relatively simple to institute because complex preparation is not required. Hypo-

volemia can easily be avoided by the rapid administration of volume through the heart-lung machine. One disadvantage of this technique is that sequestered blood contains a significant level of heparin, which requires neutralization with protamine when the blood is eventually reinfused. However, the preservation of platelets and coagulation factors by using this technique is excellent (119).

INDICATIONS

While some early studies failed to demonstrate that reinfusion of autologous blood during open heart surgical procedures had any value in reducing blood bank requirements (120, 121), numerous subsequent studies have confirmed the benefit of this technique. In fact, the majority of studies have found that intraoperative autologous blood donation with reinfusion decreases total homologous blood requirements by at least 20 to 50% (89, 96, 97, 103, 106, 119, 122, 123). In addition, a decrease in the requirement for fresh-frozen plasma, needed for control of postoperative coagulopathies, can be realized (123). Reinfusion of fresh autogolous blood that is obtained prior to exposure of the blood to the deleterious effects of the heart-lung machine has several advantages for maintaining hemostasis. Several studies have demonstrated an improvement in both the quantitative (103, 119, 124) and qualitative (125) platelet availability when compared to patients not having undergone predonation and reinfusion. In addition, postoperative coagulation factor defects are less extensive in patients receiving the reinfusion of fresh autologous blood (119).

The safety of autologous blood donation has been demonstrated repeatedly (90, 96, 97, 100, 119, 126). While transient hypotension during donation has been reported (97, 100), serious complications have not occurred when the procedure is performed properly. The use of intraoperative donation of autologous blood prior to cardiopulmonary bypass might well be indicated for any patient whose preoperative hemoglobin would allow for the necessary hemodilution associated with this technique.

Intraoperative autologous donation is highly attractive as a blood conservation technique for the majority of patients undergoing cardiac surgery. It is an inexpensive, simple method for providing fresh blood that is essentially free of risk from transmission of disease, allergic reaction, alloimmunization, and blood banking mishaps. Additionally autotransfusion does do not pose a burden on the limited blood supply. Intraoperative autologous donation appears to yield the ideal blood product for reinfusion after cardiopulmonary bypass because it not only yields red blood cells, but also fresh coagulation factors, platelets, and other essential serum components. As the results are favorable and the risks are low, intraoperative autologous blood donation and reinfusion should be considered in all patients undergoing open heart surgical procedures.

Intraoperative Blood Scavenging

HISTORIC PERSPECTIVE

One method for minimizing homologous blood usage is the intraoperative salvage of shed blood from the operative field and, after processing, reinfusion of the red blood cells. This approach is particularly advantageous during operative procedures, such as open heart surgery, where surgical blood losses constitute a significant portion of the transfusion requirement. The salvage, processing, and reinfusion of blood that is lost during a surgical procedure is called autotransfusion.

The first recorded application of autotransfusion occurred in 1818, and is credited to John Blundell, who reinfused shed blood in 10 patients with severe postpartum hemorrhage (127). William Highmore published the first scientific article in 1874 advocating the value of intraoperative autotransfusion (128), and subsequently

in 1886, John Duncan reported a case of reinfusion of shed operative blood during a leg amputation (129). In the early 1900s the development of techniques for blood storage and blood banking began to change the emphasis from autotransfusion to homologous blood usage (91, 130, 131). This was further extended during World War II when increased awareness by the public of the value of donating blood, in combination with the cumbersome nature of the techniques required for the collection of shed blood, led to a reduction in the enthusiasm for autologous blood salvage.

However, interest in autotransfusion reemerged during the 1960s with the advent of the Vietnam War. Vietnam War casualties required massive transfusions, which placed an inordinant drain on the homologous blood supply. In response, Bentley Laboratories developed a device specifically for the rapid intraoperative autotransfusion of lost blood. Shed blood was aspirated from the surgical field and collected in a reservoir. The processing of the blood entailed defoaming and filtering prior to immediate reinfusion (92, 132, 133). As much as 40 liters of blood could be reinfused during an operative procedure using this technique. Though the Bentley system was useful, disadvantages included the need to anticoagulate either the patient or the salvaged blood, the reinfusion of activated clotting factors resulting in a coagulopathy, renal failure from reinfusion of large amounts of free hemoglobin present in the filtered blood, and high risk for inadvertent but fatal air embolization during the reinfusion process.

In the 1970s the number of cardiac surgical procedures increased exponentially, which placed a tremendous burden on blood banks, since the average open heart procedure required between 8 and 12 units of blood (79, 81, 89, 96, 121). More recently, concerns about disease transmission associated with homologous blood transfusion, especially human immunodeficiency virus, have served as an additional impetus for adopting autotransfusion techniques (79, 131).

Because of the difficulties associated with the Bentley system, an alternative approach for intraoperative salvage was sought. The result was the development of red blood cell washing and reinfusing devices (132). The advantages of a red cell washing system were the removal of activated coagulation factors, free hemoglobin, and nonred blood cell debris, as well as the virtual elimination of the risk for inadvertant air embolization. Unfortunately, the washing procedure also entailed the removal of normal clotting factors and pharmacologic agents existing in the serum, including heparin (91, 134, 135). Early cell washing systems also had the disadvantage of requiring a long time interval between the time the blood was collected and the time the cells could be reinfused.

Over the past decade, the primary improvement in intraoperative salvage of blood has been in the design of the cell washing-reinfusion equipment. At present, commercially available devices from several manufacturers have reduced red blood cell processing time to as little as 3 minutes. Other improvements in equipment design include easier operation, greater reliability, and additional safety features. Present systems nearly fulfill the requirements set forth by Gilcher and Orr (136) in 1975 for the ideal autotransfusion system.

TECHNICAL CONCERNS

During open heart surgical procedures when the patient is fully heparinized, most of the shed blood can be returned to the patient through the cardiotomy suction of the heart-lung machine. However, before heparinization and after neutralization of the heparin with protamine, the use of the cardiotomy suction is not possible because of the risk for clot formation within the extracorporeal circulatory device. In order to prevent the irretrievable loss of this shed blood, other strategies had to be developed.

Autotransfusion techniques are divided into two approaches: one where the blood is recovered and filtered prior to reinfusion, and the other where the blood is recovered, filtered, and washed prior to reinfusion. In the simplest autotransfusion system the blood is collected from the operative field using a suction-based aspiration device that anticoagulates the blood as it is collected. The collected blood is filtered and stored for reinfusion. The technique is extremely simple and inexpensive. However, simply filtering the blood does not remove serum factors that can potentiate or worsen the coagulation deficits commonly seen after cardiopulmonary bypass. Because of this, simple blood retrieval and reinfusing systems during open heart surgery have been supplanted by the more advanced blood processing technique of cell washing (91, 134).

Cell washing techniques incorporate four basic steps: (a) blood harvesting from the operative site, (b) processing of the shed blood with removal of the serum, (c) storage of the red blood cells that are harvested, and (d) reinfusion of the red blood cell mass. Harvesting the shed blood is accomplished using a double-lumen suction tubing. The larger lumen provides the suction uptake of blood and the smaller lumen carries heparinized saline to the suction catheter tip (Fig. 4.16). Typically, between 10,000 and 100,000 units of heparin are added to 1 liter of normal saline and allowed to drip into a mixing chamber at the suction catheter's tip (137–139). The mixing chamber allows immediate anticoagulation of any blood aspirated from the surgical field. The anticoagulated blood is then transported to a disposable reservoir where clots and other debris are filtered out prior to further processing. The flow rate of the heparinized saline into the mixing chamber is controlled by the amount of vacuum applied by the suction apparatus and by the infusion rate set on the anticoagulant drip bag.

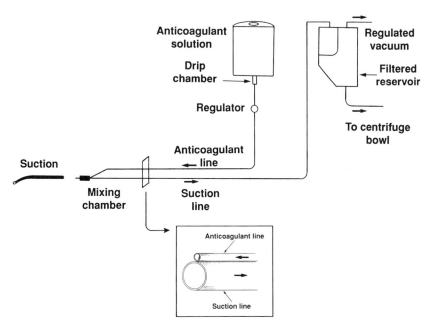

Figure 4.16. The typical blood collection system includes a suction apparatus that aspirates blood into a filtered reservoir. As blood is drawn from the surgical field, it enters a small mixing chamber to which an anticoagulant solution is added. Following mixing, the anticoagulated blood is carried to a reservoir where it is filtered and stored until centrifugation is desired. A close-up of the double-lumen suction tubing shows a small tube providing the anticoagulant solution to the mixing chamber, and a large tube serving to transport the aspirated blood.

The filtered, anticoagulated blood is processed in a centrifuge bowl, which is typically composed of two subassemblies. The inner subassembly is stationary and contains an inlet and outlet port through which fluid is able to enter or leave the processing chamber. Over the inner subassembly is positioned an outer subassembly that rotates and contains the primary processing chamber. Blood components are separated in the outer spinning centrifuge bowl based upon the differential densities of the components. The heavier, more dense blood components are centrifuged outward, toward the bowl's perimeter. The lighter, lower density components float inward, toward the bowl's center (Fig. 4.17). As blood is pumped into the spinning bowl the lighter supernatants are displaced from the bowl through the outlet and discarded. After the bowl is filled with red blood cells, normal saline wash solution is pumped into the bowl and circulated through the red cell layer. The result is dis-

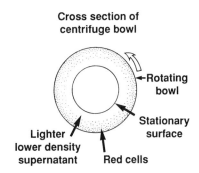

Figure 4.17. A cross-section of the centrifuge bowl is shown. As the bowl rotates, the higher density cells migrate to the outer wall while the lighter density supernatant remains more central.

placement of debris, plasma, free hemoglobin, and any anticoagulants by the wash solution through the outlet into a waste bag. Following the wash cycle, the remaining red blood cells are aspirated from the inlet port into a collection bag (Fig. 4.18). The final blood collected with this system can have a hematocrit as high as 70% (134, 139–141).

Figure 4.18. The cell saving-washing process occurs sequentially. **A.** Blood that has been collected in a reservoir from the surgical field is pumped through the inlet port of the centrifuge bowl, causing displacement of saline from the bowl out of the outlet. **B.** With centrifugation, the heavier, more dense red blood cells are spun to the periphery of the bowl and the waste plasma overflows into a waste collection bag. **C.** After the centrifuge bowl has been filled with red blood cells, the flow of blood from the reservoir is stopped and a saline wash solution is started. The saline is pumped through the layers of red blood cells, removing free hemoglobin, coagulation factors, debris, and other plasma components. **D.** Following washing of the red blood cells, the centrifuge is stopped. The washed red blood cells are aspirated from the inlet port and placed into a reinfusion bag.

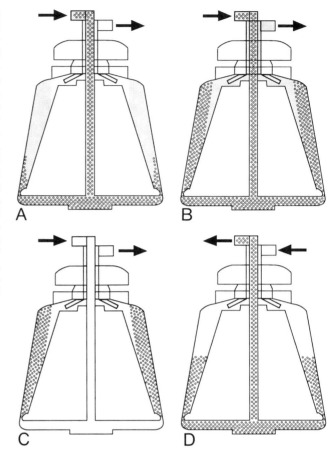

Control of the processing in all currently available devices is provided by a microprocessor, controlled by internal air detectors and solenoid valves (Fig. 4.19). The valves ensure the exact control of the fluid paths, as well as the identification of status conditions and end-points in the processing sequence. Most commonly available blood salvage systems have standard disposable equipment that includes a centrifuge bowl, reinfusion bag, and waste bag. The list price of the disposable separator, bowl, and tubing is typically in the range of $100 to $400. Other disposable materials including the reservoir, suction assembly tubing, and anticoagulant solution typically cost an additional $25 to $50. The hardware cost is in the range of $18,000 to $40,000. While the microprocessor control simplifies the operation of the equipment, qualified personnel are still necessary to set up and operate the device. Typically during open heart surgery, the equipment can be run by a perfusionist.

INDICATIONS

Intraoperative salvaging and washing of shed blood during an operative procedure has emerged as an important technique for blood conservation during cardiac surgery. The aim of intraoperative red blood cell salvage and reinfusion is a reduction in homologous blood transfusion requirements. The vast majority of studies (140–148) have demonstrated that the use of this technique is safe and effective in reducing homologous blood transfusion during open heart surgery by as much as 32 to 62%. Initially there was some concern that

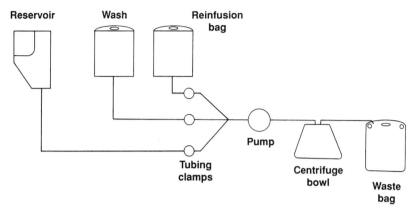

Figure 4.19. Schematic for a typical cell separator showing the reservoir bag into which aspirated anticoagulated blood is accumulated. Other portions of the apparatus include a reservoir for saline wash solution, a bag for collecting the washed blood, serial tubing clamps that are operated by a microprocessor, a pump head that allows flow in either direction (depending on which tubing clamps are open or shut), a centrifuge bowl for cell separation, and a waste bag for discarding supernatant during the washing process.

reinfusion of a platelet and coagulation factor-depleted blood product would exacerbate the extracorporeal circulatory-induced coagulation defects, but a dilutional coagulopathy was not demonstrated with the use of routine blood salvage techniques (140–142). However, a comparison between the red blood cell salvaging-washing-reinfusing technique and the ultrafiltration technique for concentrating blood remaining in the cardiopulmonary bypass circuitry after an open heart operation did indicate better postoperative hemostasis with the use of a nonred blood cell washing approach (15). Therefore, red cell washing techniques should be considered a less desirable method for salvaging and concentrating red blood cell mass in the extracorporeal circuit following bypass.

Another concern associated with the transfusion of red blood cells recovered from the operative field was that the processing might alter the cell membrane's stability and viability. However, when autologous red cell viability was compared to donor blood (139), autologous red cells were found to be more resistant to osmotic stress than the homologous blood. Red blood cells that had been collected, processed, and reinfused also had similar sur-

vival times when compared to autologous red blood cells obtained by venous puncture (140, 149, 150).

Although not universally confirmed (151), the vast majority of studies have found autologous red blood cell salvage and reinfusion to be cost-effective (141, 143, 145, 146, 152), In most evaluations of cost, the immediate cost of processing the shed blood was compared to the cost savings associated with avoidance of homologous blood usage. The cost of using blood salvage techniques was more than offset by the decreased use of blood and blood products. However, the need for trained personnel and the initial capital expense, as well as the cost of maintaining and running the equipment must be considered.

CONTRAINDICATIONS

The risks of using red cell salvaging systems can be subdivided into three areas: equipment malfunction, operator error, and blood contamination. Advances in design and microprocessor control have greatly reduced the chance that a device malfunction will result in harm to a patient. In addition, increased user experience, as well as refinements in the design of the equipment, have contributed to significant reductions in operator error. However, a persistent concern is the danger associated with the use of blood that has been contaminated on the surgical field. While current autotransfusion devices are very effective in removing damaged red blood cells and other particulate matter, they do not completely remove bacteria, malignant cells, and certain medications (92, 153, 154). The centrifugation and washing process removes a large proportion of any bacterial contamination, but unacceptable numbers of bacteria may remain within the red cell mass (155). Therefore, salvaging blood from an infected surgical site should be avoided. Similarly, blood collected from an area of malignancy should not be reinfused since malignant cells within the processed blood could, theoretically, cause diffuse metastases.

It must also be realized that blood collected from the surgical field can be contaminated with agents placed there by the operating surgical team. Certain agents used to irrigate the operative site, and bound to the red blood cell membrane, are not removed by the device and are potentially toxic if infused intravenously. Theoretically, drugs carried in the plasma are eliminated by the cell washing process, such as topical bacitracin and neomycin (156). Similarly, some topical hemostatic agents might be dangerous if given intravenously. Microfibrillar collagen hemostat is not removed during the wash cycle in scavenged blood (157). While blood exposed to thrombin from the incision is probably acceptable for salvage (158), blood exposed to Avitene (Alcon, Inc., Puerto Rico) and Surgicel (Johnson and Johnson, Arlington, TX) can potentially induce a coagulopathy if reinfused (157).

Red blood cell salvage is an important blood conservation technique during cardiac surgery. Though cost benefit and other concerns associated with the use of salvage devices must be considered, there remains a strong incentive for the use of any technique that can reasonably reduce homologous transfusion requirements.

REFERENCES

1. Brull L. Realization de l' ultrafiltration in vivo. C R Soc Biol (Paris) 1928;99:1605–1608.
2. Lunderquist A, Alwall N, Tornberg A. On the artificial kidney; XXI. The efficacy of the dialyzer ultrafilter intended for human use. Including a preliminary report on treatment of oedemic patients by means of ultrafiltration. Acta Med Scand 1952;143:307.
3. Nakamoto S. Removal of edema fluid by ultrafiltration with the disposable twin-coil artificial kidney. Cleve Clin Q 1961;28:10–15.
4. Kobayashi K, Shibata M, Kato K. Studies on the development of a new method of controlling the amount and contents of body fluids (extracorporeal ultrafiltration method.ECUM) and the application of this method for patients receiving long-term hemodialysis. Jpn J Nephrol 1972;14:1.
5. Henderson LW. Pre vs. post dilution hemofiltration. Clin Nephrol 1979;11:120.
6. Romagnoli A, Hacker J, Keats AS, Milan J. External hemoconcentration after deliberate hemodilution. Annual meeting of the American Society of Anesthesiologists, extracts of scientific papers, San Francisco, October 1976;269.
7. Darup J, Bleese N, Kalmar P, Lutz G, Pokar H, Polonius MJ: Hemofiltration during extracorporeal circulation (ECC). Thorac Cardiovasc Surg 1979;27:227–230.
8. Intonti F, Alquati P, Schiavello R, Alessandrini F. Ultrafiltration during open heart-surgery in chronic renal failure. Scand J Thorac Cardiovasc Surg 1981;15:217–220.
9. Heiss KF, Pettit B, Hirschl RB, Cilley RE, Chapman R, Bartlett R. Renal insufficiency and volume overload in neonatal ECMO managed by continuous ultrafiltration. Trans Am Soc Artif Intern Organs 1987;33:557–560.
10. Magilligan DJ. Indications for ultrafiltration in the cardiac surgical patient. J Thorac Cardiovasc Surg 1985;89:183–189.
11. Hakim M, Wheeldon D, Bethune DW, Milstein BB, English T, Wallwork J. Haemodialysis and haemofiltration on cardiopulmonary bypass. Thorax 1985;40:101–106.
12. Magilligan DJ, Oyama C. Ultrafiltration during cardiopulmonary bypass: laboratory evaluation and initial clinical experience. Ann Thorac Sur 1984;37:33–39.
13. Klineberg PL, Kam CA, Johnson DC, Cartmili TB, Brown JH. Hematocrit and blood volume control during cardiopulmonary bypass with

the use of hemofiltration. Anesthesiology 1984; 60:478–480.

14. Solem JO, Tengborn L, Steen S, Luhrs C. Cell saver versus hemofilter for concentration of oxygenator blood after cardiopulmonary bypass. Thorac Cardiovasc Surg 1987;35:42–47.

15. Boldt J, Kling D, Bormann B, Zuge M, Scheld H, Hempelmann G. Blood conservation in cardiac operations. J Thorac Cardiovasc Surg 1989;97: 832–840.

16. Boldt J, Zickmann B, Czeke A, Herold C, Dapper F, Hempelmann G. Blood conservation techniques and platelet function in cardiac surgery. Anesthesiology 1991;75:426–432.

17. Osipov VP, Lurie GO, Khodas M, Mikhailov Y, Fadejeva NV. Hemoconcentration during open heart operations. Thorac Cardiovasc Surg 1985; 33:81–85.

18. Lister G, Hellenbrand WE, Kleinman CS, Talner NS. Physiologic effects of increasing hemoglobin concentration in left-to-right shunting in infants with ventricular septal defects. N Engl J Med 1982;306:502–506.

19. Kontras S, Bodenbender J, Craenen J, et al. Hyperviscosity in congenital heart disease. J Pediatr 1970;76:214–220.

20. Wheeldon DR, Bethune DW. Blood conservation during cardiopulmonary bypass—autologous transfusion, cell saving and haemofiltration. In: Taylor KM, ed. Cardiopulmonary bypass—principles and management. Baltimore: Williams & Wilkins, 1986:289–311.

21. Salzman EW. Low-molecular-weight heparin. Is small beautiful? N Engl J Med 1986;315: 957–959.

22. Rosenberg RD, Lam L. Correlation between structure and function of heparin. Proc Natl Acad Sci 1979;76:1218–1222.

23. Holt DW, Landis GH, Dumond DA, Harden SB, Bartosik J, Miller M. Hemofiltration as an adjunct to cardiopulmonary bypass for total oxygenator volume control. J Extra-Corp Technol 1982;14:373–377.

24. Ing TS, Ashbach DL, Kanter A. Fluid removal with negative-pressure hydrostatic ultrafiltration using a partial vacuum. Nephron 1975; 14:451–455.

25. Nelson RL, Tamari Y, Tortolani AJ, Hall MH, Moccio CG. Ultrafiltration for concentration and salvage of pump blood. In: Utley JR, ed. Pathophysiology and technique of cardiopulmonary bypass. Vol 2 Baltimore: Williams & Wilkins, 1983:229–241.

26. Silverstein ME, Ford CA, Lysaght MJ, Henderson LW. Treatment of severe fluid overload by ultrafiltration. N Engl J Med 1974;291:747–751.

27. Henderson LW, Ford CN, Colton CK, Bluenle

LW, Bixler HJ. Uremic blood cleaning by diafiltration using hollow-fiber ultrafilter. Trans Am Soc Artif Intern Organs 1970;16: 107–114.

28. Nakamura Y, Masuda M, Toshima Y, et al. Comparative study of cell saver and ultrafiltration nontransfusion in cardiac surgery. Ann Thorac Surg 1990;49:973–978.

29. Karliczek GF, Tigchelaar I, Dijck L, Van Der Heide H. How much additional blood trauma is caused by haemofiltration during cardiopulmonary bypass? Life Support Syst 1986;4(suppl 1):167–173.

30. Paganini EA, Nakamoto SI. Continous slow ultrafiltration in oliguric acute renal failure. Tran Am Soc Artif Intern Organs 1980;26: 201–204.

31. Boldt T, Kling D, V Bormann B, Scheld HH, Hemplemann G. Extravascular lung water and hemofiltration during complicated cardiac surgery. Thorac Cardiovasc Surg 1987;35: 161–165.

32. Osipov VP, Lure GO, Marochnik SL, Lokshin LS. Experience in hemoconcentration by ultrafiltration in operations using artificial circulation at the all-union scientific center of surgery of the USSR Academy of Medical Sciences. Grud Serdechnososudistaia Khir 1990;7:3–6.

33. Tamari YR, Nelson R, Levy R, et al. Concentration of blood in the extracorporeal circuit using ultrafiltration. J Extracorp Technol 1983;15:133–142.

34. Hopeck JM, Lane RS, Schroeder JW. Oxygenator volume control by parallel ultrafiltration to remove plasma water. J Extracorp Technol 1981;13:267–271.

35. Page PA. Ultrafiltration versus cell washing for blood concentration. J Extracorp Tech 1990; 22:142–150.

36. Craddock PR, Fehr J, Brigham KL. Complement and leukocyte mediated pulmonary dysfunction in hemodialysis. N Engl J Med 1977; 296:769–774.

37. Abel JJ, Rowntree LG, Turner BB. On removal of diffusable substances from the circulating blood in living animals by dialysis. J Pharmacol Exp Ther 1914;5:275–316.

38. Kolff WJ, Berk HT. The artificial kidney: a dialyzer with a great area. Acta Med Scand 1944;117:121–134.

39. Alwall N. On the artificial kidney. I. Apparatus for dialysis of blood in vivo. Acta Med Scand 1947;128:317–326.

40. Kolff WJ, Watschinger B, Vertes V. Results in patients treated with coil kidney (disposable dialyzing unit). JAMA 1956;161:1433–1437.

41. MacNeill AE, Doyle JE, Anthone R, Anthone S.

Technic with parallel flow, straight tube blood dialyzer. NY State J Med 1959:4137–4149.

42. Awad JA, Brassard A, Binet J, Caron WM. Pulmonary and cardiac assistance during hemodialysis. An experimental method for the oxygenation of the blood and the support of the heart during extracorporeal dialysis. J Urol 1970; 103:388–392.

43. Lazarus JM, Lowrie EG, Hampers CL: Cardiovascular disease in uremic patients on hemodialysis. Kidney Int 1975(suppl);2:167.

44. Lindner A, Charra B, Sherrana DJ, Scribner, BH. Accelerated atherosclerosis in prolonged maintenance hemodialysis. N Engl J Med 1974; 290:697–701.

45. Hellerstedt WL, Johnson WJ, Ascher N, et al. Survival rates of 2,728 patients with end-stage renal disease. Mayo Clinic Proc 1984;59: 776–783.

46. Byrd LH, Sullivan JF. Successful coronary artery bypass in hemodialysis patients. J Dialysis 1978;2:33–42.

47. Menzoian JO, Davis RC, Idelson BA, Mannick JA, Berger RL. Coronary bypass surgery and renal transplantation: a case report. Ann Surg 1974;179:63–64.

48. Laws KH, Merrill WH, Hannon JW, Prager RL, Bender HW. Cardiac Surgery in patients with chronic renal disease. Ann Thorac Surg 1986;42:152–157.

49. Francis GS, Sharma B, Collins AJ, Helseth HK, Comty CM. Coronary artery surgery in patients with end-stage renal disease. Ann Intern Med 1980;92:499–503.

50. Sakurai H, Ackad A, Friedman HS, Lajam F, Haft JI, Stein RM. Aorto-coronary bypass graft surgery in a patient on home hemodialysis. Clin Neprol 1974;2:208–210.

51. Lamberti JJ, Cohn LH, Collins JJ. Cardiac surgery in patients undergoing renal dialysis or transplantation. Ann Thorac Surg 1975;19: 135–141.

52. Posner MA, Reves JG, Lell WA. Aortic valve replacement in a hemodialysis-dependent patient: anesthetic consideration—a case report. Anesth Analg 1975;54:24–28.

53. Chawla R, Gailiunas P, Lazarus JM, et al. Cardiopulmonary bypass surgery in chronic hemodialysis and transplant patients. Trans Am Soc Artif Intern Organs 1977;23:694–697.

54. Zamora JL, Burdine JT, Karlberg H, et al. Cardiac surgery in patients with end-stage renal disease. Ann Thorac Surg 1986;42:113–117.

55. Opsahl JA, Husebye DG, Helseth HK, Collins AJ. Coronary artery bypass surgery in patients on maintenance dialysis: long-term survival. Am J Kidney Dis 1988;12:271–274.

56. Marshall WG, Rossi NP, Meng RL, Wedige-

Stecher T. Coronary artery bypass grafting in dialysis patients. Ann Thorac Surg 1986; 42(suppl):S12–S15.

57. Deutsch E, Bernstein RC, Addonizio VP, Kussmaul WG. Coronary artery bypass surgery in patients on chronic hemodialysis. Ann Intern Med 1989;10:369–372.

58. Francis GS, Compty CM, Sharma B, Helseth HK. Myocardial revascularization in chronic renal disease patients. In: Love J, ed. Cardiac surgery in patients with chronic renal disease. New York: Futura Publishing Co, 1982:115–132.

59. Van Devanter SH, Cohn LH, Koster TK, Collins JJ. Cardiac valve replacement in chronic renal disease patients. In: Love J, ed. Cardiac surgery in patients with chronic renal disease. New York: Futura Publishing Co, 1982:151–165.

60. Monson BK, Wickstrom PH, Haglin JJ, Francis C, Comty CM, Helseth HK. Cardiac Operation and end stage renal disease. Ann Thorac Surg 1980; 30:267–272.

61. Gordon LA, Simon ER, Rukes M, Richards V, Perkins HA. Studies in regional heparinization. N Engl J Med 1956;255:1063–1066.

62. Soffer O, MacDonell RC, Finlayson DC, et al. Intraoperative hemodialysis during cardiopulmonary bypass in chronic renal failure. J Thorac Cardiovasc Surg 1979;77:789–791.

63. Zawada ET, Stinson JB, Done G. New perspectives on coronary artery disease in hemodialysis patients. South Med J 1982;75:694–696.

64. Goebel TK, Stote RM, Dubb JW, Allison NL. Intraoperative dialysis techniques. ANNA J 1987;14:121–124.

65. Murkin JM, Murphy DA, Finlayson DC, Waller JL. Hemodialysis during cardiopulmonary bypass: report of twelve cases. Anesth Analg 1987;66:899–901.

66. Paganini EP, Suhoza K, Swann S, Golding L, Nakamoto S. Continuous renal replacement therapy in patients with acute renal dysfunction undergoing intraaortic balloon pump and/or left ventricular device support. Trans Am Soc Artif Intern Organs 1986;32:414–417.

67. The kidneys. In: Goudsouzian N, Karamanian AA, eds. Physiology for the Anesthesiologist. Norwalk, Connecticut: Appleton Century Crofts, 1984:429–454.

68. Lunderquist A. On the artificial kidney for human use. Including a preliminary report on treatment of oedemic patients by means of ultrafiltration. Acta Med Scand 1952;143: 307–314.

69. Lamer C, Valleaux T, Plaisance P, et al. Continuous arteriovenous hemodialysis for acute renal failure after cardiac operations. J Thorac Cardiovasc Surg 1990;99:175–176.

70. Geronemus R, Schneider N. Continuous arteri-

ovenous hemodialysis: a new modality for treatment of acute renal failure. Trans Am Soc Artif Intern Organs 1984;30:610–613.

71. Kopman EA. Scavenging of potassium cardioplegic solution to prevent hyperkalemia in hemodialysis-dependent patients. Anesth Analg 1983;62:780–782.

72. Gailiunas P, Chawla R, Lazarus JM, Cohn L, Sanders J, Merrill JP. Acute renal failure following cardiac operations. J Thorac Cardiovas Surg 1980;79:241–243.

73. Rigden SPA, Barratt TM, Dillon MJ, DeLeval M, Stark J. Acute renal failure complicating cardiopulmonary bypass surgery. Arch Dis Child 1982;57:425–430.

74. Hilberman M, Myers BD, Carrie BJ, Derby G, Jaminson RL, Stinson EB. Acute renal failure following cardiac surgery. J Thorac Cardiovasc Surg 1979;77:880–888.

75. Abel RM, Buckley MT, Austem WG, Barnett GO, Beck CH, Fischer JE. Incidence and prognosis of renal failure following cardiac operations. Result of a prospective analysis of 500 consecutive patients. J Thorac Cardiovasc Surg 1976; 71:323–333.

76. Olinger GN, Hutchinson LD, Bonchek LI. Pulsatile cardiopulmonary bypass for patients with renal insufficiency. Thorax 1983;38:543–550.

77. Matsuda H, Hirose H, Nakano S, et al. Results of open heart surgery in patients with impaired renal function as creatinine clearance below 30 ml/min. J Cardiovasc Surg 1986;27:595–599.

78. Davis RF, Lappas DG, Kirklin JK, Buckley MJ, Lowenstein E. Acute oliguria after cardiopulmonary bypass: renal functional improvement with low-dose dopamine infusion. Crit Care Med 1982;10:852–856.

79. Tyson GS, Slanden RN, Spainhour V, et al. Blood conservation in cardiac surgery: preliminary results with an institutional commitment. Ann Surg 1989;209:736–742.

80. Utley JR, Moores WY, Stephens DB: Blood conservation techniques. Ann Thorac Surg 1981; 31:482–490.

81. Roche JK, Stengle JM. Open-heart surgery and the demand for blood. JAMA 1973;225: 1516–1521.

82. Goodnough LT, Johnston MFM, Toy PT, and the Transfusion Medicine Academic Award Group. The variability of transfusion practice in coronary artery bypass surgery. JAMA 1991; 265:86–90.

83. Milam JD. Blood transfusion in heart surgery. Clin Lab Med 1982;1:65–85.

84. Cosgrove DM, Loop FD, Lytle BW, et al. Determinants of blood utilization during myocardial revascularization. Ann Thorac Surg 1985;40: 380–384.

85. Campbell FW, Addonizio VP Jr. Platelet function alterations during cardiac surgery. In: Ellison N, Jobes DR, eds. Effective hemostasis in cardiac surgery. Philadelphia: WB Saunders, 1988:85–109.

86. Edmunds LH, Addonizio VP Jr. Platelet physiology during cardiopulmonary bypass. In: Utley JR, ed. Pathophysiology and techniques of cardiopulmonary bypass. Baltimore: William & Wilkins, 1982:106–119.

87. Gravlee GP, Hopkins MB: Blood plasma products. In: Ellison N, Jobes DR, eds. Effective hemostasis in cardiac surgery. Philadelphia: WB Saunders, 1988:69–83.

88. Grant FC. Autotransfusion. Ann Surg 1921; 74:253–254.

89. Cohn LH, Fosberg AM, Anderson RP, Collins JJ. The effects of phlebotomy, hemodilution and autologous transfusion on systemic oxygenation and whole blood utilization in open heart surgery. Chest 1975;68:283–287.

90. Tector AJ, Gabriel RP, Mateicka WE, et al. Reduction of blood usage in open heart surgery. Chest 1976;4:454–457.

91. Brzica SM, Pineda AA, Taswell HF. Autologous blood transfusion. Mayo Clin Proc 1976; 51:723–737.

92. Council on Scientific Affairs. Autologous blood transfusions. JAMA 1986;256:2378–2380.

93. Yomtovian RA. Autologous blood transfusion; past performance and current concerns. Minn Med 1986;69:353–356.

94. Hamstra RD, Block MH. Erythropoiesis in response to blood loss in man. J Appl Physiol 1969;27:503–507.

95. Newmann MM, Hamstra R, Block M. Use of banked autologous blood in elective surgery. JAMA 1971;218:861–863.

96. Hallowell P, Bland JHL, Chir B, Buckley MJ, Lowenstein E. Transfusion of fresh autologous blood in open-heart surgery. J Thorac Cardiovasc Surg 1972;64:941–948.

97. Ochsner JL, Mills NL, Leonard GL, Lawson N. Fresh autologous blood transfusions with extracorporeal circulation. Ann Surg 1973;177: 811–817.

98. Barbier-Bohm G, Desmonts JM, Couder E, et al. Comparative effects of induced hypotension and normovolaemic haemodilution on blood loss in total hip arthroplasty. Br J Anaesth 1980;52:1039–1043.

99. Cuello L, Vazquez E, Rios R, Raffucci FI. Autologous blood transfusion in thoracic and cardiovascular surgery. Surgery 1967;62:4814–818.

100. Hardesty RL, Bayer WL, Bahnson HT. A technique for the use of autologous fresh blood during open-heart surgery. J Thorac Cardiovasc Surg 1968;5:683–688.

101. Newman MM, Hamstra R, Block M. The use of banked autologous blood in elective surgery. JAMA 1971;218:861–863.
102. Dobell ARC, Mitri M, Galva R. Biologic evaluation of blood after prolonged recirculation through film and membrane oxygenators. Ann Surg 1965;4:617–622.
103. Wagstaffe JG, Clarke AD, Jackson PW. Reduction of blood loss by restoration of platelet levels using fresh autologous blood after cardiopulmonary bypass. Thorax 1972;27:410–414.
104. Kramer AH, Hertzer NR, Beven EG. Intraoperative hemodilution during elective vascular reconstruction. Surg Gynecol Obstet 1979;149: 831–836.
105. Jobes DR, Gallagher J. Acute normovolemic hemodilution. Int Anesthesiol Clin 1982;20: 77–95.
106. Lawson NW, Ochsner JL, Mills NL, Leonard GL. The use of hemodilution and fresh autologous blood in open-heart surgery. Anesth Analg 1974;53:672–683.
107. Buckley MJ, Austen WG, Goldblatt A, Laner MD. Severe hemodilution and autotransfusion for surgery of congenital heart disease. Surg Forum 1971;22:160–162.
108. Seager OA, Nesmith MA, Begelman KA, et al. Massive acute hemodilution for incompatible blood reaction. JAMA 1974;229:790–792.
109. Nahas RA, Mundth ED, Buckley MJ, et al. Effect of hemodilution on left ventricular function with regional ischemia of the heart. Surg Forum 1972;23:149–150.
110. Yoshikawa H, Powell WJ, Bland JHL, et al. Effect of acute anemia on experimental myocardial ischemia. Am J Cardiol 1973;32:670–678.
111. Pavek K, Carey JS. Hemodynamics and oxygen availability during isovolemic hemodilution. Am J Physiol 1974;226:1172–1177.
112. Messmer K, Sunder-Plasmann L, Jesch L, et al. Oxygen supply to the tissues during limited normovolemic hemodilution. Res Exp Med 1973;159:152.
113. Albert SN. Blood volume. Springfield, Illinois: Charles C Thomas, 1963:26.
114. Miller D. Normal values and examination of the blood: perinatal period, infancy, childhood and adolescence. In: Miller DR, Baechner RL, McMillan CW, Miller LP, eds. Blood diseases of infancy and childhood. St. Louis: CV Mosby, 1984:21–22.
115. Shoemaker WC. Fluids and electrolytes in the acutely ill adult. In: Shoemaker WC, Ayres S, Grevik A, et al, eds. Textbook of critical care. 2nd ed. Philadelphia: WB Saunders, 1989: 1130–1150.
116. Bick RL. Alterations of hemostasis associated with cardiopulmonary bypass, pathophysiol-ogy, prevention, diagnosis and management. Semin Thromb Hemost 1976;3:59–82.
117. de Leval MR, Hill JD, Mielke CH Jr, et al. Blood platelets and extracorporeal circulation. Kinetic studies on dogs on cardiopulmonary bypass. J Thorac Cardiovasc Surg 1975;69: 144–151.
118. Fong SW, Burns NE, Williams C, et al. Changes in coagulation and platelet function during prolonged extracorporeal circulation (ECC) in sheep and man. Trans Am Soc Artif Intern Organs 1974;20:239–247.
119. Kaplan JA, Cannarella C, Jones EL, et al. Autologous blood transfusion during cardiac surgery: a re-evaluation of three methods. J Thorac Cardiovasc Surg 1977;74:4–10.
120. Pliam MB, McGoon DC, Tarhan S. Failure of transfusion of autologous whole blood to reduce banked-blood requirements in open-heart surgical patients. J Thorac Cardiovasc Surg 1975;70:338–343.
121. Sherman MM, Dobnik DB, Dennis RC, Berger RL. Autologous blood transfusion during cardiopulmonary bypass. Chest 1976;70:592–595.
122. Silver H. Banked and fresh autologous blood in cardiopulmonary bypass surgery. Transfusion 1975;15:600–603.
123. Lilleaasen P, Froysaker T. Fresh autologous blood in open heart surgery. Influence on blood requirements, bleeding and platelets counts. Scand J Thor Cardiovasc Surg 1979; 13:41–46.
124. Iyer VS, Russell WJ. Fresh autologous blood transfusion and platelet counts after cardiopulmonary bypass surgery. Anaesth Intens Care 1982;10:348–352.
125. Dale J, Lilleaasen P, Erikssen J. Hemostasis after open-heart surgery with extreme or moderate hemodilution. Eur Surg Res 1987;19:339–347.
126. Zubiate P, Kay JH, Mendez AM, et al. Coronary artery surgery: a new technique with use of little blood, if any. J Thorac Cardiovasc Surg 1974;68:263–267.
127. Blundell J. Experiments on the transfusion of blood by the syringe. Med Chir Trans 1818; 9:56–92.
128. Highmore W. Practical remarks: overlooked source of blood-supply for transfusion in postpartum haemorrhage. Lancet 1874;1:891.
129. Duncan J. Reinfusion of blood in primary and other amputations. Br Med J 1886;1:192–193.
130. Wilson JD, Taswell HF. Autotransfusion historical review and preliminary report on a new method. Mayo Clin Proc 1968;43:26–35.
131. Yomtovian RA. Autologous blood transfusion past performance and current concerns. Minn Med 1986;69:353–356.
132. Rosenblatt R, Dennis P, Draper LD. A new

method for massive fluid resuscitation in the trauma patient. Anesth Analg 1983;62: 613–616.

133. Stehling LC, Zauder HL, Rogers W. Intraoperative autotransfusion. Anesthesiology 1975;43: 337–345.

134. Orr MD. Autotransfusion: intraoperative scavenging. Anesthesiol Clin 1982;24:97–117.

135. Umlas J, O'Neill TP. Heparin removal in an autotransfusion device. Transfusion 1981;21: 70–73.

136. Gilcher RO, Orr M. Intra-operative autotransfusion. Transfusion 1975;15:520.

137. Messick KD, Gibbons GA, Fosburg RG, Nolan PC. Intraoperative use of the haemonetics cell saver. In: 1978 Proceedings of the Blood Conservation Institute, Haemonetics, Braintree, MA.

138. Haemonetics. Cell saver plus autologous blood recovery system owner's operating and maintenance manual. Braintree, MA: Haemonetic Corporation, 1986:1–68.

139. Orr MD, Blenko JW. Autotransfusion of concentrated, selected washed red cells from the surgical field: a biochemical and physiological comparison with homologous cell transfusion. In: Proceedings of the Haemonetics Blood Conservation Institute, 1978.

140. Cordell AR, Lavender SW. An appraisal of blood salvage techniques in vascular and cardiac operations. Ann Thorac Surg 1981;31:421–425.

141. Keeling MM, Gray LA, Brink MA, Hillerich VK, Bland KI. Intraoperative autotransfusion. Experience in 725 consecutive cases. Ann Surg 1983;197:536–541.

142. Mayer ED, Welsch M, Tanzeem A, et al. Reduction of postoperative donor blood requirement by use of the cell separator. Scan J Thorac Cardiovasc Surg 1985;19:167–171.

143. Breyer RH, Engelman RM, Rousou JA, Lemeshow S. Blood conservation for myocardial revascularization. J Thorac Cardiovasc Surg 1987;93:512–522.

144. Parrot D, Lancon JP, Merle JP, et al. Blood salvage in cardiac surgery. J Cardiothorac Vasc Anesth 1991;5:454–456.

145. Pelley WB. Cost-effectiveness of blood conservation. J Extra-Corp Technol 1980;12:148–151.

146. Vertrees RA, Auvil J, Rohrer C, Rousou JH, Engelman RM. Intra-operative blood conservation during cardiac surgery. J Extra-Corp Technol 1980;12:60–62.

147. Cosgrove DM, Thurer RL, Lytle BW, Gill CG, Peter M, Loop FD. Blood conservation during myocardial revascularization. Ann Thorac Surg 1979;28:184–188.

148. Giordano GF, Goldman DS, Mammana B, et al. Intraoperative autotransfusion in cardiac operation. Effect on intraoperative and postoperative transfusion requirements. J Thorac Cardiovasc Surg 1988;3:382–386.

149. Ansell J, Parrilla N, King M, et al. Survival of autotransfused red blood cells recovered from the surgical field during cardiovascular operations. J Thorac Cardiovasc Surg 1982;84: 387–391.

150. Ray JM, Flynn JC, Bierman AH. Erythrocyte survival following intraoperative autotransfusion in spinal surgery: an in vivo comparative study and 5-year update. Spine 1986;11:879–882.

151. Winton TL, Charrette EJP, Salerno TA. The cell saver during cardiac surgery: does it save? Ann Thorac Surg 1982;33:379–381.

152. Cutler BS. Avoidance of homologous transfusion in aortic operations: the role of autotransfusion, hemodilution, and surgical technique. Surgery 1984;95:717–722.

153. Yaw PB, Sentary M, Link WJ, et al. Tumor cells carried through autotransfusion: contraindication to intraoperative blood recovery? JAMA 1975;231:490–491.

154. Klebanoff G, Phillips J, Evans W. Use of disposable autotransfusion unit under varying conditions of contamination. Am J Surg 1970;120: 351–354.

155. Boudreaux, Bornside GH, Cohn I. Emergency autotransfusion: partial cleansing of bacteria-laden blood by cell washing. Trauma 1983; 23:31–35.

156. Paravicini D, Thys J, Hein H. Rinsing the operative field with neomycin-bacitracin solution with intraoperative autotransfusion in orthopedic surgery. In: Lawin P, ed. Clinic of anesthesiology and operative intensive medicine. Munster: Westphalian Wilhelm University, 1983:1–12.

157. Robicsek F, Duncan GD, Born GVR, et al. Inherent dangers of simultaneous application of microfibrillar collagen hemostat and blood-saving devices. J Thorac Cardiovasc Surg 1986;92:766–770.

158. Blood conservation update. Electromedics, Inc. 1989;3:2.

5

HEMODILUTION AND PRIMING SOLUTIONS FOR CARDIOPULMONARY BYPASS

John R. Cooper, Jr., and Stephen Slogoff

John Gibbon (1), who developed the first heart-lung machine and performed the first successful operation using cardiopulmonary bypass (CPB), envisioned a perfusion technique employing a prime of normal composition (i.e., blood) with normal flow rates and normal blood pressure. His original techniques were continued by Kirklin et al. (2). Lillehei and his associates, first in their procedures with controlled cross-circulation (3) and then with CPB (4), employed significantly lower flow rates (30 to 35 ml/kg/min) than did Gibbon. This modification (based on the "azygos flow principle") (5) derived from the observation that dogs could survive when both the superior and inferior cava were occluded. In this situation, the azygos venous drainage of the dog, unlike that of humans, still returns to the heart because of a more central entry, and this amount of flow (10% of normal cardiac output) proved adequate for survival for up to 1 hour. This observation was rapidly accepted and applied to CPB by many who perceived the harm to blood elements by high flows and excessive suctioning. Hypothermia was added to many high and most low flow techniques to "protect" various organs, even though Lillehei's original cross-circulation procedures were done at normothermia (3). Despite lower flows, the priming solution for the extracorporeal circuit with oxygenator remained the same—whole blood, either freshly drawn and heparinized, or collected into citrated bags, but as fresh as possible.

Spurred by animal research and the occasional emergent clinical experience with asanguinous prime, surgeons around 1960 began electively using crystalloid solutions or plasma-expanding colloids to reduce or eliminate blood from the prime (Table 5.1). Hypothermia was now increasingly applied to protect organs from the "adverse effects" of not only low flow, but also hemodilution. Nevertheless, the technique of hemodilution gained increasing popularity and presently it is almost universal.

IMMEDIATE BENEFITS OF HEMODILUTION

A major reason for employing asanguinous primes was to reduce the severe strain that the use of whole blood for priming CPB circuits placed on hospital blood banks. The need for at least two units of whole blood, and possibly as many as five or six, just for prime in each patient often caused logistical nightmares for physicians trying to run an active cardiac surgical service. Many cases were postponed for lack of the correct type or amount of blood. Crystalloid primes also improved access to CPB as

Table 5.1. Historical Perspective for CPB Techniques

Surgeons	Prime	Technique
Gibbon (1)	Whole blood	High flow
Kirklin et al. (2)	Whole blood	High flow
Lillehei et al. (3)	Whole blood	Low flow
Green et al. (6)	5% Dextrose	Hemodilution and hypothermia
Panico and Neptune (7)	Saline	Hemodilution
Long et al. (8)	Dextran, 5% albumin	Hemodilution
DeWall et al. (4)	5% Dextrose	Hemodilution and hypothermia
Cooley et al. (9)	5% Dextrose	Hemodilution and normothermia

an emergency procedure by reducing the time and resources required to have a useable circuit available.

Another immediate, but unforeseen, clinical benefit of crystalloid primes was improved oxygenation during CPB. Bubble oxygenators of that period, the type most widely used, produced a high proportion of "macro" bubbles in comparison to modern devices. Compared to the modern "micro" bubbles, these bubbles were relatively inefficient in the transfer of oxygen because of the relatively small surface area of the oxygen bubbles relative to the number of red cells. Hemodilution, especially of polycythemic patients, produced an absolute reduction in the number of red cells and increased likelihood of exposure to oxygen. Arterial oxygen tension on CPB was generally higher, and additional crystalloid was given to maintain hemodilution if oxygen tension started to fall with diuresis.

Special impetus to development of nonhemic prime techniques was also provided by members of the Jehovah's Witness faith who totally refused to accept transfusion of blood or blood products even though they would allow their own blood outside their body as long as fluid continuity was constantly maintained in the CPB circuit. The use of nonhemic prime has permitted cardiac operations in over 1000 Jehovah's Witnesses at the Texas Heart Institute alone (10). These patients constitute a unique "control" group for comparison of other techniques of blood conservation.

PHYSIOLOGIC CONSEQUENCES OF HEMODILUTION

Rheology of Blood

A detailed review of the rheologic properties of blood is beyond the scope of this chapter. However, some basic definitions and concepts are required as changes in blood rheology are central to any discussion of hemodilution physiology. An exhaustive review can be found in the text by Gordon et al. (11).

A force applied to an area of a liquid confined between two plates sufficient to set the liquid in motion is known as the shear stress. The velocity at which the liquid moves in proportion to the separation of the plates is known as the velocity gradient or shear rate. The shear stress is proportional to the shear rate and the coefficient of proportionality is the fluid viscosity (equation 1).

$$\text{Shear stress} = \text{viscosity} \times \text{shear rate} \quad (1)$$

For most uniform fluids, such as water, viscosity is constant; these are known as Newtonian fluids. Blood's viscosity is not constant, but depends on the shear rate when flowing (Fig 5.1); thus blood is a non-Newtonian fluid. Lower shear rates are associated with higher viscosity as the cellular elements and plasma proteins tend to aggregate, form rouleaux, and resist flow. This aggregation at low shear rates primarily results from intracellular bridging by fibrino-

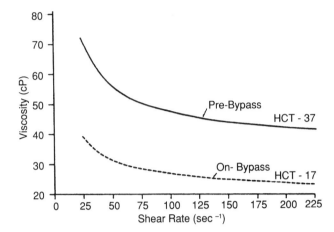

Figure 5.1. Viscosity change (in centi-Poise) plotted against shear rate (in seconds⁻¹) in a patient whose hematocrit fell from 37 to 17 after hemodilution at the initiation of CPB. (Modified from Gordon RJ, Ravin M, Rawitscher RE, Daicoff GR. Changes in arterial pressure, viscosity and resistance during cardiopulmonary bypass. J Thorac Cardiovasc Surg 1975;69:552–561.)

gen; as flow rates increase, these bridges disintegrate.

Non-Newtonian behavior of blood is also influenced by the effective cell volume (12). When solid particles (cells) are added to a fluid, they influence viscosity not only by their absolute presence, but also by their effect on the surrounding fluid. The effective cell volume is the cell volume plus the surrounding fluid that behaves as though it were a part of the cell, much like the earth and its atmosphere. Red cells are deformable, and as shear rates increase they tend to form ellipsoid shapes with the major axis aligned with flow. This latter effect, combined with disaggregation of red cells, causes blood to behave in a more Newtonian fashion at higher velocity gradients.

One further concept about behavior of fluids is important. The amount of shear stress applied to a stationary Newtonian liquid required to begin its movement is at or near zero. For the non-Newtonian blood, because of cellular geometry and aggregation, a force known as the yield stress is required to induce flow. At low shear rates the yield stress represents part of the viscous resistance and depends on both fibrinogen and hematocrit (13).

Circulatory Effects

Both organ blood flow and total cardiac output are directly proportional to perfusion pressure and inversely related to total peripheral resistance (equation 2A). This resistance to flow is proportional to vascular resistance and viscosity of the perfusate (Equation 2B).

Flow (cardiac output)

$$\propto \frac{\text{Perfusion pressure}}{\text{Total peripheral resistance}} \quad (2A)$$

Flow

$$\propto \frac{\text{Perfusion pressure}}{\text{Vascular resistance} \times \text{viscosity}} \quad (2B)$$

These relationships are often specifically expressed in the Hagen-Poiseuille equation:

$$Q = \frac{\pi \ (P1-P2) \ R^4}{8 \ \mu L} \quad (3)$$

Where Q = flow, $P_1 - P_2$ = pressure drop along a tube of radius R and length L, and μ = viscosity. Application of this equation to blood flow is limited because it is accurate only for laminar flow of Newtonian liquids in long tubes with rigid walls. It does serve to further emphasize, however, the influence of viscosity and vascular geometry on flow. In man, the aorta and larger vessels provide little impedance to blood flow; most of the vascular resistance comes from the smaller vessels: arterioles, capillaries, and venules. As vessel diameter decreases, shear rate decreases, and since blood viscosity is inversely related to shear rate, viscosity rises as flow falls. As a result, peripheral resistance also rises. Flow is lowest and viscosity highest in the postcapillary venules (14).

These physiologic effects are potentially quite harmful if CPB is used without considering viscosity. Modern CPB involves use of somewhat lower than "normal" blood flow rates in most centers: 50 ml/kg/min or 2.0 liters/m²/min. Frequently, hypothermia is also used if flow rates are further reduced to provide a bloodless operative field or, more commonly, to augment "myocardial protection." Reductions in both flow rate and perfusion pressure would tend to increase viscosity and thus peripheral resistance; this in turn would tend to decrease tissue perfusion. Hemodilution works to ameliorate the adverse effects of CPB by significantly reducing blood viscosity during bypass. There is a direct relationship between viscosity and hematocrit (15) (Fig. 5.1). Therefore, reducing hematocrit produces a marked decrease in total resistance and results in an increase in tissue perfusion (equation 2B), For example, in canine experiments a decrease in hematocrit from 42% to 25% will produce a 50% increase in flow at the same pressure (14). Extremes of hemodilution (Hct <10%) permit blood to act as a Newtonian fluid (16).

Clinically, the most noticeable effect of hemodilution is a marked drop in perfusion pressure at initiation of CPB. Gordon et al. (15) showed that when hemodilution was used to decrease hematocrit and flow rate on CPB was held constant, perfusion pressure fell in direct proportion to the change in viscosity (Fig. 5.2). Additionally, Guyton and Richardson (17) found that hemodilution increased venous return passively in dogs, probably atributable to the marked increase in small vessel flow, especially in the postcapillary venules (Fig. 5.3). This same phenomenon was noted during CPB in humans by Cooley et al. (9).

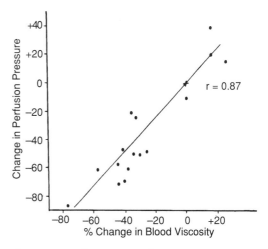

Figure 5.2. Change in perfusion pressure versus change in viscosity in a series of patients on CPB at constant flow rates. (Modified from Gordon RJ, Ravin M, Rawitscher RE, Daicoff GR. Changes in arterial pressure, viscosity and resistance during cardiopulmonary bypass. J Thorac Cardiovasc Surg 1975;69: 552–561.)

The addition of induced hypothermia to CPB further influences the rheologic behavior of blood. Temperature reduction decreases flow by inducing direct vasoconstriction and increasing viscosity (18) (Fig. 5.4). The relationship is not, however, as direct as that of hematocrit and viscosity. For example, a 10°C decrease in temperature causes about a 20 to 25% increase in viscosity. Of course, this adverse effect of hypothermia is partially or completely offset by the planned reduction in oxygen consumption. A more complete discussion of the interaction of hemodilution and hypothermia can be found in Chapter 6.

Organ blood flow during hemodilution reflects the interplay of all of these concepts. In animals, with progressive normovolemic hemodilution to a hematocrit of 19%, oxygen tension has been shown to increase in skeletal muscle, liver, pancreas, small intestine, and kidney (14). Cerebral blood flow during hemodilution has also been shown to increase 50 to 300% compared to prebypass levels (19, 20). However, since cerebral flow is also significantly influenced by local autoregulation,

Figure 5.3. Decreasing viscosity leads to increasing venous return (at a constant right atrial pressure). (From Guyton AC, Richardson TQ. Effect of hematocrit on venous return. Circ Res 1961;9: 157–163.)

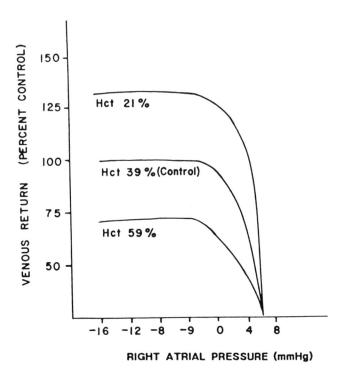

changes in carbon dioxide tension, and extremes of perfusion pressure (21), absolute statements about the regional benefits of hemodilution are difficult to make, though in general, hemodilution appears to have a salutary effect.

An exceedingly important consequence of hemodilution during CPB is an "uncoupling" of the normal relationship between perfusion pressure and blood flow. Thus, perfusion pressure cannot serve as the marker of adequacy of flow because pressure is a function of two variables: flow *and* viscosity. This pivotal concept bears directly on the incidence and causes of complications associated with the use of CPB, as will be discussed below.

HEMODILUTION, ANESTHETIC AGENTS, AND ADJUVANTS

Anesthetic agents and vasoactive adjuvant drugs may influence vascular geometry during CPB and thereby alter vascular resistance; these effects are independent of those related to hemodilution. Hemodilu-

tion may also alter the pharmacokinetics and pharmacodynamics of drugs, principally by dilution and by decreased protein binding. While there is usually a decrease in total drug concentration during CPB because of dilution, the amount of free active drug probably changes little because of decreased protein binding (22). Drug kinetics during CPB are also influenced by temperature, pH, oncotic pressure, and, sometimes, sequestration in the CPB circuit or excluded circulations like the lung. These multiple factors make study of drug activity during CPB interesting but exceedingly difficult (23). A more complete treatment of the pharmacokinetic and pharmacodynamic changes during CPB can be found in Chapter 8.

CONSIDERATIONS IN OXYGEN TRANSPORT

Hemoglobin Physiology

Oxygen transport is the movement of molecular oxygen from the atmosphere to

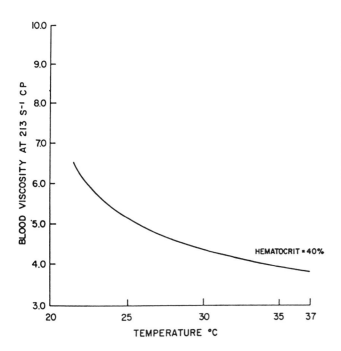

Figure 5.4. Relationship between blood viscosity (at a constant shear rate—213 sec⁻¹) and temperature. (From Rand PW, Lacombe E, Hunt HE, Austin WH. Viscosity of normal human blood under normothermic and hypothermic conditions. J Appl Physiol 1964;19:117–122, as modified by Gordon RJ, Ravin MB, Daicroff GR. Blood rheology. In: Cardiovascular physiology for anaesthesiologists. Springfield, Illinois: Charles C Thomas, 1979:27–71.)

the cellular mitochondria. This movement depends on the availability of oxygen, cardiac output, hemoglobin level, tissue perfusion, and the ability of the tissues to extract oxygen. The hemoglobin molecule provides a tremendous physiologic advantage to the process of oxygen transport by allowing relatively larger volumes of oxygen to be brought to the tissues bound to hemoglobin than could be transported were oxygen only in simple solution in the plasma.

Reduction of hemoglobin levels to below normal will still permit adequate oxygen transfer. In fact, when oxygen transport is expressed as the product of cardiac output and oxygen-carrying capacity and plotted against changes in hematocrit (Fig. 5.5), maximal delivery occurs at a hematocrit of 30%, but more importantly varies by only about 10% between hematocrits of 20 to 50 (24). This preservation obviously depends on a compensatory increase in cardiac output at lower hematocrit ranges. Hemoglobin levels are reduced as a normal consequence of CPB with hemodilution. Without an increase in cardiac output, such

a reduction will necessarily compromise oxygen delivery, but this is usually well-tolerated clinically. The lower limit to which hemoglobin can be reduced under any circumstance and not compromise a patient's safety is not known. A hemoglobin level of 10 g/dl was traditionally accepted (and institutionalized) as adequate for patients undergoing noncardiac surgery based on the above oxygen transport concepts, though now a level of 8 g/dl is documented to be associated with good outcomes (25). Anecdotal reports of patients presenting with hemoglobin levels of 3 to 4 g/dl and feeling "a little tired" are common but do not define a lower limit. In addition to increased cardiac output, various compensatory mechanisms are available to maintain oxygen transport and may be activated.

Environmental Effects

The oxygen-carrying capacity of hemoglobin is influenced by pH, P_{CO_2}, temperature, 2,3-diphosphoglycerate concentration (2,3-DPG), and hemoglobin concentration. The O_2-hemoglobin dissoci-

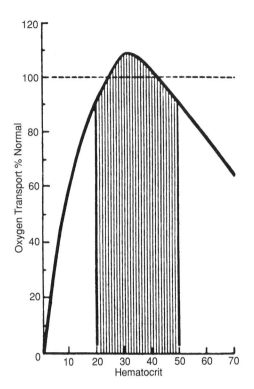

Figure 5.5. Oxygen transport versus hematocrit level showing an approximate 10% change in oxygen transport (cardiac output × oxygen-carrying capacity) between hematocrits of 20 and 50. (From LeVeen HH, Ip M, Ahmed N, et al. Lowering blood viscosity to overcome vascular resistance. Surg Gynecol Obstet 1980;150:139–149.)

ation curve may be shifted to the right by these factors (easier dissociation of oxygen from hemoglobin—higher P_{50}) or to the left (more firmly attached oxygen—lower P_{50}). Metabolic acidosis, hypercarbia, hyperthermia, increased 2,3-DPG, and anemia shift the curve to the right; while metabolic alkalosis, hypocarbia, decreased 2,3-DPG, and hypothermia shift it to the left. Abnormal hemoglobins may have normal, increased, or decreased oxygen affinity. The absolute clinical significance of each of these influences is not known.

Physiology of Chronic Anemia

Chronic anemia, or reduction in the circulating red blood cell volume, tends to develop gradually and permits compensation. These mechanisms include an increase in plasma volume to maintain a euvolemic or even hypervolemic state, an increase in heart rate and stroke volume, and the passive, but real, increase in cardiac output from decreased viscosity. In the intact human this occurs with little or no increase in myocardial oxygen extraction (14). Other compensatory mechanisms include an increased oxygen extraction by the tissues, often associated with decreased affinity of hemoglobin for oxygen produced by an increase in 2,3-DPG level in the red blood cell. Neither of these latter mechanisms are usually operative at hemoglobin levels chronically above 7 g/dl (14).

Reduction in physical activity with subsequent decrease in oxygen consumption is an important additional mechanism. The chronically anemic patient who is well-compensated may be compromised if metabolic demands are increased; e.g., by enhanced physical activity or fever or by inability to raise cardiac output from either intrinsic or acquired heart disease. In this context, an anesthetized patient will demonstrate improved tolerance to anemia because of a reduced total body oxygen consumption (overall, about 15%) and especially a reduced myocardial oxygen demand (26). Hypothermia is an important physiologic method for reducing oxygen utilization by tissues and plays a greater or lesser role, depending on the clinical circumstances. Again, anesthesia has a significant role because normal compensatory mechanisms maintaining normothermia such as shivering, which markedly increases oxygen consumption, are blocked by anesthesia and muscle relaxation.

The acute anemia produced by hemodilution coupled with lower than normal flow rates at the institution of CPB must also be associated with operative compensatory mechanisms to permit adequate oxygen delivery. These include general anesthesia and muscle relaxation, normovolemia, improved microcirculatory perfusion as a consequence of decreased viscosity, and sometimes, induced hypothermia.

HEMODILUTION AND COMPLICATIONS OF CPB

Despite early success with open heart operations using CPB, a high rate of complications was standard. Specifically, CPB was associated with postoperative neurologic, pulmonary, and renal dysfunction, and these were seen with both high and low flow rate techniques. Each was attributed to a variety of physiologic or clinical factors.

Neurologic dysfunction was thought to be associated with low perfusion pressures. Stockard et al. (27) mathematically related increased incidence of neurologic complications to degree and duration of hypotension. Pulmonary complications (postperfusion pulmonary insufficiency, "pump lung") were attributed to parenchymal hypoxia, pulmonary venous distension, the oxygenator itself, or other mechanical factors (28). Renal failure was related to low perfusion pressure and, secondarily, to low urine output during CPB (29). When Cooley et al. (9) reported their first 100 cases using hemodilution with dextrose and water prime, they anecdotally noted a reduction of postoperative cerebral, pulmonary, and renal complications. Hemodilution may have been instrumental in the reduction of morbidity associated with CPB for each of these organ systems.

The uncoupling of flow and pressure with hemodilution, as discussed above, modifies the relation between perfusion pressure and neurologic complications. The patients described by Stockard et al. (27) all had a blood prime for CPB. The relationship between perfusion pressure and an incidence of neurologic complications has disappeared since hemodilution has been universally adopted (30, 31). Subsequent reports by Govier et al. (32) and Prough et al. (33) have also demonstrated maintenance of cerebral autoregulation in

hemodiluted patients under varying levels of flow, temperature, and CO_2 tension.

Similar differences in reports of renal dysfunction with and without blood priming are also revealing. Bhat et al. (29) found bypass time, low perfusion pressure, volume of urine formation during CPB, and hemoglobinemia to be factors for postoperative dysfunction when blood priming was employed. In the same year, Abel et al. (34) found none of these factors to be predictive when hemodilution was used. It now appears that, in the absence of low cardiac output before or after CPB or excessive perioperative transfusion, preoperative renal dysfunction is the only predictor of postoperative dysfunction (31). Postperfusion respiratory failure still occurs for multiple reasons, but these are often related to extrapulmonary factors (35). The pump lung of the 1960s has markedly decreased in incidence, and this is at least partly because of hemodilution techniques (9, 36).

Another problem, referred to as the "homologous blood syndrome," was blamed for both intra- and postoperative bleeding diathesis and also contributing to postoperative cerebral, pulmonary, and renal dysfunction (37). The syndrome was sometimes thought to result from incompatibility or cross-reactions between the patient and one or more of the multiple units of donor blood used in the prime. More likely, with correct donor-patient cross-matching, it represented reaction between units of homologous blood from different donors when mixed together in the CPB circuit prior to bypass. Whatever the exact mechanism, it also disappeared with introduction of crystalloid priming.

Hemodilution alone is not solely responsible for the reduction in complications associated with CPB. Other factors such as more accurate initial diagnosis, improved anesthetic methods, better CPB equipment, and quicker recognition and treatment of ventricular failure have all contributed. Specifically, filtering of blood has helped reduce pulmonary complications

(38) (see Chapters 4 and 11), and reduction of hemolysis from decreased need for large amounts of suctioning from the surgical field has also helped reduce renal dysfunction.

PRIMING SOLUTIONS

Crystalloid Primes

The use of a crystalloid priming solution is the norm in present-day management of CPB. There is probably as much institutional variation in specific primes and components as there is in cardioplegia solutions, as they both developed in empiric fashion. In general, modern priming solutions are similar in electrolyte content to plasma and have similar osmolarity. Lactated Ringer's solution with or without glucose is a common basic priming solution; more complex commercial preparations such as Normosol are sometimes used. The addition of colloid may be justified in perfusions of long duration to prevent excessive edema formation. In addition to the institutional variation in types of priming fluids, there is also variability in the volume of priming solutions used as a consequence of differences in priming requirements for the variety of oxygenators, connecting tubing, and arterial filters that may be employed. Some institutions have a "standard" prime volume that is used on all adult patients, while others vary the volume depending on the patient's weight or body surface area. Each specific oxygenator-tubing system will obviously have a minimum "safe" priming volume; that is, one that will allow initiation of CPB without undue risk of air embolism and permit adequate flow rates with the institution of bypass.

The degree of hemodilution may be predicted by knowing the patient's weight, hematocrit, amount of intravenous fluids administered before CPB, and the oxygenator's priming volume. The patient's blood volume may be calculated by multiplying the patient's weight in kilograms by 7% (females) to 7.5% (males) (Table 5.2). If use of the intended prime volume will cause unacceptable hemodilution, then packed red blood cells may be added to the CPB circuit to compensate.

Children, and especially infants, present a special problem as most pediatric oxygenators have a minimum priming volume of 700 to 800 ml. Because this volume is larger than the infant's blood volume, blood must usually be added empirically to the prime to achieve appropriate hemodilution by most institutional protocols. The acceptable range for the hematocrit is essentially the same for children and adults.

Allowable Hemodilution

The degree of allowable hemodilution is an important consideration in the composition of the initial prime. There is also large institutional variation in the range of "acceptable" hemodilution. In general, since hemodilution has a salutary effect on perfusion and there is a theoretical decrease in microcirculatory flow with hematocrits above 30% (14), most centers try to achieve hematocrits below 30% during CPB. With priming volumes in the 1400 to 2000 ml range, this is easily achieved in most adults. Patients with large blood volumes and/or high hematocrits may require prepump

Table 5.2. Prediction of Initial Hematocrit on CPB and Potential Requirement for Addition of Blood to Priming Volume.

Predicted hematocrit on CPB	=	$\dfrac{\text{Patient's red cell volume}^2}{\text{Patient's blood volume}^1 + \text{pump prime volume} + \text{IV fluids administered prior to CPB}}$

[1] Blood volume = Patient weight × 8–8.5% (infants) or 7.5% (children, adult males) or 7.0% (adult females)
[2] Patient's red cell volume = Blood volume × hematocrit
[3] If blood needs to be added to the prime, one unit of packed red cells or one unit of whole blood contains approximately 150 ml of red blood cells. This volume can be added to the formula numerator and the total volume of the component added to the denominator. The crystalloid prime should be reduced by an equal amount.

phlebotomy or additional dilution while on CPB.

Hypothermia also influences acceptable ranges of hematocrit when employed, but guidelines are again institutional. Because of the viscosity-flow relationship, and the influence of hypothermia, it is appropriate to target a hematocrit of less than 30% if temperature is lowered to 30°C, and lower hematocrits, generally less than 25%, are preferred if temperatures are to be reduced below 25°C. There is experimental evidence that hematocrits less than 20% may be associated with abnormal distribution of flow to organs (39, 40). However, hematocrits below this level appear to be well-tolerated clinically, with values in the 15 to 18% range commonly seen during the initial stages of CPB. Physiologic compensatory mechanisms may be operative in addition to the benefits of anesthesia and hypothermia. Even extreme hemodilution to hematocrits below 15%, when used for hypothermic circulatory arrest or as is sometimes seen in Jehovah's Witness patients (10), appear to be clinically well-tolerated also (41).

Another consideration in allowable hemodilution is an acceptable hematocrit for separation from bypass. Here, too, there is much institutional variation and little hard data. Since maldistribution of coronary flow away from the subendocardium occurs experimentally with hematocrits at or below 15% (39, 42), especially if the coronary circulation is compromised, it would seem prudent to separate from bypass at hematocrits above this level. Evidence of myocardial ischemia would be further cause to add blood.

The safety of hemodilution especially with crystalloid solutions was initially questioned because of fear of increased postoperative bleeding secondary to dilutional coagulopathy. These fears proved unfounded in general, even with extreme hemodilution (43). In polycythemic patients with congenital heart disease, adequate hemodilution (Hct<30%) has been associated with a decreased incidence of postoperative coagulopathies (44).

Use of Glucose

Recently there has been considerable debate over intraoperative glucose management (45) and intraoperative use of glucose-containing fluids in general because of an association of worsened neurologic outcome with hyperglycemia in a series of noncardiac surgical cases (46). These data theoretically affect the management of CPB prime because use of glucose-containing fluids remains common practice, and blood glucose levels on bypass are commonly 500 to 800 mg/dl. Metz and Keats (47) have shown that the addition of glucose to priming solutions, by raising the osmotic pressure of the prime, significantly reduces perioperative fluid requirements and postoperative fluid retention. The seeming lack of complications from the use of glucose during CPB may relate to the putative mechanism, since both animal and human data suggest that central nervous system damage associated with hyperglycemia occurs when either global or focal injury is followed by immediate reperfusion of the ischemic area (48). Cerebral injury after cardiopulmonary bypass, in the absence of low cardiac output, is almost always embolic in origin, and areas affected would not be expected to have immediate reperfusion.

Following this line of reasoning and considering the demonstrable benefit on fluid requirements, dextrose (5%) in lactated Ringer's solution is used as the crystalloid prime for CPB at many institutions. Some centers do not use glucose in those patients who may be subject to a global central nervous system ischemia followed by reperfusion, such as arch aneurysm repair requiring circulatory arrest or descending thoracic aneurysm repair. Other centers, equally without documented support, have taken a completely opposite approach and have removed all glucose from CPB circuits.

Colloidal Primes

A consequence of hemodilution in CPB is a fall in the plasma colloidal oncotic pressure by dilution of the circulating plasma proteins. This may result, especially in the absence of glucose, in increased movement of fluid out of the vascular space into the interstitial and intracellular spaces, which could lead to postoperative edema and may be associated with dysfunction of the lung and and possibly other organs. In an effort to attenuate these changes, the addition of colloidal particles to a crystalloid prime, or even the use of a colloidal solution as the principal priming fluid have been advocated. Solutions used include albumin, 5% and 25%; dextran, 40 and 70; plasma protein fraction, 5%; hydroxyethyl starch, 6%; and human plasma. These solutions have been studied in various combinations against a crystalloid prime alone or against each other. Differences in lung water or total body water are reported between groups, most notably immediately after bypass, but these differences tend to quickly diminish in the immediate postoperative period (49, 50). The relative importance of colloid in short term CPB is, therefore, hard to judge, and individual decisions can be made on the basis of availability and cost. No significant harm is associated with synthetic or heat-treated colloid. However, human plasma should not be used without a specific indication, usually based on a clinically apparent and laboratory documented bleeding diathesis.

Other Additives

Additional components have been used in primes for varying reasons and are listed in Table 5.3, with the rationale for each. Much institutional variation exists here also.

EXPERIMENTAL PRIMING SOLUTIONS

The use of oxygen-carrying solutions in CPB has paralleled their experimental use as blood substitutes in noncardiac surgery and has been confined to two types: fluorocarbons (51) and stroma-free hemoglobin (52).

The evaluation of these liquids, which can carry relatively large amounts of dissolved oxygen, has progressed for several years. Their benefit is the ability to permit oxygen transport without blood. However, when fluorocarbons have been used in Jehovah's Witness patients who were profoundly anemic, there was no increase in survival (53). These solutions remain experimental. Substitution of hemoglobin for transfusion of red blood cells would seem ideal because of its natural oxygen-carrying capacity and because it is osmotically active. However, while several types of hemoglobin solutions have been used experimentally in animals and humans, there has been an unacceptable incidence of adverse reactions. They are still under review and are not approved for use at this time.

Table 5.3. Additional Components for CPB Prime

Component	Amount	Rationale
Heparin	10–25 mg/liter Prime	An additional safety factor if systemic heparinization is inadequate
Calcium chloride	200 mg–l g	Prevents chelation of circulating Ca^{2+} if citrated blood or packed red blood cells are added to the prime; especially important in pediatric patients
Mannitol	25–50 g	To induce diuresis; renal "protection"
Corticosteroids	Various types and amounts	Prevention or attenuation of activation of immune system by CPB

LENGTH OF BYPASS

It should be noted that essentially all of this discussion on clinical hemodilution applies to short term (<2 hours) CPB. The application of hemodilution to longer periods of bypass is discussed in Chapters 25 and 27.

ASSESSING ADEQUACY OF PERFUSION WITH HEMODILUTION

The most notable effect of the use of a modern asanguinous priming solution, as noted above, is a marked fall in perfusion pressure on institution of bypass. In almost all instances this is secondary to the resulting hemodilution and a corresponding fall in viscosity and not to either dilution of circulating catecholamines or vasodilation (Fig. 5.2). Because hemodilution results in an uncoupling of the relationship between perfusion pressure and blood flow, the assessment of adequate perfusion must be done by other means. Standard flow rates of 50 ml/kg/min or 2 liter/m²/min are a tested reference, though they may be modified by age, weight, or temperature.

Monitoring of organ perfusion is probably the most reliable method of determining perfusion adequacy during CPB with hemodilution, and the organs most sensitive to inadequate flow, the brain and kidneys, are easiest to monitor. Global cerebral function can be followed by electroencephalographic means, and urine flow shows adequate renal perfusion. Arterial blood gases will monitor oxygenator function and mixed venous oxygen tension may detect inadequate perfusion. However, normal mixed venous oxygen does not assure adequate regional perfusion because it may not reflect local organ conditions. Chapter 22 provides a complete discussion of monitoring the adequacy of perfusion.

In summary, hemodilution probably represents the most significant advance in CPB technique after the development of the pump oxygenator itself. It permits homeostatic organ maintenance under what would otherwise be often inadequate circumstances, with a resultant decrease in complications and conservation of blood resources.

REFERENCES

1. Gibbon JH. Application of a mechanical heart and lung apparatus to cardiac surgery. Minn Med 1954;37:171–180.
2. Kirklin JW, Donald DE, Harshbarger HG, et al. Studies in extracorporeal circulation. I. Applicability of Gibbon-type pump-oxygenator to human intracardiac surgery: 40 cases. Ann Surg 1956;144:2–8.
3. Lillehei CW, Cohen M, Warden HE, Ziegler NR, Varco RL. The results of direct vision closure of ventricular septal defects in eight patients by means of controlled cross circulation. Surg Gynecol Obstet 1955;101:447–466.
4. DeWall RA, Lillehei RC, Sellers RD. Hemodilution perfusions for open-heart surgery. N Engl J Med 1962;266:1078–1084.
5. Cohen M, Lillehei CW. A quantitative study of the "azygos factor" during vena caval occlusion in the dog. Surg Gynecol Obstet 1954;98: 225–232.
6. Green AE, Carey JM, Zuhdi N: Hemodilution principle of hypothermic perfusion. A concept of obviating blood priming. J Thorac Cardiovasc Surg 1962;43:640–648.
7. Panico FG, Neptune WB. A mechanism to eliminate the donor blood prime from the pump-oxygenator. Surg Forum 1959;10:605–609.
8. Long DM, Sanchez L, Varco RL, Lillehei CW. The use of low molecular weight dextran and serum albumin as plasma expanders in extracorporeal circulation. Surgery 1961;50:12–28.
9. Cooley DA, Beall AC, Grondin P. Open-heart operations with disposable oxygenators, 5 per cent dextrose prime, and normothermia. Surgery 1962;52:713–719.
10. Cooper JR. Perioperative considerations in Jehovah's Witnesses. Int Anesth Clin 1990;28: 210–215.
11. Gordon RJ. Ravin MB, Daicoff GR. Blood rheology. In: Cardiovascular physiology for anesthesiologists. Springfield, Illinois: Charles C Thomas, 1979:27–71.
12. Chien S. Present state of blood rheology. In: Messmer K, Schmid-Schoenbein H, eds. Hemodilution. Theoretical basis and clinical application. Basel: Karger, 1972:1–45.
13. Priebe H. Hemodilution and oxygenation. Int Anesth Clin 1981;190:237–255.

14. Messmer K. Hemodilution. Surg Clin N Am 1975;55:659–678.

15. Gordon RJ, Ravin M, Rawitscher RE, Daicoff GR. Changes in arterial pressure, viscosity and resistance during cardiopulmonary bypass. J Thorac Cardiovasc Surg 1975;69:552–561.

16. Laver MB, Buckley MJ. Extreme hemodilution in the surgical patient. In: Messmer K, Schmid-Schoenbein H, eds. Hemodilution. Theoretical basis and clinical application. Basel: Karger, 1972;215–222.

17. Guyton AC, Richardson TQ. Effect of hematocrit on venous return. Circ Res 1961;9:157–163.

18. Rand PW, Lacombe E, Hunt HE, Austin WH. Viscosity of normal human blood under normothermic and hypothermic conditions. J Appl Physiol 1964;19:117–122.

19. Lundar T, Froysaker T, Lindegaard K, et al. Some observations or cerebral perfusion during cardiopulmonary bypass. Ann Thorac Surg 1985;39: 381–323.

20. Lundar T, Lindegaard K, Froysaker T, Aaslid R, Wiberg J, Nornes H. Cerebral perfusion during nonpulsatile cardiopulmonary bypass. Ann Thorac Surg 1985;40:144–150.

21. Reves JG, Greely WJ. Cerebral blood flow during cardiopulmonary bypass: some new answers to old questions. Ann Thorac Surg 1989;48: 752–754.

22. Levy JH, Hug CC. Use of cardiopulmonary bypass in studies of the circulation. Br J Anaesth 1988;60:35S–37S.

23. Okutani R, Philbin DM, Rosow CE, Koski G, Schneider RC. Effect of hypothermic hemodilutional cardiopulmonary bypass on plasma sufentanil and catecholamine concentrations in humans. Anesth Analg 1988;67:667–670.

24. LeVeen HH, Ip M, Ahmed N, et al. Lowering blood viscosity to overcome vascular resistance. Surg Gynecol Obstet 1980;150:139–149.

25. Carson JL, Poses RM, Spence RK, Bonavita G. Severity of anaemia and operative mortality and morbidity. Lancet 1988;1:727–729.

26. Theye RA, Michenfelder JD. Individual organ contributions to the decrease in whole-body VO_2 with isoflurane. Anesthesiology 1975;42: 35–40.

27. Stockard JJ, Bickford RG, Schauble JF. Pressure dependent cerebral ischemia during cardiopulmonary bypass. Neurology 1973;23:521–529.

28. Tilney NL, Hester WJ. Physiologic and histologic changes in the lungs of patients dying after prolonged cardiopulmonary bypass: an inquiry into the nature of post-perfusion lung. Ann Surg 1967;166:759–766.

29. Bhat JG, Gluck MC, Lowenstein J, Baldwin DS. Renal failure after open heart surgery. Ann Intern Med 1976;84:677–682.

30. Slogoff S, Girgis KZ, Keats AS. Etiologic factors in neuropsychiatric complications associated with cardiopulmonary bypass. Anesth Analg 1982; 61:903–911.

31. Slogoff S, Reul GJ, Keats AS, et al. Role of perfusion pressure and flow in major organ dysfunction after cardiopulmonary bypass. Ann Thorac Surg 1990;50:911–918.

32. Govier AV, Reves JG, McKay RD, et al. Factors and their influence on regional cerebral blood flow during nonpulsatile cardiopulmonary bypass. Ann Thorac Surg 1984;38:592–600.

33. Prough DS, Stump DA, Roy RC, et al. Response of cerebral blood flow to changes in carbon dioxide tension during hypothermic cardiopulmonary bypass. Anesthesiology 1986;64:576–581.

34. Abel RM, Buckley MJ, Austen WG, et al. Acute postoperative renal failure in cardiac surgical patients. Surg Res 1976;20:341–348.

35. Matthay MA, Wiener-Kronish JP. Respiratory management after cardiac surgery. Chest 1989; 95:424–434.

36. Hepps SA, Roe BB, Wright RR, Gardner RE. Amelioration of the pulmonary postperfusion syndrome with hemodilution and low molecular weight dextran. Surgery 1963;54:232–243.

37. Gadboys HL, Slonim R, Litwak RS. Homologous blood syndrome: I. Preliminary observations on its relationship to clinical cardiopulmonary bypass. Ann Surg 1962;156:793–804.

38. Solis RT, Gibbs MB. Filtration of the microaggregates in stored blood. Transfusion 1972;12: 245–250.

39. Race D, Dedichen H, Schenk WG. Regional blood flow during dextran-induced normovolemic hemodilution in the dog. J Thorac Cardiovasc Surg 1967;53:578–585.

40. Brazier J, Cooper N, Maloney JV, Buckberg G. The adequacy of myocardial oxygen delivery in acute normovolemic anemia. Surgery 1974;75: 508–516.

41. Laver MB, Buckley MJ, Austen WG. Extreme hemodilution with profound hypothermia and circulatory arrest. Bibl Haematol 1975;41: 225–238.

42. Hagl S, Heimisch W, Meisner H, et al. The effect of hemodilution on regional myocardial function in the presence of coronary stenosis. Basic Res Cardiol 1977;72:344–364.

43. Niinikoski J, Laato M, Laaksonen V, et al. Effects of extreme haemodilution on the immediate post-operative course of coronary artery bypass patients. Eur Surg Res 1983;15:1–10.

44. Milam JD, Austin SF, Nihill MR, Keats AS, Cooley DA. Use of sufficient hemodilution to prevent coagulopathies following surgical correction of cyanotic heart disease. J Thorac Cardiovasc Surg 1985;89:623–629.

45. Sieber FE, Smith DS, Traystman RJ, Wollman H. Glucose: a reevaluation of its intraoperative use. Anesthesiology 1987;67:72–81.
46. Pulsinelli WA, Levy DE, Sigsbee B, Scherer P, Plum F. Increased damage after ischemic stroke in patients with hyperglycemia with or without established diabetes mellitus. Am J Med 1983; 74:540–544.
47. Metz S, Keats AS. Benefits of a glucose-containing priming solution for cardiopulmonary bypass. Anesth Analg 1991;72:428–34.
48. Lanier WL, Stangland KJ, Scheithauer BW, Milde JH, Michenfelder JD. The effects of dextrose infusion and head position on neurologic outcome after complete cerebral ischemia in primates: examination of a model. Anesthesiology 1987;66:39–48.
49. Lumb PD. A comparison between 25% albumin and 6% hydroxyethyl starch solutions on lung water accumulation during and immediately after cardiopulmonary bypass. Ann Surg 1987; 206:210–213.
50. Marelli D, Paul A, Samson R, Edgell D, Angood P, Chiu RC-J. Does the addition of albumin to the prime solution in cardiopulmonary bypass affect clinical outcome? J Thorac Cardiovasc Surg 1989;98:751–756.
51. Stone JJ, Piccione W, Berrizbeitia LD, et al. Hemodynamic, metabolic and morphological effects of cardiopulmonary bypass with a fluorocarbon priming solution. Ann Thorac Surg 1986;41:419–424.
52. Gould SA, Sehgal LR, Rosen AL, Sehgal HL, Moss GS. The efficacy of polymerized pyridoxylated hemoglobin solution as an O_2 carrier. Ann Surg 1990;211:394–398.
53. Gould SA, Rosen AL, Sehgal LR, et al. Fluosol-DA as a red-cell substitute in acute anemia. N Engl J Med 1986;314:1653–1656.

Section II

Pathophysiology of Cardiopulmonary Bypass

6

Hypothermia: Physiology and Clinical Use

Laurie K. Davies

The use of hypothermia to treat a wide variety of diseases has been advocated for centuries. Lowered body temperature has been used to combat cancer, infections, trauma, central nervous system diseases, and as a regional method to produce anesthesia for amputation (1, 2). However, it was not until 1950 that Bigelow et al. (3) demonstrated longer tolerance to inflow occlusion in hypothermic animals than in their normothermic counterparts. This work led to the first clinical application of hypothermia in cardiac surgery. Lewis and Taufic (4) used surface cooling to 28°C with 5.5 minutes of inflow occlusion to facilitate successful closure of an atrial septal defect in a 5-year-old child. In 1954, Gibbon (5) introduced the pump oxygenator to clinical practice, and in 1958, Sealy et al. (6) used hypothermia in conjunction with the cardiopulmonary bypass circuit for intracardiac repairs. The use of the pump oxygenator and hypothermia has allowed cardiac surgery to flourish. Complex lesions are repaired routinely with remarkably low mortality. A better understanding of the principles of hypothermia will maximize the advantages and safe application of this technology.

PHYSIOLOGY OF HYPOTHERMIA

One of the main difficulties in devising a reasonable strategy for application of hypothermia in humans is the fact that man is a homeotherm. A very effective homeostatic system ensures that body temperature remains consistently around 37°C regardless of changes in environmental temperatures. This tight regulation of temperature is accomplished by multiple mechanisms. Thermoreceptors in the skin sense cold, which then causes the hypothalamus to trigger a strong sympathetic nervous system response. Vasoconstriction of skin vessels to conserve heat occurs simultaneously with vasodilation of the muscle bed, augmenting muscular activity to produce heat by tensing and shivering. The endocrine system is activated; oxygen consumption is increased; and heart rate, cardiac output, and blood pressure are elevated.

Thus, one can appreciate the difficulty in understanding the appropriate response to the unnatural state of induced hypothermia in man. One must extrapolate from animal studies, biochemical equations, accidental hypothermia survivors, and normal organ temperature gradients to maximize the beneficial effects and minimize the complications of hypothermia.

Rationale for Use of Hypothermia

Why is hypothermia often employed during cardiopulmonary bypass? The major advantage to the technique is a reduction in metabolism and oxygen consumption. The

140

mechanism for this reduction is quite complex and not entirely understood. At a biochemical level, hypothermia changes the reaction rate of all biochemical processes, especially enzymatic reactions. This temperature dependence of reaction rates has been described by the concept of Q_{10}, which is defined as the increase or decrease in reaction rates or metabolic processes in relation to a temperature change of 10°C. For instance, a process with a Q_{10} of 2 will double its reaction rate with a 10°C increase in temperature or halve it with a drop of 10°C. Most reactions, including total body oxygen consumption, have a Q_{10} of 2 to 3 (7) (Fig. 6.1).

Some biochemical processes, especially those localized to cell membranes, show an abrupt change in reaction rates at certain critical temperatures. This has been termed a phase transition and is thought to be a result of a change in the cell membrane from a fluid to a gel (8). In mammalian tissues, phase transitions often occur at about 25 to 28°C, and may cause disturbed cell homeostasis.

Biophysical processes such as osmosis and water diffusion are also affected by temperature. Typically, a linear change of about 3% per 10°C is seen. Thus, this effect is minimal at clinical levels of hypothermia. However, if the freezing point of water is approached, ice is formed in the tissue, a condition that is not tolerated. The solutes concentrate in a hyperosmolar fashion in the residual nonfrozen water, causing marked fluid shifts and membrane disruption. Mammalian tissue will not regain function upon thawing from a frozen state. For this reason, there is a limit to the beneficial effects of hypothermia.

In cardiac surgery, systemic hypothermia in conjunction with cardiopulmonary bypass allows lower pump flows, better myocardial protection, less blood trauma, and better organ protection (9). Oxygen consumption (and presumably metabolic rate, since oxygen stores are minimal) predictably falls with lowered temperature. It was recognized early that lowered bypass flows could be employed in this setting and still provide adequate per-

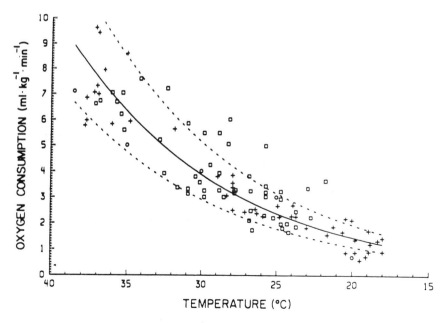

Figure 6.1. Whole body oxygen consumption ($\dot{V}O_2$) as a function of body temperature in dogs made hypothermic by surface cooling. (From Kirklin JW. Hypothermia, circulatory arrest, and cardiopulmonary bypass. In: Kirklin JW, Barratt-Boyes BG, eds. Cardiac surgery. New York: Churchill Livingstone, 1993:61–127.)

fusion as assessed by mixed venous oxygen tension and return of organ function following bypass. Relating oxygen consumption ($\dot{V}O_2$) to perfusion flow rate at various temperatures also can be valuable in assessing adequacy of tissue perfusion (Fig. 6.2). At a given temperature, a fall in oxygen consumption with a decrease in flow rate implies that oxygen delivery is not adequate. Hickey and Hoar (10) have shown in humans that a reduction in flow rate from 2.1 to 1.2 liters/min/m^2 at 25°C did not alter $\dot{V}O_2$ or tissue perfusion. Slogoff and colleagues (11) were unable to correlate low flows (<40 ml/kg/min) or pressures (<50 mm Hg) on bypass using moderate hypothermia and hemodilution with postoperative renal or central nervous system dysfunction. Lower perfusion flow rates allow better visualization by the surgeon. There will also be less venous return from the bronchial, pulmonary, and noncoronary collateral vessels. Since this returning blood is at systemic temperature, it can inappropriately warm the heart and jeopar-

dize myocardial protection. Blood trauma is minimized both because of the lower pump flows and the hemodilution employed on bypass. Because the etiology of most central nervous system damage on bypass is embolic in origin (12); lower bypass flows could minimize these focal insults. Systemic hypothermia also provides some margin of safety for organ protection if equipment failure occurs or circulatory arrest must be employed.

Acid-Base Management

One of the often discussed aspects of clinical hypothermia is appropriate acid-base management. Once again, we are faced with an artificially induced situation since the core temperature in man does not fluctuate widely except in this unnatural situation. It may be helpful to consider the behavior of blood in vitro, in exercising muscle, and in poikilothermic animals.

We have been trained to think of a pH of 7.40 and a PaCO_2 of 40 as "normal." How-

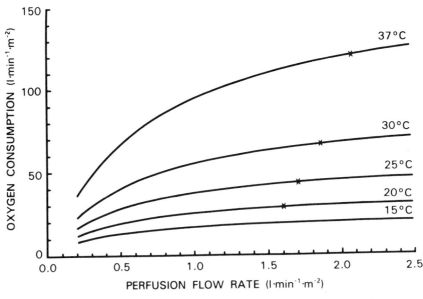

Figure 6.2. Nomogram of an equation, expressing the relation of oxygen consumption ($\dot{V}O_2$) to perfusion flow rate ($\dot{Q}$) at different temperatures (T) in animals. The x represents the perfusion flow rates used clinically at these temperatures. (From Kirklin JW. Hypothermia, circulatory arrest, and cardiopulmonary bypass. In: Kirklin JW, Barratt-Boyes BG, eds. Cardiac surgery. New York: Churchill Livingstone, 1993:61–127.)

ever, it must be kept in mind that these values are appropriate only at 37°C in blood. If one takes a sample of blood at 37°C with these values and cools it down, CO_2 becomes more soluble and Pa_{CO_2} decreases to maintain a constant CO_2 content. The ΔpH/degrees centigrade change in temperature is quite constant at about −0.015 (13). The slope of this relationship is remarkable in its similarity to the slope of the neutral pH (pN) of water (ΔpH/°C = −0.017) (Fig. 6.3). The buffer system responsible for this constant relationship of blood pH to pN with temperature changes is the imidazole moiety of protein-bound histidine. This buffer system allows a constant ratio of $[OH^-]/[H^+]$ in blood, averaging about 16:1 over a wide range of temperatures. A constant relative alkalinity with reference to the neutrality of water is preserved and no change in acid-base equilibrium occurs with this system even though the pH and P_{CO_2} values change remarkably with temperature. The important value maintained is a constant amount of H^+ *relative* to OH^-, not an absolute value of H^+ concentration.

Another way to look at this problem is to examine the behavior of blood in various locations in humans. The temperature of different tissues in man can vary considerably compared to that found in the core. For example, the skin may be at about 25°C on a cold day, while exercising muscle can achieve a temperature of 40 to 41°C. The arterial blood coming from the heart at 37°C is pumped to these tissues and behaves very much like blood in vitro as it is cooled or warmed. Total CO_2 content remains constant. Therefore, in the skin the pH is 7.60 while in the muscles it is 7.35 (Fig. 6.4). Acid-base equilibrium and a constant $[OH^-]/[H^+]$ are maintained at widely different temperatures.

In cold-blooded vertebrates, the blood pH-temperature curve also runs parallel to the pH of neutral water. Intracellular pH has also been measured in various animals and shows identical changes with temperature (14) (Fig. 6.5). The intracellular pH parallels the pN and blood pH

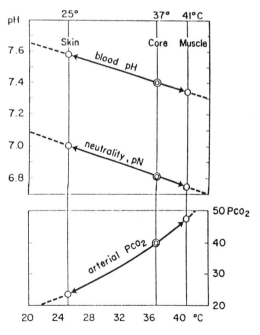

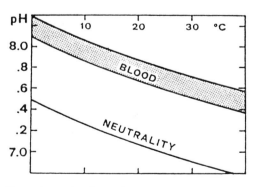

Figure 6.3. Blood pH of various ectotherms and the pH of neutral water as a function of body temperature. (From Rahn H. Body temperature and acid-base regulation [review article]. Pneumonologie 1974;151: 87–94.)

Figure 6.4. Changes in arterial pH and P_{CO_2} as 37°C blood arrives at the skin or exercising muscle at temperatures of 25 and 41°C, respectively. Neutrality of water (pN) changes in parallel with the changes in blood pH. Thus, the relative alkalinity of the blood or the ratio between $[OH^-]$ and $[H^+]$ ion remains constant. (From Rahn H. Body temperature and acid-base regulation [review article]. Pneumonologie 1974;151: 87–94.)

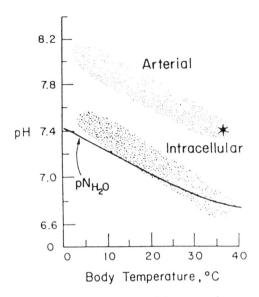

Figure 6.5. Arterial and intracellular pH as a function of body temperature in ectothermic animals. Intracellular pH closely follows the neutral pH of water; relative arterial alkalinity is maintained at all temperatures. (From Cameron DE, Gardner TJ. Principles of clinical hypothermia. Cardiac Surgery: State of the Art Reviews 1988;2:13–25).

slopes with temperature changes and differs from the extracellular pH by a constant but species-specific factor of about -0.6 to -0.8 pH units. Thus, at 37°C intracellular pH is about 6.8 to 6.9 with a 1:1 $[OH^-/H^+]$ ratio.

This constant internal milieu is accomplished predominantly by the buffering capacity of the imidazole group of histidine. As temperature changes, this imidazole protein buffer changes its pK_a in parallel with the pN of water. The fraction of unprotonated histidine imidazole groups, known as alpha, remains constant; total CO_2 remains constant; and pH changes as temperature changes. The term "alpha-stat" refers to maintenance of this constant net charge on proteins with temperature changes by keeping total CO_2 stores constant.

The alternative method of acid-base strategy is termed pH-stat. With this method, pH is the value that is maintained constant over varying temperatures. Obviously, as blood is cooled, CO_2 must be added to maintain a $Paco_2$ of 40 and a pH of 7.40. Extracellular and intracellular $[OH^-]/[H^+]$ are altered and total CO_2 stores are elevated.

Why might one strategy be chosen over another? During the first 2 decades of hypothermic bypass, pH-stat management with addition of 5% CO_2 to the oxygenator gas flow was used almost exclusively. Appreciation of the expected changes in pH with temperature seemed to be lacking and CO_2 was thought to be beneficial for cerebral vasodilation and maintenance of cerebral blood flow. In the past 15 to 20 years, this practice has been questioned, although a clear-cut answer is still not evident. On a theoretical basis, alpha-stat management may be preferable. Maintenance of constant intracellular electrochemical neutrality appears to be essential for normal cellular function (15). Depletion of intracellular metabolic intermediates of high-energy phosphates can occur if the intracellular pH changes and these metabolites lose their charged state. These substrates are then free to diffuse across lipid membranes. Most enzymes depend on optimal pH for their function. Electrochemical neutrality is also important in maintaining the Donnan equilibrium across cellular membranes, allowing normal intracellular anion concentrations and water content (16).

Poikilothermic animals whose tissues must function optimally despite wide variations in temperature follow an alpha-stat acid-base strategy. On the other hand, hibernating animals maintain a pH-stat strategy, with constant corrected blood pHa and $Paco_2$ (15). Thus, the animals hypoventilate, CO_2 stores increase, and intracellular pH becomes acidotic in most tissues. This acidotic state causes a further depression of metabolism that seems to be useful in nonfunctioning tissues such as skeletal muscle, gastrointestinal tract, and higher brain centers. However, active tissues such as heart and liver adopt a different strategy by actively extruding H^+ across their cell membranes to maintain intracellular pH at or near alpha-stat values. Thus, hibernators are able to vary their intracellular-extracellular pH gradient in different tissues, allowing different types of acid-base regulation in each. On beginning arousal, the first noticeable change is hyperventilation, which depletes CO_2 stores, raises intracellular pH, and increases metabolic rate. The animal reverts to alpha-stat control to allow tissues to regain optimal function. Thus, the issue is not clear-cut, since intracellular acid-base regulation can be independent of blood regulation both within and among different groups of animals.

Once again, we are left with the practical question of how acid-base status should be regulated during hypothermic bypass in man. The majority of animal studies would suggest that alpha-stat acid-base management is beneficial in terms of myocardial protection. McConnell et al. (17) evaluated alpha-stat regulation during hypothermia in dogs and demonstrated that significant elevations in coronary blood flow, left ventricular oxygen consumption, and lactate utilization occurred with maintenance of pH 7.7 at 28°C (alpha-stat) compared to a pH of 7.4 (pH-stat). There was also a significant increase in peak ventricular pressure when a standard preload was applied. Poole-Wilson and Langer (18) have shown greater contractility in hypothermic perfused papillary muscle when the pH of the perfusate is more alkaline than 7.4. They have also demonstrated a rapid fall in myocardial tension development as well as changes in Ca^{2+} flux with increasing the perfusate PCO_2 (19). On the other hand, Sinet et al. (20) found no effect of pH on isolated rat heart performance. The myocardium is often not perfused, but purposely made ischemic to facilitate cardiac surgery. In this setting, alkalinization of the blood before ischemia has been shown to decrease the development of acidosis in coronary sinus blood and improve contractility on reperfusion (21). It also appears that the pH of the blood reperfusing the heart may be critical to recovery of ventricular performance. Becker et al. (22) studied the myocardial effects of an acid-base strategy even more alkaline than alpha-stat. They found myocardial performance after 1 hour of circulatory arrest and cardioplegia was improved with moderate alkalinization compared to alpha-stat.

Acid-base management also appears to be important in cardiac electrophysiology. Swain et al. (23) showed that the electrical stability of the heart was increased using alpha-stat blood regulation with less spontaneous ventricular fibrillation compared to pH-stat. Kroncke et al. (24) found a 40% incidence of ventricular fibrillation in patients cooled to 24°C using pH-stat management compared to a 20% incidence in those following alpha-stat.

The appropriate acid-base management for optimal cerebral perfusion has also been questioned. Clearly, cerebral blood flow decreases significantly with hypothermia. Cerebral metabolic rate also decreases during hypothermic bypass. The response of the cerebral circulation to changes in $Paco_2$ is preserved (25); thus, alpha-stat management will result in lower cerebral flows than those seen with pH-stat management. However, because of the lowered metabolic demands, a lower cerebral blood flow may be appropriate. Govier et al. (26) demonstrated intact autoregulation in humans following alpha-stat strategy at temperatures from 21 to 29°C. Murkin et al. (27) showed coupling of cerebral blood flow and metabolism that was independent of cerebral perfusion pressure over the range of 20 to 100 mm Hg when alpha-stat management was employed. In contrast, cerebral autoregulation was abolished and cerebral blood flow varied with perfusion pressure when pH-stat strategy was used (Fig. 6.6). It has been argued that the cerebral blood flow during pH-stat hypothermia actually represents excessive blood flow and may be detrimental. Unnecessarily high blood flows may put the brain at risk for damage from excessive microemboli or high intracranial pressure.

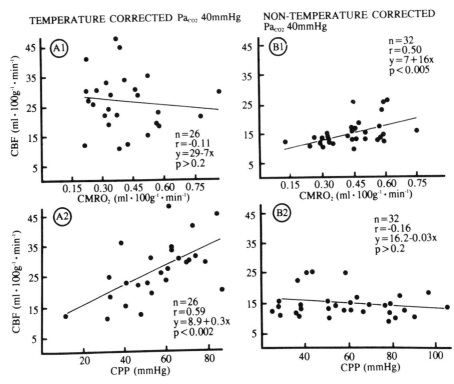

Figure 6.6. Simple linear regression of cerebral blood flow (*CBF*) versus cerebral perfusion pressure (*CPP*) or cerebral oxygen consumption (*CMRO₂*) for temperature-corrected and nontemperature-corrected groups. Upper panel: There is no significant correlation between *CBF* and *CMRO₂* in the temperature-corrected group (**A1**), whereas *CBF* significantly correlates with *CMRO₂* in the nontemperature-corrected group (**B1**). Lower panel: *CBF* is significantly correlated with *CPP* in the temperature-corrected group (**A2**), whereas *CBF* is independent of *CPP* in the nontemperature-corrected group (**B2**). (From Murkin JM, Farrar JK, Tweed WA, McKenzie FN, Guiraudon G. Cerebral autoregulation and flow/metabolism coupling during cardiopulmonary bypass: the influence of Paco₂. Anesth Analg 1987;66:825–832.)

On a microcirculatory level there is some evidence to suggest that alpha-stat management may be beneficial to the brain. Norwood et al. (28) studied the brains of hypothermic dogs perfused with anoxic blood and found a decrease in extent and magnitude of lesions when the perfusate had a higher pH. Acidic perfusate enhanced the extent of the lesions.

Hypocarbia results in a leftward shift of the oxyhemoglobin dissociation curve, causing oxygen to be less readily available to the tissues. However, more oxygen is dissolved in the plasma during hypothermia so that these two effects tend to cancel each other out. The relatively low cerebral blood flow during alpha-stat management has been shown to still be in excess of cerebral metabolic needs (27) (Table 6.1.)

A recent clinical study examined the influence of pH management on outcome in 86 patients undergoing mild hypothermic bypass (29). The authors found no differences in cardiac or neuropsychologic outcome regardless of acid-base management. However, the degree of hypothermia was not very profound (30.1°C) and the differences in Paco₂ between groups were not great (40.2 versus 47.3, uncorrected values). Their analysis looked for differences in mean group performances rather than individual patient performance. Thus, al-

Table 6.1. Different Hypothermic Acid-Base Regulatory Strategies[a]

Strategy	Aim	Total CO_2 Content	pH and Pa_{CO_2} Maintenance	Intracellular State	Alpha-Imidazole and Buffering	Enzyme Structure and Function	Cerebral Blood Flow and Coupling	Effect on Ischemic Tissue
pH-stat	Constant pH	Increases	Normal corrected values	Acidotic (excess H^+)	Excess $(+)$ charge, buffering decreased	Altered and activity decreased	Flow close to normothermic, ?Flow and metabolism uncoupled	?Lessens hypothermic protection
Alpha-stat	Constant OH^-/H^+	Constant	Normal uncorrected values	Neutral ($H^+ = OH^-$)	Constant net charge, buffering constant	Normal and activity maximal	Flow decreases (appropriate), ? Flow and metabolism coupled	?Allows full hypothermic protection
Alkaline	Alkaline pH	Decreases	Alkaline and hypocapneic uncorrected values	?Alkalotic (excess OH^-)	Decreased $(+)$ charge, buffering increased	Altered and activity decreased	?Flow decreases, ?Flow and metabolism coupling	?Augments hypothermic protection

[a]Reprinted with permission from Hickey PR, Hansen DD. Temperature and blood gases: the clinical dilemma of acid-base management for hypothermic cardiopulmonary bypass. In: Tinker JH, ed. Cardiopulmonary bypass: current concepts and controversies. Philadelphia: WB Saunders, 1989:16.

147

though this study is a welcome addition to this controversial area, further work must be done, particularly during deeper hypothermia, to determine optimal patient management.

Alterations in Organ Function

Hypothermia causes a decrease in blood flow to all organs of the body. However, some areas experience greater declines than others. Skeletal muscle and the extremities have the greatest reduction in flow, followed by the kidneys, splanchnic bed, heart, and brain. Despite these decreases in flow, arteriovenous O_2 content differences either decrease or are not changed, implying that oxygen supply is adequate to meet the metabolic requirements.

With cooling, heart rate decreases but contractility remains stable or may actually increase. Arrhythmias become more frequent as temperature decreases and may include nodal, premature ventricular beats, AV block, atrial and ventricular fibrillation, and asystole. The mechanism is unknown but may involve electrolyte disturbances, uneven cooling, and autonomic nervous system imbalance. Because coronary blood flow is well-preserved during hypothermia, it is unlikely that myocardial hypoxia plays a role in the genesis of these arrhythmias.

The pulmonary system is characterized by a progressive decrease in ventilation as the temperature is lowered. Physiologic and anatomic dead space increase from dilation of the bronchi by cold. Gas exchange is largely unaffected.

The kidney shows the largest proportional decrease in blood flow of all of the organs. Hypothermia increases renal vascular resistance, with diminished outer and inner cortex blood flow and oxygen delivery. Tubular transport of sodium, water, and chloride are decreased and concentrating ability becomes impaired. Tubular reabsorption is decreased. Urine flow may be increased with hypothermia, but this effect may be masked by anesthetic effects. The ability of the hypothermic kidney to handle glucose is impaired and glucose often appears in the urine. Hemodilution in combination with hypothermic cardiopulmonary bypass improves renal blood flow and protects the integrity of the renal tubules postoperatively.

In general, significant hepatic injury with hypothermic cardiopulmonary bypass is rare. Hepatic arterial blood flow is reduced in proportion to the fall in cardiac output. The most significant effect of hypothermia is the decrease in metabolic and excretory function of the liver. Obviously, drug actions and requirements will be modified by this change in liver function. With rewarming, hepatic efficiency reverts to normal.

Marked hyperglycemia is often a feature of hypothermic cardiopulmonary bypass. Endogenous insulin production is decreased; increased glycogenolysis and gluconeogenesis may occur because of increased catecholamines. Even if exogenous insulin is administered, its efficacy is reduced during hypothermia, and hyperglycemia may be found.

It is sometimes difficult to separate out the effects of hypothermia from those of hemodilution and cardiopulmonary bypass. Tissue water content is increased during hypothermic bypass, primarily as a consequence of hemodilution (30). Cell swelling and edema occur, which may be related to an accumulation of sodium and chloride within cells from a decrease in reaction rates of membrane Na-K adenosine triphosphatase (9). Hypothermia decreases free water clearance and causes a decrease in plasma potassium and an increase in osmolarity.

Hypothermia causes marked changes in the peripheral circulation. Systemic and pulmonary vascular resistance typically rise with cooling below 26°C (31). This increase in vascular resistance relates to increases in blood viscosity and catecholamines, hemoconcentration, cell swelling and, perhaps, active vasoconstrictor substances in the lung. In addition, arteriovenous shunts appear at low temperatures (32), and may cause a further diminution in tissue oxygen delivery. The increase in blood viscosity occurs because of fluid shifts, with loss of plasma volume from capillary leak and cell swelling. The red blood cell volume remains unchanged even though the hematocrit rises. Red blood cell aggregation and rouleaux formation can occur, further impeding blood flow. These changes can be somewhat ameliorated by adequate anesthesia, hemodilution, heparinization, and the use of vasodilators. Hypothermia also causes thrombocytopenia by a reversible sequestration of platelets in the portal circulation.

The hormonal response to hypothermia depends on the level of anesthesia. Nonanesthetized subjects demonstrate a marked sympathetic response to cold. This response can be almost ablated if deep anesthesia is used. After deep hypothermia and total circulatory arrest, a massive release of catecholamines occurs (33), which may contribute to the impaired cerebral perfusion found by Greeley and colleagues (34). Corticosteroid release is suppressed with long-term hypothermia below 28°C, but appears to be normal with short periods of hypothermia (35). Complement activation occurs during cardiopulmonary bypass and is associated with neutrophil activation. Respiratory complications correlate with the degree of complement activation (36). Hypothermia, hemodilution, and heparin reduce complement activation and subsequent neutrophil response and may protect patients from harmful sequelae. Circulating bradykinin increases during hypothermia and cardiopulmonary bypass and may contribute to altered vascular permeability and circulatory instability (37).

CLINICAL USE OF HYPOTHERMIA

Currently, hypothermia is used most commonly in cardiac surgery, although its use has also been described for major vascular procedures, intracranial surgery, and for removal of hepatic and renal tumors. For most cardiac procedures, mild to moderate systemic hypothermia (above 25°C) is used for its protective effects previously described. More profound selective myocardial hypothermia is also often used during aortic cross-clamping to aid in preservation of ischemic myocardium. Myocardial hypothermia is typically obtained in two ways: by coronary perfusion with cold cardioplegic solution, and by topical means using an ice slush or cold pericardial lavage. The optimal temperature for myocardial protection is controversial; however, most studies have demonstrated superior protection down to 2 to 4°C, as long as freezing temperatures are avoided, alkalosis is present, and the heart is promptly arrested during cooling (38).

The most dramatic application demonstrating the protective effects of hypothermia is in deep hypothermia and circulatory arrest. Systemic temperatures of 20 to 22°C or less are used to allow cessation of the circulation for periods up to 40 to 60 minutes, often without detectable organ injury (7). Deep hypothermia and circulatory arrest may be used in a variety of situations. It is quite commonly used in pediatric patients (particularly those less than 8 to 10 kg) for repair of complex congenital cardiac lesions. It is used whenever an asanguinous surgical field is necessary. It is often used in procedures requiring occlusion of multiple cerebral vessels, particularly aortic arch aneurysms. It may be used to enhance surgical exposure and speed in procedures that could lead to uncontrollable hemorrhage.

The brain is the organ at most risk for injury and limits the duration of "safe" arrest time. Cerebral metabolic activity is decreased with temperature but never ceases altogether, even at temperatures approaching 0°C. The protective effect of hypothermia may involve more than just a reduction in cerebral metabolic rate. A Q_{10} of 2.7 would predict a "safe" arrest time of only about 15 minutes at 20°C. Clinical and experimental evidence indicate, however, that 30 to 45 minutes is typically tolerated. So there appears to be a disproportionate cerebroprotective effect to profound levels of hypothermia. Other factors such as extracellular pH may play a role. Recently, Swain and colleagues (39) showed that hypothermia significantly increased the tissue energy state and intracellular pH in both the heart and brain. This increase in high-energy phosphate levels may partially explain the beneficial effects of hypothermia on organ tolerance to ischemia. On the other hand, it may be that cerebral metabolic rate of oxygen consumption decreases more precipitously with profound hypothermia than previously thought. Michenfelder and Milde (40) showed a change in Q_{10} from 2.23 between 37 and 27°C to 4.53 between 27 and 14°C. They postulated that this marked drop in oxygen consumption at lower temperatures could be explained by a primary effect of hypothermia on integrated neuronal function (as shown by suppression of the EEG).

The rate of cooling also appears to be important in the production of brain injury. Wide gradients between body and perfusate temperature in dogs correlated with brain cell necrosis and death (41). The optimal site for temperature monitoring is controversial, but it must be remembered that gradients exist among the different regions (42) (Fig. 6.7). Monitoring multiple sites to assure uniform cooling prior to arrest is advisable. Coselli et al. suggest using EEG monitoring to determine ideal depth of cooling for safe circulatory arrest (43). They advocated using electrocerebral silence as the appropriate end-point in cooling, but found that no peripheral body temperature consistently predicted this level of hypothermia. There was a wide variation in temperature among body sites when electrocerebral silence occurred.

A consequence of ischemia and anoxia is the "no-reflow" phenomenon. The cere-

bral microcirculation can shut down in multifocal areas, causing incomplete reperfusion when flow is resumed. The etiology of this problem is not completely understood but may involve increased blood viscosity, vascular smooth muscle contraction due to increased extracellular potassium, and precapillary shunting (44). It can occur with or without total circulatory arrest, and can be prevented by hypothermia (28). Microscopic cellular damage in the brain occurs to some degree following hypothermia to 18°C whether pulsatile or nonpulsatile perfusion or total circulatory arrest is employed (45).

The question of an effect on later intellectual development following hypothermic bypass with or without circulatory arrest is an unanswered one. A few studies have shown evidence of a decreased intelligence quotient and developmental capacity related to the duration of circulatory arrest (46–48). However, most studies have not been able to demonstrate an adverse effect on intellectual capacity and development when circulatory arrest times are less than 60 minutes at nasopharyngeal temperatures of about 20°C (49–51). It is difficult to interpret many of these studies because of difficulty in defining an appropriate control group. Blackwood and colleagues (52) used each child as his own control and found no difference between preoperative and postoperative scores with arrest intervals as long as 74 minutes.

Choreoathetosis and postoperative seizures are occasionally seen following deep hypothermia (7). The incidence ranges from 1 to 10% and may relate to uneven brain cooling, uneven brain reperfusion, air or particulate embolization, and excessive glycolysis. Both problems are more common following circulatory arrest, but can be seen with continuous hypothermic perfusion. Choreoathetosis usually lessens in severity with time but may persist. Seizures are usually transient and do

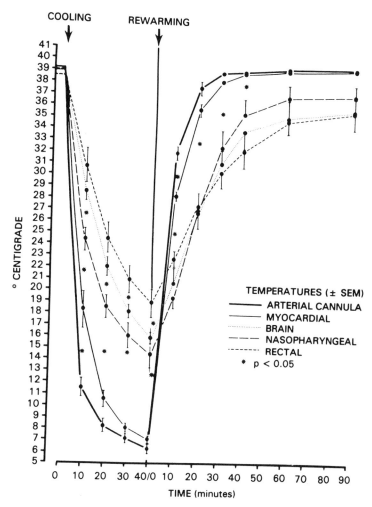

COOLING   REWARMING

TEMPERATURES (± SEM)
——— ARTERIAL CANNULA
——— MYOCARDIAL
········· BRAIN
— — — NASOPHARYNGEAL
- - - - - RECTAL
* p < 0.05

° CENTIGRADE

TIME (minutes)

Figure 6.7.   Average temperature (±SEM) of arterial cannula, myocardium, cerebral cortex, nasopharynx, and rectum during 40 minutes of cooling and 90 minutes of rewarming under cardiopulmonary bypass in six pigs. (From Stefaniszyn HJ, Novick RJ, Keith FM, Salerno TA. Is the brain adequately cooled during deep hypothermic cardiopulmonary bypass? Curr Surg 1983;40:294–297.)

not generally imply permanent brain dysfunction.

Thus, the question of "safe" circulatory arrest time is complex and cannot be answered with certainty. Hypothermia can delay but not prevent the appearance of metabolic and structural changes that occur during ischemia and lead to functional neurologic impairment. A nomogram has been devised that, although not rigorously defined, provides a best estimate of safe circulatory arrest times at three temperatures (7) (Fig. 6.8).

Cardiac surgery has advanced remarkably over the last 30 years. Hypothermia has contributed substantially toward improving patient outcome. Current efforts must be directed toward defining methods of maximizing cerebral protection and refining critical techniques.

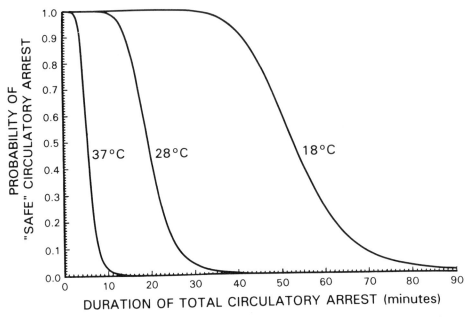

Figure 6.8.   Nomogram of an estimate (not rigorously derived) of the probability of "safe" total circulatory arrest (absence of structural or functional damage) according to the arrest time, at nasopharyngeal temperatures of 37°C, 28°C, and 18°C. (From Kirklin JW. Hypothermia, circulatory arrest, and cardiopulmonary bypass. In: Kirklin JW, Barratt-Boyes GB, eds. Cardiac surgery. New York: Churchill Livingstone, 1993:61–127.)

REFERENCES

1. Fay T. Observations on prolonged human refrigeration. NY State J Med 1940;40:1351–1354.
2. Crossman LW, Ruggiero WF, Hurley V, Allen FM. Reduced temperatures in surgery. II. Amputations for peripheral vascular disease. Arch Surg 1942;44:139–156.
3. Bigelow WG, Callaghan JC, Hopps JA. General hypothermia for experimental intracardiac surgery. Ann Surg 1950;132:531–539.
4. Lewis FJ, Taufic M. Closure of atrial septal defects with the aid of hypothermia; experimental accomplishments and the report of one successful case. Surgery 1953;33:52–59.
5. Gibbon JH. Application of a mechanical heart and lung apparatus to cardiac surgery. Minn Med 1954;37:171–180.
6. Sealy WC, Brown IW Jr, Young WG Jr. A report on the use of both extracorporeal circulation and hypothermia for open heart surgery. Ann Surg 1958;147:603–613.
7. Kirklin JW. Hypothermia, circulatory arrest, and cardiopulmonary bypass. In: Kirklin JW, Barratt-Boyes BG, eds. Cardiac surgery. New York: John Wiley & Sons, 1986:30–82.
8. Hearse DJ, Braimbridge MV, Jynge P. Protection of the ischemic myocardium: cardioplegia. New York: Raven Press, 1981.

9. Cameron DE, Gardner TJ. Principles of clinical hypothermia. Cardiac Surgery: State of the Art Reviews 1988;2:13–25.
10. Hickey RF, Hoar PF. Whole body oxygen consumption during low-flow hypothermic cardiopulmonary bypass. J Thorac Cardiovasc Surg 1983;86:903–906.
11. Slogoff S, Reul GJ, Keats AS, et al. Role of perfusion pressure and flow in major organ dysfunction after cardiopulmonary bypass. Ann Thorac Surg 1990;50:911–918.
12. Nussmeier NA, Arlund C, Slogoff S. Neuropsychiatric complications after cardiopulmonary bypass: cerebral protection by a barbiturate. Anesthesiology 1986;64:165–170.
13. Rahn H. Body temperature and acid-base regulation [review article]. Pneumonologie 1974;151: 87–94.
14. Malan A, Wilson TL, Reeves RB. Intracellular pH in cold-blooded vertebrates as a function of body temperature. Respir Physiol 1976;28:29–47.
15. Hickey PR, Hansen DD. Temperature and blood gases: the clinical dilemma of acid-base management for hypothermic cardiopulmonary bypass. In: Tinker JH, ed. Cardiopulmonary bypass: current concepts and controversies. Philadelphia: WB Saunders, 1989:1–20.
16. Reeves RB. Temperature-induced changes in blood acid-base status: Donnan r_{cl} and red cell volume. J Appl Physiol 1976;40:762–767.

17. McConnell DH, White F, Nelson RL, et al. Importance of alkalosis in maintenance of "ideal" blood pH during hypothermia. Surg Forum 1975;26:263–265.
18. Poole-Wilson PA, Langer GA. Effect of pH on ionic exchange and function in rat and rabbit myocardium. Am J Physiol 1975;229:570–581.
19. Poole-Wilson PA, Langer GA. Effects of acidosis on mechanical function and Ca^{2+} exchange in rabbit myocardium. Am J Physiol 1979;236: H525–H533.
20. Sinet M, Muffat-Joly M, Bendaace T, Pocidalo JJ. Maintaining blood pH at 7.4 during hypothermia has no significant effect on work of the isolated rat heart. Anesthesiology 1985;62:582–587.
21. Austen WG. Experimental studies on the effects of acidosis and alkalosis on myocardial function after aortic occlusion. J Surg Res 1965;5: 191–194.
22. Becker H, Vinten-Johansen J, Buckberg G, et al. Myocardial damage caused by keeping pH 7.40 during systemic deep hypothermia. J Thorac Cardiovasc Surg 1981;82:810–820.
23. Swain JA, White FN, Peters RM. The effect of pH on the hypothermic ventricular fibrillation threshold. J Thorac Cardiovasc Surg 1984;87: 445–451.
24. Kroncke GM, Nichols RD, Mendenhall JT, Myerowitz PD, Starling JR. Ectothermic philosophy of acid-base balance to prevent fibrillation during hypothermia. Arch Surg 1986;121: 303–304.
25. Prough DS, Stump DA, Roy RC, et al. Response of cerebral blood flow to changes in carbon dioxide during hypothermic cardiopulmonary bypass. Anesthesiology 1986;64:576–581.
26. Govier AV, Reves JG, McKay RD, et al. Factors and their influence on regional cerebral blood flow during nonpulsatile cardiopulmonary bypass. Ann Thorac Surg 1984;38:592–600.
27. Murkin JM, Farrar JK, Tweed WA, McKenzie FN, Guiraudon G: Cerebral autoregulation and flow/ metabolism coupling during cardiopulmonary bypass: the influence of Pa_{CO_2}. Anesth Analg 1987;66:825–832.
28. Norwood WI, Norwood CR, Castaneda AR. Cerebral anoxia: effect of deep hypothermia and pH. Surgery 1979;86:203–209.
29. Bashein G, Townes BD, Nessly ML, et al. A randomized study of carbon dioxide management during hypothermic cardiopulmonary bypass. Anesthesiology 1990;72:7–15.
30. Utley JR, Wachtel C, Cain RB, et al. Effects of hypothermia, hemodilution, and pump oxygenation on organ water content, blood flow and oxygen delivery, and renal function. Ann Thorac Surg 1981;31:121–133.
31. Cooper KE. The circulation in hypothermia. Br Med Bull 1961;17:48–51.
32. Suzuki M, Penn I. A reappraisal of the microcirculation during general hypothermia. Surgery 1965;58:1049–1060.
33. Wood M, Shand DG, Wood AJJ. The sympathetic response to profound hypothermia and circulatory arrest in infants. Can Anaesth Soc J 1980; 27:125–132.
34. Greeley WJ, Ungerleider RM, Smith LR, Reves JG. The effects of deep hypothermic cardiopulmonary bypass and total circulatory arrest on cerebral blood flow in infants and children. J Thorac Cardiovasc Surg 1989;97:737–745.
35. Blair E. Clinical hypothermia. New York: McGraw-Hill, 1964.
36. Moore FD Jr, Warner KG, Assousa S, Valeri CR, Khuri SF. The effects of complement activation during cardiopulmonary bypass: attenuation by hypothermia, heparin, and hemodilution. Ann Surg 1988;208:95–103.
37. Pang LM, Stalcup SA, Lipset JS, Hayes CJ, Bowman FO, Mellins RB. Increased circulating bradykinin during hypothermia and cardiopulmonary bypass in children. Circulation 1979;60: 1503–1507.
38. Swanson DK, Dufek JH, Kahn DR. Improved myocardial preservation at 4°C. Ann Thorac Surg 1980;30:519–526.
39. Swain JA, McDonald TJ Jr, Balaban RS, Robbins RC. Metabolism of the heart and brain during hypothermic cardiopulmonary bypass. Ann Thorac Surg 1991;51:105–109.
40. Michenfelder JD, Milde JH. The relationship among canine brain temperature, metabolism, and function during hypothermia. Anesthesiology 1991;75:130–136.
41. Almond CH, Jones JC, Snyder HM, Grant SM, Meyer BW. Cooling gradients and brain damage with deep hypothermia. J Thorac Cardiovasc Surg 1964;48:890–897.
42. Stefaniszyn HJ, Novick RJ, Keith FM, Salerno TA. Is the brain adequately cooled during deep hypothermic cardiopulmonary bypass? Curr Surg 1983;40:294–297.
43. Coselli JS, Crawford ES, Beall AC Jr. Mizrahi EM, Hess KR, Patel VM. Determination of brain temperatures for safe circulatory arrest during cardiovascular operation. Ann Thorac Surg 1988;45: 638–642.
44. Mavroudis C, Greene MA. Cardiopulmonary bypass and hypothermic circulatory arrest in infants. In: Jacobs ML, Norwood WI, eds. Pediatric cardiac surgery: current issues. Boston: Butterworth-Heinemann, 1992.
45. Molina JE, Einzig S, Mastri AR, et al. Brain damage in profound hypothermia: perfusion versus circulatory arrest. J Thorac Cardiovasc Surg 1984;87:596–604.
46. Wells FC, Coghill S, Caplan HL, Lincoln C. Duration of circulatory arrest does influence the psy-

chological development of children after cardiac operation in early life. J Thorac Cardiovasc Surg 1983;86:823–831.

47. Wright JS, Hicks RG, Newman DC. Deep hypothermic arrest: observations on later development in children. J Thorac Cardiovasc Surg 1979;77:466–468.

48. Settergren G, Öhqvist G, Lundberg S, Henze A, Björk VO, Persson B. Cerebral blood flow and cerebral metabolism in children following cardiac surgery with deep hypothermia and circulatory arrest. Clinical course and follow-up of psychomotor development. Scand J Thorac Cardiovasc Surg 1982;16:209–215.

49. Dickinson DF, Sambrooks, JE. Intellectual performance in children after circulatory arrest with profound hypothermia in infancy. Arch Dis Child 1979;54:1–6.

50. Clarkson PM, MacArthur BA, Barratt-Boyes BG, Whitlock RM, Neutz JM. Developmental progress after cardiac surgery in infancy using hypothermia and circulatory arrest. Circulation 1980;62:855–861.

51. Messmer BJ, Schallberger U, Gattiker R, Senning A. Psychomotor and intellectual development after deep hypothermia and circulatory arrest in early infancy. J Thorac Cardiovasc Surg 1976;72:495–502.

52. Blackwood MJA, Haka-Ikse K, Steward DJ. Developmental outcome in children undergoing surgery with profound hypothermia. Anesthesiology 1986;65:437–440.

7

MYOCARDIAL PROTECTION DURING CARDIAC SURGERY

Jakob Vinten-Johansen and John W. Hammon

The need to protect the myocardium from intraoperative ischemic damage predates the time of wide availability of cardiopulmonary bypass (CPB). The introduction of inflow occlusion techniques permitted the repair of simple intracardiac defects and, in many cases, the occlusion time could be increased by adding moderate systemic hypothermia (30°C) (1). After the development of clinical CPB, the recognition that simple hypothermia could protect the myocardium against ischemic injury induced by aortic cross-clamping during CPB led to the use of profound systemic hypothermia for the protection of the heart and other body organs. The development of hypothermia for organ preservation permitted longer periods of ischemic cardiac arrest for the repair of more complicated lesions. (2, 3)

Chemical arrest of the heart was first suggested by Melrose et al. in 1955 (4). He and his associates infused a 2.5% solution of potassium citrate mixed with blood proximal to the aortic cross-clamp, thereby distributing the solution specifically into the coronary circulation and achieving asystole. Unfortunately, this method produced direct myocardial injury in some cases and was subsequently abandoned (5). In a renewed effort to minimize damage during ischemia, topical cardiac hypothermia was introduced by Shumway and associates in 1959 (6, 7). Using CPB and topical hypothermia, they achieved a marked reduction in operative mortality. Nevertheless, intramyocardial temperature gradients could be measured and, therefore, these techniques were more applicable to operations where topical solutions could be used to supplement hypothermia. In the late 1960s, reports described scattered myocardial or subendocardial necrosis in patients dying after cardiac surgical operations, suggesting that current techniques of myocardial protection were inadequate (8, 9). Laboratory studies demonstrated that topical hypothermia protected inadequately against intraoperative injury, resulting in postoperative myocardial functional depression (10).

Despite early efforts to protect the heart from ischemic damage, severe postoperative damage and contracture (stone heart) were unwelcome complications (11). The call was issued to devise strategies to protect the myocardium during obligate surgical ischemia (12). Interest in chemical cardioplegia and efficient myocardial cooling was revitalized by several groups using intracellular solutions with low sodium, and subsequent reports demonstrated improved operative results (13, 14). Recognizing that the concept of cardi-

155

oplegia was meritorious, but the vehicle of implementation was suboptimal, Gay and Ebert (15) reintroduced the concept of potassium cardioplegia in 1973, emphasizing a lower concentration of potassium to avoid direct myocardial injury. This report popularized the use of potassium-based cardioplegia to achieve electromechanical arrest.

Using a different approach to chemical cardioplegia, Hearse and associates (16) at St. Thomas' Hospital in London developed an extracellular solution based on sodium as the primary element. With specific components designed to initiate cardiac arrest and maintain a soft, flaccid myocardium, their solution has become very popular internationally and represents a major advance in the area of myocardial protection.

In the late 1970s, Follette and associates (17) introduced the concept of cold-hyperkalemic blood cardioplegia. The physiologic nature of blood as well as the improved buffering and oxygen transport capacity has won this solution a wide following, with excellent results published by several independent groups (18, 19). This chapter reviews the fundamental concepts of myocardial protection during open heart surgery that have evolved and developed over the past 20 years. The concepts have changed as our understanding of the pathophysiologic determinants of ischemia and reperfusion has progressed. Early empirical observations have given way to complex biochemical and molecular interactions, which have reinforced physiologic intuition and given solid foundation to a target-specific approach of myocardial protection. This impact of science on clinical strategies for protecting the heart has prompted an in-depth description of pathophysiologic phenomena that contribute to the various phases of injury that may confront the surgical team. New directions of research that may ultimately lead to enhancement of the defenses against perioperative injury are also briefly explored.

SURGICAL ISCHEMIC AND REPERFUSION INJURY

Developing a strategy for adequately protecting the heart during elective ischemia is often problematic. The heart under consideration may present complex pictures of global or regional ischemia, differing vulnerabilities to ischemic and reperfusion injury, and various impediments to the distribution of the chosen cardioprotective solution of choice. A single cardioprotective strategy may not be adequate in all situations, and the surgical team must often mold the composition of the cardioplegic solution or its modality of delivery to conform to the requirements of the pathologic scenario at hand. The measures taken to protect the heart during elective ischemia should represent a balance struck between the requirements of the heart during aortic cross-clamp or reperfusion, with appropriate adjustments made for special considerations (hypertrophy, diffuse coronary disease), and the convenience of the anesthesia and surgical team.

Myocardial injury sustained in the surgical setting may be divided into three phases: (1) antecedent ischemia, which is precipitated prior to the institution of cardiopulmonary bypass or the delivery of cardioplegia solution (i.e., "unprotected" ischemia); (2) "protected" ischemia initiated electively by chemical cardioplegia; and (3) reperfusion injury sustained during intermittent infusions of the cardioplegic solution, after removal of the aortic cross-clamp, or after discontinuation of cardiopulmonary bypass. The stages in surgical operations where injury may be inflicted are diagrammed in Figure 7.1. Understanding the pathophysiologic mechanisms of myocardial injury occurring at these intervals and appreciating the principles of myocardial protection will help avoid injury induced by the very techniques intended to preserve the myocardium. Unlike the cardi-

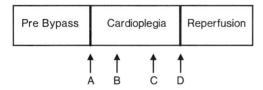

Figure 7.1. A schematic diagram representing the chronologic points where myocardial injury can be sustained. Potential injury can occur before institution of cardiopulmonary bypass (Pre Bypass) including occlusive coronary lesions or global ischemia secondary to ventricular fibrillation or severe cardiogenic shock. In these cases, the potential exists for a reperfusion injury during the induction phase of cardioplegia (point A). Intermittent infusions (B, C) represent additional intervals where injury may be sustained, particularly in newly revascularized grafts receiving cardioplegic solution for the first time. Finally, point D represents a vulnerable point because the cross-clamp is removed, often without the benefit of a terminal (warm or cold) infusion of cardioplegic solution. Also at point D there exists the cold (heart)-warm (systemic blood) interface where gas bubbles may form, and the possibility that premature reanimation of the heart may raise O_2 demands.

ologist, the surgical team has the opportunity to intervene directly to control many facets of elective ischemic and reperfusion injury to more favorably direct the outcome of the postischemic heart. The pathophysiology of ischemia and reperfusion will be described in the following sections. Interventions targeting these various pathologic processes will be discussed under "Principles of Myocardial Protection."

Determinants of Ischemic Injury

Since cardiac function depends on a continuous supply of oxygen, the conventional definition of ischemia has been an imbalance between myocardial oxygen supply and demand. However, this definition must be broadened to include the sufficient washout of tissue metabolites that can become injurious if accumulated. Ischemia can therefore be redefined as inadequate perfusion to sustain steady-state metabolism at a given level of cardiac performance (20, 21). The conventional definition has changed in two important respects: (*a*) the

acknowledgment that the accumulation of tissue metabolites (lactate, CO_2, H^+) may contribute to ischemic dysfunction and metabolic abnormalities (22, 23) and (*b*) the recognition that the coronary vasculature may not regulate the levels of perfusion appropriately in response to metabolic needs imposed by increased cardiac work.

The determinants of ischemic injury have been well documented for both regional (20) and global (24–26) normothermic ischemia. These determinants include the duration of ischemia, the extent of collateral blood flow offsetting the severity of ischemia, the ambient oxygen demands of the myocardium, and various prearrest factors (27). The distinction between global ischemia (imposed electively) and regional ischemia secondary to coronary occlusion is important because the contributions made by each of these pathologic determinants may vary in either case, and may, in turn, alter the time course of the development of injury. In addition, interventions designed to manipulate these determinants vary widely in both feasibility and benefits, and will determine to some extent the surgical management employed. Finally, the anesthesia-surgical team must think in terms of protected ischemia, which often diminishes the danger imposed by these various determinants (active under normothermic conditions) if sound principles of myocardial protection are judiciously applied. While well-planned strategies of myocardial protection counteract many determinants of ischemic injury, regional ischemia can pose a more formidable problem and may offer greater resistance to therapy than global ischemia because the dynamics of injury pathogenesis may differ, and coronary lesions prevent delivery of cardioplegic solutions.

Duration of Ischemia

In both regional and global ischemia, the potential for injury increases in proportion to the duration of warm ischemia. Irreversible injury, manifested as myocellular necrosis, occurs after as little as 30 minutes following coronary occlusion in the intact working heart, while a similar period of global ischemia produces moderate to severe functional depression without obvious necrosis. Therefore, the duration of warm ischemia (regional or global) preceding cardiopulmonary bypass, indicated as prebypass ischemia in Figure 7.1, will impose damage that may be further aggravated if myocardial protection is inadequate, and which may be avoided if prescribed strategies are applied. However, the duration of protected surgical ischemia associated with aortic cross-clamping and hypothermic cardioplegia (periods A through C, ending with release of the cross-clamp at point D in Fig. 7.1) does not demand the same anxiety as does antecedent warm unprotected ischemia because the use of arrest and hypothermia in the surgeons protective armamentarium increases myocardial tolerance to ischemia and thereby prolongs the permissible duration of ischemia (26, 28). Consequently, hypothermic cardioplegia increases the duration that aortic clamping may be safely imposed from 30 minutes or less to as much as 4 hours (28) (Fig. 7.2).

The physiologic basis underlying the greater vulnerability of the regionally ischemic myocardium to ischemic injury may be related to differences in the O_2 supply/demand status. Oxygen demands of regionally ischemic myocardium greatly exceed those of globally ischemic myocardium (29, 30) possibly because of the greater wall stress encountered in the ischemic segment during systolic paradoxical bulging. For example, 45 minutes of global normothermic ischemia followed by unmodified reperfusion may reduce postischemic function by 50 to 60% without obvious necrosis (28) (Fig. 7.2), while a similar period of regional ischemia is associated with complete dysfunction in the involved segment, and a substantial degree of subendocardial necrosis (31–33). Whereas regional ischemia

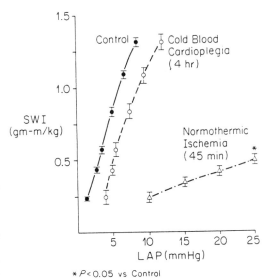

Figure 7.2. Left ventricular performance, measured by in situ Starling curves, before aortic cross-clamping (●), and after 30 minutes of reperfusion following 45 minutes of global 37°C ischemia (△) or 4 hours of protected ischemia using multidose cold blood cardioplegia (○). These data demonstrate severe dysfunction after normothermic ischemia and an increase in the duration of "tolerable" ischemia when strategies of myocardial protection are applied. *LAP,* left atrial pressure; *SWI,* left ventricular external stroke work index. (From Rosenkranz ER, Buckberg GD. 230 Myocardial protection during surgical coronary reperfusion. J Am Coll Cardiol 1983;5:1235–1246.)

may have an uncontrolled onset that is difficult to identify, as well as a prolonged duration, in most cases global ischemia is an elective process executed deliberately with precise onset and a largely premeditated duration. With global ischemia, the ischemia can be electively discontinued by removal of the cross-clamp, but can also be temporarily interrupted and pathologic consequences forestalled by episodically infusing cardioplegic solution. However, the benefits of these maneuvers must be measured against the potential for reperfusion injury.

Extent of Blood Flow Deficit

In regional ischemia, the degree of collateral blood flow will proportionally reduce the severity of ischemia and slow its pathologic time course (34). By the same token, a complete occlusion offers formidable resistance to delivery of cardioplegia, while collateral vessels will aid in this endeavor. However, during aortic cross-clamping or CPB the collateral blood flow originating from cardiac and extracardiac sources represents only 2 to 4% of normal coronary blood flow (35–37). Although this collateral supply does little to offset the severity of global ischemia, it is sufficient to wash out the cardioplegic solution, reversing cardiac hypothermia and hyperkalemia, and thereby precipitating the resumption of electromechanical activity.

Myocardial Oxygen Demands

Myocardial oxygen demands are determined by the pressure-volume area (or internal work plus potential energy), heart rate, inotropic state, and minor factors including basal metabolism, ionic homeostasis after electromechanical effort, and oxidative energy diverted to myocellular repair (38–40). Following coronary occlusion, the effect of reducing myocardial oxygen demand in the working heart upon the development of necrosis is unclear (34), possibly because the oxygen demands of dyskinetic segments are 70% of normal both during the occlusion period (29) and after reperfusion (41). However, with extracorporeal circulation and ventricular decompression, the development of necrosis may be significantly delayed. The severity of ischemia can be attenuated considerably by diminishing the denominator of the oxygen supply/demand equation. Reducing O_2 demand forms the cornerstone in strategies of myocardial protection. Decompression of the heart by venting may effectively reduce the myocardial supply/demand mismatch of both the regionally ischemic and the globally ischemic heart, thereby slowing the course of injury (42, 43). Total cardiopulmonary bypass and diastolic arrest reduce cardiac work substantially, while ox-

ygen demands are further decreased by imposing cardiac hypothermia to reduce basal energetic requirements. Each element involved in reducing the oxygen demand is fully discussed below.

DETERMINANTS OF REPERFUSION INJURY

Although the myocardium must be reperfused after either regional or global ischemia if total necrosis is to be avoided, recent studies have demonstrated that injury may be accelerated or extended by events specific to the reperfusion phase (20, 44–49). Cardiologists and scientists avidly question and emotionally dispute the very existence of this so-called "reperfusion injury" (50–52); however, evidence describing its characteristics, time course, and mechanisms are convincing. Furthermore, evidence is mounting that reperfusion injury is indeed a malleable process, amenable to modification (either extension or regression) by interventions initiated at the time of reperfusion (31, 32, 49, 53, 54). Cardiac surgeons have spoken liberally about reperfusion injury, possibly because they, unlike their cardiology colleagues, can modify the *conditions* under which reperfusion is conducted or the *composition* of the reperfusate (i.e., cardioplegia solution) with relative ease by virtue of extracorporeal technology, chemical cardioplegia, and modified reperfusates. For the present discussion, we can define reperfusion injury as pathology that is extended, accelerated, or expressed de novo from the profile observed during ischemia, resulting from events occurring after reperfusion has been initiated. This definition is rather broad in that it takes into consideration that the *rate* of injury as well as the final long-term *extent* of injury may be altered by reperfusion or by reperfusion therapy. Deceleration of the rate of reperfusion injury in the early postoperative period may be important in counteracting myocardial "stunning," which is defined as postischemic contractile dysfunction in the absence of morphologic injury or necrosis.

The concept of reperfusion injury had its genesis in the 1960s and 1970s. Jennings et al. (55) reported development of ultrastructural abnormalities after reperfusion, while Hearse and colleagues (47, 48) demonstrated that the reintroduction of oxygen and the initiation of reperfusion were associated with abrupt myocardial injury. In the following decades, a plethora of experiments were performed to describe the pathologic characteristics of reperfusion injury or "reoxygenation injury," and have striven to determine the mechanisms involved. Demonstration of reperfusion injury has involved (a) observation of morphologic, functional, metabolic, and electrophysiologic alterations, as well as changes in enzyme release beginning at the time of reperfusion, or (b) alterations in one or more of these parameters by mechanical or pharmacologic interventions initiated at the time of reperfusion. In nonsurgical models of regional ischemia, the interventions targeting some aspect of reperfusion injury may be introduced by systemic or direct intracoronary routes. In surgical models of regional ischemia (simulating revascularization of acute evolving infarction) as well as global ischemia, interventions are imposed using cardioplegia to modify the conditions and composition of the initial phases of reperfusion.

Using these approaches to study reperfusion injury, we have documented both temporal development of reperfusion injury and attenuation of postischemic injury by nonsurgical as well as surgical interventions (31, 32, 35, 36, 53, 56, 57). Figure 7.3 shows only slight accumulation of plasma creatine kinase (CK, an enzyme marker of myocellular injury) occurs during 2 hours of regional ischemia despite

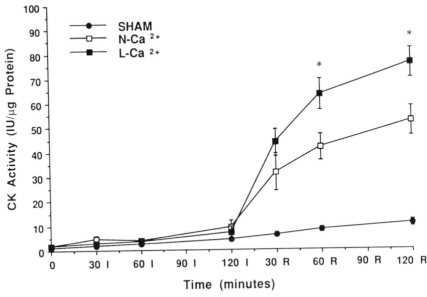

Figure 7.3. Plasma creatine kinase (*CK*) activity in sham, normocalcemic reperfused (*N-Ca²⁺*), and hypocalcemic reperfused (*L-Ca²⁺*) groups. Asterisk indicates $p < 0.05$ versus N-Ca²⁺ and sham. Time of ischemia (*I*) and reperfusion (*R*) are indicated in minutes on the abscissa. There was a very modest increase in creatine kinase activity during ischemia, a dramatic increase in creatine kinase activity during the first 30 minutes of reperfusion (with no intergroup difference), and greater creatine kinase release in the L-Ca²⁺ group after renormalization of blood [Ca²⁺] (60 and 120 minutes of reperfusion). T-bars represent SEM. (From Nakanishi K, Lefer DJ, Johnston WE, Vinten-Johansen J. Transient hypocalcemia during the initial phase of reperfusion extends myocardial necrosis after 2 hours of coronary occlusion. Cor Art Dis 1991;2:1009–1021.)

collateral blood flow sufficient to allow some degree of washout. However, CK release greatly increases during reperfusion. Secondly, the extent of CK washout can be significantly altered by reperfusion interventions. In this study, the extent of CK release as well as the infarct size were extended by regional hypocalcemia (31). In addition, there was an excellent correlation between the final postischemic creatine kinase accumulation and infarct size ($r = 0.86$). Numerous other studies have shown that injury can be reduced considerably by pharmacologic or mechanical interventions imposed during reperfusion or as an adjunct to the basic cardioplegic solution.

A number of mechanisms have been implicated in reperfusion injury, including generation of oxygen free radicals and radical metabolites from molecular oxygen (45, 58–60), activation of neutrophils and platelets, intracellular calcium accumulation, and development of microvascular injury with impaired blood flow. Pharmacologic agents or therapeutic regimens targeted specifically toward these participants in reperfusion injury must be administered before ischemia or before induction of cardioplegic arrest in order to be effective. However, it must be remembered that the stage for reperfusion injury is set by the severity of the preceding ischemia (49, 61): the more severe the ischemia (regional ischemia in evolving myocardial infarction, or poor myocardial protection stemming from failure to deliver cardioplegia beyond obstructions or failure to formulate a solution to meet specific needs), the more severe will be the ensuing reperfusion injury. Therefore, an appropriate "multitasking" strategy must be developed to prevent ischemic injury and avoid reperfusion injury.

Oxygen Radicals and Radical-Mediated Injury

Molecular oxygen (O_2, dioxygen) is relatively unreactive with biological com-

pounds by virtue of the shared electron pair in the outer molecular shell. However, oxygen-derived free radicals, defined as molecules in which one unpaired electron is added to the outer orbital shell of oxygen, are highly reactive with a broad spectrum of biological materials including sugars, amino acids, phospholipids, and DNA (60). With such a large constellation of target substrates, oxygen-derived free radicals and their metabolites are potentially toxic to cells, and are, in fact, central to the host defense and bactericidal activities of neutrophils (44). In the ischemic-reperfused myocardium, oxygen radical-induced injury includes peroxidation of lipid components of myocellular membranes leading to damage to mitochondria and sarcoplasmic reticulum (62, 63) and disruption of the vascular endothelium. These elements of myocellular injury contribute significantly to the pathologic processes leading to postischemic dysfunction (45), arrhythmias (64, 65), morphologic injury (60), and necrosis (44, 66).

SOURCES OF OXYGEN RADICALS

Molecular oxygen can undergo reduction to various radical species and related compounds by both enzymatic and nonenzymatic reactions. These reactions are listed in Table 7.1. The superoxide radical ($O_2^{\cdot}$) has a relatively high degree of reactivity with biological components, and is produced by a number of sources including mitochondria, the vascular endothelium, and activated neutrophils. The sequential univalent reduction of oxygen to H_2O (Table 7.1, equation 1) occurs in normal mitochondria of the myocyte at very low levels, but is greatly accelerated during ischemia and reperfusion (66–68). In addition, $O_2^{\cdot}$ is produced during the conversion of hypoxanthine and xanthine to uric acid by xanthine oxidase (Table 7.1, equation 2). Under normal conditions, this enzyme, which is localized in the vascular endothelium, is primarily in the dehydrogenase

Table 7.1.   Biochemical Reactions Involved in Production of Oxygen Free Radicals[a]

Equation 1:

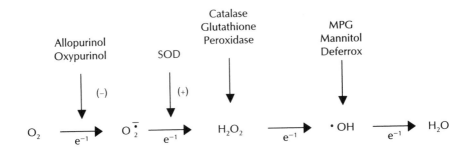

Equation 2:

(A) $Hypoxanthine + NAD^+ + H_2O \xrightarrow[\text{Dehydrogenase}]{\text{Xanthine}} Xanthine + NADH + H^+$

(B) $Hypoxanthine + H_2O + 2O_2 \xrightarrow[\text{Oxidase}]{\text{Xanthine}} Xanthine + 2O_2^{\cdot -} + 2H^+$

$Xanthine + H_2O + 2O_2 \xrightarrow[\text{Oxidase}]{\text{Xanthine}} Uric\ Acid + 2O_2^{\cdot -} + 2H^+$

Equation 3:

$Fe^{2+} + H_2O_2 \longrightarrow Fe^{3+} + {}^{\cdot}OH + H^+$

$Fe^{3+} + O_2^{\cdot -} \longrightarrow Fe^{2+} + O_2$

$H_2O_2 + O_2^{\cdot -} \longrightarrow {}^{\cdot}OH + OH^- + O_2$

Equation 4:

(A) $2O_2 + NADPH \xrightarrow[\text{Oxidase}]{\text{NADPH}} 2O_2^{\cdot -} + NADPH^+ + H^+$

(B) $2O_2^{\cdot -} + 2H^+ \longrightarrow H_2O_2 + O_2$

(C) $O_2^{\cdot -} + H_2O_2 \longrightarrow {}^{\cdot}OH + O_2 + OH^-$

(D) $H_2O_2 + C1^- \xrightarrow[\text{H}^+]{\text{Myeloperoxidase}} HOC1^- + H_2O$

Equation 5:

$LH + R^{\cdot} \longrightarrow L^{\cdot} + RH$ Initiation phase
   (i.e., peroxidation by ${}^{\cdot}OH$)

$L^{\cdot} + O_2 \longrightarrow LO_2^{\cdot}$ ⎤ Propagation
$LH + LO_2^{\cdot} \longrightarrow LOOH + L^{\cdot}$ ⎦ Phase

$L^{\cdot} + L^{\cdot} \longrightarrow LL$
$LO_2^{\cdot} + LO_2^{\cdot} \longrightarrow LOOL + O_2$ Termination
   Phase
$L_2^{\cdot} + L^{\cdot} \longrightarrow LOOL$

[a]L denotes lipid.

form and uses nicotinamide adenine dinucleotide as an electron acceptor (Table 7.1, equation 2A). During ischemia, however, two events favor the xanthine oxidase reaction: (1) hypoxanthine builds up as a result of the sequential catabolism of adenosine triphosphate (ATP) (69), and (2) the dehydrogenase form of the enzyme (70) is converted to the superoxide-producing oxidase form by a protease activated by intracellular calcium accumulation (60, 71, 72). Although xanthine oxidase is widely distributed in mammalian endothelial tissue, its presence is species-specific, and its accumulation and functional importance in man are both unclear (70, 73).

Other sources of oxygen-derived free radical production include oxidation of catecholamines, metabolism of arachidonic acid to peroxy compounds and hydroxyl radicals by the cyclooxygenase and lipoxygenase pathways, and the iron-requiring Haber-Weiss reactions. The latter series of reactions (summarized in Table 7.1, equation 3) may be important in the setting of cardiopulmonary bypass because this reaction is involved in granulocyte-mediated oxygen radical production (74). In addition, iron-containing products released by hemolysis during cardiopulmonary bypass may further facilitate any acellular formation of oxygen radicals by the Haber-Weiss reaction.

Activated neutrophils probably represent the major source of oxygen-derived free radicals, including the superoxide anion and hydrogen peroxide (74–77). Neutrophils are activated by various chemotactic factors (C3a and C5a anaphylatoxins, f-Met-Leu-Phe, interleukin 8, and platelet-activating factor) to generate a "respiratory burst" with an increase in oxygen consumption and activation of the hexose monophosphate shunt. Cardiopulmonary bypass activates the complement cascade (78, 79) with the resultant activation (80), and adherence-triggered release of cytotoxic products by neutrophils contribute to tissue injury in the ischemic-reperfused myocardium (81). During the respiratory burst that occurs seconds after stimulation, the superoxide anion is produced by a membrane-associated nicotinamide adenine dinucleotide phosphate oxidase, which transfers an electron to molecular oxygen (Table 7.1, equation 4A). Production of hydrogen peroxide (Table 7.1, equation 4B) by neutrophils or reduction of O_2^* to H_2O_2 by superoxide dismutase (SOD) provides substrate for generation of either the hydroxyl radical (Table 7.1, equation 4C) or the oxidant hypochlorous acid by myeloperoxidase (Table 1, equation 4D). Hypochlorous acid reacts with low molecular weight amines to give rise to lipophilic chloramines, which can promote membrane lipid peroxidation.

WHEN ARE OXYGEN RADICALS GENERATED?

Myocardial ischemia, whether produced globally by aortic cross-clamping or regionally by coronary artery occlusion, creates the environment necessary for generation of oxygen radicals. In addition, the tissue concentration of the endogenous antioxidants SOD, catalase, glutathione, and glutathione peroxidase are depleted during ischemia, thereby decreasing the natural defense mechanisms (58, 59, 82). Therefore, ischemia creates the biochemical setting for oxyradical production and the tissue vulnerability to oxygen radical-mediated damage. However, the primary substrate, oxygen, is in scant supply during ischemia and is not readily available until reperfusion. The appearance of oxyradical "bursts" at reperfusion is supported by both direct and indirect lines of evidence. Direct evidence of oxygen radical production in vivo has been obtained by measuring oxygen radical adducts with electron spin resonance spectroscopy using various spin trapping agents (83–85). These studies show that oxygen radicals are produced to some extent during ischemia, but that a dramatic burst of radical generation occurs during the early phase of reperfusion with a persistent production (46, 83) at a relatively lower rate for several hours thereafter (86). Indirect evidence to support this reperfusion burst comes from a wealth of data in which inhibitors or scavengers of oxygen radicals, or antineutrophil agents, were administered with beneficial effects.

Jolly et al. (87) corroborated the direct data (46, 83) that scavengers (SOD plus catalase) given before or during ischemia but before reperfusion reduced postischemic injury. In the surgical setting, the myocardium may be vulnerable to oxyradical-induced injury at several points when oxygen is potentially introduced into the myocardium: (a) the first delivery of cardioplegia to the heart suffering a period of unprotected ischemia preceding elective arrest, or the initial delivery of cardioplegia to a newly revascularized segment, (b) intermittent reinfusions of cardioplegia using a multidose regimen or with each transient reperfusion period if intermittent declamping is used, and (c) release of the cross-clamp during normothermic reperfusion and resuscitation. In addition, there are some data supporting a "late reperfusion injury" that may develop or be manifested postoperatively.

Neutrophils in Reperfusion Injury

Over the last 2 decades, an explosion of data has emerged indicating the neutrophil as a central player in myocardial ischemic-reperfusion injury (see references 88–90 for in-depth reviews). Sommers and Jennings (91) observed rapid neutrophil accumulation in ischemic-reperfused myocardium, which has also been confirmed by studies from our laboratory (Fig. 7.4A). We (31, 53, 57) and others (76, 92, 93) have demonstrated an association between the extent of postischemic injury and neutrophil accumulation within ischemic-reperfused myocardium and a reduction of postischemic injury associated with neutrophil suppression. Finally, as shown in Figure

7.4B, Lefer et al. (94) demonstrated that neutrophils accumulated within the myocardial region destined to become necrotic, and neutrophil accumulation occurred in advance of the development of necrosis, suggesting active participation in the demise of the cell rather than as a result of cell death.

The activation and migration of neutrophils to ischemic-reperfused myocardium requires interaction with chemotactic factors, most notably complement fragments (C3a and C5a), eicosanoid products such as leukotriene B_4, and platelet-activating factor. The anaphylatoxins C3a and C5a have been found in ischemic myocardium (95, 96) and have been shown to accumulate progressively during CPB (78). The level of chemotactic activity found in lymph during ischemia is proportional to the rate of neutrophil accumulation (97). Therefore, the possible activation and target-specific sequestration of neutrophils may be accentuated by cardiopulmonary bypass, myocardial ischemia, and reperfusion.

Neutrophils have a rather extensive repertoire of activity that may be recruited during delivery of blood cardioplegia or during reperfusion (after cross-clamp removal). Activated neutrophils are a primary source of deleterious oxygen radical species, including the superoxide anion, hydrogen peroxide, hydroxyl radical, and hypochlorous acid as discussed above. In addition, neutrophil activation may induce degranulation and release of proteases, proteolytic enzymes, and elastase. Third, activation of neutrophils by various chemotactic factors induces stiffening of the neutrophil, which impedes the deformability needed to negotiate passage through the microcirculation, promoting microembolization. Entrapment of neutrophils in the microcirculation may lead to impediments in regional blood flow distribution or a "no-reflow" phenomenon (89, 98, 99). Finally, neutrophils have been indirectly

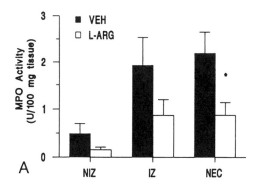

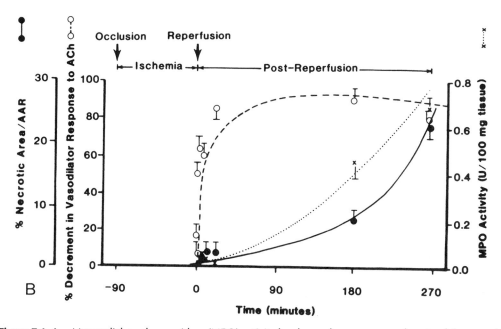

Figure 7.4. A. Myocardial myeloperoxidase (MPO) activity levels, used as a measure of neutrophil accumulation in the nonischemic zone (*NIZ*), ischemic but nonnecrotic zone (*IZ*), and ischemic necrotic (*NEC*) zone identified by triphenyltetrazolium chloride staining. The canine model of 1 hour collateral deficient (diversion of collateral blood flow) regional ischemia followed by 4.5 hours of reperfusion was used. Myeloperoxidase activity
was greater in the *IZ* and *NEC* than in the *NIZ,* and significantly reduced in dogs treated with intracoronary L-arginine (L-ARG) as precursor of endothelial nitric oxide. *VEH,* vehicle (saline). (From Nakanishi K, Vinten-Johansen
J, Lefer DJ, et al. Intracoronary L-arginine during reperfusion improves regional function and reduces infarct size.
Am J Physiol, 1992;263:H1650–H1658.) **B.** Time course (minutes) of the decrement in vasodilator responses
to acetylcholine (ACh) in isolated coronary artery rings (o----o), myocardial myeloperoxidase (MPO) activity
(x----x), and size of the necrotic area relative to the area at risk (AAR), •—•, after 90 minutes of ischemia (indicated
as 0 minutes of reperfusion) and at various intervals of reperfusion. Mean ± SEM for five to seven experiments.
(From Lefer AM, Tsao PS, Lefer DJ, MA X-L. Role of endothelial dysfunction in the pathogenesis of reperfusion injury after myocardial ischemia. FASEB J 1991;5:2029–2034.)

implicated in the etiology of postischemic edema. Edema occurs primarily
at the time of reperfusion (33, 100); the
extent of edema is roughly proportional
to the population of accumulated neutrophils (101) and agranulocytosis decreases the extent of edema (102). Interventions designed to attenuate neutro-
phil-related injury will be discussed
later.

Calcium-Related Injury

The excessive intracellular accumulation of calcium ions (Ca^{2+}) during reperfusion is a major mechanism of reperfusion injury leading to severe or lethal myocardial injury. Measurement of intracellular calcium shows little gain during moderate periods of ischemia (103, 104). However, intracellular Ca^{2+} gain occurs during reperfusion by a dramatic uncontrolled influx of Ca^{2+} and loss of sarcoplasmic reticular Ca^{2+} to the cytosol (103, 104). Accumulation of intracellular Ca^{2+} has a number of deleterious effects that may lead to severe myocellular damage or necrosis. High-energy phosphate stores may be depleted by both an acceleration in ATP utilization by Ca^{2+}-activated ATPases and a reduction in mitochondrial ATP production. In addition, increased intracellular Ca^{2+} levels may activate key enzymes that catalyze injurious processes. Examples of these processes are activation of membrane phospholipases, thereby promoting membrane disruption, and conversion of xanthine dehydrogenase to the oxygen radical-producing enzyme xanthine oxidase. Furthermore, elevated intracellular Ca^{2+} levels in the myocyte may alter Ca^{2+}-kinetics of excitation-contraction coupling or Ca cycling between the contractile apparatus and the sarcoplasmic reticulum, leading to contracture ("stone heart").

There are several mechanisms by which extracellular Ca^{2+} may enter the cell which impact on the therapeutic modality chosen to address Ca^{2+} accumulation and consequent injury: (*a*) diffusion through overt membrane disruptions or opened Ca^{2+} channels, fueled by the differential concentration gradient for Ca^{2+}; (*b*) facilitated entry via a-adrenoreceptor whose population increases and is heightened during postischemic catecholamine release; and (*c*) reversal or inhibition of the forward direction of the Na^+-Ca^{2+} exchanger driven by the intracellular accumulation of sodium (105–107) and causing a net accumulation of Ca^{2+}. The diffusion of Ca^{2+} from the extracellular space to the cytosol, and Ca^{2+} entry via the Na^+-Ca^{2+} exchange mechanism are two entry routes that may be curbed by reducing extracellular Ca^{2+} directly, i.e., chelating agents such as citrate and ethylene glycol bis(β-aminoethylether)-N,N,N',N'-tetraacetic acid. Reduction of extracellular Ca^{2+} during reperfusion would narrow the transarcolemmal concentration gradient. In addition, calcium influx via the Na^+-Ca^{2+} exchange mechanism may be prevented because the rate and direction of the exchange system are sensitive to both intracellular Na^+ and extracellular Ca^{2+} (108). As will be expanded further below, the beneficial effects of hypocalcemia by chelation may depend on the presence of hyperkalemia (31, 107).

Hydrodynamics of Reperfusion and the No-Reflow Phenomenon

In addition to the aforementioned determinants of reperfusion injury, recent studies have shown that the hydrodynamic conditions under which reperfusion is initiated (coronary pressure and blood flow) will determine in part the functional and morphologic destiny of the ischemic-reperfused myocardium (109–112). Ischemia places the microcirculation in a "leaky" state which allows both extravasation of fluid into the extravascular spaces and intracellular water accumulation. However, the absence of a significant perfusion pressure during ischemia prevents a large-scale migration of fluid out of the extravascular space, and edema fails to accumulate significantly (33). With reperfusion, the Starling forces regarding transcapillary fluid movement are altered in favor of fluid migration and accumulation in interstitial spaces (edema).

The combined effects of endothelial cell swelling and extravascular compression of capillaries by tissue edema may cause severe impairment of microvascular perfusion and precipitate a no-reflow response (98, 109). Using a canine model of 2 hours of coronary occlusion and 2 hours of reperfusion, Vinten-Johansen et al. (109, 110) showed that abrupt restoration of coronary perfusion pressure to systemic levels was associated with a progressive diminution of early microvascular reactive hyperemia to 50% of preischemic blood flow. In contrast, gradual restoration of coronary reperfusion pressure over the first 30 minutes of reperfusion preserved postischemic reactive hyperemic flow, reduced infarct size, and improved segmental systolic and diastolic function even after restoring normal perfusion pressures. Although some studies present convincing data that no-reflow is a reperfusion phenomenon that can contribute to the evolution of infarction, it is clear that control over conditions of reperfusion significantly mitigate postischemic damage (31, 32, 54, 57, 113, 114).

Manifestations of Reperfusion Injury.

Although reperfusion injury is undoubtedly a highly complex process with many pathophysiological facets, its manifestations can be grouped into several categories (20, 49).

REPERFUSION ARRHYTHMIAS

Arrhythmias precipitated following reperfusion are manifested by premature ventricular contractions and ventricular fibrillation. Failure to spontaneously resume sinus rhythm or persistence of arrhythmias requiring countershock and antiarrhythmic therapy are common consequences of poor myocardial protection either globally, in the area of the pacemaker sites, or distal to severe occlusions where cardioplegic solutions are not well distributed. A number of mechanisms have been implicated in the etiology of reperfusion arrhythmias. First, as with many reperfusion-related events, the incidence and severity of reperfusion

arrhythmias are related to the severity (blood flow deficit and duration) of the preceding ischemia. The relationship resembles a bell-shaped response curve in which maximal vulnerability to reperfusion arrhythmias occurs after short intervals of normothermic ischemia, and wanes as irreversible injury and electrical inexcitability develop with more prolonged periods of ischemia (20, 65). Second, an accumulation of intracellular calcium during ischemia may precipitate calcium cycling and hence calcium-dependent arrhythmias (115). Third, oxygen-derived free radicals such as superoxide anion and hydroxyl radical, produced as a respiratory burst during reperfusion, may damage membrane lipids and various transport proteins involved in ionic homeostasis, which in turn may precipitate reperfusion-related arrhythmias (116). Current hypotheses merge the calcium-related events and the oxygen-free radical events as "interacting triggers" for reperfusion arrhythmias (117, 118).

POSTISCHEMIC SYSTOLIC AND DIASTOLIC DYSFUNCTION

It is clear that reperfusion with unmodified blood following relatively short periods of unprotected regional (31–33, 46, 54, 56) or global (114, 119) ischemia produces a severe degree of contractile dysfunction (Fig. 7.2). Postischemic contractile function may be independent of any observable morphologic injury and may therefore be "stunned" (120) for a period of time. This postischemic dysfunction has been thought to be due to depletion of high-energy phosphate stores (i.e., ATP), although numerous studies have failed to show a direct correlation between postischemic ATP and functional recovery (32, 121, 122). The ATP turnover rate, roughly approximated by the myocardial oxygen consumption, may be more important than the static tissue level of ATP. Postischemic regional and global oxygen consumption may be near normal (41) or augmented

(35, 36, 123) despite significantly reduced levels of ATP. Although segmental work may account for these relatively elevated oxygen consumptions in the newly reperfused segment following reversible coronary occlusion, elevated global oxygen consumptions in vented bypassed (nonworking) hearts may be secondary to cellular reparative processes (123) or altered rate of internal work (internal power) against structural resistance elements. Alternatively, postischemic contractile dysfunction has been related to impairment of calcium kinetics in excitation-contraction coupling and in the sarcoplasmic reticulum (62, 63).

In addition to these pathologic etiologies of postischemic systolic dysfunction, iatrogenic impairment may occur as a result of systemic hemodilution and hyperkalemia, or as a result of systemic hypocalcemia from calcium chelating agents used in cardioplegia solutions (124). Although the use of inotropic agents immediately after removal of the aortic cross-clamp may be deleterious (125), delayed inotropic therapy or correction of systemic hypocalcemia (i.e., 15 to 30 minutes after removal of the cross-clamp) may counteract a significant portion of postischemic dysfunction without metabolic penalty (124, 126). Therefore, it may be safe to apply inotropic agents after a period of reperfusion (aortic unclamping) conducted while on total CPB, i.e., while completing proximal anastomoses, and after the most vulnerable period for reperfusion injury has passed.

Myocardial compliance, the inverse of stiffness, is highly sensitive to ischemia and reperfusion (33). In the myocardial segment subjected to ischemia, there is a rightward shift in the position of the end-diastolic pressure-segment length relations with little change in the shape or curvature of the end-diastolic pressure-length relation (Fig. 7.5, A and B), which is consistent with the concept of regional myocardial creep (31, 33, 53). In contrast to ischemia, reperfusion is associated with immediate loss of myocardial compliance character-

ized by a reversal in positional shift to the left (indicating a relative degree of "contracture") and an increase in the slope of the exponential end-diastolic pressure-length relation indicative of decreased compliance (31, 33, 53). A similar pattern is observed with global ischemia (Fig. 7.5C). In several studies, hearts made vulnerable to ischemic-reperfusion injury by 30 minutes of normothermic ischemia and subsequently protected by 1 hour of hypothermic multidose blood cardioplegia show a rightward shift in the end-diastolic pressure-dimension relations (dilation) and decreased chamber compliance (17, 35, 36, 114, 124). Avoidance of loss of compliance will be discussed later.

MYOCELLULAR NECROSIS

Whether reperfusion kills cells that at the time were reversibly damaged and theoretically salvageable before reperfusion was initiated is at the very crux of the reperfusion injury controversy. Demonstration of cell viability and "salvage" in the multidimensional and dynamic process of myocellular necrosis is fraught with its own problems. Are markers such as enzyme release (creatine kinase, lactate dehydrogenase) accurate in assessing myocardial injury in global models, as well as capable of providing chronological "repeated measures" snapshots of developing injury? Does conventional electron microscopy introduce artifactual injury to the tissue, leading to the conclusion that irreversible injury has been sustained? Does a reduction in any marker of injury represent a permanent reduction in the extent of myocellular injury or simply a delay in the progression of necrosis? This latter point is important to distinguish because some agents merely delay the time course of injury with no ultimate reduction of infarct size or salvage of myocytes (20), although a delay in myocellular demise does have important implications for the patient with a stormy postoperative course early after the discontinuation of bypass.

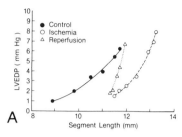

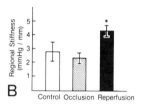

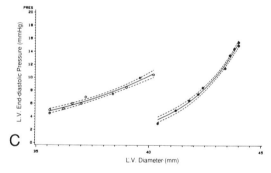

Figure 7.5. A. The curvilinear end-diastolic pressure-segment length relation before (control), after 1 hour of left anterior descending coronary artery occlusion (ischemia), and after 2 hours of reperfusion in an in situ working canine heart. Note the rightward shift in the relation without any apparent shift in the slope or contour during ischemia. After reperfusion, a more leftward position is assumed with an increase in the rate of curvature. LVEDP, left ventricular end-diastolic pressure. (From Vinten-Johansen J, Johnston WE, Mills SA, et al. Reperfusion injury after temporary coronary occlusion. J Thorac Cardiovasc Surg 1988;95:960–968.) **B.** Summary of the rate of curvature of the end-diastolic pressure-length relation when curvature was determined at an end-diastolic pressure of 4 mm Hg (termed operative muscle stiffness). Muscle stiffness significantly increased only after reperfusion. *, P < 0.05. **C.** Global normothermic ischemia produced by aortic cross-clamp was followed by 1 hour of multidose hypothermic blood cardioplegia. Global left ventricular (LV) end-diastolic pressure-minor axis di-

OTHER MANIFESTATIONS OF REPERFUSION INJURY

With severe postischemic injury, reperfusion results in incomplete restoration of myocardial perfusion to the involved myocardium. This no-reflow or "incomplete-reflow" phenomenon has been observed primarily in myocardium placed at risk by a coronary occlusion (89, 98) and localized within the necrotic tissue (109, 110), but may have a counterpart in surgical ischemia and reperfusion, particularly in revascularized myocardium. Postischemic no-reflow may develop secondary to microvascular damage and endothelial edema, microvascular embolization caused by platelets, thrombi, vascular debris or adherent neutrophils, or lastly by extravascular compression due to regional or global edema and/or contracture. Although some studies suggest that a no-reflow pathology was established before the myocardium was reperfused (127), other studies (98), including one from our laboratory (109), show that an early reactive hyperemia in subsequently infarcted tissue progressively deteriorates during the reperfusion period. Whether vascular no-reflow is a result of necrosis or a cause of "secondary" ischemia leading to a time-dependent extension of the necrotic envelope is not clear. Such a no-reflow phenomenon would be particularly relevant to surgically revascularized (coronary artery bypass grafting) evolving infarcts where strategies of myocardial protection including moderate cardioplegia delivery pressures (128), hyperosmolar

ameter (sonomicrometers) relations during gradual preload reduction in preischemic state (O) and 30 minutes after reperfusion (●). Notice the rightward shift in the postischemic relation relative to control, indicative of chamber dilation. (From Vinten-Johansen J, Chiantella V, Johnston WE, et al. Adjuvant N-(2-mercaptoproprionyl)-glycine in blood cardioplegia does not improve myocardial protection in ischemically damaged hearts. J Thorac Cardiovasc Surg 1990;100:65–76.)

composition of cardioplegia solutions, and antileukocyte therapy may limit tissue injury related to postischemic no-reflow phenomenon.

Other Victims of Ischemia and Reperfusion

The general assumption has been that the consequences of ischemic-reperfusion injury affect primarily the cardiac myocyte. However, recent data indicate that ischemia and reperfusion affect other cell types in the heart, and that the degree of injury sustained by these other tissues determines in part the severity of postischemic myocardial injury. For example, the vascular endothelium sustains significant injury from ischemia and reperfusion (129–131) and may be the primary site of complement activation and neutrophil activity after ischemia and reperfusion. In one form, the injury is expressed as an attenuated release or production of the endothelium-derived relaxing factor, nitric oxide (NO) (130), and exaggerated neutrophil-endothelial interaction. Tsao et al. (92) have shown that this endothelial dysfunction occurs primarily during the early phase (2.5 minutes) of reperfusion, and may therefore be a significant component of reperfusion injury. Nitric oxide has been implicated as a protective autocoid elaborated by the vascular endothelium (132). Nitric oxide inhibits platelet aggregation (133) and neutrophil adherence (134), and possibly neutralizes the superoxide anion. Therefore, NO may play an important role in controlling these elements of reperfusion injury; this endogenous protective capability may be lost after ischemia-reperfusion. However, the prevention or reversibility of endothelial dysfunction by reperfusion therapy is not clear. In recent studies from our laboratory, we have shown that endothelial dysfunction after short-term (60 minutes) regional ischemia can be reversed by supplementation of the NO-precursor L-arginine (53) or the NO

donor SPM-5185 (57) with an associated decrease in infarct size.

These data on endothelial protection by NO-generating agents raise a number of tantalizing possibilities for improving the outcome in ischemic-reperfusion injury secondary to global ischemia, including mechanisms prolonging patency of vascular grafts and the use of precursors and donors of NO as adjunct agents in cardioplegia solutions. The greater preservation of patency of the internal mammary artery over saphenous vein grafts (135, 136) may be related to the better endothelial function in arterial grafts (137), related to elaboration of NO by arterial endothelial cells (138), dysfunction of venous endothelium after ischemia and reperfusion (139), or mechanical distension during saphenous vein harvest (140). The addition of nitroglycerin (although a poor NO donor requiring thiol groups for release of the NO moiety) to cardioplegia may reduce postischemic injury by NO-related mechanisms in addition to its more conventional vasodilatory function. The role of the coronary vascular endothelium and NO donor agents in mitigating ischemic-reperfusion injury in the surgical setting remains to be clarified.

PRINCIPLES OF MYOCARDIAL PROTECTION

Asystole

Ischemia rapidly depletes the myocardial high-energy phosphate pool, which initiates a complex cascade of ionic, biochemical, and morphologic sequences leading to potentially lethal injury. Continued electromechanical activity after cross-clamping accelerates the rate of high-energy phosphate depletion, causing a more rapid decrease in ATP reserves before anoxic arrest ensues. Biochemical changes initiated by anoxic arrest increase the severity of ischemia and consequent reperfusion injury within a short period of time. The intentional chemical induction of diastolic arrest avoids the depletion of the high-energy phosphate pool and conserves the myocardial energy reserves (Fig. 7.6), which can be utilized during the period of ischemia to maintain ionic and metabolic homeostasis and, consequently, better tolerate ischemia. The mechanism underlying the conservation of energy stores by inducing immediate arrest is illustrated in Figure 7.7. Relative to the working heart generating normal intracavitary blood pressures and stroke volumes, induction of total electromechanical silence diminishes the oxygen demands by approximately 80 to 90%; 30 to 40% of this decrease in O_2 demands is contributed by ventricular decompression and the remainder is contributed by asystole accomplished by chemical cardioplegia. The maintenance of asystole by intermittent infusions allows the comparatively inefficient generation of ATP from anaerobic metabolism to be channeled to support cellular metabolism rather than diverted to useless contractile activity. Studies have confirmed that chemically induced cardioplegia prevents the depletion of high-energy phosphate stores caused by persistent electromechanical activity and

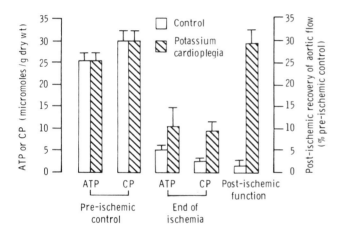

Figure 7.6. The conservation of myocardial ATP and creatine phosphate (CP) by rapid induction of diastolic arrest using chemical cardioplegia in isolated rat heart model. One group of rat hearts (n=6) were perfused with a cardioplegic solution containing 16 mmol/liter potassium (hatched bars) to induce arrest, while a second group was perfused with a normokalemic physiologic solution (open bars). Both groups were then subjected to 30 minutes of normothermic ischemia. At the end of ischemia, ATP and CP were higher in the chemical cardioplegia group compared with the anoxic arrested group, and postischemic function was superior. (From Hearse DJ. The protection of the ischemic myocardium: surgical process v clinical failure? Prog Cardiovasc Dis 1988;30:381–402.)

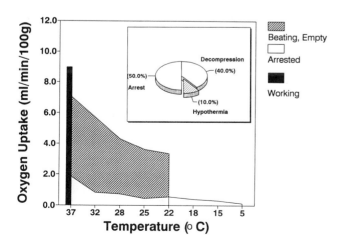

Figure 7.7. The oxygen requirements of the continuously perfused heart at 37°C at various stages of hypothermia in the decompressed beating (beating empty, hatched area) and arrested state (stippled area). Oxygen requirements of the working heart at 37°C are shown for comparison. Inset shows the percent reduction in O_2 requirements contributed by ventricular decompression, total chemical asystole, and hypothermia to 10°C relative to those of the working heart. As discussed in the text, only minor reductions in myocardial O_2 demand are accomplished by more profound hypothermia below 22°C.

allows greater postischemic functional recovery compared to ischemic (anoxic) arrest, even when intermittently applied (17, 141, 142).

Rapid asystole is induced by a number of methods, including hyperkalemia, hypermagnesemia, hypocalcemia (143) or calcium channel antagonism (144), and infusion of local anesthetic agents. Hyperkalemia is currently the most common method employed to induce cardioplegia. Exogenous potassium depolarizes the myocyte membrane, rendering the myocardium unexcitable during the time that potassium remains within the tissue. Washout of hyperkalemic cardioplegic solutions by noncoronary collateral flow permits resumption of both electrical and mechanical activity, which may escape detection and which can be counteracted by intermittent (every 20 to 30 minutes) replenishment of cardioplegic solutions. Such a multidose approach to infusion of cardioplegia solutions maintains or reestablishes electromechanical silence, restores hypothermia, temporarily provides the ischemic myocardium with oxygen and nutrients, and washes out metabolites. Potassium concentrations in cardioplegic solutions usually ranging from 12 to 30 mEq/liter are typically used to achieve cardiac standstill within 1 to 2 minutes. The optimal degree of hyperkalemia is difficult to assess because of the dependency of postischemic function, metabolism, and morphology on a multitude of interacting factors. However, hypothermia reduces the concentration of potassium required to achieve arrest. Therefore, higher potassium concentrations are used to arrest the heart with normothermic induction techniques (113, 145) or to maintain arrest during 28°C "reperfusion cardioplegia" delivered just before aortic declamping, than with intermittent infusions of 4°C cardioplegia. Potassium concentrations above 40 mEq/liter should be avoided because of the potential for tissue and vascular endothelial damage

related to calcium influx and accumulation.

The central role played by calcium in excitation-contraction coupling and ischemic-reperfusion injury have, in part, determined the evolution of myoprotective strategies. The active participation of calcium ions in the pathogenesis of ischemic-reperfusion injury has particularly enticed the greatest attention in minimizing this aspect of surgical ischemia. However, relatively little attention has been focused on dislocating the electromechanical coupling properties of calcium as a mechanism to achieve cardiac arrest. Calcium is necessary to transduce the electrical signal into a mechanical event; removal of calcium from the extracellular environment produces a negative inotropic effect, culminating in the cessation of contractile activity at extremely low levels of extracellular ionic calcium concentration (146). In 1959, Clark et al. (143) used hypocalcemic blood to initiate sustained normothermic arrest without apparent "gross evidence of damage." Others have used potassium citrate as the arresting agent (146). The "intracellular type" cardioplegic solution formulated by Bretschneider et al. (147) achieved mechanical arrest by virtue of combined hyponatremia and acalcemia. However, numerous studies in modern literature demonstrate morphologic damage to the normal myocardium resulting from extracellular ionic calcium concentrations below 0.05 mM, the so-called "calcium paradox" (148).

That the ischemic myocardium is more sensitive to calcium-related injury is emphasized by the greater extent of injury sustained compared to a nonischemic heart, or by lower extracellular Ca^{2+} concentration necessary to produce injury (31, 148, 149). The threat of precipitating such deleterious consequences with hypocalcemia for the purpose of temporarily arresting the heart may have contributed to its initial abandonment. Antagonists of the calcium slow channels, i.e., verapamil, nifedipine, diltiazem, lidoflazine, etc., may theoretically achieve electromechanical dissociation by preventing voltage-gated calcium influx through slow channels. However, the slow induction of cardioplegia, the high concentrations of blocking agents necessary to reliably achieve arrest, and the persistent half-life of the drugs would potentially create chronotropic and inotropic depression postoperatively. Therefore, calcium channel antagonism as the primary means of inducing elective cardiac arrest has found limited application. However, certain channel blockers such as verapamil have found application in supplementing asystolic arrest as well as inhibiting calcium influx in certain clinical situations (i.e., hypertrophy).

Cardiac Hypothermia

Since its introduction in the 1950s (6, 150), hypothermia has been an important component of myocardial preservation. The effects of hypothermia on the myocardium are complex and must be considered in their positive and negative aspects as summarized in Table 7.2. Many of the negative aspects of hypothermia are eliminated by using adjunctive cardioplegic arrest. For example, the paradoxical increase in inotropic state (151) and oxygen demands per beat, and the possible induction of fibrillation by hypothermia (152) are avoided when cardiac arrest is achieved before or simultaneous with the induction of hypothermia. Although a number of the physiologic effects of hypothermia listed in Table 7.2 appear to contradict the concepts of myocardial protection, the net myoprotective effects are clear: the pathogenetic tide of ischemia is stemmed and the unwelcome consequences of surgical ischemic-reperfusion injury are thereby limited.

The major myoprotective mechanisms of hypothermia are the reduction in metabolic rate and oxygen demands of the myocardium, as illustrated in Figure 7.7. Hypothermia per se (i.e., with sustained mechanical activity) may reduce myocardial oxygen consumption (MVo_2) by only 10%. However, in combination with cardiac arrest, hypothermia reduces MVo_2 by 97% if profound (4°C) cooling is achieved. The relationship between myocardial consumption and temperature is relatively exponential, as shown in Figure 7.7. Generally, the relationship conforms to Van't Hoff's law or the Q_{10} effect, whereby MVo_2 in the quiescent heart decreases by 50% for every 10°C reduction in temperature. The greatest reduction in MVo_2 in the quiescent heart occurs between 37° and 25°C, with a relatively small decrease in energy requirements achieved with lower myocardial tem-

Table 7.2. Positive and Negative Physiologic Effects of Hypothermia on the Myocardium

Positive	Negative
Decreases myocardial metabolism	Decreases rate of reparative processes
Decreases oxygen requirements	Increases myocellular swelling by altering Donnan equilibrium of Cl and inhibiting Na-K-ATPase
Decreases rate of degradative reactions	Increases inotropic state and MVo_2 per beat
Retards progression of ischemic injury	Induces fibrillation
Increases the tolerable period of ischemia	Impairs o_2 dissociation
Reduces [K^+] necessary to accomplish arrest	Impairs autoregulation
Prolongs arrest	Poses threat of epicardial and phrenic nerve "freeze injury"
Does not alter transmural blood flow distribution	Promotes rouleau formation of erythrocytes
Inhibits intracellular Ca^{2+} gain	Decreases membrane fluidity
	Inhibits sarcoplasmic reticulum sequestration of Ca^{2+}

peratures. The reduction in basal metabolic requirements of the heart during chemical cardioplegic arrest increases both the tolerance of ischemia of a given period of time as well as expands the window of safe ischemic time.

Myocardial hypothermia, by reducing the basal metabolic rate in proportion to the temperature achieved, decreases the oxygen deficit during elective ischemia and thereby retards the dynamic progression of ischemic injury. The degree of protection conferred by hypothermia is positively related to the myocardial temperatures achieved during chemically induced cardioplegia (16, 153). Figure 7.8 shows the curvilinear profile of postischemic function (aortic flow) after 60 minutes of global ischemia at the temperatures indicated on

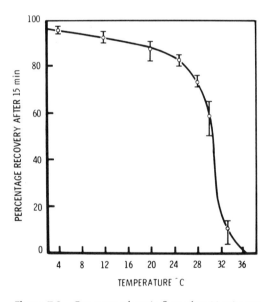

Figure 7.8. Recovery of aortic flow after 60 minutes of global ischemia induced by hyperkalemic cardioplegia at the temperature indicated on the abscissa. The model used was the isolated-perfused working rat heart, ejecting against a hydrostatic pressure of 100 cm H_2O. Notice that the greatest recovery of postischemic function occurred at temperatures below 24 to 28°C. Relatively little additional protection is gained from more profound levels (below 24°C). (From Hearse DJ. The protection of the ischemic myocardium: surgical proces?s v clinical failure? Prog Cardiovasc Dis 1988;30:381–402.)

the abscissa (16). For a given ischemic interval, the greatest preservation occurred at temperatures below 28°C, with little additional protection achieved with lower temperatures. Rosenfeldt (153) showed a similar preservation of high-energy phosphate stores at 28°C or lower. The inflection point occurring at 28°C in the temperature-functional recovery relation where the degree of protection is dramatically increased by hypothermia may be related to the greater reduction in oxygen demands that is gained between 37°C and 28°C (Fig. 7.7), but may also be related to interaction of myocardial temperature and membrane fluidity characteristics. Because the difference in o_2 demands between 22°C and 4°C are relatively minor, small differences in regional or global myocardial temperature may be well tolerated, provided that other principles of myocardial protection (reduction of o_2 demands, hypocalcemia, etc.) are observed and impediments to the delivery of cardioplegia are overcome in a timely manner. However, this should not give license to ignore the overall importance of hypothermia, because hypothermia is the primary means by which the metabolic ongoing processes are effectively limited after arrest is achieved.

Many reports suggest that hypothermia more profound than 22°C does not significantly reduce the oxygen demands of the quiescent heart (10) or fails to improve the degree of myoprotection during moderate durations of cardioplegia (16). The benefits of more profound levels of hypothermia may not be apparent unless prolonged durations of ischemia are imposed, i.e., 4 to 6 hours, as shown in Figure 7.2 (28, 153–156) Therefore, the surgeon does not need to be preoccupied with achieving the lowest levels of hypothermia possible, but must ensure a reasonable degree of myocardial cooling and ensure timely induction of local hypothermia in regions of the heart where distribution of cardioplegic solution has been compromised (i.e., infusion through grafts). Rewarming of myocardium due to heat absorption from the environment or from noncoronary collateral perfusion may be counteracted by combining intermittent reinfusions of cardioplegic solutions with topical hypothermia. However, concern has been expressed over the issue of cold injury to the heart (edema, morphologic alterations) and to extracardiac structures (phrenic nerve injury) (157–159). Hypothermia per se, when induced by infusion techniques, is not deleterious (160).

The edema observed following infusion of hypothermic cardioplegic solutions (161, 162) is of complex etiology and may in part be related to the osmolality of the solution used or to sodium accumulation secondary to a temporary inhibition of the sodium-potassium-ATPase pump. This edema may be transient and readily reversible after reperfusion (161). Topical saline slush or ice chips may be applied to resist myocardial rewarming in the intervals between infusions of cardioplegic solutions. However, application of extremely cold saline chips without saline slush (temperature <0°C) may produce severe postischemic dysfunction and mitochondrial damage in the experimental setting (153). Hypothermia may be safely maintained by coronary infusion techniques or pericardial lavage.

It must be emphasized that the benefits of diastolic arrest and hypothermia are additive (163–166), each component contributing to the total protection of the heart. Hypothermia alone, without imposing cardiac quiescence, is less effective in protecting the heart because the residual contractile activity preceding anoxic arrest elevates the oxygen requirements and places the oxygen supply/demand status in a vulnerable imbalance, which may be further aggravated by a positive inotropic effect of hypothermia (10, 151). The benefits of simultaneous diastolic arrest in hypothermia are likely derived from mechanisms that are complementary to each other, and together reduce the severity of ensuing surgical is-

chemia. While reduction of cardiac workload by combined CPB with decompression and asystole reduces o_2 demands by 90% or more (Fig. 7.7), the accrual of an oxygen debt related to continued metabolism during the ischemic interval is significantly diminished by hypothermia. Therefore, the greatest degree of myocardial protection is achieved by combining hypothermia with chemical cardioplegia. Normothermic cardioplegia may be used to overcome some of the disadvantages of hypothermia (113, 167–175) listed in Table 7.2.

Hypocalcemia

As reviewed in a previous section ("Calcium-related Injury"), calcium plays a central role in the pathogenesis of postischemic injury, probably involving changes in calcium kinetics and intracellular concentration during both the ischemic and reperfusion phases. Any therapeutic strategy targeted at alleviating calcium-related injury must take into consideration the time course of calcium involvement, particularly with regard to the potential time points of injury shown in Figure 7.1 and the routes of entry. A number of studies have established the importance of precisely adjusting the calcium content in cardioplegic solutions (114, 176–178). However, arriving at the optimal calcium content for all solutions used is virtually impossible because of compositional differences and interactions between components of various solutions used in clinical practices. The ideal concentration must be tailored to each solution used (i.e., blood versus crystalloid). First, the dose-response for calcium is a bell-shaped curve, and the window for the appropriate calcium concentration is often sharply delineated with declining protection observed on either side of the peak (114, 176). Greater injury can result if hypocalcemia is profound, i.e., below 50 µM. Second, the effects of calcium in cardioplegia or reperfusate not only depend on its concentration, but also on complex interactions with other constituents such as Na^+ (107), K^+ (31, 179), Mg^{2+} (179), the degree of hypothermia, and on catecholamine release (180), which may alter the pathogenesis of and vulnerability to ischemic-reperfusion injury.

The need to precisely control calcium is not as apparent in the in vivo or clinical settings where calcium contained in noncoronary collateral blood may alter the precisely adjusted calcium content of the solution. Jacocks et al. (181) and Engelman et al. (182) demonstrated no difference in postischemic functional recovery between calcium-free and calcium-containing crystalloid cardioplegic solutions. However, in other in vivo systems, a calcium paradox can be precipitated in ischemic myocardium by moderate hypocalcemia (31, 149) with resultant accentuated injury. For example, Nakanishi et al. (31) have shown that hypocalcemic reperfusion, without alterations in any other blood constituent, extended infarct size after reversible coronary occlusion. This observation is dramatically opposed to numerous studies attesting to the safety of hypocalcemic cardioplegia. The authors speculated that hyperkalemia may be required as an adjunct to hypocalcemia in order for the benefits of hypocalcemia to be realized. Based on studies by Tani and Neely (106), high extracellular potassium indirectly inhibits intracellular Ca^{2+} accumulation via the Na^+-Ca^{2+} exchange mechanisms. Therefore, the fortuitous interaction between hypocalcemia and hyperkalemia in cardioplegic solutions may allow maximal expression of the benefits of hypocalcemic reperfusion.

The reduction of extracellular Ca^{2+} by direct chelation is a modality that would potentially restrict transmembrane influx regardless of route of entry, and is a common practice in myocardial protective strategies employing cardioplegic solutions. Sodium citrate, often obtained in combination with phosphate and dextrose for storage of blood, is the most popular agent used to chelate Ca^{2+}. This agent, however, is relatively nonspecific for Ca^{2+} and may chelate other divalent cations as well, including Mg^{2+}. In addition, citrate is a direct inhibitor of glycolysis (183), upon which the ischemic myocardium depends when depletion of the tissue oxygen stores by ischemia limits aerobic metabolism. However, the benefits of hypocalcemia with citrate apparently override its potential negative effects since myocardial protection is adequate when citrate is used. However, alternative chelators (i.e., EGTA) should be explored as more specific chelators of Ca^{2+} in blood cardioplegic solutions.

Oxygen Radical Therapy

Therapy targeted toward reducing oxyradical-induced injury must take into consideration several factors, including the time during the operative course when oxygen radicals are generated, the source of the oxygen radicals (endothelial cell, neutrophil, myocyte), and the species of radical toward which the intervention is directed. These considerations are discussed later. In general, the choice of pharmacologic intervention should consider the cascade of oxygen radical generation shown in Table 7.1, equation 1. The therapeutic agents targeting specific oxyradical species are also represented on this scheme. Table 7.3 summarizes the various biological species of oxygen radical, their sources, and scavengers or inhibitors. Although H_2O_2 is technically not an oxygen radical, it is an important transitional molecule in the oxygen radical cascade, and is involved in ischemic-reperfusion injury.

Since the infusion of cardioplegia is a form of reperfusion during which the key sources for oxyradical production (oxygen, as well as neutrophils in blood cardioplegia) are delivered to the myocardium, scavengers and enzymes that inhibit or dismutate oxyradicals would be most effective if administered as a pretreatment therapy, or as an additive to the cardioplegic solution.

Table 7.3. Sources and Scavengers or Inhibitors of Various Species of Oxygen Free Radicals

Species	Source	Scavenger/Inhibitor[a]
$\cdot O_2^-$	Neutrophils endothelium mitochondria	SOD,[*] allopurinol, nonsteroidal antiinflammatory agents (ibuprofen, BW755C, BAY K6575, indomethacin) a-tocopherol, ascorbate,[*] MPG, NO[*]
H_2O_2	Neutrophils mitochondria	Catalase,[*] glutathione peroxidase,[*] reduced glutathione[*]
$\cdot OH$	Mitochondria Haber-Weiss	MPG, DMTU, DMSO, deferroxamine, mannitol, chlorpromazine (Thorazine), mannitol, ascorbate,[*] methionine
Lipid peroxides	Membranes	a-tocopherol, glutathione peroxidase*

[a]Asterisk denotes endogenous; MPG, N-2-mercaptopropionyl glycine; DMTU, dimethylthiourea; DMSO, dimethylsulfoxide.

An adjunct to the cardioplegic solution would allow intermittent delivery of the antioxidant agent during the period of protected arrest, with continued action in the immediate postoperative period.

Experiments using various animal models under a number of conditions relevant to the surgical setting have evaluated a host of oxygen radical scavengers and inhibitors as cardioplegic solution adjuvants (184–189). Superoxide dismutase used alone has not proven beneficial, but catalase either alone (186) or in combination with SOD (188) has demonstrated protection beyond that provided by cardioplegic solutions alone (190–194). These observations generally reflect the consensus of extensive studies in the nonsurgical literature for short-term myocardial ischemia (45, 195–197). The reason underlying the failure of SOD as the single agent to reduce oxyradical-related injury may be that the enzyme targets only the superoxide anion and fails to target other radical species distal to superoxide (i.e., H_2O_2, $\cdot OH$). In addition, the superoxide anion is released into the microenvironment at the neutrophil-endothelial cell interface, thereby preventing the anion from being exposed to circulating SOD. On the other hand, SOD plus catalase or catalase alone interrupts the accumulation of two radical species (o_2^*, H_2O_2) allowing only the $\cdot OH$ originating from sources other than the $o_2^* - H_2O_2$ cascade (i.e., Haber-Weiss reaction) to persist. However, the size of SOD and catalase molecules may limit their intracellular penetration and therefore confine their antioxidant activity to the extracellular spaces. This may allow intracellular production of oxyradicals by xanthine oxidase and mitochondria to go unchecked. The xanthine oxidase inhibitors allopurinol and oxypurinol have proven effective in improving postischemic function (36, 198). N-(2-mercaptopropionyl) glycine (MPG) is a purported scavenger of hydroxyl radicals and superoxide anions that enters the intracellular compartment. Two studies showed that MPG had no additional benefit in improving postischemic function when used as an adjuvant to cardioplegia (35, 199).

Several clinical studies support the appearance of oxygen free radicals during CPB and cardioplegic arrest (200–202). Although experimental evidence strongly supports the beneficial effects of antioxidant therapy in cardioplegia, the clinical benefits of this strategy are not yet clear. Bical et al. (203) showed no attenuation of oxygen radical metabolites in patients undergoing cardioplegic arrest using crystalloid cardioplegia with a reperfusate enhanced with allopurinol (xanthine oxidase inhibitor). This failure to reduce oxyradicals may have been related to significant compositional differences in both the crystalloid solutions and the reperfusates, or to the inclusion of allopurinol only *after* cardioplegia (as a controlled phase of reperfusion) had been delivered, thereby not preventing oxyradicals generated during cardioplegia. The latter interpretation would be consonant with the study of Jolly et al. (87), who demonstrated that delivery of scavengers after the burst of oxygen radicals had occurred in early reperfusion was not myoprotective. However, in one study in which an oxygen radical scavenger (mannitol) was delivered as an additive to the cardioplegic solution, postischemic myocardial injury in patients was reduced (204).

An appropriate strategy for alleviating oxygen radical-induced injury after bypass surgery must consider both the species of radical targeted as well as its primary source of generation. The cardioplegic vehicle must also be scrutinized for its potential to produce or exaggerate oxygen radical production. For example, crystalloid cardioplegia carries less oxygen as a substrate for oxygen radical production than its blood cardioplegia counterpart. Blood on the other hand, contains abundant oxygen, neutrophils, lipids, and iron moieties, which may generate radicals. Reducing the participation of neutrophils by depleting blood cardioplegia solutions of neutrophils or preventing their adherence to endothelium has proven to be beneficial and further highlights the role of neutrophil-mediated damage during surgical ischemia and reperfusion (205–207). However, blood also carries important endogenous "scavengers" (i.e., superoxide dismutase, catalase, and glutathione in erythrocytes) that may be important in counteracting radical-induced damage (208, 209). Further experimental and clinical studies are necessary to determine the benefits of radical scavenger therapy, and to evaluate target-specific therapy directed toward multiple radical species and their sources.

Buffering

During both normothermic and hypothermic ischemia, aerobic metabolism is short-lived, and the myocardium is reliant on the relatively low yield of ATP (2 moles per mole of glucose used) from anaerobiosis. However, tissue acidosis resulting from continued metabolism and lactate production during ischemia strongly inhibits enzymatically catalyzed metabolic reactions, further diminishing the yield of ATP. Buffering of cardioplegic solutions to counteract myocardial hydrogen ion accumulation therefore is a logical strategy for limiting the consequences of ischemia. Episodic reinfusion of cardioplegic solution would further rectify tissue acidosis by washing out metabolic byproducts to reestablish acid-base homeostasis. Buffering of acidosis can be accomplished using the cardioplegic solutions as vehicles either by exploiting the endogenous capabilities of the solution (i.e., buffering capacity of blood) or by adding exogenous buffers.

The buffering approach selected to properly manage acid-base status of cardioplegic solutions must consider the biophysical changes imposed by hypothermia as well as pharmacologic efforts to adjust acid-base balance. In aqueous solutions, the neutral pH of water (pN_{H_2O}) is temperature-dependent, increasing by 0.017 pH units per degree Celsius decrease in temperature (Fig. 7.9A). In blood, pH is alkaline relative to the neutrality point of water, but a parallel adjustment in arterial pH occurs with hypothermia (210) such that the $\Delta pH/°C$ ratio is approximately -0.0147 (i.e., the Rosenthal correction factor) (211). Therefore, a blood sample with a pH of 7.4 measured by electrodes warmed to 37°C would actually be 7.72 if temperature were 10°C during cardioplegia. In humans, changes in arterial blood pH such as those shown in Figure 7.9A occur naturally in the thermally heterogeneous structures of the body (i.e., skin at 25°C) or with changes in core temperature (212). Therefore, the question arises whether this relatively alkalotic arterial pH is appropriate for this temperature and requires no adjustment of pH or PCO_2 (i.e., alpha-stat), or whether the pH should be readjusted by adding CO_2 to the blood to conform to our concept of normal

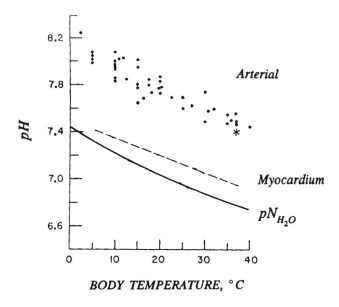

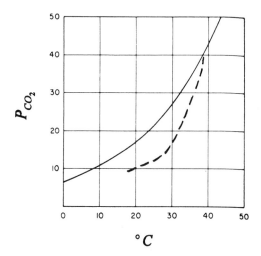

Figure 7.9. A. The relationship between pH and body temperature for arterial blood in various ectothermic invertebrate and vertebrate species (•), including man (*). Intracellular pH for turtle cardiac muscle is shown in the dashed line and is shifted downward toward more acidic values relative to arterial values. The pH-temperature relation for the neutrality point of water (pN_{H_2O}) is represented by the solid line. Note that all lines exhibit similar slope of change in pH relative to temperature. (Redrawn from White FN. A comparative physiological approach to hypothermia. J Thorac Cardiovasc Surg 1981;82:821–831.) **B.** The relationship between P_{CO_2} and temperature for human blood (CO_2 content is constant) is curvilinear and related to the increased solubility of CO_2 at lower temperatures. Clinically, more profound reduction in pH than achieved by hypothermia can be accomplished by increasing oxygen flow in the oxygenator to reduce P_{CO_2} and impose a "respiratory" alkalosis. Data points represented by dashed line are plotted from the study of Becker et al. (152), in which arterial CO_2 was manipulated to achieve a pH appropriate for temperature. (Becker H, Vinten-Johansen J, Buckberg GD, et al. Myocardial damage caused by keeping pH 7.40 during systemic deep hypothermia. J Thorac Cardiovasc Surg 1981;82:810–820.) (Solid curvilinear P_{CO_2} = temperature line redrawn from White FN. A comparative physiological approach to hypothermia. J Thorac Cardiovasc Surg 1981;82:821–831.)

for warm-blooded mammals, i.e., pH 7.4 measured by 37°C electrodes and 7.1 at 10°C (i.e., pH-stat). This dilemma has generated a dichotomy of acid-base management philosophy, with some subscribing to the alpha-stat philosophy and others to the pH-stat strategy. This controversy has encompassed a multiorgan consideration of consequences of acid-base management during hypothermic cardiopulmonary bypass (152, 213). Therefore, the surgical team has the option of following the adaptations of either poikilotherms, which regulate pH to an alkaline status with hypothermia, or those of hibernating mammals, which constrain pH to 7.4. The biophysical changes that occur as euthermic man transgresses into the hypothermic environment impacts on the biochemical adequacy of myocardial protection.

In adjusting blood pH using the Rosenthal correction, ectotherms and nonhibernating mammals act as a closed system, in that the ratio of $[OH^-]/[H^+]$ (Fig. 7.9A) and the arterial blood CO_2 *content* remain constant as temperature varies (212). With hypothermia, the P_{CO_2} falls as CO_2 solubility increases, but CO_2 content remains relatively constant. Such adjustments in blood pH are accomplished by two physiologic buffer systems: the carbonic acid-bicarbonate system, and the imidazole-containing molecules (free histidine and histidine residues of proteins), the latter being dominant (214). The constancy of $[OH^-]/[H^+]$ and CO_2 content adjusts the charge state of imidazole moieties to approximately one-half ionization (constant a value). Such adjustments in the charge state of imidazole groups in enzymes maintains a relatively stable affinity (K_m) and reaction rate for their substrates, which counteracts the metabolic depression caused by hypothermia. The physiologic consequences and benefits of temperature-adjusted acid-base balance of in vivo fluids are (a) conservation of enzyme kinetics and metabolism, (b) stabilization of Donnan equilibrium of chloride, thereby preventing ab-

normal cell volume regulation and edema, and (c) prevention of loss of ionized metabolic intermediates, which would otherwise facilitate metabolism during hypothermia. Blood used as a vehicle for hypothermic cardioplegic solutions may have a natural advantage over asanguineous solutions because temperature-related pH adjustments are made in blood by both endogenous buffer systems, thus maintaining an alkaline pH relative to the neutrality point of water and to intracellular pH (Fig. 7.9).

Alkalotic cardioplegic solutions maintain better metabolism (215, 216) and blood flow (216), and buffer intracellular as well as extracellular acidosis (152, 217–221). However, a number of reports (222–224) contradict this conclusion by suggesting that acidotic solutions decrease energy demands during ischemia and attenuate intracellular Ca^{2+} gain during ischemia and reperfusion (223–225). Further clarification of this seemingly contradictory data is warranted.

Clinically, adjustments in the acid-base balance of systemic blood as well as cardioplegic solutions can be made either by changing P_{CO_2} levels in the arterial blood (152, 213, 216), or by adding exogenous buffering agents. Figure 7.9B shows the blood P_{CO_2} changes associated with decreases in pH during progressive hypothermia. Ventilatory adjustments to lower P_{CO_2} can be made by increasing oxygenator gas flow rate to achieve even greater alkalinity than that induced by hypothermia alone (215, 216).

Various buffering agents have been used either as a primary method of pH adjustment or to supplement and amplify the intrinsic buffering capabilities of the cardioplegic solution. The ideal buffer has a dissociation constant (pK) within one pH unit of the neutrality point of the solution (sanguineous or asanguineous) used at a given temperature, should be independent of P_{CO_2} changes and be able to buffer the intracellular environment. Bicarbonate, tromethamine histidine, and phosphate buffers are used in various cardioplegic solution formulations. Bicarbonate is a weak extracellular buffer with a pK that is both outside the desirable range of physiologic pH at lower temperatures and unable to adjust appropriately to temperature. Consequently, poor results have been obtained with bicarbonate-buffered solutions (226, 227). Histidine (pK 6.04) and the active component imidazole (pK 6.7), the dominant buffer systems in blood, provide good buffering capacity with an appropriate pK range and appropriate adjustment of pK to hypothermia. Experimental studies show good preservation of high-energy phosphate stores and postischemic ventricular function with these buffers (217, 221). The imidazole-histidine buffering system may be the mechanism underlying the buffering capacity of blood cardioplegia (218, 219). Tromethamine is an excellent buffer because its pK (8.08) is nearly identical to the physiologically adjusted pH at 4 to 10°C, and buffers the intracellular as well as extracellular compartments.

Avoidance of Edema

Edema is a well-known consequence of ischemic-reperfusion injury that may be aggravated by the composition of cardioplegic solutions or the conditions of delivery (hypothermia, pressure) (33, 50, 114, 162). Edema may increase microvascular resistance to a point of impeding blood flow (no-reflow phenomenon) and oxygen delivery (increasing diffusion distance). In addition, compliance of the myocardium is lost, thereby restricting the Starling response. Edema may arise with the use of cardioplegic solutions because of (a) high delivery pressures, particularly in severely damaged myocardium; (b) hemodilution and hypo-osmolarity; and (c) physiologic changes in ionic pump systems (i.e., Na^+-K^+-ATPase) or Donnan equilibrium for chloride ions induced by hypothermia. Although normal myocardium tolerates relatively high infusion pressures (111,

162), myocardium within (109, 128) and surrounding (228) ischemic segments is vulnerable to pressure-induced edema. Consequently, the pressure at which antegrade cardioplegic solutions are infused should be restricted to below 100 mm Hg. Many blood cardioplegia users select a delivery pressure of 50 mm Hg (28, 35, 36, 56, 113, 154, 230). In addition, osmotic agents such as mannitol (162, 231) or glucose may be used to counteract edema formation. The latter component possesses the added dividend of serving as both a metabolic substrate (227, 232–234) and a potential oxygen radical scavenger. Hyperkalemia per se will contribute significantly to hyperosmolarity. Although concern is voiced over extreme hyperosmolar solutions (greater than 400 mOsm) because of the threat of myocardial dehydration or "rebound edema," Okamoto et al. (235) showed the greatest protection in a regionally ischemic revascularized segment with cardioplegic solution osmolality greater than 400 mOsm.

Amino Acid Enhancement

Cardioplegic formulations that adequately protect the myocardium of normal hearts have often been found inadequate in severely damaged hearts suffering antecedent ischemia or reperfusion injury. Failure to adequately protect these hearts may be related to the inability to maintain adequate levels of high-energy phosphates in the already energy-depleted myocardium, or failure to sustain adequate levels of glycolysis or other metabolic processes during the periods of hypothermic ischemia. Limitation of energy production by anaerobiosis during hypothermic ischemia may be in part related to depletion of key Krebs cycle intermediates and their precursors, glutamate (236) and aspartate, and to the failure of the malate-aspartate shuttle mechanism to remove protons and prevent intracellular acidosis. Both glutamate and aspartate are lost during ischemia (236) and are actively incorporated into the myocardium when exogenously supplied (237, 238). Glutamate enters into the Krebs cycle by conversion to a-keto glutarate, and aspartate enters via transamination to oxaloacetic acid. Both precursors are subsequently metabolized within the Krebs cycle to succinate with the ultimate generation of 1 mole of ATP each by substrate level phosphorylation independent of glycolysis (237, 239). Therefore, high-energy phosphates can be gained from amino acid metabolism even when the level of glycolysis is reduced during ischemia.

In addition, conversion of these substrates to succinate may also augment production of adenosine monophosphate via a salvage synthetic pathway, and thereby increase production of the cytoprotective autacoid adenosine. Substantiation of this latter mechanism is lacking, but is an important point needing clarification in view of adenosine's new emerging role in protecting the heart from ischemic and reperfusion injury (240–243). It is tempting to speculate that aspartate may also act by augmenting production of the cardioprotective substance NO (the endothelium-dependent relaxing factor) by conversion to L-arginine, the physiologic substrate for NO synthase. In addition, glutamate and aspartate may inhibit the mitochondrial accumulation of protons by sustaining the malate-aspartate shuttle, thereby preventing oxidative phosphorylation uncoupling and the generation of oxygen free radicals (244, 245). Addition of the dicarboxylic acids L-glutamate and aspartate to the cardioplegic formula has been shown to increase oxygen uptake by the myocardium during induction of cardioplegia and improve postischemic myocardial performance and oxygen utilization (154, 246) after discontinuation of cardiopulmonary bypass. The improvement observed was greater in energy-depleted hearts (154) than in normal hearts (28). The study by Rosenkranz et al. (247) suggests that glutamate and aspartate used together act synergistically by providing greater protection than either component alone. In addition, greater benefits may be obtained by combining amino acid supplementation with normothermic induction of cardioplegia, since both strategies augment oxygen uptake during induction of cardioplegia. Since amino acid supplementation acts mainly by replenishing lost Krebs cycle intermediates and facilitating both anaerobic and aerobic metabolism, the addition of glutamate and/or aspartate may be indicated in other situations where the myocardium may be extremely depressed or subjected to prolonged ischemia, such as cardiogenic shock or long-term storage for subsequent transplantation (248).

Importance of Oxygen in Cardioplegic Vehicles

Whether oxygen delivery to the cold, asystolic heart is an important function of cardioplegic solutions is still debated. The oxygen demands of the myocardium are diminished by 97% as a result of the combined effects of asystole, decompression, and hypothermia to 8 to 10°C as summarized in Figure 7.7 (113, 147). Therefore, the oxygen demands of the 4°C myocardium may average 0.3 ml/min per 100 g. Since myocardial metabolism persists at this low temperature, a considerable oxygen debt (approximately 6 ml O_2 per 100 g myocardium, 66 to 82% of normal demands of the working heart) may accumulate during a 20-minute ischemic interval between replenishment infusions of cardioplegia solution. Theoretically, oxygen delivered to the myocardium after an ischemic interval would restore tissue oxygenation, partially repay the oxygen debt built up during any antecedent ischemia or between infusions of cardioplegia, and replenish high-energy phosphate pools (155, 249). In addition, delivery of oxygen to the arrested heart just prior to release of the aortic cross-clamp may enhance the rate of cellular repair and functional recovery.

According to Table 7.4, all forms of aerated or oxygenated solutions contain sufficient oxygen to potentially meet the basal oxygen requirements of the myocardium at 10°C, assuming that all the oxygen present is extractable. However, not all solutions may be able to satisfy the oxygen debt accumulated over time at clinically acceptable volumes of solution. The bioavailability of oxygen is an important factor in the oxygen delivered by cardioplegic solutions. Bioavailability is determined not only by the oxygen content of the solution, but also by alterations in the physiologic limits of oxygen extraction (250) by the myocardium, as well as the biophysical effect of hypothermia on oxygen affinity for hemoglobin. Most studies indicate that oxygenated cardioplegia solutions produce superior results experimentally (56, 230, 251–255) and clinically (256, 257) when compared to unoxygenated or aerated solutions.

Hypothermia has a profound influence on the oxygen availability in both crystalloid and blood cardioplegia solutions. These influences can be divided into the two compartments in which oxygen is carried: the asanguineous compartment (crystalloid or blood plasma) where oxygen is dissolved, and the sanguineous (hemoglobin-containing) compartment where oxygen is bound to hemoglobin. The solubility of oxygen is temperature-dependent, increasing twofold as temperature decreases from 37 to 0°C (258). Digerness et al. (259) have shown that nearly all of the dissolved oxygen in crystalloid solutions can be released at 10°C. In blood, on the other hand, a relatively small proportion of the total oxygen content is dissolved in the asanguineous compartment, while a larger fraction of oxygen is bound to hemoglobin. Oxygen affinity for hemoglobin increases with hypothermia, which produces a leftward shift in the oxyhemoglobin dissociation curve (Fig. 7.10). Accordingly, a lower P_{O_2} is necessary at the tissue level to unload oxygen from hemoglobin to half-saturation (P_{50}), which implicates a greater difficulty in releasing oxygen to the tissues (260, 261). Therefore, the large oxygen-carrying capacity of blood cardioplegia may theoretically be counterbalanced by hemoglobin's greater affinity for oxygen at the levels of hypothermia used surgically, thereby potentially impeding the oxygen extraction by the myocardium.

In contrast to the biophysical forces interfering with dissociation of oxygen from hemoglobin at low temperatures, numerous studies have shown by direct measurement that oxygen is indeed taken up by the heart during delivery of hypothermic (4 to 8°C) blood cardioplegia (28, 35, 36, 113, 154, 230). In the myocardium not subjected to a previous period of ischemia preceding delivery of cardioplegic solution, oxygen extracted during the induction phase of cardioplegia is commensurate with the relatively small oxygen demands at that temperature (28). However, substantially greater oxygen is taken up by the heart subjected to an antecedent period of normothermic ischemia (35, 36, 113, 154, 230), presumably in order to repay the oxygen deficit. In a study reported by Magovern et al. (262), significantly greater oxygen was generally taken up with blood cardioplegia than with crystalloid cardioplegia. However, the amount of oxygen taken up with either vehicle decreased with lower infusion temperatures. In a recent

Table 7.4.   Oxygen Content of Various Cardioplegia Vehicles at 4 to 10°C

Vehicle	O_2 Content (ml O_2/100 ml)	Reference No.
Aerated crystalloid	0.5-1.0	56, 254, 259
Oxygenated crystalloid	0.86-3.5	254, 256
Blood	5.8-12	35, 36, 56, 229, 254, 268

Figure 7.10. Forces acting in the oxy-hemoglobin dissociation curve. Hypothermia shifts the curve to the left, decreasing P_{50} and making oxygen dissociation more difficult. The leftward shift may be further enhanced by alkalosis of the cardioplegic solution. However, the difficulty in oxygen unloading is opposed by increased tissue carbon dioxide (hypercarbia) and tissue acidosis. These opposing shifts in the dissociation of oxygen from hemoglobin may allow extraction of oxygen by the myocardium during infusion of cardioplegic solutions. (From Vinten-Johansen J, Julian JS, Yokoyama H, et al. Efficacy of myocardial protection with hypothermic blood cardioplegia depends on oxygen. Ann Thorac Surg 1991;52:939–948.)

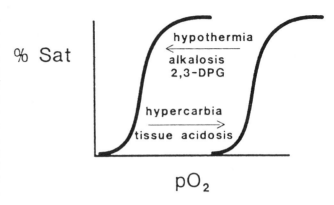

study by Vinten-Johansen et al. (35), 7.9 ± 1.7 ml O_2 was taken up by the normothermically ischemic heart during induction of cardioplegia using 791 ± 75 ml of blood cardioplegia solution. In addition, substantial oxygen was also taken up during intermittent infusions at 4 to 8°C. Because the shift in the hemoglobin dissociation curve imposes a theoretical limitation on the delivery of oxygen when blood cardioplegia is used, Vinten-Johansen et al. (229) studied whether oxygen was an important factor in the myoprotection afforded by hypothermic blood cardioplegia. The oxygen content was adjusted by controlled gas mixture in the cardioplegia delivery line to fully saturated (10.2 ± 0.6 ml O_2 per deciliter), intermediate (4.3 ± 0.5 ml O_2 per deciliter) and low (1.1 ± 0.2 ml O_2 per deciliter) levels, while other compositional attributes were held constant. The heart was subjected to 30 minutes of normothermic ischemia, and hypothermic (4°C) blood cardioplegia was delivered every 20 minutes for 1 hour of cardioplegic arrest. Postischemic left ventricular function, evaluated by pressure-volume relations, generally reflected the level of oxygen content in the cardioplegia. Postischemic left ventricular performance was well-preserved in the saturated blood cardioplegia group, moderately depressed in the intermediate oxygen-

ated group, and severely depressed in the relatively desaturated group (Fig. 7.11). It was concluded that oxygen is extracted in significant quantities from hypothermic blood cardioplegia, and that oxygen is important to the myocardial protection provided by hypothermic blood cardioplegia.

Therefore, despite the unfavorable shift in the oxyhemoglobin dissociation curve with profound hypothermia, the ischemic myocardium apparently creates an environment that counteracts these effects of hypothermia and facilitates extraction of oxygen. Figure 7.10 summarizes the forces shifting the oxyhemoglobin dissociation curve back to the right from its leftward position at lower temperatures, thereby facilitating unloading of oxygen in the ischemic myocardium. These forces include increased tissue P_{CO_2} and tissue acidosis (Bohr effect) as well as facilitated extraction due to low tissue P_{O_2} and the greater affinity of hypothermic tissue for oxygen (263). These characteristics of ischemic myocardium apparently overcome the opposition to oxygen unloading due to hypothermia, and allow extraction of oxygen from blood cardioplegic solutions. Therefore, a large and extractable source of oxygen can be added to the list of attributes of blood important to myocardial protection, which includes endogenous oxygen free

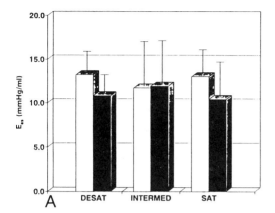

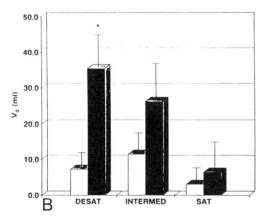

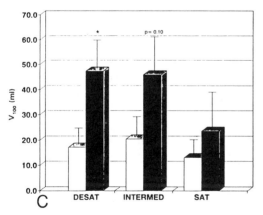

Figure 7.11. Canine hearts were subjected to 30 minutes of global normothermic ischemia followed by multidose hypothermic blood cardioplegia. **A.** Preischemic (open bars) and postischemic (filled bars) slope (E_{es}) of the end-systolic pressure-volume relation (ESPVR). **B.** The intercept of the linear ESPVR at extrapolated left ventricular pressure of 0 mm Hg (V_0). **C.** The midrange volume-axis intercept at a left ventricular pressure of 100 mm Hg (V_{100}). There were no differences in slope of the ESPVR among the three sat-

radical scavengers (209, 264), improved rheologic properties (256), and more effective buffering of acid metabolites (209, 265). To what extent this oxygen is extracted from the plasma compartment versus the hemoglobin compartment is not clear.

CARDIOPLEGIC SOLUTION DELIVERY UNITS

The evolution of myoprotective strategies using cardioplegia has grown from a simple pressure-driven system for the infusion of a single bolus of crystalloid-based cardioplegic solution to very complex devices that deliver solutions containing blood and many additives that are infused with precise volume and pressure control, and have the option for temperature variability. The decision for which clinical format to choose will depend on the sophistication and experience of the operative team, the level of patient disease, and the complexity of the perfusion system.

Crystalloid Cardioplegia Delivery Devices

The systems described above can be used to infuse crystalloid solutions as well, but are not necessary if a simple system is desired. For small patients requiring a

uration groups, indicating parallel shifts in the ESPVR. However, marked increases in both V_0 and V_{100} were observed in the desaturated and intermediate saturated blood cardioplegia groups, indicating severe and moderately severe left ventricular dilation. In contrast, hearts protected by fully oxygen saturated blood cardioplegia showed no significant dilation. SAT, saturated, 10.2 ± 0.6 vol %; INTERMED, intermediately saturated, 4.3 ± 0.5 vol %; DESAT, desaturated, 1.1 ± 0.2 vol %. (Parts reprinted from Vinten-Johansen J, Julian JS, Yokoyama H, et al. Efficacy of myocardial protection with hypothermic blood cardioplegia depends on oxygen. Ann Thorac Surg 1991;52:939–948.)

single dose of cardioplegia, a hand-held syringe will suffice. In larger patients the desired cardioplegia components can be mixed in a standard polyvinyl chloride bag with the base component (D_5W, etc.) and using a blood infusion pressure bag pumped to a pressure of 150 mm Hg, the desired amount of precooled solution can be infused using pressure regulation. Cardioplegia catheters that allow pressure measurement in the aortic root are commercially available. This can serve as a guide to infusion pressure so as not to rely on the poorly calibrated gauge on the infusion bag. If multidose cardioplegia is to be given, then it is safer to rely on a system that is integrated into the CPB equipment to avoid air or particulate emboli from bag or tubing sources and to precisely control volume, pressure, and temperature during infusion.

BLOOD CARDIOPLEGIA DELIVERY DEVICES

Typical blood cardioplegic systems must have a connection to an arterial outlet from the pump oxygenator whether the oxygenator is a membrane or bubbler type. Desired additive drugs (i.e., glutamate, aspartate, dextrose, etc.) may be manually drawn up and added to the circuit or, more commonly, drugs and solution concentrates may be continuously mixed with the cardioplegic vehicle using a double-tube system with different diameters to accomplish either 1:2, 1:3, or 1:4 dilutions of the final cardioplegia solution.

In a recirculating type of system, the desired blood volume would be continuously withdrawn from the oxygenator reservoir and mixed with drugs and concentrate, and subsequently circulated long enough to achieve the desired temperature *prior to* delivery. Heat exchange in a single-pass type of system to the desired temperature is accomplished *during* delivery. In systems including an integral heat exchanger, water of the desired temperature would be circu-

lated through the heat exchanger with the cardioplegic solution passing over the heat exchange surface. In the coil type of system, the coil (either plastic or metal) would be immersed in either warm water or an ice bath *during* delivery to achieve the desired temperature.

Single-pass blood cardioplegic systems require less volume to use because the desired quantity of cardioplegic solution does not have to be sequestered in advance. However, this system places more burden on the heat exchanger than does the recirculating type of system since desired heat transfer must be accomplished in a single pass during delivery to the heart. Systems for delivery of clear cardioplegic solutions are simpler than systems used for blood cardioplegia. Clear solution delivery units do not require a connection to a blood oxygenator outlet, may use either type of heat exchange, and be of either a single-pass or recirculating configuration.

All of these systems will utilize a roller pump on the CPB console, typically with 1/4 inch tubing. They will also include some sort of bubble trap or filter in the final delivery line to the table for protection from gaseous or particulate microemboli. In addition, some provision is made for either direct or indirect monitoring of solution temperature and pressure in the system during delivery. It should be remembered that with either type of system, absolute maximum water bath temperature is 42°C, and a 10°C maximum gradient between water bath and starting solution temperature should be observed.

SPECIAL CONSIDERATIONS IN DELIVERY AND USE OF CARDIOPLEGIC SOLUTIONS

It is obvious from the preceding discussion that adequate protection of the heart during surgical ischemia and reperfusion involves a multifaceted approach designed to address the various factors potentially contributing to ischemic and reperfusion injury. In this effort to attenuate ischemic-reperfusion injury, the composition of the cardioplegia solution and the manner in which it is delivered plays a pivotal role. The primary factors involved in the formulation and use of cardioplegia solutions are listed in Table 7.5. The individual factors are interactive in attenuating ischemic injury (i.e., during aortic cross-clamping and arrest) and thereby reducing reperfusion-related injury (i.e., during delivery of cardioplegic solutions, removal of the aortic cross-clamp). For example, both cardiac asystole and hypothermia reduce the energy demands of the myocardium and offset the severity of ischemia, thereby attenuating the potential for reperfusion injury. Likewise, hyperosmolarity and moderate infusion pressures work together to avoid interstitial edema and consequent secondary ischemia leading to no-reflow that may limit both the distribution of cardioplegic solution, particularly to the subendocardium, and blood flow once reperfusion has been established. Likewise, warm cardioplegia induction in energy-depleted hearts (i.e., cardiogenic shock) or acutely ischemic myocardium is designed to resuscitate the myocardium in order to better tolerate the subsequent period of

protected ischemia and reperfusion. The contribution of each protective factor to the overall protection of the myocardium will depend upon the severity of preoperative ischemia (if any), the duration of aortic cross-clamp, techniques of cardioplegic solution delivery (i.e., intermittent versus continuous infusions), and the adequacy of distribution of the solution. Adequate myocardial protection relies on simple and safe techniques to deliver cardioplegic solutions in a precise manner.

Method and Strategy of Antegrade Administration

In the majority of cases, the cardioplegia can be given via one of the many commerically available catheters designed for this purpose. The important features of these catheters involve ease of use, lack of significant obstruction to flow, and avoidance of trauma to the aortic intima from the jet of solution introduced. This is especially true in patients with extensive aortic atherosclerosis.

The operative team has the option of giving all of the cardioplegia via the aorta or, in some cases with extensive native coronary disease, infusions via bypass grafts as they are placed. These decisions depend on

Table 7.5. Considerations in Formulation and Use of Cardioplegia

Principle	Mechanism	Component
Reduce O_2 demand	Hypothermia	Blood, crystalloid, ice slush, lavage
	Perfusion	
	Topical	
	Asystole	KCl, $MgCl_2$, intermittent infusions
Substrate supply and utilization	Oxygen	Blood, perfluorocarbons, crystalloid (?)
	Glucose	Blood, glucose, citrate-phosphate-dextrose
	Amino acids	Glutamate, aspartate
	Buffer acidosis	Hypothermia (Rosenthal factor), intermittent infusions
	Buffers	Blood, tromethamine, histidine, bicarbonate, phosphate
	Optimize metabolism	Warm induction (37°C), warm reperfusion
Reduce Ca^{2+} overload	Hypocalcemia	Citrate, Ca^{2+}-channel blockers, K-channel openers(?)
Reduce edema	Hyperosmolarity	Glucose, KCl, mannitol
	Moderate infusion pressure	50 mm Hg

the status of the patient (emergent versus elective) and the anatomy of the coronary tree. In the emergent patient with an acute occlusion, attention to the "culprit" vessel should come first with the option of cardioplegia administration through the graft. In general, the goal of cardiac protection is to maintain myocardial temperature at 10 to 15°C and to abolish cardiac electrical activity. Substrate enhancement and other protective measures are more clinically subjective and are left to the choice of the operative team.

The therapeutic effects of a well-formulated cardioplegic solution can be exerted only if the solution is distributed throughout the myocardium. In patients with unobstructed vessels or without severe hypertrophy or aortic incompetence, distribution of the cardioplegic solution is ensured if sufficient volume is delivered at pressures ranging between 50 and 100 mm Hg. However, coronary stenoses may severely impede the antegrade distribution of cardioplegic solutions (266, 267), thereby preventing the solution from protecting the segment distal to the obstructive lesions from ischemic and reperfusion damage. Tolerance of the myocardium to ischemia is greater when provisions are made to deliver hypothermic cardioplegic solution beyond the stenoses (268). Overcoming the impediment imposed by coronary lesions in the absence of collaterals may be accomplished by (a) delivering induction or intermittent infusion of cardioplegic solutions in a retrograde fashion with or without antegrade perfusion, (b) perfusing cardioplegic solution through each graft after completion of the distal anastomoses, or (c) performing both proximal and distal grafts sequentially for individual grafts, each completion followed by an infusion of cardioplegic solution through the aortic root (268).

(a) *Retrograde infusion* has numerous advantages, including adequate distribution in vessels with diffuse lesions, avoidance of coronary ostial stenosis imposed by direct cannulation, and distribution of cardioplegic solution to vessels receiving an internal mammary graft.

(b) *Perfusion through each graft* after completion of the distal anastomoses allows unimpeded distribution to the newly revascularized segment, and allows replenishment through all grafts in multidose fashion without prolongation of cross-clamp time. Combined direct graft infusion and aortic infusion during replenishment periods ensures distribution of cardioplegic solution to grafted as well as native vessels. This technique has the added advantage that the grafted conduit can be used to selectively deliver modified reperfusates after removal of the aortic cross-clamp to severely ischemic segments if desired. This would avoid potential ischemia during completion of proximal anastomoses when blood flow is not provided to the segment during normothermic "beating empty" or fibrillating states. These modified reperfusion solutions are based on the same principles used in protecting the globally ischemic heart from ischemic-reperfusion injury during cross-clamp, with particular focus on preventing reperfusion injury. For example, normothermic blood cardioplegia can be delivered to the revascularized segment by commercially available manifold systems. Selective reperfusion is ensured while completing proximal anastomoses of an individual graft, thereby not prolonging operative procedures.

(c) Finally, sequentially completing *proximal and distal anastomoses* provides a patent conduit for delivery of cardioplegic solution via the aortic root, thereby perfusing revascularized and native coronary arteries simultaneously. Although this may prolong cross-clamp time, maldistribution of cardioplegic solution is avoided, and superior protection may counteract the consequences of shorter but less well-protected ischemic time. However, cardioplegic solution is still maldistributed to unrevascularized areas or to areas with diffusely diseased myocardium.

Delivery Pressure

While the normal myocardium not subjected to ischemic injury is tolerant of perfusion pressures in excess of 100 mm Hg (32, 111, 128), the ischemic myocardium is sensitive to perfusion pressures. The physiologic basis for this sensitivity stems from the pressure coefficient of the Starling forces of tissue fluid movement overcoming the normally intact capillary barrier and forcing the interstitial migration of fluid from the vascular compartment. Excessive perfusion pressures may cause interstitial edema, which may in turn precipitate extravascular tissue compression, impaired blood flow, and further damage related to "secondary ischemia." Accordingly, many investigators have used gentle perfusion pressures in the range of 50 mm Hg. A controlled hypotensive reperfusion in and of itself reduces reperfusion injury in ischemic myocardium (109, 110, 112, 128, 228). This applies as well to infusions of cardioplegic solutions to the global heart or into individual grafts after completion of each distal anastomosis. However, delivery of cardioplegic solutions at a given pressure will not ensure adequate distribution beyond stenoses. Appropriate caution should be exercised not to create edema in myocardium subserved by patent coronary arteries while attempting to increase the distribution of cardioplegic solutions to obstructed segments using high delivery pressures. Control over the initial reperfusion pressure where the aortic cross-clamp is removed will also avoid hydrodynamically induced injury (266). Buckberg and Rosenkranz (169) advocate removing the aortic cross-clamp while adjusting systemic perfusion pressure to 50 mm Hg. After reanimation, systemic perfusion pressure can be gradually increased to normal values.

Warm Induction of Cardioplegia

Cardioplegia delivered cold attenuates the ischemic process and prevents high-energy phosphate loss during the period of cross-clamp. However, hypothermic cardioplegia may have disadvantages in patients in whom preexisting disease (hypertrophy, ventricular failure, regional ischemia) or an event preceding CPB (ventricular fibrillation, cardiogenic shock) have reduced myocardial tolerance to ischemia. For example, hypothermia may hinder cellular repair and the restoration of metabolic homeostasis, restrict the actions of pharmacologic agents, and oppose oxygen dissociation from a blood-based vehicle. In such cases, a period of normothermic cardioplegia preceding the cold induction of arrest (113) would provide the best of both thermal worlds by curtailing the energy demands by inducing cardiac arrest, and by optimizing the energy available for repair with normothermia. Figure 7.12 shows that a delivery of warm cardioplegia increases the oxygen uptake by the heart relative to a cold infusion of the same blood cardioplegia solution in energy-depleted hearts (45 minutes of antecedent normothermic ischemia). The warm/cold induction technique resulted in improved postischemic performance over the cold induction group. Clinically, use of the warm/cold induction of cardioplegia reduced the need for postoperative inotropic therapy and mechanical support in patients presenting with cardiogenic shock (113, 167). As described by Rosenkranz et al. (113), a 5-minute period of normothermic cardioplegia is followed by 5 minutes of hypothermic cardioplegia. This brief normothermic infusion of cardioplegia solution can be accomplished easily by first circulating warm water from the heater-cooler unit over the heat exchange coils and then switching the heater-cooler unit to maximum cool at the appropriate time to initiate hypothermic cardioplegic infusion. The same advantages of normothermic cardioplegia can be used to minimize reperfusion injury and accelerate functional recovery when the heart is exposed to oxygen, systemic pressures, and normal blood constituents after removal of the aortic cross-clamp (168). Clinically, terminal warm blood cardioplegia ("hot shot") delivered in the aortic root for a period of 3 to 5 minutes (169) or at a fixed volume at controlled infusion pressure (145) improved postischemic myocardial metabolic recovery, attenuated the decrease in high-energy phosphates after reperfusion, and improved postoperative outcome (145).

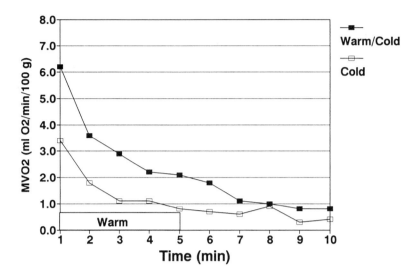

Figure 7.12. Oxygen uptake during induction of cardioplegia with cold blood cardioplegia (4°C) (open squares) and normothermic blood cardioplegia (filled squares) techniques. Hearts were subjected to 45 minutes of normothermic global ischemia, followed by 10 minutes infusion of 4°C blood cardioplegia or 5 minutes warm plus 5 minutes 4°C blood cardioplegia. (Data redrawn from Rosenkranz ER, Vinten-Johansen J, Buckberg GD, Okamoto F, Edwards H, Bugyi H. Benefits of normothermic induction of blood cardioplegia in energy-depleted hearts, with maintenance of arrest by multidose cold blood cardioplegic infusions. J Thorac Cardiovasc Surg 1982;84:667–677.)

Continuous Warm Cardioplegia

Although intermittent hypothermic cardioplegic techniques have increased the myocardium's tolerance to ischemia and reduced the potential for reperfusion injury, disadvantages remain. Protection from metabolic, morphologic, and functional consequences of ischemia are incomplete, and hypothermia alters membrane stability, volume regulation, and impedes both energy production and oxygen dissociation from hemoglobin. Continuous cardioplegia has the advantage that ischemia is never imposed, and initial results have been encouraging (170–172). The continuous delivery of warm cardioplegia overcomes the disadvantages of ischemia and hypothermia, resulting in improved postischemic systolic and diastolic performance (173) and hemodynamics, reduced perioperative complications (172, 174), and lower mortality (172). Moreover, since ischemia is largely

avoided, this technique may be particularly applicable to high-risk patients with poor preoperative myocardial function necessitating prolonged periods of cross-clamping (≥3 hours) (175). Although antegrade delivery of continuous warm cardioplegia will be difficult with aortic valve incompetence and poor distribution beyond severe coronary stenoses, the retrograde route of administration may overcome this problem. Despite the theoretical advantages of continuous warm cardioplegia, the technical problems associated with its use and the intentional or unintentional interruption of cardioplegia delivery raises the specter of ischemic and reperfusion injury in that any ischemia is unprotected. In addition, continuous cardioplegia may cause systemic hyperkalemia, hemoglobinemia, and generalized edema. The continued presence of blood in the field may hinder visualization of coronary anastomoses, valvular structures, and other aspects of cardiac anatomy.

Retrograde Cardioplegia

Administration of blood through the coronary sinus in a retrograde fashion to nourish the myocardium during operations on the aortic valve was practiced as early as 1957 to avoid the technical difficulties of antegrade coronary cannulation (269). The technique of retrograde cardioplegia has recently become popular after a laboratory study demonstrated its usefulness (270). The method has several theoretical advantages, which include even distribution of cardioplegia in diffuse coronary disease (especially when all areas cannot be revascularized), avoidance of the need for direct coronary cannulation and possible late osteostenosis in patients undergoing aortic valve replacement, and exclusion of the need for aortotomy and cannulation of the coronary ostia in patients with minimal aortic regurgitation who do not require aortic valve replacement. In addition, patients who need coronary reoperations and have a patent internal mammary artery are at some risk for inadequate myocardial protection because of the inability to infuse cold cardioplegia through the patent mammary. Although cardioplegic techniques can be cumbersome, recent advances in the design of coronary sinus cannulae permitting safe infusion of large volumes of cardioplegic solution into the coronary sinus while monitoring coronary sinus pressure have allowed the technique to become quite popular.

Coronary sinus cardioplegia alone can be quite effective; however, it may not protect the right ventricle because of problems of distribution (271). Additional efforts at right ventricular protection by topical hypothermia can be used with coronary sinus perfusion alone, or the addition of a single dose of antegrade cardioplegia combined with retrograde induction can offset these limitations (272). Recent experimental studies and clinical observations tend to support the usefulness of combined antegrade/retrograde cardioplegia in difficult coronary and valve operations, and a consensus may be developing that combined infusion techniques are preferable (273).

MYOCARDIAL PROTECTION IN THE NEONATAL AND INFANT HEART

Myocardial protection for operations in neonates and infants is of great importance in preventing perioperative morbidity and mortality and may have long-term impact on the preservation of myocardial function. Although there is laboratory evidence for greater tolerance to ischemia in the immature heart (274), clinical myocardial protection strategies and cardioplegia solutions that are effective in adult hearts may be less effective in the immature infant or neonatal heart (275). Therefore, optimal myocardial protection in the infant must address the differences in structure and function of the immature heart as well as conditions affecting the neonatal heart that are peculiar to children with congenital heart disease.

The immature heart has a denser structure than the adult heart, with a higher water and protein content per gram. As a result of the structural differences, the immature heart is less compliant and has less preload reserve, resulting in a narrower range of function closer to the peak of the Starling curve (276). Because of decreased endogenous glycogen stores, the immature heart relies more heavily on glucose metabolism and is more capable of sustained anaerobic metabolism than is the adult heart. This metabolic advantage may be the physiologic mechanism underlying the greater tolerance of the immature heart to ischemia. This increased tolerance is partly explained by less calcium sequestration during ischemia and reperfusion, as well as less catabolism and more efficient regeneration of adenosine triphosphate (277).

Because the neonatal heart exhibits a lower sarcoplasmic reticular calcium ATPase activity with less calcium sequestration, calcium-mediated excitation-contraction coupling appears to mimic that of lower vertebrates by being more dependent on extracellular calcium than that of the adult. Calcium channel blockade has been found to depress neonatal myocardial function more than that of the adult heart, suggesting a greater dependency of the neonatal heart on extracellular calcium (278). Better maintenance of postischemic biochemical and functional parameters in calcium exchange may contribute to superior postischemic myocardial function in neonatal hearts (279).

Special Situations Affecting Myocardial Protection in Children with Congenital Heart Disease

Acute and chronic conditions affecting the myocardium of neonates or children with congenital heart disease appear quite commonly in the practice of congenital cardiac surgery. Some of these conditions require special planning in the conduct of cardiac operations, especially regarding myocardial protection, and some are unique to congenital heart patients.

It is not uncommon for neonates to present for operation having suffered refractory cardiac failure or prolonged periods of hypoxia and metabolic acidosis that may increase the mortality of open cardiac operations several fold (280). Although neonatal hearts are more resistant to the effects of hypoxia than adult hearts, severe hypoxia in the neonatal heart can depress contractile function and high-energy phosphate levels (281). During long periods of anaerobic metabolism, glycogen levels fall, thus rendering the heart susceptible to further ischemic injury. Metabolic deficits, reperfusion injury, and decreased calcium uptake are the precursors of a severely damaged heart following a long intraoperative

ischemic insult in these patients. It may be much wiser to open a functionally closed ductus with a prostaglandin infusion and delay corrective surgery for several days until these deficits have been reversed, rather than subject a critically ill newborn to a long period of intraoperative ischemia. If operation is mandatory, cardioplegic techniques that emphasize substrate enhancement and that minimize reperfusion injury are of great importance (282).

Chronic cyanosis is a common condition in young children undergoing cardiac operation. Experimentally, chronic hypoxia has resulted in decreased ejection fraction, a profound drop in high-energy phosphates, and decreased recovery of systolic and diastolic function after a period of ischemic arrest and reperfusion (283–285). The reasons for these occurrences are not clear, but relate to a complex interaction between hypoxia and structural heart disease. In addition, children with decreased pulmonary blood flow have increased bronchial collateral flow between coronary, pericardial, and bronchial circulations that can markedly compromise intraoperative myocardial protection. Noncoronary collateral flow washes out cardioplegia, rewarms the heart, and causes resumption of contractile activity (286). For the reasons listed above, children with chronic cyanosis require additional planning and careful consideration of myocardial protection when undergoing long periods of intraoperative ischemia.

Patent ductus arteriosus and atrial and ventricular septal defects commonly exist in neonates and infants. Left or right ventricular pressure and/or volume overload may progress significantly before operative correction. In these particular patients, myocardial protection may be complicated by severe hypertrophy and/or dilation coupled with poor ventricular function. The realization that closure of a ventricular septal defect or ligation of a patent ductus arteriosus may subject a previously "protected" ventricle to a new postoperative stress should be realized in the preoperative evaluation, and adequate measures taken to protect this ventricle during operation.

Clinical Strategies for Protecting the Neonatal Myocardium

Hypothermia remains one of the essential features of myocardial protection in both adults and children. As previously discussed, ventricular decompression, arrest, and hypothermia work together to reduce O_2 demand. Maintenance of myocardial temperature as close to 10°C as feasible during the period of aortic cross-clamping is necessary to reduce O_2 demand optimally. Topically applied ice slush may be used as a supplementary method to achieve the temperatures. In the vast majority of infants and children to whom a cardioprotective solution is administered through the aortic root, distribution of cardioplegic solution is not hampered since the coronary arteries are normal and the aortic valve is competent. Therefore, administration of a cold solution via the aortic root is very simple and can be administered through an 18-gauge catheter inserted just prior to aortic cross-clamping. Although many surgeons use blood cardioplegia in infants, it is still reasonable to use nonblood cardioplegic solutions for cross-clamping periods of 1 hour or less, as no data have been published that prove that blood cardioplegia is definitely superior to crystalloid cardioplegia in the neonatal myocardium undergoing relatively short periods of cross-clamping. On the other hand, in a patient who has undergone a significant period of *preoperative* ischemia or a combination of hypoxia and acidosis, the cardioplegia strategy may need to be changed. Evidence is accumulating that blood cardioplegia enriched with amino acid substrates can provide superior protection in both experimental and clinical situations given these conditions (282). In such a situation, the cross-clamp should be applied early while the heart is near systemic temperature, and the heart arrested in the warm state and then gradually cooled (i.e., warm

induction). Cardioplegic solution volumes as high as 30 to 40 ml/kg of body weight may be necessary to achieve adequate hypothermia after warm induction. Delivery of the cardioplegic solution is often best controlled by the surgeon using a syringe in very small infants, but can be given via the heart-lung machine (cardioplegia delivery circuit) in older children. In the severely injured ventricle, there is evidence that a concluding dose of warm cardioplegia that maintains electromechanical arrest while again providing substrates to the myocardium can be helpful (247). There is also some evidence that the addition of other myoprotective agents, such as free-radical oxygen scavengers and calcium channel blockers, can be of value in the neonatal myocardium, although this evidence is based entirely upon experimental data (185, 287).

If the aortic valve is incompetent or if other anatomic situations preclude the safe delivery of cardioplegic solution in an antegrade fashion, cardioplegia can be delivered retrograde via the coronary sinus. In such cases a larger cardioplegia volume will be necessary and coronary sinus pressure should be monitored. At this time, there are no coronary sinus catheters specifically designed for retrograde infusion in infants and young children, so this technique cannot be specifically recommended.

In patients with increased systemic-to-pulmonary collaterals, different cardioplegia strategies must be used to counteract washout of solution and cardiac rewarming. In order to maintain myocardial hypothermia, repeat infusions of cardioplegic solution and frequent administration of topical cooling solutions may be necessary to provide continuous myocardial hypothermia. A simpler and frequently used strategy in the infant employs profound hypothermia to 18°C nasopharyngeal and/or rectal temperature and periods of low flow CPB or total circulatory arrest during the intracardiac portion of the repair. These techniques limit the amount of blood entering the left heart from the pulmonary circulation and thus avoid the deleterious effects of myocardial rewarming. Periods of up to an hour of total circulatory arrest have proven valuable in the correction of very complicated neonatal congenital defects. Using these techniques, only a single dose of cardioplegia is necessary, although a second dose of warm cardioplegia can be given at the conclusion of the aortic cross-clamping period to provide nutritive support to a previously injured or failing myocardium.

In certain situations, such as operations on the right ventricle in which the atrial septum is intact, the intracardiac portion of the defect can be repaired without cross-clamping the aorta. The left ventricle can be vented during a period of hypothermia-induced ventricular fibrillation. Because of possible introduction of air into the systemic circulation, most other congenital heart operations require aortic cross-clamping.

If multiple doses of cardioplegia are to be used, rigorous attention to removing air from the aortic root prior to the repeat infusions of cardioplegia should be observed. As in all other intracardiac operations, careful removal of air from all intracardiac chambers and the aorta prior to final cross-clamp removal is essential.

CONCLUSIONS

Our understanding of the pathophysiology of ischemia and reperfusion has evolved from relatively simple concepts to exquisitely detailed and choreographed molecular interactions involving single cell type, cell-cell, and whole organ participation. From this unraveling of a detailed and complex pathophysiologic tapestry must come applications that target the offending mechanisms yet are practical, simple, and safe. No doubt more aggressive and target-specific pharmacology will be forthcoming that exploits these molecular interactions. In this regard, prevention of neutrophil activity by monoclonal antibodies directed to-

ward neutrophil or endothelial components of adhesive glycoprotein complexes may become an important therapeutic tool to limit neutrophil participation in ischemic-reperfusion injury. In addition, compounds that act as true antiischemic agents by increasing the cell's inherent tolerance to ischemia may be on the horizon. Such agents include the ATP-sensitive potassium (K^+_{ATP})-channel openers including cromakalim, pinacidil, and nicorandil. These drugs would supplement hypothermia and rapid asystole in efforts to increase the myocardium's tolerance to ischemia. In addition, therapeutic approaches that augment the myocardium's own inherent defense mechanisms may become increasingly important. These approaches would include preserving and reinforcing the viability and secretory functions of the vascular endothelium as a means of inhibiting neutrophil and platelet activity, oxygen radical production, and limiting tissue damage as well as graft occlusion. Agents that enhance intravascular as well as interstitial adenosine (5-amino-4-imidazolecarboxamide riboside deaminase inhibitors, transport inhibitors) levels or interact specifically with adenosine receptor subtypes may assume a more eminent role in surgical myocardial protection.

It is worth repeating that these seemingly complex pharmacologic approaches need not translate into more complex cardioplegic solutions and regimens for delivery. Certainly the menu of solution formulations, additives, and supplements is enormous, which may present a smoke screen to their judicious application. However, a multifaceted approach to myocardial protection is predicated on the complex multifactorial nature of myocardial ischemic-reperfusion injury. This complex pathophysiology makes it unlikely that a single intervention or drug will be effective in preventing, delaying, or reversing clinical postischemic injury. However, a target-specific approach to myocardial protection, embracing the principles outlined here, will permit the design of myoprotective strategies that are both pragmatic and flexible, and permit better preservation of the myocardium during more prolonged procedures, in more severely damaged myocardium, or in hearts stored for transplantation.

ACKNOWLEDGMENTS

We are grateful to David Charles, C.C.P., for contributions to the section on cardioplegia delivery devices, and to Ms. Sharon Ireland for meticulous preparation of the manuscript and figures. Supported in part by grant HL36377 (Dr. Vinten-Johansen) from the National Heart, Lung and Blood Institute of the National Institutes of Health.

REFERENCES

1. Brock RC, Ross DN. Hypothermia. III: Clinical application of hypothermic techniques. Guy's Hosp Rep 1955;104:99.
2. Drew CE, Anderson IM. Profound hypothermia in cardiac surgery: report of 3 cases. Lancet 1959;1:748–750.
3. Sealy WC, Young WG Jr, Brown IW Jr, Smith WW, Lesage AM. Profound hypothermia combined with extracorporeal circulation for open-heart surgery. Surgery 1960;48:432–438.
4. Melrose DG, Dreyer B, Bentall HH, et al. Elective cardiac arrest: preliminary communication. Lancet 1955;2:21–22.
5. Helmsworth JA, Kaplan S, Clark LC Jr, McAdams AJ, Matthews EC, Edwards FK. Myocardial injury associated with asystole induced with potassium citrate. Ann Surg 1959;149:200.
6. Shumway NE, Lower RR. Hypothermia for extended periods of anoxic arrest. Surg Forum 1959;10:563–566.
7. Shumway NE, Lower RR, Stofer RC. Selective hypothermia of the heart in anoxic cardiac arrest. Surg Gynecol Obstet 1959;109:750–754.
8. Taber RE, Morales AR, Fine G. Myocardial necrosis and the postoperative low-cardiac-output syndrome. Ann Thorac Surg 1967;4:12–28.
9. Najafi H, Henson D, Dye WS, et al. Left ventricular hemorrhagic necrosis. Ann Thorac Surg 1969;7:550–561.
10. Buckberg GD, Brazier JR, Nelson RL, et al. Studies of the effects of hypothermia on regional myocardial blood flow and metabolism during cardiopulmonary bypass. I. The adequately perfused beating, fibrillating, and arrested heart. J Thorac Cardiovasc Surg 1977;73:87–94.
11. Cooley DA, Reul GJ, Wukasch DC. Ischemic contracture of the heart: "stone heart." Am J Cardiol 1972;29:575–577.
12. Katz AM, Tada M. The "stone heart": a challenge to the biochemist. Am J Cardiol 1972;29:578–580.
13. Bretschneider HJ, Hubner G, Knoll D, Lohr B, Nordbeck H, Spieckermann PG. Myocardial resistance and tolerance to ischemia: physiological and biochemical basis. J Cardiovasc Surg 1975;16:241–261.
14. Søndergaard T, Berg E, Staffeldt I, Szczepanski K. Cardioplegic cardiac arrest in aortic surgery. J Cardiovasc Surg 1975;16:288–290.
15. Gay WA Jr, Ebert PA. Functional, metabolic, and morphologic effects of potassium-induced cardioplegia. Surgery 1973;74:284–290.
16. Hearse DJ, Stewart DA, Braimbridge MV, Chir B. Cellular protection during myocardial ischemia: the development and characterization of a procedure for the induction of reversible ischemic arrest. Circulation 1976;54:193–202.
17. Follette DM, Mulder DG, Maloney JV, Buckberg GD. Advantages of blood cardioplegia over continuous coronary perfusion or intermittent ischemia. Experimental and clinical study. J Thorac Cardiovasc Surg 1978;76:604–619.
18. Cunningham JN Jr, Adams PX, Knopp EA, et al. Preservation of ATP, ultrastructure, and ventricular function after aortic cross-clamping and reperfusion. Clinical use of blood potassium cardioplegia. J Thorac Cardiovasc Surg 1979;78:708–720.
19. Olin CL, Bomfim V, Bendz R, Kaijser L, Strom SJ, Sylven CH. Myocardial protection during aortic valve replacement. comparison of different methods by intraoperative coronary sinus blood sampling and postoperative serial serum enzyme determinations. J Thorac Cardiovasc Surg 1981;82:837–847.
20. Hearse DJ. Ischemia, reperfusion, and the determinants of tissue injury. Cardiovasc Drugs Ther 1990;4:767–776.
21. Hearse DJ. Ischemia at the crossroads? Cardiovasc Drug Ther 1988;2:9–15.
22. Jennings RB. Myocardial ischemia-observations, definitions, and speculations. J Mol Cell Cardiol 1970;1:345–349.
23. Neely JR, Grotyohann LW. Role of glycolytic products in damage to ischemic myocardium. Dissociation of adenosine triphosphate levels and recovery of function of reperfused ischemic hearts. Circ Res 1984;55:816–824.
24. Silverman NA, del Nido P, Krukenkamp I, Levitsky S. Biologic rationale for formulation of antegrade cardioplegic solutions. In: Chitwood WR Jr, ed. Cardiac surgery: state of the art reviews, myocardial preservation: clinical appli-

cations. Vol 2. Philadelphia, Pennsylvania: Hanley and Belfus, Inc, 1988:181–195.

25. Buckberg GD. A proposed "solution" to the cardioplegic controversy. J Thorac Cardiovasc Surg 1979;77:803–815.

26. Hearse DJ. The protection of the ischemic myocardium: surgical success v clinical failure? Prog Cardiovasc Dis 1988;30:381–402.

27. Butchart EG, McEnany MT, Strich G, Sbokos C, Austen WG. The influence of prearrest factors on the preservation of left ventricular function during cardiopulmonary bypass. J Thorac Cardiovasc Surg 1980;79:812–821.

28. Robertson JM, Vinten-Johansen J, Buckberg GD, Rosenkranz ER, Maloney JV Jr. Safety of prolonged aortic clamping with blood cardioplegia. I. Glutamate enrichment in normal hearts. J Thorac Cardiovasc Surg 1984;88: 395–401.

29. Gayheart PA, Vinten-Johansen J, Johnston WE, et al. Oxygen requirements of the dyskinetic myocardial segment. Am J Physiol 1989;257: H1184–H1191.

30. Allen BS, Rosenkranz ER, Buckberg GD, et al. Studies of controlled reperfusion after ischemia. VII. High oxygen requirements of dyskinetic cardiac muscle. J Thorac Cardiovasc Surg 1986;92:543–552.

31. Nakanishi K, Lefer DJ, Johnston WE, Vinten-Johansen J. Transient hypocalcemia during the initial phase of reperfusion extends myocardial necrosis after 2 hours of coronary occlusion. Cor Art Dis 1991;2:1009–1021.

32. Vinten-Johansen J, Edgerton TA, Howe HR, et al. Immediate functional recovery and avoidance of reperfusion injury with surgical revascularization of short-term coronary occlusion. Circulation 1985;72:431–439.

33. Vinten-Johansen J, Johnston WE, Mills SA, et al. Reperfusion injury after temporary coronary occlusion. J Thorac Cardiovasc Surg 1988;95: 960–968.

34. Schaper W, Binz K, Sass S, Winkler B. Influence of collateral blood flow and of variations in MVO$_2$ on tissue-ATP content in ischemic and infarcted myocardium. J Mol Cell Cardiol 1987;19:19–37.

35. Vinten-Johansen J, Chiantella V, Johnston WE, et al. Adjuvant N-(2-mercaptopropionyl)-glycine in blood cardioplegia does not improve myocardial protection in ischemically damaged hearts. J Thorac Cardiovasc Surg 1990; 100:65–76.

36. Vinten-Johansen J, Chiantella V, Faust KB, et al. Myocardial protection with blood cardioplegia in ischemically injured hearts: reduction of reoxygenation injury with allopurinol. Ann Thorac Surg 1988;45:319–326.

37. Brazier J, Hottenrott C, Buckberg G. Noncoronary collateral myocardial blood flow. Ann Thorac Surg 1975;19:426–435.

38. Vinten-Johansen J, Barnard RJ, Buckberg GD, et al. Left ventricular O$_2$ requirements of pressure and volume loading in the normal canine heart and inaccuracy of pressure-derived indices of O$_2$ demand. Cardiovasc Res 1982;16:439–447.

39. Vinten-Johansen J, Duncan HW, Finkenberg JG, et al. Prediction of myocardial O$_2$ requirements by indirect indices. Am J Physiol 1982;243: H862–H868.

40. Suga H, Hayashi T, Shirahata M, Suehiro S, Hisano R. Regression of cardiac oxygen consumption on ventricular pressure-volume area in dog. Am J Physiol 1981;240:H320–H325.

41. Vinten-Johansen J, Gayheart PA, Johnston WE, Julian JS, Cordell AR. Regional function, blood flow, and oxygen utilization relations in repetitively occluded reperfused canine myocardium. Am J Physiol 1991;261:H538–H547.

42. Mills SA, Hansen K, Vinten-Johansen J, et al. Enhanced functional recovery with venting during cardioplegic arrest in chronically damaged hearts. Ann Thorac Surgery 1985;40:566–573.

43. Allen BS, Okamoto F, Buckberg GD, Bugyi H, Leaf J. Studies of controlled reperfusion after ischemia. XIII. Reperfusion conditions: critical importance of total ventricular decompression during regional reperfusion. J Thorac Cardiovasc Surg 1986;92:605–612.

44. Simpson PJ, Lucchesi BR. Free radicals and myocardial ischemia and reperfusion injury. J Lab Clin Med 1987;110:13–30.

45. Bolli R. Oxygen-derived free radicals and myocardial reperfusion injury: an overview. Cardiovasc Drug Ther 1991;5(suppl 2): 249–268.

46. Bolli R, Jeroudi MO, Patel BS, et al. Marked reduction of free radical generation and contractile dysfunction by antioxidant therapy begun at the time of reperfusion. Evidence that myocardial "stunning" is a manifestation of reperfusion injury. Circ Res 1989;65:607–622.

47. Hearse DJ. Reperfusion of the ischemic myocardium. J Mol Cell Cardiol 1977;9:605–616.

48. Hearse DJ, Humphrey SM, Chain EB. Abrupt reoxygenation of the anoxic potassium-arrested perfused rat heart: a study of myocardial enzyme release. J Mol Cell Cardiol 1973;5: 395–407.

49. Opie LH. Reperfusion injury and its pharmacologic modification. Circulation 1989;80: 1049–1062.

50. Jennings RB, Reimer KA, Steenbergen C. Myocardial ischemia revisited. the osmolar load, membrane damage, and reperfusion. J Mol Cell Cardiol 1986;18:769–780.

51. Ganz W, Watanabe I, Kanamasa K, et al. Does reperfusion extend necrosis? A study in a single territory of myocardial ischemia—half reperfused and half not reperfused. Circulation 1990;82:1020–1033.

52. Becker LC, Ambrosio G. Myocardial consequences of reperfusion. Prog Cardiovasc Dis 1987;30:23–44.

53. Nakanishi K, Vinten-Johansen J, Lefer DJ, et al. Intracoronary L-arginine during reperfusion improves regional function and reduces infarct size. Am J Physiol, 1992;263:H1650–H1658.

54. Vinten-Johansen J, Okamoto F, Rosenkranz ER, Buckberg GD, et al. Studies of controlled reperfusion after ischemia. V. Superiority of surgical versus medical reperfusion after regional ischemia. J Thorac Cardiovasc Surg 1986;92:525–534.

55. Jennings RB, Sommers HM, Smyth GA, et al. Myocardial necrosis induced by temporary occlusion of a coronary artery in the dog. Arch Pathol 1960;70:68–78.

56. Vinten-Johansen J, Edgerton TA, Hansen KJ, Carroll P, Mills SA, Cordell AR. Surgical revascularization of acute (1 hour) coronary occlusion: blood versus crystalloid cardioplegia. Ann Thorac Surg 1986;42:247–254.

57. Lefer DJ, Nakanishi K, Johnston WE, et al. Antineutrophil and myocardial protecting actions of SPM-5185, a novel nitric oxide donor, following acute myocardial ischemia and reperfusion in dogs. In: Biology of Nitric Oxide. London: Portland Press, 1992:188–190.

58. Guarnieri C, Flamigni F, Caldarera CM. Role of oxygen in the cellular damage induced by re-oxygenat?ion of hypoxic heart. J Mol Cell Cardiol 1980;12:797–808.

59. Freeman BA, Crapo JD. Biology of disease: free radicals and tissue injury. Lab Invest 1982;47:412–426.

60. McCord JM. Oxygen-derived free radicals in postischemic tissue injury. New Engl J Med 1985;312:159–163.

61. Ferrari R, Ceconi C, Curello S, et al. Intracellular effects of myocardial ischaemia and reperfusion: role of calcium and oxygen. Eur Heart J 1986;7(suppl A):3–12.

62. Krause SM, Hess ML. Characterization of cardiac sarcoplasmic reticulum dysfunction during short term, normothermic, global ischemia. Circ Res 1984;55:176–184.

63. Hess ML, Okabe E, Ash P, Kontos HA. Free radical mediation of the effects of acidosis on calcium transport by cardiac sarcoplasmic reticulum in whole heart homogenate. Cardiovasc Res 1984;18:149–157.

64. Nejima J, Knight DR, Fallon JT, Uemura N, Manders WT, et al. Superoxide dismutase reduces reperfusion arrhythmias but fails to salvage regional function or myocardium at risk in conscious dogs. Circulation 1989;79:143–153.

65. Manning AS, Hearse DJ. Reperfusion-induced arrhythmias: mechanisms and prevention. J Mol Cell Cardiol 1984;16:497–518.

66. Hammond B, Hess ML. The oxygen free radical system: potential mediator of myocardial injury. J Am Coll Cardiol 1985;6:215–220.

67. Shlafer M, Myers CL, Adkins S. Mitochondrial hydrogen peroxide generation and activities of glutathione peroxidase and superoxide dismutase following global ischemia. J Mol Cell Cardiol 1987;19:1195–1206.

68. Otani H, Tanaka H, Inoue T, et al. In vitro study on contribution of oxidative metabolism of isolated rabbit heart mitochondria to myocardial reperfusion injury. Circ Res 1984;55:168–175.

69. Jennings RB, Reimer KA. Lethal myocardial ischemic injury. Am J Pathol 1981;102:241–255.

70. Jarasch ED, Bruder G, Heid HW. Significance of xanthine oxidase in capillary endothelial cells. Acta Physiol Scand 1986;548:39–46.

71. Chambers DE, Parks DA, Patterson G, et al. Xanthine oxidase as a source of free radical damage in myocardial ischemia. J Mol Cell Cardiol 1985;17:145–152.

72. Roy RS, McCord JM. Superoxide and ischemia: conversion of xanthine dehydrogenase to xanthine oxidase. In: Greenwald R, Cohen G, eds. Oxyradicals and their scavenger systems. Vol 2. Cellular and molecular aspects. New York: Elsevier Science, 1983:145–153.

73. Downey JM, Hearse DJ, Yellon DM. The role of xanthine oxidase during myocardial ischemia in several species including man. J Mol Cell Cardiol 1988;20(suppl II):55–63.

74. Jacob HS, Vercellotti GM. Granulocyte-mediated endothelial injury: oxidant damage amplified by lactoferrin and platelet activating factor. In: Halliwell B, ed. Oxygen radicals and tissue injury. Rockville, Maryland: FASEB Publications, 1988:57–62.

75. Babior BM, Curnutte JT, McMurrich BJ. The particulate superoxide-forming system from human neutrophils. Properties of the system and further evidence supporting its participation in the respiratory burst. J Clin Invest 1976;58:989–996.

76. Romson JL, Hook BG, Rigot VH, Schork MA, Swanson DP, Lucchesi BR. The effect of ibuprofen on accumulation of indium-III labelled platelets and leukocytes in experimental myocardial infarction. Circulation 1982;66:1002–1011.

77. Ko W, Hawes AS, Lazenby WD, et al. Myocardial

reperfusion injury. platelet-activating factor stimulates polymorphonuclear leukocyte hydrogen peroxide production during myocardial reperfusion. J Thorac Cardiovasc Surg 1991; 102:297–308.

78. Chenowith DE, Cooper SW, Hugli TE, Stewart RW, Blackstone EH, Kirklin JW. Complement activation during cardiopulmonary bypass: evidence for generation of C3a and C5a anaphylatoxins. N Engl J Med 1981;304:497–503.

79. Videm V, Fosse E, Mollnes TE, Garred P, Svennevig JL. Complement activation with bubble and membrane oxygenators in aortocoronary bypass grafting. Ann Thorac Surg 1990; 50:387–391.

80. Faymonville ME, Pincemail J, Duchateau J, et al. Myeloperoxidase and elastase as markers of leukocyte activation during cardiopulmonary bypass in humans. J Thorac Cardiovasc Surg 1991;102:309–317.

81. Lucchesi BR, Mullane KM. Leukocytes and ischemia-induced myocardial injury. Ann Rev Pharmacol Toxicol 1986;26:201–224.

82. Rao PS, Cohen MV, Mueller HS. Production of free radicals and lipid peroxides in early experimental myocardial ischemia. J Mol Cell Cardiol 1983;15:713–716.

83. Zweier JL, Flaherty JT, Weisfeldt ML. Direct measurement of free radical generation following reperfusion of ischemic myocardium. Proc Natl Acad Sci USA 1987;84:1404–1407.

84. Garlick PB, Davies MJ, Hearse DJ, Slater TF. Direct detection of free radicals in the reperfused rat heart using electron spin resonance spectroscopy. Circ Res 1987;61:757–760.

85. Arroyo CM, Kramer JH, Dickens BF, Weglicki WB. Identification of free radicals in myocardial ischemia/reperfusion by spin trapping with nitrone DMPO. FEBS Lett 1987;221: 101–104.

86. Bolli R, Patel BS, Jeroudi MO, et al. Demonstration of free radical generation in "stunned" myocardium of intact dogs with the use of the spin trap alpha-phenyl N-tent-butyl nitrone. J Clin Invest 1988;82:476–485.

87. Jolly SR, Kane WJ, Bailie MB, Abrams GD, Lucchesi BR. Canine myocardial reperfusion injury. Its reduction by the combined administration of superoxide dismutase and catalase. Circ Res 1984;54:277–285.

88. Lucchesi BR, Werns SW, Fantone JC. The role of the neutrophil and free radicals in ischemic myocardial injury. J Mol Cell Cardiol 1989;21: 1241–1251.

89. Engler RL. Free-radical and granulocyte-mediated injury during myocardial ischemia and reperfusion. Am J Cardiol 1989;63:19E–23E.

90. Mullane K. Neutrophil and endothelial changes in reperfusion injury. Trends Cardiovasc Med 1991;1:282–289.

91. Sommers HM, Jennings RB. Experimental acute myocardial infarction: histological and histochemical studies of early myocardial infarcts induced by temporary or permanent occlusion of a coronary artery. Lab Invest 1964;13:1491–1503.

92. Tsao PS, Aoki N, Lefer DJ, et al. Time course of endothelial dysfunction and myocardial injury during myocardial ischemia and reperfusion in the cat. Circulation 1990;82:1402–1412.

93. Flynn PJ, Becker WK, Vercellotti GM, et al. Ibuprofen inhibits granulocyte responses to inflammatory mediators. A proposed mechanism for reduction of experimental myocardial infarct size. Inflammation 1984;8:33–44.

94. Lefer AM, Tsao PS, Lefer DJ, Ma XL. Role of endothelial dysfunction in the pathogenesis of reperfusion injury after myocardial ischemia. FASEB J 1991;5:2029–2034.

95. Pinckard RN, O'Rourke RA, Crawford MH, et al. Complement localization and mediation of ischemic injury in baboon myocardium. J Clin Invest 1980;66:1050–1056.

96. McManus LM, Kolb WP, Crawford MH, et al. Complement localization in ischemic baboon myocardium. Lab Invest 1983;48:436–447.

97. Dreyer WJ, Michael LH, West MS, et al. Neutrophil accumulation in ischemic canine myocardium. Insights into time course, distribution, and mechanism of localization during early reperfusion. Circulation 1991;84:400–411.

98. Becker LC, Ambrosio G, Manissi J, Weisman HF. The no-reflow phenomenon: a misnomer? In: Sideman S, Beyar R, eds. Analysis and simulation of the cardiac system—ischemia. Boca Raton, FL: CRC Press, Inc, 1989:289–309.

99. Engler RL, Schmid-Schonbein GW, Pavelec RS. Leukocyte capillary plugging in myocardial ischemia and reperfusion in the dog. Am J Pathol 1983;111:98–111.

100. Powell WJ Jr, DiBona DR, Flores J, Leaf A. The protective effect of hyperosmotic mannitol in myocardial ischemia and necrosis. Circulation 1976;54:603–615.

101. Engler RL, Dahlgren MD, Peterson M, et al. Accumulation of polymorphonuclear leukocytes during 3-h experimental myocardial ischemia. Am J Physiol 1986;251:H93–H100.

102. Engler RL, Dahlgren MD, Morris D, et al. Role of leukocytes in response to acute myocardial ischemia and reflow in dogs. Am J Physiol 1986; 251:H314–H323.

103. Shen AC, Jennings RB. Kinetics of calcium accumulation in acute myocardial ischemic injury. Am J Pathol 1972;67:441–452.

104. Walsh LG, Tormey JM. Subcellular electrolyte

shifts during in vitro myocardial ischemia and reperfusion. Am J Physiol 1988;255: H917–H928.

105. Pridjian AK, Levitsky S, Krukenkamp I, et al. Intracellular sodium and calcium in the postischemic myocardium. Ann Thorac Surg 1987;43:416–419.

106. Tani M, Neely JR. Mechanisms of reduced reperfusion injury by low Ca^{2+} and/or high K^+. Am J Physiol 1990;258:H1025–H1031.

107. Tani M, Neely JR. Role of intracellular Na^+ in Ca^{2+} overload and depressed recovery of ventricular function of reperfused ischemic rat hearts. Possible involvement of H^+-Na^+ and Na^+-Ca^{2+} exchange. Circ Res 1989;65: 1045–1056.

108. Langer GA. Sodium-calcium exchange in the heart. Ann Rev Physiol 1982;44:435–449.

109. Vinten-Johansen J, Johnston WE, Lefer DJ, et al. Controlled reperfusion attenuates no-reflow and reduces infarct size [abstract]. Circulation 1990;82(suppl III):286.

110. Vinten-Johansen J, Lefer DJ, Nakanishi K, et al. Controlled coronary hydrodynamics of reperfusion reduces infarct size and improves segmental systolic and diastolic function. Cor Art Dis 1992;3:1081–1093.

111. Johnson RE, Dorsey LM, Moye SJ. Cardioplegic infusion: the safe limits of pressure and temperature. J Thorac Cardiovasc Surg 1982;83: 813–824.

112. Yamazaki S, Fujibayashi Y, Rajagopalan RE, et al. Effects of staged versus sudden reperfusion after acute coronary occlusion in the dog. J Am Coll Cardiol 1986;7:564–572.

113. Rosenkranz ER, Vinten-Johansen J, Buckberg GD, Okamoto F, Edwards H, Bugyi H. Benefits of normothermic induction of blood cardioplegia in energy-depleted hearts, with maintenance of arrest by multidose cold blood cardioplegic infusions. J Thorac Cardiovasc Surg 1982;84:667–677.

114. Follette DM, Fey K, Buckberg GD, et al. Reducing postischemic damage by temporary modification of reperfusate calcium, potassium, pH, and osmolarity. J Thorac Cardiovasc Surg 1981;82:221–238.

115. Opi?e LH, Coetzee WA. Role of calcium ions in reperfusion arrhythmias: relevance to pharmacological intervention. Cardiovasc Drugs Ther 1988;2:623–636.

116. Holmburg SR, Cumming DV, Kusama Y, et al. Reactive oxygen species modify the structure and function of the cardiac sarcoplasmic reticulum calcium-release channel. Cardioscience 1991;2:19–25.

117. Hearse DJ, Tosaki A. Free radicals and calcium: simultaneous interacting triggers as determinants of vulnerability to reperfusion-induced arrhythmias in the rat heart. J Mol Cell Cardiol 1988;20:213–223.

118. Hearse DJ, Humphrey SM, Bullock GR. The oxygen paradox and the calcium paradox: two facets of the same problem? J Mol Cell Cardiol 1978;10:641–668.

119. Buckberg GD. Myocardial temperature management during aortic clamping for cardiac surgery. Protection, preoccupation, and perspective. J Thorac Cardiovasc Surg 1991;102: 895–903.

120. Braunwald E, Kloner RA. The stunned myocardium: prolonged, postischemic ventricular dysfunction. Circulation 1982;66:1146–1149.

121. Taegtmeyer H, Roberts AF, Raine AE. Energy metabolism in reperfused heart muscle: metabolic correlates to return of function. J Am Coll Cardiol 1985;6:864–870.

122. Rosenkranz ER, Okamoto F, Buckberg GD, et al. Studies of controlled reperfusion after ischemia. II. Biochemical studies: failure of tissue ATP to predict recovery of contractile function after controlled reperfusion. J Thorac Cardiovasc Surg 1986;92:488–501.

123. Krukenkamp IB, Silverman NA, Sorlie D, et al. Characterization of postischemic myocardial oxygen utilization. Circulation 1986;74(suppl III):III-125–III-129.

124. Yokoyama H, Julian JS, Vinten-Johansen J, et al. Postischemic $[Ca^{2+}]$ repletion improves cardiac performance without altering oxygen demands. Ann Thorac Surg 1990;49:894–902.

125. Lazar H, Foglia RP, Manganaro AJ, Buckberg GD. Detrimental effects of premature use of inotropic drugs to discontinue cardiopulmonary bypass. J Thorac Cardiovasc Surg 1981;82: 18–25.

126. Bixler TJ, Flaherty JT, Gardner TJ, et al. Effects of calcium administration during post-ischemic reperfusion on myocardial contractility, stiffness, edema, and ultrastructure. Circulation 1978;58(suppl I):184–193.

127. Kloner RA, Ganote CE, and Jennings RB. The "no-reflow" phenomenon after temporary coronary occlusion in the dog. J Clin Invest 1974; 54:1496–1508.

128. Okamoto F, Allen BS, Buckberg GD, et al. Studies of controlled reperfusion after ischemia. XIV. Reperfusion conditions: importance of ensuring gentle versus sudden reperfusion during relief of coronary occlusion. J Thorac Cardiovasc Surg 1986;92:613–620.

129. Mehta JL, Nichols WW, Donnelly WH, et al. Impaired canine coronary vasodilator response to acetylcholine and bradykinin after occlusion-reperfusion. Circ Res 1989;64:43–54.

130. Van Benthuysen KM, McMurtry IF, Horwitz LD.

Reperfusion after acute coronary occlusion in dogs impairs endothelium-dependent relaxation to acetylcholine and augments contractile reactivity in vitro. J Clin Invest 1987;79: 265–274.

131. Sobey CG, Dusting GJ, Grossman HJ, Woodman OL. Impaired vasodilatation of epicardial coronary arteries and resistance vessels following myocardial ischemia and reperfusion in anesthetized dogs. Cor Art Dis 1990;1:363–374.

132. Johnson G III, Tsao PS, Lefer AM. Cardioprotective effects of authentic nitric oxide in myocardial ischemia with reperfusion. Crit Care Med 1991;19:244–252.

133. Furlong B, Henderson AH, Lewis MJ, et al. Endothelium-derived relaxing factor inhibits in vitro platelet aggregation. Br J Pharmacol 1987; 90:687–692.

134. McCall T, Whittle BJR, Boughton-Smith NK, et al. Inhibition of FMLP-induced aggregation of rabbit neutrophils by nitric oxide. Br J Pharmacol 1988;95:517.

135. Loop FD, Lytle BW, Cosgrove DM, et al. Influence of the internal-mammary-artery graft on 10-year survival and other cardiac events. N Engl J Med 1986;314:1–6.

136. Grondin, CM, Campeau L, Lesperance J, Enjalbert M, Bourassa MG. Comparison of late changes in internal mammary artery and saphenous vein grafts in 2 consecutive series of pateints 10 years after operation. Circulation 1984;70:I208–I212.

137. Luscher TF, Diederich D, Siebenmann R, et al. Difference between endothelium-dependent relaxation in arterial and in venous coronary bypass grafts. N Engl J Med 1988;319: 462–467.

138. Yang ZH, Diederich D, Schneider K, et al. Endothelium-derived relaxing factor and protection against contractions induced by histamine and serotonin in the human internal mammary artery and in the saphenous vein. Circulation 1989;80:1041–1048.

139. Lefer DJ, Nakanishi K, Vinten-Johansen J, et al. Cardiac venous endothelial dysfunction after myocardial ischemia and reperfusion in dogs. Am J Physiol 1992;263:H850–H856.

140. Angelini GD, Christie MI, Bryan AJ, Lewis MJ. Surgical preparation impairs release of endothelium-derived relaxing factor from human saphenous vein. Ann Thorac Surg 1989;48: 417–420.

141. Wright RN, Levitsky S, Holland C, Feinberg H. Beneficial effects of potassium cardioplegia during intermittent aortic cross-clamping and reperfusion. J Surg Res 1978;24:201–209.

142. Roberts AJ, Abel RM, Alonso DR, et al. Advantages of hypothermic potassium cardioplegia

and superiority of continuous versus intermittent aortic cross-clamping. J Thorac Cardiovasc Surg 1980;79:44–58.

143. Clark LC Jr, Berg F, Lyons C, et al. Continuous perfusion of the arrested heart with arterialized hypocalcemic blood. Surg Forum 1959;10: 518–521.

144. Lowe JE, Kleinman LH, Reimer KA, Jennings RB, Wechsler AS. Effects of cardioplegia produced by calcium flux inhibition. Surg Forum 1977; 28:279–280.

145. Teoh KH, Christakis GT, Weisel RD, et al. Accelerated myocardial metabolic recovery with terminal warm blood cardioplegia. J Thorac Cardiovasc Surg 1986;91:888–895.

146. Weirich WL, Jones RW, Burke MF. The effect of elective cardiac arrest induced by potassium citrate and acetylcholine on ventricular function. Surg Forum 1959;10:528–532.

147. Bretschneider HJ, Hubner G, Knoll D, Lohr B, Nordbeck H, Spieckermann PG. Myocardial resistance and tolerance to ischemia: physiological and biochemical basis. J Cardiovasc Surg 1975;16:241–260.

148. Jynge P. Protection of the ischemic myocardium calcium-free cardioplegic infusates and the additive effects of coronary infusion and ischemia in the induction of calcium paradox. J Thorac Cardiovasc Surg 1980;28:303–309.

149. Kirkels JH, Ruigrok TJ, VanEchteld CJ, Meijler FL. Low Ca^{2+} reperfusion and enhanced susceptibility of the postischemic heart to the calcium paradox. Circ Res 1989;64:1158–1164.

150. Bigelow WG, Lindsay WK, Greenwood WF. Hypothermia: its possible role in cardiac surgery: An investigation of factors governing survival in dogs at low body temperatures. Ann Surg 1950;132:849–866.

151. Fukunami M, Hearse DJ. The inotropic consequences of cooling: studies in the isolated rat heart. Heart Vessels 1989;5:1–9.

152. Becker H, Vinten-Johansen J, Buckberg GD, et al. Myocardial damage caused by keeping pH 7.40 during systemic deep hypothermia. J Thorac Cardiovasc Surg 1981;82:810–821.

153. Rosenfeldt FL. The relationship between myocardial temperature and recovery after experimental cardioplegic arrest. J Thorac Cardiovasc Surg 1982;84:656–666.

154. Rosenkranz ER, Okamoto F, Buckberg GD, Vinten-Johansen J, Robertson JM, Bugyi H. Safety of prolonged aortic clamping with blood cardioplegia. II. Glutamate enrichment in energy-depleted hearts. J Thorac Cardiovasc Surg 1984;88:402–410.

155. Catinella FP, Cunningham JN Jr, Spencer FC. Myocardial protection during prolonged aortic cross-clamping. Comparison of blood and crys-

talloid cardioplegia. J Thorac Cardiovasc Surg 1984;88:411–423.

156. Harlan BJ, Ross D, MacManus A, et al. Cardioplegic solutions for myocardial preservation: analysis of hypothermic arrest, potassium arrest, and procaine arrest. Circulation 1978; 58(suppl I):I-114–I-118.

157. Speicher CE, Ferrigan L, Wolfson SK Jr, et al. Cold injury of myocardium and pericardium in cardiac hypothermia. Surg Gynecol Obstet 1962;114:659–665.

158. Rousou JA, Parker T, Engelman RM, Breyer RH. Phrenic nerve paresis associated with the use of iced slush and the cooling jacket for topical hypothermia. J Thorac Cardiovasc Surg 1985; 89:921–925.

159. Kohorst WR, Schonfeld SA, Altman M. Bilateral diaphragmatic paralysis following topical cardiac hypothermia. Chest 1984;85:65–68.

160. Shragge BW, Digerness SB, Blackstone EH. Complete recovery of the heart following exposure to profound hypothermia. J Thorac Cardiovasc Surg 1981;81:455–458.

161. Swanson DK, Myerowitz PD. Distribution of adenylates, water, potassium, and sodium within the normal and hypertrophied canine heart following 2 hr of preservation. J Surg Res 1982;32:515–525.

162. Foglia RP, Steed DL, Follette DM, et al. Iatrogenic myocardial edema with potassium cardioplegia. J Thorac Cardiovasc Surg 1979;78: 217–222.

163. Rosenfeldt FL, Hearse DJ, Cankovic-Darracott S, et al. The additive protective effects of hypothermia and chemical cardioplegia during ischemic cardiac arrest in the dog. J Thorac Cardiovasc Surg 1980;79:29–38.

164. Hearse DJ, Stewart DA, Braimbridge MV. The additive protective effects of hypothermia and chemical cardioplegia during ischemic cardiac arrest in the rat. J Thorac Cardiovasc Surg 1980;79:39–43.

165. Kay HR, Levine FH, Fallon JT, et al. Effect of cross-clamp time, temperature, and cardioplegic agents on myocardial function after induced arrest. J Thorac Cardiovasc Surg 1978; 76:590–603.

166. Kenyon NM, Litwak RS, Beck HJ, et al. Preliminary observations in isolated hypothermic cardiac asystole. Surg Forum 1959;10:567–570.

167. Rosenkranz ER, Buckberg GD, Laks H, Mulder DG. Warm induction of cardioplegia with glutamate-enriched blood in coronary patients with cardiogenic shock who are dependent on inotropic drugs and intra-aortic balloon support. J Thorac Cardiovasc Surg 1983;86: 507–518.

168. Fremes SE, Christakis GT, Weisel RD, et al. A clinical trial of blood and crystalloid cardioplegia. J Thorac Cardiovasc Surg 1984;88: 726–741.

169. Buckberg GD, Rosenkranz ER. Principles of cardioplegi?c myocardial protection. In: Roberts AJ, ed. Myocardial protection in cardiac surgery. New York: Marcel Dekker, Inc., 1987: 71–94.

170. Lazar HL, Rivers S, Cambrils M, et al. Continuous versus intermittent cardioplegia in the presence of a coronary occlusion. Ann Thorac Surg 1991;52:913–917.

171. Panos A, Christakis GT, Lichtenstein SV, et al. Operation for acute postinfarction mitral insufficiency using continuous oxygenated blood cardioplegia. Ann Thorac Surg 1989;48: 816–819.

172. Lichtenstein SV, Abel JG, Salerno TA. Warm heart surgery and results of operation for recent myocardial infarction. Ann Thorac Surg 1991; 52:455–460.

173. Yau TM, Weisel RD, Mickle DA, et al. Optimal delivery of blood cardioplegia. Circulation 1991;84(suppl 5):380–388.

174. Lichtenstein SV, Ashe KA, el Dalati H, et al. Warm heart surgery. J Thorac Cardiovasc Surg 1991;101:269–274.

175. Lichtenstein SV, Abel JG, Panos A, et al. Warm heart surgery: experience with long cross-clamp times. Ann Thorac Surg 1991;52: 1009–1013.

176. Yamamoto F, Braimbridge MV, Hearse DJ. Calcium and cardioplegia. The optimal calcium content for the St. Thomas' Hospital cardioplegia solution. J Thorac Cardiovasc Surg 1984;87:908–912.

177. Jynge P, Hearse DJ, Braimbridge M. Myocardial protection during ischemic cardiac arrest. a possible hazard with calcium-free cardioplegic infusates. J Thorac Cardiovasc Surg 1977; 73:848–855.

178. Allen BS, Okamoto F, Buckberg GD, et al. Studies of controlled reperfusion after ischemia. IX. Reperfusate composition: benefits of marked hypocalcemia and diltiazem on regional recovery. J Thorac Cardiovasc Surg 1986;92:564–572.

179. Kuroda K, Ishiguro S, Mori T. Optimal calcium concentration in the initial reperfusate for post-ischemic myocardial performance (calcium concentration during reperfusion). J Mol Cell Cardiol 1986;18:625–633.

180. Baller D, Wolpers HG, Schräder R, et al. Paradoxical effects of catecholamines and calcium on myocardial function in moderate hypothermia. Thorac Cardiovasc Surg 1983;31: 131–138.

181. Jacocks MA, Weiss M, Guyton RA, et al. Regional

myocardial protection during aortic cross-clamp ischemia in dogs: calcium-containing crystalloid solutions. Ann Thorac Surg 1981; 31:454–463.

182. Engelman RM, Auvil J, O'Donoghue MJ, Levitsky S. The significance of multidose cardioplegia and hypothermia in myocardial preservation during ischemic arrest. J Thorac Cardiovasc Surg 1978;75:555–563.

183. Randle PJ, Denton RN, England PJ. Citrate as a metabolic regulator in muscle and adipose tissue. In: Goodman TW, ed. Metabolic roles of citrate. London: Academic Press, 1968: 87–103.

184. Shlafer M, Kane PF, Wiggins VY, Kirsh MM. Possible role for cytotoxic oxygen metabolites in the pathogenesis of cardiac ischemic injury. Circulation 1982;66(suppl I):85–92.

185. Stewart JR, Blackwell WH, Crute SL, Loughlin V, Hess ML, Greenfield LJ. Prevention of myocardial ischemia/reperfusion injury with oxygen free-radical scavengers. Surg Forum 1982; 33:317–320.

186. Myers CL, Weiss SJ, Kirsh MM, Shepard BM, Shlafer M. Effects of supplementing hypothermic crystalloid cardioplegic solution with catalase, superoxide dismutase, allopurinol, or deferoxamine on functional recovery of globally ischemic and reperfused isolated hearts. J Thorac Cardiovasc Surg 1986;91:281–289.

187. Menasche P, Grousset C, Gaudel Y, Mouas C, Piwnica A. Enhancement of cardioplegic protection with the free-radical scavenger peroxidase. Circulation 1986;74(suppl III): 138–144.

188. Chambers DJ, Braimbridge MV, Hearse DJ. Free radicals and cardioplegia. free radical scavengers improve postischemic function of rat myocardium. Eur J Cardiothorac Surg 1987; 1:37–45.

189. Menasche P, Grousset C, Gaudel Y, Piwnica A. A comparative study of free radical scavengers in cardioplegic solutions. Improved protection with peroxidase. J Thorac Cardiovasc Surg 1986;92:264–271.

190. Shlafer M, Kane PF, Kirsh MM. Superoxide dismutase plus catalase enhance the efficacy of hypothermic cardioplegia to protect the globally ischemic, reperfused heart. J Thorac Cardiovasc Surg 1982;83:830–839.

191. Ytrehus K, Gunnes S, Myklebust R, Mjs OD. Protection by superoxide dismutase and catalase in the isolated rat heart reperfused after prolonged cardioplegia: a combined study of metabolic, functional, and morphometric ultrastructural variables. Cardiovasc Res 1987; 21:492–499.

192. Gharagozloo F, Melandez FJ, Hein RA, et al. The

effect of oxygen free radical scavengers on the recovery of regional myocardial function after acute coronary occlusion and surgical reperfusion. J Thorac Cardiovasc Surg 1988; 95:631–636.

193. Greenfield DT, Greenfield LJ, Hess ML. Enhancement of crystalloid cardioplegic protection against global normothermic ischemia by superoxide dismutase plus catalase but not diltiazem in the isolated, working rat heart. J Thorac Cardiovasc Surg 1988;95:799–813.

194. Das DK, Engleman RM, Rousou JA, Breyer RH, Otani H, Lemeshow S. Pathophysiology of superoxide radical as potential mediator of reperfusion injury in pig heart. Basic Res Cardiol 1986;81:155–166.

195. Werns SW, Shea MJ, Driscoll EM, et al. The independent effects of oxygen radical scavengers on canine infarct size. Reduction by superoxide dismutase but not catalase. Circ Res 1985; 56:895–898.

196. Uraizee A, Reimer KA, Murry CE, Jennings RB. Failure of superoxide dismutase to limit size of myocardial infarction after 40 minutes of ischemia and 4 days of reperfusion in dogs. Circulation 1987;75:1237–1248.

197. Shirato C, Miura T, Downey JM. Superoxide dismutase (single dose) delays rather than prevents necrosis in reperfused rabbit heart [Abstract]. FASEB J 1988;2:A918.

198. Chambers DJ, Braimbridge MV, Hearse DJ. Free radicals and cardioplegia: allopurinol and oxypurinol reduce myocardial injury following ischemic arrest. Ann Thorac Surg 1987; 44:291–297.

199. Chambers DJ, Astras G, Takahashi A, Manning AS, Braimbridge MV, Hearse DJ. Free radicals and cardioplegia: organic anti-oxidants as additives to the St. Thomas' Hospital cardioplegic solution. Cardiovasc Res 1989;23:351–358.

200. England MD, Cavarocchi NC, O'Brien JF, et al. Influence of antioxidant (mannitol and allopurinol) on oxygen free radical generation during and after cardiopulmonary bypass. Circulation 1986;74(suppl III):134–137.

201. Cavarocchi NC, England MD, Schaff HV, et al. Oxygen free radical generation during cardiopulmonary bypass: correlation with complement activation. Circulation 1986;74(suppl III):130–133.

202. Weisel RD, Mickle DAG, Finkle CD, et al. Myocardial free-radical injury after cardioplegia. Circulation 1989;80(suppl III):14–18.

203. Bical O, Gerhardt MF, Paumier D, et al. Comparison of different types of cardioplegia and reperfusion on myocardial metabolism and free radical activity. Circulation 1991;84(suppl III):375–379.

204. Ferreira R, Burgos M, Llesuy S, et al. Reduction of reperfusion injury with mannitol cardioplegia. Ann Thorac Surg 1989;48:77–84.

205. Kofsky ER, Julia PL, Buckberg GD, et al. Studies of controlled reperfusion after ischemia. XXII. Reperfusate composition: effects of leukocyte depletion of blood and blood cardioplegic reperfusates after acute coronary occlusion. J Thorac Cardiovasc Surg 1991;101:350–359.

206. O'Neill PG, Charlat ML, Michael LH, et al. Influence of neutrophil depletion on myocardial function and flow after reversible ischemia. Am J Physiol 1989;256:H341–H351.

207. Romson JL, Hook BG, Kunkel SL, et al. Reduction of the extent of ischemic myocardial injury by neutrophil depletion in the dog. Circulation 1983;67:1016–1023.

208. Julia PL, Partington MT, Buckberg GD, et al. Superiority of blood cardioplegia over crystalloid cardioplegia in limiting reperfusion damage: importance of endogenous oxygen free radical scavengers in red blood cells. Surg Forum 1988;39:221–223.

209. Bing OH, LaRaia PJ, Gaasch WH, Spadaro J, Franklin A, Weintraub RM. Independent protection provided by red blood cells during cardioplegia. Circulation 1982;66(suppl 1):81–84.

210. Rahn H, Reeves RB, Howell BJ. Hydrogen ion regulation, temperature, and evolution. Am Rev Respir Dis 1975;112:165–172.

211. Rosenthal TB. The effects of temperature on the pH of blood and plasma *in vitro*. J Biol Chem 1948;173:25.

212. White FN. A comparative physiological approach to hypothermia. J Thorac Cardiovasc Surg 1981;82:821–831.

213. Johnston WE, Vinten-Johansen J, DeWitt DS, et al. Cerebral perfusion during canine hypothermic cardiopulmonary bypass: effect of arterial carbon dioxide tension. Ann Thorac Surg 1991;52:479–489.

214. Reeves RB. An imidazole alphastat hypothesis for vertebrate acid-base regulation. Tissue carbon dioxide content and body temperature in bullfrogs. Respir Physiol 1972;14:219–236.

215. McConnell DH, White F, Nelson RL, et al. Importance of alkalosis in maintenance of "ideal" blood pH during hypothermia. Surg Forum 1975;26:263–265.

216. Buckberg GD, Becker H, Vinten-Johansen J, et al. Myocardial function resulting from varying acid-base management during and following deep surface and perfusion hypothermia and circulatory arrest. In: Rahn H, Prakash O, eds. Acid-base regulation and body temperature. Boston: Martinus Nijhoff Publishers, 1985:135–159.

217. Vander Woude JC, Christlieb IY, Sicard GA, Clark RE. Imidazole-buffered cardioplegic solution. improved myocardial preservation during global ischemia. J Thorac Cardiovasc Surg 1985;90:225–234.

218. Warner KG, Josa M, Marston W, et al. Reduction in myocardial acidosis using blood cardioplegia. J Surg Res 1987;42:247–256.

219. Warner KG, Josa M, Butler MD, et al. Regional changes in myocardial acid production during ischemic arrest: a comparison of sanguineous and asanguineous cardioplegia. Ann Thorac Surg 1988;45:75–81.

220. Geffin GA, Reynolds TR, Titus JS, et al. Relation of myocardial protection to cardioplegic solution pH: modulation by calcium and magnesium. Ann Thorac Surg 1991;52:955–964.

221. del Nido PJ, Wilson GJ, Mickle DA, et al. The role of cardioplegic solution buffering in myocardial protection. J Thorac Cardiovasc Surg 1985;89:689?–699.

222. Bernard M, Menasche P, Canioni P, et al. Influence of the pH of cardioplegic solutions on intracellular pH, high-energy phosphates, and postarrest performance: protective effects of acidotic, glutamate-containing cardioplegic perfusates. J Thorac Cardiovasc Surg 1985;90:235–242.

223. Nayler WG, Panagiotopoulos, Elz JS, Daly MJ. Calcium-mediated damage during postischaemic reperfusion. J Mol Cell Cardiol 1988;20(suppl II):41–54.

224. Kitakaze M, Weisfeldt ML, Marban E. Acidosis during early reperfusion prevents myocardial stunning in perfused ferret hearts. J Clin Invest 1988;82:920–927.

225. Mohabir R, Lee HC, Kurz RW, Clusin WT. Effects of ischemia and hypercarbic acidosis on myocyte calcium transients, contraction, and pH_i in perfused rabbit hearts. Circ Res 1991;69:1525–1537.

226. Tait GA, Booker PD, Wilson GJ, et al. Effect of multidose cardioplegia and cardioplegic solution buffering on myocardial tissue acidosis. J Thorac Cardiovasc Surg 1982;83:824–829.

227. Nugent WC, Levine FH, Liapis CD, et al. Effect of the pH of cardioplegic solution on postarrest myocardial preservation. Circulation 1982;66(suppl I):68–72.

228. Gunnes S, Ytrehus K, Sørlie D, et al. Improved energy preservation following gentle reperfusion after hypothermic, ischemic cardioplegia in infarcted rat hearts. Eur J Cardiothorac Surg 1987;1:139–143.

229. Vinten-Johansen J, Julian JS, Yokoyama H, et al. Efficacy of myocardial protection with hypothermic blood cardioplegia depends on oxygen. Ann Thorac Surg 1991;52:939–948.

230. Rosenkranz ER, Buckberg GD. Myocardial protection during surgical coronary reperfusion. J Am Coll Cardiol 1983;1:1235–1246.

231. Lucas SK, Gardner TJ, Flaherty JT, Bulkley BH, Elmer EB, Gott VL. Beneficial effects of mannitol administration during reperfusion after ischemic arrest. Circulation 1980;62(suppl I):34–41.

232. Salerno TA, Wasan SM, Charrette EJ. Glucose substrate in myocardial protection. J Thorac Cardiovasc Surg 1980;79:59–62.

233. Steinberg JB, Doherty NE, Munfakh NA, et al. Oxygenated cardioplegia: the metabolic and functional effects of glucose and insulin. Ann Thorac Surg 1991;51:620–629.

234. Salerno TA, Chiong MA. Cardioplegic arrest in pigs. effects of glucose-containing solutions. J Thorac Cardiovasc Surg 1980;80:929–933.

235. Okamoto F, Allen BS, Buckberg GD, et al. Studies of controlled reperfusion after ischemia. XI. Reperfusate composition: interaction of marked hyperglycemia and marked hyperosmolarity in allowing immediate contractile recovery after four hours of regional ischemia. J Thorac Cardiovasc Surg 1986;92:583–593.

236. Thomassen AR, Nielsen TT, Bagger JP, Henningsen P. Myocardial exchanges of glutamate, alanine and citrate in controls and patients with coronary artery disease. Clin Sci 1983;64:33–40.

237. Sanborn T, Gavin W, Berkowitz S, et al. Augmented conversion of aspartate and glutamate to succinate during anoxia in the rabbit heart. Am J Physiol 1979;237:H535–H541.

238. Wilson MA, Cascarano J. The energy-yielding oxidation of NADH by fumarate in submitochondrial particles of rat tissue. Biochim Biophys Acta 1970;216:54–62.

239. LaNoue KF, Walajtys EI, Williamson JR. Regulation of glutamate metabolism and interactions with the citric acid cycle in rat heart mitochondria. J Biol Chem 1973;248:7171–7183.

240. Toombs CF, McGee DS, Johnston WE, Vinten-Johansen J. Myocardial protection affects of adenosine: Infarct size reduction with pretreatment and continued receptor stimulation during ischemia. Circulation 1992;86:986–994.

241. Zhao ZQ, Nakanishi K, Vinten-Johansen J, McGee DS, Toombs CF. Receptor-mediated reduction of myocardial infarct size and attenuated no-reflow by endogenous adenosine during ischemia and reperfusion. Abstract. J Mol Cell Cardiol 1992;24(suppl III):S.8.

242. Thornton JD, Liu GS, Olsson RA, Downey JM. Intravenous A$_1$ selective adenosine agonists limit infarct size in the rabbit heart. Abstract. FASEB J 1991;5:A1104.

243. Keller MW, Geddes L, Spotnitz W, Kaul S, Duling BR. Microcirculatory dysfunction following perfusion with hyperkalemic, hypothermic, cardioplegic solutions and blood reperfusion. Effects of adenosine. Circulation 1991;84:2485–2494.

244. Safer B. The metabolic significance of the malate-aspartate cycle in heart. Circ Res 1975;37:527–533.

245. Safer B, Smith CM, Williamson JR. Control of the transport of reducing equivalents across the mitochondrial membrane in perfused rat heart. J Mol Cell Cardio 1971;2:111–124.

246. Rau EE, Shine KI, Gervais A, Douglas AM, Amos EC III. Enhanced mechanical recovery of anoxic and ischemic myocardium by amino acid perfusion. Am J Physiol 1979;236:H873–H879.

247. Rosenkranz ER, Okamoto F, Buckberg GD, et al. Safety of prolonged aortic clamping with blood cardioplegia. III. Aspartate enrichment of glutamate blood cardioplegia in energy-depleted hearts after ischemic and reperfusion injury. J Thorac Cardiovasc Surg 1986;91:428–435.

248. Haan CK, Lazar HL, Rivers S, et al. Improved myocardial preservation during cold storage using substrate enhancement. Ann Thorac Surg 1990;50:80–85.

249. Flaherty JT, Jaffin JH, Magovern GJ Jr, et al. Maintenance of aerobic metabolism during global ischemia with perfluorocarbon cardioplegia improves myocardial preservation. Circulation 1984;69:585–592.

250. Daniell HB. Coronary flow alterations on myocardial contractility, oxygen extraction and oxygen consumption. Am J Physiol 1973;225:1020–1025.

251. deWit L, Coetzee A, Kotze J, Lochner A. Oxygen requirements of the isolated rat heart during hypothermic cardioplegia. Effect of oxygenation on metabolic and functional recovery after five hours of arrest. J Thorac Cardiovasc Surg 1988;95:310–320.

252. Bodenhamer RM, DeBoer LW, Geffin GA, et al. Enhanced myocardial protection during ischemic arrest. oxygenation of a crystalloid cardioplegic solution. J Thorac Cardiovasc Surg 1983;85:769–780.

253. Daggett WM, Jacobs ML, Geffin GA, O'Keefe DD. The role of oxygenated solutions in cardioplegia. In: Roberts AJ, ed. Myocardial protection in cardiac surgery. New York: Marcel Dekker, 1987:295–302.

254. Engelman RM, Rousou JH, Dobbs W, Pels MA, Longo F. The superiority of blood cardioplegia in myocardial preservation. Circulation 1980;62(suppl I):I-62–66.

255. Oguma F, Imai S, Eguchi S. Role played by ox-

ygen in myocardial protection with crystalloid cardioplegic solution. Ann Thorac Surg 1986;42:172–179.

256. Daggett WM Jr, Randolph JD, Jacobs M, et al. The superiority of cold oxygenated dilute blood cardioplegia. Ann Thorac Surg 1987;43: 397–402.

257. Guyton RA, Dorsey LM, Craver JM, et al. Improved myocardial recovery after cardioplegic arrest with an oxygenated crystalloid solution. J Thorac Cardiovasc Surg 1985;89:877–887.

258. Rahn H. Aquatic gas exchange: theory, protons-proteins-temperature. In: Reeves RB, Rahn H, eds. Publications in acid-base physiology. 1977:127–138.

259. Digerness SB, Vanini V, Wideman FE. In vitro comparison of oxygen availability from asanguineous and sanguineous cardioplegic media. Circulation 1981;64(suppl IV):80–83.

260. Reeves RB, Park JS, Lapennas GN, Olszowka AJ. Oxygen affinity and Bohr coefficients of dog blood. J Appl Physiol 1982;53:87–95.

261. Astrup P, Engel K, Severinghaus JW, Munson E. The influence of temperature and pH on the dissociation of curve of oxyhemoglobin of human blood. Can J Clin Lab Invest 1965;17: 515–523.

262. Magovern GJ Jr, Flaherty JT, Gott VL, Bulkley BH, Gardner TJ. Failure of blood cardioplegia to protect myocardium at lower temperatures. Circulation 1982;66(suppl 1):60–67.

263. Longmuir IS. The effect of hypothermia on the affinity of tissues for oxygen. Life Sci 1962;7: 297–300.

264. Brown JM, Grosso MA, Terada LS, et al. Erythrocytes decrease myocardial hydrogen peroxide levels and reperfusion injury. Am J Physiol 1989;256:H584–H588.

265. Illes RW, Silverman NA, Krukenkamp IB, Levitsky S. Upgrading acellular to sanguineous cardioplegic efficacy. J Surg Res 1989; 46:543–548.

266. Robertson, JM, Buckberg GD, Vinten-Johansen J, Leaf JD. Comparison of distribution beyond coronary stenosis of blood and asanguineous cardioplegic solutions. J Thorac Cardiovasc Surg 1983;86:80–86.

267. Landymore RW, Tice D, Trehan N, et al. Importance of topical hypothermia to ensure uniform myocardial cooling during coronary artery bypass. J Thorac Cardiovasc Surg 1981;82: 832–836.

268. Becker H, Vinten-Johansen J, Buckberg GD, Follette DM, Robertson JM. Critical importance of ensuring cardioplegic delivery with coronary stenoses. J Thorac Cardiovasc Surg 1981;81:507–515.

269. Gott VL, Gonzalez JL, Suhdi ZN, et al. Retro-grade perfusion of the coronary sinus for direct vision aortic surgery. Surg Gynecol Obstet 1957;104:319–328.

270. Menasché P, Kural S, Fauchet M, et al. Retro-grade coronary sinus perfusion: a safe alternative for ensuring cardioplegic delivery in aortic valve surgery. Ann Thorac Surg 1982;34: 647–658.

271. Salter DR, Goldstein JP, Abd-Elfattah A, Murphy CE, Brunsting LA, Wechsler AS. Ventricular function after atrial cardioplegia. 1987; 76(suppl):129–40.

272. Partington MT, Acar C, Buckberg GD, Julia PL. Studies of retrograde cardioplegia. II. Advantages of antegrade/retrograde cardioplegia to optimize distribution in jeopardized myocardium. J Thorac Cardiovasc Surg 1989;97: 613–622.

273. Fiore AC, Naunheim KS, McBride LR, et al. Aortic valve replacement. Aortic root versus coronary sinus perfusion with blood cardio-plegic solution. J Thorac Cardiovasc Surg 1992;104:130–137.

274. Yano Y, Baimbridge MV, Hearse DJ. Protection of the pediatric myocardium: differential susceptibility to ischemic injury of the neonatal rat heart. J Thorac Cardiovasc Surg 1987;94: 887–896.

275. Kempsford RD, Hearse DJ. Protection of the immature myocardium during global ischemia. a comparison of four clinical cardioplegic solutions in the rabbit heart. J Thorac Cardiovasc Surg 1989;97:856–863.

276. Billingsley A, Laks H, Haas G. Myocardial protection in children. In: Baue A, Geha A, Hammond G, et al., eds. Glenn's thoracic and cardiovascular surgery. East Norwalk, CT: Appleton & Lange, 1991?:915–924.

277. Lofland GK, Abd-Elfattah AS, Wyse R, et al. Myocardial adenine nucleotide metabolism in pediatric patients during hypothermic cardioplegic arrest and normothermic ischemia. Ann Thorac Surg 1989;47:663–668.

278. Boucek RJ, Shelton M, Artman M, et al. Comparative effects of verapamil, nifedipine, and diltiazem on contractile function in the isolated immature and adult rabbit heart. Pediatr Res 1984;18:948–952.

279. Nishioka K, Nakanishi T, George BL, Jarmakani JM. The effect of calcium on the inotropy of catecholamine and paired electrical stimulation in the newborn and adult myocardium. J Mol Cell Cardiol 1981;13:511–520.

280. Bull C, Cooper J, Stark J. Cardioplegic protection of the child's heart. J Thorac Cardiovasc Surg 1984;88:287–293.

281. Jarmakani JM, Nagatomo T, Nakazawa M, Langer GA. Effect of hypoxia on myocardial high-en-

ergy phosphates in the neonatal mammalian heart. Am J Physiol 1978;235:H475–H487.

282. Kofsky E, Julia P, Buckberg G, et al. Studies of myocardial protection in the immature heart. V. Safety of prolonged aortic clamping with hypocalcemic glutamate/aspartate blood cardioplegia. J Thorac Cardiovasc Surg 1991; 101:33–43.

283. Silverman NA, Kohler J, Levitsky S, et al. Chronic hypoxemia depresses global ventricular function and predisposes to the depletion of high-energy phosphates during cardioplegic arrest. Implications for surgical repair of cyanotic congenital heart defects. Ann Thorac Surg 1984;37:304–308.

284. Lupinetti FM, Wareing TH, Huddleston CB, et al. Pathophysiology of chronic cyanosis in a ca-nine model. Functional and metabolic response to global ischemia. J Thorac Cardiovasc Surg 1985;90:291–296.

285. Visner MS, Arentzen CE, Ring WS, Anderson RW. Left ventricular dynamic geometry and diastolic mechanisms in a model of chronic cyanosis and right ventricular pressure overload. J Thorac Cardiovasc Surg 1981;81:347–357.

286. Hetzer R, Warnecke H, Wittrock H, Engel HJ, Borst HG. Extracoronary collateral myocardial blood flow during cardioplegic arrest. Thorac Cardiovasc Surg 1980;28:191–196.

287. Starnes VA, Hammon JW Jr, Lupinetti FM, et al. Functional and metabolic preservation of the immature myocardium with verapamil following global ischemia. Ann Thorac Surg 1982;34:58–65.

8

Pharmacokinetic and Pharmacodynamic Effects of Cardiopulmonary Bypass

Carl E. Rosow

Modern techniques of cardiopulmonary bypass (CPB) disrupt both pharmacokinetics and pharmacodynamics. Virtually all of the physiologic processes involved in drug absorption, distribution, metabolism, and elimination are affected. Abnormal physiologic conditions like hemodilution, hypotension, nonpulsatile blood flow, and hypothermia may alter the responses of end organs. The oxygenator and tubing may bind large amounts of some drugs. Nevertheless, the administration of drugs during and following CPB is still a largely empirical exercise. There are relatively few studies that specifically address CPB as it relates to drug levels *and* drug action. For many of our commonly used drugs we lack the information to answer basic therapeutic questions: Should more or less drug be given during CPB? Will therapeutic or toxic concentrations change? Will "normal" doses produce the expected intensity or duration of effect post-CPB?

Interest in these theoretical pharmacokinetic and pharmacodynamic issues began with examination of the stress hormonal responses to CPB about 10 years ago. Plasma concentrations of catecholamines, vasopressin, cortisol, and other stress hormones were known to increase markedly during bypass. It was not clear at the time whether these hormonal surges were deleterious, but some of them could be prevented by "deep" anesthesia (viz., high doses of opioids or high concentrations of inhalation anesthetics).

We were surprised to find that extremely high doses of the potent opioids fentanyl and sufentanil were not very effective in blocking responses during or following CPB. Early pharmacokinetic studies showed that the plasma concentration of fentanyl dropped precipitously at the start of CPB (1, 2). We hypothesized (incorrectly) that hemodilution during CPB had caused plasma concentrations of the opioids to become subtherapeutic. We also thought that low levels of opioid might account for some of the hypertensive responses seen after CPB was discontinued.

When we actually measured opioid concentrations before, during and after CPB (Fig. 8.1), it was apparent that our assumptions about hemodilution were overly simplistic (3). When sufentanil was infused up to the start of CPB, the concentration of drug decreased initially, but the fall was brief, and levels rose dramatically during rewarming. After the termination of CPB, plasma sufentanil concentration was nearly at pre-CPB levels. Subsequent studies indicate that these changes in total opioid con-

Figure 8.1. Plasma sufentanil concentrations in patients during CPB at 25°C. Group I received a bolus of sufentanil at induction of anesthesia. Groups II through IV received infusions of sufentanil that were continued up to the start of bypass. Bubble oxygenator was primed with 2 liters of Ringer's lactate. (From Okutani R, Philbin DM, Rosow CE, Koski G, Schneider RC. Effect of hypothermic hemodilutional cardiopulmonary bypass on plasma sufentanil and catecholamine concentrations in humans. Anesth Analg 1988;67:667–670.)

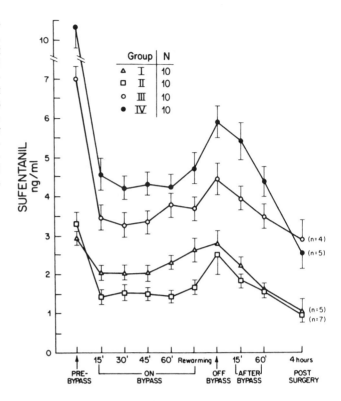

centration may not even reflect the amount of biologically active drug. (These issues will be discussed in more depth later.)

Why do we need this type of information? In the best of circumstances a drug is administered to achieve a target plasma concentration that has been shown to produce some desired therapeutic effect. It is clear that CPB can alter both drug levels and drug effects. Even very accurate pharmacologic data from normal subjects may not apply in the context of hemodilution, hypotension, and hypothermia commonly seen with CPB. For drugs like opioids, cephalosporins, and benzodiazepines, the exact plasma level is probably not critical, assuming some minimally effective concentration is reached. For other drugs like antiarrhythmics and digitalis glycosides, the difference between therapeutic and toxic doses can be very small. There is some evidence that these therapeutic windows become even smaller during and after CPB (4).

The next two sections of this chapter will describe the ways in which CPB can influence the distribution, excretion, and biological activity of drugs. The final section summarizes most of the available data for specific drug groups. For additional discussion, the reader is referred to several previous reviews (5–7). Many of the pharmacokinetic papers cited should be interpreted very cautiously. The abrupt changes in drug concentrations and intravascular volume that occur during CPB make traditional pharmacokinetic analysis very difficult. Since most CPB is relatively short in duration, it is hard to make accurate estimates of long half-lives and slow clearances. Very few of the studies cited utilize non-CPB controls, and even fewer distinguish between bound and unbound states for the drug being studied.

The references mainly reflect the materials and techniques utilized for CPB during the last 10 to 20 years. Most of these studies were accomplished with bubble oxygenators, nonpulsatile flow, and moderate hypothermia. There are only a few drug-related studies using membrane oxygenators or pulsatile flow, and fewer still using normothermic bypass.

PHARMACOKINETIC EFFECTS OF CPB

Hemodilution

When CPB is initiated with a normal crystalloid prime, there is immediate dilution of blood and a proportionate decrease in drug concentration. The effect is not necessarily a decrease in drug activity, because protein binding is altered as well. Recall that being bound to plasma proteins normally prevents a drug from crossing biological membranes and being filtered by the kidney. Except for drugs with extremely high rates of hepatic metabolism, protein-bound drugs are usually also protected from

clearance by the liver (8). Drug clearance and the intensity of biological effect are proportional to the concentration of free (unbound) drug. Protein binding of drugs is, in turn, reversible and a function of drug concentration in plasma. When CPB is begun, protein bound drug, free drug, and plasma are diluted simultaneously. Mass action, therefore, favors dissociation of drugs from protein binding sites (9). For highly protein bound drugs like propranolol, the increase in free fraction may be quite significant (Fig. 8.2).

It thus appears that hemodilution causes two opposing effects: it reduces the total drug concentration, but it also increases the proportion that is biologically active. This phenomenon was demonstrated in a study of thiopental by Morgan et al. (10) (Fig. 8.3). An exponentially declining infusion of thiopental was given in order to maintain a stable plasma concentration prior to CPB. When CPB was started, total drug concentration

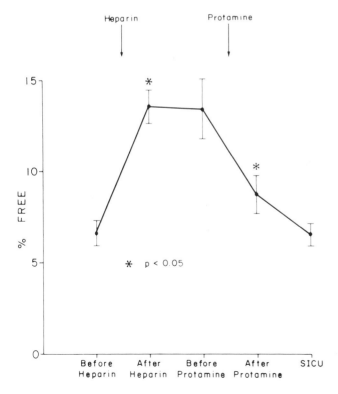

Figure 8.2. Free fraction (percent) of propranolol ($\pm$SEM), before, during, and after cardiopulmonary bypass. Comparisons are with immediately preceding values. Heparin increases free fatty acids and these compete with propranolol for binding sites. SICU, surgical intensive care unit. (From Wood M, Shand DG, Wood AJJ. Propranolol binding in plasma during cardiopulmonary bypass. Anesthesiology 1979;51:512–516.)

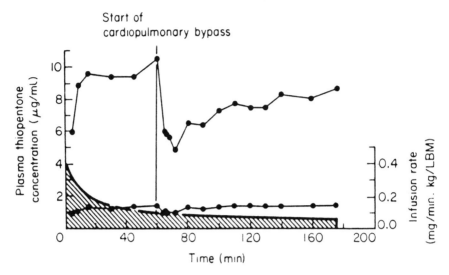

Figure 8.3.   Plasma thiopental during exponential infusion in a single patient undergoing cardiac surgery. The upper line is total drug and the lower line is unbound drug. Thiopental infusion rate is given by hatched area and the scale on the right. (From Morgan DJ, Crankshaw DP, Prideaux PR, Chang HNJ, Boyd MD. Thiopentone levels during cardiopulmonary bypass. Changes in plasma protein binding during continuous infusion. Anaesthesia 1986;41:4–10.)

dropped rapidly and then returned more slowly to prebypass levels. The concentration of unbound drug remained nearly constant throughout this period.

Why did the total concentration of thiopental decrease then increase? Drugs like digoxin, fentanyl, and thiopental have enormous volumes of distribution and are extensively bound to tissue proteins and lipids. The volumes into which these drugs are rapidly distributed are very large when compared to the volume of pump prime. This extravascular binding creates a huge reservoir of drug that can act to buffer the effects of hemodilution. When plasma concentrations fall suddenly, there is net movement of drug into the vascular compartment. Molokhia et al. (11) showed that plasma concentrations of digoxin fluctuated during CPB, but myocardial tissue concentrations remained unchanged. Massey et al. (12) described a similar effect for propofol, a highly fat-soluble anesthetic with a large distribution volume. Propofol was administered by constant-rate intravenous infusion throughout cardiac surgery, and CPB pro-

duced no measurable change in whole blood propofol concentration.

The administration of heparin can markedly affect protein binding of drugs by releasing lipoprotein lipase and thereby elevating plasma free fatty acids (FFAs). The FFAs compete for binding sites and may displace significant amounts of bound drug (8, 9, 13). After protamine reversal, FFAs are rapidly cleared, and binding is restored to original levels. Collection of heparinized blood samples may overestimate this effect, since FFA release (but not clearance) continues in vitro (14).

Drug binding may also be altered postoperatively. The stress reactant α_1-acid glycoprotein (AAG) is a major binding protein for basic drugs like lidocaine, propranolol, and meperidine (15). In the period following CPB, concentrations of AAG rise, and the binding of these drugs may increase. Holley et al. (16) found that there was a significant increase in the amount of lidocaine bound to AAG and a corresponding decrease in lidocaine clearance 3 days following CPB.

Tissue Perfusion

The combination of hypothermia, hemodilution, and nonpulsatile flow produces tremendous changes in regional blood flow. Cardiac output is redistributed at the expense of muscle and splanchnic viscera. Hepatic blood flow can be reduced by as much as 30 to 48%, and this is most likely to reduce the clearance of rapidly metabolized drugs such as fentanyl, lidocaine, and propranolol. Hepatic blood flow does not return to normal immediately following CPB, and some drugs (e.g., fentanyl) have prolonged elimination half-lives during this period (1). Interestingly, lidocaine clearance is only modestly decreased during the first 24 hours after CPB (16).

Renal blood flow is also decreased during and after CPB. As one would expect, this greatly reduces the clearance of renally eliminated drugs like digoxin and cefazolin (17, 18). Gallamine, a neuromuscular blocking drug with virtually 100% renal elimination, has only a small (and clinically unimportant) reduction in clearance on CPB (19). The differences between these drugs must be attributable to other factors like protein binding and volume of distribution.

Unlike cefazolin, the antibiotic cephalothin depends on both hepatic and renal elimination. After CPB, the hepatic clearance of this drug remains impaired, but renal elimination stays relatively intact (20).

Blood flow to muscle, liver, and kidneys may be improved by the use of pulsatile perfusion (see Chapter 13). As of this writing, there have been very few studies specifically examining the effect of pulsatile blood flow on drug disposition. Hynynen et al. (21) compared thiopental pharmacokinetics with and without pulsatile flow. They found no significant difference in distribution or elimination attributable to mode of perfusion. This might have been predicted, since thiopental is a low-clearance drug, and its elimination does not depend upon hepatic blood flow.

Hypothermia

Despite the current interest in warm bypass techniques, the majority of cases requiring CPB utilize moderate hypothermia. Decreased temperature can significantly alter drug distribution, metabolism, and excretion.

Hepatic and renal tubular enzyme systems clearly will have decreased activity in the 25 to 30°C range. A reduction in the rate of hepatic metabolism will most likely affect low-clearance drugs like diazepam and thiopental. The elimination half-life of thiopental is nearly doubled during hypothermic CPB (22).

A 7 to 10°C decrease in temperature is much less likely to affect the rate of nonenzymatic chemical processes. This seems to be an important issue in the detoxification and clearance of sodium nitroprusside (SNP). Sodium nitroprusside first reacts nonenzymatically with sulfhydryl groups to release cyanide ions, which are scavenged in the liver and kidneys by the rhodanase enzyme system. Rhodanase converts cyanide to thiocyanate. Moore and colleagues (23) gave patients SNP during CPB at 25°C and showed that the nonenzymatic release of cyanide occurred rapidly, while the enzymatic conversion of free cyanide to thiocyanate was markedly inhibited (Fig. 8.4). As a result, their patients developed significant elevations in red blood cell cyanide that persisted until rewarming. Although the amounts of SNP infused were large, they were not clinically irrelevant, and the cyanide concentrations sometimes approached levels associated with toxicity.

Cold temperature, in and of itself, can reduce organ perfusion and redistribute cardiac output. Hypothermia can markedly reduce blood flow to large vascular beds like muscle and skin. When highly distributed drugs like fentanyl or propranolol are

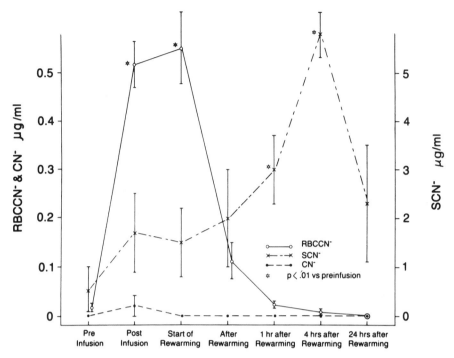

Figure 8.4. Mean (±SEM) levels of serum cyanide (CN⁻), red blood cell cyanide (RBCCN⁻), and thiocyanate (SCN⁻) for six subjects receiving an infusion of sodium nitroprusside. (From Moore RA, Geller EA, Gallagher JD, Clark DL. Effect of hypothermic cardiopulmonary bypass on nitroprusside metabolism. Clin Pharmacol Ther 1985;37:680–683.)

given to hypothermic animals, they distribute in a smaller apparent volume, and plasma concentrations are higher (24) (Fig. 8.5).

Drugs that are administered preoperatively or during the prebypass period may be extensively bound before cooling commences. The reduction in peripheral blood flow may cause large quantities of these drugs to remain sequestered in muscle and skin. When body temperature returns toward normal at the end of CPB, drug is washed out and plasma concentrations may rise. This effect is probably responsible for the secondary increases in plasma fentanyl and sufentanil seen during rewarming (3, 25) (Fig. 8.1).

Peripheral vasoconstriction that occurs during hypothermia causes a decrease in intravascular volume, and this may completely offset the increase due to pump prime. This phenomenon probably ex-plains the pharmacokinetic behavior of the neuromuscular blocking agents. d-Tubocurarine, pancuronium, and other muscle relaxants are all highly water-soluble because they are quaternary amines. These drugs do not cross membranes easily and tend to remain within the vascular space. At the onset of hypothermic CPB, intravascular volume decreases, and the plasma concentrations of *d*-tubocurarine, alcuronium, metocurine, and gallamine temporarily *increase* (Fig. 8.6) (19, 26–28).

Acid-Base Status

The management of acid-base status during hypothermic bypass could theoretically influence drug distribution, although this type of interaction has not been studied specifically. Hypothermia lowers hydrogen ion activity and may minimize the effects of local and systemic acidosis seen during CPB

EFFECT OF HYPOTHERMIA ON PROPRANOLOL KINETICS

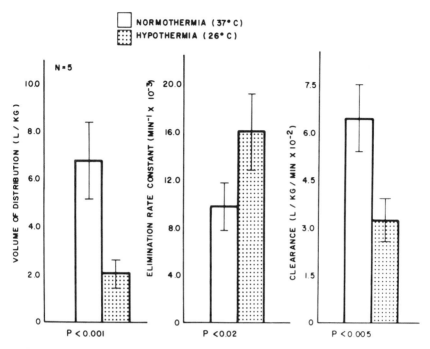

☐ NORMOTHERMIA (37°C)
▒ HYPOTHERMIA (26°C)

N=5

P <0.001   P <0.02   P <0.005

Figure 8.5. Pharmacokinetic data from five anesthetized dogs given 1 mg/kg of propranolol twice: once during normothermia and once following surface cooling in a water bath. Each bar represents the mean ± SD. (From McAllister RG Jr, Bourne DW, Tan TG, Erickson JL, Wachtel CC, Todd EP. Effects of hypothermia on propranolol kinetics. Clin Pharmacol Ther 1979;25:1–7.)

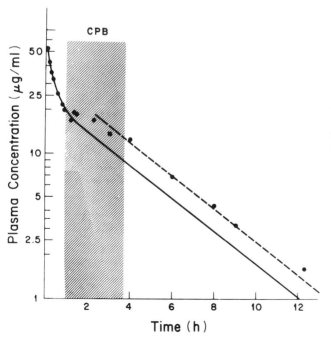

Figure 8.6. Plasma concentrations of gallamine in a cardiac patient before, during, and after hypothermic CPB. Closed circles represent measured concentrations; the solid line is the predicted concentration-time curve based upon data from noncardiac patients. (From Shanks CA, Ramzan IM, Walker JS, Brown KF. Disposition of gallamine in open-heart surgery involving cardiopulmonary bypass. Clin Pharmacol Ther 1983;33:792–799.)

(see Chapter 6). Acid conditions in tissue compartments like skeletal muscle and brain can affect the tissue partitioning of drugs by ion trapping (basic drugs should be most affected). The binding of many drugs to plasma proteins can also be affected by acidosis or alkalosis (8).

Two animal studies illustrate the complexity of these effects. In dogs subjected to significant hypercarbia and acidosis (without CPB), morphine was found to enter the central nervous system (CNS) more rapidly and remain in cerebral tissue almost twice as long (29). Brain penetration was facilitated by higher plasma morphine concentrations (a smaller apparent central volume of distribution) during hypercarbia. Acid conditions in cerebrospinal fluid and brain probably trapped morphine in its protonated form. In a very similar type of experiment, exactly the opposite results were found for fentanyl: *hypo*carbia increased penetration and retention, while hypercarbia increased the elimination of this drug (30). The differing results probably reflect the enormous difference in lipid solubility and tissue binding between the two drugs. The reduction in cerebral blood flow with hypocarbia is more likely to be rate-limiting for lipophilic drugs like fentanyl than relatively hydrophilic drugs like morphine.

Given the above, it is difficult to predict how management of acid-base status during CPB will affect drug distribution. The decision to correct pH for temperature (pH-stat versus alpha-stat) will certainly influence cerebral blood flow and may influence drug ionization as well. Recall that under pH-stat management, patients are given supplemental CO_2, and cerebral blood flow (CBF) *increases* despite a low cerebral metabolic rate ($CMRo_2$). Under alpha-stat management, CBF and $CMRo_2$ fall in parallel (31). It does not seem farfetched to propose that pH-stat management may speed the distribution of fat-soluble drugs into and out of the CNS. To my knowledge, there have been no studies investigating the effects of added CO_2 on drug kinetics or dynamics during CPB.

Drug Sequestration in the Lung

Many drugs are found in extremely high concentrations in the lung. Some are metabolically activated or inactivated there, and some are only stored temporarily and eventually reenter the systemic circulation. This uptake is particularly well-established with respect to certain neurotransmitters and basic, lipophilic drugs (32–36). Roerig and colleagues (37) have shown that 65% of an intravenous dose of fentanyl is taken up in one pass through the lung. Morphine, which is much less fat-soluble, has an uptake of only 4%. Although these drugs eventually reenter the systemic circulation, pulmonary sequestration can have considerable impact on the time-course of their effects (38). It is likely that fentanyl administered during the prebypass period remains sequestered in the lung as soon as the pulmonary circulation is interrupted. This pulmonary reservoir probably accounts for some of the increase in plasma fentanyl concentration that occurs when the lungs are reperfused.

If a drug is administered *during* CPB, exclusion of the lungs may result in a smaller apparent volume of distribution. This means that a given dose will produce a higher plasma concentration. There may also be substantial alteration in the pharmacokinetics of compounds that depend upon the lungs for biotransformation (35).

Drug Sequestration in the Oxygenator

It is well known that drugs like nitroglycerin and insulin are bound (adsorbed) in significant quantities to the surfaces of glass bottles and plastic i.v. lines. Lipophilic drugs may also dissolve in some plastics or rubber. Both bubble and membrane oxygenators provide a huge surface area for such interaction, and the quantities of drug bound may be clinically significant.

There have been several in vitro studies of opioid binding to oxygenators. Rosen et al. (39) calculated that a pediatric silicone membrane oxygenator and connecting tubes could bind 68% of a dose of fentanyl in one pass. Small pieces of the oxygenator membrane, when placed in solutions of labeled fentanyl, reached saturation after 2 hours, and bound 116 ng of fentanyl per square centimeter. No distinction was made between drug adsorbed on the surface and drug dissolved in the membrane. Similar studies were performed with the opioid sufentanil, and full saturation was found to occur by 165 minutes (40). The membrane held 11 ng/cm^2 of sufentanil at 25°C and 24 ng/cm^2 at 37°C. One would think that the majority of binding would occur at the onset of CPB when drug concentration is highest, so higher temperatures may be a fairer approximation of what occurs clinically.

If one extrapolates these data to intact oxygenators, the calculated capacity of a pediatric silicone membrane is about 750 μg of fentanyl, and the average adult membrane should hold over 2 mg (39). Of course, fentanyl given at the start of surgery will be distributed into extravascular tissues, so only a small fraction of the drug is circulating and therefore liable to be lost in the pump.

The exact amount of drug lost in this manner will depend upon the temperature, when the drug is given, the composition of the prime, and the type of oxygenator (41, 42). The binding of nitroglycerin can occur with both bubble and membrane oxygenators, the most important variable being the presence of a polyurethane defoaming sponge (43).

Drug binding is also a function of pH, since it is primarily the unionized form of the drug that binds. Skacel and colleagues (44) measured the effect of pH on alfentanil (500 ng/ml) and fentanyl (100 ng/ml) binding to a bubble oxygenator circuit

in vitro. There was appreciable loss of fentanyl when the solution was circulated through the oxygenator for 20 minutes. Alfentanil concentrations seemed to remain unchanged, although the higher concentration of this drug may have made a small amount of binding difficult to detect. Increasingly alkaline pH had little effect on alfentanil binding, but it increased the binding of fentanyl. The explanation for this difference probably lies in the difference of the pKa for alfentanil and that for fentanyl, which are 6.5 and 8.4, respectively. This means that alfentanil is already 90% unionized at pH 7.4, while fentanyl is still 90% ionized. Raising the pH will therefore produce a greater increase in the amount of uncharged (diffusible) fentanyl. The two opioids may also have more fundamental differences in their binding characteristics, since they are known to bind to different protein fractions in the blood (45).

The in vitro binding of midazolam to silicone membranes was studied by Silvasi et al. (46). When midazolam solution was circulated through an intact membrane oxygenator, 82% was absorbed in only 10 minutes. Pieces of membrane were also incubated in solutions of tritiated midazolam at room temperature, and these pieces of silicone became saturated at 11 μg/cm^2. This corresponds to 27.5 mg of midazolam in an adult oxygenator! Midazolam binding was unaffected by prior incubation of the membrane with fentanyl. One must be careful about extrapolating these data to the clinical setting, since small pieces of silicone were being exposed to extremely high concentrations of drug.

PHARMACODYNAMIC EFFECTS OF CPB

There are very few studies that specifically address the effects of CPB on drug action. As we have seen, the fact that drug levels drop when bypass is initiated does not necessarily imply a reduction in the biologically active fraction. Even if we knew the precise amount and distribution of a drug, the conditions of bypass (hypotension, hypothermia, nonpulsatile flow) might be expected to alter the sensitivity to that drug.

Hypothermia

Cold temperatures are well known to alter both the toxic and therapeutic effects of various drugs. The lethal dose of digoxin is doubled in dogs under hypothermic conditions (47). Hypothermia reduces minimum alveolar concentration (MAC) for volatile anesthetics (48) and reduces the requirements for most intravenous hypnotics.

We still do not know how much hypnosis and analgesia are actually necessary during hypothermic CPB. Anecdotal reports of recall during hypothermic CPB suggest that low temperatures do not assure hypnosis or amnesia (49). The EEG does not become isoelectric until core temperature is about 20°C, so there is still electrical evidence of cortical function at moderate hypothermia (50). Somatosensory-evoked potentials are obtainable at core temperatures as low as 19°C, although conduction times are markedly prolonged (51).

Quasha and colleagues (52) showed that only 8 mg/kg of thiopental could produce 30 minutes of EEG burst suppression at core temperatures of 25 to 30°C. Nussmeier et al. (22, 53) titrated thiopental infusions during both normothermic and hypothermic CPB to produce an isoelectric EEG. During the hypothermic phase of CPB (26 ± 2.7°C), EEG burst suppression was maintained with much lower plasma thiopental concentrations. Loomis et al. (54) found that it took arterial isoflurane concentrations of only 0.64% to produce burst suppression in CPB patients cooled to 26°C. Woodcock et al. (55) showed that patients undergoing hypothermic CPB (26.6°C) with high-dose fentanyl anesthesia required the addition of only 1.1% isoflurane to produce burst suppression.

Hypothermic CPB has also been demonstrated to alter the pharmacodynamics of muscle relaxants. The potencies of d-tubocurarine, metocurine, alcuronium, and gallamine are reduced; i.e., more drug is required for a given level of twitch depression (56–60). The results for pancuronium generally support an increase in potency during hypothermia, but a decreased response was found in one study (61). Buzello et al. (61) found that a constant rate infusion of vecuronium produced a greater effect during hypothermia (26°C). This may have reflected drug accumulation, since the duration of effect of vecuronium was prolonged fivefold at that temperature.

In the absence of muscle relaxants, hypothermic CPB (26°C) produces an increase in EMG activity, while twitch decreases modestly (62). This phenomenon is probably due to an uncoupling of excitation and contraction. During rewarming, twitch temporarily increases to supranormal levels. It is doubtful that these changes have much clinical significance.

Abnormal Blood-Brain Barrier

Certain drugs may enter the CNS more readily during CPB. Even high doses of penicillin normally produce very low concentrations in cerebrospinal fluid. Seamans et al. (63) reported a series of patients who had generalized seizure activity after receiving high doses of penicillin during CPB. The authors postulated that the blood-brain barrier had become abnormally permeable to penicillin, which is known to be epileptogenic. The cause(s) of this effect was not determined, although acidosis and hemolysis were excluded. Other experimental and clinical data indicate that penicillin-induced seizures are more likely in the presence of cerebral hypoxia or embolic injury (64). Recent animal studies suggest that cerebral vascular permeability to larger molecules (i.e., proteins) is not significantly altered by normothermic or hypothermic CPB (65). In one study using a swine model, small amounts of perivascular protein extravasation were found after pulsatile, but not nonpulsatile CPB (66).

Abnormal Blood Flow

We do not know whether nonpulsatile perfusion affects the response of the CNS to drugs. Murkin et al. (31) have shown that even normothermic, nonpulsatile perfusion decreases cerebral metabolic rate in patients while preserving the normal coupling between metabolism and cerebral blood flow. This decrease in CMR_{O_2} occurs under both volatile and opioid anesthesia, and it appears to be a primary effect (i.e., it is not secondary to a reduction in cerebral blood flow).

Arterial hypotension, by itself, will reduce the requirement for inhaled anesthetics (67), but there is some disagreement whether normothermic, nonpulsatile perfusion will do the same thing. Hall and Sullivan (68) found that dogs had a reduced requirement for enflurane following 1 hour of normothermic CPB (enflurane MAC was lower than pre-CPB control). The reasons for this change were not clear, but the authors felt that gaseous or particulate microemboli may have played a role. Antognini and Kien (69) attempted to duplicate this study but found no change in enflurane MAC either during or following CPB. Enflurane requirement did not depend upon the use of partial or total CPB, bubble or membrane oxygenators, or the administration of protamine.

Hemorrhage (or large volume shifts) have been shown to affect the pharmacodynamics of intravenous agents. Klockowski and Levy (70) showed in rats that acute blood loss (30% of blood volume) caused a marked increase in the hypnotic effect of a benzodiazepine. The change persisted for several hours, even when the blood loss was replaced immediately. Compared to controls, hemorrhaged animals required less

benzodiazepine in cerebrospinal fluid to produce a specified hypnotic effect. The authors concluded that there was a true increase in brain sensitivity, but they were unable to demonstrate any change in benzodiazepine receptor number or affinity to explain the effect.

SUMMARY

Cardiopulmonary bypass produces large and easily measured changes in the plasma concentrations of most drugs; the significance of these changes is not easy to determine. For most drug classes, the pharmacokinetic effects of CPB are qualitatively similar:

1. The total drug concentration drops initially because of hemodilution, but this may return toward normal as drug is redistributed from peripheral tissues. The amount of unbound drug increases, and in some cases the free fraction has been shown to remain constant. These changes in protein binding are most likely to be important in the case of highly bound drugs.

2. Drug is lost during CPB, but probably not in huge amounts. Renal and hepatic clearance of most drugs is decreased during CPB. Following CPB, the washout of drug from the lungs and skeletal muscle sometimes brings plasma concentrations to pre-CPB levels. The available evidence suggests that supplemental doses of digoxin, most antibiotics, and anesthetic agents are not usually necessary during hypothermic CPB.

3. Large amounts of certain drugs can be bound in vitro to oxygenators and tubing, but the amounts lost under normal clinical conditions are probably much lower. This is most likely to be important when silicone membrane oxygenators are used or when highly lipophilic drugs are administered *during* CPB.

It is difficult to generalize about the effects of CPB on pharmacodynamics. We know that hypothermia and abnormal perfusion change the relationship between drug concentration and effect. Cardiopulmonary bypass alters cerebral metabolism and may compromise the integrity of the blood-brain barrier. The sensitivity of the CNS to most anesthetic agents is increased during, and possibly following, hypothermic CPB. We do not know if this is true for normothermic CPB. Unfortunately, there is still very little information on the way CPB influences drug activity in other important tissues like myocardium, smooth muscle, liver, or kidney.

REFERENCES

1. Koska AJ, Romagnoli A, Kramer WG. Effect of cardiopulmonary bypass on fentanyl distribution and elimination. Clin Pharmacol Ther 1981;29: 100–105.
2. Koren G, Crean P, Klein J, Goresky G, Villamater J, MacLeod SM. Sequestration of fentanyl by the cardiopulmonary bypass (CPBP). Eur J Clin Pharmacol 1984;27:51–56.
3. Okutani R, Philbin DM, Rosow CE, Koski G, Schneider RC. Effect of hypothermic hemodilutional cardiopulmonary bypass on plasma sufentanil and catecholamine concentrations in humans. Anesth Analg 1988;67:667–670.
4. Morrison J, Killip T. Serum digitalis and arrhythmia in patients undergoing cardiopulmonary bypass. Circulation 1973;47:341–352.
5. Holley FO, Ponganis KV, Stanski DR. Effect of cardiopulmonary bypass on the pharmacokinetics of drugs. Clin Pharmacokinet 1982;7:234–251.
6. Buylaert WA, Herregods LL, Mortier EP, Bogaert MG. Cardiopulmonary bypass and the pharmacokinetics of drugs. Clin Pharmacokinet 1989;17: 10–26.
7. Reves JG, Croughwell N, Jacobs JR, Greeley W. Anesthesia during cardiopulmonary bypass: does it matter? In: Tinker JH, ed. Cardiopulmonary bypass: current concepts and controversies. Philadelphia: WB Saunders, 1989:69–97.
8. Wood M. Plasma drug binding: implications for anesthesiologists. Anesth Analg 1986;65: 786–804.
9. Wood M, Shand DG, Wood AJJ. Propranolol binding in plasma during cardiopulmonary bypass. Anesthesiology 1979;51:512–516.
10. Morgan DJ, Crankshaw DP, Prideaux PR, Chan HNJ, Boyd MD. Thiopentone levels during cardiopulmonary bypass. Changes in plasma protein binding during continuous infusion. Anaesthesia 1986;41:4–10.

11. Molokhia FA, Beller GA, Smith TW, Asimacopoulos PJ, Hood WB, Norman JC. Constancy of myocardial digoxin concentration during experimental cardiopulmonary bypass. Ann Thorac Surg 1971;11:222–228.
12. Massey NJA, Sherry KM, Oldroyd S, Peacock JE. Pharmacokinetics of an infusion of propofol during cardiac surgery. Br J Anaesth 1990;65: 475–479.
13. Storstein L, Nitter-Hauge S, Fjeld N. Effect of cardiopulmonary bypass with heparin administration on digitoxin pharmacokinetics, serum electrolytes, free fatty acids, and renal function. J Cardiovasc Pharmacol 1979;1:191–204.
14. Dube LM, Davies RF, Beanlands DS, et al. Dissociation of authentic and artifactual effect of circulating heparin on drug protein binding. Biopharm Drug Dispos 1989;10:55–68.
15. Piafsky KM. Disease induced changes in the plasma binding of basic drugs. Clin Pharmacokinet 1980;5:246–262.
16. Holley FO, Ponganis KV, Stanski DR. Effects of cardiac surgery with cardiopulmonary bypass on lidocaine disposition. Clin Pharmacol Ther 1984;35:617–626.
17. Coltart DJ, Chamberlain DA, Howard MR, Kettlewell MG, Mercer JL, Smith TW. Effect of cardiopulmonary bypass on plasma digoxin concentrations. Br Heart J 1971;33:334–338.
18. Miller KW, McCoy HG, Chan KKH, et al. Effect of cardiopulmonary bypass on cefazolin disposition. Clin Pharmacol Ther 1980;27:550–556.
19. Shanks CA, Ramzan IM, Walker JS, Brown KF. Disposition of gallamine in open-heart surgery involving cardiopulmonary bypass. Clin Pharmacol Ther 1983;33:792–799.
20. Miller KW, Chan KKH, McCoy HG, Fischer RP, Lindsay WG, Zaske DE. Cephalothin kinetics: before, during, and after cardiopulmonary bypass surgery. Clin Pharmacol Ther 1979;26:54–62.
21. Hynynen M, Olkkola KT, Näveri E, Palojoki R, Neuvonen PJ, Heinonen J. Thiopentone pharmacokinetics during cardiopulmonary bypass with a nonpulsatile or pulsatile flow. Acta Anaesth Scand 1989;33:554–560.
22. Nussmeier NA, Cohen NH, Stanski DR. High-dose thiopental requirement to maintain a nearly isoelectric EEG during hypothermic cardiopulmonary bypass [Abstract]. Anesthesiology 1988; 69:A91.
23. Moore RA, Geller EA, Gallagher JD, Clark DL. Effect of hypothermic cardiopulmonary bypass on nitroprusside metabolism. Clin Pharmacol Ther 1985;37:680–683.
24. McAllister RG Jr, Bourne DW, Tan TG, Erickson JL, Wachtel CC, Todd EP. Effects of hypothermia on propranolol kinetics. Clin Pharmacol Ther 1979;25:1–7.

25. Howie MB, Mortimer W, Philip J, Dumond DA, McSweeney TD. Elimination of post bypass secondary peaks of fentanyl by pulsatile cardiopulmonary bypass [Abstract]. Anesthesiology 1988; 69:3A:A60.

26. Walker JS, Shanks CA, Brown KF. Alcuronium kinetics in patients undergoing cardiopulmonary bypass surgery. Br J Clin Pharmacol 1983;15: 237–244.

27. Walker JS, Shanks CA, Brown KF. Altered d-tubocurarine disposition during cardiopulmonary bypass. Clin Pharmacol Ther 1984;35:686–694.

28. Avram MJ, Shanks CA, Henthorm TK, Ronai AK, Kinzer J, Wilkinson CJ. Metocurine kinetics in patients undergoing operations requiring cardiopulmonary bypass. Clin Pharmacol Ther 1987; 42:576–581.

29. Finck AD, Berkowitz BA, Hempstead J, Ngai SH. Pharmacokinetics of morphine: effects of hypercarbia on serum and brain morphine concentrations in the dog. Anesthesiology 1977;47: 407–410.

30. Ainslie SG, Eisele JH Jr, Corkill G. Fentanyl concentrations in brain and serum during respiratory acid-base changes in the dog. Anesthesiology 1979;51:293–297.

31. Murkin JM, Farrar JK, Tweed A, et al. Cerebral autoregulation and flow/metabolism coupling during cardiopulmonary bypass: the influence of $PaCO_2$. Anesth Analg 1987;66:825–832.

32. Vane JR. The alteration or removal of vasoactive hormones by the pulmonary circulation. In: Tedeschi DH, Tedeschi RE, eds. The importance of fundamental principles in drug evaluation. New York: Raven Press, 1968:217–235.

33. Wilson AGE, Pickett RD, Eling TE, Anderson MW. Studies on the persistence of basic amines in the rabbit lung. Drug Metab Dispos 1980;7: 402–424.

34. Jorfeldt L, Lewis DH, Lofstrom JB, Post C. Lung uptake of lidocaine in healthy volunteers. Acta Anaesth Scand 1979;23:567–584.

35. Gillis CN, Greene NM, Cronau LH, Hammond GL. Pulmonary extraction of 5-hydroxytryptamine and norepinephrine before and after cardiopulmonary bypass in man. Circ Res 1972;30: 666–674.

36. Geddes DM, Nesbitt K, Trail T, Blackburn JP. First pass uptake of ^{14}C propranolol by the lung. Thorax 1979;34:810–813.

37. Roerig DL, Kotrly KJ, Vucins EJ, Ahlf SB, Dawson CA, Kampine JP. First pass uptake of fentanyl, meperidine, and morphine in the human lung. Anesthesiology 1987;67:466–472.

38. Taeger K, Weninger E, Schmelzer F, Adt M, Franke N, Peter K. Pulmonary kinetics of fentanyl and alfentanil in surgical patients. Br J Anaesth 1988;61:425–434.

39. Rosen DA, Rosen KR, Davidson B, Nahrwold ML, Broadman L. Absorption of fentanyl by the membrane oxygenator [Abstract]. Anesthesiology 1985;63:3A:A281.

40. Rosen KR, Rosen DA. Absorption of sufentanil by the membrane oxygenator [Abstract]. Anesthesiology 1986;65:3A:A224.

41. Rosen KR, Rosen DA. Factors which affect fentanyl uptake by the membrane oxygenator [Abstract]. Anesthesiology 1986;65:3A:A225.

42. Durkan W, Lonergan M, Schwartz S, Fleming N. Effect of membrane oxygenators on sufentanil blood levels during cardiopulmonary bypass [Abstract]. Anesth Analg 1988;67:S54.

43. Booth BP, Henderson M, Milne B, et al. Sequestration of glyceryl trinitrate (nitroglycerin) by cardiopulmonary bypass oxygenators. Anesth Analg 1991;72:493–7.

44. Skacel M, Knott C, Reynolds F, Aps C. Extracorporeal circuit sequestration of fentanyl and alfentanil. Br J Anaesth 1986;58:947–949.

45. Meuldermans WEG, Hurkmans RMA, Heykants JJP. Plasma protein binding and distribution of fentanyl, sufentanil, alfentanil, and lofentanil in blood. Arch Int Pharmacodyn Ther 1982;257: 4–19.

46. Silvasi DL, Rosen DA, Rosen KR. Absorption of midazolam by the sci-med membrane oxygenator [Abstract]. Anesth Analg 1989;68:S261.

47. Beyda EJ, Jung M, Bellet S. Effect of hypothermia on the tolerance of dogs to digitalis. Circ Res 1961;9:129–135.

48. Eger EI, Saidman LJ, Branstater B. Temperature dependence of halothane and cyclopropane anesthesia in dogs: correlation with some theories of anesthetic action. Anesthesiology 1976;26: 764–770.

49. Kim CL. Awareness during cardiopulmonary bypass. AANA J 1978;46:373–383.

50. Bashein G, Nessly ML, Bledsoe SW, et al. Electroencephalography during surgery with cardiopulmonary bypass and hypothermia. Anesthesiology 1992;76:878–891.

51. Durkin MA, Hume A, Van Ess D, Kopf GS. Reliable and reproducible neurologic information using somatosensory evoked potential monitoring during hypothermic cardiopulmonary bypass [Abstract]. Anesthesiology 1985;63:3A:A72.

52. Quasha AL, Tinker JH, Sharbrough FW. Hypothermia plus thiopental: prolonged electrencephalographic suppression. Anesthesiology 1981;55:636–640.

53. Nussmeier NA, Arlund C, Slogoff S. Neuropsychiatric complications after cardiopulmonary bypass: cerebral protection by a barbiturate. Anesthesiology 1986;64:165–170.

54. Loomis CW, Brunet D, Milne B, Cervenko FW, Johnson GD. Arterial isoflurane concentration

and EEG burst suppression during cardiopulmonary bypass. Clin Pharmacol Ther 1986;40: 304–313.

55. Woodcock TE, Murkin JM, Farrar JK, Tweed WA, Guiraudon GM, McKenzie FN. Pharmacologic EEG suppression during cardiopulmonary bypass: cerebral hemodynamic and metabolic effects of thiopental or isoflurane during hypothermia and normothermia. Anesthesiology 1987;67:218–224.

56. Cannard TH, Zaimis E. The effect of lowered muscle temperature on the action of neuromuscular blocking drugs in man. J Physiol 1959; 149:112–119.

57. Horrow JC, Bartkowski RR. Pancuronium, unlike other nondepolarizing relaxants, retains potency at hypothermia. Anesthesiology 1983;58: 357–361

58. Buzello W, Schluermann D, Pollmaecher T, Spillner G. Unequal effects of cardiopulmonary bypass-induced hypothermia on neuromuscular blockade from constant infusion of alcuronium, d-tubocurarine, pancuronium, and vecuronium. Anesthesiology 1987;66:842–846.

59. Miller RD, Roderick LL. Pancuronium-induced neuromuscular blockade and its antagonism by neostigmine at 29, 37, and 41°C. Anesthesiology 1977;46:333–335.

60. Flynn PJ, Hughes R, Walton B. Use of atracurium in cardiac surgery involving cardiopulmonary bypass with induced hypothermia. Br J Anaesth 1984;56:967–72.

61. Buzello W, Schluermann D, Schindler M, Spillner G. Hypothermic cardiopulmonary bypass and neuromuscular blockade by pancuronium and vecuronium. Anesthesiology 1985;62:201–204.

62. Buzzello W, Pollmaecher T, Schluermann D,

Urbanyi B. The influence of hypothermic cardiopulmonary bypass on neuromuscular transmission in the absence of muscle relaxants. Anesthesiology 1986;64:279–281

63. Seamans KB, Gloor P, Dobell ARC, Wyant JD. Penicillin-induced seizures during cardiopulmonary bypass. A clinical and electroencephalographic study. N Engl J Med 1968;278:861–868.

64. Currie TT, Hayward NJ, Westlake G, Williams J. Epilepsy in cardiopulmonary bypass patients receiving large intravenous doses of penicillin. J Thorac Cardiovasc Surg 1971;62:1–6.

65. Laursen H, Waaben J, Gefke K, Husum B, Andersen LI, Sørensen HR. Brain histology, blood-brain barrier and brain water after normothermic and hypothermic cardiopulmonary bypass in pigs. Eur J Cardio-thorac Surg 1989;3:539–543.

66. Laursen H, Bødker A, Andersen K, Waaben J, Husum B. Brain oedema and blood-brain barrier permeability in pulsatile and nonpulsatile cardiopulmonary bypass. Scand J Thor Cardiovasc Surg 1986;20:161–166.

67. Tanifuji Y, Eger EI II. Effect of arterial hypotension on anaesthetic requirement in dogs. Br J Anaesth 1976;48:947–951.

68. Hall RI, Sullivan JA. Does cardiopulmonary bypass alter enflurane requirements for anesthesia? Anesthesiology 1990;73:249–255.

69. Antognini JF, Kien ND. Cardiopulmonary bypass does not alter canine enflurane requirements. Anesthesiology 1992;76:953–957.

70. Klockowski PM, Levy G. Kinetics of drug action in disease states. XXV. Effect of experimental hypovolemia on the pharmacodynamics and pharmacokinetics of desmethyldiazepam. J Pharmacol Exp Ther 1988;245:508–512.

Appendix

LITERATURE SUMMARY BY SPECIFIC DRUG GROUP

The following section consists of brief summaries for many of the available papers dealing with cardiopulmonary bypass as it affects drug levels or drug action. Papers focussed primarily on the pharmacologic management of CPB have not been included. Some of these references have already been discussed in the preceding text.

β-Adrenergic Blockers

Wood M, Shand DG, Wood AJJ. Propranolol binding in plasma during cardiopulmonary bypass. Anesthesiology 1979;51:512–516.

Propranolol is rapidly cleared in the liver, so its overall rate of elimination depends upon liver blood flow and is relatively independent of protein binding. In this study, CPB was initiated with a prime consisting of crystalloid (2000 ml), blood (450 ml), and Plasmanate (250 ml). Heparin (400 U/kg) was used for anticoagulation. With the onset of CPB the free fraction of propranolol increased from 6.6 to 13.5%. Plasma concentrations of free fatty acids (FFA) were dramatically increased by heparin. The authors felt that decreased propranolol binding was predominantly due to displacement by FFA, rather than just hemodilution. When heparin was reversed with protamine, propranolol binding returned to normal.

Plachetka JR, Salomon NW, Copeland JG. Plasma propranolol before, during, and after cardiopulmonary bypass. Clin Pharmacol Ther 1981;30:745–751.

Fourteen patients on chronic propranolol were studied, 7 of whom had an additional 0.1 mg/kg i.v. 100 minutes before CPB. The CPB was accomplished with a crystalloid prime and moderate hypothermia (31°C). Plasma propranolol decreased 60% with hemodilution and then dropped insignificantly during CPB. After CPB, drug levels rose and remained nearly constant for 4 hours. There were no differences attributable to the extra i.v. dose.

McAllister RG Jr, Bourne DW, Tan TG, Erickson JL, Wachtel CC, Todd EP. Effects of hypothermia on propranolol kinetics. Clin Pharmacol Ther 1979;25:1–7.

Patients receiving chronic propranolol therapy had their last dose approximately 12 hours prior to surgery. Plasma propranolol was measured before, during and after CPB at 27°C. Propranolol levels dropped on CPB, but when the values were corrected for pump prime hemodilution, levels were actually above prebypass control. Hypothermia in the absence of CPB was studied in a follow-up animal experiment. Dogs were given propranolol at 37°C, and 1 week later the experiment was repeated after surface cooling to 26°C. In the absence of CPB, plasma propranolol was consistently higher at 26°C compared with normothermia. The calculated clearance and volume of distribution were lower and the elimination half-life was prolonged.

Mantz J, Marty J, Blanchot G, Trouvin JH, Farinotti R, Desmonts JM. Acebutolol blood levels during cardiac surgery: effect of hypothermic cardiopulmonary bypass [Abstract]. Anesthesiology 1987;67:3A:A13.

Patients received long-term therapy with acebutolol until the day of surgery. Plasma levels of this drug and its major metabolite, diacetolol, were measured before, during and after CPB, but no formal pharmacokinetic analysis was performed. Plasma levels of both compounds decreased abruptly during CPB and then remained stable. Unlike propranolol, there was no increase in acebutolol concentration with rewarming or discontinuation of CPB. With chronic acebutolol therapy there was no evidence of significant washout from lung or skeletal muscle.

Miscellaneous Vasoactive Drugs

Moore RA, Geller EA, Gallagher JD, Clark DL. Effect of hypothermic cardiopulmonary bypass on nitroprusside metabolism. Clin Pharmacol Ther 1985;37:680–683.

(See text discussion and Fig. 8.4). Six patients were studied during CPB using a constant infusion of SNP at 0.45 mg/kg/hr. At 25°C, the nonenzymatic release of cyanide from SNP was not affected, but the enzymatic detoxification to thiocyanate was greatly decreased. The net effect was a significant increase in red blood cell levels of cyanide during CPB. During rewarming, cyanide levels dropped and thiocyanate increased.

Holley FO, Ponganis KV, Stanski DR. Effects of cardiac surgery with cardiopulmonary bypass on lidocaine disposition. Clin Pharmacol Ther 1984;35:617–626.

Lidocaine kinetics were studied in 5 patients before and after CPB. Clearance (C1), volume of distribution at steady-state (Vdss), and elimination half-life were not significantly different from preoperative control for the 1st day following CPB. On days 3 and 7, however, C1 and Vdss were markedly decreased, and elimination half-life had increased from 152 ± 30 minutes to 212 ± 90. These changes were accompanied by a doubling of the α_1-acid glycoprotein concentration and a decrease in lidocaine free fraction (30.2 to 16.4%).

Morrell DF, Harrison G. Lignocaine kinetics during cardiopulmonary bypass. Br J Anaesth 1983;55:1173–1177.

Various doses of lidocaine were administered *after* hypothermic CPB was started, and plasma levels were measured intermittently for 30 minutes. Lidocaine levels dropped rapidly, and the calculated distribution half-life was about 50% of the published normal value. Values for C1, Vdss, and elimination half-life were presented, but these were subject to tremendous error due to the short sampling time. The authors maintained that a normal dose of lidocaine (1.5 mg/kg) resulted in subtherapeutic concentrations ($<1.5\ \mu g/ml$) on CPB, but no data were presented to show the antiarrhythmic effect of this drug at 29°C.

Katz RI, Kanchuger MS, Patton KF, Eide TR. Effect of cardiopulmonary bypass on plasma levels of nifedipine. Anesth Analg 1990;71: 411–414.

Eight patients on chronic nifedipine therapy (10 to 20 mg p.o., every 8 hours) had their last dose approximately 1 hour before surgery, and drug levels were measured before, during, and after CPB. Plasma nifedipine was barely at therapeutic levels pre-CPB, and it declined significantly during and following CPB. In a second in vitro study nifedipine was mixed in a blood-Ringer's lactate prime and circulated through a Shiley M2000 membrane oxygenator at 23°C. There was no measurable uptake of nifedipine by the CPB circuit over the 3 hours of the experiment.

Kramer G, Romagnoli A. Papaverine disposition in cardiac surgery patients and the effect of cardiopulmonary bypass. Eur J Clin Pharmacol 1984;27:127–130.

Papaverine is a high extraction drug that is almost completely cleared in the liver. Six non-CPB and five CPB patients were studied. Papaverine in CPB patients was added to the cardioplegia solution. After CPB the elimination half-life was 2.77 ± 0.28 hours, which was significantly greater than 1.30 ± 0.25 hours for the non-CPB group. No estimate of clearance or distribution volume could be made for the CPB group. The increased half-life was attributed to decreased hepatic perfusion.

Benzodiazepines

Lowry KG, Dundee JW, McClean E, Lyons SM, Carson IW, Orr IA. Pharmacokinetics of diazepam and midazolam when used for sedation following cardiopulmonary bypass. Br J Anaesth 1985;57:883–885.

Nineteen patients received either midazolam or diazepam 5 mg i.v. every 2 hours for 14 to 15 hours following cardiac surgery. Midazolam concentrations rose and became stable within 4 to 6 hours, indicating that its clearance was not markedly prolonged post-CPB. As expected, concentrations of diazepam continued to rise throughout the period of administration.

Mathews HML, Carson IW, Lyons SM, et al. A pharmacokinetic study of midazolam in paediatric patients undergoing cardiac surgery. Br J Anaesth 1988;61:302–307.

The kinetics of midazolam were studied in children undergoing cardiac surgery with and without CPB, and in infants undergoing complete circulatory arrest. All patients were given 0.3 mg/kg midazolam; the non-CPB group received it during surgery, the other two groups received it postoperatively. A final CPB group was given an infusion of midazolam postoperatively. There were no significant differences in distribution or elimination between any of the groups, although clearance tended to be higher in the non-CPB group. Elimination was prolonged compared to historical controls.

Kanto J, Himberg JJ, Heikkilä H, Arola M, Jalonen J, Laaksonen V. Midazolam kinetics, before, during and after cardiopulmonary bypass surgery. Int J Clin Pharm Res 1985;5: 123–126.

Twelve patients were given midazolam 0.075 or 0.15 mg/kg prior to CPB. No details of CPB were given. Concentrations of midazolam dropped rapidly with hemodilution and remained stable. A small but significant rise in drug levels occurred after CPB. Elimination half-life was 281 minutes—over twice that of healthy volunteers.

Silvasi DL, Rosen DA, Rosen KR. Absorption of midazolam by the Sci-Med membrane oxygenator [Abstract]. Anesth Analg. 1989;68:S261.

As stated previously, this in vitro study showed that large amounts of midazolam could be bound to the silicone membrane of this oxygenator, and this binding was unaffected by previous saturation with fentanyl.

Aaltonen L, Kanto J, Arola M, Iisola E, Pakkanen A. Effect of age and cardiopulmonary bypass on the pharmacokinetics of lorazepam. Acta Pharmacol Toxicol 1982;51: 126–131.

Lorazepam is a drug with a low hepatic extraction ratio, so its clearance is not flow-dependent. Five patients who received 4 mg lorazepam 1 hour before CPB were compared with 14 non-CPB controls. The CPB utilized a blood-crystalloid prime and hypothermia (30°C). Total concentrations of lorazepam and its glucuronide conjugate dropped then increased on CPB. A significant increase in drug concentration occurred following CPB. Distribution and elimination half-lives were not significantly different between the two groups.

Boscoe MJ, Dawling S, Thompson MA, Jones RM. Lorazepam in open-heart surgery—plasma concentrations before, during and after bypass following different dose regimens. Anaesth Intens Care 1984;12:9–13.

Thirty-six patients were given lorazepam the night before surgery and then divided into three groups: (1) no further lorazepam, (2) additional drug during induction, (3) additional drug immediately before CPB. The CPB utilized a bubble oxygenator and clear prime (temperature not specified). Plasma concentrations of lorazepam dropped with hemodilution in all groups and increased post-CPB. It was suggested that levels in group 1 were not adequate to ensure amnesia during and post-CPB, but no actual assessments of memory were made.

Nitroglycerin

Booth BP, Henderson M, Milne B, et al. Sequestration of glyceryl trinitrate (nitroglycerin) by cardiopulmonary bypass oxygenators. Anesth Analg 1991;72:493–497.

The loss of nitroglycerin (TNG) to three bypass circuits was studied in vitro at 25°C and 37°C. At steady-state, TNG was decreased by 20.6%, 46.6%, and 67.3% with the Maxima membrane oxygenator, Cobe membrane oxygenator, and Bentley bubble oxygenator, respectively. Large amounts of TNG were adsorbed by polyurethane defoaming filters. The results did not appear to depend upon temperature.

Dasta JF, Jacobi J, Wu LS, et al. Loss of nitroglycerin to cardiopulmonary bypass apparatus. Crit Care Med 1983;11:50–52.

This in vitro study showed substantial uptake of nitroglycerin by a Cobe bubble oxygenator. Within 5 minutes arterial outlet concentrations had dropped by 70%. Relatively little drug was removed by the PVC tubing.

Dasta JF, Weber RJ, Wu LS, et al. Influence of cardiopulmonary bypass on nitroglycerin clearance. J Clin Pharmacol 1986;26:165–168.

Seven patients received TNG infusions before and during hypothermic CPB (27°C). A Bentley bubble oxygenator was used. The clearance of TNG was estimated during approximately steady-state conditions and found to increase 20% during CPB.

Digitalis Glycosides

Storstein L, Nitter-Hauge S, Fjeld N. Effect of cardiopulmonary bypass with heparin administration on digitoxin pharmacokinetics, serum electrolytes, free fatty acids, and renal function. J Cardiovasc Pharmacol 1979;1: 191–204.

Nineteen patients on maintenance digitoxin therapy underwent cardiac surgery (bubble oxygenator, crystalloid prime). Drug levels decreased by 50% after 15 minutes on CPB and then rose. By 24 hours digitoxin was at preoperative levels despite the fact that no more drug had been administered. Renal clearance of digitoxin decreased from 0.86 ml/min preoperatively to 0.45 ml/min on the 1st postoperative day. The administration of heparin raised levels of free fatty acids and decreased the protein binding of digitoxin.

Molokhia FA, Beller GA, Smith TW, Asimacopoulos PJ, Hood WB, Norman JC. Constancy of myocardial digoxin concentration during experimental cardiopulmonary bypass. Ann Thorac Surg 1971;11:222–228.

Dogs were given tritiated digoxin then anesthetized and placed on normothermic CPB for 120 minutes (blood-Ringer's prime). Plasma digoxin decreased 14% with CPB, but myocardial digoxin remained nearly constant. Very little drug was lost in the bypass circuit.

Coltart DJ, Chamberlain DA, Howard MR, Kettlewell MG, Mercer JL, Smith TW. Effect of cardiopulmonary bypass on plasma digoxin concentrations. Br Heart J 1971;33:334–8.

Eleven chronically digitalized patients underwent hypothermic CPB (28°C, blood-Ringer's prime). Plasma digoxin was slightly decreased after 2 hours of CPB and back to preoperative values by 16 hours. Urinary excretion of digoxin fell by 90% during CPB.

Morrison J, Killip T. Serum digitalis and arrhythmia in patients undergoing cardiopulmonary bypass. Circulation 1973;47:341–352.

Twenty patients receiving maintenance digoxin and four receiving digitoxin were studied. CPB utilized a dextrose-mannitol-water prime and cooling to 28°C. After an initial fall in drug concentration, levels rose, and 17 patients reached or exceeded pre-CPB levels. Eight patients receiving digoxin developed arrhythmias, and their average serum digoxin level was 1.3 ± 0.2 ng/ml during the episode. This is significantly lower than levels associated with toxicity in 77 non-CPB patients, and it suggests that myocardial sensitivity to the toxic effects of digoxin is increased after CPB.

Krasula RW, Hastreiter AR, Levitsky S, Yanagi R, Soyka LF. Serum, atrial, and urinary digoxin levels during cardiopulmonary bypass in children. Circulation 1974;49:1047–52.

Forty-two pediatric patients were divided in groups based on duration of digoxin therapy (group I, <5 days; group II, >30 days). During and following surgery serum digoxin levels were not different, but myocardial concentrations were higher in group I, and skeletal muscle concentrations were higher in group II. Incidence of arrhythmias was 25% in group I and 0% in group II.

Volatile Anesthetics

Feingold A. Crystalloid hemodilution, hypothermia, and halothane blood solubility during cardiopulmonary bypass. Anesth Analg 1977; 56:622–626.

Halothane blood/gas partition coefficients (B/G) were determined in eight patients before, during, and after CPB. The prime was 2.5 liters of Ringer's lactate, and temperatures were decreased to 28°C. The B/G was 2.8 at sternotomy and did not change during the hypothermic portion of CPB. After rewarming and shortly post-CPB the B/G was 1.6 and 1.9, respectively. The increase in B/G expected with hypothermia was antagonized by the decrease due to hemodilution. The low B/G at the end of CPB promotes the pulmonary clearance of halothane.

Sada T, Maguire HT, Aldrete JA. Halothane solubility in blood during cardiopulmonary bypass: the effect of haemodilution and hypothermia. Can Anaesth Soc J 1979;26:164–167.

Six patients were studied during normothermic CPB and six with mild hypothermia (30°C). A blood-Ringer's lactate prime (approximately 1:2) was used in a bubble oxygenator. The blood-gas partition coefficient for halothane was 1.34 at 37°C and 2.17 at 30°C. Solubility was not affected by changes in gas concentration.

Tarr TJ, Snowdon SL. Blood/gas solubility coefficient and blood concentration of enflurane during normothermic and hypothermic cardiopulmonary bypass. J Cardiothor Vasc Anesth 1991;5:111–115.

Ten patients were given constant end-tidal concentrations of enflurane before and during hypothermic CPB (24 to 26°C). A Cobe membrane oxygenator was primed with 2.5 liters of Ringer's lactate. Blood-gas solubility decreased significantly with hemodilution, but the blood concentration of enflurane rose 80% during hypothermia.

Henderson JM, Nathan HJ, Lalande M, Winkler MH, Dubé LM. Washin and washout of isoflurane during cardiopulmonary bypass. Can J Anaesth 1988;35:587–590.

Uptake and elimination of isoflurane was studied during hypothermic CPB (28 to 30°C) in 14 patients. Washin (constant 1% inspired isoflurane) was studied during hypothermia; washout was studied during both hypothermia and rewarming. Measurements were made with bubble and membrane oxygenators under both temperature conditions. The prime was 2 liters of Ringer's lactate. Washin was slow, and steady-state had not occurred by 48 minutes. Washout was rapid (50 to 70% decrease in 2 minutes; 75% by 15 minutes) and did not depend upon oxygenator type. Slightly higher washout rates occurred at higher temperatures.

Woodcock TE, Murkin JM, Farrar JK, Tweed WA, Guiraudon GM, McKenzie FN. Pharmacologic EEG suppression during cardiopulmonary bypass: cerebral hemodynamic and metabolic effects of thiopental or isoflurane during hypothermia and normothermia. Anesthesiology 1987;67:218–224.

Thirty-one patients were anesthetized with fentanyl and underwent hypothermic CPB (25 to 29°C) with EEG monitoring. They received one of three treatments during CPB: no further anesthesia, thiopental, or isoflurane. The two anesthetics were titrated to EEG burst suppression during hypothermia and during rewarming. Ce-

rebral blood flow and metabolic rate ($CMRo_2$) were determined. Thirty to 40 minutes of EEG burst suppression required 17 ± 4 mg/kg of thiopental. The same EEG effect was produced by $1.1 \pm 0.3\%$ isoflurane during hypothermia and $2.4 \pm 0.4\%$ during normothermia. The $CMRo_2$ was reduced by both anesthetics relative to control, but only thiopental reduced CBF.

Hall RI, Sullivan JA. Does cardiopulmonary bypass alter enflurane requirements for anesthesia? Anesthesiology 1990;73:249–255.

Dogs were subjected to normothermic bypass for 1 hour. Enflurane MAC was reduced by $30.1 \pm 21.5\%$ compared to a control group. This effect could not easily be related to systemic pressure, temperature, or acid-base status.

Antognini JF, Kien ND. Cardiopulmonary bypass does not alter canine enflurane requirements. Anesthesiology 1992;76:953–957.

Fourteen dogs were studied with partial CPB and either membrane ($n = 4$) or bubble ($n = 6$) oxygenators. Six more dogs were studied with total CPB and bubble oxygenators. Enflurane MAC did not change during or after 1 hour of normothermic CPB. The MAC was not influenced by partial versus total CPB, type of oxygenator, or the administration of heparin and protamine.

Loomis CW, Brunet D, Milne B, Cervenko FW, Johnson GD. Arterial isoflurane concentration and EEG burst suppression during cardiopulmonary bypass. Clin Pharmacol Ther 1986;40: 304–313.

Ten patients under fentanyl anesthesia received isoflurane through a Cobe membrane oxygenator during hypothermic CPB. Arterial pH was maintained between 7.5 and 7.55, and $Paco_2$ was between 25 and 32 mm Hg (not temperature corrected). When nasopharyngeal temperature was $26 \pm 0.61°C$, isoflurane induced burst suppression in nine patients at an average arterial concentration of only 0.64 vol%.

Nussmeier NA, Lambert ML, Moskowitz GJ, et al. Washin and washout of isoflurane administered via bubble oxygenators during hypothermic cardiopulmonary bypass. Anesthesiology 1989;71:519–525.

Hypothermia increases isoflurane solubility and therefore decreases speed of induction. Hemodilution exerts the opposite effects, since the solubility of isoflurane in saline is less than that in blood. Isoflurane (1%) was administered during hypothermic (23.4 ± 2.1°C) CPB with hemodilution (Hct 22.9 ± 2.9%). Compared to published normals, anesthetic washin was slower, but washout was comparable. The blood-gas partition coefficient was 1.39 ± 0.18—not substantially different from normal. The measured concentration of anesthetic in oxygenator exhaust gas was a reasonable approximation of the partial pressure in arterial blood during CPB.

Nussmeier NA, Cohen NH, Moskowitz GJ, Fisher DM, Eger EI II. Washin and washout of three volatile anesthetics concurrently administered during cardiopulmonary bypass [Abstract]. Anesthesiology 1988;69:3A:A84.

Four patients were given isoflurane (I), enflurane (E), and halothane (H) via a bubble oxygenator. The prime was Ringer's lactate, and moderate hypothermia (25.2 ± 0.6°C) was used. Washin was slower than normal, and I was faster than E or H. The speed of washout was greater than washin and was not different among the three anesthetics.

Stern RC, Weiss CI, Steinbach JH, Evers AS. Isoflurane uptake and elimination are delayed by absorption of anesthetic by the Sci-Med membrane oxygenator. Anesth Analg 1989;69: 657–662.

Under hypothermic conditions, the Sci-Med membrane has a capacity to absorb as much isoflurane as 17 liters of blood. This in vitro model predicts that the membrane oxygenator will markedly delay both uptake and elimination of the anesthetic.

Antibiotics

Benner EJ. Metabolism of antibiotics during cardiopulmonary bypass for open-heart surgery. Antimicrob Agents Chemother 1968;8: 373–377.

Eighteen patients undergoing valve replacement received one of three intravenous antibiotic regimens every 6 hours: (1) cephalothin (1 gram); (2) cephaloridine (1 gram); (3) pen-

icillin + methicillin + chloramphenicol (600,000 units, 1 gram, and 500 mg, respectively). Drug was given the night before and the morning of surgery. Fifteen minutes after the onset of CPB no antibiotic activity was detectable in 15/18 patients, and the level was "minimal" in the remaining three. Accumulation of cephaloridine or penicillin occurred in six azotemic patients during the postoperative period.

Eigel P, Tschirkov A, Satter P, Knothe H. Assays of cephalosporin antibiotics administered prophylactically in open heart surgery. Determination of serum and tissue levels before, during and after cardiopulmonary bypass. Infection 1978;6:23–28.

Twenty-eight patients undergoing various procedures received 2 g of cephalothin, cefazolin, or cefamandole at the start of surgery. Drug concentrations were measured in serum and tissue (right auricular appendage and pectoralis muscle). The CPB was conducted with a bubble oxygenator at 28 to 30°C (prime not specified). Bacteriocidal concentrations were maintained in tissue and blood throughout surgery. Cefazolin concentrations were still adequate 12 hours later.

Bryan CS, Morgan SL, Jordan AB, Smith CW, Sutton JP, Gangemi JD. Ceftriaxone levels in blood and tissue during cardiopulmonary bypass surgery. Antimicrob Agents Chemother 1984;25:37–39.

Fifteen patients undergoing coronary artery bypass graft (CABG) received 1 g of ceftriaxone 1 hour before skin incision. Concentrations were measured in serum, atrial appendage, and sternal bone. No details of CPB were presented. Ceftriaxone remained above minimum inhibitory concentrations (*Staphylococcus aureus, Enterobacter*) for 24 hours after a single dose.

Jungbluth GL, Pasko MT, Beam TR, Jusko WJ. Ceftriaxone disposition in open-heart surgery patients. Antimicrob Agents Chemother 1989; 33:850–856.

Ceftriaxone exhibits dose-dependent kinetics because of saturable albumin binding. Hemodilution and decreased binding markedly altered the disposition of this drug. Seven patients undergoing CABG were given a single bolus of ceftriaxone (14 mg/kg). The CPB utilized a membrane oxygenator in 6/7, crystalloid prime, and hypothermia (28°C). The CPB and heparin administration increased free fraction from 15% to 53%, and the volume of distribution doubled. Half-life increased from 7.8 to 15.4 hours. Renal filtration increased, but clearance (based on free drug) decreased.

Farber BF, Karchmer AW, Buckley MJ, Moellering RC Jr. Vancomycin prophylaxis in cardiac operations: determination of an optimal dosage regimen. J Thorac Cardiovasc Surg 1983;85:933–940.

Ten patients undergoing hypothermic CPB were given 15 mg/kg vancomycin (V) preoperatively. One hour later V levels were 30 ± 17 μg/ml. At the start of CPB, levels fell from 12 ± 6 to 7 ± 3 μg/ml and stayed relatively constant for the duration of bypass. Since 6.3 μg/ml is required to kill 50% of *S. epidermidis* strains responsible for prosthetic valve endocarditis, the authors felt that effective V prophylaxis requires a dose of at least 15 mg/kg.

Bergeron MG, Saginur R, Desaulniers D, et al. Concentrations of teicoplanin in serum and atrial appendages of patients undergoing cardiac surgery. Antimicrob Agents Chemother 1990;34:1699–1702.

Teicoplanin is a new glycopeptide antibiotic chemically related to vancomycin and with a similar spectrum of activity. Thirty-two patients undergoing CABG were given either 6 or 12 mg/kg at the start of surgery. Details of CPB were not presented. Concentrations well above those needed for most pathogens were maintained throughout surgery, and significant levels were present after 48 hours. Concentration in atrial tissue was 2.8 to 3.7 times higher than that in serum.

Miller KW, Chan KKH, McCoy HG, Fischer RP, Lindsay WG, Zaske DE. Cephalothin kinetics: before, during, and after cardiopulmonary bypass surgery. Clin Pharmacol Ther 1979;26: 54–62.

Cephalothin is actively secreted by the kidney and metabolized in the liver. Kinetics of cephalothin were determined preoperatively, during surgery, and 1 day postoperatively. During surgery cephalothin clearance was halved and elimination half-life doubled. Most of the

change was due to a decrease in hepatic clearance. Postoperatively, half-life and total clearance had returned to baseline, because renal clearance had increased markedly. Almost twice as much drug was excreted unchanged, indicating that hepatic clearance was still severely impaired.

Miller KW, McCoy HG, Chan KKH, et al. Effect of cardiopulmonary bypass on cefazolin disposition. Clin Pharmacol Ther 1980;27:550–556.

Cefazolin is excreted almost entirely by the kidney. Hypothermic (26 to 28°C) CPB did not change renal clearance from preoperative values, but total clearance was significantly less and elimination half-life was prolonged. The steady-state volume of distribution was increased, possibly due to a decrease in protein binding. The kinetics one day postoperatively were not different from preoperative.

Polk RE, Archer GL, Lower R. Cefamandole kinetics during cardiopulmonary bypass. Clin Pharmacol Ther 1978;23:473–480.

Cefamandole 20 mg/kg was administered prior to CPB with mild hypothermia (32 to 34°C) in 16 patients. Controls were 5 normal volunteers. The elimination half-life was prolonged during CPB (113 ± 37 versus 52 ± 8 minutes). Antibiotic concentrations fell during CPB, but they remained above therapeutic levels in all patients.

Opioids

Fischler M, Levron JC, Trang H, et al. Pharmacokinetics of phenoperidine in patients undergoing cardiopulmonary bypass. Br J Anaesth 1985;57:877–882.

Phenoperidine was administered as a 5 mg loading bolus 30 minutes after induction, followed by a continuous infusion of 5 mg/h. The infusion was continued until 20 to 70 min after the end of CPB. A bubble oxygenator was used, and core temperature was kept at 25.5 ± 5.8°C. Drug concentrations dropped with hemodilution then increased over the course of CPB. A further increase occurred when CPB was discontinued. During CPB, the drug concentrations in arterial and venous limbs of the circuit were almost identical, suggesting that the oxygenator did not sequester a significant amount of drug.

Howie MB, Mortimer W, Philip J, Dumond DA, McSweeney TD. Elimination of post bypass secondary peaks of fentanyl by pulsatile cardiopulmonary bypass [Abstract]. Anesthesiology 1988;69:3A:A60.

Fentanyl was given as a 50 μg/kg loading bolus and a maintenance infusion of 0.5 μg/kg/min. Temperature and composition of pump prime were not specified. Effective hepatic plasma flow was measured with indocyanine green. Patients given pulsatile flow (P-CPB) maintained hepatic flow at prebypass levels while nonpulsatile flow (NP-CPB) decreased it by 48%. In spite of this, P-CPB produced only slightly lower fentanyl levels during bypass. Only 2/9 patients given P-CPB had postbypass increases in fentanyl, compared with 12/15 given NP-CPB. This may be due to improved perfusion of muscle and other peripheral tissues with P-CPB.

Hug CC Jr, De Lange S, Burm AGL. Alfentanil pharmacokinetics in patients before and after cardiopulmonary bypass (CPB) [Abstract]. Anesth Analg 1983;62:266.

A 125 μg/kg bolus of alfentanil was administered at induction of anesthesia, and a second was given 30 minutes following CPB. The elimination half-life increased from 72 ± 6 to 195 ± 31 min, and this was due entirely to an increase in initial and steady-state distribution volume (clearance was unchanged). An increase in unbound alfentanil (due to hemodilution) contributed to the change in distribution.

Flezzani P, Alvis MJ, Jacobs JR, Schilling MT, Bai S, Reves JG. Sufentanil disposition during cardiopulmonary bypass. Can J Anaesth 1987;34: 566–569.

A computer-assisted continuous infusion device was programmed to achieve a sufentanil plasma concentration of 5 ng/ml prior to and during 90 minutes of CPB. The infusion parameters were determined using data from healthy subjects. The oxygenator and prime were not specified. Opioid levels were stable at 3.8 ± 0.4 ng/ml, dropped to 2.5 ± 0.3 with the initiation of CPB, and rose to 4.7 ± 0.4 by 90 min of CPB. Despite an exponentially decreasing infusion rate, sufentanil levels continued to climb during CPB.

Skacel M, Knott C, Reynolds F, Aps C. Extracorporeal circuit sequestration of fentanyl and alfentanil. Br J Anaesth 1986;58:947–949.

As summarized previously, fentanyl (but not alfentanil) was bound in significant quantities to a bubble oxygenator and circuit. Increasing pH did not affect alfentanil, but it increased the binding of fentanyl.

Koska AJ, Romagnoli A, Kramer WG. Effect of cardiopulmonary bypass on fentanyl distribution and elimination. Clin Pharmacol Ther 1981;29:100–105.

Twelve patients (six CPB, six non-CPB controls) were studied. All received 0.5 mg fentanyl as a single bolus. The details of CPB were not specified. Plasma concentrations of fentanyl decreased sharply with the onset of CPB but showed a normal log-linear decay post-CPB. Elimination half-life post-CPB was 5.2 ± 2.7 hours compared to 3.3 ± 1.1 hours for controls. Hepatic blood flow (estimated by indocyanine green clearance in a separate group of patients) decreased by 30% during and after CPB.

Rosen DA, Rosen KR, Davidson B, Nahrwold ML, Broadman L. Absorption of fentanyl by the membrane oxygenator [Abstract]. Anesthesiology 1985;63:3A:A281.

As discussed previously, this in vitro study showed that a Sci-Med silicon membrane oxygenator has the capacity to bind 116 ng/cm^2 fentanyl at saturation. Full saturation did not occur for over 2 hours.

Koren G, Crean P, Klein J, Goresky G, Villamater J, MacLeod SM. Sequestration of fentanyl by the cardiopulmonary bypass (CPBP). Eur J Clin Pharmacol 1984;27:51–56.

Nineteen children underwent cardiac surgery after receiving a bolus and continuous infusion of fentanyl. The CPB apparatus consisted of a silicone membrane oxygenator (Sci-Med, 0.8 m^2), an aluminum heat exchanger, PVC reservoir, and both silicone and PVC tubing. The prime was crystalloid-blood, and deep hypothermia (20°C) was used. Plasma concentration of fentanyl dropped 74 ± 8.7% on CPB, greater than expected on the basis of hemodilution alone (50.6 ± 12.0%). When fentanyl was circulated in a closed pump circuit, fentanyl concentrations fell from 120 ng/ml to 2 ng/ml within 3 minutes and then remained stable. The oxygenator was the main source of fentanyl binding.

Rosen KR, Rosen DA. Factors which affect fentanyl uptake by the membrane oxygenator [Abstract]. Anesthesiology 1986;65:3A:A225.

Fentanyl binding by a Sci-Med silicone membrane was studied in vitro. Binding was increased by warm temperature (37°C versus 25°C), unaffected by albumin, heparin, and cefazolin in the prime, and significantly decreased by the addition of packed red blood cells.

Rosen KR, Rosen DA. Absorption of sufentanil by the membrane oxygenator [Abstract]. Anesthesiology 1986;65:3A:A224.

As discussed previously, the Sci-Med silicone membrane can bind large amounts of sufentanil (11 ng/cm^2 at 25°C, 24 ng/cm^2 at 37°C). An adult membrane should hold 275 μg of sufentanil.

Durkan W, Lonergan M, Schwartz S, Fleming N. Effect of membrane oxygenators on sufentanil blood levels during cardiopulmonary bypass [Abstract]. Anesth Analg 1988;67:S54.

Sufentanil was administered before CPB utilizing either a Sci-Med II membrane oxygenator (*n* = 5) or a Maxima hollow fiber oxygenator (*n* = 3). Temperature and composition of prime were not specified. These preliminary data suggest that uptake is greater with the silicone membrane.

Okutani R, Philbin DM, Rosow CE, Koski G, Schneider RC. Effect of hypothermic hemodilutional cardiopulmonary bypass on plasma sufentanil and catecholamine concentrations in humans. Anesth Analg 1988;67:667–670.

Forty patients were given a bolus or a bolus plus infusion of sufentanil up to the time of CPB. CPB utilized a crystalloid prime, a bubble oxygenator and moderate hypothermia (25°C). The data were shown previously in Figure 8.1. Plasma concentrations of sufentanil dropped initially, then remained stable until rewarming. Levels increased during rewarming and again after CPB. Significant elevations in plasma epi-

nephrine occurred while sufentanil levels were rising, suggesting that this catecholamine response was not due to insufficient opioid.

Neuromuscular Blockers

Walker JS, Shanks CA, Brown KF. Altered d-tubocurarine disposition during cardiopulmonary bypass. Clin Pharmacol Ther 1984;35:686–694.

d-Tubocurarine (DTC) was administered to 13 patients as a 0.6 mg/kg bolus followed by a 3 μg/kg/min infusion starting one hour pre-CPB. The CPB utilized hypothermia (28°C), a bubble oxygenator, and a clear prime. Plasma DTC concentration (bound and free) rose over 400% during CPB. Free DTC rose by 27%, primarily due to hemodilution. Clearance dropped from 2.7 to 0.6 ml/min/kg, and elimination half-life increased from 172 to 633 minutes.

Shanks CA, Ramzan IM, Walker JS, Brown KF. Disposition of gallamine in open-heart surgery involving cardiopulmonary bypass. Clin Pharmacol Ther 1983;33:792–799.

Gallamine is almost totally excreted unchanged in the urine. Twenty-two patients with normal renal function were studied. The CPB was performed with a bubble oxygenator, crystalloid-blood prime, and cooling to 28°C. Plasma kinetics—particularly total clearance—did not differ markedly from previously published values in non-CPB patients. Gallamine concentrations rose with the onset of CPB, presumably because central volume had contracted.

Walker JS, Shanks CA, Brown KF. Alcuronium kinetics in patients undergoing cardiopulmonary bypass surgery. Br J Clin Pharmacol 1983;15:237–244.

Alcuronium is a muscle relaxant that is eliminated almost completely unchanged in the urine. Ten patients underwent CPB with a clear prime, bubble oxygenator, and hypothermia (25°C). Alcuronium was given as a 0.27 mg/kg bolus followed by an infusion of 1 μg/kg/min. Drug levels rose with the onset of CPB and remained elevated. Clearance was significantly decreased from pre-CPB. The elimination half-life was 532 minutes versus 199 minutes for previously published controls. The rise in alcuronium concentration was attributed to the lower clearance and a decrease in central volume.

Flynn PJ, Hughes R, Walton B. Use of atracurium in cardiac surgery involving cardiopulmonary bypass with induced hypothermia. Br J Anaesth 1984;56:967–72.

Twelve patients received a bolus of atracurium (0.6 mg/kg) followed by an infusion titrated to maintain 90 to 95% block of single twitch. During hypothermia (25 to 26°C), the relaxant requirement was 34 to 51% lower than pre-CPB. The authors felt this was due to a decrease in the Hofmann degradation of atracurium, although no breakdown products were measured. An increased sensitivity to the relaxant remains an alternative explanation.

d'Hollander AA, Duvaldestin P, Henzel D, Nevelsteen M Bomblet JP. Variations in pancuronium requirement, plasma concentration, and urinary excretion induced by cardiopulmonary bypass with hypothermia. Anesthesiology 1983;58:505–509.

Pancuronium was infused before, during, and after CPB (24 to 26°C) to maintain 90% depression of adductor pollicis twitch tension after ulnar nerve stimulation. Stable hypothermic CPB decreased pancuronium requirement from 238 to 94 μg/m²/15min. More pancuronium was needed at the onset of CPB and during rewarming.

Avram MJ, Shanks CA, Henthorm TK, Ronai AK, Kinzer J Wilkinson CJ. Metocurine kinetics in patients undergoing operations requiring cardiopulmonary bypass. Clin Pharmacol Ther 1987;42:576–581.

Metocurine (MTC) was given as a 0.3 mg/kg bolus followed by an infusion of 0.04 mg/kg/hr to non-CPB patients and patients undergoing hypothermic CPB (30°C). Plasma MTC rose with the initiation of CPB, and remained fairly stable. The level of paralysis declined during hypothermia in spite of the relatively constant levels of MTC. Clearance, half-lives, and volumes of distribution did not differ significantly from controls.

Buzello W, Schluermann D, Schindler M, Spillner G. Hypothermic cardiopulmonary bypass and neuromuscular blockade by pancuro-

nium and vecuronium. Anesthesiology 1985; 62:201–204.

Equal loading doses of pancuronium or vecuronium were administered to 20 patients, and supplements were titrated to EMG response prior to and during hypothermic CPB (26°C). During hypothermic CPB the durations of pancuronium and vecuronium were prolonged 1.8 and 5 times, respectively. Although rewarming hastened recovery, the durations of both drugs were prolonged well into the post-CPB period.

Buzello W, Schluermann D, Pollmaecher T, Spillner G. Unequal effects of cardiopulmonary bypass-induced hypothermia on neuromuscular blockade from constant infusion of alcuronium, d-tubocurarine, pancuronium, and vecuronium. Anesthesiology 1987;66:842–846.

Forty patients undergoing hypothermic CPB (26.3 ± 1.2°C) received a bolus plus constant rate infusion of *d*-tubocurarine, pancuronium, alcuronium, or vecuronium. Muscle relaxation was assessed by twitch response and evoked compound EMG. Hypothermic CPB attenuated the blockade produced by alcuronium, *d*-tubocurarine and pancuronium, but the block produced by vecuronium was enhanced.

Mark J, Wierda KH, van der Starre PJA, et al. Pharmacokinetics of pancuronium in patients undergoing coronary artery surgery with and without low dose dopamine. Clin Pharmacokinet 1990;19:491–498.

Twelve patients were given a bolus of pancuronium and studied with or without dopamine 2 μg/kg/min during and after CPB. The CPB was accomplished with a membrane oxygenator, Ringer's lactate-albumin prime, and hypothermia (28°C). Total renal clearance of pancuronium was not influenced by low-dose dopamine. Dopamine-treated patients had a greater diuresis, but pancuronium kinetics did not differ from control. Hypothermia decreased tubular reabsorption of pancuronium and thus increased its elimination.

Intravenous Anesthetics

Hynynen M, Olkkola KT, Näveri E, Palojoki R, Neuvonen PJ, Heinonen J. Thiopentone pharmacokinetics during cardiopulmonary bypass with a nonpulsatile or pulsatile flow. Acta Anaesth Scand 1989;33:554–560.

Thiopental 6 mg/kg was administered either prior to CPB or during CPB. The CPB was either pulsatile or nonpulsatile. Neither the distribution nor the elimination of thiopental was affected by the mode of perfusion. There was no evidence for lung sequestration of thiopental, since simultaneous radial artery and pulmonary artery samples were not different. An in-vitro study at 30°C and pH 7.35-7.45 showed that almost 50% of an injected dose of thiopental was lost to the bubble oxygenator circuit.

Quasha AL, Tinker JH, Sharbrough FW. Hypothermia plus thiopental: prolonged electrencephalographic suppression. Anesthesiology 1981;55:636–640.

Thirteen patients undergoing hypothermic CPB (25 to 30°C) were given either (1) no thiopental; (2) thiopental 8 mg/kg at induction, CPB, and post-CPB; (3) thiopental 8 mg/kg during CPB only. The total duration of EEG suppression (burst suppression or isoelectricity) was measured from induction to 1 hour post-CPB. The EEG suppression lasted for 4.8, 26.1, and 29.3 minutes in groups 1, 2, and 3, respectively. Periods of isoelectricity were seen only in groups 2 and 3, and only while on CPB.

Nussmeier NA, Cohen NH, Stanski DR. High-dose thiopental requirement to maintain a nearly isoelectric EEG during hypothermic cardiopulmonary bypass [Abstract]. Anesthesiology 1988;69:A91.

Thiopental was titrated to EEG response during hypothermic CPB (26°C) and blood levels were measured. Thiopental half-life was markedly prolonged (23.6 ± 9.8 hours), but hypothermia reduced the plasma level of thiopental necessary to achieve an isoelectric EEG.

Nancherla AR, Narang PK, Kim YD, et al. Sodium thiopental kinetics during cardio-pulmonary bypass [Abstract]. Anesth Analg 1986; 65:S111.

Thiopental 6 mg/kg was administered during hypothermic CPB (25 to 26°C). Total clearance was reduced by about 50% compared to previously published normal values.

Bjorksten AR, Crankshaw DP, Morgan DJ, Prideaux PR. The effects of cardiopulmonary bypass on plasma concentrations and protein binding of methohexital and thiopental. J. Cardiothor Vasc Anesth 1988;2:281–289.

Thiopental and methohexital were delivered by programmed infusion to achieve stable plasma levels before and during CPB (temperature not specified). Total concentrations of both drugs fell at the onset of CPB, and rose slowly toward pre-CPB levels. Levels of unbound drug, in contrast, remained relatively unaffected by CPB. The ratio of bound to unbound drug correlated strongly with plasma albumin.

Morgan DJ, Crankshaw DP, Prideaux PR, Chan HNJ, Boyd MD. Thiopentone levels during cardiopulmonary bypass. Changes in plasma protein binding during continuous infusion. Anaesthesia 1986;41:4–10.

Thiopental was delivered by exponentially declining infusion rate to maintain a steady plasma level before and during CPB. With the onset of CPB, total thiopental concentrations fell and then returned toward pre-CPB levels. Unbound thiopental had a decrease which was smaller and relatively short-lived. The increase in free fraction was apparently due to hemodilution and a decrease in plasma protein concentration.

Massey NJA, Sherry KM, Oldroyd S, Peacock JE. Pharmacokinetics of an infusion of propofol during cardiac surgery. Br J Anaesth 1990;65: 475–479.

A constant rate infusion of propofol (4 mg/kg/h) was administered throughout cardiac surgery. The initiation of hypothermic CPB (28°C, membrane oxygenator) produced no significant changes in whole blood concentrations of propofol. Post-CPB, clearance was not reduced, and plasma concentrations of propofol fell rapidly.

Oduro A, Tomlinson AA, Voice A, Davies GK. The use of etomidate infusions during anaesthesia for cardiopulmonary bypass. Anaesthesia 1983;38(suppl):66–69.

Etomidate was administered as a bolus plus infusion, before and during CPB. Serum concentrations of etomidate fell when CPB was initiated, then increased during the procedure. A secondary increase in drug concentration occurred when bypass was discontinued, and this may have represented release of etomidate from tissue stores or the oxygenator circuit.

Coniam SW. Alphaxalone infusion during cardiopulmonary bypass. Anaesthesia 1980;35: 576–580.

Thirteen patients were given infusions of this steroidal anesthetic before, during, and following hypothermic (28°C) CPB. Alphaxalone is rapidly cleared by hepatic metabolism and is only 20 to 40% protein bound. Drug levels dropped with hemodilution, then rose significantly during hypothermia (presumably due to decreased clearance). Levels rose again during rewarming, so there was little net change in concentration throughout the period of CPB.

Miscellaneous Drugs

Communale ME, DiNardo JA, Schwartz MJ. Pharmacokinetics of dantrolene in an adult patient undergoing cardiopulmonary bypass. J Cardiothor Vasc Anesth 1991;5:153–155.

A 76 kg male with renal failure received 200 mg of dantrolene intravenously, immediately before induction of anesthesia. He underwent CPB with a Cobe membrane oxygenator, moderate hypothermia (28°C) and hemodilution with 2 liters of crystalloid prime. Whole blood levels of dantrolene declined 17% of CPB, rose slightly with rewarming, then decreased post-CPB! Concentrations remained above suggested therapeutic levels throughout this period.

Kong AN, Jungbluth GL, Pasko MT, Beam TR, Jusko WJ. Pharmacokinetics of methylprednisolone sodium succinate and methylprednisolone in patients undergoing cardiopulmonary bypass. Pharmacotherapy 1990;10:29–34.

Six patients undergoing CPB were given 1.7 to 2.4 g of methylprednisolone sodium succinate (MPS) as part of the cardioplegia solution. The kinetics of MPS and its active metabolite, methylprednisolone (MP) were determined and compared with data from healthy volunteers. The CPB utilized hypothermia (28°C), a membrane oxygenator, and 2.5 liters of crystalloid prime. The clearances of MPS and MP were reduced by 5 and 2 times, respectively. The volume of distribution of MPS was reduced, and the elimination half-lives of both compounds were increased.

Cohen JA, Frederickson EL, Kaplan JA. Plasma heparin activity and antagonism during cardiopulmonary bypass with hypothermia. Anesth Analg 1977;56:564–570.

Plasma heparin was measured by thrombin time bioassay in 11 patients undergoing CPB with moderate hypothermia. Plasma heparin fell with hemodilution but did not decrease once hypothermia was established. Heparin levels decreased during rewarming, and the rate of decrease was dependent upon the concentration of heparin.

Green TP, Isham-Schopf B, Irmiter RJ, Smith C, Uden DL, Steinhorn RH. Inactivation of heparin during extracorporeal circulation in infants. Clin Pharmacol Ther 1990;48:148–154.

Heparin clearance was measured in 5 infants undergoing extracorporeal membrane oxygenation (ECMO). Heparin clearance was 3.8 ± 1.9 ml/kg/min during the procedure. After separation from ECMO, the isolated circuit continued to clear heparin. Measured heparin clearance in the circuit was 2.1 ± 0.8, and clearance in the infant was 1.6 ± 0.5. More than one-half of the heparin given during ECMO is eliminated by the apparatus or the blood within it.

9

THE INFLAMMATORY RESPONSE TO CARDIOPULMONARY BYPASS

James K. Kirklin, James F. George, and William Holman

Most patients who undergo operations requiring cardiopulmonary bypass (CPB) as a support technique experience few identifiable adverse sequelae and convalesce normally. It is likely, however, that nearly all patients experience a rather specific physiologic response to CPB, which can occasionally produce a deleterious response. Rarely, in their severest form, these deleterious effects may manifest as the "postperfusion syndrome," which may include one or more of the clinical signs of pulmonary dysfunction, renal dysfunction, a bleeding diathesis, increased susceptibility to infections, accumulation of increased interstitial fluid, leukocytosis, vasoconstriction, fever, and even hemolysis. We believe that CPB is inherently a pathologic condition in which blood is continuously exposed to the nonendothelial surfaces of the pump oxygenator circuit. The hypothesis has gradually evolved that CPB elicits a generalized inflammatory response, involving at least the complement, coagulation, kallikrein, and fibrinolytic cascades (1), and undoubtedly others. Precise elucidation of the mechanisms involved in this potential injury is complicated by the extreme variability of the response, and by the fact that most patients have a mild reaction to CPB. Furthermore, the same degree of variability occurs in the animal response to CPB, further confounding efforts to understand and neu-tralize these potentially damaging effects. This chapter will focus on the generalized inflammatory response to CPB.

GENERAL SCHEME OF THE DAMAGING EFFECTS

The mechanisms for damage following exposure to CPB are likely related to the general phenomena of altered arterial blood flow patterns and to the exposure of blood to abnormal surfaces, substances, and physiologic events. Altered blood flow via the nonpulsatile standard roller pump used for clinical CPB represents a marked deviation from normal physiologic pulsatile perfusion. The potential beneficial effects of pulsatile flow are numerous, and are discussed in detail in Chapter 13. During CPB, the abnormal physiologic events include exposure to shear stresses, abnormal substances, and, perhaps most importantly, exposure to unphysiologic (nonendothelial) surfaces (2).

Blood is a complex fluid composed of both formed and unformed elements. The formed elements include erythrocytes, leukocytes, and platelets. Among the unformed elements, the plasma proteins may be particularly vulnerable during CPB.

Shear stresses are generated by blood pumps, by suction devices, and by cavitation around the end of the arterial cannula.

233

Leukocytes are particularly sensitive to shear stresses, which cause destruction or functional impairments such as decreased aggregation, decreased chemotactic migration, and impaired phagocytosis (3). During CPB, an initial leukopenia develops that returns to baseline after approximately 2 hours (4). This increase occurs in part from the active movement of leukocytes out of the vascular space (5). Immediately following bypass, a leukocytosis develops that usually continues for several days (6).

During CPB, red blood cells are damaged mainly by shear stresses. This results in either immediate hemolysis with release of free hemoglobin or in a shortened red cell life span with delayed hemolysis. Hemolysis is less evident when an oxygenator is not in the system (7), and bubble oxygenators generally produce more hemolysis than membranes (8, 9). Suction (e.g., intracardiac venting) particularly damages erythrocytes. Free hemoglobin levels have been reported to increase fourfold within 10 minutes of CPB initiation (10), and the decreased erythrocyte survival time after CPB produces a progressive loss of erythrocytes during the first 3 or 4 postoperative days.

Abnormal substances incorporated into blood during CPB include air bubbles, fibrin, tissue debris, platelet thrombi, and defoaming agents. Thromboplastinogen is activated when blood makes contact with injured tissues, and this may contribute to intravascular formation of thrombin and subsequent platelet emboli. Recently, high circulating levels of plasticizing agents leached from polyvinyl chloride surfaces have been identified in patients undergoing CPB (11), and evidence for cerebral microembolization during CPB has been obtained from humans and animals (12, 13).

The greatest potential hematologic damage during CPB likely derives from exposure to unphysiologic surfaces. The surfaces of the oxygenating device probably inflict the greatest damage. The unphysiologic surfaces are gas in bubble oxygenators and the membrane itself in membrane oxy-

genation. The relative proportion of blood exposed to abnormal surfaces is much smaller in the reservoirs, tubes, and cannulae. Exposure of platelets to these foreign surfaces promotes platelet aggregation (14, 15), resulting in platelet emboli as well as a decreased platelet number (16) and function (17) after CPB. Fibrinogen is probably rapidly adsorbed to the surfaces within the bypass circuit, and platelet surface glycoproteins then bind to these sites, producing platelet aggregation (18). A portion of platelets exposed to the CPB circuit undergo degranulation and are irreversibly damaged. The precise sequence of events and proportions of impaired and destroyed platelets remain controversial (18–23). Denaturation of carrier proteins occurs during CPB with breakdown of lipoproteins and generation of fat emboli (24).

Humoral Amplification System

The humoral amplification system is a complex system of plasma proteins that respond to a local stimulus with a self-perpetuating and amplifying series of reactions. This system is critical to the generalized inflammatory response during CPB, and includes those elements and reactions that are normally involved in a localized inflammatory reaction in some areas of the body. It is likely that a major part of the deleterious effects of CPB is related to the poorly controlled generalized inflammatory response produced by the activation of the humoral amplification system during exposure of blood to nonendothelial surfaces. The four basic systems that identify with this amplification process are the coagulation cascade, the fibrinolytic cascade, the kallikrein system, and the complement system. The first three will be discussed in this section, and complement activation will be discussed separately.

Massive contact of blood with nonendothelial surfaces activates Hageman factor (factor XII) almost immediately after the onset of bypass (25, 26). This activates the coagulation cascade and also other cascades. Even with appropriate heparinization during bypass, there is evidence of ongoing microcoagulation with consumption of clotting factors (16).

The onset of bypass also activates the fibrinolytic cascade. Increased levels of plasmin (the active fibrinolytic agent) have been detected shortly after initiation of CPB (27). Plasmin may further activate prekallikrein, the complement system, and possibly Hageman factor.

The kallikrein cascade is activated by Hageman factor and undoubtedly by other events, and results in the production of bradykinin, which in turn increases vascular permeability, dilates arterioles, initiates smooth muscle contraction, and elicits pain. Kallikrein itself can activate Hageman factor and can also activate plasminogen to form plasmin, again demonstrating the complex interaction between these amplification systems. High levels of circulating bradykinin have been demonstrated during CPB (28, 29). Bradykinin is largely metabolized in the lungs, and exclusion of the pulmonary circulation during CPB acts to sustain circulating bradykinin levels. Furthermore, very young infants appear less able to eliminate bradykinin (30).

Complement

A group of circulating glycoproteins comprises the complement system and form the basic matrix of the body's response to immunologic, traumatic, infectious, or foreign body insult. Two pathways exist for complement activation (31) (Fig. 9.1). The classic pathway is usually initiated via interaction with antigen-antibody complexes. The alternative properdin pathway is activated by exposure of blood to foreign surfaces (32). In 1972, Parker and colleagues (33) noted that complement was consumed during CPB, and they hypothesized that the complement system may promote the increases in extravascular water that were frequently seen following CPB. Chenoweth

and colleagues (32) first demonstrated in 1981 that the complement anaphylatoxin C3a is increased shortly after the onset of CPB, with continuing production throughout the duration of bypass (Fig. 9.2). Although some controversy exists, it is generally acknowledged that complement is activated primarily by means of the alternative pathway at the onset of CPB (34). The anaphylatoxins C5a and C3a have similar physiologic effects observed in many patients after CPB, including vasoconstriction and increased capillary permeability (35, 36).

Although complement activation has been demonstrated during operative procedures without CPB, the magnitude of activation is small compared with that during CPB. In cardiac operations without CPB, for example, levels of C3 are essentially normal throughout the procedure (37) (Fig. 9.3). Fosse and colleagues (38) have also demonstrated increased levels of the terminal complement complex (TCC) shortly after initiation of CPB (Fig. 9.4). The TCC represents the end product of complement activation and requires splitting of C5a and C5b (38). In contrast, patients undergoing thoracotomy without CPB showed no increase in TCC levels (38).

Salama and colleagues (39) from West Germany have also demonstrated deposition of the terminal C5b-9 complement complexes on erythrocytes and neutrophils during CPB. Intravascular hemolysis was observed in all patients, and C5b-9 was demonstrated on red cell ghosts but not on intact erythrocytes, inferring a relationship between complement activation on red cells and hemolysis during CPB. In addition, granulocytes were found to nearly uniformly carry C5b-9 complexes during CPB and transiently afterward (less than 24 hours).

A prospective study at the University of Alabama at Birmingham examined variables related to CPB and their relationship to morbidity after cardiac surgery for congenital heart defects (37). Cardiac dysfunction

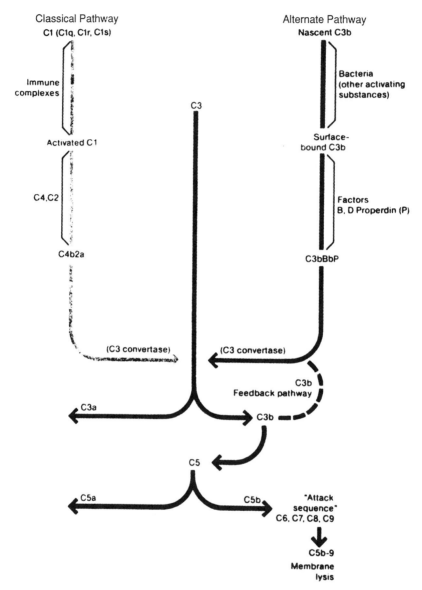

Figure 9.1.   Pathways of complement activation. (From Goldstein IM. Current concepts: complement in infectious diseases. Kalamazoo, Michigan, The Upjohn Company, 1980:7.)

within the first 24 hours after operation was significantly related to higher C3a levels 3 hours after CPB, longer duration of CPB, and younger age at operation (Table 9.1). Postoperative pulmonary dysfunction was related to the same risk factors (Table 9.2). Risk factors specific for postoperative renal dysfunction included higher C3a 3 hours after CPB and younger age (Table 9.3). An overall index of morbidity was also de-

termined, which related significantly to higher levels of C3a, longer duration of CPB, and younger age at operation (Fig. 9.5). This relationship between complement activation and morbidity observed following CPB is particularly interesting because of the similarity between the known physiologic effects of the anaphylatoxins C5a and C3a and the clinical sequelae observed in such patients (36).

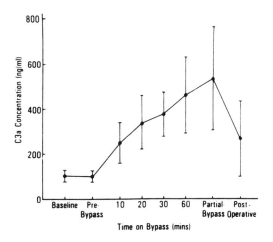

Figure 9.2. Plasma levels of C3a in patients undergoing cardiopulmonary bypass. (From Chenoweth DE, Cooper SW, Hugli TE, et al. Complement activation during cardiopulmonary bypass: evidence for generation of C3a and C5a anaphylatoxins. N Engl J Med 1981;304:497–503.)

Alterations in Microvascular Permeability

The accumulation of extravascular water is a common phenomenon following CPB, with clinical manifestations that include increased pulmonary interstitial fluid without elevation of left atrial pressure, increased tissue and peripheral edema, and, rarely, ascites. In 1966 Cleland and colleagues (40) noted progressive increases in extravascular fluid after cardiac operations that were directly related to the duration of CPB (Fig. 9.6). Despite this and other studies documenting alterations in distribution of fluid after CPB, evidence for alterations in capillary permeability was lacking until 1987, when Smith and colleagues (41) produced direct evidence for increased microvascular permeability after

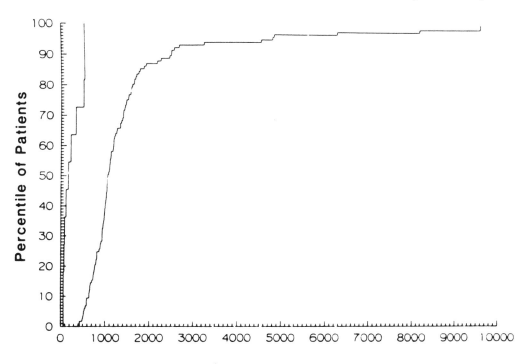

Figure 9.3. C3a levels (in nanograms per milliliter) at the end of cardiopulmonary bypass, expressed in a cumulative percentile plot. The steep vertical line on the left represents closed heart patients, 100% of whom had near-normal or normal levels. The curve on the right represents open heart patients, virtually all of whom had increased levels. Fifty percent had levels above 1000 ng·ml⁻¹ and 25% had levels above 1600 ng·ml⁻¹. (From Kirklin JK, Westaby S, Blackstone EH, et al. Complement and the damaging effects of cardiopulmonary bypass. J Thorac Cardiovasc Surg 1983;86:845–857.)

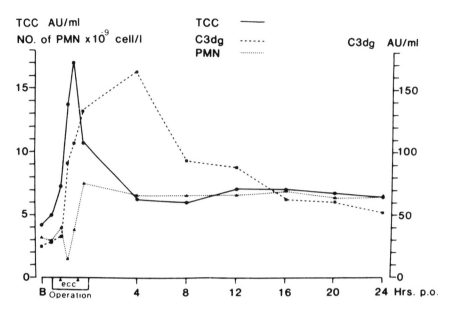

Figure 9.4. The concentration of TCC, C3dg (activation product of C3), and PMNs (polymorphonuclear neutrophils) in blood in 10 patients undergoing aorto-coronary bypass operations during extracorporeal circulation (ecc) (median values). (From Fosse E, Mollnes TE, Ingvaldsen B. Complement activation during major operations without cardiopulmonary bypass. J Thorac Cardiovasc Surg 1987;93:860–866.)

CPB. Using ultrafiltration techniques in a dog model, a segment of small intestine was isolated, its lymphatic drainage cannulated, and the segment's venous pressure progressively increased over a 3-hour period in order to increase lymphatic flow. The colloid osmotic sieving ratio, determined by the minimum lymph-plasma protein concentration ratio, was used as a measure of microvascular permeability (42). The permeability to each of six sizes of plasma proteins was measured by density gradient gel electrophoresis. A systematic increase in permeability to proteins by 2 hours of normothermic CPB was demonstrated (Fig. 9.7) and larger molecules were more permanently affected (Fig. 9.8).

These experimental findings have been corroborated by clinical studies. Breckenridge and colleagues (43) documented an increase in extracellular fluid following CPB, noting an 18% increase in the bromide space and a 33% increase in the inulin space 1 day following bypass. Brans and colleagues (44) also documented alterations in extravascular water in infants and

small children after CPB, with an increase in interstitial water of 9 to 68% over preoperative levels in all but one of 16 patients following CPB ($p=.01$).

Pulmonary Dysfunction After CPB

Although the widespread inflammatory reaction to CPB almost certainly affects all organ systems, the lung appears particularly susceptible to these effects, and it has been studied as a model for the specific organ sequelae of CPB. Although postbypass pulmonary damage is undoubtedly mediated by multiple factors, the neutrophil has perhaps generated the greatest current interest as a mediator of damage. In 1978, Chenoweth and Hugli (45) demonstrated specific C5a receptor sites on human neutrophils. Activation of the alternative pathway produces C5a that is rapidly bound to neutrophils that are then deposited in the lungs as well as in other organs. Neutrophil activation and degranulation during CPB has been demonstrated in humans (46, 47), and complement-stimulated granulocytes have been shown to secrete oxygen radicals with resultant endothelial damage (48). Flick and colleagues (49), using a sheep model, showed that leukocytes are required for the increased lung and microvascular permeability seen after microbembolization. Recently, several groups have demonstrated an association between the generation of peroxidation products during CPB and pulmonary neutrophil sequestration (50–52), as well as between oxygen-free radical generation and complement activation (53). It is hypothesized that a portion of the pulmonary dysfunction after CPB results from complement activation via the alternative pathway leading to generation of the anaphylatoxins C3a and C5a. The C5a is rapidly bound to circulating neutrophils, which are then activated and undergo depo-

sition and sequestration in the lungs as well as other organs. The activated neutrophils release superoxides and lysosomal enzymes, which in turn produce direct endothelial damage, alterations in capillary permeability, and accumulation of extravascular water (Fig. 9.9).

Protamine-Complement Interaction

The administration of protamine to neutralize heparin effects at the end of CPB is known to occasionally induce clinical syndromes characterized by decreased systemic vascular resistance, increased pulmonary vascular resistance, or possibly left ventricular dysfunction (54–58). In contrast to the anaphylatoxins C3a and C5a, which are generated by activation of either

Table 9.1. Cardiac Dysfunction After Open Operations[a]

Incremental Risk Factor	Logistic Coefficient ± SD	P Value
Higher C3a level	0.0010 ± 0.00042	0.02
Longer CPB time	0.014 ± 0.0058	0.02
Younger age	−0.06 ± 0.138	≤0.0001

[a]$n = 116$; 27 patients had events.
Modified from Kirklin JK, Westaby S, Blackstone EH, et al. Complement and the damaging effects of cardiopulmonary bypass. J Thorac Cardiovasc Surg 1983;86:845.

Table 9.2. Pulmonary Dysfunction After Open Operations[a]

Incremental Risk Factor	Logistic Coefficient ± SD	P Value
Higher C3a level	0.0025 ± 0.00094	0.008
Longer CPB time	0.025 ± 0.0111	0.02
Younger age	−1.17 ± 0.183	≤0.0001

[a]$n = 116$; 41 patients had events.
Modified from Kirklin JK, Westaby S, Blackstone EH, et al. Complement and the damaging effects of cardiopulmonary bypass. J Thorac Cardiovasc Surg 1983;86:845.

Table 9.3. Renal Dysfunction After Open Operations[a]

Incremental Risk Factor	Logistic Coefficient ± SD	P Value
Higher C3a level	0.0009 ± 0.00036	0.02
Younger age	−0.07 ± 0.142	≤0.0001

[a]$n = 116$; 24 patients had events.
Modified from Kirklin JK, Westaby S, Blackstone EH, et al. Complement and the damaging effects of cardiopulmonary bypass. J Thorac Cardiovasc Surg 1983;86:845.

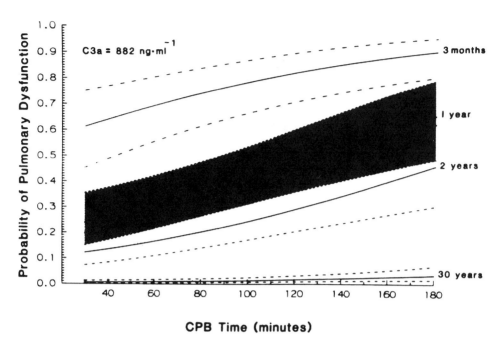

CPB Time (minutes)

Figure 9.5. Nomogram from a multivariate analysis of postoperative morbidity after cardiac surgery. The signifi-cant risk factors included C3a level (normalized as above for this figure), age at operation, and duration of CPB. The shaded areas indicate the 70% confidence limits for children 1 year of age. (From Kirklin JK, Westaby S, Blackstone EH, et al. Complement and the damaging effects of cardiopulmonary bypass. J Thorac Cardiovasc Surg 1983;86:845–857.)

Figure 9.6. Relation between time of CPB and increment in extracellular fluid minus plasma volume (ECF−PV) soon after operation (minus preoperative lev-els). x, open operation for L to R shunt; o, open operation for valvular heart disease (no congestive heart failure). (From Cleland J, Pluth JR, Tauxe WN, Kirklin JW. Blood, volume and body fluid com-partment changes soon after closed and open intracardiac surgery. J Thorac Cardiovasc Surg 1966;52:698–705.)

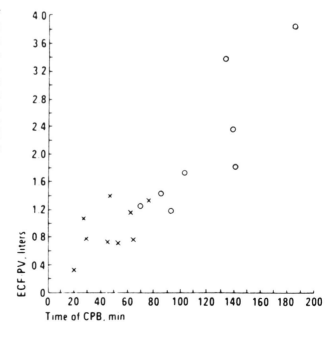

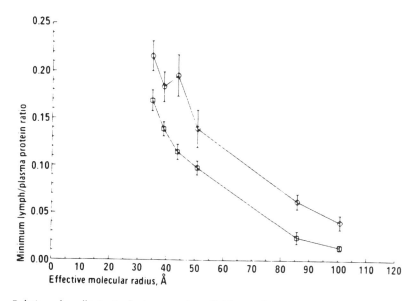

Figure 9.7.   Relation of small intestinal microvascular colloid osmotic sieving ratio, as reflected by the minimum lymph-plasma protein ratio, to molecular radius in dogs undergoing either 2 hours of nonpulsatile normothermic CPB (O) or simple hemodilution with sham CPB (□). Shown are means +1 SE for each group of seven dogs (P < 0.001). (From Smith EEJ, Naftel DC, Blackstone EH, Kirklin JW. Microvascular permeability after cardiopulmonary bypass. J Thorac Cardiovasc Surg 1987;94:225–233.)

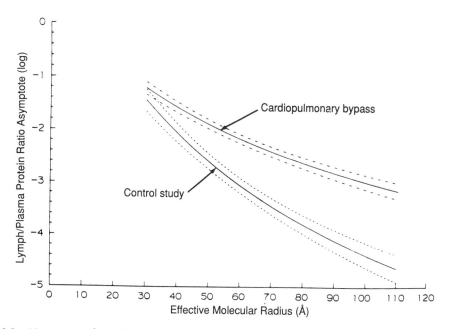

Figure 9.8.   Nomogram relating the asymptote of the lymph-plasma protein ratio (permeability ratio) to the effective molecular radius of the proteins and to the conditions of the experiments (CPB or sham procedure). The vertical axis is in logarithmic units. (From Smith EEJ, Naftel DC, Blackstone EH, Kirklin JW. Microvascular permeability after cardiopulmonary bypass. J Thorac Cardiovasc Surg 1987;94:225–233.)

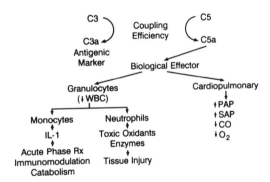

Figure 9.9. This diagram outlines the two modes of action for the human anaphylatoxins C3a and C5a produced during complement activation. The coupling efficiency refers to the relative quantity of C5a produced as compared to C3a. The coupling efficiency varies according to the activating or nonactivating character of the foreign surface in contact with blood. (From Chenoweth DE. In: Leonard EF, Turitto VT, Vroman L, eds. Blood in contact with natural and artificial surfaces. New York, The New York Academy of Sciences, 1987.)

the classic or alternative pathways, the anaphylatoxin C4a is generated only through activation of the classic pathway. In vitro studies have demonstrated that human serum containing heparin alone or protamine sulfate alone does not activate complement, but that the mixture of protamine sulfate and human serum markedly activates the classic pathway, with generation of C4a, C3a, and C5a (34) (Fig. 9.10). In patients undergoing coronary artery surgery, we found elevated C3a and nearly normal C4a levels at the end of CPB (34). With administration of protamine sulfate, marked elevation of both C3a and C4a occurred, indicating activation of the classic complement pathway (34) (Fig. 9.11). Although unproven, it is hypothesized that the occasional severe hemodynamic derangement following protamine administration results from a more vigorous activation of the classic complement pathway by the heparin-protamine sulfate interaction.

Cytokines and CPB

There is suggestive evidence that cytokines may play a significant role in mi-crovascular permeability changes after CPB (59). Cytokines are potent intercellular signaling molecules known to participate in the regulation of cellular growth, function, and differentiation. Cytokines have generally been given the name "interleukin" (IL) followed by a number (IL-1, IL-2, etc.). With the help of specific cytokines, relatively rare cells can recruit other cells, and thus, control major physiologic processes in some situations (60).

The cytokine IL-8 (originally called neutrophil chemotactic factor or T-lymphocyte chemotactic factor) is chemotactic for neutrophils, induces degranulation (61), and stimulates neutrophil attachment and transendothelial migration (62, 63). Recent studies suggest that IL-8 may play an important role in neutrophil-induced capillary permeability changes after CPB (59). Another proinflammatory cytokine, tumor necrosis factor, is released curing CPB (64) and may contribute to inflammation and induce the release of IL-8 (65).

Reduction of the Inflammatory Response to CPB

It has long been recognized that the deleterious clinical effects of CPB are of lesser magnitude and shorter duration in the presence of robust postoperative cardiac performance. This raises the possibility (a) that the same inflammatory responses attributed to CPB may be initiated within the body during or after CPB by widespread microfoci of ischemia with or without necrosis, and (b) that robust cardiac output increases the clearance of inflammatory proteins and other circulating factors. Thus, methods to improve myocardial preservation and organ perfusion during CPB may ameliorate the deleterious effects of humoral activation. Hypothermia reduces cellular metabolic activity (66, 67), but also increases red cell aggregation and blood viscosity (68). This latter effect may be counteracted by the beneficial effects of hemodilution to improve cerebral, cardiac,

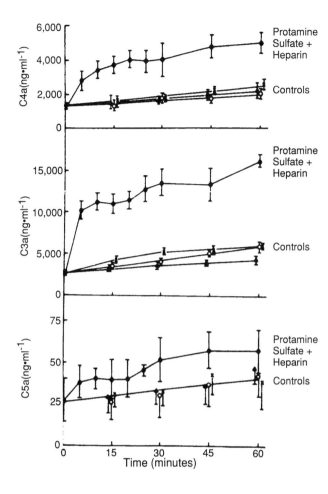

Figure 9.10. Levels of C4a, C3a, and C5a in normal human serum incubated with a mixture of protamine sulfate and heparin (●). The controls consisted of human serum alone (▲), serum-containing heparin (O), or serum-containing protamine sulfate (x). The vertical bars represent the 70% confidence limits (Reproduced with permission from The Society of Thoracic Surgeons. Kirklin JK, Chenoweth DE, Naftel DC, et al. Effects of protamine administration after cardiopulmonary bypass on complement, blood elements, and the hemodynamic state. Ann Thorac Surg 1986;41: 193–199.)

and renal blood flows during bypass (69). The potentially beneficial effects of pulsatile flow during CPB with respect to organ perfusion remain controversial, as conflicting data exist regarding the potential benefit of pulsation on lactate production and whole body oxygen consumption (70, 71).

There is increasing clinical and experimental evidence to suggest the superiority of membrane over bubble oxygenators in reducing the deleterious effects of CPB. Although animal studies have demonstrated C3a elaboration with membrane and bubble oxygenator systems (72), Cavarocchi and colleagues (73) demonstrated a reduction in C3a generation with a membrane oxygenator. The increased elaboration of C3a with a bubble oxygenator was accompanied by a significant increase in transpulmonary leukocyte sequestration following CPB (Fig. 9.12). The administration of methylprednisolone (30 mg/kg) 20 minutes before CPB in the bubble oxygenator group eliminated the difference from the membrane oxygenator group with respect to C3 elaboration and transpulmonary leukocyte sequestration. Tamiya and colleagues have also documented greater C3a and C5a production in bubble compared to membrane oxygenators (74), and membrane oxygenators have been shown to decrease pulmonary platelet and leukocyte deposition in comparison to bubble oxygenators (75).

Pharmacologic blockage of various components of the humoral amplification system have been studied, and offer hope for producing some increment of safety dur-

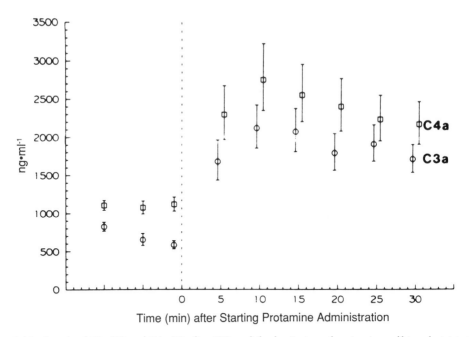

Figure 9.11. Levels of C3a (O) and C4a (□) after CPB and the beginning of protamine sulfate administration. Time 0 and the broken vertical line indicate the beginning of protamine administration, which was 10 minutes after discontinuation of CPB. Protamine was infused over 5 minutes. The vertical bars represent the 70% confidence limits. The mean normal value of C3a is 76 ng·ml⁻¹ and for C4a, 1200 ng·ml⁻¹. (Reproduced with permission from the Society of Thoracic Surgeons. From Kirklin JK, Chenoweth DE, Naftel DC, et al. Effects of protamine administration after cardiopulmonary bypass on complement, blood elements, and the hemodynamic state. Ann Thorac Surg 1986;41:193–199.)

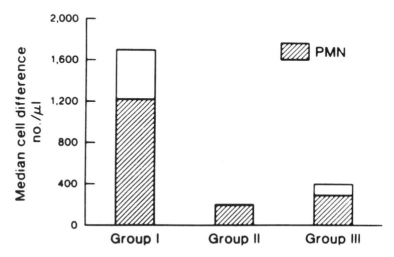

Figure 9.12. Transpulmonary leukocyte sequestration and neutropenia occurred after establishment of pulmonary circulation at conclusion of CPB. Transpulmonary leukocyte sequestration is expressed as median cell difference (MCD = WBC in right atrium − WBC in left atrium). Group I, bubble oxygenator group; Group II, bubble oxygenator group with Solu-Medrol; Group III, membrane oxygenator group. The cross-hatched area represents polymorphonuclear leukocytes and the clear area nonneutrophil WBCs. (From Cavarocchi NC, Pluth JR, Schaff HV, et al. Complement activation during cardiopulmonary bypass. J Thorac Cardiovasc Surg 1986;91:252–258.)

ing CPB. Aprotinin, a known inhibitor of plasma and kallikrein, has been shown to improve hemostasis following CPB (76–78), perhaps by preserving platelet function during CPB (79). Apart from hemostasis, however, it is likely that important amelioration of the inflammatory response by blocking one or more of the inflammation cascades will be difficult, since there appear to be multiple avenues available to initiate the inflammatory response.

A more promising approach may be the blockade of a final common pathway for the induction of endothelial damage and alterations in permeability. Although platelets and other vasoactive substances may be important, the neutrophil appears to be the critical component in this process (80–82). Removal of neutrophils by leukocyte filtration has improved organ preservation during CPB in an experimental model (83) and merits clinical investigation. Reversible blockage of neutrophil adhesion by blocking the leukocyte membrane adhesion molecule CD18 with an anti-CD18 monoclonal antibody (84) may hold promise as a transient pharmacologic means of reducing the inflammatory effects at the endothelial level.

REFERENCES

1. Blackstone EH, Kirklin JW, Stewart RW, Chenoweth DE. Damaging effects of cardiopulmonary bypass. In: Wu KK, Rossi EC, eds. Prostaglandin clinical medicine. Chicago: Year Book, 1981:355–369.
2. Addonizio VP Jr, Macarak EJ, Nicolaou KC, Edmunds LH, Coleman RW. Effects of prostacyclin and albumin on platelet loss during in vitro simulation or extracorporeal circulation. J Am Soc Hematol 1979;53:1033–1044.
3. Martin RR. Alterations in leukocyte structure and function due to mechanical trauma. In: Hwang NHC, Gross DR, Patel DJ, eds. Quantitative cardiovascular studies: clinical and research applications of engineering principles. Baltimore, University Park Press, 1979:419.
4. Kusserow BK, Larrow R, Nichols J. Perfusion and surface-induced injury in leukocytes. Fed Proc 1971;30:1516–1520.
5. Kusserow BK, Machanic B, Collins FM Jr, Clapp JF III. Changes observed in blood corpuscles after prolonged perfusions with two types of blood pumps. Trans Am Soc Artif Intern Organs 1965;11:122–126.
6. Ryhanen P, Herva E, Hollman A, Nuutinen L, Pihlajaniemi R, Saarela E. Changes in peripheral blood leukocyte counts, lymphocyte subpopulations, and invitro transformtion after heart valve replacement. J Thorac Cardiovasc Surg 1979;77:259–266.
7. Mortenson JD. Evaluation of ASAIO blood damage test. Vol I. Salt Lake City, Utah: Biomedical Test Laboratory, University of Utah Research Institute, 1977.
8. Alon L, Turina M, Gattiker R. Membrane and bubble oxygenator: a clinical comparison in patients undergoing aortocoronary bypass procedures. Herz 1979;4:56–62.
9. Clark RE, Beauchamp RA, Magrath RA, Brooks JD, Ferguson TB, Weldon CS. Comparison of bubble and membrane oxygenators in short and long perfusions. J Thorac Cardiovasc Surg 1979;78:655–656.
10. Han P, Turpie AGG, Butt R, LeBlanc P, Genton E, Gunstensen S. The use of B-thromboglobulin release to assess platelet damage during cardiopulmonary bypass. Presented at the Combined Meeting of the Royal Australasian College of Surgeons and Royal Australasian College of Physicians, February 24–29, 1980, Sydney, Australia.
11. Barry YA, Labow RS, Keon WJ, Tocchi M, Rock G. Perioperative exposure to plasticizers in patients undergoing cardiopulmonary bypass. J Thorac Cardiovasc Surg 1989;97:900–905.
12. Blauth CI, Arnold JV, Schulenberg WE, McCartney AC, Taylor KM. Cerebral microembolism during cardiopulmonary bypass. J Thorac Cardiovasc Surg 1988;95:668–676.
13. Sorenson HR, Husum B, Waaben J, et al. Brain microvascular function during cardiopulmonary bypass. J Thorac Cardiovasc Surg 1987;94:727–732.
14. Edmunds LH Jr, Saxena NC, Hillyer P, Wuilson TJ. Relationship between platelet count and cardiotomy suction return. Ann Thorac Surg 1978;25:306–310.
15. Hope AF, Lotter MG, van Reenan OR, et al. Kinetics and sites of sequestration of indium-III labeled human platlets during cardiopulmonary bypass. J Thorac Cardiovasc Surg 1981;81:880–886.
16. Kalter RD, Saul CM, Wetstein L, Soriano C, Reiss RF. Cardiopulmonary bypass. Associated hemostatic abnormalities. J Thorac Cardiovasc Surg 1979;77:427–435.
17. Bharadwaj BB, Chong G. Effects of extracorporeal circulation on structure, function and population distribution of canine blood platelets. Pre-

sented at the Combined Meeting of the Royal Australasian College of Surgeons and Royal Australasian College of Physicians, February 24–29, 1980, Sydney, Australia.

18. Gluszko P, Rucinski B, Musial J, et al. Fibrinogen receptors in platelet adhesion surfaces of extracorporeal circuit. Am J Physiol 1987;252:H615–621.

19. Dechavanne M, Ffrench M, Pages J, et al. Significant reduction in the binding of a monoclonal antibody (LYP 18) directed against the IIb/IIIa glycoprotein complex to platelets of patients having undergone extracorporeal circulation. Throm Haemost 1987;57:106–109.

20. Edmunds LH. Blood platelets and bypass [Invited Letter]. J Thorac Cardiovasc Surg 1989;97:470–471.

21. George JN, Pickett EB, Sauceman S, et al. Platelet surface glycoproteins. J Clin Invest 1986;78:340–348.

22. Mohr R, Golan M, Martinowitz U, Rosner E, Goor DA, Ramot B. Effect of cardiac operation on platelets. J Thorac Cardiovasc Surg 1986;92:434–441.

23. Zilla P, Fasol R, Groscurth P, Klepeto W, Reichenspurner H, Wolner E. Blood platelets in cardiopulmonary bypass operations. J Thorac Cardiovasc Surg 1989;97:379–388.

24. Lee WH Jr, Krumbhoar D, Fonkalsrud EW, Schjeide OA, Maloney JV Jr. Denaturation of plasma proteins as a cuase of morbidity and death after intracardiac operations. Surgery 1961;50:29.

25. Feijen J. Thrombogenesis caused by blood foreign surface interaction. In: Kenedit RM, Courtney JM, Gaylor JDS, Gilchrist T, eds. Artificial organs. Baltimore, University Park Press, 1977:235–247.

26. Verska JJ. Control of heparinization by activated clotting time during bypass with improved postoperative hemostasis. Ann Thorac Surg 1977;24:170–173.

27. Backmann F, McKenna R, Cole ER, Najafi H. The hemostatic mechanism after open-heart surgery. I. Studies on plasma coagulation factors and fibrinolysis in 512 patients after extracorporeal circulation. J Thorac Cardiovasc Sug 1975;70:76–85.

28. Ellison N, Behar M, MacVaugh Hill, Marshall BE. Bradykinin, plasma protein fraction and hypotension. Ann Thorac Surg 1980;29:15–19.

29. Pang LM, Stalcup SA, Lipset JS, Hayes CJ, Bowman FO Jr, Mellins RB. Increased circulating bradykinin during hypothermia and cardiopulmonary bypass in children. Circulation 1979;60:1503–1507.

30. Friedli B, Kent G, Olley PM. Inactivation of bradykinin in the pulmonary vascular bed of newborn and fetal lambs. Circ Res 1973;33:421–427.

31. Goldstein IM. Current concepts: complement in infectious diseases. Kalamazoo, Michigan, The Upjohn Co, 1980:7.

32. Chenoweth DE, Cooper SW, Hugli TE, et al. Complement activation during cardiopulmonary bypass: Evidence for generation of C3a and C5a anaphylatoxins. N Engl J Med 1981;304:497.

33. Parker DJ, Cantrell JW, Karp RB, Stroud RM, Digerness SB. Changes in serum complement and immunoglobulins following cardiopulmonary bypass. Surgery 1972;71:824–827.

34. Kirklin JK, Chenoweth DE, Naftel DC, et al. Effects of protamine administration after cardiopulmonary bypass on complement, blood elements, and hemodynamic state. Ann Thorac Surg 1986;41:193–199.

35. Bjork J, Hugli TE, Smedegard G. Microvasculature effect on anaphylatoxins C3a and C5a. J Immunol 1985;134:1115–1119.

36. Muller-Eberhard HJ. Complement. Am Rev Biochem 1975;44:697–724.

37. Kirklin JK, Westaby S, Blackstone EH, et al. Complement and the damaging effects of cardiopulmonary bypass. J Thorac Cardiovasc Surg 1983;86:845–857.

38. Fosse E, Molines TE, Ingvaldsen B. Complement activation during major operations without cardiopulmonary bypass. J Thorac Cardiovasc Surg 1987;93:860–866.

39. Salama A, Hugo F, Heinrich D, et al. Deposition of terminal C5b-9 complement complexes on erythrocytes and leukocytes during cardiopulmonary bypass. J Thorac Cardiovasc Surg 1985;88:101–112.

40. Cleland J, Pluth JR, Tauxe WN, Kirklin JW. Blood, volume and body fluid compartment changes soon after closed and open intracardiac surgery. J Thorac Cardiovasc Surg 1966;52:698–705.

41. Smith EEJ, Naftel DC, Blackstone EH, Kirklin JW. Microvascular permeability after cardiopulmonary bypass. J Thorac Cardiovasc Surg 1987;94:225–233.

42. Granger DM, Taylor AE. Permeability of intestinal capillaries to endogenous macromolecules. Am J Physiol 1980;238:H457–464.

43. Breckenridge IM, Digerness SB, Kirklin JW. Increased extracellular fluid after open intracardiac operation. Surgery 1970;131:53–56.

44. Brans YW, Dweck HS, Harris HB, et al. Effect of open-heart surgery on the body composition of infants and young children. Pediat Res 1981;15:1024–1028.

45. Chenoweth DE, Hugli TE. Demonstration of specific C5a receptor on intact human polymorphonuclear leukocytes. Proc Natl Acad Sci USA 1978;75:3943–3947.

46. Craddock PR, Fehr J, Brigham KL, Kronenberg RS, Jacob HS. Complement and leukocyte-mediated pulmonary dysfunction in hemodialysis. N Engl J Med 1977;296:769–774.

47. Wachtfogel YT, Kucich U, Greenplate J, et al. Human neutrophil degranulation during extracorporeal circulation. Blood 1987;69:324–330.

48. Sacks T, Moldow CF, Craddock PR, Bowers TK, Jacob HS. Oxygen radicals mediate endothelial cell damage by complement stimulated granulocytes. Am Soc Clin Invest 1978;21:1161–1167.

49. Flick MR, Perel A, Staub NC. Leukocytes are required for increased lung microvasculature permeability after microembolization in sheep. Circ Res 1981;48:344–351.

50. Braude S, Nolop KB, Fleming JS, Krausz, Taylor KM, Royston D. Increased pulmonary transvascular protein flux after canine cardiopulmonary bypass. Am Rev Respir Dis 1986;134:867–872.

51. England MD, Cavarocchi NC, O'Brien JF, et al. Influence of antioxidants (mannitol and allopurinol) on oxygen free radical generation during and after cardiopulmonary bypass. Circulation 1986;74:134–137.

52. Royston D, Fleming JS, Desai JB, Westaby S, Taylor KM. Increased production of peroxidation products associated with cardiac operations. J Thorac Cardiovasc Surg 1986;91:759–766.

53. Cavarocchi NC, England MD, Schaff HV, et al. Oxygen free radical generation during cardiopulmonary bypass: correlation with complement activation. Circulation 1986;74:130–133.

54. Nordstrom L, Fletcher R, Pavek K. Shock of anaphylactoid type induced by protamine; a continuous cardiorespiratory record. Acta Anaesthesiol Scand 1978;22:195–201.

55. Olinger GN, Becker RM, Bonchek LI. Noncardiogenic pulmonary edema and peripheral vascular collapse following cardiopulmonary bypass: rare protamine reaction? Ann Thorac Surg 1980;29:20–25.

56. Lowenstein E, Johnston WE, Lappas DG, et al. Catastrophic pulmonary vasoconstriction associated with protamine reversal of heparin. Anesthesiology 1983;59:470–473.

57. Shapira N, Schaff HV, Piehler JM, et al. Cardiovascular effects of protamine sulfate in man. J Thorac Cardiovasc Surg 1982;84:505–514.

58. Conahan TJ III, Andrews RW, MacVaugh H III. Cardiovascular effects of protamine sulfate in man. Anesth Analg 1981;60:33–36.

59. Finn A, Naik S, Klein N, Levinsky RJ, Strobel S, Elliott M. Interleukin 8 release and neutrophil degranulation after paediatric cardiopulmonary bypass. J Thorac Cardiovasc Surg In press.

60. Durum SK, Oppenheim JJ. Macrophage derived mediators: interleukin 1, tumor necrosis factor, interleukin 6, interferon, and related cytokines In: Paul WE, ed. Fundamental immunology. 2nd ed. New York: Raven Press, 1989:639–661.

61. Baggiolini M, Walz A, Kunkel SL. Neutrophil-activating peptide-1/Interleukin-8, a novel cytokine that activates neutrophils. J Clin Invest 1989;84:1045–1049.

62. Smith WB, Gamble JR, Clark-Lewis I, Vadas MA. Interleukin-8 induces neutrophil transendothelial migration. Immunology 1991;72:65–72.

63. Huber AR, Kunkel SL, Todd RF, Weiss SJ. Regulation of transendothelial neutrophil migration by endogenous Interleukin-8. Science 1991;254:99–102.

64. Jansen NJG, van Oeveren W, Broek LVD, et al. Inhibition by dexamethasone of the reperfusion phenomena in cardiopulmonary bypass. J Thorac Cardiovasc Surg 1992;102:515–525.

65. DeForge LE, Kenney JS, Jones ML, Warren JS, Remick DG. Biphasic production of IL-8 in lipopolysaccharide (LPS)-simulated human whole blood. Separation of LPS- and cytokine-stimulated components using anti-tumor necrosis factor and antil-IL-1 antibodies. J Immunol 1992;148:2133–2141.

66. Fuhrman GJ, Fuhrman FA. Oxygen consumption of animals and tissues as a function of temperature. J Gen Physiol 1959;42:715–722.

67. Treasure T, Naftel DC, Conger KA, et al. The effect of hypothermic circulatory arrest time on cerebral function morphology, and biochemistry. J Thorac Cardiovasc Surg 1985;88:101–112.

68. Eiseman B, Spencer FC. Effect of hypothermia on the flow characteristics of blood. Surgery 1961;525:32–44.

69. Utley JR, Wachtel C, Cain RB, et al. Effects of hypothermia, hemodilution, and pump oxygenation on organ water content, blood flow and oxygen delivery, and renal function. Ann Thorac Surg 1981;31:121–133.

70. Tinkle JK, Helton NE, Wood RE, et al. Metabolic comparison of a new pulsatile pump and a roller pump for cardiopulmonary bypass. J Thorac Cardiovasc Surg 1969;58:562–569.

71. Shepard RB, Kirklin JW. Relation of pulsatile flow to oxygen consumption and other variables during cardiopulmonary bypass. J Thorac Cardiovasc Surg 1969;58:694–702, 718–720.

72. Kirklin JK, Blackstone EH, Kirklin JW. Cardiopulmonary bypass: Studies on its damaging effects. Blood Purif 1987;5:168–178.

73. Cavarocchi NC, Pluth JR, Schaff HV, et al. Complement activation during cardiopulmonary bypass. J Thorac Cardiovasc Surg 1986;91:252–258.

74. Tamiya T, Yamasaki M, Maeo Y, et al. Complement activation in cardiopulmonary bypass, with special reference to anaphylatoxin production in

membrane and bubble oxygenators. Ann Thorac Surg 1988;46:47–57.

75. Gu YJ, Wang YS, Chaiang BY, Gao XD, Ye CX, Wildevuur CRH. Membrane oxygenator prevents lung reperfusion injury in canine cardiopulmonary bypass. Ann Thorac Surg 1991;51: 573–578.

76. Bidstrup BP, Royston D, Sapsford RN, Taylor KM, Cosgrove DM. Reduction in blood loss and blood use after cardiopulmonary bypass with high dose aprotinin (Trasylol). J Thorac Cardiovasc Surg 1989;97:364–372.

77. van Oeveren W, Janson NJG, Bidstrup BP, et al. Effects of aprotinin on hemostatic mechanisms during cardiopulmonary bypass. Ann Thorac Surg 1987;44:640–645.

78. van Oeveren W, Eijsman L, Roozendaal KJ, Wildevuur CRH. Platelet preservation by aprotinin during cardiopulmonary bypass. Lancet 1988;1:644.

80. Hammerschmidt DE, Stroncek DF, Bowers TK, et al. Complement activation and neutropenia dur-

ing cardiopulmonary bypass. J Thorac Cardiovasc Surg 1981;81:370–377.

81. Flick MR, Perel A, Staub NC. Leukocytes are required for increased lung microvascular permeability after microembolization in sheep. Circ Res 1981;48:344–351.

82. Craddock PR, Fehr J, Brigham KL, et al. Complement and leukocyte-mediated pulmonary dysfunction in hemodialysis. N Engl J Med 1977; 296:769–774.

83. Bando K, Schueler S, Cameron DE, et al. 12 hour cardiopulmonary preservation using donor core cooling, leukocyte depletion, and liposomal superoxide dismutase. J Heart Lung Transplantation 1991;10:304–309.

84. Byrne JG, Cohn L, Smith W, Murphy M, Couper G, Appleyard R. Complete prevention of myocrdial stunning, low reflow and edema after heart transplant by blocking leukocyte adhesion molecule during reperfusion [Abstract]. American Association for Thoracic Association Meeting, Los Angeles, California, April 26–29, 1992.

10

THE IMMUNE RESPONSE AND CARDIOPULMONARY BYPASS

Joe R. Utley

Infection in the cardiac surgery patient is often followed by death or severe morbidity. Infection of prosthetic valves or intracardiac patches is particularly dangerous. Even without infection of the intracardiac structures, infection of the sternotomy wound is followed by a prolonged period of recovery and often the need for major surgical reconstructive procedures. Cardiac surgical patients are more susceptible to infection because of the effects of cardiopulmonary bypass (CPB) on the immune system. The use of CPB also introduces some routes of infection that are unique to cardiac procedures.

THE IMMUNE SYSTEM

Alterations in virtually every component of the immune system have been described following CPB. The effects not only increase susceptibility to infection, but may also contribute to organ dysfunction in the absence of infection. Cardiopulmonary bypass has important effects on both cellular and humoral immunity.

Humoral Immunity

The immunoglobulins are the most important part of the immune system. They play a central role in allergic reactions, autoimmune responses, neutralization of tox-

ins, and defense against infection. These antibodies are the product of plasma cells, which come from bone marrow B lymphocytes. Antibody production involves a complex interaction of macrophages, T lymphocytes and B lymphocytes. The immunoglobulins are classified according to their heavy chain component as IgG, IgM, IgA, IgD, and IgE. Immunoglobulins G, M, and A are most important in resistance to infection. Antibodies may neutralize toxins of bacterial origin directly. When combined with complement, antibodies may lyse bacteria or make them more susceptible to ingestion by white cells or macrophages (opsonization).

Studies of patients' serum after CPB have shown bactericidal capacity against *Escherichia coli* to be diminished in 85% of patients and against *Staphylococcus aureus* to be diminished in 69% of patients. This depression of bactericidal capacity was accompanied by decreases in total complement. The pattern of depression of IgA, IgM, and IgG was similar to that of complement (1).

Hemodilution at the onset of bypass decreases the concentration of serum proteins in proportion to the fall in hematocrit. Concentrations of albumin and globulin continue to fall during bypass. The dilution of CPB decreases levels of complement, IgM, IgA, IgG, and opsonic capacity (Fig. 10.1) (2). During 3 hours of perfusion, se-

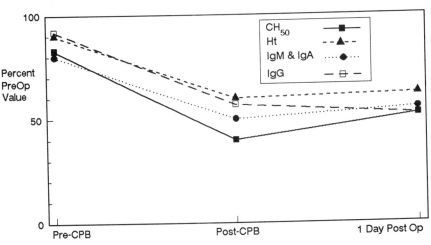

Figure 10.1.   The levels of complement (*CH₅₀*), hematocrit (*Ht*), *IgM, IgA,* and *IgG* are shown before, immediately after, and 1 day after CPB. van Velzen-Blad et al. concluded that the changes were mainly due to dilution rather than functional decreases in activity. (From van Velzen-Blad H, Dijkstra YJ, Schurink GA, et al. Cardiopulmonary bypass and host defense functions in human beings: I. Serum levels and role of immunoglobulins and complement in phagocytosis. Ann Thorac Surg 1985;39:207.)

rial studies showed diminishing concentrations of α_2-globulin and γ-globulin, while α_1-globulins and β-globulins tended to rise. It appears that serum proteins are denatured and macroaggregated by the pump oxygenator. These macroaggregates are cleared by the reticuloendothelial system. This uptake by the reticuloendothelial system causes partial reticuloendothelial blockade and bromsulphthalein retention (3).

Comparative studies of immune globulins in patients with and without CPB show several significant differences. In patients having CPB there is an increase in α_2-globulin, while α_2-macroglobulins and IgG are diminished. Immunoglobulin M is increased 6 to 8 days after bypass. The IgM elevation may represent an antibody response to exposure to a foreign protein during bypass (4).

Protein denaturation occurs at air-fluid interfaces where electrostatic surface forces cause globular proteins to align with polar groups toward the interface and nonpolar groups away from the interface. Sulf-

hydryl and hydrogen bonds are disrupted, which stabilizes the secondary and tertiary structure of the protein molecules. The unfolding of the globular molecule exposes masked chemical groups and creates a more asymmetric molecule. These changes in symmetry and chemical reactivity lead to formation of macromolecules, which tend to flocculate. During cardiopulmonary bypass, plasma viscosity increases in a manner typical of denatured proteins, although these changes are offset by the hemodilution induced by clear priming solutions. Increases in free sulfhydryl groups are found and abnormal bands of altered proteins appear on serum electrophoresis (5).

Denaturation of protein molecules involved in lipid transport may release free lipids. Changes in colloid solubility of lipids may lead, in turn, to microvascular fat emboli (6).

The disc oxygenator produces profound effects on solutions of serum proteins (7). γ-Globulin has been recommended for prophylaxis against posttransfusion non-A, non-B hepatitis following cardiac surgical procedures (8). Solutions of γ-globulin become turbid, precipitate, and react with complement after this change. The altered globulin may actually be antigenic. Antibodies to globulins are common following CPB, whereas antibodies to platelets or leukocytes are uncommon (9). γ-Globulin alterations diminish in the presence of albumin or plasma. When albumin and globulin are exposed together to the disc oxygenator, a molecular species is produced that is not produced when either is exposed alone. The investigators proposed that the unfolded globulin molecule reacts with albumin to produce the new molecular species. The precipitation of altered albumin and globulin is greater at lower temperatures (Fig. 10.2) (7). Postoperative γ-globulin prophylaxis has been shown to reduce posttransfusion non-A and non-B hepatitis in cardiac surgery patients, possibly reflecting the denaturation of endogenous γ-globulin during bypass. Other experiments have confirmed the above observations.

Exposure of plasma proteins to the pump oxygenator produces a rise in optical

density, an increase in sulfhydryl content, and an increased rate of mobility of the α_2-globulins in starch gel electrophoresis. The changes are greater with a screen oxygenator than with a membrane oxygenator. Wright et al. (10) confirmed that chemical changes represent a significant part of the alteration in immune protein function during CPB. Denatured immunoproteins may constitute one stimulus to complement activation during bypass (11,12) (see Chapter 9).

Cellular Immunity

The effect of CPB on cellular immunity is both direct effect and indirect. Leukocyte and lymphocyte counts fall with the onset of cardiopulmonary bypass. Leukocyte sequestration in tissue increases after leukocyte activation by the anaphylatoxins C3a and C5a. When bypass terminates, the concentration of leukocytes in the right atrium exceeds that in the left atrium because of leukosequestration in the pulmonary vascular bed (13–16). The activation of leukocytes is accompanied by an increase in serum concentration of elastase and lactoferrin, both of which cause tissue injury (17).

Cardiopulmonary bypass is accompanied by a decrease in the white cell count (Fig. 10.3) (18), which is more pronounced with bubble oxygenators than with membrane oxygenators (19). The immediate fall in leukocytes is followed later by leukocytosis and the appearance of immature white cells and nucleated red cells. The bone marrow shows an increase in the number of myeloid elements following CPB; thus, the bone marrow appears to be stimulated by CPB (18,20).

After bypass is discontinued, the white cell count usually increases, although levels of immunoglobulin and complement remain decreased (21). Immediately after cardiopulmonary bypass there is increased mitosis of the myelopoietic series. The number of stab cells and polymorphonu-

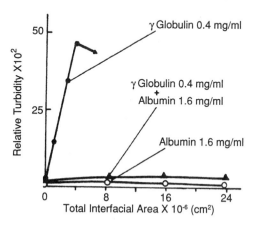

Figure 10.2. The denaturation of proteins was quantitated by the change in relative turbidity in this study. The solutions were exposed to various areas of foreign surfaces, the greatest for γ-globulins alone and least for albumins. The denaturation of γ-globulin was diminished in the presence of albumin. (From Pruitt KM, Stroud RM, Scott JW. Blood damage in the heart-lung machine. Proc Soc Exp Biol Med 1970;137:714.)

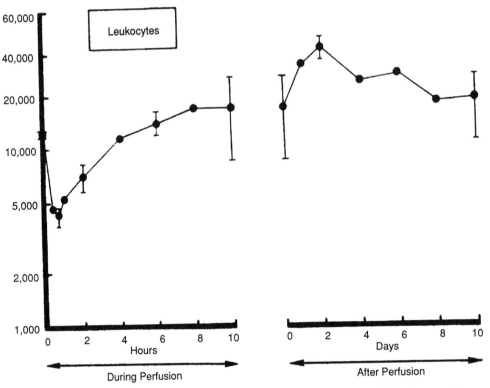

Figure 10.3. Leukocyte counts diminished immediately with the onset of CPB and then increased to supra-normal levels. (From Brinsfield EE, Hopf MA, Geering RB, Galletti PM. Hematological changes in long-term perfusion. J Appl Physiol 1962;17:531.)

clear forms diminishes for 3 days but increases by 1 week postoperatively. Cellular changes include vacuolization and nuclear lysis as well as pathologic granulation. The lymphoid cells of the bone marrow increase rapidly while the monocytes increase slightly. The phagocytic function of white cells is diminished for up to 15 days postoperatively following CPB. The erythroid series is only mildly affected (22).

When blood is exposed to the effect of the pump oxygenator without a patient in the circuit, the cells that remain after bypass have greatly altered function (23). Fewer of the remaining white cells demonstrate phagocytic activity, and those phagocytically active ingest fewer bacteria than white cells not exposed to bypass. White cells exposed to the pump oxygenator have diminished utilization of glucose and oxygen (Fig. 10.4) (23). The morphologic

changes in these cells include distortion and confluence of lobes of granulocytes. Other nuclear changes include hyaloid transformation, homogenization and vacuolization of nuclear substance, and raggedness of nuclear contour. There is loss of cytoplasm, raggedness of cytoplasmic contour, and a reduction in size of some cells. The absolute number of both polymorphonuclear and mononuclear cells diminishes, but the decrease is greater in the mononuclear cells than in the granulocytes (23–25). In both experimental animals and patients, release of white cells from the bone marrow causes the leukocytosis that may occur late in the course of cardiopulmonary bypass.

Random migration of granulocytes diminishes after CPB, but migration in response to a chemotactic stimulus increases. Depressed chemotactic migration does not return to normal for as long as 1 week postoperatively (Fig. 10.5) (26). Phagocytic function and phagocytic intracellular oxidation of ingested particles is depressed following bypass (27, 28), as is the bactericidal capacity of leukocytes (Fig. 10.6) (21, 29). The ability of neutrophils to ingest *S. albus* decreases for 1 week following cardiac surgery. Other studies show that both the phagocytic and metabolic functions of leukocytes are impaired after CPB (30, 31). Cardiotomy suction and the bubble oxygenator depress serum opsonizing capacity, while this function remains well-preserved when a membrane oxygenator is used (Fig. 10.7) (30). Similarly, membrane oxygenators preserve serum bactericidal activity better than bubble oxygenators (Fig. 10.8) (30). Another study showed that the capacity of granulocytes to kill bacteria was normal a few hours after surgery and was greater than normal on the 3rd postoperative day (31).

The quantitative nitroblue tetrazolium test (NBT) is a measure of a phagocyte's intracellular ability to produce hydrogen peroxide, which is necessary for bacterial killing. The NBT demonstrates a reduction in this ability during and after CPB (27); Schildt et al. (31) showed increased hydrogen peroxide production during the 3 days immediately following bypass. Radical staining in the NBT has produced mixed results as a monitor for potential infection after cardiac surgery. A negative test usually means no infection is present, but a positive test does not strongly predict infection (32, 33).

The total number of lymphocytes decreases in response to CPB (34, 35), including T cells, receptor cells, and B cells (35). Rosette formation and surface membrane

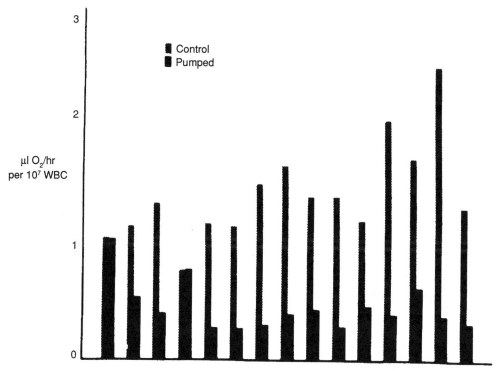

Figure 10.4.   The oxygen utilization of leukocytes exposed to a pump oxygenator is diminished compared to control leukocytes. (From Kusserow B, Larrow R, Nichols J. Metabolic and morphological alterations in leukocytes following prolonged blood pumping. Trans Am Soc Artif Organs 1969;15:40.)

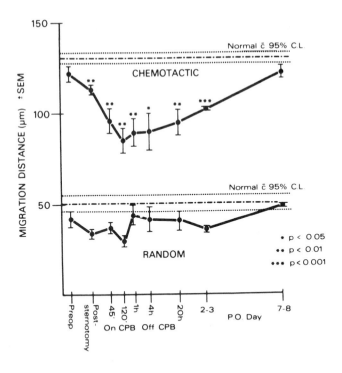

Figure 10.5. The migration of neutrophils in response to a chemotactic stimulus is diminished by CPB and does not return to normal for 7 days. (From Bubenik O, Meakins JL. Neutrophil chemotaxis in surgical patients: effect of cardiopulmonary bypass. Surg Forum 1976; 27:267.)

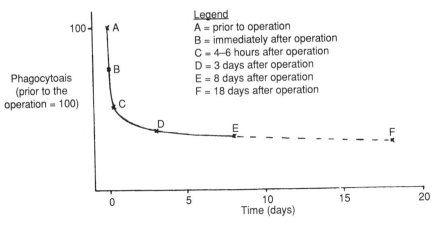

Figure 10.6. Effect of extracorporeal circulation on phagocytosis. The phagocytosis of leukocytes diminished immediately after bypass and remained depressed for 20 days in this study. (From Lundstrom M, Olsson P, Unger P, Ekestrom S. Effect of extracorporeal circulation on hematopoiesis and phagocytosis. J Cardiovasc Surg 1963;4:664.)

immunoglobulin markers also decrease. These responses return to normal by 7 days (35). Atypical lymphocytes are quite common after CPB (35). The mitogenic reaction of lymphocytes in response to phytohemagglutinin (PHA) and pokeweed mitogen were diminished 2 days postopera-tively, but exceeded preoperative levels by 5 days after operation (Fig. 10.9) (34). The diminished mitogenic response to PHA and concanavalin A may persist for up to 3 months after operation. The ability of tuberculoprotein to stimulate lymphocytes in mixed culture decreases for as long as 14

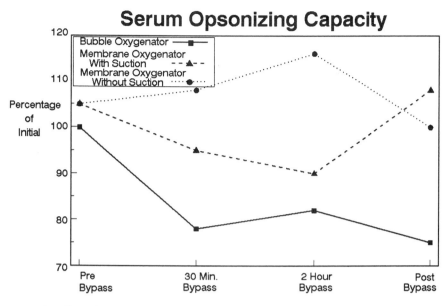

Figure 10.7.   The effect of CPB on serum opsonizing capacity is greater with the bubble oxygenator than with the membrane oxygenator, and intermediate with the membrane oxygenator and cardiotomy suction. (From van Oeveren W, Dankart J, Wildevuur CRH. Bubble oxygenation and cardiotomy suction impair the host defense during cardiopulmonary bypass: a study in dogs. Ann Thorac Surg 1987;44:523–528.)

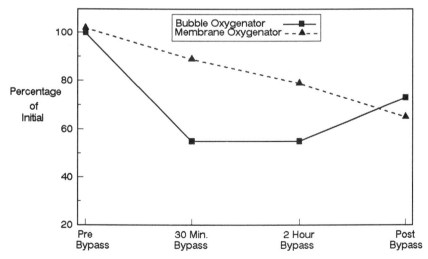

Figure 10.8.   Serum bactericidal activity is better preserved with the membrane oxygenator than with the bubble oxygenator. (From van Oeveren W, Dankart J, Wildevuur CRH. Bubble oxygenation and cardiotomy suction impair the host defense during cardiopulmonary bypass: a study in dogs. Ann Thorac Surg 1987;44: 523–528.)

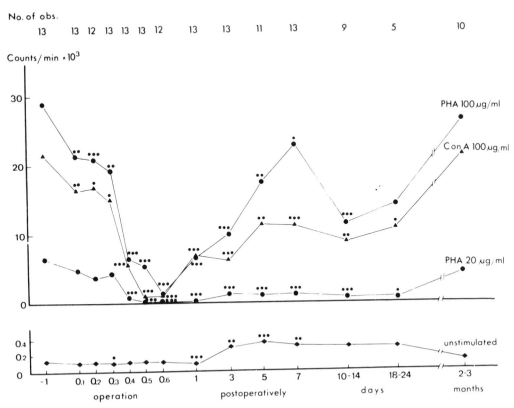

No. of obs.

Figure 10.9.   The mitogenic response of lymphocytes to PHA and con A is diminished by CPB and does not return to control values for several days. (From Salo M. Effect of anaesthesia and open-heart surgery on lymphocyte responses to phytohaemagglutinin and Concanavalian A. Acta Anaesthesiol Scand 1978;22:471.)

days postoperatively (34, 35), and the ability of lymphocytes to incorporate tritiated thymidine also diminishes (36). The latter effect is potentiated by incubation of the lymphocytes with the patient's plasma and is partially reversed by incubation with normal plasma (36).

Some lymphocyte changes observed after CPB are similar to those observed after blood transfusions. DePalma et al. (37) studied patients having CPB with and without blood transfusion and showed that some lymphocyte subpopulations are altered in response to transfusion and not bypass. Total lymphocytes and lymphocytes with markers for pan-T cells, helper-T cells, and suppressor-T cells decreased postoperatively, independent of transfusion (37). B lymphocytes decreased postoperatively in both the autologous transfusion and no transfusion groups. In contradistinction, patients receiving homologous transfusion had evidence of T-cell activation, suggesting an immune response to homologous transfusion (37). Other studies have shown lymphopenia, reduced helper-T cells, reversal of the helper/suppressor ratio, and a depressed local graft versus host reaction for as much as 6 days after bypass (38, 39). These changes may contribute to the transmission of viral-induced syndromes including the transmission of human T-cell lymphotropic virus (HTLV) III and HIV (AIDS) after CPB (38, 39).

Natural killer cells are a heterogenous subpopulation of lymphoid cells that are not T or B lymphocytes. Natural killer cells have produced cytotoxic responses in virus-infected cells, tumor cells, and normal primitive stem cells. Natural killer cells decrease in number and function after cardiopulmonary bypass (Fig. 10.10) (40, 41).

Assessment of the delayed type hypersensitivity response to common antigens before and after CPB has shown that the percentage of patients who are anergic increases from 11% preoperatively to 72% postoperatively (Figs. 10.11 and 10.12) (42).

Reticuloendothelial Function

Cardiopulmonary bypass produces a form of reticuloendothelial blockade. Blood that has been recirculated in a pump oxygenator depresses the phagocytic function of isolated perfused rat livers. This depression of phagocytic function was not accompanied by any change in bile flow, blood flow, or weight of the perfused liver. Depressed phagocytosis was produced to a lesser extent by perfusion with plasma that had been recirculated through a pump oxy-

genator. Thus the depressed phagocytosis is caused by exposure of both plasma and blood cells to the pump oxygenator (43). The authors concluded that the particles generated from both cellular breakdown and protein aggregation interfered with Kupffer cell function. The reticuloendothelial system serves the important functions of clearing circulating blood of bacteria, chylomicrons, plasma hemoglobin, thrombin, fibrin, fibrin degradation products, thromboplastin, and plasminogen activator. Other studies showed that rats that underwent CPB showed diminished phagocytic function compared to rats not operated upon or rats subjected to sham operation (Fig. 10.13) (44, 45). Similar experiments in dogs showed that animals subjected to CPB were unable to clear infused *Klebsiella aerogenes* compared to sham-operated animals. Mortality was 16% in the bypass animals and 0% in the sham-operated animals (46). One study showed that the metabolic and phagocytic function of the reticuloendothelial system returned to normal within 3 days after operation (31).

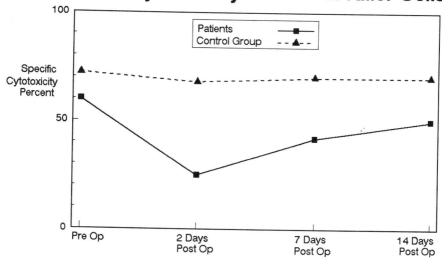

Figure 10.10.   The specific cytotoxicity of natural killer cells is diminished in patients having bypass compared to control patients. (From Rhyanen P, Huttunen K, Ilonen J. Natural killer cell activity after open heart surgery. Acta Anaesthesiol Scand 1984;28:490–492.)

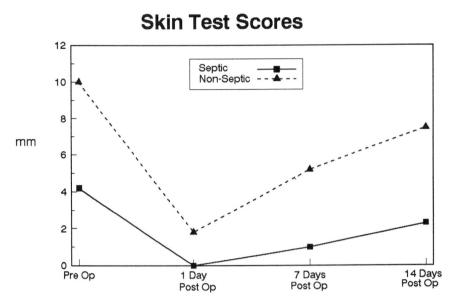

Figure 10.11. The skin test scores as manifest by the diameter of the wheal and erythema reaction (in millimeters) is less in septic compared to nonseptic patients following CPB. Both groups had depression of these scores following bypass compared to prebypass. (From Kress HG, Gehrsitz P, Elert O. Predictive value of skin testing, neutrophil migration and C-reactive protein for postoperative infections in cardiopulmonary bypass patients. Acta Anaesthesiol Scand 1987;31:398.)

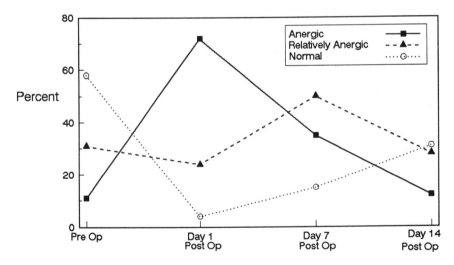

Figure 10.12. The incidence of anergy increases following bypass, while the incidence of normal skin sensitivity decreases. The incidence of patients who are relatively anergic remains essentially unchanged. (From Kress HG, Gehrsitz P, Elert O. Predictive value of skin testing, neutrophil migration and C-reactive protein for postoperative infections in cardiopulmonary bypass patients. Acta Anaesthesiol Scand 1987;31:398.)

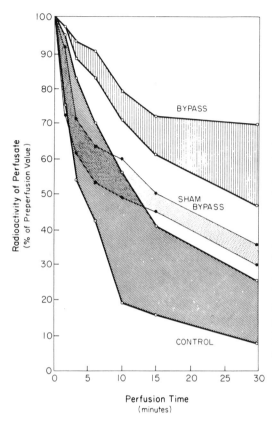

Figure 10.13. In this study the function of the reticuloendothelial system was studied by determining the rate of clearance of colloidal radioactive gold (Au[196]). CPB decreases the rate of clearance of colloidal radioactive gold. (From Subramanian V, McLeod J, Gans H. Effect of extracorporeal circulation on reticuloendothelial function. I. Experimental evidence for impaired reticuloendothelial function following cardiopulmonary bypass in rats. Surgery 1968;64:775.)

Effects of Anesthesia, Operation, and Trauma

Depression of the immune system may follow surgical operations without CPB. Drugs that depress immunity include steroids and antibiotics (47). The immune-suppressing antibiotics are tetracycline, chloramphenicol, clindamycin, oxytetracycline, streptomycin, gentamicin, kanamycin, and neomycin. The mitogenic capabilities of B- and T-cell lymphocytes are inhibited by the anesthetics halothane, cyclopropane, ether, and nitrous oxide (47). Decreases in leukocyte count have been described with barbiturate use (47). Shock and fever also depress immunity. Normal patients undergoing operation for kidney donation have been shown to have a number of immune abnormalities postoperatively, including depression of lymphocyte, B- and T-cell counts as well as diminished mitogen blastogenic response and mixed leukocyte reactivity. Response to antigenic skin testing was depressed for up to 14 days in these patients (47). Depression of opsonizing activity is present in patients following shock and trauma. Blood transfusions are immunosuppressive and may increase the risk of infection (48). It may thus be difficult to separate the nonspecific effects induced by anesthesia, operation, and trauma from those induced by the heart-lung machine in patients having cardiac surgery (27, 48).

INFECTIONS AFTER CARDIOPULMONARY BYPASS

Bacterial and Fungal Infections

The high morbidity and mortality associated with bacterial infection in cardiac surgical patients makes prevention a primary concern of the cardiac surgeon (49–52). The mortality and morbidity of bacterial and fungal infection complicating cardiac surgical procedures exceeds that from other types of operations. Factors making the risk of infection higher in cardiac surgical patients than in other types of surgical patients include the duration of the procedure; presence of a sternal osteotomy; the use of prosthetic and intravascular foreign bodies including vascular grafts, valve prostheses, pledgets, and pacemakers; postoperative immunosuppression; the contact between room air and the patient's blood stream through the cardiotomy suction and the oxygenator; the use of indwelling vascular catheters and endotracheal tubes for long periods of time; and the presence of hematoma and coagulated tissue in the area of the operation (50, 51, 53). Factors associated with lethal postoperative infection include preoperative bacterial endocarditis, bypass times greater than 3.5 hours, low cardiac output, postoperative cerebral dysfunction, and disseminated intravascular coagulation (50).

The majority of cardiac surgeons favor the use of prophylactic antibiotics to avoid the infrequent, but potentially catastrophic infection from a virulent organism highly sensitive to antibiotics. The morbidity and risk of prophylactic antibiotics are low (54, 55).

A major goal in preventing infection in cardiac surgery patients is to decrease the number and pathogenicity of microorganisms that gain access to the patient's wounds. Infections often occur in groups and are not always a random event in cardiac surgery patients. Continuous attention to the sterility of instruments and materials, the management of patients who are shedding bacteria from wounds or other sites, the avoidance of bacterial carrier states by the members of the operating team, and the rigid adherence to sterile technique while operating are important details. The risk of infection following bacteremia is greatest immediately after the operation and diminishes after 6 weeks (56). Extensive methods for improving antisepsis with heart surgery may include prophylactic antibiotics, preoperative screening for infection, housekeeping measures, and air decontamination in the operating room. Other sources of contamination may include coronary suction, heat exchanger leaks, and oxygen sources (57).

S. albus is the most common organism causing infection following cardiac surgery. Many organisms often thought to be nonpathogenic to man have caused infection in prosthetic heart valves. These organisms include *Micrococcus flavus, Pseudomonas maltophilia, Oerskoviz turbata,* and *Neisseria perflara* (58). Other orga-

nisms that may cause postoperative infection include *Klebsiella, Pseudomonas, Proteus, E. coli, Serratia,* and *Salmonella.* Fungal organisms are commonly *Candida* or *Aspergillus* (58, 59). Bacteremias after cardiac surgery are most frequently caused by Gram-negative organisms, although recent reports on this subject are lacking (60). The mycobacteria that have caused sternotomy infection have been suspected to come from bone wax or from preserved homograft valves. Determining the heterogeneity of these isolates by taxonomic groups, enzyme genotypes, plasmid profiles, and heavy metal and antibiotic resistance patterns show that they are not related to each other. This heterogeneity suggests that they are derived from local environmental sources rather than from contaminated commercial surgical material or devices (61).

Microorganisms have been cultured from the pump oxygenator in up to 75% of patients (53). The coronary suction line is the most common site of bacterial contamination. Contamination in the wound and in operating room air are the most important sources of organisms in the coronary suction line (60, 62). Contamination of cell-saver blood occurs in 20% of patients but is rarely the source of clinical infection (63). Contamination of blood, wounds, oxygenators, and cardiotomy reservoirs is related to the number of *S. aureus* organisms in the air of the operating room. Contamination with *Serratia marcescens* was greater when air was aspirated with blood into the cardiotomy suction (64). Other sources of contamination that may cause multiple episodes of infection include operating personnel who are carriers of bacteria, intravenous catheters, endotracheal tubes, and pressure transducers (65–67). Evidence of contamination has been observed from cultures of the wound, valve prosthesis, donor blood, excised cardiac valves, the pump oxygenator, bladder catheters, and chronic wounds in other areas of the body (58, 68, 69). It is estimated that 1000 bacteria settle into the sternotomy wound in the course of a 2-hour operation (58). Respirators and inhalation equipment may be a source of contamination, especially Gram-negative bacteria (65). The use of sterile disposable endotracheal tubes, suction catheters, and gloves has decreased the incidence and severity of tracheobronchial infection. Figure 10.14 is a depiction of these various sources of infection that may occur after CPB. Sternal wound infection in coronary artery operations is often related to contamination of the sternal wound from the leg wound (70). Elevated endotoxin levels during CPB are presumed to derive from the contamination that occurs during the operation (71). Patients with antiendotoxin antibodies have a lower incidence of Gram-negative infection postoperatively (72).

Air is drawn into the cardiotomy suction at the rate of 1 to 2 cubic feet per minute. The operating room air may contain 10 or more bacteria per cubic foot. The number of bacteria in the room air is influenced by the number of people in the room, the ventilation system, and the amount of time the doors are open. Fifty thousand dust particles per cubic foot were found when the operating room was not in use, and up to 824,000 dust particles per cubic foot during cardiac operations (52). Estimates are that 1200 colony-forming particles are drawn into coronary suction per hour, which would add one colony-forming unit per 6 ml of blood per hour (52). Factors important in minimizing air contamination in the operating room include air filtration, air delivery, suction control, oxygen line control, protective clothing and masks, traffic control, asepsis control, and exclusion of contaminated operations from the cardiac surgery operating rooms.

The choice of membrane or bubble oxygenator and the avoidance or use of cardiotomy suction may have significant effects on the immune system and the development of infection from airborne organisms following CPB. The use of a membrane oxygenator without cardiotomy suction maintained normal host defense mechanisms in dogs, but the addition of cardiotomy suction to a membrane oxygenator caused some changes in immune defense mechanisms (30).

The use of bubble oxygenators and cardiotomy suction caused the most serious impairment of host defense mechanisms. The studies were performed during the aerosolization of *S. aureus* into the room air. No bacteremia was observed in animals when the membrane oxygenator and no cardiotomy suction was used. More than half (8 of 15) of the animals in whom the bubble oxygenator was used developed postbypass blood stream infection with the aerosolized organisms (Fig. 10.15) (30). With the use of the membrane oxygenator the incidence of positive cultures from the wound, oxygenator, and blood during the operation was diminished. The incidence of positive cultures in the cardiotomy reservoir was similar with both types of oxygena-

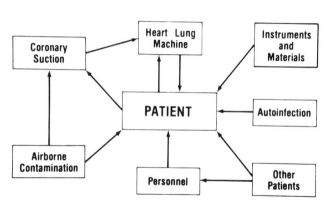

Figure 10.14. The block diagram shows the sources of infection for the cardiac surgical patient.

Figure 10.15. Infection in the wound and in heart blood of animals perfused with the bubble oxygenator is more common than those perfused with the membrane oxygenator. (From van Oeveren W, Dankert J, Wildevuur CRH. Bubble oxygenation and cardiotomy suction impair the host defense during cardiopulmonary bypass: a study in dogs. Ann Thorac Surg 1987;44:523–528.)

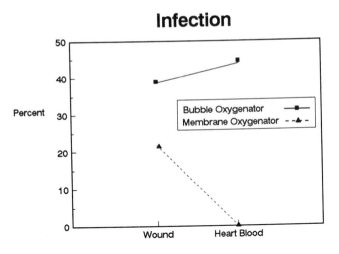

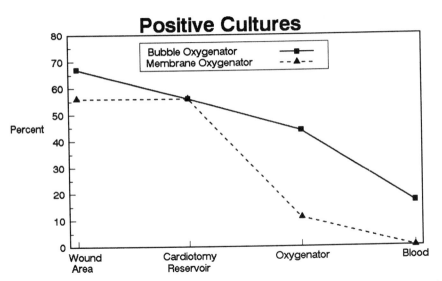

Figure 10.16. The incidence of positive cultures in the wound area and the cardiotomy reservoir is similar in animals with a membrane or bubble oxygenator. The incidence of positive cultures in the oxygenator blood or the animals' blood was significantly less with the membrane oxygenator. (From van Oeveren W, Dankert J, Wildevuur CRH. Bubble oxygenation and cardiotomy suction impair the host defense during cardiopulmonary bypass: a study in dogs. Ann Thorac Surg 1987;44:523–528.)

tors (Fig. 10.16) (30). Both wound and heart blood infections were less common in the membrane oxygenator animals after 2 weeks of survival.

When an epidemic of infection occurs in a cardiac surgical unit, a multifaceted program must be initiated to eliminate the source of contamination. Such programs are remarkably successful in decreasing the incidence of infection. Among the factors that

should be a part of such a program are operating room renovations to assure a high flow vertical unidirectional ventilation system, improvement of barriers in gowning and draping techniques, monitoring the sterility of instruments, valves, drapes, heart-lung machine, and gloves; use of local and systemic broad coverage bactericidal antibiotics, use of cardiac surgical operating rooms for only clean noncontaminated cases; admission of only clean noninfected patients to the postoperative cardiac surgery intensive care unit; and the transfer to another care unit of any patient who becomes infected. Members of the surgical team and nursing staff may be precluded from working in areas with infected and contaminated patients (73). Training of house staff and paramedical personnel in the importance of avoiding contamination of clothing and hands in the care of infected patients is important (66, 74). Such broad-based programs have decreased the incidence of deep wound infection from 2.9% to 0.6%, and the incidence of all wound infections from 6.6% to 3.3% (75).

The sources of contamination of the pump oxygenator include incomplete sterility, blood and fluids added to the machine, cardiotomy suction, oxygen and other gases, the patient, and intravascular catheters. Methods to decrease contamination in the operating room will be reflected by a lower incidence of positive cultures from the pump oxygenator. Although the incidence of positive cultures from the pump oxygenator may be from 2% to 70%, the incidence of clinical infection in patients with positive cultures is fortunately low. Patients with positive cultures from the heart-lung machine most commonly develop clinical infection if they have had infection preoperatively (76, 77).

Postoperative infection is related to a number of patient factors. Mediastinal infection is more likely with postoperative hemorrhage, early reexploration for bleeding, increased duration of the operation, and the use of a traumatic instrument (such as the Lebsche knife) for cutting the sternum. The use of the Stryker saw has lessened the incidence of sternal infection (78). A multiple regression analysis by Miholic and colleagues (79) showed that only blood transfusion, reoperation, and duration of operation were predictive factors for infection.

Changes in the immune system and the inflammatory response following by-

pass alter the relation between fever, leukocytosis, and infection in cardiac surgery patients. There is no correlation between fever, leukocytosis, and infection in the first 6 days after operation (80). After 6 days there was a correlation but still only 15% of patients with fever and leukocytosis had infection (80). Other studies showed that postoperative fever correlated with the length of CPB and with lower respiratory tract infection. Wound infection and urinary tract infection had no correlation with the duration and magnitude of postoperative fever (81).

Suppression of the immune system may contribute to the onset and exacerbation of infectious syndromes postoperatively including Behçet's syndrome and herpes zoster (82, 83).

PROPHYLACTIC ANTIBIOTICS

The value of prophylactic antibiotic therapy in cardiac surgery has been clearly demonstrated in double-blind randomized trials (84, 85). Local irrigation with antibiotics has also been shown to be effective (86). The duration of antibiotic prophylaxis is just as effective when used for 2 days as for 5 days (87). Some controversy exists concerning the use of narrow- versus broad-spectrum antibiotics. The majority of surgeons prefer the broader spectrum cephalosporins to more narrow-spectrum penicillinase-stable penicillin (88). The results of narrow- or broad-spectrum antibiotics are similar (84).

In addition to lowering the morbidity due to infection, the use of prophylactic antibiotics significantly decreases the cost of cardiac surgery by decreasing hospital stays (89).

Acknowledgment
This work was supported by the Cardiothoracic Research and Education Foundation, San Diego, California.

REFERENCES

1. Hairston P, Manos JP, Graber CD, Lee WH Jr. Depression of immunologic surveillance by pump-

oxygenation perfusion. J Surg Res 1969;9: 587–593.

2. van Velzen-Blad H, Dijkstra YJ, Schurink GA, et al. Cardiopulmonary bypass and host defense functions in human beings: I. Serum levels and role of immunoglobulins and complement in phagocytosis. Ann Thorac Surg 1985;39: 207–211.

3. Larmi TKI, Karkola P. Plasma protein electrophoresis during a three-hour cardiopulmonary bypass in dogs. Scand J Thorac Cardiovasc Surg 1974;8:152–160.

4. Wallace JW, Arai K, Blakemore WS. Comparison of postoperative glycoprotein responses in open-heart and nonopen-heart patients. J Appl Physiol 1970;28:433–438.

5. Lee WH Jr, Krumhaar D, Fonkalsrud EW, Schjeide OA, Maloney JV Jr. Denaturation of plasma proteins as a cause of morbidity and death after intracardiac operations. Surgery 1961;50:29–39.

6. Owens G, Adams JE, McElhannon FM, Youngblood RW. Experimental alterations of certain colloidal properties of blood during cardiopulmonary bypass. J Appl Physiol 1959;14: 947–948.

7. Pruitt KM, Stroud RM, Scott JW. Blood damage in the heart-lung machine. Proc Soc Exp Biol Med 1970;137:714.

8. Al-Khaja N, Roberts DG, Belboul A, et al. Gamma globulin prophylaxis to reduce post-transfusion non-A, non-B hepatitis after cardiac surgery with cardiopulmonary bypass. Scand J Thorac Cardiovasc Surg 1991;25:7–12.

9. Pretty HM, Fudenberg HH, Perkins HA, Gerbode F. Anti-γ-globulin antibodies after open heart surgery. Blood 1968;32:205–216.

10. Wright ES, Sarkozy E, Harpur ER, Dobell ARC, Murphy DR. Plasma protein denaturation in extracorporeal circulation. J Thorac Cardiovasc Surg 1962;44:550–553.

11. Parker DJ, Cantrell JW, Karp RB, Stroud RM, Digerness SB. Changes in serum complement and immunoglobulins following cardiopulmonary bypass. Surgery 1972;71:824–827.

12. Parker DJ, Cooks S, Turner-Warwick M. Serum complement studies during and following cardiopulmonary bypass. In: Junod AF, de Haller R, eds. Lung metabolism. New York: Academic Press, 1975:481–486.

13. van Oeveren W, Kazatchkine MD, Descamps-Latscha B, et al. Deleterious effects of cardiopulmonary bypass. A prospective study of bubble versus membrane oxygenation. J Thorac Cardiovasc Surg 1985;89:888–899.

14. Collet B, Alhaq A, Abdullah NB, et al. Pathways to complement activation during cardiopulmonary bypass. Br Med J 1984;289:1251–1254.

15. Cavarocchi NC, Pluth JR, Schaff HV, et al. Complement activation during cardiopulmonary bypass. Comparison of bubble and membrane oxygenators. J Thorac Cardiovasc Surg 1986;91: 252–258.

16. Royston D, Fleming JS, Desai JB, et al. Increased production of peroxidation products associated with cardiac operations. J Thorac Cardiovasc Surg 1986;91:759–766.

17. Colman RW. Platelet and neutrophil activation in cardiopulmonary bypass. Ann Thorac Surg 1990;49:32–34.

18. Brinsfield DE, Hopf MA, Geering RB, Galletti PM. Hematological changes in long-term perfusion. J Appl Physiol 1962;17:531–534.

19. Kvarstein B, Cappelen C Jr, Osterud A. Blood platelets and leucocytes during cardiopulmonary bypass. Scand J Thorac Cardiovasc Surg 1974;8:142–145.

20. Brown IW Jr, Smith WW. Hemotologic problems associated with the use of extracorporeal circulation for cardiovascular surgery. Ann Intern Med 1958;49:1035–1048.

21. Lavelle JP, Dulgnan JP, Neligan MC. The effects of cardiopulmonary bypass on immune mechanisms of man. Irish J Med Sci 1984;153: 431–436.

22. Lundstrom M, Olsson P, Unger P, Ekestrom S. Effect of extracorporeal circulation on hematopoiesis and phagocytosis. J Cardiovasc Surg 1963;4:664–670.

23. Kusserow B, Larrow R, Nichols J. Metabolic and morphological alterations in leukocytes following prolonged blood pumping. Trans Am Soc Artif Intern Organs 1969;15:40–44.

24. Kusserow B, Larow R, Nichols J. Perfusion- and surface-induced injury in leukocytes. Fed Proc 1971;30:1516–1520.

25. Kusserow BK, Larrow R. Studies of leukocyte response to prolonged blood pumping-effects upon phagocytic capability and total white cell count. Trans Am Soc Artif Intern Organs 1968; 14:261–263.

26. Bubenik O, Meakins JL. Neutrophil chemotaxis in surgical patients: effect of cardiopulmonary bypass. Surg Forum 1976;27:267–269.

27. Silva J Jr, Hoeksema H, Fekety FR Jr. Transient defects in phagocytic functions during cardiopulmonary bypass. J Thorac Cardiovasc Surg 1974; 67:175–183.

28. Taguchi K, Takamura K, Mochizuki T, Kishi D, Yokoyama T. Alteration of the phagocytic function in cardiopulmonary bypass. Hiroshima J Med Sci 1976;25:7–10.

29. Palmblad J. Activation of the bacterial capacity of polymorphonuclear granulocytes after surgery, measured with a new in vitro assay. Scand J Haematol 1979;23:10–16.

30. van Oeveren W, Dankert J, Wildevuur CRH. Bubble oxygenation and cardiotomy suction impair the host defense during cardiopulmonary bypass: a study in dogs. Ann Thorac Surg 1987; 44:523–528.
31. Schildt B, Berghem L, Holm G, et al. Influence of cardiopulmonary bypass on some host defence functions in men. Scand J Thor Cardiovasc Surg 1980;14:207–211.
32. Lerer RJ, Treat K. Nitro blue tetrazolium dye reduction test in children after cardiac surgery. Am J Dis Child 1974;127:846–849.
33. Freeman R, King B, Hambling MH. Infective complications of open-heart surgery and the monitoring of infections by the NBT test. Thorax 1973;28:617–621.
34. Salo M. Effect of anaesthesia and open-heart surgery on lymphocyte responses to phytohaemagglutinin and Concanavalin A. Acta Anaesthesiol Scand 1978;22:471–479.
35. Ryhanen P, Herva E, Hollmen A, Nuutinen L, Pihlajaniemi R, Saarela E. Changes in peripheral blood leukocyte counts, lymphocyte subpopulations, and in vitro transformation after heart valve replacement. J Thorac Cardiovasc Surg 1979;77:259–266.
36. Park SK, Brody JI, Wallace HA, Blakemore WS. Immunosuppressive effect of surgery. Lancet 1971;1:53.
37. DePalma L, Yu M, McIntosh CL, Swain JA, Davey RJ. Changes in lymphocyte subpopulations as a result of cardiopulmonary bypass. J Thorac Cardiovasc Surg 1991;101:240–244.
38. Brody JI, Pickering NJ, Fink GB, Behr ED. Altered lymphocyte subsets during cardiopulmonary bypass. Am J Clin Pathol 1987;87:626–628.
39. Pollock R, Ames F, Rubio P, Reuben J, Wong W, Mavligit G. Protracted severe immune dysregulation induced by cardiopulmonary bypass: a predisposing etiologic factor in blood transfusion-related AIDS? J Clin Lab Immunol 1987; 22:1–5.
40. van Velzen-Blad H, Dijkstra YJ, Heijnen CJ, et al. Cardiopulmonary bypass and host defense functions in human beings. II. Lymphocyte function. Ann Thorac Surg 1985;39:212–217.
41. Ryhanen P, Huttunen K, Ilonen J. Natural killer cell activity after open heart surgery. Acta Anaesthesiol Scand 1984;28:490–492.
42. Kress HG, Gehrsitz P, Elert O. Predictive value of skin testing, neutrophil migration and C-reactive protein for postoperative infections in cardiopulmonary bypass patients. Acta Anaesthesiol Scand 1987;31:398–404.
43. Subramanian V, McLeod J, Gans H. Effect of extracorporeal circulation on reticuloendothelial function. I. Experimental evidence for impaired reticuloendothelial function following cardio-

44. Subramanian V, Lowman JT, Gans H. Effect of extracorporeal circulation on reticuloendothelial function: impairment and its relationship to blood trauma. Arch Surg 1968;97:330–335.
45. Subramanian V, Lande AJ, Gans H, Lowman JT, Lillehei CW. Depression of host-defense mechanism following extracorporeal circulation. Trans Am Soc Artif Intern Organs. 1969;15: 165–171.
46. Subramanian VA, Gay WA Jr, Dineen PPA. Effect of cardiopulmonary bypass on in vivo clearance of live Klebsiella aerogens. Surg Forum 1977;28: 255–257.
47. Slade MS, Simmons RL, Yunis E, Greenberg LJ. Immunodepression after major surgery in normal patients. Surgery 1975;78:363–372.
48. Schauer PH, Lum CT, Waymack JP. Effect of perioperative blood transufsion on immune function. Surg Rounds 1989;49.
49. Engleman RM, Williams CD, Gouge TH, et al. Mediastinitis following open-heart surgery. Arch Surg 1973;107:772–778.
50. Engleman RM, Chase RM Jr, Boyd AD, Reed GE. Lethal postoperative infections following cardiac surgery: review of four years' experience. Circulation 1973;48(suppl III):31–36.
51. Hehrlein FW, Herrmann H, Kraus J. Complications of median sternotomy in cardiovascular surgery. J Cardiovasc Surg 1972;13:390–393.
52. Ochsner JL, Mills NL, Woolverton WC. Disruption and infection of the median sternotomy incision. J Cardiovasc Surg (Torino) 1972;13: 394–399.
53. Blakemore WS, McGarrity GJ, Thurer RJ, Wallace HW, MacVaugh H III, Coriell LL. Infection by airborne bacteria with cardiopulmonary bypass. Surgery 1971;70:830–838.
54. Antimicrobial prophylaxis: prevention of wound infection and sepsis after surgery. Med Lett Drugs Ther 1977;19:37.
55. Williams RW, Bradshaw MW. Prevention and treatment of infection of prosthetic valves. South Med J 1976;69:3–5.
56. Carter DR, Barney JA, Lleu J, Hanna WR, Williams GR. Endocarditis after intracardiac surgery. Am J Surg 1967;114:765–768.
57. Hughes RK. A method of improved antisepsis for open-heart surgery. Ann Thorac Surg 1966;2: 230–236.
58. Hornick RB. Source of contamination in open heart surgery. Infections of prosthetic heart valves and vascular grafts. In: Duma RJ, ed. Infections of prosthetic valves and vascular grafts—prevention, diagnosis, and treatment. Baltimore: University Park Press 1977.
59. Jamshidi A, Pope RH, Friedman NH. Fungal endo-

carditis complicating cardiac surgery. Arch Intern Med 1963;112:370–376.

60. Lockey E, Gonzalez-Lavin L, Ray I, Chen R. Bacteraemia after open-heart surgery. Thorax 1973;28:183–187.

61. Wallace RJ, Musser JM, Hull SI, et al. Diversity and sources of rapidly growing mycobacteria associated with infections following cardiac surgery. J Infect Dis 1989;159:708–716.

62. Baffes TG, Blazek WV, Fridman JL, Agustsson MH, Van Elk J. Postoperative infections in 1,136 consecutive cardiac operations. Surgery 1970;68: 791–799.

63. Schweiger IM, Gallagher CJ, Finlayson DC, Daly WL, Maher KL. Incidence of cell-saver contamination during cardiopulmonary bypass. Ann Thorac Surg 1989;48:51–53.

64. van Oeveren W, Dankert J, Boonstra PW, Elstrodt JM, Wildevuur CRH. Airborne contamination during cardiopulmonary bypass: the role of cardiotomy suction. Ann Thorac Surg 1986;41: 401–406.

65. Frater RWM, Santos GH. Sources of infection in open-heart surgery. NY State J Med 1974;74: 2386–2374.

66. Rosendorf LL, Daicoff G, Baer H. Sources of gram-negative infection after open-heart surgery. J Thorac Cardiovasc Surg 1974;67:195–201.

67. Weinstein RA, Jones EL, Schwarzmann SW, Hatcher CR Jr. Sternal osteomyelitis and mediastinitis after open-heart operation: pathogenesis and prevention. Ann Thorac Surg 1976;21: 442–444.

68. Kluge RM, Calia FM, McLaughlin JS, Hornick RB. Sources of contamination in open heart surgery. JAMA 1974;230:1415–1418.

69. Renyi-Vamos F Jr, Renyi-Vamos F Sr. Significance of asymptomatic bacteriuria in cardiac surgery. Acta Chir Acad Sci Hung 1972;13:255–261.

70. Wells FC, Newsom SWB, Rowlands C. Wound infection in cardiothoracic surgery. Lancet 1983; 28:1209–1210.

71. Nilsson L, Kulander L, Nystrom SO, Eriksson O. Endotoxins in cardiopulmonary bypass. J Thorac Cardiovasc Surg 1990;100:777–780.

72. Freeman R, Gould FK. Prevention of fever and Gram negative infection after open heart surgery by antiendotoxin. Thorax 1985;40:846–848.

73. Blouse LE, Lathrop GD, Kolonel LN, Brocket RM; Epidemiologic features and phage types associated with nosocomial infections caused by *Staphylococcus epidermidis*. Zentralbl Bakteriol [Orig A] 1978;241:119.

74. Marples RR, Hone R, Notley CM, Richardson JF, Crees-Morris JA. Investigation of coagulase-negative staphylococci from infections in surgical patients. Zentralbl Bakteriol [Orig 1] 1978;241: 140–144.

75. Clark RE, Amos WC, Higgins V, Benberg KF, Weldon CS. Infection control in cardiac surgery. Surgery 1976;79:89–96.

76. Carey JS, Hughes RK. Control of infection after thoracic and cardiovascular surgery. Ann Surg 1970;172:916–926.

77. Geldof WChP, Brom AG. Infections through blood from heart-lung machine. Thorax 1972; 27:395–397.

78. Sarr MG, Gott VL, Townsend TR. Medistinal infection after cardiac surgery. Ann Thorac Surg 1984;38:415–423.

79. Miholic J, Hudec M, Domanig E, et al. Risk factors for severe bacterial infections after valve replacement and aortocoronary bypass operations: analysis of 246 cases by logistic regression. Ann Thorac Surg 1985;40:224–228.

80. Miholic J, Hiertz H, Hudec M, Laczkovics A, Domanig E. Fever, leucocytosis and infection after open heart surgery. A log-linear regression analysis of 115 cases. J Thorac Cardiovasc Surg 1984;32:45–48.

81. Wilson APR, Treasure T, Gruneberg RN, Sturridge MF, Burridge J. Should the temperature chart influence management in cardiac operations? J Thorac Cardiovasc Surg 1988;96:518–523.

82. Paccagnella A, Turolla LM, Zanardo G, et al. Fatal progression of Behcet's disease after cardiac surgery. Thorac Cardiovasc Surg 1989;37: 320–321.

83. Dirbas FM, Swain JA. Disseminated cutaneous Herpes Zoster following cardiac surgery. J Cardiovasc Surg 1990;31:531–532.

84. Fong IW, Baker CB, McKee DC. The value of prophylactic antibiotics in aorta-coronary bypass operations. J Thorac Cardiovasc Surg 1979;78: 908–913.

85. Penkett ARL, Wansbrough-Jones MH, Wright E, Imrie F, Pepper JR, Parker DJ. Antibiotic prophylaxis for coronary artery bypass graft surgery [Letter]. Lancet 1985;29:1500–1501.

86. Sutherland RD, Miller OL, Martinez HE, Guynes WA, Fyfe T, Harkrider W. Coronary arterial bypass operations without antibiotic coverage. Chest 1979;76:174–175.

87. Hillis DJ, Rosenfeldt FL, Spicer WJ, Stirling GR. Antibiotic prophylaxis for coronary bypass grafting. J Thorac Cardiovasc Surg 1983;86: 217–221.

88. Freeman R, Gould FK. Antibiotic prophylaxis for cardiac surgery. Perfusion 1986;1:75–79.

89. Nelson RM, Dries DJ. The economic implications of infection in cardiac surgery. Ann Thorac Surg 1986;42:240–246.

11

EMBOLIC EVENTS AND CARDIOPULMONARY BYPASS

Mark Kurusz and Bruce D. Butler

The word embolus is derived from the two Greek words *en* (in) and *ballein* (to throw); the combination *embolos* originally was used to describe a wedge-shaped object or stopper. The modern standard medical definition of embolism is "a sudden blocking of an artery by a clot or foreign material which has been brought to its site of lodgment by the blood current" (1).

Embolic events associated with cardiopulmonary bypass have been a concern from the earliest clinical applications to the present time. Gross air embolism was one of the first identified risks of open heart surgery, but in the 1960s emboli composed of blood-derived material became increasingly recognized as etiologic factors in adverse postoperative sequelae. Improved techniques for anticoagulation management in the 1970s and a growing acceptance of blood filtration in the 1980s probably contributed to a decrease in morbidity and mortality during cardiopulmonary bypass. While newer technologies, such as microporous membrane oxygenation and improved arterial line filters, have decreased the incidence of microemboli even further, subtle embolic events still occur whenever cardiopulmonary bypass is used.

The production of emboli during cardiopulmonary bypass (CPB), whether gross or microscopic, has been causally linked to numerous perioperative and postoperative complications. Emboli fall into three general categories: (1) biological, (2) foreign material, and (3) gaseous. By definition, each type has the propensity to distribute into and ultimately obstruct microvessels (3 to 500 μm in diameter) of any number of tissues. Because of their small size, vast quantities (namely, hundreds of thousands to hundreds of millions) are required to cause detectable organ injury (2, 3).

Each of the three categories of emboli has been addressed to some degree by device design changes, adaptation of specific surgical or therapeutic procedures, or enhanced removal and preventive efforts by surgeons and perfusionists. These efforts have probably contributed to an appreciable decline in morbidity associated with CPB. In spite of this, emboli continue to be a topic of concern with all medical uses of extracorporeal circulation and open heart surgery. Of particular concern is the susceptibility of the brain to embolic damage. This condition is the subject of numerous reports demonstrating varying degrees of neurologic dysfunction (4–6).

The purpose of this chapter is to review the various types of emboli associated with bypass, their detection and pathophysiology, preventive measures and treatment, and future trends.

TYPES OF EMBOLI

Blood-Borne Emboli

Blood-borne microemboli associated with CPB consist primarily of autologous cellular products or aggregates of various cell types (7, 8). Cell products include microthrombi containing fibrin/fibrinogen, lipid material, protein (denatured or not), bone or muscle fragments, etc. Platelet, neutrophil, and red cell aggregates also are commonly observed during and after bypass. Blood-borne emboli can derive from homologous transfused blood. These emboli accumulate proportionately with storage time (9, 10). Fibrin formation occurs when inadequately anticoagulated blood contacts a foreign surface. Activation of factor XII to factor XIIa initiates the coagulation cascade. Heparin blocks coagulation within the cascade at multiple points, mainly by potentiating antithrombin III (11, 12) (see also Chapter 14). An initial rapid adsorption of protein material, predominantly fibrinogen, occurs on foreign surfaces (13). Fibrin deposits likely form in areas of stagnant blood flow, or where turbulence or cavitation phenomena exist, as well as on roughened surfaces (12, 14). Specific sites include intraluminal projections (15), oxygenator connectors (16), within bubble oxygenators (17), or within arterial line filters (18).

Anticoagulation therapy with heparin is usually assessed by measurement of the activated clotting time, which, if greater than 300 seconds, is considered adequate for prevention of fibrin formation within circuits (19, 20). Activated clotting time measurement is necessary because the rate of heparin metabolism may vary with different patients (21); thus, dosage or plasma levels may not accurately predict the degree of anticoagulation (22).

Macroembolic and microembolic particles of fat are generated during cardiopulmonary bypass, and are found in capillaries of the kidneys, lungs, heart, brain, liver, spleen (23) and in pericardial blood (24). These emboli are released as a result of trauma to the fat cells in the epicardium and surgical wound (25, 26) and can occur without cardiopulmonary bypass after median sternotomy or thoracotomy (25). Fat emboli may be observed directly using microscopy or possibly inferred from increases in serum levels of total lipids, free fatty acids, triglycerides, or lipases. It has been estimated that two-thirds of the fat emboli developed within a CPB circuit enter via cardiotomy suction (26). Fat emboli are commonly observed with bubble oxygenators (24, 26, 27) and to a lesser degree with membrane-type oxygenators (26), although this claim is not without challenge (28).

Fat emboli are typically formed with denaturation of plasma lipoproteins and lipids. The fat molecules that come out of solution consist of chylomicron aggregates (27) or free fat-containing triglycerides and cholesterol (26). Fat emboli may vary from 4 to 200 μm in diameter (24). A number of fatty acids and other lipid molecules have been linked with postperfusion lung parenchymal damage or alterations in surface properties (29, 30). Generation of immiscible fat, however, is reduced by hemodilution (26).

As plasma proteins come into contact with foreign surfaces within the extracorporeal circuit, denaturation can occur (27). This process results in alterations in immunologic and complement proteins (31, 32). Blood contact with foreign surfaces also activates platelets, which leads to aggregate formation and subsequent thrombocytopenia as platelets are consumed in this process (33–36). Membrane oxygenators reportedly produce fewer aggregates than bubble oxygenators (33). Platelet aggregates also are commonly observed in stored whole blood, packed red cells, and stored platelet concentrates (10). Although many aggregates are likely to disperse within the circulation (36), their embolic potential has been manifested in various organs including the brain.

Significant decreases (30 to 50%) from preoperative platelet counts are usually observed early in the procedure as the platelets adhere to the surfaces within the circuit (37) or to the gas-blood interface of gaseous microemboli (38). Functional changes and decreased platelet counts have been associated with postoperative bleeding, while the circulating aggregates may provide a causative link with postoperative neurologic dysfunction (39). Preservation of platelet numbers has been reported with prostacyclin use as well as a reduction in aggregate formation (40, 41). Reducing platelet sensitivity to aggregation with heparin (42) may be assisted with prostacyclin therapy, thus reducing the microembolic risk associated with bypass (43, 44).

Platelet aggregation is associated with release of biogenic amines such as serotonin, which not only produce vasoconstriction, but may further promote adhesiveness and aggregate formation. Release of histamine from platelets and mast cells may promote changes in microvascular membrane permeability to plasma proteins (45).

Neutrophil aggregation during CPB may lead to complement activation (32). Hicks et al. (36) and Ratliff et al. (46) found aggregated leukocytes in the lungs of dogs undergoing bypass, and their presence was difficult to prevent clinically, although damage to other organs was not reported (2). Complement-mediated neutrophil aggregation appears to depend upon the nature of the foreign material that the neutrophils contact (47). After aggregation, lysosomal enzyme release increases microvascular endothelial permeability to protein, especially in the lungs, contributing to the postperfusion lung syndrome (48).

Patients who possess cold-reacting antibodies, usually of the immunoglobulin M class, may be at risk for red cell aggregate microembolization with cold cardioplegia or other hypothermic techniques used during open heart surgery (49–51).

Foreign Material Emboli

These emboli may consist of cotton fibers, plastic or metal particles from connectors or housings of disposable devices, filter material, tubing, talc, or surgical thread. Pulmonary embolism from bone wax used as a hemostatic agent with sternotomy incisions in experimental studies has been suggested as a potential contributor to pulmonary complications following open heart surgery (52). Obviously, some of the material described above may be present on artificial surfaces that come into contact with blood during CPB or result from inadvertent inclusion within the circulating blood (53). Braun et al. (54) recently reported elevated serum aluminum levels postoperatively in patients who had undergone cardiopulmonary bypass. Such aluminum contamination was associated with use of specific manufacturers' aluminum heat exchangers. When a stainless steel heat exchanger was used, there was no elevation in plasma aluminum levels.

Microemboli that are usually relatively large in diameter (greater than 300 μm), may be released into the circuit from tubing (for example, by spallation). These emboli are more common with silicone-based rubber tubing than with tubing of polyvinyl chloride or polyurethane base (55–58). Another known foreign material is microfibrillar collagen used for surgical hemostasis. Used topically, this material has been shown to pass through autotransfusion devices and oxygenators and, although effectively removed by filtration, the ability of platelets to aggregate seems to persist. This effect has resulted in the recommendation that blood from treated patients not be returned to the extracorporeal circuit (59).

Microparticles of silicone antifoam A (Dow Corning Corp., Midland, MI) (10 μm and greater) have been observed following bypass in the adrenal gland and pancreas (60). Antifoam is composed of a liquid polymer (dimethylpolysiloxane) and particulate silica. The polymer material is the defoaming agent while the silica provides for blood dispersion.

In the early 1960s, a number of studies demonstrated anti-foam emboli in experimental animals and patients undergoing bypass. The amount of defoamer material and methods of incorporation were less understood during that period. Orenstein et al. (60) reported particle-droplet complexes incorporating antifoam in patients up to 8 months after open heart surgery. The ultimate fate of antifoam in the body is not clear. Some reports have described particles in the phagocytic cells of the spleen or lymph nodes, while others have reported continuous recirculation for prolonged periods (61). Tissue reaction to silicone or antifoam has not been reported to any significant degree. Wells et al. (62), however, reported that the antifoam polymethylsiloxane magnified the hemolytic phenomena attributed to oxygenators primarily by decreasing the resistance of red cells to mechanical stress. In earlier experimental studies on dogs, antifoam emboli were found in the brain, kidneys, and occasionally in the spleen and liver (63–65).

Gupta et al. (66) reported a significant yet transient rise in pulmonary artery pressure with antifoam injections in dogs, demonstrating the capacity of these microparticles to obstruct pulmonary microvascular blood flow. Washoff of antifoam material from the oxygenator and cardiotomy reservoir has been shown to decrease the surface tension of the precardiopulmonary bypass prime solution, which has important implications for gaseous microembolus stability or removal by arterial line filters (67). Further reductions in postcardiopulmonary bypass plasma surface tension were not observed and the values were not correlated with the duration of bypass or plasma-free hemoglobin (68). Recent design changes and a better understanding of the

amounts and methods of applications of antifoam material, as well as the use of membrane oxygenators, have enabled significant reductions in the occurrence of embolic danger from these particles. Table 11.1 summarizes the reported types of nongaseous emboli associated with CPB.

Gaseous Emboli

Gaseous microemboli originate from a number of sources during bypass; however, oxygen microbubbles generated by bubble oxygenators have historically been the most commonly reported source. Gaseous microemboli produced in these devices are usually 400 μm or less in diameter and consist primarily of oxygen, although other gases including carbon dioxide, nitrogen, or nitrous oxide may exchange with the bubbles once they are formed and perfused into the patient (69–76). Gaseous microemboli size may be quite variable, with the majority in the 10 to 100 μm range. Bubbles with diameters greater than 35 to 40 μm are reportedly associated with CPB morbidity, unlike those of smaller diameters (2, 77). In recent years, bubble oxygenators have been designed to minimize gaseous microemboli production while maintaining oxygen transfer characteristics at lower gas-to-blood flow ratios (78–81). These design changes, along with chemical defoaming agents and arterial line filtration, have significantly reduced the numbers and sizes of gaseous microemboli produced by bubble oxygenators. Gaseous microemboli with di-

Table 11.1. Nongaseous Microemboli Reported During Cardiopulmonary Bypass

Microthrombi (e.g., fibrin)	Cotton fibers
Platelet aggregates	Plastic particles
Neutrophil aggregates	Filter material
Red cell aggregates	Tubing fragments
Denatured protein	Metal
Fat or lipids	Talc
Cold-reacting antibodies	Thread
Bone fragments	Bone wax
Muscle fragments	Microfibrillar collagen
Calcium particles	Silicone antifoam

ameters below 40 μm are still reported, however, even with arterial line filtration (82, 83).

Production of gaseous microemboli depends in part on the methods of operation of the bubble oxygenator. Maintaining a low gas-to-blood flow ratio will reduce the number of bubbles released into the arterial line (84, 85). Current oxygenators operate efficiently at ratios approximating 1:1. This represents a significant advance over earlier models requiring ratios 10-fold greater (3). The enhanced efficiency is largely because of the production of smaller oxygen bubbles. The smaller size increases the total area of the contact surface of the oxygen bubble and the blood (78). These smaller microbubbles are more difficult to remove, however, and often require arterial line filtration. Arterial blood reservoir levels have been shown to be inversely related to gaseous microemboli production (70, 86, 87). With increased fluid levels, the time available for gas dissipation and defoamer action increases. Persistent gaseous microemboli often adhere to the artificial surfaces in quiescent areas of the oxygenator and reservoir, and any unnecessary jarring or abrupt shock releases these bubbles into the arterial line (71).

The production of gaseous microemboli by membrane-type blood oxygenators is significantly reduced, or by some accounts, nonexistent (70, 80, 88). Physical damage to the membrane material may allow release of gas bubbles into the blood, or areas with elevated transmembrane pressure ratios may cause bubble formation on the blood side. Graves et al. (89) described a counter-diffusion phenomenon whereby bubbles would be formed at the membrane surface.

The solubility characteristics of gases are such that the colder the solution, the greater the number of molecules dissolved within the liquid phase. The solubility of oxygen, for example, is 2.6 volume percent in water at 30°C and 4.9 volume percent at 0°C. While warming from hypothermia, gas-

eous microemboli will form in the blood if the warming gradient exceeds a certain critical threshold (90). This relationship is most evident when the subsequent rewarming gradient is in excess of 10 to 17°C (2, 88, 91, 92), which can cause gaseous microemboli to be released in the heat exchanger. Another condition could also occur, at least theoretically, whereby gaseous microemboli are released into the blood during the cooling phase when the saturated cold arterial blood exiting the heat exchanger is warmed upon mixture with the patient's warm blood (93).

The opposite situation also has been described, whereby the warm arterial blood coming from the heat exchanger is circulated into a hypothermic patient, and the increased solubility of the gases in the cold blood prevents the evolution of bubbles (94). Any existent bubbles likewise would be expected to dissolve under these conditions. Based on these principles, Edmunds and Williams (2) concluded that the greatest chance of gaseous microemboli production as a result of temperature changes most likely occurs during the cooling phase, where bubbles are released directly into the patient's circulation. Almond et al. (95) reported ischemic cerebral injury in dogs with cooling gradients of 13 to 15°C. However, their studies did not involve the search for or detection of circulating bubbles. Circumstantial evidence lending support to these phenomena has been reported clinically with rapid induction of hypothermia in patients undergoing CPB (96–98). Although currently available bubble oxygenators incorporate the heat exchanger directly into the oxygenating column, thereby enabling the defoamer action to minimize gaseous microemboli production, standard operating procedures should continue to require that heating or cooling gradients never exceed 10°C (3, 92).

Gaseous and particulate emboli are commonly reported with cardiotomy suction (34, 99). Inherent to all suctioning procedures is the mixing of air with the blood, forming relatively large bubbles, often in a foam-like matrix. These bubbles are not only larger than the gaseous microemboli produced by the oxygenator, but consist of air (mostly nitrogen) and, hence, are more stable and often associated with other blood products or aggregate material (100). The increased stability is due not only to the larger volume of gas in the bubbles that must be reabsorbed, but also to the differences in solubility of nitrogen in blood as compared to oxygen or carbon dioxide. Because of their greater stability, these bubbles present a significant risk to the patient if filtration techniques are inadequate. Previously, it has been demonstrated that bubbles can pass through a cardiotomy reservoir (101, 102); however, newer design changes incorporating improved defoamer material, unique flow patterns, and integral filters have significantly reduced the incidence of this phenomenon.

The process of suctioning results in significant blood trauma, which causes cellular aggregation and gas foam formation. Efforts to reduce the amount of air aspirated with operative field blood, as well as care in monitoring suction pump speed, will reduce blood cell trauma and decrease the likelihood of embolization.

Gaseous emboli also can be produced by processes known as gaseous or vaporous cavitation. Cavitation involves hydrodynamic phenomena that consist of bubble nucleation, growth in volume, then ultimate collapse (103). The bubbles or cavities contain gas or vapor. True vaporous cavitation is an extremely transient phenomenon. Gaseous cavitation, similar to effervescence, is more common in gas-nucleated fluids, including blood, which are subjected to tensile, ultrasonic, or supersaturating pressures (104). In these conditions, bubble growth is achieved by mass transfer of gas molecules by diffusive mechanisms and occurs with lesser pressure reductions. Vaporous cavitation occurs when a vacuous space is created in blood, for example, within the negative pressure regions that develop behind the roller pumpheads, and the sudden pressure reduction creates a drop to below liquid vapor pressure (105, 106). Early model centrifugal pumps reportedly produce fewer gaseous microemboli than roller pumpheads (107).

Similar cavitating phenomena can occur at arterial injection sites or at stenotic regions in the circuit where vortices are created with turbulent flow and negative pressures spontaneously develop (108–110). In their review of cavitation phenomena during cardiopulmonary bypass, Kuntz and Maurer (111) evaluated a number of factors involved with gaseous microemboli production at the arterial cannula site. Such factors include Reynolds' number, kinetic energy, hydrostatic and line pressure, temperature, Po_2 levels, cannula size, and fluid flow rate. The authors concluded that excess blood gas tensions should be avoided and that larger bore arterial cannulae were less likely to be associated with gaseous microemboli production at cavitating velocities. In addition to the formation of gaseous microemboli, cavitating phenomena are extremely traumatic to red cells, and can cause platelet activation, granule release, and cell lysis (103).

Air emboli can be introduced into the patient's arterial blood when the cardiac chambers are opened to the atmosphere for valvular, atrial septal, or ventricular septal repair. Pearson (75) characterized "surgical air" as that entering the arterial circulation from (a) cannulation of the heart and aorta, (b) following removal of the aortic clamp, (c) air entrainment at the site of venous cannulation, and (d) after restoration of cardiac function. Air may be introduced with insertion of the aortic, caval, or right atrial cannulae. In the presence of an atrial septal defect or with placement of a left atrial or left ventricular vent cannula, air may be introduced directly into the systemic circulation.

With open heart procedures, air often is entrained on the luminal surfaces of the heart or trapped within the muscular trabeculae. Cardiac ejection should be avoided until complete blood filling occurs. Prevention of systemic air embolism can be accomplished by insertion of a vent into the left ventricle (112) or needle aspiration of the pulmonary veins and cardiac chambers (113). Other techniques that have been proposed to reduce air embolism at the operative site include flooding the surgical field with carbon dioxide (114, 115), closure of the left atrium under blood, lung expansion to clear pulmonary venous blood, and placement of the patient in the Trendelenburg position, or allowing the right lung to collapse (116), thus preventing air from entering pulmonary veins on the right side. Details of ventricular venting have been described by Utley and Stephens (117). Both the advantages and disadvantages of venting and explicit procedures have been described by these authors for operative ways to prevent or remove "surgical air."

As previously mentioned, gaseous microemboli produced by bubble oxygenators usually consist of oxygen, and because of the solubility/diffusibility of this gas, their longevity and pathophysiology are limited to some degree. Experimentally, animals embolized intravascularly with gases of high solubility, such as carbon dioxide or oxygen, tolerate the insult better than those embolized with air or nitrogen bubbles (55, 118–120). Bubbles will pass into the systemic vasculature, causing blood flow obstruction, until the volume decreases by mass diffusion across the gas-blood interface and further movement within the microcirculation ensues. In the case of oxygen bubbles, the diffused gas will combine with unsaturated hemoglobin while carbon dioxide may be absorbed within the plasma. Yang et al. (121, 122) studied stationary and moving bubbles in whole blood and plasma and found that dissolution rates were proportional to the fluid flow rate.

The outward diffusion of the gas was largely assisted by the convective effects of the flowing blood and subsequent thinning of the boundary layer (123). A small microbubble has an increased degree of curvature that accelerates the dissolution rates as surface tension increases and pressure within the bubble rises. (Fig. 11.1)

Because gaseous microemboli are likely to occur with bypass, it has been suggested that ventilation with highly soluble gases more soluble than nitrogen, such as nitrous oxide, may cause existing bubbles to grow. Some therefore recommend that nitrous oxide be discontinued at least 10 minutes before establishing cardiopulmonary bypass (124–126). Wells et al. (127) confirmed the benefit of this practice by measuring cerebrospinal fluid markers of ischemia in 20 patients, 10 of whom received 50 to 60% nitrous oxide until CPB was begun. Lactate levels were significantly elevated in these 10 patients. Several extensive reviews cover the behavior of gas bubbles in fluids (128–134).

Free microbubbles in blood provide a foreign surface that initiates microthrombus formation (135), activates plate-

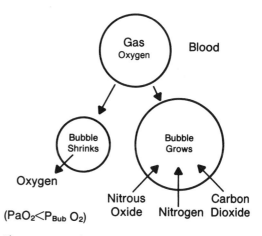

Figure 11.1. Schematic representation of a bubble in blood showing the effects of gas diffusion on size. Oxygen diffuses out, and nitrogen, carbon dioxide, and nitrous oxide diffuse in, according to partial pressure gradients. (From Butler BD. Biophysical aspects of gas bubbles in blood. Med Instrument 1985;19:59–62.)

lets and leukocytes, and alters erythrocyte count (135–137). These gas-liquid interfaces also cause the adsorption and denaturation of plasma proteins (135, 136, 138) subsequent to formation of a lipoprotein layer (139). This lipoprotein coat has been described as a layer 40 to 100 angstroms thick, within which physical forces exist that cause disruption of the secondary and tertiary protein configurations. Release of bound lipids is likely to occur as well (140). This includes phospholipids, which may have a polar attraction to the gas-liquid interface. Activation of Hageman factor and acceleration of clotting also are reported with intravascular bubbles (138).

Adherence of platelets to bubble interfaces has been observed microscopically, which apparently forms a thin outer layer that contains fibrinogen (38, 135, 141). As the first protein layered onto a bubble surface, fibrinogen has nonpolar hydrophilic groups that are exposed as possible binding sites for other blood-borne products, including fatty acids (138) and large lipid particles that may further promote platelet adhesion and spreading (142). Ultrastructural changes of microbubble-activated platelets resemble those following activation with thrombin, adenosine diphosphate, or collagen (143). Accumulation of platelets within the interstices between bubbles may also play a role in foam stabilization where excess bubbling occurs.

Microbubble-activated platelet density is greater when bubbles are 40 μm or more in diameter, suggesting a dependency on size rather than on total bubble count (142). This may be partly because of the lesser degree of curvature with larger bubbles, which could facilitate platelet adhesion and spreading (143), thereby initiating aggregate formation (138). Table 11.2 summarizes the reported causes of gaseous microemboli during CPB.

DETECTION OF EMBOLI

Detection of microemboli associated with bypass has been described using histo-

Table 11.2.   Known Causes of Gaseous Microemboli

Bubble oxygenation
High gas-to-blood flow ratio (bubble oxygenator)
Low reservoir level
Excessive cooling and heating gradients
Drug injections into circuit
Mechanical jarring of circuit
Inadequate debubbling (especially of arterial filter)
Gaseous or vaporous cavitation
Damaged membrane material
Counter-diffusion phenomena
Overoccluded roller pump
Excessive cardiotomy/vent suction
Pulsatile flow through microporous membrane
   oxygenator

logic techniques (16, 76), direct visual or optical methods (144–146), radiography (113), computed tomography (147), particle sizing using resistance or laser devices (10, 148), screen filtration pressure (149), screen sampling (33), bulk compressibility (150), fluorescein angiography (151, 152) or ultrasound (153). Each of the above techniques has afforded some degree of precision in its ability to size or count microemboli; however, more often than not, one parameter is gained at the expense of another. Optical detection devices, including particle-size analyzers and screen sampling, usually require a small sample volume obtained through a sidestream suitably narrow for light and optical through-transmission. Such techniques are fairly reliable for sizing, but not counting, the microemboli (154). Sequential sampling of aliquots of blood can be used with settling or rising chambers (in the case of gaseous microemboli) to determine bulk volume or total gas phase, but are less reliable for size determination. This same analogy applies to screen filtration techniques. Bulk compressibility takes advantage of the compressible nature of a gas bubble dispersed within a fluid to determine volume, but not size or total numbers.

Of all detection techniques, ultrasonic devices are the most commonly used today. These devices include transcranial, transesophageal, and Doppler flow devices (pulsed and continuous wave), as well as echo machines using both M- and B-modes. The enthusiasm for using ultrasound to detect microemboli is based in part on the ability to discriminate the circulating particles from the background blood flow using usually noninvasive techniques. Ultrasound devices work by emitting a sound signal from a piezoelectric crystal that is reflected from the moving blood cells. The frequency of the reflected signals differs from that of the transmitted signal in proportion to the blood velocity. With Doppler devices, these frequency shifts typically occur within the audible range (0 to 10 kHz). The audio signal contains both amplitude and frequency information, and the degree of reflection of the sound waves is a function of the difference in acoustic properties of the reflecting particles.

Microemboli, whether solid or gaseous, are more effective in scattering sound because of the difference in density between the particle and the surrounding blood or tissue. Gas bubbles are much more efficient at scattering ultrasound than more rigid particles, such as red cell aggregates or microthrombi, especially at the smaller diameters (135). This difference is due to the acoustic properties of nongaseous emboli being similar to those of blood. Additionally, gas bubbles have the propensity to resonate as the ultrasonic wave causes pressure oscillations and, hence, vibration of the gas inside the bubble. At the resonance frequency of a bubble of a particular size, the scattering of sound is maximal (155). The reflection of sound waves also is influenced by the frequency of the ultrasonic wave as it passes through the tissue and fluid, as well as by the diameter of the microembolus itself (101). Gaseous microemboli as small as 1 μm have been detected with ultrasound (155) in tissues, while other authors have detected circulating microbubbles in the 20 to 50 μm range (155–157).

Ultrasonic devices used for detection of microemboli utilize pulsed or continuous-wave transmission. With pulsed systems, short energy bursts (about 2 μsec)

are emitted at rates on the order of 1000 pulses per second. Particles along the beam path are then set in motion, reflecting the sound waves, while the regions in front of or behind it are not affected. This technique enables the operator to focus the beam to a specified depth. Using pulsed Doppler systems for microemboli detection is highly dependent upon the particle diameter (158, 159), angulation of the ultrasonic transducer (71, 101, 160), and incident pulse length (158, 159). Blood flow rate also has an important influence upon pulsed Doppler systems in that the pulse echoes usually represent the product of the pulse frequency and the time that the bubble resides within the sampling field (159). Some devices take this feature into consideration by making the pulse-repetition frequency proportional to the blood flow (161). With continuous-wave ultrasound, the emitted beam is continuous, and the particles are sonified along the entire length of beam penetration. Continuous-wave Doppler devices are currently used in a number of clinical diagnostic devices and are commonly used for microemboli detection.

Echo imaging systems have gained widespread support in recent years in detecting circulating microemboli. Transthoracic, transesophageal, and transcranial Doppler devices enable localization of microemboli within each of the respective visual fields. The B-mode enables the operator to view the emboli within the heart chambers, although some degree of quantitation may be obtained by M-mode, since the x-axis represents the time scale and relative counts are possible (162). Transesophageal echocardiography has been shown to be particularly effective in detecting gaseous microemboli during and after CPB and is useful in determining the adequacy of deairing maneuvers (163–167). Transcranial Doppler is used for detection of perioperative cerebral microemboli. These devices not only enable the detection and visualization of bubbles or particulate matter in the cranial arteries but also determine blood flow characteristics (168–170).

Quantitation of microemboli is difficult with any ultrasonic device because of certain limitations inherent to their proper operation (161, 171, 172). These limitations involve characteristics such as the frequency requirements, transducer angulation, and electrical circuitry used for signal analysis and sampling area (81, 84, 154, 161, 171). Calibration of the devices, although often overlooked, is very important. Use of solid man-made microparticles of plastic or glass is common for calibration; however, their acoustic properties are usually different than those of blood-borne or gaseous microemboli (71, 133, 173), and clumping or settling may further complicate any sort of accurate calibration. For accurate gaseous microemboli quantification, calibrated microbubbles are more reliable because of their similarities in acoustic properties (135, 148, 159, 171, 173–175). In spite of these calibration procedures, certain limitations exist with any attempt to quantitate the size or number of microemboli present in vessels or the by-pass circuit (154, 171, 176, 177) (Fig. 11.2).

PATHOPHYSIOLOGY

It is generally accepted that postoperative diffuse cerebral dysfunction following the use of CPB is largely attributable to microembolism and/or compromise of cerebral blood flow. Individual differences in patient tolerance to bypass make it difficult to universally define safe thresholds for flow, pressure, and pulsatility (178, 179). The brain has been the focus of most studies evaluating negative surgical outcome following bypass, principally because of the variety of sensitive tests capable of implicating cerebral damage. Histologic studies have also shown postcardiopulmonary bypass embolic material in the kidneys, heart, liver, lungs, and spleen (23, 24). Histology of the brains of patients who died after open heart surgery has demonstrated fibrin, fat, muscle fragments, calcium, and platelet aggregate microemboli in the vasculature (28). In these studies, fat emboli were detected in 80% of the cases and their pres-

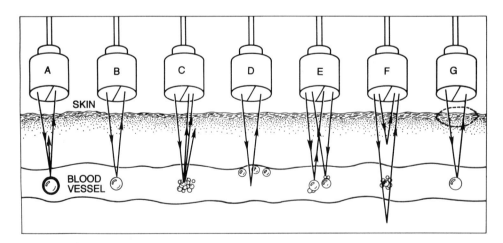

Figure 11.2. Some potential causes for signal differences from bubbles detected by Doppler ultrasound: (A) encapsulated bubble; (B) ideal condition with signal reflected back from discrete bubble; (C) multiple bubbles with scattered signals; (D) different location of bubbles within sample beam; (E) bubbles of different sizes blocking sound waves of others; (F) probe operated at different frequencies; and (G) artifact due to gross movement of skin/surface probe interface. (From Butler BD. Biophysical aspects of gas bubbles in blood. Med Instrument 1985;19:59–62.)

ence was independent of perfusion variables, whereas nonfat emboli were related to the length of perfusion time. Thus, the period of greatest risk of cerebral injury is likely to be at the beginning of CPB when the patient is susceptible to both hypotension and microemboli initially released from the perfusion circuit (180, 181).

Postoperative cerebral dysfunction following bypass, as demonstrated with psychomotor tests, may persist from a few hours to days or weeks (182–185). Some misinterpretation of the etiology of the injury may occur because similar changes in cerebral function are reported not only after microembolization but also with anxiety, sleep deprivation, drugs, cerebral edema, or hypoxemia (6, 173, 186, 187).

Additional reasons for the wide range of reported incidences of neurologic dysfunction after CPB include the variability commonly observed when comparing prospective and retrospective studies, the time lapse between pre- and postsurgical evaluation, and the thoroughness of the tests conducted (5, 188). In their retrospective evaluation of postoperative neurologic dysfunction, Bojar et al. (189) and Coffey et al. (190) reported incidence rates of 1 to 5%. This is in contrast to reported incidence rates in prospective studies as high as 30 to 61% (191–193). Incidence of stroke has been reported in approximately 5% of coronary artery bypass procedures in two prospective studies. Shaw (5), Newman (6), Smith (194), and Campbell and Raskin (195) recently have published excellent reviews on the subject of neurologic and neuropsychologic morbidity and its prevention during cardiac surgery.

Adverse neurologic outcome following bypass also has been correlated with arterial line microemboli. Lee et al. (187) found postoperative deficits in 23% of their patients after open heart surgery, 14% of whom had psychiatric findings. Carlson et al. (182) found a greater percentage of patients with decreased Bender gestalt visual motor test scores when a bubble oxygenator was used instead of a membrane-type or without use of an arterial line filter. These results correlated with ultrasonic detection of circulating microemboli. Levels of the brain-specific enzymes of creatine phosphokinase were significantly elevated in patients undergoing open heart surgery (196–198), and this effect was preventable in dogs with use of an arterial filter (199). Moody et al. (200) detected focal small cerebral capillary and arteriolar dilations in dogs and patients following bypass which they attributed to microemboli, the identity of which was suggested as either silicone antifoam (201) or air (202). They suggested that these focal dilations could be the equivalent of an anatomic correlate to neurologic deficits.

In the case of gas emboli, the topic of pathophysiology has been studied for more than 3 centuries (203). A number of reports and reviews have described the outcome of arterial air embolism with cardiac surgery involving gaseous microemboli and gross air (2, 3, 75, 171, 172, 176, 204–206). Cerebral gas embolism can cause transient changes in the electroencephalogram that may persist from seconds to hours, in addition to the neurologic dysfunction described for nongaseous microemboli. Coronary air is associated with impaired left and right ventricular function as well as with numerous electrocardiographic changes, including ventricular dysrhythmias, atrioventricular dissociation, QRS complex widening, and ST segment and T wave changes (205, 207). Clearance of coronary air while on cardiopulmonary bypass can be accomplished with the use of certain drugs, surface-active chemicals (208, 209), aortic clamping with ventricular or aortic compression, or retrograde perfusion (210, 211). Figure 11.3 illustrates the major mechanisms of air embolism as reported in 1986 (212).

Arteriolar obstruction by gaseous emboli may be associated with vascular spasm followed by hyperemia (207) and perivascular hemorrhage (213). Immediately after

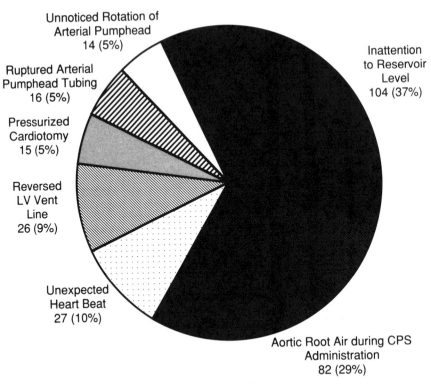

Figure 11.3. Major mechanisms of gas embolism. These were reported by survey respondents who observed 284 incidents of air embolism during clinical cases. CPS, cardioplegic solution; LV, left ventricular. (From Kurusz M, Wheeldon DR. Risk containment during cardiopulmonary bypass. Sem Thorac Cardiovasc Surg 1990;2:400–409.)

occlusion, vasodilation occurs in the arteries and venules, followed by congestion and stasis. These responses represent a direct action or injury to the vascular endothelium (206).

PREVENTION OF EMBOLI

It is unlikely today that, even with the most current bypass devices, all embolic events can be totally eliminated. However, an awareness of those factors responsible for their production and interaction with the blood (214), as previously described, may allow perfusion teams to minimize the numbers generated and consequences during clinical bypass. Undoubtedly, filtration has been the single most important technique used to reduce all types of emboli, while the current near-universal acceptance

of membrane oxygenators has led to dramatic decreases in gaseous microemboli production.

The technique of blood filtration began with the development of modern blood banking and blood transfusion practices in the 1930s (215, 216). An early blood collection/transfusion apparatus incorporating a 250-μm, reusable stainless steel filter was reported by Cooksey (217) and was later modified and used successfully on more than 11,000 transfusions.

Early laboratory experience with extracorporeal circulation confirmed the superior filtration characteristics of the pulmonary bed, and blood was often precirculated through the animal's lungs before beginning perfusion. Bjork (218) and Miller et al. (219) used filters with pores 300×300 μm in the arterial line during early clinical applications. The original Lillehei-DeWall bubble oxygenator incorporated four standard infusion set screen filters on the outflow side of the arterial settling reservoir (220). The early CPB experience of Kolff et al. (221) and Gross et al. (222) also relied on arterial filters for particulate trapping and air removal.

The seminal work of Swank and colleagues (223, 224) in the mid-1960s led to the use in 1970 by Hill et al. (225) and others of the Swank depth filter for filtration of cardiotomy blood first (225) and later arterial blood (226). The hospital mortality for patients decreased significantly in those on whom filters were used. Also in the early 1970s, Patterson and Twichell (227) described a 40-μm, pleated polyester mesh filter that functioned with low pressure drop at clinical flow rates.

Solis et al. (34) evaluated the effectiveness of both types of filters using a microparticle counter and concluded that microaggregates in the cardiotomy-suctioned blood comprised a tremendously greater volume than those found in arterial or venous blood. Further, such microaggregates found in the cardiotomy-return blood were more resistant to deaggregation and, thus, posed the greatest risk to the patient. Page et al. (228) confirmed the benefit of depth filtration of cardiotomy-suctioned blood during clinical perfusion to reduce embolus transmission to patients.

The extent of filter use by cardiac surgical teams nationwide was reported in 1983 (229). Ninety-four percent reported the practice of filtering bank blood added to the CPB circuit. Ninety-seven percent filtered cardiotomy-suctioned blood, and 78% filtered blood in the arterial line during both adult and pediatric perfusion. Because of the potential for filter occlusion with inadequate anticoagulation, several questions on this survey were asked regarding its management. Blood coagulation status was measured by greater than 95% of the respondents, who most often performed the activated clotting time at least every 30 minutes during cardiopulmonary bypass. Forty percent also reported filtration of the cardioplegic solution after earlier reports of particulate emboli contained in these solutions (230–233). The importance of rinsing and filtering the circuit with crystalloid solution prior to establishing bypass was emphasized by Reed et al. (53) in 1974 and was performed by most perfusionists in 1982 (229).

The benefit of arterial line filtration, in conjunction with either bubble or membrane oxygenation, has been confirmed in several recent reports using Doppler or transesophageal echocardiographic detection of decreased quantities of microemboli (234–238) or improved patient scores on neuropsychologic tests following CPB (239). Figure 11.4 is a photomicrograph of a trapped platelet/leukocyte embolus on the upstream side of a screen arterial filter following clinical bypass.

Pharmacologic interventions to minimize emboli during bypass consist primarily of assuring adequate heparin anticoagulation (20, 22, 240, 241). Close monitoring of the activating clotting time during CPB, as previously described, is now nearly universally practiced. Although controversial, administration of isoflurane has been shown by some to afford better tolerance for cerebral ischemia, and would therefore appear potentially useful in minimizing the effects of cerebral emboli (242–244). Barbiturates also have been used by some (245) to improve the cerebral outcome after open heart surgery, but their use as prophylaxis against emboli appears less clearly defined. Royston (246) has recently reviewed pharmacologic interventions aimed at reducing platelet and neutrophil emboli during bypass.

Acid-base management using alpha-stat was popularized in the early 1980s (247–249), and recent survey results (250) indicate its use in a majority of CPB cases. Alpha-stat management more closely maintains cerebral autoregulation in contrast to pH-stat management, during which

Figure 11.4.   Scanning electron micrograph (original magnification ×236) of 25 μm pore size, nylon screen arterial line filter after 174 minutes of blood flow. The large (>50 μm) trapped aggregate (left of center) consists of platelets and neutrophils. Singularly attached neutrophils and smaller aggregates are seen elsewhere on the woven nylon strands.

enhanced cerebral blood flow occurs. Decreased transmission of microemboli per unit volume of blood flow, therefore, might favor the alpha-stat approach to minimize the embolic "load" in perfused tissue beds (251).

Prevention of gross air embolism from either the bypass circuit or operative field has been the subject of numerous reports (211, 252, 253). A variety of safety devices with proven efficacy are available for the circuit and include arterial line filters, bubble traps, air bubble detectors, low-level alarms, and one-way valves for the vent or arterial filter purge line. The arterial line filter and air bubble detector have been reported to be highly effective in prevention of air embolism originating in the extracor-

poreal arterial line (212). Equally important in prevention of air embolism are clear lines of communication and use of protocols during CPB (254). Prebypass checklists have gained wide acceptance by teams and are effective in uncovering unsafe conditions prior to initiating bypass (255).

One other less appreciated source of emboli during cardiac surgery relates to the status of the patient's ascending aorta, which usually must be cannulated, cross-clamped, and manipulated during the procedure. Atheromatous plaques that are present may be dislodged during these maneuvers (256, 257). Alternative cannulation (258, 259) or venting sites have been proposed as well as the so-called no-touch technique (260). Intraoperative echocardiography may be helpful to define the extent of disease in the aorta, but has not been widely used to date.

TREATMENT OF EMBOLI

There is no specific treatment for microemboli per se; instead, prevention, as discussed previously, has received the most attention and appears to be the most rational approach in decreasing the risk. However, when gross air embolism occurs, definite treatment protocols have been proposed (261, 262) and used with remarkable success (263–266). The importance of having a plan for this rare event has been emphasized and can often make the difference between severe injury or death and an uneventful recovery (254). Hyperbaric oxygenation has been shown to be effective in the treatment of gross air embolism (267–272), but access to such a treatment facility may be limited (212).

The use of transesophageal echocardiography and transcranial Doppler has been reported to aid in the identification of intraventricular or intravascular bubbles, primarily during valvular procedures or when the heart chambers have been opened (168, 273). Rigorous deairing techniques may be assessed in this manner to decrease the persistence of entrapped "surgical air" emboli.

CONCLUSIONS AND FUTURE TRENDS

Currently, the subject of cerebral reactions to open heart surgery is receiving much attention (274), and further improvements in CPB techniques and patients' neurologic outcomes appear likely to emerge in the next decade. While controversy continues regarding what are the optimal specific devices, a consensus favors incorporating membrane oxygenation and filtration of blood and all fluids during bypass. The chemical modification of foreign surfaces used in extracorporeal devices, most recently by heparin-bonding, may de-

crease blood-derived microemboli, but should be approached cautiously. Leukocyte filtration is another new technology that offers potential benefits in ameliorating the inflammatory responses to CPB to which emboli contribute. The current predominance of membrane oxygenation over that of bubble oxygenation has clearly reduced gaseous microembolic phenomena in patients during bypass. Finally, research and continuing education will increase our understanding of the problems of embolic events and CPB and should further reduce levels of morbidity and mortality.

REFERENCES

1. Dorland's illustrated medical dictionary. 27th ed. Philadelphia: WB Saunders, 1988:542.
2. Edmunds LH Jr, Williams W. Microemboli and the use of filters during cardiopulmonary bypass. In: Utley JR, ed. Pathophysiology and techniques of cardiopulmonary bypass. Vol 2. Baltimore: Williams & Wilkins, 1983: 101–114.
3. Kurusz M. Gaseous microemboli: sources, causes, and clinical considerations. Med Instrument 1985;19:73–76.
4. Wong DHW. Perioperative stroke part II: cardiac surgery and cardiogenic embolic stroke. Can J Anaesth 1991;38:471–488.
5. Shaw PJ. The incidence and nature of neurological morbidity following cardiac surgery: a review. Perfusion 1989;4:83–91.
6. Newman S. The incidence and nature of neuropsychological morbidity following cardiac surgery. Perfusion 1989;4:93–100.
7. Solis RT, Kennedy PS, Beall AC, Noon GP, DeBakey ME. Cardiopulmonary bypass—microembolization and platelet aggregation. Circulation 1975;52:103–108.
8. Clark RE. Microemboli: an overview. Med Instrument 1985;19:53–54.
9. Swank RL. Alteration of blood on storage: measurement of adhesiveness of "aging" platelets and leukocytes and their removal by filtration. N Engl J Med 1961;265:728–733.
10. Solis RT, Gibbs MB. Filtration of the microaggregates in stored blood. Transfusion 1972;12:245–250.
11. Rosenberg RD. Heparin action. Circulation 1974;49:603–605.
12. Zapol WM, Levy RI, Kolobow T, Sprogg R, Bowman RL. In vitro denaturation of plasma alpha lipoproteins by bubble oxygenator in the dog. Curr Top Surg Res 1969;1:449–467.

13. Baier RE, Dutton RC. Initial events in interaction of blood with a foreign surface. J Biomed Mat Res 1969;3:191–206.

14. Kurusz M, Williams DR. Blood surfaces in the extracorporeal circuit: a scanning electron microscopic study. J Extra-Corpor Technol 1975; 7:186–198.

15. Davies GC, Sobel M, Salzman EW. Elevated plasma fibrinopeptide A and thromboxane A$_2$ levels during cardiopulmonary bypass. Circulation 1980;61:808–814.

16. Allardyce DB, Yoshida SH, Ashmore PG. The importance of microembolism in the pathogenesis of organ dysfunction caused by prolonged use of the pump oxygenator. J Thorac Cardiovasc Surg 1966;52:706–715.

17. Ashmore PG, Cvitek V, Ambrose P. The incidence and effects of particulate aggregation and microembolism in pump oxygenator systems. J Thorac Cardiovasc Surg 1968;55: 691–697.

18. Dutton RC, Edmunds LH Jr. Measurement of emboli in extracorporeal perfusion systems. J Thorac Cardiovasc Surg 1973;65:523–530.

19. Bull BS, Huse WM, Brauer FS, Korpman RA. Heparin therapy during extracorporeal circulation. II. The use of a dose-response curve to individualize heparin and protamine dosage. J Thorac Cardiovasc Surg 1975;69:685–689.

20. Young JA, Kisker CT, Doty DB. Adequate anticoagulation during cardiopulmonary bypass determined by activated clotting time and the appearance of fibrin monomer. Ann Thorac Surg 1978;26:231–240.

21. Bull BS, Korpman RA, Huse WM, Briggs BD. Heparin therapy during extracorporeal circulation. I. Problems inherent in existing heparin protocols. J Thorac Cardiovasc Surg 1975;69: 674–684.

22. Esposito RA, Culliford AT, Colvin SB, Thomas SJ, Lackner H, Spencer FC. The role of the activated clotting time in heparin administration and neutralization for cardiopulmonary bypass. J Thorac Cardiovasc Surg 1983;85:174–185.

23. Evans EA, Wellington JS. Emboli associated with cardiopulmonary bypass. J Thorac Cardiovasc Surg 1964;48:323–330.

24. Wright ES, Sarkozy E, Dobell ARC, Murphy DR. Fat globulinemia in extracorporeal circulation. Am Thorac Surg 1963;53:500–504.

25. Arrants JE, Gadsden RH, Huggins MB, Lee WH Jr. Effects of extracorporeal circulation upon blood lipids. Ann Thorac Surg 1973;15: 230–242.

26. Clark RE, Margraf HW, Beauchamp RA. Fat and solid filtration in clinical perfusion. Surgery 1975;77:216–224.

27. Lee WH Jr, Krumhaar D, Fonkalsrud E, Schjeide OA, Maloney JV Jr. Denaturation of plasma proteins as a cause of morbidity and death after intracardiac operation. Surgery 1961;50:29–39, 47.

28. Hill JD, Aguilar MJ, Baranco A, de Lanerolle P, Gerbode F. Neuropathological manifestations of cardiac surgery. Ann Thorac Surg 1969;7: 409–419.

29. Jefferson NC, Necheles H. Oleic acid toxicity and fat embolism. Proc Soc Exp Biol Med 1948;68:248–250.

30. Tieney DF, Johnson RP. Surface tension of lung extracts [Abstract]. Fed Proc 1963;22:339.

31. Clark RE, Beauchamp RA, Magrath RA, Brooks JD, Ferguson TB, Weldon CS. Comparison of bubble and membrane oxygenators in short and long perfusions. J Thorac Cardiovasc Surg 1979;78:655–666.

32. Chenoweth DE, Cooper SW, Hugli TE, Stewart RW, Blackstone EH, Kirklin JW. Complement activation during cardiopulmonary bypass. N Engl J Med 1981;304:497–503.

33. Dutton RC, Edmunds LH Jr, Hutchinson JC, Roe BB. Platelet aggregate emboli produced in patients during cardiopulmonary bypass with membrane and bubble oxygenators and blood filters. J Thorac Cardiovasc Surg 1974;67: 258–265.

34. Solis RT, Noon GP, Beall AC, DeBakey ME. Particulate microembolism during cardiac operation. Ann Thorac Surg 1974;17:332–344.

35. McKenna R, Bachmann F, Whittaker B, Gilson JR, Weinburg M Jr. The hemostatic mechanism after open-heart surgery. II. Frequency of abnormal platelet functions during and after extracorporeal circulation. J Thorac Cardiovasc Surg 1975;70:298–308.

36. Hicks RE, Dutton RC, Reis CA, Price DC, Edmunds LH Jr. Production and fate of platelet aggregate emboli during veno-venous perfusion. Surg Forum 1973;24:250–252.

37. Ward CA, Ruegsegger B, Stanga D, Zingg W. Reduction in platelet adhesion to biomaterials by removal of gas nuclei. Trans Am Soc Artif Intern Org 1974;20A:77–84.

38. Warren BA, Philp RB, Inwood MJ. The ultrastructural morphology of air embolism: platelet adhesion to the interface and endothelial damage. Br J Exp Path 1973;54:163–172.

39. Preston FE, Martin JF, Stewart RM, Davies-Jones GAB. Thrombocytosis, circulating platelet aggregates and neurological dysfunction. Br Med J 1979;2:156–158.

40. Longmore DB, Gueierrara D, Bennett G, et al. Prostacyclin: a solution to some problems of extracorporeal circulation. Lancet 1979;1: 1002–1005.

41. Aren CA, Fedderson K, Radegran K. Effects of

prostacyclin infusion on platelet activation and post-operative blood loss in coronary bypass. Ann Thorac Surg 1983;36:49–54.

42. Ellison N, Edmunds LH Jr, Colman RW. Platelet aggregation following heparin and protamine administration. Anesthesiology 1978;48: 65–68.

43. Faichney A, Davidson KG, Wheatley DJ, Davidson JF, Walker ID. Prostacyclin in cardiopulmonary bypass operations. J Thorac Cardiovasc Surg 1982;84:601–608.

44. Royston D. Aprotinin in open-heart surgery: background and results in patients having aortocoronary bypass grafts. Perfusion 1990;5 (suppl):63–72.

45. Hovig T. The role of platelets in thrombosis. Thromb Diathes Haemorrhag 1970;42 (suppl):137–153.

46. Ratliff NB, Young WG Jr, Hackel BB, Mikat E, Wilson JW. Pulmonary injury secondary to extracorporeal circulation; an ultrastructural study. J Thorac Cardiovasc Surg 1973;65: 425–432.

47. Kurusz M, Schneider B, Conti VR, Williams EH. Scanning electron microscopy of arterial line filters following clinical cardiopulmonary bypass. Proceedings of the First World Congress on Extracorporeal Technology. Brighton, UK. London: Franklin Scientific Products, 1981: 17–23.

48. Hammerschmidt DE, Stroncek DF, Bowers TK, et al. Complement activation and neutropenia occurring during cardiopulmonary bypass. J Thorac Cardiovasc Surg 1981;81:370–377.

49. Pruzanski W, Shumak KH. Biologic activity of cold-reacting autoantibodies (first of two parts). N Engl J Med 1977;297:538–542.

50. Pruzanski W, Shumak KH. Biologic activity of cold-reacting autoantibodies (second of two parts). N Engl J Med 1977;297:583–589.

51. Moore RA, Geller EA, Matthews ES, Botros SB, Jose AB, Clark DL. The effects of hypothermic cardiopulmonary bypass on patients with low-titer, nonspecific cold agglutinins. Ann Thorac Surg 1984;37:233–238.

52. Robicsek F, Masters TN, Littman L, Born AVR. The embolization of bone wax from sternotomy incisions. Ann Thorac Surg 1981;31: 357–359.

53. Reed CC, Romagnoli A, Taylor DE, Clark DK. Particulate matter in bubble oxygenators. J Thorac Cardiovasc Surg 1974;68:971–974.

54. Braun PR, L'Hommedieu BD, Klinedinst WJ. Aluminum contamination by heat exchangers during cardiopulmonary bypass. Proc Am Acad Cardiovasc Perfusion 1988;9:69–72.

55. Hubbard LC, Kletschka HD, Olsen DA, Rafferty EH, Clausen EW, Robinson AR. Spallation using roller pumps and its clinical implications. AmSECT Proc 1975;3:27–32.

56. Kurusz M, Christman EW, Williams EH, Tyers GFO. Roller pump induced tubing wear: another argument in favor of arterial line filtration. J Extra-Corpor Technol 1980;12: 115–119.

57. Israel AL, Walton RM, Crane TN, Thompson DJ, Reed CC. Comparison study of polyvinyl chloride versus silicone rubber tubing. Proc Am Acad Cardiovasc Perfusion 1983;4:47–52.

58. Uretsky G, Landsburg G, Cohn DD, Wax Y, Borman JB. Analysis of microembolic particles originating in extracorporeal circuits. Perfusion 1987;2:9–17.

59. Robicsek F, Duncan GD, Born GVR, Wilkinson HA, Masters TN, McClure M. Inherent dangers of simultaneous application of microfibrillar collagen hemostat and blood-saving devices. J Thorac Cardiovasc Surg 1986;92:766–770.

60. Orenstein JM, Sato N, Aaron B, Buchholz B, Bloom S. Microemboli observed in deaths following cardiopulmonary bypass surgery: silicone antifoam agents and polyvinyl chloride tubing as sources of emboli. Human Pathol 1982;13:1082–1090.

61. Smith WT. Cerebral lesions due to emboli of silicone antifoam in dogs subjected to cardiopulmonary bypass. J Pathol Bacteriol 1960;90: 9–18.

62. Wells R, Bygdeman MS, Shahriari AA, Matloff JM. Influence of a defoaming agent upon hematological complications of pump oxygenators. Circulation 1968;37:638–647.

63. Penry JK, Cordell AR, Johnston FR, Netsky MG. Cerebral embolism by Antifoam A in a bubble oxygenator system; an experimental and clinical study. Surgery 1960;47:84–94.

64. Cassie AB, Riddel AG, Yates PO. Hazard of antifoam emboli from a bubble oxygenator. Thorax 1960;15:22–29.

65. Thomassen RW, Howbert JP, Winn DF Jr, Thompson SW II. The occurrence and characterization of emboli associated with the use of a silicone antifoaming agent. J Thorac Cardiovasc Surg 1961;41:611–622.

66. Gupta S, Dandapat R, Maitra TK. Effects of silicone antifoam on the pulmonary vasculature. J Thorac Cardiovasc Surg 1972;63:714–719.

67. Kurusz M, Conti VR, Speer D, Butler BD. Surface tension changes of perfusates: implications for gaseous microemboli during cardiopulmonary bypass. J Extra-Corpor Technol 1985;17:138–142.

68. Butler BD, Kurusz M, Conti VR. Postbypass plasma surface tension and its role in bubble filtration. Perfusion 1986;1:187–191.

69. Jordan P Jr, Tolstedt GE, Beretta FF. Micro-

bubble formation in artificial oxygenation. Surgery 1957;43:266–269.

70. Kessler J, Patterson RH Jr. The production of microemboli by various blood oxygenators. Ann Thorac Surg 1970;9:221–228.

71. Patterson RH Jr, Kessler J. Microemboli during cardiopulmonary bypass detected by ultrasound. Surg Gynecol Obstet 1969;129:505–510.

72. Krebber HJ, Hill JD, Osborn JJ, Iatrides A. Microemboli during extracorporeal circulation. Thorac Cardiovasc Surg 1980;28:249–252.

73. Krebber HJ, Hanrath P, Janzen R, Ritoff M, Rodewald G. Gas emboli during open-heart surgery. Thorac Cardiovasc Surg 1982;30:401–404.

74. Pearson DT, Holden MP, Poslad SJ. Gaseous microemboli production of bubble and membrane oxygenators. In: Lautier A, Gille JP, eds. Extracorporeal gas exchange. Design and techniques. London: Saunders, 1986:198–234.

75. Pearson DT. Microemboli: gaseous and particulate. In: Taylor KM, ed. Cardiopulmonary bypass. Principles and management. London: Chapman and Hall, 1986:313–353.

76. Hill AG, Groom RC, Tewksbury L, et al. Sources of gaseous microemboli during cardiopulmonary bypass. Proc Am Acad Cardiovasc Perfusion 1988;9:122–130.

77. Brennan RW, Patterson RH, Kessler J. Cerebral blood flow and metabolism during cardiopulmonary bypass. Neurology 1971;21:665–672.

78. Hammond GL, Bowley WW. Bubble mechanics and oxygen transfer. J Thorac Cardiovasc Surg 1976;71:422–428.

79. Reed CC, Miller D, Stafford TB, McInnis RJ. Microemboli emission of extracorporeal oxygenators. Les Cahiers du CECEC 1984;22:35–40.

80. Pearson DT, McArdle B, Poslad SJ, Murray A. A clinical evaluation of the performance characteristics of one membrane and five bubble oxygenators: gas transfer and gaseous microemboli production. Perfusion 1986;1:15–26.

81. Pearson DT, Clayton R, Murray A, McArdle B. Blood gas control in bubble and membrane oxygenators. Proc Am Acad Cardiovasc Perfusion 1987;8:190–199.

82. Chan R, Tidwell R. Study of gaseous microemboli removal capabilities of five different arterial filters in vitro. Proc Am Acad Cardiovasc Perfusion 1983;4:53–55.

83. Massimino RM, Dyer RK, Martin J Jr, Gough JD, Stearns GT, Karlson KE. Microemboli in the arterial line and the carotid artery during perfusion with a bubble oxygenator. ASAIO J 1984; 7:155–159.

84. Pearson DT, Holden MP, Poslad SJ, Murray A, Waterhouse PS. A clinical evaluation of the gas transfer characteristics and gaseous microemboli production of two bubble oxygenators. Life Support Syst 1984;2:252–266.

85. Pearson DT. Blood gas control during cardiopulmonary bypass. Perfusion 1988;3:113–133.

86. Selman MW, McAlpine WA, Ratan RS. The effectiveness of various heart-lung machines in the elimination of microbubbles from the circulation. J Thorac Cardiovasc Surg 1967;53:613–617.

87. Clark RE, Dietz DR, Miller JG. Continuous detection of microemboli during cardiopulmonary bypass in animals and man. Circulation 1976;54:74–78.

88. Katoh S, Yoshida F. Physical factors affecting microembolus formation in extracorporeal circulation. Ann Biomed Eng 1976;4:60–67.

89. Graves DJ, Quinn JA, Smock RA. Supersaturation and bubble formation in membrane oxygenators [Abstract]. Proceedings of the 27th Annual Meeting of the Alliance for Engineering in Medicine and Biology 1974;197.

90. Severinghaus JW. Temperature gradients during hypothermia. Ann NY Acad Sci 1959;80:515–521.

91. Donald DE, Fellows JL. Physical factors relating to gas emboli in blood. J Thorac Cardiovasc Surg 1961;42:110–118.

92. Pollard HS, Fleischaker RJ, Timmes JJ, Karlson KE. Blood-brain barrier studies in extracorporeal cooling and warming. J Thorac Cardiovasc Surg 1961;42:772–778.

93. Gibbon JH Jr. Maintenance of cardiorespiratory function by extracorporeal circulation. Circulation 1959;19:646–656.

94. Gollan F. Physiology of deep hypothermia by total body perfusion. Ann NY Acad Sci 1959;80:301–334.

95. Almond CH, Jones JC, Snyder HM, Grant SM, Meyer BW. Cooling gradients and brain damage with deep hypothermia. J Thorac Cardiovasc Surg 1964;48:890–905.

96. Ehrenhaft JL, Claman MA. Cerebral complications of open-heart surgery; further observations. J Thorac Cardiovasc Surg 1961;42:514–526.

97. Ehrenhaft JL, Claman MA. Cerebral complications of open-heart surgery. J Thorac Cardiovasc Surg 1961;41:503–508.

98. Bjork VO, Hultquist G. Contraindications to profound hypothermia in open-heart surgery. J Thorac Cardiovasc Surg 1962;44:1–13.

99. Miller DR, Allbritton FF. "Coronary suction" as a source of air embolism: an experimental study using the Kay-Cross oxygenator. Ann Surg 1960;151:75–84.

100. Wright G, Sanderson JM. Cellular aggregation and trauma in cardiotomy suction systems. Thorax 1979;34:621–628.

101. Loop FD, Szabo J, Rowlinson RD, Urbanek K. Events related to microembolism during open-heart surgery: effectiveness of in-line filtration recorded by ultrasound. Ann Thorac Surg 1976;21:412–420.

102. Gallagher EG, Pearson DT. Ultrasonic identification of sources of microemboli during open-heart surgery. Thorax 1973;28:295–305.

103. Freed D, Walker WF, Dube CM, Touno T. Effects of vaporous cavitation near prosthetic surfaces. Trans Am Soc Artif Intern Org 1981;27:105–109.

104. Yount DE. On the evolution, generation, and regeneration of gas cavitation nuclei. J Acoust Soc Am 1982;71:1473–1481.

105. Bass RM, Longmore DB. Cerebral damage during open-heart surgery. Nature (Lond) 1969;222:30–33.

106. Hannemann RE, Barile RG. Bubble formation in the roller infusion pump. Am J Dis Child 1973;125:706–708.

107. Mandl JP. Comparison of emboli production between a constrained force vortex pump and a roller pump. AmSECT Proc 1977;5:27–31.

108. Ross J Jr. Factors influencing the formation of bubbles in blood. Trans Am Soc Artif Intern Org 1959;5:140–147.

109. Baird RJ, Miyagishima RT. The danger of air embolism through pressure-perfusion cannula. J Thorac Cardiovasc Surg 1963;46:212–219.

110. Kort A, Kronzon I. Microbubble formation: in vitro and in vivo observation. J Clin Ultrasound 1982;10:117–120.

111. Kuntz RA, Maurer WG. An examination of cavitation as it relates to the extracorporeal arterial infusion model. J Extra-Corpor Technol 1982;14:345–354.

112. Miller BJ, Gibbon JH Jr, Greco VR, Cohn CH, Albritten FF Jr. The use of a vent for the left ventricle as a means of avoiding air embolism to the systemic circulation during open cardiotomy with the maintenance of the cardiorespiratory function of animals by a pump oxygenator. Surg Forum 1953;4:29–33.

113. Taber RE, Maraan BM, Tomatis L. Prevention of air embolism during open heart surgery; a study of the role of trapped air in the left ventricle. Surgery 1970;68:685–691.

114. Burbank A, Ferguson TB, Burford TH. Carbon dioxide flooding of the chest in open-heart surgery. J Thorac Cardiovasc Surg 1965;50:691–698.

115. Ng WS, Rosen M. Carbon dioxide in the prevention of air embolism during open-heart surgery. Thorax 1968;23:19–26.

116. Kalkunte JR. Air embolism prevention [Letter]. Ann Thorac Surg 1988;45:586–587.

117. Utley JR, Stephens DB. Venting during cardiopulmonary bypass. In: Utley JR, ed. Pathophysiology and techniques of cardiopulmonary bypass. Vol 2. Baltimore: Williams & Wilkins, 1983:115–127.

118. Weathersby PK, Homer LD. Solubility of inert gases in biological fluids and tissues: a review. Undersea Biomed Res 1980;7:227–296.

119. Spencer MP, Oyama Y. Pulmonary capacity for dissipation of venous gas emboli. Aerospace Med 1971;42:822–827.

120. Harkins HN, Harmon PH. Embolism by air and oxygen; comparative studies. Proc Soc Exp Biol NY 1934;32:178–181.

121. Yang WJ, Echigo R, Wotton DR, Hwang JB. Experimental studies of the dissolution of gas bubbles in whole blood and plasma. I. Stationary bubbles. J Biomech 1971;4:275–281.

122. Yang WJ, Echigo R, Wotton DR, Hwang JB. Experimental studies of the dissolution of gas bubbles in whole blood and plasma. II. Moving bubbles or liquids. J Biomech 1971;4:283–288.

123. Hlastala MP, Van Liew HD. Absorption of in vivo inert gas bubbles. Resp Physiol 1975;24:147–158.

124. Munson ES, Merrick HC. Effect of nitrous oxide on venous air embolism. Anesthesiology 1966;27:783–787.

125. Bethune DW. Organ damage after heart surgery. Lancet 1976;2:1410–1411.

126. Tisovec L, Hamilton WK. Newer considerations in air embolism during operation. JAMA 1967;201:376–377.

127. Wells DG, Podolakin W, Mohr M, Buxton B, Bray H. Nitrous oxide and cerebrospinal fluid markers of ischaemia following cardiopulmonary bypass. Anaesth Intens Care 1987;15:431–435.

128. Epstein PS, Plesset MS. On the stability of gas bubbles in liquid-gas solutions. J Chem Physics 1950;18:1505–1509.

129. Liebermann L. Air bubbles in water. J Appl Physics 1957;28:205–211.

130. Turner WR. Microbubble persistence in fresh water. J Acoust Soc Am 1961;33:1223–1233.

131. Tanasawa I, Wotton DR, Yang W, Clark DW. Experimental study of air bubbles in a simulated cardiopulmonary bypass system with flow constriction. J Biomech 1970;3:417–424.

132. Hlastala MP, Fahri LE. Absorption of gas bubbles in flowing blood. J Appl Physiol 1973;35: 311–316.

133. Ward CA, Tikuisis P, Venter RD. Stability of bubbles in a closed volume of liquid-gas solution. J Appl Physiol 1975;24:147–158.

134. Feinstein SB, Shah PM, Bing RJ, et al. Microbubble dynamics visualized in the inert capillary circulation. J Am Coll Cardiol 1984;4: 595–600.

135. Philp RB, Inwood MJ, Warren BA. Interactions between gas bubbles and components of the blood: implications in decompression sickness. Aerospace Med 1972;43:946–953.

136. Philp RB. A review of blood changes associated with compression-decompression: relationship to decompression sickness. Undersea Biomed Res 1974;1:117–150.

137. Philp RB, Bennett PB, Andersen JC, et al. Effects of aspirin and dipyridamole on platelet function, hematology, and blood chemistry of saturation divers. Undersea Biomed Res 1979;6: 127–140.

138. Vroman L, Adams AL, Klings M. Interactions among human blood proteins at interfaces. Fed Proc 1971;30:1494–1502.

139. Harvey EN, Barnes DK, McElroy WD, Whiteley AH, Pease DC, Cooper KW. Bubble formation in animals. I. Physical factors. J Cell Comp Physiol 1944;24:1–22.

140. Butler BD, Hills BA. Role of lung surfactant in cerebral decompression sickness. Aviat Space Environ Med 1973;54:11–15.

141. Philp RB, Schacham P, Gowdey CW. Involvement of platelets and microthrombi in experimental decompression sickness: similarities with disseminated intravascular coagulation. Aerospace Med 1971;42:494–502.

142. Thorsen T, Brubakk A, Ovstedal T, Farstad M, Holmsen H. A method for production of N$_2$ microbubbles in platelet-rich plasma in an aggregometer-like apparatus, and effect on the platelet density in vitro. Undersea Biomed Res 1986;13:271–288.

143. Thorsen T, Dalen H, Bjerkvig R, Holmsen H. Transmission and scanning electron microscopy of microbubble-activated human platelets in vitro. Undersea Biomed Res 1987;14:45–58.

144. Tepper R, Gelman S, Lowenfelds AB, Lord JW Jr. A method for the detection of microbubbles resulting from passage of blood through heart-lung machines. Surg Forum 1958;9:171–174.

145. Selman MW, McAlpine WA, Ratan RS. The effectiveness of various heart-lung machines in the elimination of microbubbles from the circulation. J Thorac Cardiovasc Surg 1967;53: 613–617.

146. Padula RT, Eisenstat TE, Bronstein MU, Camishion RC. Intracardiac air following cardiotomy. J Thorac Cardiovasc Surg 1971;62: 736–742.

147. Muraoka R, Yokata M, Aoshima M, et al. Subclinical changes in brain morphology following cardiac operations as reflected by computed tomographic scans of the brain. J Thorac Cardiovasc Surg 1981;81:346–349.

148. Grulke DC, Marsh NR, Hills BA. Measurement of microbubbles using the Coulter counter. Br J Exp Pathol 1973;54:684–691.

149. Swank RL. The screen filtration pressure method in research: significance and interpretation. Ser Haematol 1968;1:146–167.

150. Sakauye LM, Servas FM, O'Connor KK, Cottonaro C. An in vitro method to quantitate gaseous microemboli production of bubble oxygenators. J Extra-Corpor Technol 1982; 14:445–452.

151. Blauth C, Arnold J, Kohner EM, Taylor KM. Preliminary communication. Retinal microembolism during cardiopulmonary bypass demonstrated by fluorescein angiography. Lancet 1986;2:837–839.

152. Blauth CI, Arnold JV, Schulenberg WE, McCartney AC, Taylor KM. Cerebral microembolism during cardiopulmonary bypass. Retinal microvascualr studies in vivo with fluorescein angiography. J Thorac Cardiovasc Surg 1988; 95:668–676.

153. Austen WA, Howry DH. Ultrasound as a method to detect bubbles or particulate matter in the arterial line during cardiopulmonary bypass. J Surg Res 1965;5:283–284.

154. Richardson PD. Qualitative and quantitative methods for investigating gas emboli in blood. Med Instrument 1985;19:55–58.

155. Hartveit F, Lystad H, Minken A. The pathology of venous air embolism. Br J Exp Pathol 1968; 49:81–86.

156. Rubbisow GJ, Mackay RS. Decompression study and control using ultrasonics. Aerospace Med 1974;45:476–478.

157. Butler BD, Hills BA. The lung as a filter for microbubbles. J Appl Physiol 1979;47: 537–543.

158. Hickling R. Analysis of echoes from a solid elastic sphere in water. J Acoust Soc Am 1962; 34:1582–1592.

159. Furness A, Wright G. Microbubble detection during cardiopulmonary bypass for open-heart surgery. Life Support Syst 1985;3:103–109.

160. Hatteland K, Pedersen T, Semb BKH. Comparison of bubble release from various types of oxygenators. Scand J Thorac Cardiovasc Surg 1985;19:125–130.

161. Wright G, Furness A, Haigh S. Integral pulse frequency modulated ultrasound for the detection and quantification of gas microbubbles in flowing blood. Perfusion 1987;2: 131–138.

162. Ikeda T, Suzuki S, Shinizu K, Okamoto T, Llewellyn ME. M-mode detection of microbubbles following saturation diving; a case report and proposal for a new grading system. Aviat Space Environ Med 1989;60:160–169.

163. Duff HJ, Buda AJ, Kramer R, Strauss HD, David TE, Berman ND. Detection of entrapped intracardiac air with intraoperative echocardiography. Am J Cardiol 1980;46:255–260.

164. Oka Y, Inoue T, Hong Y, Sisto DA, Strom JA, Frater RWM. Retained intracardiac air; transesophageal echocardiography for definition of incidence and monitoring removal by improved techniques. J Thorac Cardiovasc Surg 1986; 91:329–338.

165. Fukuya, Suzuki T, Okamura F, Kishi Y, Vefuji T. Detection of air embolism by transesophageal echocardiography. Anesthesiology 1983;58: 124–129.

166. Zhou JL, Chen XF, Zhang QP. Detection and removal of intracardiac residual air during open heart surgery with CPB under the guidance of echocardiography. Acta Acad Med Wuhan 1984;4:56–60.

167. Padayachee TS, Parsons S, Theobold R, et al. The detection of microemboli in the middle cerebral artery during cardiopulmonary bypass; a transcranial Doppler ultrasound investigation using membrane and bubble oxygenators. Ann Thorac Surg 1987;44:298–302.

168. Spencer MP, Thomas GI, Nicholls SC, Sauvage LR. Detection of middle cerebral artery emboli during carotid endarterectomy using transcranial Doppler ultrasonography. Stroke 1990;21: 415–423.

169. Pugsley W. The use of Doppler ultrasound in the assessment of microemboli during cardiac surgery. Perfusion 1989;4:115–122.

170. Van der Linden J, Casimir-Ahn H. When do cerebral emboli appear during open heart operations? A transcranial Doppler study. Ann Thorac Surg 1991;51:237–241.

171. Butler BD. Gaseous micro emboli: concepts and considerations. J Extra-Corpor Technol 1983;15:148–155.

172. Butler BD, Kurusz M. Gaseous microemboli: a review. Perfusion 1990;5:81–99.

173. Abts LR, Beyer RT, Galletti PM, et al. Computerized discrimination of microemboli in extracorporeal circuits. Am J Surg 1978;135: 535–538.

174. Butler BD. Production of microbubbles for use

175. Horton JW, Wells CH. Resonance ultrasonic measurements of microscopic gas bubbles. Aviat Space Environ Med 1976;47:777–781.

176. Butler BD. Biophysical aspects of gas bubbles in blood. Med Instrument 1985;19:59–62.

177. Wright G, Furness A. Gaseous microembolism—validity of bubble counting systems. Perfusion 1986;1:217–219.

178. Taylor KM. Brain damage during open heart surgery [Editorial]. Thorax 1982;37:873–876.

179. Taylor KM. Assessment of cerebral damage during cardiopulmonary bypass with particular reference to perfusion and microembolic damage. Proc Am Acad Cardiovasc Perfusion 1983; 4:110–113.

180. Branthwaite MA. Detection of neurological damage during open heart surgery Thorax 1973;28:464–472.

181. Branthwaite MA. Prevention of neurological damage during open heart surgery Thorax 1975;30:258–261.

182. Carlson RG, Lande AJ, Landis B, et al. The Lande-Edwards membrane oxygenator during heart surgery; oxygen transfer, microemboli counts and Bender-Gestalt visual motor test scores. J Thorac Cardiovasc Surg 1973;66: 894–905.

183. Savageau JA, Stanton BA, Jenkins CD, Klein MD. Neuropsychological dysfunction following elective cardiac operation. I. Early assessment. J Thorac Cardiovasc Surg 1982;84:585–594.

184. Savageau JA, Stanton BA, Jenkins CD, Frater RWM. Neurophychological dysfunction following elective cardiac operation. II. A six-month reassessment. J Thorac Cardiovasc Surg 1982;84:595–600.

185. Landis B, Baxter J, Patterson RH Jr, Tauber CE. Bender-Gestalt evaluation of brain dysfunction following open-heart surgery. J Pers Assess 1974;38:556–562.

186. Aberg T, Kilgren M. Cerebral protection during open heart surgery. Thorax 1977;32:525–533.

187. Lee WH JR, Miller W, Rowe J, Hariston P, Brady MP. Effects of extracorporeal circulation on personality and cerebration. Ann Thorac Surg 1969;7:562–570.

188. Sotaniemi KA. Cerebral outcome after extracorporeal circulation; comparison between prospective and retrospective evaluations. Arch Neurol 1983;40:75–77.

189. Bojar RM, Najafi H, Delaria GA, Serry C, Godein MD. Neurological complications of coronary revascularization. Ann Thorac Surg 1983;36: 427–432.

190. Coffey CE, Massey W, Roberts KB, Curtis S, Jores

RH, Pryor DB. Natural history of cerebral complications of coronary bypass graft surgery. Neurology 1983;33:1416–1421.

191. Breuer AC, Furlan AJ, Hanson MR, et al. Neurologic complications of open-heart surgery. Cleve Clin Q 1981;48:205–206.

192. Breuer AC, Furlan AJ, Hanson MR, et al. Neurologic complications of coronary artery bypass graft surgery: a prospective analysis of 421 patients. Stroke 1983;14:682–687.

193. Shaw PJ, Bates D, Cartlidge NEF, Heariside D, Julian DG, Shaw DA. Early neurological complications of coronary artery bypass surgery. Br Med J 1985;291:1384–1386.

194. Smith PL. Brain injury and protection. Sem Thorac Cardiovasc Surg 1990;2:381–388.

195. Campbell DE, Raskin SA. Cerebral dysfunction after cardiopulmonary bypass: aetiology, manifestations and interventions. Perfusion 1990;5:251–260.

196. Aberg T, Ronquist G, Tyden H, Ahlund P, Bergstrom K. Release of adenylate kinase into cerebrospinal fluid during open-heart surgery and its relation to postoperative intellectual function. Lancet 1982;1:1139–1142.

197. Lundar T, Stokke O. Total creatine kinase activity in cerebrospinal fluid as an indicator of brain damage during open-heart surgery. Scand J Thorac Cardiovasc Surg 1983;17:157–161.

198. Aberg T, Ronquist G, Tyden H, et al. Adverse effects on the brain in cardiac operations as assessed by biochemical, psychometric, and radiologic methods. J Thorac Cardiovasc Surg 1984;87:99–105.

199. Taylor KM, Devlin BJ, Mittra SM, Gillan JG, Brannan JJ, McKenna JM. Assessment of cerebral damage during open-heart surgery; a new experimental model. Scand J Thorac Cardiovasc Surg 1980;14:197–203.

200. Moody DM, Bell MA, Challa VR, Johnston WE, Prough DS. Brain microemboli during cardiac surgery or aortography. Ann Neurol 1990;28:477–486.

201. Williams IM, Stephens JF, Richardson EP, Stirling G, Robinson P. Brain and retinal microemboli during cardiac surgery [Letter]. Ann Neurol 1991;29:736–737.

202. Moody DM, Bell MA, Challa VR. Reply to letter. Ann Neurol 1992;30:737.

203. Boyle R. New pneumatical experiments about respiration. Phil Trans 1970;62:2011–2049.

204. Nicks R. Air embolism in cardiac surgery: incidence and prophylaxis. Aust N Z J Surg 1969;38:328–332.

205. Durant TM, Oppenheiner MJ, Webster MR, Long J. Arterial air embolism. Am Heart J 1949;38:481–500.

206. Fries CC, Levowitz B, Adler S, Cook AW, Karlson KE, Dennis C. Experimental cerebral gas embolism. Ann Surg 1957;145:461–470.

207. Utley JR, Stephens DB. Air embolus during cardiopulmonary bypass. In: Utley JR, ed. Pathophysiology and techniques of cardiopulmonary bypass. Vol 2. Baltimore: Williams & Wilkins, 1983:78–100.

208. Malette WA, Fitzgerald JB, Eiseman B. Aeroembolus: a protective substance. Surg Forum 1960;11:155–156.

209. Eiseman B, Baxter BJ, Prachuabmoh K. Surface tension reducing substances in the management of coronary air embolism. Ann Surg 1959;149:374–380.

210. Geohegan T, Lam CR. The mechanism of death from intracardiac air and its reversibility. Ann Surg 1953;138:351–359.

211. Mills NL, Ochsner JL. Massive air embolism during cardiopulmonary bypass. J Thorac Cardiovasc Surg 1980;80:708–717.

212. Kurusz M, Conti VR, Arens JF, Brown JP, Faulkner SC, Manning JV Jr. Perfusion accident survey. Proc Am Acad Cardiovasc Perfusion 1986;7:57–65.

213. Chase WH. Anatomical experimental observations on air embolism. Surg Gynecol Obstet 1934;49:569–577.

214. Royston D. Blood cell activation. Sem Thorac Cardiovasc Surg 1990;2:341–357.

215. Wilson TI, Jamieson JMM. Transfusion with stored blood. Br Med J 1938;1:1207.

216. Fantus B. The therapy of the Cook County Hospital. JAMA 1938;111:317–321.

217. Cooksey WB. New apparatus for storing, filtering and administering blood. Am J Surg 1940;49:526–527.

218. Bjork VO. An artificial heart or cardiopulmonary machine. Lancet 1948;2:491–493.

219. Miller BJ, Gibbon JH Jr, Gibbon MH. An improved mechanical heart and lung apparatus. Med Clin North Am 1953;37:1603–1624.

220. Lillehei CW, Warden HE, DeWall RA, Stanley P, Varco RL. Cardiopulmonary bypass in surgical treatment of congenital or acquired cardiac disease. Arch Surg 1957;75:928–945.

221. Kolff WJ, Effler DB, Groves LK, Peereboom G, Moraca PP. Disposable membrane oxygenator (heart-lung machine) and its use in experimental surgery. Cleve Clin Q 1956;23:69–97.

222. Gross RE, Sauvage LR, Pontius RG, Watkins E. Experimental and clinical studies of a syphon-filling disc-oxygenator system for complete cardiopulmonary bypass. Ann Surg 1960;151:285–302.

223. Swank RL, Hirsch H, Breuer M, Hissen W. Effect of glass wool filtration on blood during extracorporeal circulation. Surg Gynecol Obstet 1963;117:547–552.

224. Swank RL, Porter GA. Disappearance of micro-emboli transfused into patients during extracorporeal circulation. Surg Gynecol Obstet 1963;3:192–197.

225. Hill JD, Osborn JJ, Swank RL, Aguilar MJ, Lanerolle P, Gerbode F. Experience using a new Dacron wool filter during extracorporeal circulation. Arch Surg 1970;101:649–652.

226. Osborn JJ Swank RL, Hill JD, Aguilar MJ, Gerbode F. Clinical use of a Dacron wool filter during perfusion for open heart surgery. J Thorac Cardiovasc Surg 1970;60:575–581.

227. Patterson RW Jr, Twichell JB. Disposable filter for microemboli; use in cardiopulmonary bypass and massive transfusion. JAMA 1971; 215:76–80.

228. Page US, Bigelow JC, Carter CR, Swank RL. Emboli (debris) produced by bubble oxygenators; removal by filtration. Ann Thorac Surg 1974;18:164–170.

229. Kurusz M, Schneider B, Brown JP, Conti VR. Filtration during open-heart surgery; devices techniques, opinions, and complications. Proc Am Acad Cardiovasc Perfusion 1983; 4:123–129.

230. MacDonald JL. Is crystalloid cardioplegia a source of particulate debris? Proc Am Acad Cardiovasc Perfusion 1981;2:20–24.

231. Robinson LA, Braimbridge MV, Hearse DJ. The potential hazard of particulate contamination of cardioplegic solutions. J Thorac Cardiovasc Surg 1984;87:48–58.

232. Kurusz M, Speer D, Coughlin TR, Conti VR. Inline filtration of crystalloid cardioplegic solution. Proc Am Acad Cardiovasc Perfusion 1985; 6:123–125.

233. Palanzo DA, O'Neill MJ, Harrison LH Jr. An effective 0.2 micron filter for the administration of crystalloid cardioplegia. Proc Am Acad Cardiovasc Perfusion 1987;8:182–185.

234. Smith PLC. Interventions to reduce cerebral injury during cardiac surgery—introduction and the effect of oxygenator type. Perfusion 1989; 4:139–145.

235. Meloni L, Abbruzzese PA, Cardu G, et al. Detection of microbubbles released by oxygenators during cardiopulmonary bypass by intraoperative transesophageal echocardiography. Am J Cardiol 1990;66:511–514.

236. Sellman M, Ivert T, Stensved P, Hogberg M, Semb BKH. Doppler ultrasound estimation of microbubbles in the arterial line during extracorporeal circulation. Perfusion 1990;5:23–32.

237. Griffin S, Pugsley W, Treasure T. Microembolism during cardiopulmonary bypass: a comparison of bubble oxygenator with arterial line filter and membrane oxygenator alone. Perfusion 1991;6:99–103.

238. Abbruzzese PA, Meloni L, Cardu G, Martelli V, Cherchi A. Role of arterial filters in the prevention of systemic embolization by microbubbles released by oxygenators [Letter]. Am J Cardiol 1991;67:911–912.

239. Treasure T. Interventions to reduce cerebral injury during cardiac surgery—the effect of arterial line filtration. Perfusion 1989;4: 147–162.

240. Verska JJ. Control of heparinization by activated clotting time during bypass with improved postoperative hemostasis. Ann Thorac Surg 1977;24:170–174.

241. Cohen JA. Activated coagulation time method for control of heparin is reliable during cardiopulmonary bypass. Anesthesiology 1984;60: 121–124.

242. Newberg LA, Michenfelder JD. Cerebral protection by isoflurane during hypoxemia or ischemia. Anesthesiology 1983;59:29–35.

243. Newman B, Gelb AW, Lam AM. The effect of isoflurane-induced hypotension on cerebral blood flow and cerebral metabolic rate for oxygen in humans. Anesthesiology 1986;64: 307–310.

244. Woodcock TE, Murkin JM, Farrar JK, et al. Pharmacologic EEG suppression during cardiopulmonary bypass: cerebral heodynamic and metabolic effects of thiopental or isoflurane during hypothermia and normothermia. Anesthesiology 1987;67:218–224.

245. Nussmeir NA, Arlund C, Slogoff S. Neuropsychiatric complications after cardiopulmonary bypass: cerebral protection by a barbiturate. Anesthesiology 1986;64:165–170.

246. Royston D. Interventions to reduce cerebral injury during cardiac surgery—the effect of physical and pharmacological agents. Perfusion 1989;4:153–161.

247. White FN. A comparative physiological approach to hypothermia [Editorial]. J Thorac Cardiovasc Surg 1981;82:821–831.

248. Ream AK, Reitz BA, Silverberg G. Temperature correction of pCO_2 and pH in estimating acid base status: an example of the emperor's new clothes? Anesthesiology 1982;56:41–44.

249. Swan H. The importance of acid-base management for cardiac and cerebral preservation during open heart operations. Surg Gynecol Obstet 1984;158:391–414.

250. Groom RC, Hill AG, Akl BF, Lefrak EA, Kurusz M. Pediatric perfusion survey. Proc Am Acad Cardiovasc Perfusion 1990;11:78–84.

251. Henriksen L, Hjims E, Lindeburgh T. Brain hyperperfusion during cardiac operations. J Thorac Cardiovasc Surg 1983;86:202–208.

252. Stoney WS, Alford WC Jr, Burrus GR, Glassford DM Jr, Thomas CS Jr. Air embolism and other ac-

cidents using pump oxygenators. Ann Thorac
Surg 1980;29:36–40.

253. Kurusz M, Wheeldon DR. Risk containment
during cardiopulmonary bypass. Sem Thorac
Cardiovasc Surg 1990;2:400–409.

254. Bayindir O, Paker T, Akpinar B, et al. Case conference: a 58-year old man had a massive air
embolism during cardiopulmonary bypass. J
Cardiothorac Vasc Anesth 1991;5:627–634.

255. American Society of Extra-Corporeal Technology. Suggested pre-bypass perfusion checklist.
Perfusion Life 1990;7:76–77.

256. Tobler HG, Edwards JE. Frequency and location
of atherosclerotic plaques in the ascending
aorta. J Thorac Cardiovasc Surg 1988;96:
304–306.

257. Wareing TH, Davila-Roman VG, Barzilai B,
Murphy SF, Kouchoukas NT. Management of the
severely atherosclerotic ascending aorta during
cardiac operations. J Thorac Cardiovasc Surg
1992;103:453–462.

258. Golding LAR. Brief communications. New cannulation technique for the severely calcified
ascending aorta. J Thorac Cardiovasc Surg
1985;90:626–627.

259. Culliford AT, Colvin SB, Rohrer K, Baumann
FG, Spencer FC. The atherosclerotic ascending aorta and transverse arch: a new technique to prevent cerebral injury during bypass: experience with 13 patients. Ann
Thorac Surg 1986;41:27–35.

260. Mills NL, Everson CT. Atherosclerosis of the ascending aorta and coronary artery bypass; pathology, clinical correlates, and operative management. J Thorac Cardiovasc Surg 1991;102:
546–553.

261. Brenner WI. A battle plan in the event of massive air embolism during open heart surgery. J
Extra-Corpor Technol 1985;17:133–137.

262. Mills NL, Morris JM. Air embolism associated
with cardiopulmonary bypass. In: Waldhausen
JA, Orringer MB, eds. Complications in cardiothoracic surgery. St. Louis: Mosby Year Book,
1991:60–67.

263. Toscano M, Chiavarelli R, Ruvalo G, et al. Management of massive air embolism during open
heart surgery with retrograde perfusion of the

cerebral vessels and hyperbaric oxygenation.
Thorac Cardiovasc Surg 1983;31:183–184.

264. Hendriks FFA, Bogers AJJC, de la Riviere AB, et
al. The effectiveness of venoarterial perfusion
in treatment of arterial air embolism during
cardiopulmonary bypass. Ann Thorac Surg
1983;36:433–436.

265. Stark J, Hough J. Air in the aorta: treatment by
reversed perfusion. Ann Thorac Surg 1986;
41:337–338.

266. Brown JW, Dierdorf SF, Moorthy S, Halprin M.
Venoarterial cerebral perfusion for treatment of
massive arterial air embolism. Anesth Analg
1987;66:673–674.

267. Meijne NG, Schoemaker G, Bulterijs AB. The
treatment of cerebral gas embolism in a high
pressure chamber; an experimental study. J
Cardiovasc Surg 1963;4:757–763.

268. Takita H, Olszewski W, Schimert G, Lanphier
EH. Hyperbaric treatment of cerebral air embolism as a result of open-heart surgery; report of
a case. J Thorac Cardiovasc Surg 1968;55:
682–685.

269. Peirce II EC. Specific therapy for arterial air
embolism [Editorial]. Ann Thorac Surg 1980;
29:300–303.

270. Murphy BP, Harford FJ, Cramer FS. Cerebral air
embolism resulting from invasive medical procedures; treatment with hyperbaric oxygen.
Ann Surg 1985;201:242–245.

271. Lar LW, Lai LC, Ren LW. Massive arterial embolism during cardiac operation: successful
treatment in a hyperbaric chamber under 3 ATA.
J Thorac Cardiovasc Surg 1990;100:928–930.

272. Armon C, Deschamps C, Adkinson C, Fealey RO,
Orszulak TA. Hyperbaric treatment of cerebral
air embolism sustained during an open-heart
surgical procedure. Mayo Clin Proc 1991;66:
565–571.

273. Diehl JT, Ramos D, Dougherty F, Pandian NG,
Payne DD, Cleveland RJ. Intraoperative, two-dimensional echocardiography-guided removal
of retained intracardiac air. Ann Thorac Surg
1987;647–645.

274. Taylor KM. The cerebral consequences of cardiac surgery [Editorial]. Perfusion 1989;4:
preceding 83.

12

Neuroendocrine and Electrolyte Responses to Cardiopulmonary Bypass

John F. Butterworth IV, Joe R. Utley, and Julie A. Swain

Cardiopulmonary bypass (CPB) produces physiologic alterations not found in other major surgical procedures. During total CPB, the heart and lungs are not perfused and can neither secrete hormones nor make their normal contributions to drug metabolism. Exposure to the pump-oxygenator and its tubing traumatizes cellular blood elements and causes plasma proteins to be adsorbed and removed from the circulation. Hemodilution (from blood-free priming solutions) and the obligatory systemic heparinization alter blood concentrations of electrolytes, hormones, and serum proteins during bypass. Finally, moderate to profound hypothermia is generally used, reducing the rates of biochemical reactions and further perturbing hormonal responses.

There are additional characteristics of extracorporeal perfusion that contribute to the neuroendocrine and electrolyte alterations produced by the technique. Nonpulsatile perfusion may change the distribution of flow both among and within organs. Probably as a consequence, some hormonal alterations during CPB can be lessened or prevented by pulsatile perfusion. Nevertheless, which condition—hypothermia, hemodilution, decreased perfusion of endocrine glands, or denaturation of hormones by foreign surfaces—most contributes to the disproportionate rises in "stress" hormones characteristic of CPB remains unclear. Additionally, some hormone concentrations increase above normal levels following termination of bypass, with the return of pulsatile, warm perfusion to endocrine glands (1). In an attempt to assess the importance of these responses, a recent study has reported that attenuation or elimination of the exaggerated endocrine responses to CPB may improve the outcome (2).

The literature regarding endocrine, metabolic, and electrolyte responses to bypass is difficult to evaluate or summarize because of varying patient populations and markedly varying perfusion techniques, perfusate temperatures, contents of priming solutions, anesthetic and adjuvant drugs, and cardioplegia. Early hormone assays were often not specific for intact, active hormones. This review will emphasize, when possible, the most recent studies in which current anesthesia, cardioplegia, perfusion, and hormone measurement techniques were used. The effects of insulin and glucagon on glucose metabolism, not included here, are reviewed in Chapter 20.

PITUITARY HORMONES

The anterior portion of the pituitary gland plays a central role in the regulation

291

of the adrenal cortex, thyroid, ovaries, and testes. Many studies have shown that pituitary responses and pituitary stimulation of thyroid and adrenal cortical hormone secretion may be depressed during cardiac surgery. Limited data suggesting that anterior pituitary function is better preserved during pulsatile flow than with nonpulsatile flow during CPB will be considered in subsequent sections dealing with adrenal cortical and thyroid hormone responses. Growth hormone responses during bypass will be discussed with glucose metabolism in Chapter 20. Gonadotropin responses during CPB have not been reported.

Six cases of pituitary apoplexy, a rare but potentially devastating complication, have been reported following CPB (3). Most patients had known or occult pituitary tumors. Ischemia, hemorrhage, and edema of the gland appear to be the mechanisms for pituitary failure after bypass. These patients demonstrated varying combinations of ptosis of the eyelids, paralysis of the extraocular muscles, nonreactive and dilated pupils, decreased visual acuity, and visual field defects in addition to the characteristic hormonal deficits. In each case, the diagnosis was confirmed with cranial computed tomography. The conclusion was that hormonal replacement and neurosurgical decompression are indicated, and that the latter may be safely performed early after cardiac surgery (3).

Vasopressin

Vasopressin, or antidiuretic hormone, secreted by the posterior pituitary gland, is a potent regulator of renal water excretion (4). At high concentrations, it may increase peripheral vascular resistance and decrease cardiac contractility and coronary blood flow, which may lead to reduced cardiac output or cardiac ischemia (4, 5). Vasopressin increases renal vascular resistance, reducing renal blood flow, and potentially predisposing to renal failure (5), and stimu-

lates the release of the von Willebrand factor, *perhaps* improving hemostasis during and after cardiac surgery (see Chapter 17). Stimuli provoking vasopressin release include, most importantly, increased plasma osmolality, decreased blood volume or blood pressure, hypoglycemia, angiotensin, stress, and pain (4). General anesthesia and surgery produce moderate increases in vasopressin (6, 7). Despite striking increases in vasopressin concentration, far above those seen during other major surgical procedures, natriuresis and diuresis typically occur during cardiopulmonary bypass (7–11). Elevated concentrations of vasopressin may persist postoperatively (8–13) (Fig. 12.1).

The exaggerated vasopressin response to CPB could be initiated by any number of stimuli. However, rises in plasma osmolality and pain would seem unlikely given the widespread use of hemodilution and of large doses of narcotics to maintain anesthesia during cardiac surgery. On the other hand, volume receptors and left atrial stretch receptors influence vasopressin secretion, and these receptors may be activated by a decrease in circulating blood volume upon initiation of bypass. Left atrial pressure decreases markedly during bypass, especially with left ventricular venting, simulating volume depletion, a potent stimulus for vasopressin release. The transient hypotension normally occurring at the initiation of bypass may lead to increased vasopressin secretion. Pulsatile perfusion *during* CPB attenuates the exaggerated vasopressin response, particularly *after* bypass, but does not eliminate it (9, 11, 12) (Fig. 12.2). Pulsatile perfusion has not produced significant increases in urinary output, despite reduced vasopressor responses (11). Normothermic CPB leads to increases in vasopressin concentrations comparable to those elicited during hypothermic CPB (13).

Certain anesthetic techniques, for example, maintenance of anesthesia with

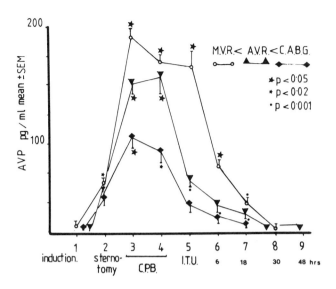

Figure 12.1. Plasma concentration of arginine vasopressin (*AVP*) during non-pulsatile bypass for mitral valve replacement (*MVR, n=8*), aortic valve replacement (*AVR, n=5*), or coronary artery bypass grafting (*CABG, n=5*). Data are presented as means ± SEM. As indicated, measurements were obtained at (1) anesthesia induction, (2) sternotomy, (3) 10 minutes after initiation of CPB, (4) 10 minutes before termination of CPB, (5) upon arrival in the critical care unit, (6) 6 hours after bypass, (7) 18 hours after bypass, (8) 30 hours after bypass, and (9) 48 hours after bypass. All three groups of patients demonstrated significant increases in *AVP* concentrations during bypass. Only at sample 5 did the mitral valve patients demonstrate significantly greater *AVP* concentration than the *CABG* patients. (From Kaul TK, Swaminathan R, Chatrath RR, Watson DA. Vasoactive pressure hormones during and after cardiopulmonary bypass. Int J Artif Organs 1990;13:293–299.)

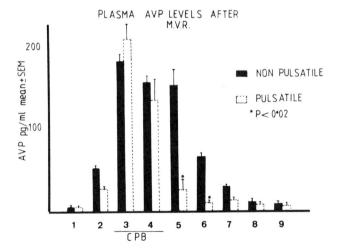

Figure 12.2. Effect of pulsatile (*n=5*) or nonpulsatile (*n=8*) perfusion on arginine vasopressin (*AVP*) responses to mitral valve replacement. See legend for Figure 12.1 for measurement times. Significant differences between the two groups were observed *after* CPB (samples 5 and 6). In this study, pulsatile bypass did not attenuate *AVP* responses during coronary bypass or aortic valve replacement. *MVR*, mitral valve replacement. (From Kaul TK, Swaminathan R, Chatrath RR, Watson DA. Vasoactive pressure hormones during and after cardiopulmonary bypass. Int J Artif Organs 1990; 13:293–299.)

large doses of synthetic opioids (fentanyl or sufentanil) or with regional anesthesia, can attenuate the hormonal responses associated with noncardiac surgical procedures; however, even high-dose narcotic anesthesia will not ablate the release of vasopressin at the onset of CPB (10, 14). Vasopressin concentrations may differ preoperatively between valve replacement and coronary artery bypass patients on the basis of the more frequent occurrence of heart failure in the former group. Unfortunately, multiple studies provide conflicting data as to which patients demonstrate the greater increases in vasopressin concentration during and after CPB (8, 9, 11) (Fig. 12.1). In summary, vasopressin concentrations increase markedly during bypass irrespective of the type of anesthesia or perfusion technique. The influence of exaggerated concentrations of vasopressin during CPB on patient outcome remains unclear.

ADRENAL HORMONES

Catecholamines

The catecholamines epinephrine and norepinephrine are products of the adrenal medulla, and (in the latter case) of sympathetic and central nerve terminals. Marked elevations of plasma epinephrine and norepinephrine concentrations occurring during CPB may underlie many of the hemodynamic sequelae of bypass perfusion, including peripheral vasoconstriction and shifts in intraorgan blood flow (12, 15–18). With hypothermia, the plasma epinephrine concentrations may increase as much as 10-fold over the prebypass concentrations; norepinephrine concentrations typically increase to a lesser extent (4-fold) (2, 12, 16, 18, 19). More profound degrees of hypothermia attenuate these rises (Table 12.1) (18, 19). Peak increases in catecholamines occur when the heart and lungs are excluded from the circulation (17, 18). Neonates, infants, and young children, much like adults, demonstrate marked increases in catecholamine concentrations during bypass (2, 20, 21).

The use of "deeper" anesthesia (large doses of the synthetic narcotic sufentanil or higher concentration of the volatile anesthetic enflurane) significantly reduces the catecholamine response of patients undergoing coronary artery bypass surgery compared to patients less deeply anesthetized (22). Likewise, deep anesthesia with large doses of sufentanil produced a lower catecholamine response to CPB and an improved outcome compared to anesthesia with morphine and halothane in critically ill neonates undergoing correction of congenital heart disease (2) (Fig. 12.3).

The effect of pulsatile perfusion on catecholamine concentrations during CPB remains controversial (12, 23). Although early studies demonstrated no significant attenuation of sympathoadrenal responses to bypass with pulsatile perfusion (12), a more recent study of elective coronary surgery patients has shown a significant reduction in epinephrine and norepinephrine concentrations during bypass when pulsatile perfusion was employed (23) (Fig. 12.4).

Elevated catecholamine concentrations during and after bypass, perhaps unavoidable to some extent, may underlie such hemodynamic alterations of the early postoperative period as hypertension, decreased cardiac output, and depressed renal function. Current studies tend to support the use of anesthetic and perfusion techniques (where feasible) that reduce the catecholamine response to surgery and bypass.

Table 12.1. Blood Pressure and Plasma Catecholamine Concentrations During Extracorporeal Perfusion In Patients Undergoing Aortocoronary Bypass Grafting[a]

Time Sequence	Before Anesthesia	After Intubation	On Bypass	Core Temp (32°C)	Core Temp (28°C)	Core Temp (24°C)
Core Temp (°C)	37.0 ± 0	36.1 ± 0.5[b]	34.7 ± 0.4[b]	31.5 ± 0.5[b]	27.8 ± 0.4[b]	24.1 ± 0.2[b]
MAP (mm Hg)	86 ± 3	76 ± 1	70 ± 4[b]	73 ± 3[b]	60 ± 3[b]	60 ± 2[b]
NE (pg/ml)	287 ± 40	360 ± 94	416 ± 83	662 ± 172[b]	540 ± 153	312 ± 86
EPI (pg/ml)	50 ± 15	29 ± 8	138 ± 47	506 ± 191[b]	267 ± 136	130 ± 62

[a]Catecholamine concentrations were not corrected for hemodilution. Core temp = rectal temperature; MAP, mean arterial pressure; NE, plasma norepinephrine concentration in picograms per milliliter; EPI, plasma epinephrine concentration in picograms per milliliter. Adapted from Reed HL, Chernow B, Lake CR, et al. Alterations in sympathetic nervous system activity with intraoperative hypothermia during coronary artery bypass surgery. Chest 1989;95:616–622.
[b]P<0.05 compared with preinduction values.

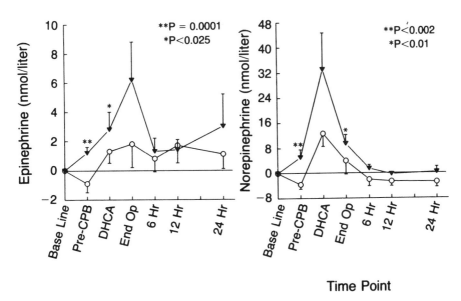

Figure 12.3. Perioperative changes in plasma epinephrine and norepinephrine in neonates undergoing cardiac surgery with either high-dose sufentanil (O; $n=30$) or halothane-morphine (▼; $n=15$) anesthesia. *Pre CPB,* before bypass; *DHCA,* after deep hypothermic circulatory arrest; *End Op,* end of operation; *6 hr, 12 hr, 24 hr* = 6, 12, or 24 hours after operation. P values determined with Mann-Whitney U test. (From Anand KJS, Hickey PR. Halothane-morphine compared with high-dose sufentanil for anesthesia and postoperative analgesia in neonatal cardiac surgery. N Engl J Med 1992;326:1–9.)

Adrenal Cortical Hormones

Secretion of cortisol is one of the central features of the metabolic stress response (14). In classic studies by Hume and colleagues (24), cortisol concentrations rose quickly to a maximum during major surgery (without bypass perfusion), then slowly returned to baseline 24 hours postoperatively. During surgery, adrenocorticotropic hormone administration failed to stimulate any further increase in cortisol concentration, indicating that the adrenal cortical response was maximal (24).

Cardiopulmonary bypass modifies cortisol responses to surgery. Several authors have measured reduced total plasma cortisol concentrations immediately upon initiation of bypass, relative to those measured before bypass (25–28) (Fig. 12.5). During bypass, cortisol concentrations return to values significantly above baseline values (2, 25–29). After CPB, patients ex-

hibit a marked elevation of absolute and hemodilution-corrected total cortisol for more than 48 hours (28–30). Free cortisol remains elevated for 24 hours. Cortisol responses during bypass appear to depend upon perfusion temperature. Taggart and colleagues (19, 31) have shown that the rise in cortisol concentration during CPB can be blunted by perfusion with blood at 20°C more so than at the more usual 28°C. Likewise, cortisol concentrations during bypass were decreased by deeper planes of anesthesia in both adults and children (2, 28, 29) (Figs. 12.5 and 12.6).

Cardiopulmonary bypass modifies adrenocorticotropic hormone responses in surgical patients. In the previously mentioned study by Hume et al. (24), surgical patients not undergoing bypass showed no rise in cortisol with administration of adrenocorticotropic hormone. In contrast, other investigators found that adrenocorticotropic hormone administration produced

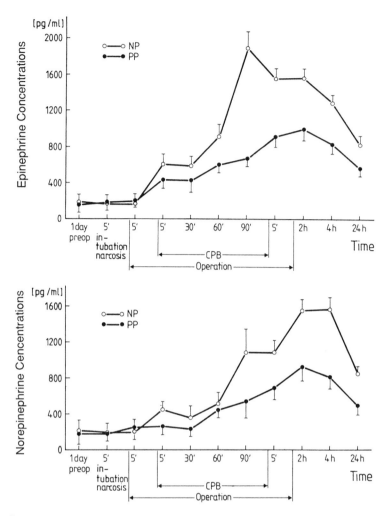

Figure 12.4.   Effects of pulsatile (*PP*) and nonpulsatile (*NP*) perfusion on catecholamine responses in 30 patients undergoing coronary artery bypass grafting. Pulsatile perfusion significantly reduced both epinephrine and norepinephrine concentrations during bypass. Values are means ± standard error. (From Minami K, Körner MM, Vyska K, et al. Effects of pulsatile perfusion on plasma catecholamine levels and hemodynamics during and after cardiac operations with cardiopulmonary bypass. J Thorac Cardiovasc Surg 1990;99:82–91.)

increased cortisol concentrations in patients undergoing extracorporeal perfusion (25). Taylor et al. (32) have measured a progressive fall in adrenocorticotropic hormone concentrations during bypass, with a subsequent increase 1 hour after pulsatile perfusion was restored. More recently, Raff et al. (27) have shown that while neither high-dose fentanyl anesthesia nor dexamethasone 40 mg significantly inhibited the increase in adrenocorticotropic hor-

mone concentration in response to cardiopulmonary bypass, concurrent administration of both fentanyl and dexamethasone significantly reduced the adrenocorticotropic hormone concentration (Fig. 12.5).

Unlike some other hormones, cortisol and adrenocorticotropic hormone responses to cardiopulmonary bypass are not significantly altered by pulsatile perfusion. One study found that total plasma cortisol rose during pulsatile bypass, but fell dramatically in patients undergoing nonpulsatile perfusion (26). This difference has not been confirmed in other studies. However, in another study, patients with and without pulsatile perfusion showed initial increases in cortisol, adrenocorticotropic hormone, and aldosterone, followed by a gradual decline in concentrations of all three hormones during bypass, then a subsequent increase in all three hormones after bypass perfusion (33). After correction for the effect of hemodilution, there was no decrease in calculated free cortisol concentrations and a slight increase in adrenocorticotropic

hormone concentrations, irrespective of whether pulsatile perfusion was used. Similarly, perfusion technique had no effect on urinary sodium excretion or urinary sodium-potassium ratio. In children undergoing bypass with either pulsatile or nonpulsatile perfusion, Pollock and colleagues (34) found that large increases in cortisol and adrenocorticotropic hormone during CPB were not modified by pulsatile perfusion. Both hormones declined toward baseline concentrations over 24 hours after both pulsatile and nonpulsatile CPB techniques (34).

Although there is no evidence for true adrenocortical hypofunction during or after bypass, Dietzman et al. (35) have shown improvement in tissue perfusion and a decrease in peripheral vascular resistance when a large dose of glucocorticoid was given just prior to bypass, possibly by reducing α-adrenergic receptor-mediated vasoconstriction or by improving cell membrane integrity (36).

In summary, current data nearly uniformly demonstrate large increases in cortisol and adrenocorticotropic hormone concentrations during bypass. Although these rises may be attenuated by deeper planes of anesthesia, pulsatile perfusion appears to yield no reduction in these exaggerated hormonal responses. Moreover, it remains unclear whether elevated corticosteroid concentrations during bypass are deleterious.

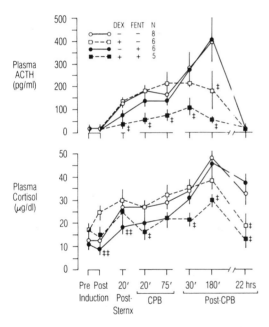

Figure 12.5. The effects of either enflurane or fentanyl (*FENT*) anesthesia with or without dexamethasone (*DEX*) treatment on cortisol and adrenocorticotropic hormone responses to cardiac surgery. All groups demonstrated significant increases in both cortisol and adrenocorticotropic hormone in response to surgery. The combination of fentanyl and dexamethasone significantly attenuated the adrenocorticotropic hormone response to surgery relative to the other three groups. (From Raff H, Norton AJ, Flemma RJ, et al. Inhibition of the adrenocorticotropin response to surgery in humans: Interaction between dexamethasone and fentanyl. J Clin Endocrinol Metab 1987; 65:295–298.)

ATRIAL NATRIURETIC FACTOR

Atrial natriuretic factor includes a family of biologically active peptides first isolated from the cardiac atria (37). These peptides, released in response to atrial distention, increase glomerular filtration, inhibit renin release, reduce aldosterone concentrations in blood, antagonize renal vasoconstrictors such as vasopressin, norepinephrine, angiotensin, and reduce blood pressure. Atrial natriuretic factor regulates

Figure 12.6. Cortisol responses during and after correction of congenital heart lesions (employing deep hypothermia and circulatory arrest (DHCA)) with either halothane-morphine (▼; $n=15$) or sufentanil (O; $n=30$) anesthesia. The sufentanil-based technique significantly attenuated the "stress" response to cardiac surgery. See legend to Figure 12.3 for Time Point guidelines. (Adapted from Anand KJS, Hickey PR. Halothane-morphine compared with high-dose sufentanil for anesthesia and postoperative analgesia in neonatal cardiac surgery. N Engl J Med 1992;326:1–9.)

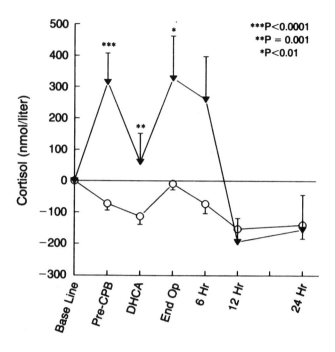

Time Point

vascular volume by increasing sodium excretion and decreasing vasomotor tone (37).

Plasma atrial natriuretic factor has been measured before, during, and following CPB with conflicting results. Patients with cardiac valve lesions, especially those with arrhythmias and congestive failure, may demonstrate elevated preoperative atrial natriuretic factor concentrations (38–41). In one study, coronary surgery patients demonstrated normal preoperative atrial natriuretic factor concentrations; no significant changes were noted during induction of anesthesia or during CPB in these patients (42). After separation from CPB, both arterial and venous concentrations of atrial natriuretic factor increased (42). However, most other studies have found significant alterations of atrial natriuretic factor concentrations during bypass, particularly during aortic cross-clamping, irrespective of the surgical procedure. Curello et al. (40) measured atrial natriuretic factor in patients undergoing either coronary artery bypass or mitral valve replacement for mitral stenosis (Fig. 12.7). Although there was no change in atrial natriuretic factor concentrations during bypass in the former group, patients undergoing mitral valve replacement demonstrated significantly reduced concentrations during CPB. After release of the aortic clamp, atrial natriuretic factor concentrations in both groups of patients rose to values equal to those found preoperatively in the mitral valve patients (40). Nearly identical responses were observed by Northridge et al. (43) in their study of 12 patients undergoing aortocoronary bypass grafting with hypothermic, nonpulsatile perfusion. In another study, arterial concentrations of atrial natriuretic factor decreased significantly after aortic cross-clamping (44). Interestingly, this study also found evidence for atrial natriuretic factor release from brain during bypass. Ashcroft et al. (39) found a significant reduction in atrial natriuretic factor concentrations during bypass, with return to baseline values postoperatively.

The lack of an effect of anesthetic induction was observed in a recent study of 16 patients undergoing aortocoronary bypass grafting or mitral valve replacement (41). In common with other studies, atrial natriuretic factor concentrations decreased significantly during hypothermic extracorporeal perfusion and aortic cross-clamping. Two recent studies comparing atrial natriuretic factor concentrations in systemic and pulmonary venous and arterial blood have identified secretion of atrial natriuretic factor into the left atrium and its clearance by the lungs in adults and children (44, 45). Thus, it is not surprising that systemic arterial and venous atrial natriuretic factor concentrations drop significantly during aortic cross-clamping (40, 43, 44).

Multiple studies of both children and adults have demonstrated a lack of correlation between atrial pressure and atrial natriuretic factor concentration during and after cardiac surgery. This is particularly apparent when patients demonstrated paradoxical increased atrial natriuretic factor concentrations during rewarming, despite reduced atrial pressure at the time (38, 40, 41, 43–46). After CPB, urine flow and sodium excretion increased concurrently with increased atrial natriuretic factor and normal vasopressin concentrations; thus, this latter diuresis is strongly influenced by atrial natriuretic factor (46). The relationship between atrial natriuretic factor concentration and atrial pressure remained abnormal in the first few hours after bypass, but returned to normal after 24 hours (38, 41). Despite no correlation between atrial

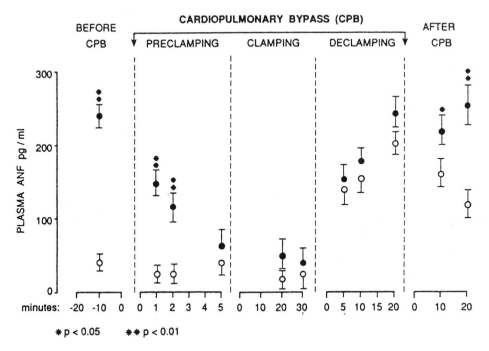

Figure 12.7. Measurements of plasma atrial natriuretic factor (*ANF*) in six patients undergoing aortocoronary bypass (O) and eight patients undergoing mitral valve replacement (●). Data are presented as means ± standard error of the mean. Despite large differences between the groups before aortic clamping, differences were minimal during and early after the ischemic period. (From Curello S, Ceconi C, De Giuli F, et al. Time course of human atrial natriuretic factor release during cardiopulmonary bypass in mitral valve and coronary artery diseased patients. Eur J Cardio-thoracic Surg 1991;5:205–210.)

pressure and atrial natriuretic factor concentrations during bypass, a 30-minute infusion of atrial natriuretic factor (1.67 µg/min) significantly increased urinary output and sodium excretion compared to placebo, indicating a preserved response to the hormone during bypass (47) (Fig. 12.8).

In summary, the preponderance of recent evidence suggests that atrial natriuretic factor concentrations are reduced during cardiopulmonary bypass, especially during hypothermia and aortic cross-clamping. Decreases in hormone concentration are most evident in patients with preoperative elevations in atrial natriuretic factor due to valvular heart disease. Most patients will demonstrate distinctly elevated atrial natriuretic factor concentrations (relative

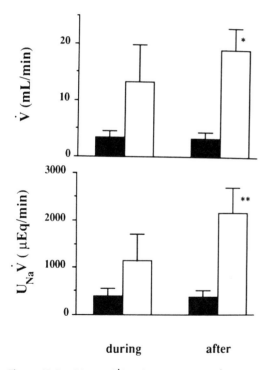

Figure 12.8. Diuresis ($\dot{V}$) and natriuresis ($U_{NA}\dot{V}$) in response to atrial natriuretic factor (*n*=6, open bars) or placebo (*n*=6, solid bars) infused during CPB. Responses were recorded during and following drug administration. (From Hynynen M, Palojoki R, Heinonen J, et al. Renal and vascular effects of atrial natriuretic factor during cardiopulmonary bypass. Chest 1991; 100:1203–1209.)

to those measured during aortic cross-clamping) during rewarming and after discontinuation of bypass. Finally, patients will fail to demonstrate the normal relationship between atrial natriuretic factor concentrations and atrial pressure during bypass and the early postoperative period.

RENIN-ANGIOTENSIN-ALDOSTERONE AXIS

The renin-angiotensin-aldosterone axis plays an important physiologic role in the control of blood pressure, intravascular volume, and electrolyte balance (48). The renal juxtaglomerular apparatus secretes renin in response to sodium depletion, falls in blood volume, or reduced renal perfusion. Conversely, factors that increase blood volume, renal perfusion, and sodium mass inhibit the release of renin. The sympathetic nervous system stimulates renin release in response to pain, emotion, and stress. Renin catalyzes the conversion of angiotensinogen to the decapeptide angiotensin I in the blood. Angiotensin-converting enzyme, present in blood vessel walls (particularly of the pulmonary vasculature), catalyzes the conversion of angiotensin I to angiotensin II (an octapeptide). Conversion of angiotensin I to angiotensin II is nearly complete during a single pass through the lungs. Angiotensin II raises blood pressure by vasoconstriction and stimulation of aldosterone secretion by the adrenal glands. Aldosterone acts on the renal distal tubules to enhance reabsorption of sodium and secretion of potassium and hydrogen ions into tubular fluid.

Serial measurements taken before, during, and after CPB have shown that renin activity increases during and shortly after CPB (49). Similarly, angiotensin II and aldosterone concentrations rise significantly during and shortly after bypass in patients undergoing nonpulsatile perfusion (49–52). Pulsatile perfusion during CPB eliminates the intraoperative and postoperative increases in plasma renin activity, and post-operative increases in both angiotensin II and aldosterone (52, 53) (Fig. 12.9).

Angiotensin-converting enzyme concentrations change markedly during and after cardiac surgery; however, if corrected for hemodilution, minimal response to bypass or hypothermia is observed (18). Absolute and corrected concentrations of angiotensin-converting enzyme are depressed during rewarming, after separation from bypass, and during the first 24 hours of recovery (18, 54, 55). By 24 hours after bypass, angiotensin-converting enzyme concentrations recover to baseline values (54, 55). Secretion of angiotensin-converting enzyme into the vascular compartment by

the lungs remains diminished in the period immediately after CPB (18, 54, 55). These studies suggest that angiotensin-converting enzyme activity is depressed by cardiopulmonary bypass, after the induction of hypothermia but before rewarming (18). Angiotensin-converting enzyme concentration may also serve as a biological marker of thyroid hormone (free T_3) action during and after cardiac surgery (55).

The role of the renin-angiotensin-aldosterone axis in the maintenance of blood pressure and peripheral vascular resistance during and after cardiopulmonary bypass remains controversial. Studies in patients undergoing aortocoronary bypass grafting have shown no effect of prostacyclin infu-

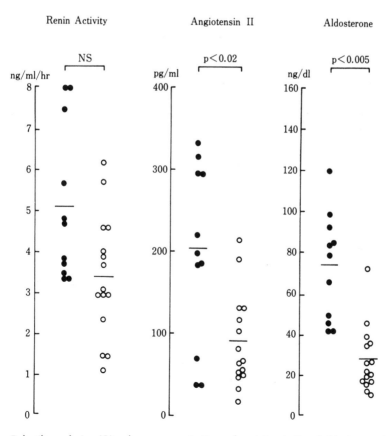

Figure 12.9.   Pulsatile perfusion (O) reduces concentrations of angiotensin II and aldosterone during CPB relative to nonpulsatile perfusion (●). (From Nagaoka H, Innami R, Arai H. Effect of pulsatile cardiopulmonary bypass on the renin-angiotensin-aldosterone system following open heart surgery. Jpn J Surg 1988;18:390–396.)

sion on blood concentrations of vasopressin or catecholamines (56). However, patients receiving prostacyclin demonstrated a significantly greater increase in angiotensin II concentrations during bypass than did patients not receiving prostacyclin (57). Preoperative administration of an angiotensin-converting enzyme inhibitor did not impair blood pressure regulation during anesthesia and CPB (57).

Postoperative hypertension occurs in up to 80% of patients following coronary bypass grafting. Two studies have documented that, despite increased concentrations of renin, angiotensin II, and aldosterone during bypass, levels of these hormones did not correlate with intraoperative or postoperative hypertension (50, 51). Hypertension seemed more closely correlated with plasma epinephrine and norepinephrine levels than with the renin-angiotensin-aldosterone axis (50). In another study, postoperative hypertension and the need for vasodilators was associated with high vasopressin concentrations, but not with angiotensin II concentrations (56). A fourth study found that postoperative hypertension could not be related to elevated renin levels, and that it could not be treated effectively by blockade of angiotensin II with saralasin (58). Moreover, preoperative administration of angiotensin-converting enzyme inhibitors failed to prevent hypertension following coronary artery bypass grafting (57). Thus, the preponderance of evidence would suggest that both intraoperative and postoperative hypertension is, at best, only loosely related to abnormal concentrations of renin, angiotensin II, or aldosterone.

THYROID

A variety of acute illnesses lead to alterations of peripheral thyroid hormone metabolism. Characteristically, serum concentrations of 3,5,3'-triiodothyronine (T_3, the active thyroid hormone species) are reduced, total thyroxine (T_4) is normal (indicating impaired peripheral conversion of T_4 to T_3) or reduced, free T_4 is reduced, and thyrotropin (thyroid-stimulating hormone or TSH) concentrations are normal, producing the so-called "sick euthyroid syndrome" (59). Although multiple studies have documented the presence of this syndrome during and after CPB, a recent study questions whether true depressing of T_3 occurs in adults during bypass (60, 61). The concentration of thyroid hormone is especially important in cardiac surgery since thyroid hormone may serve to regulate the number and agonist sensitivity of β-adrenergic receptors (59, 60).

Figure 12.10. Response of free T_3 concentration (pg/dl) to cardiovascular surgery in 14 patients. Blood samples were obtained before bypass (*Pre*), after heparin administration (*Hep*), after 5 minutes of bypass (CPB), at the nadir of cooling during CPB (*Hypo*), before termination of CPB (*warm*), and 2, 8, and 24 hours postoperatively. The T_3 declined during CPB, and then declined further during the first 24 hours after operation. (From Holland FW II, Brown PS Jr, Weintraub BD, Clark RE. Cardiopulmonary bypass and thyroid function: A "euthyroid sick syndrome." Ann Thorac Surg 1991;52:46–50.)

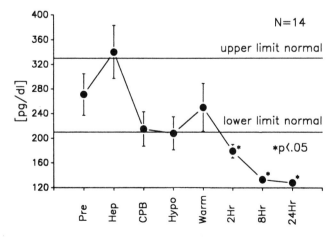

Prior to cardiopulmonary bypass, administration of heparin leads to sharp increases in free T_3 and free T_4, as heparin or nonesterified fatty acids (released by heparin) displace hormones from binding proteins (62–65). Total T_3 concentrations drop precipitously with initiation of bypass and remain depressed 24 hours after surgery (17, 18, 60, 66) (Fig. 12.10). The T_3 values corrected for hemodilution (using albumin concentration) are not altered by the initiation of bypass or by the initiation of hypothermic perfusion (18). In some studies, the measured free fraction of T_3 increases after the onset of bypass and hypothermia (18, 62). These alterations in T_3 and T_4 during bypass are independent of thyrotropin-stimulating hormone secretion since adjustments in T_3 and T_4 concentrations normally are delayed by 2 to 4 hours after a change in thyrotropin concentration (68). Absolute thyrotropin and total T_3 con-

centrations gradually return to normal after surgery.

Thyroid hormone concentrations during and after CPB in infants appear to be controlled by the extent of hemodilution and by the thyrotropin concentrations. Unlike the case for adults, there may be abnormal postoperative control of thyroid hormone concentrations in the hypothalamus or pituitary gland (69). Moreover, transcutaneous iodine absorption from povidone-iodine skin preparation may cause thyroid suppression in infants (70).

The central regulating mechanism for thyroid hormone is the thyrotropin-releasing hormone-thyrotropin axis. Thyrotropin concentrations are unchanged during normothermic bypass (62); however, thyrotropin declines upon initiation of hypothermic bypass, then steadily rises during perfusion (66) (Fig. 12.11). During the 1st postoperative day, thyrotropin concentra-

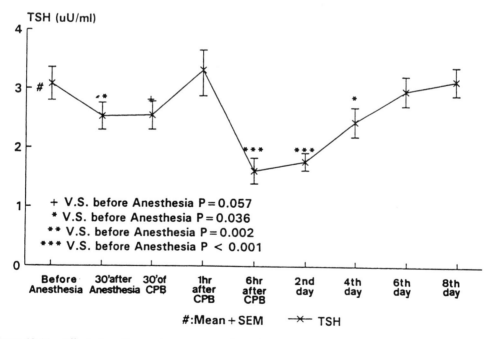

Figure 12.11. Effect of cardiovascular surgery on thyroid-stimulating hormone (TSH) concentration in 44 patients. The TSH reached its nadir 6 hours after bypass and remained low through the 4th postoperative day. V.S., versus. (From Chu SH, Huang TS, Hsu RB, et al. Thyroid hormone changes after cardiovascular surgery and clinical implications. Ann Thorac Surg 1991;52:791–796.)

tions decline below baseline values (55, 66, 71). During and shortly after CPB, the normal increase in thyrotropin concentration in responses to exogenous administration of thyrotropin-releasing hormone is blunted (71–73) (Fig. 12.12). Because of the reduced total T_3 concentrations during bypass, an increased sensitivity to thyrotropin-releasing hormone might have been anticipated. The cause of this pituitary hypofunction remains unknown; however, rises in endogenous dopamine (74) or somatostatin (75) concentrations, or nonpulsatile blood flow to the anterior pituitary gland are possible etiologies (72). Pulsatile flow during bypass reverses the abnormal pituitary response to thyrotropin-releasing hormone, and sustains normal responses of thyrotropin to exogenous thyrotropin-releasing hormone administration (73). Patients making an uncomplicated recovery from surgery demonstrated a sharp increase in thyrotropin, total T_3, and total T_4 on day 4 after surgery; patients with complications after surgery did not demonstrate such pronounced increases in these hormone concentrations (67).

These studies of thyroid function during and after CPB may have important clinical implications. The T_3 serves to regulate cardiac rate, contractility, and oxygen consumption. Moreover, thyroid hormone regulates the number and responses of β-adrenergic receptors on myocardial cell membranes (60, 76). Thus, cyclic adenosine monophosphate (AMP) production in response to β-adrenergic receptor agonists is markedly reduced in hypothyroid cardiac, adipose, and hepatic tissue. Cyclic AMP regulates intracellular calcium transients and myocardial contractility (76, 77). In some patients, poor myocardial contractility after bypass may be due to reduced T_3 concentrations. Experimental studies have shown improved myocardial contractility in pigs and baboons that received T_3 following bypass (78, 79). A beneficial response to exogenous T_3 has been found in patients undergoing elective aortocoronary bypass grafting with varying degrees of left ventricular dysfunction. Patients with preoperative left ventricular ejection fraction >40% receiving T_3 demonstrated significantly greater blood concentrations of T_3 and significantly greater cardiac outputs after CPB than control patients (Fig. 12.13). Patients with preoperative left ventricular ejection fraction <40% receiving T_3 required much less dobutamine and furosemide than did

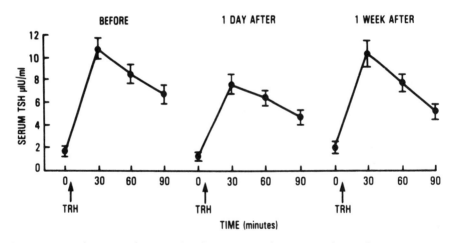

Figure 12.12. Serum thyrotropin hormone (TSH) response to thyrotropin-releasing hormone (*TRH*) in euthyroid subjects before, 1 day after, and 1 week after coronary bypass surgery with hypothermic nonpulsatile perfusion. (From Zaloga GP, Chernow B, Smallridge RC, et al. A longitudinal evaluation of thyroid function in critically ill surgical patients. Ann Surg 1985;201:456–464.)

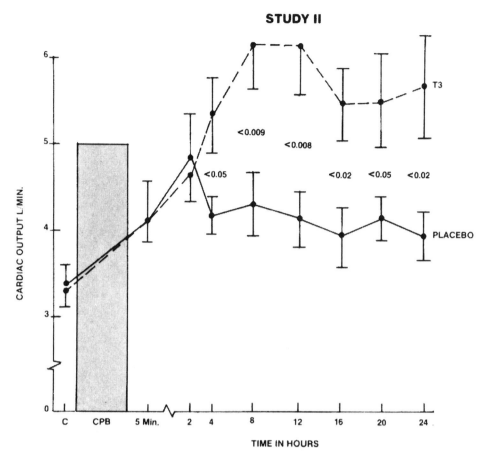

STUDY II

Figure 12.13. Effect of intravenous T_3 or placebo on cardiac output in patients with good preoperative left ventricular function undergoing coronary artery bypass grafting. Patients receiving intravenous T_3 (broken line) had significantly increased cardiac output relative to controls (solid line). (From Novitzky D, Cooper DKC, Barton CI, et al. Triiodothyronine as an inotropic agent after open heart surgery. J Thorac Cardiovasc Surg 1989;98:972–978.)

control patients (80). These studies suggest that intravenous T_3 might be of benefit to many cardiac surgery patients.

EICOSANOIDS

The lungs are actively involved in the metabolism of vasoactive substances, including eicosanoids; thus, the separation of the lungs from the circulation during extracorporeal perfusion may significantly alter the plasma concentrations and kinetics of prostaglandins and thromboxanes (81). Normally, prostaglandin H_2 is converted rapidly into prostaglandins E_2 and F_2 in the lungs. While prostacyclin and thromboxane

have been considered the main products of pulmonary arachidonic acid metabolism, the predominant prostaglandins formed in the bronchial tree and in the pulmonary vasculature are prostaglandin E_2 and prostacyclin (81, 82).

In addition to synthesis and release of prostaglandins, the lungs are a major site for metabolism of prostaglandins of the E and F types (81). These substances are nearly completely cleared during a single passage through the pulmonary circulation. Prostacyclin, a potent inhibitor of platelet aggregation, can disaggregate platelets and act as a potent vasodilator (81). Prostaglandin E_2 also serves as a vasodilator. Conversely, thromboxane A_2 potently stimulates platelet aggression and vasoconstriction.

Concentrations of 6-keto-prostaglandin F_{1a} (the stable metabolite of prostacyclin) rose significantly following aortic and atrial cannulation, and remained elevated during CPB in children and adults (82–88). The 6-keto-prostaglandin F_{1a} concentrations rose at the beginning of bypass, continued rising upon aortic clamping, but decreased progressively after termination of bypass and reperfusion of the lungs. There were no significant differences between patients undergoing cardiac surgery with or without bypass (85).

Thromboxane B_2 (the stable metabolite of thromboxane A_2) concentrations rose and reached peak arterial levels just before termination of bypass, a markedly different pattern from that seen in patients undergoing cardiac surgery without bypass (85) (Fig. 12.14). After completion of the cardiac repair and discontinuation of CPB, concentrations of prostacyclin and thromboxane metabolites decreased progressively (82–85, 87, 88). Compared with

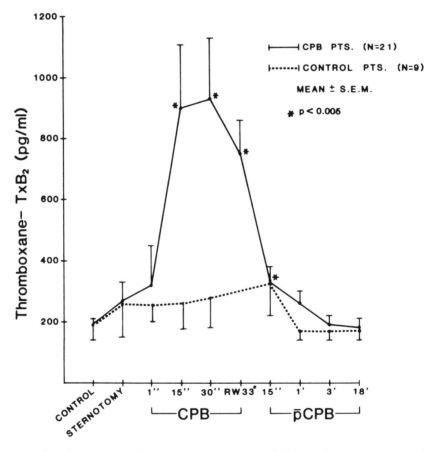

Figure 12.14. Thromboxane metabolite (*TxB₂*) concentrations in children undergoing correction of congenital heart defects either with (*n*=21) or without (*n*=9) cardiopulmonary bypass (*CPB*). Blood samples were obtained at baseline (*control*); sternotomy; 1 (*1″*), 5 (*15″*), and 30 (*30″*) minutes after initiation of CPB; during rewarming at 33°C (*RW33°*); and 15 minutes (*15″*), 1 hour (*1′*), 3 hours (*3′*), and 18 hours (*18′*) after bypass (*p̄CPB*). Patients undergoing cardiac repair without CPB had their "CPB" samples obtained 1, 15, and 30 minutes after the repair was begun. The *CPB* group demonstrated significantly elevated concentration compared to the nonbypass (control) group. (From Greeley WJ, Bushman GA, Kong DL, et al. Effects of cardiopulmonary bypass on eicosanoid metabolism during pediatric cardiovascular surgery. J Thorac Cardiovasc Surg 1988;95:842–849.)

adults, children have greater and more sustained increases in thromboxane metabolites (85, 87). Infants undergoing extracorporeal membrane oxygenation, a form of long-term CPB, demonstrate increased prostacyclin metabolite concentrations after initiation of therapy (89). With continued use of extracorporeal membrane oxygenation, prostacyclin metabolite concentrations slowly fell. Prostacyclin metabolite concentrations rose again as the patients were weaned from extracorporeal membrane oxygenation; concentrations remained elevated for about a day thereafter (89).

The surge in prostacyclin concentrations (as reflected by metabolites) at the onset of bypass appears to inhibit platelet aggregation. Although increased concentrations of prostacyclin and thromboxane during bypass may have important effects on systemic vascular resistance and vasoreac-

tivity, studies have not shown a consistent effect (82, 85). Administration of the protease inhibitor aprotinin reduced the surge in thromboxane B_2 associated with bypass, but had no effect on 6-keto-prostaglandin $F_{1\alpha}$ concentrations (86). These aprotinin-induced changes in prostaglandin metabolism were associated with better preserved platelet function, potentially significant in preventing postoperative hemorrhage.

A rapid increase in prostaglandin E_2 concentrations at the onset of CPB has been confirmed in several studies (82, 84) (Fig. 12.15). Minimal differences between arterial and venous concentrations confirm limited prostaglandin E_2 metabolism in the lungs during bypass (84). Prostaglandin E_2 concentrations fall promptly after termination of bypass and reinstitution of pulmonary perfusion. Aspiration of shed pulmonary venous blood from open pleural cavities reduces mean arterial pressure dur-

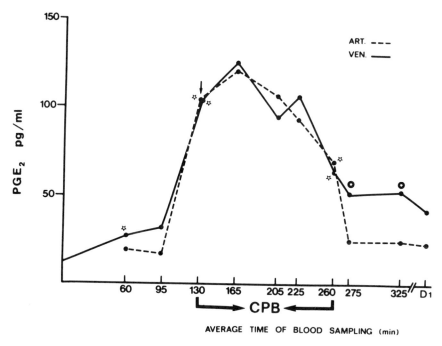

Figure 12.15. Prostaglandin E_2 (*PGE$_2$*) concentration in arterial and venous plasma samples before, during, and after cardiopulmonary bypass (*CPB*) in seven patients having coronary bypass. (From Faymonville M-E, Deby-Dupont G, Larbuisson R, et al. Prostaglandin E_2, prostacyclin, and thromboxane changes during nonpulsatile cardiopulmonary bypass in humans. J Thorac Cardiovasc Surg 1986;91:858–866.)

ing CPB and increases systemic concentrations of prostaglandin E_2 and 6-keto-prostaglandin F_{1a}, probably as a consequence of the high concentrations of prostaglandin E_2 and 6-keto-prostaglandin F_{1a} measured in shed pulmonary venous blood (90).

In summary, the role of prostanoids and thromboxanes in producing desired or adverse effects during bypass remains controversial. Perhaps most significant in maintaining this controversy is the usual practice of measuring agent concentrations in systemic blood, which ignores the importance of prostanoids and thromboxanes in local regulation of blood flow within organs.

HISTAMINE

Elevated blood concentrations of histamine may produce vasodilation and hypotension. Numerous drugs currently and formerly used during cardiac surgery induce histamine release, including narcotics (especially morphine and meperidine), muscle relaxants (especially tubocurarine), antibiotics, heparin, and protamine (91). Current anesthetic practice favors the use of agents that have negligible likelihood of inducing histamine release. (See Chapter 10 on immune responses during cardiopulmonary bypass.) In adults, plasma histamine concentrations rise at the time of systemic heparinization and remain elevated throughout the period of CPB (92). Blood products are often added to priming solutions used for pediatric CPB to limit the hemodilution (93, 94). Marath and coworkers (93) have measured pathologically elevated histamine concentrations in over 70% of blood-product-containing priming solutions *prior* to their use during pediatric bypass. Indeed, massively elevated histamine concentrations were present in over 20% of (blood-product-containing) priming solutions, prompting speculation by Marath and coworkers that the delivery of this massive histamine load to patients must have some pathologic effect. During CPB in children, particularly striking increases in histamine

concentrations occur at the time of release of the aortic cross-clamp, probably as a consequence of reperfusion of the lungs (95). Infusion of prostacyclin (to improve platelet function or systemic perfusion) during bypass diminishes the concentrations of histamine (92). Histamine concentrations in patients with the cold urticaria syndrome, a relatively rare disorder, are increased nearly 10-fold during hypothermic bypass (96). In summary, histamine may be of greatest concern when blood-containing priming solutions are used (in children) or when histamine-releasing agents must be administered. There will also be the occasional patient with a rare metabolic abnormality in which histamine concentrations will be markedly abnormal during bypass.

CALCIUM

The availability of calcium ions in the sarcoplasmic reticulum determines the extent of calcium flux during depolarizations, which influences the inotropic state of the heart (97) through calcium effects on enzyme activation, membrane permeability, and excitation-contraction coupling. Calcium ions are also necessary for normal electrical conduction and rhythm of the heart. Calcium is contained by blood in three forms: ionized ($\sim$50%), protein bound ($\sim$40%), and chelated ($\sim$10%). The free ionized fraction is the physiologically active component. In critical illnesses, the distribution of calcium among these forms can be altered; thus, measurements of total calcium may be misleading (98). The blood calcium concentration is maintained within the normal range by parathormone and 1,25-dihidroxycholicalciferol (calcitriol or vitamin D) actions on bone and kidney. Parathormone secretion is stimulated by ionized hypocalcemia and (to some extent) by mild hypomagnesemia. Parathormone secretion is suppressed by rising or normal (unchanging) ionized calcium concentrations and severe hypomagnesemia.

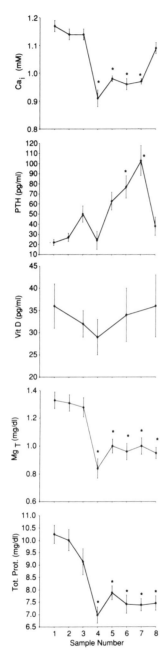

Changes in the total and ionized calcium fractions during and after CPB are influenced by the inclusion of exogenous calcium salts or blood products in the pump priming solution, and by the frequent administration of calcium salts at discontinuation of extracorporeal perfusion. Clinical studies uniformly demonstrate a fall in ionized calcium concentration upon initiation of CPB (99–112). When blood-free priming solutions are used during bypass, both total and ionized calcium decrease as a consequence of hemodilution, and (for ionized calcium) the frequent use of albumin (which chelates calcium) in priming solutions (111). Total calcium, total magnesium, ultrafilterable magnesium (an indicator for ionized magnesium, for which selective electrode monitoring is not currently available), and total protein likewise declined upon initiation of bypass (111) (Fig. 12.16).

Parathormone concentrations rise appropriately during cardiac surgery in response to declines in ionized calcium concentration. Importantly, parathormone concentrations also decline during cardiac surgery in response to rising ionized calcium concentrations. As has been demonstrated in other circumstances, the relationship between parathormone and ionized calcium concentrations demonstrates hysteresis during cardiac surgery (111–113). In brief, the change in ionized calcium concentration as well as the absolute concentration regulates parathormone secretion. When ionized calcium concentration is rising in response to increased concentrations of parathormore, secretion of parathormore will *decrease* at ionized calcium concentra-

Figure 12.16. Response of the calcium-magnesium-parathormone-calcitriol axis to coronary artery bypass grafting. *Ca*, ionized calcium; *PTH*, parathormone; *Vit D*, calcitriol; *Mg*_T, total magnesium; *Tot. Prot.*, total protein. Measurements were performed (1) before anesthesia, (2) after induction of anesthesia, (3) after heparin administration, (4) 2 minutes after initiation of bypass, (5) 5 minutes after aortic cross-clamping, (6) early during rewarming, (7) shortly before separation from bypass, and (8) during sternal closure after by-

pass. Data are presented as means ± SEM. Asterisks denote significant deviation from control values (by Scheffe's test). (From Robertie PG, Butterworth JF IV, Royster RL, et al. Normal parathyroid hormone responses to hypocalcemia during cardiopulmonary bypass. Anesthesiology 1991;75:43–48.)

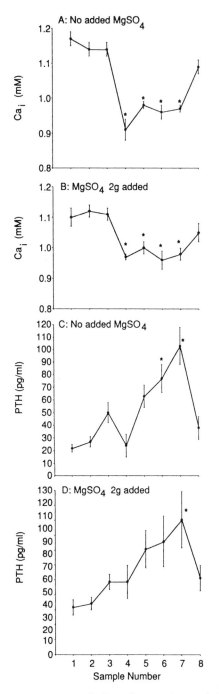

tions below "normal" that would elicit *increased* parathormone secretion if approached from a higher rather than a lower initial ionized calcium concentration.

Studies of parathormone concentrations using assays sensitive to the intact hormone have found falls at the beginning of bypass, increases to maximal concentrations during hypothermia, with a slow return toward normal values as ionized calcium concentrations approach normal values during rewarming (111, 112). It should be noted that some early studies, employing assays sensitive to both parathormone and its biologically inactive fragments, have reported falls in parathormone concentration upon initiation of bypass without appropriate increases in response to hypocalcemia thereafter (102).

Studies in adults have demonstrated that reduced magnesium concentrations do not influence the response of the calcium-parathyroid-vitamin D axis during CPB (111). Calcium and parathormone concentrations and responses were identical in patients receiving magnesium salt supplementation during bypass and in control patients in whom magnesium concentrations were permitted to fall without correction (Fig. 12.17). Calcitriol (vitamin D) is a fat-soluble vitamin; thus, it is not surprising that calcitriol concentrations are minimally altered by hemodilution and CPB and that this vitamin plays a minimal role in the alterations in calcium concentration seen during cardiac surgery (111).

Infants and young children are managed differently than adults undergoing CPB. Priming solution volumes represent a

Figure 12.17. Limited effect of magnesium repletion on parathormone (*PTH*, panels A and B) and ionized calcium (*Ca$_i$*, panels C and D) responses during bypass. Patients receiving magnesium (panels B and D) received 1 g MgSO$_4$ immediately before bypass and an additional 1 g MgSO$_4$ 30 minutes later. Total magnesium concentrations in patients receiving magne-

sium remained within the normal range during bypass. Data are presented as means ± SEM. There were no statistically significant differences between the two groups. Asterisks denote significant deviation from control values. (From Robertie PG, Butterworth JF IV, Royster RL, et al. Normal parathyroid hormone responses to hypocalcemia during cardiopulmonary bypass. Anesthesiology 1991;75:43–48.)

much greater percentage of the patient's blood volume; thus, blood products are usually included in the priming solutions for small children to avoid excessive degrees of hemodilution (74, 94). However, the responses of the calcium-parathyroid-calcitriol axis in 12 infants and 6 young children were similar to those of adults (112). Despite demonstrating much greater declines in ionized calcium concentration upon initiation of bypass than children or adults (Fig. 12.18), infants' and young children's parathyroid hormone concentrations

peaked at similar concentrations (111, 112). Moreover, parathyroid gland "sensing" of increasing and decreasing ionized calcium concentrations was also similar; infants and young children demonstrated hysteresis in a similar manner to adults (111–113). Infants and young children differed from adults in that ionized calcium concentrations did not fully recover to near-normal values before termination of CPB. This was likely a consequence of the considerably shorter duration of bypass in children compared to adults, although im-

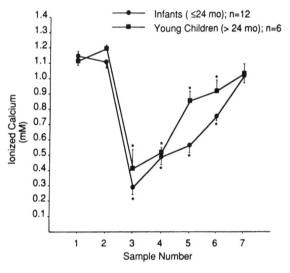

Figure 12.18. Responses of ionized calcium and parathormone in 12 infants (<24 months) and 6 young children (>24 months) undergoing correction of congenital heart defect. Data are presented as means ± SEM. There were no statistically significant differences between the two groups. Asterisks denote significant deviation from control values. (From Robertie PG, Butterworth JF IV, Prielipp RC, et al. Parathyroid hormone responses to marked hypocalcemia in infants and young children undergoing repair of congenital heart disease. J Am Coll Cardiol 1992;20:672–677.)

paired bone reabsorption in response to parathyroid hormone could not be ruled out. Most children, but almost no adults, required calcium salt supplementation to restore ionized calcium concentrations to normal at the time of separation from CPB (111, 112).

There are important clinical implications from these studies. Unlike the case for many other hormones, parathormone secretion is minimally altered by hypothermic CPB (111, 112). Ionized hypocalcemia, even to severe degrees, produced no obvious adverse effects during these studies (107, 111, 112). Moreover, during CPB, hypercalcemia may lead to accelerated adenosine triphosphate breakdown (a calcium-dependent process) and unnecessarily increase contractility and myocardial oxygen consumption (114). Systemic hypocalcemia coupled with anoxic cardiac arrest and calcium-free cardioplegia may lead to a beneficial reduction in adenosine triphosphate breakdown (119). Rewarming and reperfusion after aortic clamp removal, essential for resynthesis of high-energy phosphates, should be accompanied by minimal myocardial oxygen consumption. Exogenous calcium during this time might unnecessarily increase the inotropic state of the myocardium, leading to depletion of adenosine triphosphate.

The empirical use of calcium salts at the end of CPB supposedly for inotropic support is almost a tradition in cardiac surgery, despite limited evidence of clinical efficacy in controlled trials, a possible etiologic role in perioperative pancreatitis, and the usual absence of serious hypocalcemia in adult patients (111, 115–121). Calcium salts may also reduce the efficacy of β-adrenergic receptor agonists (116, 119). Calcium salts should be administered only when bypass is about to be terminated, ionized calcium concentration is reduced, and increased inotropy and blood pressure are needed for resumption of full myocardial activity.

MAGNESIUM

Magnesium, the second most abundant intracellular cation (after potassium), is a key cofactor regulating transmembrane electrolyte gradients, energy metabolism, synthesis of second messengers (e.g., adenylyl cyclase), ion channels, and hormone secretion and action (e.g., insulin and parathormone) (122). Much like calcium, magnesium exists in three fractions in the blood: ionized ($\sim$55%), chelated ($\sim$15%), and protein-bound ($\sim$30%). Selective electrodes are not yet commercially available for measurement of ionized magnesium concentrations; however, the ultrafilterable fraction includes only the ionized and chelated fractions, and because of the limited contribution from the chelated ions, closely approximates the ionized fraction (123). Because there is a dynamic equilibrium between intracellular and extracellular magnesium, the magnesium concentration in blood may be normal in the presence of magnesium depletion.

Cardiac surgery patients have been found to be at high risk for hypomagnesemia, which may be because of insufficient dietary intake, increased excretion secondary to diuretics, diabetes, aminoglycoside antibiotics, cardiac glycosides, ethanol abuse, pancreatic disease, or administration of citrated blood products or albumin (122, 124–126). Blood magnesium concentration decreases during and after CPB in adults and children (111, 112, 124–128) (Fig. 12.16). During bypass, total magnesium concentrations decline in concert with the ultrafilterable fraction as a consequence of chelation by albumin and other blood products and hemodilution (111). Urinary excretion of magnesium during bypass is not increased (125). Magnesium concentrations, unlike calcium concentrations, once reduced during CPB, return to normal only slowly in the absence of active treatment, because of the lack of a specific hormonal regulatory system (111, 112).

Although magnesium depletion may be manifest in the postbypass period as hyperreflexia, muscular twitching, or digitalis toxicity, the most common side effect of hypomagnesemia is cardiac arrhythmias (122, 126). Calcium and magnesium are synergistic; magnesium depletion can cause hypocalcemia refractory to exogenous calcium replacement until magnesium is administered (98). Infusion of magnesium salts prevents hypomagnesemia and its complications during and after CPB (111, 128). Side effects of magnesium salt administration are minimal. Awake patients may report a feeling of "flushing" or of "warmth." Hemodynamic responses may include a slight reduction in blood pressure (without a reduction in cardiac output) and, secondarily, a reduction in vasoconstriction from exogenous catecholamines, such as epinephrine (129). In summary, magnesium salt administration may represent a safe and appropriate measure for patients at high risk for hypomagnesemia and arrhythmias after CPB.

POTASSIUM

Maintenance of blood potassium concentration within normal values is of great importance in cardiac surgical patients. Large swings in potassium concentration may occur during cardiac surgery due to defective regulation of blood glucose concentration by insulin during and after CPB (see Chapter 20). During bypass, potassium fluxes are also influenced by anesthetic drugs, priming solutions, renal function, carbon dioxide tension, arterial pH, hypothermia, and mineralocorticoids.

Potassium depletion may be present in as many as 40% of patients having valve surgery (130, 131). Hypokalemia, the most frequent abnormality of potassium concentration observed after CPB, is more common and severe during valve operations than with coronary artery bypass grafting (132–135). Before the era of potassium cardioplegia, hyperkalemia was uncommon except in patients with diabetes or renal failure. Currently, brief episodes of hyperkalemia may be more common, especially immediately after the release of the aortic cross-clamp and with continuous warm cardioplegia.

Potassium loss during CPB is related to urine flow, implying that urine potassium concentration must remain nearly constant (136) (Fig. 12.19). Triamterene may diminish the kaliuresis (136). Bumetanide produces less kaliuresis during cardiopulmonary bypass than furosemide for a similar diuretic response (137). Increased urinary potassium loss is characteristic of the postbypass period (138).

Priming with whole blood may cause greater decreases in serum potassium than blood-free priming solutions (139). Maintenance of normocalcemia during CPB may better maintain potassium concentration than the more usual hypocalcemia (140, 141). The ionic constituents of blood-free priming solutions (other than calcium and potassium ions) have little effect on potassium concentration. Careful studies of potassium intake and output, as red blood cell potassium, rates of hemolysis, and serum hemoglobin have shown that much of the fall in serum potassium concentration is not accounted for by dilution or excretion. Likewise, repeated studies have failed to identify the organ into which blood potassium is lost (142).

In the absence of potassium cardioplegia, the fall in potassium concentration during clinical CPB appears to be proportional to the fall in body temperature (143). Conversely, potassium concentration rises with warming (144). Blood glucose rises and insulin falls during bypass (see Chapter 20). Insulin favors intracellular transport of glucose and potassium, and glycogen formation.

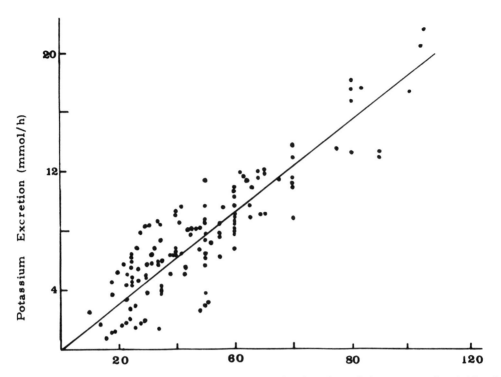

Figure 12.19.   The rate of potassium excretion (ordinate) is related in a linear fashion to urine flow (ml/hr, abscissa) during CPB. (From Patrick J, Sivpragasam S. The prediction of postoperative potassium excretion after cardiopulmonary bypass. J Thorac Cardiovasc Surg 1977;73:559–562.)

Increased concentrations of cortisol, aldosterone, and catecholamines during CPB may contribute to hypokalemia. Cortisol and aldosterone increase the urinary excretion of potassium. Catecholamines increase potassium uptake by skeletal muscle and decrease serum potassium (145). β-Adrenergic blockade with propranolol inhibits the uptake of potassium by skeletal muscle, but does not inhibit the hepatic release of potassium by β-adrenergic stimulation and may contribute to hyperkalemia (146). Hypokalemia during CPB may be lessened if albumin is added to the priming solution, because the negatively charged albumin molecules help maintain adequate blood concentrations of positively charged potassium (147).

Potassium concentrations are usually measured frequently during CPB. Several protocols have been developed for the management of potassium during bypass, although strict normokalemia need be present only when the aorta is not clamped and normal cardiac electrical activity is desired (148). Moreover, hypokalemia (requiring treatment) during bypass is less common in the current era of repeated doses of cardioplegia. The response to potassium administration during bypass is unpredictable; frequent monitoring of potassium is required (148). Because of the dangers of hyperkalemia, small frequent doses are preferred to boluses or continuous infusions. Potassium concentration should be assessed before each dose. Rises in systemic vascular resistance have been observed with infusions of intravenous potassium of 8 mEq or greater. With smaller doses, an initial fall followed by a slight rise in systemic vascular resistance is common (149).

In summary, potassium concentrations rarely remain constant during or after CPB. Hypokalemia, formerly a frequent problem during bypass, now is usually not of concern because of the widespread use of multiple doses of potassium-containing cardioplegic solutions. Postoperative potassium loss and hypokalemia continue to be common, probably as a result of elevated glucose and insulin concentrations after CPB.

ZINC, COPPER, AND IRON

Reductions in blood iron and zinc concentrations, and increases in copper concentrations occur as part of the nonspecific "acute phase reaction" to trauma, prolonged infections, burns, and major surgery (150). Patients with chronic coronary artery disease may have abnormally low concentrations of zinc in plasma. Zinc concentrations decline at the onset of CPB and remain low for 1 to 3 days postoperatively (151–153). Zinc concentrations nearly always returned to normal by the 7th postoperative day. Urinary excretion of zinc was not altered during or after cardiac surgery. Taggart et al. (154) carefully monitored iron, zinc, and copper concentrations before, during, and after coronary surgery in 20 patients perfused at either 20°C or 28°C. Significant alteration of the metal:protein molar binding ratios preceded falls in the concentrations of both ions as a consequence of the acute phase reaction to surgical trauma. Patients perfused at 20°C had less alterations of iron and zinc metabolism during surgery than those perfused at 28°C. No differences were seen after surgery, when both groups demonstrated reduced serum iron and zinc concentrations. The importance of these data may be to avoid misdiagnosis of iron deficiency anemia or zinc deficiency after cardiac surgery. Moreover, a reduced concentration of iron in blood may be advantageous. Administration of deferoxamine (an iron chelator) was associated with reduced production of free radicals during CPB (155).

Copper concentrations decrease during and after CPB. Copper concentrations fall rapidly at the onset of bypass, but usually returned to normal by the 3rd postoperative day (151, 153, 154). The alterations in copper concentration appear to be due to hemodilution (151). Zhao (152) found more transient nadir in blood copper concentration 30 minutes after perfusion, with a return to normal concentrations 1 to 2 days postoperatively, and a rise to supranormal concentrations between postoperative days 3 and 9.

CONCLUSIONS

Cardiopulmonary bypass produces widespread alterations in endocrine, humoral, and metabolic functions, some of which may be lessened by the use of pulsatile CPB or deeper planes of general anesthesia. The magnitude and direction of these changes may be influenced by the duration of bypass and the techniques employed (such as the degree of hypothermia, cardiac venting, and contents of the priming solution). For the most part, the mechanisms for these metabolic alterations during bypass are poorly understood. In selected patients, an awareness of the potential complications related to endocrine alterations may represent the difference between success and failure. Moreover, the importance of these changes may increase as longer durations of CPB, extracorporeal circulatory support, and total artificial heart replacements are considered.

REFERENCES

1. Malatinsky J, Vigas M, Jezova D, Jurcovicova J, Samel M, Vrsansky D. The effects of open heart surgery on growth hormone, cortisol and insulin levels in man. Hormone levels during open heart surgery. Resuscitation 1984; 11:57–68.

2. Anand KJS, Hickey PR. Halothane-morphine compared with high-dose sufentanil for anesthesia and postoperative analgesia in neonatal cardiac surgery. N Engl J Med 1992;326: 1–9.

3. Cooper DM, Bazaral MG, Furlan AJ, et al. Pituitary apoplexy: a complication of cardiac surgery. Ann Thorac Surg 1986;41:547–550.

4. Baylis PH. Vasopressin and its neurophysin. In: DeGroot LJ, ed. Endocrinology. 2nd ed. Vol 1. Philadelphia: WB Saunders, 1989; 213–229.

5. Heyndrickx GR, Boettcher DH, Vatner SF. Effects of angiotensin, vasopressin, and methoxamine on cardiac function and blood flow distribution in conscious dogs. Am J Physiol 1976; 231:1579–1587.

6. Cochrane JPS, Forsling ML, Gow NM, Le Quesne LP. Arginine vasopressin release following surgical operations. Br J Surg 1981;68: 209–213.

7. Knight A, Forsling M, Treasure T, Aveling W, Loh L, Sturridge MF. Changes in plasma vasopressin concentration in association with coronary artery surgery or thymectomy. Br J Anaesth 1986;58:1273–1277.

8. Wu W, Zbuzek VK, Bellevue C. Vasopressin release during cardiac operation. J Thorac Cardiovasc Surg 1980;79:83–90.

9. Philbin DM, Levine FH, Emerson CW, Coggins CH, Buckley MJ, Austen WG. Plasma vasopressin levels and urinary flow during cardiopulmonary bypass in patients with valvular heart disease: effect of pulsatile flow. J Thorac Cardiovasc Surg 1979;78:779–783.

10. Viinamaki O, Nuutinen L, Hanhela R, Karinen J, Pekkarinen A, Hirvonen J. Plasma vasopressin levels during and after cardiopulmonary bypass in man. Med Biol 1986;64:289–292.

11. Kaul TK, Swaminathan R, Chatrath RR, Watson DA. Vasoactive pressure hormones during and after cardiopulmonary bypass. Int J Artif Organs 1990;13:293–299.

12. Landymore RW, Murphy DA, Kinley CE, et al. Does pulsatile flow influence the incidence of postoperative hypertension? Ann Thorac Surg 1979;28:261–268.

13. Lehot JJ, Villard J, Piriz H, et al. Hemodynamic and hormonal responses to hypothermic and normothermic cardiopulmonary bypass. J Cardiothorac Vasc Anesth 1992;6:125–126.

14. Kehlet H. Surgical stress: the role of pain and analgesia. Br J Anaesth 1989;63:189–195.

15. Balasaraswathi K, Glisson SN, El-Etr AA, Azad C. Effect of priming volume on serum catecholamines during cardiopulmonary bypass. Can Anaesth Soc J 1980;27:135–139.

16. Hirvonen J, Huttunen P, Nuutinen L, Pekkarinen A. Catecholamines and free fatty acids in plasma of patients undergoing cardiac operations with hypothermia and bypass. J Clin Pathol 1978;31:949–955.

17. Reves JG, Karp RB, Buttner EE, et al. Neuronal and adrenomedullary catecholamine release in response to cardiopulmonary bypass in man. Circulation 1982;66:49–55.

18. Reed HL, Chernow B, Lake CR, et al. Alterations in sympathetic nervous system activity with intraoperative hypothermia during coronary artery bypass surgery. Chest 1989; 95:616-622.

19. Taggart DP, Fraser W, Gray CE, Beastall G, Shenkin A, Wheatley DJ. The effects of systemic intraoperative hypothermia on the acute-phase and endocrine response to cardiac surgery. Thorac Cardiovasc Surg 1992; 40:74–78.

20. Firmin RK, Bouloux P, Allen P, Lima RC, Lincoln JC. Sympathoadrenal function during cardiac operations in infants with the technique of surface cooling, limited cardiopulmonary bypass, and circulatory arrest. J Thorac Cardiovasc Surg 1985;90:729–735.

21. Anand KJ, Hansen DD, Hickey PR. Hormonal-metabolic stress responses in neonates undergoing cardiac surgery. Anesthesiology 1990; 73:661–670.

22. Samuelson PN, Reves JG, Kirklin JK, Bradley E Jr, Wilson KD, Adams M. Comparison of sufentanil and enflurane-nitrous oxide anesthesia for myocardial revascularization. Anesth Analg 1986;65:217–226.

23. Minami K, Körner MM, Vyska K, Kleesiek K, Knobl H, Körfer R. Effects of pulsatile perfusion on plasma catecholamine levels and hemodynamics during and after cardiac operations with cardiopulmonary bypass. J Thorac Cardiovasc Surg 1990;99:82–91.

24. Hume DM, Bell CC, Bartter F. Direct measurement of adrenal secretion during operative trauma and convalescence. Surgery 1962;52: 174–186.

25. Taylor KM, Jones JV, Walker MS, Rao S, Bain WH. The cortisol response during heart-lung bypass. Circulation 1976;54:20–25.

26. Taylor KM, Wright GS, Reid JM, et al. Comparative studies of pulsatile and nonpulsatile flow during cardiopulmonary bypass. II. The effects on adrenal secretion of cortisol. J Thorac Cardiovasc Surg 1978;75:574–578.

27. Raff H, Norton AJ, Flemma RJ, Findling JW. Inhibition of the adrenocorticotropin response to surgery in humans: interaction between dexamethasone and fentanyl. J Clin Endocrinol Metab 1987;65:295–298.

28. Flezzani P, Croughwell ND, McIntyre RW, Reves JG. Isoflurane decreases the cortisol response to cardiopulmonary bypass. Anesth Analg 1986;65:1117–1122.
29. Lacoumenta S, Yeo TH, Paterson JL, Burrin JM, Hall GM. Hormonal and metabolic responses to cardiac surgery with sufentanil-oxygen anaesthesia. Acta Anesthesiol Scand 1987;31:258–263.
30. Uozumi T, Manabe H, Kawashima Y, Hamanaka Y, Monden Y. Plasma cortisol, corticosterone, and non-protein-bound cortisol in extra-corporeal circulation. Acta Endocrinol 1972;69:517–525.
31. Taggart DP, Fraser WD, Borland WW, Shenkin A, Wheatley DJ. Hypothermia and the stress response to cardiopulmonary bypass. Eur J Cardiothorac Surg 1989;3:359–363.
32. Taylor KM, Walker MS, Rao LG, Jones JV, Gray CE. Proceedings: plasma levels of cortisol, free cortisol, and corticotrophin during cardiopulmonary by-pass. J Endocrinol 1975;67:29P–30P.
33. Kono K, Philbin DM, Coggins CH, et al. Adrenocortical hormone levels during cardiopulmonary bypass with and without pulsatile flow. J Thorac Cardiovasc Surg 1983;85:129–133.
34. Pollock EM, Pollock JC, Jamieson MP, et al. Adrenocortical hormone concentrations in children during cardiopulmonary bypass with and without pulsatile flow. Br J Anaesth 1988;60:536–541.
35. Dietzman RH, Lunseth JB, Goott B, Berger EC. The use of methylprednisolone during cardiopulmonary bypass. A review of 427 cases. J Thorac Cardiovasc Surg 1975;69:870–873.
36. Motsay GJ, Alho A, Jaeger T, Shultz LS, Dietzman RH, Lillehei RC. Effects of methylprednisolone, phenoxybenzamine, and epinephrine tolerance in canine endotoxin shock: study of isogravimetric capillary pressures in forelimb and intestine. Surgery 1971;70:271–279.
37. Atlas SA, Maack T. Effects of atrial natriuretic factor on the kidney and the renin-angiotensin-aldosterone system. In: Rosenblatt M, Jacobs JW, eds. Endocrinology and metabolism clinics of North America. Vol 16. Philadelphia: WB Saunders, 1987:107–143.
38. Dewar ML, Walsh G, Chiu RC, et al. Atrial natriuretic factor: response to cardiac operation. J Thorac Cardiovasc Surg 1988;96:266–270.
39. Ashcroft GP, Entwisle SJ, Campbell CJ, Holden MP, Keene ON. Peripheral and intracardiac levels of atrial natriuretic factor during cardiothoracic surgery. Thorac Cardiovasc Surg 1991;39:183–186.
40. Curello S, Ceconi C, De Giuli F, et al. Time course of human atrial natriuretic factor release during cardiopulmonary bypass in mitral valve and coronary artery diseased patients. Eur J Cardiothorac Surg 1991;5:205–210.
41. Kharasch ED, Yeo KT, Kenny MA, Amory DW. Influence of hypothermic cardiopulmonary bypass on atrial natriuretic factor levels. Can J Anaesth 1989;36:545–553.
42. Hedner J, Towle A, Saltzman L, et al. Changes in plasma atrial natriuretic peptide-immunoreactivity in patients undergoing coronary artery bypass graft placements. Regul Pept 1987;17:151–157.
43. Northridge DB, Jamieson MP, Jardine AG, MacArthur KJ, MacFarlane N, Dargie HJ. Pulmonary extraction and left atrial secretion of atrial natriuretic factor during cardiopulmonary bypass surgery. Am Heart J 1992;123:698–703.
44. Teran N, Rodriguez Iturbe B, Parra G, Gutkowska J. Atrial natriuretic peptide levels in brain venous outflow during cardiopulmonary bypass in humans: evidence for extracardiac hormonal production. J Cardiothorac Vasc Anesth 1991;5:343–347.
45. Pfenninger J, Shaw S, Ferrari P, Weidmann P. Atrial natriuretic factor after cardiac surgery with cardiopulmonary bypass in children. Crit Care Med 1991;19:1497–1502.
46. Schaff HV, Mashburn JP, McCarthy PM, Torres EJ, Burnett JC. Natriuresis during and early after cardiopulmonary bypass: relationship to atrial natriuretic factor, aldosterone, and antidiuretic hormone. J Thorac Cardiovasc Surg 1989;98:979–986.
47. Hynynen M, Palojoki R, Heinonen J, Tikkanen I, Harjula LJ, Fyhrquist F. Renal and vascular effects of atrial natriuretic factor during cardiopulmonary bypass. Chest 1991;100:1203–1209.
48. Miller ED Jr. The role of the renin-angiotensin-aldosterone system in circulatory control and hypertension. Br J Anaesth 1981;53:711–718.
49. Diedericks BJ, Roelofse JA, Shipton EA, Gray IP, de Wet JI, Hugo SA. The renin-angiotensin-aldosterone system during and after cardiopulmonary bypass. S Afr Med J 1983;64:946–949.
50. Weinstein GS, Zabetakis PM, Clavel A, et al. The renin-angiotensin system is not responsible for hypertension following coronary artery bypass grafting. Ann Thorac Surg 1987;43:74–77.

51. Taylor KM, Morton IJ, Brown JJ, Bain WH, Caves PK. Hypertension and the renin-angiotensin system following open-heart surgery. J Thorac Cardiovasc Surg 1977;74:840–845.

52. Nagaoka H, Innami R, Arai H. Effects of pulsatile cardiopulmonary bypass on the renin-angiotensin-aldosterone system following open heart surgery. Jpn J Surg 1988;18:390–396.

53. Canivet JL, Larbuisson R, Damas P, et al. Plasma renin activity and urine β_2-microglobulin during and after cardiopulmonary bypass: pulsatile vs. non-pulsatile perfusion. Eur Heart J 1990;11:1079–1082.

54. Gorin AB, Liebler J. Changes in serum angiotensin-converting enzyme during cardiopulmonary bypass in humans. Am Rev Respir Dis 1986;134:79–84.

55. Smallridge RC, Chernow B, Snyder R, Zaloga GP, Burman KD. Angiotensin-converting enzyme activity. A potential marker of tissue hypothyroidism in critical illness. Arch Intern Med 1985;145:1829–1832.

56. Feddersen K, Aurell M, Delin K, Haggendal J, Aren C, Radegran K. Effects of cardiopulmonary bypass and prostacyclin on plasma catecholamines, angiotensin II and arginine-vasopressin. Acta Anaesthesiol Scand 1985;29:224–230.

57. Colson P, Grolleau D, Chaptal PA, Ribstein J, Mimran A, Roquefeuil B. Effect of preoperative renin-angiotensin system blockade on hypertension following coronary surgery. Chest 1988;93:1156–1158.

58. Townsend GE, Wynands JE, Whalley DG, Wong P, Bevan DR. Role of renin-angiotensin system in cardiopulmonary bypass hypertension. Can Anaesth Soc J 1984;31:160–165.

59. Hays JH. Thyroid disease. In: Zaloga GP, ed. Problems in critical care, endocrine emergencies. Vol 4. Philadelphia: JB Lippincott, 1990: 325–341.

60. Salter DR, Dyke CM, Wechsler AS. Triiodothyronine (T_3) and cardiovascular therapeutics: a review. J Cardiol Surg 1992;7:363–374.

61. Gotzsche LS, Weeke J. Changes in plasma free thyroid hormones during cardiopulmonary bypass do not indicate triiodothyronine substitution. J Thorac Cardiovasc Surg 1992;104: 526–527.

62. Bremner WF, Taylor KM, Baird S, et al. Hypothalamo-pituitary-thyroid axis function during cardiopulmonary bypass. J Thorac Cardiovasc Surg 1978;75:392–399.

63. Saeed uz Zafar M, Miller JM, Breneman GM, Mansour J. Observations on the effect of heparin on free and total thyroxine. J Clin Endocrinol Metab 1971;32:633–640.

64. Hershman JM, Jones CM, Bailey AL. Reciprocal changes in serum thyrotropin and free thyroxine produced by heparin. J Clin Endocrinol Metab 1972;34:574–579.

65. Schwartz HL, Schadlow AR, Faierman D, Surks MI, Oppenheimer JH. Heparin administration appears to decrease cellular binding of thyroxine. J Clin Endocrinol Metab 1973;36: 598–600.

66. Holland FW II, Brown PS Jr, Weintraub BD, Clark RE. Cardiopulmonary bypass and thyroid function: a "euthyroid sick syndrome." Ann Thorac Surg 1991;52:46–50.

67. Chu S-H, Huang T-S, Hsu R-B, Wang S-S, Wang C-J. Thyroid hormone changes after cardiovascular surgery and clinical implications. Ann Thorac Surg 1991;52:791–796.

68. Lawton NF, Ellis SM, Sufi S. The triiodothyronine and thyroxine response to thyrotrophin-releasing hormone in the assessment of the pituitary thyroid axis. Clin Endocrinol 1973;2: 57–63.

69. Mitchell IM, Pollock JCS, Jamieson MPG, et al. The effect of cardiopulmonary bypass on thyroid function in infants weighing less than five kilograms. J Thorac Cardiovasc Surg 1992;103: 800–805.

70. Mitchell IM, Pollock JC, Jamieson MP, Fitzpatrick KC. Transcutaneous iodine absorption in infants undergoing cardiac operation. Ann Thorac Surg 1991;52:1138–1140.

71. Zaloga GP, Chernow B, Smallridge RC, et al. A longitudinal evaluation of thyroid function in critically ill surgical patients. Ann Surg 1985; 201:456–464.

72. Robuschi G, Medici D, Fesani F, et al. Cardiopulmonary bypass: a low T_4 and T_3 syndrome with blunted thyrotropin (TSH) response to thyrotropin-releasing hormone (TRH). Horm Res 1986;23:151–158.

73. Taylor KM, Wright GS, Bain WH, Caves PK, Beastall GS. Comparative studies of pulsatile and nonpulsatile flow during cardiopulmonary bypass. III. Response of anterior pituitary gland to thyrotropin-releasing hormone J. Thorac Cardiovasc Surg 1978;78:579–584.

74. Cooper DS, Klibanski A, Ridgway EC. Dopaminergic modulation of TSH and its subunits: in vivo and in vitro studies. Clin Endocrinol 1983;18:265–275.

75. DeRuyter H, Burman KD, Wartofsky L, Smallridge RC. Thyrotropin secretion in starved rats is enhanced by somatostatin antiserum. Horm Metab Res 1984;16:92–96.

76. Bilezikian JP, Loeb JN. The influence of hyperthyroidism and hypothyroidism on a- and

β-adrenergic receptor systems and adrenergic responsiveness. Endocr Rev 1983;4:378–388.

77. Sperelakis N, Wahler GM. Regulation of Ca^{2+} influx in myocardial cells by beta adrenergic receptors, cyclic neucleotides, and phosphorylation. Mol Cell Biochem 1988;82:19–28.

78. Novitzky D, Human PA, Cooper DK. Inotropic effect of triiodothyronine following myocardial ischemia and cardiopulmonary bypass: an experimental study in pigs. Ann Thorac Surg 1988;45:50–55.

79. Novitzky D, Human PA, Cooper DK. Effects of triiodothyronine (T_3) on myocardial high energy phosphates and lactate after ischemia and cardiopulmonary bypass. An experimental study in baboons. J Thorac Cardiovasc Surg 1988;96:600–607.

80. Novitzky D, Cooper DK, Barton CI, et al. Triiodothyronine as an inotropic agent after open heart surgery. J Thorac Cardiovasc Surg 1989;98:972–977.

81. Myers A, Uotila P, Foegh ML, Ramwell P. The eicosanoids: prostaglandins, thromboxane, and leukotrienes. In: DeGroot LJ, ed. Endocrinology. 2nd ed. Vol 3. Philadelphia: WB Saunders, 1989:2480–2490.

82. Ylikorkala O, Saarela E, Viinikka L. Increased prostacyclin and thromboxane production in man during cardiopulmonary bypass. J Thorac Cardiovasc Surg 1981;82:245–247.

83. Fleming WH, Sarafian LB, Leuschen MP, et al. Serum concentrations of prostacyclin and thromboxane in children before, during, and after cardiopulmonary bypass. J Thorac Cardiovasc Surg 1986;92:73–78.

84. Faymonville ME, Deby-Dupont G, Larbuisson R, et al. Prostaglandin E_2, prostacyclin, and thromboxane changes during nonpulsatile cardiopulmonary bypass in humans. J Thorac Cardiovasc Surg 1986;91:858–866.

85. Greeley WJ, Bushman GA, Kong DL, Newland H, Peterson MB. Effects of cardiopulmonary bypass on eicosanoid metabolism during pediatric cardiovascular surgery. J Thorac Cardiovasc Surg 1988;95:842–849.

86. Nagaoka H, Innami R, Murayama F, et al. Effects of aprotinin on prostaglandin metabolism and platelet function in open heart surgery. J Cardiovasc Surg 1991;32:31–37.

87. Watkins WD, Peterson MB, Kong DL, et al. Thromboxane and prostacyclin changes during cardiopulmonary bypass with and without pulsatile flow. J Thorac Cardiovasc Surg 1982;84:250–256.

88. Ritter JM, Hamilton G, Barrow SE, et al. Prosta-

cyclin in the circulation of patients with vascular disorders undergoing surgery. Clin Sci 1986;71:743–747.

89. Leuschen MP, Ehrenfried JA, Willett LD, et al. Prostaglandin F1 alpha levels during and after neonatal extracorporeal membrane oxygenation. J Thorac Cardiovasc Surg 1991;101:148–152.

90. Lavee J, Naveh N, Dinbar I, Shinfeld A, Goor DA. Prostacyclin and prostaglandin E2 mediate reduction of increased mean arterial pressure during cardiopulmonary bypass by aspiration of shed pulmonary venous blood. J Thorac Cardiovasc Surg 1990;100:546–551.

91. Levy JH. Anaphylactic reactions in anesthesia and intensive care. 2nd ed. Boston: Butterworth-Heinemann, 1992:51–62.

92. Man WK, Branna JJ, Fessatidis I, Beckett J, Taylor KM. Effect of prostacyclin on the circulatory histamine during cardiopulmonary bypass. Agents Actions 1986;18:182–185.

93. Marath A, Man W, Taylor KM. Histamine release in paediatric cardiopulmonary bypass—a possible role in the capillary leak syndrome. Agents Actions 1987;20:299–302.

94. Hosking MP, Beynen FM, Raimundo HS, Oliver WC Jr, Williamson KR. A comparison of washed red blood cells versus packed red blood cells (AS-1) for cardiopulmonary bypass prime and their effects on blood glucose concentration in children. Anesthesiology 1990;72:987–990.

95. Withington DE, Elliot M, Man WK. Histamine release during paediatric cardiopulmonary bypass. Agents Actions 1991;33:200–202.

96. Johnston WE, Moss J, Philbin DM, et al. Management of cold urticaria during hypothermic cardiopulmonary bypass. N Engl J Med 1982;306:219–221.

97. Reiter M. Calcium mobilization and cardiac inotropic mechanisms. Pharmacol Rev 1988;40:189–217.

98. Zaloga GP. Calcium disorders. In: Zaloga GP, ed. Problems in critical care, endocrine emergencies. Vol 4. Philadelphia: JB Lippincott, 1990;382–401.

99. Das JB, Eraklis AJ, Adams JG Jr, Gross RE. Changes in serum ionic calcium during cardiopulmonary bypass with hemodilution. J Thorac Cardiovasc Surg 1971;62:449–453.

100. Moffitt EA, Tarhan S, Goldsmith RS, Pluth Jr, McGoon DC. Patterns of total and ionized calcium and other electrolytes in plasma during and after cardiac surgery. J Thorac Cardiovasc Surg 1973;65:751–757.

101. Yoshioka K, Tsuchioka H, Abe T, Iyomasa Y.

Changes in ionized and total calcium concentrations in serum and urine during open heart surgery. Biochem Med 1978;20:135–143.

102. Gray R, Braunstein G, Krutzik S, Conklin C, Matloff J. Calcium homeostasis during coronary bypass surgery. Circulation 1980;62: 157–161.

103. Auffant RA, Downs JB, Amick R. Ionized calcium concentration and cardiovascular function after cardiopulmonary bypass. Arch Surg 1976;116:1072–1076.

104. Catinella FP, Cunningham JN Jr, Strauss ED, Adams PX, Laschinger JC, Spencer FC. Variations in total and ionized calcium during cardiac surgery. J Cardiovasc Surg 1983;24:593–602.

105. Abbott TR. Changes in serum calcium fractions and citrate concentrations during massive blood transfusions and cardiopulmonary bypass. Br J Anaesth 1983;55:753–759.

106. Hysing ES, Kofstad J, Lilleaasen P, Stokke O. Ionized calcium in plasma during cardiopulmonary bypass. Scand J Clin Lab Invest 1986; 184:119–123.

107. Westhorpe RN, Varghese Z, Petrie A, Wills MR, Lumley J. Changes in ionized calcium and other plasma constituents associated with cardiopulmonary bypass. Br J Anaesth 1978; 50:951–957.

108. Davies AB, Poole-Wilson PA. Whole blood calcium activity during cardiopulmonary bypass. Intensive Care Med 1981;7:213–216.

109. Chambers DJ, Dunham J, Braimbridge MV, Slavin B, Quiney J, Chayen J. The effect of ionized calcium, pH, and temperature on bioactive parathyroid hormone during and after open-heart operations. Ann Thorac Surg 1983; 36:306–313.

110. Heining MPD, Linton RAF, Band DM. Plasma ionized calcium during open-heart surgery. Anaesthesia 1985;40:237–241.

111. Robertie PG, Butterworth JF IV, Royster RL, et al. Normal parathyroid hormone responses to hypocalcemia during cardiopulmonary bypass. Anesthesiology 1991;75:43–48.

112. Robertie PG, Butterworth JF IV, Prielipp RC, Tucker WY, Zaloga GP. Parathyroid hormone responses to marked hypocalcemia in infants and young children undergoing repair of congenital heart disease. J Am Coll Cardiol 1992; 20:672–677.

113. Conlin PR, Fajtova VT, Mortensen RM, LeBoff MS, Brown EM. Hysteresis in the relationship between serum ionized calcium and intact parathyroid hormone during recovery from induced hyper- and hypocalcemia in normal humans. J Clin Endocrinol Metab 1989;69:593–599.

114. Tefer DJ, Nakanishi K, Johnston WE, Vinten-Johansen J. Transient regional hypocalcemia during the initial phase of reperfusion does not reduce myocardial necrosis. FASEB J 1991;5: A1048.

115. Butterworth JF IV, Royster RL, Prielipp RC, Zaloga GP. Should calcium be administered prior to separation from cardiopulmonary bypass? [Reply to letter]. Anesthesiology 1991; 75:1121–1122.

116. Zaloga GP, Strickland RA, Butterworth JF IV, Mark LJ, Mills SA, Lake CR. Calcium attenuates epinephrine's beta-adrenergic effects in postoperative heart surgery patients. Circulation 1990;81:196–200.

117. Butterworth JF IV, Strickland RA, Mark LJ, Kon ND, Zaloga GP. Calcium does not augment phenylephrine's hypertensive effects. Crit Care Med 1990;18:603–606.

118. Royster RL, Butterworth JF IV, Prielipp RC, et al. A randomized, blinded, placebo-controlled evaluation of calcium chloride and epinephrine for inotropic support after emergence from cardiopulmonary bypass. Anesth Analg 1992;74:3–13.

119. Butterworth JF IV, Zaloga GP, Prielipp RC, Tucker WY Jr, Royster RL. Calcium inhibits the cardiac stimulating properties of dobutamine but not amrinone. Chest 1992;101: 174–180.

120. Johnston WE, Robertie PG, Butterworth JF IV, Royster RL, Kon ND. Is calcium or ephedrine superior to placebo for emergence from cardiopulmonary bypass? J Cardiothorac Vasc Anesth 1992;6:528–534.

121. Castillo CF del, Harringer W, Warshaw AL, et al. Risk factors for pancreatic cellular injury after cardiopulmonary bypass. N Engl J Med 1991; 325:382–387.

122. Zaloga GP, Roberts JE. Magnesium disorders. In: Zaloga GP, ed. Problems in critical care, endocrine emergencies. Vol 4. Philadelphia: JB Lippincott, 1990:425–436.

123. Zaloga GP, Wilkens R, Tourville J, Wood D, Klyme DM. A simple method for determining physiologically active calcium and magnesium concentrations in critically ill patients. Crit Care Med 1987;15:813–816.

124. Turnier E, Osborn JJ, Gerbode F, Popper RW. Magnesium and open-heart surgery. J Thorac Cardiovasc Surg 1972;64:694–705.

125. Scheinman MM, Sullivan RW, Hyatt KH. Magnesium metabolism in patients undergoing cardiopulmonary bypass. Circulation 1969;39: 1235–1241.

126. Aglio LS, Stanford GG, Maddi R, Boyd JL III, Nussbaum S, Chernow B. Hypomagnesemia is common following cardiac surgery. J Cardiothorac Vasc Anesth 1991;5:201–208.

127. Lum G, Marquardt C, Khuri SF. Hypomagnesemia and low alkaline phosphatase activity in patients' serum after cardiac surgery. Clin Chem 1989;35:664–667.

128. Harris MN, Crowther A, Jupp RA, Aps C. Magnesium and coronary revascularization. Br J Anaesth 1988;60:779–783.

129. Prielipp RC, Zaloga GP, Butterworth JF IV, et al. Magnesium inhibits the hypertensive but not the cardiotonic actions of low-dose epinephrine. Anesthesiology 1991;74:973–979.

130. Walesby RK, Goode AW, Bentall HH. Nutritional status of patients undergoing valve replacement by open heart surgery. Lancet 1978;1: 76–77.

131. Morgan DB, Mearns AJ, Burkinshaw L. The potassium status of patients prior to open-heart surgery. J Thorac Cardiovasc Surg 1978;76: 673–677.

132. Ebert PA, Jude JR, Gaertner RA. Persistent hypokalemia following open-heart surgery. Circulation 1965;31:I137–I143.

133. Bozer AY, Ilicin G, Apikoglu A, Karamehmetoglu A, Saylam A. Serum electrolyte changes during extracorporeal circulation. Jpn Heart J 1972;13:195–200.

134. Regensburger D, Paschen K, Fuchs C. Veranderungen des Electrolyt- und Saure-Basen-Haushaltes bei Operationen mit kardio-pumonalem Bypass unter Hamdilution. Thoraxchir Vask Chir 1972;20:473–479.

135. Marcial MB, Vedoya RC, Zerbini EJ, Verginelli G, Bittencourt D, do Amaral RG. Potassium in cardiac surgery with extracorporeal perfusion. Am J Cardiol 1969;23:400–408.

136. Patrick J, Sivpragasam S. The prediction of postoperative potassium excretion after cardiopulmonary bypass. J Thorac Cardiovasc Surg 1977; 73:559–562.

137. Wilson GM, Dunn FG, McQueen MJ, Kerr IC, Thomson RM. Comparison of intravenous bumetanide and frusemide during open heart surgery. Postgrad Med J 1975;51:72.

138. Cohn LH, Angell WW, Shumway NE. Body fluid shifts after cardiopulmonary bypass. I. Effects of congestive heart failure and hemodilution. J Thorac Cardiovasc Surg 1971;62: 423–430.

139. Moffitt EA, White RD, Molnar GD, McGoon DC. Comparative effects of whole blood, hemodiluted, and clear priming solutions on myocardial and body metabolism in man. Can J Surg 1971;14:382–391.

140. Johnston AE, Radde IC, Steward DJ, Taylor J. Acid-base and electrolyte changes in infants undergoing profound hypothermia for surgical correction of congenital heart defects. Can Anaesth Soc J 1974;21:23–45.

141. Johnston AE, Radde IC, Nisbet HI, Taylor J. Effects of altering calcium in haemodiluted pump primes on sodium and potassium in children undergoing open-heart operations. Can Anaesth Soc J 1972;19:517–528.

142. Taggart P, Slater JD. Some effects of bypass surgery on myocardial and skeletal muscle electrolytes and their clinical importance. Br Heart J 1969;31:393.

143. Munday KA, Blane GF, Chin EF, Machell ES. Plasma electrolyte changes in hypothermia. Thorax 1958;13:334–342.

144. Lim M, Linton RA, Band DM. Rise in plasma potassium during rewarming in open-heart surgery [Letter]. Lancet 1983;1:241–242.

145. Weber DO, Yarnoz MD. Hyperkalemia complicating cardiopulmonary bypass: analysis of risk factors. Ann Thorac Surg 1982;34: 439–445.

146. Bethune DW, McKay R. Paradoxical changes in serum-potassium during cardiopulmonary bypass in association with non-cardioselective beta blockade [Letter]. Lancet 1978;2:380.

147. Henney RP, Riemenschneider TA, DeLand EC, Maloney JV Jr. Prevention of hypokalemic cardiac arrhythmias associated with cardiopulmonary bypass and hemodilution. Surg Forum 1970;21:145–147.

148. Manning SH, Angaran DM, Arom KV, Lindsay WG, Northrup WF III, Nicoloff DM. Intermittent intravenous potassium therapy in cardiopulmonary bypass patients. Clin Pharm 1982; 1:234–238.

149. Schwartz AJ, Conahan TJ III, Jobes DR, Andrews RW, MacVaugh H III, Ominsky AJ. Peripheral vascular response to potassium administration during cardiopulmonary bypass. J Thorac Cardiovasc Surg 1980;79:237–240.

150. Watters JM, Wilmore DW. The metabolic responses to trauma and sepsis. In: DeGroot LJ, ed. Endocrinology. 2nd ed. Vol 3. Philadelphia: WB Saunders, 1989;2367–2392.

151. Fuhrer G, Heller W, Hoffmeister HE, Sterzing T. Levels of trace elements during and after cardiopulmonary bypass operations. Acta Pharmacol Toxicol 1986;59:352–357.

152. Zhao L. Changes in blood zinc and copper and their clinical significance in patients undergoing open-heart surgery. Chung Hua I Hsueh Tsa Chih 1989;69:76–78.

153. Sjogren A, Luhrs C, Abdulla M. Changed distribution of zinc and copper in body fluids in patients undergoing open-heart surgery. Acta Pharmacol Toxicol 1986;59:348–351.
154. Taggart DP, Fraser WD, Shenkin A, Wheatley DJ, Fell GS. The effects of intraoperative hypothermia and cardiopulmonary bypass on trace metals and their protein binding ratios. Eur J Cardiothorac Surg 1990;4:587–594.
155. Menasche P, Pasquier C, Bellucci S, Lorente P, Jaillon P, Piwnica A. Deferoxamine reduces neutrophil-mediated free radical production during cardiopulmonary bypass in man. J Thorac Cardiovasc Surg 1988;96:582–589.

13

PULSATILE BLOOD FLOW

Daniel M. Philbin

The significance and contribution of the pulse has generated discussion, debate, and controversy since the very beginnings of medicine. Certainly it was present in the conflicting views of Galen, Aristotle, and Hippocrates (1). While this debate over the years periodically occupied the forefront, little in the way of laboratory studies provided the data necessary to support a given argument or thesis. Indeed, it was nearly 200 years after Harvey reported the importance of the pulse to the circulation that true laboratory studies of the pulse were performed (2, 3).

Research and interest in the function of isolated organs preceded by many years the quest for a device or system to provide total body perfusion. In many respects, perfusion devices developed for isolated organs were the forerunners to the extracorporeal systems in use today. They produced similar problems and debates about function, design, and application. The use of pulsatile flow in these early animal experiments often required cross-circulation, thus allowing the intact heart to provide the pulsation, though occasionally balloons served as suction and pressure pumps (4). However, many of the early experiments that made no attempt to produce pulsatile flow reported comparable results, suggesting that the often technically difficult and bothersome addition of pulsatility was unnecessary (5). By the turn of the century, three systems to oxygenate blood were undergoing investigation: a bubble oxygenator, a film oxygenator, and the use of an intact lung (which could provide pulsatile flow in cross-circulation). None, however, were capable of providing true extracorporeal circulation in human beings, primarily because of the formation of foam, air embolism, and hemolysis.

The modern beginning of extracorporeal circulation can be attributed to Gibbon (6–8), who was the first to develop a system clearly and purposefully intended for human application. Initial animal work began in the 1930s at the Massachusetts General Hospital. Despite the intervention of World War II, the first reports of human application appeared in the 1950s (6–8). This introduced an explosive era of cardiac surgery producing major advances so rapidly that they appear in retrospect to have been a daily phenomenon. Routine use of nonpulsatile flow soon became the established standard when early experience demonstrated generally good results without major detrimental effects attributable to the lack of pulsation (9–11). Nonetheless, interest in pulsatile flow application continued as a result of the feeling shared by many investigators that beneficial effects should accrue (12–14).

323

PHYSIOLOGIC EFFECTS OF PULSATILE FLOW

Hemodynamics

Conventional nonpulsatile flow during cardiopulmonary bypass (CPB) generally leads to increased peripheral vascular resistance (PVR). However, early studies suggested no difference in PVR with pulsatile versus nonpulsatile flow at a rate of 130 ml/kg/min (15). Indeed, Ogata and colleagues (16) reported that PVR was actually higher in patients exposed to pulsatile CPB.

In contrast, a number of workers have reported lower PVR when pulsatile CPB is employed. Mandelbaum et al. (17, 18) demonstrated lower PVR and aortic pressures during pulsatile CPB, and Nakayama and co-workers (12) reported similar results, particularly when higher flows were utilized. In a series of animal studies using the same pump to provide both types of CPB with comparable flow, a number of investigators reported lower PVR with pulsatile perfusion (13, 14, 19–21). When the Avco pulsatile pump created a pulse pressure, PVR decreased significantly in both animals and humans (22, 23). Trinkle et al. (9, 24) reported similar results while also employing hypothermia. Other studies, however, have not demonstrated any significant difference in PVR (25, 26). Additional human studies utilizing both types of perfusion also reported no apparent effect on PVR with pulsatile flow (27). Using a modified roller pump to generate pulsatility, Taylor et al. (28–30) found that such differences did exist—a finding also reported in subsequent studies by that group and others (28–32).

The majority of published reports, involving both animals and humans, demonstrate a lower PVR with pulsatile flow. This remains far from conclusive because a number of studies fail to demonstrate this difference. The differences are not easily explained, since no consistent pattern of flows, temperatures, pumps, etc., can be identified. Nonetheless, a fairly large and consistent body of literature tends to confirm and explain such a difference. Published studies have demonstrated greater carotid sinus and aortic arch baroreceptor activity with pulsatile flow than with nonpulsatile flow at the same mean pressure (33, 34). Several authors suggested that this increased baroreceptor activity could inhibit vasomotor discharge and produce a decrease in PVR (35, 36). As an example, if the pulse pressure increase was limited to the aortic arch and carotid sinus region, systemic arterial pressures decreased (35). Other investigators demonstrated a significant decrease in baroreceptor sensitivity when utilizing a high mean pressure (i.e., about 140 to 150 mm Hg) (36–38). Giron et al. (39) provided additional support for the involvement of an autonomic vasomotor mechanism in the PVR changes noted. They found that depulsation of the entire systemic arterial circuit increased PVR, but that preservation of pulsation limited to the aortic arch and carotid sinus prevented the increase in PVR. However, factors other than the autonomic nervous system are most likely involved in the decreased PVR induced by pulsatile flow. Mandelbaum and Burns (18) noted that denervation of the carotid sinus section of the vagal trunks, bilateral nephrectomy, and pharmacologic blockade of the autonomic nervous system did not abolish the PVR differences between pulsatile and nonpulsatile flow.

A number of investigators studied blood flow distribution with and without pulsatile flow and found a remarkably uniform distribution. While Nakayama et al. (12) noted slightly increased flow to the coronary and renal circulations and slightly decreased hepatic blood flow with pulsation, no statistical analysis was provided. Others, using radioactive microspheres to assess blood flow distribution with pulsatile and nonpulsatile bypass, demonstrated no differences in the distribution of flow to adrenal, hepatic, splenic, renal, or pancreatic vascular beds with either type of perfusion (19, 40). A similar lack of effect was found in comparing the effects of both types of perfusion upon hind-leg blood flow in dogs (41) or upon flow distribution to the brachiocephalic or mesenteric arterial beds (39). Thus the majority of reports agree that the PVR differences found with pulsatile flow are uniform over the numerous regional vascular beds that were examined.

Hormonal Responses

If, as the majority of investigators appear to believe, a significant difference exists between pulsatile and nonpulsatile perfusion, then most would also agree that this difference is most likely caused by different hormonal responses elicited by each type of perfusion. As with the studies on PVR, the results are somewhat varied.

CATECHOLAMINES

Animal studies reported no significant differences in catecholamine levels during pulsatile and nonpulsatile bypass (13). Landymore et al. (42) and Philbin et al. (43) noted similar results in humans. However, the latter study reported higher postoperative concentrations of catecholamines in the nonpulsatile group, which the other study did not. In contrast, Mori et al. (44), using a pulsatile assist device (PAD) to provide pulsatile flow, found a lesser increase in catecholamines with the pulsatile mode. The differences were relatively small, however, achieving statistical significance only for norepinephrine levels at 2 measurement points. In a more recent study, Minami et al. (32) also reported significant attenuation of the increases in epinephrine and norepinephrine levels both during and following bypass when pulsatile flow was employed.

RENIN-ANGIOTENSIN SYSTEM

The effects of pulsatile bypass on plasma renin activity probably depend

largely upon the preoperative drug regimen. Propranolol inhibits renin release, and when it was administered preoperatively, several investigators reported no differences in plasma renin activity with or without pulsatile flow (Fig. 13.1) (26, 27, 43). When propranolol was discontinued preoperatively, significantly lower renin activity was reported after bypass when pulsatile perfusion was utilized (42). After 45 minutes of bypass in dogs, Watkins et al. (20) also observed significantly lower plasma renin activity as well as levels of angiotensin II, a potent vasoactive end product of the renin-angiotensin system. Somewhat similar results have been reported by others (28). Canivet et al. (45) demonstrated that pulsatile flow prevented the rise in plasma renin activity seen with nonpulsatile perfusion, and concluded that pulsatility attenuated the renin response both during and after CPB.

ANTIDIURETIC HORMONE

Several investigators reported increased plasma vasopressin or antidiuretic hormone concentrations during routine nonpulsatile bypass (46–48). Subsequent studies suggested that pulsatile flow could attenuate the increases in vasopressin (Fig. 13.1) (43, 49). Since arginine vasopressin is a potent direct-acting peripheral vasoconstrictor, such an effect would contribute to the decrease in PVR often reported with pulsatile flow. Frater et al. (26) did not find that pulsatile flow attenuated the vasopressin response. However, their small study population rendered statistical evaluation difficult at best.

CORTISOL

Decreased plasma cortisol levels have also been reported during nonpulsatile bypass (50, 51). Taylor et al. (52) prevented this decrease by using normothermic pulsatile perfusion. However, using moderate hypothermia, Frater et al. (26) found no changes in cortisol levels with either pulsa-

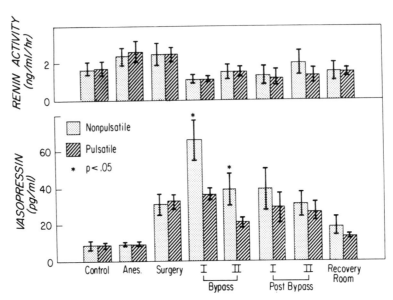

Figure 13.1. A comparison of renin activity and vasopressin responses with and without pulsatile bypass in 26 patients. Asterisk indicates statistically significant differences between groups. (From Philbin DM, Levine FH, Kono K, et al. Attenuation of the stress response to cardiopulmonary bypass by the addition of pulsatile flow. Circulation 1981;64:808–812.)

tile or nonpulsatile bypass. More recent studies have obtained similar results in adults and children, leading to the conclusion that cortisol responses to CPB are not influenced by the quality of pulsation (53–55).

PROSTAGLANDINS

Both thromboxane and prostacyclin levels appear to rise during nonpulsatile CPB (56, 57). However, pulsatile flow attenuated the increase in thromboxane while intensifying the increase in prostacyclin (58). Since thromboxane is a potent vasoconstrictor and platelet aggregator, while prostacyclin is a potent vasodilator and antithrombic agent, this effect of pulsatile flow could contribute to the decrease in PVR and improved perfusion noted by some investigators.

To summarize, the body of literature demonstrating significant differences in the hormonal responses to pulsatile and nonpulsatile CPB thus suggests a true physiologic distinction between the two. However, con-

flicting reports make it difficult to define a specific relationship between these differences and the other physiologic differences noted between pulsatile and nonpulsatile perfusion.

The Heart

The effect of CPB on the heart depends upon the state of the heart, since the beating heart provides its own pulsatile flow regardless of the type of perfusion used. Pulsatile coronary blood flow has thus been demonstrated despite nonpulsatile perfusion in the beating heart, whereas linear coronary blood flow occurs in the fibrillating heart (59, 60). The addition of systemic pulsatile flow produces pulsatile coronary flow even in the fibrillating heart.

Several investigators reported that pulsatile perfusion of the nonbeating heart increases subendocardial perfusion and/or maintains a better endocardial/epicardial flow ratio (22, 61), although Moores et al. (59, 60) found no differences in those parameters using pulsatile or nonpulsatile flow in either the beating or fibrillating heart. Grover and colleagues (62) found no change in total coronary flow, left ventricular flow, or endocardial/epicardial flow ratios with pulsatile flow in either beating or fibrillating hearts. Investigating just the beating heart, Hewitt and Weichert (63) found that pulsatile CPB did not influence coronary blood flow. However, in the presence of a critical constriction of a coronary artery, several studies provided evidence that pulsatility better maintains or improves flow (and pulsation) distal to the constriction when the heart is fibrillating (64, 65). No such changes were noted in the region of the coronary circulation supplied by a nonstenotic artery. It would appear then that pulsatile perfusion exerts little benefit to the beating heart, but that it may improve subendocardial perfusion in the fibrillating heart, particularly in the presence of a coronary stenosis.

Fibrillatory Arrest. If one examines the effect of pulsatile perfusion on myocardial metabolism, some studies suggest a beneficial effect when the heart is fibrillating. In the region beyond a stenotic coronary lesion, Schaff et al. (65) demonstrated lactate production, a decrease in oxygen tension, and an increase in CO_2 during nonpulsatile flow. When pulsatile flow was utilized, lactate was consumed, and intramyocardial oxygen and carbon dioxide tensions remained normal or nearly so. Similar results were reported by Bixler et al. (66), but these beneficial metabolic effects of pulsatile perfusion disappeared when the mean perfusion pressure was substantially increased (from a mean of 50 to 80 mm Hg). In addition, Moores et al. (59) found no significant improvement in myocardial oxygen consumption or lactate extraction with pulsatile perfusion in either fibrillating or beating hearts. Other investigators also reported a similar lack of effect on myocardial oxygen consumption, myocardial lactate levels, or myocardial adenosine triphosphate levels with pulsatile perfusion (62).

In studies utilizing intraaortic balloon counterpulsation to produce pulsatile flow during bypass in fibrillating hearts, myocardial oxygen extraction was unaffected, while lactate extraction improved (Fig. 13.2) (67). Using a similar technique, patients undergoing coronary bypass operations with routine nonpulsatile flow demonstrated marked decreases in left ventricular ejection fraction by the 1st postoperative day (68). In contrast, when pulsatile flow was used, ejection fraction increased considerably over the preoperative value the 1st postoperative day, and there was also a lower rate of intraoperative infarction. Similar findings were reported when the PAD provided pulsatile flow (69). Also utilizing the PAD, Zumbro et al. (70) detected no beneficial effect on the electrocardiograms or release of creatine phosphokinase (CPK) isoenzymes, when compared to nonpulsatile flow.

A number of studies therefore suggest that pulsatile flow better maintains subendocardial blood flow and myocardial metabolism in the fibrillating heart, which leads to better postoperative myocardial function. Unfortunately, an almost equal number of studies fail to support these conclusions, thus continuing the inconsistent pattern of results.

Cardioplegic Arrest. When employing potassium cardioplegia, Levine et al. (71) found that pulsatile flow during CPB produced no demonstrable postoperative benefit on either ejection fraction or CPK isoenzymes. Silverman et al. (72) also studied the effect of pulsatile flow during perfusion after aortic cross-clamping and found no restoration of myocardial nucleotide levels after normothermic global myocardial ischemia. However, Mori and colleagues (73) found that pulsatile reperfusion after 60 minutes of aortic cross-clamping in dogs attenuated impairment in postarrest segmental shortening, and improved left ventricular function curves and myocardial lactate extraction.

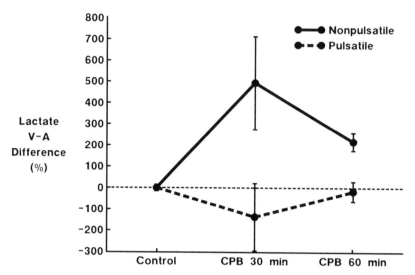

Figure 13.2.   Percent change in coronary sinus lactate difference in 14 patients undergoing pulsatile CPB compared to 13 patients undergoing nonpulsatile CPB. Cardiac arrest was with ventricular fibrillation in both groups. The coronary veno-arterial (*V-A*) differences between groups were statistically significant at *CPB 30 min* and at *CPB 60 min*. (From Pappas G, Winter SD, Kopriva CJ, Steele PP: Improvement of myocardial and other vital organ functions and metabolism with a simple method of pulsatile flow (IABP) during clinical cardiopulmonary bypass. Surgery 1975;77:34–44.)

Blood

Cardiopulmonary bypass causes hemolysis, platelet destruction, and occasional coagulopathies. A major concern has been that the addition of pulsatile flow would exacerbate these problems. Several studies, however, demonstrated either no difference or a decrease in plasma hemoglobin levels when pulsatile flow was utilized (14, 64, 74, 75). Others reported increased hemolysis but no difference in platelet levels when pulsatile flow was used in animals (19). Trinkle and colleagues (9, 24) reported reduced plasma hemoglobin levels, increased fibrinogen levels, and no difference in coagulation studies with pulsatile perfusion. Similar results were reported by Pappas et al. (67) using the intra-aortic balloon pump to provide pulsation, and by Williams et al. (76) and Bregman et al. (69) utilizing the PAD. Studies utilizing the modified roller pump for both pulsatile and nonpulsatile flow also reported no significant differences in plasma hemoglobin or platelet levels (77, 78).

The information available from human studies is thus reasonably consistent, suggesting that no increase in hematologic trauma accrues as a result of pulsatile perfusion. The conclusion can be drawn that at least some forms of pulsatile bypass produce no more damage to red cells or platelets than routine nonpulsatile bypass.

Kidney

It has long been recognized that pulsatile flow during CPB improves urinary output and presumably better maintains renal function (79, 80). Nonetheless, several investigators observed no change in kidney function or blood flow with pulsatile perfusion in the isolated kidney (81–83). Subsequent studies, however, supported the conclusions of the earlier investigators that, with kidneys in situ, urine volume was indeed related to pulse pressure amplitude, and that decreasing the pulse pressure in either or both kidneys decreased sodium excretion and urine volume (84–86). Other animal studies also reported that pulsatile perfusion improved kidney function, notably concentrating ability (74). As is frequently the case, however, other investigators could find no difference in renal function with either modality in the isolated dog kidney (87). A number of other animal studies provided varying results (14, 19, 40, 88, 89).

Clinical studies are equally confusing. A number of investigators reported an increase in urine volume (and presumably better renal function) when pulsatile flow was employed in patients undergoing CPB (23, 31, 49, 69). Other investigators, however, failed to demonstrate any effect of pulsatile flow on urine output in reasonably similar groups of patients (25, 26). In patients with preexisting renal disease, some investigators have reported improved renal function and outcome with pulsatile flow. Olinger et al. (90) reported that pulsatile flow helped to preserve renal function in patients with creatinine concentrations over 1.7 mg/100 ml. Matsuda et al. (91) reported similar beneficial effects in patients with a decreased creatinine clearance preoperatively. These conclusions are supported indirectly by studies that pulsatile perfusion provided significantly better preservation of renal function in kidneys harvested for transplantation (92, 93). Other data have demonstrated that a decrease in renal pulse pressure stimulates renin release (85, 86, 94). Such changes could affect intrarenal blood flow distribution and renal function (95). The lack of renal pulsatile perfusion can shift blood flow from the outer cortex to the juxtaglomerular areas (85, 86). In addition, ischemic histologic changes have been reported in kidneys exposed to nonpulsatile perfusion for varying periods (12, 96). Further beneficial effects of pulsatility can be found in metabolic studies, which have generally demonstrated improved renal metabolism (74). This encompasses evidence that pulsatile flow leads to lower renal vein lactate levels, greater renal oxygen consumption, and better tissue oxygen levels (97, 98). However,

another study recently failed to demonstrate any renal functional benefit from pulsatile flow (99).

The majority of studies suggest that pulsatile perfusion does maintain more normal renal metabolism, preserves outer cortical blood flow, and reduces renin release, thus better preserving renal function. Again, however, the contrasting studies fail to find evidence either experimentally or clinically of these beneficial effects.

The Brain

Somewhat surprisingly, the effect of pulsatile flow on the brain and cerebral perfusion has received little attention, perhaps because of the difficulties involved in such studies. In animal studies using nonpulsatile perfusion, cerebral blood flow varies directly with perfusion pressure, cerebral edema frequently develops, and cerebral oxygen consumption decreases (100). Others reported that pulsatile flow prevented the early ischemic changes that developed with nonpulsatile flow (101, 102). Geha et al. (21) reported that the use of pulsatile flow increased cerebrospinal fluid oxygen tension and lowered jugular venous blood lactate levels, although there was no definitive evidence of improved cerebral metabolism. Watanabe et al. (103) concluded that pulsatile flow in animals significantly increased the safety margin of bypass by preventing large changes in brain tissue pH and carbon dioxide tension and allowing a more rapid return to normal.

In a recent clinical study, Kono et al. (104) studied the effect of pulsatile flow on cerebral oxygen consumption and found no difference with that modality. They did, however, note a significant difference in cerebral arterial-venous O_2 contents and suggested that pulsatile flow minimized microcirculatory shunting during CPB and reduced cerebral vascular resistance. In contrast, Henze et al. (105) compared pulsatile and nonpulsatile flow in two groups of patients and found no difference in neurologic outcome. Those authors also reported that pulsatile flow had no effect on cerebral blood flow or cerebral metabolic rate, and concluded that pulsatile perfusion was not superior to nonpulsatile perfusion. Both of these studies involved relatively small numbers of patients, however, and considerably more research is necessary (106).

The Pancreas

Several studies have shown that serum amylase and the amylase-creatinine clearance ratio increase postoperatively after nonpulsatile bypass (107–109). In addition, acute pancreatitis after cardiac surgery has been well-documented and can be fatal (107, 109–111). The high incidence of unexplained pancreatitis detected at autopsy (or "postmortem examination") in cardiac surgical patients (112), along with the data of Warshaw and O'Hara (113), suggest that ischemia may be a significant factor. Pulsatile flow does not appear to alter total pancreatic blood flow, although it can attenuate abnormalities in serum and urinary amylase. This suggests that pulsatile flow favorably affects the pancreatic microcirculation (19, 107, 108), a theory that is supported by a recent study demonstrating the efficacy of pulsatile flow in preserving pancreatic β-cell function and tissue metabolism (114).

A number of other factors may be involved, however. Some studies suggest that the administration of drugs such as phenylephrine, norepinephrine, and steroids play a significant role (108, 115), conceivably by affecting blood flow. A recent study demonstrated that the administration of large doses of calcium chloride served as an independent predictor of pancreatic injury following bypass (116). It remains to be seen whether pulsatile flow can significantly reduce the incidence of injury.

The Lungs

The pulmonary effects of cardiopulmonary bypass with and without pulsatile flow depend to a large extent upon whether one is studying the bronchial or pulmonary circulations. Conventional CPB perfuses only the bronchial circulation, whereas with right heart bypass the pulmonary circulation receives the entire output of the extracorporeal circuit.

In studies utilizing right heart bypass with and without pulsation, no difference was noted in pulmonary function with up to 3 hours of perfusion (117). A study utilizing a similar canine preparation with normothermic perfusion demonstrated a significant increase in pulmonary vascular resistance with nonpulsatile pulmonary flow (18). The degree of increase was comparable to that seen in the peripheral resistance during conventional CPB, and was apparently not prevented by pharmacologic adrenergic or cholinergic blockade. Another animal study investigated the effects of long-term and short-term preparations with pulsatile and nonpulsatile flow (118). While this study found no difference in oxygenation with either modality, it also reported an increase in pulmonary vascular resistance during nonpulsatile flow that was not reversed by pulmonary denervation. However, in a subsequent study, other investigators found that pulsatile flow induced no difference in either pulmonary function or respiratory mechanics during right heart bypass (119).

Studies comparing pulsatile and nonpulsatile perfusion of the bronchial circulation during conventional CPB document somewhat different findings. Animal studies noted an increased incidence of pulmonary dysfunction, such as a significant increase in the alveolar-arterial oxygen gradient, alveolar hemorrhage, and pulmonary congestion, when pulsatile perfusion was employed (13, 21). However, contrary findings were reported by Dunn et al. (19), who found no difference in gas exchange or pulmonary compliance and less pulmonary congestion in the pulsatile group after bypass. Definitive clinical studies assessing any advantage to pulsatile perfusion, either bronchial or pulmonary, have yet to be performed.

NATURE OF PULSATILE FLOW

Propagation and generation of a pulse through a vascular system that is elastic and composed of many branching vessels is complex at best. To describe the entire system requires the use of a series of complex equations with multiple variables that must be solved simultaneously (120). Superimposition of disease states only serves to increase the complexity. It is thus far beyond the scope of this chapter and the ability of the author to discuss the nature of pulsatile flow in detail. Nonetheless, a few simplistic concepts are offered in the hope of providing some basic understanding of the process.

Vascular impedance, which opposes blood flow, is composed of a resistive and a reactive element. The reactive element derives primarily from the pulsatile nature of the flow and is determined mostly by compliance and vascular elasticity. This impedance serves as a measure of the ratio of instantaneous pulsatile pressure to instantaneous pulsatile flow, and depends upon the rate of pulsation. If these instantaneous measurements are not used in calculating vascular impedance, then much of the effect of cardiovascular disease on pulsatile flow will be underestimated. In addition, the variability of pulsatile flow will be missed or underrecorded.

It is also well-recognized that pulsatile flow requires more hydraulic energy than nonpulsatile flow. The additional energy required can be calculated as the product of instantaneous flow and instantaneous pressure. The use of mean rather than instantaneous values will again greatly underestimate the amount of hydraulic (cardiac) work, particularly in patients with significant cardiovascular disease. Inadequate quantification of pulsatile flow, as occurs when mean values are used for calculation, makes it impossible to correctly evaluate vascular impedance and the hydraulic energy of pulsatile flow. This, in turn, makes it virtually impossible to appreciate the differences between pulsatile and nonpul-

satile flow and between various forms of pulsatile flow. In addition, the variety of pulsatile systems in use, each with its own peculiarities and differences, further confuses the issue. Figure 13.3 demonstrates simultaneous pressures and flows in dogs with three different pulse wave configurations during CPB (121). Increasing sharpness of the pressure waveform increased a mathematically derived pulse power index, which correlated inversely with serum lactate production (Fig. 13.4) (121). This work suggests that the character of the pulsatility contributes importantly to the metabolic consequences of pulsatile bypass. The absence of a universally accepted definition of effective pulsatile flow and of accurate measurement of the pulsatile components makes comparisons an exercise in futility. This is particularly true when most of the studies on pulsatile perfusion tend to treat pulsatile flow as a single entity rather than the complex phenomenon it truly is.

SUMMARY

Given the weight of evidence available, it appears that pulsatile flow during CPB provides a more physiologic milieu and probably better tissue perfusion, presumably leading to better organ function or at least less dysfunction. Why, then, is pulsatile flow not the standard for routine use?

The explanation for this, I believe, can be found in three major areas. First, the results obtained from routine nonpulsatile bypass are very good and continue to improve from year to year. Second, providing pulsatile flow, regardless of the method used, increases costs, measured not only in dollars but also in added complexity. Third, results are inconsistent in numerous studies comparing pulsatile and nonpulsatile flow and do not clearly demonstrate the superiority of pulsatile flow. A major factor in this inconsistency is failure to recognize the true nature of pulsatile flow and its complexity. Studies that treat pulsatile flow as a uniform phenomenon and neglect to use continuous recordings of instantaneous

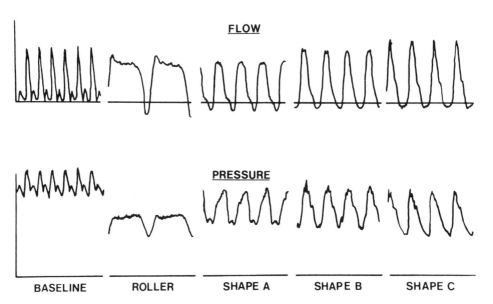

Figure 13.3. Simultaneous pressure and flow measurements before CPB (*baseline*), during traditional nonpulsatile bypass (*roller*), and with three different pulse wave configurations during bypass (*shapes A, B, and C*). Shapes B and C have sharper pulsatility, resulting in a higher pulse power index, as determined by Fourier analysis. (From Grossi EA, Connolly MW, Krieger KH, et al. Quantification of pulsatile flow during cardiopulmonary bypass to permit direct comparison of the effectiveness of various types of "pulsatile" and "nonpulsatile" flow. Surgery 1985;98:547–553.)

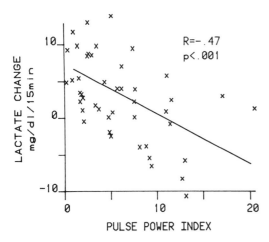

Figure 13.4. Scattergram and linear regression of rate of serum lactate production versus pulse power index in 13 dogs subjected to nonpulsatile bypass and to pulsatile bypass using the three different pulse wave configurations shown in Figure 13.3. (From Grossi EA, Connolly MW, Krieger KH, et al. Quantification of pulsatile flow during cardiopulmonary bypass to permit direct comparison of the effectiveness of various types of "pulsatile" and "nonpulsatile" flow. Surgery 1985; 98:547–553.)

flow and pressure curves only perpetuate the problem. The character of pulsatile flow produced by a single pulsatile pump varies widely under different physiologic conditions. How much greater will the variations be when two different systems are compared, particularly when different patient populations are involved?

The first obstacle to overcome, then, is to define what constitutes effective pulsatile flow and determine those physiologic states for which a given type of pulsatile flow is effective. Continuing the present simplistic approach to such a complex issue only generates needless controversy and prevents real progress. It is true that some forms of pulsatile flow are more effective and physiologic than nonpulsatile CPB. It must be determined which forms of pulsatile flow are effective and in what physiologic or pathologic states their use is justified. It is time to abandon the Humpty Dumpty approach:

"When I use a word," Humpty Dumpty said, in a rather scornful tone, "it means just what I choose it to mean—neither more nor less."

Lewis Carroll: *Through the Looking Glass.*

REFERENCES

1. Harris CRS. The heart and vascular system in ancient Greek medicine. Oxford, England: Clarendon, 1973.
2. Harvey W; Franklin KJ, trans-ed. Circulation of the blood. Oxford, England: Blackwell Scientific, 1958.
3. Hamel G. Die Bedeutung des Pulses für den Blutstrom. Ztschr Biol NSF 1889:474.
4. Jakobi C. Ein Beitrag zur Technik der künstlichen Durchblutung überlebender Organe. Arch Exp Path u Phar 1895;36:331.
5. Rodewald G. History of extracorporeal circulation. In: Hagl S, Klövekorn WP, Mayr N, Sebening F, eds. Thirty years of extracorporeal circulation. München: Deutsches Herzzentrum, 1984:25–43.
6. Gibbon JH Jr. Artificial maintenance of circulation during experimental occlusion of the pulmonary artery. Arch Surg 1937;34:1105–1131.
7. Gibbon JH Jr. The maintenance of life during experimental occlusion of the pulmonary artery followed by survival. Surg Gynecol Obstet 1939;69:602–614.
8. Gibbon JH Jr. Application of a mechanical heart and lung apparatus to cardiac surgery. Minn Med 1954;37:171–185.
9. Trinkle JK, Helton NE, Wood RC, et al. Metabolic comparison of a new pulsatile pump and a roller pump for cardiopulmonary bypass. J Thorac Cardiovasc Surg 1969;58:562–566.
10. Kirklin JW, Dushane JW, Patrick RT, Donald DE, Hetzel PS, Harshbarger HG, Wood EH. Intracardiac surgery with the aid of a mechanical pump-oxygenator system (Gibbon type): report of eight cases. Proc Staff Meet Mayo Clin 1955;30:201–206.
11. Lillehei CW, De Wall RA, Read RC, Warden HE, Varco RL. Direct vision intracardiac surgery in man using a simple disposable artificial oxygenator. Dis Chest 1956;29:1–8.
12. Nakayama I, Tamiya T, Yamamoto K, et al. High amplitude pulsatile pump in extracorporeal circulation with particular reference to hemodynamics. Surgery 1963;54:798–802.
13. Shepard RB, Kirklin JW. Relation of pulsatile flow to oxygen consumption and other variables during cardiopulmonary bypass. J Thorac Cardiovasc Surg 1969;58:694–702.
14. Jacobs LA, Klopp EH, Seamone W, Topaz SR, Gott VL. Improved organ function during cardiac bypass with a roller pump modified to de-

liver pulsatile flow. J Thorac Cardiovasc Surg 1969;58:703–712.
15. Wesolowski SA, Sauvage LR, Pinc RD. Extracorporeal circulation: the role of the pulse in maintenance of the systemic circulation during heart-lung bypass. Surgery 1955;37:663–682.
16. Ogata T, Ida Y, Nonoyama A, et al. A comparative study of the effectiveness of pulsatile and non-pulsatile flow in extracorporeal circulation. Arch Jpn Chir 1960;29:59–62.
17. Mandelbaum I, Berry J, Silbert M, et al. Hemodynamic effects of pulsatile and non-pulsatile flow. Arch Surg 1965;91:771–774.
18. Mandelbaum I, Burns WH. Pulsatile and nonpulsatile flow. JAMA 1965;191:657–660.
19. Dunn J, Kirsh MM, Harness J, et al. Hemodynamic, metabolic and hematologic effects of pulsatile cardiopulmonary bypass. J Thorac Cardiovasc Surg 1974;68:138–147.
20. Watkins L Jr, Lucas SK, Gardner TJ, Potter A, Walker WG, Gott VL. Angiotension II levels during cardiopulmonary bypass: a comparison of pulsatile and non-pulsatile flow. Surg Forum 1979;30:229–230.
21. Geha AS, Salaymeh MT, Abe T, Baue A. Effect of pulsatile cardiopulmonary bypass on cerebral metabolism. J Surg Res 1972;12:381–387.
22. Steed DL, Folette DM, Foglia R, Maloney JV, Buckberg GD. Effects of pulsatile assistance and nonpulsatile flow on subendocardial perfusion during cardiopulmonary bypass. Ann Thorac Surg 1978;26:133–141.
23. Philbin DM, Levine FH, Emerson CW, Coggins CH, Buckley MJ, Austen WG. Plasma vasopressin levels and urinary flow during cardiopulmonary bypass in patients with valvular heart disease: effect of pulsatile flow. J Thorac Cardiovasc Surg 1979;78:779–783.
24. Trinkle JK, Helton NE, Bryant LR, Griffen WO. Pulsatile cardiopulmonary bypass: clinical evaluation. Surg 1970;68:1074–1078.
25. Singh RKK, Barratt-Boyes BG, Harris EA. Does pulsatile flow improve perfusion during hypothermic cardiopulmonary bypass? J Thorac Cardiovasc Surg 1980;79:827–832.
26. Frater RWM, Wakayama S, Oka Y, et al. Pulsatile cardiopulmonary bypass: failure to influence hemodynamics or hormones. Circulation 1980; 62(suppl 1):19–25.
27. Salerno TA, Henderson M, Keith FM, Charrette EJP. Hypertension after coronary operation: Can it be prevented by pulsatile perfusion? J Thorac Cardiovasc Surg 1981;81:396–399.
28. Taylor KM, Bain WH, Russell M, et al. Peripheral vascular resistance and angiotensin II levels during pulsatile and nonpulsatile cardiopulmonary bypass. Thorax 1979;34:594–598.
29. Taylor KM. Vasopressor release and multiple

organ failure in cardiac surgery. Perfusion 1988;3:1–16.

30. Taylor KM, Bain WH, Morton JJ. The role of angiotension II in the development of peripheral vasoconstriction during open-heart surgery. Am Heart J 1980;100:935–937.

31. Levine FH, Philbin DM, Coggins CH, Emerson CW, Buckley MJ. Plasma vasopressin levels and urinary Na$^+$ excretion during CPB: a comparison of pulsatile and nonpulsatile flow. Surgical Forum 1978;29:320–322.

32. Minami K, Körner MM, Vyska K, Kleesiek K, Knobl H, Korfer R. Effects of pulsatile perfusion on plasma catecholamine levels and hemodynamics during and after cardiac operation with cardiopulmonary bypass. J Thorac Cardiovasc Surg 1990;99:82–91.

33. Ead HW, Green JH, Neil E. A comparison of the effects of pulsatile and nonpulsatile blood flow through the carotid sinus on the reflexogenic activity of the sinus baroreceptor in the cat. J Physiol (Lond) 1952;118:509–519.

34. Angell James JE. The effects of altering mean pressure, pulse pressure and pulse frequency of the impulse activity in baroreceptor fibres from the aortic arch and right subclavian artery in the rabbit. J Physiol (Lond) 1971;214:65–88.

35. Angell James JE, de Burgh Daly M. Effects of graded pulsatile pressures on the reflex vasomotor responses elicited by changes of mean pressure in the perfused carotid sinus—aortic arch regions of the dog. J Physiol (Lond) 1971;214:51–64.

36. Spickler JW, Kezdi P. Dynamic response characteristics of carotid sinus baroreceptors. Am J Physiol 1967;212:472–476.

37. Ninomiya I, Irisawa H. Aortic nervous activities in response to pulsatile and nonpulsatile pressure. Am J Physiol 1967;213:1504–1511.

38. Koushanpour E, McGee JP. Effect of mean pressure on carotid sinus baroreceptor response to pulsatile pressure. Am J Physiol 1969;216:599–603.

39. Giron F, Birtwell WC, Soroff HS, Deterling RA. Hemodynamic effects of pulsatile and nonpulsatile flow. Arch Surg 1966;93:802–810.

40. Boucher JK, Rudy LW, Edmunds LH Jr. Organ blood flow during pulsatile cardiopulmonary bypass. J Appl Physiol 1974;36:86–90.

41. Randall JE, Stacy RW. Pulsatile and steady pressure-flow relations in the vascular bed of the hind leg of the dog. Am J Physiol 1956;185:351–354.

42. Landymore RW, Murphy DA, Kinley CE, et al. Does pulsatile flow influence the incidence of postoperative hypertension? Ann Thorac Surg 1979;28:261–268.

43. Philbin DM, Levine FH, Kono K, et al. Attenuation of the stress response to cardiopulmonary bypass by the addition of pulsatile flow. Circulation 1981;64:808–812.

44. Mori A, Tabata R, Nakamura Y, Watanabe K, Onoe M, Okada Y. Effects of pulsatile cardiopulmonary bypass on carbohydrate and lipid metabolism. J Cardiovasc Surg 1987;28:621–626.

45. Canivet JL, Larbuisson R, Damas P, et al. Plasma renin activity and urine β_2-microglobulin during and after cardiopulmonary bypass: pulsatile vs nonpulsatile perfusion. Eur Heart J 1990;II:1079–1082.

46. Philbin DM, Coggins CH, Wilson N, Sokoloski J. Antidiuretic hormone levels during cardiopulmonary bypass. J Thorac Cardiovasc Surg 1977;73:145–148.

47. Simpson P, Forsling M. The effects of halothane on plasma vasopressin during cardio-pulmonary bypass. Clin Endocrinol (Oxf) 1977;7:33–39.

48. Philbin DM, Coggins CH, Emerson CW, et al. Plasma vasopressin levels and urinary sodium excretion during cardiopulmonary bypass: comparison of halothane and morphine anesthesia. J Thorac Cardiovasc Surg 1979;77:582–585.

49. Levine FH, Philbin DM, Kono K, et al. Plasma vasopressin levels and urinary sodium excretion during cardiopulmonary bypass with and without pulsatile flow. Ann Thorac Surg 1981;32:63–67.

50. Britt CI, Lloyd JR, Blizzard RM, Hamwi GJ, Sirak HD. Adrenocortical response to total body perfusion. Arch Surg 1961;82:584–591.

51. Taylor KM, Jones JV, Walker MS, Rao LGS, Bain WH. The cortisol response during heart-lung bypass. Circulation 1976;54:20–26.

52. Taylor KM, Wright GS, Reid JM, et al. Comparative studies of pulsatile and nonpulsatile flow during cardiopulmonary bypass II. The effects on adrenal secretion of cortisol. J Thorac Cardiovasc Surg 1978;75:574–578.

53. Azariades M, Wood AJ, Awang Y, Lennox SC. A qualitative analysis of pulsatile perfusion: effects on cortisol response to cardiopulmonary bypass surgery. Thorac Cardiovasc Surgeon 1986;34:163–167.

54. Kono K, Philbin DM, Coggins CH, et al. Adrenocortical hormone levels during cardiopulmonary bypass with and without pulsatile flow. J Thorac Cardiovasc Surg 1983;85:129–133.

55. Pollock EMM, Pollock JCS, Jamieson MPG, et al. Adrenocortical hormone concentrations in children during cardiopulmonary bypass with and without pulsatile flow. Br J Anaesth 1988;60:536–541.

56. Watkins WD, Moss J, Lappas DG, Levine L, Peterson MB. Vasoactive mediators and human cardiopulmonary bypass [Abstract]. Anesthesiology 1979;51:S97.

57. Davies GC, Sobel M, Salzman EW. Elevated plasma fibrinopeptide A and thromboxane B_2 levels during cardiopulmonary bypass. Circulation 1980;61:808–814.

58. Watkins WD, Peterson MB, Kong DL, et al. Thromboxane and prostacyclin changes during cardiopulmonary bypass with and without pulsatile flow. J Thorac Cardiovasc Surg 1982;84:250–256.

59. Moores WY, Hannon JP, Crum J, et al. Coronary flow distribution and dynamics during continuous and pulsatile extracorporeal circulation in the pig. Ann Thorac Surg 1977;24:582–590.

60. Moores WY, Hannon JP, Crum JD, Wilford DC. Continuous and pulsatile extracorporeal coronary perfusion in the beating and fibrillating swine myocardium: effects on left ventricular function. Surg Forum 1977;28:262–264.

61. Habal SM, Weiss MB, Spotnitz HM, et al. Effects of pulsatile and nonpulsatile coronary perfusion on performance of the canine left ventricle. J Thorac Cardiovasc Surg 1976;72:742–755.

62. Grover FL, Fewel JG, Vinas J, et al. Effects of aortic balloon pumping during cardiopulmonary bypass on myocardial perfusion, metabolism, and contractility. Chest 1979;75:37–44.

63. Hewitt RL, Weichert RF. Diastolic augmentation during heart bypass. J Thorac Cardiovasc Surg 1970;60:123–130.

64. Ciardullo R, Schaff HV, Flaherty JT, Gott VL. A new method of producing pulsatile flow during cardiopulmonary bypass using a standard roller pump. J Thorac Cardiovasc Surg 1976;72:585–587.

65. Schaff HV, Ciardullo RC, Flaherty JT, Brawley RK, Gott VL. Regional ischemia distal to a critical coronary stenosis during prolonged fibrillation—improvement with pulsatile perfusion. Circulation 1977;56(suppl 2):25–32.

66. Bixler TJ, Magee PG, Flaherty JT, Gardner TJ, Gott VL. Beneficial effects of pulsatile perfusion in the hypertrophied ventricle during ventricular fibrillation. Circulation 1979;60(suppl 1):141–146.

67. Pappas G, Winter SD, Kopriva CJ, Steele PP. Improvement of myocardial and other vital organ functions and metabolism with a simple method of pulsatile flow (IABP) during clinical cardiopulmonary bypass. Surgery 1975;77:34–44.

68. Maddoux G, Pappas G, Jenkins M, et al. Effect of pulsatile and nonpulsatile flow during cardiopulmonary bypass on left ventricular ejection fraction early after aortocoronary bypass surgery. Am J Cardiol 1976;37:1000–1004.

69. Bregman D, Bailin M, Bowman FO Jr, et al. A pulsatile assist device (PAD) for use during cardiopulmonary bypass. Ann Thorac Surg 1977;24:574–581.

70. Zumbro GL Jr, Shearer G, Fishback ME, Galloway RF. A prospective evaluation of the pulsatile assist device. Ann Thorac Surg 1979;28:269–273.

71. Levine FH, Phillips HR, Carter JE, et al. The effect of pulsatile perfusion on preservation of left ventricular function after aortocoronary bypass grafting. Circulation 1981;64(suppl 2):40–44.

72. Silverman NA, Levitsky S, Kohler J, Trenkner M, Feinberg H. Pulsatile reperfusion does not modify global myocardial ischemic injury. J Thorac Cardiovasc Surg 1982;84:406–412.

73. Mori F, Ivey TD, Itoh T, Thomas R, Breazeale DG, Misbach G. Effects of pulsatile reperfusion on postischemic recovery of myocardial function after global hypothermic cardiac arrest. J Thorac Cardiovasc Surg 1987;93:719–727.

74. Paquet KJ. Hemodynamic studies on normothermic perfusion of the isolated pig kidney with pulsatile and nonpulsatile flows. J Cardiovasc Surg (Torino) 1969;1:45–48.

75. Philbin DM, Kono K, Alban J, Moss J, Coggins CH, Buckley MJ. The hormonal and hematologic effects of pulsatile flow during cardiopulmonary bypass. In: Hagl S, Klövekorn WP, Mayr N, Sebening F, eds. Thirty years of extracorporeal circulation. Munich: C Gerber, 1984;427–434.

76. Williams GD, Seifen AB, Lawson NW, et al. Pulsatile perfusion versus conventional high-flow nonpulsatile perfusion for rapid core cooling and rewarming of infants for circulatory arrest in cardiac operation. J Thorac Cardiovasc Surg 1979;78:667–677.

77. Taylor KM, Bain WH, Maxted KJ, et al. Comparative studies of pulsatile and nonpulsatile flow during cardiopulmonary bypass. I. Pulsatile system employed and its hematologic effects. J Thorac Cardiovasc Surg 1978;75:569–573.

78. Salerno TA, Charrette EJP, Keith FM. Hemolysis during pulsatile perfusion: clinical evaluation of a new device. J Thorac Cardiovasc Surg 1980;79:579–581.

79. Hooker DR. Study of the isolated kidney: influence of pulse pressure on renal function. Am J Physiol 1910;27:24–.

80. Gesell RA. On relation of pulse pressure to renal function. Am J Physiol 1913;32:70.

81. Goodyer AVN, Glenn WWL. Relation of arterial pulse pressure to renal function. Am J Physiol 1951;167:689–697.

82. Selkurt EE. Effects of pulse pressure and mean arterial pressure modification on renal hemodynamics and electrolyte and water excretion. Circulation 1951;4:541–551.

83. Ritter ER. Pressure/flow relations in the kidney: alleged effects of pulse pressure. Am J Physiol 1952;168:480–489.

84. Judson WE, Rausch NH. Effects of acute reduction of renal artery blood pressure on renal hemodynamics and excretion of electrolytes and water [Abstract]. J Lab Clin Med 19957;50:923.

85. Many M, Soroff HS, Birtwell WC, Giron F, Wise H, Deterling RA. The physiologic role of pulsatile and nonpulsatile blood flow: II. Effects on renal function. Arch Surg 1967;95:762–766.

86. Many M, Soroff HS, Birtwell WC, Wise HM, Deterling RA. The physiologic role of pulsatile and nonpulsatile flood flow: III. Effects of unilateral renal artery depulsation. Arch Surg 1968;97:917–923.

87. Cowan GSM Jr, Padula RT, Magee JH, Camishion RC. Effects of pulsatile and nonpulsatile blood flow on renal function. Surg Forum 1968;19:389–391.

88. Senning A, Andres J, Bornstein P, Norberg B, Anderson MN. Renal function during extracorporeal circulation at high and low flow rates: experimental studies in dogs. Ann Surg 1960;151:63–70.

89. Shen J, Haneda K, Sekino Y, Arai S, Komatsu T, Mohri H. The effects of pulsatile pumping on tissue perfusion and renal function during deep hypothermic low flow perfusion. Jap J Thorac Surg 1990;43:707–711.

90. Olinger GN, Hutchinson LD, Bonchek LI. Pulsatile cardiopulmonary bypass for patients with renal insufficieny. Thorax 1983;38:543–550.

91. Matsuda H, Hirose H, Nakano S, et al. Results of open heart surgery in patients with impaired renal function as creatinine clearance below 30 ml/min. J Cardiovasc Surg 1986;27:595–599.

92. Belzer FO, Ashby BS, Huang JS, Dunphy JE. Etiology of rising perfusion pressure in isolated organ perfusion. Ann Surg 1968;168:382–391.

93. Agishi T, Peirce EC II, Kent BB. A comparison of pulsatile and non-pulsatile pumping for ex vivo renal perfusion. J Surg Res 1969;9:623–634.

94. Corcoran AC, Page IH. Renal blood flow in experimental renal hypertension. Am J Physiol 1942;135:361–371.

95. Goodman TA, Gerard DF, Bernstein EF, Dilley RB. The effects of pulseless perfusion on the distribution of renal cortical blood flow and on renin release. Surgery 1976;80:31–39.

96. Dalton ML, Mosley EC, Woodward KE, Barila TG. The effect of pulsatile flow on renal blood flow during extracorporeal circulation. J Surg Res 1965;5:127–131.

97. German JC, Chalmers GS, Hirai J, Mukherjee ND, Wakabayashi A, Connolly JE. Comparison of nonpulsatile and pulsatile extracorporeal circulation on renal tissue perfusion. Chest 1972;61:65–69.

98. Mukherjee ND, Beran AV, Hirai J, et al. In vivo determination of renal tissue oxygenation during pulsatile and nonpulsatile left heart bypass. Ann Thorac Surg 1973;15:354–363.

99. Badner NH, Murkin JM, Lok P. Renal function is not influenced by differences in pH management and pulsatile/nonpulsatile perfusion during cardiopulmonary bypass [Abstract]. Anesthesiology 1991;75:A65.

100. Halley MM, Reemtsma K, Creech O Jr. Cerebral blood flow, metabolism, and brain volume in extracorporeal circulation. J Thorac Surg 1958;36:506–518.

101. Sanderson JM, Wright G, Sims FW. Brain damage in dogs immediately following pulsatile and nonpulsatile blood flows in extracorporeal circulation. Thorax 1972;27:275–286.

102. Wright G, Sanderson JM. Brain damage and mortality in dogs following pulsatile and non-pulsatile blood flows in extracorporeal circulation. Thorax 1972;27:738–747.

103. Watanabe T, Orita H, Kobayashi M, Washio M. Brain tissue pH, oxygen tension, and carbon dioxide tension in profoundly hypothermic cardiopulmonary bypass. J Thorac Cardiovasc Surg 1989;97:396–401.

104. Kono M, Orita H, Shimanuki T, Fukasawa M, Inui K, Wasio M. A clinical study of cerebral perfusion during pulsatile and nonpulsatile cardiopulmonary bypass. J Jap Surg Soc 1990;91:1016–1022.

105. Henze T, Stephan H, Sonntag H. Cerebral dysfunction following extracorporeal circulation for aortocoronary bypass surgery: no differences in neuropsychological outcome after pulsatile versus nonpulsatile flow. Thorac Cardiovasc Surg 1990;38:65–68.

106. Campbell DE, Raskin SA. Cerebral dysfunction after cardiopulmonary bypass: aetiology, manifestations and interventions. Perfusion 1990;5:251–262.

107. Moores WY, Gago O, Morris JD, Peck CC. Serum and urinary amylase levels following pulsatile and continuous cardiopulmonary bypass. J Thorac Cardiovasc Surg 1977;74:73–76.

108. Traverso LW, Ferrari BT, Buckberg GD, Tompkins RK. Elevated postoperative renal clearance of amylase without pancreatitis after cardiopulmonary bypass. Am J Surg 1977;133:298–303.

109. Murray WR, Mittra S, Mittra D, Roberts LB, Taylor KM. The amylase-creatinine clearance ratio following cardiopulmonary bypass.

J Thorac Cardiovasc Surg 1981;82:248–253.

110. Horton EH, Murthy SK, Seal RME. Haemorrhagic necrosis of small intestine and acute pancreatitis following open heart surgery. Thorax 1968;23:438–445.

111. Panebianco AC, Scott SM, Dart CH Jr, Takaro T, Echegaray HM. Acute pancreatitis following extracorporeal circulation. Ann Thorac Surg 1970;9:562–568.

112. Feiner H. Pancreatitis after cardiac surgery: a morphologic study. Am J Surg 1976;131:684–688.

113. Warshaw AL, O'Hara PJ. Susceptibility of the pancreas to ischemic injury in shock. Ann Surg 1978;188:197–201.

114. Nagaoka H, Innami R, Watanabe M, Satoh M, Murayama F, Funakoshi N. Preservation of pancreatic betal cell function with pulsatile cardiopulmonary bypass. Ann Thoracic Surg 1989;48:798–802.

115. Rose DM, Ranson JHC, Cunningham JN Jr, Spencer FC. Patterns of severe pancreatic injury

following cardiopulmonary bypass. Ann Surg 1984;199:168–172.

116. Fernandez-Del Castillo C, Harringer W, Warshaw AL, et al. Risk factors for pancreatic cellular injury after cardiopulmonary bypass. N Engl J Med 1991;325:382–387.

117. Wesolowski SA, Fisher JH, Welch CS. Perfusion of the pulmonary circulation by nonpulsatile flow. Surgery 1953;33:370–375.

118. Clarke PC, Kahn DR, Dufek JH, Sloan H. The effects of nonpulatile blood flow on canine lungs. Ann Thorac Surg 1968;6:450–457.

119. Wemple RR, Mockros LF, Lewis JF. Pulmonary function during pulsatile and nonpulsatile right heart bypass. J Thorac Cardiovasc Surg 1969;57:190–202.

120. Bruner JMR. Handbook of blood pressure monitoring. Littleton, MA: PSG Publishing, 1978.

121. Grossi EA, Connolly MW, Krieger KH, et al. Quantification of pulsatile flow during cardiopulmonary bypass to permit direct comparison of various types of "pulsatile" and "nonpulsatile" flow. Surgery 1985;98:547–553.

Section III

Coagulation Management During Cardiopulmonary Bypass

14

ANTICOAGULATION FOR CARDIOPULMONARY BYPASS

Glenn P. Gravlee

HISTORY

Numerous events led to the first performance of surgical procedures with cardiopulmonary bypass (CPB) in Philadelphia in 1953 (1). Development of an effective and reversible method to prevent blood clotting in an extracorporeal circuit served as one impediment to this development. Heparin was discovered accidentally in 1916 by an ambitious young medical student named Jay McLean, who had been assigned to experiment with cephalin, a thromboplastic substance. McLean investigated extracts of heart and liver to determine if the thromboplastic substance found in the brain extracts might be something other than cephalin. Using similar extraction procedures, he discovered an extract that retarded plasma coagulation from both the heart (named cuorin) and the liver (named heparphosphatide initially, then changed to heparin) (2, 3). Although McLean had made an important scientific discovery at a young age, he subsequently selected a clinically oriented career that apparently precluded his participation in the development of heparin as a drug (4).

The purification of heparin proceeded in the 1920s, and a fairly crude preparation was first used to anticoagulate blood for transfusion in 1924. Febrile reactions curbed this application, and it took another 12 years to attain a heparin preparation that appeared safe for intravenous administration. During that interval, the discovery that heparin could be obtained less expensively from bovine lung than from bovine liver proved practical in the commercial development of heparin. Clinical trials in thrombotic disorders were initiated in 1935, and it was evident even then that heparin could prevent clot formation or extension although it possessed minimal ability to dissolve existing clots. Chargaff and Olson (5) discovered in 1937 that the peptide protamine dramatically neutralized heparin's anticoagulant effects. Gibbon (6) reported heparin-induced anticoagulation for CPB in animals in 1938. These events led to the selection of heparin-induced anticoagulation with protamine neutralization for the first human operation using CPB in 1953. While most other aspects of CPB practice have changed markedly since that time, the use of heparin and protamine has continued for nearly 40 years. This longevity serves as a testimonial to the astute judgment of Gibbon and his colleagues at Jefferson Medical College. Consequently, this chapter will primarily discuss the pharmacology and clinical use of heparin for this purpose. Alternatives to heparin will be presented briefly as well.

HEPARIN PHARMACOLOGY

Structural Characteristics and Biologic Function

Heparin, more specifically described as a glycosaminoglycan, is a polysaccharide that resides almost exclusively in mast cells. (7) Heparin's physiologic purpose, however, remains uncertain. Clearly, endogenous heparin plays no significant role in maintaining the fluidity of circulating blood. Heparan, a related glycosaminoglycan having a substantially lower sulfur content, dangles tantalizingly from endothelial cell membranes to irresistibly attract circulating antithrombin III (AT III) and potentiate thrombin inhibition. Physiologic anticoagulation at the blood-tissue interface thus derives not from heparin but from heparan. Heparin's primary physiologic purpose may be to participate in nonimmunologic defense against bacterial infections, with other roles likely in capillary angiogenesis and lipid metabolism (8, 9).

Most heparin preparations can be described as unfractionated, meaning that the heparin compound isolated from animal tissues contains heparin molecules of various lengths, with molecular weights ranging from 3,000 to more than 40,000 daltons. The mean molecular weight approximates 15,000 daltons (Fig. 14.1) (10, 11). The molecular weight distribution varies somewhat with the tissue source, the animal source, and the method of purification (12, 13). This variability has some clinical relevance because the spectrum of heparin's clinical actions derives in part from the molecular weight distribution of a heparin compound (14). As a result, each commercial heparin preparation represents a family of drugs whose actions and potency may vary from manufacturer to manufacturer and from batch to batch (15–17).

Heparin can be distinguished from other polysaccharides by its acid nature. It

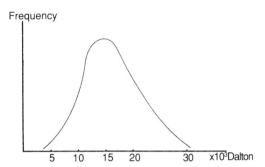

Figure 14.1. Molecular weight distribution pattern of a typical commercial unfractionated heparin preparation. (From Stiekema JCJ. Heparin and its biocompatibility. Clin Nephrol 1989;26(suppl 1):53–58.)

is the strongest macromolecular acid in the body, a characteristic that derives from abundant sulfation of its saccharide units. The basic subunit consists of a repeating disaccharide that contains a uronic acid residue linked to a glucosamine residue (Fig. 14.2) (18). Both the uronic acid and glucosamine residues can assume many different forms based upon the side groups attached to these hexose units. Sulfate groups may attach to the hexose ring via an oxygen, amino, aminoacetyl, or methane link. The result is a large molecule that bears a highly negative charge within the physiologic pH range, and which therefore attracts positively charged molecules. Specific saccharide sequences along the heparin chain determine binding sites to other macromolecules for which it has high affinity, such as AT III, thrombin, and lipoprotein lipase. In the case of antithrombin III, a specific pentasaccharide sequence binds consistently to a specific amino acid sequence on the AT III molecule (18, 19).

Tissue Source and Commercial Preparation

Heparin can be purified from several tissues and from several mammalian species. Although the name "heparin" was selected because the substance was originally

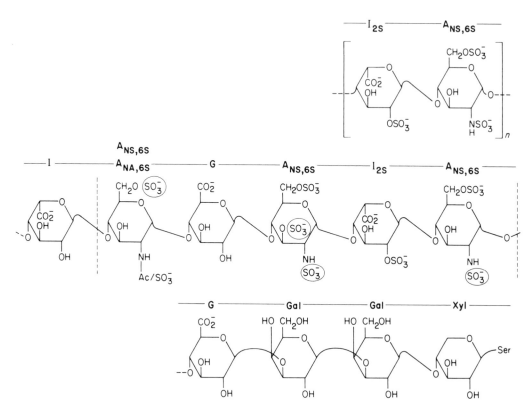

Figure 14.2.   Molecular structure of different parts of the heparin polysaccharide chain. The top row demonstrates a common repeating disaccharide subunit consisting of L-iduronic acid 2-sulfate (I_{2S}) and N-sulpho-a-D-glucosamine 6-sulfate ($A_{NS,6S}$), which represents up to 90% of beef-lung heparin and 70% of porcine mucosal heparin. On the middle row, the five saccharide units between the vertical dotted lines comprise the pentasaccharide sequence required for binding AT III ($A_{NA,6S}$ substitutes an N-acetyl-for the N-sulpho-group on $A_{NS,6S}$, G represents β-D glucuronic acid, and I represents a-L-iduronic acid). This sequence occurs in about 33% of the chains of mucosal heparin and about 20% of the chains of lung heparin. The circled sulfate groups are believed essential for high-affinity binding. The bottom row shows the typical terminal sequence of a heparin molecule (*Gal,* galactose; *Xyl,* xylose) linking to a serine amino acid residue. (From Casu B. Methods of structural analysis. In: Lane DA, Lindahl U, eds. Heparin. Chemical and biological properties, clinical applications. Boca Raton, FL: CRC Press, 1989:25–49.)

isolated from liver extracts, intestinal mucosa and lung tissue represent the most common commercial sources. Mucosal heparin tends to have a lower mean molecular weight, a more cross-linked polysaccharide structure, and a lower cost than lung heparin (15). Heparin manufacturers most often extract mucosal heparin from pigs (porcine mucosal heparin) and lung heparin from cattle (bovine lung heparin).

Differences in the tissue source influence molecular structure more than differences in the animal source (20, 21). Both porcine mucosal heparin and bovine lung heparin have been widely used as anticoagulants for CPB. Both provide effective anticoagulation and thrombosis prevention in experimental models (22, 23) and in adult volunteers (24). Investigating standardized needle punctures in exposed carotid arteries in dogs, Abbott et al. (25) found a higher incidence of delayed hemorrhage in animals anticoagulated with mucosal heparin than with lung heparin. This difference remained significant even when the anticoagulation was neutralized with protamine. Two studies prospectively compared mucosal and lung heparin for CPB in humans. Stewart and Gaich (26) found that higher doses of mucosal heparin were needed to reach the desired prolongation of the activated clotting time (ACT), a finding that might be attributable to batch-to-batch variability. Fiser et al. (27) observed greater postoperative blood loss in patients randomly assigned to receive mucosal heparin than in those who received lung heparin. Both animal and human studies indicate that mucosal heparin can be neutralized with 25% to 30% less protamine than lung heparin (21, 28). These studies used standard tests of plasma coagulation such as clotting time and activated partial thromboplastin time, which might not detect residual unneutralized inhibition of factor Xa. Because of its lower mean molecular weight, mucosal heparin more effectively inhibits factor Xa than does lung heparin (29), and protamine only partially neutralizes this effect. This might explain the greater propensity for delayed bleeding found after anticoagulation with mucosal heparin (25, 27). Fairly limited prospective comparisons and some theoretical considerations thus suggest a slight advantage to lung heparin for CPB anticoagulation.

Because of heparin's acid nature, a ligand must be bound to it when the compound is prepared for commercial use. Sodium and calcium have been used for this purpose. The two salts are indistinguishable with intravenous heparin administration, but the calcium salt retards the uptake of subcutaneously administered heparin (12, 30) and may reduce local hematoma formation with subcutaneously administered heparin (31).

Potency Standardization

Four assays have been used in recent years to determine the potency of unfractionated heparin (23, 32), including international, United States, British, and European standards. The International Standard represents the mean of the pharmacopoeial methods, which results in some variation in

potency between international units (IU) and United States Pharmacopoeia (USP) units (32). The USP assay defines 1 USP unit as the amount of heparin that maintains fluidity of 1 ml of citrated sheep plasma for 1 hour after recalcification. The British Pharmacopoeia (BP) method uses sulfated ox blood activated with thromboplastin. The BP method has been superseded by a European Pharmacopoeia (EP) method that recalcifies sheep plasma in the presence of kaolin and cephalin incubated for 2 minutes, thus constituting an activated partial thromboplastin time (APTT) for sheep plasma. The EP method rigorously standardizes the collection of sheep plasma, which might diminish the assay variability previously reported between batches of sheep plasma substrate (20). Although speculation exists about the clinical significance of batch-to-batch variability in heparin potency, it seems more likely that interpatient variability accounts for most of the observed variation in the clinical anticoagulation response to heparin. Because the relationship between mass (milligrams) and potency (units) varies among heparin preparations, it appears more sensible to record heparin doses in units than in milligrams.

Pharmacokinetics

Since heparin administration for CPB is exclusively intravenous, this discussion will be limited to that route of administration. After central venous injection of a heparin bolus, the onset of maximal ACT prolongation in the radial artery occurs within 1 minute (33, 34). Previous work (35) suggested that heparin action peaks 10 to 20 minutes after administration in cardiac surgical patients, but this finding probably represented an artifact from other factors prolonging the ACT such as hemodilution and hypothermia. Three studies clearly demonstrate that heparin's onset is much faster than that, and that a rapid redistribution effect probably accounts for a modest

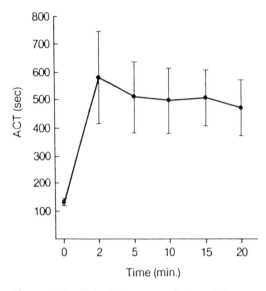

Figure 14.3. The ACT measured via radial artery blood sampling at five different intervals after injection of 300 U/kg of heparin into the right atrium. Maximum ACT prolongation was present within 2 minutes in most patients, with subsequent moderate ACT reduction likely reflecting a rapid redistribution effect. (From Gravlee GP, Angert KC, Tucker WY, Case LD, Wallenhaupt SL, Cordell AR. Early anticoagulation peak and rapid distribution after intravenous heparin. Anesthesiology 1988;68:126–129.)

reduction in heparin's anticoagulant effect, occurring 3 to 13 minutes after the peak effect. (Fig. 14.3) (33, 34, 36). It remains possible that heparin's onset would be slightly delayed in low cardiac output states or with peripheral venous injection.

DISTRIBUTION

Since heparin is macromolecular and highly polarized, one would expect minimal distribution beyond the bloodstream. Based upon these principles and upon bioassay studies of heparin kinetics, heparin's distribution was long believed to be virtually confined to the plasma compartment of the bloodstream (37, 38). Substantial in vitro evidence now points to redistribution of heparin into the endothelial cells (39–42), although this redistribution appears small in comparison to most other drugs. Some uptake into extracellular fluid, al-

veolar macrophages, splenic and hepatic reticuloendothelial cells, and vascular smooth muscle may also occur (43–45). Some or all of these tissues create a relatively small reservoir for heparin that probably contributes to delayed recurrence of heparin-induced anticoagulation (heparin rebound) after protamine neutralization of the heparin residing in the bloodstream. Defining an apparent volume of distribution for heparin remains elusive because pharmacokinetic studies in humans have used some measure of heparin effect, i.e., a bioassay, rather than direct measurement of plasma heparin concentration. Bioassays represent the most practical approach to the clinical evaluation of heparin pharmacodynamics, but these assays can only indirectly and crudely assess pharmacokinetics.

ELIMINATION AND EXCRETION.

Heparin elimination has been studied using various clotting times as bioassays, so the available information largely defines the time course of heparin's clinical activity. The clotting times differ in their sensitivities to heparin, so differences reported in heparin "elimination" kinetics under similar conditions are not necessarily inconsistent. Despite these unavoidable limitations, several aspects of heparin pharmacokinetics can be explained by existing studies. Very small doses of heparin produce minimal or no effect, suggesting a rapid initial clearance, possibly the result of heparin's affinity for endothelial membranes (46, 47). The doses used for CPB anticoagulation are very large, and heparin's biologic elimination half-life is dose-dependent (48, 49). In the only volunteer study using doses sufficient for CPB, Olsson et al. (48) found a half-life of 126 ± 24 minutes with a heparin dose of 400 U/kg. The half-lives for doses one-fourth and one-half that large were 61 ± 9 and 93 ± 6 minutes, respectively. Since CPB distorts the bioassay methods via hypothermia and hemodilution, attempts to define heparin pharmacokinetics in patients undergoing CPB are largely inapplicable. Hypothermia delays heparin elimination, with virtually constant heparin concentrations shown over 40 to 100 minutes of CPB at 25°C (50). Wright et al. (51) found a progressive decline in heparin concentrations at all temperatures, but the rate of decline was delayed in proportion to the hypothermia. Bull et al. (52) found a small decrease in the rate of ACT decline at 30°C (as compared to normothermia), although the independent prolongation of ACT by hypothermia had not been discovered at the time of that study. Severe renal impairment may also prolong heparin action, although available studies yield conflicting results (46). Liver disease apparently has little effect on heparin elimination (46). The mechanism for heparin elimination remains uncertain, but metabolism in the reticuloendothelial system and renal elimination both seem likely (43, 45, 46).

Pharmacodynamics

FIBRIN FORMATION INHIBITION

Heparin induces anticoagulation primarily by potentiating the activity of AT III, a plasma glycoprotein with a molecular weight of 58,000 daltons. Heparin attaches to AT III, thereby altering AT III configuration and rendering it much more attractive to thrombin (19, 53). Heparin thus increases the thrombin-inhibitory potency of circulating AT III by a factor of 1,000 or more. In addition to enzymatically converting fibrinogen to fibrin, thrombin activates cofactors V and VIII, thus greatly increasing the rate of fibrin clot formation via the intrinsic and common pathways. Figure 14.4 shows the plasma coagulation cas-

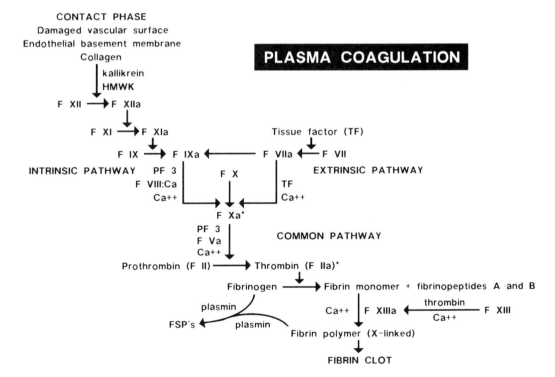

Figure 14.4. Schematic diagram of the plasma coagulation pathway, divided into intrinsic, extrinsic, and common component pathways. *F,* factor; roman numerals, different coagulation factors by number; *a,* activated coagulation factor; *Ca++,* ionized calcium; *HMWK,* high molecular weight kininogen; *PF 3,* platelet factor 3.

cade, which can be somewhat crudely divided into intrinsic, extrinsic, and common pathways. Antithrombin III also inhibits factors IXa, Xa, XIa, and XIIa (54, 55), so heparin indirectly inhibits at least seven factors or cofactors in the plasma coagulation cascade. Plasma coagulation factors vary in their sensitivity to AT III and to different heparin chain lengths. Unfractionated heparin inhibits thrombin most quickly, then inactivates Xa, IXa, XIa, and XIIa with progressively decreasing rate constants (54). Longer heparin chains inhibit thrombin more effectively than factor Xa, while the converse is true for shorter heparin chains (Fig. 14.5) (56). Thrombin inhibition involves transient simultaneous heparin binding to AT III and thrombin. Factor Xa inhibition involves heparin binding to AT III, which in turn binds to factor Xa molecules that need not bind separately to heparin, as depicted in Figure 14.5. Two-thirds or more of the heparin molecules present in commercially available preparations have no anticoagulant effect (14), which probably results from absence of the specific pentasaccharide sequence that binds to AT III.

Heparin also binds to cofactor II, a glycoprotein of molecular weight 65,000 daltons that inactivates thrombin independent of AT III (57). This reaction occurs more slowly and requires higher heparin concentrations than thrombin inhibition via the heparin-AT III interaction. The thrombin-heparin-cofactor II interaction is significantly catalyzed in vitro by plasma heparin concentrations between 0.1 and 0.4 U/ml, which is well below the heparin concentrations used for CPB. This mechanism might therefore contribute routinely to heparin's anticoagulant effect during CPB, and might assume particular importance in patients with AT III deficiency.

VARIABILITY OF PATIENT RESPONSE.

Whether measuring heparin concentration or a clotting time, the response to a fixed-dose heparin bolus varies substan-

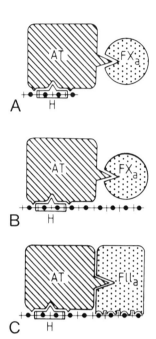

Figure 14.5. Schematic representation of the interaction between heparin (*H*) and activated factors Xa (*FX$_a$*) and IIa (thrombin, *FII$_a$*). Inhibition of factor IIa requires a heparin chain containing at least 18 saccharide units (as shown in **B** and **C**) in addition to the critical pentasaccharide sequence for antithrombin III (*AT*) binding (shown as the framed portion of H bound to AT). This occurs because the heparin molecule must simultaneously bind AT III and thrombin. Factor Xa inhibition is also accomplished with polysaccharide chains long enough to inhibit factor IIa (shown in **B**), but shorter chains can also inhibit factor Xa (shown in **A** with an octasaccharide chain), because simultaneous binding of heparin, AT III, and factor Xa are not required for Xa inhibition. (From Holmer E. Low molecular weight heparin. In: Lane DA, Lindahl U, eds. Heparin. Chemical and biological properties, clinical applications. Boca Raton, FL: CRC Press, 1989: 575–595.)

tially from patient to patient (35, 52, 58–66). The variability of clotting time responses usually exceeds the variability of blood or plasma heparin concentrations observed, as demonstrated by Monkhouse et al. (59) as early as 1953 (59, 60, 67). Bull et al. (52, 68) showed a threefold variation in ACT response to a 200 U/kg heparin bolus, and Esposito et al. (60) found a fourfold ACT range (62 to 267 sec) at that dose and a sixfold range (128 to 755 sec) after a

400 U/kg intravenous bolus. Bull et al. (52, 68) reported equally impressive ranges of heparin elimination rates during CPB using ACT as an indirect heparin assay. In vitro techniques have been introduced to predict individual patient dose-response relationships between heparin and either blood heparin concentration or ACT (HemoTec Inc, International Technidyne, Edison, NJ). The predictive accuracy of these devices has been variable (69, 70), but appears to be improving.

Table 14.1.   Acute Effects of Heparin on Platelets

Action
Serotonin release (72)
Increased adenosine diphosphate-induced aggregation (73–75)
Decreased thrombin-induced aggregation (76)
Counteraction of prostacyclin-mediated platelet inhibition (77, 78)
Increased collagen-induced aggregation (75)
Dose-dependent increase in bleeding time (79, 80)
Increased platelet factor 4 release (75)
Increased epinephrine-induced platelet aggregation (73)
Decreased platelet count (81)

SIDE EFFECTS

Plasma coagulation, the formation of a platelet plug, and fibrinolysis constitute the three major components of blood clot formation and dissolution. Heparin's therapeutic effects derive primarily from the effects on plasma coagulation described above, but heparin also affects the other two components. Heparin-induced activation of fibrinolysis has been identified in a primate model (71). Release of tissue plasminogen activator probably causes this effect, the clinical significance of which is unknown. Activation of the fibrinolytic pathway occurs during anticoagulation associated with CPB, so heparin might participate in this activation. Heparin also has numerous effects on platelets, many of which occur acutely, and would therefore be applicable in patients undergoing CPB. Table 14.1 lists these effects, which most often represent laboratory findings obtained on human platelet-rich plasma. The clinical significance of these findings is uncertain, but clearly heparin binds avidly to platelets and induces a platelet release reaction. Increased molecular chain length and increased sulfation enhance these effects, which are unrelated to AT III affinity (82–85). Moderate prolongation of bleeding time and transient decreases in platelet count have been present in some investigations and absent in others (84). Both predictable and idiosyncratic effects of heparin

on platelets have been recently reviewed by Warkentin and Kelton (84). The idiosyncratic syndrome of heparin-induced thrombocytopenia is discussed in a separate section bearing that name.

In clinical settings other than CPB, bleeding complications comprise the most common side effect of heparin, with reported incidences varying from 1% to 37% (86–89). The profound anticoagulation present during CPB probably increases surgical bleeding, but blood salvage via the cardiotomy suction usually renders this unimportant. Excessive postoperative bleeding from residual unneutralized heparin or from heparin rebound can occur after CPB (see Chapter 17).

The intravenous heparin bolus dose administered before CPB decreases arterial pressure and systemic vascular resistance approximately 10% to 20% without affecting cardiac output or heart rate (90–92). Urban et al. (91) related this change to a decrease in ionized calcium levels, and were able to prevent these changes by prophylactically administering 125 mg of calcium chloride to adult patients before giving an intravenous heparin bolus.

Heparin can induce a variety of metabolic and immunologic effects (93), thus anticoagulation with heparin might contribute to the array of abnormalities known to occur in those systems during CPB. Heparin dramatically increases plasma levels of lipoprotein lipase by releasing this enzyme from vascular endothelium. This activity bears no relation to AT III affinity, and results in triglyceride degradation and increased circulating levels of free fatty acids (9). Although the clinical significance of these effects remains unclear, they could potentially affect myocardial metabolism and the plasma free fraction of lipid-soluble drugs.

Rare acute reactions attributed to heparin include anaphylaxis, pulmonary edema (94–101), and disseminated intravascular coagulation (102). Some of these reactions have been traced to the preservatives chlorocresol and chlorbutol (96, 97, 98). Harada et al. (94) reported the uneventful use of bovine lung heparin for CPB in a child who had previously experienced anaphylaxis from porcine mucosal heparin, and Schey (103) reported resolution of a localized skin reaction to subcutaneous heparin injections when low molecular weight heparin was substituted for unfractionated heparin. Interactions with antibiotics have also been reported, notably with gentamicin and erythromycin (104, 105), although these appear unlikely to have clinical significance. Administration of heparin for weeks to months has been associated with osteoporosis, alopecia, hyperaldosteronism, and benign elevation of serum serum glutamic oxaloacetic transaminase levels (106–109).

HEPARIN DOSING AND MONITORING

For more than 2 decades of cardiac surgery with CPB, heparin dosing was accomplished empirically, with initial doses usually ranging from 200 to 400 U/kg and maintenance doses of 50 to 100 U/kg given as often as every 30 minutes or as infrequently as every 2 hours (52). The priming fluid used for the extracorporeal circuit usually contained 10,000 to 20,000 units of heparin. Heparin monitoring, defined as laboratory testing for the adequacy of blood heparin concentration or of a heparin-induced anticoagulant effect, was limited by the absence of an easily applicable test. This situation changed with the introduction of two coagulation tests that could be performed practically at the bedside using whole blood. The activated coagulation time (more appropriately called the activated clotting time in later publications) was introduced by Hattersley in 1967 (110) and the blood-activated recalcification time (BART), also termed the recalcified whole blood partial thromboplastin time, was introduced by Blakely in 1968 (111). Both of these tests were first reported for CPB heparin monitoring in 1974, BART for cardiac surgery and ACT for long-term respiratory support (63, 112). The two classic papers by Bull et al. in 1975 (52, 68) pointed out the apparent inadequacy of empiric heparin and protamine dosing protocols and recommended a structured approach using the ACT. This served as a turning point for heparin management during CPB, and the application of ACT monitoring to CPB evolved from virtually nonexistent to widespread use over the ensuing 5 years.

Laboratory Tests for Heparin Monitoring

These tests fall into two categories, clotting times and measurements of blood or plasma heparin concentration. Those who advocate clotting time measurement cite the importance of assessing a clinical heparin effect, recognizing that measuring heparin concentration alone may fail to detect patients who are markedly resistant to heparin-induced anticoagulation (60). Advocates of heparin concentration monitoring note the changing relationship between ACT and blood heparin concentration induced by CPB, especially during hypothermia (113). Jobes et al. (114) outlined ideal characteristics for a CPB anticoagulation monitor. Desirable characteristics include low cost, the use of whole blood, bedside testing capability with minimal equipment and operator attention, reproducible results that are quickly available, and shelf-stable reagents.

CLOTTING TIMES

Most plasma and whole blood tests of the intrinsic or extrinsic coagulation pathways involve measurement of the time taken to form a clot in the presence of selected coagulation stimulants. Since heparin exerts its anticoagulation effects at multiple sites along the coagulation cascade, incremental heparin doses will ultimately prolong any of these clotting times. The responsiveness of each test to heparin depends upon the reagents chosen (115–117) and upon the heparin sensitivity of the part of the coagulation cascade being tested by a particular clotting time. Table 14.2 lists several clotting times in decreasing order of heparin sensitivity. Thrombin time (TT) isolates the thrombin-mediated conversion of fibrinogen to fibrin, and the exquisite sensitivity of TT to heparin derives from thrombin's sensitivity to heparin-enhanced AT III (118). The partial thromboplastin time (PTT) and APTT are similarly very sensitive to low concentrations of heparin. These two tests are most often performed on plasma, and thus require blood collection in a citrated test tube, centrifugation to isolate plasma, then activation with an appropriate reagent followed by automated or manual measurement of the time to plasma coagulation (see Chapter 17). The TT and APTT are

so sensitive to heparin-induced anticoagulation that they become unclottable at heparin concentrations below those considered acceptable for CPB (63, 119–121). This disadvantageous feature with respect to establishing the adequacy of CPB anticoagulation converts to an advantage for detecting small residual amounts of unneutralized heparin after protamine administration (122, 123). On balance, however, TT, PTT, and APTT are inconvenient and impractical as routine monitors for heparin therapy in cardiac surgical patients.

The whole blood clotting time was the first clotting time used to measure heparin's anticoagulant effect (58, 124). A common form of this test is sometimes termed the Lee White clotting time, which simply requires the collection of a blood sample, placement of an equal volume in each of three test tubes, and manual tilting of the tubes one at a time in succession until each one clots. While offering bedside simplicity, low cost, and slightly less sensitivity to heparin than the APTT (121, 125, 126), this test requires nearly undivided attention from the operator for periods often exceeding 30 minutes in the heparinized patient, especially at the heparin doses used for CPB. Jaberi et al. (63) found this test and the APTT similarly unclottable after 400 U/kg of heparin. The ACT, BART, and BaSon tests are activated whole blood coagulation tests, a primary purpose of which is to automate and hasten the whole blood clotting time (63, 110, 119, 127, 128). The ACT and BART have heparin sensitivities appro-

Table 14.2. Clotting Times Prolonged by Heparin

Heparin Sensitivity	Test	Pathway Tested
Very sensitive	Thrombin time	Common
	Activated partial thromboplastin time	Intrinsic and common
	Whole blood clotting time	Intrinsic and common
Moderately sensitive	Saline clotting time	Intrinsic and common
	Activated clotting time	Intrinsic and common
	Blood activated recalcification time	Intrinsic and common
	BaSon clotting time	Intrinsic and common
Slightly sensitive	Prothrombin time	Extrinsic and common

priate for CPB heparin monitoring (52, 63, 64, 68). The PT is least sensitive to heparin-induced anticoagulation because heparin has little effect on the early portion of the extrinsic coagulation pathway because heparin does not inhibit factor VII, and because cephalin is such a potent coagulation activant that even small amounts of unneutralized thrombin permit a normal or near-normal PT (Fig. 14.4) (129).

ACTIVATED CLOTTING TIME (ACT)

Since the late 1970s, ACT has served as the primary workhorse for monitoring CPB anticoagulation. Like APTT, the ACT's normal range and responsiveness to heparin depend upon the equipment used and the reagents selected. The three most common types of ACT are the manual ACT, the Hemochron ACT (International Technidyne) (Fig. 14.6), and the HemoTec ACT (HemoTec Inc, Englewood, CO) (Fig. 14.7). When Bull et al. (52) introduced the ACT to cardiac surgery, they recommended the manual ACT as described by Hattersley (110), which uses diatomaceous earth (celite) as

an activant. Hattersley described prewithdrawing and discarding 1 ml or more of blood by venipuncture, then removing the tourniquet and allowing blood to flow into an evacuated and prewarmed (37°C) tube. A timer was started when blood appeared in the tube, then the tube was inverted a few times for mixing and placed in a 37°C water bath or heat block. At 1 minute and at 5-second intervals thereafter, the tube was withdrawn from the bath and tilted, and the timer was stopped at the appearance of the first unmistakable clot. Bull et al. (52) used 2 ml of blood withdrawn from an indwelling venous catheter, inverted the tube once per second for 30 seconds, placed the glass tube in a heat block warmed by a 40-watt light bulb (temperature unspecified), and rocked the tube slowly until clotting occurred. These authors used a stopwatch that was started when the blood first entered the tube and stopped when the first clearly defined clot was visible. Hattersley (110) reported a mean ACT of 107 ± 13 seconds (range, 81 to 133 seconds), whereas Bull et al. reported a mean ACT of 84 ± 13 seconds (range, 65 to 115 sec-

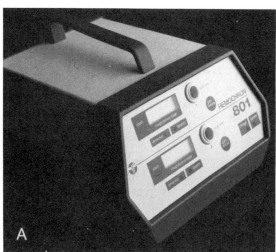
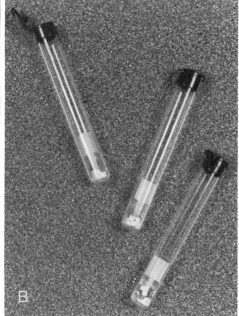

Figure 14.6. The Hemochron ACT device (**A**) and three examples of the celite-containing test tube (**B**), which is placed into one of the testing wells shown in **A** after vigorous agitation. (Photographs courtesy of International Technidyne Inc., Edison, NJ.)

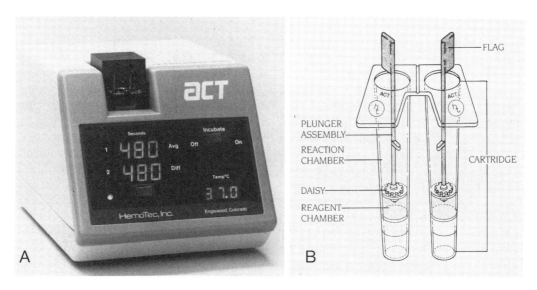

Figure 14.7. The HemoTec ACT device (**A**) and a diagram (**B**) of the dual cartridge containing the kaolin activant (initially isolated in the reagent chamber), which is placed in the well located at the top center of the ACT device. (Photograph and diagram provided courtesy of Medtronic-HemoTec Inc., Englewood, CO.)

onds). The different means and ranges reported in these two investigations could be explained by differences in technique (fresh venipuncture versus indwelling catheter, different mixing technique, water bath versus heat block) or by differences between the patient populations (5000 surgical patients screened preoperatively by Hattersley, 50 cardiac surgical patients screened preoperatively by Bull). Variations in baseline ACT values reported in different studies probably derive from factors like these as well as from instrument-, operator-, and patient-related factors (130).

The ACT decreases slightly even with surgical incision and increases if the tubes are not prewarmed (130–132). Prewarming the tubes may also improve ACT reproducibility (131). Using a manual ACT technique, Kase and Dearing (133) showed that performing the ACT without a heat block prolonged the control ACT by 50% and the CPB ACT by 100% to 150%. In blood taken from patients cooled to 24°C, Kopriva et al. (132) showed that ACT values approximating 500 seconds performed in a 37°C water bath were prolonged to over 2600 seconds when performed in a 24°C water bath. Such factors as the catheter material and the technique used for clearing residual heparin flush solution may also influence the results of ACT (134–136). Two reports indicate that one should withdraw and discard at least two times the sampling system dead space, defined as the volume contained within the system between the point of sampling and the intravascular end of the indwelling catheter (135, 137).

The ACT was designed as a bedside test initiated immediately upon blood sample withdrawal (110), although the effect of delayed test initiation upon ACT results has not been reported. Since the blood sample is drawn without anticoagulant, performing the ACT at a location remote from the patient's bedside cannot be recommended. Cugno et al. (138) reported collecting whole blood in citrate, then recalcifying the sample to perform an ACT. This technique would accommodate modest delays between blood sample collection and test initiation. Since seemingly minor variations in ACT technique can significantly influence results, it appears reasonable to define a normal range for each testing site, with the assumption that operator-related factors can be fairly well-controlled within a particular operating suite, critical care unit, angiography suite, or dialysis unit. It would not be surprising for results not to be interchangeable even between the operating room and the postoperative critical care unit. Because of test variability, duplicate tests for each ACT determination also seem advisable (139).

Manual ACT techniques have been largely replaced by automated ACT techniques, probably because automated techniques require less training and distract the operator for a shorter period, especially when the clotting times are prolonged by heparin. One report apparently links a water bath used for manual ACTs to a cluster of sternal wound infections (140). An easily overlooked aspect of automated ACT instruments is that they should receive regularly scheduled cleaning, calibration, and quality control testing (131, 141, 142). At least two automated ACT devices are commonly used in North America.

The International Technidyne Hemochron ACT (Fig. 14.6A) uses a 2-ml volume of whole blood activated by celite. A timer is started as the blood sample is placed in a test tube (Fig. 14.6B) that contains a small magnet and a plastic baffle. After vigorous manual mixing, the test tube is placed in a tilted well within a heat block and rotated continuously. The formation of a solid clot engages the magnet and causes it to leave the most dependent part of the test tube as rotation continues. This interrupts a magnetic field and automatically stops the timer. The coefficient of variation (mean divided by standard deviation $\times$ 100) of Hemochron ACT is 4% under control conditions (138, 139), but rises to 8% in the presence of blood heparin concentrations used for CPB (139). International Technidyne also offers glass tubes that lack celite and contain saline solution. These tubes can be used in the same fashion, producing a longer clotting time and a test that is slightly more sensitive to low concentrations of heparin (122).

The HemoTec ACT uses 0.4 ml of whole blood injected into each of two plastic cartridges, which are then placed in a heat block (Fig. 14.7). Each cartridge contains a plunger that is engaged by a mechanical lifting device when the test is initiated. The initial plunger movement mixes the whole blood with a kaolin activator, and the continuous rise and fall of the plunger then gently agitates each sample until clot formation retards the passive fall of the plunger after its active elevation. The absence of plunger fall, detected photo-optically, stops the timer to yield the ACT. At the relatively moderate heparin doses used with extracorporeal membrane oxygenation for pulmonary support (mean ACT 152 ± 26 seconds), Green et al. (143) found a mean coefficient of variation of 9.2% with the HemoTec ACT. The HemoTec ACT cartridges are also available with three different concentrations of kaolin to produce different sensitivities and dose-response relationships to heparin. The low-range ACT cartridge provides heparin dose-response characteristics similar to the APTT (144).

Few direct comparisons of manual or automated ACT techniques have been reported. Mabry and coauthors (145) compared manual ACT to Hemochron ACT in patients undergoing vascular surgery and found a slightly lower control ACT with the manual technique (100 ± 12 seconds) than with the Hemochron technique (117 ± 18 seconds), which is similar to the findings of Kurec et al. (121) (manual ACT 91 ± 7 seconds, Hemochron ACT 129 ± 10 seconds). These differences were not subjected to statistical analysis, and values from the two ACT techniques were indistinguishable 5 and 30 minutes after heparin administration in the study of Mabry et al. Kurec and colleagues found manual ACT more sensitive than Hemochron ACT to low concentrations of heparin (0.2 U/ml). Zahl and Ellison (146) compared the Hemochron and HemoTec ACT methods and found similar baseline ACTs, but the Hemo-

Tec ACT was much more sensitive to heparin. When the Hemochron ACT rose into the 400 to 500 seconds range, 10 of 12 HemoTec ACTs exceeded 1000 seconds. Urban and Hines (147) found directionally similar differences that were less extreme (postheparin Hemochron ACT 571 ± 44 seconds, simultaneous HemoTec ACT 742 ± 44 seconds, no difference in control ACTs). Reich at al. (148) compared Hemochron ACT with the high-range HemoTec ACT, the least heparin-sensitive of the HemoTec ACT cartridges, finding no differences at baseline and at high heparin concentrations (ACT>500 seconds, cumulative heparin dose 300 U/kg), but significantly lower HemoTec ACTs at moderate heparin concentrations (HemoTec 263 ± 51 seconds, Hemochron 338 ± 63 seconds after 120 U/kg of heparin). Stead (149) found significantly lower control ACTs with HemoTec (103 ± 5 seconds, presumably mean ± 1 standard error) than with Hemochron (147 ± 4 seconds), no difference after the initial heparin dose before starting CPB, and a significant tendency for Hemochron ACT to increase into the >700 seconds range while HemoTec ACT remained stable in the 500 to 600 seconds range. The HemoTec ACT technique used by Stead differed from the HemoTec ACT methods reported above, so that at least three different HemoTec ACT methods (differences in kaolin concentration or in blood agitation and clot detection techniques) are represented by these four comparisons between Hemochron and HemoTec. One can conclude that results differ among different ACT methods, while the clinical significance of these differences remains uncertain.

Table 14.3 lists some clinical conditions or interventions other than heparin that can affect ACT. The largest and most consistent effect is hypothermia-induced ACT prolongation, an effect that is proportionate to the level of hypothermia. Kopriva et al. (132) showed 20% to 30% longer manual ACTs at 24°C. One study suggests that experimental hypothermia in dogs re-

Table 14.3. Clinical Conditions Influencing ACT

Condition	Effect on ACT
Hypothermia	Increase (132, 150)
Hemodilution	Increase or no effect (150–153)
Thrombocytopenia	Increase or no effect (110, 152–154)
Platelet function inhibition	Increase (153, 155)
Lysed platelets	Decrease (156)
Protamine	Increase (157, 158)
Aprotinin	Increase (159, 160)
Surgical incision	Decrease (130)

leases a heparin-like factor that inhibits factor Xa, a mechanism that could potentially explain this effect (161). Hemodilution has a relatively small effect over the hematocrit range most often present during cardiac surgery (15% to 40%). Ottesen and Froysaker (151) performed in vitro hemodilution on nonanticoagulated blood from six patients, and found no convincing ACT increase in five patients until the sample contained over 70% Ringer's acetate. Results with thrombocytopenia have varied, but ACTs have been either unchanged or slightly increased with platelet counts in the 30,000 to 70,000 per microliter range. The initial report of Hattersley (110) included one patient with a platelet count of 18,000 per microliter whose ACT was prolonged (190 seconds), and another patient with a platelet count of 10,000/uL whose ACT was normal (120 seconds). Kesteven et al. (153) found a significant but relatively modest inverse correlation (r = 0.51) between platelet count and ACT during CPB anticoagulation. Substantial platelet functional impairment induced by prostacyclin or by platelet activation with ADP increases mean ACT by 50% to 60% (155). The latter study suggests that when heparin levels exceed 4 U/ml, further ACT increases depend almost entirely upon platelet functional impairment. This effect could potentially be counteracted by platelet lysis, which significantly decreased ACT in an in vitro model (156). Excessive protamine increases ACT (157, 158), as does the nonspecific protease aprotinin (159, 160). Aprotinin's effect may be specific to celite-activated ACTs.

Monitoring heparin therapy with clotting times assumes a predictable relationship between the blood heparin concentration and the clotting time response within an individual patient. Clotting times sensitive to low heparin concentrations (e.g., whole blood clotting time, APTT, TT) demonstrate a concave dose-response relationship, which converts to a straight line when plotting heparin concentration against the log of the clotting time (115, 116, 119,

124). Congdon et al. (119) demonstrated in dogs a linear dose-response relationship between heparin and ACT at the heparin doses required for CPB. The heparin management protocol recommended by Bull et al. in 1975 (52, 68) thus assumed a linear relationship between heparin dose and ACT. Bull and colleagues recommended measuring a control ACT level before surgery, administering an initial heparin dose of 200 U/kg, measuring ACT 5 minutes later, then constructing a graph with heparin dose administered on one axis and ACT on the other (Fig. 14.8A). Those authors sought an ini-

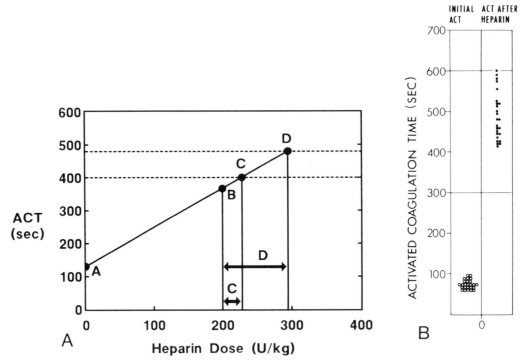

Figure 14.8.   **A.** Graph of the heparin dosing algorithm proposed by Bull et al. (68) in 1975. The control ACT is shown as point *A*, and the ACT resulting from an initial heparin bolus of 200 U/kg is shown as point *B*. The line connecting *A* and *B* is then extrapolated, and a desired ACT is selected. Point *C* represents the intersection between this line and an ACT of 400 seconds, theoretically requiring an additional heparin dose represented by the difference between points *C* and *B* on the horizontal axis (arrow *C*). Similarly, to achieve an ACT of 480 seconds (higher horizontal dotted line intersecting the ACT *versus* heparin dose line at point *D*), one would administer the additional heparin dose represented by arrow *D*. (Modified from Bull et al. (68).) **B.** The column on the left shows ACT values before heparin administration, and the column on the right shows ACT values obtained after applying a two-stage heparin administration protocol designed to produce an ACT value of 480 seconds. (From Bull BS, Huse WM, Brauer FS, Korpman RA. Heparin therapy during extracorporeal circulation. II. The use of a dose-response curve to individualize heparin and protamine dosage. J Thorac Cardiovasc Surg 1975; 69:685–689.)

tial ACT of 480 seconds, but a graphic depiction of their results suggests that the ACTs obtained from this algorithm were fairly evenly distributed between 400 and 600 seconds (Fig. 14.8**B**). In a similar study from the same group, ACT prolongation produced by this algorithm appeared to range from 380% to more than 1000% (162). The predictive accuracy of this algorithm thus falls considerably short of pinpoint. Bull et al. (52) also reported that the ACT end point became unreliable at ACTs exceeding 600 seconds, a finding that was confirmed by Stenbjerg and colleagues (62). Stenbjerg et al. found coefficients of correlation between 0.80 and 0.97 between plasma heparin concentration and ACT at ACT values below 600 seconds. Cohen (163) updated the dose-response relationship after each heparin dose by using least-squares regression, and showed good predictive accuracy (mean error 5.6 ± 14.3% and linear correlation ($r = 0.98$)) with this technique by excluding ACTs over 500 seconds and any ACTs measured in the 1st hour of CPB.

The studies of Stenbjerg et al. and of Cohen assess the linear correlation between heparin concentration (or dose) over an ACT range spanning from normal to markedly prolonged. This large range lends itself to high correlation coefficients even if the relationship between blood heparin concentration and ACT breaks down somewhat over the heparin concentration range used for CPB. Accordingly, scrutinizing Stenbjerg's data during CPB suggests a much less predictable CPB relationship between heparin concentration and ACT than their correlation coefficients suggest, although ACT prolongation by hypothermia might have caused this breakdown. Investigating the predictability of heparin dose-response in 157 patients divided into two groups with respective pre-CPB target ACTs of 480 and 600 seconds, Gravlee et al. (69) found a significantly reduced slope in the heparin dose-response relationship in the latter group (Fig. 14.9**A**). Because the groups

were demographically comparable and differed only in the size of the initial heparin bolus, this suggested a *convex* relationship between heparin concentration and ACT. This observation has been confirmed by the author in unpublished work using ex vivo heparinization of whole blood. Figure 14.9**B** contrasts this relationship to the well-established concave dose-response relationship between heparin and APTT. The dotted line continuation of the proposed heparin-ACT dose response relationship shown in Figure 14.9**B** suggests the common (but not formally documented) clinical observation that the ACT response eventually becomes concave, which might derive from platelet inhibition at high heparin concentrations (155). The relationship between blood heparin concentration and ACT thus appears more complex than early studies indicated. Factors such as intrinsic variability of the test in the anticoagulated state, platelet activation and lysis, depression of platelet function, and hypothermia probably combine to limit greatly the predictability of the ACT response to heparin during CPB. The relatively crude nature of the ACT and its response to heparin should not cause concern, however, because, except when aprotinin is used, the cumulative mechanisms leading to ACT prolongation during CPB apparently have little importance as long as sufficiently high ACTs are maintained (160, 164).

HEPARIN CONCENTRATION MONITORING

Since CPB changes the sensitivity of ACT to heparin (Fig. 14.10) (67, 165), some have advocated monitoring heparin concentration directly (113, 166, 167). Table 14.4 lists several laboratory techniques that measure whole blood or plasma heparin concentration. Protamine and polybrene titrations measure heparin concentration by identifying the reagent concentration that optimally neutralizes heparin, as judged by the fastest clot formation under standardized conditions (114, 162, 168,

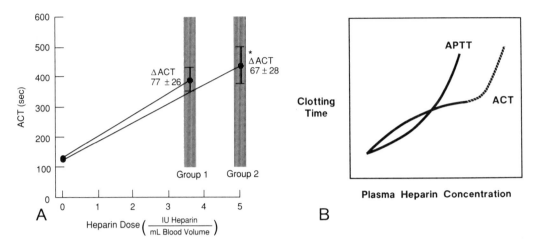

Figure 14.9.   A. The relationship between the slope of the ACT versus heparin dose relationship in two groups of 75 patients each prospectively assigned to receive heparin doses designed to produce ACT values of 480 seconds (*Group 1*) or 600 seconds (*Group 2*) by applying an ex vivo algorithm to predict heparin dose requirements. The groups differed only in initial heparin dose, yet the slope of the ACT/heparin dose relationship was significantly lower in Group 2. (From Gravlee GP, Brauer SD, Roy RC, et al. Predicting the pharmacodynamics of heparin: a clinical evaluation of the Hepcon System 4. J Cardiovasc Anesth 1987;1:379–387.) **B.** The proven relationship between *APTT* and plasma heparin concentration and a hypothesized relationship between *ACT* and plasma heparin concentration. The solid portion of the ACT curve shows the relationship suggested in Figure 14.8A and by unpublished work of Gravlee et al. The interrupted portion of the ACT curve suggests the clinical observation that infinite ACT prolongation can eventually be reached with sufficient heparin concentrations.

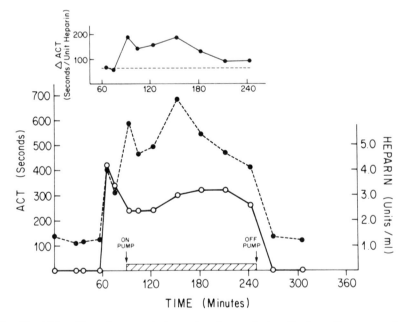

Figure 14.10.   The ACT and heparin concentration values from a single patient over the course of a cardiac surgical procedure. Once CPB began, ACT (*dotted line* connecting *solid circles*) increased while heparin concentration (*solid line* connecting *open circles*) decreased. The inset shows the changing relationship between ACT and heparin concentration over time plotted as the change in ACT concentration from the control value divided by blood heparin concentration. (From Culliford AT, Gitel SN, Starr N, et al. Lack of correlation between activated clotting time and plasma heparin during cardiopulmonary bypass. Ann Surg 1981;193:105–111.)

Table 14.4. Heparin Concentration Measurement Techniques

Protamine titration (manual or automated)
Polybrene titration
Factor Xa inhibition
Chromogenic assay (manual or automated)
Fluorogenic assay
Colorimetric assay (azure A or toluidine blue)

169). This information can be converted to a plasma or blood heparin concentration if the neutralization ratio of protamine to heparin is known (usually 1.0 to 1.2 mg protamine to 100 U heparin). Excesses of protamine and polybrene inhibit clot formation, so the tube or cartridge with the shortest clotting time represents the closest match between heparin and its neutralizing agent. These titrations are performed on whole blood, which offers a practical advantage over most other nonclotting time heparin assays. HemoTec Inc. offers automated techniques that greatly simplify bedside measurement of blood heparin concentration, and have therefore gained a popularity for heparin monitoring that is perhaps second only to ACT measurement. The reproducibility of these devices has not been scrutinized as closely as that for the various clotting times. This factor may pose a significant unexplored problem because a decisive end point for the automated heparin-protamine titration is sometimes difficult to determine.

In a fluorogenic heparin assay, plasma or diluted whole blood is mixed with pooled normal plasma, then incubated for a fixed period with a known amount of thrombin (113, 166, 170–173). This mixture is then added to a fibrin analog that is cleaved predictably by any residual thrombin (i.e., thrombin not bound by heparin or AT III) to form a quantifiably fluorescent product. Most applications of this technique require plasma, which makes the procedure impractical for the bedside. Nevertheless, some operating room laboratories have found an automated version of this test (Protopath, Dade, Miami, FL) to be feasible for CPB heparin monitoring, in part because results can be quickly obtained once the plasma has been separated (113, 172). Saleem et al. (166) showed an acceptable ($r = 0.7$) correlation between Protopath and automated protamine titration.

Other types of heparin assays rely exclusively on plasma samples and would not be practical for routine use during CPB. These tests are based upon a color change induced by binding to heparin (azure A, toluidine, and chromogenic tests) or upon heparin's ability to inhibit activated factor X (174–177).

CLINICAL ASSESSMENTS AND COMPARISONS OF HEPARIN MONITORING TECHNIQUES

Once Bull et al. (52) had outlined the potential problems with CPB heparin management using standardized dosing schemes that varied widely among institutions, numerous investigators followed up on their work by comparing clinical outcomes from ACT monitoring to those from standardized unmonitored heparin management (Table 14.5). Blood loss, blood transfusion comparisons, or both were compared in the clinical investigations shown in Table 14.5. Six of 10 studies showed decreased blood loss with ACT monitoring, and 5 of 7 showed decreased homologous blood transfusion requirements. Unfortunately, only one of these studies appeared to be completely prospective (178), and that study did not specify the method of patient assignment to the two study groups, nor was statistical analysis performed on the observed differences. Ottesen et al. (190) found no difference in postoperative blood loss between two groups that differed only in precise versus crude application of the Bull protocol for determining maintenance doses of heparin during CPB. The studies comparing transfusion requirements did not list the criteria for blood transfusion, which can vary substantially among physicians and institutions (191). From these studies it appears likely that ACT-based CPB

Table 14.5. Clinical Outcome Comparison of Different Types of Heparin Monitoring for CPB[a]

Investigators and Year	Number of Patients	Blood Loss	Transfusion	Experimental Method
A. ACT vs. No Monitoring (NM)				
Babka et al. 1977 (178)	20	ACT < NM[b]	NE	Prospective, randomized?
Verska 1977 (179)	114	ACT < NM	ACT < NM	Historical control group
Roth et al. 1979 (180)	56	ND	ND	Historical control group
Akl et al. 1980 (65)	120	ND	ACT < NM	Historical control group
Papaconstantinou and Rådegran 1981 (181)	126	ACT < NM[c]	ACT < NM[c]	Historical control group
Jumean and Sudah 1983 (182)	77[d]	ACT < NM	NE	Historical control group
Dearing et al. 1983 (183)	648	ACT < NM	ACT < NM	Retrospective, sequential grouping
Niinikoski et al. 1984 (184)	100	ACT < NM	ND	Retrospective, sequential grouping
Lefemine and Lewis 1985 (185)	61	ND	NE	Not specified[e]
Preiss et al. 1985 (186)	350	ND	ACT < NM	Retrospective, not randomized
B. Heparin Concentration vs. No Monitoring				
Jobes et al. 1981 (114)	46	ND	NE	Prospective, randomized
Bowie and Kemna 1985 (187)	150	HC < NM[b]	HC < NM[b]	Prospective, randomized
C. ACT vs. Heparin Concentration Monitoring				
Gravlee et al. 1990 (164)	21	ACT < HC[f]	NE	Prospective, randomized
Urban et al. 1991 (189)	38	ND	ND	Prospective, randomized
Gravlee et al. 1992 (188)	163	ND[g]	ND	Prospective, randomized

[a]HC, heparin concentration; ND, no difference; NE, not evaluated.
[b]No statistical analysis.
[c]Intraoperative only, no difference in postoperative period.
[d]Pediatric patients.
[e]Forty-three ACT patients, 18 NM patients.
[f]No systematic assessment of heparin rebound postoperatively.
[g]Heparin rebound systematically assessed and treated. HC > ACT for incidence of heparin rebound.

heparin management does not increase postoperative bleeding or transfusion requirement; thus, its effect on these parameters is either neutral or favorable. Limitations in experimental designs, notably the use of historical control groups, preclude a more ambitious conclusion favoring either ACT or unmonitored heparin management. Since protamine dosing may also influence postoperative bleeding (192), differences in protamine dosing might also have influenced the results of most of these studies.

Table 14.5 also lists clinical outcome studies comparing heparin concentration monitoring to no monitoring, and ACT monitoring to heparin concentration monitoring. One of two studies shows that heparin concentration monitoring decreases blood loss when compared with no monitoring

(187). This study appears to be prospective and randomized, although the method of randomization was not specified, and the unmonitored (control) group may have been historical. Three studies have compared ACT monitoring to heparin concentration monitoring (Table 14.5, part C). The two studies by Gravlee et al. (164, 188) showed conflicting results with regard to postoperative blood loss. This discrepancy might be explained by aggressive diagnosis and treatment of heparin rebound in the second study. Urban et al. (189) reported no difference between the two techniques.

Is there an optimal range for ACT or heparin concentration during CPB? Bull et al. (52) reported clinical experience that a clot does not form in the oxygenator circuit with an ACT exceeding 300 seconds. Those authors further stated the opinions that (*a*) ACTs below 180 seconds should be considered so inadequate as to be life-threatening, (*b*) ACTs between 180 and 300 seconds should be considered highly questionable, and (*c*) maintaining ACTs exceeding 600 seconds would seem unwise. They noted that a minimum ACT of 180 seconds had been suggested for patients undergoing long-term extracorporeal oxygenation for pulmonary support, and that the higher minimum ACT recommended for cardiac surgery requiring CPB was needed because of the greater amounts of tissue fluid gaining access to the circulation in that setting. While this hypothesis holds some appeal, it remains unproven. Bull et al. also recommended attaining an ACT of 480 seconds before initiating CPB, suggesting that this particular ACT value provided a safety margin over the believed minimum safe ACT of 300 seconds. It appears that many practitioners have misinterpreted their recommendation by assuming that an ACT of 480 seconds represents the minimum safe level for CPB anticoagulation, when the authors were simply offering a suggestion without scientific validation. In 1978, Young et al. (193) raised the minimum recommended ACT level of Bull et al. (300 seconds) by demonstrating fibrin formation and depletion of clotting factors, AT III, and platelets in monkeys sustaining ACTs below 400 seconds during CPB. They then applied this information to five pediatric patients undergoing CPB, finding no untoward events when ACTs over 400 seconds were maintained. They did not, however, investigate the possibility that ACTs below 400 seconds might also be safe in humans. At least six studies have reported ACT values below 400 seconds for CPB without complications (67, 114, 120, 164, 165, 194). Five of these studies report some CPB maintenance ACTs below 300 seconds (68, 114, 120, 165, 194), and Dauchot et al. (120) reported a *mean* ACT of 296 ± 51 (range, 230–437 seconds) after rewarming during CPB in 22 adults.

Metz and Keats (194) assessed the utility of ACT monitoring by administering heparin (300 U/kg) to 193 patients undergoing CPB, then blindly measuring ACT at predetermined intervals. Fifty-one of their patients had ACTs <400 seconds during CPB, with four patients having ACT values <300 seconds. No clots were visible in the extracorporeal circuits during or after CPB, and no relationship was found between lower CPB ACTs and postoperative bleeding. Cardoso et al. (195) recently reported no differences in coagulation factors, platelet counts, or membrane oxygenator performance between two groups of six pigs assigned to an ACT range of 250 to 300 seconds or of >450 seconds for 2 hours of hypothermic CPB.

Several reports suggest the safety of ACTs either in the 170 to 250 seconds range or twice normal for prolonged respiratory support with extracorporeal membrane oxygenators (112, 196–200). Defining ideal anticoagulation in that clinical setting proves difficult, however, because the patients' disease processes predispose to both thromboembolic events and disseminated intravascular coagulation, and even the relatively modest level of anticoagulation used appears to increase bleeding complications (198–200).

Two studies measuring plasma fibrinopeptide A (a sensitive marker of fibrin formation) levels found higher than normal levels during CPB for cardiac surgery, but these fibrinopeptide A (FpA) levels were still considerably lower than those measured after surgical incision alone. Davies et al. (201) noted that 54 of their 73 CPB ACT measurements in 15 patients were less than 400 seconds, and concluded (without assessing a clinical outcome) that these patients had been inadequately anticoagulated. Investigating 21 patients with two different heparin monitoring protocols, Gravlee et al. (164) found that higher heparin concentrations better suppressed FpA levels early in CPB, but that this difference was not sustained during rewarming (Fig.

14.11). Those authors found no correlation between CPB FpA levels and postoperative bleeding, although five patients exhibited CPB FpA levels more than 10 times the upper limit of normal. It thus appears that plasma FpA levels are not reliable indicators of inadequate CPB anticoagulation in humans unless the threshold for morbidity exceeds the levels reported thus far.

Is there a *maximum* safe level of anticoagulation for CPB? Exaggerating the hemorrhagic diathesis during CPB poses little difficulty as long as the blood losses are scavenged effectively into the extracorporeal circuit. One study suggests that higher blood heparin concentrations (>4 U/ml) and ACTs (>600 seconds) during CPB predispose to increased postoperative blood loss (164), although a follow-up study from the same group of investigators failed to confirm this (188). In the latter study, higher CPB heparin concentrations predisposed to postoperative heparin rebound, requiring treatment with protamine. Aside from the need for higher initial protamine doses and a higher incidence of heparin rebound, heparin doses far exceeding the minimum safe requirement for CPB confer no apparent disadvantage.

More studies purport to evaluate safe ACT levels for CPB than safe blood or plasma heparin concentrations. Jobes et al. (114) found no adverse effects with whole blood heparin concentrations exceeding 2 U/ml. The findings of Kesteven (165) were similar, except that he measured *plasma* heparin concentrations, which should be higher than whole blood heparin concentrations in proportion to the relative volumes of the two compartments. Possibly Kesteven corrected his heparin concentrations to represent whole blood levels because his patients otherwise would have sustained CPB whole blood heparin concentrations between 1.0 and 1.5 U/ml, which would likely represent inadequate anticoagulation.

In summary, the optimal ACT or heparin concentration range for CPB has not been definitively established. The ACT min-

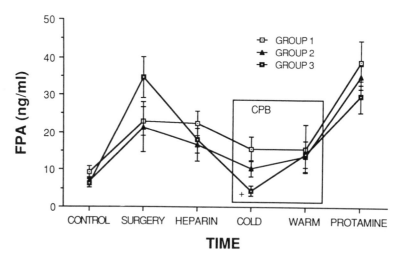

Figure 14.11. Fibrinopeptide A (*FPA*) levels during cardiac surgery in three groups of patients undergoing cardiac surgery. Patients in *Groups 1* and *2* received an initial heparin dose of 200 or 300 U/kg and additional heparin during CPB whenever ACT was below 400 seconds. *Group 3* patients received an initial heparin dose of 400 U/kg and additional heparin whenever whole blood heparin concentration was below 4.0 U/kg. The *FPA* levels peaked before heparin and after protamine, and were significantly different among the groups during hypothermic bypass (*Group 3* versus *Group 1* only). (From Gravlee GP, Haddon WS, Rothberger HK, et al. Heparin dosing and monitoring for cardiopulmonary bypass. A comparison of techniques with measurement of subclinical plasma coagulation. J Thorac Cardiovasc Surg 1990;99:518–527.)

imum of 300 seconds originally recommended by Bull et al. (52) has withstood the test of time, but it appears that lower ACTs might also be acceptable, particularly with membrane oxygenators. Hematologists sometimes question the need for anticoagulation as profound as this, citing evidence that in vitro thrombin inhibition peaks at plasma heparin concentrations below 1 U/ml (equivalent to whole blood heparin concentrations <0.5 U/ml and ACTs usually < 200 seconds) and that heparin excess stoichiometrically increases the likelihood that AT III and thrombin will bind to separate heparin chains instead of forming the desired heparin-AT III-thrombin complex (54, 202). It has not been clearly established whether it is better to monitor heparin concentration or heparin effect, but Nielsen et al. (203) reported one case of clots in both the surgical field and the extracorporeal circuit despite maintaining whole blood heparin concentrations of 4.0 U/ml or higher. The ACTs were not reported for that patient, who had a previously undiagnosed familial AT III deficiency. It seems likely that this clinical scenario could have been avoided by monitoring heparin effect (i.e., ACT) rather than heparin concentration, since there have been no reports of clots in the extracorporeal circuit with ACT >300 seconds.

Since there is no apparent advantage to maintaining ACTs lower than 300 seconds, the simplest clinical guideline is to exceed that value during CPB for cardiac surgery. Metz and Keats (194) appropriately questioned the need for any heparin monitoring, although the rare occurrences of marked heparin resistance (203) or accidental injection of a substance other than heparin suggest some virtue in doing so. There is no need to compensate for hypothermia-induced ACT prolongation by maintaining the blood heparin concentration that was present before hypothermia as long as one anticipates the expected decrease in ACT upon rewarming (163). Consequently, the author sees no clinical advantage to heparin

concentration monitoring, and has selected the following CPB heparin management protocol while recognizing that other protocols may be equally acceptable:

1. Administer heparin 300 U/kg intravenously.
2. Draw an arterial sample for ACT in 3 to 5 minutes.
3. Give additional heparin as needed to achieve ACT >300 seconds before initiating CPB, to maintain ACT >300 seconds during normothermic CPB, and >400 seconds during hypothermia below 30°C.
4. Prime the extracorporeal circuit with approximately 3 U/ml of heparin (e.g., 5000 U for a 1600 ml clear priming solution).
5. Monitor ACT every 30 minutes during CPB, or more frequently if the patient proves resistant to heparin-induced ACT prolongation.

While some prefer to select supplemental heparin doses precisely with the aid of a manual or computer-generated graphic plot as recommended by Bull et al. (68), the author believes that the relative imprecision of the ACT, the unpredictability and likely nonlinearity of the ACT-to-heparin dose-response relationship, and the lack of any proven benefit to a narrowly defined ACT end point render such maneuvers unnecessary. If ACT decreases below the desired minimum value, supplemental heparin doses of 50–100 U/kg most often prolong the ACT sufficiently without the aid of precise calculations.

Some prefer to inject heparin directly into the ascending aorta when preparing for emergency CPB during open chest cardiac massage. It seems reasonable to administer a large systemic dose of heparin (400 U/kg) in an emergency because there may be insufficient time to confirm heparin's effect with an ACT before initiating CPB. Under these circumstances, it also seems reasonable to place a larger than usual heparin dose in the extracorporeal circuit, e.g., 15,000 to 20,000 units.

HEPARIN RESISTANCE

Heparin resistance can be loosely defined as the need for higher than normal heparin doses to induce sufficient anticoagulation for the safe conduct of CPB. Many factors have been reported to alter the anticoagulation response to heparin (Table 14.6). Usually these effects are clinically insignificant (230), but they may cumulatively account for the consistent demonstration of marked interpatient variability in the anticoagulation response to a fixed heparin dose (expressed in units per kilogram). In most cases, heparin resistance can be adequately treated with increased doses of heparin. In some reports, the magnitude of the increased heparin dose and the necessity for other interventions have been exaggerated by misconceptions about the safe minimum ACT required for CPB (204, 206, 231). Clinical situations sometimes inducing noteworthy heparin resistance have included familial AT III deficiency, ongoing heparin therapy (204, 205, 216), extreme thrombocytosis (platelet count > 700,000 per microliter) (208), septicemia (66, 206), and hypereosinophilic syndrome (228). Several groups have reported an interaction between heparin and nitroglycerin in the coronary care unit setting (219, 220), but Reich et al. (232) could not confirm this interaction in the cardiac surgical setting and Amin and Horrow (233) did not find a significant in vitro interaction with AT III.

Antithrombin III deficiency can be inherited or acquired. Congenital AT III deficiency follows an autosomal dominant transmission pattern, and has an estimated prevalence of 1 for every 2000 to 20,000 people (234, 235). A reduced amount of normal AT III constitutes the most common form (235). Affected persons usually have AT III levels below 50% of normal, and they most often present between the ages of 15 and 30 years with lower limb thrombosis or pulmonary embolism. Factors precipitating this occurrence include pregnancy, infection, and surgery, so the primary clinical presentation might be either thrombosis after surgery or difficulty achieving adequate anticoagulation for CPB (203, 204, 234–236). Newborns and infants normally have AT III levels averaging 60% to 80% of adult levels and reach or exceed 90% of adult levels at approximately 3 months of age (237), which probably explains their relative heparin resistance when compared to adults (Table 14.6). For this reason, some might choose to increase the initial heparin dose (e.g., 400 U/kg) in newborns and small infants.

Acquired AT III deficiency is probably more common than inherited AT III deficiency. The multiple conditions associated with acquired AT III deficiency are listed in Table 14.7 (188, 238–243). Some other conditions listed in Table 14.6 may also be related to acquired AT III deficiency (e.g., septicemia, endocarditis, hypercoagulable states). Causes of AT III deficiency most likely in patients requiring cardiac surgery include heparin treatment and disseminated intravascular coagulation. Heparin treatment decreases AT III levels (242), but the decrease usually plateaus at levels exceeding 60% of normal. The moderate heparin resistance often observed in patients receiving preoperative heparin therapy has not been associated with decreased AT III levels (60, 244, 245). Moreover, AT III levels above 60% apparently do not predispose to thrombotic events in the nonsurgical setting (246). A critical AT III level has not been established for the surgical patient.

Antithrombin III deficiency in patients about to undergo CPB is largely a presumptive diagnosis based upon substantial heparin resistance, e.g., failure to attain an ACT >300 seconds after >600 U/kg of heparin. This condition has been shown both in vivo and in vitro to respond to fresh-frozen plasma (FFP), which contains normal concentrations of AT III (204, 207,

Table 14.6.   Factors Reported to Decrease the Anticoagulant Response to Heparin

Factor	Human Studies	Case Reports	Animal or In vitro Models
1. AT III deficiency			
A. Familial		Nielsen (203)	
		Soloway (204)	
		Marciniak (205)	
B. Acquired		Chung (206)	Reuter (207)
2. Platelets			
A. Thrombocytosis	Gravlee (69)	Wilds (208)	Conley (210)
B. Heparin-induced		Olinger (209)	
thrombocytopenia			
3. Age			
A. Pediatrics/newborns	Doty (61)		
	Dauchot (120)		
B. Increased adult age	Gravlee (69)		
4. Circadian rhythm	Schved (211)		
	Decousus (212)		
	Decousus (213)		
5. Hemoglobin concentration (Hgb)			
Decreased [Hgb]	Kase (133)		
Increased [Hgb]			Whitfield (214)
6. Preheparin ACT or PTT			
Decreased values	Esposito (60)		Bjornsson (115)
Increased values			Whitfield (214)
7. Drugs			
A. Several medications			Nelson (215)
B. Ongoing heparin therapy	Esposito (60)	Hicks (218)	
	Dietrich (216)		
	Cloyd (217)		
C. Nitroglycerin	Habbab (219)		
	Becker (220)		
8. pH and Protein effects			
A. Increased acid glycoprotein			Godal (221)
B. Decreased pH	Kase (133)		Jaques (222)
C. Antiheparin immunoglobulin		Glueck (223)	
		Pogliani (224)	
D. Neutrophil elastase			Jordan (225)
E. Increased lipoprotein levels			Bleyl (226)
9. Pregnancy	Whitfield (227)		
10. Hypereosinophilic syndrome		Hanowell (228)	
11. Sepsis/endocarditis		Mabry (66),	
		Chung (206)	
12. Autologous blood withdrawal	Mummaneni (229)		
13. Hypercoagulable states	de Takats (58)	Reuter (207)	
14. Male gender			Whitfield (214)

245, 247). Heparin resistance from AT III deficiency would be unlikely to respond to changing the biologic source of heparin from beef lung to porcine mucosa or vice versa. No guidelines or clinical studies formally establish an appropriate intervention threshold for FFP. Because of the potential risks associated with FFP (248), the author prefers to persist with additional heparin under most circumstances, perhaps administering FFP if an ACT >300 seconds cannot be achieved after 1000 U/kg of heparin. Such occurrences appear to be rare. The volume of FFP needed to raise AT III levels sufficiently to induce safe anticoagulation depends upon the magnitude of the defi-

Table 14.7. Conditions Associated with Acquired Antithrombin Deficiency

I.   Decreased synthesis from liver cirrhosis
II.   Drug-induced
      L-asparaginase
      Estrogens
      Heparin
III. Increased excretion
      Protein-losing enteropathy
      Inflammatory bowel disease
      Nephrotic syndrome
IV.   Accelerated consumption
      Disseminated intravascular coagulation
      Surgery
V.   Dilutional
      Cardiopulmonary bypass
      Autologous blood withdrawal

ciency, but 2 to 3 units appears sufficient for most adults. The ACT prolongation after administering FFP does not establish that AT III deficiency caused the heparin resistance, because increasing plasma AT III levels should increase heparin-induced anticoagulation whether or not initial AT III levels are inadequate (165, 245, 249). This might be important if the cause of heparin resistance is heparin-induced thrombocytopenia or marked thrombocytosis. In the former instance, an interaction of heparin, platelets, and an immunoglobulin G (IgG) antibody is the likely mechanism for heparin resistance. This would theoretically respond best to removal by pheresis of the patient's platelet-rich plasma, accompanied by volume replacement with FFP before CPB. After CPB and heparin neutralization, platelet concentrates would probably be needed. The treatment of marked heparin resistance from thrombocytosis would be the same, but the likely mechanism involved would be competitive heparin binding to platelets inducing an acute release of platelet factor 4, an endogenous substance capable of binding and neutralizing heparin.

The use of FFP to replace profound AT III deficiencies may become obsolete with the recent introduction (in the United States) of a human AT III concentrate (250).

This concentrate has been used successfully to treat pregnancy-induced heparin resistance and other manifestations of AT III deficiency (251), but its use for heparin resistance in cardiac surgery has not been reported. The recommended dose (in units) to increase AT III activity from 0% to 100% is 100 × body weight (in kilograms), and the half-life is approximately 22 hours (251). An average adult's AT III level would be raised by approximately 30% with 1000 units, which would probably equal the rise in AT III level accruing from 4 to 5 units of FFP. Although AT III concentrate is prepared from pooled human plasma, it has been heat-treated and should be free of infectious disease transmission risk. Consequently, AT III concentrate constitutes the theoretical treatment of choice for severe heparin resistance for which the presumptive cause is AT III deficiency (e.g., active endocarditis with low-grade disseminated intravascular coagulation). Despite the apparently low risk and absence of the waiting time required for FFP thawing, one should consider the high cost of AT III concentrate and the rare occurrence of heparin resistance requiring therapy other than increased heparin doses before selecting this therapy. The charge for 1000 units of AT III concentrate would be approximately $1800 at North Carolina Baptist Hospital.

HEPARIN-INDUCED THROMBOCYTOPENIA

As many as 28% of patients receiving heparin develop a somewhat mysterious syndrome known as heparin-induced thrombocytopenia. This syndrome most often occurs after more than 5 days of heparin administration (average onset time, 9 days) and it is most likely immune-mediated. This syndrome differs from other immune-mediated drug-induced thrombocytopenias in the following ways: (*a*) the antibodies associated with heparin-induced thrombocytopenia often become undetectable several weeks after discontinuing the drug, (*b*) the clinical syndrome does not always recur upon reexposure to the drug and sometimes resolves despite continued drug therapy, (*c*) the in vitro platelet aggregation reaction is sometimes patient-specific, and (*d*) some patients develop thrombosis and disseminated intravascular coagulation (84, 252). Most studies have found a higher incidence with bovine lung heparin than with porcine mucosal heparin (85, 252–256). Defining thrombocytopenia as a platelet count below 100,000 per microliter, the average reported incidence is 5.5% for bovine lung heparin and 1.0% for porcine mucosal heparin (84). The mechanism appears to be gradual development and binding of IgG antibodies to platelet-bound heparin, which activates platelets and induces platelet clumping. Associated immune-mediated endothelial injury and complement activation may set the stage for the activated platelets to adhere, aggregate, and form platelet clots (257, 258). When carried to an extreme, this syndrome can lead to severe morbidity or to fatal intravascular thromboembolic phenomena (259–265). The approximate incidence of thrombotic complications is 20%, which may carry a mortality rate as high as 35% (252). Both of these figures may be overestimated as a result of reporting bias, although some prospective investigations support the 20% incidence of thrombosis (84, 252).

Why would a syndrome that occurs only with prolonged heparin administration influence anticoagulation for CPB? Prophylactic continuous intravenous heparin therapy decreases the incidence of thrombotic complications from anterior myocardial infarction, of rethrombosis after percutaneous transluminal coronary angioplasty for acute coronary thrombosis, and of myocardial infarction in patients with unstable angina pectoris (88, 266–268). Because some of these patients may need subsequent surgical myocardial revascularization, the possibility exists that patients could present for urgent surgery with unrecognized heparin-induced thrombocyto-

penia. In clinical settings other than CPB, initiating therapeutic heparin doses in patients with unrecognized heparin-induced thrombocytopenia has been associated with life-threatening complications (84). Would the larger heparin doses administered for CPB induce profound thrombocytopenia or acute intravascular thrombosis in patients with unrecognized or incipient heparin-induced thrombocytopenia? Reports of such events could not be found, but thrombocytopenia disproportionate to hemodilution has been reported in such situations even in the protective presence of antiplatelet drugs (269, 270). In two patients who received preoperative heparin infusions, the author has observed profound thrombocytopenia (platelet count 30,000–35,000 per microliter) with otherwise normal coagulation tests after uneventful CPB. The preoperative platelet counts of these two patients were 110,000 and 209,000 per microliter respectively. Heparin resistance commonly occurs in patients receiving heparin infusions who have not developed thrombocytopenia, but it has also been temporally associated with heparin-induced thrombocytopenia (84, 209, 261). Consequently, unrecognized heparin-induced thrombocytopenia should possibly be considered in the differential diagnosis of intraoperative heparin resistance in patients receiving preoperative heparin therapy.

Patients with existing heparin-induced thrombocytopenia or a history of heparin-induced thrombocytopenia pose special therapeutic difficulties. In essence, a patient for whom heparin is contraindicated is placed into a clinical situation that requires the use of heparin. Several approaches to this dilemma have been taken. Olinger et al. (209) reported three patients in whom discontinuation of heparin for 4 to 8 weeks resulted in resolution of the antiplatelet antibody reaction. Those patients then tolerated the brief period of heparinization for CPB without complication and without developing thrombocytopenia beyond that expected from hemodilution. Because heparin-induced thrombocytopenia often requires 2 to 6 days to recur once the antibodies have cleared, this approach seems reasonable for patients whose need for cardiac surgery is not urgent. The antibody response might not always resolve within 8 weeks, however.

Changing the tissue source of heparin might circumvent the reaction (271), although cross-reactivity often exists, so this approach should be taken only if it can be proven safe by testing the patient's platelet-rich plasma in vitro with the alternative heparin. Some types of low molecular weight heparin (LMWH) have proven effective in heparin-induced thrombocytopenia (see below), but their use presents another set of problems, and nonreactivity with the patient's platelets should be confirmed in vitro before selecting this option (272). Low molecular weight heparinoids may prove safer than LMWHs in this setting (273). Supplementing heparin administration with pharmacologic platelet inhibition using prostacyclin, iloprost, aspirin, or aspirin and dipyridamole have been reported (269, 270, 274, 275), all with favorable outcomes. The use of iloprost titrated to a documented level of platelet functional suppression permitted heparin use without undue thrombocytopenia (274, 276), whereas aspirin or aspirin plus dipyridamole may less consistently protect against thrombocytopenia (269, 270). It seems logical that prostaglandin E$_1$ would also serve effectively in this role (277, 278), although this agent shares prostacyclin's vasodilatory side effect. Plasmapheresis acutely reduced heparin-induced platelet aggregation in two cases (279, 280). All of the above options involve maneuvers designed to reduce or eliminate the harmful effects of heparin while accepting the unavoidability of heparin-induced anticoagulation for CPB. The use of heparin could be avoided altogether by anticoagulating with ancrod or hirudin (see the next section).

ALTERNATIVES TO UNFRACTIONATED HEPARIN

Clinical situations that might call for avoidance of heparin include protamine allergy, heparin-induced thrombocytopenia, or heparin allergy. Until recently, no viable alternatives existed, but at least three intravenous alternatives to unfractionated heparin are presently available. None of these drugs has yet been approved by the Food and Drug Administration for use in the United States.

Low Molecular Weight Heparin and Heparinoids

The discovery that different components of unfractionated heparin possess differing affinities for platelets and for AT III suggested a potential advantage to fractionating heparin into different compounds for different indications (56, 281, 282). Shorter heparin chains have a lower affinity for platelets and a lesser ability to inhibit thrombin (factor IIa), while maintaining potent inhibition of activated factor X (Xa) (56, 283). Moderate inhibition of factor Xa appears to inhibit thrombus formation without impairing hemostasis as intensely as simultaneous inhibition of Xa and IIa, thus effective prophylaxis against deep vein thrombosis might occur with a lower incidence of bleeding complications (284). This potential benefit has fueled development of many different LMWH compounds, achieved either by fractionation of conventional heparins or by de novo synthesis (285). Some evidence supports the antithrombotic efficacy of Xa inhibition, yet other reports support the need for IIa inhibition to achieve the same goal (286–288). Most clinical trials indicate that LMWH prevents perioperative deep vein thrombosis at least as well as unfractionated heparin (281). Low molecular weight heparin has also been used effectively as a substitute for unfractionated heparin in hemodialysis and in the treatment of thrombosis occurring with heparin-induced thrombocytopenia (289–293). Different studies show reduced, increased, or unchanged bleeding complications with LMWH (281, 294). Some of the differences observed are probably attributable to dosing differences and to the heterogeneity of the LMWH compounds produced by different manufacturers (281, 285). Low molecular weight heparin therapy complicates heparin monitoring because APTT (and presumably ACT) is much less sensitive to Xa inhibition than to IIa inhibition. Factor Xa inhibition can be measured, but not with a simple bedside test (295–297). The difficulties imposed by Xa inhibition measurement have also complicated potency standardization of LMWH compounds (46). Recent development of a standard based upon potency of Xa inhibition should assist future comparisons of different LMWH compounds (23).

Intravenously administered LMWH has a half-life at least twice as long as that of unfractionated heparin, and possibly several times as long for some LMWH compounds (46, 284, 297). The half-life poses a potential problem with LMWH use for CPB because Xa inhibition is much less responsive to protamine neutralization than is IIa inhibition (298, 299). Some experience with LMWH for CPB has accrued. In 1983, Gouault-Heilmann et al. (300) reported LMWH use for a pulmonary embolectomy in a 66-year-old man suffering from heparin-induced thrombocytopenia and thrombosis. Apparently, no attempt was made to neutralize the LMWH after CPB, and postoperative blood loss figures were not reported. This patient survived in a situation where, in theory, the administration of a large dose of unfractionated heparin might have induced severe morbidity via further intravascular clotting. After determining that LMWH could be used safely to anticoagulate sheep for CPB, Massonnet-Castel et al. (301) used LMWH to anticoagulate six

adults undergoing elective procedures requiring CPB, decreasing the dose with each successive patient. Although no clots developed in the extracorporeal circuit, all patients bled excessively in the 6 hours following CPB. While the use of protamine was initially avoided, its use was deemed necessary in five patients, and the authors viewed heparin neutralization as only partially effective. Three of the six patients required reoperation for bleeding. One patient died 3 days later of a myocardial infarction and autopsy revealed several "spots of subperitoneal hemorrhage." The same group subsequently reported anticoagulation in 15 patients undergoing CPB using LMWH doses less than the lowest dose administered in the previous report (302). Protamine was successfully avoided in nine patients, although three of those patients bled excessively. Three different patients received protamine as treatment for excessive bleeding, and this was again considered only partially effective because two of these patients bled over 2000 ml via their mediastinal tubes in the first 24 hours. In vitro evidence supports a possible role for aminocaproic acid in this situation (298). Three patients received protamine prophylactically and they did not bleed excessively despite the lack of effective reduction in anti-Xa activity by protamine. Touchot et al. (303) successfully anticoagulated nine dogs (one died from postoperative hemorrhage) and four patients using LMWH. No clots were seen during CPB, but no postoperative data were provided. Henny et al. (304) compared unfractionated heparin to a heparinoid (a synthetic or naturally occurring heparin analog) for CPB in dogs and found that both produced satisfactory anticoagulation. The group receiving the heparinoid compound experienced less postoperative bleeding despite the absence of protamine, which was administered to the dogs receiving heparin. Many questions remain unanswered about LMWH and heparinoids for CPB, so this therapy must currently be viewed as experimental. Emergency CPB in a patient experiencing heparin-induced thrombocytopenia offers the only compelling indication, and other options may be preferred even in that setting.

Defibrinogenating Agents

Zulys et al. (305) prospectively reported the successful use of ancrod for CPB anticoagulation in 20 patients. Derived from Malayan pit viper venom, this agent lyses fibrinogen in a manner that precludes the formation of fibrin polymers. Achieving sufficient fibrinogen depletion for safe CPB anticoagulation (plasma fibrinogen concentration 0.4 to 0.8 g/liter made APTT and ACT infinite) takes at least 12 hours, and restoration of plasma coagulation after CPB requires FFP and sometimes cryoprecipitate. When compared to 20 control patients receiving heparin-induced anticoagulation, the ancrod patients experienced no difference in blood loss, but received more packed red blood cells, FFP, and cryoprecipitate. The delayed onset and the increased need for homologous blood products represent clear disadvantages to the clinical use of ancrod. An antivenom is available, but it would not assist in the regeneration of fibrinogen, which is determined by the synthetic capacity of the liver.

Defibrinogenation can also be achieved with thrombolytic agents such as streptokinase and its derivatives urokinase and recombinant tissue plasminogen activator (306). This action would accrue at the expense of increased plasmin formation and commensurate hyperfibrinolysis, which would set the stage for a potentially severe post-CPB coagulopathy. Consequently, thrombolytic agents would serve as undesirable heparin substitutes, and probably should not be considered except in an emergency when heparin is relatively contraindicated (e.g., ongoing heparin-induced thrombocytopenia with thrombosis) and other heparin substitutes are unavailable.

Hirudin

A coagulation inhibitor isolated from medicinal leeches, hirudin specifically inhibits thrombin without requiring AT III (307, 308). Currently available in some countries via recombinant genetics, this substance is a polypeptide (molecular weight of approximately 7,000 daltons) that has been used in patients suffering from chronic disseminated intravascular coagulation (307). Pharmacokinetic studies in healthy volunteers show a plasma elimination half-life of approximately 1 hour and a urinary excretion half-life of 2½ hours (308). After an intravenous bolus, the APTT prolongs markedly but transiently, returning to normal in 15 minutes, while TT remains markedly prolonged for 2 to 3 hours. The APTT prolongation correlates well with plasma hirudin levels. Walenga et al. (309) prospectively compared two hirudin dosing protocols to traditional heparin anticoagulation in 30 dogs, and found that hirudin induced satisfactory anticoagulation that appears measurable using ACT. The relatively short-lived effect of a single intravenous bolus suggests the advisability of bolus administration followed by a continuous infusion. The authors report that all clotting times returned to normal within 30 minutes of hirudin discontinuation, but one of their figures suggests moderate ACT prolongation for as much as 2 hours. The hirudin groups displayed a trend toward increased blood loss in the 150-minute observation period after CPB, but this did not reach statistical significance. Although human studies are lacking, recombinant hirudin shows greater promise than LMWH or ancrod as a substitute for heparin-induced anticoagulation.

Platelet Inhibitors

Pharmacologic platelet inhibition has been used to supplement or replace heparin for CPB anticoagulation. This technique is discussed in Chapter 16.

Coated Surfaces

The purpose of systemic anticoagulation for CPB is to prevent blood from clotting when it contacts artificial surfaces. If the artificial surfaces were nonthrombogenic, systemic anticoagulation might become unnecessary, thus reducing the risk of hemorrhagic complications with long-term CPB for pulmonary support and eliminating the need for protamine with short-term CPB for cardiac surgery (310). Heparin's strong acidity makes it possible to bind it ionically or covalently to plastic surfaces, and this has been shown to decrease thrombus formation and platelet adhesion upon the artificial surfaces (311, 312). Attachment of heparin by covalent binding appears to produce a more sustained antithrombotic effect than ionic binding to quaternary amines because heparin is gradually released into the circulation when it is ionically bound (312). Heparin bound ionically to tridodecyl methylammonium chloride (TDMAC) was used successfully in dogs and sheep for up to 6 days of extracorporeal membrane oxygenation without systemic heparin administration (313–317). A prospective comparison of systemic heparinization to TDMAC-coated surfaces in dogs found better survival with systemic heparinization (317).

More recent animal trials with a different quaternary amine (alkylbenzyldimethylammonium) dissolved in a halogenated ethane have shown promise for several days of extracorporeal membrane oxygenation in dogs, sheep, and calves (318–320). This approach effectively inhibits clotting and platelet activation and depletion while whole blood ACTs remain below 200 seconds (319, 320). Some thrombosis occurred in areas of stasis (320), which suggests that the practical application of this technique will likely require some systemic heparin, perhaps to ACTs in the 180 to 240 seconds range. Also, surfaces such as the cardiotomy reservoir, in-line filters, and the inside *and outside* surfaces of venous and arterial cannulae will require heparin coating as well. von Segesser and colleagues (321) recently used coated extracorporeal surfaces to achieve heparinless left heart bypass for thoracoabdominal aneurysm resection. Preliminary clinical trials using heparin-coated extracorporeal surfaces for cardiac surgery show some promise (322). This technique may reduce the degree of anticoagulation required for CPB while simultaneously protecting platelets from the functional deterioration commonly induced by traditional extracorporeal surfaces. If so, this will provide a welcome change in the clinical application of CPB to both cardiac surgery and pulmonary support.

Acknowledgements
The author gratefully acknowledges the editorial assistance of Kim Barnes, and careful review of the manuscript by Jan Horrow, M.D., and Faith McLellan.

REFERENCES

1. Gibbon JH Jr. Application of a mechanical heart and lung apparatus to cardiac surgery. Minn Med 1954;37:171–185.
2. McLean J. The discovery of heparin. Circulation 1959;19:75–78.
3. Howell WH, Holt E. Two new factors in blood coagulation—heparin and pro-antithrombin. Am J Physiol 1918;xlviii:328–341.
4. Best CH. Preparation of heparin and its use in the first clinical cases. Circulation 1959;19:79–86.
5. Chargaff E, Olson KB. Studies on the chemistry of blood coagulation. VI. Studies on the action of heparin and other anti-coagulants. The influence of protamine on the anticoagulant effect in vivo. J Biol Chem 1938;125:671–676.
6. Gibbon JH Jr. The maintenance of life during experimental occlusion of the pulmonary artery followed by survival. Surg Gynecol Obstet 1939;69:602–614.
7. Nader HB, Dietrich CP. Natural occurrence, and possible biological role of heparin. In: Lane DA, Lindahl U, ed. Heparin. Chemical and biological properties, clinical applications. Boca Raton, FL: CRC Press, 1989:81–96.
8. Folkman J, Ingber DE. Angiogenesis: regulatory role of heparin and related molecules. In: Lane DA, Lindahl U, ed. Heparin. Chemical and bio-

logical properties, clinical applications. Boca Raton, FL: CRC Press, 1989:317–333.

9. Olivecrona T, Bengtsson-Olivecrona G. Heparin and lipases. In: Lane DA, Lindahl U, ed. Heparin. Chemical and biological properties, clinical applications. Boca Raton, FL: CRC Press, 1989:335–361.

10. Stiekema JCJ. Heparin and its biocompatibility. Clin Nephrol 1986;26(suppl 1):S3–S8.

11. Hirsh J. Heparin. N Engl J Med 1991;324: 1565–1574.

12. Thomas DP, Barrowcliffe TW, Johnson EA. The influence of tissue source, salt and molecular weight on heparin activity. Scand J Haematol 1980;25(suppl 36):40–48.

13. Walton PL, Ricketts CR, Bangham DR. Heterogeneity of heparin. Br J Haematol 1966;12: 310–325.

14. Jaques LB, McDuffie NM. The chemical and anticoagulant nature of heparin. Semin Thromb Hemost 1978;4:277–297.

15. Rodriguez HJ, Vanderwielen AJ. Molecular weight determination of commercial heparin sodium USP and its sterile solutions. J Pharm Sci 1979;68:588–591.

16. Lasker SE. The heterogeneity of heparins. Fed Proc 1977;36:92–97.

17. Eika C. The platelet aggregating effect of eight commercial heparins. Scand J Haematol 1972; 9:480–482.

18. Casu B. Methods of structural analysis. In: Lane DA, Lindahl U, eds. Heparin. Chemical and biological properties, clinical applications. Boca Raton, FL: CRC Press, 1989:25–49.

19. Rosenberg RD. Biochemistry of heparin antithrombin interactions, and the physiologic role of this natural anticoagulant mechanism. Am J Med 1989;87(suppl 3B):2S–9S.

20. Bangham DR, Woodward PM. A collaborative study of heparins from different sources. Bull Wld Hlth Org 1970;42:129–149.

21. Novak E, Sekhar NC, Dunham NW, Coleman LL. A comparative study of the effect of lung and gut heparins on platelet aggregation and protamine neutralization in man. Clin Med 1972; 79:22–27.

22. Silverglade A. Biological equivalence of beef lung and hog mucosal heparins. Curr Ther Res 1975;18:91–103.

23. Barrowcliffe TW. Heparin assays and standardization. In: Lane DA, Lindahl U, ed. Heparin. Chemical and biological properties, clinical applications. Boca Raton, FL: CRC Press, 1989:393–415.

24. Baltes BJ, Diamond S, D'Agostino RJ. Comparison of anticoagulant activity of two preparations of purified heparin. Clin Pharmacol Ther 1973;14:287–290.

25. Abbott WM, Warnock DF, Austen WG. The rela-

tionship of heparin source to the incidence of delayed hemorrhage. J Surg Res 1977;22: 593–597.

26. Stewart SR, Gaich PA. Clinical comparison of two brands of heparin for use in cardiopulmonary bypass. J Extracorp Tech 1980;12:29–33.

27. Fiser WP, Read RC, Wright FE, Vecchio TJ. A randomized study of beef lung and pork mucosal heparin in cardiac surgery. Ann Thorac Surg 1983;35:615–620.

28. Lowary LR, Smith FA, Coyne E, Dunham NW. Comparative neutralization of lung- and mucosal-derived heparin by protamine sulfate using in vitro and in vivo methods. J Pharm Sci 1971;60:638–640.

29. Barrowcliffe TW, Johnson EA, Eggleton CA, Thomas DP. Anticoagulant activities of lung and mucous heparins. Thromb Res 1977;12:27–36.

30. Thomas DP, Sagar S, Stamatakis JD, Maffei FHA, Erdi A, Kakkar VV. Plasma heparin levels after administration of calcium and sodium salts of heparin. Thromb Res 1976;9:241–248.

31. Whitehead MI, McCarthy TG. A comparative trial of subcutaneous sodium and calcium heparin as assessed by local haematoma formation and pain. In: Kakkar VV, Thomas DP, ed. Heparin: Chemistry and clinical usage. London: Academic Press Inc, 1976:361–366.

32. Merton RE, Curtis AD, Thomas DP. A comparison of heparin potency estimates obtained by activated partial thromboplastin time and British pharmacopoeial assays. Thromb Haemost 1985;53:116–117.

33. Speight KL, Morgan GL Jr, Gravlee GP. Pharmacodynamics of intravenous heparin [Abstract]. In: Proceedings of the Society of Cardiovascular Anesthesiologists Annual Meeting, 1991: 179.

34. Skeehan TM, Heflin DW. Optimal ACT sampling interval in pediatric and adult patients after systemic heparinization [Abstract]. Anesthesiology 1989;71(suppl 3A):A289.

35. Effeney DJ, Goldstone J, Chin D, Krupski WC, Ellis RJ. Intraoperative anticoagulation in cardiovascular surgery. Surgery 1981;90: 1068–1074.

36. Gravlee GP, Angert KC, Tucker WY, Case LD, Wallenhaupt SL, Cordell AR. Early anticoagulation peak and rapid distribution after intravenous heparin. Anesthesiology 1988;68: 126–129.

37. Estes JW. The fate of heparin in the body. Curr Ther Res 1975;18:45–57.

38. Estes JW. Clinical pharmacokinetics of heparin. Clin Pharmacokinet 1980;5:204–220.

39. Hiebert LM, Jaques LB. The observation of heparin on endothelium after injection. Thromb Res 1976;8:195–204.

40. Glimelius B, Busch C, Höök M. Binding of hep-

arin on the surface of cultured human endothelial cells. Thromb Res 1978;12:773–782.

41. Bârzu T, Molho P, Tobelem G, Petitou M, Caen J. Binding and endocytosis of heparin by human endothelial cells in culture. Biochim Biophys Acta 1985;845:196–203.

42. Mahadoo J, Heibert L, Jaques LB. Vascular sequestration of heparin. Thromb Res 1977;12:79–90.

43. Jaques LB, Mahadoo J. Pharmacodynamics and clinical effectiveness of heparin. Semin Thromb Hemost 1978;4:298–325.

44. Castellot JJ Jr, Wong K, Herman B, et al. Binding and internalization of heparin by vascular smooth muscle cells. J Cell Physiol 1985;124:13–20.

45. Dawes J, Pepper DS. Catabolism of low-dose heparin in man. Thromb Res 1979;14:845–860.

46. Albada J, Nieuwenhuis HK, Sixma JJ. Pharmacokinetics of standard and low molecular weight heparin. In: Lane DA, Lindahl U, ed. Heparin. Chemical and biological properties, clinical applications. Boca Raton, FL: CRC Press, 1989:417–431.

47. de Swart CAM, Nijmeyer B, Roelofs JMM, Sixma JJ. Kinetics of intravenously administered heparin in normal humans. Blood 1982;60:1251–1258.

48. Olsson P, Lagergren H, Ek S. The elimination from plasma of intravenous heparin. An experimental study on dogs and humans. Acta Med Scand 1963;173:619–630.

49. Bjornsson TD, Wolfram KM, Kitchell BB. Heparin kinetics determined by three assay methods. Clin Pharmacol Ther 1982;31:104–113.

50. Cohen JA, Frederickson EL, Kaplan JA. Plasma heparin activity and antagonism during cardiopulmonary bypass with hypothermia. Anesth Analg 1977;56:564–570.

51. Wright JS, Osborn JJ, Perkins HA, Gerbode F. Heparin levels during and after hypothermic perfusion. J Cardiovasc Surg 1964;5:244–250.

52. Bull BS, Korpman RA, Huse WM, Briggs BD. Heparin therapy during extracorporeal circulation. I. Problems inherent in existing heparin protocols. J Thorac Cardiovasc Surg 1975;69:674–684.

53. Villanueva GB, Danishefsky I. Evidence for a heparin-induced conformational change on antithrombin III. Biochem Biophys Res Comm 1977;74:803–809.

54. Björk I, Olson ST, Shore JD. Molecular mechanisms of the accelerating effect of heparin on the reactions between antithrombin and clotting proteinases. In: Lane DA, Lindahl U, ed. Heparin. Chemical and biological properties, clinical applications. Boca Raton, FL: CRC Press, 1989:229–255.

55. Pixley RA, Colman RW. Effect of heparin on the inactivation rate of human activated factor XII by antithrombin III. Blood 1985;66:198–203.

56. Holmer E. Low molecular weight heparin. In: Lane DA, Lindahl U, eds. Heparin. Chemical and biological properties, clinical applications. Boca Raton, FL: CRC Press, 1989:575–595.

57. Ofosu FA, Fernandez F, Gauthier D, Buchanan MR. Heparin cofactor II and other endogenous factors in the mediation of the antithrombotic and anticoagulant effects of heparin and dermatan sulfate. Semin Thromb Hemost 1985;11:133–137.

58. de Takats G. Heparin tolerance. A test of the clotting mechanism. Surg Gynecol Obstet 1943;77:31–39.

59. Monkhouse FC, MacMillan RL, Brown KWG. The relation between heparin blood levels and blood coagulation times. J Lab Clin Med 1953;42:92–97.

60. Esposito RA, Culliford AT, Colvin SB, Thomas SJ, Lackner H, Spencer FC. Heparin resistance during cardiopulmonary bypass. The role of heparin pretreatment. J Thorac Cardiovasc Surg 1983;85:346–353.

61. Doty DB, Knott HW, Hoyt JL, Koepke JA. Heparin dose for accurate anticoagulation in cardiac surgery. J Cardiovasc Surg 1979;20:597–604.

62. Stenbjerg S, Berg E, Albrechtsen OK. Heparin levels and activated clotting time (ACT) during open heart surgery. Scand J Haematol 1981;26:281–284.

63. Jaberi M, Bell WR, Benson DW. Control of heparin therapy in open-heart surgery. J Thorac Cardiovasc Surg 1974;67:133–141.

64. Friesen RH, Clement AJ. Individual responses to heparinization for extracorporeal circulation. J Thorac Cardiovasc Surg 1976;72:875–879.

65. Akl BF, Vargas GM, Neal J, Robillard J, Kelly P. Clinical experience with the activated clotting time for the control of heparin and protamine therapy during cardiopulmonary bypass. J Thorac Cardiovasc Surg 1980;79:97–102.

66. Mabry CD, Read RC, Thompson BW, Williams GD, White HJ. Identification of heparin resistance during cardiac and vascular surgery. Arch Surg 1979;114:129–134.

67. Culliford AT, Gitel SN, Starr N, et al. Lack of correlation between activated clotting time and plasma heparin during cardiopulmonary bypass. Ann Surg 1981;193:105–111.

68. Bull BS, Huse WM, Brauer FS, Korpman RA. Heparin therapy during extracorporeal circulation. II. The use of a dose-response curve to individualize heparin and protamine dosage. J Thorac Cardiovasc Surg 1975;69:685–689.

69. Gravlee GP, Brauer SD, Roy RC, et al. Predicting

the pharmacodynamics of heparin: a clinical evaluation of the Hepcon System 4. J Cardiothorac Anesth 1987;1:379–387.

70. Cipolle RJ, Uden DL, Gruber SA, et al. Evaluation of a rapid monitoring system to study heparin pharmacokinetics and pharmacodynamics. Pharmacotherapy 1990;10:367–372.

71. Fareed J, Walenga JM, Hoppensteadt DA, Messmore HL. Studies on the profibrinolytic actions of heparin and its fractions. Semin Thromb Hemost 1985;11:199–207.

72. Zucker MB. Effect of heparin on platelet function. Thromb Diath Haemorrh 1974;33:63–65.

73. Thomson C, Forbes CD, Prentice CRM. The potentiation of platelet aggregation and adhesion by heparin in vitro and in vivo. Clin Sci Mol Med 1973;45:485–494.

74. Abela M, McArdle B, Qureshi M, Pearson DT. Heparin-enhanced ADP-induced platelet aggregation in patients undergoing cardiopulmonary bypass surgery. Perfusion 1986;1:175–178.

75. Cella G, Menardo A, Girolami A. Effect of heparin on in vivo platelet factor 4 (PF4) release and platelet aggregation after aspirin administration. Clin Lab Haematol 1980;2:333–338.

76. Michalski R, Lane DA, Kakkar VV. Comparison of heparin and a semi-synthetic heparin analogue, A73025. Br J Haematol 1977;37:247–256.

77. Bertelé V, Roncaglioni MC, Donati MB, de Gaetano G. Heparin counteracts the antiaggregating effect of prostacyclin by potentiating platelet aggregation. Thromb Haemost 1983;49:81–83.

78. Eldor A, Weksler BB. Heparin and dextran sulfate antagonize PGI$_2$ inhibition of platelet aggregation. Thromb Res 1979;16:617–628.

79. Heiden D, Mielke CH Jr, Rodvien R. Impairment by heparin of primary haemostasis and platelet [^{14}C]5-hydroxytryptamine release. Br J Haematol 1977;36:427–436.

80. O'Brien JR, Path FRC. Heparin and platelets. Curr Ther Res 1975;18:79–90.

81. Davey MG, Lander H. Effect of injected heparin on platelet levels in man. J Clin Pathol 1968;21:55–59.

82. Holmer E, Lindahl U, Bäckström G, et al. Anticoagulant activities and effects on platelets of a heparin fragment with high affinity for antithrombin. Thromb Res 1980;18:861–869.

83. Cella G, Scattolo N, Luzzatto G, Girolami A. Effects of low-molecular-weight heparin on platelets as compared with commercial heparin. Res Exp Med 1984;184:227–229.

84. Warkentin TE, Kelton JG. Heparin and platelets. Hematol Oncol Clin North Am 1990;4:243–264.

85. Salzman EW, Rosenberg RD, Smith MH, Lindon JN, Favreau L. Effect of heparin and heparin fractions on platelet aggregation. J Clin Invest 1980;65:64–73.

86. Cines DB. Heparin: Do we understand its antithrombotic actions? Chest 1986;89:420–426.

87. Myers TM, Hull RD, Weg JG. Antithrombotic therapy for venous thromboembolic disease. Chest 1986;89(suppl):26S–35S.

88. Kaplan K. Prophylactic anticoagulation following acute myocardial infarction. Arch Intern Med 1986;146:593–597.

89. Levine MN. Nonhemorrhagic complications of anticoagulant therapy. Semin Thromb Hemost 1986;12:63–66.

90. Seltzer JL, Gerson JI. Decrease in arterial pressure following heparin injection prior to cardiopulmonary bypass. Acta Anaesth Scand 1979;23:575–578.

91. Urban P, Scheidegger D, Buchmann B, Skarvan K. The hemodynamic effects of heparin and their relation to ionized calcium levels. J Thorac Cardiovasc Surg 1986;91:303–306.

92. Bjoraker DG, Ketcham TR. Hemodynamics and platelet release with heparin [Abstract]. Anesthesiology 1981;55:A25.

93. Jaques LB. Heparin: an old drug with a new paradigm. Current discoveries are establishing the nature, action, and biological significance of this valuable drug. Science 1979;206:528–533.

94. Harada A, Tatsuno K, Kikuchi T, et al. Use of bovine lung heparin to obviate anaphylactic shock caused by porcine gut heparin. Ann Thorac Surg 1990;49:826–827.

95. Ahmed SS, Nussbaum M. Development of pulmonary edema related to heparin administration. J Clin Pharmacol 1981;21:126–128.

96. Dux S, Pitlik S, Perry G, Rosenfeld JB. Hypersensitivity reaction to chlorbutol-preserved heparin [Letter]. Lancet 1981;1:149.

97. Hancock BW, Naysmith A. Hypersensitivity to chlorocresol-preserved heparin. Br Med J 1975;3:746–747.

98. Ainley EJ, Mackie IG, Macarthur D. Adverse reaction to chlorocresol-preserved heparin [Letter]. Lancet 1977;1:705.

99. Ansell JE, Clark WP Jr, Compton CC. Fatal reactions associated with intravenous heparin. Drug Intell Clin Pharm 1986;20:74–75.

100. Rosenzweig P, Gary NE, Gocke DJ, Saidi P, Felton SM, Eisinger RP. Heparin allergy accompanying acute renal failure. Artif Organs 1979;3:78–79.

101. Bernstein IL. Anaphylaxis to heparin sodium. Report of a case, with immunologic studies. JAMA 1956;161:1379–1380.

102. Klein HG, Bell WR. Disseminated intravascular coagulation during heparin therapy. Ann Intern Med 1974;80:477–481.

103. Schey SA. Hypersensitivity reactions to heparin and the use of new low molecular weight heparins. Eur J Haematol 1989;42:107.

104. Yourassowsky E, de Broe ME, Wieme RJ. Effect of heparin on gentamicin concentration in blood. Clin Chim Acta 1972;42:189–191.

105. Colburn WA. Pharmacologic implications of heparin interactions with other drugs. Drug Metab Rev 1976;5:281–293.

106. Levine MN, Hirsh J. Hemorrhagic complications of anticoagulant therapy. Semin Thromb Hemost 1986;12:39–57.

107. Leehey D, Gantt C, Lim V. Heparin-induced hypoaldosteronism. Report of a case. JAMA 1981;246:2189–2190.

108. Majerus PW, Broze GJ, Miletich JP, Tollefsen DM. Anticoagulant thrombolytic and antiplatelet drugs. In: Gilman AG, Rall TW, Nies AS, Taylor P, eds. Goodman and Gilman's the pharmacological basis of therapeutics. 8th ed. New York: Pergamon Press 1990;1311–1331.

109. Salomon F, Schmid M. Heparin (Letter). New Engl J Med 1991;325:1585.

110. Hattersley PG. Activated coagulation time of whole blood. JAMA 1966;196:150–436–440.

111. Blakely JA. A rapid bedside method for the control of heparin therapy. Can Med Assoc J 1968;99:1072–1076.

112. Hill JD, Dontigny L, de Leval M, Mielke CH Jr. A simple method of heparin management during prolonged extracorporeal circulation. Ann Thorac Surg 1974;17:129–134.

113. Umlas J, Gauvin G, Taff R. Heparin monitoring and neutralization during cardiopulmonary bypass using a rapid plasma separator and a fluorometric assay. Ann Thorac Surg 1984;37:301–303.

114. Jobes DR, Schwartz AJ, Ellison N, Andrews R, Ruffini RA, Ruffini JJ. Monitoring heparin anticoagulation and its neutralization. Ann Thorac Surg 1981;31:161–166.

115. Bjornsson TD, Nash PV. Variability in heparin sensitivity of APTT reagents. Am J Clin Pathol 1986;86:199–204.

116. Brandt JT, Triplett DA. Laboratory monitoring of heparin. Effect of reagents and instruments on the activated partial thromboplastin time. Am J Clin Pathol 1981;76:530–537.

117. Ts'ao CH, Galluzzo TS, Lo R, Peterson KG. Whole-blood clotting time, and activated partial thromboplastin time, and whole-blood recalcification time as heparin monitoring tests. Am J Clin Pathol 1979;71:17–21.

118. Delorme MA, Inwood MJ, O'Keefe B. Sensitivity of the thrombin clotting time and activated partial thromboplastin time to low level of antithrombin III during heparin therapy. Clin Lab Haematol 1990;12:433–436.

119. Congdon JE, Kardinal CG, Wallin JD. Monitoring heparin therapy in hemodialysis. A report on the activated whole blood coagulation time tests. JAMA 1973;226:1529–1533.

120. Dauchot PJ, Berzina-Moettus L, Rabinovitch A, Ankeney JL. Activated coagulation and activated partial thromboplastin times in assessment and reversal of heparin-induced anticoagulation for cardiopulmonary bypass. Anesth Analg 1983;62:710–719.

121. Kurec AS, Morris MW, Davey FR. Clotting, activated partial thromboplastin and coagulation times in monitoring heparin therapy. Ann Clin Lab Sci 1979;9:494–500.

122. Gravlee G, Goldsmith J, Low J, Harrison G, Branch J. Heparin sensitivity comparison of the ACT, SCT, and APTT [Abstract]. Anesthesiology 1989;71(suppl 3A):A4.

123. Hooper TL, Conroy J, McArdle B, et al. The use of the Hemochron in assessment of heparin reversal after cardiopulmonary bypass. Perfusion 1988;3:295–300.

124. Jaques LB, Ricker AG. The relationship between heparin dosage and clotting time. Blood 1948;3:1197–1212.

125. Estes JW. Kinetics of the anticoagulant effect of heparin. JAMA 1970;212:1492–1495.

126. Schriever JG, Epstein SE, Mintz MD. Statistical correlation and heparin sensitivity of activated partial thromboplastin time, whole blood coagulation time, and an automated coagulation time. Am J Clin Pathol 1973;60:323–329.

127. Hattersley PG. Progress report: The activated coagulation time of whole blood (ACT). Am J Clin Pathol 1976;66:899–904.

128. Reno WJ, Rotman M, Grumbine FC, Dennis LH, Mohler ER. Evaluation of the BART test (a modification of the whole-blood activated recalcification time test) as a means of monitoring heparin therapy. Am J Clin Pathol 1974;61:78–84.

129. Fareed J. Heparin, its fractions, fragments and derivatives. Some newer perspectives. Semin Thromb Hemost 1985;11:1–9.

130. Gravlee GP, Whitaker CL, Mark LJ, Rogers AT, Royster RL, Harrison GA. Baseline activated coagulation time should be measured after surgical incision. Anesth Analg 1990;71:549–553.

131. Jobes DR, Ellison N, Campbell FW. Limit(ation)s for ACT [Letter]. Anesth Analg 1989;69:142–144.

132. Kopriva CJ, Sreenivasan N, Stafansson S, Farrell DT, Shaffer WB Jr, Geha AS. Hypothermia can cause errors in activated coagulation time [Abstract]. Anesthesiology 1980;33:S85.

133. Kase PB, Dearing JP. Factors affecting the activated clotting time. J Extra-Corp Technol 1985;17:27–30.

134. Nichols AB, Owen J, Grossman BA, Marcella JJ, Fleisher LN, Lee MML. Effect of heparin bonding on catheter-induced fibrin formation

and platelet activation. Circulation 1984; 70:843–850.

135. Palermo LM, Andrews RW, Ellison N. Avoidance of heparin contamination in coagulation studies drawn from indwelling lines. Anesth Analg 1980;59:222–224.

136. Harper J. Use of heparinized intraarterial lines to obtain coagulation samples. Focus Crit Care 1988;15:51–55.

137. Clapham MCC, Willis N, Mapleson WW. Minimum volume of discard for valid blood sampling from indwelling arterial cannulae. Br J Anaesth 1987;59:232–235.

138. Cugno M, Colombo A, Cacciabue E, Uziel L, Agostoni A. Statistical evaluation of commonly used tets for heparin monitoring. Life Support Syst 1986;4:120–128.

139. Gravlee GP, Case LD, Angert KC, Rogers AT, Miller GS. Variability of the activated coagulation time. Anesth Analg 1988;67:469–472.

140. Richet HM, Craven PC, Brown JM, et al. A cluster of rhodococcus (Gordona) bronchialis sternal-wound infections after coronary-artery bypass surgery. N Engl J Med 1991;324: 104–109.

141. Gravlee GP. Response to "Limit(ation)s for ACT." [Letter]. Anesth Analg 1989;69:143–144.

142. Sedor FA, Mayo E, Kirvan KE. A quality-control system for the "Activated Clotting Time" test. Clin Chem 1987;33:1261.

143. Green TP, Isham-Schopf B, Steinhorn RH, Smith C, Irmiter RJ. Whole blood activated clotting time in infants during extracorporeal membrane oxygenation. Crit Care Med 1990;18: 494–498.

144. Varah N, Smith J, Baugh RF. Heparin monitoring in the coronary care unit after percutaneous transluminal coronary angioplasty. Heart Lung 1990;19:265–270.

145. Mabry CD, Thompson BW, Read RC, Campbell GS. Activated clotting time monitoring of intraoperative heparinization: our experience and comparison of two techniques. Surgery 1981;90:889–895.

146. Zahl K, Ellison N. An evaluation of three different ACT monitors. In: Proceedings of the Society of Cardiovascular Anesthesiologists, 10th Annual Meeting, 1988:158.

147. Urban MK, Hines R. ACT: A new approach. In: Proceedings of the Society of Cardiovascular Anesthesiologists 10th Annual Meeting, 1988:78.

148. Reich DL, Zahl K, Perucho H, Thys DM. An evaluation of two activated clotting time monitors during cardiac surgery. In: Proceedings of the Society of Cardiovascular Anesthesiologists 12th Annual Meeting, 1990:221.

149. Stead SW. Comparison of two methods for hep-

arin monitoring: a semi-automated heparin monitoring device and activated clotting time during extracorporeal circulation. Int J Clin Monit Comput 1989;6:247–254.

150. Cohen EJ, Camerlengo LJ, Dearing JP. Activated clotting times and cardiopulmonary bypass I: The effect of hemodilution and hypothermia upon activated clotting time. J Extra-Corp Technol 1980;12:139–141.

151. Ottesen S, Froysaker T. Use of haemonetics cell saver for autotransfusion in cardiovascular surgery. Scand J Thor Cardiovasc Surg 1982;16: 263–268.

152. Berg E, Stenbjerg S, Albrechtsen OK. Monitoring heparin and protamine therapy during cardiopulmonary bypass by activated clotting time. J Extra-Corp Technol 1979;11:229–235.

153. Kesteven PJ, Pasaoglu I, Williams BT, Savidge GF. Significance of the whole blood activated clotting time in cardiopulmonary bypass. J Cardiovasc Surg 1986;27:85–89.

154. Larach DR, Waberski W. The effect of thrombocytopenia and platelet inhibition on the activated coagulation time (ACT) in man [Abstract]. Anesthesiology 1984;61(suppl 3A):A45.

155. Moorehead MT, Westengard JC, Bull BS. Platelet involvement in the activated coagulation time of heparinized blood. Anesth Analg 1984;63: 394–398.

156. Bode AP, Eick L. Lysed platelets shorten the activated coagulation time (ACT) of heparinized blood. Am J Clin Pathol 1989;91:430–434.

157. Kresowik TF, Wakefield TW, Fessler RD II, Stanley JC. Anticoagulant effects of protamine sulfate in a canine model. J Surg Res 1988; 45:8–14.

158. Dutton DA, Hothersall AP, McLaren AD, Taylor KM, Turner MA. Protamine titration after cardiopulmonary bypass. Anaesthesia 1983;38: 264–268.

159. Dietrich W, Spannagl M, Jochum M, et al. Influence of high-dose aprotinin treatment on blood loss and coagulation patterns in patients undergoing myocardial revascularization. Anesthesiology 1990;73:1119–1126.

160. de Smet AAEA, Joen MCN, van Oeveren W, et al. Increased anticoagulation during cardiopulmonary bypass by aprotinin. J Thorac Cardiovasc Surg 1990;100:520–527.

161. Paul J, Cornillon B, Baguet J, Dureau G, Belleville J. In vivo release of a heparin-like factor in dogs during profound hypothermia. J Thorac Cardiovasc Surg 1981;82:45–48.

162. Bull MH, Huse WM, Bull BS. Evaluation of tests used to monitor heparin therapy during extracorporeal circulation. Anesthesiology 1975; 43:346–353.

163. Cohen JA. Activated coagulation time method

for control of heparin is reliable during cardiopulmonary bypass. Anesthesiology 1984;60:
121–124.

164. Gravlee GP, Haddon WS, Rothberger HK, et al.
Heparin dosing and monitoring for cardiopulmonary bypass. A comparison of techniques
with measurement of subclinical plasma coagulation. J Thorac Cardiovasc Surg 1990;99:
518–527.

165. Kesteven PJL. Blood coagulation studies during
open-heart surgery [Thesis]. London: St. Thomas'
Hospital, 1985.

166. Saleem A, Shenaq SS, Yawn DH, Harshberger K,
Diemunsch P, Mohindra P. Heparin monitoring
during cardiopulmonary bypass. Ann Clin Lab
Sci 1984;14:474–479.

167. Fox DJ, Gaines J, Reed G. Vehicles of heparin
management: a comparison. J Extra-Corp
Technol 1979;11:137–142.

168. Gomperts ED, Bethlehem B, Hockley J. The
monitoring of heparin activity during extracorporeal circulation. S Afr Med J 1977;51:
973–976.

169. Baugh RF. Detection of whole blood coagulation. Am Clin Products Rev 1984;45:38–45.

170. Anido G, Freeman DJ. Heparin assay and protamine titration. Am J Clin Pathol 1981;76:
410–415.

171. Choo IHF, Didisheim P, Doerge ML, et al. Evaluation of a heparin assay method using a fluorogenic synthetic peptide substrate for thrombin.
Thromb Res 1982;25:115–123.

172. Gauvin G, Umlas J, Chin N. Measurement of
plasma heparin levels using a fluorometric assay. Med Instrum 1983;17:165–168.

173. Savidge GF, Kesteven PJ, Al-Hasani SF, O'Brien
PF. Rapid quantitation of plasma heparin and
antithrombin III levels for cardiopulmonary
bypass monitoring, using fluorometric substrate assays. Thromb Haemost 1983;50:
745–748.

174. van Putten J, van de Ruit M, Beunis M, Hemker
HC. Automated spectrophotometric heparin assays. Comparison of methods. Haemostasis
1984;14:195–204.

175. Gundry SR, Klein MD, Drongowski RA, Kirsh
MM. Clinical evaluation of a new rapid heparin
assay using the dye Azure A. Am J Surg 1984;
148:191–194.

176. Klein MD, Drongowski RA, Linhardt RJ, Langer
RS. A colorimetric assay for chemical heparin in
plasma. Anal Biochem 1982;124:59–64.

177. Yin ET, Wessler S, Butler JV. Plasma heparin: A
unique, practical, submicrogram-sensitive assay. J Lab Clin Med 1973;81:298–310.

178. Babka R, Colby C, El-Etr A, Pifarré R. Monitoring of intraoperative heparinization and
blood loss following cardiopulmonary bypass

surgery. J Thorac Cardiovasc Surg 1977;73:
780–782.

179. Verska JJ. Control of heparinization by activated
clotting time during bypass with improved
postoperative hemostasis. Ann Thorac Surg
1977;24:170–173.

180. Roth JA, Cukingnan RA, Scott CR. Use of activated coagulation time to monitor heparin during cardiac surgery. Ann Thorac Surg 1979;
28:69–72.

181. Papaconstantinou C, Rådegran K. Use of the activated coagulation time in cardiac surgery.
Effects on heparin-protamine dosages and
bleeding. Scand J Cardiovasc Surg 1981;
15:213–215.

182. Jumean HG, Sudah F. Monitoring of anticoagulant therapy during open-heart surgery in children with congenital heart disease. Acta Haematol (Basel) 1983;70:392–395.

183. Dearing JP, Bartles DM, Stroud MR, Sade RM. Activated clotting times versus protocol anticoagulation management. J Extra-Corp Technol
1983;15:17–19.

184. Niinikoski J, Laato M, Laaksonen V, Jalonen J,
Inberg MV. Use of activated clotting time to
monitor anticoagulation during cardiac surgery. Scand J Thorac Cardiovasc Surg 1984;
18:57–61.

185. Lefemine AA, Lewis M. Activated clotting time
for control of anticoagulation during surgery.
Am Surg 1985;51:274–278.

186. Preiss DU, Schmidt-Bleibtreu H, Berguson P,
Metz G. Blood transfusion requirements in coronary artery surgery with and without the activated clotting time (ACT) technique. Klin
Wochenschr 1985;63:252–256.

187. Bowie JE, Kemna GD. Automated management
of heparin anticoagulation in cardiovascular
surgery. Proc Am Acad Cardiovasc Perfusion
1985;6:1–10.

188. Gravlee GP, Rogers AT, Dudas, LM, et al. Heparin management protocol for cardiopulmonary bypass influences postoperative heparin
rebound but not bleeding. Anesthesiology
1992;76:393–401.

189. Urban MK, Gordon M, Farrell DT, Shaffer WB.
The management of anticoagulation during cardiopulmonary bypass (CPB) [Abstract]. Anesthesiology 1991;75(suppl 3A):A437.

190. Ottesen S, Stormorken H, Hatteland K. The
value of activated coagulation time in monitoring heparin therapy during extracorporeal
circulation. Scand J Thorac Cardiovasc Surg
1984;18:123–128.

191. Goodnough LT, Johnston MFM, Toy PTCY. The
variability of transfusion practice in coronary
artery bypass surgery. JAMA 1991;265:86–90.

192. Guffin AV, Dunbar RW, Kaplan JA, Bland JW Jr.

Successful use of a reduced dose of protamine after cardiopulmonary bypass. Anesth Analg 1976;55:110–113.

193. Young JA, Kisker CT, Doty DB. Adequate anticoagulation during cardiopulmonary bypass determined by activated clotting time and the appearance of fibrin monomer. Ann Thorac Surg 1978;26:231–240.

194. Metz S, Keats AS. Low activated coagulation time during cardiopulmonary bypass does not increase postoperative bleeding. Ann Thorac Surg 1990;49:440–444.

195. Cardoso PFG, Yamazaki F, Keshavjee S, et al. A reevaluation of heparin requirements for cardiopulmonary bypass. J Thorac Cardiovasc Surg 1991;101:153–160.

196. Hickling KG. Extracorporeal CO_2 removal in severe adult respiratory distress syndrome. Anaesth Intensive Care 1986;14:46–53.

197. Kanter KR, Pennington DG, Weber TR, Zambie MA, Braun P, Martychenko V. Extracorporeal membrane oxygenation for postoperative cardiac support in children. J Thorac Cardiovasc Surg 1987;93:27–35.

198. Uziel L, Agostoni A, Pirovano E, et al. Hematologic survey during low frequency positive pressure ventilation with extracorporeal CO_2 removal. Trans Am Soc Artif Internal Organs 1982;28:359–364.

199. Heiden D, Mielke CH Jr, Rodvien R, Hill JD. Platelets, hemostasis, and thromboembolism during treatment of acute respiratory insufficiency with extracorporeal membrane oxygenation. Experience with 28 clinical perfusions. J Thorac Cardiovasc Surg 1975;70:644–655.

200. Uziel L, Cugno M, Fabrizi I, Pesenti A, Gattinoni L, Agostoni A. Physiopathology and management of coagulation during long-term extracorporeal respiratory assistance. Int J Artif Organs 1990;13:280–287.

201. Davies GC, Sobel M, Salzman EW. Elevated plasma fibrinopeptide A and thromboxane B_2 levels during cardiopulmonary bypass. Circulation 1980;61:808–814.

202. Tollefsen DM. Heparin cofactor II. In: Lane DA, Lindahl U, ed. Heparin. Chemical and biological properties, clinical applications. Boca Raton, FL: CRC Press, 1989:257–273.

203. Nielsen LE, Bell WR, Borkon AM, Neill CA. Extensive thrombus formation with heparin resistance during extracorporeal circulation. A new presentation of familial antithrombin III deficiency. Arch Intern Med 1987;147:149–152.

204. Soloway HB, Christiansen TW. Heparin anticoagulation during cardiopulmonary bypass in an antithrombin-III deficient patient. Implications relative to the etiology of heparin rebound. Am J Clin Pathol 1980;73:723–725.

205. Marciniak E, Farley CH, DeSimone PA. Familial thrombosis due to antithrombin III deficiency. Blood 1974;43:219–231.

206. Chung F, David TE, Watt J. Excessive requirement for heparin during cardiac surgery. Can Anaesth Soc J 1981;28:280–282.

207. Reuter NF. Heparin insensitivity responding to fresh frozen plasma. Minn Med 1978;61:79–81.

208. Wilds SL, Camerlengo LJ, Dearing JP. Activated clotting time and cardiopulmonary bypass, III. Effect of high platelet count on heparin management. J Extra-Corp Technol 1982;14:322–324.

209. Olinger GN, Hussey CV, Olive JA, Malik MI. Cardiopulmonary bypass for patients with previously documented heparin-induced platelet aggregation. J Thorac Cardiovasc Surg 1984;87:673–677.

210. Conley CL, Hartmann RC, Lalley JS. The relationship of heparin activity to platelet concentration. Proc Soc Exp Biol Med 1948;69:284–287.

211. Schved JF, Gris JC, Eledjam JJ. Circadian changes in anticoagulant effect of heparin infused at a constant rate. Br Med J 1985;290:1286.

212. Decousus HA, Croze M, Levi FA, et al. Circadian changes in anticoagulant effect of heparin infused at a constant rate. Br Med J 1985;290:341–344.

213. Decousus M, Gremillet E, Decousus H, et al. Nycthemeral variations of $^{99}Tc^m$-labelled heparin pharmacokinetic parameters. Nuclear Med Comm 1985;6:633–640.

214. Whitfield LR, Levy G. Relationship between concentration and anticoagulant effect of heparin in plasma of normal subjects: magnitude and predictability of interindividual differences. Clin Pharmacol Ther 1980;28:509–516.

215. Nelson RM, Frank CG, Mason JO. The antiheparin properties of the antihistamines, tranquilizers, and certain antibiotics. Surg Forum 1958;9:146–150.

216. Dietrich W, Spannagl M, Schramm W, Vogt W, Barankay A, Richter JA. The influence of preoperative anticoagulation on heparin response during cardiopulmonary bypass. J Thorac Cardiovasc Surg 1991;102:505–514.

217. Cloyd G, D'Ambra M, Koski G, Akins C. Heparin resistance in coronary artery bypass graft patients: the role of preoperative heparin therapy vs intraaortic balloon pumps. In: Proceedings of the Society of Cardiovascular Anesthesiologists 8th annual meeting, 1986:71.

218. Hicks GL Jr. Heparin resistance during cardiopulmonary bypass [Letter]. J Thorac Cardiovasc Surg 1983;86:633.

219. Habbab MA, Haft JI. Heparin resistance induced by intravenous nitroglycerin. A word of caution when both drugs are used concomitantly. Arch Intern Med 1987;147:857–860.

220. Becker RC, Corrao JM, Bovill EG, et al. Intravenous nitroglycerin-induced heparin resistance: a qualitative antithrombin III abnormality. Am Heart J 1990;119:1254–1261.

221. Godal HC. Heparin tolerance and the plasma proteins. Scand J Clin Lab Invest 1961;13:314–325.

222. Jaques LB. The pharmacology of heparin and heparinoids. Prog Med Chem 1967;6:139–198.

223. Glueck HI, MacKenzie MR, Glueck CJ. Crystalline IgG protein in multiple myeloma: identification effects on coagulation and on lipoprotein metabolism. J Lab Clin Med 1972;79:731–744.

224. Pogliani E, Cofrancesco E, Praga C. Anti-heparin activity of a macroglobulin from a patient with breast adenocarcinoma. Acta Haematol (Basel) 1975;53:249–255.

225. Jordan RE, Kilpatrick J, Nelson RM. Heparin promotes the inactivation of antithrombin by neutrophil elastase. Science 1987;237:777–779.

226. Bleyl H, Addo O, Roka L. Heparin neutralizing effect of lipoproteins. Thromb Diath Haemorrh 1975;34:549–555.

227. Whitfield LR, Lele AS, Levy G. Effect of pregnancy on the relationship between concentration and anticoagulant action of heparin. Clin Pharmacol Ther 1983;34:23–28.

228. Hanowell ST, Kim YD, Rattan V, MacNamara TE. Increased heparin requirement with hypereosinophilic syndrome. Anesthesiology 1981;55:450–452.

229. Mummaneni N, Istanbouli M, Pifarré R, El-Etr AA. Increased heparin requirements with autotransfusion. J Thorac Cardiovasc Surg 1983;66:446–447.

230. Hodby ED, Hirsh J, Adeniyi-Jones C. The influence of drugs upon the anticoagulant activity of heparin. Can Med Assoc J 1972;106:562–564.

231. Anderson EF. Heparin resistance prior to cardiopulmonary bypass. Anesthesiology 1986;64:504–507.

232. Reich DL, Hammerschlag BC, Salter O, et al. The influence of nitroglycerin on heparin anticoagulation during cardiac surgery. In: Proceedings of the Society of Cardiovascular Anesthesiologists 12th annual meeting, 1990:115.

233. Amin F, Horrow S. Nitroglycerin antagonism of heparin [Letter]. Anesthesiology 1990;73:193–194.

234. Hirsh J, Piovella F, Pini M. Congenital antithrombin III deficiency. Incidence and clinical features. Am J Med 1989;87(suppl 3B):34S–38S.

235. Thaler E, Lechner K. Antithrombin III deficiency and thromboembolism. Clin Haematol 1981;10:369–390.

236. Towne JB, Bernhard VM, Hussey C, Garancis JC. Antithrombin deficiency—a cause of unexplained thrombosis in vascular surgery. Surgery 1981;89:735–742.

237. Andrew M, Paes B, Milner R, et al. Development of the human coagulation system in the full-term infant. Blood 1987;70:165–172.

238. Büller HR, ten Cate JW. Acquired antithrombin III deficiency: laboratory diagnosis, incidence, clinical implications, and treatment with antithrombin III concentrate. Am J Med 1989;87(suppl 3B):44S–48S.

239. Arai H, Miyakawa T, Ozaki K, Sakuragawa N. Changes of the levels of antithrombin III in patients with cerebrovascular diseases. Thromb Res 1983;31:197–202.

240. Duckert F. Behaviour of antithrombin III in liver disease. Scand J Gastroenterol 1973;19(suppl):109–112.

241. Bick RL, Bick MD, Fekete LF. Antithrombin III patterns in disseminated intravascular coagulation. Am J Clin Pathol 1980;73:577–583.

242. Marciniak E, Gockerman JP. Heparin-induced decrease in circulating antithrombin-III. Lancet 1977;2:581–584.

243. Pickering NJ, Brody JI, Fink GB, Finnegan JO, Ablaza S. The behavior of antithrombin III, alpha$_2$ macroglobulin, and alpha$_1$, antitrypsin during cardiopulmonary bypass. Am J Clin Pathol 1983;80:459–464.

244. von Blohn G, Hellstern P, Köhler M, Scheffler P, Wenzel E. Clinical aspects of acquired antithrombin III deficiency. Behring Inst Mitt 1986;79:200–215.

245. Barnette RE, Shupak RC, Pontius J, Rao AK. In vitro effect of fresh frozen plasma on the activated coagulation time in patients undergoing cardiopulmonary bypass. Anesth Analg 1988;67:57–60.

246. Cosgriff TM, Bishop DT, Hershgold EJ, et al. Familial antithrombin III deficiency: its natural history, genetics, diagnosis and treatment. Medicine 1983;62:209–220.

247. Sabbagh AH, Chung GKT, Shuttleworth P, Applegate BJ, Gabrhel W. Fresh frozen plasma: a solution to heparin resistance during cardiopulmonary bypass. Ann Thorac Surg 1984;37:466–468.

248. Consensus Conference. Fresh-frozen plasma. Indications and risks. JAMA 1985;253:551–553.

249. Dietrich W, Schroll A, Göb E, Barankay A, Richter JA. Improved heparin response by substitution of antithrombin III concentrate during ex-

tracorporeal circulation. Anaesthesist 1984; 33:422–427.

250. Hoffman DL. Purification and large-scale preparation of antithrombin III. Am J Med 1989;87(suppl 3B):23S–26S.

251. Schwartz RS, Bauer KA, Rosenberg RD, et al. Clinical experience with antithrombin III concentrate in treatment of congenital and acquired deficiency of antithrombin. Am J Med 1989;87(suppl 3B):53S–60S.

252. Godal HC. Heparin-induced thrombocytopenia. In: Lane DA, Lindahl U, ed. Heparin. Chemical and biological properties, clinical applications. Boca Raton, FL: CRC Press, 1989: 533–548.

253. Cipolle RJ, Rodvold KA, Seifert R, Clarens R, Ramirez-Lassepas M. Heparin-associated thrombocytopenia: a prospective evaluation of 211 patients. Ther Drug Monit 1983;5:205–211.

254. Ansell J, Slepchuk N Jr, Kumar R, Lopez A, Southard L, Deykin D. Heparin induced thrombocytopenia: a prospective study. Thromb Hemost 1980;43:61–65.

255. Bell WR, Royall RM. Heparin-associated thrombocytopenia: a comparison of three heparin preparations. N Engl J Med 1980;303: 902–907.

256. Bailey RT, Ursick JA, Heim KL, Hilleman DE, Reich JW. Heparin-associated thrombocytopenia: a prospective comparison of bovine lung heparin manufactured by a new process, and porcine intestinal heparin. Drug Intell Clin Pharm 1986;20:374–378.

257. Cines DB, Kaywin P, Bina M, Tomaski A, Schreiber AD. Heparin-associated thrombocytopenia. N Engl J Med 1980;303:788–795.

258. Cines DB, Tomaski A, Tannenbaum S. Immune endothelial-cell injury in heparin-associated thrombocytopenia. N Engl J Med 1987;316: 581–589.

259. White PW, Sadd JR, Nensel RE. Thrombotic complications of heparin therapy. Including six cases of heparin-induced skin necrosis. Ann Surg 1979;190:595–608.

260. Towne JB, Bernhard VM, Hussey C, Garancis JC. White clot syndrome. Peripheral vascular complications of heparin therapy. Arch Surg 1979; 114:372–377.

261. Rhodes GR, Dixon RH, Silver D. Heparin induced thrombocytopenia: eight cases with thrombotic-hemorrhagic complications. Ann Surg 1977;186:752–758.

262. Kapsch DN, Adelstein EH, Rhodes GR, Silver D. Heparin-induced thrombocytopenia, thrombosis, and hemorrhage. Surgery 1979;86: 148–155.

263. Van der Weyden MB, Hunt H, McGrath K, et al. Delayed-onset heparin-induced thrombocyto-

penia. A potentially malignant syndrome. Med J Aust 1983;2:132–135.

264. Hussey CV, Bernhard VM, McLean MR, Fobian JE. Heparin induced platelet aggregation: *in vitro* confirmation of thrombotic complications associated with heparin therapy. Ann Clin Lab Sci 1979;9:487–493.

265. Kappa JR, Fisher CA, Berkowitz HD, Cottrell ED, Addonizio VP Jr. Heparin-induced platelet activation in sixteen surgical patients: diagnosis and management. J Vasc Surg 1987;5: 101–109.

266. Laskey MAL, Deutsch E, Hirshfeld JW Jr, Kussmaul WG, Barnathan E, Laskey WK. Influence of heparin therapy on percutaneous transluminal coronary angioplasty outcome in patients with coronary arterial thrombus. Am J Cardiol 1990;65:179–182.

267. Resnekov L, Chediak J, Hirsh J, Lewis D. Antithrombotic agents in coronary artery disease. Chest 1986;2(suppl):54S–67S.

268. Kander NH, Holland KJ, Pitt B, Topol EJ. A randomized pilot trial of brief versus prolonged heparin after successful reperfusion in acute myocardial infarction. Am J Cardiol 1990;65: 139–142.

269. Makhoul RG, McCann RL, Austin EH, Greenberg CS, Lowe JE. Management of patients with heparin-associated thrombocytopenia and thrombosis requiring cardiac surgery. Ann Thorac Surg 1987;43:617–621.

270. Smith JP, Walls JT, Muscato MS, et al. Extracorporeal circulation in a patient with heparin-induced thrombocytopenia. Anesthesiology 1985; 62:363–365.

271. Guay DRP, Richard A. Heparin-induced thrombocytopenia—association with a platelet aggregating factor and cross-sensitivity to bovine and porcine heparin. Drug Intell Clin Pharm 1984;18:398–401.

272. Horellou MH, Conard J, Lecrubier C, et al. Persistent heparin induced thrombocytopenia despite therapy with low molecular weight heparin [Letter]. Thromb Haemost 1984;51:134.

273. Harenberg J, Zimmermann R, Schwarz F, Kübler W. Treatment of heparin-induced thrombocytopenia with thrombosis by new heparinoid [Letter]. Lancet 1983;1:986–987.

274. Kappa JR, Horn MK III, Fisher CA, Cottrell ED, Ellison N, Addonizio VP Jr. Efficacy of iloprost (ZK36374) versus aspirin in preventing heparin-induced platelet activation during cardiac operations. J Thorac Cardiovasc Surg 1987;94: 405–413.

275. Kappa JR, Fisher CA, Todd B, et al. Intraoperative management of patients with heparin-induced thrombocytopenia. Ann Thorac Surg 1990;49:714–723.

276. Kraenzler EJ, Starr NJ. Heparin-associated thrombocytopenia: management of patients for open heart surgery. Case reports describing the use of iloprost. Anesthesiology 1988;69: 964–967.

277. Addonizio VP Jr, Macarak EJ, Niewiarowski S, Colman RW, Edmunds LH Jr. Preservation of human platelets with prostaglandin E₁ during in vitro simulation of cardiopulmonary bypass. Circ Res 1979;44:350–357.

278. Kappa JR, Musial J, Fisher KA, Addonizio VP. Quantitation of platelet preservation with prostanoids during simulated bypass. J Surg Res 1987;42:10–18.

279. Vender JS, Matthew EB, Silverman IM, Konowitz H, Dau PC. Heparin-associated thrombocytopenia: alternative managements. Anesth Analg 1986;65:520–522.

280. Brady J, Riccio JA, Yumen OH, Makary AZ, Greenwood SM. Plasmapheresis. A therapeutic option in the management of heparin-associated thrombocytopenia with thrombosis. Am J Clin Pathol 1991;96:394–397.

281. Hirsh J, Ofosu FA, Levine M. The development of low molecular weight heparins for clinical use. In: Verstraete M, Vermylen J, Lijnen HR, Arnout J, eds. Thrombosis and haemostasis. Leuven, Netherlands: International Society on Thrombosis and Haemostasis and Leuven University Press, 1987:325–346.

282. Horner AA. The nature of two components of pig mucosal heparin, separated by electrophoresis in agarose gel. Can J Biochem 1967; 45:1015–1020.

283. Hirsh J, Ofosu F, Buchanan M. Rationale behind the development of low molecular weight heparin derivatives. Semin Thromb Hemost 1985;11:13–16.

284. Salzman EW. Low-molecular-weight heparin. Is small beautiful [Editorial]? N Engl J Med 1986;315:957–959.

285. Fareed J, Kumar A, Rock A, Walenga JM, Davis P. A primate model (Macaca Mulatta) to study the pharmacokinetics of heparin and its fractions. Semin Thromb Hemost 1985;11:138–154.

286. Messmore HL. Clinical efficacy of heparin fractions: issues and answers. Crit Rev Clin Lab Sci 1986;23:77–94.

287. Ofosu FA, Blajchman MA, Modi GJ, Smith LM, Buchanan MR. The importance of thrombin inhibition for the expression of the anticoagulant activities of heparin, dermatan sulphate, low molecular weight heparin and pentosan polysulphate. Br J Haematol 1985;60: 695–704.

288. Turpie AGG, Levine MN, Hirsh J, et al. A randomized controlled trial of a low-molecular-weight heparin (Enoxaparin) to prevent deep-vein thrombosis in patients undergoing elective hip surgery. N Engl J Med 1986;315: 925–929.

289. Ljungberg B, Blombäck M, Johnsson H, Lins LE. A single dose of a low molecular weight heparin fragment for anticoagulation during hemodialysis. Clin Nephrol 1987;27:31–35.

290. Schrader J, Valentin R, Tönnis HJ, et al. Low molecular weight heparin in hemodialysis and hemofiltration patients. Kidney Int 1985;28: 823–829.

291. Roussi JH, Houbouyan LL, Goguel AF. Use of low-molecular-weight heparin in heparin-induced thrombocytopenia with thrombotic complications [Letter]. Lancet 1984;1:1183.

292. Leroy J, Leclerc MH, Delahousse B, et al. Treatment of heparin-associated thrombocytopenia and thrombosis with low molecular weight heparin (CY 216). Semin Thromb Hemost 1985;11:326–329.

293. Renaud H, Moriniere P, Dieval J, et al. Low molecular weight heparin in haemodialysis and haemofiltration -comparison with unfractioned heparin. Proc Eur Dial Transplant Assoc-Eur Renal Assoc 1984;21:276–280.

294. Bergqvist D, Burmark US, Frisell J, et al. Low molecular weight heparin once daily compared with conventional low-dose heparin twice daily. A prospective double-blind multicentre trial on prevention of postoperative thrombosis. Br J Surg 1986;73:204–208.

295. Abildgaard U, Norrheim L, Larsen AE, Nesvold A, Sandset PM, Odegaard OR. Monitoring therapy with LMW heparin: a comparison of three chromogenic substrate assays and the heptest clotting assay. Haemostasis 1990;20:193–203.

296. Mammen EF. Why low molecular weight heparin? Semin Thromb Hemost 1990;16:1–4.

297. Bara L, Billaud E, Kher A, Samama M. Increased anti-Xa bioavailability for a low molecular weight heparin (PK 10169) compared with unfractionated heparin. Semin Thromb Hemost 1985;11:316–317.

298. Fareed J. Development of heparin fractions: some overlooked considerations. Semin Thromb Hemost 1985;11:227–236.

299. Racanelli A, Fareed J, Walenga JM, Coyne E. Biochemical and pharmacologic studies on the protamine interactions with heparin, its fractions and fragments. Semin Thromb Hemost 1985;11:176–189.

300. Gouault-Heilmann M, Huet Y, Contant G, Payen D, Bloch G, Rapin M. Cardiopulmonary bypass with a low-molecular-weight heparin fraction [Letter]. Lancet 1983;2:1374.

301. Massonnet-Castel S, Pelissier E, Dreyfus G, et al. Low-molecular-weight heparin in extracor-

poreal circulation [Letter]. Lancet 1984;1: 1182–1183.

302. Massonnet-Castel S, Pelissier E, Bara L, et al. Partial reversal of low molecular weight heparin (PK 10169) anti-Xa activity by protamine sulfate: in vitro and in vivo study during cardiac surgery with extracorporeal circulation. Haemostasis 1986;16:139–146.

303. Touchot B, Laborde F, Dum F, et al. Use of low molecular weight heparin CY 222 during cardiopulmonary bypass. Experimental study and clinical application. Perfusion 1986;1: 99–102.

304. Henny CP, ten Cate H, ten Cate JW, et al. A randomized blind study comparing standard heparin and a new low molecular weight heparinoid in cardiopulmonary bypass surgery in dogs. J Lab Clin Med 1985;106:187–196.

305. Zulys VJ, Teasdale SJ, Michel ER, et al. Ancrod (Arvin[R]) as an alternative to heparin anticoagulation for cardiopulmonary bypass. Anesthesiology 1989;71:870–877.

306. Marder VJ. Comparison of thrombolytic agents: selected hematologic, vascular and clinical events. Am J Cardiol 1989;64:2A–7A.

307. Markwardt F. Pharmacology of selective thrombin inhibitors. Nouv Rev Fr Hematol 1988;30:161–165.

308. Bichler J, Fichtl B, Siebeck M, Fritz H. Pharmacokinetics and pharmacodynamics of hirudin in man after single subcutaneous and intravenous bolus administration. Arzneimittelforschung 1988;38:704–710.

309. Walenga JM, Bakhos M, Messmore HL, Fareed J, Pifarre R. Potential use of recombinant hirudin as an anticoagulant in a cardiopulmonary bypass model. Ann Thorac Surg 1991;51: 271–277.

310. Mottaghy K, Oedekoven B, Schaich-Lester D, Pöppel, Küpper W. Application of surfaces with end point attached heparin to extracorporeal circulation with membrane lungs. Trans Am Soc Artif Internal Organs 1989;35:146–152.

311. Liu LS, Ito Y, Imanishi Y. Synthesis and antithrombogenicity of heparinized polyurethanes with intervening spacer chains of various kinds. Biomaterials 1991;12:390–396.

312. Park KD, Okano T, Nojiri C, Kim SW. Heparin immobilization onto segmented polyuretha-

neurea surfaces—effect of hydrophilic spacers. J Biomed Mater Res 1988;22:977–992.

313. Eberle JW, Manton JR, Meals CR, Whitley DE, Rea WJ. Cross-linked heparin binding of a membrane oxygenator system. J Biomed Mater Res 1973;7:145–153.

314. Wakabayashi A, Woolley TO, Nakamura Y, et al. Blood coagulation studies during six day heparinless venoarterial bypass in sheep. J Surg Oncol 1976;8:299–304.

315. Hagler HK, Powell WM, Eberle JW, Sugg WL, Platt MR, Watson JT. Five-day partial bypass using a membrane oxygenator without systemic heparinization. Trans Am Soc Artif Internal Organs 1975;21:178–187.

316. Rea WJ, Whitley D, Eberle JW. Long-term membrane oxygenation without systemic heparinization. Trans Am Soc Artif Internal Organs 1972;18:316–320.

317. Fletcher JR, McKee AE, Mills M, Snyder KC, Herman CM. Twenty-four hour membrane oxygenation in dogs without anticoagulation. Surgery 1976;80:214–223.

318. Tong S-D, Rolfs MR, Hsu L-C. Evaluation of Duraflo-II heparin immobilized cardiopulmonary bypass circuits. ASAIO Trans 1990;36: M654–M656.

319. von Segesser LK, Turina M. Cardiopulmonary bypass without systemic heparinization. Performance of heparin-coated oxygenators in comparison with classic membrane and bubble oxygenators. J Thorac Cardiovasc Surg 1989; 98:386–396.

320. Toomasian JM, Hsu LC, Hirshl RB, Heiss KF, Hultquist KA, Bartlett RH. Evaluation of Duraflo II heparin coating in prolonged extracorporeal membrane oxygenation. Trans Am Soc Artif Internal Organs 1988;34:410– 414.

321. von Segesser LK, Weiss BM, Gallino A, et al. Superior hemodynamics in left heart bypass without systemic heparinization. In: Cardiothoracic surgery Berlin: Springer-Verlag, 1990:384–389.

322. Boonstra PW, Aikkerman C, Van Oeveren W, et al. Cardiopulmonary bypass with a heparin-coated extracorporeal circuit: clinical evaluation in 30 patients. In: Proceedings of the European Association of Cardiothoracic Surgery, Naples, Italy, 1990.

15

NEUTRALIZATION OF HEPARIN ANTICOAGULATION

Rita M. Moorman, Warren M. Zapol, and Edward Lowenstein

In this chapter, we present the biology of heparin neutralization, emphasizing the role of protamine, which has been used as the principal neutralization drug for over 3 decades. We also will examine other drugs that have been used to reverse heparin or are being developed for future use. The motivation behind our review is that protamine, although effective, has some serious cardiovascular side effects including life-threatening and fatal reactions.

Heparin anticoagulates indirectly by enhancing the activity of antithrombin III, a circulating proteinase inhibitor that acts on serine proteases (1). Antithrombin III neutralizes activated factors XIIa, XIa, IXa, Xa, thrombin, and XIIIa. Heparin-modified antithrombin III especially accelerates inactivation of factors Xa and thrombin (1).

BIOLOGY OF PROTAMINE

Chemistry and Uses

Protamine, a polycationic protein derived from salmon milt, posseses strong alkalinity because of an amino acid composition consisting of 67% arginine (2). In its natural state, the numerous positive charges on the protamine molecule bind with the negatively charged phosphate groups of the nucleoprotein material of salmon sperm. Heparin, a polyanion, binds ionically to

protamine to produce a stable precipitate. Protamine contains two active sites, one that neutralizes heparin and another that exerts a mild anticoagulant effect, independent of heparin.

Other clinical uses of protamine include complexing it with insulin to produce NPH insulin. This renders insulin relatively insoluble at neutral pH, extending the duration of action to approximately 24 hours. Similarly, complexing protamine with zinc forms protamine-zinc insulin, which has a duration of 36 hours. Protamine inhibits angiogenesis (3) and has been used as an antineoplastic agent on this basis (4).

The anticoagulant effect of protamine has been demonstrated in vitro (5). Debate exists as to whether this effect is clinically important and at what doses. It has been suggested that the anticoagulant effect of protamine only becomes important at doses approximately three times those required for neutralization of residual heparin (6). However, Ellison et al. (7) subsequently demonstrated only a mild, transient (30 minutes) increase in the Lee-White whole blood coagulation time with no effect on the partial thromboplastin time, despite a large excess of protamine (Table 15.1). These effects occurred at intravenous doses of up to 800 mg for a 70 kg adult. They initially proposed that the anticoagulant ef-

381

Table 15.1. Effects of Protamine on Lee-White Coagulation and Partial Thromboplastin Times (PTT) after Single Doses of 600 mg/kg in Six Volunteers[a]

	Control	Time After Injection (min)		
		5	30	60
Lee-White, three-tube (min)				
Mean	6.58	8.89[b]	6.83	6.58
SE	0.25	0.48	0.53	0.53
PTT (sec)				
Mean	41.5	40.7	41.8	40.7
SE	1.3	1.6	1.8	1.4

[a] From Ellison N, Ominsky AJ, Wollman H. Is protamine a clinically significant coagulant? A negative answer. Anesthesiology 1971;35:621–629.
[b] Mean differs significantly from control mean, P < 0.05, using two-dimensional analysis of variance.

fect of protamine appears to become clinically important only if exceedingly large amounts are infused. This relatively large therapeutic window for protamine has been confirmed by more recent studies that also examined the effects of protamine on the activated partial thromboplastin time without looking at platelet function (8).

It has since been suggested, by Ellison's group and others, that the anticoagulant effect of protamine may be due to inhibition of platelet-induced aggregation. More recent work by Ellison et al. (9) showed a decreased in vitro platelet sensitivity to adenosine diphosphate (ADP) and collagen in the presence of the heparin-protamine complex. Protamine alone has no effect on platelet aggregation. Mammen et al. (10) showed decreased platelet aggregation in response to ADP and ristocetin when protamine was administered to patients at the conclusion of cardiopulmonary bypass (CPB). They also demonstrated a decrease in platelet volume and suggested that a change in platelet surface membranes could be responsible for this altered platelet function. A human trial that administered protamine equal to the total heparin dose versus protamine given at a reduced dose based on a heparin half-life of 2 hours resulted in markedly decreased chest tube drainage, higher platelet counts, and post-

operative clotting studies closer to control values in those patients receiving the smaller protamine doses (11).

Dutton et al. (12) showed that smaller protamine doses (derived by protamine titration just prior to the discontinuation of cardiopulmonary bypass) resulted in acceptable activated clotting time (ACT) values at the conclusion of bypass with no subsequent evidence of heparin rebound. A recent dog study administering different doses of protamine (1.5, 3.0, 6.0, and 15.0 mg/kg) to heparinized and unheparinized animals showed decreasing platelet aggregation to ADP with increasing protamine doses. Significant effects on coagulation (expressed as ACT, prothrombin time, and partial thromboplastin time) became evident at excess protamine doses of 6.0 and 15.0 mg/kg in both heparinized and unheparinized animals (13). Based on these more recent studies, most patients will probably tolerate an excess protamine dose of 1 to 2 mg/kg without adverse effects on coagulation. The clinician should be aware that protamine overdose can result in further platelet dysfunction lasting several hours into the postbypass period.

ASSESSMENT OF REVERSAL OF ANTICOAGULATION

It appears desirable to test the adequacy of anticoagulation and reversal at the conclusion of CPB. Tests evaluating anticoagulation and its reversal after CPB should yield quick results and be easily performed in the operating room. The ACT, a variation of the whole blood clotting time, was introduced by Hattersley in 1966 (14), and is the most common test utilized for this purpose. This test is described in detail in Chapter 14.

Calculation of Protamine Dose

At the conclusion of CPB, the residual amount of heparin should be assessed and appropriately neutralized. The rate of heparin metabolism exhibits considerable interpatient variability, making accurate determination of residual heparin difficult (15, 16). Accurate calculation of the protamine dose for reversal is important because unneutralized heparin can increase postoperative bleeding. The role of protamine as an anticoagulant remains controversial, but is probably unimportant, even with moderate overdoses. Several inherent problems in calculating protamine dosages have been pointed out by Hurt et al. (17). These include (a) the dose of protamine necessary to neutralize heparin in vivo is not the same as that required for in vitro neutralization, (b) heparin and protamine preparations vary in their potency, and (c) the quantity of protamine required to neutralize a given heparin dose decreases over time because of heparin metabolism or excretion.

Dosage

Many different dose regimens for protamine reversal of heparin anticoagulation have been employed. Inadequate reversal, protamine anticoagulation, and adverse side effects represent the hazards of inappropriate protamine dosage.

In 1975, Bull et al. (14) demonstrated that both inadequate heparin reversal and excessive protamine administration were common in all five widely employed protamine administration protocols that they examined. The two best protocols in the group still resulted in inadequate heparinization or excessive protamine neutralization in some patients (Fig. 15.1).

Bull et al. developed a computer simulation based upon another approach to heparin administration. Heparin was administered in a quantity sufficient to raise the ACT to 480 seconds and supplemented to maintain that level every 60 minutes. Protamine was then administered in a ratio of 1.3/1 for every remaining milligram of heparin measured in the circulation at the conclusion of bypass. This method adequately compensated for marked differences in heparin and protamine requirements among their eight test patients (Fig. 15.2).

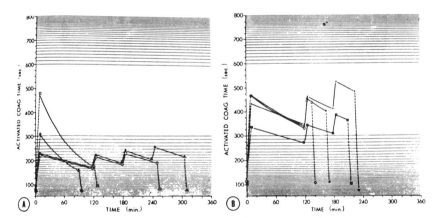

Figure 15.1.   Prior to the initiation of CPB a 300 unit per kilogram dose of heparin was given initially, with 100 units per kilogram given after 2 hours and each hour thereafter. Neutralization was accomplished with protamine, 1.5 times the total dose of heparin. For each procedure, **A** shows patients (*darkened triangles* and *open circles*) who had the least sensitivity to heparin and shortest half-life of heparin (*closed diamonds* and *open squares*). **B** shows the course of anticoagulant therapy for patients who were the most sensitive to heparin (*open diamonds* and *closed circles*) and patients who had the longest heparin half-lives (*darkened squares* and x). *Solid lines* depict the coagulation times during bypass, and the *broken lines* indicate the institution and termination of anticoagulation. (From Bull BS, Korpman RA, Huse WM, Briggs BD. Heparin therapy during extracorporeal circulation, I. Problems inherent in existing heparin protocols. J Thorac Cardiovasc Surg 1975;69:674–684.)

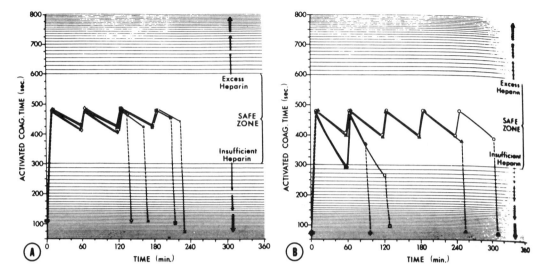

Figure 15.2. The descriptions for **A** and **B** are the same as in Figure 15. Monitoring approach (computer simulation). The activated coagulation time was raised to 8 minutes initially and was returned to that level every 60 minutes during the operation. Protamine was administered in a ratio of 1.3 mg for every 100 units of heparin remaining in the circulation at the conclusion of bypass. (From Bull BS, Korpman RA, Huse WM, Briggs BD. Heparin therapy during extracorporeal circulation, I. Problems inherent in existing heparin protocols. J Thorac Cardiovasc Surg 1975;69:674–684.)

Protamine is standardized against heparin preparations, so its potency may vary slightly. One milligram of protamine neutralizes approximately 85 units of heparin (differs slightly for porcine mucosal versus heparin lung) (15). Protamine doses are usually calculated upon the ratio of 1 mg/100 units of heparin, and it only binds effectively to circulating heparin. The extra protamine is intended to prevent heparin rebound associated with heparin release from tissue stores or from heparin-protamine aggregates and to compensate for the probable shorter biological half-life of protamine (18, 19).

Methods of Calculation of Protamine Doses

Methods utilized to determine residual heparinization at the conclusion of CPB include fixed dosing protocols, use of the ACT/heparin dose-response curve, heparin/protamine titration curves, and actual measurements of residual plasma heparin levels. Each method warrants separate analysis (Table 15.2).

FIXED PROTAMINE DOSE REGIMEN

The easiest method of calculating a protamine dose is a fixed-dose ratio of protamine to heparin. This method involves giving 1.0 to 1.3 mg of protamine for each 100 units of heparin. Either the total dose of heparin administered for the case or the heparin dose given initially defines the amount or heparin to be neutralized (14, 20). Simplicity constitutes the main advantage of this method, as no assays are required at the end of bypass and there is no need to measure the ACT. The disadvantage is the considerable variability in heparin's half-life, making it difficult to predict the status of the coagulation system immediately preceding heparin neutralization (14).

ACT/HEPARIN DOSE-RESPONSE CURVES

This technique utilizes the method described by Bull et al. (21) that involves determining three ACT values and plotting them on a graph versus heparin dose (Fig. 15.3). The calculated amount of heparin is then neutralized by giving protamine 1.3 mg/100 units of heparin at the conclusion of CPB. This method is rapid and easy to use. Other advantages of this method include (*a*) more accurate calculation of protamine dose than the fixed regimen, (*b*) a reduced quantity of protamine administered, and (*c*) possibly decreased infusion of blood, platelets, and fresh-frozen plasma (19). One disadvantage is the reliance upon the ACT, which is affected by numerous factors. Culliford et al. (22) demonstrated that CPB distorts the relationship between ACT and heparin levels, with the ACT becoming prolonged beyond what could be explained by the plasma heparin concentration. The authors also noted that protamine doses calculated by this method exceeded those calculated by measurement of plasma heparin concentration, and the amount calculated by measuring plasma heparin concentration was usually sufficient to neutralize heparin-induced anticoagulation.

HEPARIN CONCENTRATION

Precise determination of the plasma heparin concentration remaining at the conclusion of bypass is infrequently utilized. One method incubates the plasma to be analyzed for heparin with activated factor X in the presence of an excess of its inhibitor (XaI). Heparin accelerates factor Xa inhibition, and residual factor X remaining after 2 minutes is measured and converted to a heparin concentration, expressed in units per milliliter (23).

Culliford et al. (22) demonstrated decreased protamine doses after calculation by this method as opposed to ACT/heparin dose-response curves. The major disadvantage of this method is the delayed acquisition of test results. Thus, the values may not be accurate when received because the patient's heparin concentration decreases at an unknown rate while the blood specimen is being analyzed. Furthermore, the conversion of plasma heparin concentrations into a protamine dose requires an estimation of plasma volume, which is difficult to assess

Table 15.2. Comparison of Methods for Calculating Protamine Dosage

Method	Advantages	Disadvantages
Fixed dose	Simple Not reliant on ACT	Inadequate or excessive protamine Potential for increased coagulation times with standard doses
ACT/heparin dose-response curves	Rapid, easy to use in the OR	No correlation between ACT and heparin levels Relies on ACT
	More accurate protamine administration	
	Decreased blood product requirements	Dependence on plasma volume
Heparin levels	Less protamine given Not reliant on ACT	Requires peripheral laboratory Time consuming Assumes point on static curve Dependence on plasma volume
Protamine titration	Less protamine required than fixed dose	Variability between heparin-protamine preparations
	Decreased postoperative bleeding (suggested by some studies)	Dependence on blood volume estimate
	Suggested that no rebound effect seen with small protamine doses	Several steps for potential error
		Assumes point on static curve

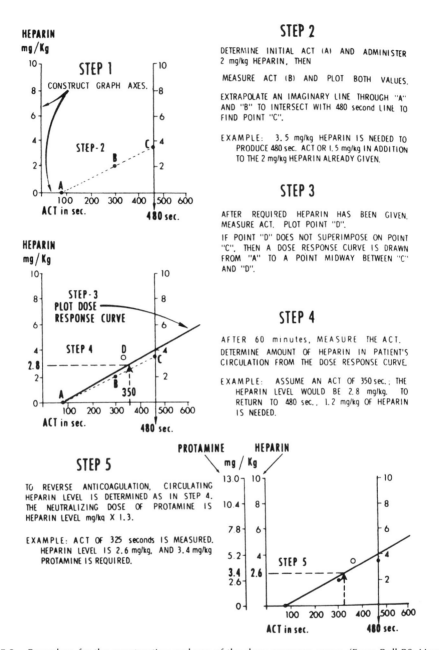

Figure 15.3. Procedure for the construction and use of the dose-response curve. (From Bull BS, Huse WM, Brauer FS, Korpman RA. Heparin therapy during extracorporeal circulation. II. The use of a dose-response curve to individualize heparin and protamine dosage. J Thorac Cardiovasc Surg 1975;69:685–689.)

at the completion of bypass (21) and there is not always good correlation between heparin levels and clotting times (24).

PROTAMINE TITRATION

Calculation of protamine dose by protamine titration was initially described by Allen and co-workers (25) and several variations of this method have been described (6, 12, 15, 16). All methods employ tubes with several dilutions of a standard protamine solution to which a fixed volume of whole heparinized blood is added. The lowest protamine concentration resulting in the shortest clotting time represents the optimal neutralization of heparin. Protamine dose is then calculated based upon an assumed neutralization ratio (e.g., 1.1 mg of protamine per 100 units of heparin) and upon estimated blood volume. Therefore, this method is actually an indirect way of estimating heparin concentrations. Advantages claimed for this method include lower protamine dose than with a fixed-dose regimen (15), absence of excessive postoperative bleeding response with this method (15), and no heparin rebound despite reduced protamine doses (12). Disadvantages include (a) the need to calculate blood volume (15, 16); (b) the variability in potency between different heparin and protamine preparations (although this can be compensated for by using the same source of protamine for dilutions as for reversal) (12); (c) manual versions of this method can be time consuming, thus when the protamine value is defined, the patient may have dropped to a lower heparin level or received an additional dose; and (d) numerous steps are involved, each incurring error (24).

arin reversal versus normal heparin decay is lacking.

Recombinant PF4 cloned in *Escherichia coli* neutralizes heparin as effectively as protamine in vitro (Fig. 15.4). Recombinant PF4 and protamine both neutralize heparin's inhibition of factor Xa and thrombin. Recombinant PF4 restored factor Xa levels more effectively than protamine (by approximately 50 to 60%) and was equipotent with human PF4 (25) (Fig. 15.5). Recombinant PF4 has been used in vivo in the rat model and was shown to be equally effective as protamine in reversing heparin anticoagulation. The PF4 injection produces normal platelet counts in this model (28).

Human or recombinant PF4 administered to Sprague-Dawley rats after heparinization had no effect upon white blood cell count, platelet count, or complement levels (Fig. 15.6). In contrast, protamine administered after heparin (0.1 mg/100 g), caused decreases of these same parameters. Furthermore, heparin neutralization by recombinant or human PF4 caused no decrease in mean arterial blood pressure or

OTHER DRUGS USED FOR REVERSAL OF ANTICOAGULATION

Platelet Factor 4

The α-granules of human platelets contain platelet factor 4 (PF4) that binds and neutralizes heparin when released during platelet aggregation (26). The PF4 is released at the site of vascular injury, binding heparin and facilitating thrombin accumulation and clot formation (25). The PF4 in platelet concentrates and fresh-frozen plasma was presumed to have been responsible for heparin reversal following CPB in two diabetics with a history of previous anaphylactic reactions to protamine (27). However, it should be noted that these patients still did have significant postbypass bleeding and actual documentation of hep-

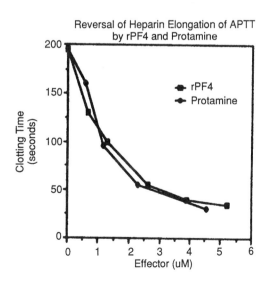

Figure 15.4. Neutralization of heparin elongation of activated partial thromboplastin time (APTT). (From Hunt AJ, Gray GS, Myers JA, Maione TE. Heparin neutralization by recombinant human PF4 in vitro [Abstract]. FASEB J 1990;4:A1991.)

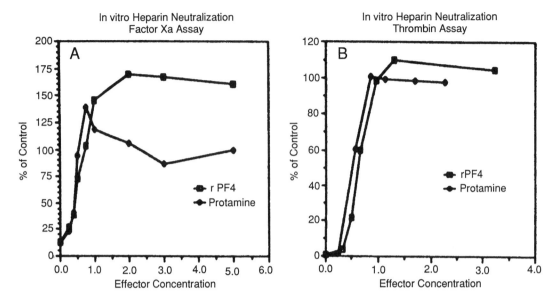

Figure 15.5. Neutralization of heparin by protamine and recombinant human PF4 (*rPF4*). With factor Xa, rPF4 and protamine were both effective, although 1 μm rPF4 could restore factor Xa activity to higher levels than protamine. Both rPF4 and protamine were equally effective (on a molar basis) at preventing inhibition of thrombin. (From Hunt AJ, Gray GS, Myers JA, Maione TE. Heparin neutralization by recombinant human PF4 in vitro [Abstract]. FASEB J 1990;4:A1991.)

pathologic pulmonary changes, whereas protamine neutralization produced these adverse effects (29).

Other drugs that have been used to neutralize heparin include the cation hexadimethrine bromide and toluidine blue. Polybrene, also known as hexadimethrine bromide, is a quaternary ammonium salt (30). At one time polybrene was commonly used to reverse heparin following CPB in humans (31, 32). Montalescot et al. (30) compared reversal of unfractionated heparin and low molecular weight heparin with both polybrene and protamine in a sheep model. They found no change in arterial blood gases and no increase in pulmonary artery pressures or thromboxane levels when low molecular weight heparin was reversed with polybrene. Polybrene reversal of unfractionated heparin, like protamine reversal of unfractionated or low molecular weight heparin, produced pulmonary vasoconstriction and thromboxane generation.

Polybrene reached the height of its popularity as a heparin antagonist during the 1950s. In 1962, the manufacturer withdrew polybrene from clinical use because of suspected nephrotoxicity (33). Polybrene has other adverse effects limiting its use. Rapid injection of clinically used doses of polybrene into heparinized dogs undergoing extracorporeal circulation consistently produced increases in pulmonary artery pressures and right heart dilation with a resultant decrease in systemic arterial pressure (34). It has also been suggested that small errors in dose calculation can result in significant polycation induced lung injury (35, 36). Toluidine blue has also been used for heparin reversal, but it is less effective than protamine and is associated with methemoglobinemia (37).

PROTAMINE REACTIONS

Adverse cardiopulmonary responses to protamine administration have been observed during the entire history of clinical cardiac surgery. This complex clinical situation has made this adverse drug reaction very difficult to define. In 1983, a specific clinical syndrome of catastrophic pulmonary vasoconstriction was described. Within 1 month, Lowenstein and co-workers (38) observed three severe protamine reactions, and in 3 more months they had collected a total of five such incidents. They observed profound increases in pulmonary arterial and central venous pressures with concurrent dramatic decreases in left atrial and systemic arterial pressures. These five patients shared certain characteristics: valvular heart disease, bolus protamine administration, a low total protamine dose (less than 0.5 mg/kg), tolerance to further protamine infusions without adverse effects, and no adverse sequelae. Since then, substantial clinical and basic science investigation has led to the recogni-

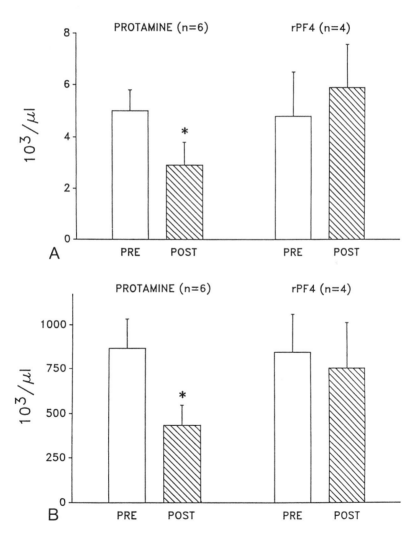

Figure 15.6. Effect of injection of protamine sulfate or recombinant PF4 (*rPF4*) on the number of circulating white blood cells (**A**) and platelets (**B**). Number of experiments in parentheses. *, $p < 0.01$, significantly different from preheparin platelet count. The values correspond to the mean +/− SEM. (From Cook JJ, Niewiarowski S, Yan Z, et al. Platelet factor 4 efficiently reverses heparin anticoagulation in the rat without adverse effects of heparin-protamine complexes. Circulation 1992;85:1102–1109.)

tion of three mechanisms producing adverse protamine reactions (Table 15.3).

It now appears that catastrophic pulmonary vasoconstriction after protamine occurs in about 1.5% of adult cardiac surgical patients (39). There are numerous suggested risk factors, including valvular heart disease (particularly mitral), preexisting pulmonary hypertension, bolus protamine administration, infusion rates greater than 5 mg/min, diabetes with prior NPH insulin exposure, specific brands of protamine, sterilization via ligation of the vas deferens, site of administration, and rate of administration. To date, none of these predisposing risk factors have been verified, but some deserve mention.

RATE OF ADMINISTRATION

The package insert for protamine suggests administering the drug no faster than 5 mg/min. Morel et al. (40) determined that the rate of protamine administration was an important factor leading to pulmonary vasoconstriction in sheep. In their study, 200 IU/kg of heparin were reversed with 2 mg/kg of protamine infused over 3 seconds, 30 seconds, 300 seconds, or 30 minutes. Sheep given protamine over 3 seconds consistently demonstrated thromboxane release, pulmonary vasoconstriction, increased pulmonary artery pressure, increased systemic vascular resistance (with no significant change in mean arterial pressures and left atrial pressures), and decreased cardiac output, whereas those given protamine over 30 minutes exhibited no change. The intermediate infusion rates showed variable and attenuated reactions.

SITE OF ADMINISTRATION

The site of protamine administration has been considered and studied as a triggering factor for protamine reactions in both humans and animals. Different studies examined various protamine injection sites including peripheral veins, inferior vena cava, left atrium, and aorta. Canine studies by Goldman et al. (41) suggest that detrimental vasoactive substances are released upon exposure of the pulmonary vasculature to protamine. Giving the drug on the left side of the circulation or via a peripheral vein with subsequent dilution were hypothesized to limit the first-pass pulmonary exposure. Casthely and co-workers (42) confirmed this hypothesis in a canine model in which protamine delivered over 4 minutes via a peripheral vein or the left atrium proved benign, whereas delivery via central venous injection decreased systemic blood pressure and systemic vascular resistance and increased pulmonary vascular resistance and pulmonary artery pressure. These results were not confirmed by Taylor et al. (43), who compared protamine administered over 30 seconds via aortic or vena caval injections in dogs and found no protection with left-sided injections, or by Rogers et al. (44), who found no differences between left- and right-sided protamine infused over 60 seconds into pigs.

Frater et al. (45) demonstrated decreased systolic blood pressure and increased plasma histamine levels in patients given protamine into the right atrium, changes that were not observed when protamine was administered into the left atrium. However, the majority of human studies to

Table 15.3. Classification of Protamine Reactions

Type	Horrow	Moorman, Zapol, Lowenstein
I.	Hypotension due to rapid administration	Pharmacologic histamine release
IIa.	Anaphylactic reactions	True anaphylaxis (IgE-mediated)
IIb.	Immediate anaphylactoid reactions	
IIc.	Delayed anaphylactoid reactions	Anaphylactoid reactions
III.	Catastrophic pulmonary vasoconstriction	Pulmonary vasoconstriction (? IgG/complement-mediated) Noncardiogenic pulmonary edema

date have not demonstrated any advantage to left-sided versus right-sided protamine administration (46, 47). The rate of infusion, and not the infusion site, appears to be the more important variable to control. Lastly, because of the risk of air embolization when a left atrial or aortic route is used, protamine is probably best administered on the right side of the circulation.

Classification or Protamine Reactions

Two classifications of protamine reactions have been proposed (Table 15.3). Horrow's classification sorts protamine reactions into type I, type II, and type III. Type I reactions result in transient systemic hypotension secondary to rapid administration. Type II reactions consist of anaphylactic and anaphylactoid reactions, which are further divided into types IIa, IIb, and IIc. Type IIa comprises true anaphylactic reactions. Immediate anaphylactoid reactions characterize type IIb, and delayed anaphylactoid (e.g., noncardiogenic pulmonary edema) are considered type IIc reactions. Type III reactions consist of catastrophic pulmonary vasoconstriction (48).

We propose an alternative classification as follows: (*a*) pharmacologic histamine release, (*b*) true anaphylaxis mediated by a specific antiprotamine immunoglobulin (Ig) IE antibody, and (*c*) thromboxane release leading to pulmonary vasoconstriction and bronchoconstriction. Thus, Horrow's type I reactions, which are characterized by systemic hypotension secondary to rapid administration, correspond in our classification to pharmacologic histamine release. Whereas Horrow includes true anaphylactic and anaphylactoid reaction in his type II, we consider them as two different types because true anaphylaxis is mediated by a specific antiprotamine IgE antibody that can be produced by protamine in the absence of heparin. The role of antiprotamine IgG antibodies is not clear. The anaphylactoid reaction is independent

of a specific IgE antibody, is associated with the heparin-protamine complex, and does not occur in the absence of heparin. Catastrophic pulmonary vasoconstriction is the most common example of the anaphylactoid reaction in our categorization, whereas Horrow classifies it separately. The rare occurrence of delayed pulmonary edema and adult respiratory distress syndrome appear to represent different manifestations of anaphylactoid responses, thus we classify them that way. In this chapter, we employ the latter classification system.

Pharmacologic Release

Basic drugs such as morphine sulphate and curare cause histamine release with rapid infusion (49). Protamine, also a basic drug, was believed to induce hypotension by this mechanism and it was demonstrated to release histamine by degranulating isolated mast cells (50). We classify protamine-induced hypotension from this mechanism as pharmacologic release. Pharmacologic release of histamine is not dependent upon heparin-protamine complexes, but can occur after the infusion of protamine alone. Its occurrence appears to depend upon the rate of infusion (51).

Stoelting et al. (51) demonstrated that the rapid administration of protamine 4.7 mg/kg over 5 minutes in heparinized humans and 4.5 mg/kg at the same rate to unheparinized dogs did not change hemodynamics or histamine levels at the conclusion of CPB. The administration of protamine 4.5 mg/kg (1) as a rapid infusion caused decreased blood pressure with parallel increases of histamine levels in dogs without prior heparinization (49).

Parsons and Mohandas (52) gave 1 mg of protamine per 1 mg of remaining heparin at a rate of 2.5 mg/sec to patients pretreated with H1 (chlorpheniramine 10 mg) and H2 (cimetidine 400 mg) histamine receptor blockers. These patients experienced a 23% decrease in mean blood pressure as opposed to a 34% decrease in patients not given pretreatment. These data again suggest a possible role of histamine in this type of reaction (52).

A greater degree of hypotension and greater increases of plasma histamine levels have been observed after rapid right-sided protamine injections as opposed to rapid left-sided administration in humans (43). These same observations have been made in animal models, which suggests a pulmonary source of the histamine released in this response (40).

Some human studies have demonstrated only a very mild, and transient decrease of blood pressure and systemic vascular resistance after rapid protamine administration (53), but clinical experience has demonstrated that rapid protamine administration can result in hypotension in humans. The variable degree of hypotension produced in many of these studies may also reflect the variability of myocardial contractile reserve. Perhaps patients with good myocardial reserve can compensate for the decreased systemic vascular resistance with a sufficient increase of cardiac index to avoid a major decline in blood pressure (51).

A direct myocardial depressant effect of protamine has been proposed as being partially responsible for this hypotension (54–56). It is difficult to determine whether depressed myocardial function is due to a reduced reserve or to direct effects of the drug on the heart (52, 57). The data on myocardial depression are far from conclusive because others have shown no changes of global myocardial metabolism or hemodynamic parameters (including cardiac index) in patients with normal left ventricular function after rapid protamine administration (58).

In summary, it appears that protamine can induce hypotension independent of the heparin-protamine complex in a fashion dependent upon the rate of administration. Thus, hypotension appears to be partly mediated by histamine release. The degree of histamine release may be greater when a right-sided injection route is utilized, possibly reflecting pulmonary histamine release, although this is controversial. This type of protamine-induced hypotension is accompanied by increased histamine levels while increased plasma thromboxane and C5a levels, and pulmonary hypertension are absent.

True Anaphylactic Protamine Reactions

True anaphylaxis to protamine (Horrow's type IIa) does not require the heparin-protamine complex and is mediated by a specific antiprotamine IgE antibody. Such reactions are perhaps the most dreaded adverse effect of protamine. True anaphylaxis requires prior protamine exposure to sensitize and produce IgE antibodies, which then bind to mast cells upon reexposure to the challenging antigen, protamine. These reactions, although uncommon, have been to date convincingly documented exclusively in diabetics receiving NPH or protamine-zinc insulin. Patients with prior protamine exposure, or patients with a fish allergy, have been suspected as candidates for these reactions, but documentation is lacking. Physiologically they are characterized by a decreased systemic arterial, pulmonary arterial, left atrial and right atrial pressures, while bronchospasm is variably present.

Using an enzyme-linked immunosorbent assay, Sharath et al. (59) showed that 53% of diabetics taking NPH insulin had elevated protamine specific IgE antibodies. They also noted that IgE levels were highest in patients taking protamine for long periods and in those who began before age 20. Nondiabetics and diabetics not using a protamine-containing form of insulin had no IgE reacting with protamine. Levy et al. (60) prospectively studied blood samples from 50 diabetic patients taking NPH insulin. They found only one sample that demonstrated an in vitro leukocyte histamine release in response to protamine challenge.

Weiss et al. (61), in a case controlled study, examined 27 diabetic and nondiabetic patients who had adverse protamine reactions. Of these 27 patients, only diabetics who received protamine-containing insulin preparations had anti-protamine IgE antibodies (Fig. 15.7). Their reactions were characterized primarily by a decreased blood pressure with the variable occurrence of bronchospasm. Some diabetics receiving protamine-insulin injections had adverse drug reactions but lacked this IgE antibody. These patients exhibited a different clinical picture characterized by increased pulmonary artery pressures, decreased systemic arterial pressure, and often by the presence of antiprotamine IgG antibody. Patients not receiving protamine insulin had reactions characterized by pulmonary vasoconstriction. These differing clinical presentations suggest two different mechanisms, one being anaphylactic and mediated by IgE antibody and the other being anaphylactoid and associated with IgG antibody. Patients may not exhibit positive skin test reactions to dilute protamine insulin preparations because of desensitization; thus, the absence of a positive skin test

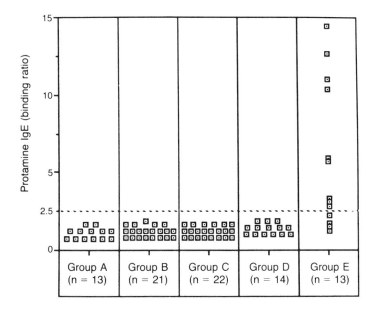

Figure 15.7. The IgE antibody to protamine. Serum levels of IgE antibody to protamine were measured with the use of the radioallergosorbent test in five patient populations. Normal subjects (*Group A*) had never been exposed to protamine in any form and included three atopic subjects with total serum IgE levels of more than 1000 ng per milliliter. *Group B* consisted of diabetic patients who had not received subcutaneous protamine-insulin injections, but who had received intravenous protamine after coronary artery bypass surgery without a reaction. *Group C* consisted of diabetic patients who were receiving daily subcutaneous injections of protamine and insulin and who had no reaction to intravenous protamine after bypass surgery. *Group D* consisted of 13 nondiabetic patients and one diabetic patient who had adverse reactions to intravenous protamine but had had no previous exposure to protamine-insulin preparations. *Group E* was composed of diabetic patients receiving daily subcutaneous injections of protamine and insulin who had adverse reactions when given intravenous protamine. The response was reported as a binding ratio (counts per minute of an unknown serum sample per counts per minute of a negative serum sample). A ratio of ≥2.5 indicated a positive response. Nine of the 13 patients in *Group E* had IgE antibodies to protamine, as compared with none of the 70 patients in the other four groups. Soluble protamine inhibited the binding of IgE antibody to the protamine-agarose complex in all nine positive serum samples. The inhibition of direct binding ranged from 60.7 to 99.5% (mean, 85.8%; data not shown). (From Weiss ME, Nyhan D, Peng Z, et al. Association of protamine IgE and IgG antibodies with life-threatening reactions to intravenous protamine. N Engl J Med 1989;320:886–892.)

does not reliably exclude an IgE or IgG anti-body-mediated protamine reaction.

There have been three reports of patients with true fish allergies experiencing adverse cardiopulmonary protamine reactions, including one patient who experienced cardiovascular collapse following protamine administration at the conclusion of CPB (62). This patient had elevated levels of IgE antibody specific for codfish antigen, peripheral eosinophilia, and a positive protamine skin test, as well as IgG, IgM, and IgE specific antibodies directed against protamine sulfate. Vertebrate fish protamines exhibit a similar nucleoprotein structure and it has been suggested that patients with a true fish allergy have antibodies that can cross-react with the protamine derived from salmon sperm, or with antigenic contaminants accompanying the protamine (63). Since shellfish and true fish are phylogenetically different, a shellfish allergy should not predispose the patient to a protamine reaction.

Vasectomized males have been suggested as having an increased risk of protamine reactions due to the development of antisperm antibodies and antibodies to protamine (64). These males with a positive complement fixation test to human protamine also fix complement in the presence of salmon protamine. It has been speculated that cross-reactivity could cause problems if exposed to protamine (65). Because human and fish protamine are similar, it is possible there could be some cross-reactivity. This possibility only remains a theoretical concern, because to date there is no documentation that protamine reactions occur more frequently in vasectomized males.

Anaphylactoid Reactions

These reactions include those formerly classified as types IIb, IIc, and III by Horrow. It is known that mediators of anaphylaxis can be liberated by pathways other than classic antigen-antibody interactions

(Fig. 15.8). Certain types of adverse responses to protamine are believed anaphylactoid in nature and mediated by complement activation with secondary release of histamine, thromboxane, and/or other vasoactive substances (66).

Protamine itself is incapable of activating complement. However, the interaction of heparin with protamine has been shown to deplete plasma C1, suggesting classic activation of the complement cascade similar to the depletion produced by antibody-antigen interactions (67).

Complement activation by the alternate pathway with increased C3a levels has been demonstrated following CPB in humans (68, 69). A second peak in C3a and C4a levels, indicating activation of the classic pathway, has also been demonstrated following protamine neutralization of heparin. The anaphylatoxins, C3a and C5a, can produce systemic inflammatory type reactions with histamine release, increased capillary permeability, leukosequestration, and hemodynamic derangements (70) manifesting as edema of the skin and mucosa, decreased systemic vascular resistance, bronchospasm, and flushing (35). Protamine has been shown to semicompetitively inhibit human plasma carboxypeptidase in vitro. This enzyme is responsible for the inactivation of anaphylatoxins and kinins. It appears that protamine can cause the activation of the complement cascade and then blocks the hydrolysis of various mediators (71). It is believed that certain types of adverse protamine reactions are caused by these mechanisms.

Adverse reactions to protamine in nondiabetic patients with prior protamine exposure have not been proven to be mediated by IgE antibodies. Our own data suggest that these reactions are anaphylactoid in nature. Levy et al. (60) reported a single case of a protamine reaction in a series of 1501 nondiabetic patients undergoing cardiac surgery with CPB. The mediator profile and antigen or antibody status of these patients were not defined. Presum-

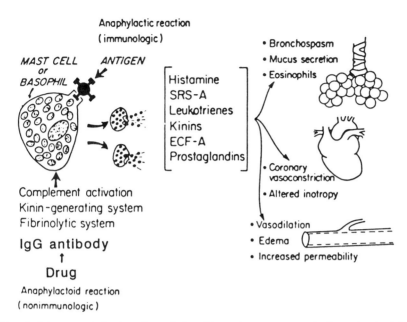

Anaphylactic reaction
(immunologic)

MAST CELL   ANTIGEN
or
BASOPHIL

Histamine
SRS-A
Leukotrienes
Kinins
ECF-A
Prostaglandins

• Bronchospasm
• Mucus secretion
• Eosinophils

• Coronary
 vasoconstriction
• Altered inotropy

• Vasodilation
• Edema
• Increased permeability

Complement activation
Kinin-generating system
Fibrinolytic system

IgG antibody
↑
Drug
Anaphylactoid reaction
(nonimmunologic)

Figure 15.8. Both true anaphylactic and anaphylactoid reactions may cause similar pathophysiologic responses including the release of many of the same mediators and end organ responses. The only reliable way of differentiating different mechanisms is by measuring specific antibody levels. The presence of IgG antibody is not specific. (Modified from Levy JH. Anaphylactic reactions in anesthesia and intensive care. Boston: Butterworths, 1986:40.)

ably, most of these patients had previously received protamine following cardiac catheterization.

Stewart and co-workers (72), in a series of 866 patients undergoing cardiac catheterization, noted two major reactions in patients with prior protamine exposure as the only apparent risk factor. Again, their antibody status was undefined. Weiss and co-workers (61) showed that patients with antiprotamine IgG antibody had an increased risk of protamine reactions, and speculated that this was due to prior exposure during cardiac catheterization. The ability of IgG antibodies to cause anaphylactoid reactions to protamine was suspected by others (73).

An additional adverse protamine reaction is characterized by noncardiogenic pulmonary edema that occurs more than 1 hour after protamine exposure. In this syndrome, a massive pulmonary capillary leak results in alveolar fluid accumulation with an accompanying decreased pulmonary compliance, wheezing, and pulmonary edema. Whether this syndrome is a modified form of protamine reaction is uncertain. Some believe it is an adverse response to an unknown substance in transfused fresh-frozen plasma (74).

Pulmonary Vasoconstrictive Reactions

The most extensively studied protamine reactions are anaphylactoid in nature and manifested by intense pulmonary vasoconstriction. Because most types of protamine reactions are heralded by the onset of systemic hypotension, it is only in recent years that the widespread use of pulmonary artery catheters, continuous hemodynamic recording, and meticulous review of these records has permitted this type of protamine reaction to be recognized. As the name implies, pulmonary vasoconstrictive protamine reactions are characterized by an increased pulmonary artery pressure due to pulmonary vasoconstriction, right ventricular failure, systemic hypotension, and decreased left atrial pressures during protamine administration at the conclusion of CPB (Fig. 15.9). This syndrome has occurred after minute doses of protamine, often less than 0.5 mg/kg and as little as 0.14 mg/kg (75).

Heparin-protamine interactions have been extensively studied in animal models in order to elucidate the possible mechanisms in humans. Much recent research has focused on anaphylactoid reactions, which can be catastrophic and are considered idiosyncratic and thus unpredictable. Compounding the idiosyncratic nature of anaphylactoid reactions is a lack of clear risk factors. This makes pulmonary vasocon-

strictive reactions especially frustrating to the clinician.

The expression of heparin-protamine reactions in animals has been very species-dependent (Table 15.4). However, recent studies have established their presence in an increasing number of mammals. The sheep model has been most extensively utilized because the ovine pulmonary vasculature is very prone to vasoconstriction. Morel et al. (76) consistently elicited pulmonary hypertension accompanied by an increased pulmonary vascular resistance, pulmonary wedge pressure, and thromboxane B2 levels, and a decreased cardiac output and stroke volume in awake sheep given heparin 200 units/kg as a bolus followed by protamine 2 mg/kg administered

Figure 15.9. An example of a pulmonary vasoconstrictive (anaphylactoid) protamine reaction. *LAP,* left atrial pressure; *RAP,* right atrial pressure; *PAP,* mean pulmonary artery pressure; *SAP,* systemic arterial pressure; *HR bpm,* heart rate, beats per minute. The two spikes on the right atrial pressure trace represent artifact from central venous sampling. *MGH,* Massachusetts General Hospital number; *DM,* diabetes mellitus on NPH insulin; *AVR,* aortic valve replacement.

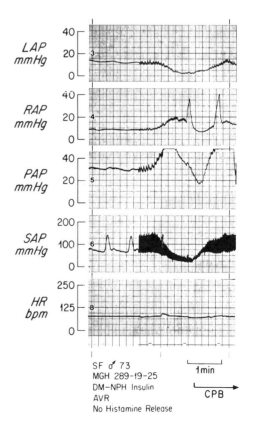

Table 15.4. Heparin-Protamine Interactions in Animal Models[a]

Author	Species	Hemodynamics	TBx Levels	Antagonist	Reaction	Coagulation
Morel, 1988	Sheep	PAP,PVR,SVR,PW increased CO,SV decreased BP,HR no change	Increased	TBx synthetase Indomethacin DMTU DMSO	Attenuated Blocked Blocked Present	Not studied
Montalescot, 1990	Sheep	PAP increased CO,SV no change	Increased	TBxA2 receptor	Blocked	BT no change
Degges, 1987	Pigs	PAP increased	Increased	Diphenhydramine Chromolyn sodium ASA	Present Present Blocked	Not studied
Schumacher, 1988	Pigs	PAP,PVR increased		TBx receptor	Blocked	Not studied
Conzen, 1989	Pigs	PAP,PVR increased MABP decreased HR no change	Increased	TBx receptor Indomethacin	Blocked Blocked	Not studied
Nuttall, 1991	Pigs	PAP increased	Increased	TBxA2 receptor (Given 2 min after protamine)	Decreased duration	BT increased in 50%, platelet aggregation inhibited

[a] TBx, thromboxane; PAP, pulmonary artery pressure; PVR, pulmonary vascular resistance; PW, pulmonary capillary wedge pressure; SVR, systemic vascular resistance; SV, stroke volume; CO, cardiac output; MABP, mean arterial blood pressure; HR, heart rate; BP, blood pressure; ASA, aspirin (acetylsalicyclic acid); BT, bleeding time.

over 10 seconds through the right atrial catheter. This response was not seen in animals given protamine without prior heparin nor was it observed in animals pretreated with indomethacin (a cyclo-oxygenase inhibitor) or a thromboxane synthetase inhibitor. Animals pretreated with dimethylsulfoxide (an OH scavenger) experienced increased pulmonary artery pressures, whereas dimethylthiourea (a H2O2 scavenger) pretreatment prevented the response (Fig. 15.10). Sheep were also found to have a profound leukopenia with the heparin-protamine interaction. Analysis of complement and histamine levels revealed a consistent increase in C3a levels but no change in plasma histamine levels during heparin-protamine interactions (76). Montalescot et al. (77) were able to prevent this reaction by pretreatment with a thromboxane receptor blocker despite un-changed levels of the plasma thromboxane metabolite. Leukopenia was not prevented by pretreatment with this agent. Heparin-protamine complex induced pulmonary hypertension with increased thromboxane B2 levels also consistently occurs in pigs (78–81).

Degges et al. (81) showed that increased thromboxane B2 release and pulmonary hypertension could be blocked by pretreating pigs with aspirin but not antihistamines. They also demonstrated the pulmonary vasoconstrictor response in isolated lungs using an acellular dextran perfusion medium, thus platelet aggregation, leukocyte sequestration, and plasma complement activation are not required.

Thromboxane A2, which is a short-lived vasoconstrictor, is rapidly hydolyzed to thromboxane B2, which is inactive and long-lived. Thromboxane A2 is known to be

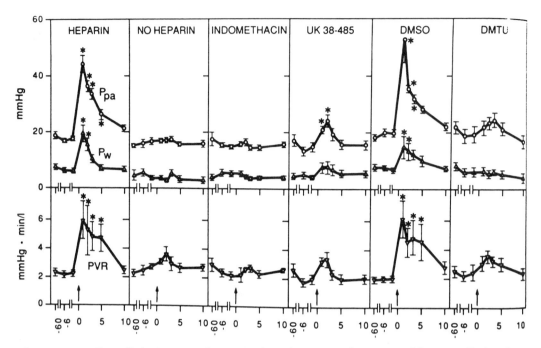

Figure 15.10. Effect of bolus injection of protamine (*arrow*) on mean pulmonary arterial pressure (*Ppa*), pulmonary capillary wedge pressure (*Pw*), and pulmonary vascular resistance (*PVR*) in the six treatment groups. Heparinized controls, n = 4; unheparinized controls, n = 10 (except for times +1 and +2 minutes for *PVR* values, where n = 6 and n = 7, respectively); indomethacin-pretreated heparinized sheep, n = 3; *UK* 38-485-pretreated heparinized sheep, n = 5; *DMSO*-pretreated heparinized sheep, n = 4; *DMTU*-pretreated heparinized sheep, n = 6. Values are the mean +/− SEM. ˙, P = 0.05 value differs from before protamine injection. DMSO, dimethylsulfoxide OH scavenger; DMTU, dimethylthiourea hydrogen peroxide scavenger; UK 38-485, thromboxane synthetase inhibitor. (From Morel DR, Lowenstein E, Nguyenduy T, et al. Acute pulmonary vasoconstriction and thromboxane release during protamine reversal of heparin anticoagulation in awake sheep. Circ Res 1988;62:905–915.)

a potent pulmonary vasoconstrictor. Pretreatment with thromboxane antagonists would seem to offer one solution to pulmonary vasoconstictive reaactions, at least in the animal model. However, thromboxane receptor antagonists can cause platelet dysfunction, which could lead to increased hemorrhage following CPB. Thus, an ultrashort acting antagonist would be required for clinical utility.

Some thromboxane receptor antagonists are known to inhibit platelet aggregation to collagen and arachidonic acid stimulation and cause a brief prolongation of bleeding times (78, 82), while other antagonists cause no increase in bleeding times even at the highest dosages used (77). Nuttall et al. (78) showed that

thromboxane A2 receptor blockade initiated 2 minutes after protamine administration shortened the duration of the pulmonary hypertensive response in pigs despite similar elevations in pulmonary artery pressures and plasma thromboxane B2 levels (Fig. 15.11).

Although thromboxane release appears to be a central factor in heparin-protamine induced pulmonary vasoconstriction, the source of thromboxane is unclear. A blood source seems doubtful as the reaction can be produced in isolated lungs perfused with acellular perfusates (79) and in platelet-depleted animals (83). Endothelial cells or more likely the pulmonary intravascular macrophage (PIM) may be the source of the thromboxane.

It has been speculated that the PIM may be the source of the thromboxane generated in pulmonary vasoconstrictive reactions (84). These lung macrophages have been described in sheep (85) and pigs (86) and occur less commonly in rats (87, 88) and dogs (89). They are five times as numerous as neutrophils in sheep lung (90) and occupy 15% of intracapillary volume (83). These macrophages respond to the infusion of various foreign particles by releasing vasoactive eicosanoids, particularly thromboxane (91). Infusion of radioactively labeled protamine into rats and sheep showed uptake primarily in the lungs of sheep with rapid development of pulmonary vasoconstriction as opposed to uptake primarily by the liver in rats. Based on these data, it has been hypothesized that the up-

take of heparin-protamine complexes by PIM causes the release of mediators, namely thromboxane, with resultant pulmonary vasoconstriction. Humans have a lesser population of these macrophages, which may partially explain the variable development of this syndrome in humans (82).

Platelet-depleted sheep still exhibit increased thromboxane B2 levels, pulmonary vascular resistance, and leukopenia when protamine is administered after heparin (81). These studies suggest that platelets do not cause this adverse response.

In summary, pulmonary vasoconstrictive protamine reactions in certain animal models result from uptake or activation in the lung, perhaps by the PIM, of the heparin-protamine complex. This interaction causes nonimmunologic activation of the

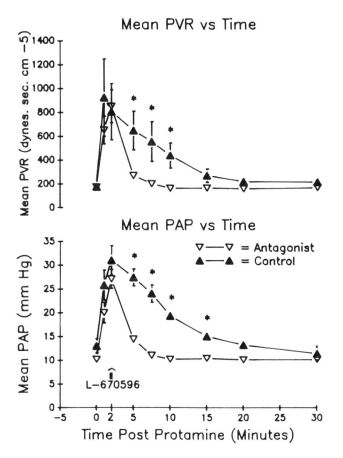

Figure 15.11. The increase in mean pulmonary vascular resistance (*PVR*) and mean pulmonary arterial pressure (*PAP*) after protamine administration at time t = 0 for control and antagonist-treated pigs. The thromboxane receptor antagonist (L-670596) was administered 2 minutes after protamine administration. Data plotted as mean +/− SEM. At lower *PAP* and *PVR* error bars are hidden by figure points. *, P ≥ 0.05. (From Nuttall GA, Murray MJ, Bowie JW. Protamine-heparin induced pulmonary hypertension in pigs; effects of treatment with a thromboxane receptor antagonist on hemodynamics and coagulation. Anesthesiology 1991;74:138–145.)

classic complement pathway with increased levels of C3a and C5a, which can release vasoconstrictor substances, most importantly thromboxane. The question of whether complement activation is merely associated with formation of heparin-protamine complexes or is a prerequisite for thromboxane generation is still unsettled. Leukocytes do not appear to play a crucial role, as evidenced by work using acellular perfusates. Histamine and platelets also do not appear to be involved. There are drugs that can block the development of this syndrome at various points of the reaction, but because of interference with coagulation or other problems these agents are not yet feasible for clinical use after CPB.

Patients who developed pulmonary vasoconstriction and bronchoconstriction following protamine administration at the conclusion of CPB had markedly elevated levels of plasma thromboxane B2 and C5a as compared to controls who did not develop adverse responses to protamine administration. The time of peak thromboxane B2 levels corresponded to the maximum pulmonary artery pressures. These data suggested that activation of complement fraction C5a was associated with thromboxane generation. It was also documented that (consistent with the animal model) leukopenia and increased C3a and C4a plasma levels were universal after protamine administration, although only patients developing pulmonary vasoconstrictive reactions had elevated levels of thromboxane and C5a (92).

One difference of the animal studies has been that catastrophic pulmonary vasoconstriction is demonstrated consistently in animal models while the incidence in humans is relatively low (1 to 2%). This fact suggests that different factors might play a role in humans. A recent study by Hobbhan and co-workers (93) examined the effects of protamine reversal of heparin in 14 noncardiac surgical patients undergoing transurethral surgery. Nine of these fourteen (64%) patients responded with in-

creases in mean pulmonary artery pressures, mean arterial pressure, pulmonary vascular resistance, and increased TxB2 and C3a levels. This work confirms the relevance of the animal model for the human reaction.

One interesting aspect of this syndrome is that although initial mediator release can cause catastrophic hemodynamic changes, there is usually no long-lasting tissue damage or sequelae if the patient can be supported through the initial event.

Diagnosis

Diagnosis of the type of protamine reaction in a patient experiencing one is based upon the clinical hemodynamic presentation, the mediators that are present, and the presence or absence of specific IgE or IgG antibodies. Screening for antibodies in insulin-dependent diabetics may be a useful way to identify patients at risk for anaphylaxis to protamine.

Skin testing is available but requires a strict protocol to give reproducible results, is unreliable in diabetics, and can give an adverse systemic response when reintroducing an antigen (94). Additionally, as stated earlier, the absence of a positive skin test does not ensure a lack of an IgE-mediated protamine reaction. Leukocyte histamine response is an in vitro test that has been used to test for protamine allergy in NPH-dependent diabetics and removes any risk to the patient of adverse reactions (58). It is a standard technique used in in vitro allergy studies that indicates specific IgE antibodies (95); however, there is little documented evidence of the usefulness of this test in screening for patients at risk for adverse protamine reactions. Serum levels of IgG or complement can be measured but are nonspecific indicators of a potential allergic reaction and are difficult to interpret post hoc because of consumption during the reaction and dilution from volume therapy during an adverse reaction (46).

The radioallergosorbent assay is a semiquantitative assay of a specific antibody described by Weiss et al. (59), who used it to determine the presence of antiprotamine IgE. The enzyme-linked immunosorbent assay involves anti-IgE tagged with an enzyme that catalyzes a photochemical reaction, and a modification was employed to determine IgG specific for protamine. Both tests described by Weiss and co-workers are probably the best currently available for the diagnosis of protamine allergy.

Therapy

Prevention of the heparin-protamine reaction would be the best strategy. Until a reliable screening test for antiprotamine antibodies is available, a history of a proven anaphylactic reaction could be helpful. We have administered hexadimethrine for successful protamine reversal in three protamine insulin-dependent diabetics who had experienced a prior protamine reaction. A compassionate use Investigational New Drug application from the Food and Drug Administration is required to gain permission to administer hexadimethrine bromide in the United States.

Protamine should be administered slowly. The protamine package insert suggests that infusion be no faster than 5 mg/min. Administration should be terminated at the first sign of any adverse reaction. Pharmacologic release reactions are rate-dependent, therefore slow administration prevents them. Protamine anaphylaxis is treated like any classic anaphylactic reaction with oxygen, fluids, and epinephrine/norepinephrine. Excessive protamine doses should be avoided since protamine has been shown to inhibit the enzyme responsible for the inactivation of anaphylatoxins and kinins, as mentioned earlier in this chapter. Also, since protamine does not inhibit angiotensin I, which can also break down these compounds, patients on angiotensin-

converting enzyme inhibitors may be at some increased risk for pulmonary hypertensive reactions to protamine (69).

Prophylactic histamine H1 and H2 blockers and/or corticosteroid administration has not reduced the incidence of pulmonary vasoconstrictor reactions. Histamine blockers are known to decrease the severity of hypotension with rapid protamine administration (50), suggesting a role in IgE-mediated reactions, but there is no evidence to support their routine use for this purpose. Therefore, we do not recommend this strategy.

A variety of supportive strategies has been used to treat acute pulmonary vasoconstriction and hypotension, including such pulmonary vasodilators as nitroglycerin and isoproterenol, and virtually all vasoactive/inotropic drugs. The comparative efficacy of different regimens for these short-lived reactions has not been documented. Reinstitution of bypass may be required. It is crucial to heparinize effectively prior to reinstitution of bypass to avoid consumption of components of coagulation and consequent disseminated intravascular coagulation. Case reports suggest that the reinstitution of bypass with heparin administration abates the reaction (96); however, it is likely that this merely represents the conclusion of a transient reaction. The role of thromboxane receptor blockade for treatment has not been studied in patients.

Inhaled nitric oxide has recently been reported as a therapy for the pulmonary vasoconstrictor reactions induced by heparin-protamine complexes in lambs (97). Nitric oxide selectively produces profound relaxation of the pulmonary vascular smooth muscle without systemic vasodilation. Breathing nitric oxide at 180 parts per million has been shown to markedly attenuate the pulmonary vasoconstrictor response in this animal model following heparin neutralization by protamine. Nitric oxide is short-lived, easily administered, and effective for treating certain types of reversible pulmonary hypertension. The value of nitric oxide inhalation for treating protamine-induced pulmonary vasoconstriction in patients has yet to be determined.

The initial pulmonary vasoconstrictive episode usually abates after a few (3) minutes. Once this occurs, continued inotropic infusion can result in a hyperdynamic heart and may need to be withdrawn. Protamine administration may be reinstituted at a rate of 5 mg/min following resolution of the episode and after resumption of hemodynamic stability.

FUTURE MANAGEMENT

To date there is no well-proven substitute for heparin anticoagulation and its reversal with protamine for the management of CPB. Research is examining such areas as total elimination of systemic heparinization by using heparin-bonded bypass circuitry (98, 99). Also, different forms of heparin, such as low molecular weight heparins and heparinoids are being investigated (see Chapter 14). Reversal of heparin by PF4, which was discussed earlier in this chapter, is currently under investigation.

The use of immobilized protamine during extracorporeal circulation has been recently reported by Yang et al. (100). Their method utilizes a "protamine bioreactor" in the bypass circuit composed of protamine bonded to the cellulose fibers of a hemodialyzer. This protamine bioreactor is placed directly into the bypass circuit to both remove and neutralize heparin in vitro. Use of this device was associated with decreased complement activation compared to the systemic administration of protamine. This device provides an interesting avenue for future investigations.

REFERENCES

1. Hunt AJ, Gray GS, Myers JA, Maione TE. Heparin neutralization by recombinant human PF4 in vitro [Abstract]. FASEB J 1990;4:A1991.
2. Ando T, Yamasaki M, Suzuki K. Protamines. In: Kleinzeller A, Springer GF, Wittman HG, eds. Molecular biology, biochemistry, and biophysics. Berlin: Springer-Verlag, 1973;12:1–30.
3. Taylor S, Folkman J. Protamine as an inhibitor of angiogenesis. Nature (Lond) 1982;297:307–312.
4. Wright JEC. Clinical trial of protamine in the treatment of malignant diseases. Br J Cancer 1968;22:415–421.
5. Chargaff E, Olson KB. Studies on the chemistry of blood coagulation. J Biol Chem 1937-38;122;153–167.
6. Perkins HA, Osborn JJ, Hurt R, Gerbode F. Neutralization of heparin in vivo with protamine; a simple method of estimating the required dose. J Lab Clin Med 1956;48:223–226.
7. Ellison N, Ominsky AJ, Wollman H. Is protamine a clinically significant anticoagulant? A negative answer. Anesthesiology 1971;35:621–629.
8. Inagaki M, Goto K, Katayama H, Benson KT, Goto H, Arakawa K. Activated partial thromboplastin time-protamine dose in the presence and absence of heparin. J Cardiothorac Anesth 1989;3:734–736.
9. Ellison N, Edmunds LH, Colman RW. Platelet aggregation following heparin and protamine administration. Anesthesiology 1978;48:65–68.
10. Mammen EF, Koets MH, Washington BC, et al. Hemostasis changes during cardiopulmonary bypass surgery. Semin Thromb Hemost 1985;11:281–292.
11. Guffin AV, Dunbar RW, Kaplan JA, Bland JW. Successful use of a reduced dose of protamine after cardiopulmonary bypass. Anesth Analg 1976;55:110–113.
12. Dutton DA, Hothersall AP, McLaren AD, Taylor KM, Turner MA. Protamine titration after cardiopulmonary bypass. Anaesthesiology 1983;38:264–268.
13. Kresowik TF, Wakefield TW, Fessler RD, Stanley JC. Anticoagulant effects of protamine sulfate in the canine model. J Surg Res 1988;45:8–14.
14. Hattersley PG. Activated coagulation time of whole blood. JAMA 1966;196:150–154.
15. Bull BS, Korpman RA, Huse WM, Briggs BD. Heparin therapy during extracorporeal circulation, I. Problems inherent in existing heparin protocols. J Thorac Cardiovasc Surg 1975;69:674–684.
16. Hawksley M. De-heparinisation of blood after cardiopulmonary bypass. Lancet 1966;1:563–565.
17. Hurt R, Perkins HA, Osborn JJ, Gerbode F. The neutralization of heparin by protamine in ex-

tracorporeal circulation. J Thorac Surg 1956;32:612–619.

18. Gervin AS. Complications of heparin therapy. Surg Gynecol Obstet 1975;140:789–796.

19. Ellison N, Beatty CP, Blake DR, Wurzel HA, MacVaugh H. Heparin rebound, studies in patients and volunteers. J Thorac Cardiovasc Surg 1974;67:723–729.

20. Akl BF, Vargas GM, Neal J, Robillard J, Kelly P. Clinical experience with the activated clotting time for the control of heparin and protamine therapy during cardiopulmonary bypass. J Thorac Cardiovasc Surg 1980;79:97–102.

21. Bull BS, Huse WM, Brauer FS, Korpman RA. Heparin therapy during extracorporeal circulation. II. The use of a dose-response curve to individualize heparin and protamine dosage. J Thorac Cardiovasc Surg 1975;69:685–689.

22. Culliford AT, Gitel SN, Starr N, et al. Lack of correlation between activated clotting time and plasma heparin during cardiopulmonary bypass. Ann Surg 1981;193:105–111.

23. Yin ET, Wessler S, Butler JV. Plasma heparin: a unique, practical, submicrogram-sensitive assay. J Lab Clin Med 1973;81:298–310.

24. Senning A. Plasma-heparin concentration in extracorporeal circulation. ACTA Chir Scand 1959;117:55–59.

25. Allen JG, Moulder PV, Elghammer RM, et al. A protamine titration as an indication of a clotting defect in certain hemorrhagic states. J Lab Clin Med 1949;34:473–476.

26. Hunt AJ, Gray GS, Myers JA, Maione TE. Heparin neutralization by recombinant human PF4 in vitro [Abstract]. FASEB J 1990;4:A1991.

27. Walker WS, Reid KG, Hider CF, Davidson IA, Boulton FE, Yap PL. Successful cardiopulmonary bypass in diabetics with anaphylactoid reactions to protamine. Br Heart J 1984;52:112–114.

28. Cook JJ, Schaffer LH, Niewiarowski S, Maione T. Heparin neutralization by protamine and platelet factor 4 in the rat. FASEB J 1990;4:A1234.

29. Cook JJ, Niewiarowski S, Yan Z, et al. Platelet factor 4 efficiently reverses heparin anticoagulation in the rat without the adverse effects of heparin-protamine complexes. Circulation 1992;85:1002–1109.

30. Montalescot G, Zapol WM, Carvalho A, Robinson DR, Torres A, Lowenstein E. Neutralization of low molecular weight heparin by polybrene prevents thromboxane release and severe pulmonary hypertension in awake sheep. Circulation 1990;82:1754–1764.

31. Keats AS, Cooley DA, Telford J. Relative antihep-

arin potency of polybrene and protamine in patients undergoing extracorporeal circulation. J Thorac Cardiovasc Surg 1959;38:362–368.

32. Weiss WA, Gilman JS, Catenacci AJ, Osterberg AE. Heparin neutralization with polybrene administered intravenously. JAMA 1958;166:603–607.

33. Haller JA, Ransdell HT, Stowens D, Rubel WF. Renal toxicity of polybrene in open-heart surgery. J Thorac Cardiovasc Surg 1962;44:486–491.

34. MacKenzie GJ, Wade JD, Davies SH, Zellos S. The circulatory effects of hexadimethrine bromide (polybrene) in dogs. Am Heart J 1961;62:511–518.

35. Schapira M, Christman BW. Neutralization of heparin by protamine, time for a change? Circulation 1990;82:1877–1879.

36. Toyofuku T, Koyama S, Kobayashi T, Kusama S, Ueda G. Effects of polycations on pulmonary vascular permeability in conscious sheep. J Clin Invest 1989;83:2063–2069.

37. Horrow JC. Protamine: a review of its toxicity. Anesth Analg 1985;64:348–361.

38. Lowenstein E, Johnston WE, Lappas DG, et al. Catastrophic pulmonary vasoconstriction associated with protamine reversal of heparin. Anesthesiology 1983;59:470–473.

39. Lowenstein E, Zapol WM. Protamine reactions, explosive mediator release, and pulmonary vasoconstriction (Editorial). Anesthesiology 1990;73:373–374.

40. Morel DR, Mo Costabella PM, Pittet JF. Adverse cardiopulmonary effects and increased thromboxane concentrations following the neutralization of heparin with protamine in awake sheep are infusion rate-dependent. Anesthesiology 1990;73:415–424.

41. Goldman BS, Joison J, Austen WG. Cardiovascular effects of protamine sulfate. Ann Thorac Surg 1969;7:459–471.

42. Casthely PA, Goodman K, Fryman PN, Abrams LM, Aaron D. Hemodynamic changes after the administration of protamine. Anesth Analg 1986;65:78–80.

43. Taylor RL, Little WC, Freeman GL, et al. Comparison of the cardiovascular effects of intravenous and intraaortic protamine in the conscious and anesthetized dog. Ann Thorac Surg 1986;42:22–26.

44. Rogers K, Milne B, Salerno TA. The hemodynamic effects of intra-aortic versus intravenous administration of protamine for reversal of heparin in pigs. J Thorac Cardiovasc Surg 1983;85:851–855.

45. Frater RWM, Oka Y, Hong Y, Tsubo T, Loubser PG, Masone R. Protamine induced circulatory

changes. J Thorac Cardiovasc Surg 1984;87: 687–692.

46. Milne B, Rogers K, Cervenko F, Salerno T. The hemodynamic effects of intaaortic versus intravenous administration of protamine for reversal of heparin in man. Can Anesth Soc J 1983; 30:347–351.

47. Cherry DA, Chiu CJ, Wynands JE, et al. Intraaortic vs intravenous administration of protamine: a prospective randomized clinical study. Surg Forum 1985;36:238–240.

48. Horrow JC. Protamine allergy. J Cardiothorc Anesth 1988;2:225–242.

49. Rosow CE, Moss J, Philbin DM, Savarese JJ. Histamine release during morphine and fentanyl anesthesia. Anesthesiology 1982;56:93–96.

50. Keller R. Interrelation between different types of cells. II. Histamine release for the mast cells of various species by cationic polypeptides of polymorphonuclear leukocytes, lysosomes and other cationic compounds. Int Arch Allergy Appl Immunol 1968;34:139–144.

51. Stoelting RK, Henry DP, Verbur KM, et al. Haemodynamic changes and circulating histamine concentrations following protamine administration to patients and dogs. Can Anaesth Soc J 1984;31:534–540.

52. Parsons RS, Mohandas K. The effect of histamine-receptor blockade on the hemodynamic responses to protamine. J Cardiothorac Anesth 1989;3:37–43.

53. Shapira N, Schaff HV, Piehler JM, et al. Cardiovascular effects of protamine sulfate in man. J Thorac Cardiovasc Surg 1982;84:505–514.

54. Sethna D, Gray R, Bussell J, Raymond M, Matloff J, Moffitt E. Further studies on the myocardial metabolic effect of protamine sulfate following cardiopulmonary bypass. Anesth Analg 1982; 61:476–477.

55. Iwatsuki N, Matsukawa S, Iwatsuki K. A weak negative ionotropic effect of protamine sulfate upon the isolated canine heart muscle. Anesth Analg 1980;59:100–102.

56. Goldman BS, Joison J, Austen WG. Cardiovascular effects of protamine sulfate. Ann Thorac Surg 1969;7:459–471.

57. Michaels IAL, Barash PG. Hemodynamic changes during protamine administration. Anesth Analg 1983;62:831–835.

58. Sethna DH, Moffitt E, Gray RJ, et al. Effects of protamine sulfate on myocardial oxygen supply and demand in patients following cardiopulmonary bypass. Anesth Analg 1982;61: 247–251.

59. Sharath MD, Metzger WJ, Richerson HB, et al. Protamine-induced fatal anaphylaxis, prevalence of antiprotamine immunoglobin E anti-

body. J Thorac Cardiovasc Surg 1985;90: 86–90.

60. Levy JH, Zaidan JR, Faraj B. Prospective evaluation of risk of protamine reactions in patients with NPH insulin-dependent diabetes. Anesth Analg 1986;65:739–742.

61. Weiss ME, Nyhan D, Peng Z, et al. Association or protamine IgE and IgG antibodies with life-threatening reactions to intravenous protamine. N Engl J Med 1989;320:886–892.

62. Knape JTA, Schuller JL, De Haan P, De Jong AP, Bovill JG. An anaphylactic reaction to protamine in a patient allergic to fish. Anesthesiology 1981;55:324–325.

63. Caplan SN, Berkman EM. Protamine sulfate and fish allergy [Letter]. N Engl J Med 1976; 295:172.

64. Samuel T, Kolk AHJ, Rumke P, Van Lis JMJ. Autoimmunity to sperm antigens in vasectomized med. Clin Exp Immunol 1975;21:65–74.

65. Samuel T, Kolk A. Auto-antigenicity of human protamines. In: Lepow IH, Crozier R, eds. Vasectomy: immunological and pathophysiologic effect in animal and man. New York: Academic Press, 1979:203–220.

66. Best N, Teisner B, Grudzinkas JG, Fisher MM. Classical pathway activation during an adverse response to protamine sulfate. Br J Anaesth 1983;55:1149–1153.

67. Rent R, Ertel N, Eisenstein R, Gewurz H. Complement activation by interaction of polyanions and polycations, I. Heparin-protamine induced consumption of complement. J Immunol 1975;114:120–124.

68. Kirklin JK, Chenoweth DE, Naftel DC, et al. Effects of protamine administration after cardiopulmonary bypass on complement, blood elements, and the hemodynamic state. Ann Thorac Surg 1986;41:193–199.

69. Cavarocchi NC, Schaff HV, Orszulak TA, Homburger HA, Schnell WA, Pluth JR. Evidence for complement activation by protamine-heparin interaction after cardiopulmonary bypass. Surgery 1985;98:525–530.

70. Grant JA, Dupree E, Goldman AS, Schultz DR, Jackson AL. Complement-mediated release of histamine from human leukocytes. J Immunol 1975;114:1101–1106.

71. Tan F, Jackman H, Skidgel RA, Zsigmond EK, Erdos EG. Protamine inhibits plasma carboxypeptidase N, the inactivator of anaphylatoxins and kinins. Anesthesiology 1989;70:267–275.

72. Stewart WJ, McSweeney SM, Kellett MA, Faxon DP, Ryan TJ. Increased risk of severe protamine reactions in NPH insulin-dependent diabetics undergoing cardiac catheterization. Circulation 1984;5:788–792.

73. Lakin JD, Blocker TJ, Strong DM, Yocum MW. Anaphylaxis to protamine sulfate mediated by a complement-dependent IgG antibody. J Allergy Clin Immunol 1978;61:102–107.

74. Hashim SW, Kay HR, Hammond GL, Kopf GS, Geha AS. Noncardiogenic pulmonary edema after cardiopulmonary bypass, an anaphylactic reaction to fresh froozen plasma. Am J Surg 1984;147:560–563.

75. Lowenstein E. Lessons from studying an infrequent event: adverse hemodynamic responses associated with protamine reversal of heparin anticoagulation. J Cardiothorac Anesth 1989; 3:99–107.

76. Morel DR, Lowenstein E, Nguyenduy T, et al. Acute pulmonary vasoconstriction and thromboxane release during protamine reversal of heparin anticoagulation in awake sheep. Circ Research 1988;62:905–915.

77. Montalescot G, Lowenstein E, Ogletree ML, et al. Thromboxane receptor blockade prevents pulmonary hypertension induced by heparin-protamine reactions in awake sheep. Circulation 1990;82:1765–1777.

78. Nuttall GA, Murray MJ, Bowie JW. Protamine-heparin-induced pulmonary hypertension in pigs; effects of treatment with a thromboxane receptor antagonist on hemodynamics and coagulation. Anesthesiology 1991;74:138–145.

79. Conzen PF, Habazettl H, Gutman R, et al. Thromboxane mediation of pulmonary hemodynamic responses after neutralization of heparin by protamine in pigs. Anesth Analg 1989; 68:25–31.

80. Schumacher WA, Heran CL, Ogletree ML. Effect of thromboxane receptor antagonism on pulmonary hypertension caused by protamine-heparin interaction in pigs. Circulation 1988; 78(suppl):II-207.

81. Degges RD, Foster ME, Dang AQ, Read RC. Pulmonary hypertensive effect of heparin and protamine interaction: evidence for thromboxane B2 release from the lung. Am J Surg 1987;154:696–699.

82. Friedhoff LT, Manning J, Funke PT, et al. Quantitation of drug levels and platelet receptor blockade caused by a thromboxane antagonist. Clin Pharmacol Ther 1986;40: 634–632.

83. Montalescot G, Kreil E, Lynch K, et al. Effect of platelet depletion on lung vasoconstriction in heparin-protamine reactions. J Appl Physiol 1989;66:2344–2350.

84. Kreil E, Montalescot G, Robinson DR, Zapol WM, Lynch KE, Lowenstein E. Adverse heparin-protamine neutralization interactions and the lung. In: Zapol WM, Lemarie F, eds. Adult respiratory distress sydrome. New York: Marcel Dekker, 1991:451–490.

85. Warner, AE, Barry BE, Brain JD. Pulmonary intravascular macrophages in sheep; morphology and function of a novel constituent of the mononuclear phagocyte system. Lab Invest 1986; 55:276–288.

86. Bertram TA, Overby LH, Danilowicz R, Eling TE, Brody AR. Pulmonary intravascular macrophages metabolize arachidonic acid in vitro. Am Rev Respir Dis 1988;138:936–944.

87. Warner AE, DeCamp MM, Molina RM, Brain JD. Pulmonary removal of circulating endotoxin results in acute lung injury in sheep. Lab Invest 1988;59:219–230.

88. Warner A, Molina A, Brain JD. Uptake of bloodborne bacteria by pulmonary intravascular macrophages and consequent inflammatory responses in sheep. Am Rev Respir Dis 1987;136:683–690.

89. Crocker SH, Eddy DO, Obenauf RN, Wismar BL, Lowry BD. Bacteremia: host-specific lung clearance and pulmonary failure. J Trauma 1981; 21:215–220.

90. Albertine KH, Decker SA, Schultz EL, Staub NC. Clearance of monastral blue by intravascular macrophages in pulmonary microvessels of sheep, goat, and pig [Abstract]. Anat Rec 1987;218:6A.

91. Bertram TA, Thigpen J, Eling TE, Brody AR. Bacterial phagocytosis and consequent arachodonic acid metabolism by pulmonary intravascular and alveolar macrophages in vitro. Am Rev Resp Dis 1989;139:A159.

92. Morel DR, Zapol WM, Thomas SJ, et al. C5a and thromboxane generation associated with pulmonary vaso- and bronchoconstriction during protamine reversal of heparin. Anesthesiology 1987;66:597–604.

93. Hobbhahn J, Conzen P, Habazettl H, Gutman R, Kellerman W, Peter K. Heparin reversal by protamine in humans-complement, prostaglandins, leukocytes, platelets, and hemodynamics. J Appl Phys 1991;71(4):1415–1421.

94. Fisher M. Intradermal testing after anaphylactoid reaction to anaesthetic drugs: practical aspects of performance and interpretation. Anaesth Intens Care 1984;12:115–120.

95. May CD, Lyman M, Alberto R, et al. Procedures for immunochemical study of histamine release from leukocytes with small volumes of blood. J Allergy 1970;46:12–20.

96. Loch R, Hessel EA. Probable reversal of protamine reactions by heparin administration. J Cardiothorc Anesth 1990;4:604–608.

97. Fratacci MD, Frostell CG, Chen TY, Wain JC, Robinson DR, Zapol WM. Inhaled nitric oxide.

A selective pulmonary vasodilator of heparin protamine vasoconstriction in sheep. Anesthesiology 1991;75(6):990–999.

98. Von Segesser LK, Turina M. Cardiopulmonary bypass without systemic heparinization. J Thorac Cardiovasc Surg 1989;98:386–396.

99. Mc Cutcheon JG, Baxter Health Care Corp., Bentley Labs Division, Irvine, CA. Presented at the American Academy of Cardiovascular Perfusion, San Francisco, CA, February 1991.

100. Yang VC, Port FK, Kim JS, et al. The use of immobilized protamine in removing heparin and preventing protamine-induced complications during extracorporeal blood circulation. Anesthesiology 1991;75:288–297.

16

PLATELET FUNCTION AND CARDIOPULMONARY BYPASS

Frederick W. Campbell and L. Henry Edmunds, Jr.

Platelet dysfunction is the hemostatic defect most commonly observed after cardiopulmonary bypass (CPB). The mechanisms producing platelet dysfunction are incompletely defined and result from blood contact with nonendothelial surfaces in the heart-lung machine and with the products of granulocytes and endothelial cells activated during CPB. Investigations of the behavior of platelets and other blood constituents during CPB have led to recognition of agents that preserve platelet numbers and function after cardiac operation. Efforts to preserve platelet function during CPB aim to decrease the incidence of hemorrhagic complications and the transfusion of homologous platelets during cardiac surgery.

PLATELET PHYSIOLOGY

Platelets normally circulate in a nonreactive state until their activation is triggered at a nonendothelialized vascular surface such as that encountered upon collision with an atherosclerotic plaque or subendothelial tissue at the site of vascular injury. A number of triggers, generated at the interface between the nonendothelial surface and blood at the site of injury, activate platelets. These include collagen and glycoprotein molecules in subendothelial tissue and adenosine diphosphate (ADP) and thrombin in the blood. When activated,

platelets contribute to thrombogenesis by adhering to the disrupted vascular surface, aggregating to form the platelet plug, contributing cofactors to the enzymatic coagulation cascade generating fibrin clot, and inducing local vascular changes.

The functional anatomy of the platelet cell is described in Figure 16.1.

Platelet-Subendothelial Interaction

Disruption of the vascular endothelium exposes blood to a subendothelial matrix, which includes collagen and several large adhesive glycoproteins including von Willebrand factor (vWF), fibronectin, and others (1). These proteins are characterized by the presence of tripeptide sequences (domains) that are recognized by specific cell surface receptors allowing interaction of platelets with the matrix. The best characterized cell-binding domain is the tripeptide sequence arginine-glycine-aspartic acid (RGD), present in many adhesive proteins. The RGD domain is recognized by the adhesive protein receptors on the platelet exterior, which are members of the integrin family of cell surface molecules.

The initial attachment of the platelet to the subendothelium is mediated by interaction of the platelet glycoprotein (GP) Ib/IX complex with vWF in the matrix. Several other adhesive interactions also occur

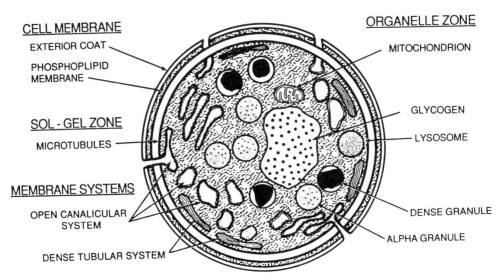

Figure 16.1. Anatomy of the platelet cell in horizontal section. Four groups of cell structures are distinguished by their roles in platelet function and their intracellular location. At the perimeter, the phospholipid *cell membrane* contains receptor sites by which extracellular agonists activate intracellular processes and platelet-to-surface adhesion and platelet-to-platelet aggregation occur. The membrane contains platelet factor 3, a phospholipid that catalyzes the coagulation cascade. The *sol-gel zone* in the peripheral cytoplasm contains microtubules responsible for the discoid shape of the normal platelet. Contractile elements in the microtubules transform the disc-shaped platelet into a sphere, extrude pseudopods, and centralize platelet secretory granules during activation. The *organelle zone* in the central cytoplasm contains three types of secretory granules, mitochondria, and glycogen particles. The *open canalicular system,* one of two intracellular membranes, is located throughout the cytoplasm and connects the cell interior with the surface, thereby increasing the cell surface area and facilitating granule secretion. The *dense tubular system* lies in the peripheral cytoplasm, and serves as a platelet calcium resevoir and as the site of prostaglandin synthesis. (From Campbell FW, Addonizio VP Jr. Platelet function alterations during cardiac surgery. In: Ellison N, Jobes JR, eds. Effective hemostasis in cardiac surgery. Philadelphia: WB Saunders, 1988:85–109.)

(Fig. 16.2, **A** and **B**). After adherence, platelets spread on the subendothelium. Spreading on collagen triggers platelet activation, an active metabolic sequence of cellular events producing platelet hemostatic actions.

The first observable response in the activation sequence is a change in platelet shape from discoid to spherical with extrusion of pseudopodia. With the initial shape change, a conformational change occurs in the surface GP IIb/IIIa receptor exposing binding sites for fibrinogen, fibronectin, vWF, and vitronectin that mediate further spreading on the subendothelial matrix as well as platelet-to-platelet aggregation (Fig. 16.2C).

Platelet aggregation results from the bridging of fibrinogen molecules between

many cells and requires the activation-dependent alteration in the GP IIb/IIIa complex to permit binding of adhesive proteins. In addition to contact with collagen in the subendothelium, exposure of GP IIb/IIIa binding sites is also induced by ADP and thromboxane A2 (TXA2), soluble agonists released from activated platelets, as well as by thrombin generated upon activation of the coagulation cascade.

Platelet activation occurs at a rate and to an extent determined by the nature and concentration of the inciting stimuli, as well as by the sensitivity of the circulating platelets. This graded platelet behavior may be observed in vitro by means of platelet aggregometry (Fig. 16.3). In the presence of potent agonists, platelet activation proceeds to completion with throm-

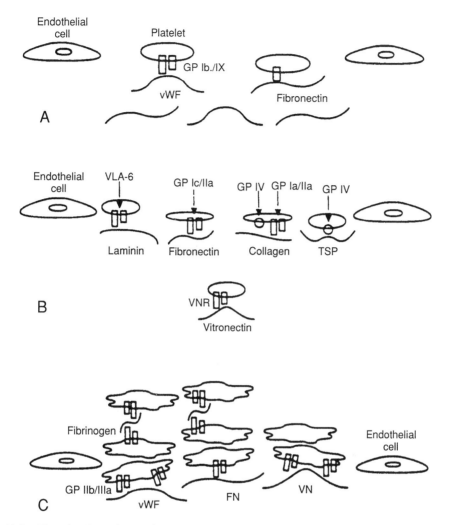

Figure 16.2.   The role of membrane glycoproteins in mediating platelet adhesion and aggregation. **A.** When flowing blood encounters an exposed subendothelial surface, platelets initially adhere to *vWF* through the membrane *GP Ib/IX* complex and to *fibronectin* through a receptor not yet identified. **B.** After these initial adherence events, platelets use several other membrane glycoprotein receptors to bind additional matrix macromolecules; *TSP,* thrombospondin; *VNR,* vitronectin receptor. **C.** The spreading of platelets on collagen, release of thromboxane A$_2$ and ADP, and presence of thrombin lead to platelet activation. Cellular activation generates a conformational change in the platelet receptor *GP IIb/IIIa* that makes it competent to bind the adhesive ligands *fibrinogen,* fibronectin (*FN*), *vWF,* and vitronectin (*VN*). The binding of the former is particularly important in supporting platelet aggregation. (From McEver RP. The clinical significance of platelet membrane glycoproteins. Hematol Oncol Clin North Am 1990;4:87–104.)

boxane synthesis (Fig. 16.4) and granule secretion. Alpha granules, dense granules, and lysosomes are extruded from the cell, releasing products that promote platelet aggregation, coagulation, and local vaso-constriction (Table 16.1). Secretion of alpha granules and dense granules are elic-ited by less potent stimuli than are required for lysosome release. Measured concentrations of the products of prosta-glandin synthesis and granule secretion provide markers that may be used to indi-cate the extent of the platelet activation process taking place.

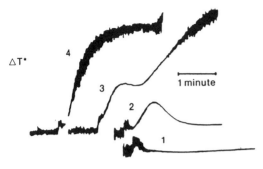

ΔT*

4

3

2

1

|—— 1 minute ——|

* ΔT—change in light transmission

Figure 16.3. The graded response of platelets to increasing concentrations of a platelet agonist is depicted in four in vitro aggregation curves. The curves were obtained by combining turbid platelet-rich plasma (PRP) with increasing amounts of an agonist (thrombin) in a platelet aggregometer. The platelet aggregometer measures the extent of platelet aggregation, an observable manifestation of platelet activation. This photo-optical instrument measures light transmittance through samples of platelet-containing plasma. Platelet-rich plasma is normally turbid and transmits light poorly. When activating agonists are added, stimulating platelet activation and causing aggregation, the turbidity of the plasma decreases. Light transmittance through the plasma sample progressively increases with the formation of increasingly large platelet aggregates. The amount of light transmitted is then recorded and produces an aggregation curve. With increasing degrees of platelet aggregation, the reduction in turbidity and change in light transmittance are greater, and the corresponding curves show larger upward deflections from the baseline. In *curve 1*, PRP is combined with thrombin 0.05 units/ml. Platelet shape change indicated by narrowing of the baseline took place within a few seconds, but aggregation did not occur. Within 10 minutes, the baseline recovers its normal amplitude as platelet discoid shape is restored (not shown). In *curve 2*, where PRP is combined with thrombin 0.1 unit/ml, upward deflection of the tracing indicates that a change in light transmittance occurred after shape change had developed. The change in light transmission coincides with an initial wave of aggregation. Platelet clumps dispersed completely in this sample, as indicated by a decrease in light transmittance and a return of the recording to baseline. Platelet discoid shape is restored and the baseline recovers its normal amplitude within 10 minutes (not shown). *Curve 3*, recorded when PRP was exposed to thrombin 0.15 unit/ml, demonstrates that an initial phase of aggregation was followed by a brief period in which disaggregation began. The pause was followed by a rapid increase in light transmission as a second wave of aggregation took place. Initiation of secondary aggregation is entirely dependent upon

The in vivo platelet plug forms as a result of the collision of circulating platelets with those activated at the subendothelial interface, where the localized presence of platelet secretory products and thrombin trigger activation of the arriving cells.

Platelet-Procoagulant Protein Interaction

Platelet function and coagulation are intimately connected. Four coagulation cofactors [fibrinogen, factor V, vWF, and high molecular weight kininogen (HMWK)] are released from platelet alpha granules. As stated above, thrombin formed during fibrin production is a potent agonist and activates platelets at the forming platelet-fibrin clot.

The initial steps of intrinsic coagulation occur on the platelet surface (Fig. 16.5). At the surface of the activated platelet, in the presence of kallikrein and HMWK, factor XI can be cleaved to factor XIa independently of factor XII (2). Thus, coagulation can begin without factor XII, a deficiency of which is often not associated with abnormal bleeding. Factor XIa remains attached to the platelet surface, serving to localize factor IX activation and subsequent coagulation reactions to the hemostatic plug. Factor X is activated at the platelet surface by a complex consisting of factor IXa, factor VIII, platelet phospholipid (platelet factor 3), and calcium. In turn,

granule contents and TXA2 extruded from platelets. *Curve 4*, was obtained when PRP was treated with thrombin 0.18 unit/ml. The first and second waves of aggregation are fused together, obscuring the biphasic nature of the platelet response. This occurred because the high concentration of agonist caused acceleration of the platelet activation sequence and rapid development of secondary aggregation. ΔT, change in light transmission. (Modified from White JG: Platelet morphology and function. In: Williams WJ, Beutler E, Ersely AJ, Lichtman MA, eds. Hematology, 3rd ed. New York: McGraw-Hill, 1983.)

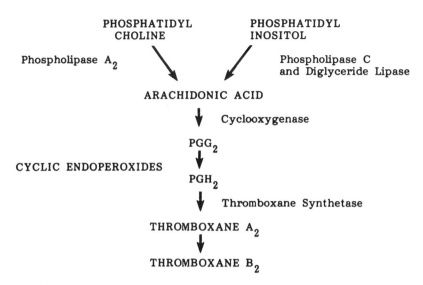

PHOSPHATIDYL
CHOLINE

PHOSPHATIDYL
INOSITOL

Phospholipase A_2

Phospholipase C
and Diglyceride Lipase

ARACHIDONIC ACID

Cyclooxygenase

PGG_2

CYCLIC ENDOPEROXIDES

PGH_2

Thromboxane Synthetase

THROMBOXANE A_2

THROMBOXANE B_2

Figure 16.4. Platelet prostaglandin synthesis. Platelet membrane phospholipids are converted to arachidonic acid by phospholipases in the stimulated platelet. Arachidonic acid is cyclo-oxygenated by the enzyme, cyclo-oxygenase, to form prostaglandin G_2 (*PGG$_2$*), which rapidly undergoes peroxidation to prostaglandin H_2 (*PGH$_2$*). These cyclic endoperoxides induce platelet aggregation. Platelet inhibitors such as aspirin and nonsteroidal antiinflammatory agents inhibit cyclo-oxygenase activity. In the platelet, the enzyme thromboxane synthetase catalyzes conversion of PGH_2 to *thromboxane A$_2$*, a platelet agonist and vasoconstrictor. Once released from the platelet, thromboxane A_2 is unstable in plasma and is rapidly hydrated to the stable, but inactive, *thromboxane B$_2$*. The latter is a measurable indicator of the more labile thromboxane A_2. (From Campbell FW, Addonizio VP Jr. Platelet function alterations during cardiac surgery. In: Ellison N, Jobes JR, eds. Effective hemostasis in cardiac surgery. Philadelphia: WB Saunders, 1988:85–109.)

factor Xa, bound via factor V to the platelet with platelet factor 3 and calcium, participates in the cleavage of prothrombin to thrombin.

Association with platelets protects the activated coagulation factors from inactivation by natural inhibitors in plasma, thus localizing the coagulation process to a nidus provided by aggregating platelets.

Regulation of Platelet Activation

Many platelet receptors mediate cell activation through stimulus-response coupling proteins in the membrane that require guanine triphosphate and, thus, are known as guanine nucleotide-binding regulatory proteins (G proteins). The G proteins interact with target enzymes or ion channels in the plasma membrane to stimulate production of second messengers or modulation of ion flux.

The G protein-mediated activation of phospholipase C cleaves phosphatidylinositol from the platelet membrane to produce a diacylglycerol (DG) and an inositol 1,4,5-triphosphate (Ins 1,4,5-P3) (3, 4). The Ins 1,4,5-P3 is thought to increase the concentration of intracellular calcium by release from the dense tubular system and endoplasmic reticulum. An influx of extracellular calcium also occurs. Calcium regulates directly, or in concert with DG or a calcium-binding regulatory protein, calmodulin, the enzymes producing platelet responses such as shape change, aggregation, prostaglandin synthesis, and granule secretion. Cyclic endoperoxides, TXA2, and ADP, which are produced during this platelet response, propagate cell activation, thereby providing positive feedback loops.

Epinephrine is an in vitro platelet agonist inducing aggregation through interaction with an a_2-adrenergic receptor on the

Table 16.1.   Contents of Platelet Secretory Granules and Their Physiologic Activities

Secretory Granules and Contents	Physiologic Activities
Alpha granules	
Coagulation factors	Co-factors for enzymatic cascade
Fibrinogen	
Factor V	
HMWK	
Glycoproteins	Participate in cell adhesion and cell-to-cell interactions
von Willebrand factor	
Thrombospondin	
Fibronectin	
Platelet-specific proteins	
Platelet factor 4 (PF4)	PF4 potentiates ADP-induced platelet aggregation and has antiheparin activity
Low affinity (LA) platelet factor 4 (β-thromboglobulin)	LA-PF4 possesses antiheparin activity
Cationic proteins	
Mitogenic factor	Stimulates vascular smooth muscle growth
Permeability factor	Increases endothelial permeability
Chemotactic factor	Attracts leukocytes
Bactericidal factor	Promotes mild antimicrobial activity
Dense Granules	
Adenine nucleotides (ADP,ATP)	ADP stimulates platelet aggregation and secretion
Guanosine nucleotides (GDP,GTP)	Function unknown
Pyrophosphate	No physiologic function
Calcium	Uncertain, promotes coagulation
Serotonin	Vasoconstriction, stimulates platelet aggregation and secretion in nonhuman species
Lysosomes	
Acid hydrolases	Hydrolytic activity in acid environments
Neutral proteases	Propagate vascular damage and promote vascular permeability

platelet surface. In vivo, epinephrine appears to potentiate other agonists but does not trigger activation alone.

In addition to these stimulatory pathways, platelets have a damping pathway that is linked to adenylate cyclase, an enzyme located in the cell membrane and coupled by G proteins to closely associated surface receptors. Adenylate cyclase activity generates cyclic AMP (cAMP), a mediator inhibiting platelet function. Increases in intracellular cAMP levels promote a calcium uptake system that lowers the concentration of cytoplasmic calcium, diminishes formation of DG and Ins 1,4,5-P3 by phospholipase C inhibition, and retards platelet prostaglandin synthesis by inhibition of phopholipase A2 and cyclooxygenase (3, 4). As a result, platelet adhesion, shape change, aggregation, and TXA2 release and granule secretion are inhibited. Platelet cAMP levels are regulated by the relative activities of adenylate cyclase and the cytoplasmic nucleotide phosphodiesterases, which degrade the mediator to inactive 5'-AMP.

Several agonists triggering platelet activation bind membrane receptors inhibiting adenylate cyclase activity and, thus, reduce cAMP production. The decreased levels of cAMP promote the platelet activation process but, in the absence of agonist interaction with other membrane receptors, are insufficient to trigger platelets to activation (4).

Platelet adenylate cyclase activity is stimulated by prostacyclin, which is synthesized by vascular endothelium. The resulting cAMP-mediated platelet inhibition is one of several natural mechanisms that explains the nonthrombogenic nature of the normal endothelial surface.

Platelet function may be altered by agents exerting actions at the surface membrane receptors, stimulus-response coupling pathways, and regulatory proteins controlling cell responses. Disintegrins are RGD-containing peptides derived from viper venoms that represent the putative platelet binding sites on the adhesive glycoprotein molecules, e.g., vWF, fibrinogen. By interacting with platelet glycoprotein receptors, including GP IIb/IIIa, these investigational agents inhibit platelet adhesion and aggregation (5). The RGD peptides of the fibrinogen molecule are also found on the plasmin-mediated degradation product, fragment D (6, 7).

Aspirin, indomethacin, and nonsteroidal antiinflammatory agents, by acetylating the enzyme, cyclo-oxygenase, impair formation of cyclic endoperoxides and TxA2 (8). The defect in platelet function induced by aspirin lasts for the life span of the cell since the anucleate platelet lacks the capacity for protein synthesis and is unable to repair the damage. Conversely, the inhibition by other nonsteroidal antiinflammatory drugs is reversed by discontinuation of the medication. While the cyclic endoperoxides and TxA2 mediate platelet aggregation and secretion, eliminating their formation by cyclo-oxygenase inhibition results in partial platelet impairment. Platelets react to collagen or thrombin (9) and to artificial surfaces (10) despite inhibition of cyclo-oxygenase by aspirin and other antiinflammatory agents.

Stimulation of adenylate cyclase activity by prostaglandins E1, D2, and I2 (prostacyclin), iloprost, and halothane (11, 12) results in an increase in intracellular cAMP levels and cell inhibition. Cyclic AMP levels

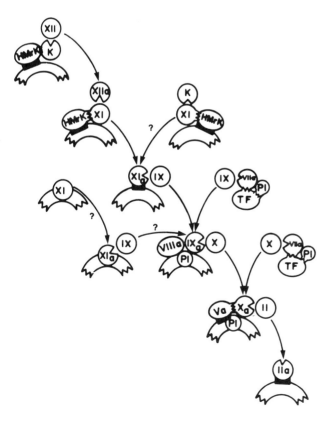

Figure 16.5. Schematic representation of platelet-mediated coagulation protein interactions. Coagulation proteins are signified by Roman numbers, with the activated forms of enzymes or cofactors designated by the subscript a. Inactive enzymes are indicated by *circles,* active enzymes by *circles with segmental scissions,* cofactors by *ellipses,* platelet membranes by *crescents,* demonstrated binding sites by *blackened areas,* and demonstrated protein-protein or protein-lipid interactions by *zigzag lines. K,* kallikrein; *HMrK,* high molecular weight kininogen; *Pl,* phospholipid; *TF,* tissue factor. *Arrows* designate conversions from inactive to active enzymes. *Question marks* indicate a postulated pathway supported by indirect evidence for which the mechanisms has not been elucidated. (From Walsh PN, Schmaier AH. Platelet-coagulant protein interactions. In: Colman RW, Hirsch J, Marder VJ, Salzman EW, eds. Hemostasis and thrombosis. Basic principles and clinical practice. 2nd ed. Philadelphia: JB Lippincott, 1987:689–708.)

are also elevated by dipyridamole, methylxanthines, and papaverine, which inhibit phosphodiesterase degradation of cAMP.

Knowledge of platelet function and regulation provides a basis for understanding platelet behavior in "unphysiologic" circumstances, including those associated with cardiac surgery. Platelet activity during extracorporeal circulation has many similarities to that observed during normal hemostasis.

PLATELETS DURING CPB

Interactions with Synthetic Surfaces

Vascular endothelial cells provide a nonthrombogenic surface due to their synthesis of prostacyclin and other chemicals and peptides; all other cells and synthetic surfaces initiate coagulation. Extracorporeal perfusion circuits are built from a variety of smooth, workable, nontoxic materials that directly activate proteins of the contact activation system and platelets.

The massive activation stimulus of CPB makes large concentrations of heparin an absolute requirement. Heparin inhibits activation of factor X and thrombin by enhancing the action of antithrombin III, therefore preventing thrombosis near the final steps of the coagulation cascade. During CPB, the early reactions of the coagulation cascade are not inhibited; thus complement, various white cells, and several other cells, including endothelial cells, are activated to produce a myriad of vasoactive substances (13) which, in turn, mediate the whole body inflammatory response associated with CPB (14).

When heparinized blood first contacts the synthetic surfaces of an extracorporeal perfusion circuit, plasma proteins adsorb onto the surface almost instantly. The composition and amounts of various adsorbed proteins do not reflect plasma concentrations (15). The chemical and physical characteristics of the surface do alter proportionate concentrations of the adsorbed

proteins, but not in a predictable way. Factor XII, vWF, fibronectin, thrombospondin, immunoglobulin G, hemoglobin, and albumin are all adsorbed (16). Fibrinogen is selectively adsorbed but the amount varies between different materials. Hydrophobic surfaces adsorb more fibrinogen than do hydrophilic surfaces (15).

The amount of adsorbed proteins changes over time. Adsorbed fibrinogen is rapidly displaced by an activated form of HMWK and to a lesser extent by factor XII (17). Other proteins are also desorbed, degraded or replaced; little is actually known about surface protein flux over time in extracorporeal perfusion systems. Nevertheless, the character of the proteinated surface, which is about 200 angstroms thick, affects subsequent platelet adhesion.

Cardiopulmonary bypass directly activates platelets by an unknown mechanism. Discoid platelets produce pseudopods (shape change) (18), adhere to synthetic surfaces, aggregate, release granular contents, synthesize and release TXA2, and fragment.

Activated platelets adhere to each other (aggregate) and adhere to surface adsorbed fibrinogen via the GP IIb/IIIa receptor complex. Fibrinogen is a necessary cofactor for aggregation, but the reaction does not occur until the receptor complex is "exposed" by ADP or another agonist. Aggregated platelets form emboli that can block arterioles and capillaries and can be trapped on filters (19). Blauth et al. (20) have observed platelet-fibrin aggregates in retinal vessels of patients during CPB.

Platelets adhere to surface-adsorbed fibrinogen at binding sites located on the alpha chain and at the C terminal domain of the gamma chain. The GP IIb/IIIa receptor is required and the GP Ib receptor is not involved (21) (Fig. 16.6). Platelets from patients with Glanzmann's thrombasthenia lack the GP IIb/IIIa receptor complex and do not adhere to the synthetic surfaces of CPB circuits, whereas platelets from patients with Bernard-Soulier's disease, that

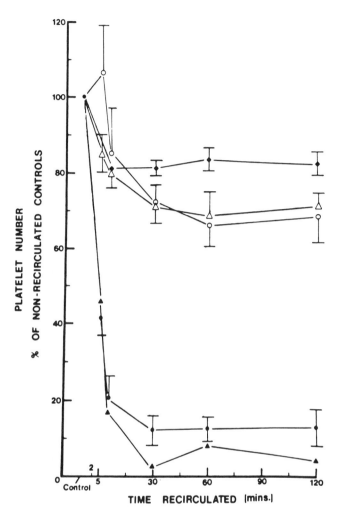

Figure 16.6. Fresh heparinized human blood was recirculated through a membrane oxygenator perfusion circuit at 37°C. Platelet count, presented as the percentage of the initial platelet count, is plotted on the Y axis (mean ± SE). •, normal blood (n=5 experiments); ▸, Bernard-Soulier blood, platelets lack the GP Ib receptors (n=2 experiments); ○, thrombasthenic blood, platelets lack the GP IIb/IIIa receptor complex (n=3 experiments); ▷, normal blood with 0.3 μm prostaglandin E_1 (PGE_1) (n=5 experiments); ♦, normal blood recirculated through the oxygenator primed with albumin (n=5 experiments). Difference between control samples and those from thrombasthenic patients was statistically significant at the <0.02 level; the difference between control samples and samples recirculated through albumin-coated circuit or samples containing PGE_1 was significant at the <0.001 level (10). (From Gluszko P, Racinski B, Musial J, et al. Fibrinogen receptors in platelet adhesion to surface of extracorporeal circuits. Am J Physiol 1987;252: H615–H621.)

lack the GP Ib receptor, adhere as completely as normal platelets (22). Surface adhesion of platelets, particularly in the oxygenator, reduces the number of circulating platelets, which are further reduced by dilution from the priming volume of the circuit.

Some adherent platelets detach and circulate as functionally compromised elements. George et al. (23) and Abrams et al. (24) have demonstrated circulation of platelet membrane fragments during CPB. Wenger and colleagues (25) have observed a 40% loss of platelet fibrinogen (GP IIb/IIIa) receptors on circulating platelets during clinical CPB. Wachtfogel and colleagues (26) have shown that platelet adrenergic re-

ceptors are also lost during in vitro perfusion of fresh, heparinized human blood in a perfusion circuit. Wenger et al. have also shown that platelet membrane fragments remain attached to the surface of the perfusion circuits in amounts greater than can be explained by adherence of "intact platelets". Thus, during CPB platelets not only adhere to synthetic surfaces, but also tear away to leave membrane fragments behind and to form circulating damaged platelets and platelet fragments with compromised function.

During CPB, platelets release granule contents (18, 27–29) and platelet sensitivity to various agonists decreases (18, 27, 29). Alpha granules release β-thromboglobulin, platelet factor 4, and various other coagulation and blood proteins. Dense granules release serotonin, ADP, and calcium. Lysosomes release a variety of acid hydrolases (30). Concentrations of released substances vary with different perfusion systems and also with rates of metabolism or clearance. In addition, platelets synthesize and release TXA2, which is a powerful local vasoconstrictor and platelet agonist (31). Platelet sensitivity to agonists is reduced. Higher concentrations of ADP, epinephrine, thrombin, and other agonists are required to induce platelet aggregation (18, 27, 29).

Scanning electron micrographs of synthetic surfaces exposed to blood show a progressive accumulation of, at first, single platelets, with extended pseudopods, then small aggregates, and finally dense accumulations of layered platelets that cover nearly the entire surface (32). Leukocytes and red cells and a few fibrin strands are included in the deposits, but platelets predominate. The density of platelet accumulation varies with the synthetic material and smoothness of the surface. Rough surfaces accumulate more platelets than smooth surfaces. Polyurethanes and hydrophilic materials accumulate far fewer platelets than hydrophobic compounds.

Transmission electron micrographs show a variety of platelet forms during in vitro recirculation studies and clinical CPB. After in vitro recirculation a few intact platelets remain, but discoid platelets are rare (Fig. 16.7). Many partially and fully degranulated platelets are present, as are platelet ghosts and fragments (33). After clinical CPB, fewer degranulated and destroyed platelets are visible in circulating blood (18). Adherence to circuit surfaces and removal of defective platelets by the reticuloendothelial system best explain the relative paucity of altered platelets in vivo as compared to in vitro.

Cardiopulmonary bypass does not destroy or alter all platelets, but produces a heterogeneous mixture of discoid and shape-changed platelets, intact platelets with reduced sensitivity to agonists, partially and completely degranulated platelets, granulated platelets with deficient membrane receptors, destroyed platelet ghosts, membrane fragments, and new platelets released from the bone marrow (34). Proportionate concentrations of the different platelet elements likely varies between patients and also varies between different bypass systems. The net result is fewer platelets that function less well. Bleeding times increase (27).

Interaction with CPB Components

Components of extracorporeal perfusion systems vary in platelet destructiveness. Rheologic factors such as shear stresses, turbulence, and stagnant flow areas in pumps and connections have less impact on platelets than on red cells, although platelet aggregates accumulate in areas of stagnant flow and turbulence. The most platelet-destructive components of extracorporeal perfusion systems are the oxygenator and the cardiotomy sucker system.

The oxygenator requires a large nonblood surface to effect gas exchange, and accounts for 50 to 85% of the surface area of various extracorporeal perfusion systems. Membrane and bubble oxygenators both reduce platelet numbers and compromise function but the time course differs. In *membrane oxygenators,* platelets react with the huge synthetic surface almost instantly. During recirculation of fresh heparinized human blood in an in vitro membrane oxygenator perfusion circuit, platelet counts decrease to approximately 20% of initial levels within 2 minutes of surface contact (33). As recirculation continues, the number of circulating platelets gradually increases to about 50% of the initial level in 2 hours as platelets detach from the surface. During in vitro circulation in polyvinylchloride circuits containing *bubble oxygenators,* the initial decline in platelet count is less severe than in membrane oxy-

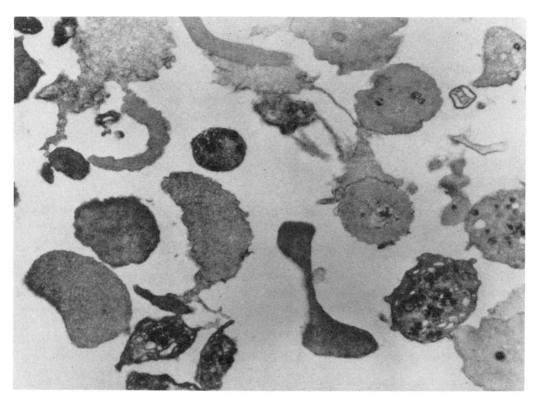

Figure 16.7.   Transmission electromicrograph of human platelets after 6 hours of simulated extracorporeal perfusion. The heterogeneous mixture consists of intact, activated platelets, partially degranulated platelets, platelet ghosts (completely degranulated platelets), and platelet fragments.

genator systems. Platelet granule release is observed, but it is less extensive initially than that in the membrane oxygenator circuit (35). In vivo, the initial platelet count decline is largely caused by hemodilution (27, 36, 37). These differences presumably reflect the fact that the bubble oxygenator contains less synthetic surface area for platelet-surface interaction. In bubble oxygenators, however, each bubble partially denatures plasma proteins at the bubble surface (37) and each new bubble exposes platelets to a new surface. In in vitro perfusion circuits that contain bubble oxygenators, the decline in platelet numbers is exponential and progressive (38); platelets do not return to circulation. During clinical perfusions lasting more than 1 hour, membrane oxygenators better preserve platelets and other blood components than bubble

oxygenator systems (27, 28). Although data are sparse, platelet counts during clinical CPB do not appear to vary significantly between sheet and hollow fiber membrane oxygenators and between membrane oxygenators and microporous "hybrid" oxygenators.

The *cardiotomy sucker* system returns blood aspirated from the surgical field to the perfusion system. This exposes platelets to air-blood and tissue-blood interfaces at which platelet activation occurs. Blood must be filtered to remove aspirated debris, fat globules, fibrin, calcium, and other potential emboli including gas emboli. A roller pump, which compresses tubing against a raceway and may be more destructive of platelets (no data are available), is required to generate the required negative pressure. During CPB, the amount of blood aspirated by the cardiotomy sucker system directly correlates with platelet loss (39).

Filters are routinely used in the arterial line of most extracorporeal perfusion systems. The need is much less with membrane oxygenators than bubble oxygenators. Bubble oxygenators produce large numbers of gaseous emboli and also more particulate emboli than membrane oxygenators (40). Particulate emboli include platelet aggregates, leukocyte emboli, occasional fibrin and fat emboli, and amorphous material. Modern filters usually have pore sizes between 25 and 40 microns. Some platelet aggregates are trapped by these filters; however, it is also likely that some platelet aggregates form on the filters and detach. Filters add surface area to the system and platelets react primarily to surfaces. The need for arterial line filters for sheet membrane oxygenator systems is debatable since these produce the fewest gaseous and particulate emboli and no filter traps the smallest emboli. However, arterial line filters are recommended for bubble and microporous oxygenators because these systems produce substantially larger numbers of gaseous emboli and also more particulate emboli (41).

The priming volume of the pump-oxygenator perfusion system averages approximately 2 liters for adults. Current practice, which emphasizes blood conservation, recommends priming with crystalloids and colloids and not blood. Priming solutions include Ringer's lactate, normal saline and dextrose solutions, albumin-containing solutions, and starch solutions. Albumin solutions are expensive; therefore, many clinicians use up to 1 liter of a starch solution as the colloid portion of the prime. The crystalloid-colloid "clear" prime spares homologous blood transfusions but significantly reduces the colloid osmotic pressure of the perfusate. The reduced colloid osmotic pressure and increase in capillary permeability caused by release of various vasoactive substances during CPB increases extracellular and extravascular water during and after CPB. Clear primes also dilute concentrations of particulate blood elements including platelets. *Dilution* is responsible for much of the thrombocytopenia that occurs during CPB (18, 27, 28); platelet adhesion, aggregation, and destruction is responsible for the remainder. During and after CPB, platelet counts are "corrected" for dilution by using the simultaneous change in hematocrit as a standard (27).

Blood aspirated into *cell saver systems* is diluted and washed before concentration into packed red cells. Such systems make no pretense for salvaging platelets, white cells, and plasma proteins and exacerbate the effects of hemodilution. In contrast to cell-saving systems, hemofiltration devices salvage plasma as well as erythrocytes. Use of hemofiltration, rather than cell saving, for hemoconcentration during bypass and for salvaging oxygenator contents after bypass preserves plasma proteins, platelet count, and aggregability, and thereby reduces postoperative blood loss and fluid requirements (42, 43).

Platelets are affected by other factors during cardiac operation. *Hypothermia,* commonly used during clinical CPB, suppresses platelet TXA2 activation (44), inhibits in vitro platelet aggregation, and prolongs bleeding times in vivo (45). *Heparin* increases the sensitivity of platelets to soluble agonists (46). Heparin-induced thrombocytopenia, an uncommon but problematic complication of heparin therapy, is discussed in Chapter 14. *Protamine* injection after CPB produces a transient reduction in platelet count and decreases platelet numbers by approximately one-third for up to 2 hours (47, 48). Platelets incubated with protamine (49) or heparin-protamine combination (46) have reduced aggregability to soluble agonists. Heparin neutralization by protamine also produces dose-related activation of complement (48, 50), which has antiplatelet actions discussed below. In rare patients, less than 0.5%, administration of protamine initiates synthesis and release of platelet TXA2 (51). The resulting pulmonary vasoconstriction may require heparin and reinstitution of CPB to overcome the intense vasoconstriction. Insertion of *nonheparin bonded pulmonary artery catheters* causes a progressive decline of the platelet count (52).

Interaction with Blood Elements and Plasmin

In addition to interaction with synthetic surfaces, platelets are affected by other processes that occur simultaneously during CPB. Blood contact with synthetic surfaces activates the four primary proteins of the contact activation system: factors XII and XI, prekallikrein (PK), and HMWK. This system initiates the "whole body inflammatory response" including intrinsic coagulation, the classic complement pathway, fibrinolysis, kinin function, and neutrophil activation during CPB. Surface-activated factor XII is cleaved into two serine proteases, factors XIIa and XIIf. In the presence of surface bound HMWK, PK, and factor XI, factor XIIa cleaves factor XI to XIa, HMWK to HWMKa plus bradykinin, and PK to kallikrein. Factor XIa cleaves factor IX to activate coagulation by the intrinsic pathway. Factor XIIf (and also plasmin) activates the first component of complement. Both kallikrein and complement activate neutrophils. Release of neutrophil cathepsin G activates platelets (53). Red cells contain high concentrations of ADP, which is released when red cells are destroyed. Platelets are also activated by release of platelet-activating factor from leukocytes, monocytes, and other sources during CPB. Conversely, HMWK, one of the four primary contact proteins, inhibits thrombin-induced platelet activation (44).

Cardiopulmonary bypass activates endothelial cells to produce tissue plasminogen activator, which cleaves plasminogen to produce the powerful fibrinolytic enzyme, plasmin. At 37°C, high concentrations of plasmin activate platelets, but low concentrations actually inhibit platelet activation by thrombin and some other platelet agonists (54). Hypothermia increases the sensitivity of platelets to activation by low or high doses of plasmin and potentiates rather than inhibits platelet activation by thrombin. At 22°C, even low concentrations of plasmin potentiate expression of platelet GP IIb/IIIa receptors, even though TXA2 synthesis is suppressed (51). Increasing evidence indicates that CPB stimulates production of plasmin (55) and fibrinolysis, and that plasmin is an important platelet agonist. There is little evidence that plasmin digests or degrades platelet membrane receptors. Cardiopulmonary bypass also stimulates release of prostaglandin I_2 (PGI_2), prostacyclin, from endothelial cells at the start of bypass (13). Prostacyclin is a strong platelet inhibitor. Platelet inhibition has been attributed to fibrinogen degradation products (56) since degradation fragments D and E bind platelet surface membrane receptors (57, 58).

PLATELET PROTECTION DURING CPB

In 1969, Zucker and Vroman (59) observed that glass slides exposed to platelets immediately after fibrinogen coating caused platelets to adhere, whereas if platelet contact was delayed 2 or 3 minutes after fibrinogen coating, platelets did not adhere to some slides. In the same year, Salzman et al. (60) found that platelets did not adhere to surfaces precoated with albumin in vitro (Fig. 16.6). Unfortunately, precoating circuits with albumin does not protect platelets during clinical CPB; the reason is not known, but presumably is due to rapid degradation or desorption of the adsorbed albumin. In 1980, Vroman et al. (61) reported that surface adsorbed fibrinogen was no longer recognized by antifibrinogen antibody a few minutes after blood contact, and that much of the adsorbed fibrinogen was displaced by HMWK. These observations suggested that platelet adhesion could be influenced by the composition of surface-adsorbed proteins, and that most of the reaction between platelets and synthetic surfaces occurred during the first few minutes of blood contact. The concept of platelet "passivated" surfaces evolved to describe surfaces that do not trigger adherence by intact circulating platelets. In support of surface "passivation," Addonizio et al. (62) reversibly inhibited platelets during in vitro recirculation of fresh human blood in a membrane oxygenator circuit with prostacyclin, which has a half-life in plasma of 2 to 3 minutes. Prostacyclin inhibited platelet adherence and function during initial blood-surface contact. Platelet function soon returned as the drug disappeared; however, the functionally intact platelets did not adhere to circuit surfaces during the 2-hour study.

Cottrell et al. (63) used iloprost, a stable analog of prostacyclin, to demonstrate that extracorporeal perfusion circuits can be passivated to platelets in vivo. In dogs, a 30-minute infusion of iloprost at the beginning of partial CPB preserved platelet numbers and prevented release of platelet thrombospondin for 2 to 3 hours after the infusion was stopped and after platelet responsiveness to ADP had returned. Shigeta and colleagues (64) confirmed the efficacy of platelet-passivated surfaces in sheep, and showed that perfusion circuit surfaces can remain passivated up to 16 hours after an initial dose of a reversible platelet GP IIb/IIIa receptor inhibitor. During 24-hour perfusions using an extracorporeal membrane oxygenator system in awake, standing sheep, a single dose of bitistatin, a disintegrin purified from snake venom, attenuated the loss of platelet numbers and release of ovine platelet factor 4, reduced adherence of platelet membrane protein to circuit surfaces, and preserved platelet responsiveness (after initial inhibition) to ADP for 12 to 16 hours. These cumulative data support the concept that temporary re-

versible inhibition of platelet function during initial contact permits circuit surfaces to become "passivated" to platelets. After surfaces are passivated, functionally intact platelets in unreduced numbers circulate and theoretically are capable of participating in wound hemostasis.

The strategy of preserving platelets by temporary inhibition during initial blood-synthetic surface contact has been extended to clinical CPB for heart surgery. Because of the need for hemostasis after completion of CPB, inhibitors must be reversible or quickly metabolized or excreted. Dipyridamole, prostanoids, and disintegrins are all reversible platelet inhibitors that act by different mechanisms.

Platelet Inhibitor Therapy

Dipyridamole inhibits platelet AMP phosphodiesterase and potentiates the inhibitory action of prostacyclin (65), but the doses required are difficult to achieve by oral administration (66). The drug has a half-life in plasma of approximately 100 minutes (66) and is a mild vasodilator. Teoh and colleagues (67) gave dipyridamole either orally before operation or intravenously during operation to low-risk patients who had coronary bypass operations. Both oral and intravenous drug significantly reduced loss of platelet numbers during and after CPB and reduced postoperative blood loss, but did not alter release of platelet factor 4 or synthesis of TXA2. Although the reduction in postoperative bleeding was significant as compared to a control group, the drug is seldom used for platelet preservation during CPB.

The *prostanoids* are eicosanoids that reversibly inhibit platelet function by stimulating adenylate cyclase to increase platelet cAMP. Prostacyclin is the natural platelet inhibitor and is more potent than PGE_1, which is effective; however, PGI_2 is 10 times less potent than the analog iloprost. In rhesus monkeys placed on CPB, infusion of PGE₁ prevents loss of platelet numbers and function, and prevents the expected increase in postoperative bleeding times (68).

Radegran and colleagues (69) and Malpass and associates (70) infused prostacyclin during operation in patients who had coronary artery bypass. Radegran et al. observed significantly higher platelet counts in patients who received prostacyclin, but Malpass et al. did not. Malpass et al. did observe reduced levels of platelet factor 4 in patients who received PGI_2. However, neither group observed a reduction in postoperative blood loss, and Malpass et al. did not observe improvement in bleeding times measured 30 minutes after stopping CPB. Both groups observed profound hypotension during the infusion, which required infusion of vasopressors.

Kappa and associates (71) infused iloprost, an investigational drug, during CPB in patients who had heparin-induced thrombosis and thrombocytopenia. In these patients, heparin acts as a powerful platelet agonist and can induce intravascular thrombosis as well as severe bleeding due to profound thrombocytopenia. An infusion of iloprost inhibited platelets in the presence of heparin and prevented the lethal manifestations of this disease. Although iloprost is less vasodilatory than prostacyclin, substantial doses of vasopressors were required to maintain blood pressure during CPB. The drug is not yet available for clinical use.

Recently a new group of *RGD-containing peptides* (disintegrins) derived from snake venom have been found to reversibly inhibit the GP IIb/IIIa membrane receptor complex of platelets. In the presence of fibrinogen, activated GP IIb/IIIa receptors are involved in platelet aggregation and adhesion. Musial and colleagues (5) demonstrated that several of these peptides preserve platelet numbers and function and suppress β-thromboglobulin release during in vitro recirculation of fresh heparinized human blood through a membrane oxygenator perfusion circuit. As noted above, Shigeta and colleagues (64) found that a single dose of bitistatin, a disintegrin, attenuates loss of platelets and release of ovine platelet factor 4, preserves platelet function, and reduces deposits of platelet membrane protein on the surfaces of the perfusion circuit during 24-hour extracorporeal membrane oxygenator perfusions in sheep. This promising group of peptides is not vasoactive and may provide a clinically useful drug for reversible platelet inhibition alone or in combination with a prostanoid.

Aprotinin

In 1988, Bidstrup and colleagues (72) found that high doses of the kallikrein and plasmin inhibitor, *aprotinin,* reduced bleeding after open heart surgery by approximately 50% (see also Chapter 17). Their observation was quickly confirmed by several European investigators who began to probe the mechanism of action. Bidstrup et al. found that the drug did not alter platelet counts during and after CPB but did reduce postoperative bleeding times. Blauhaut and her associates (73) determined that aprotinin attenuated platelet TXA2 synthesis and suppressed fibrinolysis but not complement activation. Watchfogel, Edmunds, and colleagues (unpublished data) did not observe any direct effect of aprotinin on platelet numbers during in vitro recirculation of fresh heparinized human blood; however, in this system plasmin does not form because tissue plasminogen activator is not present. These data, the clinical observations, and the known agonist properties of plasmin on platelets strongly suggest that aprotinin attenuates the platelet response to CPB by inhibiting the plasmin effect on platelets (74). The drug also inhibits kallikrein and thus attenuates activation of neutrophils during CPB.

Autologous Whole Blood Withdrawal

A portion of platelets and other blood constituents may be spared interaction with extracorporeal circuit components and other CPB-related antiplatelet factors using a process of acute normovolemic hemodilution by withdrawing blood from the patient prior to CPB and replacing the harvested volume with crystalloid or colloid solution. The autologous whole blood, containing platelets and procoagulant proteins and stored at room temperature during bypass, is reinfused into the patient after separation from CPB. Blood can be removed via arterial or central venous catheters and stored in citrated bags after anesthetic induction and prior to heparin anticoagulation. Alternatively, heparinized blood can be withdrawn via the venous cannulae after cannulation of the heart and before initiating CPB.

In clinical investigations of platelet function resulting from the intraoperative withdrawal of 10 to 25% of patient blood volume and postbypass reinfusion, platelet counts have been observed both to increase (75–79) or remain unchanged (80, 81). Qualitative platelet function has not been studied by most of these investigators, but two reports measured greater platelet adhesiveness after autologous blood administration (75, 81).

The effect of this strategy on the reduction of postoperative bleeding has been inconsistent. Reinfusion of autologous blood following CPB has resulted in significant decreases (76, 78, 81), insignificant reductions (75, 80, 82), or no difference (79, 83) in postoperative blood loss. Although 20 to 50% savings in homologous blood requirements have been reported by several investigators (77–80, 84–86), in only one report (78) is the decreased homologous blood use associated with a significant reduction in measured blood loss.

Surgical techniques, perfusion equipment, and homologous blood utilization have evolved since completion of these studies. A recent study evaluated the effects of the post-CPB reinfusion of autologous blood (10 ml/kg) withdrawn before CPB in addition to the oxygenator contents after processing in a cell separator (87). Postoperative blood loss was not decreased compared to that in patients receiving processed oxygenator content alone. Conversely, a reduction (approximately 500 ml) in homologous blood transfusion during hospitalization was observed in the patient group receiving autologous blood. This difference resulted from the decreased use of homologous blood intraoperatively after separation from bypass permitted by the availability of the autologous blood for infusion. Postoperative homologous blood use did not differ between the two patient groups.

Hemodilution resulting from the withdrawal and crystalloid or colloid replacement of autologous blood can produce unacceptably low hemoglobin levels and prohibits use of this technique in patients who have a small blood volume or preoperative anemia.

Autologous Platelet-Rich-Plasma

Harvest of platelet-rich plasma (PRP) through the process of plasmapheresis aims to sequester greater concentrations of platelets and procoagulant proteins from the adverse effects of CPB than obtained in whole blood. A plasma separator is used to collect PRP after induction of anesthesia prior to anticoagulation. Since the separated red blood cells are returned to the patient, the concentrations of platelets and clotting factors obtainable are not influenced by limits to hemodilution imposed by patient red cell mass.

Nonrandomized studies reported increased postoperative platelet counts, diminished blood loss, and reduced homologous blood use as a result of the prebypass collection and postbypass reinfusion of PRP

(88, 89). Recently, three randomized, controlled trials have been reported. Del Rossi et al. (90) observed decreased postoperative blood loss (630 ± 79 ml versus 408 ± 88 ml; P <0.05) after the reinfusion of 220 ml autologous PRP. The platelet count was greater in the PRP-treated patients immediately postoperatively, but was not different from controls by the 1st postoperative day. There was no difference in the use of homologous red blood cells between the patient groups. The PRP infusion reduced the amount of fresh-frozen plasma administered postoperatively based on elevated partial thromboplastin time (aPTT) values.

Boldt et al. (91) studied the effects of the collection and reinfusion of PRP (10 ml/kg) and platelet-poor plasma (PPP) (10 ml/kg) during coronary surgery. Postbypass PRP administration produced greater postoperative platelet counts than observed in PPP-treated patients or controls. Fibrinogen levels were better preserved in both PRP- and PPP-treated subjects than in controls, but postoperative clotting times were not different in the three patient groups. Postoperative blood loss was decreased in patients receiving either autologous plasma product (PRP, 500 ± 210 ml versus PPP, 543 ± 230 ml versus controls, 696 + 130 ml).

Jones et al. (92) administered up to 1000 ml of autologous PRP after CPB during coronary surgery. These PRP samples averaged 2.5×10^{11} platelets (30% of the circulating platelets), approximately equivalent to 5 units of platelet concentrates. Compared to control patients, PRP reinfusion resulted in insignificant preservation of postoperative platelet count, no change in coagulation times, and a decrease in red blood cell loss (1050 ± 43 ml versus 1226 ± 61 ml; P = 0.021). These hemostatic benefits, like those reported by Del Rossi et al. and Boldt et al., are not striking. Nonetheless, Jones et al. observed the homologous red blood cell requirement, based on strict hemoglobin values, was reduced in the PRP-treated patients.

POSTBYPASS PLATELET DYSFUNCTION

Diagnosis

Platelet dysfunction, producing ineffective hemostasis, may be acquired intraoperatively (Table 16.2) or originate preoperatively (Table 16.3). Knowledge of the individual patient and the hemostatic consequences of the specific operative and perfusion techniques employed may suggest that platelet dysfunction is a contributing cause of postbypass bleeding. Quantitative platelet deficiencies can be confirmed by laboratory measurement. Timely, accurate assessment of qualitative platelet function after cardiac surgery is lacking.

Table 16.2. Factors Causing Platelet Dysfunction During Cardiac Surgery, Listed by Mechanism of Action

Thrombocytopenia
 Hemodilution
  Crystalloid and colloid priming and cardioplegia solutions
  Transfusion
  Cell washing
 Transient sequestration from circulation
  Heparin (?)
  Protamine
 Platelet destruction
  Oxygenators
  Cardiotomy suction
  Filters

Qualitative Platelet Dysfunction
 Platelet interaction at nonendothelial surfaces
  Oxygenators
  Cardiotomy suction
  Filters
 Platelet interaction with blood constituents
  Endothelial plasminogen activator, plasmin release
  Factor XII, kallikrein, neutrophil activation
  Hemolysis
  Cell washing
  Heparin (potentiates activation)
 Direct inhibition
  Hypothermia
  Protamine (?)
  Halothane
  Cardiovascular drugs (see Table 16.3)

Table 16.3. Conditions and Drugs That Impair Platelet Function

Conditions
  Uremia
  von Willebrand's disease
  Platelet storage pool deficiency
  Glanzmann's thrombasthenia
  Bernard-Soulier disease
  Wiskott-Aldrich syndrome
  Thrombocytopenic purpuras
  Myeloproliferative disorders
  Dysproteinemias
  Leukemias
  Hypersplenism
  Disseminated intravascular coagulation

Drugs[a]
  Antiinflammatory agents
    Aspirin
    Nonsteroidal antiinflammatory agents
  Antimicrobials
    Penicillins
    Semisynthetic penicillins
    Cephalosporins
    Nitrofurantoin
    Hydroxychloroquine
  Cardiovascular drugs
    Dipyridamole
    Papaverine
    Prostaglandins I_2, E_1, D_2
    Iloprost
    Adenosine
    β-adrenergic agonists
    Calcium channel blockers
    Sodium nitroprusside
    Nitroglycerin
    Heparin
    Protamine
    Quinidine
    Propranolol
    Furosemide
  Anesthetic and psychotropic drugs
    Halothane
    Local anesthetics
    Heroin
    Tricyclic antidepressants
    Phenothiazines
  Other drugs
    Dextrans
    Antihistamines (H_1 receptor blockers)
    Lipid-lowering agents
    Ethanol
    Chemotherapeutic agents
    Radiographic contrast agents

[a] For a detailed listing of drugs causing abnormal platelet function, including references, see George and Shattil (93). With the exception of clinical studies demonstrating a significantly greater frequency of bleeding with aspirin, data supporting a platelet abnormality for the drugs listed are in vitro observations of altered platelet aggregation or anecdotal reports in one or a few patients (93).

PLATELET COUNT

There is no absolute relationship between platelet count and bleeding; however, spontaneous bleeding in the absence of trauma does not usually occur unless the platelet count is less than 10,000 platelets per microliter, and significant bleeding after trauma is unusual at counts above 50,000 per microliter (94). Bleeding time begins to increase when the platelet count decreases to less than 100,000 per microliter and there is a direct, inverse relationship between bleeding time and platelet counts between 100,000 per microliter and 10,000 per microliter (95). Post-CPB platelet counts are commonly 100,000 per microliter or greater (18, 27, 36, 37). Moreover, the occurrence of excessive postoperative hemorrhage does not strongly correlate with platelet count (96). This suggests that alterations in platelet function are more important than reductions in platelet count in determining the contribution made by platelets to postoperative hemostasis.

In contrast to the number of circulating platelets, platelet size, measured as mean platelet volume (MPV), and total platelet mass, i.e., plateletcrit (PCT), do correlate with the presence of bleeding after CPB (96, 97). The PCT is calculated by multipling the platelet count by the MPV. Larger platelets are younger and hemostatically more reactive than smaller, older cells. Mohr et al. (97) suggest that a PCT less than 0.1% following CPB is an indication for platelet transfusion in patients with abnormal bleeding.

BLEEDING TIME

The template bleeding time is used to evaluate platelet plug formation and reflects both platelet number and function. Strict attention to standardized technique (forearm site, skin incision length and depth, venous pressure) is required for proper measurement and validity of result. Although the test is reproducible within individuals, there is wide variation between individuals and the test is influenced by physiologic variables such as arm temperature, anxiety, and direction of the incision (98, 99).

The predictive value of the bleeding time test for intra-or postoperative bleeding problems is minimal (100). In a comprehensive review, Rodgers and Levin (99) found no correlation between bleeding time and postoperative blood loss after cardiac operations. In a clinical series that included patients receiving platelet-inhibiting drugs, preoperative bleeding time was not related to blood loss or transfusion requirement (101).

After cardiac operation, bleeding times are commonly elevated, though only a minority of patients manifest a bleeding problem. However, Harker et al. (36) observed a persistent (up to 8 hours) postoperative prolongation of bleeding time to greater than 20 minutes (despite platelet counts in excess of 100,000 per microliter) in all patients who developed postbypass hemorrhage. Postoperative bleeding time was less than 10 minutes in nonbleeding patients. Administration of platelet concentrates to the bleeding patients shortened bleeding times and cessation of hemorrhage followed. Artifact induced by inconsistent measurement technique and physiologic variables as well as conditions other than platelet abnormalities such as anemia, fibrinolysis, and some coagulation protein deficiencies that may prolong the bleeding time (99) are causes of false-positive test results.

VON WILLEBRAND FACTOR ANTIGEN

The level of vWF in plasma can be measured by immunoassay (102) and is inversely related to bleeding time in patients with deficiencies of this endothelial glycoprotein, e.g., von Willebrand's disease. Preoperative screening of vWF levels has related low vWF values to increased postoperative bleeding after cardiac surgery (103). The vWF levels and bleeding have not been correlated after CPB, however, and increasing the concentration of plasma vWF

by prophylactic administration of desmopressin acetate does not improve platelet function or reduce blood loss following cardiac operation (102). Platelet dysfunction due to mechanisms other than decreased vWF levels are not revealed by this assay.

IN VITRO PLATELET AGGREGATION

In vitro aggregation of platelets in response to agonists such as ADP, collagen, thrombin, epinephrine, and ristocetin is measured photometrically to characterize disorders of platelet function (Fig. 16.3). Impaired platelet aggregation is observed consistently after in vitro and in vivo extracorporeal circulation, but only a small number of patients develop clinical bleeding problems after CPB. Mohr et al. (96) were able to grade platelet aggregation response to ristocetin (but not to other soluble agonists) in patients after cardiac surgery and correlated more impaired grades of aggregation with the occurrence of clinical bleeding. The time-consuming and complex nature of this test, as well as its sensitivity to clinically insignificant platelet alterations, prohibits clinical usefulness.

THROMBOELASTOGRAPHY AND SONOCLOT

Thromboelastography (TEG) and Sonoclot (Sienco Inc., Morrison, CO) are qualitative tests of whole blood coagulation that measure alterations in shear elasticity and mechanical impedence, respectively, produced by the changing viscoelastic properties of forming clot. The viscoelasticity of clotting blood increases with fibrin formation, platelet-fibrin interaction, and clot retraction and it is decreased by clot lysis. Thus, abnormalities in procoagulant proteins, platelets, and fibrinolytic activity may be depicted by characteristic tracings produced and their derived parameters. In the presence of a quantitative or qualitative platelet deficiency, the TEG displays a diminished alpha angle and maximum amplitude (MA) while the ratio MA:A60 is normal

(Fig. 16.8). Abnormal Sonoclot findings characteristic of inadequate platelet number or function are reduced R2, peak, and R3 values (Fig. 16.9).

Because the TEG and Sonoclot tests are performed with whole blood, they can be performed at the bedside. Given a normal R and K time (see legend for Fig. 16.8), 20 minutes or more are required to obtain an estimate of platelet-fibrin interaction from the TEG alpha angle and MA. Son-

oclot analysis can be completed within fifteen minutes.

Thromboelastography (104, 105) and Sonoclot (105) have been shown to be more accurate predictors (greater than 85% and 74% accuracy, respectively) of postoperative hemorrhage after cardiac operation than the ACT or a battery of routine coagulation tests (platelet count, prothrombin time, elevated partial prothrombin time, fibrinogen level, fibrin split products). In

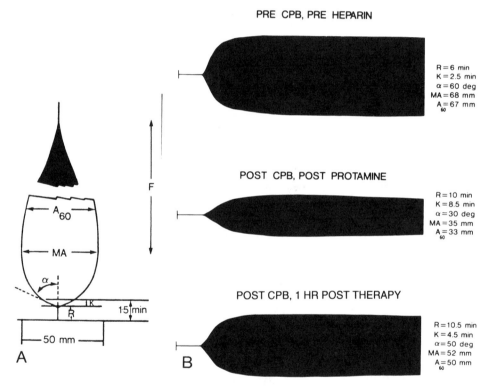

Figure 16.8. **A.** Several parameters describe the TEG representation of whole blood coagulation. The reaction time (R) (normal R, 7.5 to 15 minutes) measures the time from the placement in the cuvette until an amplitude of 1 mm is achieved, and is the time necessary for initial fibrin formation. The K value (normal K, 3 to 6 minutes) is the time interval from the end of the R value until the amplitude of the TEG is 20 mm, and is considered to be a measure of the rapidity of fibrin buildup and cross-linking. The MA, or maximum amplitude (normal MA, 50 to 60 mm), is thought to reflect the absolute strength of the fibrin clot and to depend on platelet number and function, as well as fibrinogen levels. The a value (normal a, 50° to 60°) is the slope of the outside divergence of the tracing from the point of the R value and denotes the speed at which clot is being formed and cross-linked. The parameter A_{60} denotes the amplitude 60 minutes after the MA is measured. The ratio A_{60}:MA (normal A_{60}:MA, >0.85), as well as F value (time from MA until the amplitude returns to zero) (normal F, >300 minutes), reflects loss of clot integrity over time. **B.** Perioperative TEG analysis demonstrating normal preoperative coagulation function. After CPB and protamine administration, diminished MA and a values (demonstrating platelet dysfunction) were accompanied by excessive mediastinal bleeding. Treatment was associated with normalized MA and a values and cessation of bleeding. (From Tuman KJ, Spiess BD, McCarthy RJ, Ivankovich AD. Comparison of viscoelastic measures of coagulation after cardiopulmonary bypass. Anesth Analg 1989;69:69–75.)

these studies the majority of abnormalities in TEG and Sonoclot parameters observed after CPB are those of abnormal platelet-fibrinogen interaction. Conversely, in another report, neither TEG nor routine hemostatic tests were found to offer accurate predictive information (106). Additional studies are needed to confirm the accuracy and utility of the viscoelastic tests when bleeding occurs after cardiac operation. Normative and diagnostic TEG and Sonoclot parameters need to be determined for the

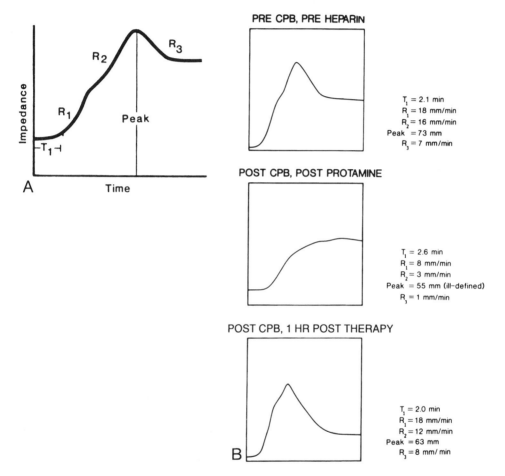

Figure 16.9. **A.** Sonoclot analysis of clot viscoelasticity. As fibrin strands form, impedance rises at various rates until a peak impedance is achieved. The onset time (T_1) reflects the beginning of fibrin formation and the primary slope (R_1) probably reflects further fibrin formation and the speed at which the clot is being formed. An inflection point is often seen, which is believed to represent the start of platelet-induced contraction of the fibrin strands. The secondary slope (R_2) is thought to reflect further fibrinogenesis and platelet-fibrin interaction. The peak impedance probably reflects completion of fibrin formation. A downward slope (R_3) is produced as platelets induce contraction of the completed clot. Platelet functionality and number are key determinants of the peak impedance and R_3 values, which are produced as platelets induce contraction of the completed clot. Clot lysis can be determined by measurement of the final impedance as a function of time, i.e., severe fibrinolysis results in a final impedance close to that at the onset of clot formation. **B.** Perioperative Sonoclot analysis of the same patient in Figure 16.8 **B.** Preoperative SCT parameters were normal; after protamine administration R_2 and R_3 markedly diminished, the peak was blunted, and its amplitude was abnormal (consistent with platelet dysfunction). Treatment was associated with improvement in R_2, R_3, and peak impedance. (From Tuman KJ, Spiess BD, McCarthy RJ, Ivankovich AD. Comparison of viscoelastic measures of coagulation after cardiopulmonary bypass. Anesth Analg 1989;69:69–75.)

cardiac surgical patient population. It is unknown whether selection of therapy based on observed TEG or Sonoclot abnormalities results in less blood loss, need for reoperation, or homologous blood requirement than treatment prescribed without TEG or Sonoclot data.

HEMOSTATOMETRY

Kovacs and colleagues (107) have recently introduced another comprehensive test of hemostatic function that uses whole blood, thus permitting its use at the bedside. In hemostatometry, blood is perfused through perforated tubing at a constant pressure. Decreases in blood flow rate produce changes in tubing pressure as the platelet-fibrin plug is formed and blood coagulates. Normal platelet-related hemostasis is observed within 5 minutes. Quantitative values may be derived from tracings of the pressure changes over time. In a preliminary report of the use of hemostatometry during cardiac surgery, post-CPB bleeding was predicted with an overall accuracy of 77% (108).

Treatment

Platelet therapy is indicated for the treatment of post-CPB bleeding in the presence of thrombocytopenia (generally less than 50,000 to 100,000 per microliter) or qualitative platelet dysfunction. Qualitative dysfunction is suggested by patient characteristics (e.g., preoperative aspirin therapy), operation-related factors (e.g., prolonged use of cardiotomy suction, bubble oxygenator), and absence of other measurable coagulation abnormalities (e.g., heparin excess indicated by ACT elevation, characteristic protamine titration, prolonged TEG reaction time value).

Hypothermia-related platelet dysfunction is corrected by warming the patient to 37°C. Serial platelet counts during massive transfusion or cell washing permit recognition of thrombocytopenia resulting from hemodilution. Although sodium nitroprus-

side (109) and nitroglycerin (110) in clinical doses are platelet inhibitors in vitro (mechanism unknown), infusion of these vasodilators to prevent hypertension-related bleeding is probably beneficial.

No pharmacologic means are available to correct the platelet dysfunction produced by cardiac surgery. Desmopressin acetate is a drug that improves platelet function and reduces elevated bleeding times in patients with nonsurgical conditions such as uremia, von Willebrand's disease, and aspirin ingestion. Administration of the drug raises circulating levels of vWF. It is not surprising that increased levels of vWF alone are not sufficient to reverse the CPB-related platelet injuries described above. Clinical investigations of desmopressin acetate use during cardiac surgery are discussed in Chapter 17.

In the absence of an effective pharmacologic therapy that restores platelet function, administration of platelets is required. If autologous whole blood or PRP is available, it is administered and hemostasis reevaluated before prescribing homologous blood products.

Homologous Platelet Transfusion

Homologous platelet transfusion is indicated for the treatment of platelet dysfunction, which produces abnormal bleeding. Thrombocytopenia or thrombocytopathy per se are not indications for platelet transfusion. Moreover, because it is difficult to predict which few patients will develop post-CPB bleeding problems, administration of any homologous blood product as preventive therapy is not justifiable. Investigators have demonstrated no benefit from prophylactic platelet transfusion following CPB (111, 112).

Platelets for transfusion are separated from fresh whole blood or harvested from single donors by platelet pheresis. Single-donor platelets are used almost exclusively for patients who are alloimmunized and refractory to platelet transfusion as a result of numerous platelet transfusions. Random- or multiple-donor platelets are more plentiful since most volunteer-donor blood is fractionated, but they provide recipients increased exposure to transfusion-related diseases.

Compatibility testing is not necessary. Platelets can be administered without regard to ABO and Rh groups unless they are heavily contaminated with red blood cells. However, because some red blood cells are present in platelet concentrates, it is preferable for Rh-negative patients to receive Rh-negative platelets to prevent Rh-immunization.

Platelets are normally stored for 5 days at 20 to 24° C, with constant gentle agitation. Platelet shape change, aggregation, alpha granule release, and loss of surface glycoproteins result from cell activation, which occurs during processing and centrifugation (113–116). There appears to be little subsequent deterioration in platelet function during 5-day storage when proper equipment and technique are used (116). Lactate accumulation and the resulting decrease in pH reduce the viability of platelets stored for periods greater than 5 days. Platelets stored at 4°C are no longer widely used because of reduced survival and function after infusion.

Platelet function after transfusion is most commonly described in terms of the percentage of infused platelets found in circulation 1 hour after transfusion (recovery) and circulating life span (survival). Five-day-old platelets have posttransfusion platelet recovery values between 40% and 58% and survivals of 5 to 7 days in normal volunteers (117) (compared to the normal 9- to 10-day platelet lifespan). Platelet alterations induced during processing produce the nonrecovered platelets, which are sequestered in the spleen. Recovery and survival of unprocessed autologous platelets are slightly greater (117). A latency period, up to 4 hours in length, between platelet transfusion and maximum improvement in bleeding time (118, 119) results from the in

vivo correction of some of the processing- and storage-induced platelet lesions.

Platelets are pooled in the blood bank when more than 1 unit is administered. Once pooled, platelets should be transfused within 6 hours. Each individual donor bag will contain 5.5×10^{10} to 7.0×10^{10} platelets. A single platelet concentrate should increase the peripheral platelet count in an adult by $6-8 \times 10^3$ per microliter (117). Thus, transfusion of 4 to 6 units of pooled platelet concentrates should provide an adequate number of functioning platelets to most patients. In pediatric patients it is common practice to infuse 0.1 unit/kg of random-donor platelets.

A standard 170 μm filter is recommended for platelet administration; filters of smaller pore size are not indicated. Pretransfusion incubation of platelets at 37° C has been used to increase the posttransfusion increment in platelet count with contradictory results (120, 121).

Fresh Whole Blood

In the 1960s, fresh whole blood was administered to correct platelet deficiencies following CPB. With improvement of fractionation techniques, use of fresh whole blood was superseded by stored blood components, including platelet concentrates. Blood banks discontinued processing fresh whole blood. Lavee et al. (122) and Mohr et al. (123) have observed that homologous fresh whole blood produces hemostatic effects equal or superior to those of platelet concentrates after routine cardiac surgery in a nonbleeding patient population. When compared to the effect of one unit of fresh whole blood, a similar increment in platelet count required 4 to 6 units of platelet concentrates; normalization of bleeding time and improved in vitro platelet aggregation required 8 to 10 units of platelet concentrates (122, 123). Postoperative blood loss was slightly decreased in patients receiving 1 unit fresh whole blood in contrast to those receiving 10 units of platelet concentrates (123). The hemostatic benefits of fresh whole blood are achieved, therefore, with a risk of transfusion-related complication one-fourth to one-tenth that provided by multiple-donor platelet concentrates. Comparative studies of fresh whole blood and platelet concentrates for treatment of hemorrhage after CPB are needed.

Although refrigerated storage of fresh whole blood for short periods would aid blood bankers' efforts to provide this product, storage at 4°C diminishes the hemostatic benefit of fresh whole blood transfusion. Administering 1 unit of fresh whole blood stored either unrefrigerated (<24 hours) or refrigerated for 5 or 24 hours, Golan et al. (124) observed that postoperative blood loss and transfusion requirements were directly related to the duration of fresh whole blood storage at 4°C. Conversely, Manno et al. (125) measured similar reductions in postoperative blood loss in children during cardiac surgery receiving either unrefrigerated fresh whole blood (<6 hours) or 24- to 48-hour-old whole blood stored at 4 to 6° C compared to children who were given stored, reconstituted components consisting of red blood cells, fresh-frozen plasma as well as 2- to 5-day-old platelets stored at 22° C (125). Differences in the hemostatic qualities of the <6-hour-old unrefrigerated fresh whole blood and the 24- to 48-hour-old refrigerated whole blood may have been compensated for by the large volume (>70 ml/kg/24 hours) of blood administered to both patient groups.

SUMMARY

Platelet interaction with synthetic surfaces, air-blood and tissue-blood interfaces in the heart-lung machine, and with other components of clinical CPB results in quantitative and qualitative platelet deficiencies. In addition, activation of complement, granulocytes, and endothelial cells during clinical CPB produces a variety of vasoactive and inflammatory mediators and plas-

min, which activate platelets or impair their function. The resulting platelet dysfunction can be ameliorated during CPB by use of short-acting platelet inhibitors and aprotinin, which are aimed at reducing platelet-synthetic surface interaction and inhibiting the antiplatelet actions of plasmin and kallikrein, respectively. Harvesting autologous whole blood or PRP before bypass offer unproven platelet protection per se during CPB.

The diagnosis of platelet dysfunction during heart surgery is hampered by the lack of rapid and specific tests. Platelet count and a high index of suspicion based on patient-, procedure-, and perfusion-related factors are clinically useful indicators of platelet dysfunction. Bedside tests of whole blood coagulation are potentially useful assays of platelet dysfunction. Transfusion of platelet concentrates or fresh whole blood are the best available means of restoring platelet function.

ACKNOWLEDGMENT

The authors wish to express their gratitude to Eleanor Grant and Myra Monahan for their valuable assistance in the preparation of this manuscript. This work was supported in part by grant HL 19055 from the National Heart, Lung, and Blood Institute, National Institutes of Health.

REFERENCES

1. McEver RP. The clinical significance of platelet membrane glycoproteins. Hematol Oncol Clin North Am 1990;4:87–104.
2. Walsh PN, Schmaier, AH. Platelet-coagulant protein interactions. In: Colman RW, Hirsh J, Marder VJ, Salzman EW, eds: Hemostasis and thrombosis. Basic principles and clinical practice. 2nd ed. Philadelphia: JB Lippincott, 1987;689–708.
3. Ashby B, Daniel JL, Smith JB: Mechanisms of platelet activation and inhibition. Hematol Oncol Clin North Am 1990;4:1–26.
4. Hawiger J, Steer ML, Salzman EW. Intracellular regulatory processes in platelets. In: Colman RW, Hirsh J, Marder VJ, Salzman EW, eds: Hemostasis and thrombosis. Basic principles and clinical practice. 2nd ed. Philadelphia: JB Lippincott, 1987;689–708.
5. Musial J, Rucinski B, Williams JA, Stewart GJ, Edmunds LH Jr, Niewiarowski S. Inhibition of

platelet adhesion to surfaces of extracorporeal circuit by disintegrins: RGD containing peptides from viper venoms. Circulation 1990; 82:261–273.

6. Kloczewiak N, Timmons S, Hawiger J: Recognition site for the platelet receptor is present on the 15-residue carboxyl-terminal fragment of the gamma-chain of human fibrinogen and is not involved in the fibrin polymerization reaction. Thromb Res 1983;29:249–255.

7. Margurerie GA, Aradillou N, Cherel G, Plow EF: The binding of fibrinogen to its platelet receptor. Biol Chem 1982;257:11872–11875.

8. Roth GJ, Siok CJ: Acetylation of the NH_2-terminal serine of prostaglandin synthetase by aspirin. Biol Chem 1978;253:3782–3784.

9. Packham MA, Kinlough-Rathbone RL, Reimers S, Mustard JF: Mechanisms of platelet aggregation independent of adenosine diphosphate. In: Silver MS, ed. Prostaglandins in hematology. New York: Spectrum, 1977;247–276.

10. Addonizio VP Jr, Smith JB, Guiod LR, Strauss JF III, Colman RW, Edmunds LH Jr. Thromboxane synthesis and platelet protein release during simulated extracorporeal circulation. Blood 1979;54:371–376.

11. Walter F, Vulliemoz Y, Verosky M, Triner L: Effects of halothane on the cyclic 3′,5′-adenosine monophosphate enzyme system in human platelets. Anesth Analg 1980;59:856–861.

12. Stengert K: Halothane-induced platelet dysfunction. Anesth Analg 1982;61:217.

13. Downing SW, Edmunds LH Jr. Release of vasoactive substances during cardiopulmonary bypass. Ann Thorac Surg 1992;54:1236–1243.

14. Blackstone EH, Kirklin JW, Stewart RW, Chenoweth DE. The damaging effects of cardiopulmonary bypass. In: Wu KW, Rossi EC, eds. Prostaglandins in clinical medicine: cardiovascular and thrombotic disorders. Chicago: Yearbook Medical Publishers, 1982:355–369.

15. Uniyal S, Brash JL. Patterns of absorption of proteins from human plasma onto foreign surfaces. Thromb Haemost 1982;47:285–290.

16. Ziats NP, Pankowsky DA, Tierney BP, et al. Absorption of Hagemann Factor (Factor XII) and other human plasma proteins to biomedical polymers. J Lab Clin Med 1990;116:687–696.

17. Brash JL, Scott CF, tenHove P, et al. Mechanism of transient absorption of fibrinogens from plasma to solid surfaces: role of the contact and fibrinolytic systems. Blood 1988;71:932–939.

18. Zilla P, Fasol R, Groskurth P, Klepetko W, Keichenspurner H, Wolner E. Blood platelets and cardiopulmonary bypass operations: recovery occurs after initial stimulation rather than continual activation. J Thorac Cardiovasc Surg 1989;97:379–388.

19. Dutton RC, Edmunds LH Jr. Measurement of emboli in extracorporeal perfusion systems. J Thorac Cardiovasc Surg 1973;63:523–530.

20. Blauth CI, Smith PL, Arnold JV, Jagoe JR, Wootton R, Taylor KM. Influence of oxygenator type on the prevalence and extent of microembolic retinal ischemia during cardiopulmonary bypass. J Thorac Cardiovasc Surg 1990;99:61–69.

21. Sheppeck RA, Bentz M, Dickson C, et al. Examination of the roles of glycoprotein Ib and glycoprotein IIb/IIIa in platelet deposition on an artificial surface using clinical antiplatelet agents and monoclonal antibody blockade. Blood 1991;78:673–680.

22. Gluszko P, Rucinski B, Musial J, et al. Fibrinogen receptors in platelet adhesion to surface of extracorporeal circuits. Am J Physiol 1987; 252:H615–H621.

23. George JN, Picket EB, Saucerman S, et al. Platelet surface glycoproteins: studies on resting and activated platelets and platelet microparticles in normal subjects and observations in patients during adult respiratory distress syndrome in cardiac surgery. J Clin Invest 1986;78:40–48.

24. Abrams CS, Ellison N, Budzynski AZ, Shattil SJ. Direct detection of activated platelets and platelet-derived microparticles in humans. Blood 1990;75:128–138.

25. Wenger RK, Lukasiewicz H, Mikuta BS, Niewarowski S, Edmunds LH Jr. Loss of platelet fibrinogen receptors during clinical cardiopulmonary bypass. J Thorac Cardiovasc Surg 1989; 97:235–239.

26. Wachtfogel YT, Musial J, Jenkin B, Niewarowski S, Edmunds LH Jr, Colman RW. Loss of platelet alpha-2 adrenergic receptors during simulated extracorporeal circulation; prevention with prostaglandin E1. J Lab Clin Med 1985;105: 601–607.

27. Edmunds LH Jr, Ellison N, Colman RW, et al. Platelet function during open heart surgery: comparison of membrane and bubble oxygenators. J Thorac Cardiovasc Surg 1982;83: 805–812.

28. Boonstra PW, Vermeulen FEE, Leusink JA, et al. Hematologic advantage of a membrane oxygenator over a bubble oxygenator in long perfusions. Ann Thorac Surg 1986;41:297–300.

29. Rinder CS, Bohnert J, Rinder HM, Mitchell J, Ault K, Hillman R. Platelet activation and aggregation during cardiopulmonary bypass. Anesthesiology 1991;75:388–393.

30. Addonizio VP Jr, Chang LK, Strauss JR III, Colman RW, Edmunds LH Jr. Release of lysosomal hydrolases during extracorporeal circulation. J Thorac Cardiovasc Surg 1982;84: 28–34.

31. Davies GC, Salzman EW, Sobel M. Elevated fibrinopeptide A and thromboxane A_2 levels during cardiopulmonary bypass. Circulation 1980;61:808–814.

32. Salzman EW, Landon J, Brier D. Surface-induced platelet adhesion, aggregation and release. In: Vroman L, Leonard E, eds. The behavior of blood and its components in interfaces. New York: Academy of Sciences, 1977:114–127.

33. Addonizio VP Jr, Macarak EJ, Niewarowski S, Colman RW, Edmunds LH Jr. Preservation of human platelets with prostaglandin E_1 during in vitro cardiopulmonary bypass. Circ Res 1979;44:350–357.

34. Laufer N, Merin G, Grover NB, Pessachowicz C, Borman JB. The influence of cardiopulmonary bypass on the size of human platelets. J Thorac Cardiovasc Surg 1975;70:727–731.

35. Addonizio VP Jr, Strauss JF III, Colman RW, Edmunds LH Jr.: Effects of prostaglandin E_1 on platelet loss during in-vivo and in-vitro extracorporeal circulation with a bubble oxygenator. J Thorac Cardiovasc Surg 1979;77: 119–126.

36. Harker LA, Malpass TW, Branson HE, Hessel EA II, Slichter SJ: Mechanism of abnormal bleeding in patients undergoing cardiopulmonary bypass: acquired transient platelet dysfunction associated with selective alpha granule release. Blood 1980;56:824–834.

37. Mammen EF, Koets MN, Washington BC, et al. Hemostasis changes during cardiopulmonary bypass surgery. Semin Thromb Hemost 1985; 11:281–292.

38. Addonizio VP Jr, Smith JB, Strauss JF III, Colman RW, Edmunds LH Jr. Thromboxane synthesis in platelet secretion during cardiopulmonary bypass with bubble oxygenator. J Thorac Cardiovasc Surg 1980;79:91–96.

39. Edmunds LH Jr, Saxena NC, Hillyer P, Wilson TJ. Relationship between platelet count and cardiotomy suction return. Ann Thorac Surg 1978;25:306–310.

40. Edmunds LH Jr, Williams W. Microemboli in the use of filters during cardiopulmonary bypass. In: Utley JR, ed. Pathophysiology and techniques in cardiopulmonary bypass. Vol 2. Baltimore: Williams & Wilkins, 1983:101–114.

41. Padayachee TS, Parsons S, Theobold R, Gosling RG, Deverall PB. The effect of arterial filtration on reduction of gaseous microemboli in the middle cerebral artery during cardiopulmonary bypass. Ann Thorac Surg 1988;45: 647–649.

42. Boldt J, Kling D, Zickmann B, Jacobi M, Dapper F, Hempelmann G: Acute preoperative plasmapheresis and established blood conservation techniques. Ann Thorac Surg 1990;50:62–68.

43. Boldt J, Zickmann B, Czeke A, Herold C, Dapper F, Hempelmann G: Blood conservation techniques and platelet function in cardiac surgery. Anesthesiology 1991;75:426–432.

44. Puri RN, Zhou F, Hu C-J, Colman RF, Colman RW. High molecular weight kininogen inhibits thrombin-induced platelet aggregation and cleavage of aggregin by inhibiting binding of thrombin to platelets. Blood 1991;77: 500–507.

45. Valeri R, Feingold H, Cassidy G, Ragano G, Khuri S, Altschule MD. Hypothermia-induced reversible platelet dysfunction. Ann Surg 1987; 205:175–181.

46. Ellison N, Edmunds LH Jr, Colman RW. Platelet aggregation following heparin and protamine administration. Anesthesiology 1978; 48:65–68.

47. Heyns A duP: Kinetics and in-vivo redistribution of 111 indium-labeled human platelets after intravenous protamine sulphate. Thromb Hemost 1980;44:65–68.

48. Kirklin JK, Chenoweth DE, Naftel DC, et al. Effects of protamine administration after cardiopulmonary bypass on complement, blood elements, and the hemodynamic state. Ann Thorac Surg 1986;41:193–199.

49. Lindblad B, Wakefield TW, Whitehouse WM Jr, Stanley JC: The effect of protamine sulfate on platelet function. Scand J Thorac Cardiovasc Surg 1988;22:55–59.

50. Best N, Sinosich NJ, Teisner B, et al: Complement activation during cardiopulmonary bypass by heparin-protamine interaction. Br J Anaesth 1984;56:339–343.

51. Lowenstein E, Lynch K, Robinson DR, Fitzgibbon CM, Zapol W. Incidence, severity and causation of adverse cardiopulmonary response to protamine reversal of heparin anticoagulation in man. Am Rev Respir Dis 1988;137(suppl):245.

52. Kim YL, Richman KA, Marshall BE. Thrombocytopenia associated with Swan-Ganz catheterization in patients. Anesthesiology 1980;53: 261–262.

53. Ferrer-Lopez P, Renesto P, Schattner M, Bassot S, Laurent P, Chignard M. Activation of human platelets by C5a-stimulated neutrophils: a role for cathepsin. Am J Physiol 1990;258: C1100-C1107.

54. Lu BH, Soria C, Cramer EM, et al. Temperature dependence of plasmin-induced activation or inhibition of human platelets. Blood 1991;77: 996–1005.

55. Stibbe J, Kluft C, Brommer EJP, Gomes M, de Jong DS, Nauta J. Enhanced fibrinolytic activity during cardiopulmonary bypass in open-heart surgery in man is caused by extrinsic (tissue-

type) plasminogen activator. Eur J Clin Invest 1984;14:375–382.

56. Bick RL: The clinical significance of fibrinogen degradation products. Semin Thromb 1982;8: 302–330.

57. Kopec M, Wegrzynowicz Z, Budzynski AZ, Latallo ZS, Lipinski B, Kowalski E: Interaction of fibrinogen degradation products (FDP) with platelets. Exp Biol Med 1968;3:73.

58. Kowalski E: Fibrinogen derivatives and their biological activities. Semin Hematol 1968; 5:45–59.

59. Zucker MB, Vroman L. Platelet adhesion induced by fibrinogen adsorbed onto glass. Proc Soc Exp Biol Med 1969;131:318–320.

60. Salzman EW, Merrill EW, Binder A, Wolf CFW, Ashford TP, Austen WG. Protein-platelet interaction on heparinized surfaces. J Biomed Mat Res 1969;3:69–81.

61. Vroman L, Adams AL, Fischer GC, Munoz PC. Interaction of high molecular weight kininogen, factor XII and fibrinogen in plasma at interfaces. Blood 1980;55:156–162.

62. Addonizio VP Jr, Macarak EJ, Nicolaou KC, Edmunds LH Jr, Colman RW. Effects of prostacyclin and albumin on platelet loss during in vitro simulation of extracorporeal circulation. Blood 1979;53:1033–1042.

63. Cottrell ED, Kappa JR, Stenach N, Fisher CAS, Tuszynski GP, Switalska HI, Addonizio VP. Temporary inhibition of platelet function with iloprost (ZK 36374) preserves canine platelets during extracorporeal membrane oxygenation. J Thorac Cardiovasc Surg 1988;96:535–541.

64. Shigeta O, Gluszko P, Downing SW, Lu W, Niewiarowski S, Edmunds LH Jr. Protection of platelets during long-term extracorporeal membrane oxygenation in sheep with a single dose of a disintegrin. Circulation 1992;86 (suppl II):398–404.

65. Fitzgerald GA. Dipyridamole. N Engl J Med 1987;316:1247–1258.

66. Pedersen AK, Fitzgerald GA. The human pharmacology of platelet inhibition: pharmacokinetics relevant to drug action. Circulation 1985;72:1164–1176.

67. Teoh KH, Christakis GT, Weisel RD, et al. Dipyridamole preserved platelets and reduced blood loss after cardiopulmonary bypass. J Thorac Cardiovasc Surg 1988;96:332–341.

68. Addonizio VP Jr, Strauss J III, Macarak EJ, Colman RW, Edmunds LH Jr. Preservation of platelet number and function with prostaglandin E_1 during total cardiopulmonary bypass in rhesus monkeys. Surgery 1978;83: 619–625.

69. Radegran K, Aren C, Teger-Nilsson A-C. Prostacyclin infusion during extracorporeal circula-

70. Malpass TW, Amory DW, Harker LA, Ivey PD, Williams DB. The effects of prostacyclin infusion on platelet hemostatic function in patients undergoing cardiopulmonary bypass. J Thorac Cardiovasc Surg 1984;87:550–555.

71. Kappa JR, Fisher CA, Bell P, Campbell FW, Ellison N, Addonizio VP. Intraoperative management of patients with heparin-induced thrombocytopenia. Ann Thorac Surg 1990; 49:713–723.

72. Bidstrup BP, Royston D, Sapsford RN, Taylor KM. Reduction in blood loss and blood use after cardiopulmonary bypass with high-dose aprotinin (Trasylol). J Thorac Cardiovasc Surg 1989;97:364–372.

73. Blauhaut B, Gross C, Necek S, Doran JE, Spaeth P, Lundsgaard-Hansen P. Effects of high-dose aprotinin on blood loss, platelet function, fibrinolysis, complement and renal function after cardiopulmonary bypass. J Thorac Cardiovasc Surg 1991;101:958–967.

74. Edmunds LH Jr, Niewiarowski S, Colman RW. Aprotinin [Invited Letter]. J Thorac Cardiovasc Surg 1991;101:1103–1104.

75. Hardesty RL, Bayer WL, Bahson HT. A technique for the use of autologous fresh blood during open heart surgery. J Thorac Cardiovasc Surg 1968;56:683–688.

76. Wagstaffe JG, Clarke AD, Jackson PW. Reduction of blood loss by restoration of platelet levels using fresh autologous blood after cardiopulmonary bypass. Thorax 1972;27:410–414.

77. Ochsner JL, Mills ML, Leonard GL, Lawson N. Fresh autologous blood transfusions with excorporeal circulation. Ann Surg 1973; 177:811–817.

78. Lawson NW, Ochsner JL, Mills NL, Leonard GL. The use of hemodilution and fresh autologous blood in open-heart surgery. Anesth Analg 1974;53:672–683.

79. Kaplan JA, Cannarella C, Jones EL, Kutner MH, Hatcher CR Jr, Dunbar RW. Autologous blood transfusion during cardiac surgery. A reevaluation of three methods. J Thorac Cardiovasc Surg 1977;74:4–10.

80. Lilleaasen P, Froysaker T. Fresh autologous blood in open-heart surgery. Influence on blood requirements, bleeding and platelet counts. Scand J Thorac Cardiovasc Surg 1979; 13:41–46.

81. Dale J, Lilleaasen P, Erikssen J. Hemostasis after open-heart surgery with extreme or moderate hemodilution. Eur Surg Res 1987;19:339–347.

82. Weisel RD, Charlesworth DC, Mickleborough LL, et al. Limitations of blood conservation. J Thorac Cardiovasc Surg 1984;88:26–38.

83. Sherman MM, Dobnik DB, Dennis RC, Berger RL. Autologous blood transfusion during cardiopulmonary bypass. Chest 1976;70:592–595.

84. Hallowell P, Bland JHL, Buckley MJ, Lowenstein E. Transfusion of fresh autologous blood in open-heart surgery. A method for reducing bank blood requirements. J Thorac Cardiovasc Surg 1972;64:941–948.

85. Cohn LH, Fosberg AM, Anderson WP, Collins JJ Jr. The effects of phlebotomy, hemodilution and autologous transfusion on systemic oxygenation and whole blood utilization in open heart surgery. Chest 1975;68:283–287.

86. Newland PE, Pastoriza-Pinol J, McMillan J, Smith BF, Stirling GR. Maximal conservation and minimal usage of blood products in open-heart surgery. J Anaesth Intens Care 1980;8:178–181.

87. Dietrich W, Barankay A, Dilthey G, Mitto HP, Richter JA. Reduction of blood utilization during myocardial revascularization. J Thorac Cardiovasc Surg 1989;97:213–219.

88. Harke H, Tanger D, Furst-Denzer S, Papachrysanthou C, Bernhard A. Einfluß and Rückwirkungen einer präoperativen Thrombocytenseparation und Aggregatbildung und Blutverlust nach Eingriffen mit extracorporaler Circulation. Anaesthetist 1977;26:64–71.

89. Giordano GF, Giordano GF, Rivers SL et al. Determinants of homologous blood usage utilizing autologous platelet-rich plasma in cardiac operation. Ann Thorac Surg 1989;47:897–902.

90. Del Rossi AJ, Cernaianu AC, Vertrees RA, et al. Platelet-rich plasma reduces postoperative blood loss after cardiopulmonary bypass. J Thorac Cardiovasc Surg 1990;100:281–286.

91. Boldt J, von Bormann B, Kling D, Jacobi M, Moosdorf JR, Hempelmann G. Preoperative plasmapheresis in patient undergoing cardiac surgery procedures. Anaesthesiology 1990;72:282–288.

92. Jones JW, McCoy TA, Rawitscher RE, Lindsley DA. Effects of intraoperative plasmapheresis on blood loss in cardiac surgery. Ann Thorac Surg 1990;49:585–590.

93. George JN, Shattil SJ. The clinical importance of acquired abnormalities of platelet function. N Engl J Med 1991;324:27–39.

94. White GC II, Marder VJ, Colman RW, Hirsh J, Salzman EW. Approach to the bleeding patient. In: Colman RW, Hirsh J, Marder VJ, Salzman EW, eds. Hemostasis and thrombosis. Basic principles and clinical practice. 2nd ed. Philadelphia: J.B. Lippincott, 1987, 1048–1060.

95. Harker LA, Slichter SJ. The bleeding time as a screening test for evaluation of platelet function. N Engl J Med 1972;287:155–159.

96. Mohr R, Golan M, Martinowitz U, Rosner E, Goor DA, Ramot B. Effect of cardiac operation on platelets. J Thorac Cardiovasc Surg 1986;92:434–441.

97. Mohr R, Martinowitz U, Golan M, Ayala L, Goor DA, Ramot B. Platelet size and mass as an indicator for platelet transfusion after cardiopulmonary bypass. Circulation 1986;74(suppl) III 153-III 158.

98. Mielke CH. Measurement of the bleeding time. Thromb Haemost (Stuttgart) 1984;52:210–211.

99. Rodgers RPC, Levin JA. Critical reappraisal of the bleeding time. Semin Thromb Hemost 1990;16:1–20.

100. Gluszko PR, Maring JK, Edmunds LH Jr. Bleeding time test [Invited Letter]. J Thorac Cardiovasc Surg 1991;101:173–174.

101. Burns ER, Billett HH, Frater RWM, Sisto DA. The preoperative bleeding time as a predictor of postoperative hemorrhage after cardiopulmonary bypass. J Thorac Cardiovasc Surg 1986;92:310–312.

102. Andersson SLG, Solem JO, Tengborn L, Vinge E. Effects of desmopressin acetate on platelet aggregation, von Willebrand and blood loss after cardiac surgery with extracorporeal circulation. Circulation 1990;81:872–878.

103. Salzman EW, Weinstein MJ, Weintraub RM, et al. Treatment with desmopressin acetate to reduce blood loss after cardiac surgery. A double-blind randomized trial. N Engl J Med 1986;314:1402–1406.

104. Spiess BD, Tuman KJ, McCarthy RJ, DeLaria GA, Schillo R, Ivankovich AD. Thromboelastography as an indicator of post-cardiopulmonary bypass coagulopathies. J Cl Monitoring 1987;3:25–30.

105. Tuman KJ, Spiess BD, McCarthy RJ, Ivankovich AD. Comparison of viscoelastic measures of coagulation after cardiopulmonary bypass. Anesth Analg 1989;69:69–75.

106. Wang JS, Lin CY, Hung WT, O'Connor MF, Thisted RA, Lee BK, et al. Thromboelastogram fails to predict postoperative hemorrhage in cardiac patients. Ann Thorac Surg 1992;53:435–439.

107. Kovacs IB, Hutton RA, Kernoff PBA. Hemostatic evaluation in bleeding disorders from native blood. Clinical experience with the hemostatometer. Am J Clin Pathol 1989;91:271–279.

108. Ratnatunga CP, Rees GM, Kovacs IB. Preoperative hemostatic activity and excessive bleeding after cardiopulmonary bypass. Ann Thorac Surg 1991;52:250–257.

109. Hines R, Barash PG. Infusion of sodium nitroprusside induces platelet dysfunction invitro. Anesthesiology 1989;70:611–615.

110. Diodati J, Theroux P, Latoru JG, et al. Effects of

nitroglycerin at therapeutic doses on platelet aggregation in unstable angina pectoris and acute myocardial infarction. Am J Cardiol 1990;66:683–688.

111. Harding SA, Skakoor MA, Grindon AJ. Platelet support for cardiopulmonary bypass surgery. J Thorac Cardiovasc Surg 1979;70:350–353.

112. Simon TL, Akl BF, Murphy W. Controlled trial of routine administration of platelet concentrates in cardiopulmonary bypass surgery. Ann Thorac Surg 1984;37:359–364.

113. George JN. Platelet membrane glycoproteins: alteration during storage of human platelet concentrates. Thromb Res 1976;8:716.

114. Slichter SJ. In vitro measurements of platelet concentrates stored at 4 and 22°C: correlation with post-transfusion platelet viability and function. Vox Sang 1981;40(suppl I):72–86.

115. Bode AP. Platelet activation may explain the storage lesion in platelet concentrates. Blood Cells 1990;16:109–126.

116. Gulliksson H, Shanwell A, Wikman A, Reppucci AJ, Sallander S, Uden AM. Storage of platelets in a new plastic container. Vox Sang 1991;61:165–170.

117. Slichter SJ. Platelet transfusion therapy. Hematol Oncol Clin North Am 1990;4:291–311.

118. Slichter SJ, Harker LA. Preparation and storage of platelet concentrates. II storage variables influencing platelet viability and function. Br J Hematol 1976;34:403–419.

119. Filip DJ, Aster RH: Relative hemostatic effec-

tiveness of human platelets stored at 4° and 22°. J Lab Clin Med 1978;91:618–624.

120. Hutchinson RE, Kunkel AD, Schell MJ, et al. Beneficial effect of brief pre-transfusion incubation of platelets at 37° C. Lancet 1989;1:986–988.

121. Hussein MA, Schiffer CA, Lee EJ. Incubation of platelet concentrates before transfusion does not improve post transfusion recovery. Transfusion 1990;30:701–703.

122. Lavee J, Martinowitz U, Mohr R, et al. The effect of transfusion of fresh whole blood versus platelet concentrates after cardiac operations. A scanning electron microscope study of platelet aggregation on extracellular matrix. J Thorac Cardiovasc Surg 1989;97:204–212.

123. Mohr R, Martinowitz U, Lavee J, Amroch D, Ramot B, Goor DA. The hemostatic effect of transfusing fresh whole blood versus platelet concentrates after cardiac operations. J Thorac Cardiovasc Surg 1988;96:530–534.

124. Golan M, Modan M, Lavee J, et al. Transfusion of fresh whole blood stored (4°C) for short period fails to improves platelet aggregation on extracellular matrix and clinical hemostasis after cardiopulmonary bypass. J Thorac Cardiovasc Surg 1990;99:354–360.

125. Manno CS, Hedberg KW, Kim HC, et al. Comparison of the hemostatic effects of fresh whole blood, stored whole blood, and components after open-heart surgery in children. Blood 1991;77:930–936.

17

MANAGEMENT OF COAGULOPATHY ASSOCIATED WITH CARDIOPULMONARY BYPASS

Jan C. Horrow

COMPONENTS OF HEMOSTASIS

Blood must remain fluid in the vessels, but congeal upon vascular disruption to prevent exsanguination. Hemostasis requires participation of platelets, coagulation proteins, and the vascular endothelium. Vessel patency depends on both hemostasis and fibrinolysis, which governs clot remodeling and breakdown. Chapter 16 dealt with aspects of platelet physiology and dysfunction and the interaction with vascular endothelium. The impact of cardiopulmonary bypass (CPB) on coagulation proteins and fibrinolysis as well as the management of bleeding associated with bypass will be covered in this chapter.

Definition of a few terms fosters an appreciation and understanding of the complexity of hemostasis. *Coagulation* refers to the formation of a clot in vitro, as occurs in the performance of routine laboratory tests. *Thrombosis* refers to formation of clot in vivo, as occurs pathologically in veins of the lower extremity or pelvis following some operations. *Hemostasis* refers to cessation of bleeding following injury (1). Thus the ideal anticoagulant is also antithrombotic, but not antihemostatic. While all components of hemostasis are essential, and the platelet response occurs first, the most fundamental part is the formation of fibrin.

FIBRIN FORMATION

The Clotting Factors and Their Activation

The liver synthesizes a series of inactive glycoproteins that circulate in the blood and lead to the production of fibrin. Activation of one of these clotting factors sequentially activates another in a series of reactions, ultimately yielding cross-linked fibrin. Fibrin formation in cellular material produces clot; when red cells and platelets are absent, it is termed gel. The sequentially activating glycoproteins earn the name "serine proteases" because their active sites, serine amino acid residues, result in cleavage of the next protein in sequence. Thus in inactive ("zymogen") form these substances serve as substrate in one reaction, and in active form as enzyme in the next reaction in sequence (2). The endothelial system, not the liver, synthesizes factor VIII. Table 17.1 summarizes important information about the clotting factors.

Roman numerals I through XIII identify the clotting factors, with an appended "a" denoting the activated form. The activa-

Table 17.1. The Clotting Factors[a]

Factor	Activated By	Acts On	Surgical Level (min)	Replacement Source	Half-life	Vitamin K Dependent?	Natural Source	Comments
I	IIa		1 g•liter^{-1}	CRYO, FFP	3–6 days	No	Liver	
II	Xa	I	20–40%	FFP, 9C	3 days	Yes	Liver	
III		X				No	Tissue	Thromboplastin
IV								Calcium ion
V	IIa	II	< 25%	FFP	12 hours	No	Liver	A cofactor
VII	Xa	X	10–20%	FFP, 9C	3 hours	Yes	Liver	
VIII	IIa	X	> 30%	CRYO, 8C, FFP	8–12 hours	No	RES	A cofactor
IX	VIIa or XIa	X	25–30%	FFP, 9C	12–14 hours	Yes	Liver	
X	VIIa or IXa	II	10–20%	FFP, 9C	30–50 hours	Yes	Liver	
XI	XIIa	IX	15–25%	FFP	48–77 hours	No	Liver	
XII	Endothelium	XI	None	Not needed	48–52 hours	No	Liver	
XIII	IIa	Fibrin	< 5%	FFP, CRYO	3–12 days	No	Liver	
vWF		VIII	see VIII	CRYO, FFP		No	Endothelium	
ProtC	IIa	Va; VIIIa			3 hours	Yes	Liver	

[a]CRYO, cryoprecipitate; FFP, fresh-frozen plasma; 9C, factor IX complex concentrate; 8C, factor VIII concentrate; RES, reticuloendothelial system; min, minimum. Note there is no factor VI. For von Willebrand factor, cryoprecipitate or FFP is administered to obtain a factor VIII coagulant activity >30%.

tion sequences do not follow numerical order, for several reasons. First, discovery of the clotting factors, which governed the numerical assignments, did not proceed in order of their activation; second, the factors interact among themselves in complex ways, rendering a strict order difficult; and third, new knowledge changes the clotting factor identities and revises their relationships. As examples, factor IV was subsequently identified as calcium ion, and is now referred to as such, while a postulated factor VI was subsequently discovered not to exist. This text will refer to the factors by their Roman numerals. However, factor I will be identified as fibrinogen, factor II as prothrombin, factor IIa as thrombin, and factor III as tissue thromboplastin, except where numerical notation is expedient.

Figure 17.1 displays a simplified version of the activation sequence of the clotting factors. Factor X occupies a central position in this scheme. Events preceding formation of factor Xa are termed either "intrinsic" or "extrinsic" based on whether the initiating stimulus arises from within or outside of the vasculature. Events subsequent to factor Xa form a "common pathway" leading to fibrin generation. Each of

these components will be considered in turn.

Intrinsic events Exposure of a negatively charged collagen matrix occurs upon disruption of the endothelial cell surface of the vasculature. Circulating factor XII binds to this matrix resulting in its activation. Factor XI also binds with assistance from high molecular weight kininogen (HMWK). On this surface, factor XIIa then cleaves a peptide fragment from factor XI to form factor XIa. In similar fashion, HMWK binds prekallikrein to the surface so that factor XIIa may split it to form kallikrein. Kallikrein accelerates the process by enhancing prekallikrein cleavage by factor XIIa. Factor XIa, however, inactivates HMWK, thus limiting this process. The term "surface activation" describes these reactions, all of which form a subset of the intrinsic events (2). Factor XIa then splits factor IX to form factor IXa. Calcium ion must be present for this process.

Factor IXa then cleaves factor X to form factor Xa. Splitting of factor X by factor IXa, a complex process, requires a phospholipid surface, calcium ion, and an accelerating cofactor, factor VIIIa. The phospholipid surface, contributed by plate-

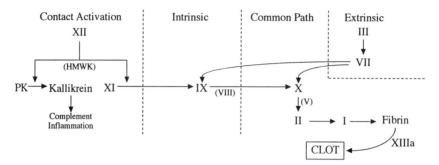

Figure 17.1. Simplified schematic of the sequence of coagulation protein activation. The *HMWK* fosters binding of *PK* (prekallikrein) and factor XI to an activating surface. Parentheses indicate cofactors.

lets and sometimes termed platelet factor 3, facilitates the molecular interactions. Calcium ions tether the substrates in this reaction to the phospholipid surface. Placement of carboxyl groups on glutamic acid residues of the substrate factors by vitamin K supplies negative charges by which the positively charged calcium ions link the factors to the phospholipid surface. Factors II, VII, IX, and X depend on vitamin K to insert these negative charges, without which factor activation does not proceed (3).

With calcium and phospholipid, factor IXa will cleave factor X slowly. In the presence of the accelerating cofactor, factor VIIIa, factor X activation proceeds rapidly. Figure 17.2 depicts this final intrinsic event leading to formation of factor Xa. The entity formed by these interacting molecules is termed the tenase ("ten-ase") complex.

Extrinsic events Tissue thromboplastin (factor III) consists of a peptide chain bound to phospholipid. When released into the vasculature from tissue damage, thromboplastin facilitates initial activation of factor X by factor VII. In a double positive feedback arrangement (Fig. 17.3), factor Xa then cleaves small amounts of factor VII to form factor VIIa. Thus activated, factor VIIa rapidly splits factor X, utilizing the phospholipid surface of thromboplastin and calcium ions (4). In a link that may be the predominant extrinsic mechanism for factor Xa formation, factor VIIa also interacts with factor IXa in the intrinsic path (2).

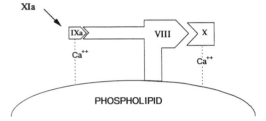

Figure 17.2. The role of factor VIII in activation of factor X. Calcium tethers factors IXa and X to the phospholipid surface (usually the platelet membrane). While factor IXa alone can activate factor X, factor VIII greatly facilitates this process. (From Horrow JC. Desmopressin and antifibrinolytics. In: Gravlee GP, ed. Blood conservation. Int Anesth Clin 1990;28: 216–222.)

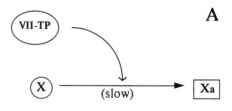

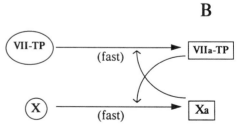

Figure 17.3. **A** depicts the initial extrinsic-mediated activation of factor X. Then a double-positive feedback loop (**B**) activates factors X and VII.

Common pathway Factor Xa splits prothrombin (factor IIa) to form thrombin (factor II), requiring a phospholipid surface and calcium ion. In analogous fashion to the role of factor VIII, a cofactor, factor Va, accelerates this "prothrombinase complex" reaction. Thrombin splits fibrinogen to form fibrin monomer.

Modulators of Coagulation

Thrombin Thrombin impacts upon every aspect of hemostasis. Its procoagulant activities include splitting fibrinogen to fibrin, activation of factors V and VIII to accelerate fibrin formation, activation of factor XIII, which cross-links soluble fibrin, and stimulation of platelet recruitment. Actions limiting clot formation include release from endothelial cells of tissue plasminogen activator (t-PA), which activates plasmin, and activation of protein C, which inactivates factors Va and VIIIa (2).

Feedback Both positive and negative feedback modulation exert a powerful influence on coagulation protein activation sequences. Positive feedback amplifies a minor molecular event to create a dramatic result. For example, the weak formation of factor Xa by factor VII and tissue thromboplastin becomes amplified by activation of factor VII by factor Xa, which then strongly activates factor X. This positive feedback permits circulating factor VII to remain harmless until tissue thromboplastin enters the vasculature. Another example is potentiation of prekallikrein cleavage by its end product, kallikrein. Negative feedback mechanisms prevent runaway coagulation factor consumption, as exemplified by factor XIa inactivation of HMWK. Note that thrombin exhibits both positive feedback (activation of factors V and VIII) and negative feedback (protein C activation) activity.

Protein C Endothelial cells release thrombomodulin, a regulatory protein that accelerates thrombin activation of protein C. Protein C, labeled such because it was the third protein eluted in an ion exchange

chromatogram, functions as an anticoagulant by inactivating factor Va and factor VIIIa and by stimulating fibrinolysis. Like other coagulation proteins, it circulates as an inactive zymogen. Thrombin cleaves a polypeptide fragment of protein C, creating the active serine protease. A cofactor, protein S, accelerates inactivation of factors Va and VIIIa by protein C. Both protein C and protein S require vitamin K for incorporation of γ-carboxyglutamate, similar to factors II, VII, IX, and X. Deficiency of protein C, an autosomal dominant trait, results in fatal neonatal thrombosis or in recurrent venous thromboses and pulmonary embolism (5).

Antithrombin Serine protease inhibitors, or "serpins," also control fibrin formation. Antithrombin III, the most important serpin, inhibits thrombin, kallikrein, and factors XIIa, XIa, Xa, and IXa by binding to their active sites at a serine residue. Antithrombin III also inhibits plasmin, a mediator of fibrinolysis (5).

von Willebrand Factor von Willebrand factor (vWF) protects factor VIII from enzymatic degradation, thus prolonging its half-life. It also tethers the platelet membrane glycoprotein Ib to exposed subendothelial matrix, thus promoting platelet adhesion (6). A massive heterogeneous molecule, vWF consists of different numbers of linked glycosylated peptides. Some of these multimers are large enough to be imaged with electron microscopy. See Chapter 16 regarding von Willebrand disease.

Fibrinogen and Fibrin

Molecular Structure Figure 17.4 depicts the six polypeptide chains which form the fibrinogen molecule—two each of Aα, Bβ, and γ subunits. Disulfide bonds link them in antiparallel fashion. Fibrinogen's three-dimensional structure features a central globular domain with twisted coils extending in opposite directions terminating in hydrophilic regions. Nonhelical protease sensitive regions interrupt the coiled-coils

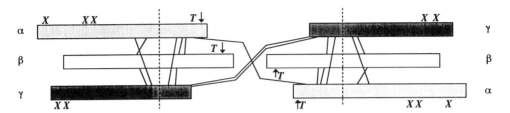

Figure 17.4. The fibrinogen molecule, composed of six polypeptide chains, one pair each of α, β, and γ. Thrombin cleaves the fibrinopeptides at sites indicated by an *arrow* and *T*. The *vertical dashed line* indicates where plasmin, formed from bound plasminogen by t-PA or other activators, cleaves the molecule. Factor XIII cross-links one fibrin molecule to another at sites designated with an *X*. *Solid lines* indicate placement of disulfide cross-linkages within the fibrinogen molecule. (Modified from Hantgan RR, Francis CW, Scherage HA, Marder VJ. Fibrinogen structure and physiology. In: Colman RW, Hirsch J, Marder VJ, Salzman EW, eds. Hemostasis and thrombosis. 2nd ed. Philadelphia: JB Lippincott, 1987:269–288.)

about midway in their length. The central "E" domain and peripheral hydrophilic "D" domains participate in fibrin polymerization (7).

Normal plasma fibrinogen concentration is 1.5 to 4.5 g/liter. An "acute phase reactant," fibrinogen increases in concentration during infection, inflammation, and stress. Thus a low normal fibrinogen concentration in a septic patient reflects fibrinogen consumption. Fibrinogen resists degradation during storage of banked whole blood, and is present in fresh-frozen plasma. Cryoprecipitate replaces fibrinogen best because each 10- to 15-ml unit contains about 20% of the fibrinogen present in one 200 to 250 ml unit of fresh-frozen plasma or one 400 to 450 ml unit of whole blood (8).

Formation and Polymerization of Fibrin   Thrombin cleaves peptide fragment A from the Aα subunit and fragment B from the Bβ subunit of fibrinogen to form fibrin. Fragment B contains the first 14 amino acid residues of the Bβ subunit. The peptide fragments, termed fibrinopeptides, serve as markers of thrombin activity. The resulting soluble fibrin monomers associate in end-to-end and staggered fashions. End-to-end linking occurs via long contact of D domains, while stacking of molecules arises from D-E staggered contacts. Figure 17.5 demonstrates formation of fibrin protofibrils via these associations. These weak mo-

lecular interactions alone do not produce an insoluble clot, however.

Factor XIII   In activated form, this coagulation factor cross-links associated fibrin monomers by covalent bonds between the α-chains and between the γ-chains. The only coagulation enzyme not a serine protease, factor XIIIa contains a cysteine active site which functions as a transamidase. Thrombin exposes the active cysteine sites of factor XIII. Calcium then separates the active enzyme, factor XIIIa, from a carrier protein moiety (9). The insoluble cross-linked fibrin so formed thickens the blood or plasma in which it is contained.

FIBRINOLYSIS

Physiologic fibrin breakdown occurs in the vicinity of clot, remodeling and dissolving clot during repair of the underlying endothelium. Pathologic fibrinolysis occurs when newly formed fibrin clots lyse prematurely, exposing damaged vessels and causing renewed bleeding. In similar fashion to fibrin formation, its breakdown proceeds by several paths. Figure 17.6 summarizes the fibrinolytic pathway.

Plasminogen and Plasmin

Lysis of fibrin depends upon activation of a cleaving enzyme, plasminogen. Hepatic synthesis results in circulating plas-

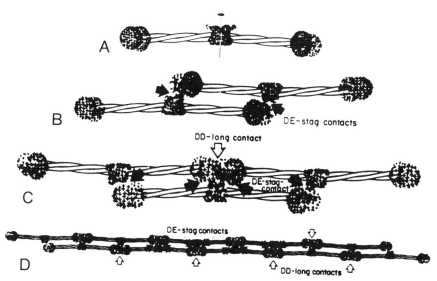

Figure 17.5. Sequence of fibrin polymerization. **A** displays the fibrin molecule as a central domain connecting with two peripheral domains via a coiled coil. In **B,** two fibrin monomers associate in staggered fashion (*DE contact*). In **C,** a third molecule joins end-to-end with the second molecule (*DD contact*) and in staggered fashion with the first molecule (*DE contact*). **D** depicts a protofibril fomed by addition of several more monomers. (From Hermans J, McDonagh J. Fibrin: structure and interactions. Semin Thromb Hemost 1982;8:11–24.)

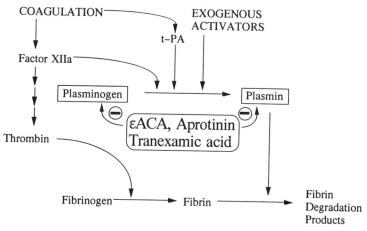

Figure 17.6. The fibrinolytic pathway. Coagulation results in formation of thrombin, which yields fibrin, and of t-PA and factor XIIa, which convert plasminogen to plasmin in the vicinity of clot. Plasmin splits fibrin. Antifibrinolytic drugs inhibit plasminogen and plasmin. Exogenous activators of fibrinolysis, such as streptokinase, may also convert plasminogen to plasmin. εACA aminocaproic acid.

minogen concentrations of 21 mg/dl in plasma or serum. The enzyme circulates as the inactive zymogen. Figure 17.7 demonstrates its molecular structure, which features five outpouchings termed "kringles," each of which contains a binding site for lysine residues of fibrinogen. Cleavage of an arginine-valine bond at residue 560 transforms the single-chain plasminogen to the two-chained plasmin molecule (10). Figure 17.4 denotes the sites at which plasminogen binds to fibrinogen. Conversion of fibrinogen to fibrin encrypts the bound plasminogen, where it awaits activation.

Figure 17.7. The structure of human plasminogen. The five outpouchings of this macromolecule are called "kringles," after a Scandanavian pastry of the same name. (From Collen D. On the regulation and control of fibrinolysis. Thromb Haemost 1980;43:77–89.)

Formation and Fate of Plasmin

Tissue plasminogen activator The physiologic activator of plasminogen is t-PA, a 527 residue serine protease synthesized in endothelial cells and released by exercise, stress, venous occlusion, and certain drugs including desmopressin and heparin. The activity of t-PA enhances 1000-fold in the presence of fibrin, essentially restricting its effect to the vicinity of clot and protecting circulating plasminogen from activation. Normally, small amounts of t-PA remodel and dissolve clots dynamically, resulting in a low level of fibrinolysis.

Factor XII The surface activation coagulation proteins (factor XII, prekallikrein, and HMWK) appear to initiate fibrinolysis by a path independent of t-PA. Conversion of prourokinase, another circulating fibrino-

lytic protein, to a potent plasminogen activator by kallikrein mediates this minor pathway, which accounts for less than half of plasma fibrinolytic activity (11).

Once plasmin is formed, it splits fibrin at parallel locations on all six peptide chains. Should plasmin reach the systemic circulation, it can also hydrolyze fibrinogen, factor V, factor VIII, complement, and some hormones. A scavenging protease, a_2-antiplasmin, binds and destroys any plasmin that circulates. Should a_2-antiplasmin be saturated, a_1-macroglobulin will perform the same function (11).

Thrombolytic Therapy

Plasminogen activators may be exogenously administered to dissolve pathologically formed intravascular clot (12). The first generation of these agents included streptokinase, an antigenic protein derived from group C β-hemolytic streptococci, and urokinase, a 411 residue nonantigenic proteolytic enzyme derived from purified human urine. Streptokinase forms a complex with plasminogen, which converts other remaining plasminogen molecules to plasmin. Activation occurs systemically without benefit of restriction to clot locations. Systemic effects combined with a long half-life (30 minutes) make bleeding complications common. Urokinase converts plasminogen to plasmin directly, but still without fibrin specificity. Its half-life in plasma is 16 minutes. Limited availability and high cost preclude its widespread clinical use.

The second generation of thrombolytic agents include anisoylated plasminogen-streptokinase activator (APSAC), single-chain urokinase plasminogen activator (scu-PA), and recombinant t-PA. The APSAC, a chemically modified streptokinase that retains antigenicity, produces a sustained lytic effect because of a prolonged half-life (≈3 hours), with fibrin specificity between that of t-PA and streptokinase. Recombinant scu-PA, like t-PA, exhibits fibrin specificity, nonreactivity in plasma, and a short half-life. It is still investigational. Recombinant t-PA enjoys wide clinical use for treatment of thrombosis. Large doses must be administered to deliver enough drug to the site of thrombosis, thus compromising fibrin specificity somewhat. Rapid elimination (3 to 5 minute half-life) and lack of antigenicity make this alternative attractive, despite its expense (1991 price, $2,200 per dose). The challenge of thrombolytic therapy is to achieve rapid clot lysis without bleeding and prevent rethrombosis with a safe and inexpensive preparation.

Products of Fibrinolysis

Breakdown of fibrin yields numerous products, best understood by first considering lysis of a fibrin monomer. The product formed after plasmin cleavage of the Aα appendage and the remaining part of the Bβ chain (residues 15 through 42) is termed fragment X. Further activity at sites midway along the coiled coils yields three kinds of products: a peripheral domain with attached polypeptide strand (fragment D), a central domain with polypeptide strands (fragment E), and the product of incomplete digestion (central domain with one peripheral domain intact, labelled fragment Y) (11). Figure 17.8 displays a two-stranded protofibril, formed after cross-linking by factor XIIIa, and its degradation products, which include a fragment containing two D domains, termed D-dimer. Tests for these various degradation products permit detection of a fibrinolytic state.

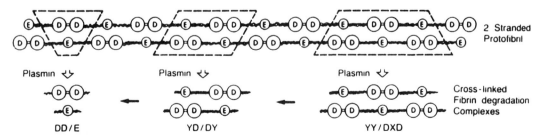

Figure 17.8. Formation of fibrin degradation products from cross-linked fibrin. Plasmin cleaves fibrin between its D and E domains at the dashed lines to yield D-dimer (*DD*), fragment Y (*DE*), fragment X (*DED*), and larger combinations (*DY, YY, DXD,* and others not shown). D-dimer serves as a specific marker for lysis of cross-linked fibrin. (From Francis CW, Marder VJ. Physiologic regulation and pathologic disorders of fibrinolysis. In: Colman RW, Hirsh J, Marder VJ, Salzman EW, eds. Hemostasis and Thrombosis. 2nd ed. Philadelphia: JB Lippincott, 1987;358–379.)

Fibrin degradation products intercalate into the forming fibrin protofibrils, preventing proper alignment of fibrin monomers for correct cross-linking by factor XIIIa. As a result, intense fibrinolysis impairs formation of subsequent clot.

Local versus Systemic Fibrinolysis

Lysis of circulating fibrinogen is not physiologic. Plasmin degradation of the fibrinogen molecule, i.e., prior to separation of the fibrinopeptides Aα (1–16) and Bβ (1–14), yields fragments X, Y, D, and E, the Aα appendage, and the Bβ (1–42) peptide fragment. This last product serves as a marker specific for fibrin*ogen*olysis. Fibrinogenolysis occurs with administration of nonselective plasminogen activators, or more rarely when release of plasminogen activator from tissues overwhelms the circulating plasmin scavengers.

Localized fibrinolysis occurring in response to intense bursts of coagulation may flood the circulation with fibrin degradation products, causing hemorrhage. In this case, fibrinogen remains intact and no plasmin circulates. In consumptive coagulopathy, formation and breakdown of fibrin in the microcirculation deplete coagulation factors and platelets and form fibrin degradation products, yielding hemorrhage.

LABORATORY TESTS OF COAGULATION

No laboratory coagulation test can duplicate the complex milieu present at an injured vessel. Merely placing a needle or catheter in a vessel initiates a host of hemostatic responses that alter measurements on the sample removed. Surface activation begins when blood leaves the protective environment of the endothelial cell and enters into collection tubes. For these reasons, one must view the results of any coagulation test as only an approximation of actual events. First this section presents the basis for the commonly used prothrombin time (PT) and

partial thromboplastin time (PTT) tests. Then tests will be presented according to temporal availability, with bedside tests considered first followed by readily available tests, then more specialized batched tests.

Common Tests: PT and PTT

The most widely utilized routine coagulation tests are the PT and PTT. Figure 17.9 illustrates the steps in performing these tests. Each test involves centrifuging a citrated specimen of blood. Citrate complexes calcium, preventing coagulation factor activation. The supernatant obtained by centrifugation, plasma, is incubated for 3 minutes with an additive that differs for the two tests. After addition of excess calcium, the time to formation of gel is clocked.

The PT, which would be labelled better as the complete thromboplastin time, incubates plasma with tissue extract

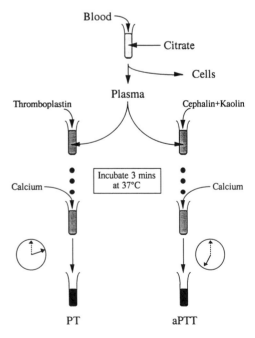

Figure 17.9. Steps in performing the prothrombin time (*PT*, left side) and the activated partial thromboplastin time (*aPTT*, right side). See text for details.

(thromboplastin). Recall that thromboplastin supplies its own phospholipid. If the plasma sample contains sufficient factor VII and factors in the common pathway, it will gel in about 12 seconds. Variations in the potency and quality of thromboplastin reagents require simultaneous determination of a control sample and comparison of the patient's result with the control result. Each batch of thromboplastin reagent is graded in potency. This grade permits calculation of the international normalized ratio, a comparison of PT results performed with one reagent with that of others. The international normalized ratio equals the ratio of the patient specimen's clotting time to control time raised to an exponent equal to the potency grade of the thromboplastin reagent. In the United States, ratios over 1.5 indicate a coagulation factor abnormality.

The PTT incubates plasma with an extract of thromboplastin that contains the phospholipid but not the tissue factor, thus preventing activation of factor VII. When dependent upon surface activation alone, gel forms slowly (73 ± 11 [SD] seconds) (13). The *activated* PTT (aPTT) utilizes a surface activation accelerator such as kaolin, ellagic acid, silica, bentonite, or celite (14). Gel formation then occurs in about 32 seconds. As with the PT, simultaneous controls are required, with abnormal patient results at 1.5 or more times control.

Coumadin therapy prolongs the PT without affecting the aPTT because factor VII is most vulnerable to lack of vitamin K. Large doses of coumadin will elevate the aPTT also. Heparin primarily affects the aPTT and not the PT because the inhibition of factors Xa and thrombin from doses of heparin commonly used to treat venous thrombosis is easily overwhelmed by the potent procoagulant action of thromboplastin. The less potent partial thromboplastin reagent, however, does not mask heparin's anticoagulant effects. Large doses of heparin will prolong the PT also.

Near-Patient Tests

Management of anticoagulation and bleeding during surgery demands that results be more rapidly obtainable than those from a centrally located hospital laboratory. Anesthesia care will benefit greatly from the current revolution in laboratory medicine based on "near-patient testing." Rapid coagulation tests on whole blood provide the clinician with immediately available insights into the complex differential diagnosis of operative hemorrhage.

The most widely known near-patient coagulation test, the activated coagulation time (ACT), has been addressed in Chapter 14. This section will not deal with the ACT or its predecessors, the whole blood clotting time and protamine titration (see Chapter 15 also). Likewise, the reader should refer to Chapter 16 regarding the bleeding time, a test of platelet function.

PT and aPTT Near-patient PT and aPTT tests employ whole blood rather than plasma. Even though platelets remain and provide phospholipid, a phospholipid reagent is added to ensure an excess. The Hemochron based tests (International Technidyne Corp., Edison, NJ) utilize citrated tubes and a true 3-minute incubation period in the Hemochron 37°C chamber, following which calcium is added and the sample timed until the magnetic detector becomes trapped in clot. For the Hemochron aPTT test, yellow-stoppered tubes containing citrate, phospholipid, and diatomaceous earth (which activates factor XII), receive 1.5 ml of blood to yield a normal range of 55 to 85 seconds. Figure 17.10 demonstrates heparin sensitivity of the ACT, bedside aPTT, and laboratory aPTT tests. Note that the whole blood aPTT lies intermediate in sensitivity between the laboratory aPTT and the ACT. For the Hemochron PT test, burgundy-stoppered tubes containing rabbit brain thromboplastin receive 2 ml of blood (normal 45 to 65 seconds). HemoTec, Inc. (Englewood, CO) also supplies cartridges for bedside determination

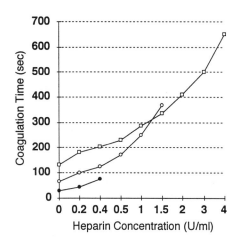

Figure 17.10. Response of three coagulation tests to heparin. Data are the mean of results from 30 volunteers. *Open squares,* Hemochron-activated coagulation time (ACT); *open circles,* Hemochron whole blood aPTT; *solid circles,* plasma aPTT. The plasma aPTT becomes unmeasurable with heparin concentrations >0.4 U/ml. Note that the whole blood aPTT is linear up to ≈1.0 U/ml, and the ACT linear up to ≈3 U/ml. Heparin concentrations are estimated from dose administered and estimated blood volume. (Data kindly supplied by F. LaDuca, PhD, and International Technidyne Corporation.)

of PT and aPTT using a stir-bar based monitor.

The Biotrack 512 coagulation monitor (Ciba-Corning Diagnostics, Medfield, MA) performs near-patient PT and aPTT tests. Cards containing reagents and a capillary tube path for blood receive one large drop of blood (about 0.1 ml). Blood moves by capillary action into a well where it picks up the reagents, then continues to move along the path. A laser detects tardy flow resulting from fibrin formation. The device then converts the actual time measured to one equivalent to that obtained from the hospital laboratory, and supplies the ratio of the patient's value to a historical control. The aPTT card utilizes soybean phosphatide as phospholipid and a sulfatide activator (15). The PT cards contain thromboplastin. Although a true 3-minute incubation does not occur with this device, the technology is extremely easy to use. In one comparison of devices in a diverse population of antico-

agulated and normal patients, the Hemochron aPTT, Biotrack coagulation monitor, and the HemoTec aPTT tests all correlated well with the laboratory-based standard (r values 0.849 to 0.963; $n = 50$) (16). All instruments proved adequate to test for reversal of heparin therapy. However, the Biotrack failed to reach an end-point for samples with reference aPTT >70 seconds and the HemoTec aPTT failed to reach an end-point in six samples.

The end-points for these near patient tests take slightly longer than in the traditional laboratory-based aPTT. Manual or automatic conversion to values obtained from the laboratory is easily accomplished. With the near-patient tests, each sample does not have a coincident control sample. Thus, periodic quality control assumes great importance to provide reproducible tests. Hospital credentials depend on adequate quality control of all patient tests. Thus, clinicians must assure routine quality control of near-patient tests they perform. Since near-patient testing technology undergoes rapid development, the reader should seek additional current information when implementing it in the operating room.

Thromboelastography This viscoelastic test on whole blood rotates a specimen in a cuvette through a small arc (9.5°) every 10 seconds. A central piston, positioned to provide a 1-mm rim of blood (0.35 ml) between it and the cuvette, remains immobile until fibrin strands couple it to the cuvette's rotatory motion. Torsion on the piston results in movement of a recording heat stylus across sensitive paper advancing at 2 mm/min. The width of the resultant tracing relates to the shear modulus (elasticity) of the specimen (17). Unfortunately, the test outcome is not calibrated in absolute units of shear modulus, but measured merely in mm of tracing width.

Figure 17.11 and Table 17.2 display the measurements obtained from the thromboelastogram (TEG) and their normal ranges. Appreciation of the overall shape of

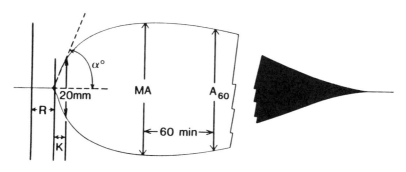

Figure 17.11. Idealized thromboelastogram, with commonly measured parameters. See text and Table 17.2 for definition and normal ranges of these measurements. (From Spiess BD, Tuman RJ, McCarthy RJ, DeLavia GA, Schillo R, Ivankovich AD. Thromboelastography as an indicator of post-cardiopulmonary bypass coagulopathies. J Clin Monit 1987;3:25–30.)

Table 17.2. Parameters Measured on the Thromboelastogram

Name	Definition	Normal Range[a]	Significance of Abnormal Values	References
R (reaction time)	Time from sample collection until pen deviation from midline	7.5–15 min	Hypercoagulability? Factor deficiency?	?
K (coagulation time)	Time from initial pen deviation from midline to amplitude of 20 mm	3 to 6 min	?	?
a (speed of clot formation)	Angle formed by midline and tangent of amplitude tracing upslope	45 to 55°	?	?
MA (maximum amplitude)	Maximum amplitude	50 to 60 mm	Hypofibrinogenemia, thrombocytopenia, platelet dysfunction	Howland et al. (21) Zuckerman et al. (22)
A_{60} (amplitude)	Tracing amplitude 60 minutes after MA	$\geq (MA - 5)$ mm	Fibrinolysis or uremia	Howland et al. (21) von Kaulla et al. (23)

[a]Normal values from Spiess et al. (20)

the TEG purportedly provides more information than these component measures. For example, a "tear-drop" shape caused by loss of clot strength may denote high fibrinolytic activity (18, 19). In fact, TEG tracings cannot diagnose specific hematologic abnormalities because they reflect a global physical property of clot formation. The TEG parameters correlate poorly with routine laboratory coagulation tests (20–23).

An abnormal TEG tracing does, however, suggest further investigation. While several investigators have shown that certain TEG parameters can predict bleeding after bypass, the information becomes available too late for appropriate clinical intervention (24, 25).

Sonoclot This viscoelastic test performed on whole blood utilizes a probe vibrating in a small sample (0.4 ml) of whole blood at 200 Hz. While the TEG displays clot shear modulus, the Sonoclot charts impedance to probe motion, which increases as coagulation events proceed. This outcome variable is also not calibrated in physical units, appearing instead in units of "percent." The curve obtained divides into several parts, termed "waves," based on the rate of increase of impedance with time (26). The manufacturer (Sienco, Inc., Morrison, CO) identifies a component analogous to the activated coagulation time ("SonAct"), as well as certain curve shapes reflecting platelet dysfunction, thrombocytopenia, and "hypercoagulability." No independent data verify these associations. In an unblinded study, the Sonoclot predicted that platelet transfusion would correct postbypass bleeding in 21 of 25 patients (27). Figure 17.12 displays Sonoclot signatures before and after aspirin administration to one of 22 volunteers. The Sonoclot failed to reflect the prolongation in bleeding time associated with aspirin (28). Hematopathologists accept neither the TEG nor the Sonoclot for diagnostic purposes, perhaps because of insufficient data linking test results with independently confirmed pathology.

Coagulation Laboratory Tests

Tests with results not always available within an hour comprise this section. Devices utilizing formation of a clot as an endpoint usually employ electrical or optical detection methods. The classic instrument, the Fibrometer (BBL Microbiological Systems, Cockeysville, MD), places a stationary and a moving probe in the sample. When fibrin strands bridge the two electrodes, conductivity increases and a timer halts (14). Laboratory PT and aPTT determinations employ this technology.

Thrombin time With the same equipment, thrombin added to a plasma sample will form fibrin within 10 seconds if (*a*) functionally active fibrinogen is present, (*b*) heparin is absent, and (*c*) fibrin degradation products are absent. Sensitivity of the thrombin time to small amounts of heparin occurs because small amounts of thrombin are added. The traditional thrombin time is relatively insensitive to fibrinogen deficiency and to fibrin degradation products: detectable prolongation requires <0.75 g/liter of fibrinogen (29) or >200 μg/ml of fibrin degradation products. Sensitivity to fibrin degradation prod-

Figure 17.12. A Sonoclot signature in a patient before (*dashed line*) and after (*solid line*) receiving four doses of 325 mg aspirin over 2 days. The initial flat portion (*SonAct*) is normally 60 to 130 seconds. R_1, R_2, and R_3 slopes of the curves, measure the rate of change in viscosity of the sample. The *TI* is the time to the first inflection point and *TP* the time to peak viscosity. Normally R_1 is 15 to 30% per minute, and TP 5 to 10 minutes. The vertical axis, called "percent," lacks calibration against a standard. (From Samra SK, Harrison RL, Bee DE, Valero V. A study of aspirin induced changes in bleeding time, platelet aggregation, and Sonoclot coagulation analysis in humans. Ann Clin Lab Sci 1991; 21:315–327.)

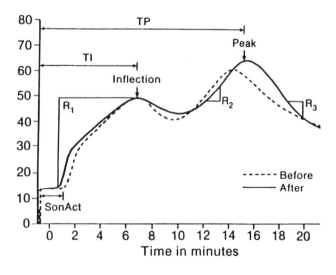

ucts improves if fibrinogen concentrations are low. Also, diluted plasma increases sensitivity of the thrombin test to fibrinogen deficiency. Hemochron supplies a near-patient thrombin time. It utilizes whole blood and pink-stoppered tubes containing lyophilized thrombin, requiring reconstitution with sterile water. Time to clot after addition of 1 ml blood is normally 39 to 53 seconds.

Reptilase time The reptilase time measures the interval between addition to plasma of venom from the South American pit viper *Bothrops jararaca* and formation of fibrin. Since this snake venom does not require thrombin to split fibrinogen, an elevated reptilase time implicates fibrinogen rather than heparin as the cause of a prolonged thrombin time (30). The reptilase time is several-fold more insensitive to fibrin degradation products than even the thrombin time. In another approach to differentiating between heparin presence and fibrinogen deficiency, heparin-containing blood added to tubes containing thrombin and protamine will produce a normal thrombin time compared to a parallel tube with thrombin alone. This "heparin-neutralized thrombin time" is available for near-patient use with the Hemochron system.

Fibrinogen Most laboratories employ the Claus method for fibrinogen determination, in which a thrombin time is performed on diluted plasma. With diluted samples, fibrinogen becomes the factor limiting clot formation, so that the clotting time varies inversely with fibrinogen activity (14). Antibody based tests for fibrinogen can distinguish among the dysfibrinogenemias.

Fibrin Degradation Products Immunologic tests provide a semiquantitative determination of the various fragments resulting from fibrin and fibrinogen degradation. The most commonly employed test (FDP) utilizes latex agglutination of serum. It provide results as either negative ($<10\,\mu g/ml$) or positive ($\geq 10\,\mu g/ml$) for antigens,

which are the breakdown products of either fibrin or fibrinogen. Serial dilutions of plasma yield more specific information when the undiluted sample is positive. More expensive quantitative analysis reveals normal serum levels of 2.1 to 2.7 $\mu g/ml$ for fibrin degradation products in the absence of exercise or stress (14). This test does not differentiate the breakdown products of fibrinogen from those of fibrin.

Sophisticated Hematology Tests

Research laboratories and a few clinical centers specializing in hemostasis and thrombosis offer a host of specialized coagulation tests. Chromogenic technology, in which a color-absorbing molecule is linked to a component of the reaction to be measured, permits quantitation of the *activity* of many hemostatic elements, such as antithrombin, t-PA, and heparin. Tests based on antibody technology include *quantitation* of fibrinopeptides A and B, the latter available for the fibrinogen split product Bβ (1–42) and for the fibrin split product Bβ 15–42; t-PA antigen; thrombin-antithrombin complex; plasmin-antiplasmin complex; and PAI-1 (pronounced "pie-one"), a naturally occurring inhibitor of plasminogen activator.

D-dimer Molecules of two linked "D" domains, a specific degradation product of cross-linked fibrin, can be detected either semiquantitatively with a latex agglutination technique (D-Di, Diagnostica Stago, Asniere-sur-Seine, France) or in a fully quantitative manner with an enzyme-linked immunosorbent assay. Many hospital coagulation laboratories offer the former method on a batched basis. The D-dimer is more specific for fibrinolysis than the FDP test. Like the FDP test, D-dimer results appear as fibrinogen equivalent units, i.e., the quantity of fibrinogen initially present that leads to the observed level of breakdown product. Normally, D-dimer is less than 0.5 $\mu g/ml$ (fibrinogen equivalent units).

BYPASS-INDUCED COAGULATION ABNORMALITIES

In the earlier days of CPB, the cellular and molecular elements of blood sustained significant mechanical trauma during perfusion, resulting in destruction of red cells and platelets, and denaturation of plasma proteins. Although the improved materials now used for bypass incite less damage, an intrinsically nonthrombogenic surface still evades discovery (31). Some heparin-coated surfaces do show promise (see Chapter 14). This section covers hemostatic abnormalities induced by bypass, except for platelet effects, which are covered in Chapter 16.

Coagulation Factors

With rare exception, normal levels for the coagulation factors range from 0.5 to 1.5 activity units/ml, corresponding to 50 to 150% of population means. (In contrast, the inhibitory proteins, such as antithrombin and protein C, adhere to a more restricted range.) When factor replacement is indicated for major surgery, the usual target, 1.0 units/ml, incorporates a threefold safety factor, since only levels below 0.3 units/ml impair the sequential enzyme activation ending with fibrin formation. The exception, factor V, retains sufficient activity at levels of 0.1 to 0.15 units/ml. Coagulation factor abnormalities induced by bypass include dilution, denaturation, deposition on extracorporeal surfaces, and hypothermia.

Dilution Hemodilution, a process now synonymous with CPB, reduces the concentrations of all coagulation factors. For adult surgery, factor levels rarely fall below 0.3 units/ml. Figure 17.13 displays the effect of bypass on factor concentrations. With neonates, even heroic efforts to reduce the priming volume of the extracorporeal circuit fail to prevent significant coagulation factor dilution.

Denaturation The air-blood interface modifies coagulation factors. Bubble oxygenators and cardiotomy suction each involve significant mechanical perturbation of blood elements. Their prolonged use

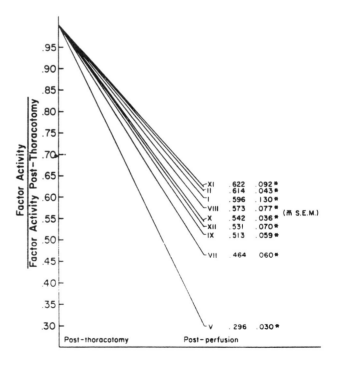

Figure 17.13. Decline in factor activity in 11 patients during bypass with a bubble oxygenator. Although factor V activity declines to only 30 ± 3% of normal, surgical hemostasis requires 15 to 25% at most. (From Kalter RD, Saul CM, Wetstein L, Soriano C, Reiss RF. Cardiopulmonary bypass. Associated hemostatic abnormalities. J Thorac Cardiovasc Surg 1979;77:427–435.)

may contribute to a coagulation factor defect (32, 33).

Deposition on extracorporeal surfaces Platelets and coagulation proteins, notably fibrinogen, deposit on the extracorporeal circuit surface. Blood proteins adsorb onto its solid surfaces (34, 35). Platelets then adhere to the adsorbed proteins.

Hypothermia In most centers, hypothermia contributes to organ preservation during bypass. Temperature-dependent enzymatic processes determine sequential activation of the coagulation factors. Since many enzymatic reactions attenuate 7% for each decrease of 1°C, fibrin formation may likewise be retarded (36). The prolongation of activated coagulation times with cold samples represents this phenomenon ex vivo (37). This anticoagulant effect of hypothermia, desirable during bypass, probably impacts on coagulation when inadequate rewarming produces postbypass core temperatures below 35°C.

Fibrinolysis

Cardiopulmonary bypass activates the fibrinolytic pathways. In the past, inadequate anticoagulation during bypass accounted for a high incidence and severity of fibrinolysis (38). With the advent of routine intraoperative coagulation testing by protamine titration or activated coagulation time, "inadequate" heparin levels (as currently defined) occur more rarely (39). Does bypass-induced fibrinolysis no longer occur, or have less impact on hemostasis?

Despite a therapeutic ACT and clinically acceptable heparin levels, thrombin formation and activity both continue during bypass, as demonstrated by relentless appearance of fibrinopeptides and thrombin-antithrombin complexes (Fig. 17.14; see also Fig. 14.11) (40–43). The foreign extracorporeal circuit provides a surface with adsorbed proteins upon which thrombin can act. Products of thrombin activity ex vivo may then be carried in vivo, where endothelium responds with release of t-PA.

dothelium responds with release of t-PA. Levels of t-PA increase during bypass, while those of its inhibitor, PAI-1, do not.

Usually, bypass-induced fibrinolysis does not achieve clinically significant proportions, with fibrin breakdown products clearing within an hour of bypass (44–46). An occasional patient, however, exhibits more marked fibrinolysis and its hemostatic consequences—renewed capillary bleeding from clot lysis and interference with polymerization of newly formed fibrin. The success of antifibrinolytic drugs in decreasing bleeding in patients undergoing cardiac surgery (see "Pharmacologic Measures") suggests that fibrinolytic mechanisms contribute to bypass-induced alterations in hemostasis.

Consumptive Coagulopathy

Disseminated intravascular coagulation, or consumptive coagulopathy, occurs rarely after CPB despite ongoing thrombin activity. This feared disorder involves activation of coagulation factors within the vasculature. Fibrin formation during bypass occurs outside the vasculature, i.e., in the extracorporeal circuit, and thus is not disseminated. Circulating a_2-antiplasmin readily scavenges plasmin that reenters the body. Thus, systemic fibrin*ogen*olysis does not occur unless heparin is seriously lacking (47). Of course, bypass does not protect patients from subsequent consumptive coagulopathy, which may occur should sepsis, shock, or a large retained clot occur (48).

TREATMENT OF COAGULOPATHY AFTER BYPASS

Identify the Cause

The diagnostic approach to hemostatic deficiency, like that of other disorders in medicine, benefits from a detailed consideration of the physiology of each component: vascular integrity, coagulation factors, platelets, and fibrinolysis.

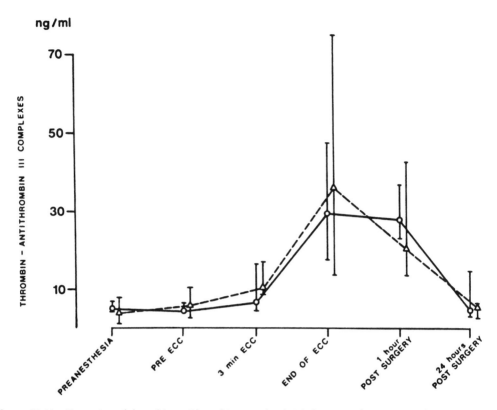

Figure 17.14. Formation of thrombin-antithrombin complex (TAT) during cardiac surgery. The TAT levels did not differ between a control group (*triangles*) and one receiving aprotinin (*circles*). Note the effect of cardiopulmonary bypass (*ECC*). (From Havel M, Teufelsbauer H, Knöbl P, et al. Effect of intraoperative aprotonin administration on postoperative bleeding in patients undergoing cardiopulmonary bypass operation. J Thorac Cardiovasc Surg 1991;101:968–972.)

Vascular integrity While properly functioning platelets and coagulation factors will successfully address capillary and small vessel trespass, more egregious vascular damage requires mechanical attention with suture or its equivalent. This "surgical" bleeding is strongly suggested by any sudden increase of 300 ml/hr or more following minimal initial chest tube drainage or by more than 10 ml/kg in the 1st hour or 20 ml/kg total over the first 3 hours after operation (49). For patients weighing less than 10 kg, more liberal criteria apply. Unfortunately, no noninvasive maneuver can indicate that sustained chest tube drainage occurs from an unattended mechanical vascular defect. Since only mediastinal exploration provides this information, one must be prepared for this intervention by providing proper depth of anesthesia, a secure airway for positive pressure ventilation, appropriate monitoring of systemic and venous pressures, continuation of any mechanical and inotropic support, and replacement of intravascular volume.

Coagulation Factors Bleeding from coagulation factor deficiency can arise from preexisting disease, excessive hemodilution, factor consumption, or unneutralized heparin. A postbypass PT or aPTT up to 1.5 times control is common. Values in excess should be treated with banked plasma products.

Platelets Both thrombocytopenia and platelet dysfunction occur after bypass. Chapter 16 presents a treatment plan for these hemostatic disorders. Maintenance of normothermia after operation contributes to proper platelet number and function. This aspect of hemostasis should not be overlooked, particularly during rapid infusion of refrigerated banked blood products to replace lost intravascular volume. A "core" temperature of at least 35°C represents a suitable goal.

Fibrinolysis Fibrinolysis causes bleeding not only by clot breakdown, but also by fibrin degradation products preventing proper association of fibrin monomers. Its treatment thus includes three aspects: halting the lytic process, removing its cause, and allowing time for reticuloendothelial clearance of fibrin degradation products. Since patients rarely suffer from an active lytic process in the postbypass period, initiation of treatment at that time with antifibrinolytic drug proves useful only in extreme cases. Treatment of fibrinolysis-induced bleeding remains of questionable efficacy, in contrast to prevention of clot lysis.

Laboratory tests Investigation should be initiated with the response as focused as possible given the limitations of time; the "shotgun" approach to therapy obfuscates final resolution of bleeding. Initial tests include platelet count, PT, aPTT, plasma fibrinogen, and fibrin degradation products. Figure 17.15 presents a first approach to the diagnosis of bleeding after bypass.

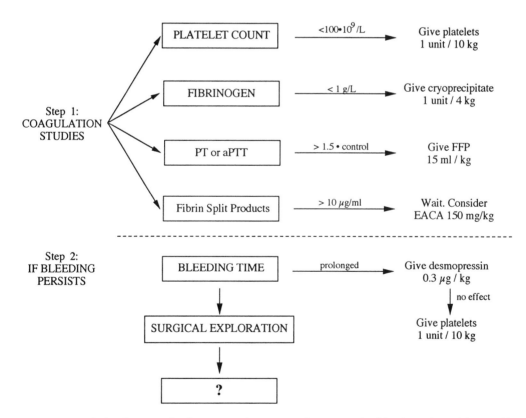

Figure 17.15.   Idealized strategy for diagnosis and treatment of postoperative bleeding. The initial tests of hemostasis include *platelet count, fibrinogen, PT,* and *aPTT.* Bleeding that persists despite normal results of these tests suggests performance of a bleeding time. Marked prolongation in the *bleeding time* (over 16 minutes) may respond to desmopressin. Otherwise, *surgical exploration* may reveal an anatomic source. Increased fibrin degradation products suggests antifibrinolytic therapy, although some would withhold that therapy until a consumptive coagulopathy is ruled out. As indicated in the text, therapy must sometimes precede definitive diagnosis.

Maintain Blood Volume and Composition

Replenishment of lost intravascular volume with clear fluids, albumin, and packed red cells progressively decreases the concentrations of platelets and coagulation factors. Thus, the etiology of bleeding quickly becomes multifactorial. Nevertheless, intravascular volume must be maintained prior to identifying the cause of bleeding. Postponement of intravascular volume restoration not only compromises cardiac output and the major organ systems, but may also create bleeding itself as a result of protracted shock initiating consumptive coagulopathy.

Banked plasma products   Dilution of coagulation factors by bypass alone to levels below which hemostasis becomes impaired (usually less than 30% of normal) occurs rarely in patients who are not neonates. Routine administration of coagulation factors via fresh-frozen plasma or cryoprecipitate after bypass constitutes not only needless waste of a valuable resource but also unnecessary exposure of the patient to potentially infectious material (50). Continued depletion and dilution that occurs with bleeding after bypass, however, validates replenishment of coagulation factors with these banked blood products. As replacement therapy for hemorrhage, platelet concentrates may suffice by themselves, since 6 units of platelets contain more than 1 unit of plasma (albeit lacking somewhat in factors V and VIII) (50). For a discussion of treatment of bleeding due to unneutralized heparin, see Chapter 15. Regardless of laboratory results, patients not actively bleeding should not receive banked plasma products or platelets.

Red cells and platelets   Adequate delivery of oxygen to tissues determines the need to administer red cells. Replacement of rapid blood loss with factor-poor, platelet-poor packed red cells does not permit enough time to verify factor and platelet defi-ciencies with coagulation tests. In noncardiac surgery, many clinicians administer platelets after 10 to 15 units of red cells. Coagulation factor dilution and partial activation of platelets by bypass demand earlier replacement in patients bleeding soon after bypass.

Hypertension   When an aortotomy has been performed, as for aortic valve replacement, avoidance of hypertension is an essential part of the treatment of postoperative hemorrhage. However, the clinician should wait until intravascular volume has been replenished and ensure adequate sedation and analgesia prior to administering vasodilators to treat hypertension.

Pharmaceuticals

Desmopressin   Figure 17.16 displays the chemical structure of this drug, modified from the nonapeptide arginine vasopressin (antidiuretic hormone, or ADH). Receptors for ADH occur on vascular smooth muscle (V_1 receptors) and the renal distal tubule (V_2 receptors). Removal of an amine group from the carboxy terminal cysteine residue of ADH protects the molecule from degradation by circulating peptidases. Replacement of D-arginine for L-arginine in the eighth position removes pressor activity. Rapid administration of desmopressin actually decreases blood pressure and systemic vascular resistance, possibly by stimulation of extrarenal V_2 receptors (51, 52).

Like ADH, epinephrine, and insulin, desmopressin releases a variety of hemostatically active substances from vascular endothelium: factor VIII, prostacyclin, t-PA, and vWF (53). Factor VIII coagulant activity increases to levels about fourfold (range, 2- to 20-fold) those of baseline within 30 to 90 minutes of desmopressin injection (54). Release of large multimers of vWF results in persistence of factor VIII activity long after desmopressin has been eliminated. Prostacyclin, by preventing platelet activation, and t-PA, by inciting fibrinolysis, both thwart hemostasis. However, the overall ef-

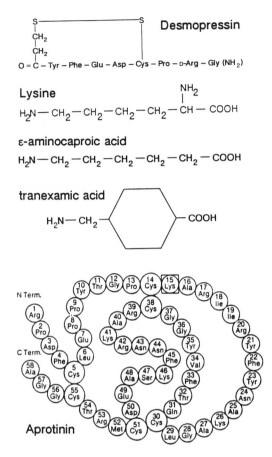

Desmopressin

Lysine

ε-aminocaproic acid

tranexamic acid

Aprotinin

Figure 17.16. Molecular structures of desmopressin, the antifibrinolytic molecules, and lysine. (Modified from Fritz H, Wunderer G. Biochemistry and applications of aprotonin, the kallikrein inhibitor from bovine organs. Drug Res 1983;33:479–494. Also modified from Horrow JC. Desmopressin and antifibrinolytics. In: Gravlee GP, ed. Blood conservation. Int Anesth Clin 1990;28:216–222.)

fect of desmopressin favors hemostasis. Conceivably, rapid administration may release sufficient prostacyclin to explain desmopressin's transient hypotension.

Desmopressin is administered in 0.3 μg/kg doses by intravenous, intranasal, or subcutaneous routes. The biologic half-life of 55 minutes belies its clinical effects, which last at least 6 hours (54). However, tachyphylaxis often occurs within 4 to 5 days, probably because of depletion of endothelial stores of vWF. In rare instances,

water intoxication may occur from inappropriate fluid therapy during repeated desmopressin administration (55). Anecdotal reports of coronary thromboses temporally associated with desmopressin administration led to concern that the drug engenders a prothrombotic state in patients with ischemic heart disease (56–58).

In several disorders characterized by a prolonged bleeding time, desmopressin demonstrates hemostatic efficacy, viz., uremia (59), cirrhosis (54), and rare platelet disorders (60). Limited data from 2 patients and 10 volunteers indicate that desmopressin may also correct aspirin-induced prolongation of the bleeding time (61). Patients with mild or moderate hemophilia A or von Willebrand's disease respond to desmopressin with increases in factor VIII and shortening of prolonged bleeding times, respectively (54). In severe factor deficiency, however, there is little endogenous factor to release, so desmopressin proves of no value. When depending on desmopressin, individual responsiveness should be determined prior to the anticipated need.

Can desmopressin treat excessive bleeding after bypass? While many investigations address the prophylactic role of desmopressin (see "Prevention of Coagulopathy"), few data assess its ability to halt established bleeding. Czer and colleagues (62) administered desmopressin 20 μg intravenously to 23 patients who demonstrated a chest tube drainage greater than 100 ml/hr for at least 2 hours after bypass. These patients received fewer blood products (15 ± 13 versus 29 ± 19 units) than a historical comparison group of 16 patients who received no drug. All patients received dipyridamole prior to surgery and bubble oxygenators during bypass, and demonstrated a bleeding time greater than 10 minutes when bleeding. Nonrandomization, lack of blinding, and methodologic bias (transfusion was not permitted for 1 hour after infusion of desmopressin) cast doubt on those results. A subsequent double-blind, prospective, randomized investigation disclosed that desmopressin provided no hemostatic effect when administered to patients with substantial mediastinal bleeding and prolonged bleeding times after cardiac surgery (63).

LoCicero and colleagues (64) retrospectively compared 74 patients who received desmopressin after bypass because of excessive bleeding as perceived by the operating surgeon with 91 matched historical controls. Although the desmopressin group bled more and received more blood products than the control group, this result should be expected since they were selected because of excessive bleeding.

Antifibrinolytics These therapeutic agents include the synthetic lysine analogs epsilon aminocaproic acid (EACA) and tranexamic acid (TA) as well as the naturally occurring protease inhibitor aprotinin (Fig. 17.16). The antifibrinolytics bind to plasminogen and plasmin, blocking the ability of the fibrinolytic enzymes to bind at lysine residues of fibrinogen. Excretion occurs renally, with urinary concentrations 75- to 100-fold those of plasma. Plasma half-life is 80 minutes. Loading doses (150 mg/kg of EACA or 10 to 20 mg/kg TA) should be followed by continuous infusions (10 mg/kg EACA or 1 to 2 mg/kg TA), adjusted for creatinine clearance (65).

Antifibrinolytics impact positively on surgical hemostasis in hemophiliacs, in patients with von Willebrand's disease and other blood dyscrasias, and after chemotherapy (66–70). Additional applications include prevention of rebleeding following subarachnoid hemorrhage, liver transplantation, and prostate surgery (18, 71–73).

Often bleeding after bypass is treated with a single 5-g dose of intravenous EACA along with a host of blood products and other modalities. Studies do not consistently demonstrate efficacy in attenuating bleeding of this subtherapeutic dose of EACA given after bypass (Table 17.3) (74–77). This lack of a salutary hemostatic response may arise from poor timing of subeffective or minimally effective doses (see "Pharmacologic Measures"). Similarly, aprotinin has no defined role as a hemostatic agent in the patient already bleeding after bypass. In contrast, antifibrinolytic drugs do decrease bleeding and blood transfusion requirements when given prophylactically. The next section addresses this aspect.

PREVENTION OF COAGULOPATHY

Compared with efforts to treat established bleeding, efforts to prevent bleeding after CPB are less costly and better rewarded. Knowledge of the mechanisms of bypass-induced coagulopathy guides the approach to its prevention. Accordingly, the following discussion focuses on coagulation factors and fibrinolysis. For aspects relating to platelet function, see Chapter 16.

Prevention includes eliminating or reducing preoperative factors that incite bleeding. Preexisting disorders of hemostasis should be effectively addressed. These include factor deficiencies, uremia,

Table 17.3. Earlier Studies of EACA to Reduce Bleeding after Cardiac Surgery

Year	Authors	N[a]	Blood Loss	Structure	Dose of EACA (g)	Timing of Dose
1967	Sterns and Lillehei (74)	240/100	34% Reduced	Retrospective	≈ 5	After bypass
1970	Gomes and McGoon (75)	202/137	No difference	Retrospective	Unknown	At sternotomy
1985	Saussine et al. (76)	29/28	No difference	Blinded; randomized	4	After protamine
1988	Vander Salm et al. (77)	31/27	18% Reduced	Blinded; randomized	5	After bypass

[a]Number of patients in the treated group/number in the control group.

hepatic compromise, and exposure to platelet-inhibiting drugs.

Physical Measures

Coagulation factors Two potential contributors to coagulation factor dysfunction are hypothermia and dilution, both essential elements of bypass in most centers. Slower enzyme kinetics may account for part of the impaired coagulation seen at temperatures below 35°C. Prevention of postbypass hypothermia requires rewarming sufficient not only to restore core temperature to 37°C or more, but also to raise a more peripherally measured temperature, such as urinary bladder, to at least 34°C (78). Since core temperature at the end of surgery usually equals the average of the core and intermediate zone (urinary bladder or rectal) temperatures when active warming is discontinued at the termination of bypass, hypothermia after surgery can be prevented by a suitable warming period during surgery (see Chapter 6). The speed of surgical closure impacts hemostasis significantly. Quicker sternal approximation limits convective heat loss, while more expedient removal of the exposed patient from the cold operating room reduces heat loss by radiation. However, speed must not compromise reasonable attention to open vessels that must be sealed to stop bleeding. Optimal management results from focused, efficient, and effective surgical attention.

Restricting the priming volume will limit hemodilution. Other methods for preserving factor levels include restriction of both intravenous fluids and cardioplegia volume, administration of diuretics when oliguria occurs, and hemoconcentration during bypass via filtration devices. Acute, preoperative plasmapheresis withdraws platelet-rich plasma for infusion following bypass. Should it be shown to have a hemostatic benefit, the mechanism will more likely be platelet, rather than coagulation factor, preservation (79).

Fibrinolysis Membrane, rather than bubble, oxygenators should be chosen when prolonged bypass is anticipated, as this will limit platelet destruction and fibrinolysis (80). Sufficient heparin doses limit thrombin activity during bypass. Since thrombin acts directly on endothelium to release plasminogen activators, inadequate thrombin inhibition fosters fibrinolysis. Prevention of bleeding thus requires frequent bedside verification of heparin activity via activated coagulation time or heparin concentration (via protamine titration) coupled with prompt effective treatment when coagulation times are not sufficiently prolonged.

Pharmacologic Measures

Heparin rebound Chapter 15 addresses the adequacy of heparin neutralization with protamine. This section will consider "heparin rebound," a term denoting the reappearance of clinical bleeding and prolonged coagulation times following complete heparin neutralization. Direct evidence supports the generally accepted notion that heparin rebound occurs from reappearance of circulating heparin (81). Explanations for this phenomenon include more rapid clearance of protamine relative to that of heparin, lymphatic-delayed return of heparin to blood, clearance of a postulated heparin antagonist, and late release of heparin sequestered in tissues (82–84). Heparin binds to endothelium; the currently favored theory involves late release of bound heparin from endothelium. Theoretically, transfusion of blood components containing antithrombin III, including fresh-frozen plasma, platelet concentrates, and whole blood, may attract heparin away from protamine, thus reactivating heparin.

Prolonged coagulation times occur as soon as 1 hour after neutralization and may persist as long as 6 hours (85–87). Should clinical bleeding not accompany a prolonged coagulation time, no intervention is necessary. Otherwise, additional 0.5 to 1 mg/kg doses of protamine usually suffice.

Clinical practice varies widely in the selection of an initial neutralizing dose of protamine, from less than 1 mg for every 100 units of remaining heparin, as determined by protamine titration, to as much as 4 mg for every 100 units of total heparin administered (88). Does a particular protamine dose scheme prevent heparin rebound? Data in the literature provide conflicting answers. Table 17.4 presents results of representative studies, which indicate no best dosing scheme to prevent heparin rebound (85, 86, 89, 90). Recent work demonstrates a role of initial heparin dose in the development of heparin rebound, albeit without a difference in bleeding after operation (91). Whether initially unneutralized or appearing as "rebound," heparin can cause bleeding after surgery. Thus, administration of protamine to neutralize remaining heparin constitutes the first pharmaceutical intervention in the treatment of a bleeding patient.

Desmopressin Can desmopressin prevent bleeding after bypass when given prophylactically? A small group of adolescents who received desmopressin during Harrington rod placement bled less and received less blanked blood compared to a control group (92). Interest in prophylactic desmopressin's hemostatic potential in cardiac surgery stems from the known acquired platelet abnormalities (see Chapter 16) and theoretical salutary effects of released vWF on platelet adhesion and in shortening prolonged bleeding times (93). Salzman and colleagues (94) initially reported a marked reduction in bleeding after bypass in patients undergoing cardiac procedures known for excess postoperative bleeding, i.e., reoperations and valve replacements. Subsequent investigations have not reproduced those results (95–101). Table 17.5 summarizes those studies.

Of course, prophylactic desmopressin finds utility for the cardiac surgical patient with a hematologic abnormality known to respond to desmopressin, such as uremia, hemophilia, or von Willebrand's disease. For other cardiac surgical patients, prophylactic desmopressin does not impart any hemostatic advantage. Recent data from vascular surgery patients agree. Of 50 patients undergoing aortoiliac surgery, 25 received

Table 17.4.   Variations in Protamine Dose to Prevent Heparin Rebound[a]

Authors	Study Group	Control Group	Results
Ellison et al. (1974) (85)	1:100 of remaining heparin by protamine titration ($n = 6$)	1:100 of total heparin given ($n = 6$)	All six study patients had heparin rebound vs. none of six control patients
Guffin et al. (1976) (89)	1:100 of remaining heparin by assuming 2 hour half-life ($n = 30$)	1:100 of total heparin given ($n = 30$)	Study group had higher platelet count, less prolonged PT and aPTT, and less bleeding
Kaul et al. (1979) (86)	Ratio = ?; protamine according to blood heparin level ($n = 27$)	Heparin: 300 U/kg then 150 U/kg hourly; protamine: 6 mg/kg ($n = 44$)	No heparin rebound in study group vs. 10/44 patients in control group
Kesteven et al. (1986) (90)	3 mg/kg protamine in divided doses; heparin levels measured at end of CPB ($n = 35$)	None	29% had heparin present 2 hours later (all had ratios less than 1.6:100)

[a]All ratios are milligram per kilogram of protamine to units per kilogram of heparin

desmopressin immediately prior to surgery without benefit of decreased bleeding or transfusion requirement (102).

Synthetic Antifibrinolytics Prophylactic administration of the synthetic antifibrinolytics decreases bleeding after bypass and reduces transfusion of homologous blood products. Table 17.6 summarizes the investigative data supporting the hemostatic efficacy of prophylactic antifibrinolytic therapy. The EACA or TA administered prior to bypass generates approximately a 30% reduction in bleeding (101, 103–108). In one investigation, TA decreased the likelihood of homologous blood transfusion from 41 to 22% (101). This salutary hemostatic effect may arise from inhibition of plasmin at platelet plasmin receptors as well as at fibrinogen

(Fig. 17.17) (109, 110). Decades ago, antifibrinolytic therapy fell into disfavor following an anecdotal report of thrombotic complications in patients with prostate carcinoma (111, 112). However, prospective studies of prophylactic antifibrinolytics during noncardiac and cardiac surgery do not substantiate fears of thrombotic complications (71, 72, 101, 103, 104). The prudent clinician withholds antifibrinolytic therapy from patients with demonstrated consumptive coagulopathy and from those with upper urinary tract bleeding. Infusion rates should be adjusted for elevated serum creatinine to account for impaired excretion.

Natural Antifibrinolytic Aprotinin, the naturally occurring antifibrinolytic, differs from its synthetic congeners with re-

Table 17.5. Prospective Studies of Desmopressin in Cardiac Surgery

Year	Authors	N[a]	Blood Loss	Structure	Population Studied
1986	Salzman et al. (94)	35/35	41% Reduced	Blinded; randomized	Reoperation or valve replacement
1988	Rocha et al. (96)	50/50	No difference	Blinded; randomized	Valve replacement; atrial septal defect
1989	Seear et al. (95)	30/30	No difference	Blinded; randomized	Children (30 of 60 cyanotic)
1989	Hackmann et al. (97)	74/76	No difference	Blinded; randomized	Elective cardiac surgery
1990	Andersson et al. (98)	10/9	No difference	Blinded; randomized	Elective coronary surgery
1990	Lazenby et al. (99)	30/30	No difference	Unblinded; consecutive	Primary coronary surgery
1991	Reich et al. (100)	14/13	No difference	Blinded; randomized	Elective cardiac surgery
1991	Horrow et al. (101)	78/81	No difference	Blinded; randomized	Elective cardiac surgery
1992	de Prost et al. (63)	47/47	No difference	Blinded; randomized	Patients bleeding after cardiac surgery

[a] Number of patients in the treated group/number in the control group.

Table 17.6. Prospective Studies of Antifibrinolytic Given Prophylactically Prior to Bypass

Year	Authors	N[a]	Blood Loss	Structure	Dose of Drug	Timing of Dose
1971	Midell et al. (107)	48/25	58% Reduced	Prospective	125 mg/kg EACA	Before bypass
1974	McClure and Izsak (108)	12/18	42% Reduced	Blinded; randomized	75 mg/kg EACA	At sternotomy
1989	DelRossi et al. (103)	170/180	30% Reduced	Blinded; randomized	5 grams EACA	Before incision
1990	Horrow et al. (104)	18/20	34% Reduced	Blinded; randomized	1 mg/kg TA	Before incision
1991	Horrow et al. (101)	77/82	30% Reduced	Blinded; randomized	1 mg/kg TA	Before incision

[a] Number of patients in the treated group/number in the control group.

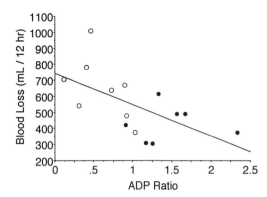

Figure 17.17. Blood loss after cardiac surgery as a function of platelet adenosine diphosphate (*ADP*), expressed as the ratio measured 2 hours after surgery to that measured before bypass. Platelet dense granules contain ADP. Each *solid circle* represents a patient who received tranexamic acid beginning prior to skin incision (prophylactic); each *open circle* represents a patient who received tranexamic acid beginning after protamine neutralization. Note that prophylactic tranexamic acid preserved platelet ADP and decreased bleeding. (From Soslau G, Horrow J, Brodsky I. The effect of tranexamic acid on platelet ADP during extracorporeal circulation. Am J Hematol 1991;38: 113–119.)

spect to size and spectrum of activity. In contrast to the smaller lysine amino acid analogs, aprotinin is a 58 residue protein derived from bovine lung. As a result, the dose of aprotinin is expressed in activity units, in a fashion similar to that of heparin. While the variation and shortcomings of heparin activity standards receive appropriate attention, these issues remain unexplored with aprotinin (113, 114). Like any foreign protein, aprotinin may cause anaphylaxis, although the incidence is only 1 per 1000 (115, 116). Likewise, fears of renal dysfunction from rapid tubular uptake have not been confirmed in clinical use (117).

Like the synthetic antifibrinolytics, aprotinin inhibits plasmin and plasminogen. In addition, aprotinin inhibits kallikrein, the contact activation protein which enhances factor XII activation (118–120). The hemostatic effect of an inhibitory action on kallikrein is difficult to predict for two reasons. First, factor XII is known to be unnecessary for clinical hemostasis (121). Second, the extent to which factor XIIa contributes to fibrinolysis is not known (2). In this regard, aprotinin-associated thrombus formation on pulmonary artery catheters remains unexplained (122). The salutary hemostatic effects of aprotinin may, in fact, derive from inhibition of plasmin alone.

Kallikrein inhibition may, however, explain prolongation of the ACT by aprotinin (123). Since this in vitro anticoagulant effect may not reflect an in vivo antithrombotic action, aprotinin compromises use of the ACT to gauge the adequacy of heparin dosing during bypass (124). Preliminary work suggests that alternative contact activators may permit use of a modified ACT when aprotinin is employed (125).

The development of aprotinin to decrease bleeding after cardiac operation parallels that of the synthetic antifibrinolytics. Initial studies failed to demonstrate a savings in blood lost or administered (107, 126). Further work revealed that higher doses of aprotinin could decrease bleeding after cardiac operations (65). Following the report of an astounding fourfold reduction in bleeding from cardiac reoperation (127), a host of clinical studies in various cardiac surgical populations has substantiated a savings in blood loss of 35 to 40% (Table 17.7) (43, 117, 128–135). As with tranexamic acid, platelet preservation during bypass appears to contribute to aprotinin's beneficial hemostatic effect (127, 128).

Cost Any prophylactic therapy entails fixed costs to prevent presumed complications. Factors that will determine the appropriateness of pharmaceuticals to prevent bleeding include the cost of the drug, the expected savings in terms of blood loss and transfusions prevented, and the estimated adverse outcome from omission of prophylaxis. Canadian data predict that a prophylactic course of aprotinin will cost over 100 times that of EACA (136). Routine aprotinin administration to all patients undergoing coronary artery bypass surgery in

Table 17.7.   Prophylactic High-Dose Aprotinin during Cardiac Surgery

Year	Authors	N[a]	Blood Loss[b]	Structure	Population Studied
1987	van Oeveren et al. (130)	11/11	47% Reduced	Unblinded; randomized	Coronary surgery
1987	Royston et al. (127)	11/11	81% Reduced	Unblinded; randomized	Repeat sternotomy
1989	Bidstrup et al. (131)	40/37	46% Reduced	Blinded; randomized	Elective coronary surgery
1989	Dietrich et al. (132)	152/317	29% Reduced	Historical controls	Elective cardiac surgery
1989	Alajmo et al. (133)	22/12	41% Reduced	Unblinded; randomized	Cardiac surgery
1990	van Oeveren et al. (128)	30/30	37% Reduced	Blinded; randomized	Elective coronary surgery
1990	Dietrich et al. (134)	19/20	49% Reduced	Blinded; randomized	Primary coronary surgery
1991	Havel et al. (43)	12/12	38% Reduced	Blinded; randomized	Primary coronary surgery
1991	Harder et al. (135)	40/40	39% Reduced	Blinded; randomized	Elective coronary surgery
1991	Blauhut et al. (117)	13/13	50% Reduced	Unblinded; sequential	Coronary surgery

[a]Number of patients who received aprotinin/number of control patients.
[b]The average reduction in blood loss, weighted by the number of patients, is 36%.

the United States could increase yearly costs by about $300 million (250,000 procedures at $1200 each). Can we afford it? Should we even pay $1 million for routine EACA prophylaxis?

Will improved screening techniques for donated blood provide greater protection from infectious diseases, making trivial the impact of bleeding prevention on patient care? Or will they merely permit elucidation of the immunosuppressive effects of transfusion and identification of yet more blood-borne transmissible diseases? The future, hopefully, will bring antithrombotic bypass techniques that preserve hemostasis and employ neither heparin nor protamine. Until these goals materialize, bypass-associated coagulopathy requires prevention and treatment.

REFERENCES

1. Fransson L-A. Heparin sulfate proteoglycans: structure and properties. In: Lane DA, Lindahl U, eds. Heparin. Boca Raton, FL: CRC Press, 1989:115–134.
2. Colman RW, Marder VJ, Salzman EW, Hirsh J. Overview of hemostasis. In: Colman RW, Hirsh J, Marder VJ, Salzman EW, eds. Hemostasis and thrombosis. 2nd ed. Philadelphia: JB Lippincott, 1987:3–17.
3. Olson RE. Vitamin K. In: Colman RW, Hirsh J, Marder VJ, Salzman EW, eds. Hemostasis and thrombosis. 2nd ed. Philadelphia: JB Lippincott, 1987:846–860.
4. Steinberg M, Nemerson Y. Activation of Factor

X. In: Colman RW, Hirsh J, Marder VJ, Salzman EW, eds. Hemostasis and thrombosis. 2nd ed. Philadelphia: JB Lippincott, 1987:112–119.
5. Hirsh J. Laboratory diagnosis of thrombosis. In: Colman RW, Hirsh J, Marder VJ, Salzman EW, eds. Hemostasis and thrombosis. 2nd ed. Philadelphia: JB Lippincott, 1987:1165–1183.
6. George J, Shattil SJ. The clinical importance of acquired abnormalities of platelet function. N Engl J Med 1991;324:27–39.
7. Hantgan RR, Francis CW, Scheraga HA, Marder VJ. Fibrinogen structure and physiology. In: Colman RW, Hirsh J, Marder VJ, Salzman EW, eds. Hemostasis and thrombosis. 2nd ed. Philadelphia: JB Lippincott, 1987:269–288.
8. van Aken WG. Preparation of plasma derivatives. In: Rossi EC, Simon TL, Moss GS, eds. Principles of transfusion medicine. Baltimore: Williams & Wilkins, 1991:323–334.
9. McDonagh J. Structure and function of factor XIII. In: Colman RW, Hirsh J, Marder VJ, Salzman EW, eds. Hemostasis and thrombosis. 2nd ed. Philadelphia: JB Lippincott, 1987: 289–300.
10. Robbins KC. The plasminogen-plasmin enzyme system. In: Colman RW, Hirsh J, Marder VJ, Salzman EW, eds. Hemostasis and thrombosis. 2nd ed. Philadelphia: JB Lippincott, 1987: 340–357.
11. Francis CW, Marder VJ. Physiologic regulation and pathologic disorders of fibrinolysis. In: Colman RW, Hirsh J, Marder VJ, Salzman EW, eds. Hemostasis and thrombosis. 2nd ed. Philadelphia: JB Lippincott, 1987:358–379.
12. Marder VJ, Sherry S. Thrombolytic therapy: current status. N Engl J Med 1988;318:1512–1520, 1585–1595.
13. Miale JB. Laboratory medicine. Hematology. 4th ed. St. Louis: Mosby, 1972:1280.

14. Koepke JA. Coagulation testing systems. In: Koepke JA, ed. Laboratory hematology. New York: Churchill Livingstone, 1984: 1113–1140.

15. Tans G, Griffin JH. Properties of sulfatides in factor-XII-dependent contact activation. Blood 1982;59:69–75.

16. O'Neill AI, McAllister C, Corke CF, Parkin JD. A comparison of five devices for the bedside monitoring of heparin therapy. Anaesth Intens Care 1991;19:592–601.

17. Bjoraker DG. The thromboelastograph D coagulation analyzer. Anesthesiol Rev 1991;18: 34–40.

18. Kang Y, Lewis JH, Navalgund A, et al. Epsilon-aminocaproic acid for treatment of fibrinolysis during liver transplantation. Anesthesiology 1987;66:766–773.

19. Spiess BD, Logas WG, Tuman KJ, Hughes T, Jagmin J, Ivankovich AD. Thromboelastography used for detection of perioperative fibrinolysis: a report of four cases. J Cardiothorac Vasc Anesth 1988;2:666–672.

20. Spiess BD, Tuman RJ, McCarthy RJ, DeLaria GA, Schillo R, Ivankovich AD. Thromboelastography as an indicator of post-cardiopulmonary bypass coagulopathies. J Clin Monit 1987;3:25–30.

21. Howland WS, Schweizer O, Goulp P. Comparison of intraoperative measurements of coagulation. Anesth Analg 1974;53:657–663.

22. Zuckerman L, Cohen E, Vagher JP, et al. Comparison of thromboelastography with common coagulation tests. Thromb Haemostas 1981; 46:752–756.

23. von Kaulla K, von Kaulla E, Wasantapruck S, et al. Blood coagulation in uremic patients before and after hemodialysis and transplantation of the kidney. Arch Surg 1966;92:184–191.

24. Tuman KJ, Spiess BD, McCarthy RJ, Ivankovitch AD. Comparison of viscoelastic measures of coagulation after cardiopulmonary bypass. Anesth Analg 1989;69:69–75.

25. Van Riper DF, Horrow JC, Osborne D. Is the thromboelastograph a clinically useful predictor of blood loss after bypass? Anesthesiology 1990;73:A1206.

26. Shenaq SA, Saleem A. Viscoelastic measurement of clot formation: the Sonoclot. In: Ellison E, Jobes DR, eds. Effective hemostasis in cardiac surgery. Philadelphia: WB Saunders, 1988: 183–193.

27. Saleem A, Blifeld C, Saleh SA, et al. Viscoelastic measurement of clot formation: a new test of platelet function. Ann Clin Lab Sci 1983;13: 115–124.

28. Samra SK, Harrison RL, Bee DE, Valero V. A study of aspirin induced changes in bleeding time, platelet aggregation, and Sonoclot coagulation analysis in humans. Ann Clin Lab Sci 1991; 21:315–327.

29. Schmaier AH. Diagnosis and therapy of disseminated intravascular coagulation and activated coagulation. In: Koepke JA, ed. Laboratory hematology. New York: Churchill Livingstone, 1984:631–658.

30. Bell WR. Defibrinogenating enzymes. In: Colman RW, Hirsh J, Marder VJ, Salzman EW, eds. Hemostasis and thrombosis. 2nd ed. Philadelphia: JB Lippincott, 1987:886–900.

31. Edmunds LE Jr. The sangreal. J Thorac Cardiovasc Surg 1985;90:1–6.

32. Kalter RD, Saul CM, Wetstein L, Soriano C, Reiss RF. Cardiopulmonary bypass. Associated hemostatic abnormalities. J Thorac Cardiovasc Surg 1979;77:427–435.

33. Thelin S, Bagge L, Hultman J, Borowiec J, Nilsson L, Thorelius J. Heparin-coated cardiopulmonary bypass circuits reduce blood cell trauma. Experiments in the pig. Eur J Cardiothorac Surg 1991;5:486–491.

34. Baier RE, Dutton RC. Initial events in interactions of blood with a foreign surface. J Biomed Mater Res 1969;3:191–206.

35. Engbers GF, Feijen J. Current techniques to improve the blood compatibility of biomaterial surfaces. Int J Artif Organs 1991;14:199–215.

36. Michenfelder JD, Theye RA. Hypothermia: effects on canine brain and whole-body metabolism. Anesthesiology 1968;29:1107–1112.

37. Jobes DR, Ellison N, Campbell FW. Limitations for ACT [Letter]. Anesth Analg 1989;69: 142–144.

38. Bick RL. Alterations of hemostasis associated with cardiopulmonary bypass: pathophysiology, prevention, diagnosis, and management. Semin Thromb Hemostas 1976;3:59–82.

39. Mammen EF, Koets MH, Washington BC, et al. Hemostasis changes during cardiopulmonary bypass surgery. Semin Thromb Hemostas 1985; 11:281–292.

40. Davies GC, Sobel M, Salzman EW. Elevated plasma fibrinopeptide A and thromboxane B_2 levels during cardiopulmonary bypass. Circulation 1980;61:808–814.

41. Tanaka K, Takao M, Yada I, Yuasa H, Kusagawa M, Deguchi K. Alterations in coagulation and fibrinolysis associated with cardiopulmonary bypass during open heart surgery. J Cardiothorac Vasc Anesth 1989;3:181–188.

42. Gravlee GP, Haddon WS, Rothberger HK, et al. Heparin dosing and monitoring for cardiopulmonary bypass. J Thorac Cardiovasc Surg 1990; 99:518–527.

43. Havel M, Teufelsbauer H, Knöbl P, et al. Effect of intraoperative aprotinin administration on

postoperative bleeding in patients undergoing cardiopulmonary bypass operation. J Thorac Cardiovasc Surg 1991;101:968–972.

44. Harker LA, Malpass TW, Branson HE. Mechanism of abnormal bleeding in patients undergoing cardiopulmonary bypass: acquired transient platelet dysfunction associated with selective α-granule release. Blood 1980;56:824–834.

45. Moriau M, Masure R, Hurlet A, et al. Haemostasis disorders in open heart surgery with extracorporeal circulation. Vox Sang 1977;32:41–51.

46. Kucuk O, Kwaan HC, Frederickson J, et al. Increased fibrinolytic activity in patients undergoing cardiopulmonary bypass operation. Am J Hematol 1986;23:223–229.

47. Ellison N, Campbell FW, Jobes DR. Postoperative hemostasis. Semin Thorac Cardiovasc Surg 1991;3:33–38.

48. Marder VJ, Martin SE, Francis CW, Colman RW. Consumptive thrombohemorrhagic disorders. In: Colman RW, Hirsh J, Marder VJ, Salzman EW, eds. Hemostasis and thrombosis. 2nd ed. Philadelphia: JB Lippincott, 1987:975–1015.

49. Kirklin JW, Barratt-Boyes BG. Postoperative care. In: Cardiac surgery. New York: Churchill Livingstone, 1986;139–176.

50. Gravlee GP. Optimal use of blood components. In: Gravlee GP, ed. Blood conservation. Internat Anesth Clinics 1990;28:216–222.

51. Bichet DG, Razi M, Lonergan M, et al. Hemodynamic and coagulation responses to 1-desamino (8-D-arginine) vasopressin in patients with congenital nephrogenic diabetes insipidus. N Engl J Med 1988;318:881–887.

52. Frankville DD, Harper GB, Lake CL, Johns RA. Hemodynamic consequences of desmopressin administration after cardiopulmonary bypass. Anesthesiology 1991;74:988–996.

53. MacGregor IR, Roberts EN, Provose CV, Broomhead AF, Ozolius M, Litka P. Fibrinolytic and haemostatic responses to desamino-D-arginine vasopressin (DDAVP) administered by intravenous and subcutaneous routes in healthy subjects. Thromb Haemostas 1988;59:34–39.

54. Mannucci PM. Desmopressin: a nontransfusional form of treatment for congenital and acquired bleeding disorders. Blood 1988;72:1449–1455.

55. Weinstein RE, Bona RD, Althman AJ, et al. Severe hyponatremia after repeated intravenous administration of desmopressin. Am J Hematol 1989;32:258–261.

56. Bond L, Bevan D. Myocardial infarction in a patient with hemophilia treated with DDAVP [Letter]. N Engl J Med 1986;314:1402–1406.

57. Byrnes JJ, Larcada A, Moake JL. Thrombosis fol-

lowing desmopressin for uremic bleeding. Am J Hematol 1988;28:63–65.

58. O'Brien JR, Green PJ, Salmon G, et al. Desmopressin and myocardial infarction [Letter]. Lancet 1989;1:664.

59. Mannucci PM, Remuzzi G, Pusineri F, et al. Deamino-8-D-arginine vasopressin shortens the bleeding time in uremia. N Engl J Med 1983;308:8–12.

60. DiMichele DM, Hathaway WE. Use of DDAVP in inherited and acquired platelet dysfunction. Am J Hematol 1990;33:39–45.

61. Kobrinsky NL, Gerrard JM, Watson CM, et al. Shortening of bleeding time by 1-deamino-8-D-arginine vasopressin in various bleeding disorders. Lancet 1984;1:1145–1148.

62. Czer LSC, Bateman TM, Gray RJ, et al. Treatment of severe platelet dysfunction and hemorrhage after cardiopulmonary bypass: reduction in blood product usage with desmopressin. J Am Coll Cardiol 1987;9:1139–1147.

63. de Prost D, Barbier-Boehm G, Hazebroucq J, et al. Desmopressin has no beneficial effect on excessive postoperative bleeding or blood product requirements associated with cardiopulmonary bypass. Thromb Haemost 1992;68:106–110.

64. LoCicero JL III, Massad M, Matano J. Effect of desmopressin acetate on hemorrhage without identifiable cause in coronary bypass patients. Am Surgeon 1991;57:165–168.

65. Verstraete M. Clinical application of inhibitors of fibrinolysis. Drugs 1985;29:236–261.

66. Williamson R, Eggleston DJ. DDAVP and EACA used for minor oral surgery in von Willebrand disease. Austr Dent J 1988;33:32–36.

67. Blombäck M, Johansson G, Johnsson H, et al. Surgery in patients with von Willebrand disease. Br J Surg 1989;76:398–400.

68. Sindet-Pedersen S, Ramström G, Bernvil S, Blombäck M. Hemostatic effect of tranexamic acid mouthwash in anticoagulant-treated patients undergoing oral surgery. N Engl J Med 1989;320:840–843.

69. Stern N, Catone GA. Primary fibrinolysis after oral surgery. J Oral Surg 1975;33:49–52.

70. Avvisati G, Büller HR, ten Cate JW, Mandelli F. Tranexamic acid for control of haemorrhage in acute promyelocytic leukaemia. Lancet 1989;2:122–124.

71. Vinnicombe J, Shuttleworth KED. Aminocaproic acid in the control of hæmorrhage after prostatectomy. Lancet 1966;2:232–234.

72. Sharifi R, Lee M, Ray P, et al. Safety and efficacy of intravesical aminocaproic acid for bleeding after transurethral resection of prostate. Urology 1986;27:214–219.

73. Schisano G. The use of antifibrinolytic drugs in

aneurysmal subarachnoid hemorrhage. Surg Neurol 1978;10:217–222.

74. Sterns LP, Lillehei CW. Effect of epsilon aminocaproic acid upon blood loss following open-heart surgery: an analysis of 340 patients. Can J Surg 1967;10:304–307.

75. Gomes MMR, McGoon DC. Bleeding patterns after open-heart surgery. J Thorac Cardiovasc Surg 1970;60:87–97.

76. Saussine M, Delpech S, Allien M, et al. Saignement après Circulation Extracorporelle et Acide Epsilon Amino-caproïque. Ann Fr Anesth Reanim 1985;4:403–405.

77. Vander Salm T, Ansell JE, Okike ON, et al. The role of epsilon-aminocaproic acid in reducing bleeding after cardiac operation: a double-blind randomized study. J Thorac Cardiovasc Surg 1988;95:538–540.

78. Horrow JC, Rosenberg H. Does urinary catheter temperature reflect core temperature during cardiac surgery? Anesthesiology 1988;69: 986–989.

79. Boldt J, Von Bormann B, Kling D, Jacobi M, Moosdorf R, Hemplemann G. Preoperative plasmapheresis in patients undergoing cardiac surgery procedures. Anesthesiology, 1990;72: 282–288.

80. van den Dungen JJ, Karliczek GF, Brenken U, et al. Clinical study of blood trauma during perfusion with membrane and bubble oxygenators. J Thorac Cardiovasc Surg 1982;83:108–116.

81. Kesteven PJ, Ahred A, Aps C, Williams BT, Savidge GF. Protamine sulphate and rebound following open-heart surgery. J Cardiovasc Surg 1986;27:600–603.

82. Perkins HA, Osborn JJ, Gerbode F. The management of abnormal bleeding following extracorporeal circulation. Ann Int Med 1959;51: 658–667.

83. Perkins HA, Acra DJ, Rolfs MR. Estimation of heparin levels in stored and traumatized blood. Blood 1961;18:807–808.

84. Frick PG, Brogli H. The mechanism of heparin rebound after extracorporeal circulation for open cardiac surgery. Surgery 1966;59: 721–726.

85. Ellison N, Beatty P, Blake DR, Wurzel HA, MacVaugh H. Heparin rebound. J Thorac Cardiovasc Surg 1974;67:723–729.

86. Kaul TK, Crow MJ, Rajah SM, Deverall PB, Watson DA. Heparin administration during extracorporeal circulation. J Thorac Cardiovasc Surg 1979;78:95–102.

87. Fiser WP, Read RC, Wright FE, Vecchio TJ. A randomized study of beef lung and pork mucosal heparin in cardiac surgery. Ann Thorac Surg 1983;35:615–620.

88. Ellison N, Ominsky AJ, Wollman H. Is prota-

mine a clinically important anticoagulant? Anesthesiology 1971;35:621–629.

89. Guffin AV, Dunbar RW, Kaplan JA, Bland JW. Successful use of a reduced dose of protamine after cardiopulmonary bypass. Anesth Analg 1976; 55:110–113.

90. Kesteven PJ, Ahred A, Aps C, Williams BT, Savidge GF. Protamine sulphate and rebound following open-heart surgery. J Cardiovasc Surg 1986;27:600–603.

91. Gravlee GP, Rogers AT, Dudas LM, et al. Heparin management protocol for cardiopulmonary bypass influences postoperative heparin rebound but not bleeding. Anesthesiology 1992;76: 393–401.

92. Kobrinsky NL, Letts M, Patel LR, et al. 1-desamino-8-D-arginine vasopressin (desmopressin) decreases operative blood loss in patients having Harrington rod spinal fusion surgery. Ann Int Med 1987;107:446–450.

93. Horrow JC. Desmopressin and antifibrinolytics. In: Gravlee GP, ed. Blood conservation. Int Anesth Clin 1990;28:216–222.

94. Salzman EW, Weinstein MJ, Weintraub RM, et al. Treatment with desmopressin acetate to reduce blood loss after cardiac surgery. N Engl J Med 1986;314:1402–1406.

95. Seear MD, Wadsworth LD, Rogers PC, Sheps S, Ashmore PG. The effect of desmopressin acetate (DDAVP) on postoperative blood loss after cardiac operations in children. J Thorac Cardiovasc Surg 1989;98:217–219.

96. Rocha E, Llorens R, Paramo JA, Arcas R, Cuesta B, Trenor AM. Does desmopressin acetate reduce blood loss after surgery in patients on cardiopulmonary bypass? Circulation 1988;77: 1319–1323.

97. Hackmann T, Gascoyne RD, Naiman SC, et al. A trial of desmopressin (1-desamino-8-D-arginine vasopressin) to reduce blood loss in uncomplicated cardiac surgery. N Engl J Med 1989; 321:1437–1443.

98. Andersson TLG, Solem JO, Tengborn L, Vinge E. Effects of desmopressin acetate on platelet aggregation, von Willebrand factor, and blood loss after cardiac surgery with extracorporeal circulation. Circulation 1990;81:872–878.

99. Lazenby WD, Russo I, Zadeh BJ, et al. Treatment with desmopressin acetate in routine coronary artery bypass surgery to improve postoperative hemostasis. Circulation 1990;82(suppl IV): 413–419.

100. Reich DL, Hammerschlag BC, Rand JH, et al. Desmopressin acetate is a mild vasodilator that does not reduce blood loss in uncomplicated cardiac surgical procedures. J Cardiothorac Vasc Anesth 1991;5:142–145.

101. Horrow JC, Van Riper DF, Strong MD, Brodsky I,

Parmet JL. The hemostatic effects of tranexamic acid and desmopressin during cardiac surgery. Circulation 1991;84:2063–2070.

102. Lethagen S, Rugarn P, Bergqvist D. Blood loss and safety with desmopressin or placebo during aortoiliac graft surgery. Eur J Vasc Surg 1991;5:173–178.

103. DelRossi AJ, Cernaianu AC, Botros S, Lemole GM, Moore R. Prophylactic treatment of post-perfusion bleeding using EACA. Chest 1989;96: 27–30.

104. Horrow JC, Hlavacek J, Strong MD, et al. Prophylactic tranexamic acid decreases bleeding after cardiac operations. J Thorac Cardiovasc Surg 1990;99:70–74.

105. Isetta C, Samat C, Kotaiche M, Jourdan J, Grimaud D. Low dose aprotinin or tranexamic acid treatment in cardiac surgery [Abstract]. Anesthesiology 1991;75:A80.

106. Karski J, Teasdale S, Carroll J, Glynn MFX. Prevention of post-bypass bleeding with cyklokapron and amicar [Abstract]. Anesthesiology 1991;75:A275.

107. Midell AI, Hallman GL, Bloodwell RD, Beall AC, Yashar JJ, Cooley DA. Epsilon-aminocaproic acid for bleeding after cardiopulmonary bypass. Ann Thorac Surg 1971;11:577–582.

108. McClure PD, Izsak J. The use of epsilon-aminocaproic acid to reduce bleeding during cardiac bypass in children with congenital heart disease. Anesthesiology 1974;40:604–608.

109. Soslau G, Horrow J, Brodsky I. The effect of tranexamic acid on platelet ADP during extracorporeal circulation. Am J Hematol 1991;38: 113–119.

110. Adelman B, Rizk A, Hanners E. Plasminogen interactions with platelets in plasma. Blood 1988;72:1530–1535.

111. Charytan C, Purtilo D. Glomerular capillary thrombosis and acute renal failure after epsilon-amino caproic acid therapy. N Engl J Med 1969;280:1102–1104.

112. Ratnoff OD. Epsilon aminocaproic acid—a dangerous weapon. N Engl J Med 1969;280: 1124–1125.

113. Barrowcliffe TW. Heparin assays and standardization. In: Lane DA, Lindahl U, eds. Heparin. Boca Raton, FL: CRC Press, 1989;393–416.

114. Coyne E, Outschoorn AS. Some thoughts on a new USP heparin assay—aren't we ready for an upgrade? Pharmacopeial Forum 1991: 1492–1495.

115. D'Ambra MN, Risk SC. Aprotinin, erythropoietin, and blood substitutes. In: Gravlee GP, ed. Blood conservation. Internat Anesth Clin 1990;28:237–240.

116. Böhrer H, Bach A, Fleischer F, Lang J. Adverse haemodynamic effects of high-dose aprotinin in a paediatric cardiac surgical patient. Anaesthesia 1990;45:853–854.

117. Blauhut B, Gross C, Necek S, Doran JE, Späth P, Lundsgaard-Hansen P. Effects of high-dose aprotinin on blood loss, platelet function, fibrinolysis, complement, and renal function after cardiopulmonary bypass. J Thorac Cardiovasc Surg 1991;101:958–967.

118. Mammen EF. Natural proteinase inhibitors in extracorporeal circulation. Ann NY Acad Sci 1968;146:754–762.

119. Fritz H, Wunderer G. Biochemistry and applications of aprotinin, the kallikrein inhibitor from bovine organs. Drug Res 1983;33:479–494.

120. Royston D. The serine antiprotease aprotinin (trasylol): a novel approach to reducing postoperative bleeding. Blood Coag Fibrin 1990; 1:55–69.

121. Schmaier AH, Silverberg M, Kaplan AP, Colman RW. Contact activation and its abnormalities. In: Colman RW, Hirsh J, Marder VJ, Salzman EW, eds. Hemostasis and thrombosis. 2nd ed. Philadelphia: JB Lippincott, 1987:18–38.

122. Böhrer H, Fleischer F, Lang J, Vahl C. Early formation of thrombi on pulmonary artery catheters in cardiac surgical patients receiving high-dose aprotinin. J Cardiothorac Vasc Anesth 1990;4:222–225.

123. deSmet AAEA, Joen MCN, van Oeveren W, et al. Increased anticoagulation during cardiopulmonary bypass by aprotinin. J Thorac Cardiovasc Surg 1990;100:520–527.

124. Royston D. High dose aprotinin therapy: the first five years' experience. J Cardiothorac Vasc Anesth 1992;6:76–100.

125. Wang J-S, Hung W-T, Karp R, Lin C-Y. Increase in ACT of heparinized blood in patients on aprotinin is caused by the celite activator [Abstract]. Richmond, VA: Society of Cardiovascular Anesthesiologists, 1991:114.

126. Tice DA, Woeth MH, Clauss RH, Reed GE. The inhibition by trasylol of fibrinolytic activity associated with cardiovascular operations. Surg Gynecol Obstet 1964;119:71–74.

127. Royston D, Taylor KM, Bidstrup BP, Sapsford RN. Effect of aprotinin on need for blood transfusion after repeat open-heart surgery. Lancet 1987;2:1289–1291.

128. van Oeveren W, Harder MP, Roozendaal KJ, Eijsman L, Wildevuur CRH. Aprotinin protects platelets against the initial effect of cardiopulmonary bypass. J Thorac Cardiovasc Surg 1990; 99:788–797.

129. Edmunds LH, Niewiarowski S, Colman RW. Aprotinin [Letter]. J Thorac Cardiovasc Surg 1991;101:1103–1104.

130. van Oeveren W, Jansen NJG, Bidstrup BP, et al. Effects of aprotinin on hemostatic mechanisms

during cardiopulmonary bypass. Ann Thorac Surg 1987;44:640–645.

131. Bidstrup BP, Royston D, Sapsford RN, Taylor KM. Reduction in blood loss and use after cardiopulmonary bypass with high dose aprotinin (Trasylol). J Thorac Cardiovasc Surg 1989;97:364–372.

132. Dietrich W, Barankay A, Dilthey G, et al. Reduction of homologous blood requirements in cardiac surgery by intraoperative aprotinin application—clinical experience in 152 cardiac surgical patients. Thorac Cardiovasc Surg 1989;37:92–98.

133. Alajmo F, Calamai G, Perna AM, et al. High-dose aprotinin: hemostatic effects in open heart operations. Ann Thorac Surg 1989;48:536–539.

134. Dietrich W, Spannagl M, Jochum M, et al. Influence of high-dose aprotinin treatment on blood loss and coagulation patterns in patients undergoing myocardial revascularization. Anesthesiology 1990;73:1119–1126.

135. Harder MP, Eijsman L, Roozendaal KJ, van Oeveren W, Wildevuur CRH. Aprotinin reduces intraoperative and postoperative blood loss in membrane oxygenator cardiopulmonary bypass. Ann Thorac Surg 1991;51:936–941.

136. Hardy G-F, Desroches J. The usefulness of natural and synthetic antifibrinolytics in cardiac surgery. Can J Anaesth 1992:353–365.

Section IV

Organ System Effects of
Cardiopulmonary Bypass

18

CARDIOPULMONARY BYPASS AND THE LUNG

Robert N. Sladen and Dan E. Berkowitz

In 1977 Pennock et al. (1) wrote, ". . . pulmonary problems remain the most significant cause of morbidity following cardiopulmonary bypass today." This statement still largely holds true, particularly in patients with preexisting lung disease or with cardiopulmonary bypass (CPB) time greater than three hours.

All patients suffer to some degree the physical consequences of lung collapse and pleural disruption. The impact of these mechanical changes depends on the patient's underlying pulmonary reserve. Furthermore, all patients suffer some degree of acute lung injury on CPB, due to a blood-mediated inflammatory response to contact activation during extracorporeal circulation. The impact of this injury may vary from microscopic changes of no clinical consequence, to a fulminating capillary leak and adult respiratory distress syndrome (ARDS). Finally, important metabolic functions provided by the lung are bypassed by extracorporeal circulation. This chapter will address the pathophysiology of these processes, correlate them with clinical pulmonary syndromes during and after CPB, and outline therapeutic approaches to the management of the lungs during CPB.

SECTION 1: MECHANICAL ALTERATIONS IN LUNG FUNCTION

Pathophysiology of Atelectasis

Atelectasis is the most common pulmonary complication after cardiac surgery, occurring in about 70% of cases. During CPB the lungs are not perfused, and are usually allowed to collapse completely. When the lungs are subsequently reexpanded and ventilated toward the end of CPB, a variable degree of pulmonary atelectasis remains. It varies in severity from microscopic (microatelectasis), which manifests as a radiographic decrease in lung volumes, to complete collapse of a lobe. Intermediate degrees of atelectasis—plate, subsegmental, and segmental—are common. Atelectasis results in deterioration of functional residual capacity (FRC), lung compliance, venoarterial admixture, and the alveolar arterial oxygen gradient (A-aDo$_2$). However, it may be difficult if not impossible to distinguish the mechanical changes in lung function induced by CPB from those related to thoracotomy, pleural resection, and pleural effusion. There are a large number of factors that predispose to postoperative pulmonary atelectasis, some of which operate during CPB, but others exist prior to surgery or occur after CPB.

FACTORS PREDISPOSING TO ATELECTASIS (TABLE 18.1)

Atelectasis is usually established during CPB in the dependent parts of the lung. However, there are conditions that exist prior to surgery that predispose to atelectasis even before CPB, and which hinder its resolution in the post-CPB period. Heavy smokers with chronic bronchitis develop metaplasia of ciliated columnar epithelium to mucin-producing goblet cells. Anterograde cilial clearance of mucus and debris is impaired, surfactant production is diminished, and small airways and alveoli tend to collapse. Obesity causes a reduction in FRC and predisposes to atelectasis before and after CPB. Patients who have preoperative or post-CPB congestive heart failure or pulmonary edema have an increase in extravascular lung water, which will exacerbate airway collapse.

During mechanical ventilation in the anesthetized, paralyzed patient the diaphragm is passively displaced cephalad by the abdominal contents, and gas flow is preferentially distributed to the nondependent regions of the lung. This causes ventilation-perfusion mismatch and promotes hypoventilation and collapse of the dependent areas. Any monotonous ventilatory pattern (i.e., one without "sighs"), such as that provided by a mechanical ventilator in the anesthetized or sedated patient, results in progressive microatelectasis of the dependent lung zones.

Pulmonary surfactant (dipalmitoyl lecithin) is a lipoprotein produced by alveolar granular epithelium (type II pneumocytes) that lowers surface tension and prevents alveolar and small airway collapse. A number of mechanisms exist that alter pulmonary surfactant during CPB. Exposure of surfactant to plasma from normal adults and children inhibits its action (2). Entrance of plasma components into air spaces through leaking lung membranes could thereby contribute to atelectasis. Mandelbaum and Giammona (3) suggested that lung distension during CPB depletes surfactant, and subsequent animal studies have confirmed that positive-pressure ventilation during CPB decreases lung compliance and increases intrapulmonary shunt after CPB (4).

During CPB the heart rests on the immobile left lower lobe. With blind bronchial suctioning, the suction catheter usually enters the more direct right mainstem bronchus, resulting in preferential right bronchial drainage. Traumatic mucosal "pitting" induced by the suction catheter at the carina causes secretions to dam up and promotes airway collapse (5). When the pleural cavity is opened, blood and fluid can enter and compress the adjacent lung. In patients undergoing coronary revascularization, dissection of the left internal mammary artery most commonly involves entry into the left pleural space. All of these factors account for the 60 to 70% preponderance of left lower lobe atelectasis after CPB (6).

Table 18.1.   Etiology of Pulmonary Atelectasis

Preoperative factors
  Smoking, chronic bronchitis (mucus cell hyperplasia, surfactant depletion)
  Obesity (decreased FRC)
  Cardiogenic pulmonary edema
Intraoperative factors
  Passive ventilation of paralyzed diaphragm
  Monotonous ventilatory pattern
CPB factors
  Surfactant inhibition—plasma, lung distension, lung ischemia
  Increased extravascular lung water (complement activation)
  Heart rests on immobile left lower lobe
  Blind bronchial suctioning—preferential right bronchial drainage, mucosal damage
  Open pleural cavity—blood, fluid

EFFECTS ON OXYGENATION

A-aDo$_2$ is consistently increased above normal after CPB (7–11). The A-aDo$_2$ increases to a maximum about 48 hours postoperatively, does not return to normal for at least 7 days, and is detectable for weeks after surgery (12). It is generally assumed that this is due to varying degrees of lung collapse on CPB, ranging from diffuse microatelectasis to lobar atelectasis. Functional residual capacity declines by about 20% after CPB (13). Although intrapulmonary shunt ($\dot{Q}_S/\dot{Q}_T$) and venoarterial admixture are increased after CPB, there is a poor correlation between decreases in measured FRC and increases in $\dot{Q}_S/\dot{Q}_T$ (3, 14).

ALTERED MECHANICAL PROPERTIES OF THE LUNG

A number of investigators have found significant changes in pulmonary mechanics induced by CPB (10, 15–19). Lung compliance (C_L) is decreased, and airway resistance (R_{AW}) and work of breathing are increased (for an explanation of the tests described, see Appendix 1). In some studies, however, alterations in pulmonary mechanics induced by CPB have been negligible (20–22).

Andersen and Ghia (10, 19) assessed the effect of CPB on total airflow resistance, total compliance of the lungs and chest wall (static thoracic compliance, C_{TH}), A-aDo$_2$, and the ratio of dead space to tidal volume (V_D/V_T). Although they did find some deterioration in these functions during CPB, they were of the same nature as those occurring in patients undergoing thoracic procedures without CPB. This study implicated active lung retraction and pleural violation, rather than CPB itself, as the major causes of disturbed lung mechanics during cardiac surgery. These authors also demonstrated a close relationship between poor preoperative pulmonary and cardiac function, and deterioration in pulmonary function in the postoperative period.

Sullivan et al. (20) attempted to exclude the impact of pleural violation, with its attendant pneumothorax and effusion, from the effects of CPB alone. They studied patients undergoing median sternotomy for correction of acquired valvular heart disease in whom neither pleural space was entered. Measurement of dynamic compliance, elastic and flow resistive work of breathing, and $\dot{Q}_S/\dot{Q}_T$ revealed no significant differences before and after CPB. Karlson et al. (22) were also not able to demonstrate any significant change in compliance, nonelastic resistance, or the work/volume ratio of the lung before and after CPB. However, there was a significant decline in lung compliance by the time patients were extubated and breathing spontaneously after surgery, compared with the preoperative level. Again, this suggests a greater contribution to pulmonary complications from the effects of anesthesia and thoracotomy than CPB itself. Cardiopulmonary bypass appears to have little adverse effect on pediatric pulmonary mechanics (21). In patients with a lesion such as an endocardial cushion defect, which causes pulmonary vascular engorgement, repair corrects the pulmonary hyperemia so that lung compliance is actually improved after CPB.

CLINICAL FEATURES

During CPB atelectasis can be directly visualized in the exposed lung, although large parts of the dependent lung fields are not in view. After the chest is closed, significant atelectasis is usually first recognised by a decrease in C_L, which results in the generation of increased peak airway pressure (P_{PK}) at normal tidal volumes (e.g., 35 cm H_2O at V_T of 10 ml/kg). This is associated with an increased A-aDo$_2$ (e.g., arterial oxygen tension [Pao$_2$] of less than 200 mm Hg on inspired oxygen fraction [FIo$_2$] of 1.0) although it will be detected by pulse oximetry only when the Pao2 falls to less than 90 mm Hg and the pulse oximetry saturation (Spo$_2$) declines below 98%. After surgery, careful auscultation of the chest reveals bronchial breathing and crackles, usually in the dependent lung fields, but clinical signs may underestimate the extent of atelectasis and radiologic confirmation is essential.

The decline in FRC and lung compliance increases the alveolar distending work of breathing. If this is severe enough it can lead to acute hypoxemic respiratory failure and continued requirement for mechanical ventilation. Collapsed airways compromise secretion clearance and predispose to pulmonary superinfection and pneumonia.

Prevention and Treatment of Atelectasis

PREVENTION

Attempts have been made to prevent atelectasis from occurring during CPB by the provision of positive-pressure ventilation, sighs, or static inflation at 5 to 10 cm H_2O pressure. However, Ellis et al. (23) found that lung compliance deteriorated during CPB, whether the lungs were mechanically ventilated, statically inflated, or allowed to deflate. Ghia and Andersen (10) claimed that the use of static inflation plus an intermittent sigh every 10 minutes to an airway pressure of 25 to 30 cm H_2O prevented a decrease in C_{TH}, and increases in R_{AW}, V_D/V_T, and A-aDo_2. Contrasting arguments were presented by Stanley et al. (4), who evaluated C_L and $\dot{Q}_S/\dot{Q}_T$ before and after CPB in 132 calves undergoing artificial heart implantation with halothane-o_2 anesthesia. The provision of positive-pressure ventilation during CPB caused a greater increase in shunt and decrease in compliance after CPB, probably through depletion of surfactant. These variables were not influenced by the gas inflating the lungs (100% o_2 or 50% o_2/N_2O). Static pulmonary inflation (continuous positive airway pressure [CPAP]) offered no advantage over allowing the lungs to remain collapsed.

Weedn et al. (24) suggested that static inflation of the lungs with oxygen may pre-

vent ultrastructural damage by sustaining cellular oxidative metabolism. In small animal studies the use of CPAP during CPB was associated with lower pulmonary lactate/pyruvate ratios and greater high-energy phosphate concentrations than the use of lung collapse (25). However, these findings have not been correlated with significant changes in gross lung function.

There is reasonable evidence that the avoidance of entry into the pleural spaces will prevent a large amount of the decrease in lung compliance seen after CPB (10, 19, 20). However, the common usage of the transpleural approach to dissection of the left internal mammary artery makes this a moot point for many patients undergoing coronary revascularization.

TREATMENT

It is possible that a series of sighs, i.e., slow, sustained inspiratory maneuvers to a P_{PK} of 25 to 30 cm H_2O, could be given just prior to weaning from CPB. This may reverse atelectasis and improve lung compliance. Identical "Valsalva" maneuvers are routinely used after open heart procedures to expel air from the left atrium and ventricle. There is a risk of disruption of an internal mammary graft by excessive distension of the left lung, or rupture of a lung bleb or weakened area. However, incision of the pericardium will allow the lung to inflate without excessive stretching of the internal mammary graft. Sighs given after separation from CPB impede venous return and add to hemodynamic instability.

Clinically, the most effective means of reversing decreased FRC and atelectasis after CPB is to provide mechanical ventilation with positive end-expiratory pressure (PEEP), which is continued into the postoperative period (14). However, the improvement in measured FRC does not directly correlate with improvement in $\dot{Q}_S/\dot{Q}_T$ or A-aDo_2. Dobbinson and Miller (13) found that FRC increased postoperatively only when levels of PEEP of 6 cm H_2O or greater were used, at the expense of cardiac performance. The adverse effects of PEEP on cardiac output can easily be overcome with modest inotropic support (e.g., dopamine 5 μg/kg/min) or preload augmentation (26, 27).

In our own experience, we have found that the combination of large tidal volumes (12 to 15 ml/kg), moderate levels of PEEP (5 to 8 cm H_2O) and, importantly, adequate time (4 to 8 hours) are successful in improving oxygenation, A-aDo_2, and C$_L$ in the vast majority of cases. A clinical guide to reasonably delivered tidal volume is provided by P$_{PK}$: ideally, it should be approximately 25 cm H_2O. If P$_{PK}$ is less than 20 cm H_2O and a system air leak has been excluded, the delivered tidal volume is probably inadequate and should be increased. If P$_{PK}$ is greater than 35 cm H_2O, either delivered tidal volume is excessive or there is another cause of high airway pressure that requires investigation (e.g., endobronchial intubation, bronchospasm, pulmonary edema). The size of the delivered tidal volume should be limited to about 12 ml/kg in patients who have undergone internal mammary grafting and where it has been noted intraoperatively that lung expansion tends to displace the graft. A large A-aDo_2 that is unresponsive to these measures (and that does not have an obvious underlying cause) is usually due to intrinsic lung disease or pulmonary edema.

SECTION 2: ACUTE LUNG INJURY AND CPB

Pathophysiology of Acute Lung Injury

Soon after the advent of CPB in the 1950s, it became apparent that a substantial proportion of deaths following cardiac surgery was related to a syndrome of acute respiratory failure referred to as "pump lung" (28). Biopsy or autopsy specimens from patients revealed striking morphologic changes (29). The lungs were diffusely congested, with intraalveolar and interstitial edema and hemorrhagic atelectasis—a picture not unlike "shock lung." Electron microscopy revealed that vessel lumina were packed with neutrophils, there was diffuse swelling of the endothelial cells, including mitochondria and the endoplasmic reticulum, and cytoplasmic swelling in the membranous pneumocytes.

THE MICROEMBOLIC THEORY

Initially it was considered that this lesion was due to embolization of particulate debris during CPB, including aggregated protein, disintegrated platelets, damaged neutrophils and fibrin, or even fat globules, a picture similar to that found with massive blood transfusion (30–35). The Dacron wool filter was introduced by Swank in 1961 (36), and Hill et al. (32) demonstrated that it could dramatically decrease the intensity of nonfat cerebral embolism. Connell et al. (34) found that Dacron wool filtration during CPB removed platelet-leucocyte aggregates and reduced the extent of the degenerative lesions in the lung: the more complete the filtration, the more normal the lungs appeared.

Despite these findings it became apparent that striking pulmonary damage could occur even when all the perfusate is filtered, suggesting other etiologies for pump lung. Indeed, the nature of the lesion we see today may be considerably different from that described in an era during which the CPB circuit was primed with whole blood that could be laden with platelet-neutrophil microaggregates, disk or bubble oxygenators caused denaturation of plasma proteins, and in-line arterial filters were rarely used.

COMPLEMENT ACTIVATION

Complement activation and the potential for pulmonary dysfunction appear to be a consistent response to contact activation of blood in extracorporeal circuits, such as leukapheresis and hemodialysis (37, 38). Some susceptible patients have developed life-threatening bronchospasm, with urticaria, angioedema, hypotension, and cardiopulmonary collapse on first use of hemodialysis.

The complement system performs three vital functions in the body's defense against invading microorganisms: leukocyte activation, cytolysis, and opsonization. The last renders bacterial cells vulnerable to phagocytosis by the adherence of opsonins or complement components. Complement is activated through two interrelated cascades termed the classical and alternate pathways, which ultimately lead to cleavage of C3, the central component of the system (Fig. 18.1). The enzyme cascade is gener-

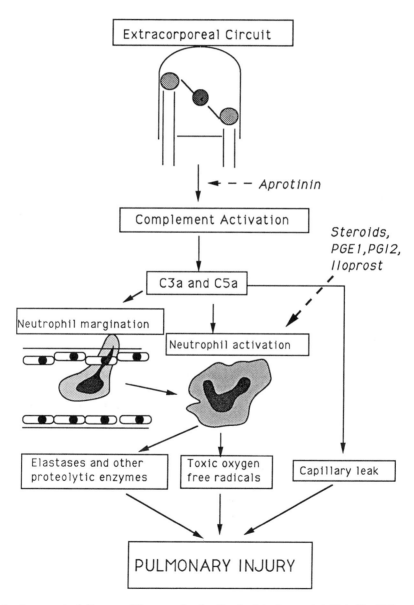

Figure 18.1. A conceptual diagram of the cascade of pathophysiologic events initiated by CPB and leading to pulmonary injury. Dashed arrows indicate inhibitory actions.

ated by the activation of enzyme precursors, which are fixed to biological membranes. Each component, a highly specialized proteinase, activates the next enzyme precursor to its catalytically active state by limited proteolysis. A small peptide fragment is cleaved and a nascent membrane binding site is exposed, so forming the next active complement enzyme of the sequence. Because each component can activate many enzyme precursors, the whole system forms an amplification cascade akin to the coagulation cascade (39).

During the activation of the complement system via either the classical or alternate pathway, C3a and C5a anaphylotoxins are generated. The C3a causes smooth muscle contraction in a wide variety of animal tissues. The C5a is 10 to 20 times more active than C3a on a molar basis and has wider biological activity. It is a major chemotactic factor for neutrophils, resulting in their margination in vessels and neutropenia. The C5a activates neutrophils by triggering the bactericidal oxidative burst, and causes the release of arachidonic acid metabolites such as leukotriene B_4, which increases vascular permeability. The C5a also provokes mast cell degranulation and smooth muscle contraction.

The striking similarities between the biological activities of anaphylotoxins C3a and C5a, and the capillary leak syndrome and organ dysfunction associated with CPB, prompted Chenoweth et al. (40) to investigate complement activation as a cause of pump lung. They demonstrated that there was a correlation between the duration of CPB, the degree of elevation of C3a levels, and post-CPB organ dysfunction. Animal studies revealed that intravenous infusion of activated complement produces pulmonary leukocyte trapping with transient leukopenia, as well as transpulmonary release of thromboxane A_2, leading to pulmonary vasoconstriction and hypertension. Concomitantly, there is an increase in the pulmonary microvascular permeability (41). This process can be at-

tenuated by superoxide dismutase, which suggests that free oxygen radicals play a role in tissue injury after activated complement infusion (42).

Hammerschmidt and Jacob (43) randomized 28 patients to CPB with membrane or bubble oxygenators, with or without steroid pretreatment. A marked leukopenia occurred in all patients. Total complement showed no decline in the 1st hour of CPB and only a slight decline in the group without steroid pretreatment. However, C3a and C5a could not be detected. The membrane oxygenator produced a significantly greater degree and duration of neutropenia, consistent with the fact that its materials include silicone, expanded Teflon, and polypropylene, which activate complement in vitro. The failure to demonstrate increased circulating C3a and C5a may have been because of their rapid clearance, the detection limits of the assay, or the fact that C5a binds so avidly to human neutrophils that it may not be detectable free in the plasma.

In contrast, Howard et al. (44) demonstrated marked increases in C3a levels within 2 minutes of the onset of CPB, an increase in C5a levels toward the end of CPB, and increased C4a levels in the postoperative period. Lung biopsy specimens that were normal before CPB were radically altered, with an increased number of neutrophils in the pulmonary arterioles and adhering to capillary walls. The finding of a transpulmonary gradient of neutrophils suggested that they were sequestrated in the pulmonary vasculature. Collett et al. (45) used sensitive assays to determine which pathway is responsible for activation of complement during CPB. They demonstrated a rapid rise in fragment Ba within 90 seconds of initiation of CPB, indicating activation of the alternate pathway. The polymers incorporated into the extracorporeal circuit are known to activate the alternate pathway in vitro (40, 46). However, there is also activation of the common pathway because C3d increases with a concomitant decline in C3.

INFLAMMATORY RESPONSE

During aortic cross-clamping on CPB, the neutrophil count in right and left atrial blood increases. After aortic cross-clamp release, and as blood flow is restored to the pulmonary vasculature, the right atrial neutrophil count increases but the left atrial count declines; neutrophils appear to be trapped in the pulmonary capillaries (46). Simultaneously, products of lipid peroxidation measured by the thiobarbituric acid reaction reach a peak. This implies a direct relationship between neutrophil trapping and oxygen free radical peroxidation of membrane lipids. Of course, reperfusion injury after ischemia generates oxygen free radicals and may also contribute to lipid peroxidation at this time. Braude et al. (41) confirmed that CPB in dogs is associated with neutrophil sequestration, and egress from the lung of products of lipid peroxidation. They also demonstrated profound pulmonary vascular permeability by finding significantly increased lung transvascular protein flux as measured by In^{113m}-transferrin.

Chenoweth et al. (40) had demonstrated that complement is activated by the nylon mesh of the bubble oxygenator and by vigorous bubbling of oxygen through the blood. Van Oeveren et al. (47) investigated whether complement activation could be lessened by the use of hollow-fiber membrane oxygenators. Hemolysis, thrombocytopenia, β-thromboglobulin release (a marker of platelet activation), and generation of reactive oxygen species in leukocytes was significantly greater with the bubble oxygenator. However, the rate of complement activation was similar with the membrane oxygenator, casting doubt on whether its use appreciably alters pulmonary morbidity on CPB.

Jansen et al. (48) noted a significant increase in C3a and elastase (evidence of activated leukocytes) after the onset of CPB, which was exacerbated after aortic cross-clamp release. This was associated with increases in leukotriene B$_4$, an eicosanoid that induces capillary leak, and tissue plasminogen activator, which enhances fibrinolysis.

The role of the eicosanoids, thromboxane, and prostacyclin in this acute inflammatory response is yet unclear (49). Thromboxane is released from platelets activated by the extracorporeal circuit, and its profound effects on vasoconstriction and platelet aggregation could further injure the microcirculation (50). Prostacyclin, which has the opposite actions, is released especially during pulsatile perfusion on CPB, perhaps because of increased shear stress on the endothelium (51). However, the benefits of pulsatile perfusion in prevention of acute lung injury during CPB remain unknown.

In summary, contact activation of the blood by the extracorporeal circuit triggers a series of amplification cascades mediated by proteolytic enzymes, especially serine proteases. It results in the activation of complement, especially C5a anaphylatoxin. The C5a is a potent bioactive molecule that normally mediates the acute inflammatory response, which has spasmogenic and leukocyte-activating properties that cause degranulation and release of toxic oxygen free radicals (52). Complement-exposed neutrophils are stimulated to adhere to surfaces and to aggregate, resulting in margination in blood vessels and leukoembolization. These neutrophils markedly increase their production of oxygen free radicals and release proteolytic enzymes, which damage endothelial cells. Complement activation and neutrophil arachidonic acid metabolites cause increased vascular permeability with capillary leak.

OTHER FACTORS CONTRIBUTING TO ACUTE LUNG INJURY

Hypoxia of Lung Parenchyma

During CPB the lungs are isolated from the pulmonary circulation. Mandelbaum and Giammona (53) demonstrated that collateral blood flow from the bronchial circulation passes through the pulmonary capillary bed and participates in cellular respiration. Attempts have been made to evaluate the nature of bronchial collateral blood flow, metabolic oxygen consumption of the lung parenchyma, and the effects of pulmonary arterial occlusion and hypoxia on the lung tissue. Balis et al. (54) found that perfusion of the canine pulmonary artery with oxygenated blood protects against hemorrhagic atelectasis during CPB. Although this suggests that hypoxia may contribute to acute lung injury, during CPB the pulmonary artery is not perfused with oxygenated blood either. Nahas et al. (55) perfused one lung with half the CPB venous return and ventilated both lungs. They observed a greater degree of damage in the perfused lung, which implied that acute lung injury is more likely to be due to humoral factors such as complement than direct tissue hypoxia.

Hemodilution

When the extracorporeal circuit is primed with colloid or crystalloid solutions there is an immediate decrease in the colloid oncotic pressure (COP) at the onset of CPB. Thereafter, an incomplete compensatory increase in COP occurs, due to an efflux of water from the intravascular to extravascular space, and to an influx of albumin from peripheral albumin stores (56). The decrease in microvascular oncotic pressure caused by hemodilution increases transcapillary fluid flux. However, double-dilution indicator techniques have indicated that as much as a 50% decrease in COP may be required to produce significant increases in pulmonary extravascular water. Byrick et al. (57) determined that accumulation of pulmonary extravascular water after coronary revascularization is not affected by priming the circuit with colloid or crystalloid solutions. Hemodilution on CPB with colloid or crystalloid does not appear to harm the lungs—indeed, it may be protective because it prevents impairment of surfactant.

Elevated Pulmonary Artery Pressure

In 1958 Kolff et al. (58) called attention to the danger of overfilling of the vascular bed as a possible cause of pulmonary complications following CPB. They wrote, "Overfilling of the pulmonary vascular bed during operations using extracorporeal circulation is most likely to occur when the heart chambers are not open. It can be avoided by placing an adequate drainage tube in the left atrium." Elevated pulmonary artery pressure during CPB was presented as the possible cause of a case of acute pulmonary edema by Byrick et al. (59) The patient had had persistent increases in pulmonary artery pressure during CPB due to inadequate venting of the left ventricle, as a result of aortic incompetence and poor left ventricular function. This was associated with a significant increase in extravascular lung water and calculated intrapulmonary shunt fraction.

Effective left ventricular venting protects the heart and lungs during CPB by reducing hydrostatic pressure in the pulmonary capillary bed. This curtails the transfer of water and electrolytes across the lung by Starling's forces in patients who are already hemodiluted and have a low COP. Increased pulmonary artery pressure is avoided if the heart is adequately vented via the pulmonary artery, right superior pulmonary vein, left atrium, left ventricle, or aortic root.

Clinical Syndromes of Acute Lung Injury

NONCARDIOGENIC PULMONARY EDEMA

Pathophysiology

Fulminant noncardiogenic pulmonary edema following CPB is an infrequent but life-threatening event, occurring in less than 1% of cases but associated with a mortality rate of 30 to 50% (60, 61). After Llamas et al. (62) reported ARDS following CPB, Olinger et al. (63) described four patients who experienced severe ARDS and peripheral vascular collapse following an otherwise uneventful CPB. Culliford et al. (64) presented three successfully treated cases in which fulminant pulmonary edema manifested within 6 hours of uneventful CPB. Since then, multiple reports have appeared in the literature that have attempted to postulate the etiology and define the therapy for this syndrome.

Noncardiogenic pulmonary edema occurs when the permeability characteristics of the alveolar capillary membrane are dramatically altered, creating a capillary leak syndrome with net migration of water and protein into the alveolar space. In its most dramatic form, it presents as the acute onset of a massive outpouring of proteinaceous fluid from the endotracheal tube. This is associated with an increase in intraalveolar fluid, pulmonary vascular resistance, intrapulmonary shunt, and hypoxemia. Lung compliance is markedly decreased. Diffuse bilateral infiltrates are seen on chest radiograph. Noncardiogenic pulmonary edema is distinguished from cardiac failure by the finding of normal or low left atrial or pulmonary artery wedge pressures, and a high protein concentration in the edema fluid (albumin concentration is > 90% of that in serum).

The most important etiologic factor is complement activation, which has been previously discussed. Noncardiogenic pulmonary edema probably occurs more often with the administration of blood products and fresh-frozen plasma *after* CPB, than during CPB itself (65–67). Although the exact mechanism of this process is unclear, antileukocyte antibodies have been isolated from both donors and recipients (68, 69). The antibodies probably bind to the leukocyte, activate the cell, and result in the release of proteolytic enzymes with subsequent endothelial damage and capillary leak. The antigen-antibody complex may

also directly activate complement and complement-mediated injury of the endothelium (43). Protamine-induced noncardiogenic pulmonary edema may be due to an immune-mediated hypersensitivity reaction (type I), to its direct activation of the complement system, or to its enhancement of heparin's ability to activate complement (63, 70).

Management

The treatment of noncardiogenic pulmonary edema following CPB must take into consideration that enormous amounts of fluid are lost from the intravascular space because of the profound capillary leak syndrome. Hashim et al. (65) point out that all three patients who died in their series of nine reactions to fresh-frozen plasma after CPB succumbed to low cardiac output syndrome rather than hypoxemia. Even in patients who have diffuse pulmonary edema with a severe intrapulmonary shunt and high A-aDo$_2$, aggressive restoration of intravascular volume with red cells, colloid, or crystalloid is required, guided by left ventricular filling pressure monitoring. Pulmonary management consists of positive pressure ventilation with high levels of airway pressure (71, 72). This may be provided as volume controlled ventilation with extrinsic positive end-expiratory pressure (PEEP$_E$), or pressure-controlled ventilation with inverse inspiratory:expiratory ratio and intrinsic or auto-PEEP (PEEP$_I$). In either event, the goals are to support the functional residual capacity, to decrease $\dot{Q}_S/\dot{Q}_T$, and to wean a high inspired oxygen fraction. Blood transfusion and inotropic support of the cardiovascular system, with calculation of oxygen derived variables, is necessary to maintain cardiac output and oxygen delivery. Steroid therapy is not indicated. Ultimate resolution involves healing of the injured lung, which is essentially a function of time.

Pilato et al. (73) reported a case of severe ARDS in which conventional treatment was inadequate and venovenous extracorporeal membrane oxygenation was instituted (73). Because of compromised cardiac function and deteriorating pulmonary function, the patient could not tolerate maximal conventional ventilator support. Extracorporeal membrane oxygenation improved oxygenation, enabling a decrease in ventilator support and a concomitant increase in cardiac output by minimizing the effects of mechanical ventilation on ventricular function. The increase in cardiac output decreased the intrapulmonary shunt with a further dramatic improvement in oxygenation.

ACUTE BRONCHOSPASM

Severe bronchospasm during CPB is an unusual event, even though many patients with chronic obstructive pulmonary disease and asthma undergo cardiac surgery.

Tuman and Ivankovich (74) reported three cases of bronchospasm on CPB. None of the patients had a history of asthma. In all cases, expiratory wheezing was heard and it was impossible to deflate the lungs on resumption of ventilation at the end of CPB. The lungs became greatly distended and bulged into the surgical field. Cardiac filling pressures were normal. In two cases, fiberoptic bronchoscopy was performed, revealing no abnormalities. No patient developed urticaria or erythema. All patients were given bronchodilator therapy (atropine, aminophylline, steroids, epinephrine, ketamine) plus halothane or isoflurane on CPB; all recovered.

Durant and Joucken (75) reported the remarkable case of an asthmatic hypertensive patient who was receiving cimetidine 400 mg b.i.d. for a gastric ulcer. The patient was given 650 mg labetalol intravenously over 15 hours for preoperative control of hypertension and unstable angina. During the 1st hour of CPB, he was given 14 mg phenylephrine for hypotension (mean arterial pressure, 40 to 45 mm Hg); during re-

warming, mean arterial pressure overshot to 150 mm Hg. On cessation of CPB, protracted bronchospasm occurred. Fiberoptic bronchoscopy revealed some mucus plugging and widespread edema. After aminophylline and steroids, the bronchospasm was finally relieved by an infusion of epinephrine. The authors questioned whether cimetidine had decreased labetalol clearance, and whether the combination of labetalol-induced β-blockade, and phenylephrine-induced α-agonism caused bronchospasm.

Casella and Humphrey (76) reported severe bronchospasm in the denervated lung of a heart-lung transplant recipient. The recipient had a history of severe exercise-induced asthma and a positive family history. The donor had no history of lung disease. The recipient developed profound airway obstruction in the donor lungs after CPB, with a peak airway pressure greater than 100 cm H_2O. The left lung could be inflated, but not deflated. Fiberoptic bronchoscopy was negative. Treatment consisted of isoproterenol, steroids, aminophylline, halothane, atropine, and furosemide. This resulted in improvement, but the patient succumbed to a fatal postoperative pneumonia.

Kyosola et al. (77) reported two cases of bronchospasm after CPB. Neither patient had a history of asthma or chronic bronchitis. In their second case, the bulging left lung disrupted the internal mammary graft, leading to a perioperative myocardial infarction, postoperative low cardiac output syndrome, pulmonary embolism, and death.

Etiology of Bronchospasm During CPB.

The most likely cause of fulminant bronchospasm on CPB is activation of human C5a anaphylatoxin by the extracorporeal circuit (52). A number of other potential causes exist. Acute cardiogenic pulmonary edema is frequently associated with bronchospasm (cardiac asthma), but there is obvious evidence of elevated left ventricular filling pressures, ventricular dysfunction, and alveolar edema. The cold urticaria syndrome is a rare disorder characterized by the release of histamine on exposure to cold, resulting in laryngospasm, bronchospasm, and hypotension. It may be prevented by pretreatment with H_1- and H_2-blockers. Bronchospasm might occur as a simple exacerbation of preexisting bronchospastic disease, or be triggered by instrumentation, secretions, or cold anesthetic gas in patients with hyperreactive airways, especially after a recent respiratory infection. β-Adrenergic blockade, even with a so-called selective (β_1) antagonist, may induce bronchospasm in susceptible individuals. Allergic reactions to antibiotics or protamine may cause acute bronchospasm in association with other manifestations of a hypersensitivity response, including hypotension, tachycardia, erythema, and urticaria. Drugs that induce histamine release, such as morphine or atracurium, are likely to exacerbate bronchospasm only when given in high doses.

Management of Bronchospasm on CPB

The most immediate response should be to attempt maximum hand ventilation with 100% oxygen—the anesthesia ventilator will not be able to cope with the rapid inspiratory flow and long expiratory time required to avoid further air trapping. Although bronchospasm may have been induced by CPB, it is important not to attempt to come off CPB—and it may be necessary to go back on CPB—until the severe attack has been broken. The airway should be examined from machine to patient, and a suction catheter passed down the endotracheal tube to exclude mechanical obstruction. Blood must be drawn for arterial blood gases because the end-tidal CO_2 will grossly underestimate arterial carbon dioxide tension (Pa_{CO_2}). A chest radiograph is obtained to exclude pneumothorax and identify pulmonary edema. Cardiac asthma is usually accompanied by elevated left atrial and pulmonary artery pressures and pulmonary edema fluid in the endotracheal tube. Fibreoptic bronchoscopy is very helpful in excluding mechanical causes for wheezing, but it may further irritate the airways and exacerbate bronchospasm.

Specific treatment includes administration of β_2 selective agonists (albuterol, metaproterenol) directly into the endotracheal tube by metered dose inhaler. Even with the use of airway adaptors, several puffs should be given because less than 15% of the metered dose of bronchodilator is delivered to the small airways with each puff. If this is not effective, small intravenous boluses of epinephrine (5 to 10 μg) may be given, followed by a continuous low-dose infusion (0.01 to 0.02 μg/kg/min). Intravenous lidocaine (1.5 mg/kg) will not reverse an acute attack, but should be given to decrease airway hyperreactivity prior to any airway manipulation.

Other pharmacologic interventions are less likely to be effective. Steroid therapy (e.g., 125 mg methylprednisolone IV) takes about 4 to 5 hours for onset of its effect. Ipratropium (Atrovent), an anticholinergic drying agent, is not effective in acute bronchospasm. Ketamine (25 to 150 mg) has bronchodilator activity and potentiates the effect of epinephrine on the airway. Addition of aminophylline, a nonselective phosphodiesterase inhibitor, is unlikely to enhance bronchodilation already achieved with albuterol or epinephrine, and has a high risk of toxic effects such as tachyarrhythmias, especially in an acidotic, hypoxemic milieu. Volatile anesthetic agents are potent bronchodilators and can be used via the anesthesia machine or the pump oxygenator. However, halothane sensitizes the myocardium to catecholamines and there is a high risk of tachyarrhythmias; the threshold is significantly lower with isoflurane or enflurane, which have equivalent bronchodilator properties. Combined administration of an H_1-blocker (diphenhy-dramine) and H_2-blocker (ranitidine) could prevent some hypersensitivity responses, but is not indicated for treatment of acute bronchospasm.

Prevention and Treatment of Acute Lung Injury

BLOOD FILTRATION

Use of extracorporeal Dacron poly-ester blood filters decreases lung damage by reducing pulmonary microembolism by microthrombi, and by filtering activated leukocytes and damaged platelets, which promote acute inflammatory responses (31–34, 78).

MEMBRANE OXYGENATORS

Membrane oxygenators avoid poten-tial damage to blood components and plasma proteins caused by gas bubbling. The risk of microembolization, sludging and capillary occlusion, hemolysis, throm-bocytopenia, and leukocyte activation, al-though not overall complement activation, is significantly less than that caused by the bubble oxygenator (47).

HEMODILUTION

Hemodilution and avoidance of ho-mologous blood prime during CPB appear to have a protective effect on lung function. One of the benefits of hemodilution may be greater preservation of surfactant. Animals in which a blood-free pump prime was used developed a significantly smaller intrapul-monary shunt than those animals in which homologous blood was used (55).

AVOIDANCE OF PULMONARY VASCULAR DISTENSION

Every effort should be made to avoid left ventricular and pulmonary vascular dis-tension, which results in pulmonary hemor-rhage and acute lung injury. Pressure can be decompressed by venting either the left

ventricle, left atrium, pulmonary veins, or pulmonary artery (58, 59).

PHARMACOLOGIC PROTECTION

Steroids

Intravenous dexamethasone and high-dose methylprednisolone are effective in inhibiting the increase in leukotriene B4 and tissue plasminogen activator after aortic cross-clamp release in patients undergoing CPB (48). However, cortico-steroids do not prevent C3a activation or leukocyte elastase release. Boscoe et al. (79) found that women receiving high-dose methylprednisolone had signifi-cantly greater complement activation than men. In a study comparing 50 pa-tients with historical controls, Coffin et al. (80) administered a single dose of methylprednisolone (30 mg/kg) at the start of anesthesia. Not only did this not confer any improvement on post-CPB lung function or complication rate, but pa-tients receiving steroids did less well with regard to blood loss, low cardiac output syndrome, and requirement for postopera-tive mechanical ventilation.

Prostaglandins

Vasodilator prostaglandins (PGs) such as PGE_1 may actually be more protec-tive on CPB than corticosteroids, with greater inhibition of intravascular pulmo-nary leukocyte aggregation, activation, and free radical production (81). The effect of PGE_1 is to increase cyclic adenosine mono-phosphate formation, which stabilizes leu-kocyte lysosomes. Administration of PGE_1, prostacyclin, or iloprost (a more stable prostacyclin analog) during CPB prevents platelet aggregation, thromboxane release, and decreases operative bleeding (82, 83). However, use of these agents is somewhat limited by their hypotensive effect, and it is not clear whether their platelet-sparing actions also protect against acute lung in-jury on CPB.

Aprotinin (Trasylol)

Aprotinin (Trasylol) is a naturally occuring 58-amino acid polypeptide that inhibits serine proteases such as plasmin and kallikrein (84). It has been known for a number of years that aprotinin infusion prevents the activation of kininogen and the formation of bradykinin on CPB (85). When CPB lasts longer than 60 minutes, the amounts of bradykinin released (4.6 to 18.0 ng/ml) are sufficient to increase capillary permeability and decrease peripheral vascular resistance, and may thereby increase extravascular lung water and lung dysfunction. Kallikrein activates leukocytes to release free oxygen radicals. In exploring the possibility that infusion of high-dose aprotinin during CPB might prevent acute lung injury, Royston and his co-workers (86) serendipitously found a dramatic reduction in surgical blood loss during the procedure. The primary mechanisms appear to be prevention of platelet aggregation and inhibition of fibrinolysis. The antifibrinolytic and hemostatic properties of aprotinin in the reduction of operative bleeding during cardiac and liver surgery have subsequently received a great deal of attention (87–91). However, its effect on the prevention of acute lung injury awaits further clarification.

SECTION 3: EFFECTS OF CPB ON LUNG METABOLIC FUNCTION

The lung plays an important function in the uptake and release of vasoactive substances. Since the lung is the only organ that receives the entire circulation, it is uniquely suited to this function. The lung is an important site for both activation and inactivation of prostaglandins. Prostacyclin (PGI_2) is primarily synthesized and released by pulmonary vascular endothelium, although it is not metabolized by the lungs. Prostaglandins of the E and F class are almost completely metabolized in a single passage through the lungs. Angiotensin-converting enzyme, located in pulmonary endothelial cells, converts the relatively inactive polypeptide, angiotensin I, to the potent vasoconstrictor and aldosterone stimulator, angiotensin II. The lung also inactivates circulating serotonin (5-hydroxy tryptamine) and bradykinin, and participates in the uptake of norepinephrine to some degree.

Pitt et al. (92) hypothesized that systemic hypertension after CPB is caused by depressed clearance of neurohumoral substances, particularly norepinephrine, by the damaged lung following CPB. Their data suggest that the diminution in the lung's ability to remove norepinephrine from the circulation was directly related to the duration of CPB. Claremont and Branthwaite (93) measured the activity of angiotensin-converting enzyme and $a1$-antitrypsin, a protease inhibitor thought to exert a protective effect on pulmonary tissue by inactivating proteases and elastases liberated from leukocytes and macrophages (93). Angiotensin-converting enzyme activity declined following CPB, possibly due to pulmonary damage. Decreased pulmonary extraction of serotonin following CPB may also play a role in postoperative pulmonary complications (94).

There is also evidence that the lungs play a role in coagulation under normal and abnormal conditions. There are a large number of mast cells containing heparin in the interstitium of the lung. The lung is able to secrete immunoglobulins in the bronchial mucus, which contribute to defense against infection. The effects of CPB on these functions have not been studied.

REFERENCES

1. Pennock J, Pierce W, Waldhausen J. The management of the lungs during cardiopulmonary bypass. Surg Gynecol Obstet 1977;145:917–927.
2. Phang P, Keough K. Inhibition of pulmonary surfactant by plasma from normal adults and from patients having cardiopulmonary bypass. Journal of Thorac Cardiovasc Surg 1986;91:248–251.

3. Mandelbaum I, Giammona S. Extracorporeal circulation, pulmonary compliance and pulmonary surfactant. J Thorac Cardiovasc Surg 1964;48: 881–889.

4. Stanley T, Liu W-S, Gentry S. Effects of ventilatory techniques during cardiopulmonary bypass on post-bypass and postoperative pulmonary compliance and shunt. Anesthesiology 1977;46: 391–395.

5. Lindholm C, Ollman B, Snyder J, et al. Flexible fiberoptic bronchoscopy in critical care medicine. Crit Care Med 1974;2:250–261.

6. Sladen R, Jenkins L. Intermittent mandatory ventilation and controlled mechanical ventilation without positive end-expiratory pressure following cardio-pulmonary bypass. Can Anaesth Soc J 1978;25:166–172.

7. Osborn JJ, Popper RW, Keith WJ, et al. Respiratory insufficiency following open heart surgery. Ann Surg 1962;156:638–647.

8. Hedley-Whyte J, Corning H, Lauer MB, et al. Pulmonary ventilation-perfusion relations after heart valve replacement or repair in man. J Clin Invest 1965;44:406–416.

9. Geha HS, Seesler HD, Kirkin JW. Alveolar-arterial oxygen gradients after open intracardiac surgery. J Thorac Cardiovasc Surg 1966;51:609–615.

10. Ghia J, Andersen N. Pulmonary function and cardiopulmonary bypass. JAMA 1970;212: 593–597.

11. Barat RE, DeVillota D, Avello F, et al. A study of the oxygenation of cardiac patients submitted to extracorporeal circulation. Br J Anaesth 1972; 44:817–824.

12. Turnbull K, Miyagishima R, Gerein A. Pulmonary complications and cardiopulmonary bypass. A clinical study in adults. Can Anaesth Soc J 1974;21:181–194.

13. Dobbinson T, Miller J. Respiratory and cardiovascular responses to PEEP in artificially ventilated patients after cardiopulmonary bypass surgery. Anaesth Intensive Care 1981;9:307–313.

14. Downs J, Mitchell L. Pulmonary effects of ventilatory pattern following cardiopulmonary bypass. Crit Care Med 1976;4:295–300.

15. Garzon AA, Seltzer B, Karlson KE. Respiratory mechanics following open-heart surgery for acquired valvular disease. Circulation 1966;33–34(suppl II):57–64.

16. Lesage A, Tsuchioka H, Young W, et al. Pathogenesis of pulmonary damage during extracorporeal circulation. Arch Surg 1966;93:1002–1008.

17. Shimizu T, Lewis F. An experimental study of pulmonary function following cardiopulmonary bypass. J Thorac Cardiovasc Surg 1966;52: 565–570.

18. Garzon A, Seltzer B, Lichtenstein S, et al. Influence of open-heart surgery on respiratory work. Dis Chest 1967;52:392–396.

19. Andersen N, Ghia J. Pulmonary function, cardiac status, and postoperative course in relation to cardiopulmonary bypass. J Thorac Cardiovasc Surg 1970;59:474–483.

20. Sullivan S, Patterson R, Malm J, et al. Effect of heart-lung bypass on the mechanics of breathing in man. J Thorac Cardiovasc Surg 1966;51: 205–212.

21. Deal C, Osborn J, Miller CJ, et al. Pulmonary compliance in congenital heart disease and its relation to cardiopulmonary bypass. J Thorac Cardiovasc Surg 1968;55:320–327.

22. Karlson K, Saklad M, Paliotta J, et al. Computerized on-line analysis of pulmonary mechanics in patients undergoing cardiopulmonary bypass. Bull de la Soc Int de Chir 1975;2:121–124.

23. Ellis E, Brown A, Osborn JJ, et al. Effect of altered ventilation patterns on compliance during cardiopulmonary bypass. Anesth Analg 1969;48: 947–952.

24. Weedn R, Coalson J, Greenfield L. Effects of oxygenation and ventilation on pulmonary mechanics and ultrastructure during cardiopulmonary bypass. Am J Surg 1970;120:584–590.

25. Hewson J, Shaw M. Continuous airway pressure with oxygen minimizes the metabolic lesion of "pump lung". Can Anaesth Soc J 1983;30:37–47.

26. Hemmer M, Suter P. Treatment of cardiac and renal effects of PEEP with dopamine in patients with acute respiratory failure. Anesthesiology 1979;50:399–403.

27. Venus B, Mathru M, Smith RA, et al. Renal function during application of positive end-expiratory pressure in swine: effects of hydration. Anesthesiology 1985;62:765–769.

28. Dodrill F. Extracorporeal Circulation. In: Allen J, ed. The effects of total body perfusion upon the lungs. Springfield, IL: Charles C Thomas, 1958:327–355.

29. Asada S, Yamaguchi M. Fine structural changes in the lung following cardiopulmonary bypass. Its relationship to early postoperative course. Chest 1971;59:478–483.

30. Jevevien E, Weiss D. Platelet microemboli associated with massive blood transfusion. Am J Pathol 1964;45:313–321.

31. Allardyce DB, Yoshida SN, Ashmore PG. The importance of microembolism in the pathogenesis of organ dysfunction caused by prolonged use of the pump oxygenator. J Thorac Cardiovasc Surg 1966;52:706–715.

32. Hill J, Osborn J, Swank R. Experience using a new Dacron wool filter during extracorporeal circulation. Arch Surg 1970;101:649–652.

33. Ashmore PG, Swank RI, Gallery R, et al. Effect of dacron wool filtration on the microemboli phenomenon in extracorporeal circulation. J Thorac Cardiovasc Surg 1972;63:240–248.

34. Connell R, Page S, Bartley T, et al. The effect on pulmonary ultrastructure of dacron wool filtration during cardiopulmonary bypass. Ann Thorac Surg 1973;15:217–229.

35. Hodge AJ, Dymock RB, Sutherland HD. A case of fatal fat embolism syndrome following cardiopulmonary bypass. J Thorac Cardiovasc Surg 1976;72:202–205.

36. Swank RL. Alteration of blood on storage: measurement of adhesiveness of "aging" platelets and leucocytes and their removal by filtration. New Engl J Med 1961;265:728–733.

37. Cradock PR, Fehr J, Brigham KL, et al. Complement and leukocyte-medicated pulmonary dysfunction in hemodialysis. New Engl J Med 1977; 296:769–774.

38. Fountain S, Martin B, Musclow E, et al. Pulmonary leukostatis and its relationship to pulmonary dysfunction in sheep and rabbits. Circ Res 1980;46:175–180.

39. Roitt IM, Brostoff J, Male DK. Immunology. Vol 7. St Louis, MO: CV Mosby, 1985:7–14.

40. Chenoweth D, Cooper S, Te H, et al. Complement activation during cardiopulmonary bypass: evidence for generation of C3a and C5a anaphylotoxins. New Engl J Med 1981;304: 497–502.

41. Braude S, Nolop K, Fleming J, et al. Increased pulmonary transvascular protein flux after canine cardiopulmonary bypass. Association with lung neutrophil sequestration and tissue peroxidation. Am Rev Resp Dis 1986;134:867–872.

42. Perkowski SW, Havill AM, Flynn JT, et al. Role of intrapulmonary release of eicosanoids and superoxide anion as mediators of pulmonary dysfunction and endothelial injury in sheep with intermittent complement activation. Circ Res 1983;53:574–583.

43. Hammerschmidt D, Jacob H. Adverse pulmonary reactions to transfusion. Adv Intern Med 1982; 27:511–530.

44. Howard R, Crain C, Franzini D, et al. Effects of cardiopulmonary bypass on pulmonary leukostatis and complement activation. Arch Surg 1988;123:1496–1501.

45. Collett B, Alhaz A, Abdullah A, et al. Pathways of complement activation during CPB. Br Med J 1984;289:1251–1254.

46. Westaby S. Complement and the damaging effects of cardiopulmonary bypass. Thorax 1983; 38:321–325.

47. Van Oeveren W, Kazatchkine M, Descamps-Latscha B, et al. Deleterious effect of cardiopulmonary bypass. A prospective study of bubble versus membrane oxygenation. J Thorac Cardiovas Surg 1985;89:888–899.

48. Jansen NJ, van OW, van VM, et al. The role of different types of corticosteroids on the inflammatory mediators in cardiopulmonary bypass. Eur J Cardiothorac Surg 1991;5:211–217.

49. Greeley W, Leslie J, Reves J. Prostaglandins and the cardiovascular system: a review and update. J Cardiothorac Anesth 1987;1:331–349.

50. Davies G, Sobel M, Salzman E. Elevated plasma fibrinopeptide A and thromboxane B2 levels during cardiopulmonary bypass. Circulation 1980; 61:808–814.

51. Watkins W, Peterson M, Kong D, et al. Thromboxane and prostacyclin changes during cardiopulmonary bypass with and without pulsatile flow. J Thorac Cardiovasc Surg 1982;84: 250–256.

52. Chenoweth DE. The properties of human C5a anaphylatoxin. The significance of C5a formation during hemodialysis. Contrib Nephrol 1987;59: 51–71.

53. Mandelbaum I, Giammona ST. Bronchial circulation during cardiopulmonary bypass. Ann Surg 1966;164:985–989.

54. Balis JU, De Villota D, Avello F, et al. The role of pulmonary hypoxia in the post-perfusion lung syndrome. Surg Forum 1969;20:205–206.

55. Nahas RA, Melrose DG, Sykes MK, et al. Postperfusion lung syndrome, role of circulatory exclusion. Lancet 1965;2:251–256.

56. Beattie HW, Evans G, Garnett ES, et al. Albumin and water fluxes during cardiopulmonary bypass. J Thorac Cardiovasc Surg 1974;67: 926–931.

57. Byrick RJ, Kay JC, Noble WH. Extravascular lung water accumulation in patients folowing coronary artery surgery. Can Anaesth Soc J 1977; 24:332–345.

58. Kolff WJ, Effler DB, Groves LK, et al. Pulmonary complications of open-heart operations; their pathogenesis and avoidance. Clevel Clin Q 1958;25:65–83.

59. Byrick RJ, Finlayson DC, Noble WH. Pulmonary arterial pressure increases during cardiopulmonary bypass, a potential cause of pulmonary edema. Anesthesiology 1977;46:433–435.

60. Fowler A, Baird M, Eberle D, et al. Attack rates and mortality of the adult respiratory distress syndrome in patients with known predispositions [Abstract]. Am Rev Resp Dis 1983;125: 77.

61. Hashim S, Kay H, Hammond G, et al. Noncardiogenic pulmonary edema after cardiopulmonary bypass: an anaphylactic reaction to fresh frozen plasma. Am J Surg 1984;147:560–564.

62. Llamas R, Forthman H. Respiratory distress in the adult after cardiopulmonary bypass. A successful therapeutic approach. JAMA 1973;225: 1183–1186.

63. Olinger G, Becker R, Bonchek L. Noncardiogenic pulmonary edema and peripheral vascular collapse following cardiopulmonary bypass. Rare

protamine reaction? Ann Thorac Surg 1980;29: 20–25.

64. Culliford A, Thomas S, Spencer F. Fulminating noncardiogenic pulmonary edema. J Thorac Cardiovasc Surg 1980;80:868–875.

65. Hashim SW, Kay HR, Hammond GL, et al. Noncardiogenic pulmonary edema after cardiopulmonary bypass. An anaphylactic reaction to fresh frozen plasma. Am J Surg 1984;147:560–564.

66. Popovsky M, Moore S. Diagnostic and pathogenetic considerations in transfusion-related acute lung injury [Abstract]. Transfusion 1984;24:433.

67. Latson T, Kickler T, Baumgarter W. Pulmonary hypertension and noncardiogenic pulmonary edema following cardiopulmonary bypass associated with antigranulocyte antibody. Anesthesiology 1986;64:106–111.

68. Levy G, Shabot M, Hart M, et al. Transfusion associated noncardiogenic pulmonary edema. Transfusion 1986;26:278–281.

69. Ward H. Pulmonary infiltrates associated with leukoagglutinin transfusion reactions. Ann Intern Med 1970;73:689–694.

70. Best N, Teisner B, Grudzinkas J, et al. Classical pathway activation during an adverse response to protamine sulphate. Br J Anaesth 1983;55:1149–1153.

71. Lloyd J, Newman J, Brigham K. Permeability pulmonary edema: diagnosis and management. Arch Intern Med 1984;144:143–147.

72. Maggart M, Stewart S. The mechanisms and management of noncardiogenic pulmonary edema following cardiopulmonary bypass. Ann Thorac Surg 1987;43:231–236.

73. Pilato MA, Fleming NW, Katz NM, et al. Treatment of noncardiogenic pulmonary edema following cardiopulmonary bypass with veno-venous extracorporeal membrane oxygenation. Anesthesiology 1988;69:609–614.

74. Tuman KJ, Ivankovich AD. Bronchospasm during cardiopulmonary bypass. Etiology and management. Chest 1986;90:635–637.

75. Durant P, Joucken K. Bronchospasm and hypotension during cardiopulmonary bypass after preoperative cimetidine and labetolol therapy. Br J Anaesth 1984;56:917–920.

76. Casella ES, Humphrey LS. Bronchospasm after cardiopulmonary bypass in a heart-lung transplant recipient. Anesthesiology 1988;69:135–138.

77. Kyosola K, Takkunen O, Maamies T, et al. Bronchospasm during cardiopulmonary bypass—a potentially fatal complication of open-heart surgery. Thorac Cardiovasc Surg 1987;35:375–377.

78. Osborn J, Swank R. Experience using a new dacron wool filter during extracorporeal circulation. Arch Surg 1970;101:649–652.

79. Boscoe MJ, Yewdall VM, Thompson MA, et al. Complement activation during cardiopulmonary bypass: quantitative study of effects of methylprednisolone and pulsatile flow. Br Med J 1983;287:1747–1750.

80. Coffin LH, Shinozaki T, DeMeules JE, et al. Ineffectiveness of methylprednisolone in the treatment of pulmonary dysfunction after cardiopulmonary bypass. Am J Surg 1975;130:555–559.

81. Bolanowski PJ, Bauer J, Machiedo G, et al. Prostaglandin influence on pulmonary intravascular leukocytic aggregation during cardiopulmonary bypass. J Thorac Cardiovasc Surg 1977;73:221–224.

82. Addonizio VP, Fisher CA, Jenkin BK, et al. Iloprost (ZK36374), a stable analogue of prostacyclin, preserves platelets during simulated extracorporeal circulation. J Thorac Cardiovasc Surg 1985;89:926–933.

83. Fish K, Sarnquist F, Van Steennis C, et al. A prospective, randomized study of the effects of prostacyclin on platelets and blood loss during coronary bypass operations. J Thorac Cardiovasc Surg 1986;91:436–442.

84. Royston D. High-dose aprotinin therapy: a review of the first five years' experience. J Cardiothorac Vasc Anesth 1992;6:76–100.

85. Nagaoka H, Yamada T, Hatano R, et al. Clinical significance of bradykinin liberation during cardiopulmonary bypass and its prevention by a kallikrein inhibitor. Jpn J Surg 1975;5:222–233.

86. Royston D, Bidstrup B, Taylor K, et al. Effect of aprotinin on the need for blood transfusion after repeat open heart surgery. Lancet 1987;2:1289–1291.

87. Bidstrup BP, Royston D, Sapsford RN, et al. Reduction in blood loss and blood use after cardiopulmonary bypass with high dose aprotinin (Trasylol). J Thorac Cardiovasc Surg 1989;97:364–372.

88. Bo L, Belboul A, al KN, et al. High-dose aprotinin (trasylol) in reducing bleeding and protecting lung function in potential bleeders undergoing cardiopulmonary bypass. Chin Med J (Engl) 1991;104:980–985.

89. Deleuze P, Loisance DY, Feliz A, et al. Reduction of pre- and postoperative blood loss with aprotinin (Trasylol) during extracorporeal circulation. Arch Mal Coeur Vaiss 1991;84:1797–802.

90. Havel M, Teufelsbauer H, Knobl P, et al. Effect of intraoperative aprotinin administration on postoperative bleeding in patients undergoing cardiopulmonary bypass operation. J Thorac Cardiovasc Surg 1991;101:968–972.

91. Mallett SV, Cox D, Burroughs AK, et al. The intra-

operative use of trasylol (aprotinin) in liver transplantation. Transpl Int 1991;4:227–230.

92. Pitt B, Gillis N, Hammond G. Depression of pulmonary metabolic function by cardiopulmonary bypass procedures increases levels of circulating norepinephrine. J Thorac Surg 1984;38: 508–613.

93. Claremont D, Branthwaite M. Metabolic indices of pulmonary damage. Anaesthesia 1980;35: 863–868.

94. Gillis LN, Greene NM, Cronau LH, et al. Pulmonary extraction of 5-hydroxtryptamine and norepinephrine before and after cardiopulmonary bypass in man. Circ Res 1972;30:666–674.

Appendix 1

Abbreviations Used in This Chapter

$A\text{-}aDO_2$	Alveolar arterial oxygen gradient	ECMO	Extracorporeal membrane oxygenation
ABGs	Arterial blood gases	FIO_2	Inspired oxygen fraction
ACE	Angiotensin-converting-enzyme	PaO_2	Arterial oxygen tension
ARDS	Adult respiratory distress syndrome	$PaCO_2$	Arterial carbon dioxide tension
AAT	Alpha-1 antitrypsin	PEEP	Positive end-expiratory pressure
C	Complement	P_{PK}	Peak airway pressure
C_{DYN}	Dynamic compliance	$\dot{Q}_S/\dot{Q}_T$	Intrapulmonary shunt
C_L	Static lung compliance	R_{AW}	Airway resistance
COP	Colloid oncotic pressure	SpO_2	Arterial oxygen saturation (pulse oximetry)
CPAP	Continuous positive airway pressure		
CPB	Cardiopulmonary bypass	V_D/V_T	Ratio of dead space to tidal volume
C_{TH}	Static thoracic compliance		

Appendix 2

Gas Equations

Alveolar-Arterial Oxygen Gradient (A-aDo$_2$)

$$A\text{-}aDo_2 = PAo_2 - Pao_2,$$
$$PAo_2 = [P_B - PH_2O]FIo_2 - Paco_2(1.25)$$

where P_B = barometric pressure, PH_2O = water vapor pressure (47 mm Hg at 37°C), and 1.25 = 1/respiratory quotient. Although the A-aDo$_2$ provides some quantitation of the degree of lung dysfunction, it is very dependent on the FIo$_2$. Normal A-aDo$_2$ ranges from 10–15 mm Hg on room air to more than 60 mm Hg on 100% oxygen.

Intrapulmonary Shunt ($\dot{Q}_S/\dot{Q}_T$)

$$\frac{\dot{Q}_S}{\dot{Q}_T} = \frac{[Cco_2 - Cao_2]}{[Cco_2 - Cvo_2]}$$

where $\dot{Q}_S$ = shunt flow, $\dot{Q}_T$ = total flow, Cco_2 = end-pulmonary capillary o$_2$ content (hemoglobin 100% saturated), Cao_2 = arterial o$_2$ content, and Cvo_2 = mixed venous o$_2$ content.

$$Cco_2 = [100\% \times Hb \times 1.34]$$
$$+ 0.0031(PAo_2)$$
$$Cao_2 = [SaO2 \times Hb \times 1.34]$$
$$+ 0.0031(Pao_2)$$
$$Cvo_2 = [SvO2 \times Hb \times 1.34]$$
$$+ 0.0031(Pvo_2)$$

where S = saturation, 0.0031-solubility coefficient of o$_2$ in blood.

Dead Space to Tidal Volume Ratio (V_D/V_T) [Bohr Equation]

$$V_D/V_T = Paco_2 - PEco_2/Paco_2$$

where $Paco_2$ is arterial co$_2$ tension and $PEco_2$ is mixed expired co$_2$ tension. Normal V_D/V_T is 0.3.

Lung Mechanics

Lung impedance describes the pressures required to effect flow and volume (Fig. 18.2). These include the pressure to effect flow through the major conducting airways, which is dependent on airway resistance (R_{AW}), and the pressure to distend the lungs, which is dependent on lung compliance (C_L).

The R_{AW} (cm H$_2$O-liters^{-1}·Vsec^{-1}) is determined by dividing the difference between peak and plateau airway pressure by air flow in liters per second:

$$R_{AW} = (\text{Peak} - \text{plateau pressure})/\text{Flow rate}$$

Conductance (G) is the reciprocal of resistance:

$$G_{AW} = 1/R_{AW}$$

The C_L reflects lung stiffness and expresses the volume of lung expanded per unit transpulmonary pressure applied. C_L (ml/cm H$_2$O) is determined by dividing the exhaled tidal volume by the difference between plateau airway pressure and end-expiratory pressure:

$$C_L = \text{Exhaled volume}/(\text{Plateau pressure} - \text{end-expiratory pressure})$$

However, unless the patient is paralyzed, the pressure required to distend the chest wall is significant. Since the lung and chest wall are mechanically in series,

$$C_{TH} = C_L + C_{CW}$$

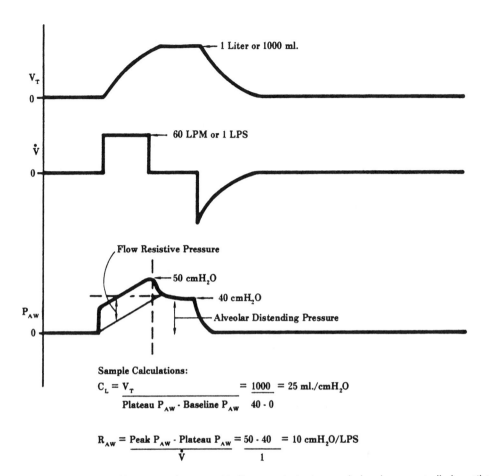

Figure 18.2.   Calculation of lung impedance. In this figure, a single time-cycled, volume-controlled ventilator breath is shown, with volume (V_T) (*top*), flow rate (V) (*middle*), and airway pressure (P_{AW}) (*bottom*). Inspiratory pause is provided at the end of inspiration. In the P_{AW} diagram, flow resistive pressure represents the pressure to overcome impedance provided by airway resistance to flow. Alveolar distending pressure represents the pressure to overcome the impedance provided by lung compliance. In this example, peak P_{AW} is 50 cm H_2O and plateau P_{AW} is 40 cm H_2O. Using V_T and V, lung compliance (C_L) and airway resistance (R_{AW}) may be calculated. (From MacIntyre N. Graphical Analysis of Flow, Pressure and Volume During Mechanical Ventilation, Bear Medical Systems, Inc.)

where C_{THP} C_L and C_{CW} are the thoracic, lung and chest wall compliances respectively.

Elastance (E) is the reciprocal of compliance:

$$E_L = 1/C_L$$

"Dynamic" compliance (C_{DYN}) is a term used, somewhat inappropriately, to describe the relationship between exhaled tidal volume and peak airway pressure:

$$C_{DYN} = \frac{\text{Exhaled tidal volume}}{\text{peak airway pressure}}$$

It cannot therefore distinguish between alterations in impedance due to airway resistance or lung compliance.

19

RENAL FUNCTION AND FLUID BALANCE WITH CARDIOPULMONARY BYPASS

Joe R. Utley

Cardiopulmonary bypass (CPB) has rather profound effects on renal function and fluid balance. The manipulations during CPB that may be of most benefit to renal function may increase extracellular fluid accumulation. The elimination of excessive interstitial fluid postoperatively greatly depends upon renal function. Thus there are many interactions between renal function and fluid balance during bypass.

Fluid shifts during CPB differ significantly from those in patients having major operative procedures without bypass. The type of cardiac disease and the status of cardiac function preoperatively have significant effects on the patient's blood volume and the accumulation of fluid during CPB. During bypass, fluid tends to accumulate in the extracellular, extravascular (interstitial) space. Fluid accumulation may be affected by temperature, flow rates, hemodilution, plasma colloid oncotic pressure, interstitial fluid pressure, capillary permeability, the capacitance of the interstitial space, and urine output. Experimentally, fluid accumulation is more pronounced in some organs than in others and may or may not be associated with organ dysfunction. The amount of fluid accumulation during CPB may be a major determinant of the postoperative need for diuretics, osmotic and oncotic agents, as well as vasoactive drugs.

RENAL FUNCTION

Abnormalities of renal function are relatively common before, during, and after CPB. Renal failure of varying degrees occurs in 1.2 to 13% of patients who have had bypass (1–6). Dialysis for renal failure is required in 4 to 7% of children following cardiac surgery. Half of the children requiring dialysis recover renal function, but 58 to 72% die (7, 8). There is a strong relationship between severity of renal failure and mortality (Fig. 19.1) (2, 3). If renal failure is severe enough to require dialysis in adult patients, the mortality is 25 to 100% (4). Common causes of death in cardiac surgery patients with renal failure are myocardial infarction, infection, and gastrointestinal bleeding. The development of renal failure correlated with bypass time, infection, and low cardiac output in one study. Renal failure was twice as common with valve surgery as with coronary artery bypass grafting (9). In another recent study, renal dysfunction was correlated with use of the intraaortic balloon pump, excessive blood loss, use of vasopressors before bypass, perioperative myocardial infarction, emergency operation, excessive transfusion, and chronic renal disease (10).

Among the factors that contribute to perioperative renal dysfunction are endocrine changes, diminished renal blood flow, alteration of cellular and humoral blood components, nephrotoxic drugs, and preexisting renal disease.

Preoperative Renal Function

In patients with renal failure before operation, postoperative renal dysfunction is more common and more severe (2, 3, 11) (Fig. 19.2). Renal function may dramatically improve if cardiac failure causing prerenal azotemia can be relieved by surgical correction of defects. Poor postoperative

cardiac function is a common cause of renal failure (Fig. 19.3) (2, 3). Renal failure is most common and severe in patients with complex cyanotic congenital heart disease and in patients requiring multiple valve procedures for rheumatic heart disease.

Patients with cyanotic congenital heart disease often have small kidneys with enlarged glomeruli, which may be the cause of benign proteinuria. Other renal abnormalities in patients with cyanotic lesions include dilation and elongation of capillary loops and afferent arterioles, hyalinization of arterioles, glomerular sclero-

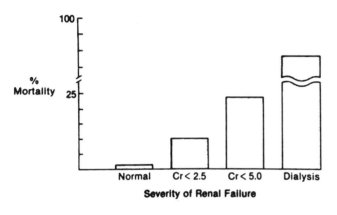

Figure 19.1. Mortality increases with increasing severity of perioperative renal failure. Perioperative renal failure was quantitated by the maximum serum creatinine concentration. Normal is less than 1.0 mg/100 ml; serum creatinine, 1.0 to 2.5 mg/100 ml; serum creatinine, 2.5 to 5.0%; and the requirement for dialysis (p < 0.05). *Cr,* maximum serum concentration. (From Abel RM, Buckley MJ, Austen WG, Barnett GO, Beck CH Jr, Fisher JE. Acute postoperative renal failure in cardiac surgical patients. J Surg Res 1976;20:341.)

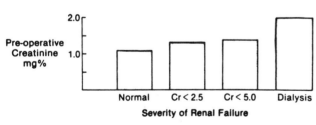

Figure 19.2. The mean preoperative serum creatinine concentration increased with increasing severity of postoperative renal failure (p < 0.05). *Cr,* maximum serum concentration. (From Abel RM, Buckley MJ, Austen WG, Barnett GO, Beck CH Jr, Fisher JE. Acute postoperative renal failure in cardiac surgical patients. J Surg Res 1976;20:341.)

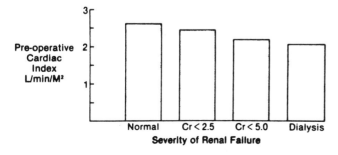

Figure 19.3. The mean preoperative cardiac index decreased with increasing severity of postoperative renal failure (p < 0.05). *Cr,* maximum serum concentration. (From Abel RM, Buckley MJ, Austen WG, Barnett GO, Beck CH Jr, Fisher JE. Acute postoperative renal failure in cardiac surgical patients. J Surg Res 1976;20:341.)

sis, thickening of glomerular basement membranes, and diminished renal blood flow as measured by *p*-aminohippuric acid clearance. The diminished flow is principally to the outer cortex of the kidney and is likely related to the greater responsiveness of children's arterioles to vasoconstrictors including catecholamines, angiotensin, and vasopressin. The abnormalities of renal blood flow in these patients do not return to normal with surgical correction of the cardiac abnormality (12–14). Diminished glomerular filtration in polycythemic patients improves with normalization of the hematocrit (15). Elevated serum uric acid levels may contribute to renal failure in children. Hyperuricemia was found in 42% of pediatric patients having cardiac surgical procedures requiring CPB. Predisposition to hyperuricemia includes young age, complex cyanotic heart disease, hypoxemia, and polycythemia. Hyperuricemia is an important contributing factor to renal failure in cyanotic congenital heart disease (16).

Patients with multiple valve abnormalities due to rheumatic fever often have prerenal azotemia because of cardiac failure. In addition, they have vascular and glomerular lesions due to the rheumatic process and emboli. Patients with bacterial endocarditis have embolic renal lesions as well as glomerular abnormalities caused by deposition of immune globulins. Renal artery obstruction and arteriolar nephrosclerosis are common in patients requiring coronary artery bypass grafting.

Nephrotoxic angiographic dyes and pharmacologic agents may contribute to preoperative renal failure. Renal failure due to angiographic dyes is associated with increasing age, renal disease, dehydration, diabetes, hyperuricemia, proteinuria, multiple myeloma, and multiple dye exposures. Antibiotics that may cause renal dysfunction include gentamicin, cephalosporins, and methicillin. Angiotensin-converting enzyme inhibitors or nonsteroidal antiinflammatory agents commonly contribute to preoperative renal failure in coro-

nary artery surgery patients (1, 17–19). Prostaglandin is a potent renal vasodilator and its synthesis is inhibited by nonsteroidal antiinflammatory drugs including aspirin (20). Angiotensin-converting enzyme inhibitors are particularly likely to cause renal failure if renal artery stenosis is present (20). In patients with serum creatinine greater than 1.5 mg/100 ml who have received nephrotoxic angiographic dyes or pharmacologic agents, operation may be delayed for 1 to 3 days while the medication is stopped and the patient is hydrated with intravenous fluids. With this form of management the creatinine will rarely rise further (1).

In patients with significant impairment of renal function with creatinine clearances less than 30 ml/min, pulsatile flow was found to have no immediate effect on creatinine clearance. The patients in whom pulsatile flow was employed did have higher creatinine clearances 1 week postoperatively. Longer periods of bypass were associated with greater diminution in creatinine clearance (21).

Operative Factors

GENERAL EFFECTS

Poor postoperative renal function has been correlated with duration of bypass in most studies (2, 3, 5, 11, 22–24). Renal blood flow, renal plasma flow, and urine output are typically diminished during bypass and the diminution increases with duration of bypass (22). The absolute values of free water clearance and creatinine clearance decrease in proportion to the duration of the procedure (25). Renal plasma flow, glomerular filtration, and sodium excretion are higher at higher flow rates and pressures than at lower flow rates and pressures (26).

Some controversy exists concerning the role of perfusion pressure in the development of postoperative renal failure. One study has shown that perfusion pressure was an important factor (11). Neither perfusion pressure, flow rates, or the presence of hemoglobinemia could be related to the development of renal failure in other studies (2, 3). In one recent study, neither low perfusion pressure or flow in absolute amounts or in intensity-duration units correlated with the development of new renal dysfunction (10). New renal failure developed in 3% of the patients. Other workers found that postoperative serum creatinine was related to lowest blood flow during CPB, age, and preoperative serum creatinine (27).

Increased concentration of urine urea has been correlated with decreased renal blood flow, and is a sensitive early indicator of renal dysfunction (28, 29). Free water clearance has been shown to be the most sensitive predictor of renal failure following bypass. Free water clearance is urine volume minus osmolar clearance. Free water clearance more negative than -20 ml/hour is rarely associated with renal failure, and less negative than -8 ml/hour (or any positive value) is almost always associated with renal failure. When mentioned elsewhere in this chapter, a reduction in free water clearance should be interpreted as a free water clearance that is less negative than the initial value. Free water clearance has been shown to allow the earlier diagnosis of renal failure following CPB than urine urea, blood urea nitrogen, serum creatinine, and oliguria (30).

In children the urinary level of β-2-microglobulin is a sensitive index of early acute renal failure following bypass. β-2-Microglobulin is filtered at the glomerulus and reabsorbed by the proximal tubule. Its appearance in the urine indicates tubular damage (31).

VASCULAR EFFECTS

The fall in blood pressure that frequently accompanies the onset of CPB may be related to several factors. The rapid hemodilution causes blood viscosity to fall and produce a fall in pressure. Catecholamines are rapidly diluted in the plasma and there is then a progressive rise in catecholamine levels during bypass. The stimulation of the renin-angiotensin-aldosterone mechanism with the onset of CPB causes increases in renal vascular resistance (32–34). Increased aldosterone levels persist longer after cardiac surgical procedures than after other types of operations (35). The high levels of vasopressin (antidiuretic hormone) observed during bypass may contribute to renal vasoconstriction as well as to the fall in urine output and free water clearance. The rise in vasopressin levels is related to the low atrial pressures, hypotension, and nonpulsatile blood flow that may accompany CPB (36). The rise in plasma cortisol levels observed during and after bypass may contribute to the sodium retention and potassium diuresis often observed after bypass. Sodium diuresis during and after CPB may be related to increases in atrial natriuretic factor (37, 38) (see Chapter 12).

Prostaglandin E1 or prostacyclin infusions have been used to inhibit platelet activation during bypass. One important side effect of these infusions is severe hypotension. Studies of the renal effects of prostaglandin infusion during CPB showed that glomerular filtration was unchanged while urine output was diminished (39). No renal failure or diminished renal function developed. The function of the proximal tubules, as measured by β-2-microglobulin in urine, was unchanged.

Pulsatile blood flow has been found to preserve flow to the kidney during bypass, especially to the outer cortex (40). Detailed experimental studies of the effect of pulsatile flow at blood flow rates of 40, 60, 80, 100, and 120 ml/min/kg body weight have shown no difference at the extremes of blood flow (41). At 80 and 100 ml/min/kg, pulsatile flow decreased systemic vascular resistance and increased renal blood flow. Pulsatile flow also diminished renal arteriovenous lactate difference. Clinical studies have shown a low incidence of postoperative renal failure in patients with preoperative creatinine of greater than 1.7 mg/100 ml when pulsatile flow was used. There were no renal deaths in 29 patients, although 1 patient died with low cardiac output (41).

HEMODILUTION

Hemodilution is one of the most important factors in protecting renal function during bypass (42, 43). It is important, however, that both the red blood cells and serum albumin be diluted to protect renal function.

Hemodilution causes a great increase in renal blood flow, which is mainly attributable to reduced blood viscosity. The increase in blood flow with lower hematocrit is particularly great to the outer cortex of the kidney (42). The increased medullary water content produced by hemodilution is an important part of the mechanism to increase urine flow and free water clearance and to counteract the effect of high vasopressin levels. Hemodilution increases renal plasma flow and the sodium, potassium, osmolar and free water clearances. Urine output is increased and urine concentrations of sodium, potassium, creatinine, and osmolality are diminished by hemodilution (42). Clinical studies have confirmed the increased urine flow and increased osmolar, creatinine, and sodium clearance with hemodilution (44, 45).

OSMOLAR AND ONCOTIC EFFECTS

The use of albumin during CPB is advocated to coat the foreign surfaces (passivation) and to diminish the interstitial fluid that accumulates during bypass. There is much evidence that diluting serum albumin concentration is important in preserving renal function during bypass. Studies of varying levels of perfusate oncotic pressure in rabbits have shown that lower levels of plasma oncotic pressure improve renal function during bypass. A correlation exists between glomerular filtration and the difference between perfusion pressure and plasma colloidal oncotic pressure. Plasma oncotic pressure is a significant antagonist

to glomerular filtration during hypotensive states (46). Other experimental studies in which red cells were hemodiluted but serum was reconstituted to normal levels show many potentially detrimental effects of restoring albumin concentration to normal.

Albumin increases flow to the inner cortex of the kidney and increases the concentration of microspheres in the medulla, suggesting vasodilation rather than an effect on blood viscosity (Figs. 19.4 and 19.5). Albumin has no effect on water content in any region of the kidney, but diminishes urine sodium and sodium, osmolar, and free water clearance (Fig. 19.6) (43). Increased plasma oncotic pressure not only diminishes glomerular filtration but also increases reabsorption of fluid from the proximal renal tubule by an osmotic mechanism (47, 48). Adding albumin to restore normal concentrations to the priming solution thus reverses many of the desired effects of hemodilution.

Another mechanism for diminished urine output despite adequate glomerular filtration is the backleak of filtrate through the tubular epithelium. Inulin backleak through the tubules has been shown to be from 5 to 50% during CPB (49).

HYPOTHERMIA

Hypothermia has important renal effects that may contribute significantly to renal dysfunction. Studies have shown depressed glomerular filtration rate, renal blood flow, and osmolar clearance while filtration fraction and potassium excretion were elevated (50). Hypothermia decreases inner and outer renal cortical blood flow in approximately equal proportions. The decreased distribution of renal microspheres in the renal medulla with hypothermia supports arteriolar vasoconstriction as part of its effect (42). Hypothermia produces significant decreases in renal tubular function (51, 52). Most of the adverse effects of hypothermia are reversed by hemodilution,

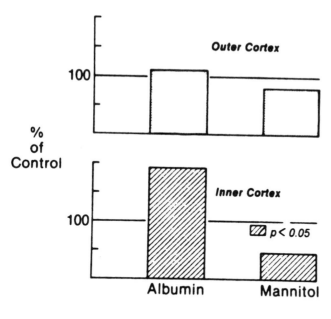

Figure 19.4. Renal blood flow to outer cortex was not affected by albumin or mannitol. Albumin increased flow to inner renal cortex; mannitol decreased inner renal cortical flow. (From Utley JR. Pathophysiology and techniques of cardiopulmonary bypass. Vol 1. Baltimore: Williams & Wilkins, 1982:51.)

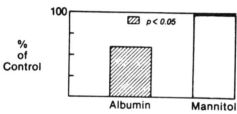

Figure 19.5. Albumin decreased urine output. Mannitol had no significant effect on urine output. (From Utley JR. Pathophysiology and techniques of cardiopulmonary bypass. Vol 1. Baltimore: Williams & Wilkins, 1982:51.)

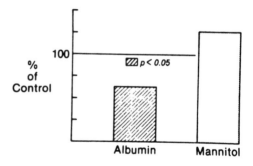

Figure 19.6. Free water clearance was diminished by albumin. Mannitol had no significant effect. (From Utley JR. Pathophysiology and techniques of cardiopulmonary bypass. Vol 1. Baltimore: Williams & Wilkins, 1982:51.)

which confirms the great importance of hemodilution when employing hypothermia during bypass.

HEMOLYSIS

Hemoglobin casts have been observed in the tubules of kidneys of patients who died of renal failure following CPB. Hemoglobin, which is released into the plasma with the destruction of red blood cells during bypass, is bound to serum proteins. Hemoglobin is bound in plasma to haptoglobin, hemopexin, and as methemalbumin. Once the hemoglobin binding proteins are saturated, hemoglobin is filtered by the glomerulus. Filtered hemoglobin may be reabsorbed by the proximal renal tubular cells and broken down into iron, globin, and porphyrin moieties. Hemoglobinuria occurs when the tubular capacity to reabsorb is exceeded (53).

In the renal tubule the charge on the hemoglobin molecule is negative above its isoelectric pH. At pH below the isoelectric point of 6.99, the charge on the hemoglobin molecule is positive. A negatively charged protein (Tamm-Horsfall protein) in the distal renal tubule combines with positively charged hemoglobin to precipitate hemoglobin-Tamm-Horsfall cast, which induces renal failure. Keeping the urine alkaline with bicarbonate infusion may thus diminish the rate of precipitation of hemoglobin casts in the tubules (54).

Free hemoglobin is cleared from the plasma faster than the hemoglobin-haptoglobin complex (Fig. 19.7) (55). Appreciable free hemoglobin is present in serum before the onset of hemoglobinuria and after hemoglobinuria ceases, indicating the continued capacity for tubular reabsorption of hemoglobin (Fig. 19.8) (55). The majority of hemoglobin is cleared from the plasma by the reticuloendothelial system rather than by renal mechanisms (55, 56).

Factors that may contribute to increased hemolysis during bypass are use of cardiotomy suction, high negative suction pressures, duration of perfusion, bubble oxygenators with high gas flow, occlusive roller pumps, and turbulent flow in the pump oxygenator (57–60).

MICROEMBOLI

Although microemboli have been more commonly implicated as a cause of postoperative cerebral dysfunction, the high levels of renal blood flow during hemodilution place the kidneys at risk of microembolic damage (See Chapter 11 on emboli). Studies of the independent and separate effects of hemodilution, hypothermia, and the CPB apparatus show that the pump oxygenator diminished blood flow and oxygen delivery to the outer cortex of the kidney (Fig. 19.9). The pump oxygenator also produced increased water content in the renal medulla and diminished sodium, osmolar, and free water clearance. Urine output fell, as did urine sodium concentration. There was a rise in urine concentration of potassium and creatinine (42).

The diminished outer cortical flow produced by the pump oxygenator may be explained by axial migration of larger microemboli. Particles tend to migrate toward the center of flow in a vessel and the axial migration is greater with larger particles. Thus particle-poor blood preferentially flows to the inner cortex while particle-rich blood preferentially flows to the end arteries of the outer cortex. Microsphere

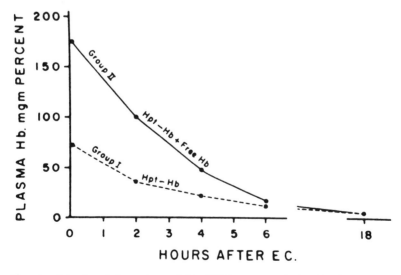

Figure 19.7. The rate of clearing of plasma hemoglobin (*Hb*) is more rapid when free hemoglobin is present. In Group 1, all plasma hemoglobin is bound to haptoglobin (*Hpt*). In Group II, free hemoglobin, in addition to hemoglobin bound to haptoglobin, is present. *EC,* extracorporeal circulation. (From Andersen MN, Mouritzen CV, Gabrieli E. Mechanisms of plasma hemoglobin clearance after acute hemolysis: studies in open-heart surgical patients. A comparative study of five different units. Ann Surg 1966;163:529.)

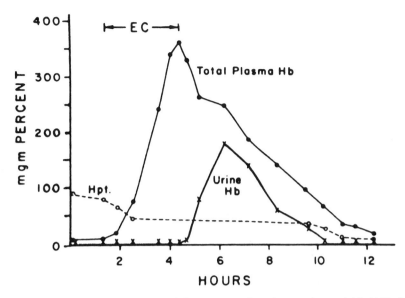

Figure 19.8.   Haptoglobin (*Hpt*) concentration falls progressively with rise in hemoglobin (*Hb*) after the beginning of bypass. Urine excretion of hemoglobin begins only after the haptoglobin is saturated and the renal tubular reabsorption is exceeded. *EC,* extracorporeal circulation. (From Andersen MN, Mouritzen CV, Gabrieli E. Mechanisms of plasma hemoglobin clearance after acute hemolysis: studies in open-heart surgical patients. A comparative study of five different units. Ann Surg 1966;163:529.)

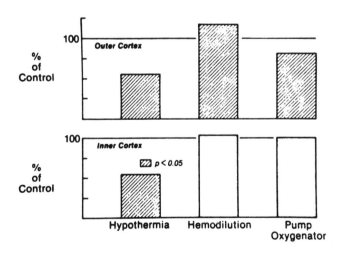

Figure 19.9.   Studies of the separate effects of hypothermia, hemodilution, and pump oxygenator show that blood flow to the outer renal cortex is diminished by hypothermia and the pump oxygenator and is increased by hemodilution. Hypothermia decreased flow to inner cortex whereas hemodilution and the pump oxygenator had no significant effects. (From Utley JR. Pathophysiology and techniques of cardiopulmonary bypass. Vol 1. Baltimore: Williams & Wilkins, 1982:45.)

studies have shown that larger microspheres tend to be delivered to the outer cortex of the kidney (61). This offers the best explanation for diminished outer renal cortical flow produced by the pump oxygenator.

Fat globules with Maltese crosses in the urine, which are evidence of renal fat emboli, have been observed during bypass (62).

RENAL PROTECTION

In a comparison of bubble and membrane oxygenators it was found that more patients had a rise of serum creatinine greater than 50 μmol/liter when the bubble oxygenator was used than when the membrane oxygenator was used. The renal dysfunction was strongly correlated with elevated levels of C3a complement, which are higher with the bubble oxygenator (63).

Furosemide reverses the effect of CPB on renal blood flow. The resulting blood flow improvement is more pronounced in the outer renal cortex than in the inner cortex or medulla (57, 64). Clinical studies show that furosemide significantly increases creatinine clearance and lowers serum creatinine in patients experiencing greater than 1 hour of bypass (57). The renal protective effects of low-dose dopamine and furosemide are synergistic (65). Verapamil reduces the incidence and severity of renal failure in experimental and clinical studies (49).

Mannitol protects renal function by increasing renal blood flow, increasing glomerular filtration, and reducing injury after ischemia (65). One study suggests that nitrous oxide, when combined with morphine, halothane, and oxygen anesthesia, lowers blood pressure and decreases free water clearance (66). Both creatinine and free water clearance were depressed postoperatively in the nitrous oxide group, although nitrous oxide use has not been correlated with postoperative renal failure.

PROGNOSIS OF RENAL FAILURE FOLLOWING CPB

Because the prevention and management of renal failure in cardiac surgery patients is improving, the overall prognosis for any degree of renal failure appears to be better. The greater age and severity of disease among coronary artery bypass surgery patients may be associated with an increasing incidence and severity of renal failure in these patients. The use of early and frequent peritoneal dialysis has lowered mortality (4). The outcome of renal failure is often not related to the status of renal function but to other factors including the patient's age and the development of other complications such as arrhythmias, cardiac failure, respiratory failure, and sepsis.

Prognosis of renal failure is much improved if urine output can be maintained and oliguric renal failure avoided. In my clinical practice, low-dose dopamine (2 to 5 μg/kg/min) is infused preoperatively, during the operation, and for many days postoperatively if the serum creatinine is greater than 2 mg/100 ml or if oliguria occurs. In oliguric postoperative cardiac surgery patients with left ventricular dysfunction, low-dose dopamine infusion has been shown to increase creatinine clearance, osmolar clearance, free water clearance, sodium excretion, and urine output. Plasma renin activity was also decreased by low-dose dopamine infusion (67). I prefer to treat oliguria aggressively with mannitol (12.5 to 25 g) and furosemide intravenously (10 to 100 mg) and to infuse a "renal cocktail" of furosemide and mannitol (500 ml 20% mannitol at 20 ml/hr and 2 g furosemide in 250 ml at 10 ml/hr) if oliguria is particularly severe and resistant to therapy (1).

FLUID BALANCE

General Considerations

Early attempts to perform cardiac surgical procedures without weight gain were fraught with problems of poor cardiac performance and hypovolemia (68–71). Deficits in plasma and blood volume were described when attempts were made to maintain constant weight during bypass procedures (72). It was recognized by the early surgeons that the edema of the postoperative patient had a different distribution than that of the patient with heart failure. After CPB the edema tended to be in the face, periorbital areas, neck, and abdomen. Weight gains of up to 2500 ml/m square body surface area, and up to 150 ml/kg body weight have been observed (73).

Both inulin and bromide space determinations have been used to determine the extent of extracellular volume expansion. Inulin space increases 33% and bromide space 18% following bypass (74). Other, more detailed studies show the volume of dilution of labeled red cells, albumin, bromide, sulfate, and water. Patients with a wide variety of conditions were studied, including those with left to right, and right to left shunts as well as patients with valve disease with and without heart failure. There is a variable plasma volume and red cell mass response in these patients. Extracellular volume is uniformly increased with a very great increase in the interstitial volume (extracellular volume minus plasma volume). The shape of labeled bromide and sulfate curves are changed after bypass, suggesting a slower equilibration of the interstitial space (74). Other studies have confirmed the increase in total body water and skeletal muscle water without increase in intracellular water (75).

Hematocrit rises progressively postoperatively due to diminishing plasma volume. Plasma volume falls during the first 24 hours postoperatively, which is related principally to urine output and less to increasing interstitial volume (74, 76). Other studies show that continuing expansion of the interstitial space may also contribute to the falling plasma volume early postoperatively (35, 77–81).

The excessive interstitial fluid volume may persist for many days postoperatively. Persistence of the volume excess has been related to preoperative congestive failure, postoperative heart failure, and poor renal function (82).

Decreasing plasma water content and rising plasma osmolarity have been observed during CPB. Insensible water loss during the procedure may occur at wound surfaces, the pump oxygenator, and skin. One study determined that the wound accounted for greater loss than the oxygenator (83, 84).

Preoperative Fluid Considerations

The patient's preoperative blood volume and body fluid composition may have significant effects on fluid balance during bypass. Patients with heart failure have increased total body water, extracellular and interstitial fluid, plasma volume, and red cell mass. Total exchangeable sodium is also increased (85–87). Patients with congenital heart disease and increased or decreased pulmonary blood flow also have increased blood volume.

In contrast to patients with heart failure, the patients with coronary artery disease and normal ventricular function have contracted blood volume. The contracted blood volume in some coronary artery patients may be due to the effect of chronic catecholamine stimulation (88). This "empty heart syndrome" seems to be less common with modern techniques of cardiac anesthesia including the use of β-adrenergic blockade and high doses of opioids (89, 90). Excessive fluid accumulation in coronary artery bypass patients has been significantly associated with increasing age, female sex, obesity, aortoiliac-femoral occlusive disease, and low ejection fraction (1).

Correction of Cardiac Defect and Fluid Balance

Surgical correction of valve and ventricular abnormalities, the relief of myocardial ischemia, and the closure of intracardiac shunts may relieve congestive failure, reduce filling pressures, and increase cardiac output. The lower postoperative filling pressures may lessen fluid accumulation. Studies have shown that the perioperative fluid accumulation is related to the preoperative cardiac abnormality. Fluid accumulation is least in patients who underwent closure of left to right shunts; intermediate in patients with coronary disease, single valve disease, and cyanotic congenital heart disease; and greatest in patients with multiple valve disease (Fig. 19.10) (73). The mean fluid accumulation ranged from 727 ml/m square body surface area in patients with left to right shunts to 2077 ml/m

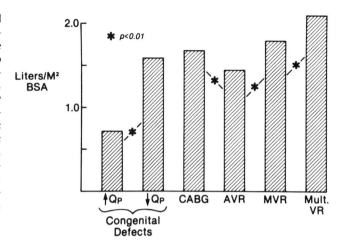

Figure 19.10. Accumulation of fluid during CPB is related to the cardiac disease. The reasons for this variation are undoubtedly complex and related to preoperative and postoperative hemodynamics and duration of bypass. *Qp,* pulmonary blood flow; *CABG,* coronary bypass grafts; *AVR,* aortic valve replacement; *MVR,* mitral valve replacement; *Mult VR,* multiple valve replacement; *BSA,* body surface area. (From Utley JR, Stephens DB. Fluid balance during cardiopulmonary bypass. In: Utley JR, ed. Pathophysiology and techniques of cardiopulmonary bypass. Vol II. Baltimore: Williams & Wilkins, 1983, p. 26.)

square body surface area in patients with multiple valve disease. The reason for these differences is undoubtedly complex, but at least partially related to preoperative body fluid composition and altered hemodynamics following surgical correction.

Operative Factors and Fluid Accumulation

Fluid accumulation is related to duration of CPB. In addition, small body size and young age are associated with excess fluid accumulation in pediatric patients (91). Other significant determinants of fluid accumulation and slow return to preoperative weight in coronary artery bypass patients were low bypass hematocrit, use of blood transfusions, number of bypass grafts, aortic clamp time, and use of the bubble oxygenator (1).

Hemodilution and Plasma Colloidal Oncotic Pressure

Hemodilution has been implicated as the cause of interstitial fluid accumulation, and its importance in comparison to hypothermia and the effect of the pump oxygenator has been determined experimentally. These studies show that hemodilution is the main cause of interstitial fluid accumulation during bypass when compared to the role of hypothermia and the pump oxygen-

ator (92). The most obvious effect of hemodilution in causing interstitial fluid accumulation is the decrease in plasma colloidal oncotic pressure. Other possible contributing factors include decreased blood viscosity, diminished oxygen-carrying capacity, and vasodilation (92).

The fall in plasma in colloidal oncotic pressure correlates most strongly with the fall in albumin concentration. The fall in colloidal oncotic pressure persists during bypass and may return to 80% of normal within 24 hours, but usually is less than normal for 7 to 14 days. The lower plasma colloidal oncotic pressure during the postoperative period contributes to increased glomerular filtration and urine output as well as to the continued shifting of fluid into the interstitial space. Both of these mechanisms contribute to the early rise in hematocrit postoperatively (77, 93, 94). Studies of Jehovah's Witnesses who receive no blood or albumin perioperatively indicate that significant amounts of albumin and protein may be mobilized into the intravascular space during and after bypass (95).

In experimental studies, hemodilution causes a significant increase in blood flow to myocardium, outer cortex of kidney, cerebral cortex, spleen, and intestine. The diminished oxygen-carrying capacity is more than compensated for by increased blood flow in all organs except kidney and spleen. Hemodilution causes increased water content in myocardium, medulla of kidney, liver, stomach, and intestine (Fig. 19.11). The increased water content correlates with increased blood flow in intestine and heart muscle. Increased tissue water content was not correlated with diminished blood flow or diminished oxygen delivery in any area. The organs that accumulate the most water experimentally do not correlate with the sites of postoperative organ dysfunction, except for myocardium (92).

The safety of hemodilution is well established (96–98). The improvement in

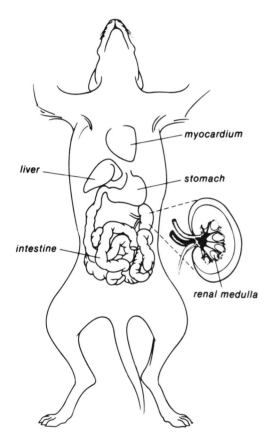

Figure 19.11. Experimental studies in dogs have shown that hemodilution is the principal cause of fluid accumulation. The organs that accumulate significant amounts of water are the myocardium, liver, stomach, intestine, and renal medulla. (From Utley JR, Stephens DB. Fluid balance during cardiopulmonary bypass. In: Utley JR, ed. Pathophysiology and techniques of cardiopulmonary bypass. Vol II. Baltimore: Williams & Wilkins, 1983, p. 28.)

blood coagulation, lung function, renal function, and myocardial function is probably related to the absence of homologous blood in the priming solution more than to the effect of decreased plasma colloidal oncotic pressure or viscosity.

Hypothermia

The effects of hypothermia on fluid balance are not as clearly defined as are the effects of hemodilution. Although the principal goal of hypothermia is to decrease oxygen consumption, it also may increase blood viscosity and cause red cell sludging, particularly in presence of cryoglobulins (99). Deceased plasma volume has been repeatedly observed during hypothermia in the absence of bypass using hemodilution (100–102). Red cells may be mobilized from the spleen during hypothermia (103). During hypothermia, as many as 25% of red cells may be part of a pool that is slow to equilibrate with the central circulation (104). The increases in plasma oncotic pressure that are observed with hypothermia may be the result of changes in the configuration of plasma proteins or the mobilization of proteins from tissue stores (105). Others observed the shifting of fluid in the intracellular space and the trapping of fluid in the peripheral vascular bed (106). Experimental study of the effect of hypothermia on regional blood flow and water content shows that hypothermia causes diminished flow to the renal cortex, cerebral cortex, and skin. These flow changes are not accompanied by any changes in water content (94). Although hypothermia protects the ischemic or injured brain from edema, no effect of hypothermia on the water content of the normal brain has been demonstrated (107, 108).

Pump Oxygenator

Contact of cellular and humoral blood components with the foreign surfaces of the pump oxygenator may contribute to the development of increased interstitial fluid. The denaturation of serum proteins and the destabilization of soluble fats may affect the colloidal properties of blood and also produce changes in capillary permeability (109).

Activation of complement, increased capillary permeability, and general inflammatory response are significant factors in the development of interstitial edema. The products of injury to white blood cells and platelets also contribute to tissue injury and edema. (see Chapter 9 on complement activation)

Although microemboli generated from the pump oxygenator may have potential effects on fluid accumulation, there have been no experimental observations that decreased blood flow due to microemboli was associated with increased water content.

Interstitial Fluid Pressure

The fall in plasma colloidal oncotic pressure that occurs at the onset of CPB is followed promptly by a rise in interstitial fluid pressure. Clinical studies show that interstitial fluid pressure rises more rapidly and to higher levels in skeletal muscle than in subcutaneous tissue during bypass (110, 111). In experimental studies significant increases in interstitial fluid pressure are observed in subcutaneous tissue, muscle, and myocardium, but not in stomach (Fig. 19.12). The greatest increase in water content occurs in myocardium and stomach rather than in muscle or subcutaneous tissue. Thus, the rise in interstitial fluid pressure does not correlate with the rise in water content.

This is undoubtedly related to differences in the relative compliance of the interstitial spaces. If the interstitial space is compliant, great amounts of fluid can accumulate without a great increase in interstitial pressure, which is the case with the stomach. Other tissues may develop significant increases in interstitial pressure without accumulating significant edema, such as skeletal muscle and subcutaneous tissue.

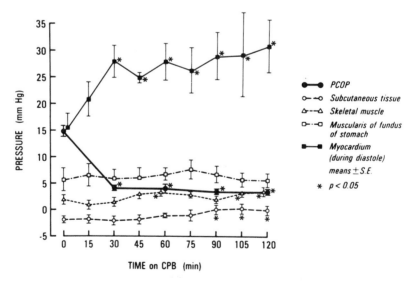

Figure 19.12. Plasma colloidal oncotic pressure (*PCOP*) and interstitial fluid pressure changes during CPB in dogs. During a 2-hour period of bypass, PCOP falls rapidly and remains low; diastolic intramyocardial pressure rises rapidly and progressively. Interstitial fluid pressure in muscle and subcutaneous tissue rises more slowly. No increase in interstitial fluid pressure in the fundus of the stomach was observed. (From Utley JR, Stephens DB. Fluid balance during cardiopulmonary bypass. In: Utley JR, ed. Pathophysiology and techniques of cardiopulmonary bypass. Vol II. Baltimore: Williams & Wilkins, 1983, p. 30.)

The different rates of rise of interstitial pressure in muscle and subcutaneous tissue may be related to difference in the pressure volume curves of the interstitial spaces of these two tissues that may derive from the rigid fascial compartment of skeletal muscle (112). Interstitial pressure rises in skeletal muscle with less than a 5% increase in tissue water content (110).

Components of Priming Solutions

Restoring the plasma colloidal oncotic pressure to normal during hemodilution CPB has detrimental effects on many parameters of renal function, although it will diminish the accumulation of interstitial fluid during bypass. Oncotically active components that have been employed include whole blood, albumin, dextran, hetastarch, and albumin. No diminished accumulation of fluid was observed in patients in whom whole blood was added to the priming solution (Figs. 19.13 through 19.15) (73). The addition of albumin to the priming solution resulted in lower hematocrits and less accumulation of fluid. Nonetheless, the addition of up to 175 g of albumin could not eliminate the accumulation of fluid during bypass.

Although albumin cannot eliminate the accumulation of interstitial fluid, the amount of fluid accumulated is inversely proportional to the concentration of serum albumin (113, 114). The amount of albumin required to return plasma colloidal oncotic pressure to normal levels would be prohibitively expensive, some of the protective effect of hemodilution on renal function would be lost, and interstitial fluid accumulation would still occur because of increased capillary permeability. There is

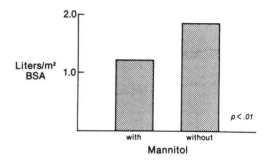

Figure 19.14.   Fluid accumulation during bypass. The addition of 12.5 g mannitol to the priming solution during bypass significantly decreases fluid accumulation. *BSA*, body surface area. (From Utley JR, Stephens DB. Fluid balance during cardiopulmonary bypass. In: Utley JR, ed. Pathophysiology and techniques of cardiopulmonary bypass. Vol II. Baltimore: Williams & Wilkins, 1983, p. 31.)

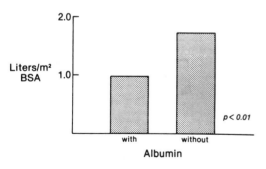

Figure 19.13.   Fluid accumulation during bypass. Comparison of fluid accumulation in patients with and without 50 g albumin in the priming solution shows a significant decrease in fluid accumulation with albumin. *BSA*, body surface area. (From Utley JR, Stephens DB. Fluid balance during cardiopulmonary bypass. In: Utley JR, ed. Pathophysiology and techniques of cardiopulmonary bypass. Vol II. Baltimore: Williams & Wilkins, 1983, p. 31.)

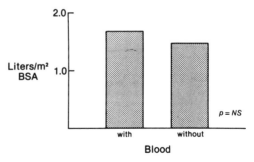

Figure 19.15.   Fluid accumulation during bypass. The use of blood in priming the pump oxygenator was not associated with significant differences in fluid accumulation during CPB. *BSA*, body surface area. (From Utley JR, Stephens DB. Fluid balance during cardiopulmonary bypass. In: Utley JR, ed. Pathophysiology and techniques of cardiopulmonary bypass. Vol II. Baltimore: Williams & Wilkins, 1983, p. 31.)

evidence that up to 40% of the rapidly exchangeable albumin may be transferred to the intravascular space during bypass (77, 78, 115).

A study of water accumulation in various organs at different albumin levels showed that fluid retention is significantly correlated with low plasma colloidal oncotic pressure and albumin levels in all tissues except liver. The relationship is strongest in intestine, muscle, myocardium, and skin and less strong in kidney, lung, and fat. The investigators noted an adverse effect on renal function from the addition of albumin (116). Another study observed increased water content in duodenum and skeletal muscle with diminished plasma oncotic pressure, while no increase was found in brain or kidney (117). This study also showed that increased fluid accumulation increased the bicarbonate requirements as well. These changes are reversed when the oncotic pressure is reconstituted with hetastarch (117). Hydroxyethyl starch and albumin have similar effects in decreasing intraoperative fluid accumulation (118). In another study, more fluid accumulation occurred with the use of hydroxyethyl starch than with albumin (119).

The addition of dextran to the priming solution may cause an osmotic diuresis because of the filtration of dextran at the glomerulus. Blood volume is better maintained with dextran, but urine flow is less than with mannitol or saline alone. Thus, dextran appears to have an effect similar to albumin in preserving plasma volume and diminishing interstitial fluid accumulation at the expense of preserving renal function (120, 121).

The infusion of hypertonic saline with hydroxyethyl starch is associated with less fluid accumulation that the infusion of hydroxyethyl starch alone (122). One study of priming solutions with and without 5% dextrose showed that the addition of dextrose is associated with less fluid accumulation during and after operation and with more rapid return to preoperative weight,

principally because of an osmotic diuresis induced by hyperglycemia (123). Another study found that the addition of glucose and lactate to the priming solution caused increased glucose and lactate, respectively, at the end of bypass. These authors recommended no glucose or lactate in the priming solution (124).

Postoperative Consequences of Fluid Accumulation and Renal Function

In coronary artery bypass patients, the time until preoperative weight is achieved is a simple function of the rapidity with which excess interstitial fluid is excreted. Slower return to preoperative weight is associated with emergency operation, operation early after recent myocardial infarction, high left ventricular end-diastolic pressure, and low postoperative hematocrit. Excessive fluid accumulation and slow return to preoperative weight are significantly correlated with postoperative death, bleeding, use of intraaortic balloon pump, and renal failure. Slow return to preoperative weight is also associated with pulmonary failure (1). Thus, the factors that preserve renal function are important contributors in the development of fluid accumulation, and intact renal function is central to the elimination of the retained fluid.

Diuretics are required postoperatively to achieve prompt excretion of the retained interstitial fluid from CPB (Fig. 19.16) (125). With the use of diuretics there is a strong correlation between the water and osmolar retention during bypass and the water and osmolar excretion the first 24 hours postoperatively. There is also a strong correlation between the preoperative creatinine clearance and the postoperative urine output and osmolar clearance. Urine osmolarity falls after bypass while urine output, osmolar output, and osmolar clearance rise during and after bypass. With hemodilution CPB the maximum urine osmolarity post-

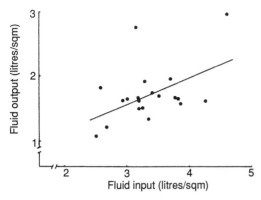

Figure 19.16. The urine output during the first post-operative night is significantly correlated with the fluid gain during bypass ($r = 0.49$, P < 0.05). The slope of the line of regression is 0.4, indicating that less than half the accumulated fluid is diuresed during this period. (From Read DH, Manners JM. Osmolar excretion after open heart surgery. Anaesthesia 1983;38: 1053–1061.)

operatively may be less than can normally be achieved. Patients usually excrete the retained water more rapidly than the retained solute postoperatively, which may account for the thirst that is common in postoperative patients.

If renal function is impaired postoperatively, the elimination of excess interstitial fluid will be greatly impaired. One of the indications for early and frequent peritoneal or hemodialysis and hemofiltration is excessive interstitial fluid causing ascites, pulmonary congestion, and total body edema (126).

Suggested indications for continuous arteriovenous hemofiltration during bypass include excessive preoperative fluid accumulation, bypass times greater than 2 hours, and the combination of low hematocrit and large reservoir volumes. Continuous arteriovenous hemofiltration may be used preoperatively and postoperatively to enable increased caloric intake in fluid-overloaded patients and to decrease fluid accumulation in diuretic-resistant patients with heart failure (127). The use of continuous arteriovenous hemofiltration in hypervolemic, oliguric children has been shown to decrease filling pressures and increase ar-

terial pressure, arterial pH, and oxygenation index (128).

Acknowledgment

This work was supported by the Cardiothoracic Research and Education Foundation.

REFERENCES

1. Utley JR. Current techniques of cardiopulmonary bypass, cardiac surgery. in: State of the art reviews. Philadelphia, PA: Hanley and Belfus, 1991;5(3):531–539.
2. Abel RM, Buckley MJ, Austen WG, Barnett GO, Beck CH Jr, Fischer JE. Acute postoperative renal failure in cardiac surgical patients. J Surg Res 1976;20:341–348.
3. Abel RM, Buckley MJ, Austen WG, Barnett GO, Beck Ch Jr, Fischer JE. Etiology, incidence and prognosis of renal failure following cardiac operations. Results of a prospective analysis of 500 consecutive patients. J Thorac Cardiovasc Surg 1976;71:32–33.
4. Gailiunas P, Chawla R, Lazarus JM, Cohn L, Sanders J, Merrill JP. Acute renal failure following cardiac operations. J Thorac Cardiovasc Surg 1980;79:241–243.
5. Krian A. Incidence, prevention, and treatment of acute renal failure following cardiopulmonary bypass. Int Anesth Clin 1976;14:87–101.
6. Ogg CS, Cameron JS. Cardiovascular surgery and the kidney. Guys Hosp Rep 1969;118: 85–103.
7. Baxter P, Rigby ML, Jones ODH, Lincoln C, Shinebourne EA. Acute renal failure following cardiopulmonary bypass in children: results of treatment. Int J Cardiol 1985;7:235–239.
8. Gomez-Campdera FJ, Maroto-Alvaro E, Galinanes M, Garcia E, Duarte J, Rengel-Aranda M. Acute renal failure associated with cardiac surgery. Child Nephrol Urol 1988–1989;9: 138–143.
9. Heikkinen L, Harjula A, Merikallio E. Acute renal failure related to open heart surgery. Ann Chir Gynaecol 1985;74:203–209.
10. Slogoff S, Reul GJ, Keats AS, et al. Role of perfusion pressure and flow in major organ dysfunction after cardiopulmonary bypass. Ann Thorac Surg 1990;50:911–918.
11. Yeboah ED, Petrie A, Pead JL. Acute renal failure and open heart surgery. Br Med J 1972;1: 415–418.
12. Aperia A, Bjarke B, Broberger O, Thoren C. Renal function in Fallot's tetralogy. Acta Paediatr Scand 1974;63:398–401.
13. Bourgeois BFD, Donath A, Paunier L, Rouge JC. Effects of cardiac surgery on renal function in children. J Thorac Cardiovasc Surg 1979;77: 283–286.

14. Gruskin AB. The kidney in congenital heart disease—an overview. Adv Pediatr 1977;24:133–139.

15. Passwell J, Orda S, Modan M, Shem-Tov A, Aladjem M, Boichis H. Abnormal renal functions in cyanotic congenital heart disease. Arch Dis Child 1978;51:803–805.

16. Yip WCL, Tay JSH, Ho, TF. Hyperuricaemia as a cause of acute renal failure complicating cardiopulmonary bypass surgery. [Letter] Arch Dis Child 1983;58:159.

17. Fillastre JP, Kleinknecht D. Acute renal failure associated with cephalosporin therapy. Am Heart J 1975;89:809–810.

18. Kiss J, Farago E, Gomory A, Homolay P, Kiss IS. Gentamycin in cardiac surgery. Acta Chir Acad Sci Hung 1977;18:133–135.

19. Olsen S, Asklund M. Interstitial nephritis with acute renal failure following cardiac surgery and treatment with methicillin. Acta Med Scand 1976;199:305–308.

20. Blythe WB. Renal autoregulation, drugs and acute renal failure. N C Med J 1985;46:413–414.

21. Matsuda H, Hirose H, Nakano S, et al. Results of open heart surgery in patients with impaired renal function as creatinine clearance below 30 ml/min: the effects of pulsatile perfusion. J Cardiovasc Surg 1986;27:595–599.

22. Moghissi K, McMillan IKR. Acute renal failure and open heart surgery. Br Med J 1972;32:228–229.

23. Moghissi K, Machell ES, Munday KA. Changes in renal blood flow and PAH extraction during extracorporeal circulation of short and long duration. Experimental study in dogs. Cardiovasc Res 1969;3:37–44.

24. Utley JR, Leyland SA, Johnson HD, et al. Correlation of preoperative factors, severity of disease, type of oxygenator and perfusion times with mortality and morbidity of coronary bypass. Perfusion 1991;6:15–22.

25. Nuutinen L, Hollmen A. Cardiopulmonary bypass and renal function. Ann Chir Gynaecol 1976;65:191–199.

26. Senning A, Andres J, Bornstein P, Norberg B, Andersen MN. Renal function during extracorporeal circulation at high and low flow rates: experimental studies in dogs. Ann Surg 1960;151:63–70.

27. Koning HM, Koning AJ, Defauw JJAM. Optimal perfusion during extra-corporeal circulation. Scand J Thor Cardiovasc Surg 1987;21:207–213.

28. Selmonosky CA. Studies on urinary urea concentration after cardiopulmonary bypass: a sensitive index of altered renal hemodynamics. Ann Surg 1970;172:226–232.

29. Selmonosky CA. Early detection of renal failure after cardiopulmonary bypass. Arch Surg 1969;99:64–68.

30. Holper K, Struck E, Sebening F. The diagnosis of acute renal failure (ARF) following cardiac surgery with cardiopulmonary bypass. Thorac Cardiovasc Surg 1979;27:231–237.

31. Fernandez F, de Miguel MD, Barrio V, Mallol J. Beta-2-Microglobulin as an index of renal function after cardiopulmonary bypass surgery in children. Child Nephrol Urol 1988–1989;9:326–330.

32. Tan CK, Glisson SN, El-Etr AA, Ramakrishnaiah KB. Levels of circulating norepinephrine and epinephrine before, during, and after cardiopulmonary bypass in man. J Thorac Cardiovasc Surg 1976;71:928–931.

33. Balasaraswathi K, Glisson SN, El-Etr AA, Azad C. Effect of priming volume on serum catecholamines during cardiopulmonary bypass. Can Anaesth Soc J 1980;27:135–139.

34. Taylor KM, Jones JV, Walker MS, Rao S, Bain WH. The cortisol response during heart-lung bypass. Circulation 1976;54:20–25.

35. Barta E, Kuzela L, Tordova E, Horecky J, Babusikova F. The blood volume and the renin-angiotensin-aldosterone system following open-heart surgery. Resuscitation 1980;8:137–146.

36. Many M, Giron F, Birtwell WC, Deterling RA Jr, Soroff JS. Effects of depulsation of renal blood flow upon renal function and renin secretion. Surgery 1969;66:242–249.

37. Dewar ML, Walsh LG, Chiu CJ, et al. Atrial natriuretic factor: response to cardiac operation. J Thorac Cardiovasc Surg 1988;96:266–270.

38. Schaff HV, Mashburn JP, McCarthy PM, Torres EJ, Burnett JC. Natriuresis during and early after cardiopulmonary bypass: relationship to atrial natriuretic factor, aldosterone, and antidiuretic hormone. J Thorac Cardiovasc Surg 1989;98:979–986.

39. Feddersen K, Aren C, Granerus G, Jagenburg R, Radegran K. Effects of prostacyclin infusion on renal function during cardiopulmonary bypass. Ann Thorac Surg 1985;40:16–19.

40. Mori A, Watanabe K, Onoe M, et al. Regional blood flow in the liver, pancreas and kidney during pulsatile and nonpulsatile perfusion under profound hypothermia. Jpn Circ J 1988;52:219–227.

41. Olinger GN, Hutchinson LD, Bonchek LI. Pulsatile cardiopulmonary bypass for patients with renal insufficiency. Thorax 1983;38:543–550.

42. Utley JR, Wachtel C, Cain RB, Spaw EA, Collins JC, Stephens DB. Effects of hypothermia, hemodilution, and pump oxygenation on organ water content, blood flow and oxygen delivery,

and renal function. Ann Thorac Surg 1981;31: 121–133.

43. Utley JR, Stephens DB, Eachtel C, et al. Effect of albumin and mannitol on organ blood flow, oxygen delivery water content, and renal function during hypothermic, hemodilution cardiopulmonary bypass. Ann Thorac Surg 1982;33: 250–257.

44. Mielke JE, Hunt JC, Maher FT, Kirlin JW: Renal performance during clinical cardiopulmonary bypass with and without hemodilution. J Thorac Cardiovasc Surg 1966;51:229–237.

45. Lilleaasen P, Stokke O. Moderate and extreme hemodilution in open-heart surgery: fluid balance and acid-base studies. Ann Thorac Surg 1978;25:127–133.

46. Schupbach P, Pappova E, Schilt W, et al. Perfusate oncotic pressure during cardiopulmonary bypass. Optimum levels as determined by metabolic acidosis, tissue edema, and renal function. Vox Sang 1978;35:332–344.

47. Brenner BM, Flachuck KH, Keimowitz RI, Berliner RW, Troy JL, Green N. The relationship between peritubular capillary protein concentration and fluid reabsorption by the renal proximal tubule. J Clin Invest 1969;48: 1519–1531.

48. Falchuk KH, Brenner BM, Tadokoro M, Berliner RW. Oncotic and hydrostatic pressures in peritubular capillaries and fluid reabsorption by proximal tubule. Am J Physiol 1971;220: 1427–1433.

49. de Torrente AD. Acute renal failure. Int Anesthesiol Clin 1984;22:83–100.

50. Kanter GS. Renal clearance of sodium and potassium in hypothermia. Can J Biochem Physiol 1962;40:113–117.

51. Terblanche J, Isaacson LC, Eales L, Barnard CN. Renal function during and immediately after profound hypothermia. Surgery 1961;50: 869–875.

52. Karim F, Reza H. Effect of induced hypothermia and rewarming on renal hemodynamics in anesthetized dogs. Life Sci 1970;9:1153–1160.

53. Thompson RB. The haemolytic anaemias. In: Thompson RB, ed. Disorders of the blood. New York: Churchill Livingstone, 1977:305–322.

54. Clyne DH, Kant KS, Pesce AJ, Pollak VE. Nephrotoxicity of low molecular weight serum proteins: physicochemical interactions between myoglobin, hemoglobin, Bence Jones proteins and Tamm-Horsfall mucoprotein. Curr Prob Clin Biochem 1979;9:299–307.

55. Andersen MN, Mouritzen CV, Gabrieli E. Mechanisms of plasma hemoglobin clearance after acute hemolysis: studies in open-heart surgical patients. A comparative study of five different units. Ann Surg 1966;163:529–536.

56. Andersen MN, Kuchiba K. Blood trauma produced by pump oxygenators. J Thorac Cardiovasc Surg 1969;57:238–244.

57. Engelman RM, Gouge TH, Smith SJ, Stahl WM, Gombos EA, Boyd AD. The effect of diuretics on renal hemodynamics during cardiopulmonary bypass. J Surg Res 1974;16:268–276.

58. Osborn JJ, Cohn K, Hait M, et al. Hemolysis during perfusion: Sources and means of reduction. J Thorac Cardiovasc Surg 1962;43:459–464.

59. Lindberg EF, Berghuis J, Theye RA, Kirklin JW. Plasma hemoglobin levels associated with use of a vertical-sheet pump-oxygenator (Mayo-Gibbon type). Surgery 1964;55:665–671.

60. McCaughan JS Jr, McMichael H, Schuder JC, Kirby CK. The use of a totally occlusive pump as a flowmeter with observations on hemolysis caused by occlusive and nonocclusive pumps and other pump-oxygenator components. Surgery 1958;44:210–219.

61. Utley JR, Marshall WG, Boatman GB, Dickerson G, Ernst CB, Daugherty ME. Trapping, nontrapping, and release of nine and fifteen micron spheres in dog kidneys. Surgery 1980; 87:222–229.

62. Lee SM. Renal fat emboli, Maltese crosses, and heart surgery. [Letter] JAMA 1986;256:40.

63. Nilsson L, Tyden H, Johansson O, et al. Bubble and membrane oxygenators—comparison of postoperative organ dysfunction with special reference to inflammatory activity. Scand J Thorac Cardiovasc Surg 1990;24:59–64.

64. Nuutinen L, Hollmen A. The effect of prophylactic use of furosemide on renal function during open heart surgery. Ann Chir Gynaecol 1976;65:258–260.

65. Kron IL, Joob AW, Meter CV. Acute renal failure in the cardiovascular surgical patient. Ann Thorac Surg 1985;39:590–599.

66. Nuutinen LS. The effect of nitrous oxide on renal function in open heart surgery. Ann Chir Gynaecol 1976;65:200–203.

67. Davis RF, Lappas DG, Kirklin JK, Buckley MJ, Lowenstein E. Acute oliguria after cardiopulmonary bypass: renal functional improvement with low-dose dopamine infusion. Crit Care Med 1982;10:852–856.

68. Litwak RS, Slonim R, Kiem Iris, Gadboys HL. Alterations in blood volume during "normovolemic" total body perfusion. J Thorac Cardiovasc Surg 1961;42:477–482.

69. Kaplan S, Edwards FK, Helmsworth JA, Clark LC. Blood volume during and after total extracorporeal circulation. Arch Surg 1960;80: 31–37.

70. McClenahan JB, Yamauchi H, Roe BB. Blood volume studies in cardiac-surgery patients. JAMA 1966;195:356–361.

71. Neville WE, Thomason RD, Hirsch DM. Postperfusion hypervolemia after hemodilution cardiopulmonary bypass. Arch Surg 1966;93:715–723.

72. Carr EA, Sloan HE, Tovar E. The clinical importance of erythrocyte and plasma volume determinations before and after open-heart surgery. J Nucl Med 1960;1:165.

73. Utley JR, Stephens DB. Unpublished data, 1979.

74. Cleland J, Pluth JR, Tauxe WN, Kirklin JW. Blood volume and body fluid compartment changes soon after closed and open intracardiac surgery. J Thorac Cardiovasc Surg 1966;52:698–705.

75. Canale SD, Fiacadori E, Medici D, et al. Effects of low flux-low pressure cardiopulmonary bypass on intracellular acid-base and water metabolism. Scand J Thorac Cardiovasc Surg 1986;20:167–170.

76. Berger RL, Body TF, Marcus PS. A pattern of blood-volume response to open-heart surgery. N Engl J Med 1964;271:59–64.

77. Beattie HW, Evans G, Garnett ES, Webber CE. Sustained hypovolemia and extracellular fluid volume expansion following cardiopulmonary bypass. Surgery 1972;71:891–897.

78. Beattie HW, Evans G, Garnett ES, Regoeczi E, Webber CE, Wong KL. Albumin and water fluxes during cardiopulmonary bypass. J Thorac Cardiovasc Surg 1974;67:926–931.

79. Reid DJ, Digerness S, Kirklin JW. Intracellular fluid volume in surgical patients measured by the simultaneous determination of total body water and extracellular fluid. Surg Forum 1967;18:29–36.

80. Beall AC, Johnson PC, Shirkey AL, Crosthwait RW, Cooley DA, DeBakey ME. Effects of temporary cardiopulmonary bypass on extracellular fluid volume and total body water in man. Circulation 1964;29(suppl):59–64.

81. Lilleaasen P, Stokke O. Moderate and extreme hemodilution in open-heart surgery: fluid balance and acid-base studies. Ann Thorac Surg 1978;25:127–133.

82. Pluth JR, Cleland J, Tauxe WN, Kirklin JW. Late changes in body fluid and blood volume after intracardiac surgery. J Thorac Cardiovasc Surg 1968;56:108–113.

83. Sturtz GS, Kirklin JW, Burke EC, Power MH. Water metabolism after cardiac operations involving a Gibbon-type pump oxygenator. Circulation 1957;16:988–1000.

84. Dordoni L, Oddi N, Schiavello R, Magalini SI, Bonoli A. Biochemical changes in extracorporeal circulation in patients. Resuscitation 1976;5:111–116.

85. Pacifico AD, Digerness S, Kirklin JW. Sodium-excreting ability before and after intracardiac surgery. Circulation 1970;2(suppl):142–146.

86. Pacifico AD, Digerness S, Kirklin JW. Regression of body compositional abnormalities of heart failure after intracardiac operations. Circulation 1970;42:999–1008.

87. Pacifico AD, Digerness S, Kirklin JW. Acute alterations of body composition after open intracardiac operations. Circulation 1970;41:331–341.

88. Cohn LH, Klovekorn P, Moore FD, Collins JJ. Intrinsic plasma volume deficits in patients with coronary artery disease. Arch Surg 1974;108:57–68.

89. Wigboldus AH, Urzua J, Viljoen JF. The "empty heart" phenomenon. J Thorac Cardiovasc Surg 1973;66:807–813.

90. Utley JR, Morgan MS, Johnson HD, Wilde CM, Bell MS. Correlates of blood volume, red cell mass and plasma volume in coronary bypass patients. Perfusion 1989;4:205–211.

91. Maehara TY, Novak I, Wyse RKH, Elliot MJ. Perioperative monitoring of total body water by bio-electrical impedance in children undergoing open heart surgery. Eur J Cardiothorac Surg 1991;5:258–265.

92. Utley JR, Wachtel C, Cain RB, Spaw EA, Collins JC, Stephens DB. Effects of hypothermia, hemodilution and pump oxygenation on organ water content, blood flow and oxygen delivery, and renal function. Ann Thorac Surg 1981;31:121–133.

93. Webber CE, Garnett ES. The relationship between colloid osmotic pressure and plasma proteins during and after cardiopulmonary bypass. J Thorac Cardiovasc Surg 1973;65:234–237.

94. English TA, Digerness S, Kirklin JW. Changes in colloid osmotic pressure during and shortly after open intracardiac operation. J Thorac Cardiovasc Surg 1971;61:338–341.

95. Gollub S, Schechter DC, Schaefer C, Svigals R, Bailey CP. Absolute hemodilution cardiopulmonary bypass: free water distribution and protein mobilization in body compartments. Am Heart J 1969;78:626–634.

96. Roe BB, Swenson EE, Hepps SA, Bruns DL. Total body perfusion in cardiac operations. Arch Surg 1964;88:128–134.

97. Neville WE, Faber LP, Peacock H. Total prime of the disc oxygenator with Ringer's and Ringer's lactate solution for cardiopulmonary bypass. Dis Chest 1964;45:320–327.

98. Cooley DA, Beall AC, Grondin P. Open heart operations with disposable oxygenators, 5 per

cent dextrose prime, and normothermia. Surgery 1962;52:713–719.

99. Eiseman B, Spencer FC. Effect of hypothermia on the flow characteristics of blood. Surgery 1962;52:532–544.

100. Fedor EJ, Fisher B. Simultaneous determination of blood volume with Cr[51] and T-1824 during hypothermia and rewarming. Am J Physiol 1959;196:703–707.

101. Oz M, Kameya S, Neville W, Clowes GHA. The relationship of blood volume, systemic peripheral resistance, and flow rate during profound hypothermia. Trans Soc Artif Intern Organs 1960;6:204–213.

102. Lofstrom B. Changes in blood volume in induced hypothermia. Acta Anaesthesiol Scand 1957;1:1–10.

103. Kanter GS. Hypothermic hemoconcentration. Am J Physiol 1968;214:856–862.

104. Chang CB, Shoemaker WC. Effect of hypothermia on red cell volumes. J Thorac Cardiovasc Surg 1963;46:117–124.

105. Svanes K, Zweifach BW, Intaglietta M. Effect of hypothermia on transcapillary fluid exchange. Am J Physiol 1970;218:981–988.

106. Kahler RL, Goldblatt A, Braunwald E. Circulatory effects of profound hypothermia during extracorporeal circulation. Am J Physiol 1962;202:523–529.

107. Clasen RA, Pandolfi S, Hass GM. Interrupted hypothermia in experimental cerebral edema. Neurology 1970;20:279–282.

108. Fenstermacher JD, Li C-L, Levin VA. Extracellular space of the cerebral cortex of normothermic and hypothermic cats. Exp Neurol 1970;27:101–108.

109. Lee WH, Krumhaar D, Fondalsrud EW, Schjeide OA, Maloney JV. Denaturation of plasma proteins as a cause of morbidity and death after intracardiac operations. Surgery 1961;50:29–39.

110. Guyton AC. Interstitial fluid pressure: II. Pressure-volume curves of interstitial space. Circ Res 1965;16:452–463.

111. Menninger FJ III, Rosenkranz ER, Utley JR, Dembitsky WP, Hargens AR, Peters RM. Interstitial hydrostatic pressure in patients undergoing CABG and valve replacement. J Thorac Cardiovasc Surg 1980;79:181–187.

112. Rosenkranz ER, Utley JR, Menninger FJ, Dembitsky WP, Hargens AR, Peters RM. Interstitial fluid pressure changes during cardiopulmonary bypass. Ann Thorac Surg 1980;30:536–542.

113. Hallowell P, Bland JHL, Dalton BC, et al. The effect of hemodilution with albumin or Ringer's lactate on water balance and blood use in open heart surgery. Ann Thorac Surg 1978;25:22–29.

114. Lilleaasen P, Stokke O, Thoresen O, Aasen A, Engesaeter L, Froysaker T. Effects of different non-haemic fluids in open-heart surgery. Scand J Thorac Cardiovasc Surg 1979;13:233–240.

115. Utley JR, Stephens DB, Wachtel C, et al. Effect of albumin and mannitol on organ blood flow, oxygen delivery, water content and renal function during hypothermic hemodilution cardiopulmonary bypass. Ann Thorac Surg 1982;33:250–257.

116. Schupbach P, Pappova E, Schilt W, et al. Perfusate oncotic pressure during cardiopulmonary bypass: optimum level as determined by metabolic acidosis, tissue edema and renal function. Vox Sang 1978;35:332–344.

117. Hindman BJ, Funatsu N, Cheng DCH, Bolles R, Todd MM, Tinker JH. Differential effect of oncotic pressure on cerebral and extracerebral water content during cardiopulmonary bypass in rabbits. Anesthesiology 1990;73:951–957.

118. Sade RM, Stroud MR, Crawford FA, Kratz JM, Dearing JP, Bartles DM. A prospective randomized study of hydroxyethyl starch, albumin, and lactated Ringer's solution as priming fluid for cardiopulmonary bypass. J Thorac Cardiovasc Surg 1985;89:713–722.

119. Saunders CR, Carlisle L, Bick, RL. Hydroxyethyl starch versus albumin in cardiopulmonary bypass prime solutions. Ann Thorac Surg 1983;36:532–538.

120. Hymes AC, Safavian MH, Arbulu A, Baute P. A comparison of Pluronic F-68, low molecular weight dextran, mannitol, and saline as priming agents in the heart-lung apparatus. J Thorac Cardiovasc Surg 1968;56:16–22.

121. Albrechtsen OK, Althaus U, Berg E, Jeyasingham K, Kim CH, Silberschmid M. Haemodilution techniques in canine extracorporeal circulation using bubble and disc oxygenators. Scand J Thorac Cardiovasc Surg 1972;6:178–183.

122. Boldt J, Zickmann B, Ballesteros M, Herold CH, Dapper F, Hempelmann G. Cardiorespiratory responses to hypertonic saline solution in cardiac operations. Ann Thorac Surg 1991;51:610–615.

123. Metz S, Keats AS. Benefits of a glucose-containing priming solution for cardiopulmonary bypass. Anesth Analg 1991;72:428–434.

124. McKnight CK, Elliott MJ, Pearson DT, Holden MP, Alberti KGMM. The effects of four different crystalloid bypass pump-priming fluids upon the metabolic response to cardiac operation. J Thorac Cardiovasc Surg 1985;90:97–111.

125. Read DH, Manners JM. Osmolar excretion after open heart surgery. Anaesthesia 1983;38: 1053–1061.

126. Yeboah ED, Petrie A, Pead JL. Acute renal failure and open heart surgery. Br Med J 1972;1: 415–418.

127. Magilligan DJ. Indications for ultrafiltration in the cardiac surgical patient. J Thorac Cardiovasc Surg 1985;89:183–189.

128. Zobel G, Stein JI, Kuttnig M, Beitzke A, Metzler H, Rigler B. Continuous extracorporeal fluid removal in children with low cardiac output after cardiac operation. J Thorac Cardiovasc Surg 1991;101:593–597.

20

METABOLIC AND SPLANCHNIC VISCERAL EFFECTS OF CARDIOPULMONARY BYPASS

Robert E. Shangraw

One of the least intensively monitored areas during surgical procedures involving cardiopulmonary bypass (CPB) is that of visceral organ perfusion and function. Major limiting factors during thoracic operations include the closed abdomen, obviating direct access to the abdominal viscera, and the cumbersome and expensive nature of available noninvasive monitoring techniques to assess splanchnic circulation, for which there is little evidence of improved clinical outcome in cardiovascular surgery. Another "system" that is not intensively monitored is the systemic metabolic and endocrine milieu, despite evidence that it is markedly altered during CPB. The purpose of this chapter is to provide a detailed review of the data available on the functional alterations, consequent to CPB, that occur in the splanchnic viscera (gastrointestinal, liver, and pancreas) along with the associated metabolic derangements.

SPLANCHNIC CIRCULATION DURING CPB

Animal Studies

The importance of adequate splanchnic circulation during CPB was underscored in the 1930s by the pathologic changes observed in "irrreversible hemorrhagic shock" (1). In a large series of experiments, Wiggers (1) and his colleagues showed that animals underwent a progressive, ultimately fatal deterioration of cardiovascular status after having initially recovered from a period of controlled hemorrhagic hypotension. At autopsy, these animals exhibited several pathologic changes in visceral organs perfused by the splanchnic circulation. Changes included capillary congestion, small hemorrhages, and early necrosis in small intestines, stomach, liver and pancreas. Therefore, animal studies on the effects of CPB focused on the adequacy of splanchnic regional perfusion during bypass to ascertain whether a shock-like state was being created (2). Cardiopulmonary bypass is often accompanied by relative hypotension and induced hypothermia, two factors that markedly affect the regional distribution of blood flow and the amount of flow that is required to maintain cellular viability.

The mechanism by which hypotension is produced is of critical importance to visceral organ viability. Studies comparing trimethaphan and controlled hemorrhage, both used to reduce systemic and total hepatic blood flow to a similar extent, revealed that hepatic energy metabolism in the trimetaphan group was maintained for 3 hours (3). In contrast, hemorrhagic hypotension produced a progressive decline in the intrahepatic ratio of adenosine triphosphate (ATP) to inorganic phosphate (ATP/

P_i), arterial ketone body ratio (which reflects the balance of reductive and oxidative metabolic reactions at the mitochondrial level), and overall energy charge (3).

Halley et al. (2) directly measured blood flow through the intestinal bed of dogs during normothermic "high-flow" and "low-flow" CPB. Intestinal blood flow was increased (45% and 27% by high- and low-flow CPB, respectively) during CPB, in association with a decrease in calculated vascular resistance across the bed. Despite the augmented flow, intestinal oxygen consumption was diminished by 20 to 30% during CPB, and did not correlate with changes in temperature or pH. In contrast, Desai et al. (4), using electromagnetic flow probes to assess hepatic blood flow in dogs, found that 60 minutes of CPB decreased blood flow through the hepatic artery (by 46%), portal vein (by 44%), and total liver (by 45%), when compared to animals undergoing thoracotomy without CPB. The decreased hepatic flow from each bed was ascribed to an *increased* vascular resistance, although the variation among animals precluded statistical significance and mean systemic blood pressure fell from 110 to 56 mm Hg. Unfortunately, the cardiac output of animals undergoing thoracotomy was not reported, precluding a comparison of total systemic flow between the two groups.

Lees et al. (5) used radiolabelled microspheres in 27 rhesus monkeys to compare regional blood flow observed during CPB with that seen in animals awake, during general anesthesia alone, or while undergoing thoracotomy without CPB. During CPB, total systemic flow was regulated to equal that of awake animals (high flow). Mean arterial pressure fell from 144 mm Hg in awake animals to 75 mm Hg during bypass, in association with a large decrease in calculated systemic vascular resistance. Compared to awake animals, bypass caused a threefold to fourfold increase in blood flow through the gastrointestinal tract, spleen, and mesentery. Oxygen-rich hepatic arterial flow decreased by 35%, although the calcu-

lated total hepatic perfusion (including portal vein) nearly doubled. There was no alteration of pancreatic perfusion during high-flow CPB. Another study, also in primates, has confirmed the increase in gastric and intestinal blood flow during high-flow CPB, but unfortunately did not measure hepatic or pancreatic flow (6).

Thus it appears that, without unanimous experimental corroboration, normothermic CPB with either high or low flows is associated with an overall increase in gastrointestinal blood flow, but with a decrease in the arterial component of hepatic blood flow and a variable effect on pancreatic perfusion.

Influence of Carbon Dioxide

Effects of arterial carbon dioxide tension ($Paco_2$) on hepatic perfusion and function are controversial. There are apparently conflicting reports on the effect of hypocapnia on hepatic artery blood flow, with a decrease reported in dogs (7), and an increase reported in monkeys (8). These differences may be reconciled, as pointed out by Gelman (8), by noting that the experiments in dogs were performed during laparotomy while those in monkeys were not, implying that surgical stimulation augmented hepatic artery flow, thus raising the baseline hepatic arterial flow in the study of Fujita et al (7). In the case of hypercapnia, cardiac output, portal, and total hepatic circulations are augmented (7). Portal venous pressure is also increased, at least partially due to the increased flow. Although there is no significant decrease in hepatic arterial flow during marked hypercapnia ($Paco_2$ = 59 mm Hg), both hepatic oxygen consumption and indocyanine green dye uptake are inhibited, indicating possible hepatocellular dysfunction during laparotomy. These studies did not control for acidosis per se, leaving unsettled the question of whether co_2 or H^+ is ultimately responsible for the observed alterations. However, the possibility exists that hypercapnia may augment shunt flow and simultaneously impair nutritional microcirculation in the liver. No studies have been reported on the influence of Pa_{CO_2} on splanchnic and hepatic circulations, and their dependent cellular functions, during CPB.

Influence of Temperature

A recent study in dogs examined liver and pancreatic blood flow during CPB, using a hydrogen gas clearance technique (9). Flow measurements were made during cooling and warming at 5°C intervals, with an intervening 40-minute period of total circulatory arrest at 20°C. During cooling, there was a progressive decrease in total hepatic perfusion, such that flow at 20°C was only 54% of that at 35°C. Similarly, pancreatic flow fell by 33% when the temperature was decreased from 35°C to 20°C. However, the pump flow rate was also decreased from 100 ml/kg/min at 35°C to 60 ml/kg/min at 20°C. It is uncertain from the presented data what effect the decreased systemic pump flow rate had on the overall perfusion pressure. Because total blood flow was not maintained throughout the study, it is impossible to determine whether the observed decrease of regional blood flow was due to comparable decreases in systemic blood flow or to changes in temperature. These data do imply, however, that neither liver nor pancreatic blood flow are autoregulated during hypothermic CPB. Unfortunately, a control experiment (similar surgery without CPB), which would have enabled a determination of whether normal splanchnic autoregulation exists or is lost secondary to CPB, was not reported.

Effect of Dopamine

Dopamine is commonly used during cardiac surgery for cardiac inotropic support or as a means of preserving renal function. However, dopamine has been shown in dogs, pigs, and humans to have a significant effect on nonrenal splanchnic circulation

(10–12). In anesthetized dogs not on CPB, a bolus of dopamine (12.8 μg/kg) directly vasodilates the superior and inferior mesenteric arteries, left gastric artery, and superior pancreatoduodenal artery (10). In contrast, dopamine fails to produce vasodilation in the canine hepatic artery, indicating a paucity or absence of dopaminergic receptors in the hepatic arterial bed (10). This interpretation is complicated, however, by a similar failure of increased blood flow through the renal arteries in the same dogs, despite the well-documented abundance of dopaminergic receptors in the canine renal artery (and an observed 50% increase in urine flow) (10). In pigs, also not undergoing CPB, dopamine also increases superior mesenteric arterial flow and, although it does not alter hepatic arterial flow, increases total hepatic flow because of augmented portal flow (12). Dopamine differs from other pressor agents in that, administered at doses producing similar effects on systemic hemodynamics, dopamine increases hepatic oxygen delivery while norepinephrine decreases it and dobutamine has no effect (12).

Lundberg et al. (11) used electromagnetic flow probes to directly assess splanchnic blood flow in nine patients undergoing abdominal aortic aneurism repair without CPB. Epidural anesthesia led to a moderate decrease in both splanchnic and systemic perfusion and perfusion pressure. Dopamine at 4 μg/kg/min, although it had no apparent effect on systemic or superior mesenteric artery hemodynamics in the absence of epidural anesthesia, reversed the impairment of splanchnic perfusion secondary to epidural anesthesia (11). Equally important, the increase in lactate production by the ischemic intestine in one patient was abolished by the dopamine infusion. Dopamine eliminated the difference between intestinal and systemic lactate production, indicating that the effect was specific for preservation of splanchnic perfusion (11). Although these studies were performed during an abdominal rather than a thoracic procedure, and were performed on subjects not undergoing CPB, they underscore the insensitivity of systemic indices for detection of regional abnormalities in the abdominal cavity, and that the splanchnic circulation can be manipulated with low-dose dopamine during surgical operation.

Problems with Clinical Monitoring

These animal studies indicate that gross splanchnic circulation is adequately maintained during CPB, but they assess neither microcirculatory adequacy nor the preservation of cellular viability and physiologic function. Furthermore, the young adult primate may not be an ideal model for circulatory efficacy in the elderly human with diffuse atherosclerotic disease, as represents a growing segment of patients undergoing CPB. One of the major difficulties in the development of CPB has been the inability to clinically monitor the integrity of perfusion and physiologic function of splanchnic organs. There have been a few attempts to assess hepatic perfusion by indicator dye (Bromosulphthalein, BSP, a dye specifically taken up by hepatocytes) uptake (13) or continuous hepatic vein oxygen saturation monitoring (14), but these have not been integrated into the routine clinical care during CPB.

Underlying the limited use of routine oximetry or dye uptake during CPB is the uncertainty of how tightly dye uptake or oxygen consumption is coupled to perfusion adequacy in the anesthetized patient (15). A second problem with hepatic vein catheterization is that it must be performed with fluoroscopic guidance, which limits its attractiveness to the clinician (14). A third monitoring technique, which has been utilized in the postoperative setting, is continuous measurement of gastrointestinal pH by tonometry (16–18). The limitation of tonometry, however, is that it is technically difficult to perform. Thus, all three of these potential methods to assess visceral perfu-

sion adequacy during CPB, despite future promise, remain relatively obscure and scarcely utilized, pending further research and/or technical development.

METABOLIC RESPONSE TO CPB

Hormonal Profile

It is important to recognize that the institution of CPB almost always occurs in an anesthetized patient already undergoing a major surgical operation. Therefore, the effects of CPB are superimposed upon a preexisting surgical stress response as modulated by general anesthesia. The hormonal response to surgery has recently been detailed in a review by Weissman (19). In general, this stress response is characterized by suppression of insulin secretion, coupled with augmented plasma levels of the so-called "counter-regulatory" hormones (catecholamines, glucagon, cortisol) (20–25). High plasma levels of pituitary hormones [growth hormone, adrenocorticotrophic hormone (ACTH), vasopressin] also occur as a result of surgical stimulation (26–28). Numerous investigators have shown that the metabolic stress response is most pronounced immediately following, rather than during, the surgical procedure itself. This perhaps indicates the ameliorating effect of general anesthesia on the metabolic and endocrine response to injury. Furthermore, the particular anesthetic technique can have a significant influence on the magnitude of stress response to surgery, with more blunting of the response occurring with a deeper level of anesthesia, an effect that may be indexed by the interaction of anesthesic depth and the hemodynamic responses to noxious stimulation (29, 30).

Roizen et al. (30) showed that the plane of anesthetic depth required to blunt the neuroendocrine response to surgery (MAC-BAR, or minimum alveolar concentration of inhaled agent required to *block adrenergic response*) is significantly deeper than that required to prevent movement on skin incision for most anesthetics. Attainment of an anesthetic depth sufficient to blunt the neuroendocrine stress response has long been considered a desirable goal in adult patients, especially in view of its effects on patients with ischemic heart disease. More recent data indicate that very young children benefit as well from an anesthetic capable of blunting the stress response (31). This complex metabolic and hormonal milieu of the stress response to noxious stimulation and its modulation by anesthesia is the background on which CPB is clinically superimposed. It must serve as the basis for further discussion of the endocrine and metabolic effects of CPB. A complete discussion of the endocrinology of CPB is found in Chapter 12. This discussion will focus on endocrine changes with significant metabolic consequences.

Carbohydrate Metabolism

INSULIN, GLUCAGON AND THE HYPERGLYCEMIA OF CPB

Insulin secretion is regulated in large part by the prevailing plasma glucose concentration. Thus, inhibition of insulin secretion is defined as either an absolute decrease in plasma concentration *or* an increase above baseline that is less marked than should occur at a given plasma glucose concentration. In an early metabolic study, 12 patients scheduled to undergo aortic valve replacement were divided into two groups, based on the planned anesthetic management (morphine 4 mg/kg, or fluroxene 2 to 4% supplanted during CPB by ketamine) (32). During the pre-CPB period, plasma insulin in both groups remained at control levels, and plasma glucose also remained unchanged in the patients receiving morphine (32). There was a modest but significant increase in plasma glucose of patients under fluroxene anesthesia, probably due to continued sympathetic activity that is known to occur with fluroxene (33). Ketamine-diazepam anesthesia has also been reported to produce a

similar stability of glucose-insulin metabolism during the pre-CPB period (34). In contrast, Abe (35) found a progressive pre-CPB hyperglycemia to 220 mg/dl accompanied by a modest rise in plasma insulin, but did not report the anesthetic technique. Children, as well as adults, may exhibit an inhibition of insulin secretion during the pre-CPB period, since plasma insulin fails to rise in response to continued glucose infusion (20, 36). However, most anesthetic techniques lead to a stable glucose-insulin millieu during the pre-CPB period.

Initiation of CPB is accompanied by development of hyperglycemia, regardless of the anesthetic technique employed (20, 32, 34, 35) (Fig. 20.1). Without glucose in the pump prime, there is a progressive hyperglycemia throughout the bypass period (37). The addition of glucose to the priming solution exacerbates the early hyperglycemia, since this represents a large glucose challenge at a time when the insulin secretory response is already inhibited by surgery (20, 32). In the study by Brandt et al. (32), all patients received 25 g of glucose in the prime, then no additional intraoperative glucose. Blood glucose rose from approximately 110 mg/dl before CPB to 250 mg/dl at commencement of CPB, and the hyperglycemia persisted for 1 to 2 hours beyond separation from CPB. The degree of hyperglycemia appeared to be related to depth of anesthesia, being more pronounced in patients with fluroxene anesthesia than in those receiving morphine 4 mg/kg. Plasma insulin concentration tends to follow that of glucose, with patients in the same anesthetic group exhibiting a more marked hyperinsulinemia in the setting of higher blood glucose levels (32). There is a temporal delay in the plasma insulin concentration relative to that of glucose during normothermic CPB. Hyperglycemia is almost maximal within the first few minutes of bypass (as the prime is distributed), while the rise in plasma insulin level is delayed, incrementing continuously throughout the CPB period (20, 34).

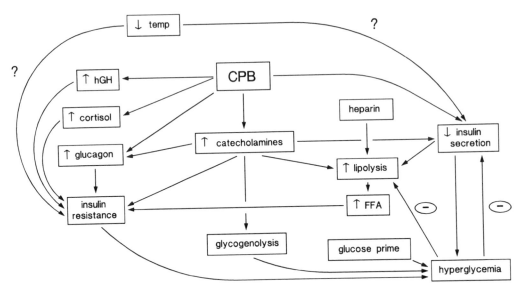

Figure 20.1.   Schematic representation of metabolic alterations during CPB. A complex system of factors contributes to development of hyperglycemia early after initiation of CPB. Hyperglycemia, in turn, provokes hyperinsulinemia later in the course of CPB and also acts to directly and indirectly restrain lipolysis. This diagram represents a core metabolic response to CPB rather than an exhaustive listing of all interactive factors playing a role in the metabolic and endocrine response to CPB; *hGH*, human growth hormone.

Although plasma insulin levels rise twofold by the end of CPB, the relatively slow response of insulin to continued hyperglycemic stimulation indicates that the secretory response is inhibited during CPB (34). One factor that may contribute to the attenuated insulin response to hyperglycemia is the direct inhibitory effect of epinephrine on the pancreatic beta cell (38), since plasma catecholamine levels are very high throughout the period of CPB (see Chapter 12).

Further exacerbation of hyperglycemia occurs during cooling to hypothermic CPB (35), a phenomenon that may be caused in part by a hypothermia-induced impairment of the peripheral glucose uptake response to insulin. However, since the hyperglycemia is not accompanied by a rise in plasma insulin concentration (35), the failure of an appropriate insulin secretory response to marked hyperglycemia indicates a second defect, a direct inhibition of insulin secretion. Good evidence is lacking to support either a direct inhibitory effect

of hypothermia on intrinsic pancreatic beta cell function in vitro, or an effect on the ability of the pancreas to secrete insulin in vivo during CPB (which requires adequate pancreatic microcirculation). However, the insulin secretory response to hyperglycemia appears to be almost completely ablated during hypothermic CPB, an effect not observed in patients undergoing normothermic CPB with similar conditions (39). During rewarming from hypothermic CPB, plasma insulin begins to increase, but never reaches the level exhibited by patients undergoing normothermic CPB (39). Hypothermia therefore appears to be a major factor responsible for the sluggish insulin response to the glucose challenge during CPB.

McKnight et al. (40), using continuous sampling of plasma during bypass, showed that hyperglycemia was also exacerbated during the rewarming period prior to termination of bypass. The etiology is unknown, but since hyperinsulinemia continues, it reflects an exacerbation of the inability of insulin to either (*a*) suppress endogenous glucose production by the liver or (*b*) stimulate tissue glucose utilization, or both.

Termination of CPB is followed by a slow but steady decline in plasma glucose, reaching preanesthesia levels several hours to several days postoperatively (32, 34). In the study by McKnight et al. (40), hyperglycemia was reversibly exacerbated by infusion of either dopamine ot isoproterenol during the initial minutes following weaning from CPB. Plasma insulin continues to remain elevated during the early postbypass period, reaching its maximal concentration 30 to 60 minutes after separation from bypass (35). Insulin levels then slowly return to baseline over the subsequent first several postoperative hours to days (20, 32, 34, 35).

It has been suggested that the insulin:glucagon ratio is more important in regulation of glucose metabolism than the absolute plasma concentration of either hormone alone (41, 42). Hyperglucagonemia might be expected during CPB because plasma concentrations of the two major humoral stimuli for glucagon secretion, catecholamines and cortisol (43, 44), are markedly elevated during and after bypass (see below). However, the 50% increase in plasma glucagon observed during CPB (39, 45) is relatively modest compared to that seen in patients with other major stresses, such as major surgery without CPB (22, 25) or severe burn injury (46), who have comparably high plasma levels of catecholamines and cortisol. Temperature management during CPB clearly influences plasma glucagon, as patients rendered hypothermic exhibit no hyperglucagonemia during or even shortly after CPB, while those undergoing normothermic bypass exhibit a nearly 100% increase above baseline during CPB that persists for at least 1 hour after CPB (39). Extended studies have revealed that peak glucagon levels are delayed until the first postoperative day (37). It remains unclear whether the blunted glucagon response associated with hypo-thermic CPB results from suppressed production and/or secretion, or from augmented plasma clearance of the hormone. To evaluate whether the blunted glucagon response occurs secondary to decreased production by the pancreatic alpha cell, the role of pancreatic perfusion adequacy should be tested.

Insulin has been administered as a therapeutic drug during cardiac surgery, in combination with glucose and potassium (GIK technique) (47). Hyperinsulinemia produced in this manner has been associated with improved ventricular performance, myocardial protection, and a decreased propensity to cardiac arrhythmias. Pretreatment with high-dose insulin prior to bypass leads to increased glycogen stores, myocardial ATP content, and an improved cellular energy charge during ischemia (48). However, aggressive potassium replacement during cardiac surgery using the GIK technique can lead to postoperative hyperkalemia and cardiac arrest, especially if postoperative renal function is suboptimal (49).

INSULIN RESISTANCE DURING CPB

There is a biphasic response to injury, which Cuthbertson (50) referred to as the "ebb" and "flow" periods, both characterized by hyperglycemia. In the initial ebb period, commonly associated with shock states, the hyperglycemia occurs secondary to elevated counterregulatory hormone levels, inhibited insulin secretion, and mobilization of free fatty acids. This is the metabolic and endocrine milieu characteristic of the first 30 minutes of CPB. The principal cause of the hyperglycemia during the ebb phase is hypoinsulinemia. Hyperglycemia is exacerbated during this time by a large glucose challenge from some pump prime solutions, prebypass intravenous fluid therapy, and often from the cardioplegia solution. During the flow phase, a more extended period associated with recovery, the hyperglycemia occurs despite a relative *hyper*insulinemia, indicating the presence of insulin resistance. The factors playing a role in development of insulin resistance during CPB are diagrammed in Fig. 20.1.

To determine the role of insulin resistance in the etiology of hyperglycemia associated with CPB, several "euglycemic clamp" studies have been conducted. The essence of the euglycemic clamp technique is that plasma glucose is regulated at a constant level by variable infusion while an elevated plasma insulin concentration is maintained by a primed, continuous intravenous insulin infusion (45, 50–53). Glucose uptake responsiveness is quantitated as the amount of glucose infusion necessary to maintain euglycemia at a fixed plasma insulin concentration, thus measuring the degree of insulin resistance. Kuntschen et al. (45) reported a steady-state glucose uptake rate of 4.6 mg/kg/min at a plasma insulin level of 2145 pmol/liter (approximately 86 mU/liter), in nine anesthetized patients during the pre-CPB period. This compares with a rate of 10.2 mg/kg/min in awake healthy volunteers, and 6.3 mg/kg/min in awake volunteers after 7 days of bed rest (53). Thus, even without CPB, the patient undergoing surgical operation under general anesthesia already has some degree of insulin resistance. However, the lessened requirement for exogenous glucose could be due to either diminished absolute glucose utilization by peripheral tissues or continued accelerated endogenous glucose production by the liver. Studies on bed rest or cortisol treatment indicate that both mechanisms may be operative at a plasma insulin concentration of less than 100 mU/liter (53, 54).

Cardiopulmonary bypass caused a further decrease in exogenous glucose uptake at plasma insulin concentration of 86 mU/liter, to approximately 3 mg/kg/min throughout the steady-state CPB period (45). By almost 1 hour after weaning from CPB, glucose uptake had returned to 4.1 mg/kg/min at a stable hyperinsulinemia (45). Similar data were obtained by the same group of investigators in patients undergoing hypothermic bypass at an identical plasma insulin concentration (39). There are several factors that could be responsible for the profound insulin resistance during CPB. The most important would be the elevated plasma cortisol and catecholamines observed during and immediately following CPB. In addition to its effect on inhibiting insulin secretion (which is irrelevant during the euglycemic clamp), epinephrine appears to inhibit glucose uptake by skeletal muscle. Neither plamsa *epinephrine* nor norepinephrine concentrations are altered by hyperinsulinemia during a euglycemic clamp (55). In awake volunteers, a comparable hyperinsulinemia decreases plasma glucagon (by 70%) and cortisol (by 50%) (55), but this has not been tested during CPB. Given the relatively modest hyperglucagonemia during bypass, it is less likely that glucagon plays a major role in the insulin resistance. However, the marked rise in plasma cortisol during bypass makes it a likely factor even if hyperinsulinemia attenuated the hypercortisolemia.

Cortisol excess has been shown to impair the ability of insulin both to stimulate peripheral glucose utilization and to arrest hepatic gluconeogenesis (54, 56). Cortisol shifts the insulin dose-response curve of glucose uptake to the right, but it does not alter the maximal response (52, 54). However, it is unknown whether the maximal glucose uptake response to insulin is altered by either hypothermic or normothermic CPB, which requires a stable plasma insulin concentration of greater than 500 mU/liter. It is possible that maximal glucose uptake is inhibited during CPB, as it appears to be impaired in the early postoperative period (57). Finally, the influence of heparin during CPB has not been evaluated. Intravenous *heparin* has been shown to decrease the glucose uptake response to exogenous glucose challenge, without altering the insulin secretory response (58). Therefore, heparin may contribute to the development of insulin resistance during CPB. Because heparin simultaneously causes a marked elevation of plasma free fatty acids, which have also been implicated in the etiology of impaired glucose metabolism, the heparin effect may be indirect, i.e., mediated through elevated plasma free fatty acid concentration (58–60). The ability of plasma free fatty acids to interfere with glucose metabolism was originally described by Randle et al. (61) as the "glucose-free fatty acid cycle". The relationship appears to be complex, however, and is influenced by the prevailing plasma glucose and insulin concentrations (59–64). More work is needed to clarify the roles of heparin and free fatty acids on glucose metabolism during CPB.

Insulin resistance might be expected to be exacerbated during hypothermia because of inhibitory effects on enzyme systems and whole-body oxygen consumption. However, a series by Kuntschen et al. (39) showed that significant hyperglycemia is delayed by hypothermia until after the rewarming process has begun. This can partly be explained by the ability of hypothermia to attenuate the rise of plasma glucagon concentration, and the consequent ability of glucagon to mobilize hepatic glucose production (56, 65). However, the ability of hepatic glucose output to increase in response to *exogenous* glucagon (glucagon stimulation test) is impaired during hypothermic bypass (39), indicating an intrinsic temperature sensitivity of hepatic gluconeogenesis. The failure of Kuntschen et al. (39) to demonstrate a difference between normothermic and hypothermic bypass in glucose uptake response to a single insulin dose does not imply that they are identical. At the plasma insulin level used in their study, cortisol may be the major cause for decreased glucose uptake. However, it is unknown whether CPB or hypothermia, unlike cortisol, will alter maximal insulin-stimulated glucose uptake.

Other questions remain about the nature of glucose metabolism during CPB. It is unclear, for example, why there is an acute exacerbation of hyperglycemia during the rewarming period from hypothermia immediately before discontinuation of CPB, which is not seen in normothermic CPB (39, 40). Whole-body studies cannot discern the contribution of individual tissues to total glucose uptake. For example, in response to a hyperinsulinemic euglycemic clamp, one-fifth of whole-body glucose uptake is normally accounted for by the liver in anesthetized dogs (65). Whether hepatic contribution to whole-body glucose uptake is altered during either normothermic or hypothermic CPB, or could serve as an index of hepatocellular function, is unknown. Also unknown is the extent to which continued hepatic glucose production decreases exogenous glucose requirements without truly reflecting any alteration in peripheral (i.e., skeletal muscle) glucose metabolism during a euglycemic clamp, although recent evidence suggests that the site of the defect in glucose utilization shortly after cardiac surgery is not in the splanchnic bed (67). Glucagon stimulation tests during bypass are suggestive that the intrinsic ability of hepatic glucose production may be impaired but not eliminated by hypothermia (39); tracer studies are needed to better understand the dynamics of basal and insulin-stimulated glucose metabolism with during either hypothermic or normothermic CPB. Finally, because a significant fraction of patients undergoing cardiac surgery have preexisting diabetes mellitus (68), it would be worthwhile to test whether the defects of glucose metabolism caused by diabetes, such as glucose intolerance and insulin resistance, are exacerbated or mimicked by CPB.

GLYCOLYSIS AND LACTIC ACID

A major end product of glucose metabolism is lactate. Neither plasma lactate nor pyruvate concentrations are altered during the prebypass period. Lactate and pyruvate levels are increased two- to threefold (to 2 to

3 mmol/liter and 100 to 150 μmol/liter, respectively), during and after normothermic CPB (45). Similar increases are observed during hypothermic CPB (37, 69). The choice of a priming solution influences the lactacemia during CPB, with plasma levels being directly related to the lactate concentration of the pump prime (37). Nevertheless, all patients exhibit a progressive increase in plasma lactate during CPB, which is maximal at 2 to 3 times baseline at the end of CPB before gradually returning to baseline by the 3rd postoperative day.

In a study by Del Canale et al. (70), CPB resulted in a greater than twofold increase in quadriceps muscle intracellular lactate content, accompanied by an even greater rise in plasma concentration. Thus, either the ability of muscle to export lactate is augmented or the increased lactate is produced elsewhere. Since lactate is thought to freely traverse the cell membrane, it is more likely that peripheral muscle is not the major source of increased plasma lactic acid during CPB.

A nonskeletal muscle source for elevated plasma lactic acid is also observed in resting human subjects during glucose or insulin infusion (71). Similarly, the rise in plasma lactate following a meal is not accompanied by increased lactate production by the forearm (72, 73). All four of these circumstances (CPB, glucose or insulin administration, and meal ingestion) therefore markedly differ from that associated with exercise, where most of the additional lactic acid load is produced by skeletal muscle (74). Thus, the major assumption that most excess lactic acid is produced by skeletal muscle has recently been called into question for a number of physiologic circumstances. More definitive work on the dynamics of lactate metabolism during CPB is clearly required to determine the tissue site(s) of elevated lactic acid production and/or diminished clearance.

Other candidate tissues for increased lactate production during CPB are splanchnic tissues (liver and intestines) (75–77), erythrocytes (78–79), skin (73), adipose tissue (80, 81) and kidney (82). None of these tissues has been tested for its contribution to whole-body lactate production during CPB.

Evidence from animal studies indicates that the use of pulsatile flow during CPB can moderate the increase in plasma lactate (83), but the mechanism (i.e., whether this is due to augmented lactate clearance or decreased lactate production) is unknown. The most striking alterations in plasma lactate concentration are observed with use of a fluorocarbon priming solution which, despite apparently good arterial and mixed venous oxygenation, leads to a 300% increase in plasma lactate concentration during and after CPB in experimental animals (84). It is unclear whether fluorocarbon-induced hyperlactatemia is due to accelerated production or enhanced washout of glycolytic products, decreased hepatic clearance, or a different combination of factors under hypothermic versus normothermic conditions.

Following cardiac surgery, there is a continued mild elevation of plasma lactate concentration, accompanied by net lactate release across the leg, which serves as an example of peripheral tissue (85). To what extent this lactate release is due to fasting or other effects of surgical trauma in general is unknown, because Svensson et al. (84) did not utilize non-CPB controls for cardiac surgery. However, the ability of insulin to moderate the lactate release by peripheral muscle and to augment lactate utilization by the myocardium appears to be intact (85).

Increased lactate release by skeletal muscle occurs at a time of decreased glucose uptake (84). There are three possible explanations for this phenomenon: (a) Glycolysis is maintained by increasing the contribution from tissue glycogen stores, (b) more glucose taken up by peripheral tissues is directed into glycolysis rather than to glycogen synthesis, or (c) impaired oxidation of glucose-derived pyruvate is coupled with decreased glycolysis as the body shifts to anaerobic-type metabolism. The prevailing metabolic and endocrine environment is compatible with any of these potential mechanisms. Since plasma pyruvate concentration tends to parallel the changes in plasma lactate (37), it is likely that the overall rate of glycolysis is maintained. Furthermore, the respiratory quotient (RQ = V_{CO_2}/V_{O_2}) is persistently elevated in patients during surgery and for several hours into the postoperative period (86, 87), indicating continued oxidative glucose metabolism.

These findings are consistent with other types of trauma, such as burn injury, which results in a 300% *increase* in glucose oxidation (88). This indicates a high level of glucose oxidation and suggests that glucose oxidation is not impaired at least in an absolute sense. Therefore, one can deduce that the net utilization of endogenous glycogen may be augmented because of the indirect evidence that glycolysis and glucose oxidation are preserved following separation from CPB, despite impaired glucose uptake. It is untested whether this net glycogen utilization occurs secondary to inhibition of glycogen synthesis or acceleration of glycogenolysis. It has recently been demonstrated that following severe burn injury, which is characterized by accelerated glycolysis despite diminished glucose uptake from plasma, the net rate of glycogen breakdown is increased sixfold compared to that of postabsorptive volunteers (88). Unfortunately, however, no studies have been reported to date on cardiac surgery patients to quantitate the glycolytic rate relative to glucose uptake during or after CPB, or determine the fractional oxidation rate of glycolysis-derived pyruvate under these conditions. Therefore, the underlying cause for increased lactate release despite poor plasma glucose utilization remains unknown.

Lipid and Protein Metabolism

FREE FATTY ACIDS, GLYCEROL, AND LIPOLYSIS

Serum free fatty acids (FFA) during the pre-CPB period, before administration of heparin, are elevated about 75 to 100% above baseline, comparable to those observed in other major intrathoracic or intraabdominal operations (22, 35). However, following heparinization and institution of CPB, serum FFA become markedly elevated, to levels 3 to 4 times baseline (32, 35, 89, 90). In patients who receive a pump prime *without* glucose, a plateau of elevated serum FFA continues throughout CPB and persists into the early postoperative hours (35). In contrast, serum FFA in patients receiving glucose-containing intravenous fluids, which stimulate insulin secretion, begin to return toward baseline values much earlier, even toward the end of the CPB period (32, 35, 90). In fact, Brandt et al. (32) found that serum FFA were actually decreased *below* baseline in the early post-CPB period, during the time of maximal hyperglycemia and hyperinsulinemia in their patients who had received intravenous glucose, before rising again as the hyperglycemia and hyperinsulinemia cleared. Regardless of whether glucose is contained in the prime, postoperative serum FFA do not decline to presurgical levels until the 7th to 10th postoperative day (35). It is noteworthy that the magnitude of FFA elevation is maximal with normothermic (35 to 36°C) CPB, with significant attenuation associated with hypothermia (<34°C) (39).

Paralleling the rise in serum FFA are an elevation in plasma free glycerol (35, 45), and a decrease in plasma triglycerides (45). Because lipolysis liberates three FFA for each glycerol, a stable relationship between serum FFA and glycerol concentrations is interpreted as a function of accelerated lipolysis, where a decrease in the FFA/glycerol ratio would be evidence for fatty acid cycling and an increase may be due to decreased hepatic uptake of FFA. Nevertheless, other factors can influence serum levels of FFA and glycerol independently, making these indirect indices suggestive, but not conclusive, that accelerated lipolysis is the principal mechanism underlying elevated FFA during CPB. Conclusive proof would require tracer studies of the rates of production of glycerol and FFA. Such studies, which would increase our understanding of the metabolic effects of CPB, remain to be done.

There are several possible mechanisms that could underlie accelerated lipolysis during and after CPB. The first candidate is heparin, which has been shown to increase plasma FFA three- to fourfold, principally via activation of endothelial-bound lipoprotein lipase (57, 90, 91). Therefore, because a large bolus of heparin is administered immediately prior to institution of CPB, a marked elevation of plasma FFA might be expected even without initiating CPB. It is noteworthy that McKnight et al. (37) observed elevated plasma glycerol levels following heparinization, which persisted throughout CPB, before abruptly decreasing to near-preheparinization levels after protamine was administered to reverse the heparin effect. Thus, the metabolic effect paralleled the hemostatic effect of heparin and protamine. Unfortunately, the authors did not report simultaneous serum FFA levels.

A second potential cause for the increased serum FFA during CPB is the increased plasma concentrations of catecholamines (particularly epinephrine), which are also known to directly stimulate lipolysis in humans (93, 94). Under normothermic conditions, the magnitude of the rise in serum FFA is directly related to elevations in plasma catecholamines (89). Catecholamines may also indirectly cause accelerated lipolysis by inhibiting insulin secretion (38, 93). A third potential stimulator of lipolysis is growth hormone, which is at least mildly elevated during CPB.

Factors moderating the FFA response are glucose and insulin (93, 95, 96). Both glucose and insulin directly inhibit the activity of lipoprotein lipase in human skeletal muscle (97). The ability of insulin to suppress lipolysis in humans is approximately 5 times as potent as its ability to stimulate glucose utilization (96, 97). Euglycemic hyperinsulinemia or glucose loading to produce hyperglycemia leads to a significant decrease in both plasma FFA and glycerol levels during and immediately following CPB (45). Not all of the effect of hyperglycemia can be ascribed to the consequent insulin secretory response, because hyperglycemia has been shown to directly inhibit lipolysis even when insulin secretion is inhibited by somatostatin (99).

In addition to having a restraining effect on lipolysis, both insulin and glucose stimulate the reesterification of FFA to storage triglycerides, another mechanism of reducing serum FFA (93, 95, 98). The sluggish rise in plasma FFA concentration during the early phase of hypothermic CPB must not involve glucose or insulin directly as these are also observed at lower plasma levels compared to normothermic CPB.

It is possible that hypothermia directly inhibits lipoprotein lipase, although this has not been reported in vivo. The fate of FFA as a function of CPB, i.e., whether they are reesterified to triglyceride (recycling), or the extent to which they are oxidized to CO_2 during and after CPB, remains unknown. The mechanism of the elevated FFA concentration during and after CPB deserves further attention because of the clinically significant impairment of myocardial contractility and increase in myocardial irritability caused by high circulating FFA levels, which can lead to significant postoperative complications (100–103).

AMINO ACID AND PROTEIN TURNOVER

Alanine and glutamine release serves as a major mechanism for peripheral tissues to dispose of amino waste associated with protein catabolism. These amino acids are taken up by the liver and the nitrogen is transferred to urea for excretion in the urine. Alanine, because of its close relationship to pyruvate, has been the amino acid most extensively studied during CPB. In the study by McKnight et al. (37), plasma alanine was diminished at the induction of anesthesia and remained low throughout surgery and CPB. There was a modest and brief rise above baseline on postoperative day 1, but otherwise no alterations were seen.

Kuntschen et al. (45) saw no changes from preanesthesia levels throughout the various stages of the surgery with CPB. At the end of CPB, or early following separation from CPB, intravenous glucose challenge stimulated alanine release (presumably via accelerated glycolysis) and euglycemic hyperinsulinemia depressed alanine release (presumably via inhibited proteolysis) (45, 103–105).

These tests verify that the normal physiologic relationship between glycolysis and alanine release is intact during and after CPB. Unfortunately, the authors did not simultaneously measure plasma concentrations of other amino acids, or perform tracer turnover studies of alanine to better analyze the dynamics underlying the gross alterations.

Glutamine turnover, which involves a complex interorgan cooperation between peripheral tissues, the gut, and the liver, has not been studied during CPB. Urea metabolism represents the final common pathway for most amino acid catabolism and requires good hepatic function for adequate synthesis. One study of urea metabolism during cardiac surgery demonstrated a stable blood urea nitrogen concentration throughout cardiac surgery with CPB, extending into the first postoperative day (86). However, these data are not particularly useful for estimating amino acid flux because, in the presence of good renal function, turnover of urea can be markedly altered despite an unchanged plasma concentration. This contention appears to hold true during cardiac surgery as well, as Chiara et al. (85) reported accelerated urinary urea nitrogen losses (net protein catabolism) during and early after CPB despite no detectable change in the blood urea nitrogen concentration. Therefore, turnover studies of urea metabolism are indicated.

Hersio et al. (107) reported that infusion of a standard hyperalimentation mixture of amino acids immediately following cardiac surgery with hypothermic CPB did not influence peripheral utilization of plasma glucose, pyruvate, or FFA. Unfortunately, however, these authors did not simultaneously quantitate protein synthesis or catabolism. In human volunteers, protein synthesis is stimulated by infusion of amino acids, either in the presence or absence of hyperinsulinemia (108). Similarly, Kunschen et al. (45) did not measure amino acid or urea fluxes during euglucemic hyperinsulinemia during CPB. Insulin has been shown in normal humans to have a powerful restraining effect on protein catabolism (104–106). Furthermore, the effect of insulin on protein and amino acid metabolism can be preserved even in the setting of "insulin resistance" as indexed by glucose metabolism (109).

The effect of cardiac surgery with CPB on protein metabolism, in general, has received scant attention to date. Rennie and MacLennan (110) performed stable isotopic tracer studies of leucine metabolism in a series of patients undergoing coronary artery bypass grafting. They found that leucine flux (an index of proteolysis) was decreased 36% and whole-body protein synthesis was decreased 43% after induction of anesthesia alone. Therefore, net negative protein balance occurs even before surgical manipulation begins. Unfortunately, the study was terminated before institution of CPB, leaving unanswered the question of the effect of CPB itself on protein dynamics. The importance of protein metabolism cannot be overestimated because it is the principal determinant of coagulation status, immunocompetence, and wound healing in the postoperative course. Therefore much important work remains to be done.

Energy and Acid-Base Metabolism

OXYGEN CONSUMPTION, CARBON DIOXIDE PRODUCTION, AND METABOLIC RATE

Indirect calorimetry is commonly used to measure the indices of energy metabolism, oxygen consumption ($\dot{V}_{O_2}$) and carbon dioxide production ($\dot{V}_{CO_2}$). Technical factors preclude accurate measurement of $\dot{V}_{O_2}$ by indirect calorimetry at inspired F_{IO_2} of greater than 60%, because the Haldane transform used to calculate $\dot{V}_{O_2}$ in all indirect calorimeters renders the measurement exquisitely sensitive to small changes in measurements of oxygen tension, leading to large errors in estimation of V_{O_2} at higher F_{IO_2}.

In addition, indirect calorimetry requires that pulmonary ventilation is the mechanism for gas exchange. For these reasons, indirect calorimetry is not useful to assess energy metabolism during cardiac surgery at 100% F_{IO_2} with extracorporeal blood gas exchange. Studies therefore depend on use of the Fick principle to determine these parameters, which requires accurate measurement of blood flow as well as arteriovenous gas gradients.

During the cardiac surgery but prior to institution of CPB, oxygen consumption, carbon dioxide production, and resting energy expenditure are not different from those exhibited by the anesthetized patient prior to incision (87). Institution of hypothermic CPB, however, results in a rapid decline of greater than 50% in $\dot{V}_{O_2}$, V_{CO_2} and energy expenditure (70, 86, 87). Decreased oxygen consumption occurs comcomitantly with decreased oxygen extraction ($\dot{V}_{O_2}$/A-V O_2 difference), indicating than even in the setting of low pressure-low flow hypothermic CPB, $\dot{V}_{O_2}$ is apparently not perfusion-limited (70).

Although many anesthetic agents are known to depress $\dot{V}_{O_2}$ at normothermia, their effects during hypothermic CPB are considered to be minimal, especially in relation to the profound effects of hypothermia (111). Unique among anesthetic agents, however, propofol has been shown to decrease whole-body $\dot{V}_{O_2}$ during hypothermic CPB (69). Further studies are needed to determine the regional implications of this depression in whole-body $\dot{V}_{O_2}$ caused by propofol.

Damask et al. (87) reported an 80% decline in V_{CO_2}, and a marked decrease in respiratory quotient (RQ) during CPB. Such a low RQ (0.48) is consistent with accelerated fat oxidation coupled with a profound block in glucose oxidation. However, Chiara et al. (86) found a much more modest drop in RQ from 0.96 to 0.91, which indicates continued oxidation of predominantly glucose as well as lipid. One explanation for the observed difference in RQ values could be the different techniques, including the more profound hypothermia in the Damask et al. series compared to that of Chiara et al. (21°C versus 28°C) (86, 87). Another possibility is technical problems in the study of Damask et al., leading to loss of CO_2 during sampling and analysis: it is extremely rare to see RQ values less than 0.60 in humans.

Institution of pulsatile flow does not appear to influence $\dot{V}_{O_2}$ during CPB, although its effect on V_{CO_2}, and therefore RQ, is unknown (112). Rewarming leads to some recovery of whole-body $\dot{V}_{O_2}$ and V_{CO_2}, but only to rates approximately 50% of those during the pre-CPB period (86, 87). Although both energy expenditure and body temperature rise during the rewarming period, Chiara et al. (86) were unable to establish a correlation between body temperature and energy expenditure.

Skeletal muscle ATP stores are maintained during CPB, but there is a 15 to 20% depletion of cellular phosphocreatine in skeletal muscle (113). It is important to recognize that skeletal muscle is resistant to effects of ischemia, however, and that the maintenance of high-energy phosphate stores in other tissues more sensitive to ischemia (i.e., liver, pancreas, and intestine) remains to be determined.

Two pH management strategies are employed during hypothermic CPB, alphastat or pH-stat. In the former, "ventilation" is altered such that the blood pH is raised by 0.0147 pH units for each degree Centigrade decrease in body temperature, the Rosenthal (114) correction factor. The latter dictates that blood pH is maintained constant at 7.40 regardless of temperature. Using nuclear magnetic resonance spectroscopy or a fiberoptic pH probe to monitor intracellular pH and high-energy phosphate status during hypothermic bypass, Swain et al. (115) found that both heart and brain intracellular pH are regulated according to alpha-stat principles, with a progressive rise in pH with decreasing temperature down to 20°C. Furthermore, they found that intracellular pH is regulated much more independently of changes in blood pH than previously thought, with a continued pH gradient maintained across the cell membrane. This is consistent with two recent studies on nonanesthetized animals demonstrating that intravenous administration of sodium bicarbonate fails to alkalinize intracellular pH of cardiac or skeletal muscle despite a marked rise in plasma pH (116, 117). The choice of either alpha-stat or pH-stat management strategy had no effect on the high-energy phosphate stores of either heart or brain (115). This topic is discussed in detail in Chapter 6.

After weaning from CPB, there is a significant 10 to 15% *increase* above prebypass values in both $\dot{V}_{O_2}$ and V_{CO_2}, beginning as early as 30 minutes after separation from CPB and maintained at a plateau over the next 90 minutes (87). Even more dramatic increases in $\dot{V}_{O_2}$ and V_{CO_2}, as well as an increase in energy expenditure, occur after termination of anesthesia and transfer of the patient to the intensive care unit (86, 118). The early postoperative increase in energy metabolism was up to 70% above that predicted by the Harris-Benedict equation (hypermetabolic response) (86). This occurred approximately 3 hours following arrival to the intensive care unit, corresponding to the time of peripheral rewarming and fluid resuscitation.

Repayment of a theoretical "oxygen debt," shivering, and mechanical ventilation have all been considered as underlying causes of the hypermetabolic response. However, there is little evidence that a true limitation of oxygen supply exists during CPB. An elevated RQ persists for several hours into the postoperative period, consistent with a preferential oxidation of glucose over lipid (86). This indicates that glucose oxidation is not impaired, at least in an absolute sense. Hersio et al. (107) were unable to modify the hypermetabolic response after hypothermic CPB with amino acid infusion, despite the theoretical advantage of amino acids in stimulating thermogenesis.

Energy and acid-base metabolism of patients undergoing normothermic CPB has not been reported. It is therefore impossible to distinguish the effects of CPB from those of profound hypothermia, on the parameters of energy and acid-base metabolism. It is possible that hypothermia is a major factor underlying many of the alterations of energy metabolism during hypothermic CPB, but this remains to be tested in a controlled study.

MINERAL METABOLISM

Extrarenal Potassium Metabolism

Potassium (K$^+$) homeostasis is effected by (*a*) regulating the plasma K$^+$ concentration and (*b*) determining the compartmental distribution of K$^+$ in the body. The first mechanism is largely accomplished by the kidney, which responds to alterations of plasma K$^+$ concentration by either reabsorbing or secreting K$^+$ to maintain normokalemia. Renal control of K$^+$ homeostasis is discussed in detail in the Chapter 19. Because 98% of total body K$^+$ resides in the intracellular compartment, however, the more important acute regulator of total body and even circulating K^+ is that which determines compartmentation of the electrolyte. Transmembrane shifts of K^+ resulting in a very large change in plasma K^+ (at least acutely) would be accompanied by an immeasurably small difference in total intracellular K^+ content.

Abe et al. (119) examined plasma K^+ levels during and after CPB in 20 patients. They found that plasma K^+ rose briefly during the initiation of CPB, corresponding to the time of cooling and administration of cardioplegia solution. Thereafter, normokalemia resumed throughout the hypothermic CPB period. Plasma K^+ began to fall during rewarming, although still remaining within normal limits, but hypokalemia developed 60 to 90 minutes following separation from CPB. These investigators ruled out dilution

and acid-base disturbances as potential causes of the hypokalemia. There was an increase in K^+ excretion during and after CPB (6 to 8 mEq/m/hr), but 26 mEq/m² of K^+ was calculated to have moved from the extracellular to the intracellular compartment by 1 hour after CPB (119). This indicates that the more important mechanism for the decrease in plasma K^+ following CPB was through redistribution in the body rather than permanent loss in the urine.

Two independent endocrine systems contribute to movement of K^+ from the extracellular to the intracellular compartment: insulin (120, 121) and β-adrenergic stimulation (122, 123). Cardiopulmonary bypass causes marked elevation of both plasma insulin and catecholamine levels, particularly during the late rewarming period and early after discontinuation of CPB. As illustrated in Fig. 20.2, however, com-

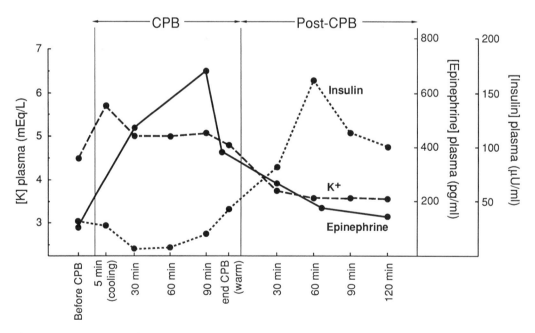

Figure 20.2. Time course for the changes in plasma insulin, epinephrine, and K^+ before, during and after hypothermic CPB. Alterations in plasma norepinephrine tend to parallel those of epinephrine. The peak in plasma epinephrine occurs soon after release of the aortic cross-clamp and thereafter approaches a level close to that seen prior to CPB. In contrast, the peak in plasma insulin, and nadir of hypokalemia, are delayed until approximately 1 hour after separation from CPB. (Data points are adapted from Reves JG, Karp RB, Buttner EE, et al. Neuronal and adrenomedullary catecholamine release in response to cardiopulmonary bypass in man. Circulation 1982;66:49–55. Data points are also adapted from Abe T, Nagata Y, Yoshioka K, Iyomasa Y. Hypopotassemia following open heart surgery by cardio-pulmonary bypass. J Cardiovasc Surg 1977;18:411–419.)

parison of the time courses of plasma insulin and catecholamines with that of plasma K^+ leads one to conclude that the more likely mediator of post-CPB hypokalemia is insulin rather than catecholamine stimulation (61, 119).

Insulin mediates cellular K^+ uptake via direct activation of a membrane-bound Na^+-K^+ ATPase located in close proximity to the insulin receptor. Furthermore, insulin-stimulated K^+ uptake, both in vivo and in vitro, is mutually independent from insulin-stimulated glucose uptake (120, 125). The K^+ uptake responsiveness to insulin, moreover, can be completely intact despite the presence of a profound clinical "insulin resistance" of glucose metabolism in humans (52). Therefore, the marked insulin resistance of glucose metabolism that accompanies CPB may not affect the responsiveness of K^+ metabolism to insulin whatsoever.

It is important to remember that the significant hypokalemic action of hyperinsulinemia during the glucose-insulin-potassium technique occurs via redistribution rather than secretion of potassium: Bohrer et al. (126) reported a case of postoperative cardiac arrest resulting from rebound hyperkalemia, secondary to potassium reentering the plasma compartment as the hyperinsulinemia cleared. Whether insulin stimulates renal potassium excretion is controversial. Rossetti et al. (127), using a euglycemic-normokalemic clamp technique, reported increased K^+ excretion during hyperinsulinemia, but Furuya et al. (128), directly examining rabbit collecting ducts, found that insulin inhibited K^+ secretion in vitro.

Although the time course of catecholamine excess does not parallel the alterations in plasma K^+ concentration associated with CPB (119), catecholamines can also exert important effects during cardiac surgery with CPB. Catecholamines also act via stimulation of Na^+-K^+ ATPase, independently of insulin (122, 129). Several investigators have shown that catecholamine-induced hypokalemia is mediated by the β_2-agonist receptor, and that epinephrine or

dopamine can be used for treatment of acute hyperkalemia (123, 129). Therefore, it is not surprising that effective β-adrenergic blockade decreases the tendency to develop the intraoperative or postoperative hypokalemia of cardiac surgery (131). Pederson et al. (132), using labelled $^{42}K^+$, demonstrated that propranolol increases plasma K^+ by causing a shift of K^+ from the intracellular to the extracellular compartment, without any effect on renal K^+ excretion. The role of the kidney in catecholamine-induced hypokalemia is paradoxical: epinephrine infusion promotes handling of an intravenous KCl challenge, despite causing a 50 to 100% inhibition of renal K^+ secretion; while pretreatment with propranolol interferes with disposal of a KCl challenge despite augmented renal K^+ excretion (122).

The liver appears to be a major storage organ for plasma K^+ uptake, accounting for almost 80% of insulin-stimulated, whole-body K^+ uptake in humans (122, 133). It is possible that the failure of significant hypokalemia to develop during hypothermic CPB may be due in part to an inability of the cooled hepatocytes to respond to adrenergic stimulation (134). However, the direct influence of hypothermia on K^+ homeostasis during CPB remains to be tested.

CALCIUM HOMEOSTASIS

Calcium homeostasis during cardiac surgery has been a subject of recent controversy. Calcium has positive inotropic effects, and maintenance of normocalcemia has been associated with preservation of myocardial contractility (135). Because of a decrease in ionized calcium concentration during the bypass period (136, 137), many practitioners have in the past considered calcium chloride ($CaCl_2$) administration a virtual requirement for separation from CPB, in an attempt to promote better hemodynamic stability. However, inclusion of 250 mg $CaCl_2$ in the 2 liters of pump prime increases ionized calcium levels during CPB to supranormal levels compared to preoperative values (138). Subsequent $CaCl_2$ challenge at the time of weaning from CPB leads to an almost 50% increase in ionized calcium at 30 minutes post-CPB, with continued elevation persisting for 20 hours (138). Because of this effect, calcium is rarely included in the prime at most institutions.

Recently, Robertie et al. (137) studied 28 patients undergoing nonvalvular cardiac surgery using a blood-free prime without supplemental calcium. They found that, although there is a mild depression (to 0.93 mM) during bypass, plasma ionized calcium returns to pre-CPB levels by the time of chest closure without any exogenous $CaCl_2$. Furthermore, these authors found that the recovery mechanism appeared to involve an appropriate pituitary response of parathyroid hormone (PTH) secretion. The etiology of the delayed rise of PTH levels in response to the initial hypocalcemia is unknown. It may involve a combination of factors, including hemodilution or inhibition of pituitary function (e.g., by hypothermia or nonpulsatile flow).

Hypercalcemia has been shown to compromise the inotropic effectiveness of epinephrine in both rats and humans (88, 89). The myocardial response to dobutamine is also impaired by iatrogenic hypercalcemia (141). In addition, $CaCl_2$ administration has recently been identified as a risk factor for development of postoperative pancreatitis (142). It is unclear from the data on patients exhibiting postoperative pancreatic injury (142) whether it was calcium loading or underlying hypotension that was truly responsible for pancreatic injury. However, there are numerous other clinical circumstances where hypercalcemia without hypotension is associated with pancreatic injury (143–147).

Elevated *intracellular* calcium has been implicated in the exacerbation of ischemic cellular injury to cardiac and neuronal tissue (147–149). However, it is unclear whether elevation of extracellular ionized calcium (hypercalcemia) is neces-

sarily accompanied by a parallel rise in its intracellular concentration. Furthermore, the intracellular compartmentation of calcium is very important in determining the toxic potential of intracellular calcium (148, 150). Much work remains to be conducted on the physiologic and pathologic roles of calcium during and after CPB. In the meantime, it seems prudent to correct only moderate-to-severe hypocalcemia which interferes with weaning from CPB, because the mild hypocalcemia more typical during CPB appears to be a self-limited process.

LIVER FUNCTION AND CPB

The liver serves many different functions, participating in (*a*) Cori cycle activity, with glucose production and lactate clearance; (*b*) synthesis of plasma proteins, such as coagulation factors and plasma cholinesterase; (*c*) immune function and clearance of intravascular debris, by intrahepatic Kupffer cells; and (*d*) drug metabolism, principally by the cytochrome P_{450} system. Because of multiple distinct functions of the liver, it is difficult to assess global liver function with a single method during or after CPB. Therefore, markers of hepatocellular damage have been selected on the basis of enzyme leak from injured tissue, although their exact relationship to preserved liver function remains unclear.

Hepatic Substrate Metabolism

Waldhausen et al. (151) studied the relationship between hepatic blood flow and hepatic oxygen consumption in dogs undergoing normothermic CPB. They found that hepatic oxygen consumption is preserved at pump flow rates as low as 2.2 liter/m^2/min. Below this rate of perfusion, which corresponded to a liver flood flow of approximately 110 ml/100 g liver per minute, hepatic oxygen consumption (and blood flow) was markedly curtailed. These authors did not assess consequent hepatocellular damage as a result of liver hypoperfusion during CPB. It is unclear whether these relationships between systemic flow, liver perfusion, and oxygen consumption are maintained under hypothermic conditions.

A major role of the liver is to regulate plasma glucose concentration by varying its rate of glucose production. Kuntschen et al. (39) demonstrated that, during CPB in humans, the ability of exogenous glucagon to induce hyperglycemia is impaired. However, their conclusion that this occurs secondary to compromised hepatic glucose output was based on a failure to achieve an expected glucagon-induced hyperglycemia rather than a direct measure of glucose production by isotope dilution. It is possible that glucose production is already markedly stimulated on the basis of hypercortisolemia and elevation of plasma catecholamines (152).

In the absence of direct assessment, it is unclear that hepatic glucose production is abnormal during CPB. Even if glucose output was diminished, it remains to be tested whether this represents a change in gluconeogenesis or glycogenolysis. Glycogenolysis is likely to be stimulated by catecholamines, even in the absence of exogenous glucagon stimulation (152). The role of potential underlying mechanisms, such as hypothermia and nonpulsatile or reduced hepatic blood flow, can only be speculated on at this point. Furthermore, general anesthesia alone (with pentobarbital) has been shown to cause a 30% decrease of hepatic glucose production in rats (153).

It is unclear whether the rise in lactic acid associated with CPB (154) is caused by increased lactate production (partially splanchnic in origin), decreased lactate clearance (largely hepatic), or some combination of these dynamics. In a study on the effect of CPB in dogs, Anderson et al. (13) demonstrated that hepatic lactate removal is maintained despite a rising plasma concentration, consistent with increased peripheral lactate production during bypass.

However, the conditions of bypass used by Anderson et al. differed from common clinical practice in that they maintained normothermia and a high mean arterial pressure (75 to 110 mm Hg) with high pump flow (50 to 60 ml/kg/min).

Hepatic lactate clearance and lactate production rates remains to be tested under hypothermic, low-flow conditions. Alterations in glucose-lactate cycling (the Cori cycle) as a result of CPB have only received scant attention to date, although this is a potential probe for examining preservation of overall hepatic function under the unusual physiologic circumstances presented by CPB.

Hepatic Protein Synthesis

An iatrogenic heparin-induced coagulopathy is currently a clinical standard prior to CPB. Subsequently, commencement of CPB leads to a largely dilutional decrease of almost all coagulation factors (155). The only factors not subject to an approximately 40% decrease are factors VIII and XI (155). With administration of protamine, the functional coagulopathy is completely reversed. However, the decrease in plasma coagulation factor concentrations persists into the early postoperative period (155). Parenthetically, the decrease in procoagulant factors was paralleled by decreased plasma concentrations of antithrombin and plasminogen (155). In the postoperative setting, there was great variability of plasma fibrinogen in the study of Wolk et al. (155), the result being that a greater than 50% average reduction in plasma fibrinogen concentration did not achieve statistical significance.

The question arises as to whether the decreased plasma fibrinogen concentration reflects increased consumption or decreased hepatic synthesis in the affected patients. It would be interesting to compare plasma fibrinogen concentrations with standard liver function tests, such as serum glutamate-pyruvic transaminase (SGPT) or bilirubin. They could also be performed simultaneously with an assessment of hepatic fibrinogen synthesis (156, 157), to determine the extent to which liver injury and functional impairment contribute to decreased coagulation factor levels following CPB.

Plasma fibronectin is a glycoprotein that facilitates phagocytic clearance of debris and microorganisms from the vascular compartment. Although it can be synthesized by many tissues in vitro, the principal tissue responsible for synthesizing plasma fibronectin in vivo appears to be the liver (158). Several investigators (159–164) have shown that plasma fibronectin concentration is decreased by CPB, but the etiology remains uncertain. The potential mechanisms responsible for this decrease involve "losses" through hemodilution, blood loss, and redistribution into extravascular fluids (164). In addition, fibronectin is consumed as it binds to heparin, fibrin, and cellular debris to facilitate phagocytosis (164).

Another mechanism contributing to plasma fibronectin deficiency is intravascular proteolysis by abnormally high levels of serum proteases (165). However, the influence of hypothermic CPB on fibronectin synthesis is unknown. Fibronectin has a fractional synthetic rate of approximately 30% per day indicating a very high turnover rate in normal humans (156, 157). Furthermore, fibronectin synthesis is exquisitely sensitive to altered physiologic states such as trauma (156), exercise (157), and starvation (166). The mechanism by which normal plasma fibronectin levels are restored in the hours after separation from bypass is equally complex. Extravascular stores of fibronectin can be remobilized into the vascular space (164), and urinary diuresis reverses the effects of hemodilution. Studies examining the role of hepatic fibronectin synthesis following CPB remain to be performed.

Plama cholinesterase levels are also decreased during CPB, which is at least partially due to hemodilution (167). Although the role of hepatic synthesis was not tested directly, the recovery of normal plasma cholinesterase levels by postoperative days 1 and 2 is more consistent with fluid diuresis from the vascular compartment than hepatic biosynthesis of the enzyme, because (unlike fibronectin) synthesis of plasma cholinesterase is relatively slow (167, 168).

The conclusion to be drawn from the currently available data is that although there may be some mild and temporary impairment of plasma protein synthesis associated with hypothermic CPB, it does not appear to have clinical significance in the short term. Furthermore, it also appears to be completely reversed, at least by indirect assessment, by the first postoperative day. Further work is necessary to determine if recovery of apparently normal levels of plasma proteins occurs secondary to accelerated hepatic synthesis or another mechanism.

Hepatic Drug Metabolism

Many drugs administered to patients undergoing cardiac surgery are metabolized by the liver. Clearance of these or other drugs could serve as another index of hepatic function during and after CPB (169). Barstow and Small (169) have recently reviewed a number of clinical liver function tests that assess different aspects of hepatic drug metabolism. These include metabolite formation of allopurinol, caffeine, lidocaine, methacetin, and aminopyrine. Many of these tests could potentially be applied to the cardiac surgery patient, but have not as yet.

On the other hand, hepatic metabolism of fentanyl and midazolam appears to be decreased by hypothermic cardiopulmonary bypass (169–173). Koren et al. (173) reported that metabolism of fentanyl in children is virtually arrested during bypass at 20°C, over a period of up to 2 hours. There have been several attempts to dissect the effect of hypothermia from that of CPB. Koska et al. (170) correlated the increased plasma half-life ($t_{1/2}$) of fentanyl with a comparable 30% decrease in hepatic blood flow during normothermic CPB. Alternatively, Koren et al. (173) demonstrated that hypothermia decreased fentanyl clearance by over 70% in piglets, without superimposed CPB, concomitant with a 42% decrease in hepatic blood flow.

Unlike fentanyl, metabolism of theophylline, a low-extraction drug, is relatively unaffected by hypothermia (175). It is possible that (a) high hepatic-extraction drugs such as fentanyl (or sorbitol) are more sensitive to temperature-induced changes in hepatic blood flow, or (b) different hepatic enzyme systems have different temperature sensitivities. Midazolam clearance is also decreased following CPB, in both adults and children (172, 173). The role of hypothermia has not been separately addressed in the metabolism of midazolam, nor are there data on the duration of impaired hepatic drug metabolism in the postoperative period after CPB.

Hepatic metabolism of nitroglycerin and lorazepam is not decreased by CPB. Dasta et al. (176) found a 20% increase in apparent clearance of nitroglycerin associated with CPB, although they could not exclude the possibility of nonhepatic factors such as adhesion of nitroglycerin to elements of the bypass circuit and metabolism by erythrocytes and endothelial cells. In contrast to midazolam, no CPB-induced increase in the elimination $t_{1/2}$ of lorazepam has been observed (176). It is possible that the impairment of midazolam but not lorazepam during CPB is related to their different mechanisms of hepatic metabolism: lorazepam is primarily conjugated intact with glucuronide (a process relatively resistant to liver disease), while midazolam must first be oxidized by hepatic mixed function oxidase prior to conjugation. Thus, identification of the particular enzyme system is important when attempting to evaluate hepatic function. Fentanyl appears to be a good candidate for assessing liver metabolism because its metabolism appears quite sensitive to changes associated with CPB and hypothermia, but others must be tested to probe different enzyme systems as well (169).

Markers of Hepatocellular Injury

There is no autoregulation of hepatic blood flow during CPB (9), although the hepatic oxygen consumption is maintained at systemic flows as low as 2.2 liters/m^2/min (151). There is no currently accepted monitor for on-line assessment of adequate hepatic perfusion other than by careful regulation of systemic flow during CPB. The traditional method for determination of adequate liver function, the "liver function tests," include plasma levels of bilirubin and enzymes found in high concentration in the liver. However, the time course for appearance of hyperbilirubinemia in relation to a hepatic ischemic insult is unknown. This makes intraoperative assessment of hepatic function difficult. Welbourn et al. (178) followed plasma enzyme patterns in 22 patients during and after CPB with "mild" hypothermia (nadir range, 19 to 34°C). These authors reported that, especially when corrected for hemodilution, plasma levels of lactic dehydrogenase, hydroxybutyrate dehydrogenase, isocitrate dehydrogenase, and glutamic oxaloacetic transaminase all rise during CPB and remain elevated postoperatively (178). However, the source of the enzyme leak could not be ascribed to the liver, and appeared to be largely due to myocardial damage. Serum glutamic pyruvic transaminase (SGPT) and ornithine carbamoyltransferase, considered more specific markers of liver damage, are not elevated during or after CPB (178, 179).

Intraoperative serum bilirubin levels have not been reported. Use of a dye uptake technique, such as BSP or indocyanine green, which are specifically taken up by the liver, has been used to assess the effects of CPB (13). However, it is difficult to distinguish between the effects of hepatic hypoperfusion and hepatocellular dysfunction despite "adequate" perfusion using a dye uptake technique alone. Under normal circumstances, BSP uptake is considered a better marker of hepatic perfusion, but this has not been verified under conditions of hypothermic CPB. Alternatively, estimation of hepatic blood flow from bolus indocyanine green clearance correlates poorly with that directly measured by flowmeter in either healthy volunteers or subjects with liver disease (15). Therefore, dye uptake methods for assessing either liver perfusion or function must be carefully validated before they are applied to patients undergoing CPB. From a purely clinical perspective, there is no evidence that CPB is detrimental to the liver in the majority of patients, but that does not necessarily exclude the need for hepatic monitoring during cardiac surgery.

Postoperative liver dysfunction is often clinically heralded by the appearance of jaundice ("postpump jaundice"), which has an incidence of 10 to 20% (179–181) Postpump jaundice usually occurs secondary to conjugated (direct) hyperbilirubinemia (182), suggesting that the defect is in biliary excretion of bilirubin rather than a more proximal hepatocellular process. The underlying hyperbilirubinemia is maximal at postoperative day 2 and resolves in most patients within the first week. In a prospective study of 248 patients, Collins et al. (182) found that the incidence of postpump jaundice was not associated with preoperative ethanol intake or occurrence of intraoperative hypoxia, hypotension, or hypothermia. It occurred far more frequently in patients undergoing multiple valve procedures (with higher right atrial pressures), and was associated with higher transfusion requirements and longer pump times.

Hyperbilirubinemia can be caused by hepatocellular failure in clearing a normal bilirubin challenge or by excessive bilirubin load overwhelming the normal he-patic functions. Therefore, the role of excessive bilirubin challenge secondary to massive transfusion must be considered as a possible contributor in some patients who develop postpump jaundice, who otherwise do not exhibit evidence of hepatic injury or failure.

Long duration of CPB, in addition to being a risk factor for postpump jaundice, is also associated with other specific markers of hepatocellular damage, such as high plasma levels of isocitrate dehydrogenase (178). However, postpump jaundice can also occur in patients who underwent uncomplicated operations, raising the question of how better intraoperative monitoring of hepatic function could reduce the incidence of this phenomenon. Appearance of jaundice following cardiac surgery is accompanied by a 25-fold increment in incidence of mortality (182), while progression to fulminant hepatic failure is uniformly fatal (183).

Frank hepatic trauma during cardiac surgery has been reported. The mechanism can involve inadvertent placement of thoracostomy tubes (184) or direct manipulation to augment venous return to the heart during placement of right atrial lines (185). Hepatic trauma can rapidly lead to unexplained hypovolemia, and thus requires immediate abdominal exploration.

PANCREATIC FUNCTION AND CPB

Exocrine and Endocrine Pancreas

The pancreas has two broad functions, defined as "exocrine" and "endocrine" in nature. Exocrine pancreatic function involves the synthesis and secretion of digestive enzymes and other alimentary factors. A key enzyme in this system is amylase, which is released as a proenzyme and activated in the pancreatic duct. Amylase is normally detected in low concentration in the circulation, but since pancreatic *injury* leads to intravascular leak of the enzyme, serum amylase is an index of pancreatitis. For maximal utility, pancreatic amylase must be distinguished from its isoenzyme, salivary amylase. It has been proposed that the relationship between amylase and creatinine clearance (amylase:creatinine clearance ratio, ACCR) is a more specific indicator of pancreatic injury (186). However, this method has been criticized, as CPB-associated alterations in ACCR may be produced by alterations in renal function rather than pancreatic injury (187). There are no good assessments of pancreatic exocrine *function* per se in the acute intra- and postoperative settings.

Endocrine pancreatic function involves secretion of insulin (from the beta cell) and glucagon (from the alpha cell). As discussed in the section, "Metabolic Response to CPB," both insulin and glucagon secretion are suppressed during hypothermic CPB (20, 34, 36, 39, 45). Factors that may play a role in the inhibition of hormones (insulin and glucagon) are hypothermia (35, 39) and altered perfusion. In addition, high circulating catecholamines may specifically inhibit insulin release (38), which is not a sign of poor pancreatic function but rather an intact physiologic control mechanism. This contrasts with glucagon release, which is normally stimulated by catecholamines (43). Recovery of "appropriate" insulin secretion occurs within 1 hour after separation from CPB (35), and impairment of insulin secretion does not recur postoperatively (20, 32, 34, 35). In contrast, peak glucagon levels are delayed until the first postoperative day (37). It is unclear whether the slower response of circulating glucagon vis-à-vis insulin represents a difference of functional recovery of the alpha cell as compared to the beta cell from the effects of CPB, hypothermia or general anesthesia.

Markers of Pancreatic Cellular Injury

The pancreas resembles the liver in that it (*a*) has a high metabolic rate (188), (*b*) has no intrinsic autoregulation of blood flow during bypass (9, 189), and (*c*) intraoperative monitoring of its perfusion and function are difficult. There appears to be a variable spectrum of pancreatic injury associated with CPB. Nonpulsatile, hypothermic CPB is followed by asymptomatic hyperamylasemia in 30 to 70% of patients (142, 190–192). Similarly, an elevation in ACCR is observed in 31 to 90% of patients undergoing normothermic CPB (193). Alterations in ACCR, however, may reflect alteration in renal function rather than pancreatic injury (187). Serum levels of the pancreatic isoamylase were elevated in 27%, and pancreatic ribonuclease in 13%, of 30 postoperative patients without clinical pancreatitis studied by Haas et al. (194). In the largest series studied to date, Fernandez-del Castillo et al. (142) prospectively followed 300 consecutive patients undergoing CPB and found a 27% incidence of pancreatic cellular injury, defined as hyperamylasemia accompanied by a rise in pancreatic isoamylase (30%), lipase (10%), or both (60%). Ninety-nine percent of these patients were completely asymptomatic.

The incidence of clinical pancreatitis ("postpump pancreatitis") is 0.1 to 1% by either prospective or retrospective analysis (142, 194, 195). Nonsurviving cardiac surgery patients more commonly exhibit pathologic evidence of pancreatitis. In a study of 209 patients who died within 10 days of cardiac surgery, Feiner (195) reported that the incidence of pancreatitis was 16%, while Warshaw and O'Hara (197) found an 11% incidence in 101 autopsies (197). The pathology in both series was consistent with intraoperative pancreatic ischemia.

Risk factors for development of postpump pancreatitis include prolonged duration of CPB, perioperative hypotension, low postoperative cardiac output, and perioperative administration of calcium (142, 194). It is unclear whether the association with calcium administration is an independent risk factor or whether it is merely associated with the treatment of hypotension. However, pancreatitis has been reported secondary to hypercalcemia in a variety of medical conditions not accompanied by hypotension, such as multiple myeloma (143), hyperparathyroidism (144), breast cancer (145), iatrogenic calcium overload (146), and vitamin D intoxication (147). Reber (146) has suggested that calcium-mediated pancreatic enzyme leak into the plasma may be caused by increased permeability of the pancreatic duct secondary to hypercalcemia (198). Thus, injudicious use of calcium which results in hypercalcemia, rather than approproate correction of (measured) hypocalcemia appears to be a risk factor for pancreatitis. Hypothermia has been considered as a potential cause of pancreatitis, but the studies suggesting this link (199, 200) have involved accidental hypothermia, rather than the more controlled conditions present during hypothermic CPB.

Implications of postpump pancreatitis are serious. Among patients exhibiting severe pancreatitis, the mortality is 67 to 100%, and even mild forms of postoperative pancreatitis have a 26 to 70% mortality rate (142, 195). Today there exists a real difficulty in the intraoperative (and even postoperative) (194) diagnosis of pancreatic injury occurring with cardiac surgery.

GASTROINTESTINAL COMPLICATIONS

There are neither good indicators of gastrointestinal (GI) function nor specific enzymes that indicate gastrointestinal injury in the perioperative period. This has precluded intraoperative diagnosis of gastrointestinal ischemia and dysfunction. Even postoperatively, the signs of GI injury are very subtle, which contributes to delayed diagnosis and treatment. Thus, assessment of the effects of CPB on the GI system has been limited to case reports of severe injury—often resulting in patient death or resection of infarcted tissue. Several retrospective analyses of over 13,000 bypass cases have revealed an overall incidence of GI complications following cardiac surgery of 1 to 2% (183, 201–203). Thus, GI complications occur at roughly the same rate as pancreatitis.

The most frequent complication is GI bleeding, usually duodenal or gastric in origin, which accounts for 25 to 60% of overall GI complications (183, 201–204). Mortality associated with GI hemorrhage is 33 to 53% (183, 202, 203). Less common are duodenal ulcers, diverticulitis, colonic pseudo-obstruction, intestinal ischemia or infarction, and splenic infarction (183, 205, 206). Mortality associated with these complications is comparable to that observed with GI hemorrhage. In contrast, acalculus cholecystitis, which occurs in 5 patients per 1000, has a mortality of 86% (183).

Risk factors for development of GI complications include prolonged duration of CPB, low perioperative cardiac output, and valve surgery (with possible portal congestion) (183, 203, 207). These risk factors have also been identified for postpump jaundice and postpump pancreatitis (see sections on "Liver Function" and "Pancreatic Function"). Not surprisingly, then, there is a high coincidence of pancreatitis in patients with postpump GI complications (183, 201).

The intestine serves as a barrier to keep intraluminal bacteria and endotoxin from migrating into the vasculature. Rocke et al. (208) reported that plasma endotoxin levels were increased transiently after release of the aortic cross-clamp. Their nine patients had an uneventful intraoperative and perioperative course, therefore preventing an analysis of the role of endotoxin in subsequent development of postoperative sepsis. However, it is noteworthy that the degree and time course of endotoxemia in these patients closely resembles the effect of 1-hour superior mesenteric artery occlusion in cats (209). Furthermore, the magnitude of endotoxemia was directly related to duration of CPB (208). Obviously more work needs to be done on the effect of CPB on intestinal endotoxin barrier function.

Intestinal permeability to proteins is also affected by CPB: extravasation of plasma proteins into the interstitial space is increased as much as fourfold during nonpulsatile, normothermic CPB at 2.2 liters/m^2/min in dogs (210). This increased permeability was most pronounced for large molecules. Thus, CPB produces an abnormal bidirectional increase in material flux across the intestinal wall. The significance of increased endotoxin leak into the circulation is that this may occur in patients with the longest CPB times, which already poses an increased risk of GI and hepatic injury. These factors may all contribute to development of postoperative sepsis and multiple system organ failure.

One problem that has not been addressed is the *mechanism* by which prolonged CPB is associated with hepatic, pancreatic and GI injury. A second problem, which may be related, is determining what constitutes adequate visceral perfusion, and how this might be monitored intraoperatively during CPB. One approach that has been reported is to monitor the intraluminal pH of either stomach or colon by tonometry (16–18). Acidosis of either stomach or colon has been shown to be reasonably predictive of tissue ischemia (16–18). However, tonometry is relatively difficult to master from both the technical and interpretive viewpoints at this time. Perhaps continued development would allow it to be simplified into a more practicable clinical tool, as has been the case with pulse oximetry.

SUMMARY

Cardiopulmonary bypass produces marked alterations in the splanchnic circulation, and produces a complex physiologic response of the endocrine and metabolic enviroment. Today, most of these alterations are invisible to the anesthesiologists and surgeons caring for the patient because of significant limitations in patient monitoring in terms of regional blood flow and substrate utilization. Because most patients appear to do well postoperatively, there has not been a rush to improve the system of monitoring. However, the changes in perfusion and in metabolic function are profoundly important and must be understood to advance the level of care in the future. In terms of splanchnic perfusion and cellular viability, improved monitoring would be expected to reduce the incidence of visceral complications from the present 1 to 2% of patients. While the relative number of patients affected appears at first to be small, the absolute number is substantial, and the consequences of visceral complications can be very serious.

Understanding the metabolic environment, on the other hand, will prove to be important because proper manipulation of the complex alterations could reduce the incidence of stroke (by better glycemic control), hypertension, postoperative arrhythmias, and impaired myocardial performance (by directing myocardial substrate utilization). Specific optimization of protein metabolism will promote wound healing, immune function, and recovery of normal coagulation status. However, as outlined in the chapter, most of the important work remains to be done.

REFERENCES

1. Wiggers CJ. The present status of the shock problem. Physiol Rev 1942;22:74–117.
2. Halley MM, Reemtsmak, Creech O Jr. Hemodynamics and metabolism of individual organs during extracorporeal circulation. Surgery 1959;46:1128–1134.
3. Yokoyama T, Okamoto R, Yamamoto Y, et al. Hepatic energy status in hypotension of different aetiologies In dogs. Clin Sci 1991;81:627–633.
4. Desai JB, Mathie RT, Taylor KM. Hepatic blood flow during cardiopulmonary bypass in the dog: a comparison between pulsatile and nonpulsatile perfusion. Life Support Systems 1984;2(supp 1):303–305.
5. Lees MH, Herr RH, Hill JD, Morgan CL, Oschner

AJ III, Van Fleet DL: Distribution of systemic blood flow of the rhesus monkey during cardiopulmonary bypass. J Thorac Cardiovasc Surg 1971;61:570–586.

6. Rudy LW Jr, Heymann MA, Edmunds LH Jr. Distribution of systemic blood flow during cardiopulmonary bypass. J Appl Physiol 1973; 34:194–200.

7. Fujita Y, Sakai T, Ohsumi A, Takaori M. Effects of hypocapnia and hypercapnia on splanchnic circulation and hepatic function in the beagle. Anesth Analg 1989;69:152–157.

8. Gelman S. Carbon dioxide and hepatic circulation. Anesth Analg 1989;69:149–151.

9. Mori A, Watanabe K, Onoe M, et al. Regional blood flow in the liver, pancreas and kidney during pulsatile and nonpulsatile perfusion under profound hypothermia. Jpn Circ J 1988;52:219–227.

10. Van Kesteren RG, van Alphen MMA, Charbon GA. Effects of dopamine on intestinal vessels in anesthetized dogs. Circ Shock 1988;25:41–51.

11. Lundberg J, Lundberg D, Norgren L, Ribbe E, Thorne J, Werner O. Intestinal hemodynamics during laparotomy: effects of thoracic epidural anesthesia and dopamine in humans. Anesth Analg 1990;71:9–15.

12. Noldge GFE, Priebe H-J, Armbruster K, Muller W, Haberstroh J, Geiger K. Discrepancy between total and splanchnic O_2 deliveries during dobutamine, dopamine and norepinephrine. Anesthesiology 1991;75:A556.

13. Anderson MN, Norberg B, Senning A. Studies of liver function during extracorporeal circulation with low flow rate. Surgery 1958; 43:397–407.

14. Kainuma M, Fujiwara Y, Kimura N, Shitaokoshi A, Nakashima K, Shimada Y. Monitoring hepatic venous hemoglobin oxygen saturation in patients undergoing liver surgery. Anesthesiology 1991;74:49–52.

15. Skak C, Keiding S. Methodological problems in the use of indocyanine green to estimate hepatic blood flow and ICG clearance in man. Liver 1987;7:155–162.

16. Fiddian-Green RG, Amelin PM, Herrmann JB, et al. Prediction of the development of sigmoid ischemia on the day of aortic operations. Indirect measurements of intramural pH in the colon. Arch Surg 1986;121:654–660.

17. Fiddian-Green RG, Baker S. Predictive value of the stomach wall pH after cardiac operations: comparison with other monitoring. Crit Care Med 1987;15:153–156.

18. Gutierrez G, Bismar H, Dantzker DR, Silva N. Comparison of gastric intramucosal pH with measures of oxygen transport and consumption in critically ill patients. Crit Care Med 1992; 20:451–457.

19. Weissman C. The metabolic response to stress: an overview and update. Anesthesiology 1990; 73:308–327.

20. Allison SP, Prowse K, Chamberlain MJ. Failure of insulin response to glucose load during operation and after myocardial infarction. Lancet 1967;1:478–481.

21. Butler MJ, Britton BJ, Wood WG, Mainwaring-Burton R, Irving MH. Plasma catecholamine concentrations during operation. Br J Surg 1977;64:786–790.

22. Göschke H, Bär E, Girard J, et al. Glucagon, insulin, cortisol, and growth hormone levels following major surgery: their relationship to glucose and free fatty acid elevations. Horm Metab Res 1978;10:465–470.

23. Holter JB, Pflug AE, Porte D. Mechanism of plasma catecholamine increases during surgical stress in man. J Clin Endocrin Metab 1977;45:936–940.

24. Holter JB, Pflug AE. Effects of anesthesia and surgical stress on insulin secretion in man. Metabolism 1980;29:1124–1127.

25. Russell RCG, Walker CJ, Bloom SR. Hyperglucagonaemia in the surgical patient. Br Med J 1975;1:10–12.

26. Chernow B, Alexander HR, Smallridge RC, et al. Hormonal responses to graded surgical stress. Arch Intern Med 1987;147:1273–1277.

27. Cochrane JPS, Forsling ML, Gow NM, Lequesne LP. Arginine vasopressin release following surgical operations. Br J Surg 1981;68:204–213.

28. Knight A, Forsling M, Treasure T, Aveling W, Loh L, Sturridge MF. Changes in plasma vasopressin concentration in association with coronary artery surgery or thymectomy. Br J Anaesth 1986;58:1273–1277.

29. Yakaitis RW, Blitt CD, Angiulo JP. End-tidal halothane concentration for endotracheal intubation. Anesthesiology 1977;47:386–388.

30. Roizen MF, Horrigan RW, Frazer BM. Anesthetic doses blocking adrenergic (stress) and cardiovascular responses to incision-MAC BAR. Anesthesiology 1981;54:390–398.

31. Anand KJS, Hickey PR. Halothane-morphine compared with high-dose sufentanyl for anesthesia and postoperative analgesia in neonatal cardiac surgery. New Engl J Med 1992; 326:1–9.

32. Brandt MR, Korshin J, Hansen AP, et al. Influence of morphine anaesthesia on the endocrine-metabolic response to open-heart surgery. Acta Anaesth Scand 1978;22:400–412.

33. Price HL. General anesthetics. In: Goodman LS, Gilman A, eds. The pharmacological basis of therapeutics. 5th ed. New York: Macmillan, 1975:95–96.

34. Malatinsky J, Vigas M, Jezova D, Jurcovicova J, Samel M, Vrsansky D. The effects of open heart

surgery on growth hormone, cortisol and insulin levels in man. Hormone levels during
open heart surgery. Resuscitation 1984;11:
57–68.

35. Abe T. Influence of cardiac surgery using cardio-pulmonary bypass on metabolic regulation.
Jpn Circ J 1973;38:13–21.

36. Benzing G III, Francis PD, Kaplan S,
Helmsworth JA, Sperling MA. Glucose and insulin changes in infants and children undergoing hypothermic open-heart surgery. Am J
Cardiol 1983;52:133–136.

37. McKnight CK, Elliott MJ, Pearson DT, Holden
MP, Alberti KGMM. The effect of four different
crystalloid bypass pump-priming fluids upon
the metabolic response to cardiac operation. J
Thorac Cardiovasc Surg 1985;90:97–111.

38. Porte D Jr, Graber AL, Kuzuya T, Williams RH.
The effect of epinephrine on immunoreactive
insulin levels in man. J Clin Invest 1966;
45:228–236.

39. Kuntschen F, Galletti PM, Hahn C. Glucose-insulin interactions during cardiopulmonary bypass. Hypothermia versus normothermia. J
Thorac Cardiovasc Surg 1986;91:451–459.

40. McKnight CK, Elliott M, Pearson DT, Alberti
KGMM, Holden MP. Continuous monitoring of
blood glucose concentration during open-heart
surgery. Br J Anaesth 1985;57:595–601.

41. Parilla R, Goodman MN, Chernick SS. Effect of
glucagon:insulin ratios on hepatic metabolism.
Diabetes 1974;23:725–731.

42. Unger RH. Alpha- and beta-cell interrelation-
ships in health and disease. Metabolism 1974;
23:581–593.

43. Gerich JE, Karam JH, Forsham PH. Stimulation
of glucagon secretion by epinephrine in man. J
Clin Endocrinol Metab 1973;37:479–481.

44. Marco J, Galle C, Roman D, Diaz-Fierros M,
Vallanueva ML, Valverde J. Hyperglucagonism
induced by glucocorticoid treatment in man.
New Engl J Med 1973;288:128–131.

45. Kuntschen FR, Galletti PM, Hahn C, Arnulf JJ,
Isetta C, Dor V. Alterations of insulin and glucose metabolism during cardiopulmonary bypass under normothermia. J Thorac Cardiovasc
Surg 1985;89:97–106.

46. Wilmore DW, Moylan JA, Pruitt BA Jr, Lindsay
CA, Faloona GR, Unger RH. Hyperglucagonaemia after burns. Lancet 1974;1:73–75.

47. Haider W, Eckersberger F, Wolner E. Preventive
insulin administration for myocardial protection in cardiac surgery. Anesthesiology 1984;
60:422–429.

48. Haider W, Benzer H, Schutz W, Wolner E. Improvement of cardiac preservation by preoperative high insulin supply. J Thorac Cardiovasc
Surg 1984;88:294–300.

49. Bohrer H, Fleischer F, Krier C. Hyperkalemic

cardiac arrest after cardiac surgery following
high-dose glucose-insulin-potassium infusion
for inotropic support. Anesthesiology 1988;
69:949–953.

50. Cuthbertson DP. Post-shock metabolic response. Lancet 1942;1:433–437.

51. DeFronzo RA, Tobin JD, Andres RA. Glucose
clamp technique: a method for quantifying insulin secretion and resistance. Am J Physiol
1979;237:E214–E223.

52. Shangraw RE, Jahoor F, Miyoshi H, et al. Differentiation between septic and postburn insulin
resistance. Metabolism 1989;38:983–989.

53. Stuart CA, Shangraw RE, Prince MJ, Peters EJ,
Wolfe RR. Bedrest-induced insulin resistance
occurs primarily in muscle. Metabolism 1988;
37:802–806.

54. Rizza RA, Mandarino LJ, Gerich JE. Cortisol-in-
duced insulin resistance in man: impaired suppression of glucose production and stimulation
of glucose utilization due to a postreceptor defect of insulin action. J Clin Endocrinol Metab
1982;54:131–138.

55. Schmitz O, Alberti KGMM, Christensen NJ,
Hjollund E, Beck-Nielsen H, Orskov H. Aspects
of glucose homeostasis in uremia as assessed by
the hyperinsulinemic euglycemic clamp technique. Metabolism 1985;34:465–473.

56. Lecavalier L, Bolli G, Gerich J. Glucagon-cor-
tisol interactions on glucose turnover and lactate gluconeogenesis in normal humans. Am J
Physiol 1990;258:E569–E575.

57. Nilsson F, Bake B, Berglin W-OE, et al. Glucose
and insulin infusion directly after cardiac surgery: effects on systemic glucose uptake, catecholamine excretion, O_2 consumption and CO_2
production. JPEN (Journal of Parental and Enteral Nutrition) 1985;9:159–164.

58. Pelkonen R, Miettinen TA, Taskinen M-R,
Nikkila EA. Effect of acute elevation of plasma
glycerol, triglyceride and FFA levels on glucose
utilization and plasma insulin. Diabetes
1968;17:76–82.

59. Ferrannini E, Barrett EJ, Bevilacqua S, DeFronzo
RA. Effect of fatty acids on glucose production
and utilization in man. J Clin Invest 1983;
72:1737–1747.

60. Lee KU, Lee HK, Koh CS, Min HK. Artificial induction of intravascular lipolysis by lipid-hep-
arin infusion leads to insulin resistance in man.
Diabetologia 1988;31:285–290.

61. Randle PJ, Newsholme EA, Garland PB. Regulation of glucose uptake by muscle. 8. Effects of
fatty acids, ketone bodies and pyruvate, and of
alloxan-diabetes and starvation, on the uptake
and metabolic fate of glucose in rat heart and
diaphragm muscles. Biochem J 1964;93:
652–665.

62. Jenkins AB, Storlien LH, Chisholm DJ, Kraegen

EW. Effects of nonesterified fatty acid availability on tissue-specific glucose utilization in rats in vivo. J Clin Invest 1988;82:293–299.

63. Walker M, Fulcher GR, Sum CF, Orskov H, Alberti KGMM. Effects of glycemia and nonesterified fatty acids on forearm glucose uptake in normal humans. Am J Physiol 1991;261:E304–E311.

64. Yki-Jarvinen H, Puhakainen I, Koivisto VA. Effect of free fatty acids on glucose uptake and nonoxidative glycolysis across human forearm tissues in the basal state and during insulin stimulation. J Clin Endocrinol Metab 1991; 72:1268–1277.

65. Del Prato S, Castellino P, Simonson DC, DeFronzo RA. Hyperglucagonemia and insulin-mediated glucose metabolism. J Clin Invest 1987;79:547–556.

66. Baba H, Xiao-jun Z, Kunkel K, Jahoor F, Wolfe RR. Hepatic role in glucose metabolism by means of hepatectomized dog model [Abstract]. FASEB J 1990;4:A281.

67. Nilsson F, Ekroth R, Milocco I, et al. Splanchnic glucose balance and insulin resistance in the early postoperative phase of cardiac surgery. JPEN (Journal of Parenteral and Enteral Nutrition) 1988;12:574–578.

68. Alberti KGMM, Gil GV, Elliott MJ. Insulin delivery during surgery in the diabetic patient. Diabetes Care 1982;5(suppl 1):65–77.

69. Laycock GJA, Alston RP. Propofol and hypothermic cardiopulmonary bypass. Anaesthesia 1992;47:382–387.

70. Del Canale S, Fiaccadori E, Vezzani A, et al. Cell metabolism response to cardiopulmonary bypass in patients undergoing aorto-coronary grafting. Scand J Thorac Cardiovasc Surg 1988; 22:159–164.

71. Yki-Jarvinen H, Bogardus C, Foley JE. Regulation of plasma lactate concentration in resting human subjects. Metabolism 1990;39: 859–864.

72. Jackson RA, Blix PM, Matthews JA, Morgan LM, Rubenstein AH, Nabarro JDN. Comparison of peripheral glucose uptake after oral glucose loading and a mixed meal. Metabolism 1983; 32:706–710.

73. Jackson RA, Hamling JB, Sim BM, Hawa MI, Blix PM, Nabarro JDN. Peripheral lactate and oxygen metabolism in man: the influence of oral glucose loading. Metabolism 1987;36:144–150.

74. Katz A. Regulation of lactic acid production during muscle contraction. Stockholm, Sweeden: Huddinge University Hospital, 1986. Thesis.

75. Clark B, Sherratt HSA. Glycolysis and oxidation in preparations from small-intestinal mucosa of four species. Comp Biochem Physiol 1967; 20:223–243.

76. Felig P, Wahren J, Hendler R. Influence of oral glucose ingestion on splanchnic glucose and gluconeogenic substrate metabolism in man. Diabetes 1975;24:468–475.

77. Davis MA, Williams PE, Cherrington AD. Effect of a mixed meal on hepatic lactate and gluconeogenic precursor metabolism in dogs. Am J Physiol 1984;247:E362–E366.

78. Kriesberg RA. Glucose-lactate inter-relations in man. New Engl J Med 1972;287:132–137.

79. Hotchkiss RS, Song S-K, Ling CS, Ackerman JJH, Karl IE. Sepsis does not alter red blood cell glucose metabolism or Na^+ concentration: a ^2H-, ^{23}Na-NMR study. Am J Physiol 1990;258: R21–R31.

80. Marin P, Rebuffe-Scrive M, Smith U, Björntorp P. Glucose uptake in human adipose tissue. Metabolism 1987;36:1154–1160.

81. Newby FD, Sykes MN, DiGirolamo M. Regional differences in adipocyte lactate production from glucose. Am J Physiol 1988;255: E716–E722.

82. Wahren J, Felig P. Renal substrate exchange in human diabetes mellitus. Diabetes 1975;24: 730–734.

83. Jacobs LA, Klopp EH, Seamone W, Topaz SR, Gott VL. Improved organ function during cardiac bypass with a roller pump modified to deliver pulsatile flow. J Thorac Cardiovasc Surg 1969;58:703–712.

84. Stone JJ, Piccione W Jr, Berrizbeitia LD, et al. Hemodynamic, metabolic, and morphological effects of cardiopulmonary bypass with a fluorocarbon priming solution. Ann Thorac Surg 1986;41:419–424.

85. Svensson S, Ekroth R, Milocco I, Nilsson F, Ponten J, William-Olsson G. Glucose and lactate balances in heart and leg after coronary surgery: influence of insulin infusion. Scand J Thorac Cardiovasc Surg 1989;23:145–150.

86. Chiara O, Giomarelli PP, Biagioli B, Rosi R, Gattinoni L. Hypermetabolic response after hypothermic cardiopulmonary bypass. Crit Care Med 1987;15:995–1000.

87. Damask MC, Weissman C, Askanazi J, Rosenbaum SH, Elwyn D, Hyman AI. Do oxygen consumption and carbon dioxide production affect cardiac output after cardiopulmonary bypass? Arch Surg 1987;122: 1026–1031.

88. Wolfe RR, Jahoor F, Herndon DN, Miyoshi H. Isotopic evaluation of the metabolism of pyruvate and related substrates in normal adult volunteers and severely burned children: effect of dichloroacetate and glucose infusion. Surgery 1991;110:54–67.

89. Hirvonen J, Huttunen P, Nuutinen L, Pekkarinen A. Catecholamines and free fatty acids in plasma of patients undergoing cardiac opera-

tions with hypothermia and bypass. J Clin Pathol 1978;31:949–955.

90. Teesalu RV, Keis UE, Kallikorm AP, Tsilmer KZ, Kuusk AE. The dynamics of content of insulin, of somatotropic hormone, glucose and free fatty acids in the blood during the operation of direct revascularization of the myocardium under neuroleptanalgesia [in Russian]. Kardiologiia 1981;21:97–100.

91. Borensztajn J, ed. Lipoprotein lipase. Chicago: Evener Publishing, 1987.

92. Pradines-Figueres A, Vannier C, Ailhaud G. Lipoprotein lipase stored in adipocytes and muscle cells is a cryptic enzyme. J Lipid Res 1990;31:1467–1476.

93. Jensen MD, Haymond MW, Gerich JE, Cryer PE, Miles JM. Lipolysis during fasting. Decreased suppression by insulin and increased stimulation by epinephrine. J Clin Invest 1987;79:207–213.

94. Wolfe RR, Peters EJ, Klein S, Holland OB, Rosenblatt J, Gary H Jr. Effect of short-term fasting on lipolytic responsiveness in normal and obese human subjects. Am J Physiol 1987;252:E189–E196.

95. Wolfe RR, Peters EJ. Lipolytic response to glucose infusion in human subjects. Am J Physiol 1987;252:E218–E223.

96. Henderson AA, Frayn KN, Galasko CSB, Little RA. Dose-response relationships for the effects of insulin on glucose and fat metabolism in injured and control subjects. Clin Sci 1991;80:25–32.

97. Farese RV, Yost TJ, Eckel RH. Tissue-specific regulation of lipoprotein lipase activity by insulin/glucose in normal-weight humans. Metab Clin Exp 1991;40:214–216.

98. Bonadonna RC, Groop LC, Zych K, Shank M, DeFronzo RA. Dose-dependent effect of insulin on plasma free fatty acid turnover and oxidation in humans. Am J Physiol 1990;259:E736–50.

99. Shulman GI, Williams PE, Liljenquist JE, Lacy WW, Keller U, Cherrington AD. Effect of hyperglycemia independent of changes in insulin or glucagon on lipolysis in the conscious dog. Metab Clin Exp 1980;29:317–320.

100. Opie LH. Metabolism of free fatty acids, glucose and catecholamines in acute myocardial infarction. Am J Cardiol 1975;36:938–953.

101. Liedtke AJ, Nellis SH, Neely JR. Effects of excess free fatty acids on mechanical and metabolic function in normal and ischemic myocardium in swine. Circ Res 1978;43:652–661.

102. Vik-Mo H, Mjos OD. Influence of free fatty acids on myocardial oxygen consumption and ischemic injury. Am J Cardiol 1981;48:361–365.

103. McVeigh JJ, Lopaschuk GD. Dichloroacetate stimulation of glucose oxidation improves re-

covery of ischemic rat hearts. Am J Physiol 1990;259:H1079–H1085.

104. Fukagawa NK, Minaker KL, Rowe JW, et al. Insulin-mediated reduction of whole body protein breakdown: dose-response effects on leucine metabolism in postabsorptive men. J Clin Invest 1985;76:2306–2311.

105. Tessari P, Trevisan R, Inchiostro S, et al. Dose-response curves of effects of insulin on leucine kinetics in humans. Am J Physiol 1986;251:E334–E342.

106. Shangraw RE, Stuart CA, Prince MJ, Peters EJ, Wolfe RR. Insulin responsiveness of protein metabolism in vivo following bedrest in humans. Am J Physiol 1988;255:E548–E558.

107. Hersio K, Takala J, Kari A, Huttunen H. Changes in whole body and tissue oxygen consumption during recovery from hypothermia: effect of amino acid infusion. Crit Care Med 1991;19:503–508.

108. Tessari P, Inchiostro S, Biolo G, et al. Differential effects of hyperinsulinemia and hyperaminoacidemia on leucine-carbon metabolism in vivo. Evidence of distinct mechanisms in regulation of net amino acid deposition. J Clin Invest 1987;79:1062–1069.

109. Shangraw RE, Jahoor F, Miyoshi H, Neff WA, Stuart CA, Wolfe RR. Regulation of protein and amino acid catabolism by insulin in septic or severely burned patients [Abstract]. Anesthesiology 1988;69:A182.

110. Rennie MJ, MacLennan P. Protein turnover and amino acid oxidation: The effects of anaesthesia and surgery. In: Garrow JS, Halliday D, eds. Substrate and energy metabolism in man. London: John Libbey, 1985:213–221.

111. Morray JP, Pavlin EG. Oxygen delivery and consumption during hypothermia and rewarming in the dog. Anesthesiology 1990;72:510–516.

112. Shepard RB, Kirklin JW. Relation of pulsatile flow to oxygen consumption and other variables during cardiopulmonary bypass. J Thorac Cardiovasc Surg 1969;58:694–702.

113. Del Canale S, Fiacodori E, Medici D, et al. Effects of low flux-low pressure cardiopulmonary bypass on intracellular acid-base and water metabolism. Scand J Thorac Cardiovasc Surg 1986;20:167–170.

114. Rosenthal MB. The effect of temperature on pH of blood and plasma in vitro. J Biol Chem 1948;173:25–32.

115. Swain JA, McDonald TJ Jr, Robbins RC, Balaban RS. Relationship of cerebral and myocardial intracellular pH to blood pH during hypothermia. Am J Physiol 1991;260:H1640–H1644.

116. Thompson CH, Syme PD, Williams EM, Ledingham GG, Radda GK. Effect of bicarbonate administration on skeletal muscle intracellular pH in the rat: implications for acute ad-

ministration of bicarbonate in man. Clin Sci 1992;82:559–564.

117. Zahler R, Barrett E, Majumdar S, Greene R, Gore JC. Lactic acidosis: effect of treatment on intracellular pH and energetics in living rat heart. Am J Physiol 1992;262:H1572–H1578.

118. Raison JCA, Osborn JJ, Beaumont JO, Gerbode F. Oxygen consumption after open heart surgery measured by a digital computer system. Ann Surg 1969;171:471–484.

119. Abe T, Nagata Y, Yoshioka K, Iyomasa Y. Hypopotassemia following open heart surgery by cardio-pulmonary bypass. J Cardiovasc Surg 1977;18:411–419.

120. Andres R, Baltzan MA, Cader G, Zierler KL. Effect of insulin on carbohydrate metabolism and on potassium in the forearm of man. J Clin Invest 1962;41:108–115.

121. DeFronzo RA, Felig P, Ferrannini E, Wahren J. Effect of graded doses of insulin on splanchnic and peripheral potassium metabolism in man. Am J Physiol 1980;238:E421–E427.

122. Rosa RM, Silva P, Young JB, et al. Adrenergic modulation of extrarenal potassium disposal. N Engl J Med 1980;302:431–434.

123. DeFronzo RA, Bia M. Extrarenal potassium homeostasis. In: Seldin DW, Giebisch G, eds. The kidney: physiology and pathophysiology. New York: Raven Press, 1985:1179–1205.

124. Reves JG, Karp RB, Buttner EE, Tosone S, Smith LR, Samuelson PN, Kreusch GR, Oparil S: Neuronal and adrenomedullary catecholamine release in response to cardiopulmonary bypass in man. Circulation 1982;66:49–55.

125. Zierler KL. Effect of insulin on potassium efflux from rat muscle in the presence and absence of glucose. Am J Physiol 1960;198:1066–1070.

126. Böhrer H, Fleisher F, Krier C. Hyperkalemic cardiac arrest after cardiac surgery following high-dose glucose-insulin-potassium infusion for inotropic support. Anesthesiology 1988;69:949–953.

127. Rossetti L, Klein-Robbenhaar G, Giebisch G, Smith D, DeFronzo RA. Effect of insulin on renal potassium metabolism. Am J Physiol 1987;252:F60–F64.

128. Furuya H, Tabei K, Muto S, Asano Y. Effect of insulin on potassium secretion in rabbit cortical collecting ducts. Am J Physiol 1992;262:F30–F35.

129. Clausen T, Flatman JA. The effect of catecholamines on Na-K transport and membrane potential in rat soleus muscle. J Physiol (Lond) 1977;270:383–414.

130. Vitez TS. Treatment of hyperkalemia with epinephrine. Anesthesiology 1986;65:350–351.

131. Todd EP, McAllister RG, Campbell HC, et al. Ef-

fect of propanolol on hypokalemia induced by cardiopulmonary bypass. Circulation 1977;55(suppl 3):222–228.

132. Pedersen G, Pedersen A, Pedersen EB. Effect of propanolol on total exchangeable body potassium and total exchangeable body sodium in essential hypertension. Scand J Clin Lab Invest 1979;39:167–170.

133. Shangraw RE, Hexem JG. Maximal insulin-stimulated glucose and potassium uptakes during liver transplantation [Abstract]. Anesth Analg 1992;74:S279.

134. Sprung J, Cheng EY, Bosnjak ZJ. Hypothermia and serum potassium concentration. Anesthesiology 1991;75:164.

135. Yokoyama H, Julien JS, Vinten-Johansen J, et al. Postischemic [Ca^{2+}] repletion improves cardiac performance without altering oxygen demands. Ann Thorac Surg 1990;49:894–902.

136. Fuhrer G, Heller W, Hoffmeister HE, Sterzing T. Levels of trace elements during and after cardiopulmonary bypass operations. Acta Pharm Toxicol 1986;59(suppl 7):352–357.

137. Robertie PG, Butterworth JF IV, Royster RL, et al. Normal parathyroid hormone responses to hypocalcemia during cardiopulmonary bypass. Anesthesiology 1991;75:43–48.

138. Westhorpe RN, Varghese Z, Petrie A, Wills MR, Lumley J. Changes in ionized calcium and other plasma constituents associated with cardiopulmonary bypass. Br J Anaesth 1978;50:951–957.

139. Zaloga GP, Willey S, Malcolm D, Chernow B, Holaday JW. Hypercalcemia attenuates blood pressure response to epinephrine. J Pharmacol Exp Ther 1988;247:949–952.

140. Zaloga GP, Strickland RA, Butterworth JF IV, Mark LJ, Mills SA, Lake CR. Calcium attenuates epinephrine's β-adrenergic effects in postoperative heart surgery patients. Circulation 1990;81:196–200.

141. Butterworth JF IV, Zaloga GP, Prielipp RC, Tucker WY Jr, Royster RL. Calcium inhibits the cardiac stimulating properties of dobutamine but not of amrinone. Chest 1992;101:174–180.

142. Fernandez-del Castillo C, Harringer W, Warshaw AL, et al. Risk factors for pancreatic cellular injury after cardiopulmonary bypass. N Engl J Med 1991;325:382–387.

143. Meltzer LE, Palmon FP Jr, Paik YK, Custer RP. Acute pancreatitis secondary to hypercalcemia of multiple myeloma. Ann Intern Med 1962;57:1008–1012.

144. Mixter CG Jr, Keynes M, Cope O. Further experience with pancreatitis as a diagnostic clue to hyperparathyroidism. N Engl J Med 1962;266:265–272.

145. Gafter U, Mandel EM, Har-Zahav L, Weiss S.

Acute pancreatitis secondary to hypercalcemia: occurrence in a patient with breast carcinoma. JAMA 1976;235:2004–2005.

146. Izsak EM, Shike M, Roulet M, Jeejeebhoy KN. Pancreatitis in association with hypercalcemia in patients receiving total parenteral nutrition. Gastroenterology 1980;79:555–558.

147. Waele BD, Smitz J, Willems G. Recurrent pancreatitis secondary to hypercalcemia following vitamin D poisoning. Pancreas 1989;4: 378–380.

148. Choi DW. Calcium-mediated neurotoxicity: relationship to specific channel types and role in ischemic damage. Trends Neurosci 1989; 11:465–469.

149. Opie LH. Reperfusion injury and its pharmacologic modification. Circulation 1989;80: 1049–1062.

150. Siesjo BK, Bengtsson F. Calcium fluxes, calcium antagonists, and calcium-related pathology in brain ischemia, hypoglycemia, and spreading depression: a unifying hypothesis. J Cereb Blood Flow Metab 1989;9:127–140.

151. Waldhausen JA, Lombardo CR, McFarland JA, Cornell WP, Morrow AG. Studies of hepatic blood flow and oxygen consumption during total cardiopulmonary bypass. Surgery 1959; 46:1118–1127.

152. Meyerholz H-H, Gardemann A, Jungermann K. Control of glycogenolysis and blood flow by arterial and portal adrenaline in perfused liver. Biochem J 1991;275:609–616.

153. Penicaud L, Ferre P, Kande J, Leturque A, Issad T, Girard J. Effect of anesthesia on glucose production and utilization in rats. Am J Physiol 1987;252:E365–E369.

154. Toffaletti J, Christenson RH, Mullins S, Harris RE. Relationship between serum lactate and ionized calcium on open-heart surgery. Clin Chem 1986;32:1849–1853.

155. Wolk LA, Wilson RF, Burdick M, et al. Changes in antithrombin, antiplasmin and plasminogen during and after cardiopulmonary bypass. Am Surg 1985;51:309–313.

156. Thompson C, Blumenstock FA, Saba TM, et al. Plasma fibronectin synthesis in normal and injured humans as determined by stable isotope incorporation. J Clin Invest 1989;84: 1226–1235.

157. Carraro F, Hartl WH, Stuart CA, Layman DK, Jahoor F, Wolfe RR. Whole body and plasma protein synthesis in exercise and recovery in human subjects. Am J Physiol 1990;258: E821–E831.

158. Tamkun JW, Hynes RO. Plasma fibronectin is synthesized and secreted by hepatocytes. J Biol Chem 1983;258:4641–4647.

159. Gandhi JG, Vander Salm T, Szymanski IO. Effect of cardiopulmonary bypass on plasma fibronectin, IgG, and C3. Transfusion 1983;23: 476–479.

160. Snyder EL, Barash PG, Mosher DF, Walter SD. Plasma fibronectin level and clinical status in cardiac surgery patients. J Lab Clin Med 1983;102:881–889.

161. Pourrat E, Sie PM, Desrez X, et al. Changes in plasma fibronectin levels after cardiac and pulmonary surgery: role of cardiopulmonary bypass. Scand J Thorac Cardiovasc Surg 1985; 19:63–67.

162. Labrousse F, Dequirot A, Sos P, Le Quang NT. Plasma fibronectin depletion after cardiac surgery in children with or without cardiopulmonary bypass. J Clin Chem Clin Biochem 1986;24:441–444.

163. Gotta AW, Carsons S, Abrams L, Keany AE. Fibronectin levels during cardiopulmonary bypass. N Y State J Med 1987;87:493–496.

164. Saba TM. Fibronectin deficiency following cardiopulmonary bypass. N Y State J Med 1987; 87:487–490.

165. Haniuda M, Morimoto M, Sugenoya A, Iida F. Suppressive effect of ulinastatin on plasma fibronectin depression after cardiac surgery. Ann Thorac Surg 1988;45:171–173.

166. Howard L, Dillon B, Saba TM, Hofmann S, Cho E. Decreased plasma fibronectin during starvation in man. JPEN (Journal of Parenteral and Enteral Nutrition) 1984;8:237–244.

167. Roelofse JA, van der Bijl P. Plasma cholinesterase levels during cardiopulmonary bypass. A report on 10 cases. S Afr Med J 1987; 71:662–664.

168. Eicher O, Farah A. Cholinesterases and anticholinesterase agents. New York: Springer-Verlag 1963:78.

169. Barstow L, Small RE. Liver function assessment by drug metabolism. Pharmacotherapy 1990; 10:280–288.

170. Koska AJ, Romagnoli A, Kramer WG. Effect of cardiopulmonary bypass on fentanyl distribution and elimination. Clin Pharmacol Ther 1981;29:100–105.

171. Holley FO, Ponganis KV, Stanski DR. Effect of cardiopulmonary bypass on the pharmacokinetics of drugs. Clin Pharmacokinet 1982; 7:234–251.

172. Kanto J, Himberg JJ, Heikkila H, Arola M, Jalonen J, Laaaksonen V. Midazolam kinetics before, during and after cardiopulmonary bypass surgery. Intern J Clin Pharm Res 1985;2:123–126.

173. Koren G, Barker C, Goresky G, et al. The influence of hypothermia on the disposition of fentanyl-human and animal studies. Eur J Clin Pharmacol 1987;32:373–376.

174. Mathews HML, Carson IW, Lyons SM, et al. A pharmacokinetic study of midazolam in paediatric patients undergoing cardiac surgery. Br J Anaesth 1988;61:302–307.

175. Koren G, Barker C, Bohn D, Kent G, Biggar WD. Influence of hypothermia on the pharmacokinetics of gentamycin and theophilline in piglets. Crit Care Med 1985;13:844–847.

176. Dasta JF, Weber RJ, Wu LS, et al. Influence of cardiopulmonary bypass on nitroglycerin clearance. J Clin Pharmacol 1986;26:165–168.

177. Aaltonen L, Kanto J, Arola M, Iisalo E, Pakkanen A. Effect of age and cardiopulmonary bypass on the pharmacokinetics of lorazepam. Acta Pharmacol Toxicol 1982;51:126–131.

178. Welbourn N, Melrose DG, Moss DW. Changes in serum enzyme levels accompanying cardiac surgery with extracorporeal circulation. J Clin Pathol 1966;19:220–232.

179. Norberg B, Senning A. A study of serum enzymes during and after surgery with the Crafoord-Senning heart-lung machine. Acta Chir Scand 1959;245(suppl):275–284.

180. Lockey E, McIntyre N, Ross DN, Brokes E, Sturridge MF. Early jaundice after open-heart surgery. Thorax 1967;22:165–169.

181. Sanderson RG, Ellison JH, Benson JA, Starr A. Jaundice following open heart surgery. Ann Surg 1967;165:217–224.

182. Collins JD, Ferner R, Murray A, et al. Incidence and prognostic importance of jaundice after cardiopulmonary bypass surgery. Lancet 1983;1:1119–1123.

183. Krasna MJ, Flancbaum L, Trooskin SZ, et al. Gastrointestinal complications after cardiac surgery. Surgery 1988;104:773–780.

184. Robinson G, Brodman R. Going down the tube. Ann Thorac Surg 1981;31:400–401.

185. Eugene J, Ott RA, Stemmer EA. Hepatic trauma during cardiac surgery. J Cardiovasc Surg 1986;27:100–102.

186. Warshaw AL, Fuller AF. Specificity of increased renal clearance of amylase in diagnosis of acute pancreatitis. N Engl J Med 1975;292:325–328.

187. Smith CR, Schwartz SI. Amylase:creatinine clearance ratios, serum amylase, and lipase after operations with cardiopulmonary bypass. Surgery 1983;94:458–463.

188. Harper SL, Pitts VH, Granger DN, Kvietys PR. Pancreatic tissue oxygenation during secretory stimulation. Am J Physiol 1986;250:G316–G322.

189. Kvietys PR, McLendon JM, Bulkley GB, Perry MA, Granger DN. Pancreatic circulation: intrinsic regulation. Am J Physiol 1982;242:G596–G602.

190. Moores WY, Gago O, Morris JD, Peck CC. Serum and urinary amylase levels following pulsatile and continuous cardiopulmonary bypass. J Thorac Cardiovasc Surg 1977;74:73–76.

191. Missavage AE, Weaver DW, Bouman DL, Parnell V, Wilson RF. Hyperamylasemia after cardiopulmonary bypass. Am Surg 1984;50:297–300.

192. Rattner DW, Gu Z-Y, Vlahakes GJ, Warshaw AL. Hyperamylasemia after cardiac surgery. Ann Surg 1989;209:279–283.

193. Murray WR, Mittra S, Mittra D, Roberts LB, Taylor KM. The amylase-creatinine clearance ratio following cardiopulmonary bypass. J Thorac Cardiovasc Surg 1981;82:248–253.

194. Haas GS, Warshaw AL, Daggett WM, Aretz HT. Acute pancreatitis after cardiopulmonary bypass. Am J Surg 1985;149:509–515.

195. Rose DM, Ranson JHC, Cunningham JN, Spencer FC. Patterns of severe pancreatic injury following cardiopulmonary bypass. Ann Surg 1984;199:168–172.

196. Feiner H. Pancreatitis after cardiac surgery. A morphologic study. Am J Surg 1976;131:684–688.

197. Warshaw AL, O'Hara PJ. Susceptibility of the pancreas to ischemic damage in shock. Ann Surg 1978;188:197–201.

198. Reber HA. Acute pancreatitis—another piece of the puzzle? N Engl J Med 1991;325:423–425.

199. MacLean D, Morrison J, Griffith PD. Acute pancreatitis after accidental hypothermia and hypothermic myxoedema. Br Med J 1973;4:757–761.

200. Savides EP, Hoffbrand BI. Hypothermia, thrombosis and acute pancreatitis. Br Med J 1974;1:614–617.

201. Hanks JB, Curtis SE, Hanks BB, Andersen DK, Cox JL, Jones RS. Gastrointestinal complications after cardiopulmonary bypass. Surgery 1982;92:394–400.

202. Heikkinen LO, Ala-Kulju KV. Abdominal complications following cardiopulmonary bypass in open-heart surgery. Scand J Thorac Cardiovasc Surg 1987;21:1–7.

203. Leitman IM, Paull DE, Barie PS, Isom OW, Shires GT. Intra-abdominal complications of cardiopulmonary bypass operations. Surg Gynecol Obstet 1987;165:251–254.

204. Decker GAG, Josselsohn E, Svensson L, Schein M. Acute gastroduodenal complications after cardiopulmonary bypass surgery. S Afr J Surg 1984;22:261–264.

205. Burton NA, Albus RA, Graeber GM, Lough FC. Acute diverticulitis following cardiac surgery. Chest 1986;89:756–757.

206. Evora PRB, Moraes MMFS, Ribeiro PJF, et al. Nonocclusive intestinal ischemia and necrosis after correction of interatrial communication

with cardiopulmonary bypass. J Cardiovasc Surg 1989;30:1002–1005.

207. Moneta GL, Misbach GA, Ivey TD. Hypoperfusion as a possible factor in the development of gastrointestinal complications after cardiac surgery. Am J Surg 1985;149:648–650.

208. Rocke DA, Gaffin SL, Wells MT, Koen Y, Brock-Utine JG. Endotoxemia associated with cardiopulmonary bypass. J Thorac Cardiovasc Surg 1987;93:832–837.

209. Garthiram P, Gaffin SL, Wells MT, Brock-Utne JG. Superior mesenteric artery occlusion shock in cats: modification of the endotoxemia by antilipopolysaccharide antibodies. Circ Shock 1986;19:231–237.

210. Smith EEJ, Naftel DC, Blackstone EH, Kirklin JW. Microvascular permeability after cardiopulmonary bypass. An experimental study. J Thorac Cardiovasc Surg 1987;94:225–233.

21

NEUROLOGIC EFFECTS OF CARDIOPULMONARY BYPASS

Anne T. Rogers, Stanton P. Newman, David A. Stump, and Donald S. Prough

For patients experiencing cardiopulmonary bypass (CPB), overall cardiovascular morbidity and mortality have been declining steadily in recent years (1). However, because of changing population demographics, more elderly patients are now presenting for cardiac surgery. These older patients have a greater risk and incidence of stroke (1, 2).

This observation has led to intense scientific interest in the neurologic effects of cardiopulmonary bypass. Cardiac surgical patients develop more frequent, more severe brain injury than patients with comparable preoperative risk factors undergoing noncardiac surgery (3–5). Severe brain injury leading to death or frank stroke (e.g., hemiparesis or aphasia) occurs in relatively few patients ($\leq5\%$) (1–3, 6, 7). However, more detailed testing, e.g., with a battery of neuropsychologic tests indicates that more than 50% of patients are affected by subtle brain injury (3, 8–10). Some authors have stated that neuropsychologic tests lack sufficient specificity to detect subclinical focal brain damage (11), but this viewpoint is being challenged as further studies are published (12).

Those who suffer neurologic injury have a substantially prolonged hospital stay, with an attendant increase in cost (13). With regard to neuropsychologic deficits, some resolve with time, but a high proportion persist to disable patients by impairing memory, concentration, and hand-eye coordination, with a predictably negative impact on life-style (3, 14). The extent to which these changes affect the quality of life will in part depend upon activity level prior to surgery and the extent to which a patient is involved in intellectual pursuits.

MEASURES AND INCIDENCE OF NERVOUS SYSTEM INJURY

Severe Nervous System Damage

Stroke, defined as a focal central nervous system deficit of relatively sudden onset that lasts for more than 24 hours, is the major cause of severe neurologic disability following cardiac surgery. Incidence estimates vary from 1 to 5% (1, 2, 6, 7). Approximately 70% of these strokes occur intraoperatively; 30% occur early in the postoperative period (15–17). A proportion of affected patients die in the hospital because of persistent coma or multiorgan dysfunction with inability to be weaned from mechanical ventilation (13).

The diagnosis of major stroke is relatively clear-cut if patients receive a comprehensive neurologic examination before and after surgery (6); most observers agree on the presence or absence of such major stroke indicators as visual field defects, aphasia, sensory deficits, and hemiparesis. More commonly, in clinical situations, patients have a brief neurologic assessment during their admission history and physical examination, and are later monitored in the intensive care unit using the Glasgow Coma Scale or equivalent measure. Clearly, examiner bias and training will influence reporting, thus partially explaining differing event rates among investigations. Importantly, retrospective series are known to identify a lower incidence of major neurologic deficits than prospective studies (18), a discrepancy that shows the need to define study conditions precisely.

A few studies have used brain imaging techniques to determine whether it is possible to detect brain injury not apparent by clinical examination (Fig. 21.1). Aberg et al. (4) subjected 54 patients to computerized cranial tomography (CCT) and to a

limited set of three cognitive tests before and after surgery. The CCT identified two new brain infarcts, but neither had clinical neurologic changes; one had a decrement on neuropsychologic testing. Fish et al. (19) found no CCT abnormality in 85 patients either before or after coronary artery bypass surgery. Using the more sensitive technique of magnetic resonance imaging, other studies have revealed a high proportion of patients with preoperative abnormalities. In a study of 20 patients, Newman et al. (unpublished data, 1992) found that 80% had magnetic resonance imaging abnormalities prior to surgery for myocardial revascularization. Eight days postsurgery, repeat scans were performed and 30% of patients showed significant new changes.

Subtle Nervous System Damage

Careful clinical neurologic testing will identify less profound manifestations

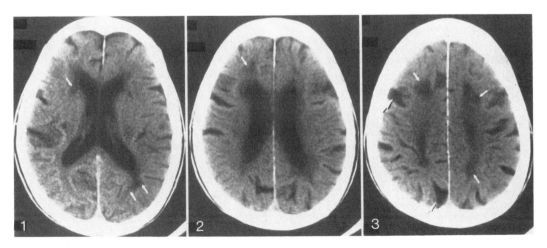

Figure 21.1. Computed tomography of the brain, done preoperatively, showing diffuse degenerative vascular disease. Multiple areas of wedge-shaped peripheral hypoattenuation are seen (*arrows* with shadowing seen on left side of panel 3), compatible with small remote cortical infarcts. The striking examples of confluent hypoattenuation in the deep white matter (*white arrows* seen in all three panels) are believed to be demyelination secondary to chronic ischemic change. The patient was a 71-year-old female presenting for "redo" myocardial revascularization. The admitting house officer reported her neurologic examination as unremarkable other than noting the presence of bilateral carotid bruits. A neurologic specialist found abnormal deep tendon reflexes and abnormal tandem gait. Cerebral arteriography performed 2 years previously revealed only some atherosclerosis of the cavernous portion of both internal carotid arteries and some intracranial atherosclerotic changes not amenable to surgical correction. (CT scan provided by Dr. Dixon Moody, Department of Radiology, Bowman Gray School of Medicine, Winston-Salem, NC.)

of nervous system damage that fall short of stroke, such as loss of vibration sense, abnormal reflexes, altered gait, etc. (3). Additionally, detailed neuro-ophthalmologic examination may reveal abnormalities of visual and oculomotor function. Visual field defects result from either posterior cortical ischemia or retinal lesions. Shaw et al. (17) noted retinal abnormalities in 25% of 312 coronary artery bypass patients, with areas of retinal infarction found in 54 (17%).

Peripheral nerve injury of the upper extremity occurs in 6% of patients undergoing median sternotomy (20, 21) and must be differentiated from central lesions such as watershed infarction (22). The most common mechanism of injury is stretching of the lower trunk or medial cord of the brachial plexus secondary to sternal retraction. More than 90% of these symptoms resolve within 3 months (20). Other nerves reported to have been injured after cardiac surgery include the phrenic, ulnar, radial, saphenous, facial, and recurrent laryngeal nerves (20).

Neuropsychologic assessment offers a method for detecting subtle central nervous system functional changes that may not be apparent using other methods (Fig. 21.2). In the clinical care setting, such an assessment is pursued to examine whether some-

one with a known or suspected brain lesion, e.g., following head injury, shows objective evidence of cognitive disturbance. Studies of the neuropsychologic impact of cardiac surgery focus on the change in performance by examining two or more measurement intervals (pre- and postoperative). These assessments take place under time constraints imposed by the clinical environment, making the selection of tests extremely important. Testing must offer objectivity, reproducibility, discrimination, and control for practice effects (improved performance on repeat testing), yet the battery must be brief to limit patient fatigue. Methodologic issues that affect the reported incidence of deficits include the number, sensitivity, and range of tests used. Tests selected by some researchers lack sufficient sensitivity to detect the subtle disturbances of patients undergoing cardiac surgery (23). Importantly, studies using only a few tests have reported lower neuropsychologic deficit rates in contrast to those employing a greater number. The least effective assessments are those designed to give a quick overview of cognitive functioning such as the Mini-Mental Status Examination (24).

It should not be assumed that neurologic and neuropsychologic examinations will be in agreement, or that they are mea-

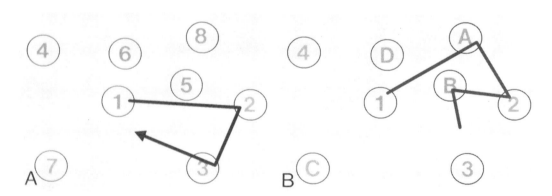

Figure 21.2. Examples of neuropsychological tests. Trail-Making A (depicted in **A**), and Trail-Making B (**B**) assess attention and concentration. In Trail-Making A, the patient must join 1 to 2 to 3, etc. In Trail-Making B, the patient must join 1 to A, to 2, to B, to 3, to C, etc. The time taken to complete the form is measured, along with the number of errors. The test can be administered in a pencil and paper form, or in a computerized form using a computer-assisted design board.

suring the same type of brain damage. Both are subject to measurement error and are influenced by many different factors. A number of studies have reported no agreement between neurologic and neuropsychologic findings (25, 26) although others have found a positive correlation (27, 28). Frank neurologic disturbances such as stroke may reflect a mechanism such as macroembolization, whereas the more subtle changes detected by neuropsychologic testing may be due to microembolization or anesthetic effects.

The study of neuropsychologic changes related to CPB involves a number of pitfalls that have produced some confusing results (29). In a number of studies, the analysis of neuropsychologic data has followed traditional experimental design by examining group data over time. This mode of analysis assumes deficits in all patients and ignores the possibility of learning. To take a hypothetical example, if approximately 20% of patients show deterioration and approximately 60% show some learning effects, with the remainder showing no change, then the overall trend will be toward some improvement. Many data have shown this overall tendency (30). This analysis, however, fails to detect those patients who have sustained deficits. In order to identify those individuals who are performing at a level significantly lower than preoperatively, a different form of analysis is required, i.e., examining changes in individual performance over time. Thus each patient serves as his or her own control. In order to use this approach, one must precisely define a neuropsychologic deficit (9, 31). One way of doing this is as follows:

1. The standard deviation for each test is calculated for the study group as a whole at the preoperative interval.
2. A difference score is computed for each subject on each test by subtracting his or her postoperative score from his or her preoperative score.

3. If individual performance has deteriorated by more than one standard deviation as calculated in (1.), then the subject is considered to have a significant deterioration in that test.
4. A subject is considered to have a neuropsychologic deficit if two or more tests show significant deterioration.

Another approach is to interpret a decrement of 20% in individual test performance from the preoperative level to denote a significant deterioration (32). It is critical to note that when most neuropsychologic tests are repeated on the same individual, improvement is usually observed. It is against this expected practice effect that deteriorations are to be considered. In tests performed on nonsurgical volunteers and patients undergoing noncardiac thoracic surgery, 96% of subjects improved performance by at least 10% (32). In contrast, 69% of coronary bypass patients had deteriorated by >20% on postoperative days 5 through 7.

Changes in neuropsychologic performance occurring in the days shortly after surgery have been reported in a number of studies (3, 9, 33–40). The incidence of neuropsychologic morbidity in these studies ranges from 13 to 79% (Table 21.1). Other than potential surgical differences between institutions, the variation in these reported figures are attributable to a number of factors including the number and type of tests used, the definition of a deficit, and the type of patients selected for surgery. Clearly, some coronary artery bypass patients do suffer from short-term neuropsychologic changes in almost all studies. There have been fewer studies on valvular surgery patients. Bethune (33) examined 30 patients undergoing valve surgery with one memory test of delayed recall. Six days after surgery, 90% of patients were found to have a decrement in their memory performance. While this study indicated a high incidence of deficits, it should not be assumed that neuropsychologic morbidity is more

Table 21.1. Neuropsychologic Changes Following Cardiac Surgery

Author(s)	Subjects[a]	No. of Tests Performed	Postoperative Intervals	% Deficit[b]
Bethune (33)	8 CABG	1	8 days	13
	30 CVS	1	6 days	90
Savageau et al. (68)	172 CABG	3	9 days	28
	29 CVS			
	26 Combined			
Savageau et al. (34)	245	3	6 months	19
Garvey et al. (35)	37 CABG	1	7 days	18
	7 CVS			
Shaw et al. (3)	298 CABG	10	7 days	79
	50 PVS	10	7 days	31
Shaw et al. (204)	259 CABG	10	6 months	22[c]
Nevin et al. (37)	65 CABG	10	7 days	20
Newman et al. (9)	67 CABG	10	8 days	73
	24 PVS and	10	8 days	50
	7 thoracic			
Newman et al. (9)	67 CABG	10	2 months	37
	24 PVS and	10	2 months	46
	thoracic			
Newman et al. (29)	66 CABG	10	12 months	29
Hammeke and Hastings (38)	46 CABG	12	10 days	54[c]
Sotaniemi et al. (27)	49 CVS	7	2 months	27
Mattlar et al. (51)	64 CABG	7	2 months	0
Stump et al. (32)	27 CABG	8	7 days	56

[a] CABG, coronary artery bypass surgery; CVS, cardiac valvular surgery; Combined, CABG/CVS; PVS, peripheral vascular surgery.
[b] Deficit defined as a deterioration in two or more tests.
[c] Authors used another definition in original publication.

quent after valve replacement than aorto-coronary bypass, as appropriate comparison studies with the same surgical team have not been performed (41).

The major recovery after bypass-related brain damage occurs in the first few months. Despite some reviews to the contrary (42), a number of long-term studies suggest that a proportion of patients experience persistent neuropsychologic problems (Table 21.1). Newman et al. (29) followed 66 patients for 12 months after surgery; 29% of patients had neuropsychologic deficits compared to an incidence of 73% 8 days postoperatively. Other studies (Table 21.1) have also concluded that a significant proportion of deficits observed shortly after myocardial revascularization persist. In valve replacement surgery, Sotaniemi et al. (27) examined the outcome of 49 patients and found that approximately 27% had deficits 2 months

postoperatively. Those undergoing mitral valve surgery had the poorest outcome compared with other types of valvular surgery. Forty-four of these patients were followed for 5 years postoperatively (43); although many of the early deficits were mild, they persisted at the 5-year assessment.

It is critical to recognize that studies relying on complaints spontaneously voiced by patients will grossly underestimate the true deficit rate, since many will not report functional changes. Thus, subjective reports do not correlate with objective assessments of cognitive function. What appears to underlie patients' *subjective* complaints is mood state (10); i.e., anxious patients and those with a depressed mood are more likely to complain spontaneously of their cognitive deterioration while those with a more normal mood state simply do not report subtle changes.

Quality of Life

The term quality of life has been used in a variety of ways including psychological well-being, disability, return to work, return to social and leisure activities, or overall satisfaction with the surgical procedure.

Magni et al. (44) instructed the relatives of cardiac surgery patients to complete a global scale that examined a range of behaviors and feelings including mood, worries, interests, initiative, energy, and dependence. Significant improvements over the preoperative state had occurred in 75% of patients when followed up 12 months after surgery.

High rates of satisfaction have also been reported by patients themselves following myocardial revascularization. Kornfeld et al. (45) reported that 60% of patients were extremely pleased and only 4% reported displeasure with their surgical experience. Other self-reports have yielded a high frequency of positive responses, with 71% of subjects reporting without qualifications that they would undergo surgery again (46) and 70% reporting that they were very pleased with the operation (47).

While levels of depressed mood intensify in some patients following surgery (46, 48–50), these are short-lived and in most studies the mood level improves over that seen preoperatively. It is, however, significant that for a small number of individuals the depressed mood persists. Mattlar et al. (51) reported that in the months following surgery, about 25% of patients may need some treatment for depression.

The influence of preoperative anxiety upon physical and psychologic function following surgery has long interested psychologists, anesthesiologists, and surgeons (52) because high anxiety levels impair recovery. Besides informing patients about the procedures they will undergo and what they should expect following surgery, there are a range of more formal psychologic interventions to reduce preoperative anxiety

(52). Kulik and Mahler (53) found that having a preoperative patient share a room with a postoperative patient who had undergone a similar procedure was highly effective in reducing anxiety and hastening recovery. In general, when compared to preoperative anxiety levels, patients usually show an initial increase in anxiety followed by a decline in the months following surgery (46, 48).

Because of its simplicity and focus on economic factors, the ability to return to work has often been used as an indicator of the success of a procedure (54). However, its ease of assessment belies the complexity of any interpretation that can be placed on the data. Return to work depends upon many factors including the nature of employment, the level of seniority, economic support such as pensions, housing, and the general level of economic activity. As a result, research on return to work following cardiac surgery has produced mixed findings. Anderson et al. (55) reported 90% of patients under 55 years of age returning to work, Westaby et al. (56) found 73% returning to work, and Bass (57) 75%. Kornfeld et al. (45) reported high rates of return to work in coronary artery bypass patients: 76% were working 9 months postsurgery and 65% were working at the 3.5-year follow-up. In contrast, Gundle et al. (58), working in a rural and impoverished area, found 83% unemployed 1 to 2 years after surgery.

The complexity of issues is further illustrated by the failure to find a direct relationship between symptoms and return to work in some studies, confirming the difficulty of using this indicator to define the functional success of a procedure (47, 59). Regardless of the data, it is clear that the long-term repercussions of failing to return to work after surgery can be dramatic. Jenkins et al. (46) reported that 20% of families showed significant deterioration in income. These changes in family income may have broader implications for individuals' social functioning as well as their psychological well-being.

Studies on both valve replacement and aortocoronary bypass have found patients more physically active following cardiac surgery (46, 47, 60, 61), as would be expected with the removal or reduction of symptoms and the customary advice given to increase activity levels.

Difficulties in sexual functioning among males is a frequent clinical report following cardiac surgery. Gundle et al. (58) found that 57% of male patients reported sexual dysfunction, while Kornfeld et al. (45) found a considerable drop in reports of sexual activity 9 months after surgery, which persisted in many when followed up 3.5 years after surgery. Corresponding data are not available for women. This area of life may have important repercussions for personal relationships, and relatively little attention has been paid to it with regard to intervention.

MECHANISMS OF INJURY

For decades, investigators have debated the etiology of nervous system dysfunction after cardiopulmonary bypass (Table 21.2). The central controversy is, do specific bypass variables such as blood pressure and perfusion flow rate influence outcome or is the fate of the brain determined by cerebral embolization? If perfusion methods do have an effect, is this secondary to their impact on the adequacy of global cerebral perfusion, or because of their effect on the total embolic load delivered to the brain? In 1974, Stockard et al. (62) drew attention to an association between intraoperative hypotension and poor neurologic outcome after cardiac surgery. More recently, the etiologic role of global cerebral hypoperfusion has been questioned, while emphasis has been placed on systemic embolization as the primary causative factor (11, 28). Sophisticated technical devices are now available to measure cerebral blood flow and metabolism (63, 64) and to detect and quantitate cerebral em-

Table 21.2. **Possible Mechanisms of Postoperative Neurologic, Neuropsychologic, and Neuro-ophthalmologic Deficits**

Embolism
  Microembolism
    Gas
    Fat
    Cellular aggregates
    CPB circuit material
  Macroembolism
    Air
    Particulate matter
      Atheroma
      Calcific debris
      Thrombus
Cerebral hypoperfusion
  Systemic hypotension
  Low pump flow
  Nonpulsatile flow
  Incorrect cannula placement (arterial or venous)

boli (65). New studies will define the relative importance of these hypotheses.

The etiologic role of cerebral ischemia seems obvious in the case of frank stroke, but subtle brain dysfunction detected in the early postoperative period might reflect, in part, residual anesthetic effects. However, as discussed above, the persistence of a significant proportion of these abnormal findings at remote postoperative intervals (from 30 days to 1 year), confirms their organic nature (29, 66). Aberg et al. (4) reported that more than 50% of patients undergoing bypass had an increase in the brain-specific enzyme adenylate kinase of sufficient magnitude to suggest neural cell injury, whereas no increase occurred in patients undergoing lung resection.

Moody and colleagues (67) recently reported numerous microvascular lesions in the brains of patients dying soon after cardiac surgery and of dogs that had undergone CPB. These lesions were demonstrated using a histochemical method that employs a stain specific for alkaline phosphatase, a native enzyme present in the endothelium of capillaries, arterioles, and the smallest arteries but not veins. Lesions consisted of focal small capillary and arteriolar dilations known colloquially as SCADs (Fig. 21.3).

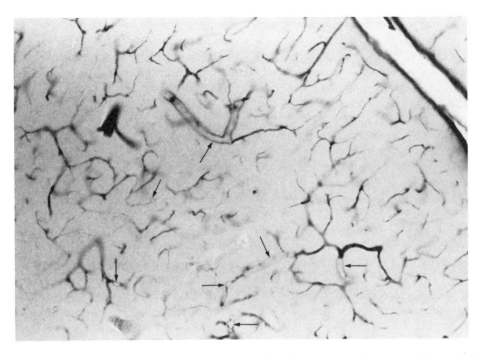

Figure 21.3.   Multiple brain microemboli in a patient who died shortly after cardiac surgery. This is a photomicrograph of cerebral cortex with alkaline phosphatase stain, and celloidin embedding in a section 100 μm thick that reveals seven small capillary and arteriolar dilations (*arrows*) (SCADs) (67). These are believed to be the "footprint" of a soluble embolic agent previously removed by the solutions used in tissue processing. Small-daughter emboli have been identified downstream from the large sausage-shaped ones. It is postulated that since the emboli can deform to assume the shape of the lumen of a large arteriole, it would be possible for the agent to deform and pass through an arterial line micropore filter in the extracorporeal circuitry. (Photomicrograph provided by Dr. Dixon Moody, Department of Radiology, Bowman Gray School of Medicine, Winston-Salem, NC.)

Such changes were not seen in numerous brains examined from both humans and dogs not undergoing either CPB or major proximal arterial manipulation. The authors postulated that small capillary and arteriolar dilations may be the anatomic correlate of postoperative cognitive dysfunction.

PATIENT FACTORS INFLUENCING OUTCOME

Age

Gardner et al. (1) reported a rise in stroke rate following myocardial revascularization from 0.57% in 1979 to 2.4% in 1983, an observation attributed to an increase in the mean age of patients (55.1 years versus 59.2 years). Combining data from 1974 through 1983, they noted that stroke rates correlated dramatically with the age of the patient (0.23% for those <45 years old versus 7.14% for those >75 years old). Acinapura and colleagues (2) have confirmed this association, reporting a stroke rate of 1% in patients younger than 70 years, in contrast to 4% in those older than 70 years. Older patients show a greater incidence of neuropsychologic deficits after both valvular and coronary artery bypass procedures (9, 27–29, 68).

Gender

Male patients constitute the majority (~80%) of those undergoing myocardial revascularization (69) and approximately 50% of the valvular surgical population. In patients subjected to myocardial revascularization, cardiovascular morbidity and mortality are reportedly higher for women than men, although some controversy exists (70). Two studies report postoperative neuropsychiatric impairment more frequently in women than men (27, 28). Women are older than men when they present for myocardial revascularization, a fact that may reflect some protective effect of female sex hormones or a difference in referral patterns. Thus, any observed differences in deficit rates may be because of age rather than gender per se. Intense interest has recently focused on health care issues for women, as we come to understand that conclusions based on clinical trials conducted in men may not be applicable to female subjects (71).

Cardiac Disease

Historically, open cardiac procedures (valvular repair, valvular replacement, and left ventricular aneurysmectomy) have been associated with a two- to threefold higher incidence of neurologic sequelae than coronary artery bypass grafting procedures (27, 28, 72, 73). Other factors contributing to an increased stroke risk include the presence of left ventricular thrombus (74), the severity of valvular calcification (73), and the extent of atherosclerosis in the ascending aorta (1).

Cerebrovascular Disease

The relationship between preexisting cerebrovascular disease and stroke has generated significant debate. Interpretation of data is confounded by the fact that, in any reported study, the percentage of patients with preexisting symptomatic cerebrovascular disease is small (~20%). In addition, the spectrum includes (a) symptomatic versus asymptomatic cerebrovascular lesions; (b) extracranial versus intracranial cerebrovascular lesions; and (c) hemody-

namically significant stenoses versus intimal irregularity. An additional factor to consider is whether the cerebrovascular disease was documented by noninvasive Doppler sonography or cerebral angiography (75).

Gardner and colleagues (1) reported a positive correlation between perioperative stroke and a prior history of stroke, transient ischemic attacks, or carotid endarterectomy compared to patients with no such history (3.3-fold increase in risk). This association has been confirmed by many other investigators (76–81).

Other studies have explored the relationship between asymptomatic carotid bruits, hemodynamically significant carotid stenoses, and postoperative complications. Furlan and colleagues (82) found that *asymptomatic* unilateral stenosis (50 to 90%) of an internal carotid artery or unilateral carotid occlusion does not increase stroke risk after myocardial revascularization. Other investigators have reported no association between *asymptomatic* carotid bruits and neurologic sequelae (79, 80). The investigations of Jones et al. (83) and of Reed et al. (81) have examined the overall influence of preoperative carotid bruit (symptomatic and asymptomatic): both authors reported a positive association between carotid bruit and postoperative stroke. However, both reports comment that the overall risk of stroke is small and comparable to the reported risk of stroke from carotid endarterectomy alone (84). Harrison et al. (14) found that the incidence of postoperative neuropsychologic deficits was similar in patients with angiographically detectable carotid artery disease, compared to patients with no evidence of vessel wall disease.

In summary, preoperative symptomatic cerebrovascular disease appears to increase stroke risk in myocardial revascularization patients. An asymptomatic carotid bruit per se may not alter risk in the absence of clinical symptomatology. If the neurologic history and examination reveals symptoms or signs suggestive of cerebrovascular insufficiency, ultrasonography or angiography may be appropriate. Clinical and laboratory data should then be carefully reviewed to assess the need for sequential or combined carotid endarterectomy and aortocoronary bypass. The practice of combining myocardial revascularization and carotid endarterectomy during one procedure continues to be controversial, because such an operative strategy is not necessarily protective to the brain.

In one series of 115 patients with bilateral carotid disease who underwent unilateral carotid endarterectomy combined with aortocoronary bypass, eight perioperative strokes (7%) occurred, of which six were ipsilateral to the endarterectomy (82). Jones et al. (83) reported on a group of patients who had combined carotid/coronary procedures in whom the stroke rate was similar to a group having only coronary artery bypass grafting. In a report by Gravlee et al. (85), three patients with bilateral total occlusion of the internal carotid arteries underwent myocardial revascularization: no patient suffered a stroke perioperatively or during the follow-up period even though no carotid surgery was performed. Gravlee et al. suggested that neurologic outcome is better predicted by the functional state of the cerebral collateral circulation, as judged by preoperative neurologic symptoms, than by the specific occlusive anatomy of the extracranial carotid arteries. Jones et al. recommended that (*a*) combined procedures be performed in neurologically symptomatic patients with bilateral carotid disease in association with unstable angina, left main obstruction, or diffuse multivessel disease; (*b*) staged procedures be performed in patients with stable angina and symptomatic carotid lesions; and (*c*) coronary artery grafting alone be performed for most patients with asymptomatic bruit, mild-to-moderate carotid artery obstruction, or prior stroke, with the caveat that the risk of neurologic injury is higher in the presence of previous stroke.

Hypertension

Neither chronic hypertension nor the use of antihypertensive drugs seems to affect the incidence of stroke after cardiac surgery (1, 73).

CEREBRAL PHYSIOLOGY AND INTRAOPERATIVE MONITORING

Electroencephalography

The value of routine electroencephalographic (EEG) monitoring during cardiac surgery is controversial. Widespread clinical acceptance is limited by the duration of monitoring required, the multiplicity of confounding variables, and pronounced electrical artifact (86). Bashein et al. (87) have pointed out that much of the data supporting its use are derived from anecdotal reports, serial experiences, and retrospective analyses. Using the raw, unprocessed EEG signal is essential for recognition of seizure and burst suppression patterns. However, this unprocessed method generates huge volumes of data that require expert interpretation. Clinical use is simplified by computer processing of the raw signal, which reduces the amount of data to be examined and facilitates interpretation (Fig. 21.4).

Several forms of processed electroencephalography are being used in surgical practice, including the Cerebral Function Monitor, the Compressed Spectral Array (Fig. 21.4), and the Density Modulated Spectral Array (88). Typically, these formats use only one or two channels, permitting gross global measurements or hemispheric comparisons, but with the potential to miss ischemic brain areas distant from the leads.

The premedicated patient lying with eyes closed typically has a preponderance of alpha rhythm (8 to 13 Hz) with periods of theta (4 to 8 Hz) and delta (<4 Hz) activity during drowsy moments. During induction of anesthesia with high-dose opioids and benzodiazepines, there is marked

Figure 21.4. An example of EEG monitoring using a compressed spectral array format (right and left hemispheres). Shown at the top of the arrays are the channel designations and the frequency scale in hertz. Superimposed on the arrays are the spectral edge frequencies (*x*) and the median power frequencies (*o*). The real-time scale is found between the arrays. On the right side are plotted the esophageal temperature (*x*) and the mean arterial pressure (*o*), with their respective scales shown at the top. Along the left margin, the numeral *1* indicates the time of induction of anesthesia; *2* indicates the start of surgery; *3,* the start of bypass; and *4,* the start of aortic occlusion. The second *3* indicates the end of aortic occlusion, and the second *2* the end of bypass. (From Bashein G, Nessly ML, Bledsoe SW, et al. Electroencephalography during surgery with cardiopulmonary bypass and hypothermia. Anesthesiology 1992;76:878–891.)

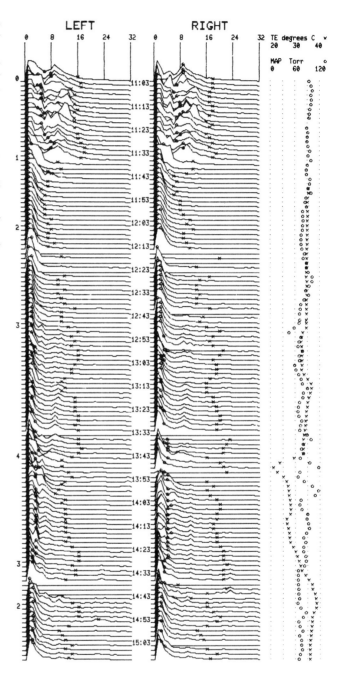

slowing of the EEG; alpha rhythm disappears and a delta rhythm predominates. During moderate systemic hypothermia, there is mainly diminution in wave amplitude with some further slowing. If thiopental or isoflurane is used, or if temperatures are lowered further, burst suppression may supervene, progressing to an isoelectric pattern. Cerebral ischemia is also manifested by reduced amplitude and frequency.

Unlike carotid endarterectomy, no discrete event during cardiac surgery is expected to have a close temporal relationship with the onset of cerebral ischemia. Electroencephalographic abnormalities do occur as a consequence of brain ischemia during cardiac surgery (87), but accurate interpretation is difficult. Changes at the onset of CPB are common and may not be clinically important; rather, they may reflect the effects of hemodilution and hypothermia. Certainly the appearance of any new abnormality should alert the team to the possibility of inadequate cerebral perfusion. When a period of marked systemic hypoperfusion occurs, e.g., due to a venous air lock, marked bilateral slowing of the EEG recording is readily apparent. However, during profound hypothermia ($<20°C$), spontaneous electrical activity may be completely abolished without impairing neuronal cellular integrity.

In an uncontrolled clinical trial using a historical control group, Arom et al. (89) reported that modification of $PaCO_2$ or mean arterial pressure in response to EEG abnormalities was associated with improved neurologic outcome. Edmonds and colleagues (90) reported a similar, nonrandomized study in which EEG changes were predictive of adverse postoperative outcome in a historical control group; a later group of patients managed with higher mean arterial pressure during bypass had fewer EEG findings and a lower rate of "disorientation" (4% versus 29%).

Bashein et al. (87) reanalyzed a prospective study by Witoszka et al. (91) and concluded that, using a prevalence rate of 10% for postoperative deficits, the false-positive fraction of EEG abnormalities is 60% and the false-negative 75%. For a 5% postoperative deficit rate, the figures would rise to 76% false-positive and 87% false-negative. Of 118 patients in a study by Salerno et al. (92), 22 (19%) had an EEG abnormality during CPB, but only 2 had clinical evidence of neurologic injury. Two patients with a normal EEG throughout surgery had hemispheric infarcts identified in the recovery room; the authors concluded that these occurred after surgery.

In summary, 1 to 4 channel EEG recordings can be used clinically to monitor

the expected effects of hypothermia and anesthetic agents such as thiopental (11). Such a method may also detect global cerebral hypoperfusion during marked decreases in systemic perfusion flow rate or hemispheric asymmetry in patients with cerebrovascular disease. More discrete regional discrimination will require a greater number of recording channels and correction for the effects of body temperature and electrical artifact. Despite persuasive rhetoric from the manufacturers of monitoring devices, no prospective, controlled, randomized studies document the clinical efficacy of EEG monitoring in reducing perioperative brain injury (93, 94). Those few uncontrolled studies that have reported a correlation between EEG parameters of cerebral ischemia and outcome (89, 90) have found improved outcome with higher blood pressure during bypass, contradicting the bulk of published work (see below). This disparity will require further elucidation.

Regional Cerebral Blood Flow and Metabolism

Although no data link cerebral blood flow and metabolism to neurologic and neuropsychologic outcome, extensive clinical and experimental studies have helped to clarify cerebral physiology during extracorporeal circulation. In particular, various reports have elucidated actual cerebral changes induced by changes in pump flow rate, blood pressure, etc. Such information helps us understand mechanisms of brain injury and explain the impact of various management strategies. Sarnquist (95) has emphasized how important these issues are—because every day in the operating room, we are faced with practical dilemmas about optimal perfusion management for our patients. If postoperative brain injury is found to be related to the total embolic load delivered to the cerebral circulation intraoperatively

(96), knowledge gained from these physiologic studies may assist us to modify the conduct of bypass accordingly.

Cerebral physiologic changes during bypass have been studied mainly using xenon-133 clearance techniques in which dissolved isotope is injected into the systemic circulation either directly or via the extracorporeal circuit. A flexible helmet containing multiple gamma detectors (1 to 12 per hemisphere) fits around the head to record the rate at which xenon-133 concentrations decline within adjacent brain tissue (Fig. 21.5) (63), and clearance curves are displayed and analyzed on-line to derive regional cerebral blood flow in both hemispheres simultaneously.

Precisely speaking, the term "global cerebral blood flow" derives from the Kety-Schmidt inert gas method (actually hemispheric flow), while the xenon-133 clearance method measures *regional* cerebral blood flow, i.e., the brain blood flow directly under each gamma detector. However, mean global cerebral blood flow can be stated as the average of regional values derived from each detector (63).

Cerebral oxygen consumption is a derived variable, calculated from the product of mean global cerebral blood flow and the cerebral arteriovenous oxygen content difference stated as:

$$CMRo_2 = CBF \times a\text{-}jvDo_2$$

where $CMRo_2$ = cerebral oxygen consumption, CBF = mean global cerebral blood flow, and a-jvDo$_2$ = the cerebral arteriovenous oxygen content difference. Cerebral venous blood is sampled from a catheter inserted percutaneously into the internal jugular vein and advanced in a retrograde fashion into the jugular bulb (97).

In awake, normotensive, normothermic humans, cerebrovascular resistance and therefore cerebral blood flow are normally regulated by Pao$_2$, Paco$_2$, pressure autoregulation, and the level of metabolic demand (Fig. 21.6) (98, 99). Normal awake values are listed in Table 21.3.

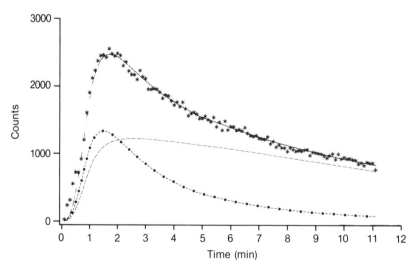

Figure 21.5. Xenon-133 head clearance curve after intravenous injection. The *asterisks* represent actual counted gamma emissions with the computer-fitted smoothed curve superimposed. The fast compartment (predominantly gray matter flow) [• – – •] and the more slowly clearing compartment (white matter and extracerebral tissues) [–] are also shown. (From Rogers AT, Stump DA. Cerebral physiologic monitoring. Crit Care Clin 1989;5:845–861.)

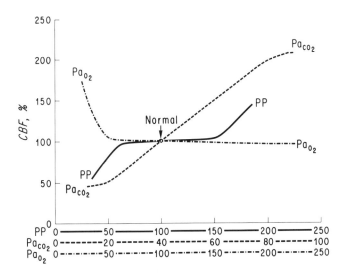

Figure 21.6. The relationship of cerebral blood flow (*CBF*) to perfusion pressure (*PP*), PaCO_2, and PaO_2 in awake, normothermic man. Units on the abscissa are in millimeters of mercury. (From Michenfelder JD. The awake brain. In: Michenfelder JD, ed. Anesthesia and the brain. Clinical, functional, metabolic, and vascular correlates. New York: Churchill Livingstone 1988:3–21.)

Table 21.3.   Cerebral Metabolism and Oxygen Delivery (Normothermic Awake Man)[a]

	Awake Values
CMRO_2 [CMRO_2 = CBF × (CaO_2 − CjvO_2)]	3.5 ml/100 g/min
CBF	50 ml/100 g/min
CaO_2	20 ml/100 ml
CjvO_2	13 ml/100 ml
CDO_2 [CDO_2 = CBF × CaO_2]	10 ml/100 g/min

[a]CMRO_2, cerebral oxygen consumption; CBF, cerebral blood flow; CaO_2, arterial oxygen content; CjvO_2, cerebral venous oxygen content; CDO_2, cerebral oxygen delivery.

CARBON DIOXIDE

In awake, normothermic man, carbon dioxide inhalation causes arteriolar dilation in the brain, whereas hypocapnia results in vasoconstriction (98) (Fig. 21.6).

In the current clinical practice of CPB, two distinct strategies exist for management of arterial carbon dioxide levels and blood pH during hypothermic bypass, i.e., *alpha-stat* and *pH-stat* (Table 21.4) (100–104). The intriguing question of which approach is preferable has been addressed in a variety of ways, including empiric debate (100, 101) and extrapolation of data from species for whom hypothermia is a more "normal" physiologic state than

Table 21.4.   Alpha-Stat and pH-Stat levels of PaCO_2 at Moderate Hypothermia

	PaCO_2 at 28.5°C[a] (mm Hg)	PaCO_2 at 37°C[b] (mm Hg)
pH—stat	40	60
Alpha—stat	27	40

[a]Body temperature.
[b]Blood gas analyzer temperature.

man (103, 105, 106). This controversy has been summarized in a recent editorial by Prough and colleagues (107).

In 1966, Wollman et al. (108) reported that CO_2 responsiveness was preserved during bypass with mild-to-moderate systemic hypothermia. Since then, the majority of studies have agreed with their conclusions (63, 64, 109–111) (Fig. 21.7). However, some controversy exists: in 1983, Henriksen and colleagues (112) reported that PaCO_2 responsiveness is virtually absent during extracorporeal circulation; in 1989, using an argon saturation and desaturation method, Soma and coworkers (113) failed to find a correlation between carbon dioxide blood levels and cerebral blood flow. Significantly, both of these studies used carbon dioxide levels in the higher range, equivalent to the pH-stat strategy. Perhaps because of specific patient or anesthesia factors, study subjects already

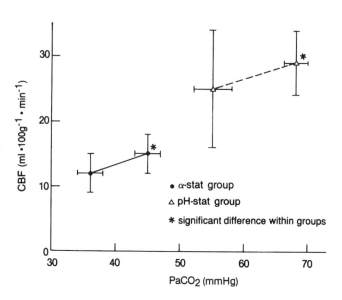

Figure 21.7. Relation between mean ± SD cerebral blood flow (*CBF*) (xenon-133 clearance) and mean ± SD partial pressure of CO_2 uncorrected for temperature (PaCO_2) in patients during CPB. •, group 1 (n=13); △, group 2 (n=12). *, $p<0.05$ different from low PaCO_2 within group by two-way repeated-measures analysis of variance. (From Prough DS, Rogers AT, Stump DA, Mills SA, Gravlee GP, Taylor C. Hypercarbia depresses cerebral oxygen consumption during cardiopulmonary bypass. Stroke 1990;21:1162–1166.)

had maximal cerebral vasodilation, with no further arteriolar response possible upon increasing carbon dioxide concentrations. Alternatively, these conflicting conclusions may relate to differences in cerebral blood flow methods.

Prough et al. (111) found that cerebral oxygen consumption is depressed by high levels of temperature-uncorrected PaCO_2 equivalent to extreme pH-stat management in humans during bypass at 28°C. The mechanism may involve the anesthetic/narcotic effect of carbon dioxide potentiated by hypothermia and narcotic agents. Hypercarbia depresses cerebral oxygen consumption in normothermic, anesthetized animals (114–116). Studies in head injury patients reported by Obrist et al. (117) have also suggested a relationship between CMRO_2 and PaCO_2.

TEMPERATURE

In animals undergoing hypothermic CPB, cerebral blood flow and cerebral oxygen consumption decrease with falling systemic temperatures (118, 119). Similarly, in humans, cerebral blood flow and cerebral oxygen consumption are decreased (63, 109–111, 120). During

systemic rewarming, cerebral blood flow increases once more to approximate prebypass levels (109, 110).

BLOOD PRESSURE

Cerebral perfusion is governed by the formulas

$$CBF = \frac{CPP}{CVR}$$

$$CPP = MAP - (ICP \text{ or } JVP)$$

where *CBF* = cerebral blood flow, *CPP* = cerebral perfusion pressure, *MAP* = mean arterial pressure, *ICP* = intracranial pressure, *JVP* = jugular bulb venous pressure, and *CVR* = cerebrovascular resistance.

In awake man, autoregulation maintains global brain perfusion constant over a wide range of mean arterial blood pressures, from 50 to 150 mm Hg (Fig. 21.6) (98). Hypercarbia induces changes consistent with impairment of autoregulation, i.e., cerebral blood flow becomes "pressure passive" (121, 122).

Early studies of cerebral autoregulation during moderately hypothermic nonpulsatile CPB in humans resulted in disagreement (110, 112, 123). Differing acid-base management accounts for these conflicting results: Govier et al. (110) adjusted $Paco_2$ to approximately 40 mm Hg, *uncorrected for body temperature* (alpha-stat) and reported preservation of autoregulation down to a mean arterial pressure of 30 mm Hg. In contrast, Lundar et al. (123) used a *temperature-corrected* $Paco_2$ of 37.5 mm Hg (pH-stat) and concluded that brain blood flow was pressure-passive.

Murkin et al. (109) confirmed that with alpha-stat management, cerebral blood flow is independent of cerebral perfusion pressure over a range of 20 to 100 mm Hg, whereas during pH-stat bypass, cerebral blood flow varies directly with perfusion pressure. Rogers et al. (124) reported cerebral blood flow responses to phenylephrine infusion in alpha-stat and pH-stat patients. Over the range of pressures studied (mean arterial pressure, 55 to 85 mm Hg) alpha-stat patients showed no significant change in cerebral blood flow during phenylephrine infusion (Fig. 21.8). In contrast, during pH-stat bypass, cerebral blood flow increased with rising mean arterial pressure. Collectively, these data suggest that the pH-stat method of managing $Paco_2$ and pH produces cerebral effects analogous to acute hypercarbia.

Profound hypothermia (18 to 20°C) and deep hypothermic circulatory arrest may induce a different physiologic profile than moderate hypothermia. Such conditions may induce cerebral vasoparesis, resulting in pressure-dependency of cerebral blood flow even with alpha-stat management (125).

PUMP FLOW RATE

Recent experimental and clinical investigations provide conflicting conclusions regarding the relationships among pump flow rate, cerebral blood flow, and cerebral oxygen consumption during CPB (110, 113, 126–130). Interpretation of

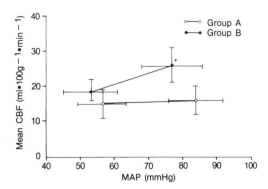

Figure 21.8. Cerebral blood flow (*CBF*) response (xenon-133 clearance) to phenylephrine infusion in patients in *Group A* ($Paco_2$ 41 mm Hg, uncorrected for body temperature) and *Group B* ($Paco_2$ 54 mm Hg, uncorrected for body temperature) patients, corrected for the effect of elapsed time between measurement intervals. $^*p<0.001$ for CBF within Group B. *MAP*, mean arterial pressure. (Reprinted with permission from Rogers AT, Stump DA, Gravlee GP, et al. Response of cerebral blood flow to phenylephrine infusion during hypothermic cardiopulmonary bypass: influence of $Paco_2$ management. Anesthesiology 1988; 69:547–551.)

these studies requires careful consideration of the species studied, the methods used, and the precise bypass conditions. In particular, the effects of variations in systemic *flow rate* must be differentiated from those due to the influence of *perfusion pressure*.

Using similar methods and anesthetic techniques in various clinical studies, Govier et al. (110), Murkin et al. (127), Rogers et al. (126), and Venn et al. (64) varied perfusion flow rate from 1 to 2.25 liters/min/m² during both alpha-stat and pH-stat bypass and found no correlation between perfusion flow rate and cerebral blood flow or cerebral oxygen consumption. In contrast, Soma et al. (113) studied patients during stable pH-stat bypass and concluded that perfusion flow rate and cerebral blood flow are directly proportional. In addition, Soma and colleagues found no correlation between cerebral blood flow, $Paco_2$ level, and mean arterial pressure— observations that differ markedly from those of most other investigators. In the clinical study by Rogers et al. (126), during both alpha-stat and pH-stat bypass, alterations in systemic flow rate between 1.75 and 2.25 liters/min/m² did not cause corresponding changes in mean arterial pressure; rather, systemic vascular resistance varied with perfusion flow rate in a reciprocal fashion, accommodating variations in systemic flow without accompanying changes in systemic arterial pressure. Importantly, as systemic flow rate increased, there was no corresponding change in cerebral perfusion, an observation that might have important implications for the distribution of emboli.

Studies in profoundly hypothermic animals have shown a direct relationship between pump flow rate and cerebral blood flow; however, mean arterial pressure appeared to vary as systemic flow rate was changed (128, 129). Thus, these findings may reflect impairment of pressure autoregulation under profoundly hypothermic conditions.

OXYGEN

In awake volunteers, hypoxemia (Fi_{O_2} = 0.1) increases cerebral blood flow by 35% (Fig. 21.6); less well known is the fact that *hyperoxia* constricts the cerebral vasculature, causing a 15% decrease in blood flow (98, 131). Thus, cerebral oxygen delivery is preserved, a form of autoregulation. Hypocapnia, which usually causes cerebral vasoconstriction, cannot override this protective mechanism during hypoxemia (131). Studies of hypoxemia during otherwise steady-state bypass in humans are lacking for obvious ethical reasons. One clinical study by Rogers et al. (132) documents cerebrovascular changes associated with hyperoxic conditions as Pa_{O_2} was changed randomly within a range of approximately 125 to 300 mm Hg. During alpha-stat bypass management, with other variables held constant, cerebrovascular responsiveness to Pa_{O_2} was preserved: higher Pa_{O_2} levels were associated with cerebral blood flow levels approximately 15% lower than those found under normoxic conditions. Corresponding data for pH-stat conditions are not available.

AGE

Advancing age has been associated with decreases in cerebral blood flow and cerebral oxygen consumption in awake, normothermic subjects (133). In a large study of cardiac surgical patients without symptomatic cerebrovascular disease, Roy and co-workers (134) found that cerebral blood flow was not affected by age, while cerebral oxygen consumption decreased slightly with advancing age. They concluded that advanced age per se does not predispose to global cerebral ischemia during hypothermic, nonpulsatile CPB. The same group of investigators concluded that advanced age does not affect the relationship between carbon dioxide tension and cerebral blood flow (135), or the preservation of cerebral autoregulation under alpha-stat conditions (136). Similarly, Brusino et al. (137) found that age did not affect cerebral pressure autoregulation. As a consequence, recommendations for higher mean arterial pressures (>70 mm Hg) in elderly patients may be unnecessary, but without further study, such conclusions should not be extrapolated to patients with symptomatic cerebrovascular disease.

CEREBROVASCULAR DISEASE

In awake normothermic patients, cerebrovascular disease is associated with persistent but reduced cerebral responsiveness to Pa_{CO_2} (133, 138). During carotid endarterectomy, Pa_{CO_2} may influence the regional distribution of cerebral blood flow as well as the overall level: hypercarbia may cause an intracerebral "steal" whereby global cerebral vasodilation diverts blood flow from brain regions at high ischemic risk to well-perfused regions during carotid occlusion (139). It is interesting to speculate whether the same phenomenon would be observed during pH-stat bypass. Although most studies of cerebral hemodynamics during bypass have been confined to patients without clinical evidence of cerebrovascular disease, some data are available. In a series of nine patients with a past history of stroke, transient ischemic attacks, or previous carotid endarterectomy, Gravlee et al. (140) observed no regional maldistribution of cerebral blood flow in association with increases in Pa_{CO_2}. Specifically, no regional inhomogeneity (steal) was seen at higher levels of Pa_{CO_2}.

ANESTHETICS

Most reports in cardiac surgical patients have used high-dose opioid anesthesia with various combinations of oxygen, nitrous oxide, and benzodiazepines. Measurements recorded in the interval between induction of anesthesia and onset of bypass at mild systemic hypothermia (34 to 36°C) typically indicate cerebral blood flow and oxygen consumption levels that are approximately 50% of those observed in normothermic awake subjects (64, 110, 120, 140). During moderately hypothermic nonpulsatile bypass, blood flow and oxygen consumption decrease further (64, 110, 111). Woodcock and colleagues (120) have studied the cerebral physiologic effects of both thiopental and isoflurane when used to induce electroencephalographic burst suppression in fentanyl-anesthetized bypass patients. Both thiopental-treated and isoflurane-treated patients had significantly lower cerebral oxygen consumption than fentanyl-treated subjects. However, the two treatment groups differed with respect to cerebral blood flow rates. Thiopental-treated patients had lower cerebral blood flow rates than fentanyl-anesthetized subjects, whereas isoflurane patients had cerebral blood flow rates comparable to those receiving only fentanyl.

INFLUENCE OF TIME

Using two different study designs, Prough, Rogers, and colleagues et al. concluded that cerebrovascular resistance changes over time during stable hypothermic nonpulsatile bypass (124, 141). First, in 12 patients (6 alpha-stat, 6 pH-stat), two sequential cerebral blood flow measurements separated by 20 to 30 minutes were obtained under steady-state conditions with no change in other controlled variables such as Pa_{CO_2}, blood pressure, temperature, etc. (124); all subjects had a fall in cerebral blood flow with time (0.7 to 1% per min) (Fig. 21.9). Second, in another study that examined cerebrovascular reactivity to the vasodilating effect of carbon dioxide, the duration of bypass altered cerebrovascular reactivity such that cerebral blood flow failed to increase in response to rising Pa_{CO_2} levels (141). This time-dependent effect was not accompanied by a concomitant fall in cerebral oxygen consumption, so progressive brain cooling cannot account for the progressive increase in cerebrovascular resistance. Stump et al. (142) confirmed this time-dependent effect using transcranial Doppler measurements of middle cerebral artery flow velocity.

This decline in cerebral blood flow at a constant mean arterial pressure could be attributed to progressive vasoconstriction (from unidentified factors) or to microvascular obstruction (e.g., from accumulating embolic debris). Govier et al. (110) found no relationship between cerebral blood flow and duration of CPB. This discrepancy may be explained by differences in experimental design and statistical analysis, since Govier et al. studied multiple data points in an extensive series of patients and subjected the results to factor analysis. Additionally, their patients did not experience a period of stable hypothermia. Because of the profound effects of Pa_{CO_2} and temperature on cerebral blood flow, subtle effects, such as those attributable to bypass duration, might

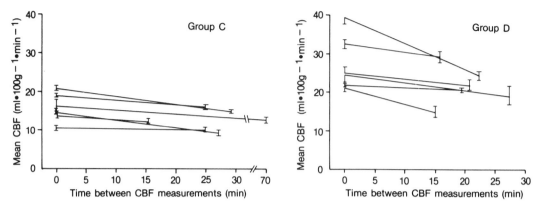

Figure 21.9. Spontaneous decline in cerebral blood flow (*CBF*) (xenon-133 clearance) during CPB for patients in *Group C* (Pa_{CO_2} 40 mm Hg, uncorrected for body temperature) and *Group D* (Pa_{CO_2} 58 mm Hg, uncorrected for body temperature). Data points represent mean global CBF for individual patients at each time interval, ±SD of the 16 regional values. (Reprinted with permission from Rogers AT, Stump DA, Gravlee GP, et al. Response of cerebral blood flow to phenylephrine infusion during hypothermic cardiopulmonary bypass: influence of Pa_{CO_2} management. Anesthesiology 1988;69:547–551.)

be overshadowed in the latter type of analysis.

Doppler Sonography

Transcranial Doppler techniques that measure flow velocity in the middle cerebral artery (143) have been used as a qualitative index of cerebral perfusion to confirm directional changes already established by xenon-133 clearance (142, 144, 145). An important development has been the use of Doppler sonography for the detection and quantification of systemic emboli (Fig. 21.10). Emboli moving past an ultrasonic transducer have a higher acoustic contrast with plasma than red blood cells and produce Doppler signals of higher amplitude than normal blood flow (146). Several reports demonstrate a high incidence of embolic events in the middle cerebral artery during weaning from bypass (147–149). An alternative method that places a transducer over the common carotid artery has also demonstrated a high incidence of embolic events, especially during manipulation of the aorta and initiation of cardiac ejection (65) (Table 21.5). Preliminary data indicate that the number of microem-

bolic events detected may correlate with postoperative neuropsychologic deficit rates (Table 21.6).

Retinal Fluorescein Angiography

Using fluorescein angiography to visualize retinal vessels <30 µm, Blauth and colleagues (150, 151) have observed diffuse retinal microembolism in cardiac surgical patients (Fig. 21.11): in 21 patients undergoing coronary artery bypass grafting with bubble oxygenators, 100% of intraoperative fluorescein angiograms were abnormal. In most cases, the changes resolved by the 8th postoperative day. Psychometric testing was more frequently abnormal in those patients with extensive microvascular lesions. In a canine model of CPB, these occlusions were shown histologically to be intravascular platelet-fibrin microaggregates (150).

Transcranial Oximetry

Recently, considerable interest has been shown in a noninvasive device that monitors brain oxygen metabolism (152–154), a concept originally developed by

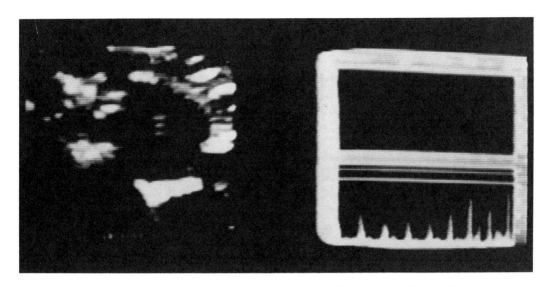

Figure 21.10. Arterial sonography in a canine model of systemic embolization. The *left panel* is a coronal view of canine aorta, (B-mode image) showing 200 micron polystyrene microspheres within the lumen. The *right lower panel* shows continuous wave Doppler with corresponding flow velocity signals. (Provided by Dr. David A. Stump, Department of Anesthesia, Bowman Gray School of Medicine, Winston-Salem, NC.)

Table 21.5.   Number of Emboli Detected in Hospitalized Patients Using a Carotid Emboli Monitoring Device[a]

Patient Type	No.	Total No. of Emboli Detected		
		Mean (SEM)	Fewest Detected	Most Detected
Asymptomatic health[b]	5	0 (0.0)	0	0
Coronary artery bypass graft[c]	8	61.8 (9.0)	23	107
Valve replacement[c]	8	1339 (546.3)	38	4455

[a] From Stump DA, Stein CS, Tegeler CH, et al. Validity and reliability of an ultrasound device for detecting carotid emboli. J Neuroimag 1991;1:18–22.)
[b] No. of emboli observed during 1 hour of monitoring.
[c] No. of emboli observed during surgery; significantly greater than the number observed in a healthy group ($p < 0.05$).

Jobsis et al. (155). Briefly, a dual spectrophotometer is applied across the cranium to estimate hemoglobin saturation, using a frequency close to the infrared range. Smith et al. (153) have emphasized that the device is sensitive to all hemoglobin in the tissue of interest (arterial, arteriolar, capillary, venular, and venous), and thus differs from pulse oximetry that measures only arterial hemoglobin. The clinical role of this technique and the degree of correlation with outcome have yet to be established.

Table 21.6.   Relationship Between Microembolic Events and Neuropsychologic Outcome 8 Weeks After Cardiac Surgery[a]

MEE[b] Count During CPB	No. of Patients	No. with Deficit	% with Deficit
<200	58	5	9
201–500	13	3	23
501–1000	16	5	31
>1000	7	3	43

[a] From Newman S. Neuropsychological and psychological changes following cardiac surgery. In: Smith P, Taylor K, eds. The brain and cardiac surgery. London: Edward Arnold, 1992.
[b] Microembolic event.

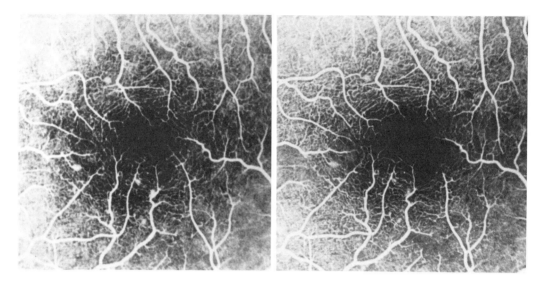

Figure 21.11. Retinal fluorescein angiograms. The *left panel* is a normal preoperative study. The dark central area is the macula. A repeat angiogram (*right panel*) after bypass using a bubble oxygenator. Comparison with the preoperative study shows areas of nonperfusion around the macula at 6 o'clock and from 9 to 12 o'clock, associated with truncation of the retinal arterioles in those areas. (Reprinted with permission from Blauth C. Assessment of cerebrovascular microembolism by retinal fluorescein angiography. Perfusion 1989;4:123–129.)

IMPACT OF INTRAOPERATIVE MANAGEMENT ON NERVOUS SYSTEM INJURY

Surgical Factors

Cerebral emboli resulting from manipulation of a diseased ascending aorta are thought to be a major cause of neurologic morbidity after aortocoronary bypass (1, 156). Preoperatively, calcification of the aorta may be noted on chest roentgenogram, cineangiography, or computed axial tomography of the chest (156). Intraoperatively, the surgeon usually palpates the proposed aortic cannulation site to delineate the presence and extent of atherosclerotic plaque. Findings range in severity from a normal aortic wall to the so-called porcelain aorta (157), and adjustments in the cannulation site are generally made according to these findings. However, clinical appreciation of atherosclerosis in the ascending aorta may be relatively insensitive (156, 158), and Culliford et al. (156) have commented that even gentle palpa-

tion of a severely diseased aorta may be hazardous.

Barzilai and colleagues (158) used Doppler ultrasonography intraoperatively to characterize the proximal aorta before placing the aortic inflow cannula or the aortic cross-clamp. In 8 of 33 patients, atheromatous or calcific lesions were identified by ultrasound at the clinically selected sites. Typically, plaques not palpable by clinical examination were noncalcified, containing loose necrotic debris with the potential for systemic embolization (Fig. 21.12). Although this ultrasound technique may decrease stroke risk, no data exist to document cost-effectiveness.

Severe disease in the ascending aorta may necessitate considerable modification of the surgical plan, e.g., retrograde cardioplegic techniques or suturing proximal aortocoronary anastomoses while the aorta remains cross-clamped to avoid side clamp application. More severe generalized disease (e.g., porcelain aorta) may preclude conventional approaches to revascularization altogether. Alternative strategies include the use of internal mammary artery grafting, femoral arterial cannulation sites, or even deep hypothermic circulatory arrest (156, 159).

Historically, several series have documented a higher incidence of stroke after open ventricle procedures than following myocardial revascularization (28, 72, 73). Serial data from one institution document a marked decline in neuropsychiatric complications after open ventricle procedures between 1982 and 1986 (from 13.3% to 7.5%) even in the absence of any neuroprotective agent (11, 28). Refinements in surgical technique including meticulous debridement, irrigation of cardiac chambers, and evacuation of air prior to the resumption of cardiac ejection may have contributed to this decline (11). Despite such precautions, 80 to 100% of patients have intravascular air at the termination of bypass, detectable by transesophageal echo- cardiography (160) or an ultrasonic transducer placed over the carotid artery (65, 161).

Duration of CPB

The vast majority of reports have linked the duration of extracorporeal circulation with neurologic and neuropsychologic deterioration (1, 5, 11, 31, 68, 72, 78). This may reflect the deleterious effect of bypass per se, or an increase in risk due to patient factors such as severity of atherosclerosis, valvular calcification, etc.

Oxygenator Type

With regard to stroke rate, no data compare membrane and bubble oxygenators. Blauth et al. (151) noted significantly fewer retinal microvascular lesions in patients undergoing coronary artery bypass

Figure 21.12. Ultrasonic backscatter images of potential cannulation sites in the ascending aorta of patients undergoing cardiac surgery (transverse views). *Right panel,* image from a patient with widespread atherosclerotic disease. *Narrow arrowhead* depicts calcified plaque, while *broader arrowhead* denotes a region with no discernable calcification. *Left panel,* image from a patient with a homogenous calcified plaque (*arrowhead*). (Reprinted with permission from Barzilai B, Marshall WG Jr, Saffitz JE, Kouchoukos N. Avoidance of embolic complications by ultrasonic characterization of the ascending aorta. Circulation 1989;80:I-275–I-279.)

grafting using a membrane oxygenator as compared to a bubble oxygenator (50% versus 100%). No large-scale clinical trials are available to document significant differences in cerebral outcome among various types of oxygenators. However, at least three studies with relatively small numbers of patients have shown a trend toward improved neuropsychologic outcome using membrane oxygenators compared to bubble oxygenators (72, 78, 151).

Arterial Filters

Taylor et al. (162) demonstrated a significant reduction in levels of creatine kinase (brain fraction) in the cerebral spinal fluid if arterial filtration was used during bypass in dogs. Using transcranial Doppler, Pugsley et al. (149) reported markedly reduced microemboli counts in patients when a filter was used, with an associated lesser tendency toward postoperative neuropsychologic deterioration. Several authors have concluded that arterial filtration can reduce neuropsychologic dysfunction following cardiac surgery (163–166). Some controversy still exists (35): Aris et al. (167) found no significant difference in the incidence of nervous system dysfunction with or without the use of arterial line filtration.

Hypothermia

During cardiac surgical procedures, moderate hypothermia (25 to 30°C) may be induced to facilitate myocardial cooling and protection. Conventional wisdom dictates that such a maneuver also provides cerebral protection while the brain is subjected to the insult of nonpulsatile bypass. For treatment of complex congenital heart disease or repair of the thoracic aorta, deep hypothermia (<20°C) may be induced to provide neuroprotection for periods of total circulatory arrest (168, 169). Considerable experimental evidence supports the concept of cerebral protection by hypother-

mia, with the mechanism generally attributed to a progressive decrease in cerebral oxygen consumption with falling temperature (170). However, a more complex interrelationship may be at work (171, 172). For example, Swain et al. (173) have shown that hypothermia not only alters the energy state of brain cells, but increases intracellular pH. Since intracellular acidosis contributes to brain cell injury and death (174), hypothermia may work by altering the degree of pH change rather than simply by metabolic suppression.

For most patients undergoing myocardial revascularization or valvular procedures, the brain is at risk not only during hypothermic bypass, but also during normothermic periods when cerebral embolization is known to occur (11, 149, 175). The greatest risk of macroembolization from the surgical field occurs with aortic manipulation and resumption of left ventricular ejection, so hypothermia during bypass conveys little benefit. Microemboli do occur during stable extracorporeal perfusion (149), but are most frequently observed in close temporal relationship to aortic manipulation, onset of bypass, and separation from bypass (149, 175). Despite the use of moderate hypothermia, persisting neuropsychologic deficit has been detected in over one-third of cardiac surgical patients (9, 23). No prospective clinical trials have compared hypothermic and normothermic bypass in relation to either neurologic or neuropsychologic outcome. With the recent interest in warm cardioplegic techniques (176), we may be forced to defend moderate hypothermia as a clinically effective neuroprotective tool, or abandon it. For children undergoing complex cardiac repairs under total circulatory arrest, profound hypothermia is likely to remain an essential adjunct (177).

Acid-Base Management

Bashein et al. (178) studied patients undergoing a combination of valvular and coronary artery bypass procedures and found no difference in neurologic or neuropsychologic outcome with either pH-stat or alpha-stat management. One possible explanation is that only a subset of patients in each treatment group is vulnerable to nervous system injury (107). A subset of patients in the alpha-stat group might be vulnerable to cerebral hypoperfusion; a subset of patients in the pH-stat group may be exposed to an excess microembolic load, the so-called "luxury perfusion syndrome" (Fig. 21.13). Alternatively, the results may reflect the lack of any real difference in blood gas values between groups during normothermic intervals of risk. Third, the relatively small sample size may have limited the predictive power of this study. Fourth, as discussed above, the use of group mean data to compute a postoperative deficit rate may mask those patients who suffered a deterioration in performance, because some patients improve with practice.

Mean Arterial Pressure

Early studies suggested an association between hypotension during bypass and brain injury after cardiac surgery (26, 62, 76, 77, 179). Stockard and co-workers (62)

coined the phrase "tm50," arbitrarily defined as the integral of mean arterial pressure <50 mm Hg over time in minutes. A tm50 of 100 mm Hg-minutes was considered to be the critical threshold for ischemic brain damage. In marked contrast is the bulk of recently published work suggesting that no such association exists, for either neurologic or neuropsychologic outcome (1, 11, 19, 28, 34, 72, 73, 78, 178, 180, 181). Stockard et al. recommended a lower threshold of 50 mm Hg for blood pressure during bypass in typical cases, with a higher level (>70 mm Hg) for older patients and those with preexisting neurologic disease. In light of more recent data, such recommendations may lack substance, although no prospective studies have randomly assigned patients to either higher or lower blood pressure management during bypass to assess impact on postoperative brain function.

Pump Flow

Conventionally, pump flow rates are maintained in the range of 1.75 to 2.5 liters/min/m² (45 to 65 ml/kg/min) during hypothermia. However, the use of lower flow rates (1 to 1.75 liters/min/m²; 25 to 45 ml/kg/min) carries several potential

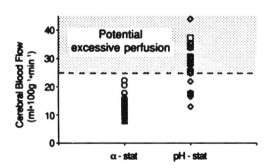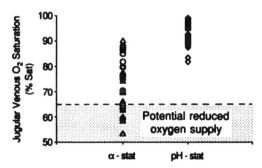

Figure 21.13. *Left panel,* individual patient values for cerebral blood flow (xenon-133) during α-stat and pH-stat bypass (moderate hypothermia). These overlap considerably, although the highest values are in the pH-stat group. *Right panel,* individual patient values for jugular venous oxygen saturation during alpha-stat and pH-stat bypass. By knowing Paco₂, one cannot predict individual levels of cerebral blood flow or cerebral oxygen extraction. (Reprinted with permission from Prough DS, Stump DA, Troost BT. $PaCO_2$ management during cardiopulmonary bypass: intriguing physiologic rationale, convincing clinical data, evolving hypothesis? Anesthesiology 1990;72:3–6.)

benefits, including decreased trauma to blood cells and platelets, and reductions in noncoronary collateral flow. No prospective controlled studies have been published that compare "low-flow" bypass with conventional flow rates in this context. Many studies of postoperative outcome do not specifically distinguish between perfusion pressure and pump flow rate in reporting their results, thus confounding interpretation. Two studies provide some information, that of Kolkka and Hilberman (72), and that of Ellis and co-workers (180). Ellis et al. examined 30 coronary artery bypass patients with neurologic and neuropsychologic testing before and after surgery using flow rates <40 ml/kg/min. Some deterioration in performance was noted in 17% of patients, which the authors considered comparable to other reports in the literature. In addition, those patients with evidence of brain injury experienced flow rates and perfusion pressures comparable to those who did not. Kolkka and Hilberman studied 204 patients under similar conditions, but included various cardiac surgical procedures. They concluded that patients with postoperative deficits had similar flows and pressures compared to patients with no deficit, and that the overall incidence was comparable to other studies using more conventional perfusion techniques.

Blood Glucose Concentration

Considerable experimental evidence suggests that preexisting hyperglycemia exacerbates ischemic brain injury (182, 183). The extent of cerebral damage correlates with blood glucose (184) and brain glucose concentrations (185). Corresponding clinical data are available, but are largely anecdotal in nature because of a lack of prospective controlled trials (183, 186). During cardiac surgery, blood glucose concentrations rise progressively, with dramatic increases noted during systemic rewarming and separation from bypass, even in nondiabetic patients (187). The mechanism is a combination of insulin resistance and hypothermic suppression of insulin secretion (187).

Metz and Keats (188) have recommended using glucose-containing priming solutions during bypass to improve perioperative fluid balance, stating that such a practice does not affect the incidence of major stroke. Lanier (183) has condemned this recommendation in a careful review of the cardiovascular and neurologic implications. No randomized clinical studies currently determine whether blood glucose should be tightly controlled during cardiac surgery or whether this might affect postoperative morbidity.

Barbiturates

In 1982, Slogoff and associates (28) reported the use of thiopental for neuroprotection during coronary artery bypass grafting and open ventricle procedures. This was a logical extension of animal studies showing that thiopental reduced brain injury in models of focal cerebral ischemia (189, 190). Pre- and postoperative testing included a neurologic and psychiatric examination; limited neuropsychologic testing was also done (Trail-Making A & B). In patients given thiopental (15 mg/kg) prior to initiation of bypass, fewer neuropsychiatric complications were detected compared to patients receiving diazepam (0.15 mg/kg), but the difference was not statistically significant.

A similar study, reported from the same institution in 1986, used a more rigorous protocol (11): only open ventricle procedures were included and the dose and duration of thiopental administration were increased, such that EEG burst suppression was maintained from before aortic cannulation until after weaning from bypass. Total doses of thiopental averaged 40 ± 8 mg/kg. Thiopental-treated patients had an incidence of transient (early) neuropsychiatric abnormalities similar to control patients (5.6% versus 8.6%, not significant). However, at 10 days postoperatively, thiopental-treated patients were free of abnormalities, while 7.5% of control patients were still affected. Other differences were noted between treatment groups, including a more frequent need for inotropic infusions (7% versus 1%), prolonged awakening time, and prolonged ventilatory support (19 ± 8 hours versus 14 ± 5 hours) in thiopental-treated subjects. Interestingly, 27% of patients with no clinically detectable abnormality displayed deterioration in test scores on Trails A and B; thiopental and control groups were equally affected. The authors recommended routine adoption of this preventive strategy for open ventricle procedures, and the study was hailed as the first determination that thiopental offered brain protection in a clinical setting (191). Todd (12) urges caution, however, in widely extrapolating results from this study performed with bubble oxygenators, normothermia, and no arterial line filtration.

In an attempt to avoid undesirable side effects, Metz and Slogoff (192) compared thiopental given as a single bolus dose (15 mg/kg) prior to aortic declamping with the previously described continuous infusion method (total dose, 36 ± 10 mg/kg). Only open ventricle procedures were included; neurologic and psychiatric examinations were similar to the two previous studies from the same institution; no neuropsychologic tests were administered. The incidence of persistent neuropsychiatric dysfunction at 10 days was extremely low (<2%) and comparable in both groups. Inotropic support was required in a similar number of cases in both treatment groups. Patients receiving bolus dose thiopental were, however, extubated sooner than infusion patients (16 ± 5 hours versus 18 ± 6 hours; P < 0.05). Since the authors consider it unethical to deny thiopental neuroprotection to patients undergoing open ventricle procedures, no control group was studied in this report. Metz and Slogoff concluded that since bolus administration of thiopental sodium is associated with no

more frequent central nervous system deficits than the infusion technique, the bolus should be adopted as a clinical standard of care.

In an accompanying editorial, Prough and Mills (193) discussed the general applicability of these conclusions. Acceptance of these recommendations necessitates several assumptions: first, that cannulation of the aorta per se does not entail significant neurologic risks; second, that maintenance of bypass is not associated with a progressive risk of microembolic damage; and third, that important neurologic injury occurs primarily from ejection of macroemboli from the heart and that other potential sources are relatively unimportant. Available data, although inconclusive, do not warrant these assumptions. In addition, the very low incidence of gross neurologic deficits reported by Metz and Slogoff suggest that potential therapeutic interventions can be studied only in extraordinarily large series. An alternative would be to include the more subtle and sensitive neurologic and cognitive deficits that have been reported by many investigators.

Thiopental neuroprotection for coronary artery bypass graft patients has been addressed by Zaidan and colleagues (7): 300 patients were randomized to receive either placebo or thiopental by continuous infusion from before aortic cannulation until after weaning from bypass. Thiopental-treated subjects required more frequent inotropic and vasopressor support, and had a longer time to awakening and (6 ± 4 hours versus 4 ± 2 hours) tracheal extubation (22 ± 18 hours versus 17 ± 10 hours), compared with placebo patients. No difference was seen in the incidence of major stroke between groups (3.3% thiopental versus 1.3% placebo; not significant), although thiopental patients had a higher incidence of lethargy in the early postoperative period. No neuropsychologic testing was included. In an accompanying editorial, Todd (12) concluded that thiopental therapy has no place in the routine management of patients undergoing myo-cardial revascularization.

Calcium Channel Antagonists

Nimodipine, a calcium channel antagonist that penetrates the blood-brain barrier, has been found to be neuroprotective in several experimental and clinical models of acute cerebral ischemia (194–196). Postulated mechanisms include cerebral vaso-dilation with prevention of postischemic hypoperfusion (197) or attenuation of ischemia-induced intracellular acidosis (198).

Forsman et al. (199) reported a small study of 39 patients undergoing a variety of cardiac surgical procedures who received nimodipine. Neuropsychologic testing 6 months after operation suggested some benefits from treatment, but the authors con-cluded that the small number of patients studied precluded firm recommendations. Larger studies in more homogenous patient populations will determine the place of ni-modipine in our therapeutic armamen-tarium.

Prostacyclin

It has been postulated that cerebral microembolization by platelet aggregates may contribute to bypass-related brain injury. Fish et al. (19) conducted a random-ized, double-blind study to investigate whether inhibition of platelet aggregation by infusion of prostacyclin during bypass reduces neuropsychologic and neurologic dysfunction after coronary artery bypass grafting. No differences were detected be-tween treatment and placebo groups. Inter-estingly, since prostacyclin is also a vasodi-lator, mean arterial pressure was signifi-cantly lower in prostacyclin-treated pa-tients, apparently without adverse conse-quences. The work of Aren and colleagues (200) supports these findings.

CONCLUSION

Since the mid-1960s, a vast body of scientific work has been published docu-menting the incidence and nature of brain injury following cardiac surgery. During the last decade, we have markedly refined our measurement tools, encompassing neuro-psychologic testing as a sensitive, objective measure of subtle brain dysfunction that serves as a vital adjunct to careful neuro-logic examination. We have begun to under-stand the crucial importance of conducting prospective clinical studies and random-ized, controlled clinical trials in large series of patients, asking focused and specific questions. In our desire to conduct clinical trials that will answer questions about feasi-bility, safety, efficacy, and cost effectiveness of interventions, we must not forget that many questions relating to mechanism of injury remain unanswered. Thus, physio-logic studies in smaller groups of patients and animal models will continue to appear.

The next decade promises even more exciting developments. Will we be able to answer definitively the question of whether brain injury is caused by embolization or hypoperfusion? Will we improve the tech-nology of bypass further? Will we develop pharmacologic agents that can be used prophylactically, such as free radical scav-engers (201), that have favorable cost-benefit and risk-benefit ratios? Will totally new techniques, such as "cerebroplegia" (202, 203) be adopted into widespread clinical practice? Will hypothermic bypass come to be considered a relic of the Dark Ages? By the year 2000, will more extensive preoperative screening be done routinely in cardiac surgical candidates to assess "brain reserve," and quantify perioperative risk factors more precisely? This is a fascinating time to participate in the care of patients undergoing cardiopulmonary bypass.

Dedication

This chapter is dedicated in loving memory of the late Dr. Mary A. Bell, D.Phil, a colleague who ex-

emplified intelligence, industry, integrity, dedication, and humor.

Acknowledgments
Dr. Rogers wishes to acknowledge David Charles, CCP, and his perfusion staff at North Carolina Baptist Hospital, Winston-Salem, North Carolina, for their dedication in patient care and collaboration in research activity. She also wishes to thank Faith McLellan, Wilson Somerville, and their editorial staff for preparation of this manuscript.

REFERENCES

1. Gardner TJ, Horneffer PJ, Manolio TA, et al. Stroke following coronary artery bypass grafting: a ten-year study. Ann Thorac Surg 1985; 40:574–581.
2. Acinapura AJ, Rose DM, Cunningham JN Jr, Jacobowitz IJ, Kramer MD, Zisbrod Z. Coronary artery bypass in septuagenarians. Analysis of mortality and morbidity. Circulation 1988; 78(suppl I):I-179–I-184.
3. Shaw PJ, Bates D, Cartlidge NEF, et al. Neurologic and neuropsychological morbidity following major surgery: comparison of coronary artery bypass and peripheral vascular surgery. Stroke 1987;18:700–707.
4. Aberg T, Ronquist G, Tydén H, et al. Adverse effects on the brain in cardiac operations as assessed by biochemical, psychometric, and radiologic methods. J Thorac Cardiovasc Surg 1984;87:99–105.
5. Smith PL, Treasure T, Newman SP, et al. Cerebral consequences of cardiopulmonary bypass. Lancet 1986;1:823–825.
6. Breuer AC, Furlan AJ, Hanson MR, et al. Central nervous system complications of coronary artery bypass graft surgery: prospective analysis of 421 patients. Stroke 1983;14:682–687.
7. Zaidan JR, Klochany A, Martin WM, Ziegler JS, Harless DM, Andrews RB. Effect of thiopental on neurologic outcome following coronary artery bypass grafting. Anesthesiology 1991; 74:406–411.
8. Campbell DE, Raskin SA. Cerebral dysfunction after cardiopulmonary bypass: aetiology, manifestations and interventions. Perfusion 1990; 5:251–260.
9. Newman S, Smith P, Treasure T, Joseph P, Ell P, Harrison M. Acute neuropsychological consequences of coronary artery bypass surgery. Curr Psychol Res Rev 1987;6:115–124.
10. Newman S, Klinger L, Venn G, Smith P, Harrison M, Treasure T. Subjective reports of cognition in relation to assessed cognitive performance following coronary artery bypass surgery. J Psychosom Res 1989;33:227–233.
11. Nussmeier NA, Arlund C, Slogoff S. Neuropsychiatric complications after cardiopulmonary bypass: cerebral protection by a barbiturate. Anesthesiology 1986;64:165–170.
12. Todd M. Barbiturate protection and cardiac surgery: a different result. Anesthesiology 1991; 74:402–405.
13. Weintraub WS, Jones EL, Craver J, Guyton R, Cohen C. Determinants of prolonged length of hospital stay after coronary bypass surgery. Circulation 1989;80:276–284.
14. Harrison MJG, Schneidau A, Ho R, Smith PLC, Newman S, Treasure T. Cerebrovascular disease and functional outcome after coronary artery bypass surgery. Stroke 1989;20:235–237.
15. Coffey CE, Massey EW, Roberts KB, Curtis S, Jones RH, Pryor DB. Natural history of cerebral complications of coronary artery bypass graft surgery. Neurology 1983;33:1416–1421.
16. Martin WRW, Hashimoto SA. Stroke in coronary bypass surgery. Can J Neurol Sci 1982;9:21–26.
17. Shaw PJ, Bates D, Cartlidge NEF, Heaviside D, Julian DG, Shaw DA. Early neurological complications of coronary artery bypass surgery. Br Med J 1985;291:1384–1387.
18. Sotaniemi KA. Cerebral outcome after extracorporeal circulation. Comparison between prospective and retrospective evaluations. Arch Neurol 1983;40:75–77.
19. Fish KJ, Helms KN, Sarnquist FH, et al. A prospective, randomized study of the effects of prostacyclin on neuropsychologic dysfunction after coronary artery operation. J Thorac Cardiovasc Surg 1987;93:609–615.
20. Morin JE, Long R, Elleker MG, Eisen AA, Wynands E, Ralphs-Thibodeau S. Upper extremity neuropathies following median sternotomy. Ann Thorac Surg 1982;34:181–185.
21. Roy RC, Stafford MA, Charlton JE. Nerve injury and musculoskeletal complaints after cardiac surgery: influence of internal mammary artery dissection and left arm position. Anesth Analg 1988;67:277–279.
22. Gravlee GP, Hudspeth AS, Toole JF. Bilateral brachial paralysis from watershed infarction after coronary artery bypass. A report of two cases and review of the predisposing anatomic and physiological mechanisms. J Thorac Cardiovasc Surg 1984;88:742–747.
23. Newman S. The incidence and nature of neuropsychological morbidity following cardiac surgery. Perfusion 1989;4:93–100.
24. Freeman AM III, Folks DG, Sokol RS, et al. Cognitive function after coronary bypass surgery: effect of decreased cerebral blood flow. Am J Psychiatry 1985;142:110–112.
25. Lee WH, Miller W, Rowe J, Hairston P, Brady MP. Effects of extracorporeal circulation on person-

ality and cerebration. Ann Thorac Surg 1969; 7:562–570.

26. Tufo HM, Ostfeld AM, Shekelle R. Central nervous system dysfunction following open-heart surgery. JAMA 1970;212:1333–1340.

27. Sotaniemi KA, Juolasmaa A, Hokkanen ET. Neuropsychologic outcome after open-heart surgery. Arch Neurol 1981;38:2–8.

28. Slogoff S, Girgis KZ, Keats AS. Etiologic factors in neuropsychiatric complications associated with cardiopulmonary bypass. Anesth Analg 1982;61:903–911.

29. Newman S, Klinger L, Venn G, Smith P, Harrison M, Treasure T. The persistence of neuropsychological deficits twelve months after coronary artery bypass surgery. In: Wilner A, Rodewald G, eds. Impact of cardiac surgery on the quality of life. New York: Plenum Press, 1990: 173–179.

30. Klonoff H, Clark C, Kavanagh-Gray D, Mizgala H, Muno I. Two-year follow-up study of coronary bypass surgery: psychologic status, employment status, and quality of life. J Thorac Cardiovasc Surg 1989;97:78–85.

31. Newman S, Pugsley W, Klinger L, Harrison M, Aveling W, Treasure T. Neuropsychological consequences of circulatory arrest with hypothermia—a case report. J Clin Exp Neuropsychol 1989;11:529–538.

32. Stump D, Newman S, Coker L, Phipps J, Miller C. Persistance of neuropsychological deficits following CABG [Abstract]. Anesthesiology 1990;73:A113.

33. Bethune DW. Focal neurological lesions and diffuse brain damage in open-heart surgery patients. In: Becker R, Katz J, eds. Psychopathological and neurological dysfunctions following open heart surgery. Berlin: Springer-Verlag 1982:300–306.

34. Savageau JA, Stanton B-A, Jenkins CD, Frater RWM. Neuropsychological dysfunction following elective cardiac operation. II. A six month reassessment. J Thorac Cardiovasc Surg 1982;84:595–600.

35. Garvey JW, Willner A, Wolpowitz A, et al. The effect of arterial filtration during open heart surgery on cerebral function. Circulation 1983;68(suppl II):II-125–II-128.

36. Smith PL, Treasure T, Newman SP, Joseph P, Ell PJ, Schneidau A, Harrison MJ. Cerebral consequences of cardiopulmonary bypass. Lancet 1986;1:823–825.

37. Nevin M, Adams S, Colchester ACF, Pepper JR. Evidence for involvement of hypocapnia and hypoperfusion in aetiology of neurological deficit after cardiopulmonary bypass. Lancet 1987;2:1493–1495.

38. Hammeke TA, Hastings JE. Neuropsychologic

39. Van Foreest M. Neuropsychological functioning following cardiopulmonary bypass. In: Wilner A, ed. Impact of cardiac surgery on the quality of life. New York: Plenum Press, 1990: 181–189.

40. Feys-Dunne N, Wilner AE. Changes in psychometric test scores after cardiac surgery. In: Wilner AE, Rodewald G, eds. Impact of cardiac surgery on the quality of life. New York: Plenum Press, 1990:167–171.

41. Mills SA, Prough DS. Neuropsychiatric complications following cardiac surgery. Sem Thorac Cardiovasc Surg 1991;3:39–46.

42. Allen C. Cabbages and CABG. Br Med Bull 1988;297:1485–1486.

43. Sotaniemi KA, Mononen H, Hokkanen TE. Long-term cerebral outcome after open-heart surgery. A five-year neuropsychological follow-up study. Stroke 1986;17:410–416.

44. Magni G, Unger H, Valfre C, et al. Psychosocial outcome one year after heart surgery. Arch Intern Med 1987;147:473–477.

45. Kornfeld D, Heller S, Frank K, Wilson S, Malm J. Psychological and behavioral responses after coronary artery bypass surgery. Circulation 1982;66:24–28.

46. Jenkins CD, Stanton BA, Savageau JA, Denlinger P, Klein MD. Coronary artery bypass surgery: physical, psychological, social, and economic outcomes six months later. JAMA 1983;250: 782–788.

47. Mayou R, Bryant B. Quality of life after coronary artery surgery. Q J Med 1987;62:239–248.

48. Strauss B, Paulsen G. Psychiatric methods of the international study: Hamilton Depression and Anxiety Scales. In: Wilner A, ed. Impact of cardiac surgery on the quality of life. New York: Plenum Press, 1990:19–26.

49. Speidel H. Psychiatric issues: simple frequencies pre- and postoperatively. In: Wilner A, ed. Impact of cardiac surgery on the quality of life. New York: Plenum Press, 1990:27–37.

50. Rodewald G, Wilner A. Introduction. In: Wilner A, Rodewald G, eds. Impact of cardiac surgery on the quality of life. New York: Plenum Press, 1990:1–5.

51. Mattlar CE, Engblom E, Vanttinen E, Knuts LR. Neuropsychological findings and personality structure associated with coronary artery bypass surgery (CABS). J Clin Exp Neuropsychol 1988;10:329.

52. Newman S. Anxiety, hospitalization, and surgery. In: Fitzpatrick R, ed. The experience of illness. London: Tavistock Press, 1984: 133–153.

53. Kulik J, Mahler H. Effects of preoperative room-

mate assignment on preoperative anxiety and recovery from coronary bypass surgery. Health Psychol 1987;6:525–543.

54. Walter P. Return to work after coronary artery bypass surgery. In: Walter P, ed. Return to work after coronary artery bypass surgery: psychosocial and economic aspects. Berlin: Springer-Verlag, 1985.

55. Anderson A, Barboriak J, Hoffman R, Mullen D. Retention or resumption of employment after aortocoronary bypass operations. JAMA 1980; 243:543–545.

56. Westaby S, Sapsford R, Bentall II. Return to work and quality of life after surgery for coronary artery disease. Br Med J 1979;2: 1028–1031.

57. Bass C. Psychosocial outcome after coronary artery by-pass surgery. Br J Psychiatry 1984; 145:526–532.

58. Gundle M, Reeves B, Tate S, Raft D, McLaurin L. Psychosocial outcome following coronary artery sugery. Am J Psychiatry 1980;137: 1591–1594.

59. LaMendola W, Pelligrini R. Quality of life and coronary artery bypass patients. Soc Sci Med 1979;13:457–461.

60. Stanton B, Jenkins C, Savageau J, Thurer R. Functional benefits following coronary artery bypass graft surgery. Ann Thorac Surg 1984; 37:286–290.

61. Lucia W, McGuire L. Rehabilitation and functional status after surgery for valvular heart disease. Arch Intern Med 1970;126:995–999.

62. Stockard JJ, Bickford RG, Schauble JF. Pressure-dependent cerebral ischemia during cardiopulmonary bypass. Neurology 1973;23:521–529.

63. Prough DS, Stump DA, Roy RC, et al. Response of cerebral blood flow to changes in carbon dioxide tension during hypothermic cardiopulmonary bypass. Anesthesiology 1986;64: 576–581.

64. Venn GE, Sherry K, Newman S, Harrison M, Treasure T. Cerebral blood flow determinants and their clinical implications during cardiopulmonary bypass. Perfusion 1988;3: 271–280.

65. Stump DA, Stein CS, Tegeler CH, et al. Validity and reliability of a device for detecting carotid emboli. J Neuroimaging 1991;1:18–22.

66. Blauth C, Griffin S, Harrison M, et al. Neuropsychologic alterations after cardiac operation. J Thorac Cardiovasc Surg 1989;98:454–459.

67. Moody DM, Bell MA, Challa VR, Johnston WE, Prough DS. Brain microemboli during cardiac surgery or aortography. Ann Neurol 1990; 28:477–486.

68. Savageau JA, Stanton B-A, Jenkins CD, Klein MD. Neuropsychological dysfunction following elective cardiac operation. I. Early assessment. J Thorac Cardiovasc Surg 1982;84:585–594.

69. Gardner TJ, Horneffer PJ, Gott VL, et al. Coronary artery bypass grafting in women: a ten-year perspective. Ann Surg 1985;201:780–784.

70. King KB, Clark PC, Hicks GL Jr. Patterns of referral and recovery in women and men undergoing coronary artery bypass grafting. Am J Cardiol 1992;69:179–182.

71. Cotton P. Is there still too much extrapolation from data on middle-aged white men? JAMA 1990;263:1049–1050.

72. Kolkka R, Hilberman M. Neurologic dysfunction following cardiac operation with low-flow, low-pressure cardiopulmonary bypass. J Thorac Cardiovasc Surg 1980;79:432–437.

73. Slogoff S, Reul GJ, Keats AS, et al. Role of perfusion pressure and flow in major organ dysfunction after cardiopulmonary bypass. Ann Thorac Surg 1990;50:911–918.

74. Breuer AC, Franco I, Marzewski D, Soto-Velasco J. Left ventricular thrombi seen by ventriculography are a significant risk factor for stroke in open-heart surgery. Ann Neurol 1981;10: 103–104.

75. Furlan AJ, Craciun AR. Risk of stroke during coronary artery bypass graft surgery in patients with internal carotid artery disease documented by angiography. Stroke 1985;16: 797–799.

76. Stockard JJ, Bickford RG, Myers RR, Aung MH, Dilley RB, Schauble JF. Hypotension-induced changes in cerebral function during cardiac surgery. Stroke 1974;5:730–746.

77. Javid H, Tufo HM, Najafi H, Dye WS, Hunter JA, Julian OC. Neurological abnormalities following open-heart surgery. J Thorac Cardiovasc Surg 1969;58:502–509.

78. Sotaniemi KA. Brain damage and neurological outcome after open-heart surgery. J Neurol Neurosurg Psychiatry 1980;43:127–135.

79. Turnipseed WD, Berkoff HA, Belzer FO. Postoperative stroke in cardiac and peripheral vascular disease. Ann Surg 1980;192:365–368.

80. Breslau PJ, Fell G, Ivey TD, Bailey WW, Miller DW, Strandness DE Jr. Carotid arterial disease in patients undergoing coronary artery bypass operations. J Thorac Cardiovasc Surg 1981;82: 765–767.

81. Reed GL III, Singer DE, Picard EH, DeSanctis RW. Stroke following coronary-artery bypass surgery: a case-control estimate of the risk from carotid bruits. N Engl J Med 1988;319: 1246–1250.

82. Furlan AJ, Breuer AC. Central nervous system complications of open heart surgery. Stroke 1984;15:912–915.

83. Jones EL, Craver JM, Michalik RA, et al. Com-

bined carotid and coronary operations: when are they necessary? J Thorac Cardiovasc Surg 1984;87:7–16.

84. Ropper AH, Wechsler LR, Wilson LS. Carotid bruit and the risk of stroke in elective surgery. N Engl J Med 1982;307:1388–1390.

85. Gravlee GP, Cordell AR, Graham JE, et al. Coronary revascularization in patients with bilateral internal carotid occlusions. J Thorac Cardiovasc Surg 1985;90:921–925.

86. Rogers AT, Stump DA. Cerebral physiologic monitoring. Crit Care Clin 1989;5:845–861.

87. Bashein G, Bledsoe SW, Townes BD, Coppel DB. Tools for assessing central nervous system injury in the cardiac surgery patient. In: Hilberman M, ed. Brain injury and protection during heart surgery. Boston: Martinus Nijhoff, 1988:109–136.

88. Levy WJ, Grundy BL, Smith NT. Monitoring the electroencephalogram and evoked potentials during anesthesia. In: Saidman LJ, Smith TY, eds. Monitoring in anesthesia. Boston: Butterworth, 1984:227–267.

89. Arom KV, Cohen DE, Strobl FT. Effect of intraoperative intervention on neurologic outcome based on electroencephalographic monitoring during cardiopulmonary bypass. Ann Thorac Surg 1989;48:476–483.

90. Edmonds HL Jr, Griffiths LK, van der Laken J, Slater AD, Shields CB. Quantitative electroencephalographic monitoring during myocardial revascularization predicts postoperative disorientation and improves outcome. J Thorac Cardiovasc Surg 1992;103:555–563.

91. Witoszka MM, Tamura H, Indeglia R, Hopkins RW, Simeone FA. Electroencephalographic changes and cerebral complications in open-heart surgery. J Thorac Cardiovasc Surg 1973;66:855–864.

92. Salerno TA, Lince DP, White DN, Lynn RB, Charrette EJ. Monitoring of electroencephalogram during open-heart surgery. A prospective analysis of 118 cases. J Thorac Cardiovasc Surg 1978;76:97–100.

93. Bashein G, Nessly ML, Bledsoe SW, et al. Electroencephalography during surgery with cardiopulmonary byass and hypothermia. Anesthesiology 1992;76:878–891.

94. Levy WJ. Monitoring of the electroencephalogram during cardiopulmonary bypass. Know when to say when. Anesthesiology 1992;76:876–877.

95. Sarnquist FH. Neurological outcome after "low flow, low pressure" cardiopulmonary bypass. In: Hilberman M, ed. Brain injury and protection during heart surgery. Boston: Martinus Nijhoff Publishing, 1988:13–25.

96. Murkin JM. Cerebral hyperperfusion during

cardiopulmonary bypass: the influence of $PaCO_2$. In: Hilberman M, ed. Brain injury and protection during heart surgery. Boston: Martinus Nijhoff, 1988:47–66.

97. Shenkin HA, Harmel MH, Kety SS. Dynamic anatomy of the cerebral circulation. Arch Neurol Psychiatry 1948;60:240–252.

98. Lassen NA. Cerebral blood flow and oxygen consumption in man. Physiol Rev 1959;39:183–237.

99. Michenfelder JD. The awake brain. In: Anesthesia and the brain. New York: Churchill Livingstone, 1988:3–21.

100. Tinker JH, Campos JH. Blood gases should be corrected for temperature during hypothermic cardiopulmonary bypass: pH-stat mode. J Cardiothorac Anesth 1988;2:701–704.

101. Murkin JM. Con: blood gases should not be corrected for temperature during hypothermic cardiopulmonary bypass: α-stat mode. J Cardiothorac Anesth 1988;2:705–707.

102. Williams JJ, Marshall BE. A fresh look at an old question. Anesthesiology 1982;56:1–2.

103. Ream AK, Reitz BA, Silverberg G. Temperature correction of P_{CO_2} and pH in estimating acid-base status: an example of the emperor's new clothes? Anesthesiology 1982;56:41–44.

104. Rahn H, Reeves RB, Howell BJ. Hydrogen ion regulation, temperature, and evolution. Am Rev Respir Dis 1975;112:165–172.

105. Williams GD, Seifen AB, Lawson NW, et al. Pulsatile perfusion versus conventional high-flow nonpulsatile perfusion for rapid core cooling and rewarming of infants for circulatory arrest in cardiac operation. J Thorac Cardiovasc Surg 1979;78:667–677.

106. White FN. A comparative physiological approach to hypothermia. J Thorac Cardiovasc Surg 1981;82:821–831.

107. Prough DS, Stump DA, Troost BT. $PaCO_2$ management during cardiopulmonary bypass: intriguing physiologic rationale, convincing clinical data, evolving hypothesis? Anesthesiology 1990;72:3–6.

108. Wollman H, Stephen GW, Clement AJ, Danielson GK. Cerebral blood flow in man during extracorporeal circulation. J Thorac Cardiovasc Surg 1966;52:558–564.

109. Murkin JM, Farrar JK, Tweed WA, McKenzie FN, Guiraudon G. Cerebral autoregulation and flow/metabolism coupling during cardiopulmonary bypass: the influence of $PaCO_2$. Anesth Analg 1987;66:825–832.

110. Govier AV, Reves JG, McKay RD, et al. Factors and their influence on regional cerebral blood flow during nonpulsatile cardiopulmonary bypass. Ann Thorac Surg 1984;38:592–600.

111. Prough DS, Rogers AT, Stump DA, et al. Hyper-

carbia depresses cerebral oxygen consumption during cardiopulmonary bypass. Stroke 1990; 21:1162–1166.

112. Henriksen L, Hjelms E, Lindeburgh T. Brain hyperperfusion during cardiac operations. J Thorac Cardiovasc Surg 1983;86:202–208.

113. Soma Y, Hirotani T, Yozu R, et al. A clinical study of cerebral circulation during extracorporeal circulation. J Thorac Cardiovasc Surg 1989;97:187–193.

114. Artu AA, Michenfelder JD. Effects of hypercarbia on canine cerebral metabolism and blood flow with simultaneous direct and indirect measurement of blood flow. Anesthesiology 1980;52:466–469.

115. Kliefoth AB, Grubb RL, Raichle ME. Depression of cerebral oxygen utilization by hypercapnia in the rhesus monkey. J Neurochem 1979;32: 661–663.

116. Berntman L, Dahlgren N, Siesjö BK. Cerebral blood flow and oxygen consumption in the rat brain during extreme hypercarbia. Anesthesiology 1979;50:299–305.

117. Obrist WD, Clifton GL, Robertson CS, Langfitt TW. Cerebral metabolic changes induced by hyperventilation in acute head injury. Cerebral Vasc Dis 1987;6:251–255.

118. Johnston WE, Vinten-Johansen J, DeWitt DS, O'Steen WK, Stump DA, Prough DS. Cerebral perfusion during canine hypothermic cardiopulmonary bypass: effect of arterial carbon dioxide tension. Ann Thorac Surg 1991;52: 479–489.

119. Hindman BJ, Funatsu N, Cheng DCH, Bolles R, Todd MM, Tinker JH. Differential effect of oncotic pressure on cerebral and extracerebral water content during cardiopulmonary bypass in rabbits. Anesthesiology 1990;73:951–957.

120. Woodcock TE, Murkin JM, Farrar JK, Tweed WA, Guiraudon GM, McKenzie FN. Pharmacologic EEG suppression during cardiopulmonary bypass: cerebral hemodynamic and metabolic effects of thiopental or isoflurane during hypothermia and normothermia. Anesthesiology 1987;67:218–224.

121. Harper AM. The inter-relationship between $PaCO_2$ and blood pressure in the regulation of blood flow through the cerebral cortex. Acta Neurol 1965;41(suppl):94–103.

122. Raichle ME, Stone HL. Cerebral blood flow autoregulation and graded hypercapnia. Eur Neurol 1972;6:1–5.

123. Lundar T, Froysaker T, Lindegaard KF, et al. Some observations on cerebral perfusion during cardiopulmonary bypass. Ann Thorac Surg 1985;39:318–323.

124. Rogers AT, Stump DA, Gravlee GP, et al. Response of cerebral blood flow to phenyleph-rine infusion during hypothermic cardiopulmonary bypass: influence of $PaCO_2$ management. Anesthesiology 1988;69:547–551.

125. Greeley WJ, Ungerleider RM, Smith LR, Reves JG. The effects of deep hypothermic cardiopulmonary bypass and total circulatory arrest on cerebral blood flow in infants and children. J Thorac Cardiovasc Surg 1989;97:737–745.

126. Rogers AT, Prough DS, Roy RC, et al. Cerebrovascular and cerebral metabolic effects of alterations in perfusion flow rate during hypothermic cardiopulmonary bypass in man. J Thorac Cardiovasc Surg 1992;103:363–368.

127. Murkin JM, Farrar JK, Cleland A, MacDonald JL, Mayer R. The influence of perfusion flow rates on cerebral blood flow and oxygen consumption during hypothermic cardiopulmonary bypass [Abstract]. Anesthesiology 1987;57:A9.

128. Fox LS, Blackstone EH, Kirklin JW, Bishop SP, Bergdahl LAL, Bradley EL. Relationship of brain blood flow and oxygen consuption to perfusion flow rate during profoundly hypothermic cardiopulmonary bypass. J Thorac Cardiovasc Surg 1984;87:658–664.

129. Miyamoto K, Kawashima Y, Matsuda H, Okuda A, Maeda S, Hirose H. Optimal perfusion flow rate for the brain during deep hypothermic cardiopulmonary bypass at 20°C. J Thorac Cardiovasc Surg 1986;92:1065–1070.

130. Rebeyka IM, Coles JG, Wilson GJ, et al. The effect of low-flow cardiopulmonary bypass on cerebral function: an experimental and clinical study. Ann Thorac Surg 1987;43:391–396.

131. Kety SS, Schmidt CF. The nitrous oxide method for the quantitative determination of cerebral blood flow in man: Theory, procedure and normal values. J Clin Invest 1948;27:476–483.

132. Rogers AT, Stump DA, Prough DS, Angert KC, Wallenhaupt SA. Cerebrovascular responsiveness to PaO_2 is preserved during hypothermic cardiopulmonary bypass. Anesthesiology 1987; 67(suppl):A12.

133. Yamamoto M, Meyer JS, Sakai F, Yamaguchi F. Aging and cerebral vasodilator responses to hypercarbia: responses in normal aging and in persons with risk factors for stroke. Arch Neurol 1980;37:489–496.

134. Roy RC, Prough DS, Stump DA, Gravlee GP. Effect of advancing age on cerebral blood flow and $CMRO_2$ during hypothermic cardiopulmonary bypass [Abstract]. Anesthesiology 1989; 71:A37.

135. Rogers AT, Roy RC, Gravlee GP, Taylor C, Prough DS. Age does not affect CO_2 reactivity during hypothermic cardiopulmonary bypass in man [Abstract]. Anesthesiology 1989;71:A36.

136. Roy RC, Rogers AT, Prough DS, Stump DA, Taylor C, Daniels T. Age does not affect cerebral auto-

regulation during hypothermic cardiopulmonary bypass in man [Abstract]. Anesth Analg 1990;70:S1–S338.

137. Brusino FG, Reves JG, Prough DS, Stump DA, Croughwell ND. The effect of age on cerebral blood flow autoregulation during hypothermic cardiopulmonary bypass [Abstract]. J Thorac Cardiovasc Surg 1988;67(3A):A10.

138. Bullock R, Mendelow AD, Bone I, Patterson J, MacLeod WN, Allardice G. Cerebral blood flow and CO_2 responsiveness as an indicator of collateral reserve capacity in patients with carotid arterial disease. Br J Surg 1985;72:348–351.

139. Boysen G, Ladegaard-Pedersen HJ, Henriksen H, Olesen J, Paulson OB, Engell HC. The effects of $PaCO_2$ on regional cerebral blood flow and the internal carotid arterial pressure during carotid clamping. Anesthesiology 1971;35:286–300.

140. Gravlee GP, Roy RC, Stump DA, Hudspeth AS, Rogers AT, Prough DS. Regional cerebrovascular reactivity to carbon dioxide during cardiopulmonary bypass in patients with cerebrovascular disease. J Thorac Cardiovasc Surg 1990;99: 1022–1029.

141. Prough DS, Rogers AT, Stump DA, et al. Cerebral blood flow decreases with time while cerebral oxygen consumption remains stable during hypothermic cardiopulmonary bypass in humans. Anesth Analg 1991;72:161–168.

142. Stump DA, Rogers AT, Prough DS, Hudspeth AS. Cerebral blood flow declines independently of metabolism during hypothermic cardiopulmonary bypass. In: Wilner AE, Rodewald G, eds. Impact of cardiac surgery on the quality of life. New York: Plenum Press, 1990;265–271.

143. Bishop CCR, Powell S, Rutt D, Browse NL. Transcranial Doppler measurement of middle cerebral artery blood flow velocity: a validation study. Stroke 1986;17:913–915.

144. Stump DA, Roy RC, Rogers AT, Prough DS, Hileman R. Time, temperature and brain blood flow during hypothermic cardiopulmonary bypass [Abstract]. Anesth Analg 1989;68:S283.

145. Vannelli T, Murkin JM, Lee D. The influence of pH-management on mean blood flow velocity in the middle cerebral artery during hypothermic cardiopulmonary bypass [Abstract]. Anesthesiology 1991;75:A56.

146. Padayachee TS, Parsons S, Theobold R, Linley J, Gosling RG, Deverall PB. The detection of microemboli in the middle cerebral artery during cardiopulmonary bypass: a transcranial doppler ultrasound investigation using membrane and bubble oxygenators. Ann Thorac Surg 1987;44:298–302.

147. Albin MS, Hantler CB, Mitzel H, Bunegin L, Grover F. Aeric microemboli and the transcranial doppler (TCD): episodic frequency and

timing in 62 cases of open heart surgery [Abstract]. Anesthesiology 1991;75(3A):A53.

148. van der Linden J, Casimir-Ahn H. When do cerebral emboli appear during open heart operations? A transcranial doppler study. Ann Thorac Surg 1991;51:237–241.

149. Pugsley W, Klinger L, Paschalis C, et al. Microemboli and cerebral impairment during cardiac surgery. AJR 1990;34–43.

150. Blauth CI, Arnold JV, Schulenberg WE, McCartney AC, Taylor KM, Loop FD. Cerebral microembolism during cardiopulmonary bypass. Retinal microvascular studies in vivo with fluorescein angiography. J Thorac Cardiovasc Surg 1988;95:668–676.

151. Blauth CI, Smith PL, Arnold JV, Jagoe JR, Wootton R, Taylor KM. Influence of oxygenator type on the prevalance and extent of microembolic retinal ischemia during cardiopulmonary bypass. Assessment by digital image analysis. J Thorac Cardiovasc Surg 1990;99:61–69.

152. Tamura M. Non-invasive monitoring of brain oxygen metabolism during cardiopulmonary bypass by near-infrared spectrophotometry. Jpn Circ J 1991;55:330–335.

153. Smith DS, Levy W, Maris M, Chance B. Reperfusion hyperoxia in brain after circulatory arrest in humans. Anesthesiology 1990; 73:12–19.

154. Prough DS, Scuderi PE, Lewis G, Stump DA, Goetting M. Initial clinical experience using in vivo optical spectroscopy to quantify brain oxygen saturation [Abstract]. Anesthesiology 1990;73:A424.

155. Jobsis FF, Keizer JH, LaManna JC, Rosenthal M. Reflectance spectrophotometry of cytochrome $aa3$ in vivo. J Appl Physiol 1977;43:858–872.

156. Culliford AT, Colvin SB, Rohrer K, Baumann FG, Spencer FC. The atherosclerotic ascending aorta and transverse arch: a new technique to prevent cerebral injury during bypass: experience with 13 patients. Ann Thorac Surg 1986; 41:27–35.

157. Coselli JS, Crawford ES. Aortic valve replacement in the patient with extensive calcification of the ascending aorta (the porcelain aorta). J Thorac Cardiovasc Surg 1986;91:184–187.

158. Barzilai B, Marshall WG Jr, Saffitz JE, Kouchoukos N. Avoidance of embolic complications by ultrasonic characterization of the ascending aorta. Circulation 1989;80(suppl I):I-275–I-279.

159. Peigh PS, DiSesa VJ, Collins JJ Jr, Cohn LH. Coronary bypass grafting with totally calcified or acutely dissected ascending aorta. Ann Thorac Surg 1991;51:102–104.

160. Oka Y, Inoue T, Hong Y, Sisto DA, Strom JA, Frater RWM. Retained intracardiac air. Transe-

sophageal echocardiography for definition of incidence and monitoring removal by improved techniques. J Thorac Cardiovasc Surg 1986;91:329–338.

161. Pearson DT, Holden MP, Waterhouse PS, Clark JI. Gaseous microemboli during open heart surgery: detection and prevention. Proc Am Acad Cardiovasc Perfusion 1983;4:103–109.

162. Taylor KM, Devlin BJ, Mittra SM, Gillan JG, Brannan JJ, McKenna JM. Assessment of cerebral damage during open-heart surgery. A new experimental model. Scand J Thorac Cardiovasc Surg 1980;14:197–203.

163. Aberg T, Kihlgren M. Cerebral protection during open-heart surgery. Thorax 1977;32: 525–533.

164. Carlson RG, Landé AJ, Landis B, et al. The Landé-Edwards membrane oxygenator during heart surgery: oxygen transfer, microemboli counts, and Bender-Gestalt visual motor test scores. J Thorac Cardiovasc Surg 1973;66: 894–905.

165. Treasure T. Interventions to reduce cerebral injury during cardiac surgery—the effect of arterial line filtration. Perfusion 1989;4:147–152.

166. Pugsley WB, Klinger L, Paschalis C, Newman S, Harrison M, Treasure T. Does arterial line filtration affect the bypass related cerebral impairment in patients undergoing coronary artery surgery. Clin Sci 1988;76:30–31.

167. Aris A, Solanes H, Cámara ML, Junqué C, Escartin A, Caralps JM. Arterial line filtration during cardiopulmonary bypass. Neurologic, neuropsychologic, and hematologic studies. J Thorac Cardiovasc Surg 1986;91:526–533.

168. Greeley WJ, Kern FH, Ungerleider RM, et al. The effect of hypothermic cardiopulmonary bypass and total circulatory arrest on cerebral metabolism in neonates, infants, and children. J Thorac Cardiovasc Surg 1991;101:783–794.

169. Tan PSK, Aveling W, Pugsley WB, Newman SP, Treasure T. Experience with circulatory arrest and hypothermia to facilitate thoracic aortic surgery. Ann R Coll Surg Engl 1989;71:81–86.

170. Steen PA, Newberg L, Milde JH, Michenfelder JD. Hypothermia and barbiturates: individual and combined effects on canine cerebral oxygen consumption. Anesthesiology 1983;58: 527–532.

171. Michenfelder JD, Milde JH. The relationship among canine brain temperature, metabolism, and function during hypothermia. Anesthesiology 1991;75:130–136.

172. Todd MM, Warner DS. A comfortable hypothesis reevaluated. Cerebral metabolic depression and brain protection during ischemia. Anesthesiology 1992;76:161–164.

173. Swain JA, McDonald TJ Jr, Balaban RS, Robbins

RC. Metabolism of the heart and brain during hypothermic cardiopulmonary bypass. Ann Thorac Surg 1991;51:105–109.

174. Siesjö BK. Mechanisms of ischemic brain damage. Crit Care Med 1988;16:954–963.

175. Stein CS, Stump DA, Hager RA, Rogers AT, Prough DS, Tegeler CH. Microemboli detection in the carotid artery during cardiac surgery [Abstract]. Anesth Analg 1991;72(suppl):S277.

176. Engelman RM. Retrograde continuous warm blood cardioplegia. Ann Thorac Surg 1991;51: 180–181.

177. Mitchell D, Hilberman M. Brain function after hypothermic circulatory arrest. In: Hilberman M, ed. Brain injury and protection during heart surgery. Boston: Martinus Nijhoff Publishing, 1988:157–170.

178. Bashein G, Townes BD, Nessly ML, et al. A randomized study of carbon dioxide management during hypothermic cardiopulmonary bypass. Anesthesiology 1990;72:7–15.

179. Gilman S. Cerebral disorders after open-heart operations. N Engl J Med 1965;272:489–498.

180. Ellis RJ, Wisniewski A, Potts R, Calhoun C, Loucks P, Wells MR. Reduction of flow rate and arterial pressure at moderate hypothermia does not result in cerebral dysfunction. J Thorac Cardiovasc Surg 1980;79:173–180.

181. Stanley TE, Smith LR, White WD, et al. Effect of cerebral perfusion pressure during cardiopulmonary bypass on neuropsychiatric outcome following coronary artery bypass grafting [Abstract]. Anesthesiology 1990;73(3A):A93.

182. Sieber FE, Smith DS, Traystman RJ, Wollman H. Glucose: a reevaluation of its intraoperative use. Anesthesiology 1987;67:72–81.

183. Lanier WL. Glucose management during cardiopulmonary bypass: cardiovascular and neurologic implications. Anesth Analg 1991;72: 423–427.

184. LeMay DR, Gehua L, Zelenock GB, D'Alecy LG. Insulin administration protects neurologic function in cerebral ischemia in rats. Stroke 1988;19:1411–1419.

185. Lanier WL, Stangland KJ, Scheithauer BW, Milde JH, Michenfelder JD. The effects of dextrose infusion and head position on neurologic outcome after complete cerebral ischemia in primates: examination of a model. Anesthesiology 1987;66:39–48.

186. Steward DJ, Da Silva CA, Flegel T. Elevated blood glucose levels may increase the danger of neurological deficit following profoundly hypothermic cardiac arrest. Anesthesiology 1988;68:653.

187. Rogers AT, Zaloga GP, Prough DS, Butterworth JF IV, Robertie P, Ward KA. Hyperglycemia during cardiac surgery: central vs. peripheral

mechanisms [Abstract]. Anesth Analg 1990;70: S328.

188. Metz S, Keats AS. Benefits of a glucose-containing priming solution for cardiopulmonary bypass. Anesth Analg 1991;72:428–434.

189. Michenfelder JD, Milde JH, Sundt TM Jr. Cerebral protection by barbiturate anesthesia. Arch Neurol 1976;33:345–350.

190. Smith AL, Hoff JT, Nielsen SL, Larson CP. Barbiturate protection in acute focal cerebral ischemia. Stroke 1974;5:1–7.

191. Michenfelder JD. A valid demonstration of barbiturate-induced brain protection in man—at last. Anesthesiology 1986;64:140–142.

192. Metz S, Slogoff S. Thiopental sodium by single bolus dose compared to infusion for cerebral protection during cardiopulmonary bypass. J Clin Anesth 1990;2:226–231.

193. Prough DS, Mills SA. Should thiopental sodium administration be a standard of care for open cardiac procedures? J Clin Anesth 1990;2: 221–225.

194. Hara H, Nagasawa H, Kogure K. Nimodipine prevents postischemic brain damage in the early phase of focal cerebral ischemia. Stroke 1990;21(suppl IV):IV-102–IV-104.

195. Gelmers HJ, Hennerici M. Effect of nimodipine on acute ischemic stroke. Pooled results from five randomized trials. Stroke 1990;21(suppl IV):IV-81–IV-84.

196. Triggle DJ. Calcium antagonists. History and perspective. Stroke 1990;21(suppl IV):IV-49–IV-58.

197. Prough DS, Furberg CD. Nimodipine and the "no-reflow phenomenon"—experimental triumph, clinical failure? Anesth Analg 1989;68: 431–435.

198. Bielenberg GW, Burniol M, Rösen R, Klaus W. Effects of nimodipine on infarct size and cerebral acidosis after middle cerebral artery occlusion in the rat. Stroke 1990;21(suppl IV): IV-90–IV-92.

199. Forsman M, Olsnes BT, Semb G, Steen PA. Effects of nimodipine on cerebral blood flow and neuropsychological outcome after cardiac surgery. Br J Anaesth 1990;65:514–520.

200. Aren C, Blomstrand C, Wikkelso C, Radegran K. Hypotension induced by prostacyclin treatment during cardiopulmonary bypass does not increase the risk of cerebral complications. J Thorac Cardiovasc Surg 1984;88:748–753.

201. Schmidley JW. Free radicals in central nervous system ischemia. Stroke 1990;21:1086–1090.

202. Bachet J, Guilmet D, Goudot B, et al. Cold cerebroplegia: A new technique of cerebral protection during operations on the transverse aortic arch. J Thorac Cardiovasc Surg 1991; 102:85–94.

203. Robbins RC, Balaban RS, Swain JA. Intermittent hypothermic asanguineous cerebral perfusion (cerebroplegia) protects the brain during prolonged circulatory arrest. A phosphorus 31 nuclear magnetic resonance study. J Thorac Cardiovasc Surg 1990;99:878–884.

Section V

Clinical Applications and Management of Cardiopulmonary Bypass

22

CONDUCT AND MONITORING OF CARDIOPULMONARY BYPASS

Richard F. Davis, Jeri L. Dobbs, and Henry Casson

The focus of this entire text is a comprehensive discussion of the clinical management of cardiopulmonary bypass (CPB). One might, therefore, justifiably question the need for a separate chapter to discuss the conduct and monitoring of CPB. Indeed, many of the topics that would reasonably be included in a clinically oriented conduct and monitoring of CPB discussion are themselves the topics of full chapters in this text. For example, perfusion circuitry, blood pumps, filters, and cannulation techniques (Chapter 3), anticoagulation (Section III, Chapters 14 to 17), temperature control (Chapter 6), hemodilution and priming solutions (Chapter 5), hemofiltration (Chapter 4), blood flow patterns (Chapter 13), pharmacokinetic and pharmacodynamic effects of CPB (Chapter 8), other physiologic responses to CPB (Section II, Chapters 7, 9 to 12) and specific organ system pathophysiology produced by CPB (Section IV, Chapters 18 to 21) are all the subjects of one or more chapters in the preceding text. The purpose of this final section of the text is integrative, to synthesize the foregoing sections within the context of the clinical uses of CPB. This chapter specifically is designed to integrate the previous chapters into a discussion of the conduct and monitoring of CPB.

Within the U.S.A. it is currently estimated that more than 400,000 surgical procedures are completed annually that require some sort of mechanical cardiovascular assistance, ranging in degree of cardiopulmonary support from simple arteriovenous hemofiltration or venovenous (nonoxygenator) bypass often used in hepatic transplantation, to total CPB in support of complex intracardiac surgical procedures. The degree of patient dependence on satisfactory performance of the perfusion follows a similar spectrum. In most circumstances of venovenous and partial left (or less commonly, right) heart bypass, the patient's intrinsic cardiac function remains capable of supporting the circulation in the event of perfusion failure. However, as it is commonly applied in aortocoronary bypass surgery, even partial CPB must provide total cardiopulmonary support for a significant proportion of the CPB interval. In this regard, the distinction between total CPB (which requires bicaval cannulation with caval tourniquets for total diversion of systemic venous return toward the oxygenator) and partial CPB (the use of a two-stage single venous drainage cannula theoretically precludes total diversion of venous return and is therefore always associated with partial CPB) becomes largely semantic.

Cardiac surgery, in general, renders the patient totally dependent upon the life-sustaining functions of the CPB apparatus and its use. Indeed, in the circumstance of profound hypothermia and circulatory arrest (see Chapters 6, 23, and 24), the patient [hypothermic, no cardiac function, and an electrically silent central nervous system (CNS)] meets most of the clinical criteria defining death. In all of these cases the degree of dependence of the patient on the CPB apparatus and the skill of the entire team involved in its use (perfusionist, surgeon, and anesthesiologist) for moment to moment life-sustaining cardiopulmonary support is without equal in the practice of medicine. Thus, the monitoring of patient physiologic functions and equipment performance during CPB, and the readiness to respond to both the common and the unusual problems that arise are the primary elements in the conduct of CPB and are of critical importance to a successful clinical outcome following CPB. This chapter will focus on the important elements of patient and equipment monitoring during CPB and the routine clinical conduct of CPB.

PATIENT PHYSIOLOGIC MONITORING DURING CPB

Monitoring of the patient's physiologic functions during CPB differs little in principle from normal intraoperative physiologic monitoring practices for non-CPB supported surgery of similar magnitude. Because CPB occupies only a portion of the total operative interval, management of patients for surgical procedures requiring CPB must include physiologic monitoring appropriate to the patient's condition, in addition to the routine monitoring associated with all anesthetic procedures. For example, the pre- and post-CPB course for a patient undergoing a second aortocoronary bypass surgery with a left ventricular aneurysmectomy should be expected to be more complex than that for an otherwise healthy child undergoing repair of a secundum atrial septal defect. Accordingly, the intensity of physiologic monitoring should be

based on patient condition, procedural requirements, and expected problems rather than on some arbitrary routine. This section presents elements of patient monitoring commonly used to assess abnormalities produced specifically, by CPB, rather than a more generalized discussion of patient monitoring for cardiac surgery.

Cardiovascular Monitoring

BLOOD FLOW AND PERFUSION PRESSURE

Maintenance of cardiovascular stability during CPB requires the obvious interplay of machine (pump) function for blood flow and patient factors such as systemic vascular resistance and venous compliance. Yet, despite the ease of blood flow control and the sophisticated pharmacologic agents available for manipulation of vascular smooth muscle tone, there is no uniformly accepted standard for either blood flow rate or perfusion pressure during CPB. Any discussion of optimum flow rates and perfusion pressure during CPB should be based on an understanding of oxygen consumption, blood flow distribution, and intrinsic autoregulatory capability of specific vascular beds. Fortunately in some of these areas a reasonable body of knowledge has developed over the nearly 40-year history of clinical CPB. Unfortunately there are large gaps in the data. For example, *clinically* the regional distribution of blood flow during hypothermic CPB and the regional vascular autoregulatory capability remain relatively poorly understood, with some notable exceptions as discussed below.

Minute oxygen consumption ($\dot{V}_{O_2}$) is the major determinant of blood flow requirement normally and during CPB. The well-known Fick equation describes $\dot{V}_{O_2}$ in the readily understandable and clinically measurable terms of cardiac output and arteriovenous oxygen content difference.

$$\dot{V}_{O_2} = \dot{Q}\,(C_{(a\text{-}\bar{v})}O_2)$$

where $C_{(a\cdot\bar{v})}O_2 = (S_{(a\cdot\bar{v})}O_2)(1.34)(Hb) + (P_{(a\cdot\bar{v})}O_2)(.0031)$ and $\dot{V}O_2$ = minute oxygen consumption (ml·min⁻¹), $\dot{Q}$ = cardiac output (liter·min⁻¹). Also, Hb = hemoglobin concentration (g·liter⁻¹), 1.34^a = hemoglobin oxygen content (ml O_2·gm⁻¹) at 100% saturation (ml·g⁻¹), $S_{(a\cdot\bar{v})}O_2$ = arteriovenous hemoglobin oxygen saturation difference (ml·liter⁻¹), $P_{(a\cdot\bar{v})}O_2$ = arteriovenous oxygen partial pressure difference (mm Hg), and 0.0031 = solubility of oxygen in blood (ml O_2·mm Hg⁻¹·100 ml blood⁻¹, at 37°C) increased by hypothermia.

Thus, knowledge of $\dot{V}O_2$ allows reasonable prediction of effective flow requirement during CPB for any given level of hemoglobin concentration (hemodilution) and arteriovenous oxygen content difference (oxygen extraction). Two important caveats apply to this simplistic approach. First there is a requirement for accurate knowledge of $\dot{V}O_2$ and second, the operative phrase is "effective flow."

During CPB effective blood flow is blood flow from the oxygenator that actually results in tissue perfusion. It is easy to understand that arterial blood aspirated from the surgical field represents a loss of effective flow from total CPB flow. In this context, all physiologic and anatomic shunting of arterialized blood around capillary beds to the venous circulation also detracts from effective perfusion. For exam-

[a]The precise value for the hemoglobin oxygen content of whole blood at 100% saturation is not definitely known and may not be a constant. Pure hemoglobin in solution (molecular weight 64,458) can combine with 1.39 ml of O_2 per gram, but whole blood contains other hemoglobin subtypes such as methemoglobin, carboxyhemoglobin, etc., that decrease the net oxygen-carrying capacity (1). The value of 1.34 is commonly cited, but, in fact, one study has shown that 1.306 ml O_2 per gram hemoglobin was the most applicable number clinically (2, 3).

tracts from effective perfusion. For example, bronchial blood flow, which is normally the major component of "physiologic" right to left shunting of blood (2 to 4% of cardiac output), may be significantly increased in certain congenital lesions associated with decreased pulmonary arterial blood flow and correspondingly increased pulmonary collateral blood flow. In adults with significant chronic obstructive lung disease, bronchial blood flow may also be significantly increased. At a total flow rate of 4 to 5 liters/min during CPB, this physiologic shunting may normally be 250 to 500 ml/min that is lost from effective systemic perfusion and pathologic increases in bronchial or pulmonary collateral flow may substantially increase that amount of lost effective blood flow.

Left atrial, left ventricular or aortic root vents are another common source of loss of effective flow. Blood returned to the oxygenator from these vent lines is lost from effective systemic perfusion. Parenthetically, the requirement for such vents is largely created by the existence of physiologic and anatomic shunts. Finally, if the microcirculation is inhomogenously perfused, for example because of an increased interstitial fluid compartment either locally or systemically, then the net result is an increased effective diffusion distance for oxygen from the capillaries to the cells that results in a loss of effective perfusion. Thus, determination of effective flow is not altogether straightforward and it may be at times significantly less than total pump output.

Total systemic $\dot{V}O_2$ is primarily a function of age, size (body surface area or lean body mass), and temperature. In the newborn infant, $\dot{V}O_2$ in proportion to body weight is approximately twice that of the average adult (8 ml/kg/min vs 4 ml/kg/min). This proportion rises over the first 2 months of life to a peak of 9 to 10 ml/kg/min. Thereafter there is an exponential decline in $\dot{V}O_2$ per unit mass, as age increases, that parallels the change in cardiac index with age.[b] The relationship between $\dot{V}O_2$ and size is similar to that for $\dot{V}O_2$ and age in that as body mass increases (beyond an age of approximately 6 months), the $\dot{V}O_2$ per unit mass actually decreases. The influence of temperature on $\dot{V}O_2$ was fully discussed in Chapter 6. In the present context it is important to remember that the relation is nonlinear and $\dot{V}O_2$ approaches a minimum of 10 to 15% of the normothermic value at approximately 15°C (Fig. 22.1). Importantly however, this decline in $\dot{V}O_2$ with decreasing temperature may not be the same in all organs. For example the duration of "safe" circulatory arrest time at 18°C is 45 to 60 minutes regarding neurologic outcome, yet for renal function at 18°C the safe limit is significantly longer. The transplantation literature would suggest even longer "circulatory arrest" times for transplanted organs (4 to 5 hours for the heart, 24 or more hours for the kidney and the liver), recognizing of course that graft organs are stored at more profound levels of hypothermia than are clinically applied in CPB (<4°C). However, factors other than decreased $\dot{V}O_2$—for example, variable, tissue-specific tolerance for hypoxia—may also contribute to the variability of safe arrest time in different organs maintained at the same temperature.

Autoregulation of blood flow to various organ vascular beds during CPB obvi-

ously pertains to any discussion of blood flow rate and perfusion pressure requirements during CPB. Physiologically, autoregulation of blood flow refers to the ability of organ vasculature, through neural, chemical, and direct smooth muscle effects, to regulate local resistance in order to maintain relatively constant flow despite significant changes in perfusion pressure (7). This capability is preserved in some organ vascular beds during CPB despite the superimposition of a nonpulsatile flow pattern, hemodilution, and hypothermia. For example, Govier et al. (8), Prough et al. (9), and Murkin et al. (10) have independently examined cerebral blood flow responsiveness to changed perfusion pressure and carbon dioxide tension during CPB. The conclusion from these studies is that CO_2 responsiveness of the cerebral vasculature is maintained during CPB even at 20°C. Also, autoregulation of cerebral blood flow to changes in perfusion pressure is preserved during CPB and the response curve may even be shifted to the left, indicating a decrease of the autoregulatory pressure threshold from the normal of about 50 mm Hg to approximately 30 mm Hg. As discussed by Thomson (11), this lowering of the pressure threshold for autoregulation is linked to the decreased cerebral metabolic rate for oxygen produced by hypothermia. The cerebral perfusion pressure intercept with the maximal vasodilation blood flow line would be expected to be lower as temperature decreases if blood flow and metabolic rate remain coupled during hypothermia, as has been shown by Murkin et al. (10) for alpha-stat pH management (Fig. 22.2).

The effects of CPB on autoregulation in other organs is clinically less well documented. Likewise, the effect of CPB on distribution of blood flow to (and within) specific organs requires further study in man despite nearly 40 years of clinical experience with CPB, and a substantial experimental data base. Experimentally, with per-

---

[b]There is disagreement regarding the declining cardiac output with increasing age that may also apply to the relationship of $\dot{V}O_2$ to increasing age. Early studies demonstrated a clear inverse relationship between increasing age and cardiac output (4). However the study populations were unselected and the increasing prevalence of cardiovascular disease with advancing age makes the interpretation of the data unclear. More recent studies have confirmed the earlier data for sedentary individuals, but show well-preserved cardiac function, including cardiac output, in physically fit elderly persons free of overt cardiovascular disease (5, 6).

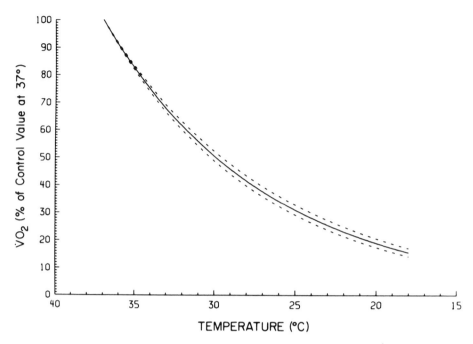

Figure 22.1. The nomogram depicts the relationship between oxygen consumption ($\dot{V}O_2$), as a percent of the value at 37°C, and body temperature. The dotted lines show the 70% confidence limits. (From Kirklin JW, Barratt-Boyes BG. Cardiac Surgery. New York: John Wiley & Sons, 1986:32.)

fusion circuit blood flow in the range of 2 to 2.5 liters/min/m², systemic blood flow distribution remains essentially normal (12). Experimentally, hypothermia during CPB is associated with altered local $\dot{V}O_2$ and the associated change in vascular resistance tends to promote regional blood flow distribution in proportion to the local $\dot{V}O_2$ produced by hypothermia.

Systemic measurements that may indicate the adequacy of total blood flow relative to total $\dot{V}O_2$ during CPB include $S_{\bar{v}}O_2$, pH, and lactate concentration. The latter two are closely linked because accumulation of lactic acid in blood leads to hydrogen ion accumulation through dissociation. ($CH_3CHOHCOOH \longleftrightarrow CH_3\text{-}CHOHCOO + H^+$). However, there are other sources of hydrogen ion production during oxygen (blood flow) deprivation such as on-going glycolysis (anaerobic glucose metabolism) and continued adenosine triphosphate hydrolysis, both of which produce a net accumulation of hydrogen ion.

Measurement of hemoglobin oxygen saturation in the venous return (or venous oxygen partial pressure) during CPB has the same significance as the corresponding pulmonary artery (mixed venous) measurement during normal circulation. Given steady-state conditions of hemoglobin concentration, P_{50} (primarily a function of 2,3-diphosphoglyceric acid concentration, temperature, and pH) and arterial oxygenation, then $S_{\bar{v}}O_2$ will change in direct proportion to systemic blood flow at constant $\dot{V}O_2$. Unfortunately the inverse relationship between $S_{\bar{v}}O_2$ and $\dot{V}O_2$ (predictable from the Fick equation) confounds the simple interpretation of $S_{\bar{v}}O_2$ data. For example, if blood flow and arterial oxygen content are held constant, then $S_{\bar{v}}O_2$ will *increase* as $\dot{V}O_2$ *decreases* (13). In the case of a capillary bed that is underperfused relative to the local level of $\dot{V}O_2$, the contribution to the systemic $S_{\bar{v}}O_2$ (or pH or lactic acid concentration, for that matter) is a function of the ratio between systemic blood flow volume and the local area blood flow volume. Importantly, an intense hypoxic insult in a focal area of considerable clinical importance (brain, heart, kidney, etc.) may well not produce a major change in $S_{\bar{v}}O_2$. Accordingly, although monitoring $S_{\bar{v}}O_2$ during CPB is a common practice, a normal or increased $S_{\bar{v}}O_2$ value during CPB does not ensure that the perfusion is necessarily meeting regional oxygen delivery requirements. However, a low $S_{\bar{v}}O_2$ during CPB does indicate a problem with systemic oxygen delivery that may be due to insufficient blood flow, hemoglobin function or concentration, arterial oxygenation, or excessive oxygen consumption due to inadequate anesthesia or hyperthermia.

One method for individualizing blood flow volume relative to $\dot{V}O_2$ during CPB was termed oxygen consumption plateauing by its original describers, Mandl and Motley (14). Using this method, $\dot{V}O_2$ is calculated during CPB and the perfusion is increased until there is no further increase in $\dot{V}O_2$, the $\dot{V}O_2$ plateau. Perfusion is then maintained at this level until an intervention occurs that would be expected to alter $\dot{V}O_2$, for example rewarming, at which point the plateau must be reestablished. One theoretical advantage to this technique is that it calls attention to variables other than flow that have an effect on $\dot{V}O_2$. For example, pharmacologic manipulation of perfusion pressure, if excessive vasoconstriction or vasodilation exist, may improve $\dot{V}O_2$ presumably by improving perfusion to previously under perfused areas. The concept then becomes

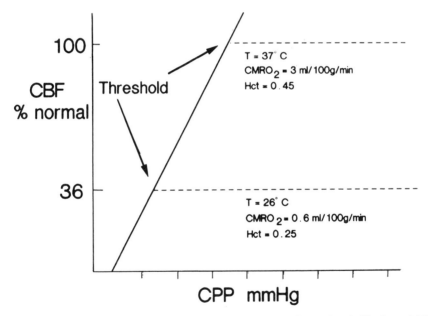

Figure 22.2. Theoretical effect of hypothermic bypass on the autoregulatory threshold. The *solid line* is the pressure flow relation for the maximally vasodilated state. The autoregulatory threshold is the point where the autoregulatory plateau (represented by the *dashed lines*) intersects the maximal vasodilation pressure flow relation. Given maintained coupling between cerebral metabolic rate and blood flow, a decreased metabolic rate such as that produced by hypothermia will effectively produce a leftward shift of the autoregulatory threshold (lower dashed line, solid line intersection). *CBF*, cerebral blood flow; *CPP*, cerebral perfusion pressure. (From Murkin JM, Farrar JK, Tweed A, et al. Cerebral autoregulation and flow/metabolism coupling during cardiopulmonary bypass: the influence of carbon dioxide. Anesth Analg 1987;61:825.)

one of $\dot{V}O_2$ optimization. The chief difficulty of the technique is the lack of a "gold
standard" against which to compare any
given clinical $\dot{V}O_2$ calculation during CPB.
The steady-state awake or anesthetized
prebypass value may be calculated and used
as the baseline for CPB, when corrected for
the expected temperature effect, but using
the uncorrected awake $\dot{V}O_2$ as the baseline
would yield excess perfusion during CPB.
The anesthetized, paralyzed, mechanically
ventilated patient has a substantially lower
$\dot{V}O_2$ than the awake patient state. Another
difficulty is that clinically there is not as
clear a plateau to $\dot{V}O_2$ as would be theoretically predicted. Optimization of $\dot{V}O_2$ during
CPB may provide the best means of assessing adequacy of perfusion during CPB; however, this represents an untested hypothesis,
at least as measured against the standard of
clinical outcome.

What then are reasonable flow recommendations for CPB? In adults at normothermia, progressive acidosis and increased

lactate production are seen with total flows
less than 1.6 liters/min/m² or 50 ml/kg/
min (15, 16). Clinical and experimental
data support a total flow of 1.8 liters/min/
m² as predictive of the $\dot{V}O_2$ plateau in normothermic adults (17, 18). Kirklin and
Barratt-Boyes (19) have recommended flow
in the 2.2 to 2.5 liters/min/m² as "more securely adequate" in normothermic adults.
During hypothermia, various nomograms
have been proposed (Fig. 22.3) that predominantly rely on the plateauing of $\dot{V}O_2$ to
indicate overall adequacy of perfusion for
any given temperature. The recommended
flow in infants and children is higher, 80 to
125 ml/kg/min.

Perfusion (arterial) pressure during
CPB, like blood flow, remains a topic of
some controversy in the management of
CPB. In general, blood flow probably outweighs perfusion pressure as a guide to adequacy of perfusion during CPB especially
with hemodilution, but solid data supporting this contention are lacking. Perfu-

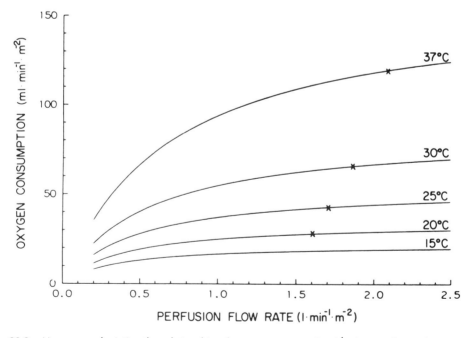

Figure 22.3. Nomogram depicting the relationship of oxygen consumption ($\dot{V}O_2$) to perfusion flow rate and temperature. The small Xs represent commonly clinically used flow rates at the various temperatures. (From Kirklin JW, Barratt-Boyes BG. Cardiac surgery. New York: John Wiley & Sons, 1986:35.)

sion pressure is determined by the interaction of blood flow and overall arterial impedance. Impedance, in this case, is primarily related to actual friction resistance since the steady-state nonpulsatile nature of most CPB largely negates the elastance, inertial, and reflection components that influence aortic input impedance during pulsatile flow. Friction resistance is primarily a function of the vasomotor tone (cross-sectional area of the arterial system) and blood viscosity. Viscosity, in turn, is a function of temperature (see Chapter 6) and the degree of hemodilution (see Chapter 5). The interaction of temperature and hematocrit with regard to viscosity is depicted graphically in Figure 22.4.

For any given level of hematocrit, viscosity (and, therefore, resistance to blood flow) increases substantially as temperature decreases. Normal viscosity at 37°C and a hematocrit of 40 approximates that seen at 25°C with hematocrit of 25. This relationship indicates the importance of hemodilution in CPB, especially with hypothermia. With the onset of CPB, using an asanguineous prime solution there is an immediate fall in systemic vascular resistance that is not seen with a blood prime (Fig. 22.5). This drop in resistance with the onset of CPB is primarily due to the acute decrease in viscosity produced by the hemodilution from the prime solution (20). Fortunately, this usually transient hypotension appears to have little clinical effect.

A more complex phenomenon pertaining to perfusion pressure during CPB is the increasing vascular resistance seen over time. Because of the third space equilibration of crystalloid prime solutions and the hemoconcentrating effect of the diuresis commonly seen during CPB, the initial drop in viscosity is corrected as the excess crystalloid is removed from the vasculature. Add to this the physical increase in viscosity produced by even moderate hypothermia

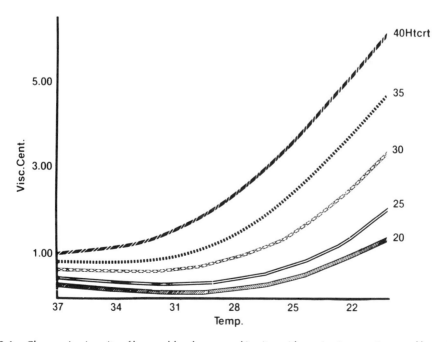

Figure 22.4.   Changes in viscosity of human blood measured in vitro with varying temperatures and hematocrit (*Htcrt*). (From Robicsek F, Martens TN, Nieshuchowski W. Vasomotor activity during cardiopulmonary bypass. In: Utley JR, ed. Pathophysiology and techniques of cardiopulmonary bypass. Baltimore: Williams & Wilkins, 1983:1–12.)

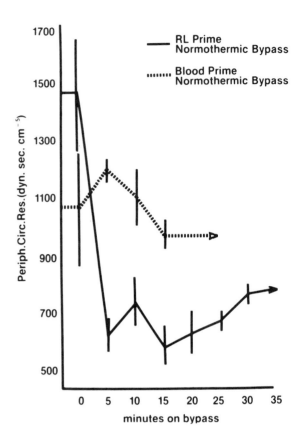

Figure 22.5. Changes in circulatory resistance comparing data from 15 patients undergoing normothermic bypass with a crystalloid prime (*solid line*) to 8 patients undergoing normo- thermic bypass with a blood prime. *RL,* Ranger's lactate solution. (From Robiscek F, Martens TN, Nieshuchowski W. Vasomotor ac- tivity during cardiopulmonary bypass. In: Utley JR, ed. Pathophysiology and techniques of car- diopulmonary bypass. Baltimore: Williams & Wilkins, 1983:1-12.)

(Fig. 22.4) and it would seem attractive to accept that viscosity change accounts for both the precipitous drop in vascular resis- tance with the onset of CPB and the steady increase of resistance over time during CPB. However, even if temperature and blood composition (viscosity) are held constant during CPB, calculated vascular resistance still increases with time (20).

The increase in circulating catechola- mines that occurs during CPB is well docu- mented and is, to some extent, modifiable by the type and depth of the anesthetic, but there remains in most clinical circum- stances a significant increase in plasma cat- echolamines during CPB (21, 22). This cat- echolamine release is but one manifestation of a major stress response elicited by CPB (see Chapters 9 and 12). It is likely that the additive vasomotor effects of circulating catecholamines and other vasoactive media- tors of the stress response are responsible

for the increased vascular resistance found during and after CPB. Indirect evidence that reflex sympathetic neural activation may also play a role in this response is provided by the observation that unilateral stellate ganglion blockade ameliorates the hyper- tensive response following CPB (23).

Another important point regarding perfusion pressure during and immediately after CPB is the relatively common occur- rence of significant measurement artifacts. Especially when hypothermia has been em- ployed during CPB, a significant underesti- mation of central aortic pressure is seen in measured radial artery pressures, some- times by as much as 30 to 40%. This is counter to the normal state where actual radial artery systolic pressure exceeds cen- tral aortic pressure by 10 to 15% or more, largely due to the amplification of effects of pressure waves reflected from the periph- ery (24).

This artifact is associated with rewarming at the end of CPB and often continues for 30 minutes or more into the post-CPB interval. The physiologic cause of the artifact is not completely understood. In the past, persistent vasoconstriction was often stated to be the cause. However, sufficient proximal conductance vessel constriction to dampen the radial pressure is unlikely and the effect of distal constriction should be an enhancement of the normal gradient. A more likely explanation is that rewarming initiates uneven vasodilation and intense skeletal muscle vasodilation in the forearm and hand may have the effect of a large arteriovenous shunt and thereby decrease the pressure measured at the radial artery (25). The final solution to this interesting puzzle remains. But the important clinical message is that apparent hypotension, as measured at the radial artery, at the conclusion of CPB should be confirmed, preferably by a central aortic or femoral arterial pressure measurement, before instituting inotropic or vasoconstrictor therapy. This is easily accomplished using an 18- or 20-gauge needle with pressure tubing connected to a transducer, usually the arterial catheter transducer. As an alternative, use of a Doppler probe placed over the brachial artery in conjunction with an ordinary blood pressure cuff and manometer may provide more accurate measurement of arterial pressure than a radial catheter in this situation.

Other common causes of low pressure artifact from the radial artery measurement include surgical retraction and patient size. Significantly obese patients positioned with the arms tucked to the sides will frequently have enough tissue compression of the axillary artery to cause dampening of the radial artery waveform. Even with nonobese patients, the "arms at the sides" positioning coupled with aggressive use of a sternal retractor for internal mammary artery dissection can lead to axillary artery compression and radial artery waveform dampening. For completeness, the potential disaster of aortic dissection must be mentioned (see Chapter 29 for a complete discussion). A sudden precipitous drop of radial artery pressure (either left or right, but more classically left) coincident with the onset of CPB should at least raise the question of aortic dissection caused by aortic cannula malposition at the onset of perfusion. Fortunately, the associated findings of a tensely distended aorta with obvious intramural hematoma formation are sufficiently pronounced to make the diagnosis of the problem relatively straightforward. Unfortunately, the treatment of the problem is substantially more complex (see Chapter 24).

Less common, but of equal or greater importance, is the artifact of radial artery pressure measurement during CPB caused by inappropriate aortic perfusion cannula placement so that the flow of blood out of the cannula is directed preferentially into one of the great vessels of the aortic arch. The artifact produced is a high and very pulsatile radial arterial pressure when the radial catheter is ipsilateral to the inadvertent cannulation in the case of either the innominate or left subclavian artery (Fig. 22.6). Another clinical sign of this same complication is lateralized blanching of the face with the onset of CPB in the case of the left carotid artery perfusion (26). The clinical problem presented is one of gross overperfusion of the cerebral arterial system leading to cerebral edema or frank neurologic injury and also the probability of significant systemic underperfusion. Awareness of the potential problem by perfusionists, surgeons, and anesthesiologists coupled with vigilance for these signs is the key to preventing this potential disaster.

PULMONARY ARTERY AND LEFT ATRIAL PRESSURE MONITORING

Both pulmonary artery (PA) and left atrial (LA) pressure monitoring have a major role in clinical care decisions in cardiac surgical patients. The most important

Figure 22.6. The figure is a drawing of the left radial artery pressure waveform during CPB. The high pulsatile pressure is due to the arterial cannula inadvertently directed into the left subclavian system. At the *arrow,* the cannula was redirected into the aortic lumen. (From McCleskey CH, Cheney FW. A correctable complication of cardiopulmonary bypass. Anesthsiology 1982;36:214–216.)

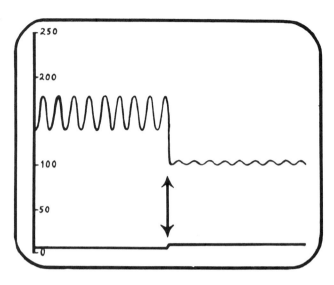

components of this role are found in the pre- and post-CPB intervals, and both measurements feature prominently in decisions regarding weaning from CPB (see Chapter 30). However, both monitors can be useful during CPB. The LA pressure and, less directly, PA pressure give the same information regarding left ventricular filling during CPB as off CPB. But rather than the usual clinical context of using the measured LA or PA pressure to guide the adjustment of ventricular filling to appropriate physiologic levels, during CPB the expectation is that both PA and LA pressure should be near zero and the monitoring is used to prevent overdistension of the left ventricle. For example, a patient with markedly increased bronchial blood flow due to chronic lung disease or cyanotic congenital heart disease can markedly overdistend the left ventricle if venting is not adequate. Another example is the patient with aortic valve insufficiency. As left ventricular emptying decreases (on CPB and cooling) or stops (on CPB and fibrillation), massive overdistension can rapidly result from blood flow through the incompetent aortic valve. In fact, during ventricular fibrillation on CPB, surgical manipulation of the heart can result in significant imcompetence of even an anatomically normal aortic valve. In most cases, this type of abnormal filling of the left ventricle during CPB can be detected by monitoring either the LA or PA pressure. Importantly, however, because of compliance variation among patients, there is no quantitative predictability of left ventricular volume based on LA or PA pressure. Therefore, one should expect near zero pressures and be wary of any increase during CPB.

As with radial artery catheter pressure measurement, one must be aware of measurement artifacts during CPB in LA and PA pressures. Both LA and PA catheters can be inadvertently kinked or obstructed; LA catheters are more vulnerable to inadvertent dislodgement than are PA catheters, but both are vulnerable. There is a tendency during CPB for a PA catheter that has been properly positioned in the prebypass period to migrate distally into the PA by 3 to 5 cm or more as blood volume is taken from the right ventricle into the venous reservoir and the heart empties with initiation of CPB. This can produce a "permanent wedge" phenomenon that has been implicated in PA rupture or pulmonary infarction. Often this malposition is indicated by a distinct increase in the PA pressure reading or $S_{\bar{v}}O_2$ in the case of an oximeter PA catheter. This malposition is sufficiently predictable that it may be clinically prudent to arbitrarily withdraw the PA catheter by 3 to 5 cm at the commencement of CPB. The routine use of a catheter introducer and a sterile protective sheath allows sterile repositioning of the PA catheter at the end of CPB. Some experienced clinicians recommend withdrawal of the PA catheter further, into the SVC, during CPB. However, refloating the PA catheter at the end of CPB is not always easily accomplished, and difficulty is most likely in the low output management problems where the PA catheter is most useful. Despite the seemingly sound arguments for withdrawing the PA catheter during CPB, it has not been conclusively shown that this practice decreases the already small incidence of PA catheter-induced PA rupture.

Central venous pressure measurement is also helpful in guiding clinical decisions during CPB. As with LA and PA pressures, the expectation is that pressure in the vena cava [both superior vena cava (SVC) and inferior vena cava (IVC)] should be at or near zero or even slightly negative during CPB. In contrast to LA and PA pressure increase, an increased SVC or IVC pressure is not usually associated with cardiac distension. Rather, the increased venous pressure indicates impaired venous drainage to the venous reservoir due to either venous cannulae of insufficient size, malpositioned venous cannulae, venous cannulae or drainage line obstruction, or insufficient vertical distance between the heart and the venous reservoir to promote an adequate siphon effect.

The major adverse physiologic effect of elevated venous pressure during CPB is a reduction in effective perfusion pressure for critical organs such as brain, kidneys, and abdominal viscera, (especially the liver) and an enhanced tendency for edema production. For example, if the mean arterial pressure is 60 mm Hg during CPB and if SVC and IVC pressures are near zero then the brain, the kidneys, and the splanchnic arterial bed have an effective perfusion pressure of 60 mm Hg. However, if SVC or IVC pressure is elevated to 20 mm Hg, for

example, then the net perfusion pressure in these same areas is only 40 mm Hg and the increased back pressure will promote accumulation of edema. From this perspective, the liver is theoretically particularly vulnerable because approximately 75% of hepatic blood flow occurs at venous pressure via the portal vein. An elevated venous outflow pressure (i.e., IVC pressure) could theoretically have a major adverse effect on hepatic blood flow during bypass.

It is important to recognize that SVC and IVC pressures are not necessarily equal during CPB even with a single two-stage venous drainage cannula. Moreover, there is little visible evidence of IVC engorgement with a median sternotomy incision. Especially with cardiac retraction and a single two-stage venous cannula, it is common to have venous drainage impairment and an increased measured central venous pressure. Venous pressure measurement is also subject to significant artifact during bypass. For example, during total CPB (bicaval cannulation with tourniquets around the cavae) the venous catheter may be entrapped in the tourniquet. If the venous catheter is occluded, the constant flush infusion device on the transducer will rapidly overpressurize the transducer. On the other hand, if the catheter remains patent and passes beyond the tourniquet then, with the heart open, an artifactually low venous pressure will be measured. In this situation SVC and IVC pressure can each vary independently. A further central venous pressure measurement artifact, not specific for CPB, is produced when the pressure port of a PA catheter remains within the lumen of the introducer sheath; then an infusion into the sheath via the sidearm can produce a pressure in excess of SVC pressure that is measured at the right atrial port of the PA catheter (Fig. 22.7) (27).

Mixed venous hemoglobin oxygen saturation $S_{\bar{v}}O_2$, as measured from a PA catheter, loses most of its clinical utility during CPB because of the diversion of venous return into the venous reservoir. However, as

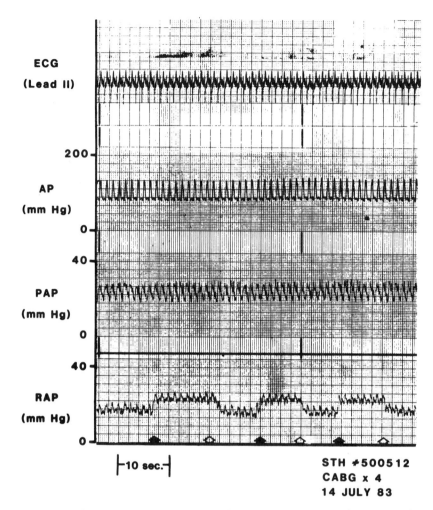

Figure 22.7.   Right atrial pressure (*RAP*) is increased at the onset of the venous infusion port infusion (*solid arrow*) and returns to the preinfusion level when the infusion stops. *AP,* arterial pressure; *PAP,* pulmonary artery pressure; *CABG,* coronary artery bypass graft. (From Davis RF. Yet another CVP artifact. Anesthesiology 1984;60:262.)

previously mentioned, a very high PA catheter $S_{\bar{v}}O_2$ can be an indicator of a catheter in "wedged" position during CPB. The value of $S_{\bar{v}}O_2$ measurement of venous blood drained into the venous reservoir is considerable, having much the same significance as the corresponding PA catheter measurement off bypass. As described above in the section on blood flow and perfusion pressure requirements during CPB, if one is aware of the major determinants of the $S_{\bar{v}}O_2$ value (hemoglobin concentration, blood flow, hemoglobin P_{50}, arterial oxygenation,

and systemic oxygen consumption) then the $S_{\bar{v}}O_2$ can be used as a guide to adequacy of flow during CPB.

Other Cardiovascular Monitors

Another increasingly commonly used clinical cardiovascular monitor is transesophageal echocardiography (TEE). Unfortunately, a substantial portion of TEE utility is lost during CPB. Blood loss from the cardiac chambers obscures the ultrasound definition of the chambers; there is little or no cavity, therefore little or no ultrasound contrast to define cardiac structures. Likewise, during CPB there is little or no intracardiac blood flow, so that Doppler information on blood flow velocity and direction and on valvular function is largely irrelevant. However, as the heart is filled at the conclusion of CPB, TEE regains its ability to visually display intracardiac structures, wall motion, and blood flow direction and velocity.

Electrocardiographic monitoring must be continued during CPB. During periods of cardioplegic arrest it is important to verify that the ECG is isoelectric. Following the surgical repair, the ECG should return to the baseline state before weaning from CPB (see Chapter 30). Abrupt changes of the ST segment deviation from isoelectric should raise the immediate question of intracoronary embolization of air or particulates. Persistent ST segment deviation should raise the question of ongoing ischemia that should be investigated and corrected prior to terminating CPB. One should not overlook the value of direct observation of the heart as an adjunct to ECG diagnosis, especially in patients with arrhythmia problems.

Neurologic Monitoring

Neurologic monitoring during CPB is directed primarily toward the myoneural junction to confirm adequacy of muscle paralysis and toward the CNS to detect functional abnormalities developing during CPB. The former is straightforward and needs little attention here except to say that unnecessary oxygen consumption and CO_2 production during moderate hypothermic CPB are decreased when a complete level of skeletal muscle paralysis is maintained. This, coupled with the decreased effective concentration of neuromuscular blocking agents produced by the blood volume expansion from the CPB priming volume (see Chapter 8), explain the common clinical recommentation to re-dose relaxants with

approximately one-half of an expected "intubating dose" at the time of initiating CPB. In this regard there is perhaps some theoretical advantage to the use of d-tubocurarine because its ganglionic blocking side effects may help control the increase in vascular resistance during hypothermia and CPB.

Central nervous system monitoring has traditionally relied on electrophysiologic measurement of neurologic activity measured from the body surface and exemplified by the electroencephalogram (EEG). An enhancement of this passive measurement is the evoked potential. Typically, an evoked potential is measured as the surface electrophysiologic manifestation of the transmission of a stimulus along a given neural pathway. Other, nonelectrophysiologic CNS monitoring includes transcranial Doppler and reflectance spectrometry. Transcranial Doppler ultrasound measures blood flow velocity in major arterial segments in the brain and can detect transient artifacts in the velocity signal attributable to particulate or gas emboli. Reflectance spectrometry developments now allow measurement of the signal produced by the mean venous oxygen hemoglobin saturation at discrete loci in the brain. Although the CNS monitoring capabilities applicable to patients undergoing CPB are significant, the clinical use is relatively small compared to the total scope of CPB monitoring. Also, the ability of more intensive CNS monitoring to decrease the frequency of adverse neurologic outcome after CPB remains largely untested.

ELECTROPHYSIOLOGIC MONITORING

Recording of a full standard EEG electrode montage on a strip chart with an experienced EEG analyst observing the signals is the gold standard for EEG recordings. The value of this approach intraoperatively is debated for certain procedures such as carotid endarterectomy; however, application of such technique to CPB is rarely seen outside of specific focused clinical investigation. The processed EEG, either compressed spectral array or density modulated spectral array, provides a smaller volume of data than the raw EEG, but the data are presented in a much more user-friendly format, that allows clinicians to detect lateralized (or global) change in both the dominant frequency and the power of the EEG even with intermittent observation of the record. Excellent, comprehensive reviews of this subject are readily available (28–30).

The process of CPB presents many physiologic changes that markedly complicate the interpretation of the EEG. The primary changes in the EEG indicating hypofusion or hypoxia are slowing of the dominant frequency and loss of power in the signal, and similar changes can be produced in the EEG by hemodilution, hypothermia, anesthetics, perfusion changes, and pulsatility changes, in addition to any imputed hypoxic CNS insult (28). For example, anesthetics have well-known EEG effects, including the ability to produce burst suppression or an isoelectric pattern with barbiturates and with the volatile anesthetic isoflurane. Mild hypothermia itself produces slowing of the EEG, which proceeds through burst suppression to an isoelectric pattern as temperature is further decreased. However, comparing temperature-related EEG changes to hypoxia, there are differences that may become clinically useful (31). Significant hypoxia is marked by a rapid decrease in high-frequency EEG activity. Also, while the burst suppression pattern of hypothermia tends to be regular, that seen with hypoxia is more irregular. Perhaps the situation is analogous to ST segment depression in the electrocardiogram. Here, the unproven but hopeful hypothesis is that there exist discrete EEG patterns, detectable during CPB and distinguishable from other effects, that reliably indicate CNS hypoxia at a treatable point prior to frank cytologic injury.

Currently the use of evoked potentials during CPB is largely limited to surgery involving the descending thoracic aorta, generally repair of aortic coarctation, aortic dissection and aortic aneurysm repair. Because of the anatomy of the major blood supply to the spinal cord (the anterior spinal artery and the communicating artery of Adamkewicz) (Fig. 22.8), the spinal cord is at risk of ischemic injury when the descending thoracic aorta is clamped to permit surgical repair. By monitoring the progress of an evoked signal at several sites from the periphery to the cerebral cortex one can monitor the function of each component of the transmission sequence from peripheral nerve through the spinal cord to the cerebral cortex. Theoretically, observation of increased latency or decreased amplitude of the evoked potential signal at any site along the path would allow intervention prior to neurologic injury. In aortic coarctation, for example, observation of an abnormal evoked potential after application of the aortic clamp could then trigger removal and replacement of the clamp or some other (pharmacologic) maneuver to increase perfusion pressure or cardiac output in an attempt to improve spinal cord blood flow before the repair is undertaken. Unfortunately, the caveats regarding the interaction of CPB, hypothermia, anesthesia, hemodilution, and the EEG also apply to evoked potentials. Also, the predominant type of evoked potential used clinically is currently the sensory evoked potential. In the case of the somatosensory evoked potential, the motor component of the spinal cord is relatively silent. Cases exist of dense motor paraplegia following thoracic aortic surgery despite persistently normal somatosensory evoked potentials throughout the aortic cross-clamp interval (32).

Temperature Monitoring

Because of the integral relationship between temperature control (manipulation) and CPB, it is fair to say that temperature measurement is a core physiologic monitor during CPB. A major difficulty,

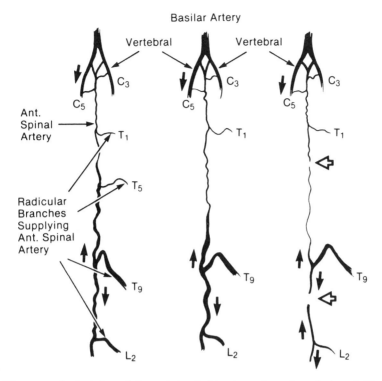

Figure 22.8. Diagrammatic depiction of the variation in blood supply to the spinal cord. The variation diagramed on the right presents a higher risk for spinal cord ischemia with descending aortic surgery. (From Dembitsky WP. Central nervous system injury during surgery of the descending aorta. Ch 8. In: Utley JR, ed. Pathophysiology and techniques of cardiopulmonary bypass. Vol 1. Baltimore: Williams & Wilkins, 1982:80.)

however, is the simple definition of "core" temperature. The technology available for temperature measurement during CPB is nothing less than abundant. The problem is not how to measure; the technological capability exceeds the clinical need for accuracy or adaptability. Measurement of nasopharyngeal, esophageal, tracheal, mixed venous blood, bladder urine, rectal (fecal), tympanic membrane, and even great toe temperature are readily available for clinical use. In many cardiac surgical units measurement of two or more of these is common practice. But, what is core temperature? The concept of a single core body temperature is just that, a concept rather than a reality. Figure 22.9 is instructive in this regard. The expectation is that especially during cooling or rewarming, temper-

ature is site-specific, and the variability from site to site is significant.

Temperatures are measured during cooling to assure that the organs felt most vulnerable to potential underperfusion actually receive the benefit of the desired degree of hypothermia. In this regard the brain is usually the target, and nasopharyngeal (not airway), tympanic membrane, or esophageal (below tracheal bifurcation) are the usually accepted best estimates of brain temperature. Tympanic membrane temperature monitoring is less popular because of the occurrence of probe-related tympanic membrane injury. Mixed venous temperature in the extracorporeal circuit is a reasonable indicator of average body temperature directly analogous to an $S_{\bar{v}}O_2$ measurement.

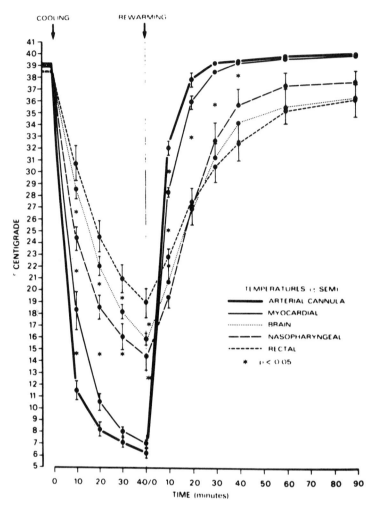

Figure 22.9. The figure diagrammatically shows the relationships of temperatures measured at various sites over time during cooling and rewarming from cardiopulmonary bypass. (From Stefaniszyn HJ, Novick RJ, Keith FM, Salerno TA. Is the brain adequately cooled during deep hypothermic cardiopulmonary bypass? Curr Surg 1983;40:294–297.)

During rewarming, the target, obviously, is a normothermic patient at the end of CPB. Success is both time-dependent as well as measured temperature-dependent. For example, the total caloric loss in a series of adult patients cooled to 30°C for 130 minutes on CPB was calculated at 238 kilocalories (33). The net return during rewarming was approximately 160 kilocalories, leaving a heat debt of 78 kilocalories or approximately the equivalent of 1.5 hours of the basal metabolic heat output. This deficit is likely the explanation for the

common clinical observation of rebound hypothermia, sometimes termed afterdrop, following termination of CPB. In this regard, the use of vasodilators, nitroprusside, or nitroglycerin to force a vasodilation during CPB theoretically promotes a more uniform rewarming, and has been clinically shown to decrease the incidence and severity of rebound hypothermia after CPB (34).

Important considerations for temperature measurement during rewarming are prevention of effervescence and blood damage. Because of the inverse relationship between gas solubility in blood (or any liquid) and temperature, dissolved gases tend to come out of solution as a fluid is warmed. If this happens clinically the consequences of gaseous embolization (even microemboli) can be significant. In general, maintenance of a temperature gradient from the heat exchanger to the venous blood of not more than approximately 10°C will prevent significant microbubble formation. Although heat exchangers are highly efficient, there is a temperature gradient produced within the heat exchanger. A boundary layer forms immediately adjacent to the heat exchanger in which blood temperature will equal heat exchanger temperature, while blood farther away from the exchange surface will not fully equilibrate with exchanger temperature. Because blood damage (both cellular elements and protein denaturation) increases with temperature greater than 42°C, this temperature forms the practical upper limit to temperature within the heat exchanger (35). But as previously mentioned, the minimum exchanger temperature, approximately 4°C, appears not to damage blood.

Urinary Volume-Renal Function

A detailed discussion of the effect of CPB on renal function is found in Chapter 19. Most cardiac surgical units closely follow the urine flow of patients during CPB as an indicator of normal renal function. While a brisk flow of urine during CPB may be comforting and may, in fact, facilitate fluid management during CPB, existing clinical data do not support a close relationship between urine flow while on CPB and postoperative renal function. In the mid 1970s Abel and associates (36) examined a large number of patients for factors predictive of postoperative renal failure. Two major factors emerged as significant correlates of postoperative renal failure, time on bypass and preexisting renal failure. Other factors including urine volume on bypass were not significantly related to postoperative renal failure.

What is the place of diuretic medications either osmotic (i.e., mannitol) or loop (i.e., furosemide and congeners) diuretics in the management of the oliguric patient during CPB? Several considerations are pertinent. The first is to assure catheter patency. This may seem an absurd comment, but clinical experience indicates that the bladder is very compliant and that pharmacologic diuresis will rarely fill it to a pressure sufficient to overcome an obstructed catheter. In general, a physiologic urine volume of 0.5 to 1.0 ml/kg/hr requires no treatment. Oliguric or anuric patients may or may not benefit from diuretic therapy. Again, available clinical data do not relate urine volume during CPB to postoperative renal dysfunction. However, oliguria or even normal urine flow in the face of hyperkalemia, hemoglobinemia (presumed hemolysis), or suspected volume overload (excessive hemodilution) are indications for diuresis. Theoretically, in the case of hyperkalemia, loop diuretics would provide the greatest potassium loss. In the case of hemoglobinuria, a large volume of alkaline urine is desired, so either loop or osmotic diuretics (or both) may be useful.

Coagulation

Coagulation monitoring is an obviously major area of patient monitoring during CPB. Section III, Chapters 14 to 17, provide a detailed review of all relevant aspects of coagulation and CPB.

Laboratory Data

The frequency and type of laboratory data monitored during CPB are relatively institution-specific, but laboratory support should minimally include blood gas and pH measurement and rapid access to electrolytes, especially potassium and calcium, as well as glucose and perhaps lactate. Whether these data are available from a satellite laboratory in close proximity to the operating room, from "in line" or "in room" monitors, or from the main hospital laboratory is less important than the rapid availability of data. The rapidity and magnitude of intraoperative changes in these parameters in cardiac surgical patients makes their rapid (5 to 10 minute) availability a virtual requirement for safe cardiac surgery.

A common area of controversy in blood gas data interpretation during CPB is the management of P_aCO_2 and pH during hypothermia. The discussion of alpha-stat versus pH-stat management schemes is well presented in Chapters 6 and 21 and does not need to be recapitulated here. The use of potassium-based cardioplegic solutions mandates the capability for rapid and accurate assessment of serum potassium concentration. The metabolic consequences of CPB, especially those involving glucose utilization (see Chapter 20), create the requirement for frequent glucose (and optimally lactate) measurement during and after CPB.

Emerging technologies for "on line" or local laboratory measurements include cartridge-based electrode systems and intravascular, usually fluorochrome, catheter-based technology. The latter generally couples intensity of fluorescence of the fluorochrome when stimulated by light at a specific wavelength to fiberoptic technology for transmission of the emitted fluorescent light to an analytic instrument. The intensity of fluorescence is proportional to the concentration of the parameter being measured (P_aO_2, P_aCO_2, pH). Current capabilities in this area include systems that will pass through a 20-gauge catheter, are capable of giving near continuous P_aO_2, P_aCO_2, and pH data at ambient patient temperature and still permit pressure measurement via the same catheter. Depending on institutional practices regarding frequency of blood gas analysis and cost of the testing, this new approach may prove to be cost-

effective, but the clinical value of the continuous measurement of blood gas data (as opposed to intermittent sampling) remains to be established.

The cartridge electrode systems are more conventional in that electrochemical reactions form the basis for measurement. The novelty (advantage) is that the cartridge is a self-contained unit with electrodes and calibration solutions capable of making a defined number of measurements over a defined time span. For institutions capable of using the full capacity of the cartridge within its life span, the result is also often very cost-effective. Cartridge-based systems are often small enough to be physically attached to the CPB machine and may be equipped with automatic sampling capability. Although this is not actually a continuous measurement, the sampling frequency is programmable and limited only by the time required for the actual electrode measurement. These instruments also may provide quality management functions such as documentation of quality control testing and control over instrument use by uncertified or untrained individuals, in addition to providing needed laboratory data.

EQUIPMENT MONITORING DURING CPB

Oxygenator Function

Arguably, the single most important item of equipment in the CPB set-up is the oxygenator. Whether membrane (hollow fiber or true membrane) or bubble (see Chapter 2), the oxygenators in current use are manufactured as single use, disposable items subject to stringent quality control. Problems do occur nevertheless, although rarely. The immediate life-sustaining function of the oxygenator is oxygenation of the blood; ventilation follows. Therefore, the single best monitor of oxygenator function is oxygenation. As just discussed, a variety of instrumentation is available for blood gas (P_aO_2, in this case) analysis ranging from laboratory benchmark instruments to in-line catheter based systems. The point is that the adequacy of oxygenation must be reliably determined both early and through-out the CPB course. The emphasis on labo-ratory determination does not discount clinical observation. A cyanotic surgical field should get everyone's attention quickly! Having established adequate initial oxygenator function, it is prudent to reas-sess blood gases at regular intervals throughout CPB. Also, recalling the earlier discussion of the value of $S_{\bar{v}}O_2$ measure-ment to guide perfusion adequacy, venous drainage line oximetry is useful.

Air Detection

Massive air embolism during CPB is a catastrophe that hopefully few ever experi-ence, but it calls attention to the problem of air detection in CPB circuitry. The prob-lem is not limited to massive embolism, as both macro- and microbubbles can lead to circulatory obstruction in discrete vascular beds that can produce devastating organ damage. Air detection and embolism pre-vention methods fall within several catego-ries. The first category is the simple alarm. This might be, for example, a blood level sensor on the venous reservoir. The func-tion of this alarm is to simply call attention to a reservoir level that has fallen below a preselected threshold, in order to allow time for corrective action before risking air entrainment into the pumping apparatus. The time factor is not insignificant. For ex-ample, a volume alarm at the 500-ml resid-ual volume point on a venous reservoir gives only 6 seconds to zero volume when flow rate is 5 liters min. The type of pump used is significant in this regard. Conven-tional roller pumps easily pump air; centrif-ugal pumps are less able to do so, but will readily push a blood-foam mixture. The second category of air detection device

couples the alarm to a functional result. For example, the reservoir alarm is linked to the flow control so that triggering the alarm stops flow or produces a programmable flow reduction (perhaps to 50% or 25% of the prealarm flow). The not-so-subtle disad-vantage of this type of integrated alarm is the functional impediment caused by the inevitable false alarm. Nevertheless, a pro-grammed machine response may convey a clinical safety advantage. A third category of air detection device is the simple, func-tional, float valve that is capable of stop-ping blood flow rapidly and effectively in the event of massive air entrainment. Unfor-tunately it is largely ineffective for small en-trained volumes because there must be enough air entrained to allow the valve float to seat and seal. The disadvantage of such a simple system is that although air entrain-ment into the pump head may be pre-vented, the perfusion system is stopped and the "fix" (i.e., refilling the reservoir and un-seating the valve) is time-consuming. Such a safety device is not suitable as the primary safety device on the arterial limb of conven-tional CPB, but may be a very useful safety feature in simpler systems, for example venovenous bypass, or on rapid transfusion devices.

The last type of air detection device is actually a trap, namely, an arterial line fil-ter. Micropore filters prevent passage of gas-eous emboli through a combination of ad-hesive and cohesive forces. Hydrophilic filter materials attract and hold a layer of liquid in direct contact with the filter mate-rial (adhesive force). This thin layer of liquid then attracts further liquid that fills the pores in the filter mesh (cohesive force). This combination of forces resists displacement of liquid from the filter mesh by gas bubbles but permits net transport of liquid through the mesh. Thus gas bubbles are trapped by the filter mesh while liquid flows through the mesh. This tendency to resist gas bubble passage is a function of the pressure change across the filter. The "bubble point pressure" (BPP) is the pressure change across the filter at which point gas bubbles pass through the filter. Bubble point pressure is approximated by the following equation (37):

$$BPP=\frac{4\delta\cos\Theta}{d}$$

where δ is the surface tension of the liquid (cohesion), Θ is the wetting angle of the liquid/solid interface (adhesion), and d is the pore diameter of the filter. The pressure difference across most arterial filters is on the order of a few millimeters of mercury so that BPP is not exceeded, even with high flows, and significant air volumes can be retained by the filter before enough filter area is occluded to cause the pressure difference to exceed the BPP. The efficacy of such filters is further enhanced by venting the filter to allow the perfusion pressure to purge retained air before BPP is exceeded. This vent

can be connected to the cardiotomy reservoir to permit continuous purging of the filter, recognizing that this component of the flow from the pump is lost to the patient. When using a filter it is prudent to arrange a bypass circuit around the filter (Fig. 22.10). The bypass circuit is kept occluded unless a problem develops with the filter, at which point the filter can be effectively removed from the circuit using the bypass limb. Further discussion of the use of arterial filters and other types of filters may be found in Chapter 3.

The clinical value of arterial line filtration is a controversial issue. Opponents of the routine use of arterial line filters argue the absence of conclusive clinical data showing improved outcome with their use. However, there are clinical data demonstrating improved neurologic outcome after CPB associated with the use of arterial line filtration (38–41). Proponents of arte-

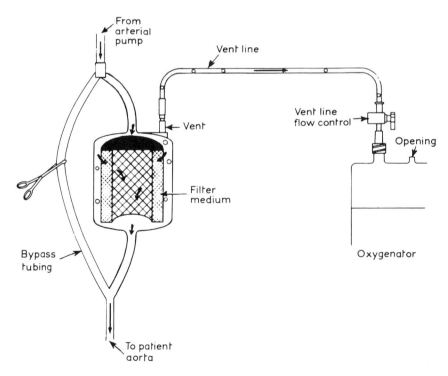

Figure 22.10. The figure depicts appropriate current connections for use of an arterial filter during CPB. (From Berman L, Marin F. Micropore filtration during cardiopulmonary bypass. Ch. 19. In: Taylor KM, ed. Cardiopulmonary bypass, principles and management. Baltimore: Williams & Wilkins, 1986:362.)

rial line filtration argue that filters remove particulate matter from the circuit and trap (and remove when vented) undissolved gas from circulation. Berman and Marin (37) have provided an excellent review of micropore filtration during CPB.

CONDUCT OF CPB

Although it may seem self-evident, it is important to establish a cardiopulmonary perfusion protocol to include at least acquisition of key clinical data by the perfusionist, a prebypass checklist, and a system of record-keeping to insure that important features of the perfusion become part of the patient's clinical record. The clinical data base necessary for safe conduct of CPB begins with a review of the patient's clinical record for pertinent data. Past cardiac history and present state of heart disease are pertinent to an understanding of the proposed surgical intervention and to anticipation of difficulties with CPB. Social history is often pertinent. For example, a patient of the Jehovah's Witnesses faith may refuse blood products and therefore require more intensive efforts to maximize intraoperative blood salvage. A history of previous cardiac surgery should lead to the question of potential cannulation difficulty and the anticipation of potential hemorrhage during sternotomy and mediastinal dissection. Allergy history and physical parameters such as height and weight are obviously important to the conduct of CPB.

The perfusion record should be a standardized medical document retained as a component of the medical record. In this regard it is analogous to the anesthetic record and often takes much the same physical appearance with a graphic component and a chart component plus a section for text. And like the anesthetic record, the perfusion record should be a clearly legible, accurate reflection of the key components of the perfusion. Important components are event timing (CPB start and stop times, arrest times, cross-clamp times, among others) perfusion pressure, flow rates, urine volumes, temperature, medications (including vasoactive infusions and anesthetic vaporizer use), and the timing, volume, and type of cardioplegia solution infused. All personnel involved in the procedure should be noted. Finally, it is reasonable to establish a perfusion data base using key elements from the perfusion record to permit a cross-referenced review of past experience to guide future decisions.

The preperfusion checklist is an important safety component that with greater or lesser formality is virtually universally completed. Most formally, this is a specific written checklist that is completed prior to each perfusion and is directly analogous to the preflight checklist in aviation. The use of such a checklist forces all necessary components of CPB to be verified as being present and functional prior to commencing bypass. An example of this type of checklist is shown in Table 22.1. While the components of the checklist may vary, the function of the list, verification of readiness before initiation of CPB, is critical.

Initiation of CPB is normally accomplished by simply opening the venous drainage cannula and initiating forward flow from the oxygenator through the arterial cannula into the patient. Observation of flow direction is obviously critical and, in

Table 22.1.   Prebypass Checklist

Circuit
   Priming
   Cannulation
   Tubing Integrity
Pump
   Function
   Direction
   Occlusion (for roller pumps)
Oxygenator
   Gas supply verified
   Prime volume
   Functional check
Patient
   Anticoagulation
   Anesthesia
   Relaxants

this regard, a stepwise approach to starting CPB is prudent. One approach is to initiate either forward flow or venous drainage first, observe for the expected flow pattern, then begin the second step and again observe for the result. This type of approach should virtually eliminate the rare but real tragedy of directionally inappropriate perfusion. Most often, the perfusion flow rate is gradually brought up to the targeted rate as venous drainage and reservoir volumes permit. Coordination between perfusionist and anesthesiologist is important at this time, as ventilation should continue until there is verification of adequate drainage, perfusion flow, and oxygenation. After this point, mechanical ventilation should generally stop and the airway should be opened to atmospheric pressure. A possible exception to this practice is that when there is significant left ventricular ejection during CPB, it is prudent to at least maintain oxygen insufflation sufficient to allow oxygenation of the residual pulmonary blood flow. This will prevent ejection of desaturated blood from the left ventricle and the potential of coronary perfusion with unarterialized blood. It is prudent to verify the overall function of the perfusion early after the onset of CPB by direct measurement of arterial and venous blood gas tensions, pH, hematocrit, and perhaps glucose and potassium.

Anesthesia is easily maintained during CPB using either intravenous or volatile anesthetics. It is common practice to include an anesthetic vaporizer in the CPB gas sup-

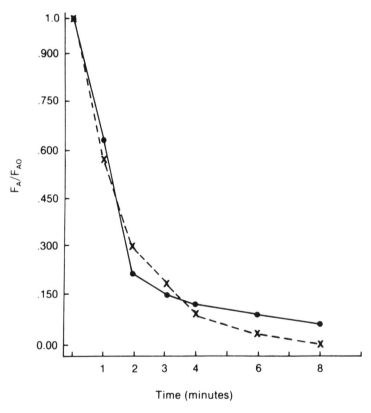

Figure 22.11. Actual (*solid line*) and predicted (*dashed line*) isoflurane washout curves for one patient during CPB. F_A, measured isoflurane concentration; F_{AO}, measured baseline isoflurane concentration. (From Price SL, Brown DL, Carpenter RL, et al. Isoflurane elimination via a bubble oxygenator during extracorporeal circulation. J Cardiothorac Anesth 1988;2:41–44.)

ply to allow direct administration of the anesthetic via oxygenator gas flow. If this is done, it is reasonable to include a bypass gas line so the vaporizer can be functionally removed from the gas supply in the event of malfunction. The inadvertent contact of liquid volatile anesthetics and the plastics of the oxygenator has produced disastrous oxygenator failure due to near explosive cracking of the plastic casing (42). Clearly, if a vaporizer is to be used during CPB it should not be placed near the oxygenator, and liquid anesthetics must be kept away from the oxygenator. For reasons that have not been fully elucidated, the removal of volatile anesthetics from the patient-CPB circuit during CPB is perhaps more efficient than by pulmonary ventilation. In the case of isoflurane, approximately 10 minutes of perfusion time is sufficient to eliminate the agent before separation from CPB (Fig. 22.11) (43). The pharmacokinetic effects of CPB are complex for the intravenous agents; a complete discussion can be found in Chapter 8. As previously mentioned, it is appropriate to maintain complete neuromuscular blockade throughout the CPB interval. Careful attention to patient physiologic and machine monitoring, as discussed, will facilitate a smooth perfusion.

REFERENCES

1. Leigh JM. Oxygen therapy at ambient pressure. Ch 5. In: Scurr C, Feldman S, eds. Scientific foundations of anaesthesia. 2nd ed. Chicago: Medical Yearbook Publishers, 1974:254.
2. Guyton AC. Textbook of medical physiology. 7th ed. Philadelphia: WB Saunders, 1986:497.
3. Gregory IC. The oxygen and carbon monoxide capacities of fetal and adult blood. J Physiol (Lond) 1974;236:625–634.
4. Brandfonbrenner M, Landowne M, Shock NW. Changes in cardiac output with age. Circulation 1955;12:557–566.
5. Gerstenblith G, Renlund DG, Lakatta EG. Cardiovascular response to exercise in younger and older men. Fed Proc 1987;46:1834–1839.
6. Rodeheffer RJ, Gerstenblith G, Becker LC, et al. Exercise cardiac output is maintained with advancing age in health human subjects: cardiac

7. Guyton AC. Textbook of medical physiology. 7th ed. Philadelphia: WB Saunders, 1986:234.
8. Govier AV, Reves JG, McKay RD, et al. Factors and their influence on regional cerebral blood flow during nonpulsatile cardiopulmonary bypass. Ann Thorac Surg 1984;38:592–600.
9. Prough DS, Stump DA, Roy RC, et al. Response of cerebral blood flow to changes in carbon dioxide tension during hypothermic cardiopulmonary bypass. Anesthesiology 1986;64:576–581.
10. Murkin JM, Farrar JK, Tweed A, et al. Cerebral autoregulation and flow/metabolism coupling during cardiopulmonary bypass: the influence of carbon dioxide. Anesth Analg 1987;66:825–832.
11. Thomson IR. The influence of cardiopulmonary bypass on cerebral physiology and function. Ch 2. In: Cardiopulmonary bypass, current concepts and controversies. Philadelphia: WB Saunders, 1989:28.
12. Rudy LW, Heymann MA, Edmunds H. Distribution of systemic blood flow during cardiopulmonary bypass. J Appl Physiol 1973;34:194–200.
13. Harris EA, Seelye ER, Barratt-Boyes BG. On the availability of oxygen to the body during cardiopulmonary bypass in man. Br J Anesth 1974;46:425–431.
14. Mandl JP, Motley JR. Oxygen consumption plateauing: a better method of achieving optimum perfusion. J Extra-corpor Technol 1979;11:69–77.
15. Clowes GHA, Neville WE, Sabga G, Shibota Y. The relationship of oxygen consumption, perfusion rate, and temperature to acidosis associated with cardiopulmonary bypass. Surgery 1958;44:220–225.
16. Diesh G, Flynn PJ, Marable SA, et al. Comparison of low (azygous) flow and high flow principles of extracorporeal circulation employing a bubble oxygenator. Surgery 1957;42:67–72.
17. Moffitt EA, Kirlin JW. Physiologic studies during whole-body perfusion in tetralogy of Fallot. J Thoracic Cardiovasc Surg 1962;44:180–188.
18. Levin MB, Theye RA, Fowler WS, Kirlin JW. Performance of the stationary vertical-screen oxygenator (Mayo-Gibbon). J Thorac Cardiovasc Surg 1960;39:417–426.
19. Kirklin JW, Barratt-Boyes BG. Cardiac Surgery. New York: John Wiley & Sons, 1986:45.
20. Robicsek F, Masters TN, Nieshuchowski W. Vasomotor activity during cardiopulmonary bypass. Ch 1. In: Utley JR, ed. Pathophysiology and techniques of cardiopulmonary bypass. Vol II. Baltimore: Williams & Wilkins, 1983:1–12.
21. Hine IP, Wood WG, Mainwaring-Buton RW, et al.

The adrenergic response to surgery involving cardiopulmonary bypass, as measured by plasma and catecholamine concentrations. Br J Anaesth 1976;48:355–363.

22. Wallach R, Karp RB, Reves JG, et al. Pathogenesis of paroxysmal hypertension developing during and after coronary artery bypass surgery: a study of hemodynamic and humoral factors. Am J Cardiol 1980;46:559–565.

23. Fouad FM, Estafanous FG, Bravo EL. Possible role of cardioaortic reflexes in post-coronary bypass hypertension. Am J Cardiol 1979;44:866–872.

24. Murgo JP, Westerhof N. Arterial reflections and pressure waveforms in humans. Ch 6. In: Yin FCP, ed. Ventricular vascular coupling. Berlin: Springer Verlag, 1987:144–146.

25. Stern DH, Gerson JI, Allen FB, Parker FB. Can we trust the radial artery pressure immediately after cardiopulmonary bypass? Anesthesiology 1985; 62:557–561.

26. Chapin JW, Nance P. Facial paleness. Anesth Analg 1982;61:475.

27. Davis RF. Yet another CVP artifact. Anesthesiology 1984;60:262.

28. Levy WJ. Intraoperative EEG patterns: implications for EEG monitoring. Anesthesiology 1984;60:430–434.

29. Levy WJ. Automated EEG processing for intraoperative monitoring. Anesthesiology 1980;53: 223–236.

30. Levy WJ. Central nervous system monitoring. In: Kaplan JA, ed. Cardiac anesthesia. 2nd ed. New York: Grune & Stratton, 1987:319–338.

31. Levy WJ. Quantitative analysis of EEG changes during hypothermia. Anesthesiology 1984; 60:291–297.

32. Ginsburg HH, Shetler AG, Raudzeus PA. Postoperative paraplegia with preserved intraoperative somatosensory evoked potentials. J Neurosurg 1985;63:296–300.

33. Kirklin JW, Barratt-Boyes BG. Cardiac surgery. New York: John Wiley & Sons, 1986:51.

34. Noback CR, Tinker JH. Hypothermia after cardiopulmonary bypass in man. Anesthesiology 1980;53:277–280.

35. Kirklin JW, Barratt-Boyes BG. Cardiac surgery. New York: John Wiley & Sons, 1986:46.

36. Abel RM, Buckley MJ, Austen WG, et al. Etiology, incidence and prognosis of renal failure following cardiac operations. Results of a prospective analysis of 500 consecutive patients. J Thorac Cardiovasc Surg 1976;71:323–333.

37. Berman L, Marin F. Micropore filtration during cardiopulmonary bypass. Ch 19. In: Taylor KM, ed. Cardiopulmonary bypass, principles and management. Baltimore: Williams & Wilkins, 1986:362.

38. Brantwaite MA. Prevention of neurologic damage during open heart surgery. Thorax 1975;30: 258–61.

39. Carlson RG, Lande AJ, Landis B, et al. The Lande-Edwards membrane oxygenator during heart surgery. Oxygen transfer microemboli counts, and Bender-Gestalt visual motor test scores. J Thorac Cardiovasc Surg 1973;66:894–905.

40. Aberg T. Effect of open heart surgery on intellectual function. Scand J Thorac Cardiovasc Surg 1974;15(supp l):1–63.

41. Willner AE, Caramarte L, Garvey J, et al. The relationship between arterial filtration during open heart surgery and mental abstraction ability. Proc Am Acad Cardiovasc Perfusion 1983;4: 56–59.

42. Maltry DE, Eggers GWN. Isoflurane-induced failure of the Bentley-10 oxygenator. Anesthesiology 1987;66:100–101.

43. Price SL, Brown DL, Carpenter RL, et al. Isoflurane elimination via a bubble oxygenator during extracorporeal circulation. J Cardiothorac Anesth 1988;2:41–44.

23

CARDIOPULMONARY BYPASS IN INFANTS AND CHILDREN

Richard N. Gates, Christine K. Cushen, and Hillel Laks

Having performed the first successful repair of a congenital heart defect using total cardiopulmonary bypass (CPB) in 1953, Gibbon (1) is credited for his foresight and perseverance in the development of CPB. Unfortunately, the next four patients expired, and he became discouraged with the technique. Shortly thereafter, Lillehei and his associates began an amazing series of operations using cross-circulation with children's mothers as oxygenators (2). However, with the further development of mechanical oxygenators, human cross-circulation was abandoned. By 1955, Kirklin et al. (3) reported the first series of congenital heart defects repaired using total bypass. Since that time, important advances in CPB have been made. The development of miniaturized extracorporeal circuits, deep hypothermia and circulatory arrest, and moderate hypothermia with low-flow bypass have facilitated the performance of complex procedures with improved results in neonates and infants.

Cardiopulmonary bypass for neonates and infants must be considered separately from bypass for adults. These patients *are not* small adults. Their cardiovascular system is structurally and functionally distinct from that of the adult. Adaptation of many mechanical and technical components of the extracorporeal circuit is necessary for its use with neonates and infants. In this chapter we will discuss both the theoretical and practical aspects of cardiopulmonary bypass for the neonate and infant as practiced at the UCLA Medical Center.

LOW-FLOW CPB AND CIRCULATORY ARREST

In 1950, Bigelow et al. (4) proposed that hypothermia could lower the body's metabolic rate to such a degree that the circulation could be temporarily arrested while a cardiac operation was performed. Shortly thereafter, they reported experiments indicating that 15 minutes of circulatory arrest at 20°C was feasible (5). Ten years later, Weiss et al. (6) reported the first clinical use of deep hypothermia and circulatory arrest. By 1955, Kirklin et al. (3) had published the first clinical report of intracardiac operations performed utilizing total CPB. However, early extracorporeal circuits were cumbersome and engineering technology made them unsatisfactory for the low-flow perfusion requirements of small infants and neonates. Thus, necessity led to the development and refinement of techniques for deep hypothermia and circulatory arrest, as reported by Barratt-Boyes et al. (7). Throughout the seventies, the use of circulatory arrest served as the optimum approach to neonatal and infant surgery. Subsequent technical advances in the miniaturization of extracorporeal circuits have allowed for the integration of hypothermia and low-flow CPB into the extracorporeal circuitry applied to neonates and infants (8). Today, the surgeon and perfusionist must determine which technique, or combination thereof, is most ideally suited to their patient's operation. A thorough understanding of neonatal and infant physiology, as well as a knowledge of the advantages and limitations of each technique, should lead to the proper approach.

The Physiology of Hypothermia

Hypothermia progressively decreases the metabolic rate of tissues and whole-body oxygen consumption. However, the metabolic rate of the patient never reaches zero and hypothermic cells still require some oxygen for metabolic work. Failure to maintain adequate oxygen delivery results in ischemia. Ischemic tissues must rely on anaerobic metabolism and adenosine triphosphate (ATP) stores in order to maintain cellular integrity. Ongoing ischemia eventually depletes these energy stores and subsequent cellular disruption leads to organ dysfunction or failure. During bypass, the adequacy of tissue perfusion may be assessed by examining oxygen consumption, lactate production, acid-base balance, mixed venous P_{O_2}, and mixed venous oxygen saturations (9). Adequate tissue perfusion at any temperature is determined by the observation of minimal lactate production, normal pH, and normal mixed venous P_{O_2} and oxygen saturation. Inadequate tissue perfusion is manifested by increased lactate production, decreased pH, and decreased mixed venous P_{O_2} and oxygen saturation. Capillary beds that are inadequately perfused will demonstrate decreased oxygen consumption and thereby increased anaerobic metabolism. As perfusion diminishes, some capillary beds may fail to be perfused at all, thus producing areas of ischemia relying solely on anaerobic metabolism for energy. Because such areas of par-

tial circulatory exclusion exist, decreases in pH and increases in lactate production may not linearly reflect the degree of systemic hypoperfusion. Laboratory assessment of perfusion thus suffers from these practical limitations. Nonetheless, when oxygen consumption falls in the presence of increasing serum lactate, decreasing pH, and a falling mixed venous P_{O_2} and mixed venous O_2 saturation, one should consider the possibility of generalized tissue hypoperfusion.

The cardiac index of infants and neonates is approximately 25 to 50% higher than that of adults. Normal cardiac index for an infant or neonate is approximately 2.8 to 3.2 liters/min/m². Normothermic flow rates in the range of 80 to 100 ml/kg, or 2.4 to 2.8 liters/min/m², normally meet the metabolic demands of anesthetized neonates and infants (10). Infants and neonates demonstrate lower perfusion pressures than adults because of the increased compliance of their vasculature. Temperature must be carefully monitored in infants and neonates during bypass because their high ratio of surface area to body weight and immature thermal autoregulatory center predisposes them to wide temperature fluctuations. Flow rates during the induction of hypothermia should be maintained in the range of 2.0 to 2.4 liters/min/m² in order to prevent uneven cooling between organs and tissues (10). Once the desired degree of hypothermia is obtained, flow rates may be reduced. Clinical studies indicate that at 20°C, flow rates of approximately 1.2 liters/min/m² are required to avoid generalized tissue hypoperfusion (11).

Optimizing general tissue perfusion should be the primary goal during CPB. However, one must take into account the frequent necessity to decrease blood flow in order to optimize operating conditions. Because of hypothermia, reduced tissue perfusion is well tolerated by most organs. The notable exception is the brain. Indeed, the development of significant cerebral ischemia during hypothermic low-flow bypass or deep hypothermia with circulatory arrest places a limit on their clinical utility. Because of this, much of the work in the field of low-flow bypass and circulatory arrest has concentrated on determining what conditions create cerebral ischemia, how to determine when cerebral ischemia exists, and when it remains reversible.

Cerebral Pathophysiology

LOW-FLOW CPB

Like many other organs, the brain is capable of autoregulating blood flow in order to prevent ischemia. The cerebrum appears to maintain this ability during moderate hypothermia (12). Autoregulation of cerebral blood flow is influenced by arterial pH and pco_2 concentrations. During hypothermia, pco_2 may be regulated by alpha-stat acid-base management (which is uncorrected for the temperature of blood) or by pH-stat acid-base management (which is corrected for the temperature of blood). Currently, most surgeons and perfusionists manage the pco_2 using the alpha-stat method as this appears to improve the ability of the brain to autoregulate (13). Cerebral blood flow at a given hypothermic flow rate is higher using pH-stat control (14). The technique of pH-stat management causes an alteration in cerebral autoregulation such that flow consistently exceeds demand (15). Such cerebral overperfusion might be deleterious, as the increased blood flow carries more microemboli, which may cause cerebral damage. Regardless of the acid-base management system used, cerebral autoregulation appears to be lost at temperatures of 18 to 22°C (16). At these temperatures, cerebral autoregulation fails and cerebral blood flow becomes dependent upon systemic pressure. There is also evidence that neonates possess an immature and ineffective cerebral autoregulatory center. The high rate of cerebral hemorrhage commonly associated with extracorporeal membrane oxygenation circulatory support may be ex-

plained by cerebral vasodilation and excessive cerebral flow (17). Thus, there is still a need to determine safe maximum and minimum flow rates for neonates during extracorporeal support at various degrees of hypothermia.

The deleterious effects of noncoronary collateral circulation include myocardial warming, washout of cardioplegia, and blood return obscuring the operative field. Therefore, during deep hypothermia and low-flow CPB, it is beneficial to have extracorporeal flow rates as low as possible. However, this must be balanced against the potential development of cerebral ischemia with very low extracorporeal flow rates. This has led to the concept of the "optimum low-flow rate." The optimum low-flow rate may be defined as the minimum flow rate where cerebral ischemia is not produced. Such a state will provide the surgeon with the best possible operating conditions without compromising the cerebrum.

Using nuclear magnetic resonance spectroscopy, sheep on CPB at various flow rates were monitored for the development of intracellular acidosis and the depletion of ATP levels at a nasopharyngeal temperature of 15°C. The minimum flow rate where cerebral ischemia did not occur was 10 ml/kg/min (18). Depletion of ATP levels during ischemia has been correlated with the loss of somatosensory evoked responses (SSER) (19). Thresholds for the loss of SSER in dogs were between 0.25 and 0.75 liters/min/m² (20). Continuous SSER may provide one method for determining the optimal hypothermic low-flow rate. Acceptable flow rates are likely to vary from patient to patient, but flow rates of approximately 0.5 liters/min/m² at 20°C probably represent safe low-flow rates. Nonetheless, a margin a safety should be added and we maintain flow at 1.0 to 1.2 liters/min/m². Such an approach to neonatal and infant surgery should allow for maximum patient safety and the best possible operative field for the surgeon.

CIRCULATORY ARREST

In 1968, Kramer et al. (21) demonstrated that brain ATP levels during circulatory arrest correlated with subsequent function. Once ATP levels reached 20% of normal, subsequent recovery was not observed. In dogs, at a 25°C cerebral cortical temperature, the arrest period during which this occurred was approximately 60 minutes. The brains of Mongolian gerbils have been studied for levels of ATP, pyruvate, lactate, and alanine after various circulatory arrest periods at 18°C. Plain histology and electron microscopy were studied as well. Elevations in the levels of pyruvate, lactate, and alanine were all noted, as were decreases in ATP levels that were directly related to the duration of arrest. Histologic and clinical neurologic abnormalities were noted after approximately 45 minutes of hypothermic circulatory arrest (22). These experimental studies have correlated well with the clinical experience of a "safe" deep hypothermic arrest period being about 45 minutes. In the report of Kirklin et al. (23) of 219 patients undergoing circulatory arrest at 18 to 20°C, there was an average arrest time of 42 ± 14 minutes for 211 patients without neurologic sequelae. For the 8 patients with neurologic sequelae, the average arrest time was 59 ± 10 minutes. Neurologic complications after deep hypothermia and circulatory arrest may include seizures, transient hemiparesis, choreoathetosis, or impaired intellectual development. An ongoing study at the Boston Childrens Hospital is evaluating many of these complications, and the results of this study are anxiously awaited.

Factors associated with the development of choreoathetosis are somewhat unclear. In general, cerebral hypothermia below 17°C and prolonged circulatory arrest times are considered risk factors (24). Other factors may include age beyond infancy, cyanotic heart disease with systemic to pulmonary collaterals, and rapid cooling (25). Complete and even cooling of the brain is critical to cerebral protection during circulatory arrest. Although unproven, most pediatric cardiac surgeons believe that for optimum protection the brain's temperature should be kept in the range of 17 to 20°C. Nasopharyngeal, tympanic, rectal, or "core" temperatures are good monitoring parameters; however, they may prove unreliable in reflecting the true cortical temperature. Electrocerebral silence on an electroencephalogram (EEG) is a reliable method of determining a cerebral temperature of less than 20°C and may be used to determine when circulatory arrest may be initiated (26). In the absence of an EEG, one may assume cerebral quiescence when tympanic membrane and nasopharyngeal temperatures are below 20°C. However, cooling on bypass should continue for a period of at least 20 minutes in order to assure uniform cerebral cooling. Adherence to established techniques of controlled deep hypothermia and circulatory arrest should allow for successful operations with a low incidence of permanent neurologic sequelae. However, one should be aware that there is no currently available method to accurately predict a safe period of circulatory arrest for individual patients.

Although gross neurologic function is generally well-preserved after deep hypothermia and circulatory arrest, the intellectual developmental outcome of infants undergoing the technique is less clear. This is a difficult subject to assess, as up to one-third of children with congenital heart defects will develop neurologic changes that are not associated with surgery (27). Blackwood et al. (28) studied infants before and after the performance of deep hypothermia and circulatory arrest. They could not find any deleterious effects on future intellectual development of children whose arrest times were between 10 and 74 minutes. This study was commended because patients served as their own controls. However, this study was also criticized because of the difficulty in reliably assessing the potential for intellectual developmental outcome in children less than 2 years of age. The report of Clarkson et al. (29) of Barratt-Boyes' patients supports the concept that periods of circulatory arrest between 45 and 60 minutes do not result in subsequent intellectual impairment. Nonetheless, Wells et al. (30) have reported that the time of circulatory arrest correlates linearly with a decline in future intelligence quotient (IQ). The study of Wells et al. used comparison groups of similarly matched patients undergoing continuous low-flow CPB with moderate hypothermia as well as siblings of both groups. This study concluded that IQ dropped 0.5 points per minute of circulatory arrest. Further, unsuspected cerebral atrophy, hypoxic-ischemic encephalopathy, and subdural hematomas have been demonstrated in patients who underwent uneventful circulatory arrest (31).

There is recent evidence that circulatory arrest results in the loss of cerebral autoregulation during rewarming (32). Cerebral blood flow after circulatory arrest was found to be significantly reduced compared to cerebral blood flow after hypothermia and low flow perfusion. Based on the balance of clinical evidence and laboratory work, there is probably some degree of permanent neurologic injury that unpredictably occurs with hypothermic circulatory arrest despite appropriate technique. The degree of neurologic damage appears to be related to the length of the arrest period and may be particularly severe when the duration exceeds 60 minutes.

Recently, many of the concepts of myocardial protection have been experimentally applied to cerebral protection. Studies by Ueda and associates (33, 34) have demonstrated the feasibility of utilizing retrograde cerebral perfusion without damaging the blood-brain barrier. In the future, such techniques may allow for intermittent or continuous retrograde perfusion of the cerebrum with oxygenated solutions and cerebral protective agents that may allow for the nonischemic preservation of the brain during a period of circulatory arrest. If ret-

rograde "cerebroplegia" techniques are demonstrated to be effective, this could provide improved intraoperative protection of the brain while simultaneously extending the clinical utility of circulatory arrest.

Choice of Technique and Technical Considerations

Acceptance of the above information, along with technological advances in the miniaturization of extracorporeal circuits that allow safe and effective low-flow bypass, have led us to a philosophy of avoiding circulatory arrest. We now restrict circulatory arrest to operations that can not be satisfactorily performed utilizing deep hypothermia and low-flow CPB. Many procedures previously believed to require circulatory arrest can be managed with deep hypothermia, low-flow bypass, and very brief periods of circulatory arrest. This approach should reduce the risk of an adverse neurologic outcome. Drawbacks to this philosophy include the necessity for cannulae in the operative field and the potential for bronchial and noncoronary collateral blood flow to obscure the operative field. In addition, noncoronary collateral flow washes out cardioplegia. In patients with chronic and severe systemic hypoxia, extensive noncoronary collateral flow may be present. In these cases, one should carefully assess the degree of collateral flow. If excessive, it may preclude utilizing the low-flow approach. Nonetheless, many theoretical problems with low-flow CPB can be minimized by the use of appropriate cannulation techniques, optimizing low-flow states, and employing appropriate myocardial protection.

While deep hypothermia and low-flow bypass appear to afford greater safety than circulatory arrest, the surgeon should be aware that cerebral deficits may occur with both techniques. Therefore, when technically possible, congenital heart operations should be performed using moderate hypothermia (24 to 28°C) with full calculated flow rates. This can frequently be accomplished in patients weighing more than 7 kg who do not have significant cyanosis and increased noncoronary collateral flow.

The following three sections review the clinical approach to bypass for infants and children at the UCLA Medical Center. Included are clinical examples that reflect an integration of the previously presented theoretical and experimental data.

CIRCULATORY ARREST

The two approaches used for induction of deep hypothermia and circulatory arrest are surface cooling and core cooling. In either case, patients are initially anesthetized with a potent inhalation agent and endotracheally intubated with the aid of a nondepolarizing neuromuscular blocker. Anesthesia is commonly maintained with high doses of opioids. Surface cooling techniques have been shown to give superior uniformity of cooling between tissues and organs. Cooling begins with the skin and muscle and then progresses toward central organs. However, there are major clinical drawbacks to surface cooling techniques, which include prolonged anesthetic time, the cumbersome apparatus, the possibility of skin damage, and the potential for ventricular fibrillation with an uncontrolled arrest of the heart. Because of this, most centers employ core cooling. The major disadvantage of core cooling is that temperature gradients develop between tissues and organs based on differential flow rates (35). Low-flow tissues, such as the muscle and skin, tend to remain at higher temperatures than the high-flow organs such as the liver and kidney. This problem can be greatly diminished by using slower rates of cooling and maintaining high-flow rates until the desired temperature is reached. A period of no less than 20 minutes should be used to cool the patient to a temperature of 20°C. Rectal or bladder, nasopharyngeal, and tympanic membrane temperatures should be monitored during the induction of hypothermia to ensure uniform cooling. Gradients between the extracorporeal water bath temperature and venous blood temperature should not exceed 8 to 10°C in both the cooling and rewarming phases of hypothermia. For core cooling, temperature drops should be no more than 0.5°C per minute.

We employ a technique that primarily utilizes core cooling and is supplemented with some surface cooling. For the surface cooling component, we employ a cooling blanket under the patient and ice packs about the head. Great care must be taken to separate the skin from direct contact with ice, since failure to do so may result in subcutaneous fat necrosis. While the ice packs are applied and as the cooling blanket circulates, sternotomy and cannulation are performed. If the operation is to be performed with circulatory arrest alone, the right atrium is cannulated with a single venous cannula. However, when low flow with periods of circulatory arrest are planned, standard bicaval cannulation or single atrial cannulation may be employed. The combination of surface cooling and slow core cooling allows for even and effective cerebral cooling. Despite the theoretical advantages of pure surface cooling, core cooling offers practical advantages by virtue of having the patient on partial bypass during cooling. One such advantage is the ability to control the state and substance of the circulation during cooling. In many patients initiation of partial bypass allows for the correction of preexisting hypoxemia and hypoperfusion. Perhaps the most significant advantage of the core cooling technique is the ability to create a controlled cardiac arrest. Allowing the heart to "beat itself to sleep" under conditions of decreased stroke work greatly benefits myocardial protection.

The patient is therefore cooled using a flow rate of 2.0 to 2.4 liters/min/m². Once the patient is at 25°C, we perform a controlled blood cardioplegia arrest. This is generally a substrate-enriched, warm blood cardioplegia arrest as will be described in "Myocardial Protection." During this time, core cooling continues from 25°C to 18°C degrees tympanic membrane temperature and to 18°C to 20°C rectal temperature. Before discontinuing perfusion, a supplemental dose of a nondepolarizing neuromuscular blocker such as pancuronium is advised in order to avert muscular activity during circulatory arrest. At this point, blood flow may be terminated, the patient exsanguinated into the pump oxygenator, and the venous cannula removed. After completion of the procedure, the venous cannula is reinserted and warming begins with a perfusate from the extracorporeal circuit that has been buffered and warmed as needed.

Careful attention must be given to acid-base balance during the rewarming phase. Acidosis frequently develops from the wash-out of lactic acid produced during the circulatory arrest period. During rewarming, it is common to utilize flow rates as high as 3.2 liters/min/m². Aggressive vasodilation will help to reduce the development of temperature gradients between the central and peripheral arterial beds. Patience is important during rewarming. Premature separation from bypass before adequate rewarming of the periphery leads to elevated peripheral vascular resistance in the early postoperative period. This places an undue strain on the myocardium and may increase the requirement for postoperative inotropic support. The venous oxygen saturation of the extracorporeal circuit should be carefully monitored during rewarming. A decreasing venous oxygen saturation may indicate an inadequate level of anesthesia or muscle relaxation, with impending shivering or the need to increase blood flow. Overuse of bicarbonate during rewarming is discouraged as an alkalemia may later result. This may lead to arrhythmias, which can be difficult to control.

An illustrative example of this approach to circulatory arrest is that of a full-term neonate weighing 3.5 kg. Shortly after birth, this patient became mildly cyanotic and severely acidotic secondary to low cardiac output. The child then required intubation for rapidly developing respiratory failure. Echocardiogram and cardiac catheterization revealed supracardiac total anomalous pulmonary venous connection with obstruction of the vertical vein behind the pulmonary artery. The patient was resuscitated and prepared for operation. The decision was made to perform the procedure using deep hypothermia and circulatory arrest. Factors that influenced this decision were the need to provide a completely bloodless field during the entire procedure (which consists of an anastomosis between the transverse vein and the back of the left atrium) and the ability to almost always perform the repair in less than 40 minutes.

DEEP HYPOTHERMIA AND LOW-FLOW CPB

Patients who undergo deep hypothermia with low-flow CPB are treated similarly to patients undergoing circulatory arrest. Patients are induced with an inhalation anesthetic and placed on a cooling blanket. If a brief period of circulatory arrest is planned, ice packs are placed about the head, as described in "Circulatory Arrest." Core cooling is initiated with flow rates of 2.0 to 2.4 liters/min/m². Once corporeal temperatures have reached 25°C, a controlled blood cardioplegia arrest is performed. Core cooling at the above flow rate is then continued until the patient's tympanic membrane and nasopharyngeal temperature are 18°C. Rectal or bladder temperature should be in the range of 18 to 20°C. At this point, flow may be lowered to 0.8 to 1.2 liters/min/m². Using this approach to low-flow bypass, brief periods of circulatory arrest or decreased flow may be safely used. Rewarming of patients undergoing deep hypothermia and low-flow bypass should follow the same principles outlined in "Circulatory Arrest."

An example of this approach to deep hypothermia and low-flow bypass is that of a full-term infant weighing 4 kg. This patient developed severe cyanosis and mild cardiac failure shortly after birth. Echocardiography revealed transposition of the great arteries with an intact ventricular septum. Cardiac catheterization confirmed the diagnosis and demonstrated normal coronary artery anatomy. A balloon atrial septectomy was performed and the patient was medically stabilized. An arterial switch operation was planned using deep hypothermia and low-flow bypass with a short period of circulatory arrest. Sternotomy was performed and a single right atrial cannula inserted. The patient was cooled to a rectal temperature of 20°C and a tympanic membrane temperature of 18°C using a flow rate of 2.0 to 2.4 liters/min/m². As in the previous case, a controlled cardioplegic cardiac arrest was performed at 25°C and the intracardiac portion of the operation was then initiated. Once the hypothermia target temperature was achieved, flow was dropped to 0.8 to 1.2 liters/min/m² and maintained at this level. After completion of the arterial reconstruction, flow was stopped and the patient exsanguinated. The atrial cannula was removed and the atrial septectomy repaired. The cannula was then reinserted and rewarming instituted. The arterial switch procedure is an operation that is frequently performed exclusively using circulatory arrest. However, with careful cannulation and appropriate venting, a technically satisfactory procedure can be performed using the approach described above. Other procedures that may be performed using predominantly deep hypothermia and low-flow CPB include repair of truncus arteriosis and tetralogy of Fallot.

MODERATE HYPOTHERMIA

Many noncomplex pediatric open heart procedures performed on noncyanotic infants weighing over 7 kg may be done using moderate hypothermia and full calculated flow rates. We use this approach whenever technically feasible. Factors to consider include the degree of cyanosis and noncoronary collateral flow, the degree of bronchial arterial collateral flow and the ability to effectively vent this return, the time anticipated to complete the repair, and the overall anatomic complexity of the procedure. An illustrative example of this approach was a 1½-year-old child weighing 10 kg who was asymptomatic despite a moderate-sized perimembranous ventricular septal defect. This patient had a Q_p/Q_s (pulmonary to systolic blood flow ratio) of 2.8 and mildly elevated pulmonary artery pressures. Therefore, he was scheduled to undergo elective closure of the defect. In this patient, moderate hypothermia (25°C) with full calculated flow rates were used for extracorporeal support. After sternotomy and bicaval cannulation, the patient was cooled to 25°C with flow rates of 2.2 liters/min/m². At this point, the flow rate was dropped to 1.4 liters/min/m² concurrent with the transatrial repair of the ventricular septal defect. Once the defect had been closed, flow rates were increased to 2.5 to 3.0 liters/min/m² and rewarming was initiated.

Tremendous advancements have been made in the equipment and techniques available for the performance of hypothermic low-flow CPB. It is now possible to apply the original concept of Sealy et al. (8) of hypothermic low-flow bypass to a degree capable of sustaining critical organ function without irreversible ischemic damage in patients less than 5 kg. In combination with circulatory arrest, this provides the surgeon with powerful tools that allow more complicated surgical repairs to be achieved in ever younger patients. Future advancements in cerebral protection through cerebroplegia may allow greater periods of circulatory arrest with a lower risk of cerebral injury.

MYOCARDIAL PROTECTION

The development of advanced techniques of myocardial protection has permitted successful performance of complicated open heart procedures on younger and sicker pediatric patients. Myocardial preservation is critical in infants and neonates, as 50% of hospital deaths in this patient group may be related to inadequate protection of the heart during operation (36). The structural and functional differences of the neonatal myocardium, when combined with the frequent metabolic and physiologic derangements encountered at the time of surgery, present a unique challenge to the pediatric cardiac surgeon. A carefully planned approach to myocardial protection must take the above into consideration, as well as the need to optimize surgical exposure in order to facilitate an accurate operative repair.

Structure and Function of the Neonatal Heart

To develop better methods of neonatal myocardial protection it is important to be aware of the inherent differences between the neonatal and adult heart. A newborn sheep's heart comprises 0.73% of body mass, as opposed to 0.49% in the adult. This is predominantly because of the increased mass of the right ventricle and the higher percentage of water found within the myocardium. There is a smaller percentage of collagen components per gram of wet weight heart in the newborn period (37). Further, noncontractile structural elements make up a greater percentage of the heart's overall weight (38). Functionally, this results in less compliant right and left ventricles. These ventricles are less responsive to changes in preload and afterload than their adult counterparts. In addition, the neonatal heart has a limited contractile reserve that appears to be related to its baseline hyperadrenergic state (39). Therefore, the neonatal heart is more susceptible to congestive heart failure caused by increases in either preload or afterload.

The neonatal heart has fewer mature mitochondria and a lower oxidative capacity (40). However, the normal neonatal heart has increased glycogen stores and a three- to fourfold higher ability to produce glycolytically derived ATP (41). This is probably responsible for the well-documented ability of a normal neonatal heart to withstand prolonged ischemia (42). Indeed, after comparable periods of ischemia, healthy puppies have significantly less reduction in compliance and myocardial edema than adult dogs (43). After a 60-minute hypoxic insult, reoxygenated neonatal rabbit hearts are able to regain mitochondrial function, while adult hearts are not (44). Moderately hypoxic newborn dog hearts are temporarily able to maintain normal contractility, while adult hearts fail to do so. These properties of the neonatal myocardium are felt to be related to increased energy flux through glycolytic anaerobic pathways (45).

Unfortunately, the pediatric cardiac surgeon rarely operates upon a normal and healthy neonatal heart. Most neonates and infants requiring surgery have significant hemodynamic and metabolic conditions associated with their congenital heart disease. Frequently, the young heart is subject to volume overload, acute hypoxia, or chronic hypoxia. These conditions place stress on the heart, which leads to its metabolic depletion. Congestive heart failure leads to a chronically stressed and energy-depleted myocardium.

Acute hypoxia, particularly when combined with acidosis, has been demonstrated to decrease myocardial contractility in newborn lambs. This reduction in contractility may be partially alleviated by the maintenance of a normal pH (46). Nonetheless, if the period of acute hypoxia is prolonged, glycogen depletion will occur. Prolonged hypoxia in the glycogen-depleted heart causes irreversible myocardial damage. The avoidance of severe hypoxia in the preoperative and early intraoperative period prior to controlled cardiac arrest is critical to ensure a state where good myocardial protection can be induced.

Far more insidious, but equally deleterious, are the effects of chronic hypoxia on the young heart. Canine models have demonstrated that chronic hypoxia globally depresses myocardial function and predisposes the myocardium to an accelerated depletion of ATP during controlled arrest (47). Patients exposed to chronic hypoxia are prone to cardiac decompensation when stressed by acute ischemic episodes (48). Great care must be taken to avoid ischemic stress in these patients during the pre- and early intraoperative period prior to controlled cardiac arrest.

Ventricular hypertrophy secondary to outflow tract obstruction or pulmonary artery banding leads to hypertrophic changes within myocytes (49). In adults, myocardial hypertrophy has been associated with depressed ATP levels within myocytes (50). It is important to recognize the potential for such conditions preoperatively and to ensure optimal pre- and intraoperative hemodynamic support and oxygenation. Inadequate management during this critical time may lead to the inability of the neonatal myocardium to tolerate an ischemic arrest period. This may cause postoperative myocardial failure, which as mentioned above, is a factor in postoperative death in up to 50% of neonatal patients (36). Optimizing hemodynamics and oxygen delivery prior to a controlled cardiac arrest, along with the subsequent delivery of effective myocardial protection, provides the foundation for successful pediatric open heart surgery.

Techniques of Myocardial Protection

There are several methods available for myocardial protection during cardiac operations. These include continuous perfusion, intermittent aortic cross-clamping, topical hypothermia, and intermittent or continuous cardioplegia. In addition, cardioplegia may be blood-based or crystalloid-based, and delivery can be either antegrade or retrograde. Selection of an appropriate approach should be based on the following: (*a*) an understanding of the

unique properties of the young myocardium, (*b*) the current metabolic and hemodynamic state of the heart, (*c*) the anticipated exposure required, (*d*) the time required to perform the procedure, and (*e*) consideration of the proposed approach to bypass (i.e., circulatory arrest versus deep hypothermia with low-flow bypass versus moderate hypothermia with full calculated flow rates).

CONTINUOUS PERFUSION

Simple operations performed on the right side of the heart may be conducted using continuous perfusion. This technique protects the myocardium by direct coronary perfusion with oxygenated blood delivered from the extracorporeal circuit. Aortic cross-clamping is not necessary and partial bypass may be instituted with bicaval cannulation and either aortic or femoral artery cannulation. When femoral artery cannulation is used, procedures may be performed through a right posterolateral thoracotomy. By combining hypothermia with the technique, ventricular fibrillation may be induced, thus facilitating operative precision. However, redistribution of blood flow away from the endocardium during fibrillation will lead to suboptimal myocardial protection (51). Major drawbacks to continuous perfusion include the risk of air emboli, the difficulty of operating on a heart that is beating, and a continuous coronary sinus return that makes visualization suboptimal. When compared to current cold cardioplegia techniques, continuous perfusion provides inferior exposure and myocardial protection (52). Continuous perfusion is mainly of historic interest, but on occasion, the technique may be applicable.

INTERMITTENT AORTIC CROSS-CLAMPING

Intermittent aortic cross-clamping was frequently used in pediatric open heart surgery prior to the development of current cardioplegia techniques. This technique produces a fairly bloodless field. However, the heart continues to contract and there is little myocardial relaxation. There is a substantial risk for air emboli and it is difficult to gauge appropriate time intervals for removal of the cross-clamp to reperfuse the heart. As with continuous perfusion, hypothermia and fibrillation may be added to facilitate the technical aspects of the procedure, but again, this is suboptimal for endocardial protection. There is both theoretical and laboratory evidence that this method is inferior to current cardioplegia techniques (53). Nonetheless, some centers selectively employ intermittent cross-clamping.

HYPOTHERMIA

Systemic and local hypothermia are the cornerstones of myocardial protection. The protective effects of hypothermia are directly related to the decrease in metabolic activity it induces (54). A 90 to 95% reduction in oxygen consumption can be achieved by maintaining myocardial temperature at approximately 15°C (55). Systemic hypothermia is particularly important in infants as chronic cyanosis has been shown to increase noncoronary collateral flow flow to the heart (56). Significant collateral flow will wash out cardioplegic solutions and rewarm the heart. Systemic

cooling does not affect collateral flow, but it decreases myocardial warming by lowering the temperature gradient between the heart and systemic blood. Further, systemic hypothermia allows reduced extracorporeal flow rates, thereby lowering myocardial collateral flow. Local hypothermia may be achieved by topically applied cold saline or by cold antegrade- or retrograde-delivered cardioplegia. The efficacy of ischemic arrest induced by aortic cross-clamping in the presence of topical hypothermia has been demonstrated both experimentally and clinically (57, 58). This technique permits surgery to be performed on a motionless and flaccid heart.

Whereas direct topical hypothermia appears to be adequate for many pediatric procedures, hearts with hypertrophied ventricles may experience nonuniform cooling, which results in suboptimal myocardial protection (59). Topical hypothermia may damage the phrenic nerves and great care must be taken to avoid too low a temperature within the pericardium. We have used an infant cardiac insulation pad to help protect the phrenic nerves and reduce temperature loss through the pericardium (Cardiac Insulation Pad-Pediatric, Shiley, Irvine, CA) (Fig. 23.1). Delivery of hypothermic cardioplegia through the aortic root results in a more uniform cooling of the myocardium than does topical hypothermia. The combi-

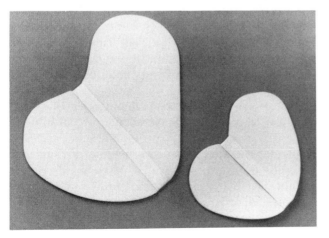

Figure 23.1. Adult and infant cardiac insulation pads.

nation of hypothermia and cardioplegic arrest provides optimal myocardial protection. As such, ischemic arrest and topical hypothermia are infrequently used today.

CARDIOPLEGIA

The development of cardioplegic solutions have greatly advanced the field of cardiac surgery. Cardioplegia produces a dry, still, and relaxed heart, thus facilitating performance of a precise operation. Hypothermic and hyperkalemic cardioplegia causes a diastolic electromechanical arrest, which greatly lowers the heart's metabolic rate. The efficacy of potassium cardioplegia has been demonstrated both experimentally and clinically (60, 61). Hypothermic, hyperkalemic cardioplegia may be considered the "gold standard" for myocardial protection.

Two major types of hyperkalemic cardioplegia have been developed, crystalloid-based and blood-based. Chapter 7 discusses the theoretical, experimental, and clinical advantages of both methods. We have found blood to be an excellent vehicle for cardioplegia delivery in the pediatric population. The oxygen-carrying capacity, buffering ability, osmotic properties, inherent antioxidant capacity, and natural substrate content underlie our choice of blood to deliver cardioplegia.

At the UCLA Medical Center, the standard cold arrest and maintenance cardioplegia solution is composed of 500 ml of 5% dextrose/0.2 molar normal saline, 200 ml of 0.3 molar Tham, and 50 ml of standard CPD solution (citrate, phosphate, dextrose). This is mixed with 60 mEq of KCl for the initial arresting solution, or 30 mEq of KCl for the maintenance solution (Table 23.1). The crystalloid-based cardioplegia solution is mixed in a 1 to 4 ratio with blood from the extracorporeal circuit to create blood cardioplegia. The final sanguineous solution has a potassium concentration of 18 to 20 mEq/liter for the initial arresting solution, and 8 to 10 mEq/

Table 23.1. Crystalloid Components of Blood Cardioplegia

Solution	Composition[a]
Standard maintenance	500 ml 0.2 M NS, 200 ml 0.3 M Tham, 50 ml CPD,[b] 30 mEq KCl
Standard arrest	500 ml 0.2 M NS, 200 ml 0.3 M Tham, 50 ml CPD,[b] 60 mEq KCl
Warm induction	500 ml 0.2 M NS, 200 ml 0.3 M Tham, 50 ml CPD,[b] 60 mEq KCL, 250 ml 0.46 M monosodium glutamate/aspartate

[a] NS, normal saline; Tham, tromethamine; CPD, citrate, phosphate, dextrose.
[b] In neonates and small infants, the amount of added CPD may be reduced to 15 ml (see text).

liter for the maintenance solution. Both solutions have a pH of 7.6 to 7.7, an ionized calcium level of 0.5 to 0.6 μM/liter, and an osmolality in the range of 320 mOsm. Based on experimental evidence showing improved myocardial function in neonates after using cardioplegia with higher calcium levels (0.8 to 1.2 μM/liter), we have decreased the amount of CPD added to the cardioplegia solution utilized for neonates (58, 62). The neonatal patient displays an increased sensitivity to hypocalcemic cardioplegia solutions, which is contrary to the situation in the adult. This may be accounted for by the structural and metabolic differences of the neonatal myocardium. Specifically, for neonates and infants who demonstrate a depletion of myocardial reserves, we reduce the amount of CPD added to the cardioplegia solution to 15 ml. Cardioplegia solutions should be mixed daily to prevent bacterial colonization and contamination. Laboratory sampling to verify results should be performed prior to administration.

Cold (4°C), high potassium blood cardioplegia is delivered at an initial infusion pressure of 80 to 100 mm Hg until arrest is obtained. Once the heart is arrested, the pressure is lowered to 50 to 60 mm Hg and delivery is maintained for 3 minutes. Cardioplegia is delivered by pressure and time, not volume. Cardioplegia should be delivered from the extracorporeal circuit under the operation of the cardiovascular perfusionist. However, for infants less than 5 kg body weight, cardioplegia is best delivered by the surgeon using a hand-held syringe. The maintenance solution of cold (4°C), low potassium blood cardioplegia is infused at a pressure of 70 to 80 mm Hg for 2 minutes. This should be repeated every 15 to 20 minutes or whenever electromechanical activity returns to the heart.

WARM INDUCTION CARDIOPLEGIA

The standard cold blood cardioplegia solution allows for excellent myocardial protection for most elective pediatric open heart surgery. However, many pediatric procedures are emergent and performed on compromised hearts. As discussed previously, these energy-depleted hearts are acutely sensitive to ischemic episodes. For this group of patients, our initial cardioplegia infusion is provided for "resuscitation" of the heart. This is achieved by the delivery of warm, substrate-enriched, blood cardioplegia prior to the beginning of cold blood maintenance cardioplegia. In energy-depleted adult and neonatal hearts, this technique has been shown to significantly improve functional recovery after ischemic periods (63). The theoretical background for this approach is quite convincing and has been well-discussed by Buckberg (64).

In brief, after cross-clamp application and decompression of the ventricle, a warm cardioplegic arrest is achieved. In this state, the baseline metabolic requirements of the heart are greatly reduced. During this time, by supplying substrate-enriched, fully oxygenated warm blood, the heart is able to replete its metabolic stores prior to the induction of hypothermia. This allows myocardial preservation to be initiated in a state where the myocardium is no longer ischemic and the heart is undergoing aerobic metabolism, which is believed less likely to result in a significant myocardial reperfusion injury. Currently, we prepare warm

induction blood cardioplegia by combining the standard high potassium cardioplegia solution with a preparation of 250 ml of 0.46 molar monosodium aspartate/glutamate monohydrate. The resulting concentration of glutamate/aspartate is 13 μM/liter. To resuscitate the heart, warm (37°C), high potassium blood cardioplegia is delivered until arrest is achieved and then continued for 1 minute. This is followed by cold (4°C), low potassium blood cardioplegia delivered for 2 minutes. Controlled pediatric trials to demonstrate the efficacy of warm induction cardioplegia have not been performed. However, experimental evidence strongly supports this approach for myocardial protection in hearts with severe metabolic depletion. We have adopted this technique in procedures where a metabolically depleted and stressed heart is suspected (i.e., systemic hypoxia, congestive heart failure, pressor dependence, metabolic acidosis, etc.) and for all procedures where circulatory arrest is planned.

MANAGEMENT OF REPERFUSION INJURY: LEUKOCYTE DEPLETION

The majority of damage resulting from suboptimal myocardial protection is realized during reperfusion. Experimental evidence gained from research on long-term myocardial preservation for cardiac transplantation supports the concept that reperfusate modification can lead to subsequent improvements in myocardial function. In particular, leukocyte depletion with blood filters has been demonstrated to significantly enhance the functional recovery of donor hearts preserved for 12 hours with Stanford solution (65). In a rabbit heart model employing 2 hours of global ischemia, both pharmacologic leukocyte inhibition and mechanical leukocyte filtration during reperfusion resulted in improved ventricular function and decreased cellular edema, mitochondrial injury, and capillary injury (66). The mechanisms responsible for improved function are unclear, but they are likely related to the reduction of leukocyte-mediated oxidant damage. Ko et al. (67) have demonstrated that elevated levels of platelet-activating factor (which leads to leukocyte stimulation) are present during reperfusion. The rise in platelet-activating factor parallels a rise in leukocyte hydrogen peroxide production. Hence, platelets (which are also variably filtered by leukocyte filters) also appear to play an important role in reperfusion injury.

In cases where the myocardium is believed to be in an energy-depleted state prior to arrest (where warm blood induc-tion cardioplegia will be used), or when there has been concern about inadequate myocardial protection during operation, we perform a controlled reperfusion of the heart with leukocyte-depleted, substrate-enriched blood cardioplegia at 37°C. Leukocyte filters are commercially available and easily insert into the extracorporeal circuit for filtration (Pall RC 100, Pall Biomedical Products, East Hills, NY) (Fig. 23.2). The modified reperfusate is delivered at a pressure of 50 to 60 mm Hg for 3 to 5 minutes. This is followed by perfusion with warm (37°C) unmodified blood from

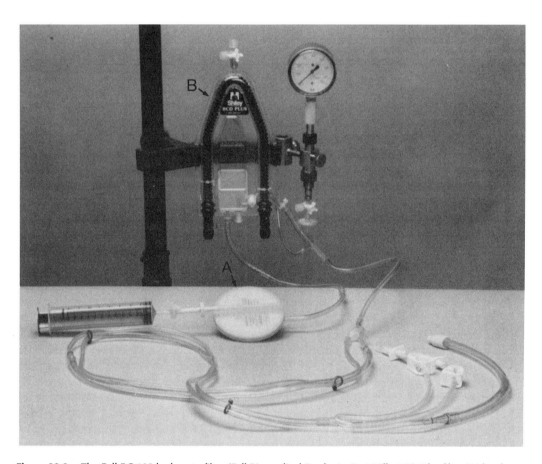

Figure 23.2. The Pall RC 100 leukocyte filter (Pall Biomedical Products, East Hills, NY). The filter (**A**) has been attached to a blood cardioplegia device (*BCD* plus) (**B**) (Shiley, Irvine, CA). Modified blood cardioplegia (4 parts blood, 1 part crystalloid cardioplegia solution composed of 500 ml 0.2 M normal saline, 200 ml 0.3 M Tham, 50 ml CPD, 250 ml 0.46 M monosodium glutamate/aspartate monohydrate, and 30 mEq/liter KCl) is passed through the leukocyte filter and then through the blood cardioplegia device for warming to 37°C. Delivery pressure is monitored from the BCD by the attached manometer.

the extracorporeal circuit prior to the removal of the aortic cross-clamp.

WARM HEART SURGERY

Recently, the concept of continuous warm blood cardioplegia has been introduced for myocardial protection during adult cardiac surgery. Initial results have demonstrated excellent recovery of ventricular function with a decreased perioperative infarction rate (1.7% versus 6.8%), decreased use of the intraaortic balloon pump (0.9% versus 9.0%), and decreased prevalence of low cardiac output syndrome (3.3% versus 13.3%) (68), as compared to a historical cohort. The concept of continuously maintaining metabolism in order to avoid ischemia and prevent a subsequent reperfusion injury is quite attractive. However, successful continuous coronary perfusion requires that the aortic valve remain competent, which limits positioning of the heart. Further, continuous coronary perfusion leads to a continuous coronary sinus effluent. These technical problems may limit the application of continuous antegrade warm blood cardioplegia for pediatric procedures. Retrograde delivery of warm continuous blood cardioplegia alleviates many of the technical problems associated with antegrade delivery and may allow continuous warm blood cardioplegia to become a more useful technique for pediatric myocardial protection.

ANTEGRADE AND RETROGRADE DELIVERY

A final consideration in myocardial protection is the route of cardioplegia delivery. Standard antegrade cardioplegia delivery affords sufficient protection for the majority of pediatric procedures. However, certain operations may be facilitated by utilizing retrograde techniques. The major benefit of retrograde cardioplegia in pediatric procedures is the ability to operate on the aortic root or aortic valve without the interruption required to perform ostial

perfusion. Further, the heart may be placed in any position during retrograde cardioplegia. The technique of retrograde cardioplegia is simple and does not require isolation of the right heart (69). The efficacy of this approach has been demonstrated in animals and humans (70, 71). Retrograde, cold (4°C), low potassium maintenance cardioplegia should be delivered at a pressure of 30 to 40 mm Hg for a minimum of 2 to 3 minutes. The intervals between delivery should be approximately every 10 to 12 minutes. Greater volumes of retrograde cardioplegia should be delivered when compared to antegrade cardioplegia because as much as two thirds of retrograde solutions may be shunted through thebesian veins into the right ventricle (personal observation). As previously noted, delivery of cardioplegia in neonates less than 5 kg is facilitated by hand perfusion on the operative field.

An Integrated Approach To Myocardial Protection

The surgeon and perfusionist must plan an approach to myocardial protection that incorporates knowledge of the current metabolic and hemodynamic state of the heart, the anticipated operative exposure required, the length of the procedure required, and that is easily integrated with the approach used for CPB. The approach used for myocardial protection in the three previously presented cases will now be reviewed to demonstrate an integrated approach to myocardial protection.

The first patient presented was a cyanotic, acidotic newborn infant with obstructed supracardiac total anomalous pulmonary veins. This patient was repaired using deep hypothermia and circulatory arrest. By instituting partial bypass and core cooling, the circulation was rapidly controlled and the patient's acidosis and hypoperfusion corrected. Partial bypass allowed the myocardium to be partially unloaded, and as hypothermia was induced, myocardial oxygen supply exceeded oxygen demand. At 25°C the aortic cross-clamp was applied and high potassium, 37°C, substrate-enriched blood cardioplegia was infused antegrade, and the heart was resuscitated. Subsequently, low potassium, cold (4°C) blood cardioplegia was infused antegrade to cool the heart. As this procedure involved the region about the coronary sinus, the use of retrograde cardioplegia was not a consideration. Therefore, maintenance, low potassium, cold (4°C) blood cardioplegia was intermittently infused antegrade at approximately 20-minute intervals. Just prior to removal of the cross-clamp, a final dose of cardioplegia consisting of low potassium, 37°C leukocyte-depleted blood cardioplegia was infused antegrade.

The second patient presented was a newborn infant with transposition of the great arteries. This patient had undergone a balloon septectomy and had been medically stabilized with good cardiac output and moderate systemic desaturation. This patient was repaired using deep hypothermia and low-flow CPB with a brief period of circulatory arrest at the conclusion of the procedure. As for the above patient, systemic desaturation was corrected during the period of partial bypass used for the induction of hypothermia. Once a temperature of 25°C was reached, a high potassium, warm (37°C), substrate-enriched blood cardioplegia arrest was attained. Next, low potassium, cold (4°C) blood cardioplegia was infused antegrade. All subsequent maintenance blood cardioplegia was low potassium, cold blood cardioplegia. Because of the small size of the coronary sinus in newborns and the use of a single atrial cannula, retrograde cardioplegia was not practical in this instance. Therefore, subsequent doses of maintenance blood cardioplegia were delivered by ostial cannulation once the aorta was transected and the coronary buttons removed. After the LeCompte maneuver (which brought

forward the true pulmonary artery) the coronary arteries were reimplanted into the neoaorta and cardioplegia was given via the neoaortic root (72). After the period of circulatory arrest used to close the atrial septectomy, systemic rewarming was reinstituted and the pulmonary artery anastomosis performed. Prior to removal of the aortic cross-clamp, low potassium, warm (37°C) substrate-enriched blood cardioplegia was administered.

The final patient presented was a 1½-year-old child with a ventricular septal defect. This patient was asymptomatic, but had a Qp/Qs of 2.8 and mildly elevated pulmonary artery pressures. Elective repair was scheduled and performed using moderate hypothermia (25°C) and a full calculated flow rate of 1.4 liters/min/m². Initial arrest was performed using high potassium, cold (4°C) blood cardioplegia. Intermittent maintenance cardioplegia was delivered approximately every 12 to 15 minutes using alternating retrograde and antegrade low potassium, 4°C blood cardioplegia. Prior to removal of the cross-clamp, a single dose of low potassium, warm (37°C) substrate-enriched blood cardioplegia was given. These three examples represent an integrated approach to myocardial protection that considers the technique of bypass employed, the functional and metabolic status of the myocardium, and the anticipated operative exposure and time required to perform the procedure.

The field of neonatal and infant myocardial protection is rapidly advancing and has paralleled the ability to successfully repair more complicated congenital lesions in ever younger patients. Future progress is likely to be made in deducing factors required for the optimal resuscitation of the impaired pediatric heart and in determining factors responsible for reperfusion damage and their subsequent limitation. Continuous warm blood cardioplegia may play a significant role in the future of myocardial protection.

CANNULATION

Arterial

Virtually any major artery may be cannulated with successful flow to its run-off bed (73). Hence, the selection of an arterial cannulation site should take into account the assurance of adequate cerebral flow, coronary flow, visceral flow, and convenience of position. In most cases, the ascending aorta is cannulated just proximal to the innominate artery. In special cases, such as an interrupted aortic arch, the ascending aorta and pulmonary artery, descending aorta, or femoral artery may be cannulated. In the hypoplastic left heart syndrome, the pulmonary artery may be cannulated alone. When multiple arterial cannulae are employed, the percentage of flow directed through each cannula must be reflected in the size difference between the two cannulae. As flow through a cylinder is related to the fourth power of its radius, small changes in French scale sizing are reflected by large changes in flow. For example, at a constant transcannula gradient of 60 mm Hg, a 14 French cannula carries 100% more blood flow than a 10 French cannula. Neonates have a greater percentage of their circulating blood volume directed to the upper extremities and head than adults do. Therefore, this knowledge needs to be reflected in the size of the cannula selected for the head and upper extremity.

Minimization of turbulent flow exiting the arterial catheter can be achieved by limiting the pressure drop across the cannula to less than 100 mm Hg. This is a particularly important consideration in infants as their arteries are smaller, thinner, and more vulnerable to flow-related trauma. Flow gradients vary from cannula to cannula because of design differences and varying methods of sizing. The surgeon and perfusionist should be aware of anticipated gradients by reviewing standard gradient charts (74).

Because of the small size of pediatric great arteries, the intralumenal position of arterial catheters must be carefully controlled. The tourniquet used to secure the aortic pursestring suture around the cannula should be made of thin and firm silastic when small 10 to 14 French cannulae are used. The use of large rubber catheters in these cases may compromise the arterial lumen. Innominate artery obstruction can easily occur in the neonate, with resulting potential for cerebral hypoperfusion. One can ensure that an arterial cannula is unobstructed and in the true lumen of the aorta by monitoring the patient's perfusion pressure directly via the aortic cannula. A tube off of the aortic cannula may be easily connected to an extracorporeal circuit transducer or aneroid manometer. This is done by attaching the pressure manometer to a four-way stopcock at the arterial filter port via drug infusion tubing. Arterial infusion line pressure may then be easily monitored while access to the circuit is gained for the purpose of sampling or drug infusion. In pediatric patients, pulsatile flow is best demonstrated when the pressure is monitored by an aneroid manometer. As with adults, perfusion inflow (or line pressure) should be carefully monitored during the initiation of bypass and placement of the aortic cross-clamp. Significant increases or decreases in pressure across the cannula must be noted and corrective action taken immediately.

For pediatric arterial cannulation, a sturdy catheter with a high ratio of internal diameter to external diameter is desirable. We frequently employ THI angled aortic perfusion cannulae (Argyle, St. Louis, MO) (Fig. 23.3). For the main perfusion pump, the tubing size we use is ¼ inch for patients 15 kg and under, and ⅜ inch for patients 15 to 50 kg. The arterial and venous tubing sizes we have selected are listed in Table 23.2. Appropriate tube sizing will minimize pressure gradients and greatly re-

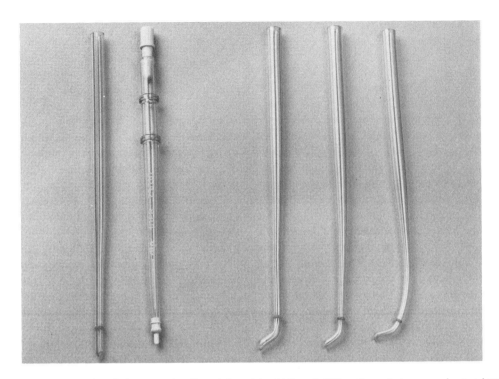

Figure 23.3. Arterial perfusion cannulae. From left to right, 14 French THI aortic perfusion cannula-straight tip (Argyle, St. Louis, MO); 10 French straight tip arterial cannula (DLP, Grand Rapids, MI); and 14, 12, and 10 French THI aortic perfusion cannula (angled) (Argyle).

Table 23.2.   Tube Sizing for Infants and Neonates

Weight (kg)	Perfusion Pump (inch)	Arterial (inch)	Venous (inch)
Less than 5	1/4	1/4	1/4
5–15	1/4	1/4	3/8
16–25	3/8	1/4	3/8
26–50	3/8	3/8	3/8

duce the chance of excessive pressure developing within the extracorporeal circuit.

Venous

As with arterial cannulation, the approach to venous cannulation is dictated by the proposed procedure. In most operations for infants, bicaval cannulation of the superior and inferior vena cavae facilitates operative exposure. Purse-string sutures placed on the cavae, combined with tapes around these vessels, allow for the exclusion of the right atrium. One should be aware that an increased proportion of venous return is from the superior vena cava in neonates and infants, which should be reflected in the size ratio of the superior to inferior vena cavae cannulae selected. Several special venous cannulation issues may arise in neonates and infants. A persistent left superior vena cava may require cannulation or division prior to bypass. Patients with an interrupted inferior vena cava are best served by femoral vein cannulation with a special extended length cannula that lies within the abdomen. The superior vena cava may need to be cannulated at the innominate junction for the performance of a Glenn shunt. In cases where circulatory arrest is planned, a single atrial cannula facilitates drainage of the patient.

As venous return of blood from the body depends on gravity, the choice and size of venous cannulae are extremely important. Prior to the development of modern cannulae, effective venous drainage was highly dependent upon the height of the operating table in relation to the entry of venous blood into the extracorporeal circuit. However, design improvements now allow for large wire-reinforced venous cannulae to be employed with excellent venous return. Pressure drops across these cannulae should not be allowed to exceed 30 mm Hg. Figure 23.4 demonstrates the right-angled venous cannulae (DLP, Grand Rapids, MI) that we frequently employ. Venous drainage is most safely done by gravity; however, pump-driven systems are available that may decrease the priming volume of the extracorporeal circuit.

Venous pressure should not be allowed to become negative within these systems as this collapses and obstructs the great veins (75). Obstruction of venous return may also occur if the cannulae selected are too large. The side ports of oversized venous cannulae may be continuously occluded by an overstretched vein wall and thereby paradoxically decrease overall venous return. This complication may be avoided by selecting appropriately sized cannulae based on anticipated extracorporeal flow rates and a review of the manufacturer's flow/gradient charts. Frequent monitoring of the patient's venous pressure should alert the surgeon or perfusionist of a potential venous obstruction.

Intracardiac Suction and Venting

The basic principles of adult intracardiac suction devices apply to the infant and neonate and are discussed in Chapter 3. Venting of the left ventricle carries increased significance in the infant and neonate because a greater proportion of pediatric procedures are intracardiac and cyanotic patients have greater bronchial arterial collateral flow. Good venting improves operative exposure to facilitate expedient surgery. Ineffective venting may lead to ventricular distension and its detrimental results. The left ventricle is generally vented from the right atrium through a created atrial septal defect or patent foramen ovale. The left side of the heart may also be vented through the left superior pulmonary vein, left atrium, or left ventricle. Many pediatric venting cannulae are available for clinical use. Figure 23.5 shows the DLP infant vent catheters (DLP, Grand Rapids, MI) and a small 6 French urinary catheter (Akron, Chippewa Lake, OH), which we commonly employ. These vents are attached to ¼-inch tubing that should be made as short as possible. The minimization of vent tubing is important because it is not uncommon to have up to 30% of a neonate's circulating volume held within the suction system. The perfusionist must be keenly

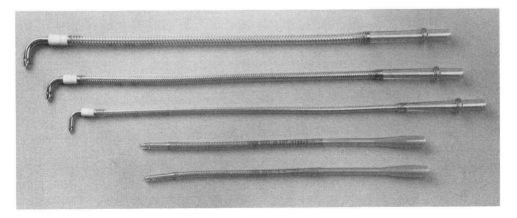

Figure 23.4. Venous cannulae. From bottom to top, 14 and 16 French William Harvey pediatric cannulae (Bard, Santa Ana, CA); and 12, 16, and 20 French venous cannulae (DLP, Grand Rapids, MI).

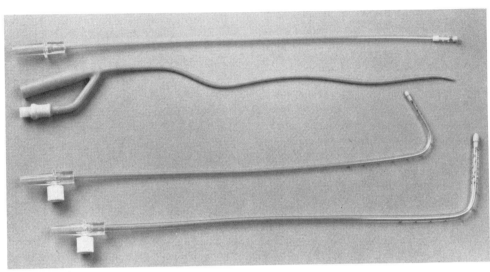

Figure 23.5. Intracardiac venting catheters. From top to bottom, 12 French pediatric intracardiac sump (DLP, Grand Rapids, MI); 6 French 3 ml pediatric Foley catheter (Akron, Chippewa Lake, OH); and 10 and 13 French infant vent catheter (DLP).

aware of the return volume entering through the venting system. Dislodging or kinking of the vent can quickly lead to unsafe volumes within the venous reservoir. Whenever possible, a pressure relief valve should be placed within the venting circuit to release the high negative pressures that may develop when an occlusion occurs. This will eliminate undue trauma to cardiac structures and help to maintain a continuous return to the extracorporeal circuit.

Cardioplegia Cannula

For delivery of antegrade cardioplegia we place a Teflon Angiocath catheter (Deseret Medical, Sandy, UT) with a side port into the aortic root. We apply a piece of autoclaved tape to the proximal end of these 2-inch catheters in order to secure them to the operative field. A 4-inch intravenous extension tubing is then connected to the catheter prior to connecting this assembly to the cardioplegia delivery tubing. A three-way stopcock present at the proximal end of the 4-inch extension tubing provides an extra port for pressure monitoring during cardioplegia adminis-

tration. For infants weighing less than 5 kg, an 18-gauge catheter is used, whereas a 16-gauge catheter is used for infants weighing 5 to 10 kg. For infants weighing between 10 and 20 kg, a 14-gauge catheter is used, and a 12-gauge DLP cardioplegia cannula is employed for patients larger than that. Direct perfusion of the coronary ostia may be performed using a Jehle coronary perfusion catheter (Pilling, Fort Washington, PA) (Fig. 23.6).

In neonates, retrograde cardioplegia may be delivered by a large coronary perfusion cannula such as the 27-cm no. 210804 Mayo balloon (Polystan, Copenhagen, Denmark). Infants may receive retrograde cardioplegia via the commercially available pediatric retroplegia coronary sinus cardioplegia cannula (Research Medical Inc., Midvale, UT) (Fig. 23.7). Retrograde catheters should be gently introduced into the coronary sinus and the balloon inflated just past the eustachian valve. During delivery, it is common for a small amount of cardioplegia to escape around the balloon and enter the atrium. As long as pressure is maintained in the coronary sinus, adequate retrograde perfusion will continue. Particu-

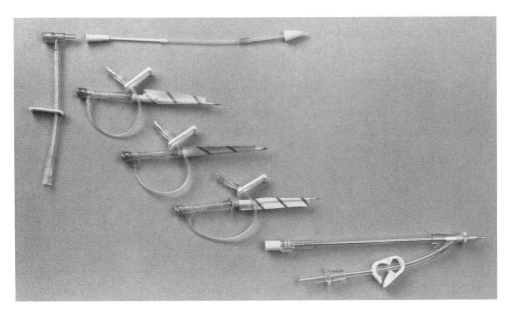

Figure 23.6.   Antegrade cardioplegia catheters. From top to bottom, Jehle 11/32 inch coronary perfusion catheter (Pilling, Fort Washington, PA); 14-, 16-, and 18-gauge catheter (Angiocath) with T-connector intravenous extension (Desert Medical, Sandy, UT); and 14-gauge aortic root cannula (DLP, Grand Rapids, MI).

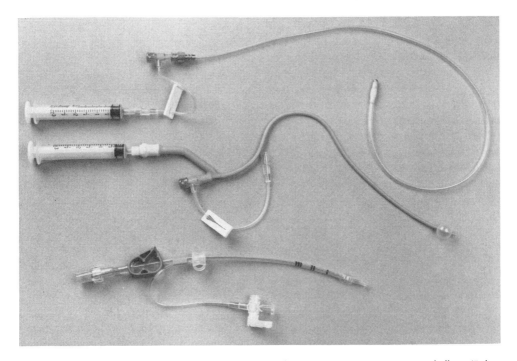

Figure 23.7.   Retrograde cardioplegia catheters. From top to bottom, 27 cm no. 210804 Mayo balloon (Polystan, Copenhagen, Denmark); 6 French 3 ml pediatric Foley catheter (Akron, Chippewa Lake, OH); and pediatric retroplegia coronary sinus cardioplegia cannula (Research Medical, Midvale, UT).

larly in infants, attempting to create a water-tight seal with a circumferential purse-string suture may result in transient or permanent heart block that is completely avoidable. Under some circumstances, a 270° purse-string suture may be useful if great care is taken to avoid the conduction tissue.

THE EXTRACORPOREAL CIRCUIT PRIMING SOLUTION

The composition of the extracorporeal circuit priming solution gathers increasing significance as patients become smaller, because the percentage of total circulating volume contributed by the patient during bypass diminishes as body weight decreases. The typical adult has a blood volume of approximately 65 ml per kilogram of body weight. The following guidelines are useful in estimating total blood volume in relation to age: 1 to 3 years, 70 to 75 ml/kg; 1 to 12 months, 75 to 85 ml/kg; newborn, 90 ml/kg; and premature, 100 ml/kg (Table 23.3). Thus, a 3-kg neonate will contribute only 270 ml to the total circulating blood volume during bypass.

It is desirable to avoid blood in the extracorporeal circuit prime whenever possible in order to reduce the risk of transmitting human immunodeficiency virus (HIV), hepatitis B or C, and of developing transfusion reactions (76). This is frequently possible in children and polycythemic infants because hematocrits between 16% and 28% are desirable during hypothermic bypass. Several factors are involved in the se-

lection of a hematocrit for hypothermic bypass. These include oxygen delivery, rheology, and oncotic properties. Oxygen delivery is related to the oxygen saturation of hemoglobin, hemoglobin concentration, and cardiac output. With extracorporeal circuits, all three of these variables are under the direct control of the perfusionist. Hemoglobin saturation is maintained at 100% and blood flow rates are varied to meet oxygen consumption demands. Hematocrit can then be varied to optimize oncotic and rheologic properties. An increased incidence of renal failure and renal dysfunction has been documented after hypothermic CPB without hemodilution (77). Hemodilution counteracts the increase in blood viscosity associated with progressive hypothermia and thus facilitates blood flow by reducing systemic vascular resistance, which has a viscosity component and a vascular component. The major negative effect of hemodilution is the loss of oncotic activity; therefore, tissue edema increases as hemodilution progresses (78). This can be limited by the careful selection of priming components. In order to determine the volume of red blood cells needed to prime the extracorporeal circuit, the following formula may be applied:

$$\text{Volume required} = \frac{[(PBV+ECCV) \times CPB\ Hct] - (PBV \times Pt\ Hct)}{\text{Hct of donor blood}}$$

where, PBV = patient's blood volume, $ECCV$ = extracorporeal circuit volume, $CPB\ Hct$ = the desired hematocrit on bypass, and $Pt\ Hct$ = patient's pre-CPB hematocrit.

The noncellular components of the prime consist of crystalloid and colloid solutions. Both of these components have significant effects on organ function and metabolism during and after bypass. In adults, extracellular fluid accumulation during CPB has been shown to be significantly

Table 23.3. Estimate of Total Blood Volume by Age

Age	Estimate (cc/kg)
Adult	65
3 years	70
1 year	75
6 months	80
1 month	85
Newborn	90
Premature	100

lower when albumin or mannitol was added to the extracorporeal circuit prime (79). There is an inverse relationship between colloid oncotic pressure and edema formation during bypass when studied in laboratory pigs (80). However, despite the positive effects of increased albumin on fluid balance, a negative effect on renal function is noted if the concentration of albumin becomes too high. From the analysis of such studies, the optimal oncotic pressure for the prime of the extracorporeal circuit is probably about 16 mm Hg (81). Crystalloid components of the prime are also important. When crystalloid components are added in excess, hyperglycemia, lactic acidosis, and osmolar flux may occur (82). These effects may be mitigated by the judicious selection of crystalloid components.

When stored blood is added to the extracorporeal circuit prime, sodium bicarbonate and calcium chloride are usually required for buffering of the blood and to offset the effect of citrate on free serum calcium levels. Approximately 200 units of heparin, 3 mEq of sodium bicarbonate, and 50 mg of calcium chloride should be added to the extracorporeal circuit prime for every 50 ml of stored packed red blood cells. The addition of these agents may lead to a hypernatremic prime. Hence, whenever possible, fresh blood should be used for the neonatal extracorporeal circuit prime. The more stable condition of cell membranes in unstored blood accounts for their ability to withstand CPB with a lower rate of hemolysis. Unfortunately, fresh blood is difficult to obtain, so one must prepare for the adverse effects of stored blood. As such, we use the following components to make up the extracorporeal circuit prime (Table 23.4).

Plasmalyte A (Baxter Healthcare, Deerfield, IL). This is the initial crystalloid solution for recirculating and debubbling of the extracorporeal circuit. This solution has a composition of Na, 140 mEq; K, 5 mEq; Cl, 98 mEq; Mg, 3 mEq; glucose, 23 mEq; and acetate, 27 mEq. The solution has an osmolality of 294 mOsm and a pH of about 6.7. Once the desired bypass hematocrit is determined, excess plasmalyte is removed and the components listed below are added.

25% Normal Serum Albumin. The volume added should result in an albumin concentration of 10%.

Packed Red Blood Cells. Using the previously mentioned formula, the volume of blood required for the desired hematocrit is determined and added.

Sodium Bicarbonate. Add 20 mEq/350 ml of packed red blood cells. Additional amounts may be required as noted by the pH.

Heparin. Add 1000 units/unit of packed red blood cells. If a clear prime is used, add 1000 units/1000 ml of pump volume.

Mannitol. Add 0.5 g/kg body weight. For circulatory arrest cases, we prefer to add this upon rewarming in order to optimize osmotic diuresis at that time.

Table 23.4. Composition of the Prime[a]

Blood: Volume required $= \dfrac{[(PBV + ECCV) \times CPB\ Hct] - (PBV \times Pt\ Hct)}{\text{hematocrit of donor blood}}$

25% Serum albumin: The volume required to have 10% albumin in the final solution
Plasmalyte A: Volume required = ECCV − (blood volume + 25% serum albumin volume)
Sodium bicarbonate: 20 mEq/350 ml of packed red blood cells, additional amounts as required by pH
Heparin: 1000 units/unit of packed red blood cells.
1000 units/1000 ml of prime if a clear prime is used.
Mannitol: 0.5 g/kg (for circulatory arrest, add upon rewarming)

[a] Abbreviations: PBV, patient's blood volume; ECCV, extracorporeal circuit volume; CPB Hct, CPB hematocrit; Pt Hct, patient's hematocrit.

Before initiation of bypass, the prime components should be checked to verify their appropriate concentrations. Acceptable ranges are shown in Table 23.5.

Additionally, steroids (methylprednisolone 30 mg/kg) may be introduced into the extracorporeal circuit prime in order to promote membrane stabilization, etc., during circulatory arrest or prolonged bypass. This practice has not been demonstrated to provide superior results in the form of a randomized clinical trial. However, the debate regarding the value of steroids continues on a theoretical basis. We have found it unnecessary to add plasma clotting factors to the extracorporeal circuit prime. It is believed that, as patients are anticoagulated on bypass, the addition of fresh-frozen plasma serves no purpose other than oncotic. This oncotic effect may be more efficiently obtained by using albumin or a synthetic colloid. Further, plasma proteins are destroyed to a variable extent during CPB, which renders them less efficient once anticoagulation is reversed.

THE EXTRACORPOREAL CIRCUIT

The Venous Reservoir

As with all aspects of extracorporeal support used for neonates and infants, an attempt to limit transfusion requirements is secondary in importance only to safety.

Table 23.5. Acceptable Values for the Prime

Component	Value
pH	7.35–7.45
P_{O_2}	80–300 mm Hg
P_{CO_2}	35–45 mm Hg
Sodium	<140 mEq
Potassium	3.5–5.0 mEq
Calcium (ionized)	Approximately 1.0 mmol
Glucose	<200 mg/dl
Hematocrit	Depends on anticipated degree of hypothermia
Oncotic pressure	13–16 mm Hg
Osmotic pressure	Approximately 300 mOsm

Hence, a desirable venous reservoir allows for safe operation with a relatively low volume. Bubble oxygenators combine reservoir function and oxygenation in the same chamber and a venous reservoir is not required. Oxygenation and temperature change occur within the same chamber, whereas in membrane oxygenators temperature changes occur in the venous reservoir prior to oxygenation. Most commonly used membrane oxygenators require a separate venous reservoir. Volume may be reduced in these reservoirs by employing vacuum as opposed to gravity drainage (83). Such systems must be carefully monitored, as excessive venous suction pressures may collapse the great veins and induce paradoxic obstruction. To maintain safety while decreasing priming volumes, the diameter of the reservoir may be reduced (84). In general, the above considerations promote the use of a membrane oxygenator, which has an integrated venous reservoir, in bypass for neonates and infants.

The Oxygenator

No oxygenator can compete with the delicate efficiency of the human lung. Nonetheless, the goal of oxygenators is to maximize gas transfer while minimizing trauma to blood. Oxygenators employed for pediatric cases must be able to function with wide fluctuations in hematocrit, temperature, and the delivery of oxygen. The mechanics of gas transfer by bubble and membrane oxygenators have been discussed in Chapter 2. As the question of whether membrane or bubble oxygenators are less traumatic to blood elements is not completely resolved (85, 86), the choice of an oxygenator should be based on the overall perfusion requirements of each individual patient. Nonetheless, we prefer the Cobe VPCML membrane oxygenator (Cobe, Lakewood, CO)(Fig. 23.8) for use in all circuits designed for neonates, infants, and children. This oxygenator works on a parallel plate-designed membrane and integrates a

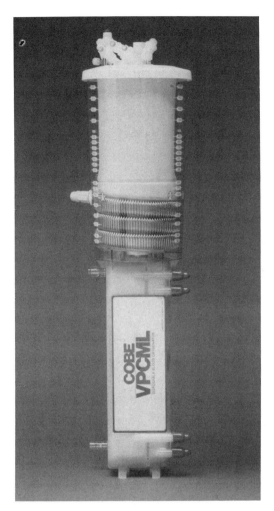

Figure 23.8. The Cobe VPCML membrane oxygenator (Cobe, Lakewood, CO).

venous reservoir and the capacity for a filtered suction return. This allows for a relatively low priming volume. The division of the membrane into one third and two thirds oxygenating capacity permits the single unit to be utilized for patients in the weight range of premature to 50 kg. Other advantages include a manifold for blood sampling and drug administration, a low pressure drop between the inlet and outlet of the membrane, a defoamer with "open" reservoir, and arterial and venous temperature monitoring sites. As with any membrane oxygenator, the selection of this unit re-

flects many considerations specific to the needs of pediatric open heart surgery.

Heat Exchangers and Filters

These have been discussed in detail in Chapters 2 and 3. A highly efficient heat exchanger should be employed. Temperature gradients between the patient and the heater/cooler should not exceed 8 to 10°C. Higher gradients may cause gas to come out of solution (87). The temperature of the water bath should not exceed 42°C, as temperatures above 44°C cause red blood cell destruction.

Arterial filters should be used regardless of the type of oxygenator employed. Formation of microemboli has been demonstrated to occur with both membrane and bubble oxygenators (88). The filter also serves as a bubble trap, which is an added measure of safety. Pediatric filters that require a small volume to prime are available. Our preference is the ¼-inch inlet Pediatric Intersept arterial filter (Medtronic, Anaheim, CA) (Fig. 23.9). These filters may be continuously purged; however, in neonates and infants, the purging line must be kept small in order to prevent a significant diversion of flow.

The Pump

Both roller and centrifugal pumps are available for pediatric perfusion. The current trend toward safer extracorporeal circuits has heightened interest in the use of centrifugal pumps. These pumps offer some advantages over roller pumps. They are less likely to pump air, have a lower priming volume, and will not generate high pressures if the arterial tubing becomes accidentally obstructed. Nonetheless, each type of pump offers certain advantages that must be evaluated for their significance to each clinical pediatric practice. Recently, counterpulsation has been made available for use with some roller pumps. Intraaortic balloon counterpulsation has not been

Figure 23.9.   The ¼-inch inlet Pediatric Intersept arterial filter (Meditronic, Anaheim, CA)

proven beneficial in children. The technical problems of a high heart rate, small peripheral arteries, and difficulties in determining an appropriately sized balloon have contributed to disappointing clinical results. Pump-delivered counterpulsation may reduce some of these problems; however, no clinical studies yet support its use in infants or neonates.

The lower flow volumes used during pediatric bypass demand accurate flow calibration and monitoring. A 200-ml/min flow difference may mean little in a 75 kg patient; however, such a discrepancy can be disastrous in a 5 kg neonate. In roller pumps, this translates into ensuring that the roller mechanism synchronizes properly with the blood flow sensor. Belt slippage can lead to an inaccurate determination of flow. Routine maintenance and frequent calibration should avoid this pitfall. Centrifugal pumps rely on transducers for flow measurements. These, too, should be serviced and calibrated regularly.

Ultrafiltration

Also known as hemoconcentrating, ultrafiltration removes water and solutes from blood within the extracorporeal circuit. Its application is gaining in pediatric perfusion, to which it is well suited. When used in adults as a means for processing residual blood in the oxygenation circuit after discontinuing bypass, studies have demonstrated the superiority of ultrafiltration over red cell separation with respect to maintenance of plasma proteins and colloid oncotic pressure (89, 90). In our experience, ultrafiltration may be particularly useful in neonates and infants, as these patients display increased capillary permeability and are particularly susceptible to edema formation when colloid oncotic pressure drops. Ultrafiltration effectively removed free water after CPB in volume-overloaded, critically ill children (91). In institutions where crystalloid cardioplegia is used during prolonged procedures, ultrafiltration may be very helpful during bypass, and it has also been used to "wash" extracorporeal circuit prime solutions to reduce undesirable levels of lactate and glucose (92). The Hemocor Plus (Minntech, Minneapolis, MN) (Fig. 23.10) is an example of an effective pediatric hemoconcentrator that may be used when blood cardioplegia and hypothermia are employed during CPB.

Safety Devices

The safety characteristics of the extracorporeal circuit play a major role in the optimum care of the pediatric patient. As with adult patients, safety comes first. Safety features that we believe should be mandatory for pediatric bypass procedures include an air bubble detector, a blood reservoir level detector, and a pressure sensor with a high-pressure limit.

Since pediatric extracorporeal circuits have decreased priming volumes, the error margin for maintaining an acceptable minimum operating reservoir volume is reduced. The shorter length of arterial tubing may also permit more rapid air transfer through the circuit and into the patient. All of these factors translate into the necessity of using reliable and rapidly sensing safety monitors in pediatric extracorporeal circuits. The alarm systems for these circuits should also be durable, easy to operate, and precise.

Safety features for the improvement of bypass advance at a steady rate. Perfusionists and physicians should stay abreast of these advances through journals, symposia, and promotional literature. Many safety devices require adaptation for application to pediatric CPB. The perfusionist performing the adaptation should rigorously test the modification prior to its clinical use and be familiar with the technical specifications of all equipment used.

The following are the application and modification of the three basic safety devices used at the UCLA Medical Center. These should serve as representative examples, not as definitive guidelines. The Sarns air bubble detector (Sarns/3M Health Care, Ann Arbor, MI) has a cylindrical compartment through which the arterial extracorporeal tubing passes. An electronic eye monitors flow through the tubing and will detect large air bubbles. Once air is sensed, the alarm activates an audible and visible warning, which interrupts arterial flow

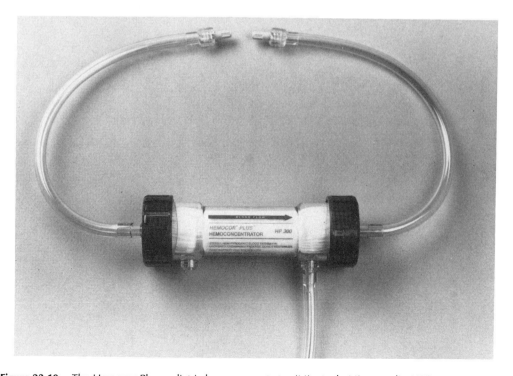

Figure 23.10.   The Hemocor Plus pediatric hemoconcentrator (Minntech, Minneapolis, MN).

until the sensor is reset. The tubing compartment size is ⅜ inch, as this is the most frequently used tubing size for adults. This can be modified to sense ¼-inch tubing (which is used for neonates) by simply wrapping a longitudinally split piece of ⅜-inch tubing around the ¼-inch tubing and inserting this into the sensor (Fig. 23.11). This has proven to be an easy and cost-effective modification.

The minimum operating level of the venous reservoir may be monitored by devices utilizing an electronic eye or a Doppler probe. The necessity to securely fix the level sensor to the curvature of the venous reservoir imposes a challenge in utilizing this device. When the device is affixed by suction, a back-up system should be applied to prevent unexpected dislodgement. This can include taping, banding, or structural fixation. When sensing gel is required, as with Doppler transducers, one must ensure that the sensing material does not dry out or

drop out of place. We believe that a pressure transducer that shuts off flow when the pressure exceeds a preset limit should also be considered mandatory. This device will detect excessive pressure developing from an obstruction to flow and will stop forward blood flow prior to a damaging event such as rupture at a tubing connection site. With the equipment used in our practice, a 300 mm Hg pressure cut-off appears appropriate, although this may vary and should be applied according to the manufacturers' guidelines.

Monitoring

Monitoring may be divided into three major categories: hemodynamic monitoring, extracorporeal circuit monitoring, and laboratory monitoring of the physiologic parameters of the patient. Hemodynamic and physiologic monitors used during bypass for the neonate and infant should in-

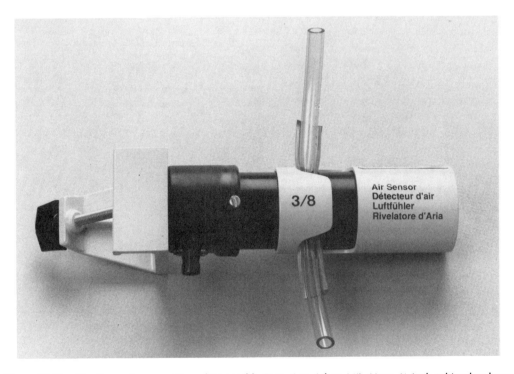

Figure 23.11. The Sarns air sensor (Sarns/3M Health Care, Ann Arbor, MI). Here, ¼-inch tubing has been wrapped with a longitudinally split piece of ⅜-inch tubing in order to fit the ⅜-inch compartment size.

clude the following: electrocardiogram, arterial blood pressure (umbilical, femoral, or brachial), central venous pressure, urine output, temperature (tympanic or nasopharyngeal and bladder or rectal), and at times EEG. Monitoring of the extracorporeal circuit is performed by the perfusionist using the operational safety devices described above as well as the interpretation of available mechanical and technical information.

Various laboratory tests are necessary to evaluate the metabolic response of the patient to perfusion and anesthesia. The laboratory monitoring of blood and serum during extracorporeal circulation should probably include arterial and mixed venous blood gases, hematocrit or hemoglobin, potassium, glucose, ionized calcium, and activated clotting time. We also monitor platelet count, serum lactate, osmotic and oncotic pressures. Activated clotting times should be maintained as in adults (see Chapter 14). In pediatric patients, initial

heparin dosages used range from 250 to 300 U/kg in addition to the heparin used to prime the extracorporeal circuit. There are many devices available for the laboratory monitoring of CPB. Significant advances have been made in minimizing the blood volume required for ex vivo analysis and in the development of noninvasive monitoring. Continuous, on-line, arterial and venous PO_2, PCO_2, and pH may now be noninvasively monitored (Fig. 23.12). These devices are not meant to replace standard arterial blood gas analyzers, but rather to complement them. Standard machine-based blood gas monitoring is still required.

Hypothermic bypass has been demonstrated to decrease renal blood flow, glomerular filtration rate, and free water clearance (93). Neonates and young infants can not effectively concentrate urine when compared to adults. As such, these patients are easily under- or overhydrated, thus frequent laboratory and hemodynamic moni-

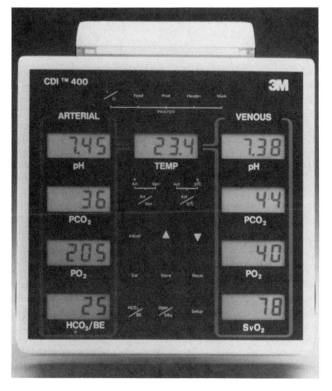

Figure 23.12. The CDI system 400 extracorporeal blood gas monitoring system (CDI/3M Health Care, Tustin, CA).

toring should be utilized to optimize volume status. Separation of the neonate or infant from CPB is facilitated by judicious volume and temperature management. In summary, careful monitoring of the extracorporeal circuit and of the patient will produce maximum patient safety and improved clinical results with cardiac surgical procedures using extracorporeal circulation in children.

REFERENCES

1. Gibbon JH. Application of a mechanical heart and lung apparatus to cardiac surgery. Minn Med 1954;37:171–185.
2. Warden HE, Cohen M, Read RC, et al. Controlled cross-circulation for open intracardiac surgery. J Thorac Surg 1954;28:331–343.
3. Kirklin JW, Dushane JW, Patrick RT, et al. Intracardiac surgery with the aid of a mechanical pump-oxygenator (Gibbon-type): report of eight cases. Mayo Clin Proc 1955;30:201–206.
4. Bigelow WG, Callaghan JC, Hopps JA. General hypothermia for experimental intracardiac surgery. Ann Surg 1950;132:3;531–539.
5. Bigelow WG, Lindsay WK, Greenwood WF. Hypothermia: its possible role in cardiac surgery. Ann Surg 1950;132:5;849–866.
6. Weiss M, Piwnica A, Lenfant C, et al. Deep hypothermia with total circulatory arrest. Trans Am Soc Artif Intern Organs 1960;6:227–239.
7. Barratt-Boyes BG, Simpson MM, Neutze EA, et al. Intra-cardiac surgery in neonates and infants using deep hypothermia. Circulation Suppl 1970;61 & 62(suppl III);III-73.
8. Sealy WC, Brown IW, Young Jr, WG, et al. Hypothermia, low flow extracorporeal circulation and controlled cardiac arrest for open heart surgery. Surg Gynecol Obstet 1957;441–450.
9. Hickey RF, Hoar PF. Whole body oxygen consumption during low-flow hypothermic cardiopulmonary bypass. J Thorac Cardiovasc Surg 1983;86:903–906.
10. Reed CC, Kurusz M, Lawrence Jr AE. Safety and techniques in perfusion. Stafford, Texas: Quali-Med, Inc., 1988:154.
11. Fox LS, Blackstone EH, Kirklin JW. The relationship of whole-body oxygen consumption to perfusion flow rate during hypothermic bypass. J Thorac Cardiovasc Surg 1982;83:239–248.
12. Govier AV, Reves JG, McKay RD, et al. Factors and their influence on regional cerebral blood flow during nonpulsatile cardiopulmonary bypass. Ann Thorac Surg 1984;38:592–600.
13. Murkin JM, Farrar JK, Tweed WA, et al. Cerebral autoregulation and flow/metabolism coupling during cardiopulmonary bypass: the influence of PCO_2. Anesth Analg 1987;66:825–832.
14. Soma Y, Hirotani T, Yozu R, et al. A clinical study of the cerebral circulation during extracorporeal circulation. J Thorac Cardiovasc Surg 1989;97:187–193.
15. Johnsson P, Messeter K, Ryding E, et al. Cerebral vasoreactivity to carbon dioxide during cardiopulmonary perfusion at normothermia and hypothermia. Ann Thorac Surg 1989;48:769–775.
16. Greeley WJ, Ungerleider RM, Kern FH, et al. Effects of cardiopulmonary bypass on cerebral blood flow in neonates, infants, and children. Circulation 1989;80(suppl I):209–215.
17. Van De Bor M, Walthers FJ, Gangitano ES, et al. Extracorporeal membrane oxygenation and cerebral blood flow velocity in newborn infants. Crit Care Med 1990;18:10–13.
18. Swain JA, McDonald TJ, Giffith PK, et al. Low-flow hypothermic cardiopulmonary bypass protects the brain. J Thorac Cardiovasc Surg 1991;102:76–84.
19. Rebeyka IM, Coles JG, Wilson GJ, et al. The effect of low-flow cardiopulmonary bypass on cerebral function: an experimental and clinical study. Ann Thorac Surg 1987;43:391–396.
20. Wilson GJ, Rebeyka IM, Coles, JG. Loss of somatosensory evoked response as an indicator of reversible cerebral ischemia during hypothermic, low-flow, cardiopulmonary bypass. Ann Thorac Cardiovasc Surg 1988;45:206–209.
21. Kramer RS, Sanders AP, Lesage AM, et al. The effect of profound hypothermia on preservation of cerebral ATP content during circulatory arrest. J Thorac Cardiovasc Surg 1968;56:5;700–709.
22. Treasure T, Naftel DC, Conger KA, et al. The effect of hypothermic circulatory arrest time on cerebral function, morphology, and biochemistry. J Thorac Cardiovasc Surg 1983;86:761–770.
23. Kirklin JK, Kirklin JW, Pacifico AD. Deep hypothermia and circulatory arrest. In: Arcinegas E, ed. Pediatric cardiac surgery. Chicago: Yearbook Medical Publishers, 1985.
24. Pearl JM, Laks H. Review & critique. Cardiac Chronicle 1991;5:6;10–11.
25. Wong PC, Jonas RA, Barlow CF, et al. Factors associated with choreathetosis following circulatory arrest in children with heart disease [abstract]. Circulation 1991;84(suppl II):121.
26. Coselli JS, Crawford ES, Beall Jr AC, et al. Determination of brain temperatures for safe circulatory arrest during cardiovascular operations. Ann Thorac Surg 1988;45:638–642.
27. Puntis JWL. Neurological complications of heart disease in children. Br J Clin Pract 1990;43:2170–2220.

28. Blackwood MJA, Haka-Irke K, Steward MB. Developmental outcome in children undergoing surgery with profound hypothermia. Anesthesiology 1986;65:437–440.

29. Clarkson PM, MacArthur BA, Barratt-Boyes B, et al. Developmental progress after cardiac surgery in infancy using profound hypothermia and circulatory arrest. Circulation 1980;62:855–861.

30. Wells FC, Coghill S, Caplin HL, et al. Duration of circulatory arrest does influence the psychological development of children after cardiac operation in early life. J Thorac Cardiovasc Surg 1983;86:823–831.

31. Ferry PC. Neurologic sequelae of open-heart surgery in children. Am J Dis Child 1990;144:369–373.

32. Greeley WJ, Kern FH, Ungerleider RM, et al. The effect of hypothermic cardiopulmonary bypass and total circulatory arrest on cerebral metabolism in neonates, infants, and children. J Thorac Cardiovasc Surg 1991;101:783–794.

33. Ueda T, Yamamoto L, Takara E, et al. Tolerance of the cerebral venous system to retrograde perfusion pressure in focal cerebral ischemia in rats. Stroke 1989;20:378–385.

34. Ueda T, Yamamoto L, Diksic M. Transvenous perfusion of the brain with verapamil during focal cerebral ischemia in rats. Stroke 1989;20:501–506.

35. Rudy LW Jr, Boucher JK, Edmunds LH Jr, et al. The effects of deep hypothermia and circulatory arrest on the distribution of systemic blood flow in rhesus monkeys. J Thoracic Cardiovasc Surg 1972;64:706–712.

36. Bull C, Cooper J, Stark J. Cardioplegic protection of the child's heart. J Thorac Cardiovasc Surg 1984;88:287–293.

37. Romero T, Covell J, Friedman W. A comparison of pressure-volume relations of the fetal, newborn, and adult heart. Am J Physiol 1972;555:5;1285–1290.

38. Romero T, Friedaman W. Limited left ventricular response to volume overload in the neonatal period: a comparative study with the adult animal. Pediat Res 1979;13:910–915.

39. Teitel DF, Sidi D, Chin T, et al. Developmental changes in myocardial contractile reserve in the lamb. Pediat Res 1985;19:9;948–955.

40. Tomec RJ, Hoppel CL. Carnitine palmitotranserase in bovine fetal heart mitochondria. Arch Biochem & Biophys 1975;170:716–723.

41. Rolph TP, Jones CT. Regulation of glycolytic flux in the heart of the fetal guinea pig. J Dev Physiol 1983;5:31–49.

42. Dawes GS, Mott JC, Shelley HJ. The importance of cardiac glycogen for the maintenance of life in foetal lambs and new-born animals during anoxia. J Physiol 1959;146:516–538.

43. Yee ES, Ebert PA. Effect of ischemia on ventricular function, compliance, and edema in immature and adult canine hearts. Surg Forum 1979;30:250–252.

44. Young HH, Shimizu T, Nishioka K, et al. Effect of hypoxia and reoxygenation on mitochondrial function in neonatal myocardium. Am J Physiol 1983;245:998–1006.

45. Jarmakani JM, Nakazawa M, Nagatomo T, et al. Effect of hypoxia on mechanical function in the neonatal mammalian heart. Am J Physiol 1978;235:469–474.

46. Downing SE, Talner NS, Gardner TH. Influences of arterial oxygen tension and pH on cardiac function in the newborn lamb. Am J Physiol 1966;211:1203–1208.

47. Silverman NA, Kohler J, Levitsky S, et al. Chronic hypoxemia depresses global ventricular function and predisposes to the depletion of high energy phosphates during cardioplegic arrest: implications for surgical repair of cyanotic congenital heart defects. Ann Thorac Surg 1984;37:4;304–308.

48. Scheuer, J. Studies in the human heart exposed to chronic hypoxemia. Cardiology 1971;56:215–222.

49. Laks H, Morday F, Garner D, et al. Temporal changes in canine right ventricular volume mass, cell size, and sarcomere length after banding the pulmonary artery. Cardiovasc Res 1974;8:106–111.

50. Peyton RB, Hones RN, Attarian D, et al. Depressed high-energy phosphate content in hypertrophied ventricles of animal and man. Ann Surg 1982;196:3;278–284.

51. Buckberg GM, Hottenrott CE. Ventricular fibrillation: its effect on myocardial blood flow, distribution, and performance. Ann Thorac Surg 1975;20:76–85.

52. Braimbridge MV, Chayen J, Bitensky L, et al. Cold cardiopegia or continuous coronary perfusion? Report on preliminary clinical evidence as assessed cytochemically. J Cardiovasc Thorac Surg 1977;71:900–906.

53. Adappa MG, Jacobson LB, Hetzer R, et al. Cold hyperkalemic cardiac arrest versus intermittent aortic cross-clamping and topical hypothermia for coronary bypass surgery. J Thorac Cardiovasc Surg 1978;75:2;171–178.

54. Buckberg GD, Brazier JR, Nelson RH, et al. Studies on the effect of hypothermia on regional myocardial blood flow and metabolism during cardiopulmonary bypass. I: the adequately perfused beating, fibrillating, and arrested heart. J Thorac Cardiovasc Surg 1977;73:87–94.

55. Chitwood WR, Sink JD, Hill RC, et al. The effects of hypothermia on myocardial oxygen consumption and transmural coronary blood flow in the

potassium-arrested heart. Ann Surg 1979; 190:106–116.

56. Zreikat, HY. Collateral vessels between the coronary and bronchial arteries in patients with cyanotic congenital heart disease. Am J Cardiol 1980;45:599–603.

57. Lamberti JJ, Cohn LH, Laks H, et al. Local cardiac hypothermia for myocardial protection during correction of congenital heart disease. Ann Thorac Surg 1975;20:4;446–455.

58. Corno AF, Bethencourt DM, Laks H, et al. Myocardial protection in the neonatal heart. J Thorac Cardiovasc Surg 1987;93:2;163–172.

59. Schactner A, Schmiimert G, Lajos TS, et al. Selective intercavitary and coronary hypothermia cardioplegia for myocardial preservation. Arch Surg 1976;111:1197–1209.

60. Saw HS, Juggi JS, Ganendran A, et al. The efficacy of potassium-induced cardioplegia and topical hypothermia in the correction of congenital cardiac lesions. Aust N Z Surg 1981;51:3;264–270.

61. Hammon JW, Graham TP, Boucek RJ, et al. Myocardial adenosine triphosphate content as a measure of metabolic and functional myocardial protection in children undergoing cardiac operation. Ann Thorac Surg 1987;44:467–470.

62. Crawford FA, Barnes TY, Heath BJ. Potassium-induced cardioplegia in patients undergoing corection of congenital heart defects. Chest 1980;78:316–320.

63. Rosenkranz ER, Vinten-Johansen J, Buckberg GD. Benefits of normothermic induction of blood cardioplegia in energy depleted hearts, with maintenance of arrest by multidose cold blood cardioplegic infusions. J Thorac Cardiovasc Surg 1982;84:667–677.

64. Buckberg GD, Myocardial protection during adult cardiac operations. In: Baue AE, Geha AS, Hammond GL, et al, eds. Glenn's thoracic and cardiovascular surgery. East Norwalk, CT: Appleton and Lange, 1991:1417–1442.

65. Breda MA, Drinkwater DC, Laks H. Prevention of reperfusion injury in the neonatal heart with leukocyte-depleted blood. J Thorac Cardiovasc Surg 1989;97:654–665.

66. Chang-Chun C, Matsuda H, Sawa Y, et al. Effects of a cyclic adenosine monophosphate phosphodiesterase inhibitor, DN-9693, on myocardial reperfusion injury. Ann Thorac Surg 1991;52: 495–499.

67. Ko W, Hawes AS, Lazenby D, et al. Myocardial reperfusion injury. J Thorac Cardiovasc Surg 1991;102:297–308.

68. Lichtenstein SV, Ashe KA, El Dalati H, et al. Warm heart surgery. J Thorac Cardiovasc Surg 1991;101:269–274.

69. Drinkwater DC, Laks H, Buckberg GD. A new simplified method of optimizing cardioplegic delivery without right heart isolation. J Thorac Cardiovasc Surg 1990;100:56–63.

70. Grundy SR, Kirsh MM. A comparison of retrograde cardioplegia versus antegrade cardioplegia in the presents of coronary artery obstruction. Ann Thorac Surg 1984;38:124–127.

71. Snyder HE, Smithwick W, Wingard JT, et al. Retrograde coronary sinus perfusion. Ann Thorac Surg 1988;46:389–390.

72. Lees MH, Herr RH, Hill JD, et al. Distribution of systemic blood flow of the rhesus monkey during cardiopulmonary bypass. J Thorac Cardiovasc Surg 1971;61:570–586.

73. LeCompte Y, Zannini L, Hazan E, et al. Anatomic correction of transposition of the great arteries: a new technique without use of a prosthetic conduit. J Thorac Cardiovasc Surg 1981;82: 629–638.

74. Broadman R, Siegel H, Lesser M, et al. A comparison of flow gradients across disposable arterial perfusion catheters. Ann Thorac Surg 1985; 39:3;225–233.

75. Wenger RK, Bavaria JE, Patrick RT, et al. Flow dynamics of peripheral venous catheters during extracorporeal membrane oxygenation (ECMO) with a centrifugal pump. J Thorac Cardiovasc Surg 1988;96:478–484.

76. Verska JJ, Ludington LG, Brewer LA. A comparative study of cardiopulmonary bypass with a nonblood and blood prime. Ann Thorac Surg 1974; 18:72–80.

77. Mielke JE, Hunt JC, Maher FT, et al. Renal performance during clinical cardiopulmonary bypass with and without hemodilution. J Thorac Cardiovas Surg 1966;51:229–237.

78. Utley JR, Watchel C, Cain RB, et al. Effects of hypothermia, hemodilution and pump oxygenation on organ water content, blood flow and oxygen delivery and renal function. Ann Thorac Surg 1981;31:121–133.

79. Utley JR, Stephens DB, Fluid balance during cardiopulmonary bypass. In: Utley JR, ed. Pathophysiology and techniques of cardiopulmonary bypass. Baltimore: Williams & Wilkins, 1983; 23–35.

80. Lilleaasen P, Stokke O, Thoresen O, et al. Effects of different nonhaemic fluids in open-heart surgery. Scand J Thorac Cardiovasc Surg 1979;13: 233–240.

81. Schupbach P, Pappova E, Schilt W, et al. Perfusate oncotic pressure during cardiopulmonary bypass: optimum level as determined by metabolic acidosis, tissue edema, and renal function. Vox Sang 1978;35:332–344.

82. Ratcliffe JM, Wyse RKH, Hunter S, et al. The role of priming fluid in the metabolic response to

cardiopulmonary bypass in children less than 15 kg body weight undergoing open-heart surgery. Thorac Cardiovasc Surg 1988;36:2;65–74.

83. Wabeke E, Elstrodt JM, Mook PH, et al. Clear prime for infant cardiopulmonary bypass: a miniaturized circuit. J Cardiovasc Surg 1988; 29:117–122.

84. Ochsner JL, Horowitz MD, Ballantyne R. A venous reservoir for cardiopulmonary bypass in newborns and small infants. Ann Thorac Surg 1988;45:686.

85. Williams DR, Tyers GFO, William EH, et al. Similarity of clinical and laboratory results obtained with microporous teflon membrane oxygenators and bubble-film hybrid oxygenators. Ann Thorac Surg 1978;25:30–35.

86. Addonizio Jr VP, Strauss JF, Coleman RW, et al. Effects of prostaglandin E1 on platelet loss during in vitro cardiopulmonary bypass. Circ Res 1979; 44:350–357.

87. Almond CH, Jones JC, Synder HM, et al. Cooling gradients and brain damage with deep hypothermia. J Thorac Cardiovasc Surg 1964;48:890–897.

88. Dutton RC, Edmunds Jr LH, Hutchinson JC, et al. Platelet aggregate emboli produced in patients during cardiopulmonary bypass with membrane and bubble oxygenators and blood filters. J Thorac Cardiovasc Surg 1974;67:258–265.

89. Boldt J, Kling D, von Borman B, et al. Blood conservation in cardiac operations. Cell separation versus hemofiltration. J Thorac Cardiovasc Surg 1989;97:832–840.

90. Nakamura Y, Masuda M, Toshima Y, et al. Comparative study of cell saver and ultrafiltration nontransfusion in cardiac surgery. Ann Thorac Surg 1990;49:973–978.

91. Zobel G, Stein JI, Kuttnig M, et al. Continuous extracorporeal fluid removal in children with low cardiac output after cardiac operations. J Thorac Cardiovasc Surg 1991;101:593–597.

92. Ridley PD, Ratcliffe JM, Alberti KG, et al. The metabolic consequences of a "washed" cardiopulmonary bypass pump-priming fluid in children undergoing cardiac operation. J Thorac Cardiovasc Surg 1990;100:528–537.

93. Utley JR, Renal effects of cardiopulmonary bypass. In: Utley JR, ed. Pathophysiology and techniques of cardiopulmonary bypass. Baltimore: Williams & Wilkins, 1982:40–54.

24

PERFUSION FOR THORACIC AORTIC SURGERY

Nicholas T. Kouchoukos, Nabil Abboud, and William R. Klausing

Technological advances and increased understanding of the pathophysiology of cardiopulmonary bypass (CPB) have increased the safety of operations that require repair or replacement of segments of the thoracic aorta. Optimal protection of the brain and spinal cord, the heart, and other organs as well as the avoidance of excessive bleeding and coagulopathies are important objectives during these procedures, which are often lengthy and complex. Specific recommendations about techniques represent those chosen by the authors. These are not necessarily the only acceptable clinical approaches.

SURGERY OF THE ASCENDING AORTA

Preinduction and Anesthetic Management

Venous access is accomplished with a 14-gauge central and two large-bore peripheral venous catheters. A 20-gauge catheter for monitoring of blood pressure and arterial blood gases is placed in a radial artery. The left radial artery is used for procedures that involve the ascending aorta and aortic arch because the innominate artery may be occluded during the procedure. When aortic dissection is present, both radial arteries are cannulated in order to detect reductions in pressures that may occur after establishing retrograde perfusion from the femoral artery. These reductions in pressure may reflect reduced or absent cerebral blood flow as a result of compression of the true lumen of the aorta by the false lumen or by flaps of dissected aortic or brachiocephalic arterial tissue. Leads II and V_5 of the electrocardiogram are continuously monitored. A pulmonary artery catheter is placed for monitoring of pulmonary artery pressure and mixed venous oxygen saturation. Thermistor probes are placed for measurement of nasopharyngeal and rectal or bladder temperatures. A bladder catheter and nasogastric tube are also inserted.

Anesthesia is induced with intravenous midazolam (0.1–0.2 mg/kg), fentanyl (75 to 100 μg/kg), and pancuronium (0.15 mg/kg). After intubation, anesthesia is maintained with fentanyl and isoflurane. Heparin 350 U/kg is administered prior to cannulation. The level of anticoagulation is measured 3–5 minutes after administration of the heparin using the activated clotting time (ACT) and direct heparin-protamine titration. The ACT is maintained at 450 seconds or greater. The ACT is determined every 45 minutes during bypass, and additional heparin is administered to maintain the ACT above this level.

Cannulation

A median sternotomy incision is made and the pericardium is divided. For primary procedures that involve replacement of the aortic root or the ascending aorta, venous drainage is established with a single two-stage cannula placed into the right atrium and inferior vena cava through the right atrial appendage. For reoperative procedures, separate cannulas are placed into the superior and inferior vena cavae. If the distal ascending aorta or proximal aortic arch is normal, arterial return from the pump oxygenator is established by insertion of a 21 to 24 French flexible short soft-tipped polyvinyl chloride catheter into the ascending aorta. If the aorta cannot be safely cannulated, either common femoral artery is exposed through a vertical incision and an 18 to 22 French polyvinyl chloride cannula is inserted and connected to the pump oxygenator circuit.

Perfusion

Currently, our preferred system for CPB consists of polyvinyl chloride tubing, roller pumps, and a microporous polypropylene membrane oxygenator with an integral heat exchanger. The circuit is primed with 2000 ml of lactated Ringer's solution, 25 g of mannitol, and 2000 U of heparin. No glucose is added to the pump prime and administration of solutions containing glucose is kept to a minimum. Experimental studies indicate that increased blood glucose levels are associated with central nervous system ischemia or injury at normothermia (1–3). Blood glucose levels are measured at regular intervals during the operative procedures and values greater than 150 to 200 mg/dl are treated with intravenous insulin.

Cardiopulmonary bypass is established at flows of 2.2 to 2.4 liters/min/m². The temperature of the perfusate is gradually decreased to 20° to 24°C and nasopha-ryngeal and rectal/bladder temperatures are reduced to 24° and 28°C, respectively. Temperature gradients between the water bath of the heat exchanger and the blood and between the blood and the tissues are maintained at less than 12°C (4). The hematocrit of the perfusate is kept between 20% and 25%. The alpha-stat method is used for regulation of acid-base balance. When the heart fibrillates, the aorta is clamped just upstream from the aortic cannula. A venting catheter is placed into the left ventricle through the right superior pulmonary vein. Intermittent suction is maintained on this catheter using a separate roller pump and the blood is returned to the venous reservoir.

Rewarming of the perfusate and the patient is begun as the aortic procedure is being completed. When the rectal/bladder temperature reaches 34°C and the nasopharyngeal temperature is 37°C, blood is slowly infused into the patient to permit ejection of blood from the ventricles, air is evacuated from the cardiac chambers and the ascending aorta, the left ventricular venting catheter is removed, and bypass is discontinued. Protamine sulfate (1.3 mg/100 U of circulating heparin, as estimated by heparin assay) is slowly administered through the peripheral venous cannula following a test dose of 20 mg. The arterial and venous cannulas are removed, bleeding is controlled, and after insertion of drainage catheters, the incision is closed.

Myocardial Protection

The hypothermia induced prior to aortic clamping provides some myocardial protection. However, adjunctive measures are usually necessary. When the heart fibrillates during the initial period of cooling, the ascending aorta is clamped. If the aortic valve is competent, blood cardioplegia is administered through a large-bore needle in the ascending aorta proximal to the clamp. If the aortic valve is incompetent, the aorta can be opened and the coronary arteries are individually cannulated and perfused. Alternatively, the cardioplegic solution can be administered retrogradely through a balloon-tipped catheter inserted into the coronary sinus. If the aortic valve is competent, we currently administer the blood cardioplegic solution (temperature 4°C) both antegradely (2 minutes) and retrogradely (2 minutes) at a flow of 250 ml/min. Myocardial temperature is measured with a thermistor probe in the anterior interventricular septum. The infusion is discontinued when the myocardial temperature reaches 10° to 12°C or after 4 minutes, whichever occurs first. Additional cardioplegic solution is infused every 20 to 30 minutes for 2 to 3 minutes at the same flow rate, usually retrogradely. After closure of the aorta and before removal of the aortic clamp, warm blood cardioplegia (600 ml at 150 ml/min) is infused either antegradely or retrogradely (5). Retrograde infusion is preferable because it results in evacuation of air from the coronary arteries and facilitates evacuation of air from the aortic root. When the duration of myocardial ischemia is likely to exceed 60 minutes, a cooling jacket is placed around the ventricles to prevent rewarming of the myocardium.

Special Situations

AORTIC DISSECTION

In patients with ascending (DeBakey type I) aortic dissections, cannulation of the femoral artery and establishment of retrograde flow followed by placement of an occlusive clamp on the ascending aorta may result in compression of the true lumen by the intimal flap, since the proximal communication between the true and false lumens is excluded. This may severely impair perfusion of the brain and other organs (Fig. 24.1, A and B) during the time the aorta is clamped. Compression of the true lumen may persist after graft replacement of the ascending aorta, since the distal suture line of the graft will keep the proximal

edges of the dissected aorta together (Fig. 24.1C). If undetected or untreated, this complication can result in irreversible brain damage (6).

The occurrence of this complication can be detected by simultaneous monitoring of femoral and both radial artery pressures. A decrease in one or both radial artery pressures relative to the femoral artery pressure at the onset of CPB indicates that perfusion of the brachiocephalic vessels may be inadequate. If electroencephalographic monitoring is used, a significant change in the signals after onset of bypass would also suggest impaired perfusion of the brain. Doppler ultrasonography of the carotid arteries may also detect alterations in carotid artery flow after the onset of bypass (7).

Several options are available to manage this complication. If it occurs after placement of the aortic clamp, the clamp should be immediately removed. If there is no significant aortic valve incompetence, profound hypothermia and circulatory arrest can be used (see below) and an open anastomosis can be performed between the ascending aorta and the aortic graft. After completion of this anastomosis, an 8-mm collagen-impregnated Dacron graft is sutured to the aortic graft adjacent to the aortic anastomosis. The femoral arterial cannula is clamped and the arterial line from the pump oxygenator is disconnected from the femoral artery cannula and is attached to the 8-mm graft. Blood is slowly infused to evacuate air from the 8-mm graft, the aortic graft, the descending aorta, and the brachiocephalic vessels. A clamp is placed on the aortic graft just proximal to the smaller graft connected to the arterial line, and the antegrade flow is established. The proximal anastomosis of the aortic graft to the ascending aorta is completed while the patient is rewarmed. This is our preferred technique.

In the presence of aortic valve incompetence, use of the above technique is not possible since the heart will fibrillate and

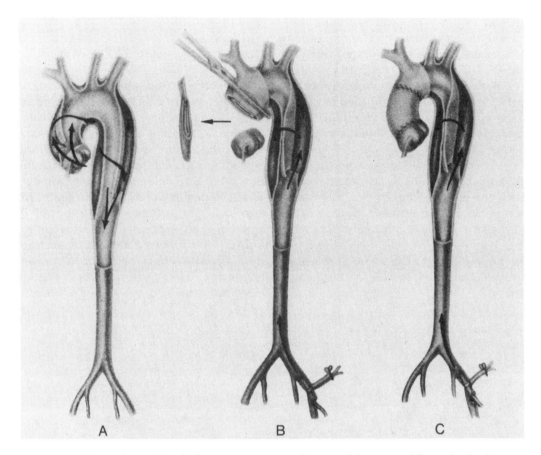

Figure 24.1.   The mechanism by which, in extensive type I dissection **(A)**, an intimal flap at the distal reentry may steer the entire perfusion into the false channel following aortic cross-clamping (*arrow*) **(B)**. The situation will persist even after completion of the graft-to-aorta anastomosis if the heart is in asystole and retrograde perfusion continues **(C)**. (From Robicsek F, Guarino RL. Compression of the true lumen by retrograde perfusion during repair of aortic dissection. J Cardiovasc Surg 1985;26:36–40.)

distend with cooling. In this situation, we prefer to establish circulatory arrest immediately after the heart fibrillates, open the ascending aorta and proximal aortic arch, and perfuse the brachiocephalic arteries directly with cold blood (8). A separate arterial line connected to a roller pump is added to the perfusion circuitry and a Y-connector is attached. Balloon catheters are attached to the Y-connector and are carefully inserted into the innominate and left carotid arteries. The left subclavian artery is occluded with a clamp or a balloon catheter. Flows of 500 to 800 ml at perfusion pressures of 40 to 60 mm Hg are used. The aorta can be clamped distal to the left

subclavian artery or can be occluded with a large balloon catheter. Flow can then be resumed through the femoral artery, and systemic cooling can also be achieved. When cooling is completed (nasopharyngeal temperature 12° to 14°C), circulatory arrest is established, the balloon catheters are removed, and the operation is completed as described above.

An alternative technique, described by Robicsek and Guarino (6), involves the use of a perfusion cannula that is inserted through an opening into the ascending aortic graft and then into the widely opened aorta into the true lumen of the aortic arch. The cannula is secured to the aorta using a special clamp. The graft is then anasto-mosed to the distal aorta after approxi-mating the divided layers of the aorta (Fig. 24.2). The remainder of the procedure is completed as described above. Antegrade perfusion can also be established by passing a cannula from the left ventricular apex through the aortic valve into the ascending aorta.

If compression of the true lumen of the aorta by the intimal flap does not occur until the aortic clamp has been removed, several options are available to achieve flow in the true lumen. A portion of the aortic wall between the true and false lumens (the "septum") distal to the aortic graft can be excised during a period of circulatory arrest.

SEVERE AORTIC VALVE INCOMPETENCE AND ASSOCIATED ANEURYSMAL DISEASE OF THE ASCENDING AORTA

If severe aortic valve incompetence is present, the left ventricle may become se-verely distended when the heart fibrillates during cooling, and decompression by the intracardiac vent may be inadequate. If the ascending aorta can be safely clamped, the procedure is completed as described above. If the ascending aorta is markedly an-eurysmal and a clamp cannot be safely applied, then alternative strategies are re-quired. Our preferred method of manage-ment involves direct perfusion of the in-nominate and left common carotid arteries. Circulatory arrest is established as soon as

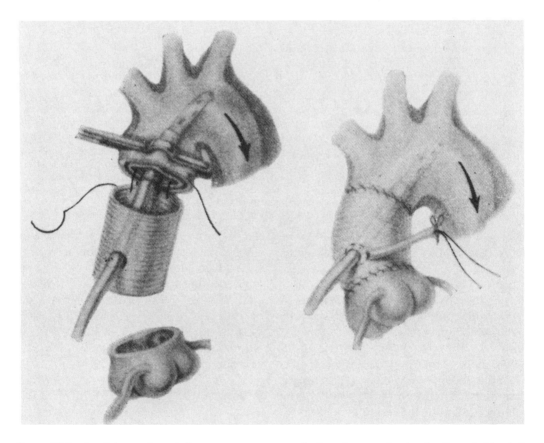

Figure 24.2. Special cannula and clamp to restore antegrade flow. See text for details. (From Robicsek F, Guarino RL. Compression of the true lumen by retrograde perfusion during repair of aortic dissection. J Cardiovasc Surg 1985;26:36–40.)

the heart fibrillates, and the ascending aorta and aortic arch are opened. A large balloon catheter is inserted into the descending thoracic aorta at or beyond the level of the left subclavian artery and is inflated. Cardiopulmonary bypass is reestablished and cooling is continued. Balloon catheters are attached to the Y-connector of a separate arterial line and are placed in the innominate and left carotid arteries. The left subclavian artery is clamped or occluded with a balloon catheter. Perfusion of these arteries with cold blood is then established at the pressures and flow rates described above (see "Aortic Dissection"). When the appropriate nasopharyngeal and rectal/bladder temperatures are achieved, total circulatory arrest is established, the balloon catheters are removed, and the operation is completed.

REOPERATION FOR PSEUDOANEURYSM

Pseudoaneurysms resulting from separation of suture lines between aortic tissues and previously inserted Dacron grafts may reach large size and impinge on the undersurface of the sternum. When reoperation is required, entry into the false aneurysm during sternotomy can result in fatal hemorrhage. Computerized tomographic scanning is useful in determining the size of such aneurysms and their proximity to the sternum. When reoperation for such aneurysms is required, the common femoral artery and vein are cannulated prior to opening the sternum. If the probability of entering the aneurysm during sternotomy is high, heparin is administered and CPB is established before opening the sternum; profound cooling is carried out. When the nasopharyngeal and rectal/bladder temperatures reach the appropriate levels, circulatory arrest is established. The patient is placed in a steep Trendelenburg position and the sternum is opened. If a segment of distal ascending aorta can be isolated circumferentially, it is occluded with a clamp, bypass is reestablished, the temperature of the patient is raised to 24 to 28°C,

and the procedure is completed. If this is not possible, anastomosis of a graft to the distal ascending aorta or aortic arch is completed during the interval of circulatory arrest. Retrograde arterial flow is then reestablished, a clamp is placed on the graft proximal to the innominate artery after removal of air from the arch, and the procedure is completed while the patient is being rewarmed.

If the left ventricle becomes distended after the heart fibrillates, as evidenced by a substantial increase in the pulmonary artery pressure, but before optimal cooling of the brain can be achieved, the sternum is immediately opened, the aorta is entered, and direct cannulation and perfusion of the innominate and left subclavian arteries with cold blood are carried out. The procedure is then completed as described above.

Results

The early results of our experience with aortic root and ascending aortic replacement during a recent 7-year period using the techniques described above are shown in Table 24.1. The complications are summarized in Table 24.2. The need for

Table 24.1. Operations on the Ascending Aorta, 1985 to 1991

Procedure	No. of Patients	Hospital Mortality No.
Replacement of ascending aorta and aortic valve with composite graft	59	5
Aneurysm 42		
Dissection 17		
Replacement of ascending aorta and aortic valve with aortic allograft or pulmonary autograft	30	1
Aortic valve disease 26		
Dissection 4		
Replacement of ascending aorta and aortic valve (separate)	18	0
Aneurysm 17		
Dissection 1		
Replacement of ascending aorta	6	2
Total	113	8

prolonged (>48 hours) mechanical ventilation was the most frequent postoperative complication. The transfusion requirements for the intraoperative and early postoperative periods are shown in Table 24.3.

SURGERY OF THE AORTIC ARCH

Protection of the central nervous system and avoidance of diffuse or focal neurologic injury are critical components of surgical procedures on the thoracic aorta that involve the aortic arch. Several methods for cerebral protection have been developed and employed clinically. Hypothermic circulatory arrest is a widely used technique, and is our current method of choice.

Preinduction and Anesthetic Management

The techniques for venous and arterial access and for monitoring are similar to

Table 24.2. Complications Following Operations on the Ascending Aorta (N = 113)

	No. of Patients	%
Low output syndrome	2	1.8
Intraaortic balloon pump	5	4.4
Reoperations for bleeding	3	2.7
Permanent neurologic deficit	2	1.8
Renal dysfunction/failure	4	3.5
Prolonged mechanical ventilation	12	10.6
Deep wound infections	0	0

Table 24.3. Transfusion Requirements for Operations on the Ascending Aorta

	Number of Units	
Operation	Mean ± SD	Range
Intraoperative		
Red blood cells	2.2 ± 2.8	0–17
Fresh-frozen plasma	1.5 ± 2.5	0–14
Platelets	4.1 ± 6.5	0–32
Postoperative		
Red blood cells	1.4 ± 1.9	0–10
Fresh-frozen plasma	0.4 ± 1.1	0–6
Platelets	0.8 ± 3.4	0–30

those used for operations on the ascending aorta (see previous discussion). The drugs used for induction and maintenance of anesthesia are also similar.

Pharmacologic Adjuncts

Methylprednisolone (7 mg/kg) is administered intravenously at the beginning of cooling when a period of total circulatory arrest is anticipated. Although the protective effects of glucocorticoids on the central nervous system when hypothermic circulatory arrest is used are not conclusively established, the absence of significant side effects or complications with this dose of methylprednisolone and the potential benefits justify its use. Because patients in whom circulatory arrest is used are placed in a steep Trendelenburg position, some degree of brain edema probably occurs. This can be inferred from the marked facial edema that is present in these patients. Glucocorticoids appear to be effective in the treatment of cerebral edema (9). The dose of methylprednisolone we use is lower than that generally recommended (30 mg/kg), but is probably effective under conditions of deep hypothermia; the lower dose may reduce the incidence of side effects.

Thiopental (7 to 15 mg/kg) is also administered intravenously prior to establishing circulatory arrest. Barbiturates exert a protective effect on the central nervous system when it is rendered ischemic that is additive to the protection afforded by hypothermia, but only when electrical activity is present (10). In the absence of electrical activity, little or no additional protection is provided because barbiturates eliminate only the portion of cerebral metabolism and oxygen consumption that is related to neuronal electrical activity (11). In adult patients undergoing aortic surgery, the level of hypothermia achieved (12 to 15°C) usually results in electrical quiescence. The relatively small dose of thiopental administered is sufficient to ensure electrical silence, and avoids the myocardial depressant effects and prolonged anesthesia that are common with larger doses (12).

Isoflurane is administered continuously during the cooling period through a vaporizer in line with the oxygen supply to the membrane oxygenrator. Isoflurane may exert effects similar to those of the barbiturates on cerebral metabolism and oxygen consumption (13). Because it is not used toward the end of rewarming and is rapidly eliminated, isoflurane provides cerebral protection during the period of circulatory arrest and does not add to the myocardial depression and prolonged anesthesia potentially produced by barbiturates. In addition, its systemic vasodilatory effects may enhance the speed of cooling.

Mannitol (0.3 to 0.4 g/kg) and furosemide (100 mg) are administered intravenously prior to establishing circulatory arrest to preserve renal function (14). Mannitol promotes osmotic diuresis, decreases blood viscosity, and improves renal cortical blood flow. Furosemide results in increased free water and sodium excretion and in the release of intrarenal prostaglandin E_1, which produces dilation of the afferent renal arteries.

Insulin is given intravenously to keep the blood glucose level below 200 mg/dl. Elevated blood glucose levels have been associated with an increased incidence of central nervous system dysfunction following deep hypothermia and circulatory arrest (15).

Cannulation

A median sternotomy incision is used and a common femoral artery is exposed for cannulation. If the aortic disease also involves the proximal one-half or more of the descending thoracic aorta, provisions should be made to perform a left lateral thoracotomy incision or to convert the median sternotomy incision to a T-incision through the fourth left intercostal space. This permits better access to the descending tho-racic aorta and reduces manipulation of the left lung. After dividing and retracting the pericardium, a small polyvinyl catheter is placed through the right superior pulmonary vein for monitoring of left atrial pressure. A woven Dacron graft of the appropriate size is immersed in a 25% albumin solution and is autoclaved at 270°C for 3 minutes (16). This renders the graft impervious to blood and substantially reduces blood loss through the interstices of the graft.

After administration of heparin, the femoral artery is cannulated, a single two-stage venous cannula is inserted into the right atrium through the appendage, and CPB is established at 2.2 liters/min/m². A venting catheter is inserted into the left ventricle through the right superior pulmonary vein.

Technique of Cooling

Cooling is initiated once the left ventricular vent is in place. The nasopharyngeal, rectal/bladder, and perfusate temperatures are continuously monitored. Temperature gradients between the water bath of the heat exchanger and the blood, and between the blood and the tissues are maintained below 12°C (4). To reduce blood viscosity, patients with large estimated circulating blood volumes (>6000 ml) and acceptable hemoglobin concentrations (generally >11.5 g/dl) undergo phlebotomy prior to establishing bypass. Five hundred to 1000 ml of blood are removed and stored in transfusion bags for reinfusion at the end of the procedure. The hematocrit of the perfusate is maintained between 15 and 20%. Slow cooling probably results in more uniform cooling of the brain and may be associated with fewer neurologic complications postoperatively (17). The head of the patient is not packed in ice unless a prolonged period of circulatory arrest (>50 to 60 minutes) is anticipated. When the nasopharyngeal temperature reaches 12 to 15°C and the rectal/

bladder temperature reaches 15 to 18°C, circulatory arrest is established. The patient is placed in a steep Trendelenburg position and 20 to 25% of the calculated blood volume of the patient is withdrawn from the venous cannula into the reservoir of the oxygenator. The venous and arterial cannulas are then clamped. Removal of a larger amount of blood increases the probability of aspiration of air into the cerebral circulation through the open arteries. The brachiocephalic arteries are not clamped.

Myocardial Protection

During operations on the aortic arch, myocardial protection is accomplished using the techniques described for operation on the ascending aorta (see previous discussion).

Hypothermic Circulatory Arrest

Aneurysms of the aortic arch vary in size and extent and the techniques for repair are variable. In general, the aorta is opened beneath the brachiocephalic vessels and the extent of the aortic disease is assessed. Atherosclerotic debris is removed from inside the aorta, taking care not to dislodge fragments that may enter the descending thoracic aorta or the brachiocephalic vessels. If the entire arch is involved, a cuff of descending thoracic aorta distal to the left subclavian artery is fashioned and the Dacron graft is sutured to this cuff with a continuous polypropylene suture. The graft is then placed under tension and an oval segment is excised with a wire cautery that conforms to the size of the cuff of aortic tissue surrounding the brachiocephalic arteries. The graft is sutured to this cuff of aorta with a continuous suture.

Occasionally, the aneurysm is small and has a discrete communication with the aorta. In this case, the defect in the wall of the aorta is repaired with a Dacron patch. If the aneurysm only involves the proximal and inferior portion of the arch, a single anastomosis can be performed beneath the brachiocephalic vessels by bevelling the graft and the aortic incision.

After these suture lines are completed, the arterial pump flow is turned up slowly until blood enters the Dacron graft. The graft and the brachiocephalic vessels are gently massaged to evacuate air. A clamp is then placed on the graft just proximal to the innominate artery. Cardiopulmonary bypass is established at 1.6 liters/min/m² and rewarming of the patient is begun.

If there is concern that atherosclerotic debris has been dislodged into the descending thoracic aorta, an 8-mm collagen-impregnated Dacron graft is anastomosed to an opening in the aortic graft in the arch on the anterior or inferior undersurface. The arterial line from the pump-oxygenator is disconnected from the femoral artery cannula and connected to this graft. The 8-mm graft, the aortic graft, and the brachiocephalic vessels are gently massaged to evacuate air. A clamp is placed on the aortic graft proximal to the innominate artery and bypass is established. The resulting antegrade flow in the arch and descending thoracic aorta should eliminate the possibility of embolization of dislodged atherosclerotic debris into the brachiocephalic vessels.

Safe Duration of Circulatory Arrest

Although the safe duration of circulatory arrest at brain temperatures of 15 to 18°C is not known with certainty, experimental and clinical studies suggest that periods of arrest of 45 to 60 minutes infrequently result in focal neurologic signs indicative of cerebral injury (18–21). However, confounding factors exist in patients who undergo operations in the aortic arch for atherosclerotic aneurysm or dissection. These include the potential for embolization of debris from the aortic lumen and the presence of extracranial cerebrovascular occlusive disease (20). Following operations on the aortic arch, reversible central nervous system dysfunction manifested by confusion, lethargy, and delirium occurs in 15 to 20% of patients, and is more common if the duration of circulatory arrest exceeds 50 minutes (21, 22). Increasing age is also a risk factor for this reversible dysfunction. Focal neurologic deficits are more likely to be the result of embolization (20, 21).

Technique of Rewarming

Rewarming of the patient is accomplished using the same temperature gradients (12°C or less between the water bath of the heat exchanger and the blood, and between the blood and the tissues) that are used during cooling. The perfusate flow is slowly increased as the temperature of the patient increases, to a maximum of 2.4 to 2.6 liters/min/m². The acid-base status of the patient is determined at intervals (20 to 30 minutes) during rewarming. Base deficits of greater than 4 mEq/liter are treated with sodium bicarbonate. If the circulatory arrest time exceeds 30 minutes, sodium bicarbonate (0.5 mEq/kg) is given when bypass is reestablished. Sodium nitroprusside is also infused to facilitate rewarming. Systemic vascular resistance is maintained at 1000 dynes/sec/cm⁻⁵ or less.

During the period of rewarming, the aortic graft is anastomosed to the ascending aorta. If either aortic valve or aortic root replacement is required, it is performed during this interval. If aortic root replacement is necessary, the tubular portion of the composite graft is sutured to the aortic arch graft with a continuous polypropylene suture after the graft has been attached to the aortic annulus and the coronary arteries. A 14-gauge rigid needle is then inserted into the graft through a small stab wound and is secured with a mattress suture and pledgets. It is connected to 1/4 inch tubing, and gentle suction is applied. The aspirated blood is returned to the pump-oxygenator system using a separate pump head. The aortic clamp is removed and is placed in a partially occluding position to permit perfusion of the coronary arteries.

When rewarming is completed (rectal/bladder temperature 34°C, nasopharyngeal temperature 37°C), suction is increased on the aortic catheter, the left ventricular vent is removed, air is aspirated from the left-sided cardiac chambers, and bypass is discontinued. Decannulation is then effected, and protamine is administered. Appropriate pacing wires and drainage tubes are placed and the incisions are closed.

Platelets, fresh-frozen plasma, and other clotting factors are not routinely administered. Pharmacologic agents that may reduce the severity of diffuse bleeding (ε-aminocaproic acid, desmopressin acetate, and aprotinin) are used selectively. Red blood cells are infused to maintain the hematocrit between 22 and 27%.

Alternative Methods of Cerebral Protection

ANTEGRADE CEREBRAL PERFUSION

This technique was first successfully used by DeBakey and associates (23) for resection of aortic arch aneurysm. Recent experience with cerebral perfusion has involved the use of moderate hypothermia (26 to 28°C) with direct cannulation and perfusion of the innominate and left carotid arteries or the innominate artery alone (24). Profound hypothermia of the brain produced by direct cannulation of the innominate and left carotid arteries and perfusion with blood at 10 to 12°C to produce "cerebroplegia" combined with systemic perfusion at 27 to 28° has also been used (8). Currently, there are no conclusive data to indicate that cerebral perfusion with either of these techniques provides protection of the brain that is superior to that provided by hypothermic circulatory arrest. Its use will be limited or even contraindicated in patients with atherosclerosis or dissection involving the brachiocephalic arteries, with large aneurysms where exposure of the brachiocephalic arteries is difficult or not possible, and in patients in whom circulatory arrest is implemented prior to sternotomy.

RETROGRADE CEREBRAL PERFUSION

Intermittent or continuous retrograde perfusion of the brain through the superior vena cava in combination with hypothermic circulatory arrest has also been used to provide protection of the brain during operations that involve the aortic arch (25, 26). Experience with this technique is limited. Substantial differences in oxygen content between the perfused blood and the blood draining from the arch vessels ranging up to 5 mg/dl have been observed (26). This suggests continuing metabolic activity of the brain despite hypothermic perfusion. The percentage of retrograde flow through the superior vena cava that actually perfuses the brain has not been determined in humans.

MALPERFUSION SYNDROMES

These syndromes are managed similarly to those which occur during operations on the ascending aorta (see "Special Situations" under "Surgery of the Ascending Aorta").

Results

The early results of our experience with aortic arch replacement alone or in conjunction with operations on the adjacent thoracic aorta and the aortic valve using hypothermic circulatory arrest are shown in Table 24.4. Aneurysm formation secondary to degenerative disease was the most frequent indication for operation. Seventeen of the 62 procedures (27%) were performed for acute or chronic aortic dissection. The durations of cooling, circulatory arrest, rewarming, myocardial ische-

mia, and CPB are shown in Table 24.5. The complications are summarized in Table 24.6. The transfusion requirements for the intraoperative and early postoperative periods are shown in Table 24.7.

Table 24.4. Operations on the Aortic Arch Employing Hypothermic Circulatory Arrest, 1985 to 1991

Procedure		No. of Patients	Hospital Mortality No.
Replacement of ascending aorta and aortic arch		59	5
Isolated	13		
+ CABG[a]	31		
+ Aortic root replacement and CABG	8		
+ Aortic valve replacement and CABG	7		
Replacement of ascending aortic arch and proximal one-half of descending aorta		3	0
Total		62	5

[a]Coronary artery bypass grafting.

Table 24.5. CPB Data (N = 62)

Times	Mean (min)	Range (min)
Cooling	48	20–79
Arrest	33	5–73
Rewarming	86	45–179
Myocardial ischemic	111	0–233
Duration of bypass[a]	146	59–258

[a]Period of circulatory arrest excluded.

Table 24.6. Complications Following Operations on the Aortic Arch (N = 62)

Complication	No. of Patients	%
Low output syndrome	11	17.7
Intraaortic balloon pump	4	6.5
Reoperations for bleeding	1	1.6
Permanent neurologic deficit	3	4.8
Renal dysfunction/failure	2	3.2
Prolonged mechanical ventilation	16	25.8
Deep wound infections	0	0

Table 24.7. Transfusion Requirements for Operations on the Aortic Arch

Operation	Number of Units	
	Mean ± SD	Range
Intraoperative		
Red blood cells	3.1 ± 2.6	0–12
Fresh-frozen plasma	2.2 ± 2.4	0–14
Platelets	6.1 ± 5.5	0–26
Postoperative		
Red blood cells	2.2 ± 3.8	0–27
Fresh-frozen plasma	0.7 ± 1.5	0–6
Platelets	1.4 ± 3.1	0–30

SURGERY OF THE DESCENDING THORACIC AND THORACOABDOMINAL AORTA

Distal Perfusion

Distal perfusion with an extracorporeal circuit is not universally employed for operations on the descending thoracic and thoracoabdominal aorta. Simple aortic clamping without distal perfusion has been employed by some groups (27, 28). Passive shunts from the proximal to the distal aorta during aortic clamping have been used by others (29). Distal perfusion with either a passive shunt or an extracorporeal circuit permits effective decompression of the arterial bed above the aortic clamp and reduces left ventricular afterload (30, 31). Although this can be accomplished by intravenous infusion of a vasodilator (sodium nitroprusside or nitroglycerin) when simple aortic clamping is used, reduction of proximal aortic pressure by this method also results in reduction of the distal aortic pressure, and may reduce arterial perfusion of the spinal cord. This may accentuate the spinal cord ischemia that results from aortic clamping (32, 33). During resection of aneurysms that involve the descending thoracic aorta, distal perfusion provides blood flow to the lower intercostal and lumbar arteries and may reduce the severity of the spinal cord ischemia that results during exclusion of segments of the descending thoracic aorta by clamping. Distal aortic

perfusion will also provide perfusion and protection of the kidneys, liver, and gastrointestinal tract if the aortic disease does not extend below the celiac or superior mesenteric artery.

Indications

We believe that distal aortic perfusion provides important protection of the spinal cord and abdominal organs and that it should be employed, if technically feasible, for all operations on the descending thoracic aorta. Evidence is accumulating that suggests that, for aortic disease that also involves the abdominal aorta, distal perfusion combined with hypothermia may offer important protection as well (34).

Methods

LEFT ATRIUM TO FEMORAL ARTERY BYPASS

Following a left thoracotomy and incision of the pericardium, the left atrium is cannulated using a 28 to 32 French straight or angled cannula, which is inserted through a purse-string suture in the left atrial appendage. The left common femoral artery is exposed through a vertical incision and is cannulated with a 20 or 22 French cannula. Alternative sites for cannulation proximally include the left ventricular apex, the left inferior pulmonary vein, or the aorta above the involved segment. Alternative distal cannulation sites include the external iliac artery or the aorta below the involved segment. Tubing connected to these cannulas is passed through a roller pump or connected to a centrifugal pump. The centrifugal pump offers the advantages of trapping air bubbles in the center of the vortex within the pump head, which reduces the possibility of embolization, and of minimizing trauma to the blood elements. A reservoir can be added to the circuit to compensate for rapid shifts in blood volume. Full heparinization is not required. Low doses of heparin are administered to maintain the activated clotting time between 150 and 200 seconds. A heat exchanger can be incorporated into the circuit to induce hypothermia and facilitate rewarming. Flows of up to 2.0 to 2.2 liters/min/m² can usually be achieved with this technique. After aortic clamping, aortic pressure above the excluded aortic segment can be maintained at normal levels by adjustment of flow and use of sodium nitroprusside. The mean distal aortic perfusion pressure should be maintained at or above 60 mm Hg to minimize the possibility of ischemic injury to the spinal cord (35).

Because only low doses of heparin are required, this technique is particularly advantageous for the management of patients with multiple injuries who require operation for acute aortic transection. It has also been used for repair of arteriosclerotic aneurysms and dissections that involve the descending thoracic aorta (36).

FEMORAL VEIN TO FEMORAL ARTERY BYPASS

The common femoral artery and vein (usually the left) are exposed through a vertical incision in the groin. A 28 to 32 French long (60 cm) cannula is passed into the right atrium from the femoral vein. A 20 to 22 French cannula is placed in the left femoral artery. The left external iliac artery or the aorta distal to the involved segment can also be used. Full heparinization is required and an oxygenator is incorporated into the perfusion circuit. Flows of up to 1.5 liters/min/m² are used. If adequate flow cannot be achieved because of limited venous drainage, the pericardium is incised and a 28 to 32 French right-angled cannula is placed through a purse-string suture into the main pulmonary artery and positioned in the right ventricle. The cannula is connected to the venous return line with a Y-connector. The perfusate is cooled, and body temperature can be reduced to 32 to 34°C. Lower temperatures may result in ventricular

fibrillation. Pressures above and below the excluded aortic segment are maintained at levels identical to those with left atrium to femoral artery bypass. Shed blood is returned to the bypass circuit by suction.

HYPOTHERMIC CPB AND CIRCULATORY ARREST

Spinal cord ischemic injury with resultant paraparesis or paraplegia is a major complication following extensive resections of the thoracic and thoracoabdominal aorta. Among patients who have undergone resections of all or most of the descending thoracic aorta and a part or all of the contiguous abdominal aorta without the use of adjuncts to prevent ischemia, the reported incidence of neurologic injury has ranged from 10 to 28% (37). Significant renal dysfunction or failure is also a serious complication after extended periods of aortic occlusion, which are often required for these operations (38).

Hypothermia has been shown in experimental studies to have a marked protective effect on spinal cord function during periods of aortic occlusion (39–42). Recent clinical reports have demonstrated the feasibility and safety of bypass, hypothermic circulatory arrest, and posterolateral exposure for operations on the thoracic and thoracoabdominal aorta for a variety of indications (34, 43–45). These studies suggest that hypothermia may reduce the frequency and severity of spinal cord injury after extensive aortic resections. Hypothermia also provides protection of the myocardium, the kidneys, and the abdominal viscera.

Preinduction and Anesthetic Management

Venous access, monitoring, and drugs for induction and maintenance of anesthesia are similar to those used for operations on the ascending aorta and aortic arch. The right radial artery is used for monitoring proximal arterial pressure because the left subclavian artery may be temporarily occluded or sacrificed during the procedure. Distal aortic pressure is monitored with a cannula in the right femoral artery. A double lumen endobronchial tube is used to permit collapse of the left lung.

Pharmacologic Adjuncts

Methylprednisolone and thiopental at the dosages described above (see "Surgery of the Aortic Arch") are administered for their potential protective effects on the central nervous system.

Cannulation

Exposure of the entire descending thoracic and abdominal aorta is obtained with a left thoracoabdominal incision through the bed of the resected fifth or sixth rib. The diaphragm is incised radially and the abdominal viscera and the left kidney are retracted medially after incision of the peritoneum in the left gutter. Minimal dissection is used and the collapsed left lung is gently retracted anteriorly to minimize injury. If access to the pulmonary artery is needed, the pericardium is incised vertically anterior to the left phrenic nerve.

The left common femoral artery and vein are cannulated as described above for femoral vein to femoral artery bypass. If full flow (>2.0 to 2.2 liters/min/m²) cannot be achieved, a 28 to 32 French right-angled cannula is placed in the main pulmonary artery and positioned in the right ventricle. It is then connected to the venous return line with a Y-connector (Fig. 24.3).

Technique of Cooling

Cooling is initiated immediately after establishing full CPB. The technique is identical to that described above for procedures involving the aortic arch. Cooling is

continued until the nasopharyngeal temperature reaches 12 to 15°C and the rectal/bladder temperature reaches 15 to 18°C. During the period of cooling, if possible, the aorta is circumferentially isolated proximal and distal to the aortic segment that will be resected. The heart fibrillates when the myocardial temperature (measured with a thermistor probe) reaches 28 to 30°C. If the pulmonary artery pressure increases or the left ventricle distends, indicating the presence of aortic valve incompetence, the left heart is vented through the left atrial appendage or through the apex of the left ventricle. After circulatory arrest is established, the patient is placed in the Trendelenburg position and 20 to 25% of the calculated blood volume is withdrawn from the venous cannula into the reservoir of the oxygenator.

Hypothermic Circulatory Arrest

The techniques for surgical repair of the aortic disease vary according to the location and extent of the aortic disease. If the disease involves the distal aortic arch, the proximal anastomosis is performed using an open technique. No clamps are placed on the proximal aorta or the brachiocephalic vessels. The aorta is clamped distally at a convenient location. A cuff of aorta is fashioned at the appropriate level, usually beneath the origin of the left carotid and left subclavian arteries, and a woven Dacron graft that has been preclotted with albumin and autoclaved is anastomosed to the aorta with a continuous polypropylene suture. After this anastomosis is completed, a perfusion cannula that is connected to a separate arterial tubing, oxygenator, and roller pump (Fig. 24.3) is inserted into the graft through a small incision (Fig. 24.4). Alternatively, an 8-mm collagen-impregnated Dacron graft can be sutured to the aortic graft and connected to the arterial line. With the head of the patient in a deeply dependent position, blood is slowly infused into this line and into the aortic graft to re-

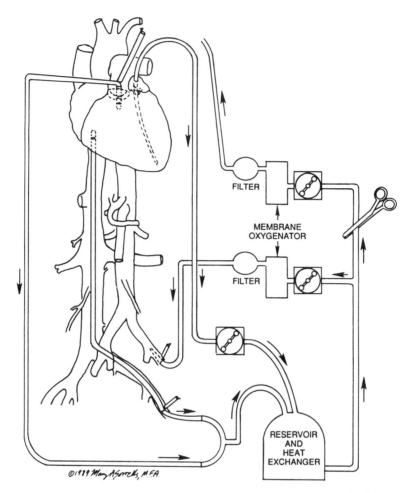

Figure 24.3. Extracorporeal circuit for hypothermic CPB and circulatory arrest using the left thoracotomy approach. The figure shows a single venous reservoir and heat exchanger. Venous drainage is obtained by cannulation of the inferior vena cava and the pulmonary artery. The left ventricle is vented through the left atrial appendage. Cardiopulmonary bypass is initiated through the left common femoral artery. After the interval of circulatory arrest, a separate arterial tubing, roller pump, membrane oxygenator, heat exchanger, and filter are used to regulate flow to the upper and lower parts of the body. (From Kouchoukos NT, Wareing TH, Izumoto H, Klausing W, Abboud N. Elective hypothermic cardiopulmonary bypass and circulatory arrest for spinal cord protection during operations on the thoracoabdominal aorta. J Thorac Cardiovasc Surg 1990;99:659–664.)

move air from the aorta. The distal aorta is simultaneously perfused to facilitate filling of the heart and aortic arch with blood and removal of air. The graft is then occluded with a clamp distal to the cannula and proximal flow is reestablished (Fig. 24.4). Thirty-five percent of the arterial flow is directed through the proximal arterial line and 65% through the distal line. Total flow is maintained in the range of 1.0 to 1.5 liters/min/m² at the low temperatures.

Hypothermic Perfusion

The remainder of the procedure on the aorta is completed during a period of hypothermic perfusion and low flow. The temperature of the perfusate is adjusted to maintain the rectal/bladder temperature below 20°C. During the period of hypothermic low flow, buttons of aorta containing the lower intercostal and upper lumbar arteries, and the orifices of the ce-

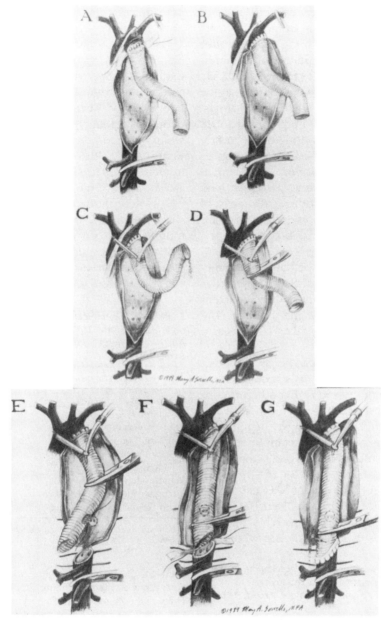

Figure 24.4.   A and **B**. After occlusion of the aorta between the left subclavian and carotid arteries, and occlusion of the left subclavian artery and the abdominal aorta, the graft is anastomosed to the proximal aorta during circulatory arrest. This anastomosis can be performed with an open technique if clamping of the aorta is not possible (**C**). A second arterial perfusion cannula is inserted into the graft and blood is infused to remove air (**D**). The graft is occluded below the cannula and flow is reestablished through both arterial lines (**E**). A button of aorta containing pairs of intercostal and lumbar arteries is sutured to the graft (**F**). The aortic clamp is repositioned to permit perfusion of intercostal arteries (**G**). The distal aortic clamp is removed and air is removed from the graft. (From Kouchoukos NT, Wareing TH, Izumoto H, Klausing W, Abboud N. Elective hypothermic cardiopulmonary bypass and circulatory arrest for spinal cord protection during operations on the thoracoabdominal aorta. J Thorac Cardiovasc Surg 1990;99:659–664.)

liac, superior mesenteric, and renal arteries when indicated, are anastomosed to the graft (Fig. 24.4). Rewarming is begun after completion of the anastomosis of the intercostal and lumbar arteries to the graft. Early reperfusion of these latter arteries may be important to the prevention of spinal and ischemic complications. The proximal aortic clamp is repositioned below these anastomoses and the anastomosis of the graft to the distal aorta is performed. Air is evacuated from the graft with an 18-gauge needle. After completion of the anastomosis of the graft to the distal aorta, all clamps are removed. When the rectal/bladder temperature reaches 34°C, bypass is discontinued. The heart usually defibrillates spontaneously when the myocardial temperature reaches 28 to 30°C, but a direct current countershock is occasionally required. The cardiac vent and the arterial and venous cannulas are then removed.

If all anastomoses can be performed in less than 45 minutes, this is accomplished during a single period of hypothermic circulatory arrest and hypothermic perfusion is not required. Rewarming is begun after all anastomoses have been completed.

The results using this technique in 19 patients are shown in Table 24.8. Hypothermic circulatory arrest was used routinely in all cases that involved the aortic arch, and selectively for patients who required extensive resections and who were

considered to be at risk for spinal cord ischemic injury. The 30-day mortality was 15.8% (three patients). Spinal cord ischemic injury occurred in only 1 of the 17 patients (5.9%) who were judged to be at risk for this complication (Table 24.9). Reoperation for bleeding was required in one patient. Prolonged mechanical ventilation was required in a substantial number of patients (47%); this has also been observed by others (45). The transfusion requirements are shown in Table 24.10.

Severe pulmonary dysfunction, extensive coronary artery disease, and more than minimal aortic valve incompetence are relative contraindications to use of this technique. Coronary artery bypass grafting and aortic valve replacement may be necessary

Table 24.9.   Complications Following Operations on the Descending Thoracic and Thoracoabdominal Aorta Employing Hypothermic CPB and Circulatory Arrest (N = 19)

Complication	No. of Patients	%
Low output syndrome[a]	2	10.5
Intraaortic balloon pump[a]	2	10.5
Reoperations for bleeding	1	5.3
Permanent neurologic deficit	3	15.8
Stroke 2		
Paraplegia 1		
Renal dysfunction/failure	4	21.1
Prolonged mechanical ventilation	9	47.4
Deep wound infections	1	5.3

[a] The first two complications listed are for the same two patients.

Table 24.8.   Operations on the Descending Thoracic and Thoracoabdominal Aorta Employing Hypothermic CPB and Circulatory Arrest, 1985 to 1991

Procedure	No. of Patients	Hospital Mortality No.
Arch and proximal descending thoracic aorta	2	0
Arch and entire descending thoracic aorta	1	0
Entire descending thoracic aorta	2	0
Arch and thoracoabdominal aorta	2	1
Thoracoabdominal aorta	12	2
Total	19	3

Table 24.10.   Transfusion Requirements for Operations on the Descending Thoracic and Thoracoabdominal Aorta Employing Hypothermic CPB and Circulatory Arrest (N = 19)

Transfusion Requirements (units)	Number of Units	
	Mean ± SD	Range
Intraoperative		
Red blood cells	6.3 ± 4.1	1–21
Fresh-frozen plasma	3.7 ± 2.9	0–12
Platelets	9.3 ± 9.6	0–40
Postoperative		
Red blood cells	3.3 ± 3.9	0–13
Fresh-frozen plasma	1.8 ± 2.7	0–10
Platelets	1.4 ± 2.7	0–8

to correct these conditions before elective aortic resection is undertaken. Additional experience with the technique of hypothermic CPB and circulatory arrest will be required in patients judged to be at high risk for the development of spinal cord ischemic injury before it can be concluded that the technique provides better protection of the spinal cord than alternative techniques. However, it is an extremely useful technique in situations where proximal control of the aorta cannot be obtained or when it is contraindicated.

REFERENCES

1. D'Alecy LG, Lundy EF, Barton KJ, Zelenock GB. Dextrose containing intravenous fluid impairs outcome and increases death after eight minutes of cardiac arrest and resuscitation in dogs. Surgery 1986;100:505–511.
2. Cole DJ, Shapiro HM, Drummond JC, Zivin JA. Halothane, fentanyl/nitrous oxide, and spinal lidocaine protect against spinal cord injury in the rat. Anesthesiology 1989;70:967–972.
3. Kraig RP, Petito CK, Plum F, Pulsinelli WA. Hydrogen ions kill brain at concentrations reached in ischemia. J Cereb Blood Flow Metab 1987; 7:379–386.
4. Reed CC, Stafford TB. Cardiopulmonary Bypass. 2nd ed. Woodland, TX: Surgimedics/Texas Medical Products, 1985:327.
5. Buckberg GD. Antegrade/retrograde blood cardioplegia to ensure cardioplegic distribution: operative techniques and objectives. J Cardiac Surg 1989;4:216–238.
6. Robicsek F, Guarino RL. Compression of the true lumen by retrograde perfusion during repair of aortic dissection. J Cardiovasc Surg 1985;26: 36–40.
7. Antona C, Agrifoglio M, Alamanni F, Spirito R, Polvani GL, Biglioli P. Aortic dissection type A surgery: Doppler sonography to evaluate correct carotid artery perfusion during cardiopulmonary bypass. J Cardiovasc Surg 1991;32: 307–309.
8. Bachet J, Guilmet D, Goudot B, et al. Cold cerebroplegia: a new technique of cerebral protection during operations on the transverse aortic arch. J Thorac Cardiovasc Surg 1991;102: 85–94.
9. Klatzo I. Presidential address. Neuropathological aspects of brain edema. J Neuropathol Exp Neurol 1967;26:1–14.
10. Lafferty JJ, Keykhah MM, Shapiro HM et al: Cerebral hypometabolism obtained with deep pentobarbital anesthesia and hypothermia (30°C). Anesthesiology 1978;49:159–164.
11. Steen PA, Newberg L, Milde JH et al: Hypothermia and barbiturates: individual and combined effect on canine cerebral oxygen consumption. Anesthesiology 1983;58:527–532.
12. Hickey PR, Anderson NP: Deep hypothermic circulatory arrest: a review of pathophysiology and clinical experience as a basis for anesthetic management. J Cardiothorac Anesth 1987;1: 137–155.
13. Newberg LA, Michenfelder JD: Cerebral protection by isoflurane during hypothermia or ischemia. Anesthesiology 1983;59:29–35.
14. Kwika G, Kidney S, Nugent M: Renal preservation during aortic anesthesia. In: Kaplan JA, ed. Vascular anesthesia. New York: Churchill Livingstone, 1991:386–387.
15. Steward DJ, Da Silva CA, Flegel T. Elevated blood glucose levels may increase the danger of neurological deficit following profoundly hypothermic cardiac arrest [Letter to the Editor]. Anesthesiology 1988;68:653.
16. Kouchoukos NT, Marshall WG Jr. Treatment of ascending aortic dissection in the Marfan's Syndrome. J Cardiac Surg 1986;1:333–346.
17. Busto R. Dietrich WD, Globus MY-T, Valdes I, Scheinberg P, Ginsberg MD. Small differences in intraischemic brain temperature critically determine the extent of ischemic neuronal injury. J Cereb Blood Flow Metabol 1987;7:729–738.
18. Mohri H, Barnes RW, Winterscheid LC, Dillard DH, Merendino KA. Challenge of prolonged suspended animation: a method of surface induced deep hypothermia. Ann Surg 1968;168: 779–787.
19. Treasure T, Naftel DC, Conger KA, Garcia JH, Kirklin JW, Blackstone EH. The effect of hypothermic circulatory arrest time on cerebral function, morphology, and biochemistry. An experimental study. J Thorac Cardiovasc Surg 1983;96:761–770.
20. Coselli JS, Crawford ES, Beall AC Jr, Mizrahi EM, Hess KR, Patel VM. Determination of brain temperatures for safe circulatory arrest during cardiovascular operation. Ann Thorac Surg 1988;45: 638–642.
21. Griepp RB, Ergin MA, Lansman SL, Galla JD, Pogo G. The physiology of hypothermic circulatory arrest. Semin Thorac Cardiovasc Surg 1991;3: 188–193.
22. Wragg RE, Dimsdale JE, Moser KM, Daily PO, Dembitsky WP, Archibald C. Operative predictors of delirium after pulmonary thromboendarterectomy. A model for postcardiotomy delirium? J Thorac Cardiovasc Surg 1988;96: 524–529.

23. DeBakey ME, Crawford ES, Cooley DA, Morris GC: Successful resection of fusiform aneurysm of aortic arch with replacement by homograft. Surgery 1957;105:657.

24. Frist WH, Baldwin JC, Starnes VA, et al. A reconsideration of cerebral perfusion in aortic arch replacement. Ann Thorac Surg 1986;42:273–281.

25. Lemole GM, Strong MD, Spagna PM, Karmilowicz NP. Improved results for dissecting aneurysms. Intraluminal sutureless prosthesis. J Thorac Cardiovasc Surg 1982;83:249–255.

26. Ueda Y, Miki S, Kusuhara K, Okita Y, Tahata T, Yamanaka. Deep hypothermic systemic circulatory arrest and continuous retrograde cerebral perfusion for surgery of aortic arch aneurysm. Eur J Cardiothorac Surg 1992;6:36–41.

27. Najafi H, Javid H, Hunter J, et al. Descending aortic aneurysmectomy without adjunct to avoid ischemia. Ann Thorac Surg 1980;30:326–335.

28. Crawford ES, Walker HS, Saleh SM, et al. Graft replacement of aneurysm in descending thoracic aorta: results without bypass or shunting. Surgery 1981;89:73–75.

29. Gott VL. Heparinized shunts for thoracic vascular operation. Ann Thorac Surg 1972;14:219.

30. Hug HR, Taber RE. Bypass flow requirements during thoracic aneurysmectomy with particular attention to the prevention of left heart failure. J Thorac Cardiovasc Surg 1969;57:203–213.

31. Kouchoukos NT, Lell WA, Karp RB, Samuelson PN. Hemodynamic effects of aortic clamping and decompression with a temporary shunt for resection of the descending thoracic aorta. Surgery 1979;85:25–30.

32. Cunningham JN Jr, Laschinger JC, Spencer FC. Monitoring of SEP during surgical procedures on the thoracoabdominal aorta: IV. Clinical observations and results. J Thorac Cardiovasc Surg 1987;94:275.

33. Laschinger JC, Owen J, Rosenbloom M, Cox JL, Kouchoukos NT. Detrimental effects of sodium nitroprusside on spinal motor tract perfusion during thoracic aortic cross-clamping. Surg Forum 1987;38:195–202.

34. Kouchoukos NT, Wareing TH, Izumoto H, Klausing W, Abboud N. Elective hypothermic cardiopulmonary bypass and circulatory arrest for spinal cord protection during operations on the thoracoabdominal aorta. J Thorac Cardiovasc Surg 1990;99:659–664.

35. Laschinger JC, Cunningham JN Jr, Ctainella FP, et al. Detection and prevention of intraoperative spinal cord ischemia after cross-clamping of the thoracic aorta: use of somatosensory evoked potential. Surgery 1982;92:1109–1117.

36. Borst HG. In discussion: von Segesser LK, Weiss BM, Garcia E, Turina M. Perfusion with low systemic heparinization during resection of descending thoracic aortic aneurysms. Eur J Cardiothorac Surg 1992;6:246–250.

37. Crawford ES, Crawford JL, Safi HJ, et al. Thoracoabdominal aortic aneurysms: preoperative and intraoperative factors determining intermediate and long-term results in 605 patients. J Vasc Surg 1986;3:389–402.

38. Svensson LG, Coselli JS, Safi HJ, Hess KR, Crawford ES. Appraisal of adjuncts to prevent acute renal failure after surgery on the thoracic or thoracoabdominal aorta. J Vasc Surg 1989; 10:230–239.

39. Pontius RG, Brockman L, Hardy EG, Cooley DA, DeBakey ME. The use of hypothermia in the prevention of paraplegia following temporary aortic occlusion: experimental observations. Surgery 1954;36:33–38.

40. Owens JC, Prevedel AE, Swan H. Prolonged experimental occlusion of thoracic aorta during hypothermia. Arch Surg 1955;70:95–97.

41. Robertson CS, Foltz R, Grossman RG, Goodman JC. Protection against experimental ischemic spinal cord injury. J Neurosurg 1986;64: 633–642.

42. Colon R, Frazier OH, Cooley DA, McAllister HA. Hypothermic regional perfusion for protection of the spinal cord during periods of ischemia. Ann Thorac Surg 1987;43:639–643.

43. Mahfood S, Qazi A, Garcia J, Mispireta L, Corso P, Smyth N. Management of aortic arch aneurysm using profound hypothermia and circulatory arrest. Ann Thorac Surg 1985;39:412–417.

44. Massimo CG, Poma Ag, Viligiardi RR, Duranti A, Colucci M, Favi PP. Simultaneous total aortic replacement from arch to bifurcation: experience with six cases. J Texas Heart Inst 1986;13: 147–151.

45. Crawford ES, Coselli JS, Safi HJ. Partial cardiopulmonary bypass, hypothermic circulatory arrest, and posterolateral exposure for thoracic aortic aneurysm operation. J Thorac Cardiovasc Surg 1987;94:824–827.

25

EXTRACORPOREAL LIFE SUPPORT FOR RESPIRATORY FAILURE

Robert E. Cilley and Robert H. Bartlett

The short-term application of extracorporeal circulation using a mechanical pump and an artificial means of gas exchange to substitute for heart and lung function ushered in the modern era of cardiac surgery. Extracorporeal circulation was initially limited to several hours' duration and was therefore not applicable as a form of extended life support. The development of membrane oxygenators that utilize a gas permeable surface to avoid direct contact between blood and gas phases opened the door to long-term extracorporeal life support. The past 20 years have seen two major developments in extracorporeal life support: (1) The technology of extracorporeal life support has progressed to the point where injured lungs can be easily supported for several days and, if necessary, even for several weeks in newborns, children, and adults. (2) Specific patient populations with potentially reversible respiratory failure have been identified in whom extracorporeal life support can be used with reasonable hope of lung recovery (1, 2).

The acronym ECMO (for extracorporeal membrane oxygenation) has previously been used to describe prolonged extracorporeal circulation without thoracotomy. Since prolonged extracorporeal circulation may involve all lung functions and may not utilize solely "membrane" oxygenators, ex-

tracorporeal life support (ECLS) has become the preferred terminology.

HISTORY

The development of a mechanical device to substitute for the function of the heart and lungs—a "heart-lung machine"—is reviewed in Chapter 1. The earliest devices exposed blood directly to gas mixtures to provide oxygenation and carbon dioxide removal. Extracorporeal circulation was provided by the insertion of cannulae directly into the heart or great vessels. These devices worked and resulted in the development of the disposable, single-use, gas-interface oxygenators used for cardiac surgery. Extracorporeal circulation using these devices was limited to several hours' duration. A time-dependent pathologic response occurred that resulted in thrombocytopenia, hemolysis, coagulopathy, generalized edema, and multiorgan failure. This response appeared to result from direct exposure of blood to gaseous oxygen (3, 4), which of course does not occur in the native lung. The first attempts to separate the blood phase from the gas phase (similar to what occurs in the native lung) utilized semipermeable membranes such as cellophane or polyethylene. These plastics have low gas permeability and thus required very large surface areas to achieve adequate gas exchange (5, 6). The development of silicone rubber membranes (dimethylpolysiloxane) with much greater permeability to oxygen and carbon dioxide allowed practical membrane oxygenators to be built in the 1960s (7).

As a result of animal experimentation and the collaboration of medical industry, several membrane oxygenators became available for clinical use in the 1960s (8–11). These early developments showed that membrane oxygenators could achieve adequate gas exchange to conduct extracorporeal circulation free of a direct blood-gas interface. In the absence of direct gas exposure to blood, extracorporeal circulation could be carried out for weeks without hemolysis, significant capillary leak, or organ deterioration.

The use of partial heparinization was an important development in ECLS. Heparin anticoagulation sufficient to produce an infinite clotting time had been used since the development of the first heart-lung machines. Bartlett et al. (12) demonstrated that much lower doses of heparin could be used safely. Heparin administration could then be regulated to prevent thrombosis in the extracorporeal circuit with a prolonged but measurable clotting time, thereby reducing bleeding complications.

The concept of intensive care units developed during the 1960s and early 1970s as sicker and sicker patients were being treated. Many had respiratory failure as part of their illness and required mechanical ventilator support to maintain adequate oxygenation and ventilation. The clinical application of arterial blood gas analysis provided the "normal" values for Pao_2 and $Paco_2$ that were sought during mechanical ventilation. Native lungs were subjected to greater pressures and volumes in an effort to provide adequate gas exchange (13). A new pathology, adult respiratory distress syndrome, came to be recognized at about that same time. Failure of the lungs, either as a primary pathology or as one organ among multiple failing organs, caused or contrib-

uted to most intensive care unit deaths. Just as hemodialysis was a form of extracorporeal circulation to support the failing kidney until recovery occurred or an organ transplant was performed, extracorporeal circulation with an artificial lung was a possible solution to the problem of life-threatening respiratory failure.

The first successful use of extracorporeal respiratory support was reported by Hill et al. in 1972 (14). Key events in the history of ECLS are presented in Table 25.1. The concept of a method to support the failing lungs had such far-reaching implication that enormous interest was generated in developing these techniques.

The year 1975 was a key year in the history of extracorporeal respiratory support. In that year many of the investigators studying prolonged extracorporeal support met near Copenhagen and produced a benchmark publication (20). Likewise in that year, the National Institutes of Health ECMO study, a multicenter, prospective, randomized study of ECMO in life-threatening respiratory failure, was begun. This study was completed in 1979 and reported in 1980 (21). It included only extremely high-risk patients and was dominated by patients with influenza pneumonia. During ECMO many patients remained on very high pressure mechanical ventilation, which may have contributed to ongoing lung injury. The study was terminated at 92 patients (less than a third of the projected study size) when survival of the ECMO and control groups were both less than 10%. Death was frequently the result of technical complications, and autopsies uniformly revealed extensive pulmonary fibrosis (i.e., an irreversible injury). As a result of the study findings, ECMO therapy for adults essentially stopped in this country. The commonly drawn conclusion was that ECMO does not work. The correct conclusions of the study would be better stated as (*a*) application of ECMO to patients who already have irreversible pulmonary fibrosis does not work—application to patients with re-

Table 25.1. Key Events in the History of ECLS for Respiratory Failure

Date	Event
1965–1975	Unsuccessful attempts to support infants with both bubble and membrane oxygenators by Rashkind et al. (15), Dorson et al. (16), White et al. (17), Pyle et al. (18)
1972	First successful treatment of adult respiratory distress syndrome with ECMO using partial venoarterial bypass for 3 days by Hill et al. (14)
1975	First neonatal ECMO survivor at University of California, Irvine, by Bartlett et al. (19)
1975	Copenhagen meeting of ECMO investigators hosted by Zapol and Qvist (20)
1975–1979	National Institutes of Health ECMO study of adults with respiratory failure shows 10% survival in treatment and control groups (21)
1979	First neonatal ECMO seminar leading to development of ECMO research teams in Richmond, Pittsburgh, and Detroit
1980	Neonatal ECMO project moves from California to University of Michigan in Ann Arbor
1982	45 newborn cases with 23 survivors reported by Bartlett et al. (22)
1985,1989	Randomized prospective studies of ECMO for neonatal respiratory failure show superiority to conventional therapy (23, 24)
1986	Gattinoni et al. (25) report 49% survival using extracorporeal carbon dioxide removal in the adult respiratory distress syndrome; others report similar results (26–30)
1988	Treatment of select adult patients resumes in United States
1988	ECMO registry report: 795 cases at 18 centers with greater than 80% survival (31)
1989	Extracorporeal Life Support Organization (ELSO) study group formed
1990	Overall survival rate of 83% in 3500 newborns (32)

versible lung injury may yet work; (*b*) technical conduct of ECMO is critically important, and complications on ECMO are often life-threatening and must be reduced to a minimum if ECMO is to be "successful"; and (*c*) lungs will not heal when exposed to extremely high ventilator pressures.

Extracorporeal life support has been applied to adults since that time (1975) primarily in Europe. Gattinoni et al. (25) of Milan (in collaboration with Kolobow at the NIH) used the technique of extracorporeal carbon dioxide removal and apneic oxygenation of the native lung, reporting a 50% survival in patients with severe adult respiratory distress syndrome. Other European and Japanese investigators corroborated these results (26–30). In light of these results, there is currently a renewed interest in ECLS application to adult patients.

While Gattinoni et al. studied ECLS in adults, Bartlett and co-workers (19) foresaw the application of the technique to a select population of patients with life-threatening, "fatal" respiratory failure that was reversible. Neonates with respiratory failure characterized by pulmonary hyper-

tension with right-to-left hypoxic shunting were amenable to ECLS treatment. The nature of respiratory failure in neonates was such that there was a rapid progression to death prior to irreversible lung injury (i.e., before mechanical ventilation had been used for an extended period of time with its resultant injury). The technique of neonatal ECLS involved the extrathoracic cannulation of the right internal jugular vein and right common carotid artery for partial venoarterial cardiopulmonary bypass (CPB). Partial heparinization using whole blood activated clotting time was used to prevent circuit thrombosis and minimize hemorrhagic complications. The most physiologically significant concept to come from this experience was that of "lung rest." It became apparent that even profoundly injured lungs could recover if allowed to heal without the application of high-pressure mechanical ventilation.

More recently, venovenous extracorporeal support using a single cannula placed in the internal jugular vein has been used to provide extracorporeal support with excellent results in newborns (33). With the success of ECLS in newborns in defining a population with reversible respiratory failure, ECLS is now being applied to both pediatric and adult patients for respiratory support at some centers. The ECLS techniques have also been used for prolonged cardiac support on a more limited basis in patients of all ages.

PHYSIOLOGY OF ECLS

Hemodynamics and Characteristics of Different Methods of ECLS

VENOARTERIAL BYPASS

During venoarterial ECLS, venous blood is drained from the central circulation, pumped through an artificial lung, and returned to a central artery (Fig. 25.1A). Blood bypasses the pulmonary circulation. Both cardiac and pulmonary function can be supported with venoarterial bypass. The total aortic blood flow reflects a combination of the pump flow and the native cardiac output. Arterial oxygen content and Po_2 in systemic arteries result from the relative contribution of oxygen delivery from these two sources. During venoarterial bypass, essentially nonpulsatile flow is delivered by the extracorporeal circuit into the aorta or its branches. The resulting pulse contour of the arterial pressure wave is dampened. It is, however, unusual for the arterial pressure trace to be flat. Under most circumstances, 10 to 50% of the total aortic flow is contributed by the native cardiac output, resulting in pulsatile aortic flow. It is probably more important to achieve adequate total systemic oxygen delivery than for this flow to be pulsatile.

VENOVENOUS BYPASS

In this technique, venous blood is circulated through the artificial lung and returned to the venous circulation (Fig. 25.1B). Techniques initially utilized another large vein with a separate cannula for blood return. The common femoral vein has been used for this purpose. Other ingenious methods have been used to provide extracorporeal support utilizing a single cannula. A single lumen catheter system that alternates venous drainage with the reinfusion of oxygenated blood has been developed by Kolobow et al. (34). A single catheter with two lumens that allows continuous drainage and reinfusion has been developed for newborn ECLS, and is now used routinely (33).

During venovenous bypass, oxygenated venous blood is returned to the venous circulation and mixed with systemic venous blood, thus raising its oxygen content. Some of the mixed blood returns to the extracorporeal circuit (i.e., recirculates), while some enters the right ventricle and traverses the pulmonary vasculature, or is shunted, to the left heart and finally to the systemic arterial circulation. Venovenous ECLS is limited by the amount of systemic venous return that can be "captured" in the extracorporeal circuit. If insufficient systemic venous return is removed by the venous cannula, adequate support may not be achieved. Venovenous ECLS depends solely upon the cardiac output to provide flow and is most useful in pure respiratory failure or when respiratory failure is accompanied by cardiac failure that is solely attributable to hypoxia or to the excessive intrathoracic pressures generated by mechanical ventilation.

Arteriovenous bypass has not yet found practical clinical application. The concept of an "artificial placenta" is appealing and has been investigated in lambs (35, 36).

Oxygen Delivery to Tissues During Extracorporeal Support

Management of ECLS requires a thorough understanding of oxygen delivery and oxygen consumption physiology. Oxygen consumption (Vo_2) reflects the aerobic

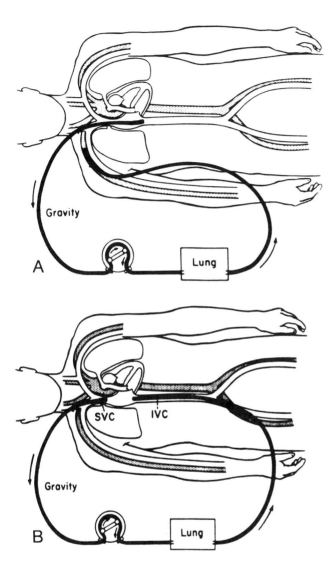

Figure 25.1. Two modes of extracorporeal circulation. **A.** Venoarterial access. **B.** Venovenous access. *SVC*, superior vena cava; *IVC*, inferior vena cava. (From Bartlett RH. Extracorporeal life support for cardiopulmonary failure. Curr Probl Surg 1990;27:635.)

metabolic activity of tissues. Newborns use 5 to 8 ml/kg/min of oxygen, children use 4 to 6 ml/kg/min, and adults use 3 to 5 ml/kg/min. Oxygen consumption is decreased by hypothermia, sedation, and complete paralysis. Oxygen consumption is increased by exercise, shivering, catacholamines, hyperthermia, and infection. Under normal steady-state conditions, the amount of oxygen taken up across the lungs into the pulmonary blood is equal to the amount of oxygen consumed by the tissues. This concept, the Fick principle, is summarized by the following equation:

$$Vo_2 = (\text{Cardiac Output}) \times (Cao_2 - Cvo_2)$$

where Cao_2 = arterial oxygen content and Cvo_2 = mixed venous oxygen content.

The amount of oxygen delivered to the tissues($\dot{D}o_2$) is the product of the cardiac output and Cao_2. Oxygen consumption, under most circumstances, is independent of oxygen delivery. Normally, oxygen delivery exceeds oxygen consumption by a factor of about 4 to 1. If arterial blood is nearly saturated, this corresponds to a mixed venous oxygen saturation of 75%. When oxygen delivery is reduced significantly in mammalian species, oxygen consumption becomes supply-limited and falls, resulting in acidosis, hypotension, and a rise in blood lactate (i.e., shock). This constitutes a physiologic definition of shock. The ratio of oxygen delivery to oxygen consumption is more important than the absolute quantities of the individual components of oxygen delivery, namely hemoglobin, arterial oxygen saturation, and cardiac output (37, 38).

Extracorporeal life support is most often applied to treat low oxygen delivery in the face of arterial hypoxia (hypoxic shock). Systemic oxygen delivery during ECLS is then a combination of oxygen delivery from the extracorporeal circuit and oxygen delivery across the native lung. This is most easily understood when applied to the situation of venoarterial ECLS. Here total oxygen delivery is expressed as:

$$
\begin{aligned}
\text{Total } D o_2 = \\
(EC \text{ flow}) \times (Ca o_2 \text{ postmembrane lung}) \\
+ (\text{native cardiac output}) \\
\times (Ca o_2 \text{ left ventricle})
\end{aligned}
$$

This concept must be appreciated in order to interpret the arterial blood gases sampled from the patient while on venoarterial ECLS. An example is illustrative:

A patient with a hemoglobin of 15 g/dl is on 50% extracorporeal support with minimal lung function. Perfusate blood is 100% saturated ($P o_2$ = 500, $Ca o_2$ = 22 mlo_2/dl). Right atrial, left atrial, and left ventricular blood is 75% saturated ($P o_2$ = 35, $Cv o_2$ = 15 mlo_2/dl). Systemic arterial blood will have an oxygen content of (0.5 × 22 mlo_2/dl) + (0.5 × 15 mlo_2/dl) = 18.5 mlo_2/dl. ($P o_2$ approximately 50; saturation, 88%). A rise in systemic arterial $P o_2$ at constant extracorporeal flow may reflect very different physiologic conditions. Improving lung function will result in greater oxygen saturation of left ventricular blood and correspondingly improving $P o_2$ in systemic arterial blood. However, decreased native lung blood flow will likewise result in a rising $P o_2$ as more of the systemic arterial blood is being contributed by the extracorporeal circuit. These patterns might be seen under conditions of pneumothorax, hemothorax, or pericardial tamponade.

The best monitor of the adequacy of tissue oxygenation is the mixed venous oxygen saturation. Continuous venous oxygen monitoring is performed routinely during ECLS. In venovenous bypass, $Pa o_2$ will be identical to the mixed right atrial $P o_2$, assuming there is no contribution from native lung gas exchange. Because of the return to the right ventricle of unsaturated blood not captured by the venous drainage catheter, right atrial saturation can rarely be raised to greater than 80 to 90%. The resulting $Pa o_2$ in arterial blood may be as low as 40 mm Hg. The patient will thus be relatively hypoxic and even cyanotic, but if the cardiac output is normal and hemoglobin adequate, oxygen delivery will be adequate and recovery can occur. Under these circumstances, recovery will be heralded by an increase in arterial $P o_2$ as the native lung contributes oxygen to the pulmonary blood flow.

An interesting physiologic property of lung function has been recognized with the application of ECLS. Even the most severely injured lungs (as might be found in severe adult respiratory distress syndrome) can support oxygenation if they are not required to provide any ventilatory function. This is the rationale behind extracorporeal carbon dioxide removal and so-called "apneic oxygenation" as developed by Gattinoni et al. (25). The lungs are inflated to moderate pressures (15 to 20 cm H_2O) and oxygen concentration is reduced, while carbon dioxide is removed by low flow partial venovenous bypass.

During ECLS, oxygen delivery is controlled primarily by the extracorporeal flow rate. Extracorporeal flow is set at the minimum amount that results in a normal $Sv o_2$. Pump flow is increased to treat falling $Pa o_2$ and $Sv o_2$. Pump flow may be decreased as $Pa o_2$ rises when $Sv o_2$ is normal, usually indicating lung recovery. Air-oxygen sweep gas mixtures can be employed to reduce the $P o_2$ of the perfusate if significant arterial hyperoxia is present.

Carbon Dioxide Removal During Extracorporeal Support

Metabolic production of carbon dioxide approximates oxygen consumption (respiratory quotient = 1). Excretion of carbon dioxide across normal native lungs is exquisitely sensitive to alveolar ventilation with the rate and depth of breathing controlled to maintain Pa_{CO_2} at about 40 mm Hg. During extracorporeal circulation the major determinants of carbon dioxide removal are the surface area of the artificial lung and the flow rate and composition of the sweep gas. Carbon dioxide removal is more efficient than oxygen transfer under most circumstances. Since an extracorporeal circuit is designed to meet oxygen consumption needs, it will normally be capable of removing excessive amounts of carbon dioxide. Practically speaking, carbon dioxide removal is often excessive when artificial lungs are ventilated with oxygen or oxygen/air mixtures. Dangerous levels of hypocarbia are avoided by adding carbon dioxide to the ventilating gas for the artificial lung, allowing the Pa_{CO_2} to be set at any desired level.

Control of Coagulation

Blood in the extracorporeal circuit is exposed to a number of synthetic materials including silastic, polyvinylchloride, polyurethane, and polycarbonate, as well as stainless steel and aluminum. Whenever blood contacts any foreign surface, enzymatic cascades are initiated that result in the production of fibrin, complement, kinins, and plasmin. The most clinically significant event is the activation of the coagulation cascade which, if not modified, will result in thrombosis of the extracorporeal circuit.

As long as very high flows are maintained and there are no stagnant areas, extracorporeal circulation can be conducted for long periods of time without heparin (39–41). However, systemic heparinization is customarily used to prevent thrombosis. Unlike CPB for cardiac surgery where heparin administration is designed to achieve nearly infinite clotting times (total anticoagulation), long-term ECLS seeks to maintain the minimum allowable level of anticoagulation and thus limit hemorrhagic complications over long periods of time.

The concept of partial heparinization was first introduced by Bartlett et al. (12). As currently practiced, it involves smaller loading doses of heparin than are given for cardiac surgery (40 to 150 units/kg) followed by continuous heparin infusions of 20 to 70 units/kg/hr. Heparin effect is monitored by whole blood activated clotting time. Although thrombocytopenia and procoagulant depletion will also prevent circuit thrombosis, they are associated with hemorrhagic complications. Thrombocytopenia must be prevented by platelet transfusions as necessary to maintain platelet counts greater than $100,000/mm^3$. Fibrinogen levels and prothrombin time should be near normal and fibrin degradation products should not appear in excess, allowing heparin effect alone to maintain anticoagulation. Fresh-frozen plasma and/or cryoprecipitate may be necessary to achieve this. The currently accepted practice for prolonged extracorporeal circulation is to maintain the whole blood activated clotting time at about 200 seconds (1.5 to 2 times the normal clotting time of 120 seconds).

Two properties of heparin are particularly important with regard to prolonged partial heparinization. Heparin is excreted in the urine and bound to platelets. Heparin administration must therefore be increased during periods of diuresis and platelet transfusion. This is particularly important with partial heparinization during prolonged extracorporeal circulation when the risk of overheparinization may be catastrophic bleeding, while underheparinization may result in circuit thrombosis.

Effects of ECLS on Other Organ Systems

EFFECTS OF ECLS ON FORMED BLOOD ELEMENTS

Whereas red blood cell destruction occurs after several hours of bypass using a bubble oxygenator, there is negligible red cell loss attributable to the use of modern membrane lungs. The surface of the extracorporeal circuit becomes "pacified" because of the dense protein monolayer that forms on the membrane lung and other circuit surfaces in the first few minutes of blood contact. Potential sources of red blood cell damage during long-term ECLS include mechanical injury from the pumping device and the occurrence of negative pressure surges within the circuit. These are minimized by having the roller pump adjusted to be nearly occlusive and the use of servoregulation to interrupt circuit pumping if inadequate venous return occurs. Plasma free hemoglobin levels are usually less than 40 mg/dl and urine is clear during ECLS. Transfusions are needed to maintain hematocrit, replacing blood losses from wounds and blood sampling as well as from the small amount of red cell destruction that does occur.

Platelets adhere to the prosthetic surface within minutes of exposure. They tend to adhere most to areas where fibrinogen has been deposited. Adenosine diphosphate and serotonin release attracts other platelets, causing platelet aggregates to form. These "clumps" of platelets, which also include some white cells (and red cells in more stagnant areas of the circuit), are released into the circulating blood and infused into the patient. They subsequently dissaggregate and are eventually removed by the reticuloendothelial system (42, 43). Platelets are continuously consumed during ECLS. If consumption is balanced by increased production, platelet counts will stabilize in the 30,000 to 60,000 range (1). In newborns and children, platelet production does not match destruction, and platelet transfusion is almost always required.

The effects of prolonged ECLS on white blood cells are less well known. Total and differential white blood cell count are nearly normal during ECLS (44, 45). Bacterial infections generally resolve with antibiotic treatment, providing evidence that white cell function is adequate. Total white blood cell counts during ECLS range from 5,000 to 15,000/mm³ under most circumstances.

FLUID AND ELECTROLYTES

Increased capillary permeability resulting from complement activation occurs to some degree when ECLS is initiated (46). There is often an initial weight gain and visible edema after ECLS is started. Whether this is a result of CPB itself or a reperfusion phenomenon is unknown. Edema usually resolves within 1 or 2 days and diuresis results in a return to the baseline weight (47). Hemofiltration may be necessary if renal function is abnormal or edema is significant.

Although it is rarely a problem, significant amounts of free water are lost from the membrane lung. Cool, dry, sweep gas exits the lung warmed and saturated with water vapor. An infant can lose more than 150 ml/day of free water in this fashion.

Serum-ionized calcium may fall to dangerous levels when extracorporeal circulation is started and result in cardiac dysfunction if not treated (48). This is most important when venovenous ECLS is initiated and can result in significant hypotension from low cardiac output. It is unclear whether this is due to the citrate present in banked blood or a dilutional phenomenon. There are no other electrolyte abnormalities that are peculiar to ECLS. Electrolytes are monitored as they would be in any critically ill patient and requirements are administered with parental nutrition solutions.

GASTROINTESTINAL

Although gastrointestinal function may be normal, it is not customary to use enteral nutrition during prolonged ECLS. With the recent emphasis on the beneficial effects of luminal nutrition on the integrity of the intestinal mucosa, this practice may change.

RENAL FUNCTION

Renal function is usually normal during ECLS. Both loop diuretics and osmotic agents can be used to treat fluid overload or edema. Preexisting renal failure may be treated by dialysis using a hemofilter placed within the circuit.

CENTRAL NERVOUS SYSTEM

Function appears to be unaffected by prolonged ECLS. Infants may be awake, alert, and even playful, and adults may be communicative during ECLS. Inorganic emboli related to an aluminum heat exchanger that is no longer sold have been found in the brain and other tissues of newborns treated with ECLS (49). The effect of microembolization from the extracorporeal circuit, although potentially dangerous, seems to be of less practical importance. Organ function remains nearly normal for many weeks and tissue infarcts are not found at autopsy.

The Physiology of the Native Lung During ECLS

During venoarterial ECLS, left ventricular outflow falls proportionate to the extracorporeal flow, resulting in a decreased pulse pressure. If cardiac arrest occurs during venoarterial ECLS, the left ventricle will continue to fill from thebesian veins and bronchial blood flow. Very high left atrial pressures will result if there is no left ventricular ejection, resulting in high pulmonary pressures and pulmonary edema. Left heart decompression is required under these circumstances.

During venoarterial bypass, a significant portion of the pulmonary blood flow is diverted through the extracorporeal circuit. There appear to be no major deleterious effects of reduced pulmonary blood flow unless normal ventilation is maintained. With normal ventilation of the native lungs during bypass, pulmonary capillary pH can be as high as 8.0. Hemolysis and pulmonary hemorrhage can result even without marked systemic hypocarbia (50, 51). When ECLS is initiated, ventilator settings are rapidly decreased to prevent further damage from overdistention, as well as to prevent local tissue alkalosis. There is no standard approach to management of the native lung during ECLS. It may not be important whether a low respiratory rate and normal inspiratory pressure are chosen or the patient is placed on continuous positive airway pressure (or whether the patient is taken off the ventilator entirely). A few sustained inflations above the alveolar opening pressure are provided periodically to prevent total lung collapse.

During venovenous bypass, right ventricular output is normal and probably higher than prior to instituting ECLS, since cardiac output increases after severe hypoxemia is corrected. This may have the salutary effect of exposing the pulmonary arterioles to blood with a relatively high Po_2, which may be beneficial in the treatment of pulmonary hypertension.

Very severely injured lungs can recover if placed "at rest" using ECLS. The period necessary for recovery spans from several days to several weeks. The presence of extensive fibrosis currently precludes recovery. If ECLS is initiated before fibrosis occurs or is irreversibly initiated, recovery can be expected unless technical complications ensue. The x-ray appearance of a typical newborn with meconium aspiration before, during, and after ECLS is shown in Figure 25.2.

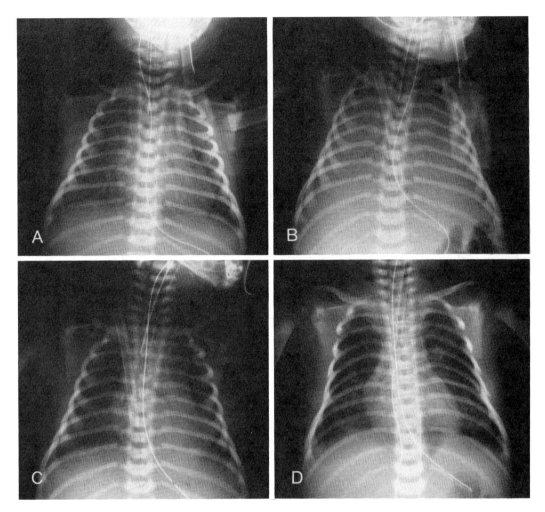

Figure 25.2.   X-ray appearance of a newborn with meconium aspiration syndrome. **A.** Appearance prior to institution of ECLS of a patient on maximal ventilator settings; $Pa_{O_2} = 35$. **B.** The 2nd day on ECLS, ventilator settings reduced for lung rest, double lumen venovenous cannula is in the right atrium, and there is a typical white-out appearance of the lungs. **C.** Lung recovery after 4 days of ECLS with the ventilator still at low settings. **D.** The patient as maintained on low ventilator settings after decannulation from ECLS.

TECHNICAL ASPECTS OF PROLONGED ECLS

The management of extracorporeal circuit flow, membrane lung function, and anticoagulation are the most critical aspects of prolonged ECLS. These topics have been discussed in the previous section.

Logistics and Cost of Prolonged ECLS

Providing ECLS requires a significant investment of personnel, time, and financial support. It requires extensive laboratory training and should not be undertaken lightly. The best examples of establishing

ECLS centers come from the neonatal ECMO experience. Guidelines for neonatal ECMO have been proposed and provide some insight into the support structure required to perform safe ECLS (52).

Extracorporeal life support should be based in a tertiary care center with an appropriately staffed intensive care unit for support. The ECLS centers should be geographically located where they can expect patient treatment population of at least one per month. Each center needs a medical director, and an ECLS coordinator is usually required to supervise staff training, equipment maintenance, and data recording. Most centers have found that a specially trained perfusionist, nurse, or respiratory therapist is necessary to manage the extracorporeal circuit. The primary responsibility of this technical specialist is to regulate blood flow, control membrane lung function, and adjust anticoagulation. Perhaps most importantly, they must also diagnose and treat patient and circuit emergencies (circuit disruption, membrane lung failure, power loss, and thrombosis). Under most circumstances each patient will also have a one-on-one intensive care unit nurse in addition to the ECLS technical specialist. A follow-up team of neonatologists, neurologists, or developmental specialists is needed.

Dedicated intensive care unit space with on-site backup equipment for all ECLS components, as well as operating capability within the intensive care unit itself, are required. The ECLS centers need a well-defined program for staff training and certification. This requires didactic teaching, laboratory training with live animals, and bedside training. The ECLS system thus is a team undertaking that requires institutional support, personal commitment from the leadership, and continuous updating and training.

Equipment

CIRCUIT DESCRIPTION

A basic ECLS circuit, used in its most common application, neonatal venoarterial ECLS, is depicted in Figure 25.3. Venous blood, from a centrally placed catheter, drains via gravity through a collapsible "bladder" and then to a roller pump. Servoregulation prevents negative pressure application to the venous side of the circuit by interrupting pump flow if venous return is inadequate. Blood is pumped through the artificial lung and subsequently through a heat exchanger (oriented vertically as a "macrobubble trap") and then returned to the patient. Components of the circuit are affixed to a mobile cart (Fig. 25.4). The oxygenated blood is returned to the patient through a major artery during venoarterial bypass or to a major vein during venovenous bypass. Standard priming techniques include flushing the circuit with carbon dioxide, vacuum application to the membrane lung gas phase, and crystalloid priming. The circuit is then coated with albumin, followed by blood priming. Circuit electrolytes and gas partial pressures are measured and adjusted in preparation for initiation of ECLS.

TUBING AND CATHETERS/USE OF THE M-NUMBER

The ECLS circuits are made of the same components used in operative CPB including polyvinylchloride tubing and polycarbonate connectors. As long as the patient's blood volume is adequate, the venous drainage catheter limits extracorporeal flow. Venous catheters, tubing, and reinfusion catheters must be chosen to allow adequate blood flow to support any given patient. Although the pressure/flow characteristics of straight tubes with known diameters can be calculated, most catheters and circuit components have irregular diameters and may have side holes, curves, and tapered areas that invalidate these calculations. A standardized system to describe the pressure/flow relationship of blood access devices has recently been described and has been termed the "M-number" (53, 54). If

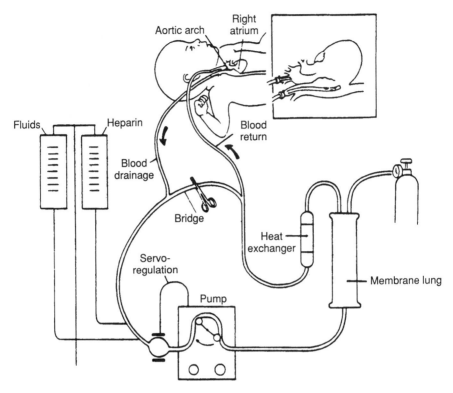

Figure 25.3. The ECLS circuit for newborn venoarterial bypass using jugulocarotid cannulation. (From Bartlett RH, Andrews AF, Toomasian JM, Haiduc NJ, Gazzaniga AB. Extracorporeal membrane oxygenation for newborn respiratory failure: 45 cases. Surgery 1982;92:426.)

the M-number of a particular catheter or tubing is known, then the pressure/flow characteristics can be determined from a nomogram or chart (Figs. 25.5 and 25.6). Conversely, if specific flows are needed to support a given patient, an arterial and venous cannula can be chosen that will support flow at acceptable pressures.

An example is illustrative. A typical 3.5-kg newborn needing venoarterial bypass might easily be cannulated with a 14-French venous catheter and a 10-French arterial catheter. The Bio-Medicus (Medtronics Biomedicus Inc., Eden Prairie, MN) 14-French venous catheter has an M-number of 3.35 and would be expected to support flows in excess of 1 liter/min across a 50 mm Hg pressure drop. The 14-French Axiom catheter (M = 4.25) on the other hand, would allow only 450 ml/min under similar conditions. If all that could be

placed was an 8-French catheter because of a small vein, the Bio-Medicus catheter would support 400 ml/min of flow and would most likely be adequate. The use of the M-number does not guarantee success, but it can be helpful to avoid failure due to inadequate catheter size.

ARTIFICIAL LUNGS

The characteristics and performance of membrane lungs and hollow fiber oxygenators are presented in Chapter 2. A few points about gas transfer merit mention. Silicone rubber used in commercially available membrane lungs has gas transfer capabilities of 200 to 400 mlO_2/min/m^2 when ventilated with oxygen at 1 atmosphere pressure. However, oxygen diffusion through the thin film of venous blood is the limiting factor that determines a membrane lung's oxygenating capacity. Oxygen diffuses through venous blood at a rate of approximately 100 mlO_2/min/m²/100 micron blood film thickness. Thus, for membrane lungs with a blood film of approximately 200 micron (the practical limits of blood film thickness in a membrane lung), about 50 ml of oxygen might be transferred each minute per square meter of oxygenator surface. Practically speaking, a newborn weighing 4.0 kg, supported by a 0.8 m² SciMed (Avecor Cardiovascular, Plymouth, MN) lung at 400 ml/min of flow would require 20 to 30 ml/min

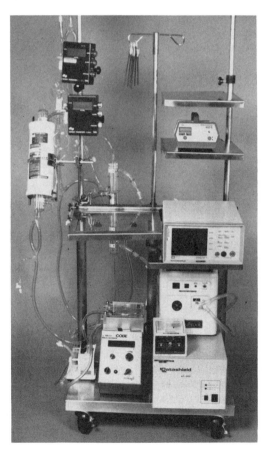

Figure 25.4. A mobile ECLS cart includes membrane lung, line pressure monitors, bladder box servoregulation unit, roller pump, heater and heat exchanger, venous saturation monitor, activated clotting time tester, and portable power supply.

of oxygen to meet its metabolic requirements. This is somewhat below the theoretical gas transfer capability for a lung of this size. Since carbon dioxide transfer is much more efficient than oxygen transfer, provision must be made to add carbon dioxide to the sweep gas of the membrane lung. This is accomplished by mixing in "carbogen" (5% carbon dioxide, Pco_2 = 38 mm Hg) to give 2 to 4% carbon dioxide. Alternatively, carbon dioxide may be directly added to the sweep gas using a regulator. If the latter is done, continuous carbon dioxide monitoring of the sweep gas should be performed.

An ideal membrane lung would have low thrombogenicity, high oxygen transfer per unit surface area, a relatively large gas space to minimize water condensation within the membrane lung, low blood path resistance, and small priming volume. It should also be relatively inexpensive and easy to prime. The most widely used membrane lung for ECLS is the SciMed-Kolobow lung, consisting of a long, spirally wound envelope of silicone rubber. Gas circulates within the envelope and blood passes lengthwise between the windings of the spiral. This device requires high perfusion pressures to overcome its high resistance; however, excellent gas exchange and low priming volume are achieved.

Hollow fiber oxygenators have also been used for ECLS. Microporous capillaries, around which the blood flows, conduct the sweep gas. These devices have low resistance and low priming volumes, but their use for this clinical application has been limited by a tendency to leak plasma into the gas phase after 24 to 48 hours.

PUMPING SYSTEMS

Most ECLS centers use direct drive roller pumps. The theoretical disadvantages of these pumps include (*a*) they provide only nonpulsatile flow; (*b*) they can generate extreme negative pressures if venous return is inadequate; (*c*) they generate very

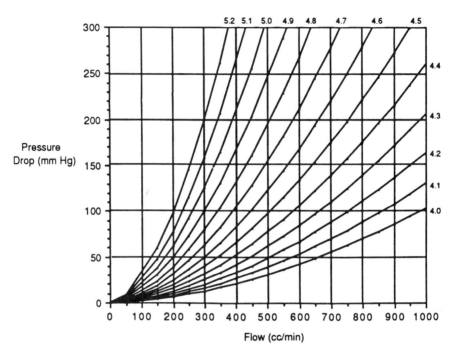

Figure 25.5. The pressure/flow characteristics of small vascular access devices with M-numbers greater than 4.0. See text for details.

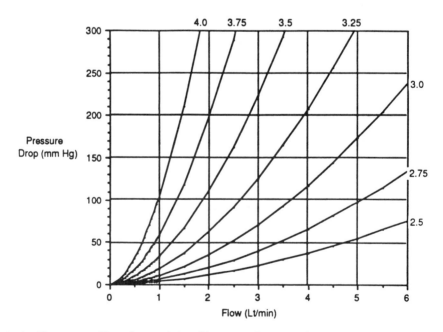

Figure 25.6. The pressure/flow characteristics of large vascular access devices with M-numbers less than 4.0. See text for details.

large positive pressures when outflow is occluded, sufficient to cause circuit rupture; (*d*) roller occlusion can contribute to red cell damage and hemolysis; and (*e*) tubing fatigue of the raceway segment can result in catastrophic raceway rupture. In spite of these potential problems, with proper servoregulation (see below) these pumps are relatively safe, very reliable, and cause minimal blood damage.

The "constrained vortex" or centrifugal pump is used by some centers; however, they have not gained widespread acceptance. These pumps can generate sufficient negative pressure to cause hemolysis when venous flow is limited. Likewise, when outlet resistance rises, the revolutions per minute must be increased to maintain flow, and significant hemolysis can result.

Another pumping system worthy of mention is the Rhone Poulenc pump (Collin-Cardio, Arcueil, France) (55). This pump is not approved for use in the United States. It consists of three rollers situated between two plates. A flaccid but distensible segment of oval silicone rubber tubing is stretched over the rollers. As the pump rotates, segments of the tubing are sequentially compressed over the rollers. The tubing fills passively without generating negative pressure and will not fill if venous return is inadequate. When venous return is adequate, the tubing fills and blood flow occurs. Pressure plateaus at about 300 mm Hg, with flow decreasing above this level, lessening the chance of high-pressure blowouts.

SERVOREGULATION AND MONITORING

When a roller pump is used, it is critical that it not apply high negative pressure to the venous filling line. Even small amounts of negative pressure can cause significant hemolysis and air entrainment within the circuit. Right atrial and superior vena cava damage may occur if they are sucked into the catheter. Unlike cardiac surgery, during long-term ECLS, a large venous reservoir where blood is relatively stagnant cannot be used because this will lead to thrombosis under the conditions of partial heparinization.

The problem of regulating pump flow to venous return is addressed by including a small collapsible bladder in the venous return line at its lowest point, prior to the roller pump. When the bladder collapses from inadequate venous return, a switch is activated that stops the roller pump and sounds an alarm. The pump restarts instantly when the bladder fills. Alternatively, a pressure monitor in the venous line can be used to servoregulate the pump. As long as venous return is adequate, the desired pump flow is delivered. Inadequate venous return may result from hypovolemia, high intrapericardial pressure (pericardial effusion, hemopericardium), high intrathoracic pressure (tension pneumothorax, tension hemothorax, excessive airway pressure), and catheter kinking. A commercially available "bladder box/servoregulator" is manufactured for long-term ECLS use by the Seabrook Medical Systems Company (Cincinnati, OH).

Premembrane/postmembrane pressure monitors should be included within the circuit. Excessive preoxygenator pressure may indicate membrane lung thrombosis and impending circuit failure. Pressure monitoring on the arterial side of the circuit can be used to servoregulate the pump to avoid circuit disruption if inadvertent arterial occlusion occurs (usually by tubing kinking or a misplaced clamp).

Continuous venous oxygen saturation monitoring is typically employed during ECLS. Venous oximetry during venoarterial bypass provides the best method of measuring the adequacy of tissue oxygenation, with venous oxygen saturations of 70 to 80% seen during adequate support. During venovenous bypass, recirculation of already oxygenated blood gives a falsely high "venous oxygen saturation" and patient arterial blood saturation monitoring is more help-ful. Trends in changes of the oxygen deliv-ery/oxygen consumption relationship can be identified from venous oximetry during venovenous ECLS.

Continuous monitoring of the oxygen concentration and carbon dioxide concen-tration of the membrane lung sweep gases adds another measure of safety to the con-duct of ECLS.

HEAT EXCHANGERS, HEATERS, AND POWER SUPPLIES

During the rapid rewarming required for cardiac surgery, it may be important to place the heat exchanger proximal to the oxygenator in the extracorporeal circuit; however, in long-term ECLS, normothermia is maintained. The best position for the heat exchanger is after the membrane lung, so blood can be returned to body temperature after the cooling that occurs in the mem-brane lung. Membrane lung ventilating gases cool when expanded from high pres-sures, and there is significant evaporative heat loss as the dry ventilating gases become saturated with water vapor. In larger chil-dren and adults, heat exchanger position is less important.

Because of problems with corrosion in aluminum heat exchangers resulting in blood leaks and circuit contamination, stainless steel heat exchangers are now used. Counter-current water flow from the heater must warm the blood to body temperature without excessive localized heating that might result in hemolysis.

Since transportation may be required for diagnostic studies, and power failures occur, a portable battery pack serves as an integral component of the ECMO cart. All critical equipment including the pump, servoregulator, and heater are plugged into the battery pack.

HEMOFILTRATION

Incorporation of a hemofilter within the extracorporeal circuit can be used to meet a number of physiologic needs (56). In fluid overloaded patients who are unre-sponsive to diuretics but still require signif-icant volumes of parenteral fluids, a hemo-filter can provide slow continuous ultrafil-tration. The volume of extracellular fluid to be removed is regulated by simply control-ling the ultrafiltrate flow from the hemo-filter using an accurate intravenous pump. Continuous arteriovenous hemofiltration provides some clearance of uremic toxins by replacing the continuous output of the hemofilter with a plasma-like electrolyte solution. When catabolic acute renal failure and uremia requiring high solute clearance are present, continuous arterial venous he-mofiltration with dialysis can be employed. Here the hemofilter ultrafiltrate compart-ment is perfused with a dialysis solution.

The hemofilter may be placed any-where in the circuit where there is a suffi-cient pressure gradient to provide filtration pressure. One such gradient is the pressure drop across the membrane lung itself. This site has the disadvantage of creating a "hy-poxic shunt" and is therefore not used. The preferred location is to place the hemofilter between a postroller pump site (either be-fore or after the membrane lung) and a preroller pump venous sampling port. This creates a retrograde "flow shunt," and pump speed must be increased to overcome this shunt. The pump speed may be readjusted by use of a flow meter or by calculations made from oxygen saturation measurements taken from various points in the circuit.

Long-term ECLS patients may have suf-fered from poor perfusion prior to the ECLS and may have some degree of acute renal failure. They are often very edematous and are inadequately nourished. No further vas-cular access is required and the patients are already heparinized, making hemofiltration ideal for these patients.

Cannulation

Cervical cannulation is the site of choice for most ECLS applications. The largest cannula that can be inserted in the internal jugular vein will almost always permit adequate venous drainage for ECLS. Historically, drainage of the cephalad portion of the vein has not been employed. There is concern that the increased intracranial pressure from ligation of this vessel may increase the risk of intracranial hemorrhage, especially in premature newborns. A cephalad drainage catheter is now being employed in these high risk neonates of less than 35 weeks' gestation.

Although ligation of the common carotid artery is unappealing, most patients (from newborn to adult) have sufficient collateral circulation that the risk of acute stroke is minimal. With an experience of several thousand common carotid artery ligations, there have been minimal neurologic sequelae that can be attributed to ligation of this vessel (1, 2). Other venous and arterial access sites that may be used are summarized in Table 25.2 (57).

As described above, the M-number can be used to predict attainable flow from a given cannula. In general, the largest cannula that will fit into the internal jugular vein and common carotid artery will provide adequate flow for almost every patient. Cannulation is performed as an operative procedure in the intensive care unit where ECLS is to be performed. (Anesthesia con-

Table 25.2. Access for ECLS[a]

Vessel	Advantages	Disadvantages	Comments
Common carotid artery (CCA)	1. Single incision if combined with jugular vein cannulation 2. Excellent perfusion of aortic arch vessels	1. Potential cerebral blood flow compromise	1. Minimal sequela attributed to CCA ligation in adult or pediatric patients 2. Arterial access of choice in all ages
Axillary artery	1. CCA ligation is avoided 2. Excellent perfusion of aortic arch vessels	1. Dissection is time-consuming 2. Distal perfusion required 3. Artery repair following ECLS is required	1. Secondary choice for arterial access in adults if arch perfusion is essential
Common femoral artery (CFA)	1. CCA ligation is avoided	1. Poor perfusion of aortic arch vessels 2. Distal perfusion required 3. Artery repair following ECLS is required	1. Too small in children <5 years old 2. Secondary choice for arterial access in older children
Common iliac artery	1. CCA ligation is avoided	1. Requires extensive dissection for required retroperitoneal approach	1. Secondary choice after CCA in children 2 to 5 years old
Internal jugular vein (IJV)	1. Single incision and dissection if combined with CCA cannulation 2. May be ligated 3. Large vein with easy access to right atrium	1. Concern for intracranial pressure increase and associated hemorrhage with ligation	1. Venous access of choice in all ages 2. Cephalad cannula may be added
Common femoral vein	1. Accessible vein for reinfusion during venovenous bypass 2. Percutaneous access easy	1. Requires second incision 2. Venous repair following ECLS is required 3. Distal cannula drainage required during ECLS unless saphenofemoral access used	1. Too small in children <5 years old 2. Secondary choice for venous access after IJV in all but young children

[a] Modified from Hirschl RB. Cannulation techniques for ECLS. Extracorporeal life support for pediatric and adult cardiorespiratory failure: an introduction to ECLS. In: EL50 course manual. Ann Arbor, MI: University of Michigan, 1991:20.

sists of locally infiltrated xylocaine, intravenous morphine, and a neuromuscular blocker.) Complete operating room staffing is optimal, including a scrub nurse or technician and a circulating nurse. Electrocautery and headlights are brought to the intensive care unit. Cannulation occurs concurrently with circuit preparation and priming.

Cannulation technique involves minimal handling of the vessels, especially the vein, to avoid spasm. In the neonate, intimal stay sutures are placed to prevent dissection of the delicate arterial intima upon introduction of the catheter. The artery is mobilized even when venovenous bypass is anticipated in case a rapid conversion to venoarterial bypass is required. Electrocautery is used liberally to minimize bleeding. Catheters are secured within the vessels using sutures. A short segment of silicone rubber tape ("vessel-loop") is included within the suture. When removing the catheter, the suture can be cut against the silicone rubber tape, avoiding damage to the native vessels.

Repair of the carotid artery and jugular vein is possible after ECLS, and has been advocated by some (58, 59). Greater experience is needed to define the long-term benefit of vessel reconstruction, and whether it can be performed without complication.

General Intensive Care Unit Care of the Patient on Prolonged ECLS

Like any critically ill patient, ECLS patients require one-on-one nursing, but they also require a technical specialist to regulate the extracorporeal circuit. After being placed on ECLS and recovering from the insult of tissue hypoxia, these critically ill patients may actually become "normal," permitting discontinuation of muscle relaxants and resumption of spontaneous movement. Both adults and children may become communicative; newborns will open their eyes and interact with parents and care givers. Sedation and analgesia are provided as necessary.

The feared complication of intracranial hemorrhage (occurring in 14% of neonatal ECLS patients) may be heralded by obvious neurologic deterioration or seizures, an unexplained increase in platelet consumption, or may be clinically silent. In neonates, cranial ultrasound is useful for assessing intracranial hemorrhage and is performed daily throughout their time on ECLS.

Parenteral nutrition is continued and easily increased to meet nutritional requirements. Caloric and protein needs may be met without fear of excess fluid administration because of the ease with which hemofiltration can be performed on ECLS.

Routine electrolytes including sodium, chloride, bicarbonate, phosphorus, and magnesium are monitored daily, or more frequently if changes are occurring. More frequent monitoring may be required during periods of high-volume hemofiltration. Glucose, urea nitrogen, creatinine, albumin, hepatic transaminases, and bilirubin are also measured daily. Hematologic values including blood count, fibrinogen, fibrin degradation products, and serum hemoglobin are checked as well. Potassium, calcium, hematocrit, and platelets require more frequent monitoring and correction. Patient arterial, pre-, and postoxygenator blood gas tensions are checked periodically. In the past, large numbers of patient blood gas determinations were made; now, with a greater reliance on continuous venous oximetry and universal application of pulse oximetry, these are only checked a few times throughout the day.

Since the patient is partially heparinized and will bleed excessively from minor wounds, some areas of routine care are altered; no intramuscular injections are given. No percutaneous arterial or venous samples are obtained. New intravenous catheters are not started, and all intravenous lines are capped and left in place if nonfunctional. "Capillary blood gases," requiring heel or digital puncture, are not performed. Urethral catheters are neither inserted nor removed, if possible. Endotracheal tubes may be changed with extreme care. Tracheal suctioning should be done gently with soft catheters, if possible.

Patients remain on broad-spectrum parenteral antibiotics throughout the time that ECLS is used. Specific infections mandate specific antibiotic treatment. It is surprisingly uncommon to have a patient deteriorate during ECLS from an infection. Topical antifungal agents are used liberally.

Critically ill patients and their families always require emotional support and sensitivity. Extracorporeal life support adds another factor to the emotional turmoil that families experience. Most centers provide information booklets to help families understand this treatment. The patient who was sick enough to die, and in fact may have been dying when ECLS was initiated, often becomes "well" and may appear almost normal. If treatment proceeds with resolution of the disease and recovery, the results are gratifying to all. If, however, the lungs fail to recover, life support must either be terminated or allowed to continue until a fatal complication results. This kind of outcome can be emotionally devastating to all involved. Support from nursing personnel, social workers, and the clergy is helpful.

Surgical Procedures on ECLS/Management of Bleeding

Minor surgical procedures may be required during ECLS and should not be taken lightly. Significant bleeding complications have occurred after seemingly trivial procedures. Arterial cutdown may be needed if appropriate access could not be obtained prior to starting ECLS or if the access was lost. Tube thoracostomy may be required to drain hemothorax or pneumothorax. Cannulation sites may bleed, requiring reexplo-

ration. When these procedures are performed, electrocautery should be available. Skin incisions can be made with the cutting mode of an electrocautery instrument. Muscles should be cauterized, and not torn (this is especially important during chest tube insertions). "Fibrin glue" (cryoprecipitate, calcium, and thrombin solution) applied to wounds will decrease bleeding complications.

Major operative procedures can be performed on ECLS either to treat the primary pathology or to deal with complications (usually bleeding). Table 25.3 lists some of the operative procedures that have been performed on ECLS. Although bleeding may be a significant problem, liberal use of cautery, application of fibrin glue, and a low threshold for reexploration permit nearly any procedure to be performed.

When bleeding occurs during ECLS, several strategies may be employed. Laboratory evaluation may reveal correctable forms of coagulopathy. Prothrombin time should be normal and, if not, corrected with fresh-frozen plasma. Low fibrinogen levels (<100 mg/dl) are corrected with cryoprecipitate. Platelet counts should be elevated to greater than 150,000 by platelet transfusion. Activated clotting times are allowed to fall to the 160- to 180-second

Table 25.3. Surgical Procedures Performed on ECLS

Thoracotomy for intrathoracic bleeding
Transthoracic repair of congenital diaphragmatic hernia
Ligation of patent ductus arteriosus
Open lung biopsy
Lung lobectomy for bronchopleural fistula
Lung lobectomy for arteriovenous malformation
Lung lobectomy for cystic adenomatoid malformation
Pericardial window to release tamponade
Repair of aortic puncture wound
Tracheal reconstruction
Laparotomy for gastrointestinal perforation
Gastrectomy for bleeding
Transabdominal repair of congenital diaphramatic hernia
Splenectomy for bleeding
Exploratory laparotomy for hemoperitoneum

range. High circuit flow rates should be maintained during times when the activated clotting time is low. Activated clotting time can be further lowered to the 120- to 140-second range and heparin discontinued for several hours if bleeding persists. When ACTs are this low, a back-up, saline-primed circuit should be immediately available in the intensive care unit. If these measures fail to stop the bleeding, operative therapy is indicated. A rule of thumb is to explore the appropriate body cavity or wound for bleeding that exceeds one-half a blood volume in 24 hours.

Weaning/Discontinuation of ECLS Support

The return of pulmonary gas exchange heralds lung recovery in patients treated with ECLS (60). This is usually seen as an increase in venous saturation and arterial Po_2 or as a decrease in arterial Pco_2 without a change in ventilator settings or level of ECLS. Pulmonary compliance will improve and the chest x-ray will clear. Serial compliance measurements may provide a means to easily quantify lung recovery (61). Extracorporeal flow is progressively decreased, allowing more pulmonary blood flow. When low levels of support have been achieved (approximately 25% of the initial flow), the patient should be "trialed off" with moderate ventilator support, and if stable, decannulated. The weaning procedure is oftentimes more of a "discovery" that the patient has improved sufficiently to no longer require ECLS. In patients who are unable to be taken off of ECLS at low ventilator settings, sequential trials off of ECLS at moderately high ventilator settings are performed once or twice daily. Continued improvement with serial trials indicates that ECLS should be continued. Failure to improve after several trials off may indicate residual, static, lung disease and ECLS should be discontinued, anticipating that prolonged mechanical ventilation will be required. During prolonged trials off of by-

pass, anticoagulation of both the patient and circuit must be maintained.

The decision to discontinue ECLS is made in a similar fashion during venovenous bypass. Here a trial off of ECLS may be accomplished much more simply. Capping the oxygenator gas inlet port allows the circuit oxygen to be consumed and equilibrate the entire extracorporeal circuit with the patient's mixed venous blood. A 300-ml circuit with a hemoglobin of 15 mg/dl has approximately 15 ml of available oxygen when equilibrated to a mixed venous oxygen saturation of 75%. Extracorporeal flow and anticoagulation need not be changed; there is no concern about circuit, catheter, or patient thrombosis. Hemodynamics remain constant, without the abrupt changes in pulmonary blood flow and aortic pressure associated with initiating and stopping venoarterial bypass. Patient management during ECLS is summarized in Table 25.4.

CLINICAL APPLICATIONS OF ECLS

Neonatal Respiratory Failure

Neonatal respiratory failure can be severe, progressive, and rapidly fatal. These characteristics make it ideally suited for a treatment such as ECLS. The severity and potential for mortality justifies the use of extraordinary life-saving means. The rapidity with which neonatal respiratory failure can progress ensures that the "sick lungs" will not be irreversibly injured by the application of mechanical ventilation for many days by the time ECLS is used.

Although there are a number of distinct causes of respiratory failure in newborns, they share a common pathophysiologic mechanism: pulmonary artery hypertension. Hypoxia, hypercarbia, and acidosis cause pulmonary vasoconstriction that results in right-to-left shunting at the atrial, ductal, and intrapulmonary levels. Shunting worsens the hypoxia, which in turn increases pulmonary vascular resistance, creating a vicious cycle. The ECLS and "lung

Table 25.4. Summary of Patient Management During Extracorporeal Life Support

Patient identified meeting criteria for ECLS; no contraindications present
Cannulation of vessels in the intensive care unit; preparation of the ECLS circuit
ECLS is initiated
ECLS management
    Extracorporeal circuit flow adjusted using arterial oxygen tension, mixed venous oxygen saturation to provide
        adequate oxygen delivery
    Sweep gas flow and composition adjusted to normalize arterial carbon dioxide tension
    Ventilator placed at rest settings
    Systemic blood pressure regulated by volume administration and inotropes as necessary
    Hemoglobin maintained at 14–15 g/dl by transfusion and ultrafiltration if necessary
    Platelet count maintained greater than 100,000
    Activated clotting time maintained at 200 seconds by continuous heparin infusion
    Central nervous system function, nutrition, renal function monitored and supported
Native lung recovery occurs (chest x-ray improved, rising PaO_2, lower ECLS flow, appearance of CO_2 in
    endotracheal tube)
"Trial off" at moderate or low ventilator settings
Decannulation, ventilator weaning, extubation

rest" provide one method to break this cycle when it will not respond to conventional means. Conventional methods for treating pulmonary artery hypertension have included mechanical ventilation with paralysis, induced respiratory alkalosis, and sometimes vasodilators. Up to 5% of neonates will not respond to conventional treatment and may benefit from the period of lung rest that can be achieved with ECLS to allow the lung to heal (62).

INDICATIONS AND CONTRAINDICATIONS

Earlier in the history of neonatal ECLS, ECMO was offered as a salvage therapy in patients who were believed moribund and unlikely to survive (19). More objective criteria have evolved over the ensuing years. The two most widely used objective measures are the alveolar-arterial oxygen gradient ($AaDO_2$) and the oxygenation index (OI) (63–65):

$$AaDO_2 =$$

$$\frac{1}{F_iO_2}\left[\left(P_{atm} - pH_2O - \frac{PaCO_2}{R}\right) - PaO_2\right]$$

where P_{atm} = atmospheric pressure, pH_2O = vapor pressure of water at 37°C (47 mm Hg), R = respiratory quotient, $PaCO_2$ = ar-

terial PCO_2, PaO_2 = arterial PO_2, and OI = (mean airway pressure $\times FiO_2/PaO_2) \times 100$.

An $AaDO_2$ greater than 610 for 8 hours defines a mortality risk of about 80%. Oxygenation index consistently greater than 25 defines an approximately 50% mortality risk, while an oxygenation index greater than 40 defines a 80% mortality in our experience (66). Each center performing neonatal ECLS should corroborate the applicability of objective criteria to their own neonatal population.

Contraindications to neonatal ECLS include profound neurologic impairment, congenital anomalies incompatible with prolonged or meaningful survival, and irreversible lung disease already present (such as bronchopulmonary dysplasia). Mechanical ventilation of greater than 7 days' duration is a relative contraindication, while mechanical ventilation for more than 10 days is an absolute contraindication.

Whenever possible, prior to instituting ECLS a cranial ultrasound should be obtained to rule out intracranial hemorrhage. In addition an echocardiogram should be obtained to rule out significant structural heart disease. It is noteworthy that total anomalous pulmonary venous return can present with apparent respiratory failure meeting "ECLS criteria."

The high risk of intracranial hemorrhage in the early newborn experience (approximately 30%) was associated with gestational age less than 35 weeks (67). It has also been noted that when intracranial hemorrhage is present, it may rapidly expand under the condition of partial heparinization. The presence of an intracranial hemorrhage by ultrasound or gestational age less than 35 weeks constitute relative contraindications to ECLS in the newborn. We have, however, returned to treating premature newborns ($\geq$32 weeks) on an individualized basis using higher platelet counts, lower activated clotting times, and a cephalad jugular venous drainage catheter with encouraging results (68).

COMPLICATIONS, RESULTS, AND OUTCOME

The complications of ECLS fall into three main categories: (a) bleeding associated with heparin anticoagulation, (b) mechanical failure of circuit components, and (c) long-term neurologic and pulmonary sequelae. Bleeding complications occur in 30% of all patients, with intracranial hemorrhage and bleeding from an operative site each accounting for nearly half of those complications and gastrointestinal bleeding accounting for the remainder. The incidence of intracranial hemorrhage and technical complications has fallen as experience has progressed (2). Jugular and carotid ligation is surprisingly well tolerated. Symptoms of right hemispheric dysfunction have been minimal (66, 69, 70).

Survival advantage using ECLS in newborn respiratory failure has been shown in two randomized prospective studies (23, 24). However, since these patients are selected from a population with high mortality risk ($\sim$80%), there is no control group to which they may be compared (for follow-up). Approximately one-fourth of the newborns with severe respiratory failure treated by mechanical ventilation alone, without extracorporeal support, will have developmental or neurologic impairment (71, 72). Follow-up data from experienced neonatal ECLS centers shows the majority of patients to be normal (73, 74). Two hundred forty-five of 322 patients (74%) are essentially normal at follow-up of 6 months to 13 years (2).

There are currently over 70 centers using ECLS for the treatment of newborn respiratory failure in North America. With more then 5000 newborn cases reported, the overall survival rate is 83% (Table 25.5) (75).

Pediatric and Adult Respiratory Failure

The favorable experience with neonatal ECLS has renewed interest in the application of ECLS to older children and adults. Currently, approximately 15 centers offer ECLS for respiratory failure in children and adults. The early adult ECMO experience

Table 25.5.   Neonatal Cases and Survival by Diagnosis (1973–1991)[a]

Primary Diagnosis	Total	No. of Survivors	% Surviving
Meconium aspiration syndrome	2067	1919	93
Respiratory distress syndrome	788	666	85
Congenital diaphragmatic hernia	996	608	61
Pneumonia/sepsis	752	578	77
Air leak syndrome	22	13	59
Persistent pulmonary hypertension of the newborn	692	606	88
Other	162	132	81
Totals	5479	4522	83

[a] Data from ELSO registry, Extracorporeal Life Support Organization, Ann Arbor, MI.

demonstrated that life support could be provided for days or weeks, but nearly 90% of the patients died from pulmonary fibrosis (irreversible lung disease) or the complications of ECMO. As currently applied to children and adults, ECLS is indicated in acute, potentially lethal respiratory failure that does not respond to conventional therapy when the underlying condition is reversible. Extracorporeal life support is currently used as "salvage" therapy in children and adults, when survival would otherwise not be expected. Further studies are needed to define its place in the treatment of respiratory failure outside the newborn period. The severity of the lung disease can be defined objectively by a transpulmonary shunt fraction greater than 30% and a static lung compliance less than 0.5 ml/cm H_2O/kg (2).

In children and adults, it is much more difficult to identify underlying conditions that are reversible. Unlike neonates, older children and adults are more likely to have irreversible disease from interstitial inflammation leading to pulmonary fibrosis. It is perhaps unfortunate that these patients can be treated with high pressure mechanical ventilation successfully for so long. Acceptable arterial blood gases may be generated at the expense of ongoing lung injury from the application of high pressure mechanical ventilation. The rapid progression to lethality and earlier application of ECLS in newborns protect their lungs from the injuries that often result from many days of mechanical ventilation. High-pressure mechanical ventilation is clearly injurious and may be as much the culprit as the cure in the pathophysiology of lung injuries (76).

It is important that ECLS be initiated early in the course of disease. Patient selection should include a short period of acute illness (less than 5 days). There may be a place for pharmacologic therapy to prevent or minimize pulmonary fibrosis. Current results of ECLS in children and adults are shown in Tables 25.6 and 25.7 (75). These

Table 25.6. Pediatric Respiratory Cases and Survival by Diagnosis (1982–1991)[a]

Respiratory Diagnosis	Total	No. of Survivors	% Surviving
Bacterial pneumonia	23	9	39
Viral pneumonia	92	44	48
Intrapulmonary hemorrhage	3	3	100
Aspiration	31	19	61
Pneumocystis	5	2	40
Adult respiratory distress syndrome	79	33	42
Others	52	25	48
Totals	285	135	47

[a] Data from ELSO registry, Extracorporeal Life Support Organization, Ann Arbor, MI.

Table 25.7. Adult Respiratory Cases and Survival by Diagnosis (1988–1991)[a]

Respiratory Diagnosis	Total	No. of Survivors	% Surviving
Bacterial pneumonia	3	1	33
Viral pneumonia	7	6	86
Intrapulmonary hemorrhage	1	0	0
Aspiration	2	0	0
Adult respiratory distress syndrome	12	8	67
Other respiratory	7	2	29
Totals	32	17	53

[a] Data from ELSO registry, Extracorporeal Life Support Organization, Ann Arbor, MI.

patients were generally treated with ECLS on the basis of their progressive deterioration in spite of maximal ventilator support, including jet ventilation where applicable. Thus, their predicted mortality is nearly 100%.

In 1990 most institutions should count on start-up costs approaching $100,000. This includes salary and benefits of a full-time clinical coordinator ($40,000 to 50,000) as well as primary and back-up equipment ($20,000 × 2). In addition, laboratory animal training exercises must be conducted and disposables purchased. The ECMO costs per day adds approximately $2000 above and beyond the cost of a newborn in a neonatal intensive care unit on a mechanical ventilator. There is evidence that this cost is offset by a shorter neonatal intensive care unit stay and ultimately less significant residual lung disease. (Bartlett RH, unpublished data.) Actual per day cost of ECMO depends somewhat upon the volume of cases performed at a particular institution. Some institutions have used dedicated full-time employees as ECLS technical specialists, while others have trained a group of technical specialists used only when cases are performed. Most third party payers are now reimbursing for the expenses of ECLS including cannulation procedures, operative procedures performed on ECLS, and the care of the patient on extracorporeal circulation on a daily basis.

FUTURE DIRECTIONS

In 1989 the active ECLS centers joined together to form a study group called the Extracorporeal Life Support Organization (ELSO).

The purpose of this group is to maintain the data registry, conduct clinical studies on extracorporeal support and serve as the communication center for research and clinical practice of extracorporeal life support (2).

The future of ECLS for respiratory failure is uncertain. When properly applied, this technology can be life-saving. Safer ECLS may find earlier application and more widespread use in the treatment of moderate respiratory failure, (for example, percutaneously placed venous catheters used for venovenous ECLS and a nonthrombogenic circuit that does not require systemic heparinization). Alternatively, ECLS may be supplanted by safer, less injurious mechanical ventilation. Improved drug therapies to relax pulmonary arterioles are needed to reliably break the cycle of pulmonary artery hypertension, as are drugs to control of the deleterious effects of pulmonary inflammatory responses (see Chapter 18).

REFERENCES

1. Bartlett RH, Gazzaniga AB. Extracorporeal circulation for cardiopulmonary failure. Curr Probl Surg 1978;15:1–96.
2. Bartlett RH. Extracorporeal life support for cardiopulmonary failure. Curr Probl Surg 1990; 27:621–705.
3. Lee WH Jr, Krumhaar D, Fonkalsrud EW, et al. Denaturation of plasma proteins as a cause of morbidity and death after intracardiac operations. Surgery 1961;50:29–39.
4. Dobell ARC, Mitri M, Galva R, et al. Biologic evaluation of blood after prolonged recirculation through film and membrane oxygenators. Ann Surg 1965;161:617–622.
5. Kolff WJ, Effler DB. Disposable membrane oxygenator (heart-lung machine) and its use in experimental and clinical surgery while the heart is arrested with potassium citrate according to the Melrose technic. Trans Am Soc Artif Intern Organs 1956;2:13–21.
6. Clowes GHA Jr, Hopkins AL, Neville WE. An artificial lung dependent upon diffusion of oxygen and carbon dioxide through plastic membranes. J Thorac Surg 1956;32:630.
7. Kammermeyer K. Silicone rubber as a selective barrier. Ind Eng Chem 1957;49:1685.
8. Kolobow T, Bowman RL. Construction and evaluation of an alveolar membrane artificial heart lung. Trans Am Soc Artif Intern Organs 1963; 9:238.
9. Landé AJ, Dos SJ, Carlson RG, et al. A new membrane oxygenator-dialyzer. Surg Clin North Am 1967;47:1461–1470.

10. Pierce EC II. A modification of the Clowes membrane lung. J Thorac Cardiovasc Surg 1960; 39:438–448.

11. Bramson ML, Osborn JJ, Main FB, et al. A new disposable membrane oxygenator with integral heat exchange. J Thorac Cardiovasc Surg 1965;50: 391–400.

12. Bartlett RH, Drinker PA, Burns NE, et al. The toroidal membrane oxygenator: design, performance and prolonged bypass testing of a clinical model. Trans Am Soc Artif Intern Organs 1972;18:369–374.

13. Kolobow T. Extracorporeal respiratory gas exchange: a look into the future. ASAIO Trans 1991; 37:2–3.

14. Hill JD, O'Brien TG, Murray JJ, et al. Prolonged extracorporeal oxygenation for acute post-traumatic respiratory failure (shock-lung syndrome): use of the Bramson Membrane Lung. N Engl J Med 1972;286:629–634.

15. Rashkind WJ, Freeman A, Klein D, et al. Evaluation of a disposable plastic, low volume, pumpless oxygenator as a lung substitute. J Pediatr 1965;66:94–102.

16. Dorson W Jr, Meyer B, Baker E, et al. Response of distressed infants to partial bypass lung assist. Trans Am Soc Artif Intern Organs 1970; 16:345–351.

17. White JJ, Andrews HG, Risemberg H, et al. Prolonged respiratory support in newborn infants with a membrane oxygenator. Surgery 1971; 70:288–296.

18. Pyle RB, Helton WC, Johnson FW, et al. Clinical use of membrane oxygenator. Arch Surg 1975; 110:966–970.

19. Bartlett RH, Gazzaniga AB, Jefferies R, et al. Extracorporeal membrane oxygenation (ECMO) cardiopulmonary support in infancy. Trans Am Soc Artif Intern Organs 1976;22:80–93.

20. Zapol WM, Qvist J, eds. Artificial lungs for acute respiratory failure. New York: Academic Press, 1976.

21. Zapol WM, Snider MT, Hill JD, et al. Extracorporeal membrane oxygenation in severe acute respiratory failure. JAMA 1979;242:2193–2196.

22. Bartlett RH, Andrews AF, Toomasian JM, et al. Extracorporeal membrane oxygenation for newborn respiratory failure: 45 cases. Surgery 1982; 92:425–433.

23. Bartlett RH, Roloff DW, Cornell RG, et al. Extracorporeal circulation in neonatal respiratory failure: a prospective randomized study. Pediatrics 1985;76:479–487.

24. O'Rourke PP, Crone R, Vacanti J, et al. Extracorporeal membrane oxygenation and conventional medical therapy in neonates with persistent pulmonary hypertension of the newborn: a prospective randomized study. Pediatrics 1989;84: 957–963.

25. Gattinoni L, Pesenti A, Mascheroni D, et al. Low-frequency positive-pressure ventilation with extracorporeal CO_2 removal in severe acute respiratory failure. JAMA 1986;256:881–886.

26. Knoch M. Treatment of severe ARDS with extracorporeal CO_2 removal. In: Gille JP, ed. Neonatal and adult respiratory failure: mechanisms and treatment. Paris: Elsevier, 1989:123.

27. Falke K, Schulte HD. Extracorporeal CO_2 elimination with low frequency ventilation for the treatment of severe acute pulmonary failure. Dtsch Med Wochenschr 1985;110:663–664.

28. Bindslev L. Extracorporeal circulation using surface heparinized equipment. In: Gille JP, ed. Neonatal and adult respiratory failure: mechanisms and treatment. Paris: Elsevier, 1989:97.

29. Morioka T, Terasaki H. Present status of extracorporeal lung assist (ECLA as ECMO or extracorporeal CO_2 removal) in Japan. In: Gille JP, ed. Neonatal and adult respiratory failure: mechanisms and treatment. Paris: Elsevier, 1989:147.

30. Gille JP: Neonatal and adult respiratory failure: mechanisms and treatment. Paris: Elsevier, 1989.

31. Toomasian JM, Snedecor SM, Cornell R, et al. National experience with extracorporeal membrane oxygenation (ECMO) for newborn respiratory failure: data from 715 cases. ASAIO Trans 1988;34:140–147.

32. Stolar CJ, Snedecor SS, Bartlett RH. Extracorporeal membrane oxygenation and neonatal respiratory failure: experience from the extracorporeal life support organization. J Pediatr Surg 1991;26:563–571.

33. Anderson HL, Otsu T, Chapman RA, Bartlett RH. Venovenous extracorporeal life support in neonates using a double lumen catheter. ASAIO Trans 1989;35:650–653.

34. Kolobow T, Borelli M, Spatola R, Tsuno K, Prato P. Single catheter veno-venous membrane lung bypass in the treatment of experimental ARDS. ASAIO Trans 1988;34:35–38.

35. Griffith BP, Borovetz HS, Hardesty RL, et al. Arteriovenous ECMO for neonatal respiratory support: a study in perigestational lambs. J Thorac Cardiovasc Surg 1979;77:595–601.

36. Schmidt S, Dudenhausen JW, Langner K, et al. A new perfusion circuit for the newborn with lung immaturity: extracorporeal CO_2 removal via an umbilical arterio-venous shunt during apneic O_2 diffusion. Artif Organs 1984;8:478–480.

37. Cilley RE, Polley TZ, Zwischenberger JB, Toomasian JM, Bartlett RH. Independent measurement of oxygen consumption and oxygen delivery. J Surg Res 1989;47:242–247.

38. Cilley RE, Scharenberg AM, Bongiorno PF, Guire

KE, Bartlett RH. Low oxygen delivery produced by anemia, hypoxia and low cardiac output. J Surg Res 1991;51:425–433.

39. Whittlesey GC, Kundu SY, Salley SO, et al. Is heparin necessary for extracorporeal circulation? ASAIO Trans 1988;34:823–826.

40. Wakabayashi A, Chen CC, Mullin PJ, et al. Successful prolonged heparinless venoarterial bypass in sheep. J Thorac Cardiovasc Surg 1976; 71:648–658.

41. Fletcher JR, McKee AE, Herman CM. Membrane oxygenation in baboons without anticoagulants. J Surg Res 1977;22:273–280.

42. Hicks RE, Dutton RC, Ries CA, et al. Production and fate of platelet aggregate emboli during venovenous perfusion. Surg Forum 1973;24: 250–252.

43. Dutton RC, Edmunds LH Jr, Hutchinson JC, et al. Platelet aggregate emboli produced in patients during cardiopulmonary bypass with membrane and bubble oxygenators and blood filters. J Thorac Cardiovasc Surg 1974;67:258–265.

44. Hocker JR, Wellhausen SR, Ward RA, Simpson PM, Cook LN. Effect of extracorporeal membrane oxygenation on leukocyte function in neonates. Artif Organs 1991;15:23–28.

45. DePalma L, Short BL, Van Meurs K, Luban NLC. A flow cytometric analysis of lymphocyte subpopulations in neonates undergoing extracorporeal membrane oxygenation. J Pediatr 1991;118: 117–120.

46. Westfall SH, Stephens C, Kesler K, Connors RH, Tracy TF, Weber TR. Complement activation during prolonged extracorporeal membrane oxygenation. Surgery 1991;110:887–891.

47. Anderson HL III, Coran AG, Drongowski RA, Ha HJ, Bartlett RH. Extracellular fluid and total body water changes in neonates undergoing extracorporeal membrane oxygenation (ECMO). J Pediatr Surg 1992;27:1003–1008.

48. Meliones JN, Moler FW, Custer JR, et al. Hemodynamic instability after the initiation of extracorporeal membrane oxygenation: role of ionized calcium. Crit Care Med 1991;19(1):1247–1251.

49. Vogler C, Sotelo-Avila C, Lagunoff D, Braun P, Schreifels JA, Weber T. Aluminum-containing emboli in infants treated with extracorporeal membrane oxygenation. N Engl J Med 1988; 319:75–79.

50. Kolobow T, Spragg RG, Pierce JE. Massive pulmonary infarction during total cardiopulmonary bypass in unanesthetized spontaneously breathing lambs. Int J Artif Organs 1981;4:76–81.

51. Foster AH, Kolobow T. A potential hazard of ventilation during early separation from total cardiopulmonary bypass [Letter]. J Thorac Cardiovasc Surg 1987;93:150–151.

52. American Academy of Pediatrics Committee on Fetus and Newborn: Recommendations on extracorporeal membrane oxygenation. Pediatrics 1990;85:618–619.

53. Montoya JP, Merz SI, Bartlett RH. A standardized system for describing flow/pressure relationships in vascular access devices. ASAIO Trans 1991;37:4–8.

54. Sinard JM, Merz SI, Hatcher MD, Montoya JP, Bartlett RH. Evaluation of extracorporeal perfusion catheters using a standardized measurement technique—the M-number. ASAIO Trans 1991; 37:60–64.

55. Durandy Y, Chevalier JY, Lecompte Y. Single-cannula venovenous bypass for respiratory membrane lung support. J Thorac Cardiovasc Surg 1990;99:404–409.

56. Heiss KF, Pettit B, Hirschl RB, Cilley RE, Chapman R, Bartlett RH. Renal insufficiency and volume overload in neonatal ECMO managed by continuous ultrafiltration. ASAIO Trans 1987; 33:557–560.

57. Hirschl RB. Cannulation techniques for ECLS. Extracorporeal life support for pediatric and adult cardiorespiratory failure: an introduction to ECLS. In: ELSO course manual. Ann Arbor, MI: University of Michigan, 1991:20.

58. Moulton SL, Lynch FP, Cornish JD, Bejar RF, Simko AJ, Krous HF. Carotid artery reconstruction following neonatal extracorporeal membrane oxygenation. J Pediatr Surg 1991;26: 794–799.

59. Spector ML, Wiznitzer M, Walsh-Sukys MC, Stork EK. Carotid reconstruction in the neonate following ECMO. J Pediatr Surg 1991;26:357–361.

60. Cilley RE, Wesley JR, Zwischenberger JB, Toomasian JM, Bartlett RH. Pulmonary recovery predicted by measurement of pulmonary and membrane lung gas exchange during extracorporeal membrane oxygenation. Surg Forum 1985;36:294–296.

61. Garg M, Lew CD, Ramos AD, Platzker ACG, Keens TG. Serial measurement of pulmonary mechanics assists in weaning from extracorporeal membrane oxygenation in neonates with respiratory failure. Chest 1991;100:770–774.

62. Graves ED, Redmond CR, Arensman RM. Persistent pulmonary hypertension in the neonate. Chest 1988;93:638–641.

63. Krummel TM, Greenfield LJ, Kirkpatrick BV, et al. Alveolar-arterial oxygen gradients versus the neonatal pulmonary insufficiency index for prediction of mortality in ECMO candidates. J Pediatr Surg 1984;19:380–384.

64. Beck R, Anderson KD, Pearson GD, Cronin J, Miller MK, Short BL. Criteria for extracorporeal membrane oxygenation in a population of in-

fants with persistent pulmonary hypertension of the newborn. J Pediatr Surg 1986;21:297–302.

65. Hallman M, Merritt TA, Jarvenpaa AL. Exogenous human surfactant for treatment of severe respiratory distress syndrome: a randomized prospective trial. J Pediatr 1985;106:963–969.

66. Bartlett RH, Gazzaniga AB, Toomasian J, Coran AG, Roloff D, Rucker R, Corwin AG. Extracorporeal membrane oxygenation (ECMO) in neonatal respiratory failure; 100 cases. Ann Surg 1986; 204:236–245.

67. Cilley RE, Zwischenberger JB, Andrews AF, Bowerman RA, Roloff DW, Bartlett RH. Intracranial hemorrhage during extracorporeal membrane oxygenation in neonates. Pediatrics 1986;78:699–704.

68. Bui KC, LaClair P, Vanderkerhove J, Bartlett RH. ECMO in premature infants: review of factors associated with mortality. ASAIO Trans 1991; 37:54–59.

69. Glass P, Miller M, Short B. Morbidity for survivors of extracorporeal membrane oxygenation: neurodevelopmental outcome at 1 year of age. Pediatrics 1989;83:72–78.

70. Schumacher RE, Barks JDE, Johnston MV, et al. Right-sided brain lesions in infants following extracorporeal membrane oxygenation. Pediatrics 1988;82:155–161.

71. Brett C, Dekl M, Leonard CH, et al. Developmental follow-up of hyperventilated neonates: preliminary observations. Pediatrics 1981; 68:588–591.

72. Cohen RS, Stevenson DK, Malachowski N, et al. Late morbidity among survivors of respiratory failure treated with tolazoline. J Pediatr 1980; 97:644–647.

73. Hofkosh D, Thompson AE, Nozza RJ, Kemp SS, Bowen A, Feldman HM. Ten years of extracorporeal membrane oxygenation: neurodevelopmental outcome. Pediatrics 1991;87:549–555.

74. Schumacher RE, Palmer TW, Roloff DW, LaClaire PA, Bartlett RH. Follow-up of infants treated with extracorporeal membrane oxygenation for newborn respiratory failure. Pediatrics 1991;87: 451–457.

75. Extracorporeal life support organization registry. Ann Arbor, MI: University of Michigan Press, October 1991.

76. Kolobow T. Acute respiratory failure: on how to injure healthy lungs (and prevent sick lungs from recovering). ASAIO Trans 1988;34:31–34.

26

Extracorporeal Cardiopulmonary Support for Resuscitation and Invasive Cardiology Outside the Operating Suite

Thomas X. Aufiero and Walter E. Pae, Jr.

HISTORICAL BACKGROUND

It was the lack of a rapid effective treatment for moribund patients with pulmonary embolus that led John Gibbon to begin his pioneering work with extracorporeal cardiopulmonary support. Gibbon himself was never able to treat such a patient, but in 1961, Cooley et al. (1) utilized emergency cardiopulmonary bypass (CPB) to support a patient with a massive pulmonary embolus. The patient was eventually transported to the operating theater, where the embolus was removed with cardiopulmonary support, and ultimately survived to be discharged from the hospital. In this case report, Cooley and his co-workers suggested the need for a less cumbersome system specially adapted for use in emergency and resuscitative situations. The early years of CPB saw many other reports on the use of this modality as a resuscitative device (1–3).

Stuckey (2) in 1958 reported a series of three patients treated with CPB for cardiogenic shock following acute myocardial infarction. Despite criteria that patients be moribund before inclusion, one patient survived to ultimate hospital discharge. This was a time when open chest cardiopulmonary resuscitation (CPR) was limited mostly to the operating room, and closed chest CPR and cardiac resuscitation was just beginning to become an accepted practice (4).

In the 1960s there was an explosion of new operative techniques, permitted by the new and rapidly improving technology of CPB. Investigators continued to explore the role of CPB as a resuscitative tool (3, 5). In 1966, Proctor (6) evaluated the technique, being interested in whether the left side of the heart could be adequately decompressed, a question that remains today. He concluded, "there appears to be no insoluble problem in the use of the technique of closed-chest, venoarterial bypass by peripheral cannulation in acute myocardial infarction with severe shock or cardiac arrest." However, the technique was not immediately grasped and put into widespread use.

May et al. (7), in 1971, suggested that the technology could be utilized in the growing number of community hospitals. They reported 10 patients who required resuscitation and support with CPB during noncardiac emergency operations. These included pulmonary embolectomy, traumatic rupture of the aorta, aortopulmonary fistula, and an aortic arch injury. Nine of the 10 patients were transferred while on CPB, from as far away as 75 miles. However, during the next 20 years, there was only sporadic interest in using CPB as a resuscitative measure. Most investigators were discouraged with the overall poor clinical outcome, due mainly to the long periods of time necessary to institute CPB. The skill required to perform femoral artery cutdowns, as well as the time and difficulty encountered during the performance of CPR were limiting factors (8). Furthermore, the equipment necessary was cumbersome.

More recently, several developments have caused a resurgence of interest in extracorporeal cardiopulmonary support for resuscitation outside the operating room environment, and elective use in assisted angioplasty. Cannulae have been developed that allow rapid percutaneous placement using the Seldinger technique, providing adequate systemic flow and venous drainage to decompress the heart. Commercial compact portable bypass systems have been developed that use vortex pumps without venous reservoirs (Figure 26.1).

TECHNIQUES

The institution of CPB in the emergency setting by cannulation of the femoral vessels has been accepted since the early days of bypass. This was initially done with direct visualization of the vessels through a groin incision. There are limitations to this technique. Although a skilled surgeon can rapidly isolate and cannulate the vessels, the technique is cumbersome to carry out

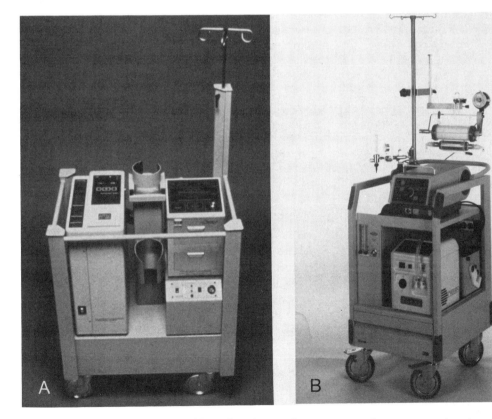

Figure 26.1. **A.** The Bard CPS portable cardiopulmonary bypass system. (Photo courtesy of Bard Cardiopulmonary Division, Billerica, MA.) **B.** The Sarns PERcart unit. (Photo courtesy of Sarns 3M Health Care, Ann Arbor, MI.)

while conventional CPR is being performed. Resuscitative cardiopulmonary
support was also dependent on a surgeon
being available to perform the cutdown.
This may have excluded many patients from
the technique, or unnecessarily delayed the
institution of CPB. In addition, the early
cannulae used did not always allow satisfactory flow rates or venous drainage. Philips
et al. (9) have suggested using thin-walled
sheaths for the rapid percutaneous institution of CPB. Using two 30-cm 12 French venous cannulae and a single 15-cm 12
French arterial cannula, they were able to
achieve flow rates of 2 to 2.5 liters/min.
Several manufacturers now package systems
designed for the rapid institution of CPB
(e.g., Bard Cardiopulmonary, Billerica, MA;
Biomedicus Medtronics, Inc., Minneapolis,
MN). (Figs. 26.2 and 26.3). The cannulae
range in size from 12 to 19 French for arterial cannulation and from 17 to 24 French
for venous cannulation, providing flow
rates up to 5 liters/min using a vortex pump
without a venous reservoir.

Insertion Techniques

PERCUTANEOUS

After both groins have been sterilized
and prepared with an antiseptic solution,
local anesthesia is utilized as necessary. The
femoral artery and vein are then punctured
using a thin-walled needle and a guide wire
is placed. When performed in the catheterization laboratory, fluoroscopy can be utilized to assist in cannulation. In elective settings, a femoral arteriogram is performed to
define the anatomy and ensure the patency
and caliber of the femoral artery. The skin is
then incised and the patient is systemically
heparinized with heparin, 300 units per
kilogram. Activated whole blood clotting
times are measured and maintained at
>300 seconds (we choose >475 seconds
in our practice) with additional doses of
heparin as needed. The vessel is then suc-
cessively dilated with 8, 12, and 14 French
dilators passed over a long stiff guide wire.
The cannulae are now exchanged over the

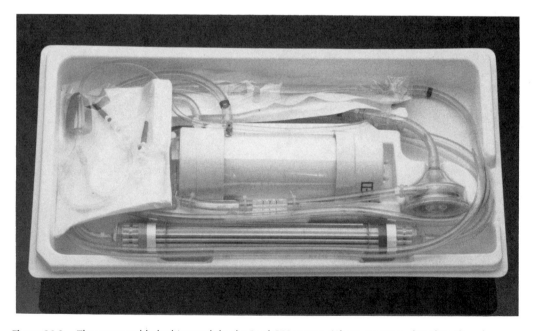

Figure 26.2. The preassembled tubing pack for the Bard CPS system. (Photo courtesy of Bard Cardiopulmonary Division, Billerica, MA.)

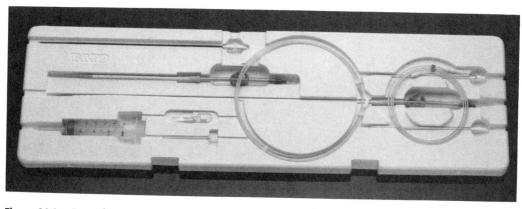

Figure 26.3. Prepackaged cannulae for percutaneous bypass, available from Bard Cardiopulmonary. (Photo courtesy of Bard Cardiopulmonary Division, Billerica, MA.)

guide wire. A 19-cm long 20 French multi-hole venous cannula and 17 or 18 French short arterial cannulae are most commonly utilized. The cannulae are then allowed to fill with blood and clamped until connected to the bypass circuit (Fig. 26.4).

DIRECT VISUALIZATION

Cannulation of the femoral artery and vein under direct vision and removal with repair of the puncture site is preferred to percutaneous cannulation except in emergency situations, or when a prolonged support period is anticipated, as in the case of extracorporeal membrane oxygenation. Under aseptic conditions and with suitable local anesthesia, a longitudinal incision is made from the inguinal ligament inferiorly for approximately 15 cm, and the femoral artery and vein exposed. For arterial cannulation, the common femoral, profunda femoral, and superficial femoral arteries are isolated with Dacron tapes. Following the administration of heparin, the superficial and profunda femoral arteries are clamped with noncrushing vascular clamps. A Rummel tourniquet is placed around the common femoral artery and a transverse arteriotomy is performed. A 17 or 19 French arterial cannula is then passed and secured with the Rummel tourniquet. Venous cannulation with a long 19 or 20 French multi-holed cannula is performed in a similar

fashion. Alternatively, the Seldinger technique can be used with the vessels in direct vision without isolation. This eliminates the time needed to encircle the vessels and perform an arteriotomy, thus allowing for more rapid insertion.

The Bypass Circuit

The early emergency pump oxygenator circuits used for resuscitation were simply scaled down versions of the pump oxygenator circuit used in the operating room, with a battery pack attached. The development of smaller, more efficient, and less traumatic membrane oxygenators, as well as widespread acceptance of centrifugal pumps, has added much to the resurgence of interest in emergency extracorporeal circulation. It is not in the scope of this chapter to discuss the pros and cons of membrane versus bubble oxygenators, or roller pumps as opposed to vortex pumps. However, the most commonly used systems for emergency extracorporeal support consist of a hollow fiber membrane oxygenator and a centrifugal pump head (Fig. 26.5). No venous reservoir bag is utilized. The system can be rapidly primed by any trained individual, allowing set-up while the perfusionist is still enroute to the hospital. The absence of a venous reservoir in the circuit allows improved flow rates since venous

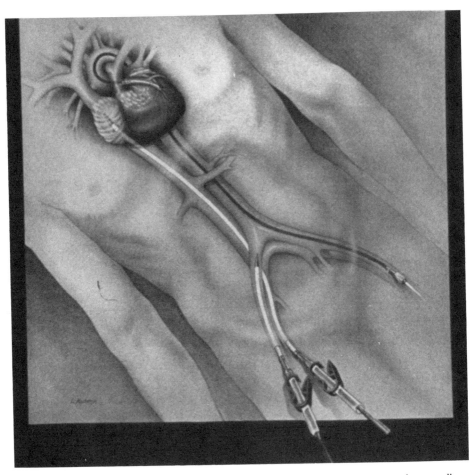

Figure 26.4. An artist's rendition showing percutaneously placed arterial and venous cannulae as well as an angioplasty catheter. Cannulation of the right groin permits easier positioning of the venous catheter. (Photo courtesy of Bard Cardiopulmonary Division, Billerica, MA.)

drainage is by suction rather than by conventional gravity drainage. The vortical pumps employed also provide a certain edge of safety in preventing the pumping of massive amounts of air. Because of the aspirating nature of venous return, however, care must be taken that all central venous lines are closed to air, and no central venipunctures should be attempted while on bypass.

Initiation of Bypass

Prior to initiating bypass, it is imperative to ascertain that all central catheters are closed to air, and to confirm that heparin has been given by measuring activated clotting time. The venous line is opened first. The arterial line is then opened, while pump flow is increased to prevent retrograde flow. When the clamp is fully opened, pump speed is increased until a corresponding increase in blood flow cannot be seen. Pulmonary ventilation should continue, especially if the left ventricle is ejecting. In these bypass systems without venous reservoirs, the need for peripheral vasoconstrictors is observed to be much less than for conventional bypass. "Venous chatter" and decreasing pump flows are often the effect of intravascular hypovolemia and can be improved by administration of fluid.

Although fluid can be rapidly transfused via the priming line, care must be taken not to introduce air when doing so. This route is best reserved for situations where large volumes are needed immediately to maintain adequate pump flows. Small amounts of air may diffuse out through the membrane lung, and large amounts may be trapped in the centrifugal pump, but care should still be exercised not to admit any to the circuit inadvertently.

Once the patient has been stabilized on CPB, attempts to correct the underlying problems can begin. If the patient has been in intractable ventricular fibrillation, defibrillation should again be attempted. Continued CPR may be of value to further decompress the heart. A pulmonary artery catheter should be used to confirm that the heart is decompressed. Kolobow et al. (10) have suggested that a percutaneously placed spring-like device, directed into the pulmonary artery, could be used to aid in decompression of the left heart. Aortic insufficiency is a relative contraindication to this

technique because of the massive ventricular distension that will occur with retrograde flow in the aorta and an incompetent aortic valve. Additionally, in some patients with ventricular fibrillation, left ventricular decompression will be difficult to achieve with closed chest bypass and the lack of direct ventricular venting.

Cardiac catheterization and/or angioplasty can now be performed as indicated. In elective angioplasty situations, central venous catheters should be placed prior to the initiation of bypass. In emergency situations, extreme care must be used not to allow air to be aspirated into the system while positioning and flushing the cannulae. Patients can be transported while on bypass, whether from the nursing unit to the catheterization laboratory, catheterization laboratory to operating room, or rarely from hospital to hospital. Hill et al. (11) have had three patients who required that CPB be instituted at the referral hospital and were then transported utilizing combinations of ground transport and helicopter

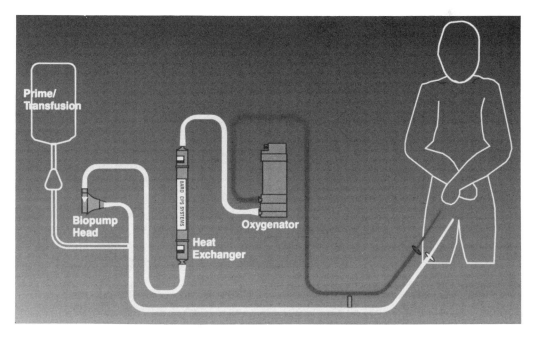

Figure 26.5.   A schematic diagram of an emergency bypass system utilizing a vortex pump and without a venous reservoir. (Photo courtesy of Bard Cardiopulmonary Division, Billerica, MA.)

or fixed wing aircraft. Prior to transporting patients, a secure and transportable oxygen source and a reliable battery must be available. It is also mandatory to carefully secure the bypass lines to the patient to prevent dislodgement during transport. Transport demands prior planning to ensure that patient, equipment, and personnel will all fit safely and that the personnel are familiar with the transportation vehicles.

Weaning from Bypass and Decannulation

By reducing the blood pump speed, blood flow through the system is gradually reduced while the patient's hemodynamic status is monitored. The need for inotropic and/or intraaortic balloon pump support is assessed by the pulmonary capillary wedge pressure, cardiac output, systemic blood pressure, and calculated systemic vascular resistance. When flow through the vortex pump reaches 0.5 liters/min, the arterial line is clamped. When bypass is discontinued in the operating room, protamine sulfate is always given to reverse the heparin, and the cannulae are removed under direct vision with operative repair. Some (12) have suggested when the procedure is performed in the catheterization laboratory that the cannulae not be removed initially, but that they be removed in the intensive care unit several hours after the last heparin dose, after confirming that the activated clotting time is less than 240 seconds. The cannulae are then removed and a C-clamp device left in place in the groin for several hours. We have found that this practice carries an inordinately high risk of complication referable to the cannulation site, and suggest that placement and removal under direct vision and repair offer the best chance of avoiding these complications (13). Complications requiring operative intervention have occurred in as many as 10% of patients who have had percutaneous cannulae placed and removed without di-

rect visualization and repair of the vessels (14).

INDICATIONS

The indications for the use of CPB outside the operating room can be grouped into two broad categories, assisted angioplasty and resuscitation. Certainly there is some overlap between these two groups, as patients resuscitated from cardiac arrest have undergone subsequent cardiac catheterization and angioplasty while on extracorporeal support. Also, the most uniformly successful results for survival following resuscitation with bypass have been observed in patients whose arrest occurred in or near the catheterization laboratory. Other indications, such as multiple trauma, severe exposure hypothermia, and drug overdoses, have been anecdotally reported.

Assisted Angioplasty

When angioplasty was first introduced in 1977(14), it was applied to stable patients with preserved left ventricular function and single vessel coronary artery disease. Since that time, the application of the technique has exploded dramatically to encompass patients with multivessel disease as well as impaired left ventricular function. Despite advances in techniques, coronary angioplasty still carries a 5% risk of acute vessel closure (15), often requiring emergency CPB and coronary bypass surgery. This emergency surgery has been associated with higher rates of morbidity and mortality (16).

Coronary angioplasty has also been expanded to include a group of patients who are not considered to be candidates for coronary artery bypass. These include patients with severely depressed left ventricular function (ejection fraction <25%), lack of suitable conduits or target vessels for coronary bypass, and multiple noncardiac diseases. However, many of these patients also would not tolerate transient vessel occlusion associated with balloon inflation, or would not tolerate the delay associated with the institution of CPB and surgical revascularization should acute vessel occlusion occur. Multiple techniques have been suggested to support this type of patient during coronary angioplasty (17). These include intraaortic balloon counterpulsation, antegrade coronary perfusion either with a "bailout" catheter or a perfusion balloon catheter, coronary sinus retroperfusion, and cardiopulmonary support.

Kanter et al. (18) extrapolated the use of CPB as a resuscitative tool into the catheterization laboratory in 1988. They reported six patients resuscitated from cardiac arrest or cardiogenic shock with CPB. Shawl and his group (19, 20) have reported a number of patients who have had cardiopulmonary support in both the emergency and elective situations of high-risk angioplasty and valvuloplasty (19). These include 35 patients who had percutaneous cardiopulmonary support instituted prior to angioplasty (20). A national registry of 14 centers performing elective supportive angioplasty has reported 105 patients who underwent supported angioplasty in 1988 (21). Their entrance criteria included ejection fractions less than 25%, a target vessel that supplied more than one-half of the myocardium, severe or unstable angina, and the presence of at least one vessel likely to be dilatable. In this group, the angioplasty success rate was 95%; however, 27 patients suffered a complication referable to vessel cannulation, while 14 had postangioplasty ischemia or infarction. Although no patients became bypass-dependent, there were eight (7.6%) in-hospital deaths. With the growth of interventional cardiology, and the introduction of atherectomy and laser devices, the use of assisted angioplasty is expected to increase. Two major issues that remain unresolved are patient selection for assisted angioplasty, and means of ensuring ventricular decompression.

In elective situations such as most supported angioplasties, the patient usually remains awake or lightly sedated. Supplemental oxygen and sedation with benzodiazepines (e.g., midazolam) and opiates (e.g., fentanyl) are commonly provided by an anesthesiologist. Some centers opt for general anesthesia and endotracheal intubation with mechanical ventilation for these procedures. While perhaps providing a more controlled situation, clinical experience indicates that this latter approach is not required.

Patients with acute myocardial infarction and cardiogenic shock are poor candidates for medical (thrombolytic) reperfusion. Percutaneous transluminal coronary angioplasty has been utilized with a 56% survival rate in selected patients (22). Certainly the optimal therapy in these patients is lacking, and as knowledge accumulates regarding reperfusion injury, perhaps more suitable strategies and results will follow. For example, Okamoto et al. (23) have proposed a system to allow for assisted angioplasty and controlled reperfusion with substrate-enriched blood cardioplegia during total vented bypass without thoracotomy. Their proposed system includes institution of bypass early to slow infarction and direct left ventricular venting with a transaortic cannula. This is then followed by angioplasty and direct reperfusion. This constitutes an interesting concept with future promise.

Resuscitation

Since the early 1960s, closed-chest massage for CPR has been used routinely (24). Despite the advancement of cardiac life support and the modification of techniques (25), the survival rate after CPR for in-hospital cardiac arrest has remained disappointingly low (26). In 1813, LeGallois proposed that organ function could be supported by an external source of oxygenated blood (27). Modern heart-lung machine technology represents an outgrowth of this concept. However, when extracorporeal cardiopulmonary support has been employed as a resuscitative measure, the results have not been uniformly successful. The recent development of systems specifically designed for resuscitation may allow for improvement upon these results.

Patients who have suffered cardiac arrest in or near the cardiac catheterization laboratory or intensive care unit have benefitted most from emergency cardiopulmonary support. Mooney et al. (28) have reviewed the literature on this topic and demonstrated a markedly improved survival when using this technique in patients who arrested in the catheterization laboratory when compared to patients whose arrest occurred outside the catheterization laboratory. Several reasons are proposed to account for these results including a better knowledge of the patient and the underlying pathology, as well as a more precise timing of the event. The immediate availability of personnel capable of initiating CPB probably also improved survival in these patients.

Other Indications

Emergency CPB has been utilized as a resuscitative adjunct for several other groups of patients. In 1976, Mattox and Beal (29) expanded on the earlier work of Cooley et al. (30) and reported 39 patients who had emergency bypass instituted outside the operating room. Thirteen of 19 patients with massive pulmonary embolus survived operation. Twenty-six of the 39 were able to be weaned from CPB and 15 were considered to be long-term survivors. In this report, 10 patients were placed on portable bypass because of massive thoracic trauma. Only one patient in this group survived to discharge. The use of CPB in the setting of massive trauma has been reported since this time (31, 32), but because of the need for systemic heparinization, it has remained disappointing. Recently, however,

Bennett et al. (33) have reported support of a patient with multiple trauma using heparinless bypass and a heparin-coated circuit. This patient was on bypass for over 5 hours and underwent multiple diagnostic procedures as well as a splenectomy and a nephrectomy. He was able to be discharged from the hospital 85 days later. It is possible that this technology will open these techniques to a whole new group of patients.

Cardiopulmonary bypass with active rewarming has been used to salvage patients with severe hypothermia secondary to environmental exposure. Since many of these patients die as a result of ventricular arrhythmias or circulatory collapse, CPB is an attractive method of rewarming. The introduction of rapid femoral cannulation techniques (34) should lead to greater utilization and easier application for these patients.

CONCLUSIONS

The use of emergency CPB systems is expanding rapidly because of the increasing availability of compact commercial systems and femoral catheters with more acceptable flow characteristics. Familiarity with these systems has also improved with the increasing numbers of assisted angioplasties. As these two factors have developed, the indications for cardiopulmonary support have also expanded. Still, most individual centers do not have large enough numbers of similar patients to form solid conclusions regarding which patients will be most apt to benefit from the use of emergency bypass. Presently, two separate registries exist to evaluate data from multiple centers.

Both groups have recently reported updates. Hill et al. (35) reported 187 patients from 17 centers. The majority of patients required bypass for cardiac arrest (125) or cardiogenic shock (44). Thirty percent of patients were successfully weaned from bypass with a 21% survival at 30 days. Importantly, there were no survivors from unwitnessed arrests, and 77% of survivors had a major therapeutic intervention performed while on bypass. Overlie et al. (36) similarly reported 153 patients who were placed on CPB for cardiac arrest (120) or cardiogenic shock (33). They reported a similar survival of 27%. Long-term follow-up of patients who underwent high-risk supported angioplasty was reported by Shawl et al. (37). At 25 months, 121 of 142 patients had survived, with 86% remaining asymptomatic or in New York Heart Association Class 1 (37).

Emergency CPB systems can provide meaningful survival to a select group of patients who were previously considered unsalvageable. Still, certain guidelines appear necessary. Patients with unwitnessed cardiac arrest who are not profoundly hypothermic are not candidates. Those patients who have correctable underlying pathologies, whether anatomic or metabolic, have improved survival. A prolonged period of conventional CPR (greater than 30 minutes) is a relative contraindication to the use of CPB. Presently, patients with multiple trauma or intracranial hemorrhage are poor candidates because of the necessity for anticoagulation. The use of heparin-bonded circuits may further improve survival and increase the usefulness of extracorporeal life support in these groups.

The increasing ease of set-up and initiation of bypass, coupled with the greater availability of portable bypass systems, will tempt those not now familiar with CPB to initiate emergency bypass. This may become an acceptable reality in the future, but at present it appears that continuing to limit the technique to application by cardiac surgeons and selected interventional cardiologists is prudent.

REFERENCES

1. Cooley DA, Beal AC, Alexander JK. Acute massive pulmonary embolism—successful surgical treatment using temporary cardiopulmonary bypass. JAMA 1965;193:117–118.
2. Stuckey JA. The use of the heart lung machine in selected cases of acute myocardial infarction. Surg Forum 1958;8:342–344.
3. Joseph WL, Maloney JV Jr. Extracorporeal circulation as an adjunct to resuscitation of the heart. JAMA 1965;193:117–118
4. Kouwenhoven WB, Jude JE, Knickerbocker GG. Closed chest cardiac massage. JAMA 1960; 173:1064–1067.
5. Kennedy JH. The role of assisted circulation in cardiac resuscitation. JAMA 1965;197:97–100.
6. Proctor E. Closed-chest circulatory support by pump-oxygenator in experimental ventricular fibrillation at normal temperature. Thorax 1966; 21:385–390.
7. May IA, Hardy KL, Samson PC. Emergency bypass for the community. Am J Surg 1971;122: 256–259.
8. Phillips SJ, Zeff RH, Kongtahworn C. Percutaneous cardiopulmonary bypass: application and indication for use. Ann Thorac Surg 1989; 47:121–123.
9. Philips SJ, Ballentine B, Slonine D, et al. Percutaneous initiation of cardiopulmonary bypass. Ann Thorac Surg 1983;36:223–225.
10. Kolobow T, Rossi F, Borelli M, et al. Long-term closed chest partial and total cardiopulmonary bypass by peripheral cannulation for severe right and/or left ventricular failure, including ventricular fibrillation. Trans Am Soc Artif Intern Organs 1988;34:485–489.
11. Hill JG, Bennett J, Parson J, et al. Personal communication, 1991.
12. Shawl FA, Domanski MJ, Wish MH, et al. Percutaneous cardiopulmonary bypass support in the catheterization laboratory: technique and complications. Am Heart J 1990;120:195–203.
13. Davis PK, Iams WB, Myers JL. Clinical experience with a new portable rapid access cardiopulmonary support (CPS) system. Unpublished results, presented at the Circulatory support Topical meeting of the Society of Thoracic Surgeons, 1988, St. Louis, MO.
14. Gruentzig A. Transluminal dilatation of coronary artery stenosis. Lancet 1978;1:263–265.
15. Cowley MJ, Dorros G, Kelsey SF, et al. Acute coronary events associated with percutaneous transluminal coronary angioplasty. Am J Cardiol 1984;53:12C–16C.
16. Roubin GS, Talley JD, Anderson HV, et al. Morbidity and mortality associated with emergency bypass graft surgery following elective coronary angioplasty [Abstract]. J Am Coll Cardiol 1987;9:124A.
17. Lincoff AM, Popura JJ, Ellis SG, et al. Percutaneous support devices for high risk or complicated coronary angioplasty. J Am Coll Cardiol 1991;17:770–780.
18. Kanter KR, Pennington DG, Vandormael M.

Emergency resuscitation with extracorporeal membrane oxygenation for failed angioplasty [Abstract]. J Am Coll Cardiol 1988;11:149.

19. Shawl FA: Percutaneous cardiopulmonary support in high-risk angioplasty. Cardiol Clin 1989; 7:865–875.

20. Shawl FA, Domanski MS, Punja S, et al. Percutaneous cardiopulmonary bypass to support high-risk elective coronary angioplasty [Abstract]. J Am Coll Cardiol 1989;13:160A.

21. Vogel RA, Shawl F, Tommaso C, et al. Initial report of the national registry of elective cardiopulmonary bypass supported coronary angioplasty. J Am Coll Cardiol 1990;15:23–29.

22. Hibbard MD, Holmes DR, Gersh BJ, et al. Coronary angioplasty for acute myocardial infarction complicated by cardiogenic shock [Abstract]. Circulation 1990;82:III–511.

23. Okamoto F, Allen BS, Buckberg GD, et al. Studies of controlled reperfusion after ischemia VII. Regional blood cardioplegic reperfusion during total vented bypass without thoracotomy: a new concept. J Thorac Cardiovasc Surg 1986;92: 553–563.

24. Kouwenhoven WB, Jude JR, Knickerbocker GG. Closed chest cardiac massage. JAMA 1960; 173:1064–1067.

25. American Heart Association. Standards and guidelines for cardiopulmonary resuscitation and emergency cardiac care. JAMA 1980;244: 462–468.

26. Bedell SH, Delbanco TL, Cook EF, et al. Survival after cardiopulmonary resuscitation in the hospital. N Engl J Med 1983;309:569–608.

27. Nelson RM. Era of extracorporeal respiration. Surgery 1975;78:685–693.

28. Mooney MR, Arom KV, Joyce LD, et al. Emergency cardiopulmonary bypass support in patients with cardiac arrest. J Thorac Cardiovasc Surg 1991;101:450–454.

29. Mattox KL, Beal AC Jr. Resuscitation of the moribund patient using portable cardiopulmonary bypass. Ann Thorac Surg 1976;22:436–442.

30. Cooley DA, Beall AC Jr, Alexander JL. Acute massive pulmonary embolism: successful surgical treatment using temporary cardiopulmonary bypass. JAMA 1961;177:283–286.

31. Reichman RT, Joyo CI, Dembitsky WP. Improved patient survival after cardiac arrest using a cardiopulmonary support system. Ann Thorac Surg 1990;49:101–105.

32. Phillips SJ. Percutaneous cardiopulmonary bypass and innovations in clinical counterpulsation. Crit Care Clin 1986;2:297–318.

33. Bennett J, Hill J, Bruhn P, et al. Heparin-free cardiopulmonary support, utilizing a carmeda coated circuit, for a patient with pulmonary hemorrhage and multiple trauma. J Extra-Corpor Technol 1992;23:86–89.

34. Lamb GW, Banaszak D, Kupferschmid J. Percutaneous cardiopulmonary bypass for the treatment of hypothermic circulatory collapse. Ann Thorac Surg 1989;47:608–611.

35. Hill J, Bruhn P, Cohen S, et al. Emergent applications of cardiopulmonary support: a multi institutional experience. Presented at the Southern Thoracic Surgical Association 38th Annual Meeting, 1991, Orlando, FL.

36. Overlie PA, Vogel RA, O'Neill WW, et al. Emergency cardiopulmonary bypass: initial report of the national registry of supported angioplasty participants. Circulation 1991;84:II–132.

37. Shawl F, Domanski M, Wish M. Cardiopulmonary bypass supported PTCA: long term follow up in 142 high risk patients. Circulation 1991;84: II–132.

27

CIRCULATORY ASSIST DEVICES: APPLICATIONS FOR VENTRICULAR RECOVERY OR BRIDGE TO TRANSPLANT

Francisco A. Arabia, Jack G. Copeland, Douglas F. Larson,
Richard G. Smith, and Marilyn R. Cleavinger

CLINICAL APPLICATIONS AND MANAGEMENT

At the present time, orthotopic heart transplantation is acknowledged as the best therapy for end-stage congestive heart failure. It is estimated that 164,000 people in the United States die each year as a result of end-stage heart disease. About 20 to 40% of potential cardiac recipients die while waiting for a heart transplant (1). Approximately 1600 to 2000 heart transplants are performed every year under the current procurement system (2, 3). The discrepancy between the possible recipients and the available donors generates a realistic need for circulatory support systems for cardiac support and replacement.

The first indication for use of mechanical circulatory assist was for the treatment of postcardiotomy cardiogenic shock (4–7). This category encompasses approximately 2000 patients who cannot be weaned from cardiopulmonary bypass (CPB) (8). Some circulatory devices were designed for this purpose, "pending recovery of the natural heart." Some of these systems, and others, are currently being used for a second indication: temporary cardiac support until a donor heart becomes

available for transplantation or "bridge to transplantation" (9–13). As progress continues to be made in the medical and engineering sciences, there is no doubt that permanent assist devices or devices that will totally replace the heart will some day become available.

The spectrum of devices discussed in this chapter ranges from the intraaortic balloon pump (IABP) to the total artificial heart (TAH). Each system is described in detail.

PATIENT SELECTION, INITIATION OF SUPPORT, OUTCOME

Patients with severe cardiac failure are at once diverse, with each patient having a unique constellation of medical history and organ dysfunction, and homogeneous with each patient also sharing many aspects of congestive heart failure, low output syndrome, and cardiogenic shock. They frequently have been treated with maximal medical inotropic and afterload reduction therapy and often have had treatment with an intraaortic balloon pump as well. For those who continue to decompensate, a number of possible solutions are available.

Patient selection is the most important factor in determining survival with mechanical circulatory assistance (6, 14, 15). The younger the patient, the better the survival. The experience with the use of postcardiotomy devices for cardiac recovery has shown that patients younger than 60 years have a survival rate of 21 to 31%, patients older than 60 years have a survival of 12%. The survival rate for patients over 70 years is 6%. Other factors that contribute to the success of these devices include the performance and selection of the device, and the skill, experience, and judgment of the surgeon who is using these devices (16).

A variety of criteria have been used in the past as guidelines for placement of ventricular assistance (Table 27.1). The aggregate of these criteria functions as a definition of cardiogenic shock (17). These criteria are presented as the basic guidelines and are not exclusive of other considerations, such as (*a*) requirement for high-dose catecholamine support with or without adjuvant drugs such as phosphodiesterose III inhibitors, (*b*) systemic hypotension (mean arterial pressure <60, systolic <80 mm Hg), (*c*) respiratory distress, (*d*) waxing and waning state of consciousness, (*e*) failure to separate from bypass, and (*f*) metabolic acidosis, etc. Common to all of these patients is a global picture indicating inadequate perfusion of organs and tissues as a result of cardiac failure. Prompt institution of mechanical circulatory assistance is of great importance. Prolonged hypotension (>12 hours) is associated with multisystem failure and poor recovery (16). In order to simultaneously assess the physiologic need and the results of circulatory support, the cardiac output and direct atrial pressures should be measured. In this context, direct left atrial pressure is preferable to pulmonary capillary wedge pressure measurement as an index of left ventricular failure since the latter may be less accurate in face of pulmonary edema. The need for univentricular or biventricular support should also be addressed very early in the process of determining the degree of support. Patients who are bridge to transplant candidates often require biventricular support. Patients who have a low right atrial pressure, normal or slightly elevated pulmonary vascular resistance, and no ventricular arrhythmias may benefit from left ventricular support only. Approximately 20% of patients who receive left ventricular support ultimately require right ventricular support as well (18–20). A large number of patients require inotropes for right ventricular support during the first 48 hours after implantation of a left ventricular device. The current criteria most often used to differentiate between the need for univentricular or biventricular support are summarized in Table 27.2.

The merits of paracorporeal biventricular support versus left ventricular support may be disputed, but once the decision to provide support is made, there is little technically to separate the two approaches. The only requirements for biventricular support are two extra cannulae and a few extra minutes of operating time. Biventricular support is not associated with a higher incidence of thrombotic, infectious, cannulation, and mechanical problems as compared to univentricular assist (21). It appears that mortality is higher in the patients receiving biventricular support; however, whether this is due to the degree of preexisting myocardial damage that dictates biventricular rather than univentricular support rather than to

Table 27.1.   Criteria for Placement of VAD[a]

Cardiac index <2.0 liters/min/m^2
Systemic vascular resistance >2100 dyn-sec/cm^{-5}
Atrial pressure >20 mm Hg
Urine output <20 ml/hr with
  Optimal preload
  Maximal drug therapy
  Corrected metabolism
  IABP

[a]Adapted from Pennington DG, Swartz LD, Pae WE, Burkholder JA. Circulatory support symposium 1988: patient selection. Ann Thorac Surg 1989;47:77–81.

Table 27.2. Criteria of Support[a]

Right ventricular failure: right VAD and IABP
  Left atrial pressure <15 mm Hg
  Right atrial pressure >20 mm Hg
  Few or no arrhythmias
  Near normal left ventricle function by
    echocardiogram, ventriculogram, or MUGA[b]
Left ventricular failure: left VAD only
  Left atrial pressure >20 mm Hg
  Right atrial pressure <15 mm Hg
  Few or no arrhythmias
  Near normal pulmonary vascular resistance
  Normal right ventricle function by echocardiogram,
    ventriculogram, or MUGA[b]
Biventricular failure: right VAD plus left VAD ± IABP
  Right and left atrial pressures, ≥20 mm Hg
  Ventricular tachycardia or fibrillation
  Severely impaired right and left ventricular function
    by echocardiogram, ventriculogram or MUGA[b]

[a] Adapted from Pennington DG, Reedy JE, Swartz MT, et al. Univentricular versus biventricular assist device support. J Heart Lung Transplant 1991;10:258–263.
[b] Multigated acquisition scan.

the extent of support per se has not been established. The need for univentricular versus biventricular support should be individualized for each patient.

Another factor that has to be taken into consideration once the need for support has been established is whether a continuous flow or pulsatile device should be used. The use of prolonged continuous flow has been associated with end-organ dysfunction (14). The use of an intraaortic balloon pump in addition to a continuous flow device (centrifugal pump) appears to improve end-organ function (22). If a device that provides pulsatile flow is chosen, then selection must be made between synchronous or asynchronous contractions of the device with the native heart. Synchronous counterpulsatile flow has been postulated to improve myocardial recovery when reversible damage is suspected and a need to augment blood flow to the endocardium is desired. Asynchronous pulsatile flow may be used when there is irreversible myocardial damage and maximal blood flow is required to maintain end-organ function. Other considerations may also be important, such as the inability to track the ECG

in tachyarrythmias and chaotic rhythms, desirability of controlling rate to optimize device filling or to decrease the amount of device-related hemolysis, and the mode of device filling may dictate a counter-pulsating pumping mode. Each device has its own peculiarities in this area.

AVAILABILITY OF DEVICES

In 1976, an amendment to the Food, Drug and Cosmetics Act gave the Food and Drug Administration (FDA) the responsibility to oversee clinical trials. Inherent in this regulation is the requirement that the FDA must ensure that anticipated benefits to the individual patient, and to society at large, outweigh the risks involved in subjecting patients to an unproven device. Before any clinical trials begin, the FDA reviews an application known as an Investigational Device Exemption (IDE) submitted by the sponsor of the proposed study. The IDE application contains information such as a description of the device; materials and manufacturing; a description of any bench and animal testing; results and conclusions from these tests; a protocol of the proposed clinical trial including indications, criteria for patient selection, methods proposed to evaluate the results, and a patient-informed consent document (23). Studies are overseen by an institutional review board at each site where the study is to take place. The institutional review board is expected "to apply local community attitudes and ethical standards in making a judgment that the benefits to subjects and the knowledge to be gained outweigh the risks" (24).

Because devices that existed before 1976 did not require an IDE application, any device that could show "substantial equivalence" to a preamendment device could be exempted from the IDE requirement by filing a request for exemption (510k). Importantly, the device categories of balloon pumps, centrifugal pumps, and resuscitative systems do not require an IDE because similar technology existed prior to

1976. Although centrifugal pump technology existed prior to the amendment, its use for ventricular assistance did not. Because of the absence of a rigorous clinical study with these exempted devices, issues involving patient selection, complications, and informed consent are unclear (25). Once the IDE study is concluded, the accumulated data are submitted to the FDA for premarketing approval. The FDA staff and a panel of non-FDA experts review all data presented by the IDE sponsor. Approval at this point is the prerequisite to marketing any new device.

COMPLICATIONS OF CIRCULATORY SUPPORT SYSTEMS

Bleeding

Bleeding can be quite significant at the time of placement of an intrathoracic device, especially if CPB has taken more than 2½ hours. Activation of platelets and the coagulation system by exposure of the blood to artificial surfaces and turbulent flow patterns of the heart-lung machine may lead to a severe coagulopathy characterized by platelet dysfunction (26) (see Chapter 16). Once control of surgical bleeding has been obtained, control of bleeding from suture lines, conduits, and raw surfaces as a result of deficiencies in the coagulation system become the next major clinical undertaking. Clear professional communication between the surgeon, anesthesiologist, hematologist, and blood bank may prove to be life-saving if persistent bleeding continues. Prompt control of bleeding is necessary to decrease the incidence of end-organ dysfunction as a result of transfusions.

The bleeding time becomes greater than 30 minutes after 2 hours of CPB (27). It appears that the platelets become dysfunctional when they interact with the oxygenator surfaces, either bubble or membrane. Normalization of this platelet function impairment appears to begin 30 minutes after termination of CPB. A platelet count above $100,000/\mu l$, with normally functioning platelets, should provide clinically adequate hemostasis. A platelet count below this level, at the completion of CPB, will most often require exogenous platelet administration. Prolonged bleeding time with a platelet count above $100,000/\mu l$ indicates platelet dysfunction and may also require exogenous administration of platelets. Desmopressin, a synthetic analog of the hormone arginine vasopressin, has been very useful in augmenting platelet function to improve hemostatic plug formation (28–30). Its mode of action is mediated by factor VIII complex; therefore, adequate levels of factor VIII are required. It is administered intravenously at a dose of 0.3 $\mu g/kg$ over 10 minutes. A response, a decrease in bleeding time, may be measured 30 to 90 minutes after administration.

The dilution of the coagulation factors to less than one-half of normal concentration as a result of the nonblood prime appears not to adversely affect hemostasis. However, the persistent dilution by more than 50% coupled with the consumption that is encountered during prolonged operations requires administration of coagulation factors, either in fresh-frozen plasma or cryoprecipitate. The use of cell saver devices will help in returning red cells from the operative field back to the circulation, but contributes to the hemodilution and platelet dysfunction in that any procoagulant factors and platelets are lost in the washing process.

In the postoperative period, brisk bleeding or tamponade can decrease cardiac filling and thus prevent filling of any circulatory assist device. The same criteria for reoperation used for routine operations should be used when devices are implanted. Evidence of tamponade in the face of rapid bleeding or sudden decrease on chest tube drainage, or ongoing bleeding of over 200 ml/hour for more than 3 to 4 hours are commonly accepted criteria for reoperation.

Bleeding may also become a significant problem at the time of removal of assist devices. Dense, immature adhesions between the device and intrathoracic organs tend to cause diffuse hemorrhage.

THROMBOEMBOLISM

The formation of macroscopic thrombus in circulatory assist devices is commonly seen at explant even when the patient has had "adequate anticoagulation." Anticoagulation regimens differ among institutions using devices, mainly because no one regimen seems more effective than the others. Many anticoagulants have been used at different times after implantation and in combination. These agents include low molecular weight (LMW) dextran, aspirin, heparin, warfarin, and dipyridamole. A typical US regimen would institute intravenous LMW dextran at 25 ml/hr and dypiridamole 100 mg every 6 hours via the nasogastric tube on the 1st postoperative day (31). A continuous intravenous infusion of heparin to maintain partial thromboplastin time at 50 to 60 seconds is appropriate after bleeding has ceased, usually by postoperative day 2 or 3. At the time heparin is started, dextran should be discontinued. Subsequently, the patient should be maintained on heparin and dypiridamole unless problems with heparin are encountered or a relatively long implant time is anticipated. In either of these cases, warfarin might be favored over heparin with maintenance of a prothrombin time of 17 to 18 seconds. In case of clinically evident embolism or transient ischemic attack (TIA), aspirin might be added at a dose of 65 to 325 mg/day.

Most types of devices have specific internal sites that are more prone to the formation of thrombus. Centrifugal pumps tend to form thrombus at the cones (18). We know from our own experience that the Novacor (Division of Baxter Healthcare Co., Oakland, CA) left ventricular assist device may form clots around the inflow valve. If the inflow site for the Novacor is the left ventricular apex, thrombus can form within the ventricle and then embolize in and out of the device (32). The CardioWest AVAD is prone to the formation of thrombus on the diaphragm housing junction near the outflow valve (31). The AVAD system is designed to provide parallel blood flow between its chambers and the heart. This division of flow may predispose to thrombus formation within the native heart. It has also been noticed that thrombus plaques form more commonly on the right rather than the left ventricular assist device. Warfarin appears to decrease the incidence of these plaques (33). Examination of the Jarvik 7 revealed deposits of platelets on the valve housing junctions, in the groove formed by the graft-valve housing, and at the junction of the diaphragm with the device housing (32, 34).

Other factors that appear to be involved in the development of thrombus within devices are a low or reduced blood flow and infection. The low flow state and the contact of blood with an artificial surface may accelerate thrombus formation. Infection can lead to a hypercoagulable state with activation of inflammatory cells and mediators, leading to the formation of thrombus. Infection within a device, on valves, or adherent thrombus, is more likely to be seen after prolonged periods of support. The risk of this complication in "nonpermanent" implants appears to be low.

The brain is by far the most sensitive organ to thromboembolism, and therefore also appears to be the most common organ affected by thromboembolism. Fortunately, irreversible neurologic damage has not been a common clinical observation during the use of circulatory assist devices. Transient ischemic attacks have been among the more frequently reported events. Embolism to the kidneys, ophthalmic artery, lung, and heart via the coronaries has also been documented. Embolism to other organs, such as the liver, should be expected to be more difficult to document. Based on current experience, thrombosis, thromboembolism, and infections are increasingly common beyond 30 days and may be interrelated (32).

INFECTION

Patients who need circulatory assistance are at risk for developing infections not only because of the presence of a large foreign body, but also because they are most often debilitated and malnourished. Improvement of the nutritional status of the patient should be considered of great importance. Prophylactic antibiotics should be routinely used during the perioperative period. The combined use of vancomycin and gentamicin from before surgery until chest tubes are removed is a common practice.

Infection rate is directly related to duration of circulatory support. It appears that pneumonia and mediastinitis are the most prevalent infections encountered. In one series using the Thoratec VAD (Berkeley, CA), sepsis as a result of nosocomial pneumonia with Gram-negative bacilli was the most common infection (35). Other common infectious complications include infection involving not only the support device and inflow and outflow conduits, but also the drive lines. These infections require systemic antibiotics and surgical debridement. Fungal infections, with *Candida* and *Aspergillus* organisms, have been reported in immunosuppressed patients who required circulatory support (18, 32). The occurrence of an infection in these patients increases the morbidity and mortality (2.5 to 31%). However, many of these patients can be successfully treated with antibiotics and become good candidates for cardiac transplantation. Prior im-

munosuppression should be a relative contraindication for the use of a TAH because sepsis from mediastinitis and pneumonia appear to be the most common infections leading to death in patients with TAH (36, 37).

HEMOLYSIS

Hemolysis is commonly observed during extended bypass. Chronic hemolysis can be associated with anemia and requirement for transfusions, which may sensitize a potential transplant patient to tissue antigens, thus creating a less compatible potential recipient. Chronic hemolysis may also be associated with chronic renal failure. None of the currently approved investigational devices, when used as recommended, produce excessive hemolysis (free hemoglobin, >10 mg/dl). Most clinical hemolysis is related to patient-specific, not device-specific parameters (18). In the bridge to transplant setting, drive parameters of devices should be set to minimize blood trauma while accepting a blood flow index of 2.5 liters/min/m². Blood transfusion should not be given unless the hematocrit falls below 20, and then blood that is less than 1 week in storage should be used and administered using a white blood cell filter.

MULTIORGAN FAILURE

Multiorgan failure is multifactorial. Many "device patients" are in some degree of cardiogenic shock preoperatively. This may persist if the device fails to produce the desired increase in cardiac output. Many of these patients have clinically significant bleeding during placement of the device, requiring large amounts of blood products. Postoperatively, many will require inotropic support for the first 24 to 48 hours to maintain an adequate output. The presence of sepsis compounds multiorgan failure. Infection and multiorgan failure are the two most common causes of mortality in patients who undergo placement of a total artificial heart (36).

Renal failure in this patient population is associated with mild azotemia and abnormal free water clearance. Its onset is associated with a high mortality. The onset of acute renal failure in patients who had received the Thoratec device was associated with a mortality >90% (38). The management of renal failure by hemodialysis, ultrafiltration, peritoneal dialysis, or a combination of these did not affect the outcome. Massive transfusions may be associated with adult respiratory distress syndrome. Hypoxemia is usually one of the first manifestations of pulmonary failure. Increased intrapulmonary shunt and decreased compliance are common clinical accompaniments. Jaundice is the most common evidence of liver failure. Although an elevated bilirubin may represent hemolysis, elevations in the liver enzymes may help make the diagnosis of liver failure. Gastrointestinal failure presents itself as bleeding from the gastrointestinal tract. Also, we have occasionally seen prolonged ileus. The outcome of patients with multiorgan failure is very well known from others fields in medicine. The more organs involved in failure, the higher the mortality.

WEANING AND BRIDGING

The goal of all of these devices is that the patient will be successfully weaned from mechanical support or that a heart transplant will be performed. When these devices are used as a bridge to transplantation, the potential recipient should meet all normal transplant selection criteria before elective cardiac transplantation. It appears that 35 to 70% of patients who received a mechanical support device are either successfully weaned or receive a heart transplant (33, 39).

CONCEPTS OF CIRCULATORY ASSIST DEVICES

Intraaortic Balloon Pump

The IABP is the simplest and most frequently used circulatory assist device in use today (1). It was first introduced by Moulopoulos et al. (40) in 1962 and then described clinically by Kantrowitz et al. (41) in 1968. Its offers the least complicated means of circulatory assistance. Operation of the balloon is timed with the electrocardiogram or aortic pressure waveform. It inflates during diastole (counterpulsation) propelling blood into the coronary arteries and the periphery. The effects of the IABP on the circulation (Fig. 27.1) include augmentation of diastolic pressure, a decrease in afterload, and a decrease in myocardial oxygen consumption (42). Use of the IABP improves cardiac function, augmenting cardiac output by approximately 10% or 500 to 800 ml/min. It is usually used in combination with inotropic agents that are usually at near maximal levels at the time of IABP insertion.

The IABP has many therapeutic uses in modern medicine. It is widely used in left ventricular failure following CPB for revascularization or valve replacement. It is also used in patients in cardiogenic shock on maximal inotropic support awaiting cardiac transplantation (43), cardiogenic shock following myocardial infarction, or intractable angina. Other limited uses include left main coronary disease, ventricular arrhythmias, right ventricular failure (44), septic shock, and pulmonary embolus. In cases of right ventricular failure, the IABP can be placed in the pulmonary artery. This is performed in the operating room with the heart and great vessels exposed (44).

Contraindications for the use of the IABP include aortic valve insufficiency, aortic aneurysm, and severe aortoiliac or femoral disease precluding the insertion of the balloon. Augmentation of the diastolic

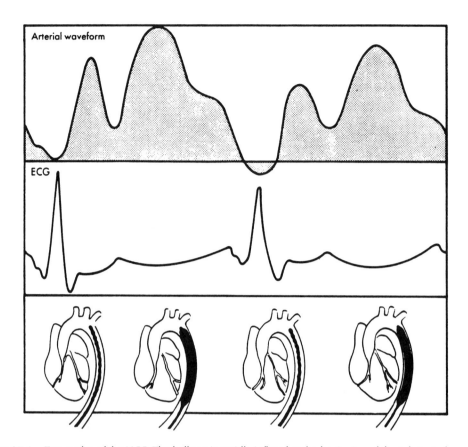

Figure 27.1.   Two cycles of the IABP. The balloon is rapidly inflated at the beginning of diastole just after aortic valve closes. Rapid deflation follows before next systole. (From Quaal SJ. Balloon's effect on a failing heart. In: Norwitz BE, ed. Comprehensive intra-aortic balloon pumping. St. Louis: CV Mosby, 1984:81.)

pressure will cause an increase in regurgitant flow across an incompetent aortic valve, resulting in left ventricular distension. The same augmentation or passage of the balloon may cause perforation of the aortic wall in patients with an aortic aneurysm.

The IABP is usually inserted percutaneously in one of the femoral arteries using the Seldinger technique (45) and advanced into the descending aorta just distal to the origin of the left subclavian artery (Fig. 27.2). If the femoral artery pulse is not palpable, especially after bypass, insertion may require a femoral artery cutdown. In cases of severe obstruction of the iliac and femoral vessels, the IABP may be placed while in the operating room directly into the as-

cending aorta and advanced into the descending aorta.

The advantages of the IABP are (*a*) non-IDE device, (*b*) inexpensive ($35,000 per console and $650 to $750 per balloon), (*c*) easy to insert and use, (*d*) large experience/minimal required surveillance (physicians, perfusionist, nurses), and (*e*) anticoagulation not absolutely necessary (recommended during weaning). The disadvantages are (*a*) a complication rate of 20%, (*b*) limited increase in cardiac output, (*c*) no effective preload reduction, and (*d*) limited effectiveness with tachycardia, dysrhythmias, and right ventricular failure (25).

Complications related to the IABP occur during insertion, pumping, removal or shortly after. These include dissection of the aorta, perforation, compromised blood flow to the lower extremity (when placed in the femoral artery) leading to ischemia, bleeding, thrombosis, embolism, thrombocytopenia, and infection. Peripheral pulses should be monitored frequently and on a regular schedule to document adequate blood flow to the extremity where the IABP was placed. Monitoring of the arterial pressure is required to verify maximal augmentation of diastolic pressure. This will result in a decrease in the afterload and myocardial oxygen consumption.

Axial Flow Pump

The Hemopump or Nimbus pump (Johnson and Johnson, Rancho Cordova, CA) is a device that can provide nonpulsatile flow rates up to 3.5 liters/min and shares some of the simplicity of the IABP. The device is actually a miniature axial flow pump at the end of a catheter. The pump is inserted through a 12-mm woven graft that is sutured to a femoral or iliac artery. The cannula is advanced into the aorta, across the aortic valve, and the tip is positioned at the apex of the left ventricle under fluoroscopic guidance (Fig. 27.3). The axial pump actually sits in the descending aorta (46) in a 7- $\times$ 16-mm cylindrical housing at the end of a 20-cm long flexible inflow cannula. It aspirates blood from the left ventricle and pumps it directly into the descending aorta. The pump generates 3 liters/min when rotating at 24,500 rpm, discharging into an output load of 100 mm Hg

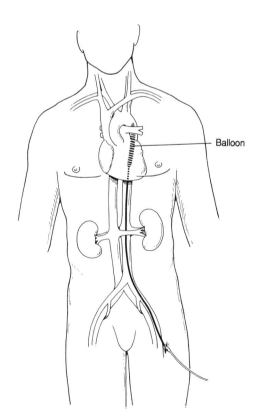

Figure 27.2. The IABP is usually inserted via the femoral arteries. The tip of the balloon should be placed just distal to the origin of the left subclavian artery.

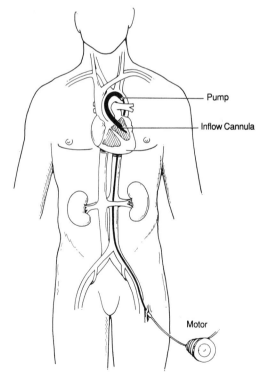

Figure 27.3. The Hemopump is inserted via the femoral arteries. The inflow to the pump sits in the left ventricle and the outflow in the proximal descending aorta.

pressure (47). Stationary blades provide directional flow of the blood as it exits the axial pump. The Hemopump is a disposable, one-time use device. The average time for insertion has been approximately 20 minutes.

Indications for placement are similar to those of the IABP. These include cardiogenic shock despite maximal medical support and pulmonary capillary wedge pressure (PCWP) >18 mm Hg, and cardiac index <2 liters/min/m². The Hemopump has been used in patients with refractory cardiogenic shock after coronary artery bypass grafting (48), acute myocardial infarction, ischemic cardiomyopathy, postpartum cardiomyopathy, and rejection of a transplanted heart (49). Contraindication for the use of the Hemopump is severe aortoiliac disease that will prevent introduction of the inflow cannula and pump into the aorta. Advantages of the Hemopump are (a) insertion without sternotomy, (b) less invasive, (c) costs comparable to IABP, and (d) small size. Disadvantages are (a) it cannot provide right ventricular support; (b) it is used for short duration; (c) IDE is required at present; (d) complication with insertion, injury to the aortic valve, hemolysis, bleeding, and ischemic injury to the extremity used for placement; and (d) requires an artery with a 7 to 10 mm lumen, which may in turn require a retroperitoneal approach to the iliac artery. The time range for its use has been 13 to 120 hours.

Internal Ventricular Assist Devices

The Novacor ventricular assist device and Thermedics ventricular assist device (Thermo Cardiosystem, Inc., Woburn, MA) represent prototypes of implantable devices for cardiac assist that took over 20 years of research and development funded by the National Institutes of Health. These devices work in a similar fashion and both provide pulsatile assistance to the failing left ventricle. They represent a family of univentricular assist devices. These VADs

are used in profound cardiogenic shock that is unresponsive to maximal inotropic support and IABP.

The Novacor LVAS (left ventricular assist system) is an electrically driven pump that energizes a solenoid that moves a dual-pusher plate to propel blood into the aorta. It was initially described in 1983 to provide long-term assistance, and may well become the first totally implantable "permanent" left VAD (50). It has been used to support patients in profound cardiogenic shock after cardiac surgery, but its main application has been as a bridge to heart transplantation (51). The device is implanted in the left upper quadrant of the abdomen, anterior to the fascia of the rectus abdominis muscle (Fig. 27.4). It weighs approximately 3.3 kg and occupies a volume of about 400 ml. The inflow to the device comes via a low porosity Dacron conduit that is anastomosed to a hole cored in the apex of the left ventricle. The outflow is also via a similar Dacron conduit that usually goes to the ascending aorta, but it may

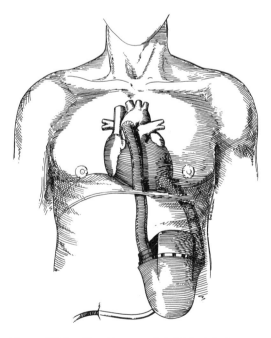

Figure 27.4. The Novacor left VAD (electromechanical).

also be anastomosed to the abdominal aorta. Bioprosthetic inflow and outflow valves maintain unidirectional flow. The blood pump is made of a seamless, smooth-surfaced polyurethane sac. The power line and a vent travel subcutaneously and exit the patient in the right lower quadrant of the abdomen. A series of sensors are attached to the pump mechanism and exit the body in the same line. These connect to a console where there are two controllers, one serving as a back-up. Information about filling and stroke volumes, pump rate, and energy usage are displayed on the console for analysis. This device can provide flows up to 8 liters/min (52). The Novacor VAD can be triggered in three different settings: (a) at a fixed rate independent of the intrinsic cardiac activity, (b) following the native QRS complex of the ECG, or (c) following changes in the rate of pump filling. It is most widely used in the latter setting. This allows ventricular systole to fill the VAD and trigger device ejection. However, the device has been used in patients who are in ventricular fibrillation. In this case, filling of the device occurs by a pressure gradient; 10 mm Hg is the minimum required.

The Thermedics left VAD is a totally implantable, pneumatically driven dual-chamber pump in a rigid titanium housing. A polyurethane, flexible diaphragm sits between the air and blood chambers. The remainder of the blood chamber is made of sintered titanium microspheres. This surface promotes coating the lining with the patient's own blood while minimizing clot formation (53). This device has been used since 1985 (54). This VAD is positioned intraabdominally in the left upper quadrant of the abdomen. The inlet low porosity Dacron conduit is anastomosed to a hole cored in the apex of the left ventricle. A longer outlet Dacron conduit goes to the aorta. Porcine valves sit at the inlet and outlet of the device, and provide unidirectional flow. The pneumatic drive line travels subcutaneously and exits the skin at a dis-

tance from the device; it then connects to the console. Triggering of this device also has the three settings similar to those described for the Novacor VAD. This device can also generate blood flows up to 8 liters/min.

Indications for placement of the Novacor VAD or Thermedics VAD are similar. The following criteria must be met: (a) approved transplant candidate, (b) systolic blood pressure ≤80 mm Hg or mean blood pressure ≤60 mm Hg with a PCWP ≥20 mm Hg and a cardiac index ≤2.0 liters/min/m², (c) maximal inotropic support, and (d) IABP support. Exclusion criteria that will contraindicate the use of these devices include: (a) weight <50 kg, (b) body surface area <1.5 m², (c) age >65 years, (d) chronic renal insufficiency requiring hemodialysis within 1 month prior to surgery, (e) unresolved pulmonary infarction secondary to pulmonary embolism, (f) severely depressed right ventricular function with estimated ejection fraction <10%, (g) fixed pulmonary hypertension with pulmonary vascular resistance >6 Wood units after a trial of prostaglandin E₁ or inhalation oxygen therapy, (h) severe hepatic failure with total bilirubin >10 mg/dl or biopsy-proven cirrhosis, (i) unresolved malignancy, (j) severe blood dyscrasia, (k) severe cerebrovascular or peripheral vascular disease, (k) history of strokes, TIAs, (l) acute systemic infection, and (m) positive HIV antibody test.

The advantages of implantable VADs are pulsatile flow, good mobilization of patients is possible, long periods of support are possible, and high cardiac output capability. The disadvantages are (a) they require a median sternotomy with extension into the upper abdominal wall or abdominal cavity, (b) fit problems are possible in smaller patients, (c) they cannot support the right ventricle, (d) IDE is required, (e) anticoagulation is required, (f) expense ($65,000 per console and $24,000 per pump), and (g) complications of bleeding, infection, or thromboembolism can occur.

Postimplantation Management of the Novacor VAD

Frequent monitoring of the cardiovascular, respiratory, hepatic, and renal systems is performed according to established protocols required of each institution. Bleeding from drainage tubes and coagulation profiles are serially determined to establish the requirement for blood products. Stroke volume and cardiac output are displayed on the left VAD monitor; inotropic support is given as needed to support the right ventricle. Of great concern is the development of right ventricular failure manifested by low device output, peripheral edema, hepatic congestion, a high central venous pressure, and a decrease in the PCWP. In this case, a centrifugal right VAD may be necessary. A euvolemic state should be maintained for proper functioning of the VAD.

Low molecular weight dextran is usually started within 24 hours of implant. Dipyridamole 100 mg every 6 hours is given via a nasogastric tube in the immediate postoperative period, and continued for the duration of the implant. Chest tube drainage is monitored, and heparin replaces dextran as soon as bleeding has completely stopped and a "hemostatic plug" is present. Chest tubes are removed as soon as minimal drainage is noticed. Ventilatory support is weaned, leading to extubation and early mobilization of the patient. Prophylactic broad-spectrum intravenous antibiotics are recommended for the first 24 to 48 hours. If evidence of sepsis or acute infection is determined, cultures from all body fluids, including chest tubes, are obtained and appropriate antibiotics are started. All central, monitoring, and peripheral lines are removed as early as possible.

Early nutritional support is of extreme importance. It is initiated, preferably via the gastrointestinal route, with tube feedings or by mouth. Frequent calorie counts may be required. Examination of all wounds, especially the cable exit site, is performed for early detection of infections. To avoid formation of cytoxic antibodies, strategies that minimize giving the patient blood products are used. Blood is drawn using "microtechnique" (small tubes such as used for neonates), only single-donor platelets are given, and white blood cell filters are utilized. The patients' hematocrit is allowed to fall to 18 to 20% before blood is replaced. Iron supplements and erythropoietin are utilized when appropriate. When blood is required, the freshest (less than 7 days old) possible units are administered to minimize hemolysis associated with these devices (33). Recommended chronic anticoagulation with the Thermo Cardiosystems Inc. left VAD consists of aspirin alone.

UNI- OR BIVENTRICULAR DEVICES

Centrifugal Pumps

This family of pumps utilizes centrifugal force to generate a nonpulsatile flow. The flow rate depends on the rotational speed of the pump. Blood enters the pump at the apex and is accelerated outward. Currently there are three manufacturers for this type of pump: Medtronic-Biomedicus (Eden Prairie, MN), Sarns, Inc. (Ann Arbor, MI), and Aries Medical (Chelmsford, MA). These pumps can be used to assist either the left or right ventricle, or both (55). The inflow cannula to the pump originates from the left or right atrium and the outflow goes to the aorta or pulmonary artery. The centrifugal pump is extracorporeal, with the inflow and outflow cannulae passing through the chest wall (Fig. 27.5). The pump is electromagnetically coupled to a motor that connects to the control console (56). This makes the pump console completely sealed from blood contacting surfaces in the "pump head."

Flows ranging from 2 to 5 liters/min are obtained with these devices. The current adult centrifugal pumps should not be run below outputs of 0.5 liters/min. It is recommended that the activated clotting

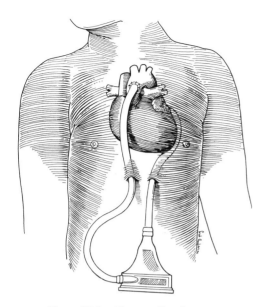

Figure 27.5.   The centrifugal pump.

time be maintained at 1.5 times normal with continuous heparin infusions. During weaning of these devices, the dosage of heparin should be increased to decrease the potential for thrombus formation (39).

Indications for the use of the centrifugal pumps are similar to those described above. They have been used in cardiogenic shock (57), as a bridge for transplantation (58, 59), to support a failing heart after transplantation (60), and in patients that were unweanable from bypass (61).

The advantages of centrifugal pumps are (*a*) non-IDE device, (*b*) comparatively inexpensive ($11,000 per console and $150 per disposable pump head), (*c*) used for left or right ventricular support or both simultaneously, (*d*) small console size, and (*e*) flow probe provides feedback on the pump flow. The disadvantages include (*a*) intensive monitoring, usually requiring a perfusionist present at all times; (*b*) full anticoagulation needed; (*c*) patient immobilization; (*d*) support limited to a few days, so use for bridge to transplant is limited; (*e*) hemolysis, bleeding, infection, and thromboembolism are potential complications; and (*f*) pump head requires changing every 24 to 48 hours.

Pulsatile Paracorporeal Pumps

The family of paracorporeal pumps provides uni- or biventricular pulsatile flow. A system of 2 or 4 cannulae provide inflow and outflow to the blood pumps. The most commonly used devices have been Cardio-West (previously known as Symbion) AVAD (Tucson, AZ), Thoratec (Berkeley, CA), Abiomed (Danvers, MA), and Sarns, Inc.

The CardioWest AVAD consists of a rigid housing made of two compartments separated by a flexible diaphragm. Each ventricle can be used for right or left sides of the heart. Two units provide complete biventricular support (Fig. 27.6). The inflow cannula, a 51 French bullet tip cannula without side holes, sits in the right or left atrium. Unidirectional mechanical valves sit at the inflow and outflow ports of the device. The outflow conduit connects with a Dacron graft that is anastomosed to the ascending aorta or pulmonary artery (62). The diaphragm in the unit is pro-

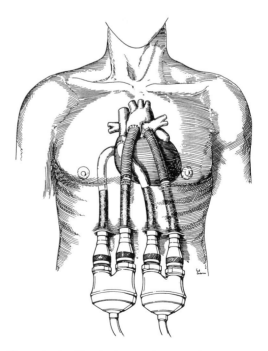

Figure 27.6.   The CardioWest biventricular assist device (pneumatic).

pelled by compressed air that comes from a control console. A computer provides readout stroke volumes and outputs that are calculated from air flow out of the ventricles. Implantation of the device usually requires the use of CPB. This system provides average outputs of about 5 liters/min; slightly higher outputs can be obtained by increasing the vacuum applied to the diaphragm, thus sucking blood into the prosthetic ventricle. The unit can pump at a rate that is determined by ECG sensing, but we use it at a rate of about 80 per minute independent of the patient's heart rate.

Anticoagulation is initiated immediately in patients who have received the CardioWest AVADs. Deposits of tiny platelet thrombi have been observed in the outflow portion of the unit, presumably because of uneven flow characteristics and asymmetrical movement of the diaphragm related to gravity and to inflow patterns. Upon serial examination of these tiny plaques, usually a few millimeters, they seem to come and go without any associated evidence of thromboembolism. These plaques are more frequent in the right than in the left VAD (31).

The Thoratec VAD is a pneumatically driven paracorporeal prosthetic ventricle. This system has been very successful when used as a bridge for cardiac transplantation (63). Inflow and outflow cannulae may be positioned in a manner similar to that used with the CardioWest device (Fig. 27.6). Better left device filling is obtained if the left pump inflow cannula comes from the patient's left ventricular apex. Björk-Shiley valves sit at the inlet and outlet of each ventricle and provide unidirectional flow. A polyurethane sac divides the blood chamber from the air chamber within the prosthetic ventricle. When the device is used as a bridge to transplantation and sacrifice of a sizable portion of left ventricular apex will thus have no long-term consequence, the inflow to the left ventricular device may be anastomosed to an apical left ventriculotomy (64). The stroke volume

from each paracorporeal ventricle is about 65 ml. The pneumatic drive lines connect to a console a few feet from the patient. This system can be triggered in a similar fashion to the one described above. A similar anticoagulation regimen is recommended.

The Abiomed BVS 5000 system is also a paracorporeal, pulsatile, pneumatic device that can provide biventricular support (Fig. 27.7). Each blood pump, right or left heart support, consists of two polyurethane chambers. Each chamber is separated from the other with trileaflet polyurethane valves. Blood flows continuously in both pump systole and diastole by gravity from the patient's atrium to the first chamber within the blood pump. From there, it flows passively across an inlet valve into the active ventricle-like chamber where it is pneumatically propelled into the patient's great vessel composite cannula with distal Dacron conduit. The pumps are operated by

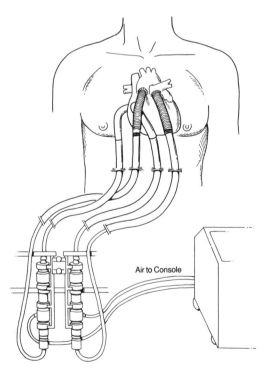

Figure 27.7. The Abiomed circulatory support system is shown with the inflow and outflow cannulae, prosthetic ventricles, and console.

a console that determines the pulsatile rate and the systole/diastole ratio based on the compressed air flow into and out of the chambers. The system maintains a stroke volume of 82 ml (65). This system has been designed as a support system for hearts that have sustained reversible damage, particularly in failure to wean from CPB situations. Patients must be kept at bed rest with this pump. It can be used as uni-or biventricular support. In this instance, anticoagulation was maintained with the use of intravenous heparin during the full duration of assist, keeping the activated coagulation time at 150 to 200 seconds (66).

The advantages of the paracorporeal systems are (*a*) right, left, or biventricular support; (*b*) pulsatile flow; (*c*) patient mobilization (patients cannot be mobilized with the Abiomed system); (*d*) versatility for bridge to transplant; (*e*) useful on smaller patients; (*f*) long periods of support are possible; (*g*) feedback and control of device cardiac output; (*h*) easier implantation; and (*i*) commercial availability. The disadvantages of these systems include (*a*) cannulae limit flow to 4 to 6 liters/min; (*b*) complications of hemolysis, thromboembolism, bleeding, and infection; (*c*) anticoagulation is required; and (*d*) expense ($40,000 to $70,000 per console and $11,000 to $13,000 per device).

Total Artificial Heart

The TAH provides complete support of the circulation, but requires removal of the native heart. This device has been used to provide permanent support; however, its most important role is to serve as a bridge to cardiac transplantation. The first implantable experimental design was introduced in 1958 (67, 68). The first clinical use of an artificial heart was performed in 1969 by Cooley et al. (69), when they implanted the Liotta heart, supporting a patient for 64 hours until a donor heart became available. The use of the TAH as a permanent device was initiated by DeVries et al. (70). In 1982

they implanted the Jarvik-7 in Dr. Barney Clark (71). The patient survived 112 days. The first successful use of the Jarvik TAH as a bridge for cardiac transplantation was performed by Copeland et al. (72) in 1985 in a 25-year-old male with idiopathic cardiomyopathy (73–75). The TAH has also been used by the same group in patients with viral and ischemic cardiomyopathies as well as in adults with congenital heart disease (73–76). Total artificial hearts are currently manufactured by CardioWest and Hershey Medical Center (Hershey, PA).

The CardioWest C-70 (Symbion, Jarvik J-7) is a pneumatically driven biventricular device (Fig. 27.8). Placement of a TAH requires a median sternotomy. Blood is withdrawn prior to heparinization for preclotting the Dacron outflow grafts. Following heparinization, double atrial and single ascending aortic cannulations are performed. Cardiopulmonary bypass is established and fibrillation is induced electrically. The ascending aorta is cross-clamped and a cardiectomy at the atrioventricular level is performed. The great vessels are transected just superior to the commissures of the semilunar valves. The polyurethane/Dacron atrial cuffs are then sutured in place

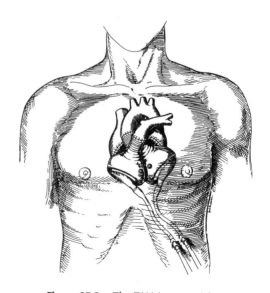

Figure 27.8. The TAH (pneumatic).

with 3-0 polypropylene. The aortic graft anastomosis and pulmonary artery anastomosis are also performed with 3-0 polypropylene. The drive lines are tunneled subcutaneously. The left ventricle is then prefilled with saline and snapped to the atrial and aortic connection. Air is then removed from the ventricle. The technique of implanting the right ventricle is identical to the left (75, 77).

The prosthetic ventricles are made of polyurethane. Mechanical heart valves (Medtronic-Hall, Minneapolis, MN) sit at the inlet and outlet of the ventricles to provide unidirectional flow. Blood and air are separated by a four-layer segmented polyurethane diaphragm. This diaphragm retracts during diastole and is displaced forward by compressed air during systole, propelling blood out of the prosthetic ventricle.

Each console has a primary and backup controllers, as well as pressurized air tanks for back-up and patient transport (78). The controller provides adjustment of the heart rate, systolic duration, and drive line pressures for each of the ventricles. A personal computer monitors the mechanical function of the TAH. It displays the stroke volume and cardiac output for each of the ventricles. The CardioWest C-70 is set so that there is incomplete filling, but complete emptying with each stroke. The atrial pressure on each side determines ventricular filling. As atrial pressure increases, a higher stroke volume and cardiac output are obtained. An atrial pressure of 5 mm Hg provides a cardiac output of 4 to 5 liters/min, while an atrial pressure of 10 to 15 mm Hg may result in a cardiac output as high as 12 liters/min at the same heart rate.

The Penn State (Hershey, PA) heart is a pneumatically driven device that also requires removal of the native ventricles. It consists of two prosthetic ventricles that are anastomosed to the respective atria and great vessels. Each ventricle contains two chambers, one where the blood enters and is pressurized. The other chamber is filled with compressed CO_2. A polyurethane diaphragm separates the two chambers within the prosthetic ventricle. The stroke volume is about 70 ml. Mechanical valves at the inlet and outlet provide unidirectional flow. The left system is set to maintain a given aortic pressure by increasing or decreasing the rate of contraction. The right system is set to maintain a given left atrial pressure by also changing the rate of contraction (79).

CONSIDERATIONS FOR CHOOSING A DEVICE

Circulatory assist devices have become more common and more accessible in the last few years. At the same time, a larger number of devices with overlapping purposes have become available. The considerations presented here should only serve as guidelines. It is expected that newer and more complicated devices will be developed within the next years.

The Novacor left VAD requires implantation of the device in the subcutaneous or intramuscular planes in the abdomen. The device should fit between the costal margin and the superior iliac spine on the left side. The patient should probably weigh a minimum of 50 kg to avoid size incompatibility. The possible problem of right ventricular failure, or increase in pulmonary vascular resistance, must be considered before implanting such a device. The necessity for right ventricular support should be anticipated. The Novacor should be used as a device for bridging to transplant in view of the obligatory excision and ischemia (from sutures) of the left ventricular apex. At the present time, the Novacor is recommended for transplantable patients over 50 kg and under the age of 45. The patient should also have normal pulmonary vascular resistance and probably no right ventricular failure.

The CardioWest AVAD or Thoratec VAD are clearly the devices of choice when the cardiac pathology is felt to be reversible. Implantation of these devices may not require bypass. They can be used as the next step after IABP. The maximal cardiac output with these devices appears to be approximately 5 liters/min. Thus, in order to provide an adequate blood flow index (≥ 2.5 liters/min/m^2), the patient should be less than 80 kg.

The TAH should be used when there is global cardiac decompensation that is not likely to be reversible. The best candidate for TAH is a patient who weighs over 75 kg, is under the age of 45, and rapidly decompensates while waiting for a transplant. This should be done in a setting where the wait for a donor is not extended, and preferably transplantation can be expected within the first 3 to 4 weeks after implantation (33).

FUTURE DIRECTIONS

Congestive heart failure affects approximately 4 million people in the US. Approximately 3 to 10% of these patients will die per year as a result of the complications of congestive heart failure. It is estimated that $3.1 billion per year would be required to support every patient needing a circulatory support system. It is thought that by treating patients with circulatory assist devices, these patients may return to the work force and contribute to society an income greater in value than the total investment (80). Many new models of assist devices will appear during the next few years. The TAH with electrical motors are under study (81). The first fully portable left VAD was recently implanted at St. Luke's Episcopal Hospital (Houston, TX) in a patient awaiting heart transplantation. This represents a giant step in the development of these devices. Research and periodic reevaluation of current and new systems should continue, as well as the development of a permanent circulatory assist device (82). The concept of xenotransplantation, or the use of a donor heart from another species to be used in a human recipient, continues to be controversial and biologically impossible. However, this al-

ternative continues to be explored (83). The technology that has been developed and the knowledge that has been acquired with all types of circulatory assist devices represent one of man's great achievements. The quest for new materials, new power supplies, and better devices will undoubtedly open new frontiers that will change human life as we know it.

REFERENCES

1. Levinson MM, Copeland JG. The artificial heart and mechanical assistance prior to heart transplantation. In: Cerrilli CJ, ed. Organ transplantation and replacement. Philadelphia: JB Lippincott, 1987:661–679.
2. Iglehart JK. Transplantation: the problem of limited resources. N Engl J Med 1983;309:123–128.
3. Evans RW, Manninen DL, Garrison LP Jr, Maier AM. Donor availability as the primary determinant of the future of heart transplantation. JAMA 1986;255:1892–1898.
4. Pierce WS, Parr GVS, Myers JL, Pae WE, Bwi AP, Waldhausen JA. Ventricular-assist pumping in patients with cardiogenic shock after cardiac operations. N Engl J Med 1981;305:1606–1010.
5. Pae WE, Pierce WS, Pennock JL, Campbell DB, Waldhausen JA. Long-term results of ventricular assist pumping in postcardiotomy cardiogenic shock. J Thorac Cardiovasc Surg 1987;93:434–441.
6. Pennington DG, McBride LR, Swartz MT, et al. Use of the Pierce-Donachy ventricular assist device in patients with cardiogenic shock after cardiac operations. Ann Thorac Surg 1989;47:130–135.
7. Rose DM, Conolly M, Cunningham JN, Spencer FC. Technique and results with a roller pump left and right heart assist device. Ann Thorac Surg 1989;47:124–129.
8. DePaulis R, Riebman JB, Deleuze P, Olsen DB. The total artificial heart: indications and preliminary results. J Cardiac Surgery 1987;2:275.
9. Pennock JL, Pierce WS, Campbell DB, et al. Mechanical support of the circulation followed by cardiac transplantation. J Thorac Cardiovasc Surg 1986;92:994–1004.
10. Carpentier A, Perier P, Brugger JP, et al. Heterotopic artificial heart as a bridge to cardiac transplantation. Lancet 1986;2:97–98.
11. Hill JD, Farrar DJ, Hershon JJ, et al. Use of a prosthetic ventricle as a bridge to cardiac transplantation for postinfarction cardiogenic shock. N Engl J Med 1986;314:626–628.

12. Farrar DJ, Hill JD, Gray LA, et al. Heterotopic prosthetic ventricles as a bridge to cardiac transplantation. A multicenter study in 29 patients. N Engl J Med 1988;318:333–340.
13. Pennington DG, Codd JE, Merjavy JP, et al. The expanded use of ventricular bypass systems for severe cardiac failure and as a bridge to cardiac transplantation. J Heart Transplant 1984; 3:170–175.
14. Ott RA, Mills TC, Eugene J, Gazzaniga AB. Clinical choices for circulatory assist devices. ASAIO Trans 1990;36:792–798.
15. Hill JD. Bridging to cardiac transplantation. Ann Thorac Surg 1989;47:167–171.
16. Hill JD, Hardesty RL, Baumgartner WA, Rose DM. Intraoperative management. Ann Thorac Surg 1989;47:82–87.
17. Pennington DG, Swartz LD, Pae WE, Burkholder JA. Circulatory support symposium 1988: patient selection. Ann Thorac Surg 1989;47: 77–81.
18. Pierce WS, Gray LA, McBride LR, Frazier OH. Other postoperative complications: circulatory support—1988. Ann Thorac Surg 1989;47: 96–101.
19. Portner PM, Oyer PE, Pennington DG, et al. Implantable electrical left ventricular assist system: bridge to transplantation and the future. Ann Thorac Surg 1989;47:142–150.
20. Kormos RL, Borovetz HS, Gasior T, et al. Experience with univentricular support in mortally ill cardiac transplant candidates. Ann Thorac Surg 1990;49:261–272.
21. Pennington DG, Reedy JE, Swartz MT, et al. Univentricular versus biventricular assist device support. J Heart Lung Transplant 1991;10: 258–263.
22. Ott RA, Joyce L, Emery RW. Current status of mechanical circulatory assistance. Bull Minn Heart Inst Found 1988;6:13–18.
23. Acharya A. Development of PMA guidance for ventricular assist devices and total artificial heart. IEEE Eng Med Biol 1988;7:90–91.
24. Federal Register. January 18, 1980;45: 3732–3747.
25. Smith RG, Cleavinger M. Current perspectives on the use of circulatory assist devices. AACN AACN Clin Issues Crit Care Nurs 1991;3:488–499.
26. Joist JH, Pennington DG. Platelet reactions with artificial surfaces. ASAIO Trans 1987;33: 341–343.
27. Copeland JG, Harker LA, Joist JH, DeVries WC. Bleeding and anticoagulation. Ann Thorac Surg 1989;47:88–95.
28. Czer LS, Bateman TM, Gray RJ, et al. Treatment of severe platelet dysfunction and hemorrhage after cardiopulmonary bypass: reduction in

blood product usage with desmopressin. J Am Coll Cardiol 1987;9:1139–1147.
29. Seear MD, Wadsworth LD, Rogers PC, Sheps S, Ashmore PG. The effect of desmopressin acetate (DDAVP) on postoperative blood loss after cardiac operations in children. J Thorac Cardiovasc Surg 1989;98:217–219.
30. Salzman EW, Weinstein MJ, Weintraub RM, et al. Treatment with desmopressin acetate to reduce blood loss after cardiac surgery: a double-blind randomized trial. N Engl J Med 1986;314: 1402–1406.
31. Icenogle TB, Smith RG, Cleavinger M, et al. Thromboembolic complications of the Symbion AVAD system. Artif Organs 1989;13:532–538.
32. Didisheim P, Olsen DB, Farrar DJ, et al. Infections and thromboembolism with implantable cardiovascular devices. ASAIO Trans 1989;35:54–70.
33. Copeland JG, Smith RG, Cleavinger MR, Icenogle TB, Sethi GK, Rosado, LJ. Bridge to transplantation indications for Symbion TAH, Symbion AVAD and Novacor LVAS. In: Akutsu T, ed. Artificial heart 3. Proceedings of the 3rd International Symposium on Artificial Heart and Assist Device. Tokyo: Springer-Verlag, 1991: 303–308.
34. Levinson MM, Smith RG, Cork RC, et al. Thromboembolic complications of the Jarvik-7 total artificial heart: case report. Artif Organs 1986;10:236–244.
35. McBride LR, Ruzevich SA, Pennington DG, et al. Infectious complications associated with ventricular assist device support. ASAIO Trans 1987;33:201–202.
36. Muneretto C, Solis E, Pavie A, et al. Total artificial heart: survival and complications. Ann Thorc Surg 1989;47:151–157.
37. Griffith BP. Interim use of the Jarvik-7 artificial heart: lessons learned at Presbyterian-University Hospital of Pittsburgh. Ann Thorac Surg 1989; 47:158–166.
38. Kanter KR, Swartz MT, Pennington DG, et al. Renal failure in patients with ventricular assist devices. ASAIO Trans 1987;33:426–428.
39. Magovern GJ, Golding LAR, Oyer PE, Cabrol C. Weaning and bridging. Ann Thorac Surg 1989; 47:102–107.
40. Moulopoulos SD, Topaz S, Kolff W. Diastolic balloon pumping (with carbon dioxide) in the aorta—a mechanical assistance to the failing circulation. Am Heart J 1962;63:669.
41. Kantrowitz A, Tjonneland S, Freed PS, Phillips SJ, Butner AN, Sherman JC. Initial clinical experience with intraaortic balloon pumping in cardiogenic shock. JAMA 1968;203:113–118.
42. Quaal SJ. Balloon's effect on a failing heart. In: Norwitz BE, ed. Comprehensive intra-aortic

balloon pumping. St. Louis: CV Mosby, 1984: 84–94.

43. Hardy MA, Dobelle W, Bregman D, et al. Cardiac transplantation following mechanical circulatory support. Am Soc Artif Intern Organs 1979; 25:182–185.

44. Park SB, Lieblet GA, Burkholder JA, et al. Mechanical support of the failing heart. Ann Thorac Surg 1986;42:627–631.

45. Seldinger SI. Catheter replacement of the needle in percutaneous arteriography: a new technique. Acta Radiol 1953;39:368–376.

46. Roundtree WD. The hemopump temporary cardiac assist device. AACN Clin Issues Crit Care Nurs 1991;3:562–574.

47. Butler KC, Moise JC, Wampler RK. The Hemopump—a new cardiac prosthesis device. IEEE Trans Biomed Eng 1990;37:193–196.

48. Phillips SJ, Barker L, Balentine J, et al. Hemopump support for the failing heart. ASAIO Trans 1990;36:M629–632.

49. Deeb GM, Bolling J, Nicklas RS, et al. Clinical experience with the Nimbus pump. ASAIO Trans 1990;36:M632–M636.

50. Portner PM, Oyer PE, Jassawalla JS, Miller PJ, et al. An alternative in end-stage heart disease: long-term ventricular assistance. Heart Transplant 1983;3:47–59.

51. Portner PM, Oyer PE, Pennington DG, et al. Implantable electrical left ventricular assist system: bridge to transplantation and the future. Ann Thorac Surg 1989;47:142–150.

52. Shinn JA. Novacor left ventricular assist system. AACN Clin Issues Crit Care Nurs 1991;3: 575–586.

53. Abou-Awdi NL. Thermo cardiosystems left ventricular assist device as a bridge to cardiac transplant. AACN Clin Issues Crit Care Nurs 1991; 3:545–551.

54. Bernhard WF, Clay W, Gernes D, et al. Temporary and permanent left ventricular bypass: laboratory and clinical observations. World J Surg 1985;9:54–64.

55. Drinkwater DC, Laks H. Clinical experience with centrifugal pump ventricular support at UCLA Medical Center. ASAIO Trans 1988;34:505–508.

56. Quaal SJ. Centrifugal ventricular assist devices. AACN Clin Issues Crit Care Nurs 1991;3: 515–526.

57. Park SB. Mechanical support of the failing heart. Ann Thorac Surg 1986;42:627–631.

58. Golding LAR, Stewart RW, Sinkenwich M, Smith W, Cosgrove DM. Nonpulsatile ventricular assist bridging to transplantation. ASAIO Trans 1988; 34:476–479.

59. Bolman RM, Cox JL, Marshall W, et al. Circulatory support with a centrifugal pump as a bridge to cardiac transplantation. Ann Thorac Surg 1989;47:108–112.

60. Hooper TL, Odom NJ, Fetherston GJ, Waterhouse P, Hilton CJ, Dark JH. Successful use of the left ventricular assist device for primary graft failure after heart transplantation. J Heart Transplant 1988;7:385–387.

61. Joyce LD, Kiser JC, Eales F, King RM, Toninato CJ, Hansen J. Experience with the Sarns centrifugal pump as a ventricular assist device. ASAIO Trans 1990;36:M619–623.

62. Ganzel BL, Gray LA, Slater AD, Mavroudis C. Surgical techniques for the implantation of heterotopic prosthetic ventricles. Ann Thorac Surg 1989;47:113–120.

63. Farrar DJ, Lawson JH, Litwak P, Cederwall G. Thoratec VAD system as a bridge to heart transplantation. J Heart Transplant 1990;9:415–423.

64. Ley SJ. The Thoratec ventricular assist device: nursing guidelines. AACN Clin Issues Crit Care Nurs 1991;3:529–544.

65. Dixon JF, Farris CD. The Abiomed BVS 5000 system. AACN Clin Issues Crit Care Nurs 1991; 3:552–561.

66. Champsaur G, Ninet J, Vigneron M, Cochet P, Neidecker J, Boissonnat P. Use of the Abiomed BVS 5000 as a bridge to cardiac transplantation. J Thorac Cardiovasc Surg 1990;100:122–128.

67. Akutsu T, Kolff WJ. Permanent substitutes for valves and hearts. Trans ASAIO 1958;4:230–235.

68. Akutsu T, Houston CS, Kolff WJ. Artificial hearts inside the chest, using small electric motors. Am Soc Artif Intern Organs 1960;6:299.

69. Cooley DA, Liotta D, Hallman GL, Bloodwell RD, Leachman RD, Milam JD. First human implantation of cardiac prosthesis for staged total replacement of the heart. Trans ASAIO 1969;15: 252–263.

70. Jarvik RK, Smith LM, Lawson JH, et al. Comparison of pneumatic and electrically powered total artificial heart in vivo. Am Soc Artif Intern Organs 1978;24:593–599.

71. DeVries WL, Anderson JL, Joyce LD, et al. Initial human application of the Utah total artificial heart. N Engl J Med 1984;310:273–278.

72. Copeland JG, Levinson MM, Smith R, Icenogle TB, Vaughn C, Cheng K, Ott R, Emery RW. The total artificial heart as a bridge to transplantation. JAMA 1986;256:2991–2995.

73. Copeland JG, Smith RG, Icenogle T, et al. Orthotopic total artificial heart bridge to transplantation: preliminary results. J Heart Transplant 1989;8:124–138.

74. Levinson MM, Smith RG, Cork RC, et al. Three recent cases of the total artificial heart before transplantation. J Heart Transplant 1986;5: 215–228.

75. Levinson MM, Copeland JG. Technical aspects of the total artificial heart implantation and temporary applications. J Cardiac Surg 1987;2:3–19.
76. Copeland JG, Smith RG, Icenogle TB, Ott RA. Early experience with the total artificial heart as a bridge to cardiac transplantation. Proceedings of the 2nd International Symposium on Artificial Heart and Assist Device, 1987:217–223.
77. DeVries WC, Joyce LD. The artificial heart. Clin Symp 1983;35:1–32.
78. Barker LE. The total artificial heart. AACN Clin Issues Crit Care Nurs 1991;3:587–597.
79. Magovern JA, Pierce WS. Mechanical circulatory assistance before heart transplantation. In:

Baumgartner WA, Reitz BA, Achuff SC, eds. Heart and heart-lung transplantation. Philadelphia: WB Saunders, 1990:73–85.
80. Poirier VL. Can our society afford mechanical hearts? ASAIO Trans 1991;37:540–544.
81. Davis PK, Rosenberg G, Snyder AJ, Pierce WS. Current status of permanent total artificial hearts. Ann Thorac Surg 1989;47:172–178.
82. Poirier VL. The quest for the permanent LVAD. We must continue. We must push forward. ASAIO Trans 1990;36:787–788.
83. Bailey LL. Biologic versus bionic heart substitutes. Will xenotransplantation play a role? ASAIO Trans 1987;33:51–53.

28

Noncardiovascular Applications of Cardiopulmonary Bypass

Michael J. Murray

The development of cardiopulmonary bypass (CPB) during the 1950s for repair of cardiac anomalies stimulated an appraisal of its potential in assisting with the management of other disease processes. Complications associated with this technique tempered the initial enthusiasm for bypass for noncardiac applications. With time, however, a more reasoned approach to the use of CPB for noncardiovascular applications has developed, and many of the early problems and complications have been overcome.

Interestingly, physicians and scientists from noncardiac disciplines helped advance the development of CPB. For example, neurosurgeons and neuroanesthesiologists with expertise in brain protection and monitoring made significant contributions to the management of all patients undergoing bypass. The development of CPB was secondary to many advances in not only surgery, but also physiology, anesthesiology, cardiology, and bioengineering (1).

The current applications of CPB for noncardiovascular use involve four main areas. First, bypass is used to induce profound hypothermia so that circulatory arrest can be instituted, thereby providing a bloodless surgical field for the repair of vascular abnormalities such as intracranial aneurysms and resections of tumor/thromboses of the vena cava/right atrium. Prior to the availability of CPB, surgeons did use hypother-

mia, with a safe limit of 28 to 30°C (2), in conjunction with cardiac inflow occlusion to manage some of these cases. Cardiopulmonary bypass is necessary, however, to institute the degree of hypothermia that circulatory arrest requires.

Second, CPB, though primarily thought of as a means to facilitate operations on the heart, also bypasses the lungs. In fact, Gibbon developed his pump oxygenator in order to operate on patients with pulmonary embolism (3). Patients with significant pulmonary disease in whom bypass allows a bloodless pulmonary field constitute the second largest group of patients benefiting from CPB for noncardiovascular applications.

A third group of patients includes those in whom operations on the inferior vena cava necessitate a bypass procedure to return blood to the heart. Occasionally, venoarterial bypass can be utilized in these patients, but more frequently, venovenous bypass is instituted. This technique uses advances and knowledge gained with the development of CPB.

Last, patients who have unusual disease processes may also benefit from the use of bypass techniques in managing their illness.

The experience and techniques gained in the application of CPB to the "traditional" cardiovascular patient are used in managing all of these situations.

Anesthetic Considerations

The anesthetic considerations for non-cardiovascular applications of CPB are similar to those used for patients undergoing cardiac surgery. It is important to note, though, that bypass in and of itself can adversely affect the same organ system, whether it is the brain, lung, or kidney, upon which the surgery is being performed (4). Therefore, special care must be taken to provide protection to these vital organs when they themselves are being operated upon in conjunction with the use of CPB. These considerations will be discussed in greater detail below.

Surgical Considerations

While the preferred technique for the use of CPB in cardiac surgery is a midline sternotomy with cannulation of the right atrium and ascending aorta (5), certain circumstances require the institution of bypass using lower extremity access (6), most frequently, femorofemoral bypass (7, 8). Access via the upper extremities is not possible because the blood vessels are too small to accept sufficiently large cannulae (9). Although the access site depends primarily on the surgery being planned, femorofemoral bypass is used more often in CPB for noncardiovascular than for cardiac applications.

The degree of hemodilution (10, 11), degree of hypothermia (12–16), pump flows (17), and type of oxygenator (18), are similar to what has previously been described for the more common uses of CPB.

Complications

Patients undergoing CPB for noncardiovascular applications experience similar complications to those that cardiac surgical patients experience. Neurologic (19, 20), pulmonary (21, 22), gastrointestinal (23), cardiac (24), bleeding (25, 26), immunologic (27, 28), and infectious (29) complications are at least as prevalent in this noncardiac population as they are in the traditional patient population. Because patients undergoing noncardiovascular applications of CPB often do not have significant cardiac disease, they theoretically should have less cardiac risk. Although the incidence of cardiac complications should be lower, if hypothermia and circulatory arrest are used or if the pump time is too long, the risk for dysrhythmias and/or left ventricular dysfunction does, indeed, increase (30). Personnel in the operating room involved in the surgery, monitoring, and anesthetic management must be well versed and experienced in the implementation and use of CPB (31).

CARDIOPULMONARY BYPASS WITH PROFOUND HYPOTHERMIA AND CIRCULATORY ARREST

Hypothermia

HISTORICAL PERSPECTIVE

In 1958, Sealy and colleagues (32) described open heart surgery using hypothermia as an adjunct to CPB. By the following year, they had used the technique to operate on 95 patients, with an overall survival rate of 83% (33). Also in 1959, Drew and Anderson (16) reported three cases in which they used cardiac bypass with profound hypothermia and circulatory arrest. Unique to their technique was the use of the patient's own lungs to provide oxygenation during surgery. Although one child died during the perioperative period from heart block following correction of an atrioventricular canal defect, their technique caused minimal complications from hypothermia.

During that same year (1959), Woodhall, working with Sealy's group, used the technique to repair an intracranial vascular aneurysm (34). Several other techniques had been used to repair these intracranial vascular malformations, but there were problems with all of them. Before 1959, surface cooling to 28 to 30°C was used (to avoid inducing ventricular fibrillation), but this limited the maximum vascular occlusion time to 8 to 10 minutes (35). Isolated cerebral perfusion techniques in which the brain is selectively cooled have also been described (36), but it is difficult to provide cooling for the entire brain by cannulating just the carotid arteries. Extracorporeal perfusion with profound hypothermia and circulatory arrest became the preferred technique for repairing a number of neurovascular abnormalities.

Initially there was a great deal of enthusiasm for induction of hypothermia and circulatory arrest, not only for use in neurosurgical procedures, but also for repair of intracardiac lesions. As expertise with membrane oxygenation improved, the majority of cardiac cases were repaired using CPB, an oxygenator, and moderate hypothermia, to approximately 25 to 30°C. This temperature provided a 50% reduction in metabolic rate, and, therefore, extended the safe ischemic time for not only the brain and heart but all organ systems. There continue to be surgical cases, however, that can be managed most effectively with profound hypothermia and circulatory arrest.

MANAGEMENT OF HYPOTHERMIA

When using profound hypothermia, one cools the patient to 15°C before establishing circulatory arrest. Monitoring core temperature and neurologic function (37) intraoperatively is very important. In patients undergoing a craniotomy, thereby making electroencephalographic documentation of neurologic function technically difficult, it is even more important to document core temperature. Because thoracotomy is not always surgically indicated, bypass is often established using the femoral artery and vein for access (38, 39). Initially the Q_{10} for humans was thought to be approximately 2 (the metabolic rate dou-

bles for every 10°C increase in temperature). Recently Michenfelder and Milde (40) have demonstrated that below 27°C, the Q_{10} is greater than 2, not only because of hypothermia's effect on metabolic rate, but also because of its effect on cerebral function per se, which is independent of its effect on metabolic rate. This effectively doubles the impact of hypothermia on the brain. Cooling from 37°C to less than 17°C would, therefore, decrease the metabolic rate by 87½%, not by 75% as more commonly thought.

The lower the temperature, the lower the cerebral metabolic rate (41). Since electrocerebral silence occurs frequently at 20°C, some authors have cooled patients to 20°C and then instituted circulatory arrest with satisfactory results (42). Circulatory arrest is most often instituted, however, with a core temperature of 15°C because the brain cools more slowly than the body core (43) (Fig. 28.1), and within the brain there are temperature gradients of between 2 and 5°C (44). Of some importance is the maintenance of hypothermia throughout the entire brain. In those situations in which it can be used, external cranial cooling is suggested as an important means to the maintenance of hypothermia within the central nervous system during circulatory arrest (45). Surface cooling of the brain alone, however, provides inadequate cerebral protection during circulatory arrest (46). Therefore, a method that directly cools the blood and decreases the core temperature, in conjunction with surface cooling of the brain, may provide the best means of prolonging the safe neurologic ischemic time (47). The majority of reports have indicated that a nasopharyngeal temperature of between 15 and 18°C should be achieved before circulatory arrest is induced (Table 28.1). Temperatures of less than 10°C are associated with a higher incidence of complications (61, 62).

The longer the circulatory arrest, the greater the incidence of neurologic complications even with adequate levels of hypo-

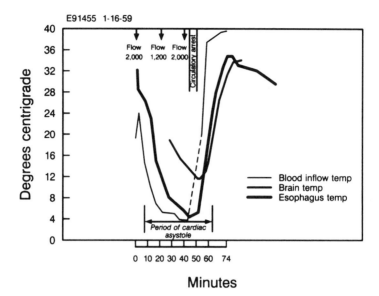

Figure 28.1. Temperature recorded via an esophageal temperature probe, from the arterial inflow cannula and from a probe placed in the parietal cortex after bypass was instituted. (Modified from Woodhall B, Sealy WC, Hall KD, Floyd WL. Craniotomy under conditions of quinidine-protected cardioplegia and profound hypothermia. Ann Surg 1960;152:37–44.)

thermia. Neurologic dysfunction correlates better with the degree of hypoxia that occurs with extended circulatory arrest than it does with the lack of perfusion per se (63). The safe ischemic time can be prolonged, therefore, by preliminary hyperbaric oxygenation, but this is not usually practical (64). The safe time limit for circulatory arrest has, however, not been fully delineated (65). Early reports demonstrated a reluctance to use circulatory arrest for more than 30 minutes (66). The majority of more recent reports suggest that a core temperature of 15°C will provide up to 60 minutes of safe ischemic time during circulatory arrest (Table 28.1).

MANAGEMENT OF CIRCULATORY ARREST

Although hypothermia itself should provide maximum cerebral protection (67), drugs such as a long-acting muscle relaxant (pancuronium) or antibiotics should be given prior to circulatory arrest since it will be impossible to administer these agents once the bypass machine is turned off. There is new experimental evidence that tissue acidosis after circulatory arrest is decreased if hyperventilation and mild hypocapnia are induced prior to circulatory arrest (68). After the patient is on bypass, during the induction and documentation of hypothermia, a barbiturate should be administered for its neuroprotective effects only if there is evidence of cerebral electrical activity on the electroencephalogram (69, 70). Barbiturates may be indicated for those patients who do not have electroencephalographic monitoring or in whom a central nervous system temperature of 15°C cannot be documented, but this is controversial, as noted (71). Corticosteroids and mannitol are often empirically given in an attempt to decrease neurologic complications, but there are no studies of patients undergoing circulatory arrest that have demonstrated an improved outcome with these drugs.

Table 28.1.   Use of CPB with Profound Hypothermia and Circulatory Arrest for Neurosurgical Procedures

Author[a]	No. of Patients	Year	Diagnosis	Anes-thesia[b]	Access[c]	Hypo-thermia[d]	Duration of Circulatory Arrest[e]	Compli-cation
Woodhall (34)	1	1959	Subcortical tumor cyst	I		E11	10	
Uihlein (48*)	2	1960	Intracranial aneurysms	I	Open	E14 B15.5	25–44	Bleeding
Patterson (38)	7	1962	Intracranial aneurysms	I	Closed	E~4–7 B~14–17	9–42.5	Bleeding
Drake (49)	10	1964	Intracranial aneurysms		8-open 2-closed	E 9.6–16.8 B 5–18	5–18	Spasm (5/10)
Patterson (50)	8	1965	Intracranial aneurysms		Closed	E 4–14	9–29	
Neville (51)	4	1966	Intracranial aneurysms (3), vascular malignancy (1)		Closed	B <15	<40	
Uihlein (52*)	67	1966	Intracranial aneurysms		17-open 49-closed	E <15		
Sundt (53)	1	1972	Basilar artery aneurysm		Closed	Surface cooling E 13	30	
McMurtry (54)	12	1974	Basilar artery aneurysms	I	Open	Surface cooling E 28–29	1–28	
Patterson (55)	1	1975	Hemangioblastoma brain stem		Open	E 10	19	
Silverberg (56)	1	1980	Giant cerebral aneurysm		Closed	E 20	28	
Baumgartner (57)	14	1983	Middle cerebral artery aneurysm (8), internal carotid artery aneurysm (3), basilar artery aneurysm (2), hemangioblastoma (2)	N	Closed	E 16–20	5–51	
Gonski (58)	40	1986	Intracranial aneurysms		Open	E <17.5	5–39	
Richards (59)	11	1987	Intracranial aneurysms	I				
Williams (60)	10	1991	Intracranial aneurysms (4), glomus tumors (3), arteriovenous malformations (2), hemangioblastoma (1)	N + I	Closed	E 10–12	1–60	Edema, swelling

[a] Name of first author only given, to conserve space. *Same institution.
[b] I, inhalational; N, narcotic.
[c] Access refers to whether cannulation was performed through an "open" chest vs. the groin (closed).
[d] B, brain; E, esophageal; expressed in degrees Centigrade.
[e] Expressed in minutes.

Use in Neurosurgery

In the late 1950s, there were multiple, simultaneous developments in the field of CPB. The studies of hypothermia in dogs by Bigelow et al. (72) stimulated other investigators who used the animal work to serve as a basis for clinical experimentation. In 1960, Woodhall and colleagues (34) at Duke University reported the first use of bypass and profound hypothermia using quinidine to protect the myocardium. With a 10-minute period of circulatory arrest, they drained a subcortical tumor-like cyst involving the left parietal lobe. Their case stimulated Uihlein and colleagues (48) at the Mayo Clinic to use extracorporeal circulation with profound hypothermia and circulatory arrest to repair intracranial aneurysms in two patients. Although the basic principles were the same, the reports highlight the anesthetic and surgical differences that can be found between physicians and institutions utilizing these techniques.

Other investigators, notably Patterson and Ray (38), expanded the technique and instituted closed-chest extracorporeal circulation. Using cannulae that were advanced into the vena cavae via the internal jugular and a femoral vein, respectively, they drained venous blood, and placed the arterial cannula in a femoral artery. This technique solved some of the technical difficulties in performing a simultaneous thoracotomy and craniotomy and was quickly adopted by other groups. The decision to use thoracic or femoral cannulation sites should be made following consultation between the members of the neurologic and cardiac teams.

By 1966, Uihlein and colleagues (52), using the new technique since 1961, had operated on a total of 66 patients with intracranial aneurysms. The mortality rate, though relatively high, was thought acceptable given the alternative. Not everyone, however, was enamored with this technique for repair of intracranial aneurysms. Using the closed-chest technique, Drake and colleagues (49) in London, Ontario, Canada, had difficulties in the 10 patients they operated on for intracranial aneurysm. They ran into technical problems because of the poor venous return using cannulae in large central veins. More importantly, from their perspective, arterial spasm, always a problem with ruptured cerebral aneurysms, continued to present difficulties; 5 of their 10 patients died within 2 to 3 months of the operative procedure. They abandoned this technique and developed other surgical techniques that dramatically changed the way neurosurgeons approached intracranial aneurysms. These techniques, simultaneously developed by Thor Sundt et al. (53) from the Department of Neurosurgery at the Mayo Clinic, led this group to also abandon the use of profound hypothermia and circulatory arrest for management of intracranial pathology.

At the same time, Michenfelder was pioneering work in the field of neuroanesthesia, which would also impact on the management of these patients (73). The refinements of the surgical approach to aneurysms, including the operating microscope, withdrawal of cerebrospinal fluid, controlled hypotension, and sophisticated neuroanesthesia made surgery for most intracranial pathology much safer without the use of extracorporeal circulation. Beginning in 1965, the majority of neurosurgical centers in the United States and Canada had abandoned the intraoperative use of profound hypothermia and circulatory arrest.

In 1972, however, Sundt, et al. (53) reported a case in which a giant aneurysm of the basilar artery, otherwise inoperable, was managed successfully with CPB, profound hypothermia, and circulatory arrest. It was the first case using this technique at the Mayo Clinic since 1964. The repair went well, and over the intervening 20 years, several reports have delineated the limited, but important, role of bypass, hypothermia, and circulatory arrest in managing neurosurgical pathology.

INDICATIONS

Since 1972, the majority of cases employing circulatory arrest have been for surgical treatment of giant basilar and cerebral aneurysms and of hemangioblastomas, frequently of the brain stem. In current practice, hypothermia and circulatory arrest allow the only chance for resection in this subgroup of patients. Baumgartner et al. (57) used a modified hypothermic approach in managing all forms of intracranial aneurysms, but this technique has not been utilized elsewhere.

ANESTHETIC MANAGEMENT

The successful management of these difficult patients mandates frequent, open communication between the neuro- and cardiovascular surgical and anesthesia teams. Unlike most patients presenting for cardiac surgery, many of these patients are young and have no coronary artery disease. The majority, however, do have vascular pathology, frequently a ruptured cerebral aneurysm in which careful management of the hemodynamics preoperatively to avoid hypo- and hypertension is as important as it is in the cardiac patient undergoing CPB. Many of these patients, therefore, should receive vasoactive drugs, most frequently β-blockers, to attenuate hemodynamic instability.

Positioning these patients can also be a major problem. While the literature shows that most people prefer closed-chest techniques, there are some circumstances in which the cranial pathology can only be approached posteriorly, mandating that the patient be in a prone position. Under these circumstances, femoral cannulation is difficult and a posterolateral thoracotomy, allowing access to the atria for venous cannulation, may be necessary. Monitoring for these patients includes a pulmonary artery catheter and an intrathecal catheter. A pulmonary artery catheter is placed because myocardial dysfunction can be a problem even in the absence of coronary artery dis-

ease when prolonged circulatory arrest is used. Furthermore, during circulatory arrest, if the pulmonary vasculature is not vented, as is frequently the case in closed-chest CPB, pulmonary edema can be a serious complication. The placement of a pulmonary artery catheter can be an important adjunct in managing these patients once bypass is reinstituted after circulatory arrest.

Occasionally, drainage of cerebrospinal fluid helps the surgeon better visualize the vascular pathology. This benefit must be weighed against the risk of an epidural hematoma in a heparinized hypothermic patient. Drainage is often achieved with a malleable needle, but in current practice, catheters designed for epidural use can be placed in the intrathecal space by the use of an 18- or 17-gauge Tuohy needle. The catheter is then taped to the patient's back, allowing for the monitoring of cerebrospinal fluid pressure and withdrawal of fluid. The larger the catheter, the better the dynamic response for pressure monitoring and the easier it is to withdraw cerebrospinal fluid. Some catheters have a spiral wire incorporated into their walls that prevents kinking and facilitates pressure monitoring and fluid withdrawal.

The maintenance of stable hemodynamics in the immediate preoperative period is a most important component of the anesthetic protocol. Therefore, a neuroanesthetic technique that employs β-blockers and controlled hypotension using nitroprusside is often used. When intracranial hypertension is a problem, controlled hyperventilation and the use of an anesthetic agent such as isoflurane are preferred. As pointed out, the majority of these patients do not have coronary artery disease, and an inhalation anesthetic, as was frequently described in early case reports, can be used. More recent case reports have described the use of a narcotic technique and, most likely, the choice of an inhalation versus a narcotic technique should be decided after careful consideration of the tracranial pathology and the patients' cardiac status.

Neurologic dysfunction is a major postoperative concern, but since these patients are undergoing craniotomy and because of the presence of anesthetic agents and hypothermia, there is no effective way to intraoperatively monitor neurologic function. Careful attention to detail in managing the hemodynamic response to anesthetic induction and surgery, as well as controlling $Paco_2$ and core temperature, are the most important adjuncts in improving outcome in these patients. Following the surgical procedure, early neurologic assessment of function in the operating room is also important and will sometimes dictate the choice of anesthetic agents. The use of propofol in these cases has not been fully explored, but based on its short half-life, might be a reasonable agent to achieve these goals if the incidence of hypotension associated with its use can be decreased.

COMPLICATIONS

Complications experienced by these patients are similar to those experienced by other patients undergoing CPB. Unique to these patients, however, are the coagulopathy and the neurologic dysfunctions that are frequently associated with bypass. These patients are at increased risk for coagulopathy for several reasons including the heparinization necessary for institution of bypass, the hypothermia that has its own effects on coagulation function beginning at approximately 30 to 32°C (74), and the vascular reactivity of the intracerebral arterial system. Many case reports underscore the major morbidity that these patients experience secondary to postoperative bleeding (Table 28.1). It is, therefore, incumbent that the surgeon establish surgical hemostasis. The anesthesiologist must establish baseline coagulation function on the patient's arrival in the operating room and monitor to identify any coagulation defects

as the patient comes off CPB. These defects include transfusion-related thrombocytopenia and decreased coagulation factors that may necessitate the use of transfused platelets, fresh-frozen plasma, or cryoprecipitate. The use of thrombin glue by the neurosurgical team, though it does have identified risks, might be of benefit in managing these patients.

The incidence of neurologic dysfunction following bypass can run as high as 70% depending upon the sensitivity of the neuropsychiatric test to evaluate neurologic function (20). Of more concern than neuropsychiatric dysfunction are the gross neurologic deficits that these patients may have on presentation to the operating room. The goal is to not worsen any preexisting deficits and, certainly, not to create any new ones. Management of hemodynamics, controlled hypotension, and induced hyperventilation may have a role in the management of these patients. Also important is the documentation of core temperature. A protective degree of hypothermia needs to be achieved in the brain prior to the institution of circulatory arrest. Several studies have documented the temperature gradients of 2 to 5°C that may exist within the brain during profound hypothermia. More importantly, brain temperature may lag behind core temperature (Fig. 28.1). A temperature probe may be necessary to document that the temperature of the brain is, indeed, less than 15°C, the temperature most frequently cited as allowing maximal cerebral protection.

Use in Urologic Surgery

The use of CPB techniques to facilitate resection of malignancies arising in the kidney came about serendipitously. Whereas the benefits of bypass with deep hypothermia and cardiac arrest were quickly appreciated and utilized for resection of intracranial aneurysms, it was not until 1970, over 10 years after the use of CPB in neuro-surgical procedures, that reports began to appear describing the technique of bypass with hypothermia and circulatory arrest for removal of tumor thromboemboli that had invaded the inferior vena cava with right atrial extension. It had been recognized for some time that patients with renal cell car-cinomas extending into the inferior vena cava had a poor prognosis (75), but if the tumor could be resected in its entirety, then prognosis was more favorable (76). The critical aspect of surgery, therefore, was the removal of the tumor with a technique that did not significantly increase morbidity. In 1970, Marshall and colleagues (77) re-ported several cases of hypernephromas ex-tending into the inferior vena cava, includ-ing a case in which they had attempted to isolate the inferior vena cava and kidney. The patient sustained a cardiac arrest fol-lowing occlusion of the vena cava for re-moval of the tumor thrombus. The patient was diagnosed as having a pulmonary embo-lism and quickly underwent a thoracotomy with cardiac massage, and a pulmonary arteriotomy was made to permit removal of a pulmonary thromboembolus. Based on this experience, in the next case, the authors placed two femoral vein catheters below the obstructing tumor, which were connected to a cannula in the internal jugular vein that had been advanced into the superior vena cava. No blood pump was used initially, since the distal venous pressure was suffi-ciently elevated to allow adequate flow from the femoral vein to the proximal caval site. During the procedure, however, the sys-temic arterial pressure began to fall, so extra-corporeal circulation was begun. This was the first time that venovenous bypass was used in resection of kidney tumors ex-tending into the right atrium.

The second report in which bypass was utilized was in a patient with a right atrial tumor. Thinking that it was a myxoma, the patient was placed on full bypass, the tumor resected from the atrium, and to everyone's surprise, the pathologic report returned "hypernephroma" (78).

INDICATIONS

The main indication for CPB is for tu-mors of the kidney, primarily renal cell car-cinoma or hypernephromas, which extend into the inferior vena cava superiorly past the diaphragm. In children, Wilms' tumors can present in this same way (79). Tumors that do not extend into the right atrium or above the diaphragm can frequently be re-sected using current surgical techniques without the necessity of a bypass proce-dure. Depending upon the degree of exten-sion of the tumor, venovenous bypass can occasionally be used to shunt blood from the inferior to the superior vena cava. Many, however, have found that collateral circula-tion is sufficient, so that this is not usually necessary. The main use for CPB is for the institution of hypothermia to allow exsan-guination into the pump with circulatory arrest for resection of caval tumors that ex-tend into the right atrium. Since complete removal of the tumor is critical to survival, several authors have commented that a quiet, motionless, bloodless right atrium al-lows the best chance for complete resection of the tumor (80–82). In addition, given the high incidence of pulmonary artery em-bolization, bypass is occasionally instituted in those patients who sustain a pulmonary embolism intraoperatively (77, 83, 84) and in whom pulmonary embolectomy offers the only chance for survival.

MANAGEMENT

The successful management of these patients requires full cooperation between the cardiac and urologic teams. The anes-thetic management of these cases has been infrequently described, but in the reports that have described the anesthetic manage-ment, it is obvious that a narcotic anesthetic technique predominates (85). This should not necessarily be the case, however. A standard intravenous induction with thiopental and succinylcholine has been used, followed by maintenance of anesthesia with inhalation agents, enflurane and nitrous oxide (84). Standard monitoring of the electrocardiogram, pulse oximeter, esophageal temperature, and systemic arterial pressures was utilized. A pulmonary artery catheter may be relatively contraindicated in these patients, depending on the extent and location of the tumor thrombus. Many patients with documented extension of the tumor into the right atrium will have cardiac symptoms and signs present prior to the surgical procedures (82, 86). Several case reports have documented that in positioning the patient, the tumor can apparently become dislodged or displaced further into the right atrium with a precipitous drop in blood pressure. The left lateral decubitus position seems to be the position in which this is most likely to occur (81, 84).

After the induction of anesthesia, either a thoracoabdominal or a midline abdominal incision extended into a sternotomy is made. While the cardiac and urologic surgical teams can begin their procedure simultaneously, the patient is not heparinized for bypass (in order to avoid excessive bleeding) until the urologic surgeons have the kidney and inferior vena cava dissected free. Once the urologists are ready, the patient is placed on CPB and, when necessary, cooled to 15°C. Some physicians report packing the patient's head in ice to keep the patient's brain at a sufficiently low temperature (87, 88), perhaps a worthwhile technique given the gradients between core and cerebral temperature (Fig. 28.1). However, there are centers in which circulatory arrest is instituted with only moderate degrees of hypothermia (approximately 25°C) (84). From the literature, however, it is apparent that the time necessary to resect the caval and right atrial tumor ranges from 10 to 45 minutes (Table 28.2). Therefore, hypothermia to 15°C should be instituted when circulatory arrest is contemplated.

During institution of bypass, a double filter can be placed in the bypass arterial line to prevent the embolization to the patient of tumor emboli (89). Because of the concern about emboli, these patients have not been considered candidates for the use of an intraoperative cell saver (84), though the latter recommendation is not based on any reported adverse sequelae. There does not appear to be contraindication to the use autotransfusion since the tumor is already in the bloodstream; furthermore, if cardiotomy suckers are used on bypass, autotransfusion, in effect, is used already.

COMPLICATIONS

The difficulties using this technique are similar to those described for the repair of intracranial aneurysms. The problem of neurologic dysfunction is difficult to quantify in this patient population since the majority of reports are of single cases. There are only 2 series in which more than 10 patients were studied. Bleeding, especially from retroperitoneal beds, was the major perioperative complication in both of these series (96, 104). Once the inferior vena cava is resected, many patients will develop postoperative ascites and lower extremity edema until adequate collateral flow is established. This is not a problem in most cases, however, because collateral flow is usually sufficient. In fact, in a large series from the Cleveland Clinic, when bypass was instituted, only the superior vena cava was cannulated for venous return because the collaterals around the inferior vena cava were sufficient to maintain venous flow to the proximal site throughout the period of cross-clamping the inferior vena cava (85). Other complications, including postoperative pulmonary dysfunction and sepsis, are similar to those with standard CPB. Since most of these cases include a nephrectomy, postoperative renal failure is common. The intravenous contrast agents used preoperatively to establish the diagnosis of renal cell carcinoma and inferior vena cava occlusion may contribute to this high incidence of postoperative renal dysfunction. It is important, however, for the anesthesiologist to avoid the administration of any nephrotoxic drugs, to monitor urine output and central venous pressure carefully, and to intervene as appropriate if either decreases below safe levels.

CARDIOPULMONARY BYPASS WITHOUT CIRCULATORY ARREST FOR PULMONARY PROCEDURES

In 1959, the same year in which Woodhall and colleagues (34) utilized CPB for excision of an intracranial aneurysm, Woods et al. (105) used bypass for resection of a carinal tumor. The procedure went well but was complicated by postoperative bleeding. An obstructing blood clot was emergently suctioned from the tracheostomy and was attributed to the combination of the operative procedure and the sequelae of bypass. As in other uses of CPB, problems with coagulation remained formidable. Nissen (106) used bypass combined with hypothermia to resect a malignant adenoma of the trachea. A third case was reported by Adkins and Izawa (107) in which a cylindroma was resected using bypass. In their case report, they emphasized the importance of having the CPB machine primed and ready and the patient's groin prepared. If, during the induction of general anesthesia, the patient's airway was obstructed because of the intratracheal tumor, femoral CPB could be instituted immediately.

In 1965, Neville and colleagues (108) reported using bypass for tracheal resections. Depending on the location of the tumor, they used either a right, left, or anterior thoracotomy. They cannulated the superior vena cava from the right atrium, drained the inferior vena cava via a catheter in the femoral vein, and returned blood to their patients via a cannula in the femoral artery. Of the 11 patients they studied, they

used CPB in 8 and partial CPB in 3. Of their 11 patients, 2 died from complications from hemorrhage, 4 from pulmonary complications, and 1 from a myocardial infarction. The authors had attempted to minimize bleeding by completing the major portion of the operation before instituting bypass. As demonstrated in their results, however, this did not sufficiently obviate the bleeding complications frequently seen following bypass. In addition, as noted during CPB for cardiac and vascular procedures, postoperative pulmonary complications were common. Other individuals continued to advocate CPB for pulmonary bypass based on the ease with which sterility was maintained (no manipulation of a tumor or carina around a contaminated endotracheal tube), the unencumbered nature of the surgical incision, and the ease of performance (109).

While CPB continues to be used occasionally for tracheal surgery, primarily in infants and small children in whom adequate ventilation with traditional endotracheal tubes is difficult to maintain (110), current management of tracheal and carinal pathology was pioneered by Grillo and his colleagues (111) at the Massachusetts General Hospital. In 1969, they reported the cases of 31 patients who underwent tracheal resection over a 7-year period in which bypass was not utilized. They emphasized the importance of advances in surgical techniques, anesthetic practice, and management of perioperative complications. For tracheal lesions, anesthesia is induced and an oral endotracheal tube is placed, the chest opened, the trachea transected distally to the lesion, and the distal tracheal segment intubated through the operating field (Fig. 28.2). The tracheal lesion can then be resected, and the trachea reanastomosed as shown. For more distal lesions, including lesions of the carina, Grillo et al. advocated intubating one of the mainstem bronchi through the operative field with obstruction of the contralateral pulmonary artery to optimize ventilation and perfusion

Table 28.2.   Use of CPB for Patients with Renal Tumor

Author[a]	No. of Patients	Year	Type	Anesthesia[b]	Access[c]	Technique[d]	Complications[e]	Arrest Time (min)
Marshall (77)	4	1970		ND	V-FV, SVC	Standard CPB	Cardiac arrest in 1 patient, no circ. arrest in 2 patients	
Adrekani (78)	1	1971	Renal cell	ND	ND	CPB		
Gleason (89)	1	1972	Renal cell	ND	V-SVC, FV A-FA			
Utley (79)	1	1973	Wilms'	ND	V-SVC	CPB with circ. arrest		ND
Murphy (90)	1	1973	Wilms'	ND		CPB with circ. arrest		
Paul (86)	1	1975		ND	V-SVC, IVC A-FA			
Bissada (91)	1	1977	Renal cell	ND	V-SVC, right common iliac vein A-ND			
Farooki (92)	1	1976	Wilms'	ND	ND			
Vaughan (93)	1	1977	Nephroblastoma		V-SVC A-FA	CPB		
Theman (80)	2	1978	Wilms' adrenal carcinoma	ND	V-SVC A-aorta	CPB	Systolic hypertension	43 15
Choh (81)	1	1982	Renal cell	ND	V-SVC, FV A-aorta	CPB		
Prager (82)	1	1982	Renal cell Adrenal carcinoma	ND	V-SVC A-aorta	Standard CPB		ND
Klein (94)	4	1984	Renal cell	ND	V-SVC A-aorta, FA	CPB 25°C	1 patient with filter extrusion, hemorrhage	ND
Krane (95)	1	1984	Renal cell	ND	V-SVC A-aorta, FA	CPB 11°C		32
Montie (96)	13	1984	Renal cell	ND	V-SVC A-aorta	CPB 18–20°C	Bleeding, DVT	12–47
Marshall (87)	1	1984	Renal cell	ND	V-SVC A-aorta	CPB 19.5°C		41
Novick (97)	1	1980	Renal cell	ND	V-SVC A-aorta, FA	CPB	None	
Farrell (98)	1	1974	Renal cell	ND	V-SVC, FV A-FA	CPB 31°C	None	
Daughtry (83)	1	1977		ND	ND	ND	Pulmonary embolism intraop	

Table 28.2. *continued*

Author[a]	No. of Patients	Year	Type	Anesthesia[b]	Access[c]	Technique[d]	Complications[e]	Arrest Time (min)
Wilkinson (84)	1	1986		Pentothal succinylcholine Enflurane N$_2$O	V-SVC A-aorta	ND	Sepsis, pulmonary embolism intraop	
Turini (99)	1	1986	Renal cell	ND	V-SVC, FV A-aorta	CPB 28°C		
Lachance (88)	1	1987	Renal cell	ND	V-SVC A-aorta	CPB 15°C	None	14
Hedderich (100)	4	1987	Renal cell	ND	V-SVC, FV A-aorta	1 with CPB with arrest, 3 without CPB		
Marshall (101)	9	1988	Renal cell	ND				
Hunt (102)	1	1988	Wilms'	"Cardiac surgery anesthetic"	ND	CPB 15°C		37
Wickey (103)	1	1988	Renal cell	IV fentanyl (Induction and maintenance)		CPB 20°C		27
Welch (85*)	20	1989	95% with renal cell	Narcotic technique	V-SVC A-aorta	CPB 15.8°C	Bleeding, pulmonary dysfunction	12–44
Novick (104*)	43	1990	39 with renal cell	Thiopental				10–44

[a] Name of first author only given, to conserve space. *Same institution.
[b] ND, not described; IV, intravenous
[c] V, venous cannula; FV, femoral vein; SVC, superior vena cava; A, arterial cannula; FA, femoral artery;
[d] circ, circulatory
[e] DVT, deep venous thrombosis.

during resection of the carinal lesion (Fig. 28.3).

It is currently unusual, then, to use CPB for carinal or tracheal lesions (112). In those circumstances in which it might be used, the experiences from past reports would be appropriate for today's practice in that obstruction of the airway following induction of general anesthesia is a potential problem of great concern, and though we are better able to manage the bleeding and pulmonary complications following by-

pass, they are still potential major complications.

Pulmonary Embolectomy

As noted previously, Gibbon initially developed CPB to manage massive pulmonary embolism (3). It was not until 1961, however, that Cooley et al. (113) reported the first successful use of bypass to resect a pulmonary embolus. Previously, pulmonary embolectomy was occasionally per-

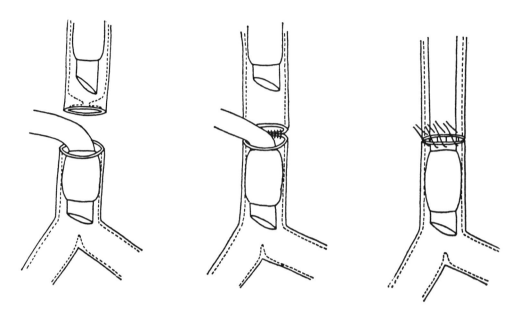

Figure 28.2.   Procedure for resection of high tracheal lesion. After the trachea is transected below the lesion, the distal tracheal segment is intubated through the operating field. After resection of the lesion, as the trachea is reanastomosed, the distal endotracheal tube is removed and the anastomosis completed. (Modified from Geffin B, Bland J, Grillo H. Anesthetic management of tracheal resection and reconstruction. Anesth Analg 1969;48:884–890.)

formed using cardiac inflow occlusion under general body hypothermia, the same technique that had been used to resect cardiac lesions. It was obvious to the authors that CPB had important advantages for resection of pulmonary emboli, otherwise a uniformally fatal obstruction. In 1966, Rosenberg and colleagues (114) reviewed the experience with CPB for pulmonary embolectomy and made several recommendations. Based on earlier experiences, if pulmonary embolectomy was to be successful, time was of the essence, and resection must be attempted within 2 hours of the embolization.

In 1967, Beall and Cooley (115) summarized their experience at the Texas Heart Institute using CPB for resuscitation and treatment of pulmonary emboli. Their success rate was only 33% for long-term survival, but they believed that the technique was indicated because, otherwise, the mortality rate would have been, in their estimation, 100%.

Sautter (116), at the Marshfield Clinic, also reported similar survival rates (4 of 11) and, based on his experience, recommended using CPB only for those patients who were hypotensive and whose lives were immediately threatened. His technique used hypothermic low-flow hemodilution because no blood was required to prime the bypass machine. Because large cannulae were unnecessary, peripheral cannulization could be used to facilitate the emergent implementation of bypass, which he believed was most important in managing patients and improving survival. In his experience, mortality had more to do with the underlying disease process than with technique. He strongly recommended that bypass for pulmonary embolectomy be instituted as rapidly as possible when the patient's cardiopulmonary condition was still reversible, before a series of events began from which resuscitation was impossible.

Garcia and colleagues (117), recognizing the importance of the early use of

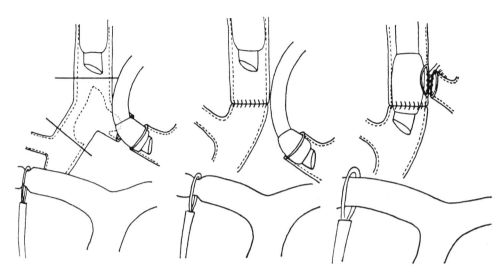

Figure 28.3. Procedure for resection of carinal lesion, similar to what was described for Figure 28.2. (Modified from Geffin B, Bland J, Grillo H. Anesthetic management of tracheal resection and reconstruction. Anesth Analg 1969;884–890.)

CPB to resuscitate patients, advocated partial bypass for resuscitation, and then, employing a combined approach, total bypass for resection of the pulmonary embolus. In current practice, transthoracic pulmonary embolectomy without bypass has met with such limited success that the procedure has been all but abandoned. Cardiopulmonary bypass for open pulmonary embolectomy should be utilized for those patients who are hypotensive (systolic pressure less than 90 mm Hg), have a Pao_2 of less than 60 mm Hg on 100% oxygen, and have a urinary output of <20 ml/hr (118). These guidelines were developed more than 20 years ago, but are still being used today (119). There are no prospective, controlled studies comparing pulmonary embolectomy with and without bypass, nor are such studies likely to be performed in the future. Pulmonary catheter embolectomy is a new technique that has been advocated for managing these critically ill patients, but its role is still being investigated (120).

In summary, in those patients in whom CPB is indicated, it should be instituted as soon as possible for resuscitation of the patient, frequently via the groin, and then with the bypass in effect, the thromboembolus should be resected. Problems with bleeding and postoperative pulmonary complications (pulmonary edema, atelectasis, etc.) must be managed aggressively. Despite the best efforts, based on previous reports, a mortality rate of approximately 70% in the first 30 days postoperatively is not unusual.

Pulmonary Transplantation

At this point in time, single-lung transplantation, frequently transplanting the donor lung into the recipient's left chest, is the most frequently utilized approach. This can be achieved 70 to 80 percent of the time without CPB. During resection of the native lung, the contralateral lung is ventilated while the donor lung is implanted in the chest and the pulmonary artery anastomosed; the donor lung is ventilated via an endotracheal tube inserted through the operative field. In some patients, however, it is impossible to ventilate and oxygenate the patient because of the disease process in the remaining contralateral native lung. In these circumstances, CPB is used. Insertion of the arterial and venous cannulae is usually through the groin, keeping the chest free of cannulae in order to improve the surgical field for the transplant surgeon (121).

In addition to the occasional use of bypass for management of pulmonary transplantation, CPB has also been used for "domino" procedures in which one recipient patient's heart and lungs are removed, en bloc, with the (normal) heart given to a second recipient while the first recipient then receives a heart-lung transplant (122). Also increasingly, donors are placed on bypass for procurement of combined heart-lung preparations, allowing the rapid induction of hypothermia, viewed as an optimal preservation technique for multiorgan procurement (123, 124).

Other Uses

There have been a few case reports in which CPB is used for pulmonary lesions that cannot be managed by any other means. Shuman (125) reported a sarcoma of the lung with extension into the left atrium that was successfully managed using bypass, similar to the experience reported for resection of renal cell carcinomas that extended into the right atrium (125). Pulmonary artery aneurysms and fistulae have also been successfully resected using bypass (126). Previous comments regarding the use of bypass for the induction of anesthesia in the management of obstructing carcinomas of the trachea also pertain to life-threatening tracheal obstructions that cannot be otherwise managed (127, 128). Maharaj et al. (129) reported a case in which a patient was placed on bypass and an intratracheal foreign body removed. Finally, in the management of alveolar proteinosis, several case reports have described the use of this technique for bilateral lung lavage (130, 131). In most cases, however, alveolar proteinosis can be effectively managed without the use of CPB (132). Even patients with a single-lung and alveolar pro-

teinosis have been managed by more conservative techniques (133).

VENOVENOUS BYPASS

Marshall and colleagues (77) used a passive venovenous bypass to manage a patient with renal cell carcinoma extending into the inferior vena cava and right atrium in 1970. The need for such a bypass technique that could drain blood from the lower extremities and portal system was obvious in the 1960s, but the first clinical trials for liver patients utilizing passive bypasses, however, were unsuccessful. Either the bypasses clotted and did not function or, far worse, clots formed and released from the bypass tubing, causing lethal pulmonary emboli. In cases in which heparinization was used, the addition of anticoagulant therapy to patients with liver-associated coagulopathy produced unacceptable bleeding, leading to increased morbidity and mortality. It was not until the early 1980s that venovenous bypass came into practice using heparin-bonded circuits with a centrifugal pump (134, 135) instead of systemic heparinization with a roller pump.

DEFINITION

Venovenous bypass differs from CPB in many ways: (a) an oxygenator is not used in the circuit; (b) the arterial system is not perfused, therefore pressures within the system are lower; and (c) the circuit, in essence, is serving as only a conduit for blood from one or more regions of the body to the right heart. Therefore, venovenous bypass frequently utilizes flows less than those seen on cardiac bypass, and, though occasionally flows as high as 6 liters/min can be achieved, flows between 1 and 2 liters/min are most frequently used, which are significantly lower than those achieved on the systemic side.

INDICATIONS

Venovenous bypass is used for the treatment of respiratory failure (extracorporeal CO_2 removal, see Chapter 25), and in the management of surgical procedures on the liver, most frequently for liver transplantation during the anhepatic phase; and for combined resections of the liver *and* vena cava.

MANAGEMENT

When instituting venovenous bypass, depending upon the organ bed to be bypassed, the cannula is usually placed in one femoral vein and advanced into the bifurcation to drain the inferior vena cava. In circumstances in which the portal system must be drained, a second catheter is placed in the portal vein. The drainage from these catheters is then directed to a centrifugal pump, with return to the patient most frequently via an axillary or internal jugular vein. (The use of centrifugal pumps is discussed in Chapter 3.) For procedures involving the liver, no heparin is used. For extracorporeal CO_2 removal, more aggressive heparinization is mandatory.

As stated previously, since venovenous bypass in this context is intended only to return blood to the heart without support of oxygenation, CO_2 removal, or perfusion of the entire body, flows much lower than those seen on classic CPB are employed. In our own practice, flows are considered adequate as long as they are not less than 1 liter/min (136) and cardiac preload is maintained. Decreased flows usually indicate a problem with the cannulae or some other obstruction to the venous system.

Complications of venovenous bypass are few. The new techniques that obviate the need for heparin by using heparin-bonded catheters, tubings, and pumps, and the use of centrifugal pumps (137) have decreased the complications of clotting that were previously reported. Air embolism can occur in venovenous bypass (138, 139), just as in CPB, with potentially lethal sequelae. In studies of venovenous bypass, no clinically significant coagulopathy has

been described (134, 140). However, decreases in core temperature, heart rate, and arterial pressure with increases in central venous pressure have been reported (140). The blood volume becomes concentrated as evidenced by increases in hematocrit, colloid oncotic pressure, serum osmolality, and serum sodium. These data, along with an accumulating base deficit, suggest that venovenous bypass is associated with less than optimal perfusion of the abdomen and lower extremities. Flow-dependent, third-space fluid accumulation (141) is most likely responsible for decreasing cardiac output and pump flow during the bypass. These limitations, however, while of importance, do not limit the use of venovenous bypass for those surgical procedures in which it has clearly proven to be beneficial.

Liver Transplantation

It is possible to carry out liver transplantation successfully without venovenous bypass (142), but many centers report a higher incidence of complications and associated morbidity and mortality when venovenous bypass is not used (143, 144). The surgical team at the University of Pittsburgh decided that the liver transplantation procedure would be improved by the use of a bypass technique that would shunt blood from the lower extremities and mesenteric beds to the right atrium. In 1982, Dr. Henry Bahnson, a cardiac surgeon at the University of Pittsburgh, assisted with a liver transplantation operation in which venovenous bypass was used. In this patient, heparin was administered to facilitate bypass. In the next several patients in whom heparin was used, the bleeding from the raw surfaces of the operative wound was so great and the heparin effect reversed with such difficulty, that the value of venovenous bypass in liver transplantation was again questioned. However, within the same year, work done at the University of Pittsburgh demonstrated that it was indeed possible to use venovenous bypass without heparinization (145). Concerns about the possibility of clot formation in the bypass tubing and consequent pulmonary embolization remained a concern, but subsequent studies and experiences demonstrated that these concerns were ill-founded (143). It is possible, as stated previously, to perform liver transplantation without venovenous bypass, and in some liver transplant centers, especially in Europe, this is still the method of choice (142). Other centers have reported the use of partial or total CPB, including systemic heparinization with an oxygenator in the pump circuit (146–148).

The majority of liver transplant centers throughout the United States and Europe do, however, utilize venovenous bypass (142, 149–151). It is the ability to use this technique that has greatly facilitated the development of liver transplantation. Use of venovenous bypass for up to 4 to 5 hours without obvious harm to the recipient has extended the surgeon's time, allowing for the modification of many of the aspects of recipient operation. With the hemodynamic stability afforded by venovenous bypass, it is possible for the surgeon to perform the resection of the native liver in a more determined and careful manner. Once the liver has been isolated and resected, all of the raw surfaces that were created during the hepatectomy are closed. This extremely important aspect of the surgical procedure, in which the surgeon can utilize the additional time to obtain surgical hemostasis, has significantly decreased the bleeding problems associated with liver transplantation.

MANAGEMENT

Venovenous bypass has been suggested for venous decompression, improved hemodynamic stability, and decreased intraoperative blood loss during the anhepatic phase of liver transplantation. Since hypothermia with its effect on coagulation is a problem, the maintenance of normothermia during the operative procedure is important. In many centers, patients are positioned on a heating blanket on the operating table. In our own practice, an air-warming device is placed over the lower and upper extremities during surgery. Routine hemodynamic monitoring should include electrocardiography for measurement of heart rate and for the presence of ischemia; a core temperature probe; pulse oximetry; an arterial cannula for continuous monitoring of systemic arterial pressure; a pulmonary artery catheter for measurement of cardiac filling pressures and cardiac outputs; and metabolic monitoring including arterial blood gases, sodium, potassium, ionized calcium, blood glucose, and coagulation (through the use of a thromboelastogram and, increasingly, a prothrombin and activated partial thromboplastin time). These measurements are obtained at baseline and then repeated at discrete intervals during the operative procedure.

As stated in the introductory section, liver transplantation necessitates the drainage of both the systemic and portal systems. This is frequently done with cannulae in the femoral and portal veins. In those circumstances in which the portal vein cannot be easily cannulated, catheters placed in the mesenteric venous system of the abdomen have been described (149). During the recipient hepatectomy, following the abdominal laparotomy, and when bypass is ready for implementation, the surgeon ligates the hepatic artery and common duct and mobilizes the liver. The portal vein and femoral cannulae are inserted, allowing both the splanchnic and systemic venous drainage to be brought into the venovenous circuit. Entry into the proximal systemic venous system is usually via the axillary or internal jugular vein. The surgeon then proceeds with mobilization of the liver, dividing all structures, including the infrahepatic vena cava.

Following the initiation of bypass, there is frequently a transient decrease in hemodynamics that rarely persists for more than 15 to 30 seconds. In one study, with the initiation of bypass, there was a 4°C decrease in core temperature, a statistically significant decrease in heart rate, systemic arterial pressure; and an increase in the central venous pressure (140). Electrocardiographic changes, attributable to the effects of temperature and alterations in potassium, were also noted. It is important to monitor and treat hypothermia aggressively during the transplant procedure since heparinless venovenous bypass cannot use a classic heat exchanger because of the large, potentially thrombogenic surface area that could lead to fibrin deposition and release of emboli into the patient.

When bypass is discontinued, it is important that coagulopathies are corrected. This is accomplished through the infusion of platelets, fresh-frozen plasma, and cryoprecipitate based on the findings of the thromboelastogram and other clotting studies. Calcium, potassium, and glucose abnormalities must be monitored and treated. Hypocalcemia is readily corrected with the intravascular administration of calcium chloride; hyperkalemia is usually transient. Hyperglycemia is infrequently treated intraoperatively since many of these patients become hypoglycemic within 6 to 10 hours of the operative procedure.

Caval Resections

INDICATION

As surgical and anesthetic techniques common to transplantation of the liver improved, these advances were used in procedures on the liver (for resections) (152), the vena cava (for relief of obstructions) (153), and for combined hepatic and inferior vena caval resections (154). Leiomyosarcomas of the vena cava, in which isolated resection of the inferior cava is indicated (155), and the use of bypass for surgical correction of the Budd-Chiari syndrome (156, 157) and to repair traumatic disruption of the vena cava (158), have been reported, but in most cases, venovenous bypass is indicated for combined hepatic and vena caval resections. Frequently, it is impossible to isolate the liver and achieve acceptable cancer-free margins without resecting the inferior vena cava (154).

MANAGEMENT

During a combined liver and vena caval resection, decompression of the portal system is not necessary. The cross-clamp time is usually only 15 to 30 minutes, and it would be unusual for the bowel and mesentery not to tolerate venous outflow obstruction for this period of time. It is, however, necessary to shunt the lower systemic circulation. In these circumstances, the systemic circulation is drained via a catheter in the inferior vena cava, and the venous effluent is returned to the patient through a large-bore, internal jugular cannula. Most of these patients are operated on in a thoracoabdominal position, and unlike the supine position used for liver transplantation, the thoracoabdominal position makes access to the axillary vein more difficult to achieve. During bypass, a flow of greater than 1 liter/min is the goal. As with liver transplantation, the use of venovenous bypass permits better surgical exposure, allowing more meticulous dissection, resection of the tumor mass and vena cava, and insertion of a polytetrafluoroethylene graft (GORE-TEX, WL Gore, Flagstaff, AZ) when indicated.

CARDIOPULMONARY AND VENOVENOUS BYPASS FOR OTHER INDICATIONS

Use of CPB for Anesthetic Problems

Prior to the clinical use of dantrolene, malignant hyperthermia was treated with support therapies including hyperventilation and systemic cooling of the patient. In one case in which these maneuvers were unsuccessful, CPB with hypothermia was instituted via a femorofemoral approach

(159). The patient was cooled from 41°C to 37°C with excellent outcome. The development of dantrolene made such maneuvers generally unnecessary; however, malignant hyperthermia remains a problem, and occasionally patients will present to surgery with diagnosed (160) or undiagnosed malignant hyperthermia. One such patient with unknown malignant hyperthermia underwent repair of a ventricular septal defect (161). Anesthesia included nitrous oxide and halothane and the only difficulty during bypass was the need for an increased fresh gas flow through the oxygenator (minute ventilation) to maintain an acceptable Pa_{CO_2}. At the completion of bypass, the patient became febrile and tachycardic. Upon arrival in the intensive care unit, the patient's temperature was greater than 40°C. Malignant hyperthermia was suspected, and the patient was successfully managed with an intravenous injection of dantrolene. Malignant hyperthermia more commonly presents intraoperatively than postoperatively. In patients such as this or in short procedures where the intraoperative temperature is normal and the hyperthermia develops postoperatively in the recovery room or intensive care unit, sepsis is more commonly the concern, but occasionally, patients will be febrile secondary to the development of malignant hyperthermia.

Cardiopulmonary Bypass and Accidental Hypothermia

Accidental hypothermia has been a problem for millennia. Only in the 20th century did the realization come that many patients who might otherwise be declared dead could be resuscitated. In 1967, Kugelberg and colleagues (162) described the management of a patient who presented to their hospital with a core body temperature of 21.7°C. Concerns about gradually warming the patient and the risk of cardiac arrest from ventricular fibrillation stimulated the

authors to rewarm the patient rapidly with bypass using a heat exchanger and oxygenator. This was performed using the left femoral artery and vein for cannulation. The patient was successfully rewarmed without the development of ventricular fibrillation. The postoperative period was complicated by bronchopneumonia and renal failure, but the patient eventually had a complete recovery. The authors highlighted the use of bypass for the management of accidental hypothermia based on their observations that the patient can be more rapidly rewarmed; there was diminished risk of ventricular fibrillation; and in the event of ventricular fibrillation, circulation and oxygenation could be supported until the heart was defibrillated (frequently once the core temperature was greater than 28°C). In other circumstances, patients have been more emergently managed, usually while profoundly hypothermic, and partial bypass has been instituted while the patient underwent cardiopulmonary resuscitation for ventricular fibrillation.

Several series have examined the use of CPB in accidental hypothermia. Following a tragedy on Mount Hood in Oregon in which 11 patients presented to the hospital emergency department profoundly hypothermic, 10 of the patients were warmed via bypass, and there were 2 long-term survivors (163). There were no survivors among those patients who presented with a core temperature less than 22°C. This would substantiate previous reports in which successes were rarely observed if the core temperature was this low. The two survivors had spontaneous respiratory activity on admission to the hospital.

The issue of age in identifying patients who are candidates is controversial. Based on the Bellevue experience, youth itself is not protective when core temperatures are below 26°C (164). In a series reported from England, Duguid et al. (165) described an 87% mortality rate in 23 elderly patients treated via active external warming and concluded that elderly patients should not be actively rewarmed. A review of the literature since the initial report in 1967 from Kugelberg et al. would indicate a much higher success rate (approximately 70%). The poor success rate with the Mount Hood victims may have been because the exposure was substantially longer than in other studies. The decision of whether or not to initiate rewarming should not be made on the basis of initial temperature alone until the human limits are further defined.

A review of the previous reports would indicate, however, a dire prognosis for core temperatures less than 16°C. The length of time of the hypothermic insult, independent of core temperature, is another factor in determining the prognosis. Furthermore, prognosis for patients without some evidence of respiratory activity, with chronic health problems, or who are elderly is sufficiently poor that aggressive rewarming with bypass needs to be carefully considered in these particular circumstances. In managing these patients, hemoconcentration, electrolyte abnormalities, hyperkalemia, hypokalemia, and pulmonary and cardiac problems have been reported, and renal failure secondary to myoglobinuria is a major concern.

Whether or not CPB is useful in these profoundly hypothermic patients remains, however, controversial. A recent study from New York described 16 patients with core temperatures of between 25 and 32°C. All were successfully managed using warmed intravenous fluids, heated aerosol masks, and, occasionally, warm peritoneal dialysis (166). The decision of whether to use bypass to warm a profoundly hypothermic patient is best made by the physicians managing the patient and is based on their assessment of the patient's status and availability of resources.

Several case reports have indicated that patients who are hypothermic fol-

lowing an overdose with barbiturates can also be successfully resuscitated using bypass (167). In contrast to patients who experience accidental hypothermia, the patients with barbiturate-induced comas have higher core temperatures and tend to be older patients. Outcome is improved if the patient can be rewarmed, and one of the advantages of bypass is the ability to include a filter to dialyze barbiturates (168).

Vascular Procedures

While uncommon, bypass with and without hypothermia has been used for a number of rare and exotic vascular problems. These reports all include the presence of a fistula or aneurysm that would not be amenable to repair without circulatory arrest or require the ability to isolate the affected vessel and preserve organ function through the use of the degree of hypothermia that bypass affords. There are reports of repairs of aortovenous fistulas affecting the aorta and vena cava (169), and the aorta and renal vein (170) using bypass, hypothermia, and circulatory arrest. Also reported have been repairs of a variety of aneurysms and fistulas (171–173), hemangiomas (174, 175), and vascular malformations of the face (176). Interestingly, in management of renal artery abnormalities, though surgical repair is commonly performed in situ, occasionally autotransplantation with or without extracorporeal surgery is performed. In cases in which extracorporeal surgery is performed, the kidney can be cooled, either with the intraarterial perfusion of a plegic solution or occasionally utilizing a pulsatile unit with oxygenated albumin perfusate (177, 178).

Orthopaedic Procedures

In the 1950s and 60s, bypass techniques were used to administer high concentrations of chemotherapeutic agents to discrete regions of the body (179, 180). These were most frequently administered to patients with neoplasms of the lower extremities. A bypass technique was used employing a small oxygenator in which the artery and vein that supplied the tumor area were isolated and cannulated with cannulae of appropriate size. For the lower extremities, the common femoral artery and vein were most frequently cannulated. The arm could likewise be treated utilizing an axillary artery and vein. Complete isolation of the limb was accomplished by applying a tourniquet proximal to the cannulae. Perfusion was usually brief, lasting from 15 to 30 minutes. While this technique held promise, other treatment modalities have largely supplanted regional perfusion techniques. Some centers continue to use this technique experimentally, however.

Extracorporeal Filtration of *Schistosoma*

Several reports in the late 1960s described a bypass procedure in which the portal system was drained via a cannula placed in the splenic vein and advanced into the portal vein (181–184). The blood was filtered to trap schistosomes, with a roller pump in the circuit to infuse blood back into a femoral vein. Heparinization was required for this procedure. Complications were minimal, though the technique was not always successful. Several hundred patients were treated with this technique, but newer antiparasitic drugs make it unnecessary today.

SUMMARY

Despite enthusiasm in the 1960s for the use of CPB as an adjunct in a variety of surgical cases, the primary use today is to facilitate the surgical correction of cardiac and aortic lesions. However, bypass techniques developed for these procedures have indications in other cases where they are clearly life-saving. Certain neurosurgical and urologic procedures can only be undertaken and completed with success when circulatory arrest, implemented with the use of CPB and profound hyperthermia, is used. Furthermore, certain procedures on the lungs can only be achieved when systemic oxygenation is supplied via CPB. The principles developed for CPB have led to the development of effective venovenous bypass techniques that have been used in hepatic transplantation and in other procedures involving the abdominal viscera. There are other uncommon conditions in which CPB and venovenous bypass can be used that improve patient survival and decrease morbidity.

It is imperative that the surgical and anesthetic teams have the necessary experience to use these techniques, which are frequently gained in using CPB for cardiac procedures. A well-trained, experienced, and knowledgeable team significantly decreases morbidity and improves survival.

REFERENCES

1. Burchell HB. Contributions of the basic sciences to successful clinical application of cardiopulmonary bypass. Mayo Clin Proc 1980; 55:754–757.
2. Stephen CR, Bourgeois-Gavardin M, Dent S, Brown IW Jr, Sealy WC. Anesthetic management in open-heart surgery: electroencelphalographic and metabolic findings in 81 patients. Anesth Analg 1959;38:198–205.
3. Curtis LE. An early history of extracorporeal circulation. J Cardiovasc Surg 1966;7: 240–247.
4. Norlander O, Pitzele S, Edling I, Norberg B, Crafoord C, Senning A. Anesthesiological experience from intracardiac surgery with the Crafoord-Senning heart-lung machine. Acta Anaesth Scand 1958;2:181–210.
5. Serry C, Najafi H, Dye WS, Javid H, Hunter JA, Goldin MD. Superiority of aortic over femoral cannulation for cardiopulmonary bypass, with specific attention to lower extremity neuropathy. J Cardiovasc Surg 1978;19:277–279.
6. Berger RL, Barsamian EM. Iliac or femoral vein-to-artery total cardiopulmonary bypass. An experimental and clinical study. Ann Thorac Surg 1966;2:281–289.

7. Berger RL, Saini VK, Dargan EL. Clinical applications of femoral vein-to-artery cannulation for mechanical cardiopulmonary support and bypass. Ann Thorac Surg 1973;15:163–169.

8. Smith CR, Getrajdman GI, Hsu DT. Venous cannulation for high-flow femorofemoral bypass. Ann Thorac Surg 1990;49:674–675.

9. Abouna GM. Brachial arteriovenous shunts for hemodialysis and extracorporeal procedures. Eur Surg Res 1973;5:390–400.

10. Lilleaasen P, Stokke O. Moderate and extreme hemodilution in open-heart surgery: fluid balance and acid-base studies. Ann Thorac Surg 1978;25:127–133.

11. Kawashima Y, Yamamoto Z, Manabe H. Safe limits of hemodilution in cardiopulmonary bypass. Surgery 1974;76:391–397.

12. Kabat H, Dennis C, Baker AB. Recovery of function following arrest of the brain circulation. Am J Physiol 1941;132:737–747.

13. Rosomoff HL, Holaday DA. Cerebral blood flow and cerebral oxygen consumption during hypothermia. Am J Physiol 1954;179:85–88.

14. Swan H, Zeavin I, Holmes JH, Montgomery V. Cessation of circulation in general hypothermia. I. Physiologic changes and their control. Ann Surg 1953;138:360–376.

15. Parkins WM, Jensen JM, Vars HM. Brain cooling in the prevention of brain damage during periods of circulatory occlusion in dogs. J Thorac Cardiovasc Surg 1954;140:284–287.

16. Drew CE, Anderson IM. Profound hypothermia in cardiac surgery. Report of three cases. Lancet 1959;1:748–750.

17. Garman JK. Optimal pressures and flows during cardiopulmonary bypass. Pro: a low-flow, low-pressure technique is acceptable. J Cardiothorac Vasc Anesth 1991;5:399–401.

18. van Oeveren W, Kazatchkine MD, Descamps-Latscha B, et al. Deleterious effects of cardiopulmonary bypass. A prospective study of bubble versus membrane oxygenation. J Thorac Cardiovasc Surg 1985;89:888–899.

19. Silverstein A, Krieger HP. Neurologic complications of cardiac surgery. Arch Neurol 1960;3:601–605.

20. Shaw PJ, Bates D, Cartlidge NEF, Heaviside D, Julian DG, Shaw DA. Early neurological complications of coronary artery bypass surgery. Br Med J 1985;291:1384–1387.

21. Barnhorst DA. Extracardiac thoracic complications of cardiac surgery. Surg Clin North Am 1973;53:937–944.

22. Maggart M, Stewart S. The mechanisms and management of noncardiogenic pulmonary edema following cardiopulmonary bypass. Ann Thorac Surg 1987;43:231–236.

23. Welling RE, Rath R, Albers JE, Glaser RS. Gastrointestinal complications after cardiac surgery. Arch Surg 1986;121:1178–1180.

24. Hermens WT, Willems GM, van der Vusse GJ. Minimal myocardial injury after uncomplicated coronary bypass surgery. Various sources of over estimation. Clin Chim Acta 1988;173:243–250.

25. Gomes MMR, McGoon DC. Bleeding patterns after open-heart surgery. J Thorac Cardiovasc Surg 1970;60:87–97.

26. Woodman RC, Harker LA. Bleeding complications associated with cardiopulmonary bypass. Blood 1990;76:1680–1697.

27. Westaby S. Organ dysfunction after cardiopulmonary bypass. A systemic inflammatory reaction initiated by the extracorporeal circuit. Intensive Care Med 1987;13:89–95.

28. Moore FD Jr, Warner KG, Assousa S, Valeri CR, Khuri SF. The effects of complement activation during cardiopulmonary bypass. Attenuation by hypothermia, heparin, and hemodilution. Ann Surg 1988;208:95–103.

29. Bell DM, Goldmann DA, Hopkins CC, Karchmer AW, Moellering RC Jr. Unreliability of fever and leukocytosis in the diagnosis of infection after cardiac valve surgery. J Thorac Cardiovasc Surg 1978;75:87–90.

30. Reed WA, Kittle CF. Survival rate and metabolic acidosis after prolonged extracorporeal circulation with total cardiopulmonary bypass. J Thorac Cardiovasc Surg 1958;148:219–225.

31. Tinker JH. Cardiopulmonary bypass: current concepts and controversies. Philadelphia: WB Saunders, 1989.

32. Sealy WC, Brown IW Jr, Young WG Jr. A report of the use of both extracorporeal circulation and hypothermia for open heart surgery. Ann Surg 1958;147:603–613.

33. Sealy WC, Brown IW Jr, Young WG Jr, Smith WW, Lesage AM. Hypothermia and extracorporeal circulation for open heart surgery: its simplification with a heat exchanger for rapid cooling and rewarming. Ann Surg 1959;150:627–639.

34. Woodhall B, Sealy WC, Hall KD, Floyd WL. Craniotomy under conditions of quinidine-protected cardioplegia and profound hypothermia. Ann Surg 1960;152:37–44.

35. Botterell EH, Lougheed WM, Scott JW, Vandewater SL. Hypothermia, and interruption of carotid, or carotid and vertebral circulation, in the surgical management of intracranial aneurysms. J Neurosurg 1956;13:1–42.

36. Bachet J, Guilmet D, Goudot B, et al. Cold cerebroplegia. A new technique of cerebral protection during operations on the transverse aor-

tic arch. J Thorac Cardiovasc Surg 1991; 102:85–94.

37. Coselli JS, Crawford ES, Beall AC Jr, Mizrahi EM, Hess KR, Patel VM. Determination of brain temperatures for safe circulatory arrest during cardiovascular operation. Ann Thorac Surg 1988; 45:638–642.

38. Patterson RH, Ray BS. Profound hypothermia for intracranial surgery: laboratory and clinical experiences with extracorporeal circulation by peripheral cannulation. Ann Surg 1962;156: 377–393.

39. Michenfelder JD, Kirklin JW, Uihlein A, Svien HJ, MacCarty CS. Clinical experience with a closed-chest method of producing profound hypothermia and total circulatory arrest in neurosurgery. Ann Surg 1964;159:125–131.

40. Michenfelder JD, Milde JH. The relationship among canine brain temperature, metabolism, and function during hypothermia. Anesthesiology 1991;75:130–136.

41. Michenfelder JD, Milde JH. The effect of profound levels of hypothermia (below 14C) on canine cerebral metabolism. J Cerebral Blood Flow Metab 1992;12:877–880.

42. Rittenhouse EA, Mohri H, Dillard DH, Merendino KA. Deep hypothermia in cardiovascular surgery. Ann Thorac 1974;17:63–98.

43. Stefaniszyn HJ, Novick RJ, Keith FM, Salerno TA. Is the brain adequately cooled during deep hypothermia cardiopulmonary bypass? Curr Surg 1983;40:294–297.

44. Olsen RW, Hayes LJ, Wissler EH, Nikaidoh H, Eberhart RC. Influence of hypothermia and circulatory arrest on cerebral temperature distributions. J Biochem Eng 1985;107:354–360.

45. Crittenden MD, Roberts CS, Rosa L, et al. Brain protection during circulatory arrest. Ann Thorac Surg 1991;51:942–947.

46. Michenfelder JD, Terry HR Jr, Daw EF, Uihlein A. Induced hypothermia: physiologic effects, indications and techniques. Surg Clin North Am 1965;45:889–898.

47. Lim RA, Rehder K, Harp RA, Dawson B, Kirklin JW. Circulatory arrest during profound hypothermia induced by direct blood-stream cooling: an experimental study. Surgery 1961;49: 367–374.

48. Uihlein A, Theye RA, Dawson B, et al. The use of profound hypothermia, extracorporeal ciculation and total circulatory arrest for an intracranial aneurysm. Preliminary report with reports of cases. Staff Meet Mayo Clin 1960;35: 567–576.

49. Drake CG, Barr HWK, Coles JC, Gergely NF. The use of extracorporeal circulation and profound hypothermia in the treatment of ruptured intra-

cranial aneurysm. J Neurosurg 1964;21: 575–581.

50. Patterson RH Jr, Bronson SR. Profound hypothermia for intracranial surgery using a disposable bubble oxygenator. J Neurosurg 1965;23: 184–190.

51. Neville WE, Thomason RD, Peacock H, Colby C. Cardiopulmonary bypass during noncardiac surgery. Arch Surg 1966;92:576–587.

52. Uihlein A, MacCarty CS, Michenfelder JD, Terry HR Jr, Daw EF. Deep hypothermia and surgical treatment of intracranial aneurysms. A five-year survey. JAMA 1966;195:127–129.

53. Sundt TM Jr, Pluth JR, Gronert GA. Excision of giant basilar aneurysm under profound hypothermia. Report of case. Mayo Clin Proc 1972; 47:631–634.

54. McMurtry JG III, Housepian EM, Bowman FO Jr, Matteo RS. Surgical treatment of basilar artery aneurysms. Elective circulatory arrest with thoracotomy in 12 cases. J Neurosurg 1974;40: 486–494.

55. Patterson RH Jr, Fraser RAR. Vascular neoplasms of the brainstem: a place for profound hypothermia and circulatory arrest. Adv Neurosurg 1975;3:425–428.

56. Silverberg GD, Reitz BA, Ream AK, Taylor G, Enzmann DR. Operative treatment of a giant cerebral artery aneurysm with hypothermia and circulatory arrest: report of a case. Neurosurgery 1980;6:301–305.

57. Baumgartner WA, Silverberg GD, Ream AK, Jamieson SW, Tarabek J, Reitz BA. Reappraisal of cardiopulmonary bypass with deep hypothermia and circulatory arrest for complex neurosurgical operations. Surgery 1983;94: 242–249.

58. Gonski A, Acedillo AT, Stacey RB. Profound hypothermia in the treatment of intracranial aneurysms. Aust N Z J Surg 1986;56:639–643.

59. Richards PG, Marath A, Rice Edwards JM, Lincoln C. Management of difficult intracranial aneurysms by deep hypothermia and elective cardiac arrest using cardiopulmonary bypass. Br J Neurosurg 1987;1:261–269.

60. Williams MD, Rainer G, Fieger HG Jr, Murray IP, Sanchez ML. Cardiopulmonary bypass, profound hypothermia, and circulatory arrest for neurosurgery. Ann Thorac Surg 1991;52: 1069–1075.

61. Björk VO, Hultquist G. Brain damage in children after deep hypothermia for open-heart surgery. Thorax 1960;15:284–291.

62. Edmunds LH Jr, Folkman J, Snodgress AB, Brown RB. Prevention of brain damage during profound hypothermia and circulatory arrest. Ann Surg 1963;157:637–649.

63. Norwood WI, Norwood CR, Castaneda AR. Ce-

rebral anoxia: effect of deep hypothermia and pH. Surgery 1979;86:203–209.

64. Smith G, Ledingham IM, Norman JN, Douglas TA, Bates EH, Lee FD. Prolongation of the time of "safe" circulatory arrest by preliminary hyperbaric oxygenation and body cooling. Surg Gynecol Obstet 1963;117:411–416.

65. Kondo Y, Turner MD, Bebin J, Hardy J. Body responses and recovery after 2½ hour hypothermic circulatory arrest. Surgery 1974;76: 439–446.

66. Kirklin JW, Dawson B, Devloo RA, Theye RA. Open intracardiac opertions: use of circulatory arrest during hypothermia induced by blood cooling. Ann Surg 1961;154:769–776.

67. Hickey PR, Andersen NP. Deep hypothermic circulatory arrest: a review of pathophysiology and clinical experience as a basis for anesthetic management. J Cardiothorac Anesth 1987;1: 137–155.

68. Watanabe T, Miura M, Inui K, et al. Blood and brain tissue gaseous strategy for profoundly hypothermic total circulatory arrest. J Thorac Cardiovasc Surg 1991;102:497–504.

69. Lafferty JJ, Keyhah MM, Shapiro HM, Van Horn K, Behar MG. Cerebral hypometabolism obtained with deep pentobarbital anesthesia and hypothermia (30C). Anesthesiology 1978; 49:159–164.

70. Quasha AL, Tinker JH, Sharbrough FW. Hypothermia plus thiopental: prolonged electroencephalographic suppression. Anesthesiology 1981;55:636–640.

71. Michenfelder JD. Hypothermia plus barbiturates: apples plus oranges? Anesthesiology 1978;49:157–158.

72. Bigelow WG, Mustard WT, Evans JG. Some physiologic concepts of hypothermia and their applications to cardiac surgery. J Thorac Surg 1954;28:463–480.

73. Tinker JH. ASA Award: John D. Michenfelder. Anethesiology 1990;73:596–598.

74. Valeri CR, Cassidy G, Khuri S, Feingold H, Ragno G, Altschulte MD. Hypothermia-induced reversible platelet dysfunction. Ann Surg 1987;205:175–181.

75. Myers GH Jr, Fehrenbaker LG, Kelalis PP. Prognostic significance of renal vein invasion by hypernephroma. J Urol 1968;100:420–423.

76. Riches EW. Factors in the prognosis of carcinoma of the kidney. J Urol 1958;79:190–195.

77. Marshall VF, Middleton RG, Holswade GR, Goldsmith EI. Surgery for renal cell carcinoma in the vena cava. J Urol 1970;103:414–420.

78. Ardekani RG, Hunter JA, Thomson A. Hidden hypernephroma simulating right atrial tumor. Ann Thorac Surg 1971;11:371–375.

79. Utley JR, Mobin-Uddin K, Segnitz RH, Belin RP,

Utley JF. Acute obstruction of tricuspid valve by Wilms' tumor. J Thorac Cardiovasc Surg 1973; 66:626–628.

80. Theman T, Williams WG, Simpson JS, Radford D, Rubin S, Stephens CA. Tumor invasion of the upper inferior vena cava: the use of profound hypothermia and circulation arrest as a surgical adjunct. J Pediatr Surg 1978;13:331–334.

81. Choh JH, Gurney R, Shenoy SS, Upson J, Lajos TZ. Renal-cell carcinoma. Removal of intracardiac extension with aid of cardiopulmonary bypass. NY State J Med 1981;81:929–932.

82. Prager RL, Dean R, Turner B. Surgical approach to intracardiac renal cell carcinoma. Ann Thorac Surg 1982;33:74–77.

83. Daughtry JD, Stewart BH, Golding LAR, Groves LK. Pulmonary embolus presenting as the initial manifestation of renal cell carcinoma. Ann Thorac Surg 1977;24:178–181.

84. Wilkinson CJ, Kimovec MA, Uejima T. Cardiopulmonary bypass in patients with malignant renal neoplasms. Br J Anaesth 1986;58: 461–465.

85. Welch M, Bazaral MG, Schmidt R, et al. Anesthetic management for surgical removal of renal carcinoma with caval or atrial tumor thrombus using deep hypothermic circulatory arrest. J Cardiothorac Anesth 1989;3:580–586.

86. Paul JG, Rhodes DB, Skow JR. Renal cell carcinoma presenting as right atrial tumor with successful removal using cardiopulmonary bypass. Ann Surg 1975;181:471–473.

87. Marshall FF, Reitz BA, Diamond DA. A new technique for management of renal cell carcinoma involving the right atrium: hypothermia and cardiac arrest. J Urol 1984;131:103–107.

88. Lachance SL, Murray GF. Surgical management of renal cell carcinoma involving the hepatic vena cava. WV Med J 1987;83:378–380.

89. Gleason DM, Reilly RJ, Anderson RM, O'Hare JE, Kartchner MM, Komar NN. Removal of hypernephroma and inferior vena cava. Arch Surg 1972;105:795–797.

90. Murphy DA, Rabinovitch H, Chevalier L, Virmani S. Wilms tumor in right atrium. Am J Dis Child 1973;126:210–211.

91. Bissada NK, Finkbeiner AE, Williams GD, Weiss JB. Successful extraction of intracardiac tumor thombus of renal carcinoma. J Urol 1977;118: 474–475.

92. Farooki ZQ, Green EW, Arciniegas E. Echocardiographic pattern of right atrial tumour motion. Br Heart J 1976;38:580–583.

93. Vaughan ED Jr, Crosby IK, Tegtmeyer CJ. Nephroblastoma with right atrial extension: preoperative diagnosis and management. J Urol 1977;117:530–533.

94. Klein FA, Smith MJV, Greenfield LJ. Extracorpo-

real circulation for renal cell carcinoma with supradiaphragmatic vena caval thrombi. J Urol 1984;131:880–883.

95. Krane RJ, deVere White R, Davis Z, Sterling R, Dobnik DB, McCormick JR. Removal of renal cell carcinoma extending into the right atrium using cardiopulmonary bypass, profound hypothermia and circulatory arrest. J Urol 1984; 131:945–947.

96. Montie JE, Jackson CL, Cosgrove DM, Streem SB, Novick AC, Pontes JE. Resection of large inferior vena caval thrombi from renal cell carcinoma with the use of circulatory arrest. J Urol 1988;139:25–28.

97. Novick AC, Cosgrove DM. Surgical approach for removal of renal cell carcinoma extending into the vena cava and the right atrium. J Urol 1980;123:947–950.

98. Farrell RM, Bloch J, Marshall VF. Caval umbrella to trap emboli in patients with renal cell carcinoma. Surg Gynecol Obstet 1974;139: 835–839.

99. Turini D, Selli C, Barbanti G, Beneforti P, Calamai G. Removal of renal cell carcinoma extending to the supradiaphragmatic vena cava with the aid of cardiopulmonary bypass. Urol Int 1986;41:303–306.

100. Hedderich GS, O'Connor RJ, Reid EC, Mulder DS. Caval tumor thrombus complicating renal cell carcinoma: a surgical challenge. Surgery 1987;102:614–621.

101. Marshall FF, Dietrick DD, Baumgartner WA, Reitz BA. Surgical management of renal cell carcinoma with intracaval neoplastic extension above the hepatic veins. J Urol 1988;139: 1166–1172.

102. Hunt TM, Firmin RF, Johnstone MJS. Management of a patient with Wilms's tumour extending into the right heart chambers: a case report and a review of other published reports. Br Heart J 1988;60:165–168.

103. Wickey GS, Martin DE, Larach DR, Belis JA, Kofke A, Hensley FA Jr. Combined carotid endarterectomy, coronary revascularization, and hypernephroma excision with hypothermic circulatory arrest. Anesth Analg 1988;67: 473–476.

104. Novick AC, Kaye MC, Cosgrove DM, et al. Experience with cardiopulmonary bypass and deep hypothermic circulatory arrest in the management of retroperitoneal tumors with large vena caval thrombi. Ann Surg 1990;212:472–477.

105. Woods FM, Neptune WB, Palatchi A. Resection of the carina and main-stem bronchi with the use of extracorporeal circulation. New Engl J Med 1961;264:492–494.

106. Nissen VR. Extrakorporelle zirkulation für

langdauernde (30 minuten) Atemunterbrechung zur operation bifurkationsnaher trachealgeschwülste. Schweiz Med Wschr 1961;91: 957–960.

107. Adkins PC, Izawa EM. Resection of tracheal cylindroma using cardiopulmonary bypass. Arch Surg 1964;88:405–409.

108. Neville WE, Langston HT, Correll N, Maben H. Cardiopulmonary bypass during pulmonary surgery. Preliminary report. J Thorac Cardiovasc Surg 1965;50:265–276.

109. Crastnopol P, Platt N, Phillips WR, Mesbah M, Henry EI, Aaron RS. Resection of solitary tracheal papilloma using cardiopulmonary bypass. NY State J Med 1967;67:1166–1169.

110. Louhimo I, Leijala M. Cardiopulmonary bypass in tracheal surgery in infants and small children. Prog Pediatr Surg 1987;21:58–63.

111. Geffin B, Bland J, Grillo HC. Anesthetic management of tracheal resection and reconstruction. Anesth Analg 1969;48:884–890.

112. Mathisen DJ, Grillo HC. Carinal resection for bronchogenic carcinoma. J Thorac Cardiovasc 1991;102:16–23.

113. Cooley DA, Beall AC Jr, Alexander JK. Acute massive pulmonary embolism. Successful surgical treatment using temporary cardiopulmonary bypass. JAMA 1961;177:283–286.

114. Rosenberg DML, Schmidt R, Warren S, Cohen S, Stern F. Partial circulatory support in massive pulmonary embolism. Ann Thorac Surg 1966; 2:217–225.

115. Beall AC Jr, Cooley DA. Use of cardiopulmonary bypass for resuscitation and treatment of acute massive pulmonary embolism. Pac Med Surg 1967;75:67–70.

116. Sautter RD. The technique of pulmonary embolectomy with the use of cardiopulmonary bypass. J Thorac Cardiovasc 1967;53:268–274.

117. Garcia JB, Barankay A, Grimshaw VA, Deac R, Ionescu MI, Wooler GH. Pulmonary embolectomy using heart-lung by-pass. Report of successful case. J Cardiovasc Surg 1969;10: 165–171.

118. Sasahara AA. Clinical studies in pulmonary thromboembolism. In: Sasahara AA, Stein M, eds. Pulmonary embolic disease. New York: Grune & Stratton, 1965.

119. Del Campo C. Pulmonary embolectomy: a review. Can J Surg 1985;28:111–113.

120. Greenfield LJ. Catheter pulmonary embolectomy. Chest 1991;100:593–594.

121. Lee BS, Sarnquist FH, Starnes VA. Anethesia for bilateral single-lung transplantation. J Cardiothorac Vasc Anesth 1992;6:201–203.

122. Baumgartner WA, Traill TA, Cameron DE, Fonger JD, Birenbaum IB, Reitz BA. Unique aspects of

heart and lung transplantation exhibited in the "domino-donor" operation. JAMA 1989;261: 3121–3125.

123. Stewart LM, McCarthy H, Fabian JA. Use of cardiopulmonary bypass in organ transplantation. In: Fabian JA, ed. Anesthesia for organ transplantation. Philadelphia: JB Lippincott, 1992: 159–174.

124. Adachi H, Ueda K, Koyama I, et al. Donor core cooling for multiple organ retrieval: new application of portable cardiopulmonary bypass for transplantation. Transplant Proc 1989;21: 1200–1202.

125. Shuman RL. Primary pulmonary sarcoma with left atrial extension via left superior pulmonary vein. J Thorac Cardiovasc Surg 1984;88: 189–192.

126. Murphy JP, Adyanthaya AV, Adams PR, McArthur JD, Walker WE. Peripheral pulmonary artery aneurysm in a patient with limited respiratory reserve: controlled resection using cardiopulmonary bypass. Ann Thorac Surg 1987;43: 323–325.

127. Hall KD, Friedman M. Extracorporeal oxygenation for induction of anesthesia in a patient with an intrathoracic tumor. Anesthesiology 1975;42:493–495.

128. Bricker DL, Parker TM, Dalton ML Jr. Cardiopulmonary bypass in anesthetic management of resection. Arch Surg 1979;114:847–849.

129. Maharaj RJ, Whitton I, Blyth D. Emergency extracorporeal oxygenation for an intratracheal foreign body. Anaesthesia 1983;38:471–474.

130. Seard C, Wasserman K, Benfield JR, Cleveland RJ, Costley DO, Heimlich EM. Simultaneous bilateral lung lavage (alveolar washing) using partial cardiopulmonary bypass. Report of two cases in siblings. Am Rev Respir Dis 1970; 101:877–884.

131. Zapol WM, Wilson R, Hales C, et al. Venovenous bypass with a membrane lung to support bilateral lung lavage. JAMA 1984;251:3269–3271.

132. Moazam F, Schmidt JH, Chesrown SE, et al. Total lung lavage for pulmonary alveolar proteinosis in an infant without the use of cardiopulmonary bypass. J Pediatr Surg 1985;20:398–401.

133. Heymach GJ III, Shaw RC, McDonald JA Vest JV. Fiberoptic bronchopulmonary lavage for alveolar proteinosis in a patient with only one lung. Chest 1982;81:508–510.

134. Brenner WI, Engelman RM, Williams CD, Boyd AD, Reed GE. Nonthrombogenic aortic and vena caval bypass using heparin-coated tubes. Rev Surg 1974;31:132–134.

135. van der Hulst VPM, Henny CP, Moulijn AC, et al. Veno-venous bypass without systemic heparini-

zation using a centrifugal pump: a blind comparison of a heparin bonded circuit versus a non-heparin bonded circuit. J Cardiovasc Surg 1989;30:118–123.

136. Shaw BW Jr, Martin DJ, Marquez JM, et al. Advantages of venous bypass during orthotopic transplantation of the liver. Sem Liv Dis 1985;5: 344–348.

137. Memsic L, Quinones-Baldrich W, Kaufman R, Rasool I, Busuttil RW. A comparison of porcine orthotopic liver transplantation using a venous-venous bypass with and without a nonpulsatile perfusion pump. J Surg Res 1986;41:33–40.

138. Khoury GF, Mann ME, Parot MJ, Abdul-Rasool IH, Busuttil RW. Air embolism associated with veno-venous bypass during orthotopic liver transplantation. Anesthesiology 1987;67: 848–851.

139. Prager MC, Gregory GA, Ascher NL, Roberts JP. Massive venous air embolism during orthotopic liver transplantation. Anesthesiology 1990; 72:198–200.

140. Paulsen AW, Whitten CW, Ramsay MAE, Klintmalm GB. Considerations for anesthetic management during veno-venous bypass in adult hepatic transplantation. Anesth Analg 1989;68:489–496.

141. Demling RH, Hicks RE, Edmunds LH Jr. Changes in extravascular lung water during venovenous perfusion. J Thorac Cardiovasc Surg 1976;71: 291–294.

142. Wall WJ, Grant DR, Duff JH, Kutt JL, Ghent CN, Bloch MS. Liver transplantation without venous bypass. Transplantation 1987;43:56–61.

143. Shaw BW, Martin DJ, Marquez JM, et al. Venous bypass in clinical liver transplantation. Ann Surg 1984;200:524–534.

144. Starzl TE, Iwatsuki S, Esquivel CO, et al. Refinements in the surgical technique of liver transplantation. Sem Liv Dis 1985;5:349–356.

145. Denmark SW, Shaw BW Jr, Starzl TE, Griffith BP. Venovenous bypass without systemic anticoagulation in canine and human liver transplantation. Surg Forum 1983;34:380–382.

146. Calne RY, Rolles K, Farman JV, Kneeshaw JD, Smith DP, Wheeldon DR. Veno-arterial bypass in orthotopic liver grafting. Lancet 1984; 2:1269.

147. Calne RY, Smith DP, McMaster P, Craddock GN, Rolles K. Use of partial cardiopulmonary bypass during the anhepatic phase of orthotopic liver grafting. Lancet 1979;2:612–614.

148. Campbell Cree I, Hayashi T, Bernardez DB. Liver transplantation following extracorporeal hypothermia. Can J Surg 1968;11:452–563.

149. Persson NH, Brown M, Goldstein R, et al. Inferior mesenteric vein cannulation for veno-ve-

nous bypass during liver transplantation: alternative access in difficult hilar dissection. Transplant Proc 1990;22:174.

150. Ringe B, Bornscheuer A, Blumhardt G, Bechstein WO, Wonigeit K, Pichlmayr R. Experience with veno-venous bypass in human liver transplantation. Transplant Proc 1987; 19:2416.

151. Rakela J, Perkins JD, Gross JB Jr, et al. Acute hepatic failure: the emerging role of orthotopic liver transplantation. Mayo Clin Proc 1989; 64:424–428.

152. Bismuth H, Castaing D, Garden OJ. Major hepatic resection under total vascular exclusion. Ann Surg 1989;210:13–19.

153. Bergan JJ, Yao JST, Flinn WR, McCarthy WJ. Surgical treatment of venous obstruction and insufficiency. J Vasc Surg 1986;3:174–181.

154. Miller CM, Schwartz ME, Nishizaki T. Combined hepatic and vena caval resection with autogenous caval graft replacement. Arch Surg 1991;126:106–108.

155. Kieffer E, Bahnini A, Koskas F. Nonthrombotic disease of the inferior vena cava: surgical management of 24 patients. In: Bergan JJ, Yao JST, eds. Venous disorders. Philadelphia: WB Saunders, 1991:501–16.

156. Evans WE, Turnipseed WD, Vasko JS. Surgical correction of the Budd-Chiari syndrome. Vasc Surg 1976;10:230–237.

157. Murphy JP, Gregoric I, Cooley DA. Budd-Chiari syndrome resulting from a membranous web of the inferior vena cava: operative repair using profound hypothermia and circulatory arrest. Ann Thorac Surg 1987;43:212–214.

158. Launois B, de Chateaubriant P, Rosat P, Kiroff GK. Repair of suprahepatic caval lesions under extracorporeal circulation in major liver trauma. J Trauma 1989;29:127–128.

159. Ryan JF, Donlon JV, Malt RA, et al. Cardiopulmonary bypass in the treatment of malignant hyperthermia. New Engl J Med 1974;290: 1121–1122.

160. Byrick RJ, Rose DK, Ranganathan N. Management of a malignant hyperthermia patient during cardiopulmonary bypass. Can Anaesth Soc J 1982;29:50–54.

161. MacGillivray RG, Jann H, Vanker E, Gemmell L, Mahomedy AE. Development of malignant hyperthermia obscured by cardiopulmonary bypass. Can Anaesth Soc J 1986;33:509–514.

162. Kugelberg J, Schüller H, Berg B, Kallum B. Treatment of accidental hypothermia. Scand J Thor Cardiovasc Surg 1967;1:142–146.

163. Hauty MG, Esrig BC, Hill JG, Long WB. Prognostic factors in severe accidental hypothermia: experience from the Mt. Hood tragedy. J Trauma 1987;27:1107–1112.

164. White JD. Hypothermia: the Bellevue experience. Ann Emerg Med 1982;11:417–424.

165. Dugid H, Simpson RG, Stowers JM. Accidental hypothermia. Lancet 1961;2:1213–1219.

166. Shields CP, Sixsmith DM. Treatment of moderate-to-severe hypothermia in an urban setting. Ann Emerg Med 1990;19:1093–1097.

167. Kennedy JH, Barnett J, Flasterstein A, Higgs W. Experimental barbiturate intoxication: treatment by partial cardiopulmonary bypass and hemodialysis. Cardiovasc Res Cent Bull 1976; 14:61–68.

168. Fell RH, Gunning AJ, Bardhan KD, Triger DR. Severe hypothermia as a result of barbiturate overdose complicated by cardiac arrest. Lancet 1968;1:392–394.

169. Gutierrez-Perry L, Boland JP, Burke A, Figueroa E. Repair of traumatic arteriovenous fistula of the aortic arch. WV Med J 1987;83:219–221.

170. Griffin LH Jr, Fishback ME, Galloway RF, Shearer GL. Traumatic aortorenal vein fistula: repair using total circulatory arrest. Surgery 1977; 81:480–483.

171. Anagnostopoulos CE, Kabemba JM, Stansel HC Jr. Control of a bleeding intercostal aneurysm with the aid of partial pump-oxygenator bypass. Ann Thorac Surg 1969;8:358–360.

172. Fletcher JP, Klineberg PL, Hawker FH, et al. Arteriovenous fistula following lumbar disc surgery—the use of total cardiopulmonary bypass during repair. Aust N Z J Surg 1986;56: 631–633.

173. Schwentker EP, Bahnson HT. Total circulatory arrest for treatment of advanced arteriovenous fistula. Ann Surg 1972;175;70–74.

174. Milligan NS, Edwards JC, Monro JL, Atwell JD. Excision of giant haemangioma in the newborn using hypothermia and cardiopulmonary bypass. Anaesthesia 1985;40:875–878.

175. Little KET, Cywes S, Davies MRQ, Louw JH. Complicated giant hemangioma: excision using cardiopulmonary bypass and deep hypothermia. J Pediatr Surg 1976;11:533–536.

176. Mulliken JB, Murray JE, Castaneda AR, Kaban LB. Management of a vascular malformation of the face using total circulatory arrest. Surg Gynecol Obstet 1978;146:168–172.

177. Dubernard JM, Martin X, Gelet A, Mongin D. Aneurysms of the renal artery: surgical management with special reference to extracorporeal surgery and autotransplantation. Eur Urol 1985;11:26–30.

178. Martinez-Piñeiro JA, Gonzalez Martin M. Extracorporeal repair of the renal artery for renovascular hypertension. A case report. Eur Urol 1975;1:165–169.

179. Edlich RF, Buchin RJ, Tsung MS, Martini D,

Matson CJ. Blood flow to a canine sarcoma during regional perfusion. J Surg Res 1968;8:438–446.

180. Creech O, Krementz ET, Ryan RF, Winblad JN. Chemotherapy of cancer: regional perfusion utilizing an extracorporeal circuit. Ann Surg 1958;148:616–632.

181. Goldsmith EI, Carvalho FF, Prata A, Kean BH. Surgical recovery of schistosomes from the portal blood. JAMA 1967;199:235–240.

182. Kean BH, Goldsmith EI. Schistosomiasis Japonica. Treatment by extracorporeal hemofiltration. Am J Med 1969;47:546–552.

183. Carvalho Luz FF. Extracorporeal filtration of portal blood for the removal of *Schistosoma mansoni*: analysis of 100 operations. Proc R Soc Med 1969;62:115–118.

184. Kessler RE, Amadeo JH, Tice DA, Zimmon DS. Extracorporeal filtration of schistosomes in unanesthetized man. Surg Forum 1970;21:378–380.

29

MANAGEMENT OF UNUSUAL PROBLEMS ENCOUNTERED INITIATING AND MAINTAINING CARDIOPULMONARY BYPASS

David R. Hockmuth and Noel L. Mills

Occasionally, while evaluating a patient for cardiopulmonary bypass (CPB) surgery, an unusual complicating problem may be encountered. Often the experience of a single surgeon or group of surgeons may be inadequate to form a plan of management for these problems. This chapter examines several infrequently encountered conditions, and attempts to develop an approach to CPB in patients with cryoproteins, pregnancy, hemoglobinopathy, pneumonectomy, acquired immunodeficiency syndrome (AIDS), and malignant hyperthermia.

Cryoproteins

Cold agglutinins can be defined as serum antibodies that become active at decreased blood temperature and produce agglutination or hemolysis of red blood cells. These antibodies are classically directed against I or i antigens on the red blood cells. They can also be nonspecific. Cold agglutinins can be characterized in a number of ways. The most important characteristic applicable to cardiac surgery is thermal amplitude, the temperature below which the antibodies become activated. As the temperature drops below the thermal amplitude, antibody activity increases exponentially. In general, this activity reverses as

rewarming occurs (1). The thermal amplitude is typically measured in a laboratory at several different temperatures, for example, 4°, 15°, room temperature (approximately 22°C), and 37°C. A positive result at 4 and 15°C, but a negative result at room temperature and 37°C would predict a thermal amplitude between 15°C and room temperature. Additionally, an important factor in assessing cold agglutinins is the titer or concentration. High titer cold agglutinins are more clinically significant than low titer antibodies. There is no general definition for high versus low titer; however, Lee et al. (2) have suggested low titer as being less than 1:32 and high titer as greater than 1:128.

Hemolysis in patients with cold agglutinin antibodies is produced by activation of the complement system. For hemolysis to occur the cold agglutinin and complement activities must overlap. In other words, the temperature must be low enough for the cold agglutinins to activate but warm enough for a complement fixation to occur. Cold agglutination due to lowering the temperature below the thermal amplitude may be reversed by warming to back above the thermal amplitude.

Clinical symptoms related to cold agglutinins that are not associated with hypo-

742

thermic bypass are uncommon because activation generally occurs at a temperature below the ambient or body temperature. Clinical symptoms may occur, however, during cold exposure or hypothermic bypass. With cold exposure, a common finding may be acrocyanosis of digits, tip of the nose, or ears, secondary to agglutination and ischemia. Most commonly, immediate treatment by warming the affected areas will reverse the agglutination and thus the ischemic syndrome. Failure to reverse the process may result in gangrene. A patient with prolonged hypothermic bypass would be at risk for multiorgan damage due to gangrene from prolonged vascular occlusion with red cell agglutination (3). This would be an uncommon but catastrophic consequence of failure to recognize and treat the presence of cold agglutinins.

Diagnosis

If patients undergo screening for cold agglutinins, a diagnosis can be easily be made based on results of laboratory tests. If screening at 4°C is negative, no further screening is needed. If the screen is positive at 4°C, thermal amplitude should be determined and the titer determined for each temperature at which the screen was positive. This will give more precise information for dealing with the cold agglutinin antibodies. In patients who are not initially screened for cold agglutinins, a diagnosis may be made by astute observation. Intraoperatively, during hypothermic bypass, agglutination within the vessels may be noted, as may hemolysis by hemoglobinuria, usually recognized by pink or red discoloration of the urine. The latter occurrence is relatively common even in the absence of cryo-agglutination, however, and one should consider the diagnosis of inadequate anticoagulation when intravascular agglutination is observed. If a blood cardioplegia reservoir is used, the perfusionist may note agglutination as the blood cardioplegia is mixed and cooled. In addition, immediate

agglutination of blood in a syringe during phlebotomy may indicate the presence of cold agglutinins. Many cold agglutinins will cause agglutination of a routine cross-match done at room temperature. Any of the above findings suggest the presence of clinically significant cold agglutinins, and steps should be taken to prevent adverse reactions during CPB (4–6).

The Ehrlich finger and palm test is a clinical method for determining the presence and significance of cold agglutinins. The finger test may be performed by placing venous tourniquets on the index fingers and placing the fingers in a 4°C water bath for 15 minutes. The palm test may be performed by placing an ice cube in the palm of one hand for 15 minutes and checking for acrocyanosis in both palms (1). Hemolysis seen in a hematocrit obtained from the cold-immersed fingers would constitute a positive test.

Clinical Relevance

As noted above, it is unusual for cold agglutinins to become clinically apparent in a patient unless the patient is undergoing hypothermic bypass. However, the importance of cold agglutinins in a patient undergoing hypothermic bypass is potentially great (7–10). With prolonged exposure of the entire body to hypothermic temperatures below the thermal amplitude and with significant titers, hemolysis or agglutination with prolonged sludging and multiorgan infarction may occur.

Monoclonal and polyclonal forms of the antibodies are seen. The monoclonal types usually associated with lymphoreticular neoplasms are generally nonreversible. The polyclonal antibodies are often associated with acute infectious diseases such as mycoplasma, infectious mononucleosis, or cytomegalovirus (3). Production of polyclonal cold agglutinins is typically transient and may remit spontaneously in weeks, but when present, it may be associated with acute life-threatening intravascular hemolysis (3). Leach et al. (4) have developed a comparison of clinically significant and insignificant cold agglutinins (Table 29.1). An important point in assessing the need to screen for cold agglutinins is that a failure to screen may lead to an adverse outcome, for example, myocardial infarction, stroke, or acute renal failure, and without the knowledge of the presence of cold agglutinins, these adverse outcomes may be attributed to another cause; hemolysis may be attributed to, for example, mechanical trauma to blood (11). The fact that 14 of 15 letters, articles, and abstracts regarding this subject state that cold agglutinins may be of clinical significance suggests some clinical relevance to cold agglutinins. One scientific abstract states that mechanical trauma to blood may be more important than cold-reacting autoantibodies when the thermal amplitude is less than 22°C (12).

Treatment

Treatment of cold agglutinin disease during CPB essentially consists of prevention of complement activation and ultimately of agglutination or hemolysis. Treatment is based on the etiology and the severity of the problem. In the case of cold agglutinins caused by acute infection (e.g., a recent viral illness), elective cardiac surgery should be postponed for several weeks, by which time the antibody may have disappeared (11). In addition, in a mild case of cold agglutinins (i.e., a case in which there is a very low thermal amplitude, such as 4°C) and/or a low titer of antibodies, minor or no changes in surgical technique and in some cases treatment with corticosteroids to avoid hemolysis have been advised (13). Concerning patients with low titer, nonspecific antibodies (and only these patients), Moore et al. (1) concluded the following: heparinization has no protective effect against agglutination; dilution with pump prime or cardioplegic solution has little effect on hemolysis or agglutination; hypothermic bypass can be performed on these patients without increased risks of hemolytic or agglutination crises; and some hemolysis occurs in all patients during hypothermic bypass, especially during the rewarming phase, whether or not cold agglutinin antibodies are present.

In a case with clinically significant cold agglutinins, high thermal amplitude, high titer, positive Ehrlich's test, clinical symptoms, etc., a number of changes in surgical technique have resulted in successful surgery using bypass. The most important technique is using either normothermia or mild hypothermia with temperatures continuously maintained above the thermal amplitude to avoid the active temperature

Table 29.1.   Characteristics of Cold Agglutinins[a]

Clinically Significant[b]	Clinically Insignificant[c]
1. Lytic (cause hemolysis)	1. Nonlytic (causes reversible red blood cell agglutination only)
2. Active in saline at 20°C	2. Peak activity 0–4°C
3. Almost always IgM[d] antibodies	3. Seldom IgM antibodies (IgG, IgA or nonimmunoglobulin)
4. Wide thermal range (4–32°C)	4. Low thermal range 0–6°C
5. Bind complement	5. Seldom bind complement
6. Agglutination irreversible	6. Agglutination reversible
7. Enhance agglutination when incubated at 30°C in albumin	7. Agglutination is not enhanced when incubated at 30°C in albumin.

[a] Adapted from Leach AB, Van Hasselt GL, Edwards JC. Cold agglutinins and deep hypothermia. Anaesthesia 1983;38:140–143.
[b] These are commonly associated with chronic cold hemagglutinin disease, neoplasm of lymphoid origin, and mycoplasma pneumonia.
[c] These are commonly associated with viral infections (e.g., cytomegalovirus infections and mononucleosis).
[d] Ig, immunoglobulin.

range of agglutination (7, 11, 14, 15). Hence, the presence of cryoagglutinins with high titer or high thermal amplitude may represent a reasonable indication for the use of warm cardioplegia myocardial protection techniques while maintaining normothermic systemic temperatures. When selecting cold cardioplegic myocardial protection, we recommend using initial wash-out of blood from the coronary circulation with warm followed by cold cardioplegia and rewarming the heart with warm cardioplegia ("hot shot") to prevent agglutination from blood exposed to a cold heart. Refinements of this latter technique consist of bicaval cannulation with tightening of caval tapes to avoid cooling of large amounts of blood in the heart and placement of a sump catheter in the right atrium to retrieve cardioplegia until the coronary sinus effluent is clear. The effluent would then be discarded. In addition, low systemic flows during bypass may be used to decrease the noncoronary collateral flow and subsequent cooling of this blood.

If it is uncertain whether this noncoronary collateral flow will cause problems, the heart may be maintained at a temperature above the thermal amplitude (16). Venting the left ventricle will avoid cooling and stagnation of blood in the left ventricular cavity. Crystalloid cardioplegia is used rather than blood cardioplegia to avoid agglutination of the cells in the solution when delivered at low temperature (17). Adjuncts may include an insulation pad to prevent cooling of blood in structures adjacent to the mediastinum. Significant activation of cold agglutinins may be prevented by using a septal temperature probe in the myocardium to keep the myocardial temperature greater than the thermal amplitude, and in addition warming of fluids, blood, plasma, inspired gases, and bolus injections (11) should be considered in the periods preceding and following bypass, especially if the cryoagglutinin has a high thermal amplitude. Such measures should not be needed during bypass, since the heat exchange in the circuit should compensate adequately for any of these factors. Dilution of antibodies by extracorporeal circuit primary solution may be an important factor in reducing the tendency for activation of high titer cold agglutinins (Rock W, personal communication, 1991), although this differs from the earlier suggestion of Moore et al. (1). It seems reasonable to assume that hemodilution during bypass will reduce the concentration of the cryoagglutinin 30 to 50%; thus little protection would appear likely unless the cold agglutinin titer is very low (1:2 or less).

The literature contains descriptions of successful cardiac surgery after plasmapheresis (18) or total exchange transfusions in patients with high titer, high thermal amplitude cold agglutinins. There is some evidence that the patient's own red cells may be protected from hemolysis, and if transfusions are required, autologous packed red cells may be advantageous (11). In the case of unexpected agglutination encountered at the time of surgery, several techniques may be useful: verification by the blood bank that cold agglutination is present rather than an unrecognized alloantibody, the use of crystalloid cardioplegia to dilute the antibody in the coronary circulation, or use of noncardioplegic techniques and maintenance of systemic temperatures greater than 28 to 30°C at which significant amounts of agglutination are unlikely to occur. In addition, the extracorporeal circuit and oxygenator should be inspected carefully for cell aggregates. Arterial filters should be used in all cases.

Summary

In summary, evidence exists that patients about to undergo hypothermic bypass should be screened for cold agglutinins (7–10). If an initial screen is positive, the cold agglutinins should be characterized as to thermal amplitude and titer. Clinical symptoms, as suggested by a positive Ehrlich's test, should also be sought. A patient with low titer, low thermal amplitude, clinically asymptomatic cold agglutinins with a negative Ehrlich's test, can tolerate bypass with moderate hypothermia at very low risk with little or no alteration in technique. For clinically significant cold agglutinins with high thermal amplitude and/or titer, if due to a transient viral illness, elective surgery may be postponed several weeks in the hope that this will decrease cold agglutinins to insignificant levels. However, in severe cases in which the high titer, high thermal amplitude cold agglutinins are not transient, precautions should be taken as outlined above

to prevent an agglutination or hemolytic crisis (Fig. 29.1).

PREGNANCY

Although the rate of cardiovascular disease in pregnancy has steadily declined over the past several decades, it remains a topic of interest because of the high rate of fetal mortality when an operation requiring CPB is needed. The incidence of all maternal cardiovascular disease during pregnancy is currently about 1.5% (19). The most frequently performed procedures in-

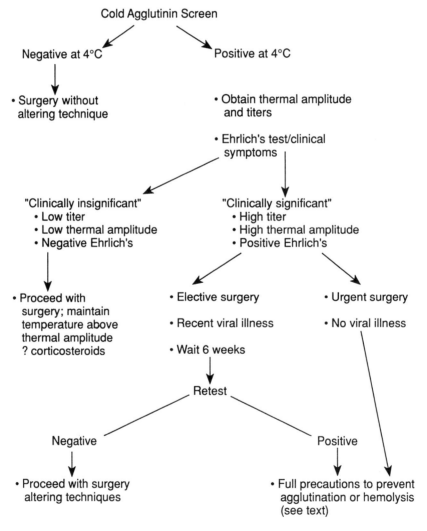

Figure 29.1. Algorithm for cold agglutinins in CPB.

clude closed mitral commissurotomy, open mitral commissurotomy, mitral valve replacement, and aortic valve replacement (20). Other cardiac problems associated with pregnancy in which operation may be necessary are atrial septal defect, patent ductus arteriosus, ventricular septal defect, and idiopathic hypertrophic subaortic stenosis (21). Because of intravenous drug abuse, infectious endocarditis assumes an increasing role among cardiovascular diseases in pregnancy.

A number of fundamentals in the physiology of pregnancy affect the timing and use of bypass in the pregnant patient. The first trimester is the trimester of organogenesis. Therefore, any injury to the embryo during this period may result in teratogenesis. This is particularly true of drugs. An important example is warfarin, a well-known teratogen. Because of the small size of the warfarin molecule, it can cross the placenta. The neonatal morbidity and mortality for patients taking warfarin throughout their pregnancy may be 40% or greater. For this reason, patients undergoing warfarin therapy are often changed to heparin when pregnancy is diagnosed. The large heparin molecule cannot cross the uteroplacental barrier (22). However, the rate of spontaneous abortion increases with heparin (23).

Other factors associated with bypass that may lead to teratogenesis include hypoxemia and decreased perfusion. During the second trimester of pregnancy, the period of organogenesis is finished; therefore, teratogenesis is not seen. The risk of premature labor is much less than in the third trimester, when the risk rises significantly. The hypervolemia and anemia of pregnancy also are less in the second trimester than in the third trimester, as are the hemodynamic demands because of the smaller size of the fetus and less uterine blood flow.

Numerous physiologic changes occur during pregnancy. Because there is no autoregulation of uterine blood flow, nonpulsatile flow during CPB may compromise

fetal blood supply. After the 28th to 32nd week of gestation, the patient's blood volume has increased by 30 to 50%. Heart rate increases 10 to 15% and stroke volume increases 30 to 35% with an associated 15% decrease in systemic vascular resistance. During pregnancy, uterine blood flow represents 10 to 15% of the cardiac output, as compared to only 1% in a nonpregnant female (21).

The lowest risk for bypass surgery is believed to occur during the second trimester, with maternal risk during this time varying from 1.8 to 5% (20, 24–27). In particular, a survey of Society of Thoracic Surgery members who had performed bypass surgery on pregnant women revealed only 1 maternal mortality in 68 cases. In general, the maternal risk is probably not increased over that in a nonpregnant patient. Fetal risk, however, is quite high, ranging from 10 to 50% (21, 24–26, 28). The survey of STS members revealed a 20% fetal mortality in the same 68 CPB cases.

A closer examination of the causes of fetal risk reveals multiple factors. There are numerous possible causes for fetal hypoxia. Low perfusion flows or hypotension during bypass can result in fetal hypoxia because of the lack of autoregulation of the uterine blood flow. Low hemoglobin oxygen saturation and possibly the lack of pulsatile flow, uterine arteriovenous shunts, or uterine arterial spasm may contribute to fetal hypoxia. Hypoxia may result from particulate or bubble embolization to the uteroplacental bed (29). Uterine blood flow may also be compromised by venous obstruction of the inferior vena cava resulting from improper cannula placement (30).

Hypoxia is best diagnosed by noting fetal heart rate decelerations. The normal fetal heart rate (FHR) is between 120 and 160 beats per minute (bpm). The fetal heart rate may decrease to 80 to 100 bpm with hypothermia, but FHRs less than 60 bpm suggest a high probability of life-threatening fetal distress. Acidosis may contribute to fetal bradycardia. Fetal bradycardia, defined as FHR less than 120 bpm at normothermia and FHR <80 bpm at hypothermia, may be treated by increasing the bypass flow rate, which usually increases the heart rate toward normal (28, 31, 32). However, one problem that may occur is a temporary increase in the heart rate followed by a heart rate reduction that does not respond to increased flow. For this reason, time on CPB is a significant factor and should be minimized.

The initiation of uterine contractions most frequently causes fetal death (28). Detection of uterine contractions can be monitored by a tocodynamometer. When the FHR is monitored simultaneously, the FHR pattern may show late decelerations with each uterine contraction, indicating hypoxia. This usually indicates that blood flow across the myometrium stops as uterine contraction pressure increases to exceed the uteroplacental arteriolar pressure. Most uterine contractions resolve after the termination of bypass. Risk of initiation of uterine contractions does not end, however, with the bypass period; therefore, it is recommended that uterine contractions be monitored postoperatively for 72 hours (26). The rewarming cycle during bypass is associated with the onset of uterine contractions (26). The dilution of progesterone during CPB secondary to hemodilution may constitute another etiology (28). Uterine contractions are treated with tocolytic agents (see below). Progesterone may also be useful.

Perfusion problems constitute a potential source of fetal complications. These include nonpulsatile perfusion, inadequate perfusion pressure, inadequate perfusion flow, embolic phenomena to uteroplacental circulation, or alterations in placental blood flow secondary to cannulation. Meffert and Stansel (22) noted an increase in fetal mortality when mitral valve replacement was performed, as compared to that resulting from mitral commissurotomy. Those authors believed that this difference resulted from bypass times required

for mitral valve replacement. Fetal mortality rate has been noted to increase with an increase in bypass time.

A number of strategies have evolved for avoidance of complications, and techniques have been devised to reduce the rate of fetal complications. Because of the marked increase in cardiac output during pregnancy, normal cardiac output during the third trimester of pregnancy may be 6 liters/min; therefore, a perfusion flow of 4 liters/min represents only two-thirds that of the normal flow and could result in fetal hypoperfusion. Bubble and particulate emboli are minimized by using a membrane oxygenator and a filter on the arterial side of the extracorporeal circuit. Fetal heart rate can be adequately maintained by perfusion at either normothermia or mild hypothermia. In pregnant patients, some sources recommend perfusion pressures ranging from 60 to 75 mm Hg, preferably accomplished with high perfusion flows rather than with a-adrenergic agonists. Fetal heart rate monitoring should be used to detect the decreases in heart rate associated with poor fetal perfusion. Since FHR correlates with bypass flow, fetal bradycardia should be treated with an increase in perfusion flow rate. Both FHR and uterine activity monitoring should be maintained for 48 to 72 hours postoperatively.

In the third trimester of pregnancy, particularly because of the increased rate of premature labor, expectant management of the patient allowing the fetus to stay in utero as long as possible plays an increasing role. Options may include expectant management of the mother with delivery or cesarean section followed by maternal cardiac surgery, maternal surgery with the fetus remaining in utero, or simultaneous cesarean section and maternal cardiac surgery. The approach selected should balance the maturity of the fetus with the severity of maternal cardiac disease and the risk of labor and delivery with uncorrected cardiac disease. If uteroplacental insufficiency is present (suggested by fetal bradycardia), delivery of the fetus prior to bypass should be considered. Although the exact role is not known, avoidance of bypass by using a closed procedure such as closed mitral commissurotomy or balloon valvuloplasty may be an option in patients at particularly high risk for undergoing bypass.

Fetal complications could also be theoretically attributed to nonpulsatile perfusion, hyperoxygenation, or anticoagulation with heparin. At present, none of these factors has been clearly identified as the cause of fetal problems. Hypothermia also causes FHR decelerations; therefore, normothermia or mild hypothermia ($32°C$) is generally used. Most sources believe that a hematocrit exceeding 20 to 25% should be maintained as well as a perfusion flow index of 3 liters/min/m². To avert the potential effects of aortocaval compression by the gravid uterus, central cannulation is preferable to femoral arterial or venous cannulation. Late in pregnancy the right flank should be elevated to prevent aortocaval compression (22).

When necessary, tocolytic agents are used. At term, the uterus is more (26) responsive to tocolytic agents than it is earlier in pregnancy. A number of tocolytic agents are available. The agent should be chosen because of its effectiveness as well as its lack of side effects. A number of tocolytic agents may have cardiovascular side effects, particularly β-adrenergic agonists such as terbutaline (21, 26, 33). Ritodrine and magnesium sulfate have proven most effective in clinical trials (25). Other approaches include ethanol or a combination of a β-adrenergic agonist and progesterone (28). Because of limited side effects, magnesium sulfate may be the best tocolytic agent for pregnant patients undergoing bypass associated with diabetes mellitus or hypertension.

If measures to avoid or treat fetal complications fail and fetal distress occurs, measures must be taken to correct this problem. If fetal distress can be prevented, fetal mortality will decline. Metabolic acidosis,

when present, is treated with sodium bicarbonate. Glucose is given to replenish decreased fetal glycogen stores, and reduced blood oxygen saturation is promptly corrected by increasing perfusion flow, hemoglobin concentration, or oxygen flows as indicated (31). Inotropic or vasopressor agents should be avoided when other treatments may be substituted. For example, if the patient has lost blood and needs volume replacement, transfusion would be preferred over vasopressor agents. Epinephrine has been recommended because of its rapid onset, brief duration, and few unwanted side effects at moderate doses. At high doses, epinephrine predominantly manifests α-adrenergic effects. Since blood flow to the gravid uterus is primarily under α-adrenergic control, α-adrenergic agonists will decrease uterine blood flow in normotensive pregnant patients. Drugs that exhibit a combination of α- and β-adrenergic activity are most useful because they increase maternal blood pressure without reducing uterine blood flow (29, 34). Examples of such drugs are ephedrine and moderate-dose epinephrine. A reduction in uterine blood flow has been seen in animal studies in which hypotension was treated with dopamine or hypertension was treated with nitroprusside. In addition, nitroprusside crosses the placenta in animals and may liberate free cyanide ions and result in metabolic acidosis. Large doses of nitroprusside in gravid ewes uniformly result in maternal and fetal death (19, 29).

In summary, CPB during pregnancy is associated with a low rate of maternal complications but a high risk to the fetus. If possible, bypass surgery should be avoided during pregnancy. If the disease process dictates that surgery is necessary, the first and third trimester are best avoided in order to minimize teratogenesis or premature initiation of uterine contractions and labor. It appears likely that fetal distress and complications can be avoided by maintaining a high mean arterial pressure, high perfusion flows, normothermia or mild hypothermia, by the use of fetal monitoring, and by early treatment of FHR decelerations and uterine contractions. If fetal distress does become apparent, corrective measures must be taken.

HEMOGLOBINOPATHY AND ERYTHROCYTE DISORDERS

Sickle Cell Trait and Disease

In the normal adult, hemoglobin A is the predominant form of hemoglobin comprising 96 to 97% of all hemoglobin. Hemoglobin A consists of two alpha and two beta chains. Sickle cell hemoglobinopathy is a single gene recessive abnormality that may be present in a heterozygous recessive form, which is sickle cell trait, or in a homozygous recessive form, which is expressed as the sickle cell disease. The percentage of hemoglobin S and hemoglobin A varies with the individual, but more hemoglobin S is present in patients who are homozygous recessive and express the sickle cell disease. These individuals have a predominance of hemoglobin S, which may account for 80 to 98% of the hemoglobin present. This homozygous state is found in 0.15% of American blacks and is associated with clinical sickle cell disease manifesting as severe hemolytic anemia and vaso-occlusive phenomena, resulting from the increased blood viscosity that occurs when sickle cells aggregate (34). When this occurs, the red blood cells are often described as sickled, which describes the shape they assume. Sickled cells also deliver little oxygen to the tissues.

In contrast, patients with the sickle cell trait have a lower percentage of hemoglobin S, accounting for 20 to 45% of their total hemoglobin. About 8% of American blacks carry the heterozygous recessive trait. These individuals have few clinical problems and, except for severe or provoked conditions, they rarely experience sickle cell crises. Red blood cell sickling re-

sults from deoxyhemoglobin formation. The tendency toward sickling increases with hypoxemia, acidosis, increased concentrations of 2,3-diphosphoglyceric acid, infection, hypothermia, and capillary stagnation. A hypertonic environment that may lead to crenation of normal red blood cells also will lead to sickling in the abnormal cells. The abnormal hemoglobin changes properties of the cell membrane and also cell metabolism. Osmotic and mechanical fragility increase, making hemolysis more likely. A hypotonic environment will lyse red blood cells with increased osmotic fragility.

In patients with sickle cell disease, some sickling begins to appear at 85% hemoglobin oxygen saturation, and sickling of red blood cells is complete at 38% saturation. In patients with sickle cell trait, sickling begins at hemoglobin oxygen saturations of approximately 40%. To a degree, sickling is reversible but if it is repeated, the sickled cells become permanently damaged, resulting in markedly increased fragility and a shortened cell life span. In addition to increased blood viscosity potentially causing vascular occlusion, sickling can cause endothelial cell injury in the microvasculature. This may activate the intrinsic clotting system and exacerbate the vaso-occlusive phenomenon (19, 35).

Operative Management

The operative strategy in sickle cell patients is to prevent sickling, and thereby prevent hemolysis or vaso-occlusive phenomena intraoperatively and postoperatively. Since sickling results from decreased hemoglobin oxygen saturation, maintaining adequate arterial oxygen tension assumes paramount importance. Adequate capillary perfusion with short capillary transit times and avoidance of low output states (to prevent low mixed venous oxygen saturations) are also important (36–38). Continuous measurement of arterial and mixed venous oxygen saturations help to maintain adequate oxygen saturations. Because sickle crises are frequent when high concentrations of hemoglobin S are present (i.e., homozygous patients), marked reduction of sickling can be achieved by relative dilution of hemoglobin S with respect to hemoglobin A. This can be accomplished by using preoperative or intraoperative exchange transfusions.

Preoperative exchange transfusions, particularly applicable in patients who are already anemic, not only increase the prevalence of hemoglobin A relative to hemoglobin S but also suppress the production of hemoglobin S. This therapy improves the oxygen-carrying capacity of the blood by correcting the anemia and deficiency of hemoglobin A. In nonanemic patients, exchange transfusion may be accomplished intraoperatively. This type of transfusion is usually performed by sequestering the initial bypass venous drainage from the patient after priming the extracorporeal circuit with whole blood containing hemoglobin A. Therefore, initiating bypass replaces the blood initially removed by venous drainage (19, 38). The goal of exchange transfusion is to achieve a hemoglobin A fraction of 60 to 70%, which is also the level sought when treating a major sickle cell crisis (37).

Acidosis shifts the oxyhemoglobin dissociation curve to the right, which increases the tendency toward sickling. This holds true particularly in venous blood, where sickling is most often initiated. Arterial and mixed venous blood gases should be measured frequently and acidosis aggressively treated with sodium bicarbonate (37, 38). Hypoperfusion may result from hypothermia, dimished intravascular volume, poor patient positioning, tourniquets, low perfusion flows, or low cardiac output states. It is important to avoid hypoperfusion because of the tendency of blood to desaturate during the capillary and venous phase of circulation, resulting in low hemoglobin oxygen saturation and red blood cell

sickling. Hypoperfusion can usually be prevented by maintaining adequate flow on bypass, and avoiding low cardiac output states both before and after bypass.

Localized sickling may occur in the heart during aortic cross-clamping because of the absence of coronary blood flow. This phenomenon may be avoided by washing hemoglobin S out of the heart using either crystalloid cardioplegia or blood cardioplegia with a high fraction of hemoglobin A. Because mechanical prosthetic valves may predispose the patient to increased hemolysis, such valves are not recommended in these patients (38). Other means of avoiding mechanical blood trauma include using a centrifugal pump rather than a roller pump and minimizing the use of cardiotomy suction. Especially in patients with sickle cell disease, it appears advisable to minimize or avoid hypothermia during extracorporeal circulation. Despite the risks involved, numerous successful open heart surgeries have been performed using the above techniques in patients with homozygous sickle cell disease (23, 39–41).

HEREDITY SPHEROCYTOSIS

Heredity spherocytosis, an autosomal dominant defect in red blood cell membranes, results in spherically shaped red blood cells that have increased osmotic and mechanical fragility. The usual treatment for heredity spherocytosis resulting in hemolysis is splenectomy, which corrects the hemolysis and increases the shortened life span of the red blood cells to normal, although the cells retain their abnormal properties. Data describing CPB in these patients are quite limited; one case report describes a nonsplenectomized patient undergoing bypass with no apparent increase in blood destruction or in osmotic fragility over the baseline level (42). In addition, in a patient who had previously undergone splenectomy, no increase in hemolysis was noted during or after bypass, despite triple valve replacement using Bjork-Shiley mechanical valves (43).

MISCELLANEOUS

Cardiopulmonary bypass in association with other abnormalities relating to hemoglobinopathy or red blood cell abnormalities are briefly mentioned in the literature. However, data on these abnormalities are sparse enough to be of limited use. Thalassemia minor patients exhibit no increase in red blood cell fragility; therefore, one would expect no hemolysis. Anemia in these patients is treated with transfusions. Hemolysis has been induced by a number of drugs in patients with glucose-6-phosphate dehydrogenase deficiency (44). This sex-linked inherited deficiency is present in 10–15% of American black males. Susceptible individuals may develop explosive hemolysis when they receive drugs such as antimalarials, quinidine, phenacetin, or sulfonamides. These drugs should be avoided in susceptible patients undergoing surgery, including those undergoing bypass. Heredity elliptocytosis is a condition thought to be similar to heredity spherocytosis: there is infrequent hemolysis and anemia, and no specific precautions are recommended in these patients (34, 44).

Acute methemoglobinemia may result from increased production of methemoglobin to levels far exceeding the usual amount, which is less than 1% of the total circulating hemoglobin. Secondary or acquired methemoglobinemia is almost always caused by poisoning with chemicals or drugs classified either as direct oxidants such as nitrites or indirect oxidants such as benzocaine. Other such medications include methylene blue, nitroglycerin, nitroprusside, prilocaine, silver nitrate, sodium nitrate, and sulfonamides. The diagnosis of methemoglobinemia is made when cya-

nosis occurs in the presence of an adequate arterial oxygen tension, and is supported by a chocolate brown color of blood rather than the usual dark blue of cyanosis. Confirmation of the diagnosis can be made by spectrophotometry specific to methemoglobin. This absolute diagnosis takes some time, therefore, treatment should begin immediately. First, all probable offending drugs should be withdrawn. Next, there should be confirmation that oxygen delivery to the patient is adequate and that the oxygen tension is high. If cyanosis persists in the presence of high arterial oxygen tension, pharmacologic treatment should begin. The drug of choice in the management of acute methemoglobinemia is methylene blue, 1 to 3 mg/kg administered in a 1% solution, which converts methemoglobin to active hemoglobin. The response to methylene blue is usually excellent, and because the treatment is relatively innocuous, its use should not be delayed. Methylene blue may cause methemoglobinemia when a dose greater than 7 mg/kg is administered. If the patient fails to respond to methylene blue, the next line of treatment consists of high-dose vitamin C and if necessary, exchange transfusion (45).

CARDIOPULMONARY BYPASS AFTER PNEUMONECTOMY

Cardiopulmonary bypass techniques for patients who have undergone prior pneumonectomy have not been specifically addressed in the literature. The technical aspects of conducting perfusion in such patients are not significantly different from those in patients who have had lobectomy or no pulmonary resection. Our combined experience includes seven patients, and what follows is the treatment protocol we have chosen for these patients. Unfortunately, prospective studies evaluating different management protocols for these patients are not available.

Preoperative Data

Routine sputum cultures are obtained to assess the patient's resident flora. A right heart catheterization with measurements of pulmonary artery pressures aids our selection of patients for cardiac surgery who have had a pneumonectomy. We have uniformly selected postpneumonectomy patients having a pulmonary artery systolic pressure less than 40 mm Hg for cardiac surgery, believing that this level is a realistic upper limit in this subset of patients. In a treatise on the right heart, Morris and Wechsler (46) noted that a variety of factors hinder understanding of right ventricular hemodynamic function and that suitable parameters to quantitatively assess right ventricular performance are lacking. Therefore, extensive studies of the right ventricle, including ejection fraction, dp/dt, loading conditions, etc., would be of questionable help in assessing a patient with a single lung for cardiac surgery (46).

Preoperative pulmonary function tests are mandatory. The problem arises in choosing minimal acceptable parameters to select patients capable of avoiding respirator dependence after operation or CPB. Our requirements for CPB surgery in postpneumonectomy patients are forced expiratory volume per 1 second of 40% predicted or 800 ml, resting Pco_2 $\leq$50 mm Hg and co diffusion capacity greater than 50% predicted.

Granulocytes and Complement

White cell adherence to capillary endothelium during bypass has been linked to alveolar cell damage (47). Inhibition of granulocyte activation with nifedipine or with oral calcium channel blockers has been reported (48). Ibuprofen has also been reported to reduce white cell accumulation in the lungs during bypass. Leukocyte filtration can be incorporated into the arterial infusion line from the extracorporeal circuit, which represents a recent development that might especially benefit postpneumonectomy patients undergoing bypass. Methylprednisolone at doses of 30 mg/kg administered before bypass has been associated with reduced anaphylatoxin levels (49). The mechanisms of complement activation resulting in pulmonary injury have yet to be completely elucidated; however, it appears rational to be especially aggressive in attempting to avoid generation of the potent inflammatory anaphylotoxins (C3a and C5a) as much as possible in accordance with our current level of scientific knowledge.

Blood Products, Hemodilution

Hemodilution for CPB has been associated with a decrease in postoperative pulmonary problems theoretically from dilution of noxious blood elements or from avoidance of noxious elements, e.g., microaggregates present in homologous blood. However, excessive hemodilution may predispose to edema, which might be addressed by limiting hemodilution to a hematocrit fraction of >20% in postpneumonectomy patients.

Blood transfusions are avoided not only because of potential infections or transfusion reactions, but also because of possible pulmonary damage from such elements as platelets and white blood cells. Washed packed red blood cells appear more appropriate when transfusion is indicated, and we avoid the return of shed blood in patients undergoing bypass after pneumonectomy. We believe that when platelet transfusion is indicated, steroids and diphenhydramine should be used as pretreatment, and that leukocyte filters (Pall Biomedical Products, Easthills, NY) designed for platelet concentrates should be used.

Operative Considerations

Technically, the position of the heart may be distorted because of contracted fibrothorax and/or hyperinflation of the remaining lung. This may lead to technical difficulty for exposure, especially after left pneumonectomy. Remote cannulation from the femoral vessels has been helpful in some of our patients. Monitoring of pulmonary artery pressure, as well as left atrial pressure, with possible left ventricular venting is important. We believe that strict control of the level of pulmonary capillary hydrostatic pressure is critical both operatively and postoperatively to prevent pulmonary edema that might rise from even transient acute rises in pulmonary capillary pressure. Air emboli in the pulmonary circuit would seemingly be less well tolerated, and this is addressed by standard techniques. Cardiopulmonary bypass time is directly related to postoperative lung water; therefore, at times, a less complete coronary revascularization may be preferable to incurring a long bypass time. Complement activation is increased not only in extremes of age, but with long perfusion runs.

Postoperative Considerations

We are much less tolerant of the mild degrees of pleural effusion that occur in the usual coronary bypass patient because these may critically impair gas exchange in the postpneumonectomy patient. Daily weights, diuretics, and consultation with an experienced pulmonologist are routinely employed. Incisional pain is a major cause of postoperative decrease in lung volume (50), thus minimizing pain by surgical technique and optimizing analgesia with postoperative opioids, are particularly important to these patients. As opposed to the usual intercostal route, pleural tubes, when indicated, are routed through the mediastinum into the appropriate hemithorax as there is a definite decrease in chest wall pain with that technique. Using these guidelines, we have extubated our patients who have one lung and have undergone cardiac surgery within 24 to 48 hours postoperatively and have avoided any significant postoperative pulmonary problems.

ACQUIRED IMMUNODEFICIENCY SYNDROME (AIDS)

A modern epidemic has emerged that is unlike previously known epidemics in that the disease may lie clinically silent for 10 years or more after the organism is introduced. In June 1979, a 32-year-old man in New York City, infected with the human immunodeficiency virus (HIV), appeared at first to be a medical curiosity, but the syndrome was rapidly recognized, and by June 1983, over 1600 cases had been reported in the United States. Healthcare workers have always lived with the risks associated with contracting potentially fatal diseases; however, rarely in the course of history has a disease provoked such an emotional response, intense debate, and such a plethora of research efforts. The apparently uniform fatal outcome of clinical AIDS mandates introspection and close scrutiny of any invasive procedures performed by healthcare workers. At the time of this writing, debate rages on, significant research advances are few, and guidelines and statutes will definitely change. This section will briefly discuss the management of patients harboring an HIV infection who undergo cardiac surgery.

Exposure

Homologous blood should be considered a toxic substance. For those associated with bypass, exposure to blood is a daily risk. Gerberding et al. (51) studied the risks of exposure in 1307 consecutive surgical procedures and reported that accidental exposure to blood occurred in 84 instances. The incidence of exposure increased when procedures lasted more than 3 hours and when blood loss exceeded 300 ml. Their data supported the practice of double-gloving and the use of waterproof garments and face shields. Blood contact events were reported in 28% of 684 operations at the University of New Mexico (52). The authors concluded that most contacts were preventable and reflected indifference to universal precautions that were part of their standard operating room policy.

The so-called "universal precautions" advised by the Centers for Disease Control (CDC) in Atlanta did not address the unique problems that occur in the operating room (53). Cardiothoracic cases (54) revealed a 58% contact ($p < 0.001$) with blood by personnel and multiple contacts in 12 cases. Although no case of operating room transmission of HIV had yet been documented, the authors concluded it had no doubt occurred and would certainly be documented in the future.

Preoperative Testing

Acquired immunodeficiency syndrome has clearly become a national obsession. The National Commission on AIDS 133-page document recorded that mass screening programs would interfere with doctor-patient relationships and would encourage a false sense of security. This is because a 6- to 12-week window period normally occurs between infection with the HIV virus and seropositivity with traditional HIV screening tests. The medicolegal ramifications of testing patients present a significant problem, although in part this may be obviated by complying with local statutes for informed consent. No solution has been developed for the emergency patient who must rapidly undergo CPB when there is not sufficient time to obtain test results; thus the CDC "universal precautions" urge that *all* patients be treated as potentially infected. It is our policy to test all patients who undergo bypass as it is our belief that we have an ethical obligation to maintain, as much as possible, an environmentally safe workplace.

The extent to which blood must be considered a toxic substance is realized when one studies the history of a nurse healthcare worker infected in Iowa. The worker was infected during a resuscitative effort on an HIV-positive patient when blood seeped from an IV line onto her gloveless left index finger, which had been previously cut during gardening. She became HIV-positive 3 months later. If a patient develops clinical AIDS after heart surgery, he or she will likely blame the surgery, its personnel, etc., when in fact, a positive HIV test may have predated the surgery, a further indication of the prudent approach to establish the status of each patient before elective open heart surgery.

Testing of the Healthcare Worker

In October 1991, Congress passed legislation directing states to enact regulations requiring healthcare workers to adhere to guidelines intended to prevent transmission of the HIV virus to patients. States that do not comply will forfeit federal funds granted under the Public Health Service Act. An amendment dropped from the bill would have made it a federal crime for an HIV-infected healthcare worker to perform invasive procedures on patients without disclosing his or her HIV status. Patient confidentiality arguments have now taken a 180-degree turn to "healthcare worker confidentiality." In December 1991, the first hospital in the United States began mandatory HIV testing of its physicians with the requirement of an annual test for continued staff membership and privileges. The federal CDC in Atlanta recommends voluntary testing, but has stopped short of advising mandatory testing for AIDS. The CDC estimates that one million people in the United States have the HIV virus and 130,000 have died of AIDS since 1981. As of June 30, 1991, 6782 healthcare workers were known to have the AIDS virus. There were 1441 nurses, 989 technicians, and 728 doctors, of which 46 were surgeons.

Laboratory Testing

The Elisa screening test, which may be completed in a few hours, has few false-negative results, but a significant number of false-positives. The confirmatory test is the Western Blot, which has a low false-positive rate. Patients confirmed positive with this test should have adequate counseling, which is available in most hospital settings at this time.

Ethics in Refusing Care to HIV Patients

The American Medical Association and the American College of Physicians have endorsed statements that doctors may not ethically refuse to treat a patient solely because the patient has AIDS or is seropositive for HIV infection. To date, the American Society of Extra-Corporeal Technology, Inc., has not taken a position on this problem. The subcommittee on AIDS of The American College of Surgeons Governors Committee does not currently recommend discontinuation of practice for HIV-positive surgeons (55). Much public concern has focused on the risk of doctor-to-patient transmission after a Florida dentist who died of AIDS had five patients become HIV-positive. No other HIV transmissions from healthcare worker to patient have been reported. Patient-to-healthcare worker transmission has been reported and appears to be much more frequent than the reverse. The Society of Thoracic Surgeons Committee on AIDS has made the following recommendations to thoracic surgeons: (a) Prior to elective surgery, make every attempt to identify patients who are positive for infection with the HIV by voluntary testing. In doing so, be careful to comply with any applicable confidentiality statutes and informed consent statutes. (b) Use "universal precautions" against exposure to blood and other body fluids in the operating room and throughout the hospital, regardless of whether the status of the HIV serology is known. (c)

Take a leadership role to encourage easing the current restrictions on HIV testing in order that we may learn about the risk of transmission of HIV, the role that positive HIV status may play in affecting the results of treatment of other disease processes, and the possibility that surgery and bypass may accelerate the development of AIDS in the HIV-positive patient. (d) Encourage hospital laboratories to develop the capability of providing rapid screening of patients for HIV.

In summary, the AIDS epidemic has positively and negatively affected the use of CPB. Healthcare workers have become much more cautious since the identification of its etiology. The modes of HIV transmission have been established with a high degree of certainty and, in infected patients, viral presence has been established in virtually all body fluids (semen, vaginal secretions, blood, urine, saliva, cerebrospinal fluid, mother's milk, and almost certainly, feces). Although the true incidence of conversion of medical healthcare workers after most work-related exposures to HIV infection remains unknown, the incidence of a healthcare worker seroconverting after a hollow needle puncture is in the range of 1 in 150 exposures. All hospitals should have the drug azidothymidine immediately available for healthcare workers who experience an injury from an HIV-positive patient. There is laboratory evidence that azidothymidine given within 15 minutes of such injury can prevent HIV viral migration into the injured worker's cells. Full-blown AIDS is 100% fatal in spite of intense research efforts to control the disease. Healthcare professionals working in the bypass environment have an obviously increased risk of exposure, and "universal precautions" to provide barriers cannot be overemphasized. Cardiopulmonary bypass material (oxygenators, reservoirs, tubing, etc.) used in a known HIV-positive patient should have 10% formaldehyde circulated within all aspects of the unit before the prescribed discard protocol.

Malignant Hyperthermia

Malignant hyperthermia is a syndrome of acute hyperthermia (core temperatures may exceed 42°C) and/or myotonic reactions initiated by a hypermetabolic state of skeletal muscle. This syndrome can be triggered by administration of potent inhalation anesthetics (e.g., halothane, enflurane, and isoflurane) and succinylcholine. The syndrome was originally described in 1962 (56). The incidence is approximately 1 in 15,000 children and 1 in 50,000 adults. Early on, management of patients with malignant hyperthermia consisted of copious amounts of chilled IV Ringer's lactate solution, lavage of stomach and bladder with iced solutions, and large IV doses of procainamide or procaine (57). Currently, dantrolene sodium from 1 to 10 mg/kg is the treatment of choice, along with some of the active cooling measures listed above. Unlike previous pharmacologic measures (e.g., procainamide), dantrolene specifically addresses the causative mechanism, which is impaired reuptake of ionized calcium from the cytosol into storage sites located in the sarcoplasmic reticulum of skeletal muscle myocytes. Prior to the introduction of dantrolene, mortality was greater than 60% (58). Before dantrolene was available, CPB had been used unsuccessfully and later successfully as a method of controlled cooling in the treatment of malignant hyperthermia (59).

Byrick et al. (60) described the anesthetic management of a patient with biopsy-proven malignant hyperthermia who underwent coronary artery bypass grafting. Measures included pretreatment with dantrolene, venting of the oxygenator, removal of the halothane vaporizer from the oxygenation-inspired gas pathway, and the use of high-dose fentanyl for anesthesia and pancuronium for muscle relaxation. Cold potassium (10 mEq/liter) cardioplegia was used; inotropic agents and calcium (possible trigger agent) were avoided. The patient continued to receive dantrolene every 6

hours for 24 hours after the operation. No evidence of malignant hyperthermia was encountered.

The diagnosis of malignant hyperthermia may be complicated or delayed by the coincidental use of bypass, and may require an increased index of suspicion in the presence of high temperatures persisting more than 8 hours after the operation and markedly elevated creatine phosphokinase (CPK) levels. At least one patient believed to have had malignant hyperthermia presenting late during bypass has been successfully treated with a single dose of dantrolene (1 mg/kg) (61). Early recognition and treatment of malignant hyperthermia is important because the marked hypermetabolism outstrips the oxygen delivery capacity of the oxygenator, especially at normothermia. During bypass, unexpected hyperthermia or temperature rises and unexplained metabolic and respiratory acidosis would provide the most likely clues to the diagnosis. When suspected, it appears sensible to induce or maintain hypothermia while awaiting dantrolene-induced resolution of the clinical syndrome. Repeated doses of dantrolene may be required. Dantrolene is known to cause skeletal muscle weakness and causes myocardial depression in animals; caution is advised in its use in cardiac patients (60, 61).

REFERENCES

1. Moore RA, Geller EA, Mathews ES, Botros SB, Jose AB, Clark DL. The effect of hypothermic cardiopulmonary bypass on patients with low-titer, nonspecific cold agglutinins. Ann Thorac Surg 1984;37:233–238.
2. Lee M-C, Chang C-H, Hsieh M-J. Use of a total wash-out method in an open-heart operation. Ann Thorac Surg 1989;47:57–58.
3. Pruzanski W, Shumak KH. Biologic activity of cold-reacting autoantibodies (Second of Two parts). N Engl J Med 1977;297:583–589.
4. Leach AB, Van Hasselt GL, Edwards JC. Cold agglutinins and deep hypothermia. Anaesthesia 1983;38:140–143.
5. Dake SB, Johnston MFM, Brueggeman P, Barner HG. Detection of cold hemagglutination in a

blood cardioplegia unit before systemic cooling of a patient with unsuspected cold agglutinin disease. Ann Thorac Surg 1989;47:314–315.

6. Pruzanski W, Shumak KH. Biologic activity of cold-reacting autoantibodies (First of Two parts). N Engl J Med 1977;297:538–542.

7. Berreklouw E, Moulijin AC, Pegels JG, Meijne NG. Myocardial protection with cold cardioplegia in a patient with cold autoagglutinins and hemolysins. Ann Thorac Surg 1982;33:521–522.

8. Klein HG, Faltz LL, McIntosh CL, Appelbaum FR, Deisseroth AB, Holland PV. Surgical hypothermia in a patient with a cold agglutinin. Transfusion 1980;20:354–357.

9. Wertlake PT, McGinniss MH, Schmidt PJ. Cold antibody and persistent intravascular hemolysis after surgery under hypothermia. Transfusion 1969;9:70–73.

10. Williams AC. Cold agglutinins: Cause for concern? Anaesthesia 1980;35:887–889.

11. Shahian DM, Wallach SR, Bern MM. Open-heart surgery in patients with cold-reactive proteins. Surg Clinics N Am 1985;65:315–322.

12. AuBuchon JP, Stofan BA, Davey RJ. Hemolysis during extracorporeal circulation: significance of cold-reactive auto-antibodies and mechanical trauma [Abstract]. Blood 1983;62(suppl 1):42a.

13. Schreiber AD, Herskovitz BS, Goldwein M. Low-titer cold-hemagglutinin disease: Mechanism of hemolysis and response to corticosteroids. N Engl J Med 1977;296:1490–1494.

14. Diaz JH, Cooper ES, Ochsner JL. Cardiac surgery in patients with cold autoimmune diseases. Anesth Analg 1984;63:349–352.

15. Blumberg N, Hicks G, Woll J, et al. Successful cardiac bypass surgery in the presence of a potent cold agglutinin without plasma exchange [Letter]. Transfusion 1983;23:363–364.

16. Landymore R, Isom W, Barlam B. Management of patients with cold agglutinins who require open-heart surgery. Can J Surg 1983;26:79–80.

17. Holman WL, Smith SH, Edwards R, Huang ST. Agglutination of blood cardioplegia by cold-reacting autoantibodies. Ann Thorac Surg 1991; 51:833–836.

18. Paccagnella A, Simini G, Nieri A, DaCol U, Frugoni C, Valfre C. Cardiopulmonary bypass and cold agglutinin [Letter]. J Thorac Cardiovasc Surg 1988;95:543.

19. Naulty JS, Cefalo RC, Lewis P. Fetal toxicity of nitroprusside in the pregnant ewe. Am J Obstet Gynecol 1980;139:708–711.

20. Becker RM. Intracardiac surgery in pregnant women. Ann Thorac Surg 1983;36:453–458.

21. Werch A, Lambert HM, Cooley D, Reed CC. Fetal monitoring and maternal open heart surgery. South Med J 1977;70:1024.

22. Meffert WG, Stansel HC Jr. Open heart surgery during pregnancy. Am J Obstet Gynecol 1968; 102:1116–1120.

23. Heiner M, Teasdale SJ, David T, Scott AA, Glynn MFX. Aortocoronary bypass in a patient with sickle cell trait. Can Anaesth Soc J 1979; 26:428–434.

24. Izquierdo LA, Kushnir O, Knieriem K, Wernley JA, Curet LB. Effect of mitral valve prosthetic surgery on the outcome of a growth-retarded fetus. A case report. Am J Obstet Gynecol 1990; 163:584–586.

25. Caritis SN, Edelstone DI, Mueller-Heubach E. Pharmacologic inhibition of premature labor. Am J Obstet Gynecol 1979;133:557–578.

26. Lamb MP, Ross K, Johnstone AM, Manners JM. Fetal heart rate monitoring during open heart surgery. Br J Obstet Gynecol 1983;88:669–674.

27. Pedersen H, Finster M. Anesthetic risk in the pregnant surgical patient. Anesthesiology 1979; 51:439–451,669–674.

28. Korsten HHM, Van Zundert AAJ, Mooij PNM, De Jong PA, Bavinck JH. Emergency aortic valve replacement in the 24th week of pregnancy. Acta Anaesth Belg 1989;40:201–205.

29. Conroy JM, Bailey MK, Hollon MF, Cooke JE, Baker JD 3d. Anesthesia for open heart surgery in the pregnant patient. South Med J 1989;82: 492–495.

30. Harrison EC, Roschke EJ. Pregnancy in patients with cardiac valve prostheses. Clin Obstet Gynecol 1975;18:107–123.

31. Koh KS, Friesen RM, Livingstone RA, Peddle LJ. Fetal monitoring during maternal cardiac surgery with cardiopulmonary bypass. Can Med Assoc J 1975;112:1102–1104.

32. Reisner LS. Cardiac dysfunction: special considerations during pregnancy. In: Utley JR, ed. Pathophysiology and techniques of cardiopulmonary bypass. Vol III (Cardiothoracic Surgery Series). Baltimore: Williams & Wilkins, 1985:15–29.

33. Ravindran R, Viegas OJ, Padilla LM, LaBlonde P. Anesthetic considerations in pregnant patients receiving terbutylline treatment. Anesth Analg 1980;59:391–392.

34. Rolbin SH, Levinson G, Shnider SM, Biehl DR, Wright RG. Dopamine treatment of spinal hypotension decreases uterine blood flow in the pregnant ewe. Anesthesiology 1979;51:37–40.

35. Szentpetery S, Robertson L, Lower RR. Complete repair of tetralogy associated with sickle cell anemia and G-6-PD deficiency. J Thorac Cardiovasc Surg 1976;72:276–279.

36. Chun PKC, Flannery EP, Bowen TE. Open-heart surgery in patients with hematologic disorders. Am Heart J 1983;105:835–842.

37. Fox MA, Abbott TR. Hypothermic cardiopulmonary bypass in a patient with sickle-cell trait. Anaesthesia 1984;39:1121–1123.

38. Ingram CT, Floyd JB, Santora AH. Aortic and mitral valve replacement after sickle cell crisis [Letter]. Anesth Analg 1982;61:802–803.

39. Yacoub MH, Baron J, Et-Etr A, Kettle F. Aortic homograft replacement of the mitral valve in sickle cell trait. J Thorac Cardiovasc Surg 1970;59:568–573.

40. Riethmuller R, Grundy EM, Radley-Smith R. Open heart surgery in a patient with homozygous sickle cell disease. Anaesthesia 1982;37:324–327.

41. Harris LC, Haggard ME, Travis LB. The coexistence of sickle cell disease and congenital heart disease: a report of three cases with repair under cardiopulmonary by-pass in two. Pediatrics 1964;33:562–570.

42. Craenen J, Kilman J, Hosier DM, Weinberger M. Mitral valve replacement in a child with sickle cell anemia. J Thorac Cardiovasc Surg 1972;63:797–799.

43. Moyes DG, Holloway AM, Hutton WS. Correction of Fallot's tetralogy in a patient suffering from hereditary spherocytosis. S Afr Med J 1974;48:1535–1536.

44. deLeval MR, Taswell HF, Bowie EJW, Danielson GK. Open heart surgery in patients with inherited hemoglobinopathies, red cell dyscrasias and coagulopathies. Arch Surg 1974;109:618.

45. Robicsek F. Acute methemoglobinemia during cardiopulmonary bypass caused by intravenous nitroglycerin infusion. J Thorac Cardiovasc Surg 1985;90:931–933.

46. Morris JJ, Weschsler AS. Right ventricular function: the assessment of contractile performance. In: Fiske RL, ed. *The right heart*. Philadelphia: FA Davis Co, 1987:3–18.

47. Rabello RC, Oleveirash, Tanka H, Weigl DR, Vergenelli G, Zerrini EJ. The influence of the nature of the prime on post perfusion pulmonary changes. J Thorac Cardiovasc Surg 1973;66:782–793.

48. Komer C. In: Casthely PA, Bregman D, eds. Cardiopulmonary bypass: physiology, related complications, and pharmacology. Mt. Kisco, NY: Futura Publishing, 1991:37–84.

49. Cavarocchi NC, Pluth JR, Shaft HV, et al. Complement activation during cardiopulmonary bypass. J Thorac Cardiovasc Surg 1986;91:252–528.

50. Peters RM. Effects of cardiopulmonary bypass on lung function. In: Utley JR, ed. Pathophysiology and techniques of cardiopulmonary bypass. Vol II. Baltimore: Williams & Wilkins, 1983;167–174.

51. Gerberding JL, Littell C, Tarkington A, et al. Risks of exposure of surgical personnel to patient's blood during surgery at San Francisco General Hospital. New Engl J Med 1990;322:1788–1793.

52. Popejoy SL, Fry DE. Blood contact and exposure in the operating room. Surg Gynecol Obstet 1991;172:480–483.

53. Centers for Disease Control. Recommendation for preventing transmission of infection with human T-lymphotropic virus Type III/lymphadenopathy—associated virus in the workplace. MMWR 1985;35:681–686,691–695.

54. Centers for Disease Control. Recommendation for preventing transmission of infection with human T-lymphotropic virus Type III/lymphadenopathy—associated virus in the workplace. MMWR 1986;35:21–23.

55. Subcommittee on AIDS of The American College of Surgeons Governors Committee. 1991 Clinical Congress highlights: statement on the surgeon and HIV infection. ACS Bulletin Dec 1991;76:28–31.

56. Denborough MA, Foster VFA, Lovell RRH, Mapleston PA, Villiers JD. Anaesthetic deaths in a family. Br J Anaesth 1962;34:395–396.

57. Ryan JF, Kerr WS Jr. Malignant hyperthermia: a catastrophic complication. J Urol 1973;109:879–883.

58. Britt BA, Kalow W. Malignant hyperthermia, a statistical review. Can Anaesth Soc J 1970;17:293–301.

59. Ryan JF, Donlon JV, Malt RA, et al. Cardiopulmonary bypass in the treatment of malignant hyperthermia. New Engl J Med 1974;290:1121–1122.

60. Byrick RJ, Rose DK, Ranganathan. Management of a malignant hyperthermia patient during cardiopulmonary bypass. Can Anaesth Soc J 1982;29:50–54.

61. MacGillivray RG, Jann H, Vanker E, Gemmel L, Mahomedy AE. Development of malignant hyperthermia obscured by cardiopulmonary bypass. Can Anaesth Soc J 1986;33:509–514.

30

TERMINATION OF CARDIOPULMONARY BYPASS

Hugh C. Hemmings, Jr., and Stephen J. Thomas

The return of the heart and lungs to the circulation following cardiopulmonary bypass (CPB) for myocardial revascularization, valve replacement or repair, or surgery for repair of congenital heart defects represents a period of potential stress for the heart, the success of which depends on thorough planning and preparation. The anesthesiologist facilitates this transition by assessing cardiac function and, if inadequate, providing appropriate pharmacologic support to ensure separation. The termination of bypass is a team effort; communication between surgeon, perfusionist, and anesthesiologist is mandatory.

Cardiopulmonary bypass is associated with several major physiologic insults including cardiac arrest (diastolic arrest or ventricular fibrillation), hypothermia, hemodilution, anticoagulation, electrolyte abnormalities, and high endogenous catecholamine levels, among others. Prior to the conclusion of CPB, these factors must be thoroughly evaluated. Termination of CPB is usually uneventful following careful preoperative and intraoperative assessment and planning. This chapter will review the factors that determine the successful termination of CPB and the methods involved.

PREPARING FOR SEPARATION

Preparation for separation from CPB must be based on a clear understanding of the patient's preoperative condition and the events of the operative course. Most preparations are routine and common to all cardiac surgical cases, while certain situations demand specific preparations, e.g., inotropic therapy for predicted postoperative ventricular dysfunction.

Rewarming

Before termination of CPB, the patient must be rewarmed if hypothermia was employed. Moderate hypothermia (25 to 30°C) is often used to slow myocardial rewarming following cold cardioplegia and perhaps reduce central nervous system complications; occasionally deep hypothermia (16 to 25°C) with circulatory arrest is needed for repairs of certain congenital defects or aortic arch aneurysms. This process is facilitated by the heat exchanger in the bypass circuit. Temperature measurement must include the arterial and venous blood (it is customary to keep the gradient less than 10°C; see Chapter 22 for further discussion) and one or more patient sites such as nasopharyngeal, esophageal, rectal, bladder, or great toe. Rewarming is initiated so that its completion coincides as much as possible with completion of the surgical procedure. Criteria for rewarming vary between institutions, but usually require a nasopharyngeal or esophageal temperature of 37°C, bladder or rectal temperature of 35°C, or great toe temperature of 30°C. Palpation of the patient's head and shoulders can be helpful in assessing the degree of peripheral perfusion and rewarming. However, the high blood flow to tissue mass ratio of the head and neck region will result in more rapid rewarming of these areas, and this clinical assessment can therefore underestimate the adequacy of rewarming in other areas.

Inadequate rewarming while on CPB can result in a considerable (2 to 3°C) drop in patient temperature during sternal closure and transport to the intensive care unit. This fall in temperature can result in shivering, with increased oxygen consumption, cardiac rhythm disturbances, and increased peripheral vascular resistance. Nitroprusside-induced vasodilation during CPB may facilitate rewarming and decrease the postbypass fall in temperature (1). Shivering should be anticipated and prevented with muscle relaxants until ventilator weaning is appropriate.

LAMPS

Following rewarming, the major factors that must be considered routinely prior to the termination of CPB can be recalled using the mnemonic LAMPS for *l*aboratory data, *a*nesthesia machine, *m*onitors, *p*atient/*p*ump, and *s*upport (Table 30.1).

LABORATORY DATA

Cardiopulmonary bypass results in numerous metabolic abnormalities, which should be normalized prior to termination of bypass when possible. Arterial blood gases and pH should be measured and corrective action taken, if necessary. Particular attention should be paid to arterial pH, especially in prolonged cases where metabolic acidosis with a considerable base deficit is likely to occur. Acidemia, from respiratory and/or metabolic acidosis, should be corrected because of its depressant effects on myocardial function, its interference with the action of inotropes, and its ability to increase pulmonary vascular tone (2–4). Serum sodium and potassium should be checked. Hemodilution and repeated dosing of hyperkalemic cardioplegia solution frequently result in significant electrolyte abnormalities, especially in the presence of poor renal function. Potassium has pronounced effects on cardiac conduction, and residual cardioplegia may result in atrioventricular conduction block, particularly in the presence of hyperkalemia (5). In this circumstance, atrioventricular pacing should be routinely available. However, the hyperkalemia can be treated with insulin (10 to 20 units IV) and glucose (50 g IV) or furosemide (5 to 10 mg IV), if severe. It is usually unnecessary to treat mild hyperkalemia ($K^+ \leq 6.0$ mEq/liter) in the presence of normal renal function, since serum potassium continues to fall following bypass, and hypokalemia may result.

Hypokalemia should be avoided following bypass and should be treated promptly since ventricular and atrial arrhythmias may be more common in the presence of acute hypokalemia, particularly in the patient receiving digoxin. Ideally, serum ionized calcium and glucose should also be determined. Hypocalcemia resulting from hemodilution and transfusion of albumin or citrate-containing blood products should be corrected with $CaCl_2$ (dosage range, 3 to 5 mg/kg) to improve myocardial contractility (in the presence of hypocalcemia) and peripheral vascular tone. Hyperglycemia, which is common following CPB, usually returns to normal shortly after termination of CPB, but should be treated with insulin in diabetic patients. Moderate hyperglycemia (<300 mg/dl) is probably inconsequential, and should be monitored for further increases. More severe hyperglycemia increases serum osmolarity and can cause osmotic diuresis and central nervous system dysfunction, and may increase the susceptibility of the brain to hypoxic damage. Treatment should include small incremental intravenous doses or continuous infusion of regular insulin,

Table 30.1.   Mnemonic for Preparations Prior to Termination of CPB

Laboratory data
pH, P_{CO_2} of arterial blood
S_{O_2} of venous blood
Serum Na^+, K^+, Ca^{2+}, glucose
Hematocrit
Activated clotting time, heparin concentration, thromboelastogram

Anesthesia/Machine
Analgesia - supplemental opioid
Amnesia - benzodiazepine
Muscle relaxation - supplemental neuromuscular blocking agent
Airway - Functional oxygen delivery system
   Anesthesia machine on
   Adequate oxygen supply
   Breathing circuit intact
   Endotracheal tube connected, unkinked
   Ventilator functional
   Ability to ventilate both lungs confirmed
   Vaporizers off

Monitors
Invasive blood pressure monitors - zeroed and calibrated
   Arterial catheter - radial, femoral or aortic
   Pulmonary artery catheter
   Central venous (right atrial) catheter
   Left atrial catheter
Electrocardiogram
   Rate - pacing capability
   Rhythm
   Conduction
   Ischemia
Bladder catheter - urine output
Pulse oximeter
Capnometer/mass spectrometer
Safety monitors - oxygen analyzer, circuit pressure alarm, spirometer
Transesophageal echocardiography
Temperature (37°C nasopharangeal, 35°C rectal or bladder)

Patient/Pump
The heart
   Cardiac function - contractility, size
   Rhythm
   Ventricular filling
   Air removed
   Vent removed
The lungs
   Inflation/deflation
   Compliance
The field
   Bleeding
   Oxygenation - blood color
   Movement - inadequate anesthesia

Table 30.1.   *continued*

Support
Pharmacologic
   Inotropes
   Vasodilators
   Vasoconstrictors
   Antiarrhythmics
Electrical
   Atrial and/or ventricular pacing
Mechanical
   Intraaortic balloon counterpulsation
   Left and/or right ventricular assist device

with close monitoring of blood glucose and potassium levels, to avoid the possibility of hypoglycemia and/or hypokalemia as a result of insulin therapy.

Hemodilution is induced during hypothermic CPB to reduce blood viscosity and improve systemic circulation. (A complete discussion of hemodilution is in Chapter 5.) The optimal hemoglobin concentration during CPB is usually 6 to 8 g/dl, although there is no proven minimum safe level. Healthy adult patients rarely need homologous blood transfusion with appropriate blood conservation measures, although the chronically ill patient may require red cell transfusion. This can be accomplished efficiently while still on CPB. Heparin-induced anticoagulation should be monitored during rewarming and additional heparin given if necessary because of the increased metabolism of heparin at higher body temperatures and the potential consequences of inadequate anticoagulation. Marked abnormalities in coagulation and platelet function occur following CPB (6). Platelet transfusions are occasionally required, especially in patients with thrombocytopenia or chronic renal failure, receiving aspirin therapy, or requiring reoperation or a lengthy procedure. Fresh-frozen plasma and cryoprecipitate should be available for treating factor deficiencies or coagulopathies, but are rarely required. Postoperative bleeding is usually due to one of three factors: inadequate surgical hemostasis, inadequate heparin reversal, or platelet dysfunction. Desmopressin, an analog of arginine vasopressin, can also be used to improve platelet function and hemostasis in the presence of renal failure or factor VIII deficiency, and may also decrease bleeding in normal patients following CPB (7, 8). Initial reports that desmopressin decreased bleeding following cardiac surgery have not been substantiated (8–12). However, a recent study indicated that prophylactic treatment with tranexamic acid, a potent antifibrinolytic agent, significantly reduced blood loss and homologous blood transfusion following cardiac surgery (13).

ANESTHESIA/MACHINE

The requirements for anesthetics and muscle relaxants are greatly reduced during CPB because of the anesthetic effects of hypothermia and decreased metabolism of most drugs (14). However, rewarming reverses these effects, and care must be taken to ensure adequate anesthetic depth and muscle relaxation in order to prevent patient awareness and shivering. It is prudent to administer supplementary anesthetic agents (usually a benzodiazepine and opioid) and muscle relaxant empirically when rewarming is initiated. Occasionally, volatile anesthetic agents are used to induce vasodilation and facilitate rewarming; these agents should be discontinued 10 minutes prior to termination of CPB to eliminate their circulatory depressant effects, which could impair ventricular function during emergence from bypass (15, 16). The vaporizers on the anesthesia machine and the bypass pump should be turned off. The anesthesia machine should also be checked; oxygen should be flowing through the machine and the airway circuit should be properly connected. Failure to wean from CPB has occurred because of the inadvertent administration of a cardiodepressant volatile anesthetic during the weaning process.

The lungs should be inflated manually to evaluate compliance and eliminate macroatelectasis. Inspection of the lungs may suggest poor deflation, unilateral inflation, pneumothorax, or pleural fluid accumulation, which should be corrected. When this is observed clinically, the prophylactic use of bronchodilators such as epinephrine should be seriously considered. Rarely, endotracheal suction will be required to clear the endotracheal tube; this should be done carefully in the anticoagulated patient. At this point, mechanical ventilation with 100% oxygen and an adequate tidal volume should be initiated and the anesthesiologist's attention focussed on additional factors.

MONITORS

It is important to quickly survey all routine monitors including the pulse oximeter, capnometer, the apnea alarm, and the oxygen monitor, and return to operation any that may have been turned off during CPB. Pulse oximeter probes placed on the extremities frequently do not function immediately following CPB because of peripheral hypoperfusion; a probe placed on the ear lobe or lip may perform better. There is usually a larger gradient between the Pa_{CO_2} and end tidal P_{CO_2} ($P_{ET}CO_2$) following CPB than present preoperatively. Adequate ventilation should be maintained during termination of CPB to prevent hypercapnia and respiratory acidosis with resultant pulmonary hypertension (17, 18). Clinically, mild hyperventilation (Pa_{CO_2} approximately 30 mm Hg) is a useful adjunct in the treatment of increased pulmonary vascular resistance.

Pressure transducers should be zeroed and calibrated with the operating table in its neutral position. Frequently the radial arterial pressure does not reflect the central aortic pressure following CPB (19–21). If there appears to be a discrepancy between the transduced radial arterial pressure and the aortic pressure estimated by palpation, the aortic pressure can be transduced from a needle in the aorta. This central aortic pressure can then be used during termination of CPB to avoid the unnecessary administration of vasoactive drugs. Alternatively, a femoral arterial catheter can be placed that will more closely reflect the central aortic pressure. Central and peripheral arterial pressures usually equilibrate shortly after CPB is discontinued. If a difficult separation from CPB is anticipated, preparations should be made to measure left ventricular filling pressures, especially in patients difficult to wean from CPB. Pulmonary artery catheters frequently migrate distally during manipulation of the heart during cardiac surgery. If the waveform reflects pulmonary artery occlusion pressure, the catheter should be pulled back until pulmonary artery pressure appears. The left atrial catheter is a useful monitor of left ventricular filling pressure and can be used as a route for inotrope administration (see below). The central venous pressure should be measured, especially in those patients with pulmonary hypertension or right ventricular failure. The appropriate right/left ventricular function balance is an important variable in successful weaning.

The electrocardiogram should be carefully assessed for rate, rhythm, conduction changes, and evidence of ischemia. Sinus rhythm or a rate of 70 to 90 bpm appears to be ideal for termination of CPB in the adult, while higher rates are desirable in the case of congenital lesions or other cases when stroke volume is fixed (e.g., following left ventricular aneurysm repair, when LV chamber size and compliance are reduced).

Following hyperkalemic diastolic arrest, slow heart rates are commonly observed due to sinus bradycardia, atrial fibrillation with a slow ventricular response, or atrioventricular conduction block. These abnormalities are usually transient. Sinus bradycardia is easily treated with atrial pacing, which can be discontinued when an adequate rate or normal conduction returns following CPB. Atrial pacing can be used for sinus or junctional bradycardia with normal conduction. Sequential atrioventricular pacing is indicated for atrioventricular conduction block or significant first-degree heart block. This preserves the atrial contribution to ventricular filling, a significant advantage in the presence of a noncompliant hypertrophied ventricle (hypertension, aortic stenosis) or enlarged ventricle (aortic or mitral regurgitation). Ventricular pacing is used only when the ventricular rate is too slow and atrial or atrioventricular pacing is not feasible; e.g., atrial fibrillation or flutter with a very slow ventricular response.

Tachycardia (>120 bpm in the adult) prior to termination of CPB is more difficult to manage. In the patient with good ventricular function, sinus tachycardia often slows with ventricular filling and increased arterial pressure; in such a case, termination of CPB may solve the problem. Patients with poorly functioning ventricles often have persistently rapid rates. It is important to consider and treat other common causes of tachycardia, including hypoxemia, hypercapnia, anemia, inadequate anesthesia, and effects of medications (e.g., β-adrenergic agents or pancuronium). Once these causes are eliminated and myocardial function is adequate, the rate can be reduced with appropriate doses of beta or calcium channel blocking drugs. Supraventricular tachycardias are best treated with cardioversion; however, therapy with propranolol, edrophonium, verapamil (in divided doses of 2.5 mg IV), or adenosine (6 to 12 mg IV bolus centrally) may be effective when cardioversion fails. Digoxin is also useful, especially in patients treated with digoxin preoperatively, but its effects may be delayed.

Ventricular fibrillation is common during reperfusion, and usually responds to direct current defibrillation. Sustained or recurrent ventricular fibrillation increases myocardial oxygen consumption and may result in ventricular distension, which can produce irreversible myocardial damage. Potential causes, including hypothermia, hypoxemia, acidosis, hypocalcemia, hypomagnesemia, hypotension, or myocardial ischemia, should be addressed and corrected. Recurrent ventricular fibrillation should be treated with class I and/or III antiarrhythmics (lidocaine, procainamide, bretylium) and repeat defibrillation. β-Adrenergic blockers (propranolol 1 mg or esmolol 20 mg by intraaortic injection) are remarkably effective for facilitating defibrillation in resistant cases. Premature ventricular contractions are common following CPB. This condition can be treated by correcting hypokalemia, overdrive pacing to a higher heart rate, or antiarrhythmic agents.

All available electrocardiogram leads should be examined and compared to a preoperative tracing prior to terminating CPB to detect evidence of ventricular damage or ischemia. Ventricular pacemakers, if present, should be momentarily discontinued to make the evaluation. Transient ST segment elevation is common during emergence from CPB, but usually resolves over time (22). Persistent ST segment elevation suggests myocardial ischemia, which may require surgical treatment (i.e., revision of a graft or placement of an additional graft). Other possible causes include (a) intracoronary artery air embolism, which occurs with open heart procedures, usually involves the right coronary artery and frequently improves after a period of increased perfusion pressure; (b) coronary artery or internal mammary artery spasm, which may improve with intravenous nitroglycerin or calcium channel blockers or elevated perfusion pressure; or (c) residual cardioplegia-induced changes, which may improve with additional reperfusion on CPB.

Urine output is routinely monitored during CPB, but does not predict postoperative renal dysfunction (23). Nevertheless, patients with preoperative renal dysfunction or low urine output during or following CPB are often treated with low-dose dopamine infusion (1 to 3 kg/min) for its natriuretic and renal vasodilatory effects (24, 25). Although dopamine has been shown to be a more effective diuretic and natriuretic than dobutamine in adults following CPB, dopamine does not appear to be more effective than dobutamine in protecting renal function in children following CPB (25, 26). It is not known whether prophylactic use of dopamine preserves renal function. Following termination of CPB and the resumption of pulsatile blood flow, many patients exhibit a marked diuresis, particularly if mannitol has been added to the pump prime. In such cases, serum potassium should be monitored frequently and replenished as needed to maintain levels greater than 4.0 mEq/liter, especially in patients receiving digoxin or with arrhythmias.

Most CPB pumps include an in-line monitor of venous oxygen saturation. Changes in this parameter may reflect the adequacy of systemic perfusion and oxygen delivery or increases in oxygen consumption (e.g., shivering) while on CPB. Prior to terminating CPB, the venous saturation and pump flow should be checked. A low saturation may indicate the need for additional muscle relaxant, red cell transfusion, or vasodilator therapy prior to weaning from bypass.

Fiberoptic oximeter pulmonary artery catheters that allow continuous measuring of mixed venous oxygen saturation may be useful guides when titration of vasodilator and inotrope therapy of severe left ventricular failure is necessary following CPB (27).

Transesophageal echocardiography provides information that can be very useful when terminating CPB. The left ventricular short axis view provides a useful indicator of left ventricular size and filling. Regional wall motion abnormalities may provide an important indicator of myocardial ischemia, including the failure of a specific coronary artery bypass graft, although this has not been confirmed in the post-CPB period where regional wall motion abnormalities may also be due to residual effects of cardioplegia and inhomogeneous myocardial temperature. Perhaps the most useful application of transesophageal echocardiography in preparing for the termination of CPB is in evaluating valvular function after valve replacement or repair (28). Epicardial and transesophageal echocardiography have also proven to be useful in evaluating the repair of complex congenital heart defects (29, 30).

PATIENT/PUMP

With all of the attention placed on the electrocardiogram and invasive pressure monitors, it is easy for the novice to overlook one of the most important indicators of cardiac function, direct observation of the heart itself. Inspection of the heart will provide valuable information concerning contractility, rhythm, and ventricular filling. Contractility can be assessed by observing the speed of contraction in comparison to that present before CPB, as well as the size of the heart. A poorly contracting heart will dilate as diastolic volume increases to increase stroke volume. Sinus rhythm can frequently be determined by observing sequential atrial and ventricular contractions even if P waves are not evident on the electrocardiogram. Right ventricular filling and ejection can be easily observed since the right ventricle is on the anterior surface of the heart; this parameter is a useful monitor for guiding volume infusions from the pump when terminating CPB. It is also important to continually monitor the lungs for bilateral inflation and deflation. An indication of ongoing blood loss can also be obtained by observing the surgical field and the pump suction prior to protamine administration. This blood can be replaced by infusions from the pump while the arterial cannula is still in place.

Once CPB has been discontinued, direct observation of the heart remains as an important monitor of ventricular function until the chest is closed, and is invaluable in guiding volume infusions and the titration of inotropic agents. Observation of blood color is also important, but is obviously a late monitor of hypoxemia. The effectiveness of heparin reversal by protamine can also be determined by observing clot formation in the surgical field. Bronchospasm, secondary to reactive airway disease or rarely to protamine administration, may be evident as lung hyperinflation. *The importance of direct observation of the patient in the conduct of cardiac anesthesia cannot be overemphasized.*

SUPPORT

The need for pharmacologic support following CPB is usually assessed by reviewing the ECG and all available hemodynamic data. However, other information available before and during bypass relating to ventricular function is of value in preparing for separation. Such data consist of the primary cardiac diagnosis, including the extent of myocardial dysfunction and the patient's status relative to the natural history of the disease, the effectiveness of intraoperative myocardial protection, and the adequacy of surgical repair.

Preoperative myocardial dysfunction frequently presages difficulty with termination of CPB. Preoperative ventricular dysfunction is usually the result of ischemia (coronary artery disease), pressure overload (valvular stenosis or hypertension), volume overload (valvular regurgitation), or cardiomyopathy. The underlying cause of the preoperative ventricular dysfunction has considerable impact on the predicted postoperative ventricular function. Ventricular function is almost always impaired to some extent by aortic cross-clamping. The ischemia imposed by aortic cross-clamping can result in considerable myocardial stunning, which is a condition of prolonged reversible postischemic ventricular dysfunction of viable myocardium that follows reperfusion, and which may exacerbate preexisting irreversible ventricular dysfunction (31). In the case of acute myocardial ischemia, successful myocardial revascularization may improve ventricular function by restoring perfusion. However, improvements in ventricular function can be delayed for hours to days because of myocardial stunning, or for weeks in the case of prolonged ischemia resulting in "hibernating" myocardium (32). Improved ventricular function is usually obtained following valve replacement and relief of the pressure overload in aortic stenosis, a condition in which the compensatory response to chronic pressure overload is a concentric hypertrophy of the ventricular wall that tends to normalize wall stress and avoid an overall decrement in contractility (33). In contrast, irreversible myocardial dysfunction is frequently present in the patient with mitral regurgitation. Here, the acute afterload mismatch produced by replacing the mitral valve usually results in postoperative ventricular dysfunction (33, 34). The degree of postoperative dysfunction is less predictable in patients with mitral stenosis or aortic regurgitation, but myocardial depression may exist because of the cardiomyopathy of rheumatic heart disease or eccentric ventricular hypertrophy, respectively. Previous myocardial infarction is an obvious cause for irreversible myocardial dysfunction. Ventricular dysfunction can also result from cardiomyopathy, which may be ischemic (congenital or acquired), viral, hypertrophic (secondary to pressure or volume overload or idiopathic), or drug-induced (e.g., adriamycin). Evidence of preoperative myocardial dysfunction is provided by a history of poor exercise tolerance, congestive heart failure, or recent myocardial infarction, and/or by evidence of ongoing myocardial ischemia, increased ventricular filling pressures, cardiomyopathy, or a decreased ejection fraction (35).

Adequate myocardial protection during CPB is essential for successful cardiac surgery. Preoperative ventricular hypertrophy or coronary artery stenosis predisposes the myocardium to ischemic damage during CPB, as do ventricular distention, coronary artery embolism, persistent ventricular fibrillation, and inadequate myocardial perfusion occurring during CPB (36). Inadequate myocardial preservation following aortic cross-clamping can result from numerous causes (see Chapter 7) including inadequate cardioplegia solution delivery or amount, incorrect cardioplegia solution composition, inadequate or poorly maintained myocardial cooling, aortic valve or cross-clamp insufficiency, or extensive noncoronary collateral blood flow. Clues to the adequate delivery of cardioplegia include "normal" coronary perfusion pressure during administration, rapid electrical and mechanical arrest without prolonged prearrest ventricular fibrillation, and rapid myocardial cooling. Prolonged aortic cross-clamping can lead to impaired postoperative ventricular function, especially when cross-clamp time is greater than 120 minutes (37, 38).

The adequacy of the surgical repair will also have an impact on postoperative ventricular function. For coronary artery bypass grafting, the number of lesions bypassed, the quality of the distal anastomoses, and the presence of small distal vessels or distal coronary artery disease (as in diabetes mellitus) are important factors. For valvular surgery or surgery to repair congenital defects, the specific valvular or anatomic defect, the adequacy of the valvular or anatomic repair, competency of valve replacements, and resultant changes in intracardiac pressures and flows are important. Procedures requiring ventriculotomy have a profound impact on postoperative ventricular function. Transection of important coronary artery branches or resection of viable myocardium can have important detrimental effects.

The surgeon is an important source for information regarding the adequacy of the surgical procedure. Objective evidence of the adequacy of the surgical repair can be obtained prior to the termination of CPB by flowmeter determination of coronary artery bypass graft flows, by esophageal or epicardial echocardiographic assessment of intracardiac structures, color-flow Doppler assessment of transvalvular flows, and shunts and measurement of intracardiac pressures with a needle or catheter connected to a pressure transducer (e.g., to determine the gradient across a repaired valve or outflow tract).

Evaluation of the factors discussed above prior to the termination of CPB will give some idea of the need for circulatory support after CPB. If right or left ventricular failure is anticipated, plans should be made for the institution of pharmacologic and/or mechanical support, including inotropes, vasodilators, and/or ventricular assist devices. If needed, pharmacologic therapy should be begun in advance of discontinuation of CPB to allow the drug to take effect and to titrate the dose. The capacity to pace the heart using atrial and/or ventricular pacing electrodes with a sequential atrioventricular pacemaker should be available. A period of partial bypass may benefit cases of severe ventricular dysfunction by allowing the gradual recovery of cardiac function from the effects of ischemia and cardioplegia, and the titration of vasoactive drugs. When preoperative left ventricular function is disturbingly reduced, it is wise to apply a second set of electrocardiogram leads prior to draping the patient in the event that intraaortic balloon counterpulsation is required. If cardiac function is inadequate and unresponsive to therapy after terminating CPB, it is prudent to reinstitute bypass to prevent ventricular distension and possible ischemic damage. This allows extra time for the heart to recover and for a reassessment of the situation and formulation of a revised plan.

SEPARATION FROM CPB: TECHNIQUE AND PROBLEMS

Termination of CPB

Physiologically, separation from bypass converts a circulation in series (venae cavae → oxygenator → aorta) to one in parallel (venae cavae → *both* oxygenator *and* right ventricle/lungs/left ventricle → common return to aorta), and finally to one in series (vena cavae → heart/lungs → aorta). The duration of the transitional period of parallel circulations (partial bypass) is determined by ventricular function. The better the ability of the left ventricle (or, less commonly, the right) to sustain the entire cardiac output, the more rapidly bypass can be terminated. Conversely, poor left ventricular function mandates a period of partial bypass while preload is "optimized" by carefully adjusting venous return, and contractility is improved by judicious selection of inotropes. During separation, ventricular distension should be avoided and coronary perfusion pressure should be maintained.

A general approach to the termination of CPB is shown in Fig. 30.1. Separation is accomplished by gradual occlusion of the venous line, which decreases flow to the pump and leaves more blood in the patient. Arterial flow rate from the pump is then reduced (e.g., to 2 liters/min). Hemodynamics are assessed and appropriate drugs administered, if necessary. Flow can then be reduced further and hemodynamics reassessed. This process is then cycled until separation from CPB is complete. During this period, it is also essential to observe that the lungs are being adequately ventilated with appropriate peak inspiratory pressures. Hemodynamic management for every patient focusses on regulating four primary determinants of cardiac function: rate and rhythm, arterial blood pressure, preload or ventricular volume (ventricular filling pressure), and contractility (stroke volume). An algorithm for the diagnosis and treatment of hemodynamic abnormalities at the termination of CPB is shown in Figure 30.2.

Rate and rhythm are controlled as much as possible prior to separation. Atrial, ventricular, or atrioventricular sequential pacing should be instituted when needed. Blood pressure is then assessed, and preload and contractility are altered as

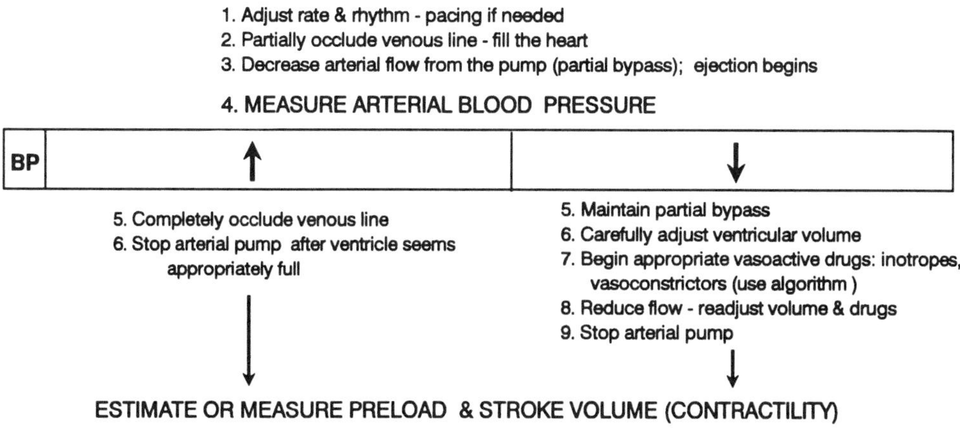

1. Adjust rate & rhythm - pacing if needed
2. Partially occlude venous line - fill the heart
3. Decrease arterial flow from the pump (partial bypass); ejection begins

4. MEASURE ARTERIAL BLOOD PRESSURE

BP	↑	↓

5. Completely occlude venous line
6. Stop arterial pump after ventricle seems
    appropriately full

5. Maintain partial bypass
6. Carefully adjust ventricular volume
7. Begin appropriate vasoactive drugs: inotropes,
    vasoconstrictors (use algorithm)
8. Reduce flow - readjust volume & drugs
9. Stop arterial pump

ESTIMATE OR MEASURE PRELOAD & STROKE VOLUME (CONTRACTILITY)

Figure 30.1.   General approach to the termination of CPB. (Modified with permission from Amado WJ, Thomas SJ. Cardiac surgery: intraoperative management. In: Thomas SJ, ed. Manual of cardiac anesthesia. 2nd ed. Ch. 17. New York: Churchill Livingstone, 1993.)

appropriate. If both ventricular volume and inotropic state are adequate, use of vasoconstrictors or vasodilators for blood pressure control is warranted. If blood pressure is too low, a search for the etiology of the postbypass ventricular dysfunction is mandatory before beginning vasoactive drugs. Filling of the heart is assessed by direct inspection of the right ventricle, pulmonary artery diastolic pressure, central venous pressure, and/or left atrial pressure. It is important to recognize that right ventricular filling and central venous pressure may not accurately indicate left ventricular volume. The pulmonary artery occlusion or diastolic pressure is frequently used to guide volume infusion at the conclusion of CPB. However, the pulmonary artery occlusion pressure has been found to correlate poorly with left ventricular end diastolic volume after coronary artery bypass surgery, possibly because of acute changes in left ventricular compliance (39). With poor left or right ventricular function, a direct measure of left ventricular filling pressure is helpful to better guide volume infusion. Ideal left atrial pressure will vary; however, a value of 10 to 15 mm Hg is almost always adequate in patients following isolated coronary artery bypass surgery. Higher pressures may be

required in patients with valvular disease. Transesophageal echocardiography, if available, provides the best estimate of ventricular volume.

It is best to keep the filling pressure on the lower side to avoid ventricular distension. Following termination of CPB, volume can be infused directly from the pump through the aortic cannula as long as it is in place. The need for additional volume can be judged by evaluating the response to volume infused from the pump. While repeated cardiac output measurement and stroke volume calculation are the best way to judge this Frank-Starling effect of volume expansion, for practical purposes the arterial pressure effect is also useful. This is true because over a short time frame (1 to 2 minutes) following the infusion, one can assume an unchanged vascular resistance so that a pressure increment produced by the volume infusion relates directly to a flow (stroke volume) increment.

The goal following CPB is to have an adequate arterial pressure (90 to 100 mm Hg; higher in patients with renal, cerebrovascular or hypertensive disease) and cardiac output (>3.0 liters/min) with a left atrial pressure of 10 to 15 mm Hg (15 to 20 mm Hg in patients with chronic preopera-

BP								
VFP								
SV								
DX	Too full	?↓Contractility ↑SVR	Hyperdynamic	↑↑SVR ± Hypovolemic	Too full ↓SVR	Big trouble ↓↓Contractility	↓↓SVR	Hypovolemia ??RV failure ↑CVP (>LAP)
RX	Wait Diuretic Venodilator	Inotrope prn Vasodilation	Wait Anesthetics	Volume or Vasodilation	Wait Vasoconstrict if BP too low	1. Adjust preload if necessary 2. Inotrope 3. Vasodilator (arteriolar) 4. Repeat 1,2,3 prn 5. Return to CPB if necessary 6. IABP 7. LVAD	Vasoconstrict	Volume If rt heart failure 1. Return to CPB if necessary 2. Inotrope 3. Maintain perfusion pressure 4. If PA pressure ↑ vasodilator (PGE1, NO) 5. IABP, RVAD

Figure 30.2. Algorithm for the diagnosis and treatment of hemodynamic abnormalities at the termination of CPB. *BP,* systemic blood pressure; *VFP,* ventricular filling pressure; *SV,* stroke volume; *Dx,* diagnosis; *Rx,* treatment; *SVR,* systemic vascular resistance; *CVP,* central venous pressure; *LAP,* left atrial pressure; *IABP,* intraaortic balloon pump; *LVAD,* left ventricular assist device; *RVAD,* right ventricular assist device; *PA,* pulmonary artery; *PGE$_1$,* prostaglandin E$_1$; *NO,* nitric oxide; *RV,* right ventricle. (Modified with permission from Amado WJ, Thomas SJ. Cardiac surgery: intraoperative management. In: Thomas SJ, ed. Manual of cardiac anesthesia. 2nd ed. Ch. 17. New York: Churchill Livingstone, 1993.)

770

tive volume or pressure overload). It is important to have adequate coronary perfusion pressure, especially in the presence of coronary artery disease or ventricular hypertrophy. Frequently the arterial pressure is low and the filling pressure is moderately high shortly after terminating CPB. If there is no reason to suspect severe ventricular dysfunction, this condition usually responds to a single bolus of an inotrope such as epinephrine (4 to 8 µg IV), ephedrine (10 mg IV), or $CaCl_2$ (5 mg/kg IV; see below), or a short infusion of an inotrope (e.g., epinephrine 1 to 5 µg/min IV). Hypotension may also be due to vasodilation and hypovolemia, particularly if the patient has been rewarmed for a long period. This condition is identified by low arterial pressure and filling pressures with an adequate cardiac output, and is effectively treated with an α-adrenergic agonist (e.g., phenylephrine 50 to 100 µg IV or an infusion at 10 to 50 µg/minute). If the situation does not improve rapidly, and cardiac function is worse than anticipated, additional support may be required; if additional inotropes and vasodilators are not already prepared or if the patient's condition continues to deteriorate, partial bypass should be reinstituted while therapy is optimized. Additional time on partial CPB will allow more time for the postischemic recovery of ventricular function (40).

Left Ventricular Failure

Ventricular failure or dysfunction can be defined as inadequate cardiac pump performance, despite appropriate adjustments of preload and afterload, due to a decrease in myocardial contractility that can be either acute (as in ischemia) or chronic (as in cardiomyopathy). A subacute form of ventricular dysfunction, known as "stunning," may also develop following episodes of ischemia and may progress to postischemic ventricular dysfunction (31). Stunned myocardium exhibits recovery of contractile function that is delayed after restoration of

coronary blood flow. This phenomenon has been observed following coronary artery bypass grafting and may improve with inotropic therapy (40, 41).

INOTROPIC THERAPY

Initial therapy of left ventricular dysfunction is usually achieved with an inotrope. A comparison of mild ventricular dysfunction following separation from CPB and the result of inotropic treatment, as analyzed by pressure-volume loops, is shown in Fig. 30.3B. Calcium chloride or calcium gluconate (Tables 30.2 and 30.3) have a positive inotropic effect in the presence of hyperkalemia or hypocalcemia, but are ineffective with normocalcemia and may actually be harmful because of the detrimental effects of elevated intracellular Ca^{2+} in ischemic cells following reperfusion (42). β-Adrenergic receptor agonists are the most potent and widely used inotropes. They work by binding to and stimulating β-adrenergic receptors that are coupled to the formation of the intracellular messenger, adenosine 3':5'monophosphate (cyclic AMP). A number of different β-adrenergic agonists are available (Table 30.2) including the natural catecholamines epinephrine, norepinephrine, and dopamine, and the synthetic catecholamines dobutamine and isoproterenol. These drugs have varying actions at β_1-, β_2- and α-receptors and are initially selected based on their relative actions at each receptor type.

Severe ventricular failure usually requires the maximal potency of epinephrine or norepinephrine, frequently in combination with vasodilator therapy (see below). Epinephrine and norepinephrine are also useful when ventricular dysfunction is accompanied by peripheral vasodilation, since they are also potent α-receptor agonists. The vasopressor effect of norepinephrine is greater than that of epinephrine because of the greater potency of epinephrine at β_2-receptors, which produce considerable vasodilation in skeletal muscle. Dobu-

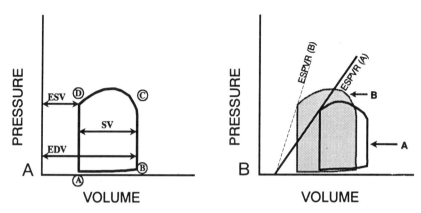

Figure 30.3. **A.** Idealized pressure-volume loop with corresponding events of the cardiac cycle under normal conditions. A, mitral valve opens and ventricular filling begins; B, mitral valve closes: end-diastolic volume (*EDV*) and pressure (*EDP*). C, aortic valve opens following isovolumic contraction; D, aortic valve closes, end-systolic volume (*ESV*) and pressure (*ESP*). The stroke volume (*SV*) is EDV-ESV. **B.** Pressure-volume loop demonstrating mild ventricular dysfunction following separation from CPB. Loop *A* shows an increase in end-diastolic volume (*EDV*), a reduced end-systolic pressure-volume relationship (*ESPVR*), and reduced stroke volume. Inotropic therapy will usually increase contractility as illustrated by the shift from *ESPVR* (A) to *ESPVR* (B). Stroke volume increases, end-systolic and end-diastolic volumes decrease. (Modified with permission from Amado WJ, Thomas SJ. Cardiac surgery: intraoperative management. In: Thomas SJ, ed. Manual of cardiac anesthesia. 2nd ed. Ch. 17. New York: Churchill Livingstone, 1993.)

tamine and dopamine are useful when moderate inotropic support is desired. Dobutamine is a β_1-receptor agonist with only minimal α-receptor activity, and is therefore useful when further vasoconstriction is undesirable. Dopamine is unique in that it stimulates renal dopamine receptors and causes an increase in both renal blood flow and sodium excretion; it is especially useful in patients with renal dysfunction (24, 25). Use of dopamine as an inotrope at higher doses (>10 µg/kg/min) is complicated by its activity at α-adrenergic receptors, which may produce undesirable increases in systemic vascular resistance, and by its tendency to increase ventricular filling pressures and to induce tachycardia and atrial arrhythmias (43, 44). The partial dependence of the inotropic effects of dopamine on endogenous catecholamines may also limit its efficacy in patients with chronic ventricular dysfunction and following CPB.

Isoproterenol is a nonselective β-receptor agonist that is a potent inotrope (β_1-effect) and peripheral vasodilator (β_2-effect). The potent chronotropic effect of isoproterenol (β_1 and β_2) is not compensated for by the baroreceptor-mediated reflex bradycardia that occurs with β-receptor agonists that also possess intrinsic α-receptor activity such as epinephrine and norepinephrine. Isoproterenol or dobutamine may be useful in patients with severe pulmonary hypertension and right ventricular failure, because α-receptor stimulation is a potent mechanism producing pulmonary vasoconstriction. Isoproterenol is also useful for the treatment of slow ventricular rates or atrioventricular conduction disturbances when other methods have failed because of the positive chronotropic and dromotropic effects of β-adrenergic stimulation. These effects are also clinically useful in cardiac transplantation dealing with the acutely denervated transplanted heart.

In general, epinephrine appears to be the most useful inotrope for adult cardiac surgical patients with its combined β_1, β_2, and α actions, while dopamine and isoproterenol are favored in the pediatric population because of advantages of a higher heart rate in this group. However, patterns of inotrope use show institutional variations, and many would choose dopamine or dobutamine as their first agent of choice for inotropic stimulation when weaning from CPB. In critically ill adults with severe ventricular dysfunction and low urine output, it is probably advantageous to use a low-dose dopamine infusion (100 to 200 μg/min) to optimize renal perfusion, combined with a second inotrope (e.g., dobutamine) to increase contractility without increasing ventricular filling pressure, as can be seen with higher doses of dopamine (45, 46). The use of dopamine or epinephrine as an inotrope in severe left ventricular dysfunction is limited by dose-dependent increases in afterload and preload. These undesirable side effects are the basis for the frequent clinical use of combined inotropic stimulation and afterload reduction with direct acting vasodilators such as nitroprusside or nitroglycerin (47).

A relatively recent addition to available inotropes is amrinone, a selective inhibitor of fraction III of cyclic nucleotide phosphodiesterase (PDE III). This agent produces two actions that are beneficial in the treatment of ventricular dysfunction, namely a decrease in afterload and an increase in contractility without significant tachycardia or arrhythmias (48). The inotropic activity of amrinone appears to be synergistic with that of β-adrenergic agents, and may not be associated with increased myocardial oxygen consumption; these properties have made this agent particularly useful in patients with severe left ventricular dysfunction (49, 50). Advantage can be taken of the inotropic activity of amrinone without its vasodilatory activity by combining it with an α-adrenergic vasoconstrictor, usually norepinephrine (51, 52). Another important application of amrinone and its congeners in combination with adrenergic agonists is its use in patients with antecedent congestive heart failure. The de-

sensitization of β-adrenergic receptors that occurs in congestive heart failure significantly limits the efficacy of β-adrenergic agonists. Combined therapy with phosphodiesterase inhibitors enhances the inotropic effect of β-adrenergic receptor agonists by potentiating the rise in intracellular cyclic AMP and may permit use of a lower dose of β-adrenergic agonist. Inhibitors of phosphodiesterase also have a positive lusitropic, or myocardial relaxation, effect (53). This positive lusitropic effect enhances diastolic myocardial relaxation, improves ventricular compliance, facilitates ventricular filling, and decreases ventricular filling pressure and perhaps end-diastolic wall tension at any given filling volume. Thus, myocardial O_2 consumption may be decreased while stroke volume is increased.

Few studies have compared the use of various inotropic agents during emergence from CPB, although numerous studies have investigated the effects of various inotropes in patients following cardiac surgery. This topic was recently reviewed by Di Sesa (54). In a study of patients considered candidates for inotropic support, the hemodynamic effects of dopamine, dobutamine, and epinephrine were compared during termination of CPB (43). All three agents increased cardiac output, although a flat dose-response curve was observed for both dopamine and dobutamine when compared to epinephrine. No significant problems with tachycardia, arrhythmias, or vasodilation were observed with any of these drugs at the doses studied. In contrast, a study comparing dobutamine with isoproterenol during emergence from CPB had to be terminated early because of problems with tachycardia and arrhythmias in the isoproterenol group (55). Dobutamine was found to increase both cardiac output and mean arterial blood pressure. Thus epinephrine, dopamine, and dobutamine each have been shown to be effective in terminating CPB, although epinephrine is more efficacious at higher doses.

Table 30.2. Inotropes Used in the Termination of CPB[a]

Drug	Dose	Mechanism	Actions	Indications	Contra-indications	Adverse Effects
Calcium chloride or calcium gluconate	2–10 mg/kg IV bolus effects last 10–20 minutes	↑ Ca_i^{2+}	Inotrope if hypocalcemic Vasopressor if normocalcemic	Hypocalcemia (from CPB, albumin, citrate) Hyperkalemia Hypotension (e.g., secondary to protamine) Myocardial depression (e.g., secondary to residual cardioplegia or hypocalcemia) Calcium channel blocker overdose	Hypercalcemia Pancreatitis Digitalis toxicity	Coronary artery spasm (?) Pancreatitis
Epinephrine	Low-dose infusion 1–2 μg/min, primarily β Moderate dose infusion 2–10 μg/min, mixed α and β High-dose infusion 10–20 μg/min, primarily α; potent vasoconstriction 2–8 μg IV bolus	α_1-receptor (↑ Ca_i^{2+}) β_1-receptor (↑ cAMP) β_2-receptor (↑ cAMP)	Inotrope - β_1-effect Vasopressor - α_1-effect at higher doses Vasodilator - β_2-effect primarily in muscle Chronotrope - β_1-effect Bronchodilation - β_2-effect	Ventricular dysfunction Vasodilation Anaphylaxis Bronchoconstriction	Idiopathic hypertrophic subaortic stenosis (relative) Tetralogy of Fallot (with RV outflow tract obstruction, relative)	Vasoconstriction (splanchnic, renal) Arrhythmias
Norepinephrine	4–16 μg/min	β_1-receptor (↑ cAMP) α_1-receptor (↑ Ca_i^{2+})	Inotrope - β_1-effect Vasopressor - α_1-effect Chronotrope - β_1-effect	Ventricular dysfunction Vasodilation Anaphylaxis Shock	See epinephrine	Vasoconstriction (splanchnic, renal) Arrhythmias

Drug	Dose	Mechanism	Effect	Indication		Side effects
Dopamine	0.5–2 μg/kg/min (activation of DA_1 receptors) >2 μg/kg/min (activation of β_1 receptors) >5 μg/kg/min (activation of α_1 receptors)	α_1-receptor ($\uparrow Ca_i^{2+}$) β_1-receptor ($\uparrow$cAMP) DA_1-receptor ($\uparrow$ cAMP)	Inotrope - β_1-effect Vasopressor - α_1-effect Renal vasodilator and natriuretic-DA_1 effect Chronotrope - β_1-effect	Ventricular dysfunction Vasodilation Renal dysfunction/ oliguria	See epinephrine	Tachycardia Peripheral vasoconstriction Arrhythmias
Dobutamine	2–20 μg/kg/min	β_1-receptor ($\uparrow$cAMP) α_1-receptor ($\uparrow Ca_i^{2+}$)	Inotrope - β_1-effect Vasodilator - β_2-effect Chronotrope - β_1-effect	Vasoconstriction	See epinephrine	Tachycardia
Isoproterenol	1–5 μg/min	β_1-receptor ($\uparrow$cAMP) β_2-receptor ($\uparrow$cAMP)	Inotrope - β_1-effect Vasodilator - β_2-effect Bronchodilation - β_2-effect Chronotrope - β_1-effect	Ventricular dysfunction, especially RV Bronchoconstriction Bradycardia - profound β-blockade, AV block, cardiac transplant Pulmonary hypertension - primary, secondary	See epinephrine	Tachycardia Vasodilation $\uparrow MVO_2$
Amrinone	0.5–1.5 mg/kg IV bolus (slow) 5–30 μg/kg/min infusion	PDE III inhibition ($\uparrow$ cAMP) ($\uparrow Ca_i^{2+}$)	Inotrope - due to $\uparrow$ cAMP Vasodilator - due to $\uparrow$ cAMP	Ventricular dysfunction Vasoconstriction	Thrombocytopenia	Vasodilation
Ephedrine	5–10 mg IV bolus	α_1-effect ($\uparrow Ca_i^{2+}$) β_1-effect ($\uparrow$ cAMP)	Vasopressor - α_1-effect Inotrope - β_1-effect $\downarrow$ Venous capacitance	Ventricular dysfunction Vasodilation	See epinephrine	Tachycardia

775

[a]cAMP, cyclic adenosine monophosphate; RV, right ventricular; DA, dopamine; MVO_2, myocardial O_2 consumption; AV, atrioventricular; Ca_i^{2+} intracellular ionized calcium; PDE, phosphodiesterase

Table 30.3. Comparative Effects of Supportive Therapies Used to Facilitate Termination of CPB[a]

Therapy	Preload	SVR	PVR	Contractility	Conduction	Rate	Rhythm	MVO$_2$
Calcium salts	↑ LVEDP	↑	—	↑ dP/dt ↑ SV	↓ AV conduction	↓	Arrhythmogenic	↑
Epinephrine	↑ PAOP	↑	↑	↑ dP/dt ↑ CO	Enhanced	↑	Arrhythmogenic	↑
Norepinephrine	↑ PAOP	↑	↑	↑ dP/dt ↑↓ CO	Enhanced	Reflex ↓	Arrhythmogenic	↑
Dopamine	↑ PAOP	↑ (at high doses)	↑	↑ dP/dt ↑ CO	±	↑	Arrhythmogenic	↑
Dobutamine	↓ PAOP, ↓ LVEDP	↓	↓	↑ dP/dt ↑ CO	Enhanced	↑	↑ Automaticity	± or ↓
Isoproterenol	↓ PAOP	↓	↓	↑ dP/dt ↑ CO	Enhanced	↑↑	↑ Automaticity Arrhythmogenic	↑
Amrinone	↓ PAOP	↓	↓	↑ dP/dt ↑ CO	Enhanced	±	±	± or ↓
Ephedrine	↑ CVP	↑	↑	↑ dP/dt ↑ CO	Enhanced	↑	±	↑
Sodium nitroprusside	↓ PAOP, ↓ CVP	↓	↓	± dP/dt ↑ CO	±	Reflex ↑	±	↓
Nitroglycerin	↓ LVEDP, ↓ PAOP, ↓ CVP	↓	↓	± dP/dt ↑↓ CO	±	Variable	±	↓
Phenylephrine	↑ PAOP, ↑ CVP	↑	↑	± dP/dt ↑↓ CO	±	Reflex ↓	±	± or ↓
Intraaortic balloon counterpulsation	↓ PAOP, ↓ CVP, ↓ LAP	↓ LV afterload	—	↑ CO	±	±	±	↓

[a]SVR, systemic vascular resistance; PVR, pulmonary vascular resistance; MVO$_2$, myocardial O$_2$ consumption; LVEDP, left ventricular end-diastolic pressure; SV, stroke volume; AV, atrioventricular; PAOP, pulmonary artery occlusion pressure; CO, cardiac output; CVP, central venous pressure; LAP, left atrial pressure; LV, left ventricular; dP/dt, first time derivative of ventricular pressure.

VASODILATORS

While positive inotropes are useful in improving the contractile state of the failing ventricle, vasodilators can improve ventricular function by optimizing its loading conditions (Table 30.3). Indeed, severe heart failure is characterized by both poor left ventricular function (decreased cardiac output with elevated filling pressure) and elevated systemic vascular resistance, and added therapeutic benefit may be obtained by treating both abnormalities (56). Thus, the effects of inotropes and vasodilators are additive in augmenting cardiac output and decreasing filling pressures in the treatment of severe left ventricular failure.

Sodium nitroprusside and nitroglycerin are the most useful vasodilators in cardiac anesthesia because of their potency, rapid onset, and short duration of action (Table 30.3). These properties make them ideal for rapid titration of arterial pressure. Other vasodilators that are used occasionally but which have slower onsets and longer durations of action include hydralazine and phentolamine (an α_1-adrenergic antagonist). Sodium nitroprusside is a potent arterial vasodilator as well as venodilator, while nitroglycerin is a potent venodilator but is less potent as an arterial vasodilator. This is clinically evident in the greater efficacy of sodium nitroprusside in reducing arterial pressure in normovolemic patients, while both agents are effective in reducing ventricular filling pressures. Nitroglycerin, and to a lesser extent sodium nitroprusside, are also effective pulmonary vasodilators and inhibitors of hypoxic pulmonary vasoconstriction (hence, the increased pulmonary shunt frequently observed with their use). Other pulmonary vasodilators useful for the acute control of right ventricular afterload include prostaglandin E1, prostacyclin, and inhaled nitric oxide (see below). Nitroglycerin also exhibits potent effects on coronary blood flow, and is useful in treating myocardial ischemia.

In the perioperative period, sodium nitroprusside (0.5 to 10 μg/kg/min) and nitroglycerin (0.5 to 4 μg/kg/min) are useful in treating ventricular dysfunction with elevated filling pressures, pulmonary hypertension, and systemic hypertension. Sodium nitroprusside appears to be particularly effective in producing systemic vasodilation during rewarming on CPB, treating postoperative hypertension in patients with hyperdynamic circulations and in reducing afterload and preload in patients with poor ventricular function and acceptable arterial blood pressure. Concurrent volume infusion may be required to maintain adequate filling pressures and achieve increased stroke volume (Fig. 30.4). Both sodium nitroprusside and nitroglycerin have also been used to offset the vasoconstriction produced by inotropes with intrinsic α-adrenergic activity. The use of sodium nitro-

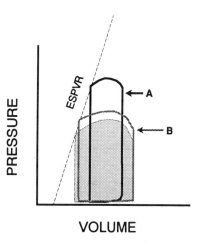

Figure 30.4. Systemic vasoconstriction and hypertension with concomitant hypovolemia following CPB (loop *A*) results in decreased stroke volume. Administration of additional intravascular volume and of a vasodilator results in loop *B*, in which end-diastolic volume and stroke volume have returned toward normal (shaded loop) as the blood pressure is reduced. The end-systolic pressure volume relationship (*ESPVR*) is unchanged. (Modified with permission from Amado WJ, Thomas SJ. Cardiac surgery: intraoperative management. In: Thomas SJ, ed. Manual of cardiac anesthesia. 2nd ed. Ch. 17. New York: Churchill Livingstone, 1993.)

prusside is complicated by the potential for cyanide toxicity at higher doses, while nitroglycerin has the advantage of being relatively nontoxic.

VASOCONSTRICTORS

Vasoconstrictors work by increasing systemic vascular resistance (afterload) and decreasing venous capacitance (increasing preload) due to their action at α-adrenergic receptors (Fig. 30.5). Both phenylephrine and methoxamine are pure α_1-agonists useful in the treatment of hypotension secondary to vasodilation, while ephedrine and metaraminol act to release endogenous catecholamines and thereby activate both α- and β-receptors. In general, the use of pure α-agonists to increase arterial blood pressure in patients with poor ventricular function or pulmonary hypertension is best avoided because increased afterload with-

out a compensatory increase in contractility results in a decreased stroke volume. If significant arterial vasodilation is combined with poor left ventricular function, norepinephrine, which possesses less β_2-adrenergic activity than epinephrine, may be appropriate. Pure α-receptor agonists are useful in the treatment of hypotension in patients with good ventricular function; the beneficial increase in coronary perfusion pressure usually outweighs the negative effects of decreased cardiac output and increased filling pressures in the patient with coronary artery disease or ventricular hypertrophy. Short-term use of a vasopressor is frequently required when terminating CPB in the vasodilated patient; this is easily accomplished with small boluses of phenylephrine (50 to 100 µg IV).

MECHANICAL SUPPORT

If ventricular function remains inadequate despite appropriate inotropic and vasodilator therapy, the addition of mechanical support may be required to allow termination of CPB (57). Intraaortic balloon counterpulsation (IABP) (Table 30.3) in addition to inotropic and vasodilator therapy should be considered early in the patient with poor preoperative ventricular function and postoperative low cardiac output syndrome; a need for this device can be anticipated in the patient with severe preoperative left ventricular dysfunction (58). Patients who require IABP prior to surgery are probably best managed by arbitrarily reinstituting IABP prior to weaning from CPB. If difficulty or failure is encountered terminating CPB despite maximal pharmacologic therapy, this device should be inserted while still on bypass. Further discussion of mechanical modes of ventricular support can be found in Chapter 27.

Right Ventricular Failure

This condition may occur as a result of right coronary artery damage, occlusion or embolism, inadequate intraoperative right

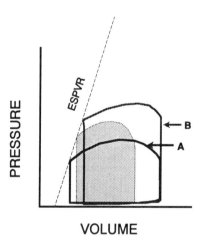

Figure 30.5. Hypotension due to systemic vasodilation despite hypervolemia results in increased stroke volume and decreased end-systolic volume. (*A*) Administration of an arterial vasoconstrictor increases blood pressure and end-systolic volume. (*B*) Stroke volume is reduced while the end-systolic pressure-volume relationship (*ESPVR*) is unchanged. Vasoconstriction is indicated only when systemic blood pressure is unacceptably low. Shaded loop represents normal hemodynamics. (Modified with permission from Amado WJ, Thomas SJ. Cardiac surgery: intraoperative management. In: Thomas SJ, ed. Manual of cardiac anesthesia. 2nd ed. Ch. 17. New York: Churchill Livingstone, 1993.)

ventricular protection, or in patients with pulmonary hypertension (e.g., secondary to chronic mitral stenosis, left-to-right shunts, massive pulmonary embolism, or a reaction to protamine administration). Classic signs include elevated pulmonary artery pressure and central venous pressure, decreased arterial pressure and cardiac output, and a bulging right ventricle. Pulmonary artery occlusion pressure or left atrial pressure will be low or normal if right ventricular failure is associated with normal left ventricular function, but may be elevated if right and left ventricular dysfunction coexist. The therapeutic goals in treating right ventricular dysfunction are similar to those in treating left ventricular dysfunction: increase right ventricular contractility and decrease afterload (pulmonary artery pressure), while maintaining adequate preload (central venous pressure) and coronary perfusion pressure. It is more difficult to achieve these objectives, however, given the pulmonary vasoconstriction induced by most inotropes when administered via the right atrium. It is critical to maintain adequate systemic arterial pressure in the presence of right ventricular failure in order to provide adequate coronary perfusion pressure to the distended right ventricle, which has an elevated end diastolic pressure.

The goal in right ventricular failure is maintenance of a normal systemic arterial (coronary perfusion) pressure, an increased ventricular contractility, and a decreased right ventricular afterload. These effects may be best achieved by selective infusion of pulmonary vasodilators into the right atrium and vasopressors into the left atrium. This has been achieved by infusing prostaglandin E_1 (32 to 50 ng/kg/min) into the right atrium, and norepinephrine into the left atrium in patients with refractory right heart failure following mitral valve replacement (59). Alternatively, nitroglycerin can be infused into the right atrium as the pulmonary vasodilator. Inhaled nitric oxide has been used experimentally as a se-

lective pulmonary vasodilator with encouraging results (60).

If a left atrial catheter is not available, isoproterenol or dobutamine can be infused into the right atrium. Isoproterenol may be useful for increasing right ventricular contractility without significantly increasing pulmonary artery pressure (afterload), although problems with tachycardia and arrhythmias may occur. Use of dobutamine may avoid these problems. Amrinone is a promising agent for the treatment of right ventricular dysfunction and pulmonary hypertension following CPB because of its ability to increase right ventricular contractility and reduce pulmonary vascular resistance (61).

Other manipulations to decrease pulmonary vascular resistance include hyperventilation to induce hypocapnia, a reduction in tidal volume and inspiratory time, and avoidance of hypoxemia and acidemia. If these measures fail, intraaortic balloon counterpulsation may help maintain coronary perfusion pressure. Finally, a right ventricular assist device can be used in severe refractory cases (see Chapter 27).

Problem Situations Following CPB

VASODILATION AND HYPOTENSION

Systemic vascular resistance progressively decreases with rewarming and continues to decrease during the period following CPB. In some but not all cases, pronounced vasodilation at the termination of CPB appears to be related to the duration of rewarming; the systemic vascular resistance can be quite low and the cardiac output high if this period is protracted. This condition is effectively treated with a vasopressor such as phenylephrine to restore arterial blood pressure and maintain coronary perfusion pressure.

VASOCONSTRICTION AND HYPERTENSION

In the patient with good ventricular function, this condition can occur with inadequate rewarming or in the immediate postbypass period as the core body temperature drops with thermal equilibration. The cardiac output is usually reduced and the ventricular filling pressure may be low, normal, or high. Treatment is with vasodilator therapy, usually sodium nitroprusside at low doses (0.25 to 0.5 μg/kg/min IV) with volume replacement as necessary to maintain preload. Hydralazine (in 2.5- to 5-mg IV increments) may also be employed in the stable patient.

HYPOXEMIA

Hypoxemia can be a serious problem in the immediate postbypass period if not quickly recognized and treated. Possible etiologies include atelectasis (corrected by vigorous lung expansion and occasionally the addition of positive end-expiratory pressure); bronchospasm, due to preexisting pulmonary disease or secondary to protamine administration and recognized by high peak inspiratory pressures, poor lung deflation and a shallow slope on the expiratory phase of the capnogram (treated with aerosolized β_2-agonists, volatile anesthetic agents if ventricular function is satisfactory, or intravenous epinephrine or isoproterenol); right-to-left intracardiac shunt, which may occur with congenital heart disease or in otherwise normal patients with a patent foramen ovale and elevated right atrial pressure; low cardiac output, especially when accompanied by right-to-left shunting, high oxygen consumption, and/or low oxygen delivery (anemia); vasodilator therapy, which increases intrapulmonary shunting due to inhibition of hypoxic pulmonary vasoconstriction; noncardiogenic pulmonary edema, usually secondary to allergic reactions to drugs or blood products; pneumothorax, hemothorax, or hydrothorax, usually evident as distended pleurae visible in the surgical field; and other causes not specific to cardiac surgery including inadequate ventilator settings, circuit disconnections, endobronchial intubation, kinking or obstruction of the endotracheal tube, etc. An arterial blood gas should be checked soon after the termination of CPB to assess the adequacy of ventilation and oxygenation, especially when the pulse oximeter is not functional and problems are encountered in the postbypass period.

SUDDEN HEMODYNAMIC DETERIORATION

This critical situation can result from a number of causes, but is usually due to an early or late reaction to protamine, or to the adverse hemodynamic effects of pericardial or chest closure. The latter can result in compression of the heart producing a tamponade effect, which may improve with volume infusion or inotropic support as the heart adjusts to the altered loading conditions. Otherwise, the pericardium may need to be reopened or the sternum may have to be left open for closure at a later date. Another cause of sudden hemodynamic deterioration is ischemia associated with kinking, clotting, or embolization of a vascular graft that may require surgical revision and is usually associated with changes in the electrocardiogram, or with coronary or internal mammary artery spasm or embolization, also usually associated with ST segment elevation and occasionally followed by arrhythmias. Treatment of spasm includes nitroglycerin or calcium channel blockers. Other causes of acute hemodynamic deterioration include arrhythmias, which may be secondary to new myocardial ischemia, other metabolic or electrolyte abnormalities, or to atrial decannulation, and surgical manipulation of the heart, which should be obvious.

PROGRESSIVE HEMODYNAMIC DETERIORATION

The hemodynamic status of most patients gradually improves following the termination of CPB as the residual effects of myocardial ischemia and cardioplegia abate, even in patients requiring aggressive inotropic therapy. If this is not the case, or if requirements for vasoactive drugs actually increase, correctable causes such as myocardial ischemia or valvular dysfunction should be sought. Early institution of intra-aortic balloon counterpulsation may be advantageous to improve myocardial perfusion and salvage ischemic myocardium, otherwise a return to partial CPB may be necessary to allow further recovery of cardiac function and optimization of pharmacologic therapy.

Controversial Issues in the Termination of CPB

CALCIUM ADMINISTRATION

Most anesthesiologists do not recommend the routine administration of calcium salts at the end of CPB except in those patients with evidence of hyperkalemia or hypocalcemia. The incidence of hypocalcemia is common during CPB, but ionized Ca^{2+} usually approaches normal values immediately prior to termination of bypass (62). Moreover, considerable evidence suggests that elevated intracellular Ca^{2+} is correlated with increased cell death and injury during ischemia and reperfusion, as occurs frequently during cardiac surgery (42). Nevertheless, calcium salts are still frequently administered during termination of CPB for their vasopressor and inotropic effects. A recent study suggests that $CaCl_2$ administration during emergence from CPB in patients with good ventricular function has no significant effect on cardiac index (63). Use of calcium salts at the conclusion of bypass should be guided by determination of ionized Ca^{2+} levels; significant increases in ventricular function are produced experimentally by Ca^{2+} administration in the presence of hypocalcemia (64). Calcium salts should probably not be administered to patients with good ventricular function in the absence of hypocalcemia or hyperkalemia because of the potential detrimental effects

of iatrogenic hypercalcemia; whether this is true in cases of impaired ventricular function is unknown.

USE OF INOTROPES

Concern exists that inotropic stimulation of the myocardium may have deleterious effects because of increased energy consumption (65). This may be particularly relevant following cardiac surgery with ischemic cardiac arrest, especially in the presence of residual myocardial ischemia caused by disproportionate increases in myocardial oxygen consumption relative to supply (66). Animal data suggest that catecholamines should be avoided in the reperfusion period immediately following release of the aortic cross-clamp to facilitate metabolic recovery of the myocardium (67). Exogenous positive inotropic agents may also potentiate damage because of the already high endogenous catecholamine levels during cardiac surgery (68). Inotropic agents are clearly useful in discontinuing CPB, and may even expedite the recovery of stunned myocardium (41). Given their potential to increase myocardial damage, however, their use should probably be delayed until the heart has had a chance to recover from the ischemia immediately following aortic cross-clamp release. Animal data suggest that in the presence of ventricular dysfunction, the potentially deleterious effects of inotropic stimulation on oxygen consumption may be reduced by afterload-reducing agents (69).

REFERENCES

1. Novack CR, Tinker JH. Hypothermia after cardiopulmonary bypass in man. Anesthesiology 1980; 53:277–280.
2. Cingolani HE, Faulkner SL, Mattiazzi AR, et al. Depression of human myocardial contractility with "respiratory" and "metabolic" acidosis. Surgery 1975;77:427–432.
3. Houle DB, Weil MH, Brown EB, et al. Influence of respiratory acidosis on ECG and pressor responses to epinephrine, norepinephrine and metaraminol. Proc Soc Exp Biol Med 1957;94:561–564.

4. Rudolph AM, Yuan S. Response of the pulmonary vasculature to hypoxia and H+ ion concentration changes. J Clin Invest 1966;45:399–441.

5. Ettinger PO, Regan TJ, Oldewurtel HA. Hyperkalemia, cardiac conduction, and the electrocardiogram: a review. Am Heart J 1974;88:360–371.

6. Harker LA, Malpass TW, Branson HE, et al. Mechanism of abnormal bleeding in patients undergoing cardiopulmonary bypass: acquired transient platelet dysfunction associated with selective alpha-granule release. Blood 1980;56:824–834.

7. Mannucci PM. Desmopressin, a nontransfusional form of treatment for congenital and acquired bleeding disorders. Blood 1988;72:1449–1455.

8. Salzman EW, Weinstein MJ, Weintraub RM, et al. Treatment with desmopressin acetate to reduce blood loss after cardiac surgery: a double blind randomized trial. N Engl J Med 1986;314:1402–1406.

9. Czer LSC, Bateman TM, Gray RJ, et al. Treatment of severe platelet dysfunction and hemorrhage after cardiopulmonary bypass: reduction in blood product usage with desmopressin. J Am Coll Cardiol 1987;9:1139–1147.

10. Rocha E, Llorens R, Paramo JA, Arcas R, Cuesta B, Martin Trenor A. Does desmopressin acetate reduce blood loss after surgery in patients on cardiopulmonary bypass? Circulation 1988;77:1319–1323.

11. Hackman T, Gascoyne RD, Naiman SC, et al. A trial of desmopressin (1-desamino-8-D-arginine vasopressin) to reduce blood loss in uncomplicated cardiac surgery. N Engl J Med 1989;321:1437–1443.

12. Frankville DD, Harper GB, Lake CL, Johns RA. Hemodynamic consequences of desmopressin administration after cardiopulmonary bypass. Anesthesiology 1991;74:988–996.

13. Horrow JC, Van Riper DF, Strong MD, Brodsky I, Parmet JL. Hemostatic effects of tranexamic acid and desmopressin during cardiac surgery. Circulation 1991;84:2063–2070.

14. Buylaert WA, Herregods LL, Mortier EP, et al. Cardiopulmonary bypass and the pharmacokinetics of drugs: an update. Clin Pharmacokin 1989;7:234–251.

15. Price SL, Brown DL, Carpenter RL. Isoflurane elimination via a bubble oxygenator during extracorporeal circulation. J Cardiothorac Anesth 1988;2:41–44.

16. Nussmeier NA, Lambert ML, Moskowitz GJ, et al. Washin and washout of isoflurane administered via bubble oxygenators during hypothermic cardiopulmonary bypass. Anesthesiology 1989;71:519–525.

17. Bermudez J, Lichtiger M. Increases in arterial to end-tidal CO$_2$ tension differences after cardiopulmonary bypass. Anesth Analg 1987;66:690–692.

18. Salmenperä M, Heinonen J. Pulmonary vascular responses to moderate changes in PaCO$_2$ after cardiopulmonary bypass. Anesthesiology 1986;64:311–315.

19. Stern DH, Gerson JI, Allen FB, Parker FB. Can we trust the direct radial artery pressure immediately following cardiopulmonary bypass? Anesthesiology 1985;62:557–571.

20. Mohr R, Lavee J, Goor DA. Inaccuracy of radial artery pressure measurement after cardiac operations. J Thorac Cardiovasc Surg 1987;94:286–290.

21. Gallagher JD, Moore RA, McNicholas KW, Joge AB. Comparison of radial and femoral arterial blood pressure in children after cardiopulmonary bypass. J Clin Monitoring 1985;1:168–171.

22. Thomson IR, Rosenbloom M, Cannon JE, Morris A. Electrocardiographic ST-segment elevation after myocardial reperfusion during coronary artery surgery. Anesth Analg 1987;66:1183–1186.

23. Abel RM, Birkley MJ, Austen WG, Barnett GO, Beck CH Jr, Fischer JE. Etiology, incidence and prognosis of renal failure following cardiac operations. Results of a prospective analysis of 500 consecutive patients. J Thor Cardiovasc Surg 1976;71:323–333.

24. Davis RF, Lappos DG, Kirklin JK, Birkley MJ, Lowenstein E. Acute oliguria after cardiopulmonary bypass: renal functional improvement with low dose dopamine infusion. Crit Care Med 1982;10:852–856.

25. Hilberman M, Moseda J, Stimson EB, et al. The diuretic properties of dopamine in patients after open-heart operation. Anesthesiology 1984;61:489–494.

26. Weinstone R, Campbell JM, Booker PD, McKay R. Renal function after cardiopulmonary bypass in children: comparison of dopamine with dobutamine. Br J Anaesth 1991;67:591–594.

27. Jastremski MS, Laksmipathi C, Beney KM, Bailly RT. Analysis of the effects of continuous on-line monitoring of mixed venous saturation on patient outcome and cost effectiveness. Crit Care Med 1989;17:148–153.

28. Cahalan MK, Litt L, Botvinick EH, et al. Advances in noninvasive cardiovascular imaging: implications for the anesthesiologist. Anesthesiology 1987;66:356–372.

29. Ungerleider RM, Greeley WJ, Sheikh KH, et al. Routine use of intraoperative epicardial echocardiography and Doppler color flow imaging to guide and evaluate repair of congenital heart lesions. A prospective study. J Thorac Cardiovasc Surg 1990;100:297–309.

30. Greeley WJ, Ungerleider RM. Echocardiography

during surgery for congenital heart disease. In: DeBruijn NP, Clements FM, eds. Intraoperative use of echocardiography, Philadelphia: JB Lippincott, 1991:129–175.

31. Braunwald E, Kloner RA. The stunned myocardium: prolonged, postischemic ventricular dysfunction. Circulation 1982;66:1146–1149.

32. Rahimtoola SH. The hibernating myocardium. Am Heart J 1989;117:211–221.

33. Ross J Jr. Afterload mismatch in aortic and mitral valve disease: implications for surgical therapy. J Am Coll Cardiol 1985;5:811–826.

34. Ross J Jr. Left ventricular function and the timing of surgical treatment in valvular heart disease. Ann Intern Med 1981;94:498–504.

35. Mangano DT. Biventricular function after myocardial revascularization in humans: deterioration and recovery patterns in the first 24 hours. Anesthesiology 1985;62:571–577.

36. Lell WA, Huber S, Buttner EE. Myocardial protection during cardiopulmonary bypass. In: Kaplan JA, ed. Cardiac anesthesia. Philadelphia: WB Saunders, 1987:927–962.

37. Floyd RD, Sabiston DC, Lee KL, et al. The effect of duration of hypothermic cardioplegia on ventricular function. J Thorac Cardiovasc Surg 1983; 85:606–611.

38. Levitsky S, Wright RW, Rao KS, et al. Does intermittent coronary perfusion offer greater myocardial protection than continuous aortic crossclamping? Surgery 1977;82:51–59.

39. Hansen RM, Viguerat CE, Matthay MA, et al. Poor correlation between pulmonary arterial wedge pressure and left ventricular end-diastolic volume after coronary artery bypass graft surgery. Anesthesiology 1986;64:764–770.

40. Takeishi Y, Tono-Oka I, Kubota I, et al. Functional recovery of hibernating myocardium after coronary bypass surgery: does it coincide with improvement in perfusion? Am Heart J 1991; 122:665–670.

41. Ellis SG, Wynne J, Braunwald E, et al. Response of reperfusion-salvaged, shinned myocardium to inotropic stimulation. Am Heart J 1984;107:13–19.

42. Elz JS, Panagiotopoulos S, Nayler WG. Reperfusion-induced calcium gain after ischemia. Am J Cardiol 1989;63:7E–13E.

43. Steen PA, Tinker JH, Pluth JR, et al. Efficacy of dopamine, dobutamine and epinephrine during emergence from cardiopulmonary bypass in man. Circulation 1978;57:378–384.

44. Salomon NW, Plachetka JR, Copeland JG. Comparison of dopamine and dobutamine following coronary artery bypass grafting. Ann Thor Surg 1982;33:48–54.

45. Richard C, Ricome JL, Rimailho A, Bottineau G, Auzepy P. Combined hemodynamic effects of do-

pamine and dobutamine in cardiogenic shock. Circulation 1983;67:620–626.

46. Loeb HS, Bredakis J, Gunnar RM. Superiority of dobutamine over dopamine for augmentation of cardiac output in patients with chronic low output cardiac failure. Circulation 1977;55: 375–381.

47. Hess W, Klein W, Muller-Busch C, Tarnow J. Haemodynamic effects of dopamine and dopamine combined with nitroglycerin in patients subjected to coronary bypass surgery. Br J Anesth 1979;51:1063–1068.

48. Goenen M, Pedemonte O, Baele P, et al. Amrinone in the management of low cardiac output after open heart surgery. Am J Cardiol 1985; 56:33B–38B.

49. Gage J, Rutman H, Lucido D, et al. Additive effects of dobutamine and amrinone on myocardial contractility and ventricular performance in patients with severe heart failure. Circulation 1986;74:367–373.

50. Benotti JR, Grossman W, Braunwald E, et al. Effects of amrinone on myocardial energy metabolism and hemodynamics in patients with severe congestive heart failure due to coronary artery disease. Circulation 1980;62:28–34.

51. Robinson RJS, Tchervenkow C. Treatment of low cardiac output after aortocoronary bypass surgery using a combination of norepinephrine and amrinone. J Cardiothorac Anesth 1987;1: 229–233.

52. Lathi KG, Shulman MS, Diehl JT, Stetz JJ. The use of amrinone and norepinephrine for inotropic support during emergence from cardiopulmonary bypass. J Cardiothorac Anesth 1991;5: 250–254.

53. Wynands JE. Amrinone: is it the inotrope of choice? J Cardiothoracic Anesthesia 1989; 3(suppl 2):45–52.

54. DiSesa VJ. The rational selection of inotropic drugs in cardiac surgery. J Cardiac Surg 1987; 2:385–406.

55. Tinker JH, Tarhan S, White RD, et al. Dobutamine for inotropic support during emergence from cardiopulmonary bypass. Anesthesiology 1976; 44:281–286.

56. LeJemtel TH, Sonnenblick EH. Should the failing heart be stimulated? N Engl J Med 1984;310: 1384–1385.

57. Sturm JT, Fuhrman TM, Sterling R, et al. Combined use of dopamine and nitroprusside therapy in conjunction with intra-aortic balloon pumping for the treatment of postcardiotomy low-output syndrome. J Thorac Cardiovasc Surg 1981;82:13–17.

58. Feola M, Weiner L, Walinsky P, et al. Improved survival following coronary artery bypass sur-

gery in patients with poor left ventricular function: role of intraaortic balloon counterpulsation. Am J Cardiol 1977;39:1021–1026.

59. D'Ambra MN, LaRaia PJ, Philbin DM, et al. Prostaglandin E$_1$: a new therapy for refractory right heart failure and pulmonary hypertension after mitral valve replacement. J Thorac Cardiovasc Surg 1985;89:567–572.

60. Frostell C, Fratacci MD, Wain JC, Jones R, Zapol WM. Inhaled nitric oxide: a selective pulmonary vasodilator reversing hypoxic vasoconstriction. Circulation 1991;83:2038–2047.

61. Hess W, Arnold B, Veit S. The haemodynamic effects of amrinone in patients with mitral stenosis and pulmonary hypertension. Eur Heart J 1986; 7:800–807.

62. Robertie PG, Butterworth JF, Royster RL, et al. Normal parathyroid hormone responses to hypocalcemia during cardiopulmonary bypass. Anesthesiology 1991;75:43–48.

63. Royster RL, Butterworth JF, Prielipp RC, et al. A randomized, blinded, placebo-controlled evaluation of calcium chloride and epinephrine for inotropic support after emergence from cardiopulmonary bypass. Anesth Analg 1992;74:3–13.

64. Drop LJ, Geffin GA, O'Keefe DD, et al. Relation between ionized calcium concentration and ventricular pump performance in the dog under hemodynamically controlled conditions. Am J Cardiol 1981;47:1041–1051.

65. Katz AM. Potential deleterious effects of inotropic agents in the therapy of chronic heart failure. Circulation 1986;73(suppl 3):184–190.

66. Lazar HL, Buckberg GD, Foglia RP, et al. Detrimental effects of premature use of inotropic drugs to discontinue cardiopulmonary bypass. J Thorac Cardiovasc Surg 1981;82:18–25.

67. Ward HB, Einzig S, Wang T, et al. Comparison of catecholamine effects on canine myocardial metabolism and regional blood flow during and after cardiopulmonary bypass. J Thorac Cardiovasc Surg 1987;87:452–465.

68. Reves JG, Buttner E, Karp RB, et al. Elevated catecholamines during cardiac surgery: consequences of reperfusion of the postarrested heart. Am J Cardiol 1984;53:722–728.

69. Dyke CM, Lee KF, Parmor J, et al. Inotropic stimulation and oxygen consumption in a canine model of dilated cardiomyopathy. Ann Thorac Surg 1991;52:750–758.

INDEX

Page numbers followed by t, f, and n denotes tables, figures, and notes, respectively.